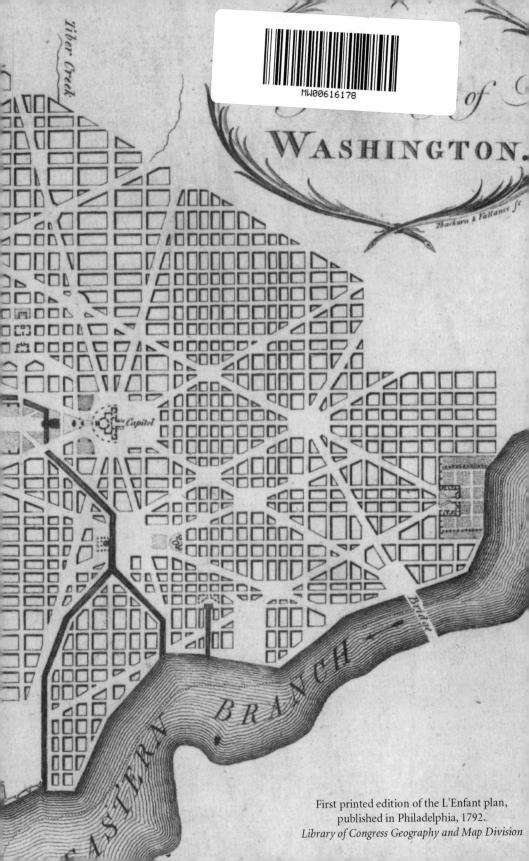

WASHINGTON.

Thackara & Vallance sc

Tiber Creek

Capitol

EASTERN BRANCH

Bridge

First printed edition of the L'Enfant plan,
published in Philadelphia, 1792.
Library of Congress Geography and Map Division

UNDERSTANDING
THE TIMES

Also by William P. Grady:

*FINAL AUTHORITY: A Christian's
Guide to the King James Bible*

*WHAT HATH GOD WROUGHT!: A Biblical
Interpretation of American History*

UNDERSTANDING THE TIMES
VOLUME ONE

HOW SATAN TURNED AMERICA AGAINST GOD

William P. Grady, Ph.D.

GRADY
PUBLICATIONS, INC.

DISCLAIMERS

The opinions expressed in this book are solely those of the author and do not necessarily reflect the views of the individuals who were interviewed and/or quoted.

While the author has made every effort to provide accurate Internet addresses at the time of publication, neither the publisher nor the author assumes any responsibility for errors, or for changes that occur after publication.

All quoted material is cited exactly (including misspellings) as it appears in printed sources. Within the quoted matter, including Bible verses, italicized material is emphasized by the source, bold print indicates emphasis by the author of this book.

Publisher has exhausted every effort to locate M. Brun.

ISBN 0-9628809-3-0
Library of Congress Control Number: 2005920431
First Printing, April 2005

For information, address:
GRADY PUBLICATIONS, INC.
P.O. Box 5217
Knoxville, TN 37928
(865) 219-5990
(800) 596-0767
william.grady@gradypublications.com
www.gradypublications.com

Dedication

This volume is lovingly dedicated to my children and their families—
"I have no greater joy than to hear that my children walk in truth."

(III JOHN 4)

Daniel

Michelle

Hunter

Shaelyn

Abigail

Sara

Larry

Sammi

Jessie

Caleb

Dixie

Paul

Emily

Joshua

Leah

and those who follow after . . .

"Keep *them* safe till the storm passes by."

Table of Contents

Preface

ACCORDING TO REVELATION 3:17, the great danger of the last days stems from a prevailing spiritual blindness within the Body of Christ. This very condition was foreshadowed by the fall in the Garden. (Genesis 3:6) Paul's depiction of Jesus as the *"last* Adam" (I Corinthians 15:45) made Eve the first major type of the Church in Scripture. In order to rescue their brides, *both* "Adams" would have to forfeit a perfect environment; lay aside their lordship; take upon sin; and endure separation from the Father. While the *first* Adam "blew it," the *last* Adam would make everything right! (Romans 5:12-21) Charles Wesley set this doctrine to music with the words, "Second Adam from above, reinstate us in thy love."

In I Timothy 2:14, Paul gives us the key to fully appreciate this beautiful picture of man's redemption: *"And Adam was not deceived, but the woman being deceived was in the transgression."* While Eve was tricked into eating the fruit, her husband did so with a full understanding of the consequences. (Romans 5:14; Genesis 5:1-5)

The all-important verse that connects this typology to the present Laodicean apostasy is Ecclesiastes 1:9a: *"The thing that hath been, it is that which shall be; and that which is done is that which shall be done . . ."* Thus, the history of mankind will undoubtedly end the same way it began—*with a bride being deceived!*

More specifically, with regard to Japheth's spiritual destiny, the collapse of the Church in its westernmost theater of enlargement will also follow the predictable pattern of a precise historical antecedent. As the fall of Rome (not to mention the calamitous Dark Ages) was set in motion when the "Religious Right" of the fourth century embraced the grossly compromised testimony of a pagan professional politician (Emperor Constantine "The Great"), you might want to watch for a similar generation of naive Christians getting snookered by *another* "born-again" con man.

But of course, this is merely wishful thinking on my part; the Scripture has already spoken on the matter—*"There is no remembrance of former things; neither shall there be any remembrance of things that are to come with those that shall come after"* (Ecclesiastes 1:11). As even the heathen know, "The only lesson that men ever learn from history is that men never learn from history; therefore, history is doomed to repeat itself." This is the essence of *déjavu*. And *whatever* you do, don't let the fact that the *initial* deception took place in *Iraq* bother you (Genesis 2:14); it's probably just a "coincidence."

Introduction

O VER FIVE YEARS before the Twin Towers were destroyed, 230 men, women and children perished when TWA Flight 800 went down off the coast of Long Island, New York, on July 17, 1996. After a $43 million investigation, the Federal Bureau of Investigation (FBI) and the National Transportation Safety Board (NTSB) concluded that the crash was initiated by an explosion of fuel in the plane's center tank.

In 1998, Admiral Thomas H. Moorer, USN Ret., issued an ominous mailing to the American people. The former Naval aviator and *chairman of the Joint Chiefs of Staff* expressed his concern over

> a great deal of important evidence bearing on the crash that apparently has not been given the attention that it deserves by either the official investigators or the news media. The most obvious and inexplicable example is the evidence provided by **183 eyewitnesses interviewed by the FBI who saw a streak of light heading toward the plane immediately before the explosion.**[1]

While conducting a revival meeting in Texas in January 2002, I shared this amazing letter with the congregation. The following evening a church member returned and asked to speak with me about the matter. After introducing himself, the man stated that he was a graduate of the Air Force Academy and had worked in Air Force Intelligence for eighteen years, attaining the rank of major, before transferring to inactive status. To my amazement, he gave me a copy of a highly technical, non-classified, 126-page dossier by another retired Naval officer. The cover sheet read:

Interim Report
on the
Crash of TWA Flight 800
and the
Actions of the NTSB and the FBI
by
Cmdr. William S. Donaldson, USN Ret.
In cooperation with
Associated Retired Aviation Professionals
For The
Committee on Transportation & Infrastructure
Subcommittee on Aviation
U.S. House of Representatives
Washington, D.C.
July 17, 1998
Copyright © 1998 William S. Donaldson, III

Among other things, Commander Donaldson took issue with the Central Intelligence Agency (CIA) over a video they produced in a desperate attempt to discredit the numerous eyewitnesses who testified that a missile destroyed the ill-fated airliner.

Defying the laws of physics, aerodynamics, and jet engine mechanics, the video has the aircraft center wing tank mysteriously exploding, the plane flying along for awhile as the explosion sound makes its way toward shore. The nose falls off and the plane climbs vertically 3,000 feet trailing fire just in time for observers ashore to hear the sound and look seaward to observe a large, slow moving, Boeing 747 morph into a streaking anti-aircraft missile!

It would be easy to understand why 10 year olds watching this cartoon on Saturday morning would believe it on face value, but it is perplexing to think network news producers, who are responsible for providing national news, would be suckered without checking the facts first.[2]

Commander Donaldson, a career military man, labeled the present time as "perplexing." The King James translators chose a more profound word when rendering the prophetic truth in II Timothy 3:1, *"This know also, that in the last days **perilous** times shall come."*

Four of the thirty-four conclusions contained in the commander's report are as follows:

4. TWA Flight 800 was destroyed by an airbursting anti-aircraft missile.

6. The preponderance of evidence strongly points to a hostile attack by enemies of the United States.

32. Officials in the White House, Justice Department and the NTSB appear to be withholding information from the American people and the United States Congress that protects the identity and motives of those who attacked TWA FL800.

34. Based on the fact that TWA Flight 800 was the likely target of a State Sponsored terrorist attack, which is an Act of War, and the fact that the Administration has covered up this act for political expediency prior to the 1996 election, the Congress should do one or more of the following:
    a. Hold Congressional Hearings into the cause of the crash of TWA Flight 800.
    b. Request the Justice Department appoint an Independent Counsel to investigate.[3]

The passage in II Timothy 3 also explains why it will be perfectly normal for national leaders to mislead the American people in the closing days of the Church Age. Verse four lists "traitors" as one of the signs of the times.

However, there is another cultural phenomenon that is more dangerous than intentional governmental deception. You might call it *intentional citizen stupidity*. On page 9-A of *USA Today* for September 19, 2002, the following headline appeared in bold, inch-high letters—"Warnings not passed down, 9/11 inquiry says."

Highlights from the declassified intelligence report include:

June 1998: Intelligence officials learned from several sources that Osama bin Laden was considering attacks in the USA, including Washington, D.C., and New York.

August 1998: Officials learned that a group of unidentified Arabs planned to fly an explosive-laden plane from a foreign country into the World Trade Center.

July 2001: A person returning from Afghanistan told the CIA, "Everyone is talking about an impending attack."[4]

(This unprecedented negligence within the intelligence community would be substantiated during the 2004 9/11 Commission hearings, particularly with regard to the critical President's Daily Brief, or PDB, of August 6, 2001.)

Do you suppose that such an alarming revelation in "the nation's newspaper" provoked an outcry from the public sector? *Are you kidding?* The average American today is too busy watching Ozzie Osbourne and Jerry Springer to be distracted by matters of national security, etc. Just as Europe entered the Dark Ages when the text of the King James Bible was abandoned and later emerged with Erasmus and the A.V. 1611, America is presently experiencing her own benighted demise for the identical reason.

An appropriate Scripture to explain this end-day "space cadet" mentality is given in II Thessalonians 2:11, *"And for this cause God shall send them strong delusion, that they should believe a lie."* Our passage in II Timothy 3, adds in verse 13, *"But evil men and seducers shall wax worse and worse, deceiving, and being deceived."*

Now, it is one thing to be dense concerning the threatening agenda of those who manipulate various segments of our government, but it is quite another to be unaware of imminent judgment from God Himself! Do you know that America is currently engaged in a sin far more threatening than abortion? Consider the words of the prophet Zechariah:

> *And in that day will I make Jerusalem a burdensome stone for all people: all that burden themselves with it shall be cut in pieces, though all the people of the earth be gathered together against it. . . .* ***And it shall come to pass in that day, that I will seek to destroy all the nations that come against Jerusalem.*** *(Zechariah 12:3,9)*

Has anyone noticed that our celebrated "War on Terrorism" has *never* applied to the non-stop murders of defenseless Israeli citizens by the treacherous Palestinian Authority? I assure you that the God of Israel is up to speed on the hypocritical situation. Whatever happened to that providential bond between Israel and America? Is it mere coincidence that the center letters in the name "Jerusalem" just happen to be "USA"? Appropriately enough, conclusion number eight in Commander Donaldson's report confirms:

> 8. The United States was warned by Israeli intelligence of a terrorist risk to TWA FL800 prior to the event.[5]

But can we really expect the secular leaders of America to rise any higher than the so-called point men of evangelical Christianity? Whereas conspiracy author Texe Marrs believes that Monica Lewinsky was a "servant of the Israeli Mossad spy agency,"[6] prophecy "expert" Jack Van Impe, media "missionary" Jerry Falwell and Christian "psychologist" James Dobson all speak positively about Israel while simultaneously praising her traditional nemesis—the pope! The rank and file within the hodge-podge of Laodicean apostasy (including what is left of the Independent Baptist movement) have chosen to look the other way as well. Although "Brother" Bush has twice ridden into the White House on a wave of euphoric adulation from his "Christian coalition," he and his State Department have since conspired to extinguish God's *"burning bush!"*

As this book was going to press, the world was being assured that a "Road Map to Peace" would stabilize the Middle East by 2005. One would certainly have to admit that the collective "wisdom" displayed by the U.S.A., U.N. and Vatican State was practically supernatural. For Israel's willingness to "merely" give up the West Bank and East Jerusalem, the rest of us could finally realize that elusive dream—*"on earth peace, good will toward men"* (Luke 2:14).

However, there is one small problem with this proposition; *Jesus Christ is planning to ride through the Eastern Gate in the immediate future to establish Jerusalem as the capital of His universe.* Therefore, it must remain closed until He appears.

> *Then he brought me back the way of the gate of the outward sanctuary which looketh toward the east; and it was shut.*
> *Then said the LORD unto me; This gate shall be shut, it shall not be opened, and* **no man** *shall enter in by it; because the LORD, the God of Israel, hath entered in by it, therefore it shall be shut.*
> *It is for the prince; the prince, he shall sit in it to eat bread before the LORD; he shall enter by the way of the porch of that gate, and shall go out by the way of the same.* (Ezekiel 44:1-3)

You see, unbeknownst to those 183 ambassadors in the U.N., the land in question actually belongs to God and He doesn't appear open to the idea of subdividing.

*I will also gather all nations, and will bring them down into the valley of Jehoshaphat, and will plead with them there for my people and for my heritage Israel, whom they have scattered among the nations, **and parted my land**.* (Joel 3:2)

This book deals with *negative reality* ("How Satan Turned America Against God") as opposed to *positive fantasy* ("God Bless America"; "revival is just around the corner," etc.). Consequently, it will not be carried in the average "Christian" bookstore. It reveals America's main purpose for existence, her tragic repudiation of that role and how the process was orchestrated by Satan. The United States is about to commit national suicide for daring to move against the nation of Israel. The so-called "Road Map to Peace" will end in *"sudden destruction"* (I Thessalonians 5:3), for an *"understanding of the times"* has always been for one purpose— *"to know what Israel ought to do"* (I Chronicles 12:32).

To the kindly influence of Christianity we owe that degree of civil freedom and political and social happiness which mankind now enjoys. In proportion as the genuine effects of Christianity are diminished in any nation, either through unbelief, or the corruption of its doctrines, or the neglect of its institutions; in the same proportion will the people of that nation recede from the blessings of genuine freedom and approximate the miseries of complete despotism.

DR. JEDEDIAH MORSE
Father of inventor Samuel F. B. Morse

1

Land For Peace

*"They have said, Come, and let us cut them off from
being a nation; that the name of Israel may be no more
in remembrance. . . . So persecute them with thy
tempest, and make them afraid with thy storm."*
(Psalm 83:4,15)

ON OCTOBER 30, 1991, a fateful "peace" conference was
convened in Madrid, Spain, by President George Bush. From
that moment until now, the panacean pipe dream for a lasting
solution to the Israeli-Palestinian conflict has been called—"land for
peace." President Bush set the pace from the opening bell. An excerpt
from his speech follows:

> Throughout the Middle East, we seek a stable and enduring settlement.
> We've not defined what this means. Indeed, I make these points with no
> map showing where the final borders are to be drawn. **Nevertheless we
> believe territorial compromise is essential for peace.**[1]

The Arab position was articulated by Egypt's foreign minister, Amr
Moussa. Three of his four points involved the "land for peace" scam.
He said:

> Secondly, the West Bank, Gaza and the Golan Heights are occupied
> territories.
> Thirdly, settlements established in territories occupied since '67, including
> Jerusalem are illegal, and more settlements will foreclose potential progress
> toward real peace and cast doubts on the credibility of the process itself.

> Fourthly, the holy city of Jerusalem has its special status. . . . The occupying power should not exercise monopoly or illegal sovereignty over the holy city. It should not persist in unilateral decisions declared to annex the holy city as this lacks validity or legitimacy.[2]

While President Bush was speaking in Madrid, a portentous atmospheric phenomenon began to occur in the North Atlantic Ocean. A powerful storm developed off the coast of Nova Scotia packing sustained winds of 73 mph (only one mph short of hurricane status). This was quite unusual, as most hurricanes originate in the tropics (after forming off the west coast of Africa). And while the normal weather pattern for America is westward to eastward, *this* storm would travel over a thousand miles in the opposite direction! You might say it had a mind of its own.

The following day (October 31), the tempest decided to come ashore for some "trick-or-treating." It abruptly smashed its way into New England with waves in excess of one hundred feet—the highest on record! The storm was initially called a "monster," as it was literally hundreds of miles wide. It then proceeded down the coast all the way to Florida, causing multiplied millions of dollars in damage.

The nation's meteorologists were astonished by their own data. The extremely rare weather patterns that coalesced to create this "Halloween Monster" can only happen about once every century. They concluded that it was one of the most powerful storms to have ever occurred. These findings resulted in a book being written about the event, followed by a feature length Hollywood film; both entitled *The Perfect Storm.*

The front-page headlines of *The New York Times* and *USA Today* newspapers featured the Madrid peace conference and the Perfect Storm stories right next to each other! The adjacent articles in *USA Today* were titled "One-on-one peace talks next" and "East Coast hit by rare storm."[3]

However, to gain the ultimate spiritual perspective, you might want to read an article that appeared in the *Maine Sunday Telegram* for November 3, 1991.

Bush Surveys Storm Damage to Home

By Tom Raum
Associated Press

KENNEBUNKPORT—President Bush surveyed the devastating damage that a fierce Atlantic storm dealt his turn-of-the-century ocean-side home on Saturday and proclaimed: "The sea won this round."

But as he stood in a yard littered with stones, mud, broken glass and overturned furniture, the president vowed to rebuild the three-story home that has been in his family since 1903.

"It's devastating . . . but everything can be repaired," Bush said as he led a group of reporters on a tour of the damage.

He said he had some insurance, but that it wouldn't come close to the amount needed to restore the imposing house and its furnishing. The home was assessed last year at $2.2 million. Local realtors, however, have said it is worth considerably more.

Bush said many years' accumulation of books and personal belongings had been destroyed or washed out to sea in the storm that ravaged the Atlantic seaboard on Wednesday and Thursday.

At the height of the storm, 30-foot waves crashed over the house and the rocky point on which it sits, the president said.

The front, first floor of the three-story, stone-and-shingle home was ripped open to the sea, revealing the remains of what had been the Bushes' living room, a bedroom and a family sitting room.

"The main part of the house is severely damaged," Bush said as he and a group of reporters stepped gingerly over broken glass and twisted pieces of wood and metal that had once been the Bush's [sic] living room.

"All that nice living room went out to sea," an obviously pained Barbara Bush told reporters.

But, she added philosophically: "We are very lucky, we Bushes. A lot worse things happen in life."

The president said he couldn't believe the extent of the damage, "and I've been around the ocean a long time. Most who have lived around here all their lives have never seen anything like it."

"Unfortunately, the sea won this round. We'll see how we go on the next one," he said. . . .

At one point, Bush ducked through a bent, open French door between jagged shards of glass to get from one room to the other.

Outside, he looked for personal belongings in the littered yard. He picked up a soggy book, looked at it and shook his head. Earlier, he had found a small framed picture of his father, the late Sen. Prescott Bush of Connecticut, lying in the mud.

"I had four pairs of binoculars that I had for years. I found one of them—and it was full of water," Bush said sadly.

"This was solid water. It looked like part of the ocean," Bush said, standing on his debris-strewn lawn.

The stone pier Bush uses as a boat dock lay in ruins. . . .

Asked if he planned to rebuild the house exactly as it had been, Bush said: "I don't know. We're waiting to talk to the adjusters and the building guys. . . ."

Nevertheless, there are no plans to move to higher ground. "It means something to us," Bush said of the house. "It's our family strength."[4]

I was able to interview one of the carpenters who helped repair the president's home. When I asked him to relate his outstanding memory of the damage, he recalled how everyone was dumbfounded that the force of the storm had obliterated the massive retaining wall designed to protect the property. He said that although the wall was three to four feet thick and anywhere from fifteen to twenty feet high, it was no match for storm tides at least twenty feet higher than normal. He distinctly remembered that even the foundation for the new wall had to be poured again. His second most vivid recollection was that the ocean had swept through half the house, leaving seaweed, sand, and other debris in its wake.

The Bible explanation for this dramatic cause and effect sequence is so vital to comprehend that your very life may be hanging in the balance. In Deuteronomy 32:10, God described the nation of Israel as *"the apple of his eye."* After twenty centuries of displacement the Jews are finally back in their own land. Anyone stupid enough to mess with them now would be playing with "spiritual nitroglycerin."

> *And I will bring again the captivity of my people of Israel, and they shall build the waste cities, and inhabit them; and they shall plant vineyards, and drink the wine thereof; they shall also make gardens, and eat the fruit of them.*
>
> *And I will plant them upon their land, **and they shall no more be pulled up out of their land which I have given them**, saith the LORD thy God.* (Amos 9:14-15)

You say, "Dr. Grady, that 'Perfect Storm' business was just an unusual coincidence, that's all." Help yourself, son!

On August 23, 1992, President Bush moved the deadly Madrid peace conference to American soil. The theme for the Washington, D.C.-based talks remained the same—"land for peace." The U.S. representative was acting Secretary of State, Lawrence Eagleburger. In an interview with Eagleburger, *The New York Times* reported that the peace negotiations were resuming "in the context of an Israeli Government that is prepared to be far more forthcoming."[5] Better duck, America!

That very day Hurricane Andrew devastated southern Florida, causing $30 billion in property damage and leaving 180,000 homeless (with another 25,000 displaced in Louisiana), *making it the worst natural disaster in American history!* The National Hurricane Center described Andrew as a 25 to 30-mile-wide tornado! Andrew was so furious it even destroyed the wind-measuring device, making it impossible to confirm the storm's top wind speed. The last recorded figure was 175 mph, though officials have rendered estimates as high as 200 mph!

Once again, the Madrid peace conference and "Mother Nature's response" shared front-page coverage in the national press. The headlines for *USA Today* on August 24 were, "1 Million flee Andrew," "This will make Hugo look weak," and "Monster storm targets Fla." Also on page one was an article entitled, "Mideast peace talks to resume on positive note."

The New York Times had similar dual front-page coverage on August 26, but with an added "bonus." Directly to the left of the Madrid peace conference story was an article about President Bush's ratings crashing in the polls.[6] Less than one year after attaining an incredible ninety-two percent approval rating following the Iraqi defeat in February, 1991, Bush was spiraling to reelection defeat for coming against God's nation. (Genesis 12:3)

The United States of America is literally teetering on the brink of divine annihilation; yet no one seems to have a clue, *including the professing born-again believers!* Tell me—have the leaders of *your* particular "camp" or "movement" warned *you* of this imminent national catastrophe? Most of the pastors with whom I am acquainted are too pre-occupied with "fanning the flames of revival," holding politically-correct "God and Country" rallies, or constructing $100 million auditoriums to have noticed that deadly sword of Damocles hanging over their unsuspecting congregations.

The land in question belongs to Israel and no sorry Gentile is going to get away with redistricting a single square inch!

But you say, "Dr. Grady, you're just trying to intimidate me with *more* coincidences. Don't you realize that storms and hurricanes are normal occurrences?" Well, yes, I understand your point of view completely.

On January 16, 1994, President Bill Clinton and Syria's President Hafez Assad met in Geneva to discuss more "land for peace" arrangements. This time Israel would have to return the Golan Heights to Syria. Clinton was quoted in the press as stating, "Israel must make concessions that will be politically unpopular with many Israelis."[7] *Less than twenty-four hours later, a 6.9 earthquake pulverized southern California.* The quake, centered in Northridge, became the second-most deadly "natural" disaster to come against America. (For added emphasis, the quake's epicenter just happened to strike in the very district where 95 percent of America's pornographic films are produced.)

The source for these amazing "coincidences" is a well-researched book entitled *Israel: The Blessing or the Curse*, by co-authors John McTernan and Bill Koenig. Mr. McTernan is a retired federal agent who served for twenty-six years with the Treasury Department while Mr. Koenig is a White House correspondent, residing in the Washington, D.C., area. These men are to be highly commended for producing such a timely and insightful warning on America's coming judgment.

Their perspective on the late Yasser Arafat's "visits" to America is beyond incredible. If the Hebrew, Moses, was commanded to remove his shoes after being *invited* to enter the Promised Land, how do you think Jehovah would react to some Egyptian psychopath with a NASCAR checkered flag draped on his head *bursting in unannounced*?

The Results of Meeting with Yasser Arafat

September 1, 1993: President Clinton announces he will meet Arafat and Rabin on September 13 in Washington, D.C., to begin the Oslo peace accords. After nearly a week of meandering in the Atlantic Ocean, Hurricane Emily hits North Carolina on this day.

March 2, 1997: Arafat meets with President Clinton in Washington, D.C. The same day, awesome tornado storms unleash tremendous damage in Arkansas and flooding in Kentucky and Ohio. Arkansas and Kentucky declared disaster areas.

January 21, 1998: President Clinton is waiting to meet with Arafat at the White House. At this exact time, the president's sex scandal breaks.

September 27, 1998: Arafat is meeting with the president in Washington. Hurricane George hits Alabama and stalls. The hurricane stalls until Arafat leaves and then it dissipates. Parts of Alabama declared a disaster area.

October 17, 1998: Arafat comes to the Wye Plantation meeting. Incredible rains fall on Texas, which cause record flooding. Parts of Texas are declared a disaster area.

November 23, 1998: Arafat comes to America. He meets with President Clinton who is raising funds for the Palestinian state. On this day the stock market fell 216 points.

December 12, 1998: On this day the U.S. House of Representatives votes to impeach President Clinton. At the very time of the impeachment, the president is meeting with Arafat in Gaza over the peace process.

March 23, 1999: Arafat meets with Clinton in Washington, D.C. Market falls 219 points that day. The next day Clinton orders attack on Serbia.

September 3, 1999: Secretary of State Albright meets with Arafat in Israel. Hurricane Dennis comes ashore on this very day after weeks of changing course in the Atlantic Ocean.

September 22, 1999: Arafat meets with Clinton in Washington, D.C. The day before and after the meeting, the market falls more than 200 points each day. This was the first time in history the market lost more than 200 points for two days in a week. The market lost 524 points this week.

June 16, 2000: Arafat meets with President Clinton. The market falls 265 points on this day.

July 12-26, 2000: Arafat at the Camp David meetings. Powerful droughts throughout the country. Forest fires explode in West into uncontrollable fires. By the end of August, 7 million acres are burnt.

November 9, 2000: Arafat meets with President Clinton at the White House to try and salvage the peace process. This was just two days after the presidential election. The nation was just entering into an election crisis which was the worst in over one hundred years.

November 11, 2001: Arafat speaks at the U.N. General Assembly and condemns Israel. He later meets with Secretary of State Colin Powell. On this day, Saddam threatens the U.S. with nuclear weapons. Within twenty-four hours of meeting with Powell, an airplane crashes in NYC killing two hundred sixty-five people. The crash was fifteen miles from where Arafat spoke.[8]

"BROTHER" BUSH VS. THE BURNING BUSH

During his 2000 election campaign, George W. Bush stated in a debate with Al Gore, "I want everyone to know, should I be the president, Israel's going to be our friend. *I'm going to stand by Israel.*"[9] Has "Brother" Bush delivered the goods? After the land for the American

Embassy in Jerusalem was given to Washington, D.C., in 1991, Congress authorized the relocation from Tel Aviv. Yet, Mr. Clinton refused to facilitate the transfer. Bush promised Jewish voters that he would move the Embassy to Jerusalem if elected president. This has yet to be done. Do you think Israel's God is impressed with rhetoric?

On June 6, 2001, President Bush sent CIA director George Tenet to Israel to broker a cessation of construction projects in the disputed settlement areas. (The president was going to "stand by Israel," etc.) Well, while Mr. Tenet was en route, a funny thing happened out in the Gulf of Mexico. Tropical Storm Allison formed within a day and headed off to visit the president's home state. Allison had never heard the expression, "Don't mess with Texas." She was more familiar with the concept—"Don't mess with *Israel*."

One of the heaviest rainfalls in U.S. history drenched numerous portions of Texas between June 5-11. More than two feet of rain closed *Bush* Intercontinental Airport for nearly two days. Houston received over twenty-eight inches in a single twenty-four hour period alone. The city was forced to shut down for three days. An estimated 25,000 homes and businesses were damaged or destroyed as well as 50,000 automobiles and trucks.[10]

Allison's ten-day "visit" left Texas in shambles. Twenty-eight counties were declared a disaster area (along with fourteen parishes in Louisiana). The price tag for Tenet's attempt to pressure Israel was $3 billion in Houston and another $4 billion statewide. Once again, the two stories shared front-page news coverage. In the June 13, 2001, issue of *The New York Times*, one article was titled "Flood Tunneled into Houston's Cultural Heart." The second title read, "Two Sides in Mideast Accept U.S. Plan for a Cease-Fire."[11]

On October 2, 2001, President Bush issued his first public statement in favor of a Palestinian State; that same day the national anthrax terrorist attack began in Florida.[12] While America's clinics scrambled for vaccine, the Bush administration assured the world that a Mideast peace plan was just around the corner.

Since the tragic events of 9/11, America has been reaping what she has sown. As *we* pressured Israel to forfeit *her* sovereignty, the identical force has now returned upon *us*. McTernan and Koenig provide these striking parallels:

At the same time the Israeli government was destabilized in late 2000, so was America's.

Almost a year to the day that the intense terrorism began against Israel, America was attacked by the same kind of terrorists.

Jerusalem, the capital of Israel, was under terrorist attack and Washington, D.C., was also under attack by terrorists.

Israel was in a low-grade war with Muslims. America also entered into a low-grade war with Muslims.

Israel's capital, Jerusalem, was attacked by terrorists. America's capital, Washington, D.C., was also attacked by terrorists.

Americans had come under the same fear that the Israelis live under.

Israel's economy suffered because of the terrorism. The American economy fell under the same pressure.

The tourist industry collapsed in Israel because of the terrorism. The tourism industry in America collapsed after the terrorist attacks.[13]

The same principle applies with regard to the many casualties sustained in the Iraqi War. For having slapped Israel's hand whenever she attempted to retaliate against the PLO for over 100 bombings since President Bush declared his "War on Terror," our leaders were forced to contend with a steady arrival of body bags at Dover Air Force Base.

The explanation for this amazing sequence of events can only be found in the Bible. (The *Koran* would be the *last* place to look.) *"Be not deceived; God is not mocked: for whatsoever a man soweth, that shall he also reap"* (Galatians 6:7).

In his epistle to the church in Rome, Paul wrote: *"What advantage then hath the Jew? or what profit is there of circumcision? Much every way: chiefly, because that unto them were committed the oracles of God"* (Romans 3:1-2). It has been said that "Judaism is the stalk on which the rose of Christianity bloomed." As a result of Israel's temporary blindness, the Body of Christ has become the guardian of the "Mosaic tablets." On August 15, 2003, Judge Roy Moore announced on the *O'Reilly Factor* program that he had "no intention" of obeying the federal court order to remove his Ten Commandments monument from Alabama's state judicial building. Millions of potential viewers were unable to watch the *O'Reilly Factor* that night as the largest electrical brownout in American history had pulverized much of the Northeast at 4:00 p.m.

The following day, CNN's *Headline News* channel reported that Israel would comply with the "Road Map to Peace" timetable by surrendering Jericho, Ramallah, Qualqilia and Talkarem to the Palestinian

Authority. The very next story announced that Tropical Storm Erika was headed for Brownsville, Texas! A headline on page 3A of *USA Today* for November 4, 2003, read, "Judicial panel ousts Ala.'s chief justice." A second headline on the same page stated, "Winds knock socks off Northeast; 2 dead, about 1 million lose power."

Because her citizens are beset by ignorance and apathy, America remains a nation under siege. Since our leaders have literally opted to challenge the God of Israel over a real estate matter, the so-called "Road Map to Peace" (announced in April 2003) will inevitably take us over the cliff. In view of this reality, you might want to pull over on the shoulder for a moment to consider the Apostle Paul's admonition.

> *Examine yourselves, whether ye be in the faith; prove your own selves. Know ye not your own selves, how that Jesus Christ is in you, except ye be reprobates?* (II Corinthians 13:5)

If you're not a born-again believer, then repent and accept Jesus Christ as your personal Lord and Saviour. (Romans 10:13) And if I were you, I wouldn't put it off. Things are only going to get worse in the near future for *any* nation that comes against Jerusalem:

> *Then shall the LORD go forth, and fight against those nations, as when he fought in the day of battle. . . .*
> ***And this shall be the plague wherewith the LORD will smite all the people that have fought against Jerusalem;*** *Their flesh shall consume away while they stand upon their feet, and their eyes shall consume away in their holes, and their tongue shall consume away in their mouth.* (Zechariah 14:3,12)

And talk about hurricanes, tornadoes, earthquakes and *tsunamis*—you haven't seen *anything* yet!

> *And the second angel sounded, and as it were a great mountain burning with fire was cast into the sea: and the third part of the sea became blood:*
> *And the third part of the creatures which were in the sea, and had life, died; and the third part of the ships were destroyed. . . .*
> *And the same hour was there a great earthquake, and the tenth part of the city fell, and in the earthquake were slain of men seven thousand: and the remnant were affrighted, and gave glory to the God of heaven.* (Revelation 8:8, 9; 11:13)

If you *are* a Christian, then you had better be sure that you are totally right with God! And yes, I do believe in a *pre-Tribulation Rapture.* I am not worried about entering that seven-year *eruption* of divine wrath because of the blessed *interruption* promised in I Thessalonians 4:16. However, I'm not so sure about a possible *disruption* occurring this side of the *interruption* as a consequence of all the *corruption* sown by the modern Bible movement. *The prevailing oblivion displayed by professing Christians toward America's subtle betrayal of Israeli sovereignty constitutes the paramount symptom of this apostasy.*

The problem in the last days is that the remnant of sincere Bible-believers reflecting "Philadelphia" Church Age values are greatly outnumbered by their apostate "Laodicean" brethren. The danger lies in the fact that the blatant hypocrisy of this carnal/natural majority has given *"great occasion to the enemies of the LORD to blaspheme"* (II Samuel 12:14a). America's subsequent cultural degeneration and abandonment of Israel has now given God the justification to dump *her* upon the junk pile of nations.

One of the best ways to prepare for whatever disruption may be coming is to apply an important principle found in Ezekiel, chapter 9. Before Israel is converted at the end of the Tribulation, God Himself will bring severe chastisement on Jerusalem. He will do so by dispatching six angels, each with *"a slaughter weapon in his hand"* (verse 2). However, one of the "heavenly hit men" will also have a *"writer's inkhorn by his side"* (verse 2). The spiritual principle contained in the Lord's instructions could one day save your life as well as any loved ones who heed your example.

> *And the LORD said unto him, Go through the midst of the city, through the midst of Jerusalem, **and set a mark upon the foreheads of the men that sigh and that cry for all the abominations that be done in the midst thereof.***
>
> *And to the others he said in mine hearing, Go ye after him through the city, and smite: let not your eye spare, neither have ye pity:*
>
> *Slay utterly old and young, both maids, and little children, and women: **but come not near any man upon whom is the mark;** and begin at my sanctuary. Then they began at the ancient men which were before the house.*
>
> *And he said unto them, Defile the house, and fill the courts with the slain: go ye forth. And they went forth, and slew in the city.* (Ezekiel 9:4-7)

Because the Lord's *nature* never changes (Malachi 3:6), He might also be predisposed to preserve the Christians who are found *"sighing and crying"* for *"all the abominations that be done"* in *America* during the closing days of the Church Age. As the song title goes, "Tears are a language God understands." (Isaiah 38:5) After all, He wrote the book on "smart bombs." If God could find the Jews in Goshen (Exodus 8:22-23) and Rahab's house on the wall (Joshua 6:22-23), what makes you think that He couldn't find *you*? Why worry about anthrax when you've got Psalm 91:7 for comfort? *"A thousand shall fall at thy side, and ten thousand at thy right hand; but it shall not come nigh thee."*

Thus the all-important key to physical survival in the days ahead is having the right attitude toward Israel. *"Pray for the peace of Jerusalem: they shall prosper that love thee"* (Psalm 122:6). And yet, herein lies the precise "Catch-22" that confronts the modern Christian in our land; *one cannot be found weeping for America's sin and pending judgment while simultaneously participating in her post-9/11 revival of neo-patriotism.* It is impossible to ride the fence on this one. The question of the hour is as timely today as it was in 1491 BC: *"Then Moses stood in the gate of the camp, and said, Who is on the LORD's side? let him come unto me"* (Exodus 32:26a).

However, because it would be cultural suicide to even *hint* that II Chronicles 7:14 demands humility, repentance and confession of sin, the majority of emotionally correct, "militant" Laodiceans have opted to join with their neighbors and co-workers in singing "God Bless America," waving American flags and sporting those incredible "Power of Pride" bumper stickers.

The Bible clearly warned that this expedient defection would take place in the last days:

> *For the time will come when they will not endure sound doctrine; but after their own lusts shall they heap to themselves teachers, having itching ears;*
> *And they shall turn away their ears from the truth, and shall be turned unto fables.* (II Timothy 4:3)

If you're still undecided about standing with the Lord, just start watching the Weather Channel before retiring each night. (As the humanistic advertisement for the program *StormWatch* puts it, "Experience people at their best and Nature at its worst.") Then pull those covers snugly against your chin. You won't have to worry about anything stirring out there in the dark—*until* the next mile marker is reached on the "Road Map to Peace." *Nighty-night!*

"For when they shall say, Peace and safety; then sudden destruction
cometh upon them, as travail upon a woman with child;
and they shall not escape."
(I Thessalonians 5:3)

2

Goldenah Medinah

"And I will bless them that bless thee,
and curse him that curseth thee . . ."
(Genesis 12:3a)

IN THE AFTERMATH of 9/11, America experienced her greatest revival of patriotism since the dark days of World War II. To date, no amount of petty negativity has been allowed to dampen the spirits of the "pumped" ("Let's roll!" etc.). I mean, so what if our *Pledge of Allegiance* has been declared unconstitutional—*twice*? And why get rattled just because Judge Roy Moore was not allowed to keep a Ten Commandments memorial in his own courthouse? Didn't Russia and Red China do okay without them? And what's the big deal about a sodomite bishop being sanctioned by a mainline "Christian" denomination? Didn't Jesus tell us to love our neighbor?

As previously noted, many Baptist churches have opted to "cash in" on the prevailing phenomenon. Besides, to do otherwise could get you stoned (Acts 7:58). Therefore, it should come as no surprise that these same congregations are woefully ignorant of God's sovereign purpose for the United States of America.

Most of the brethren would say that America was raised up for world evangelism. Although the mission field is certainly a high priority with God, it was not the *primary* reason for our nation's engenderment. The Gospel had already been spread for seventeen centuries before the United States came into being.

Others would contend that America's destiny was to glorify God by unleashing the power of the King James Bible in a land pioneered by born-again Christians. Again, this was definitely *a* purpose but not *the* purpose. There will be plenty of time for the Lord to reclaim His glory in the millennial kingdom, not to mention throughout all eternity. (Ephesians 2:7)

LESS THAN NOTHING

Thanks to Satan, the essential reason for our national existence remains one of the best kept secrets in "Christian America." So many believers spend their lives in front of the "boob tube" that they are seriously out of touch with Biblical truth, especially regarding the last days. Therefore, an appropriate place to begin our search for America's destiny would be the following Scriptures:

> *Behold, the nations are as a drop of a bucket, and are counted as the small dust of the balance: behold, he taketh up the isles as a very little thing. . . .*
> *All nations before him are as nothing; and they are counted to him less than nothing, and vanity.* (Isaiah 40:15,17)

The key to a proper "exegesis" of this passage is the word "All." According to *Webster's Dictionary,* "All" would have to include the United States. (Remember, humility is good for the soul.) However, despite this clear pronouncement, America has experienced a continual flow of unprecedented and unrivaled prosperity. The hymnist, Samuel A. Ward, put it this way—"America! America! God shed His grace on thee."

Yet, even more startling, it appears that America has also been granted divine immunity from judgment. Consider *Roe* v. *Wade* in light of the following statute contained in the Mosaic code: *"So ye shall not pollute the land wherein ye are: for blood it defileth the land: and the land cannot be cleansed of the blood that is shed therein, but by the blood of him that shed it"* (Numbers 35:33). If God could hear the *voice* of Abel's blood crying out to him from the ground (Genesis 4:10), do you suppose he has missed the cries of those 50,000,000 infants who've been butchered in America since 1973?

However, while Cain was immediately cursed for committing a *single* murder (Genesis 4:11), America seems to be getting by with harboring a network of serial killers known as "abortion providers." The explanation for this disconcerting scenario is provided by a pair of qualifying passages in the Old Testament. The first of these "spiritual loopholes" establishes a major dichotomy within the so-called "community of nations," as one race is found to be unequivocally exempt from the "All" of Isaiah 40:17. After a Moabite king solicited Baalam to place a curse on Israel, the hireling prophet prudently declined the contract as his knees began smiting one another at the prospect, stating:

> How shall I curse, whom God hath not cursed? or how shall I defy, whom the LORD hath not defied? For from the top of the rocks I see him, and from the hills I behold him: **lo, the people shall dwell alone, and shall not be reckoned among the nations.** (Numbers 23:8-9)

Thus, while *"All nations before him are as nothing"* (Isaiah 40:17a), Jehovah made it clear that the physical posterity of Abraham, Isaac and Jacob would *"not be reckoned among the nations."*

The second qualifier is God's specific promise to bless *any* nation that would look after Israel. This amazing offer is found in three separate passages:

> Now the LORD had said unto Abram, Get thee out of thy country, and from thy kindred, and from thy father's house, unto a land that I will shew thee: And I will make of thee a great nation, and I will bless thee, and make thy name great; and thou shalt be a blessing: **And I will bless them that bless thee, and curse him that curseth thee:** and in thee shall all families of the earth be blessed. (Genesis 12:1-3)

> Let people serve thee, and nations bow down to thee: be LORD over thy brethren, and let thy mother's sons bow down to thee: **cursed be every one that curseth thee, and blessed be he that blesseth thee.** (Genesis 27:29)

> He couched, he lay down as a lion, and as a great lion: who shall stir him up? **Blessed is he that blesseth thee, and cursed is he that curseth thee.** (Numbers 24:9)

Therefore, though *"All nations before him are as nothing"* and even *"less than nothing"* (Isaiah 40:17), *any* nation wise enough to befriend the *one* nation that *"shall not be reckoned among the nations"* (Numbers 23:9b), would automatically be delivered from global inconsequentiality. Such a nation would be placed in a category by itself. Seen from Jehovah's perspective, an appropriate saying might be, "Any friend of Israel's is a friend of mine."

It is the central thesis of this chapter that America's true destiny cannot be discerned apart from her unique relationship to Israel. The historical fulfillment of Biblical prophecy confirms that America's providential mission was to assist Israel in her transition from *exile* to *restoration.* The United States would serve as the geographic half step between the Diaspora and Zionism. In the late 1800s, as waves of Europe's Jewish émigrés caught their first glimpse of Ellis Island, jubilant cries of "Goldenah Medinah" would fill the air. To a remnant exhausted by eighteen centuries of tenuous subsistence, America was eagerly perceived as a "Golden Land" indeed.

The first phase of America's special relationship with God's covenant people was to provide them with a place to literally catch their breath. Due to a fervent Baptist lobby in Virginia, America became the first nation in history predicated on total religious liberty. Henceforth, pogroms would be outlawed by the glorious Bill of Rights.

This, in turn, enabled another Scriptural truth to impact America's progress. Not only would the United States be blessed for sheltering the Jew, but the Jewish presence would trigger a second blessing as well. King David wrote, *"Pray for the peace of Jerusalem: **they shall prosper that love thee"*** (Psalm 122:6). With the advent of Zionism, thousands of American Jews experienced a renewal of devotion for their ancient homeland. Jeremiah's exhortation, *". . . let Jerusalem come into your mind"* (Jeremiah 51:50b), took on new meaning. The same would apply to Psalm 137:5, *"If I forget thee, O Jerusalem, let my right hand forget her cunning."* As these sons of Abraham reaped the blessings promised in Psalm 122:6, their Gentile neighbors gleaned the residual effect. (Genesis 30:30)

The second stage of our support for Israel commenced with her long-anticipated return to nation status. In the afternoon of May 14, 1948 (the day on which the British mandate over Palestine expired), the *Declaration of the Establishment of the State of Israel* was ratified and signed by members of the National Council gathered at the Tel Aviv Museum. David Ben-Gurion (the Prime Minister-designate) then formally read the historic document proclaiming the existence of a Jewish state called *Israel*, to begin on May 15, 1948. At the stroke of midnight (Tel Aviv time), the British mandate ended and the State of Israel came into being.

Just *eleven* minutes later (at precisely 6:11 p.m., Eastern Standard Time, May 14), President Harry Truman's press secretary, Charlie Ross, issued the following statement:

> This government has been informed that a Jewish state has been proclaimed in Palestine, and recognition has been requested by the provisional government thereof. The United States recognizes the provisional government as the de facto authority of the new State of Israel.

From a Bible perspective, this magnanimous act would constitute America's finest hour. That the first diplomatic recognition of Israel occurred in the *eleventh* minute of her existence was also a sign that the "times of the Gentiles" were drawing to a close, *eleven* being the number in Scripture for *crisis* or *disintegration*, as in American Airlines flight *11* striking the first of the *Twin Towers* on September *11* in New York City (*eleven* letters), the state of New York being the *eleventh* to join the Union, etc. (See: Genesis 42:32; II Kings 25:2; Matthew 20:6, 9; Acts 2:14.)

The following day, Egypt, Syria, Lebanon, Iraq and Transjordan attacked Israel on her Sabbath. On page one of the May 16 edition of *The Palestine Post* (the first issue printed since the proclamation), the main headline—"STATE OF ISRAEL IS BORN"—was accompanied by several others, the two most portentous appearing side-by-side: "Egyptian Air Force Spitfires Bomb Tel Aviv; One Shot Down" and "U.S. Recognizes Jewish State." Two other wars would follow in 1967 and 1973. Throughout these turbulent years, American aid and diplomacy not only enabled Israel to survive, but to attain the status of a nuclear power as well.

Two Kingdoms

Because today's Christians are subjected to a self-indulgent society ("*You* deserve a break today;" "Have it *your* way;" "Has anyone done anything for *you* lately?"etc.), many cannot see the big picture. How else can you explain why so many Baptist ministers were willing to publicly endorse "Brother" Bush while he and his Powell/Rice "tag team" were plotting to dismember the tiny Jewish State?

The main flaw that continues to plague most Baptists is their inability to rightly divide between the *Kingdom of Heaven* and the *Kingdom of God* (II Timothy 2:15). A basic law of logic states, "Things that are different are not the same." The last time I checked, birds were flying in the heavens, not in God.

The *Kingdom of Heaven* is an earthly, tangible domain; the *Kingdom of God* is purely spiritual in nature. While King Jesus will one day rule the universe from a literal throne (Matthew 25:31), He proclaimed to His disciples, *"The kingdom of God is within you"* (Luke 17:21). Paul adds, *"For the kingdom of God is not meat and drink; but righteousness, and peace, and joy in the Holy Ghost"* (Romans 14:17).

When these kingdoms are viewed as distinct entities, another amazing truth will unfold. Contrary to popular opinion, the inspired, infallible Bible is more of a *history* book than a *theological* volume. It is the only "religious" book in the world that dictates the course of entire nations, often before they come into existence. While being passed off as just another treatise on morality, it tells *what* will happen in history, *how* it will take place and *why* it will take place. The "Holy" Koran makes no such revelations.

The theme that occupies the most paper and ink in Scripture is one of *physical kingdoms*, not the "church." After 4,000 years of Old Testament kingdoms (recorded in such books as I and II Samuel, I and II Kings, and I and II Chronicles), the Body of Christ shows up for a 2,000-year interlude, followed by a 1,000-year Jewish kingdom. I have often said that the King James Bible is only two-sevenths Baptist.

When the entire scope of Biblical truth is considered, the "Church Age" appears as a blip on the screen. Handel wrote, "And He shall reign forever and ever." Yet, the eternality of the Saviour's kingdom is not limited to *duration* alone. The prophet wrote, *"Of the **increase** of his government and peace there shall be no end, upon the throne of David, and upon his kingdom, to order it, and to establish it with judgment and with justice from henceforth even forever"* (Isaiah 9:7a). You might keep in mind that the physical universe would be about the only place big enough to contain Abraham's spiritual progeny. (See Genesis 15:5; 22:17; 26:4; Exodus 32:13; Deuteronomy 1:10; 10:22; 28:62; I Chronicles 27:23; Nehemiah 9:23.)

Another insight concerning the difference between the two kingdoms can be gleaned from a simple study of the word "holy." While the religious world has a multiplicity of usage for this word (*holy* father; *holy* church; *holy* Koran; etc.), the Bible renders a radically different perspective. With regard to the hermeneutical principle of the "law of first mention," the first time the word "holy" appears in Scripture the object in question is—*dirt*. *"And he said, Draw not nigh hither: put off thy shoes from off thy feet, for the place whereon thou standest is **holy ground"** (Exodus 3:5).

How "irreligious" can you get? The first thing that the Bible calls "holy" is a parched piece of ground on the Sinaitic peninsula. It is declared to be "holy" because one day a *literal* Jewish king will sit upon a *literal* throne in a *literal* city atop a *literal* mountain to receive the *literal* worship of all who survive a *literal* Tribulation period. Of course, such a prospect will *literally* blow the minds of everyone from the Vatican to the United Nations.

> *And it shall come to pass, that every one that is left of all the nations which came against Jerusalem shall even go up from year to year to worship the King, the LORD of hosts, and to keep the feast of tabernacles.*
>
> *And it shall be, that whoso will not come up of all the families of the earth unto Jerusalem to worship the King, the LORD of hosts, even upon them shall be no rain.*
>
> *And if the family of Egypt go not up, and come not, that have no rain; there shall be the plague, wherewith the LORD will smite the heathen that come not up to keep the feast of tabernacles.*
>
> *This shall be the punishment of Egypt, and the punishment of all nations that come not up to keep the feast of tabernacles.* (Zechariah 14:16-19)

This abstract doctrine of "holy dirt" was certainly understood by Naaman the Syrian after he was miraculously healed of his leprosy by the God of Israel. Before returning to his heathen homeland, the converted captain implored Elisha:

> *Behold, now I know that there is no God in all the earth, but in Israel . . .*
>
> *. . . Shall there not then, I pray thee, be given to thy servant two mules' burden of **earth**? for thy servant will henceforth offer neither burnt-offering nor sacrifice unto other gods, but unto the LORD.* (II Kings 5:15b and 17a)

HEBREW HISTORY

If one must understand the nation of Israel to properly comprehend America, a brief review of Hebrew history is in order. Israel's story begins with a manifestation of God's gracious, unmerited election:

> *For thou art an holy people unto the LORD thy God: the LORD thy God hath chosen thee to be a special people unto himself, above all people that are upon the face of the earth.*
>
> *The LORD did not set his love upon you, nor choose you, because ye were more in number than any people; for ye were the fewest of all people:*
>
> *But because the LORD loved you, and because he would keep the* **oath** *which he had sworn unto your fathers, hath the LORD brought you out with a mighty hand, and redeemed you out of the house of bondmen, from the hand of Pharaoh king of Egypt.* (Deuteronomy 7:6-8)

The "oath" in verse eight is a reference to one of the most important teachings in all the Bible. On no less than *five* separate occasions, the Lord promised to give a piece of real estate to Abraham's descendants (through Isaac and Jacob, that is) with absolutely *no* strings attached.

> *And the LORD said unto Abram, after that Lot was separated from him, Lift up now thine eyes, and look from the place where thou art northward, and southward, and eastward, and westward:*
>
> *For all the* **land** *which thou seest, to thee will I give it, and to thy seed forever.*
>
> *And I will make thy seed as the dust of the earth: so that if a man can number the dust of the earth, then shall thy seed also be numbered.*
>
> *Arise, walk through the* **land** *in the length of it and in the breadth of it; for I will give it unto thee.* (Genesis 13:14-17)

> *In the same day the LORD made a covenant with Abram, saying, Unto thy seed have I given this* **land**, *from the river of Egypt unto the great river, the river Euphrates:* (Genesis 15:18)

> *And I will give unto thee, and to thy seed after thee, the land wherein thou art a stranger, all the* **land** *of Canaan, for an everlasting possession; and I will be their God.* (Genesis 17:8)

> *And the angel of the LORD called unto Abraham out of heaven the second time,*

*And said, By myself have I sworn, saith the LORD, for because thou
hast done this thing, and hast not withheld thy son, thine only son:*

*That in blessing I will bless thee, and in multiplying I will multiply
thy seed as the stars of the heaven, and as the sand which is upon the sea
shore; and thy seed shall possess the **gate of his enemies***;

*And in thy seed shall all the nations of the earth be blessed; because
thou hast obeyed my voice.* (Genesis 22:15-18)

*The LORD God of heaven, which took me from my father's house, and
from the **land** of my kindred, and which spake unto me, and that sware
unto me, saying, Unto thy seed will I give this **land**; he shall send his
angel before thee, and thou shalt take a wife unto my son from thence.*
(Genesis 24:7)

The "international community" has vehemently repudiated these
five unconditional promises to Israel. Yet, you really can't blame them
in light of their professed ideological convictions such as love, peace,
tolerance, brotherhood, etc. For instance, consider *how* Israel obtained
her land in the first place. The "dirt" in question was never known as
"the land of Palestine;" the Bible calls it *"the land of **Canaan**."* (Genesis
17:5) The Lord simply had Joshua "confiscate" it from Canaan's
descendants and give it to Jacob's descendants (like the land that was
transferred from the Patuxets to the Pilgrims). Given the fact that God
"rarely" checks with anyone before doing something, a humanist might
say that the Lord took the land for "selfish motives." *"For the LORD
hath chosen Zion; he hath desired it for his habitation"* (Psalm 132:13).

An indication of how rough things were about to get was given in
the following words: *"And the captain of the LORD'S host said unto
Joshua, Loose thy shoe from off thy foot; **for the place whereon thou
standest is holy.** And Joshua did so"* (Joshua 5:15).

Here we go again! Over 3,000 people get slaughtered on the *first*
piece of "holy ground" (Exodus 32:28) and now another 500,000 will
be destroyed on the *second* piece of "holy ground." Isn't this a strange
way for a "religious book" to get started? And how much more
"intolerant" can you get than *genocide*? *"And they utterly destroyed all
that was in the city, **both man and woman, young and old**, and ox, and
sheep, and ass, with the edge of the sword"* (Joshua 6:21).

Now although God gave the land to Abraham's seed for an *everlasting*
possession, his offer of material blessings and security was *conditional*
on Israel's obedience to the Law. The land was unconditional; the

blessings were conditional. *The importance of this distinction cannot be overstated.*

> *For what nation is there so great, who hath God so nigh unto them, as the LORD our God is in all things that we call upon him for?*
>
> *And what nation is there so great, that hath statutes and judgments so righteous as all this law, which I set before you this day?* (Deuteronomy 4:7-8)

> *The LORD shall cause thine enemies that rise up against thee to be smitten before thy face: they shall come out against thee one way, and flee before thee seven ways.*
>
> *The LORD shall command the blessing upon thee in thy storehouses, and in all that thou settest thine hand unto; and he shall bless thee in the land which the LORD thy God giveth thee.*
>
> *The LORD shall establish thee an holy people unto himself, as he hath sworn unto thee, **if thou shalt keep the commandments of the LORD thy God, and walk in his ways.***
>
> *And all people of the earth shall see that thou art called by the name of the LORD; and they shall be afraid of thee.* (Deuteronomy 28:7-10)

The shallow Christian who ridicules dispensational truth will note that Israel's singular mandate for national survival was strict obedience to the Mosaic Law. (See also: Deuteronomy 17:18-19; 15:5; 8:3; 5:30-33; 6:4-7; 4:2 and 18:18-19.) Apart from latent typology, there is not one "sermon" in the Old Testament about "looking forward to the cross" (as New Testament believers "look *back* to the cross"). *This is why the apostles themselves were completely oblivious to the death, burial, and resurrection of Jesus Christ as late as the night before it occurred.* (Luke 18:34 and 24:11; I Corinthians 2:8; Colossians 1:25-27)

Because the Bible is a supernatural history book, the Author "went out on a limb" by announcing *ahead of time* that the Jew would eventually break his part of the *conditional* covenant. Consequently, Israel's penalty for *rejection* of the *law* was *ejection* from the *land.*

> *I call heaven and earth to witness against you this day, that ye shall soon utterly perish from off the land whereunto ye go over Jordan to possess it; ye shall not prolong your days upon it, but shall utterly be destroyed.*

And the LORD shall scatter you among the nations, and ye shall be left few in number among the heathen, whither the LORD shall lead you. (Deuteronomy 4:26-27)

*As the nations which the LORD destroyeth before your face, so shall ye perish; **because ye would not be obedient unto the voice of the LORD your God.*** (Deuteronomy 8:20)

*Hear, O earth: behold, I will bring evil upon this people, even the fruit of their thoughts, **because they have not hearkened unto my words, nor to my law, but rejected it.*** (Jeremiah 6:19)

THE DIASPORA

Israel's first dispersion was to Babylon in 586 B.C. and lasted seventy years. Their later exile was global and would extend for nineteen centuries. Isaiah wrote:

*And it shall come to pass in that day, that the LORD shall set his hand **again the second time** to recover the remnant of his people, which shall be left, from Assyria, and from Egypt, and from Pathros, and from Cush, and from Elam, and from Shinar, and from Hamath, and from the islands of the sea.*
*And he shall set up an ensign for the nations, and shall assemble the outcasts of Israel, **and gather together the dispersed of Judah from the four corners of the earth.*** (Isaiah 11:11-12)

The second dispersion was occasioned by Israel's rejection of her national Messiah. Again, because the Bible is primarily an "inspired history book," the Lord revealed to Moses:

I will raise them up a Prophet from among their brethren, like unto thee, and will put my words in his mouth; and he shall speak unto them all that I shall command him.
And it shall come to pass, that whosoever will not hearken unto my words which he shall speak in my name, I will require it of him. (Deuteronomy 18:18-19)

When confronted before Pilate's judgment hall with the ultimate watershed of their entire existence, the Jews gave two fatal replies that would trigger nearly 2,000 years of surreal consequences: *"Then answered all the people, and said, His **blood** will be on us, and on our children"* (Matthew 27:25), and, *"The chief priests answered, We have no king but **Cæsar"*** (John 19:15b).

It is at this point in our study that things become more than a little heavy. Not only are the unregenerate incapable of accepting what happened next (I Corinthians 2:14), but the typical Laodicean apostate as well (II Timothy 4:3).

First of all, the "God of *Love*" that all the beaming "born-againers" like to rap about down at the local "Christian" bookstore, wanted rebellious Israel to know exactly how He felt about them—*". . . my soul shall **abhor** you"* (Leviticus 26:30b). The definition for "abhor" in the 1828 *American Dictionary of the English Language* reads: "to hate extremely, or with contempt; to loathe, detest or abominate." (See also: Psalm 2:12; Proverbs 6:16; Ecclesiastes 3:8; Malachi 1:3; John 3:36; Romans 9:13 and I John 2:15.)

They were also notified that He would amplify their judgment sevenfold (Leviticus 26:24) while tracking them down like wild animals (i.e., "You may run, but you can't hide").

> *Behold, I will send for many fishers, saith the LORD, and they shall fish them; and after will I send for many hunters, and they shall hunt them from every mountain, and from every hill, and out of the holes of the rocks.*
>
> *For mine eyes are upon all their ways: they are not hid from my face, neither is their iniquity hid from mine eyes.* (Jeremiah 16:16-17)

Other "delicate" prophecies would include: *"And ye shall eat the flesh of your sons and the flesh of your daughters shall ye eat."* (Leviticus 26:29); *"And I will . . . cast your carcases upon the carcases of your idols . . ."* (Leviticus 26:30b); and *"they shall be an execration . . ."* (Jeremiah 44:12d).

Next, because the Lord's innate holiness requires a righteous pretext for judgment (Psalm 51:4), He "fixed" things so the Jew could not obey his own Law while in exile. *"For the children of Israel shall abide many days without a king, and without a prince, and without a sacrifice, and without an image, and without an ephod, and without teraphim"* (Hosea 3:4).

After being told what would happen if they disobeyed the Law (Deuteronomy 28; Leviticus 26; Ezekiel 20:1-3), the Jews woke up one morning to discover that they would now have to violate their very oracles in order to survive. Like the devil said, *"Skin for skin, yea, all that a man hath will he give for his life"* (Job 2:4). For example, God had expressly forbidden His nation to be under Gentile authority. (Deuteronomy 17:14-15) Another statute prohibited them from intermarriage with the heathen. (Nehemiah 13:26) They were also obligated to offer animal sacrifices on the altar before their temple in Jerusalem. The only way out of their dilemma was to be cleansed from the *old* covenant by coming under a *new* one. This, unfortunately, they adamantly refused to do. The Bible makes it clear that Israel's problem was a *heart* problem:

> *Therefore speak unto them, and say unto them, Thus saith the Lord GOD; Every man of the house of Israel that setteth up his idols in his heart, and putteth the stumblingblock of his iniquity before his face, and cometh to the prophet; I the LORD will answer him that cometh according to the multitude of his idols;*
>
> *That I may take the house of Israel in their own heart, because they are all estranged from me through their idols.* (Ezekiel 14:4-5)

Because the Lord is *"a discerner of the thoughts and intents of the heart"* (Hebrews 4:12b), He provided Israel with a couple of convenient Scriptures to justify their rejection of His Son. While the Lord commanded Moses, *"And thou shalt say unto Pharaoh, thus saith the LORD, **Israel is my son, even my firstborn**"* (Exodus 4:22), He added in Isaiah, *"I the LORD have called thee in righteousness, and will hold thine hand, and will keep thee, and give thee for a covenant of the people, **for a light of the Gentiles**"* (Isaiah 42:6). So the Bible "obviously" taught that God's true son and light to the Gentiles was *Israel* and not Jesus, etc.

Thus, with His own alibi firmly in hand, the "God of Love" proceeded to lower the boom! One of several game plans that He followed may be viewed in Deuteronomy 28:

> *And ye shall be left few in number, whereas ye were as the stars of heaven for multitude; because thou wouldest not obey the voice of the LORD thy God.*
>
> *And the LORD shall scatter thee among all people, from the one end of the earth even unto the other; and there thou shalt serve other gods, which neither thou nor thy fathers have known, even wood and stone.*
>
> *And among these nations shalt thou find no ease, neither shall the sole of thy foot have rest: but the LORD shall give thee there a trembling heart, and failing of eyes, and sorrow of mind:*

And thy life shall hang in doubt before thee; and thou shalt fear day and night, and shalt have none assurance of thy life:

In the morning thou shalt say, Would God it were even! and at even thou shalt say, Would God it were morning! for the fear of thine heart wherewith thou shalt fear, and for the sight of thine eyes which thou shalt see. (Deuteronomy 28: 62, 64-67)

By now it should be evident that the most hateful, bigoted, anti-Semitic literature ever written was penned by *Jews*—not by Nazis, Catholics or Muslims. No "hate literature" by *anyone* could match Ezekiel, chapters 16 and 23; Deuteronomy, chapters 28, 29, 32; and Leviticus, chapter 26. Less than half of the anti-Semitic material between Genesis and Malachi would include:

Exodus 32:7-10; Numbers 16:19-22, 44, 45; 21:5-6; 14:11-12; Deuteronomy 9:4-8, 12-14, 19-20; 29:22-28; 30:16-19; 31:16-18, 27; 32:16-25; Isaiah 1:4, 10, 15; 2:6; 3:1-4, 8, 25-26; Jeremiah 5:29-31; 6:8, 11-12, 19; 7:13-16, 20, 28; 8:1-3, 10, 13; 9:11, 22; 11:7-10, 14, 17, 22; Ezekiel 2:1-4; 5:5-11, 16-17; 7:8-9, 23, 25; 8:18; 14:12-16, 16:35-43; 20:6, 8, 13, 16, 21, 27, 33-34, 45-48; 21:1-5; 22:19-22, 30-31; 24:6, 9, 12, 14, 21; Amos 3:1, 3, 14-15; 4:6-8, 11-12; 5:12, 16, 21, 23, 27; 6:7-9, 11; 7:16-17; 9:7-10; Micah 3:1-4, 8-9.[1]

The Bible teaches that God's judgment upon his own people was intended as a sober object lesson for the Gentiles. (Romans 11:20-21) Not only would the heathen take note when Israel was being blessed (Psalm 126:2), but also when she was passing under the rod:

Even all nations shall say, Wherefore hath the LORD done thus unto this land? what meaneth the heat of this great anger?

Then man shall say, Because they have forsaken the covenant of the LORD GOD of their fathers, which he made with them when he brought them forth out of the land of Egypt. (Deuteronomy 29:24-25)

With the destruction of Jerusalem in 70 A.D. by Emperor Titus, the Jews began an odyssey of death and misery that would last for nearly two millennia. Their days became darker than your nights. The following list of atrocities represents a mere sample of the voluminous historical record.

A.D. 600: Jews were forced to "convert" to the Moslem faith (Antioch) or get killed. There were only *ten* Jewish families left in Antioch in 1928.

A.D. 850: They were heavily taxed in Iraq.

A.D. 1050: The synagogues in Tripoli were converted into mosques. In 1939, there were only four Jewish families left in Tripoli.

A.D. 1190: Jews committed suicide rather than surrender to the Crusaders (in York, England). Eighteen were killed, in Lincoln, on murder charges.

A.D. 1281: In Exter (England), the synods forbade Jews to hold public office; 5,000 were expelled from England and driven out to Flanders and France.

A.D. 1321: Jews in France were buried, dead or alive, in pits.

A.D. 1333: All the synagogues in Baghdad were looted and then destroyed.

A.D. 1349-1360: All Jews were expelled from Hungary; they were expelled from the Arimea (1016, 1350), from Portugal (1497), France (1306, 1394, 1420), and also from Austria (1421) and Sardinia (1492).

A.D. 1355-1391: Fifty-thousand were murdered in Palms (Spain), more than 12,000 were murdered by mobs in other parts of Spain.

A.D. 1388: No Jews were allowed to settle in Strasbourg. The Austrian government slaughtered 100,000 Jews in the fourteenth century alone. After being blamed for the Black Death, forty-six Jewish communities in Germany were razed to the ground.

A.D. 1399: Thousands of Jews were tortured and burned alive in Posen (Poland).

A.D. 1391-1471: Over 40,000 Jews murdered during Catholic pogroms in Italy.

A.D. 1420: An entire Jewish community was annihilated in Toulouse, France.

A.D. 1494: Thousands of Jews restricted to ghettoes in Cracow.

A.D. 1500: All Jews expelled from the Rhineland. The same occurred in Genoa, Cremona and Naples.[2]

One of the best types of the Jew in Scripture is Cain—the first man who thought he could merit God's favor *without a blood sacrifice.* (Genesis 4:1-9) His prideful disobedience gave rise to the expression "trying to get blood from a turnip."

Before Cain *murdered his brother* (John 1:11) he was living off the land. However, after Abel's blood hit the ground, Cain was forced to become the world's first "city slicker" (Genesis 4:17; Isaiah 14:21). He could no longer earn a living as a farmer or shepherd because *something went wrong with a piece of dirt.*

As a "marked man" (Genesis 4:14), Cain became a *fugitive*; one who fled from the *Torah* (the Law). For the heinous crime of *murdering his brother*, Cain was also condemned to spend the rest of his existence as a *vagabond*; one who wandered around in a "Diaspora" (in *circles*).

The only "positive" note in our story is that Cain received God's personal assurance of *supernatural preservation.* (Genesis 4:15) Henceforth, he would be like that burning bush that could not be extinguished.

THE HOLOCAUST

The apex of "Cain's" suffering was the infamous Holocaust of World War II. The genocide of 6,000,000 helpless victims has become the definitive manifestation of man's inhumanity to his fellow man. (I can *still* recall my own revulsion after visiting the Auschwitz death camp as a teenager in 1971.)

However, there is a major "sticky wicket" issue that must be addressed—Who *really* authorized the "Final Solution?" Don't look for any insights from the typical modern Christian, as the topic is too politically incorrect for him to handle. The following passage contains a most unwelcome implication:

> *Therefore thus saith the LORD of hosts; Because ye have not heard my words,*
>
> *Behold, I will send and take all the families of the north, saith the LORD, and* **Nebuchadrezzar the king of Babylon, my servant,** *and will bring them against this land, and against the inhabitants thereof, and against all these nations round about,* **and will utterly destroy them, and make them an astonishment, and an hissing, and perpetual desolations.**
> (Jeremiah 25:8-9) [See also Jeremiah 27:6, 43:10 and Ezekiel 29:19-21.]

Now if God raised up Nebuchadnezzar to bring the Jew to "perpetual desolations," *what makes you think he didn't do the same thing with Adolf Hitler?* Were they not sufficiently warned, *"And if ye will not yet for all this hearken unto me, then I will punish you* **seven times more** *for your sins"* (Leviticus 26:18)? Besides, the Jews were burning their own children long before they entered Hitler's crematoriums: *"And they have built the high places of Tophet, which is in the valley of the son of Hinnom,* **to burn their sons and their daughters in the fire;** *which I commanded them not, neither came it into my heart"* (Jeremiah 7:31).

Despite these horrific judgments, the Jew refused to repent. Nellie Sachs, a Jewish poet who won the Nobel Prize for Literature in 1966, believed that the smoke from the stacks of Auschwitz and Treblinka (where 3,000,000 Jews were cremated) just may have been a "ray of sunlight." Rather than bow the knee, the Jew preferred to interpret the curses pronounced against him as proof of divine favor!

> O the chimney's freedomway for Jeremiah and Job's dust!
> Who devised you and laid you stone upon stone; the road
> for refugees of smoke?
> O the chimneys on the ingeniously devised habitations of death!
> When Israel's body drifted as smoke through the air,
> Was welcomed by a star; the chimney sweep—
> A star turned black, **or was it a ray of sunlight**?[3]

The problem with Nobel Prize winners is their willful ignorance of the only "history book" in the world that predicts the future with infallible accuracy. The ovens of the Third Reich were merely another fulfillment of Bible prophecy:

> *And the people shall be as the **burnings** of lime: as thorns cut up shall they be **burned** in the fire.* (Isaiah 33:12)

The party line developed among modern Jewish apologists was that "persevering Israel" would eventually become the world's messiah: that "light of the Gentiles" from Isaiah 42:6. A sample of their nonsense follows:

> The purpose of the Dispersion (A.D. 70-A.D. 1948) was for the purpose of Israel teaching *monotheism* to the Gentiles and to teach *them* about the "Brotherhood of Man." **It had nothing to do with** *God punishing them for anything*.
> *Genesis is a myth.* The Jew *enriches* each civilization that he enters, and that civilization is impoverished when *he* leaves it. In the end, their own unique way of thinking about *themselves* produced their history. Israel's history will end by them converting the world to an international brotherhood and the Messianic AGE of "man" on earth. . . .
> How is one to explain the miracle of survival in Jewish history? How did it happen? By what *inner strength* and through what good fortune? Their will to live; their *"elan vital,"* as a people, surged powerfully within them . . . they managed to outlive their enemies who sat in the sun. The most powerful preserver was their religion, which was a synthesis of every group drive, social ideal, and cultural striving of the Jewish people.[4]

However, for the ultimate exposé of Jewish recalcitrance, consider the following poem by Michael Pinto of Flushing, New York, *age eleven*. The theme of this amazing poem reveals why Israel today, *after twenty-six devastating centuries of sorrow, reproach, exile, torture and death,* is no closer to the God of Abraham, Isaac and Jacob than she was in II Kings 17, more than seven hundred years before her Messiah was born.

> Jewish families gather around, while Germans come to run their town.
> Who used to have shops, now have nothing.
> Who used to have families, now have nothing.
> People stripped of what they owned; Germans treating Jews like dirt.
> Who had money, now have nothing.
> Who had houses, now have nothing.
> People shouting for help; people hiding their precious possessions.
> Who had clothing, now have nothing.
> Who had food, now have nothing.
> German boots banging on the cement; mirroring
> the beating of people's hearts.
> Who had hope, now have nothing. [Deuteronomy 28:65,67]
> Who had friends, now have nothing. [Deuteronomy 28:53-56]
> But there is **one** thing the Germans couldn't take!
> That is **pride** in who **we** are! [Romans 2:19-28]
> Who have nothing, still have **pride**.
> [Proverbs 16:18, 29:23; Ezekiel 28:17]
> Who has **pride** [Satan: Isaiah 14:12-14],
> now has **faith**. [Deuteronomy 32:20, 28][5]

You have just reviewed the religious manifesto of a secular humanist. The only thing more accurate than Michael's naive poem is the following inspired statement by the wisest man who ever lived: *"Pride goeth before destruction, and an haughty spirit before a fall."* (Proverbs 16:18)

With these incredible egotistical fantasies serving as spiritual "shock absorbers," you will be better prepared to examine the scariest verse in all of Scripture. While it is bad enough to think of Adolph Hitler as an unwitting "servant of the Lord," there is something far more bizarre than even this. It has to do with God's *attitude* throughout the Jewish holocaust.

Have you ever read *The Diary of Anne Frank*? Well, keep the pathos of her ordeal in mind as you read the following bloodcurdling statement:

> *And it shall come to pass, that as the* LORD *rejoiced over you to do you good, and to multiply you;* **so the** LORD **will rejoice over you to destroy you, and to bring you to nought**; *and ye shall be plucked from off the land whither thou goest to possess it.* (Deuteronomy 28:63)

Solomon presented the same ghastly theme in the opening chapter of Proverbs:

> *Because I have called, and ye refused; I have stretched out my hand, and no man regarded;*
> *But ye have set at nought all my counsel, and would none of my reproof:*
> ***I also will laugh at your calamity; I will mock when your fear cometh;***
> *When your fear cometh as desolation, and your destruction cometh as a whirlwind; when distress and anguish cometh upon you.*
> *Then shall they call upon me, but I will not answer; they shall seek me early, but they shall not find me:*
> *For that they hated knowledge, and did not choose the fear of the* LORD:
> *They would none of my counsel: they despised all of my reproof.*
> *Therefore shall they eat of the fruit of their own way, and be filled with their own devices.* (Proverbs 1:24-31)

Sadly, Anne's ancestors missed the Lord's personal admonition:

> *O that there were such an heart in them, that they would **fear** me, and keep all my commandments always, that it might be well with them, and with their children for ever!* (Deuteronomy 5:29)

ROME USURPS ISRAEL

When the Jewish mob cried out, *"We have no king but Cæsar";* the Lord replied, "You've got a deal." History confirms that *Roman* Catholic popes and kings have killed more Jews than anyone else.

It all began with the fall of the Roman Empire in 476 A.D. With Caesar having been run out of town by the barbarians, the Roman bishop "humbly" stepped forward to fill the vacuum of leadership. In similar fashion, the cardinals replaced the Roman Senate; the archbishops became the imperial governors; the bishops and metropolitans were the new provincial governors; and, the Catholic priests became the Roman *"civitas."*

The entire framework of the Roman Catholic Church is a carbon copy of ancient Rome, including the "vestal virgins" (replaced by the nuns). Absolutely *nothing* can be found that resembles the true New Testament Church as laid out in the book of Acts. This is one of the main reasons why Catholics have been discouraged from reading their own "Bible."

There are many obvious indications that the pope considers himself a literal king in the tradition of Constantine. His "pastorate" is inaugurated with an ostentatious *coronation.* He *rules* from a *throne* in the Vatican *state.* He carries a *scepter* and wears a *crown.* The "faithful" *kiss* his toes and hand. He no more emulates Paul's example (I Corinthians 11:1) than do Michael Jackson or Jesse Jackson. He also claims the identical title of Constantine the Great—*Pontifex Maximus* (chief priest of the Roman state religion).

The pope is able to masquerade as a religious politician because the "Holy See" has been successful in usurping Israel's role in the Kingdom of Heaven. *With the Jews removed from their land, the emerging Roman Catholic monstrosity was free to take Israel's place by misappropriating the entire Old Testament.* Though the *Levitical* priesthood was gone, "Father" O'Riley would be only too happy to keep those sacrifices going down at the local Catholic parish. And the *Roman* priest would even throw in Saturday night Bingo as a bonus.

Rome's focus on the material Kingdom of Heaven also enabled the pope to advance "God's work" by employing the various military campaigns in the Hebrew Old Testament. Millions of Christians, Jews and Muslims were subsequently dispatched by the "sword of the Lord." (Judges 7:18)

The Scriptural doctrine of Premillennialism was conveniently trashed by Augustine's *City of God.* According to him, Rome was the "New Jerusalem" and the Kingdom was *definitely* underway despite a few plagues, famines, incursions and other momentary distractions. ("Pay no attention to that man behind the curtain.")

Now in order for the pope to retain his bogus dominion, he would have to insure that the rightful owners were eliminated. ("Dead men tell no tales," etc.) And so, while "His Holiness" was busy exterminating all the Bible-believing Christians within reach, he also spent considerable energy persecuting the Jews. Pope Gregory IX ordered all copies of the *Talmud* confiscated under pain of death. The Roman Catholic Fourth Latern Council decreed that all Jews must wear the "Star of David." Pope Gregory VI forbade "Christians" to work for Jews. Pope Paul IV stated that all Jews in Rome had to be "ghettoized."[6]

THE DARK AGES

So, try to guess how rough it was going to get on the European theater with the Bible expelled and the pope killing Christians and Jews alike. Do you suppose the Lord had a sufficient alibi for judgment? As most Bible teachers believe the seven churches of Revelation (chapters 2 and 3) give a panoramic view of the entire Church Age, a number of significant insights to medieval "Christianity" can be gleaned from John's epistle to the Thyatirans. The predominant theme of the "Dark Ages" is *Death, Death, Death* and *more Death*.

> *And I gave her space to repent of her fornication; and she repented not. Behold, I will cast her into a bed, and them that commit adultery with her into great tribulation, except they repent of their deeds.*
> *And I will **kill** her children with **death**; and all the churches shall know that I am he which searcheth the reins and hearts: and I will give unto every one of you according to your works.* (Revelation 2:21-23)

By every indication imaginable, *"the Son of God, who hath his eyes like unto a flame of fire"* (Revelation 2:18), was determined to *kill* Jezebel's children with *death!* Over fifty percent of Europe's population would die before their thirteenth birthday. Children in the Dark Ages were not even given names until they had reached the age of seven. The life expectancy for females was only twenty-four years; males being slightly higher.

The leading causes of death were starvation and disease, with the former facilitating the latter. The Continent's "famine formula" called for at least one year in every four. With the disappearance of iron, peasants had to struggle with primitive wooden plows. Weather patterns became increasingly unpredictable. Seasons of drought would be followed by severe flooding: mildly dry winters by bitterly cold and wet ones. The skeletons exhumed from this period would tell their own tale of misery and woe. Abnormally worn teeth gave evidence of a diet that included grass as a major staple for years on end. (Daniel 4:32) Bark, roots and even white clay served as delicacies for others. Bones were often deformed by rickets. The black horse of Revelation 6:5 and 6 was a pervasive foe indeed. *"A measure of wheat for a penny, and three measures of barley for a penny,"* was beyond the reach of most. In *A World Lit Only by Fire*, author William Manchester relates how hunger drove some impoverished peasants to sell the very clothes off their backs for food, remaining naked year round as a result.[7] The occasional traveler or stranger was at high risk of being killed and cannibalized. Gallows were often dismantled in a frenzy to provide warm, raw meat.

Disease followed hard on the heels of famine. Bodies already weakened by hunger and toil were no match for a myriad of germs and infection. Dysentery, epilepsy, malaria, tuberculosis, influenza, diphtheria, scurvy, typhoid, scabies, scrofula, impetigo, and a host of other maladies were as common then as the common cold is today. Bathing was unheard of. Man and beast lived under the same roof. In a time when neither forks nor handkerchiefs existed, table guests were reminded to blow their noses with the hand that held the knife, rather than the one holding the food. Having outlawed the Bible with its numerous medical facts— *"the life of all flesh is the blood thereof"* (Leviticus 17:14b); *and he shall put a covering upon his upper lip, and shall cry, Unclean, unclean"* (Leviticus 13:45b), etc.—would-be physicians were reduced to primitive witch doctors. Barbara Tuchman writes that ringworm was treated by washing the scalp with a boy's urine, gout by a plaster of goat dung mixed with rosemary and honey. Believing that latrine attendants were immune, many patients visited the public "outhouse" on the theory that foul odors were efficacious.[8] Manchester graphically illustrates the overall repulsiveness of the age with the popular story of a peasant's first (and nearly last) visit to one of the few cities in existence. Passing by a row of perfume shops, the poor fellow fainted at the unfamiliar scent and could not be revived until a shovel of excrement was held under his nose![9]

These dire conditions were only exacerbated by a foreboding isolation. Dark Age peasants could not even avail themselves of the adage: "Misery loves company." Approximately 75 million of them (80 to 90 percent of Europe's entire population) subsisted in primitive villages of fewer than a hundred people scattered anywhere from fifteen to twenty-five miles apart.

The limitations of their benighted facilities bordered on the incredulous. Due to the absence of calendars and geography, the average person never knew *where* he was or *when* he was. (He barely knew *if* he was.) Adults could not discern their own age. Few ventured more than twenty-five miles from the place of their birth for fear of getting lost. (Remember Hansel and Gretel's breadcrumbs?) As to "Who's afraid of the big, bad wolf?," the answer in the Middle Ages was, "Just about *everyone!*" (Ditto: "Lions and tigers and bears! Oh, my!") Most hamlets were situated in the Black Forest and other heavily wooded areas that stretched from Russia to the Atlantic. Peasants lived in constant terror of bears, boars, bandits, wolves, witches, trolls, hobgoblins and demons. "Tree huggers" were nowhere to be found. Since the devil's darkness is the only alternative to the light of God's word, the "Black Forest" of Germany was certainly given an appropriate name. According to Tacitus's *de Germania*, Julius Caesar interviewed a team of explorers who had trekked through the Black Forest from Poland to Gaul. They testified to having completed their two-month journey without a single glimpse of sunlight![10] Such a world harbored a criminal element far in excess of Robin's "Merry Men." Vlad the Impaler, Prince of Walachin (we know him as Count Dracula, or "son of the devil"), impaled, skinned, strangled, boiled and roasted over 50,000 people during his ten-year Romanian reign of terror from 1466 to 1476!

Without the precious Word of God, life continued to be a cheap commodity. Capital punishment could be meted out for over a hundred different crimes. According to Tuchman, the mainstay of atrocity tales occurred on May 28, 1358, when a band of peasants in revolt captured a French knight and his family. The contemporary account declares that the unfortunate knight was "killed and roasted on a spit before the eyes of his wife and children. Then, after ten or twelve of them violated the lady, they forced her to eat some of her husband's flesh and then killed her."[11] Unbridled sin would *have* to be rampant in an age depicted by darkness. (John 3:19) One historian summarized, "Sodomy was frequent, prostitution general and adultery almost universal."[12] As late as the sixteenth century, Andreas Musculus, a Lutheran minister, despaired, "Nobody cares about heaven or hell; nobody gives a thought to either God or the Devil."[13]

Having merely surveyed the general character of this period, time and space preclude an extended review of the really big killing fields of Thyatira. A short list would include the Islamic and Viking invasions, the "Holy Wars" (including the insane Children's Crusade), the Hundred Years War, and the Black Death that wiped out one-third of Europe's population in the fourteenth century alone. Manchester concludes, ". . . the portrait which emerges is a mélange of incessant warfare, corruption, lawlessness, obsession with strange myths, and an almost impenetrable mindlessness."[14]

In consequence of Rome's attempt to arrogate the Jewish Kingdom of Heaven, the curse of Genesis 12:3 fell upon her unsuspecting parishioners. For having seduced *"the kings of the earth"* to join her in perennial pogroms against Abraham's seed, *"the great whore's"* own offspring were *"made drunk with the wine of her fornication."* (Revelation 12:1-2) Preferring a *papal toe* to a *nail-scarred foot*, Europe's benighted inhabitants got to experience the "joy" of a Satanic Millennium. Messing with that "burning bush" had consigned untold millions to "a world lit only by fire."

THE "JEWISH CONSPIRACY"

Throughout the protracted havoc of the Dark Ages, the Jew became the designated scapegoat. His God-given propensity to excel in the financial arena only facilitated that belief. Of course, the Vatican has been instrumental in the majority of anti-Semitic slander with *The Protocols of the Learned Elders of Zion* remaining the definitive forgery.

This is not to say that certain Jews have *not* been involved with conspiratorial intrigue. Karl Marx and Leon Trotsky were Jews; however, Lenin, Stalin, Tito, Mao and Castro were not! The enduring image of "Hymie" as the "ubiquitous revolutionary" has been fostered by every pope in history. You could call it "job security."

On the other hand, how would *you* be inclined to act if *your* race was under constant subjection by the powers that be? To the average Jew, "Christianity" has been equated primarily with Roman Catholicism. So why should anyone be surprised to discover that some Jews may have plotted to overthrow their "Christian" tormentors? (If I'm not mistaken, a bunch of Gentiles did the same thing in 1776, and with a lot less provocation!)

However, the party line that Jewish international bankers have controlled the world for centuries is a myth. The Rothschilds are to banking what Marx was to Communism. Although the House of

Rothschild has exerted considerable influence on the banking industry, so has the "House of Rockefeller." J.P. Morgan and Andrew Carnegie were Gentiles—so is Bill Gates, the richest man in the world!

The greatest argument against the theory that world revolution has been financed essentially by a giant "Jewish Conspiracy" is contained in the Jewish Old Testament itself. In one of those numerous "anti-Semitic" passages, Israel was told exactly what would happen if she violated her covenant. The promise in Deuteronomy 15:6 would be reversed:

> *The stranger that is within thee shall get up above thee very high; and thou shalt come down very low.*
> ***He shall lend to thee, and thou shalt not lend to him****: he shall be the head, and thou shalt be the tail.* (Deuteronomy 28:43-44)

Could that possibly have been worded any clearer? The bottom line concerning Jews and money is simple. *God gave them unique abilities in the area of finance to ensure their survival in the Diaspora.* (Malachi 3:16) These gifts were never designed to let the "tail wag the dog". (Deuteronomy 28:44) Their sole purpose was to keep the "eternal flame" burning. (Genesis 31:12; Exodus 12:36; Matthew 2:11-14; Revelation 11:6) And given the nature of his transitory existence, a particular expertise in precious stones enabled the Jew to always "travel light." (Exodus 12:11) Predictably, these endowments were a constant source of irritation to their Catholic antagonists.

With his arrival in *Goldenah Medinah*, the Jew reached his full potential down on Wall Street. (Much of this wealth would later find its way to the fledgling state of Israel.)

The Jew is often criticized for his excessive materialism (although the average American synagogue *pales* in comparison to the growing trend among extravagant Independent Baptist church auditoriums). While gold will take the place of concrete in the New Jerusalem, the unfortunate reality is that the Jewish exile found his security in "filthy lucre." And old habits are hard to break.

It is also regrettable that America's decline in morality (caused by apostate Christianity) has increased the potential for profits from sin, whether legalized or otherwise. This explains the significant percentage of Jews in Hollywood, pornography and even illicit crime. A pastor friend of mine who grew up in a Jewish neighborhood in Brooklyn, New York, told me that the initial reason so many Jews entered vaudeville was to sublimate traditional Gentile anti-Semitism to laughter. ("You see, we're not such bad people after all.")

As for a concerted "Jewish conspiracy against Christianity," most Baptist churches are split by either backslidden or lost members, not Jews. Although the early church was beset by Jewish opposition (I Thessalonians 2:14-16), Jews in America love money more than they hate Bible-believing Christians. Though evangelical leaders engaged in vice-related litigation often find themselves confronted by a typical Jewish lawyer from the satanic American Civil Liberties Union (A.C.L.U.), his underlying "motive" is generally his paycheck. Yet, a few like Alan Dershowitz are obviously more consumed with the damnable tenets of secular humanism.

Whatever the degree of Jewish complicity in conspiratorial matters, a *safe* rule of thumb for Christians to follow is that amazing admonition in Paul's epistle to the Romans: *"As concerning the gospel, they are enemies for your sakes: but as touching the election, they are beloved for the fathers' sakes"* (Romans 11:28).

THE BALFOUR DECLARATION

When Frederick the Great asked a Christian if he could offer any proof that the Bible was inspired, the humble believer gave a simple two-word answer: "The Jew." According to that amazing "history book" ("disguised" as a religious book), the Jew would one day return to his land. *"Therefore say, Thus saith the Lord GOD; I will even gather you from the people, and assemble you out of the countries where ye have been scattered, and I will give you the land of Israel"* (Ezekiel 11:17).

The "history book" also recorded *when* this would occur according to the Bible's own timetable: *"But, beloved, be not ignorant of this one thing, that one day is with the Lord as a thousand years, and a thousand years as one day"* (II Peter 3:8). The application, with regard to Israel's return, is found in Hosea 6:1-2: *"Come, and let us return unto the LORD: for he hath torn, and he will heal us; he hath smitten, and he will bind us up. **After two days will he revive us: in the third day he will raise us up, and we shall live in his sight.**"*

In 1967, Israel fought and won its second major war against Arab coalition forces. This time, however, the spoils included the nation's ancient capital of Jerusalem. Do you think it mere coincidence that the name of the war came to be called *The Six-Day War*? (Hebrews 4:1-9; Revelation 20:2)

The Bible implies that Israel's return from exile would be even more spectacular than her original exodus from Egypt.

> *Therefore, behold, the days come, saith the LORD, that it shall no more be said, The LORD liveth, that brought up the children of Israel out of the land of Egypt; But, The LORD liveth, that brought up the children of Israel from the land of the north, and from all the lands whither he had driven them: and I will bring them again into their land that I gave unto their fathers.* (Jeremiah 16:14-15)

And what a spectacular miracle it was! Not only did Israel survive two thousand years of nonstop persecution, but she outlived every single one of her original contemporaries as well!

Moabites, Jebusites, Amorites, Phillistines, Babylonians, Persians, and the ancient Greeks, Romans, Egyptians, Canaanites, Hittites, Ammonites, Medes, etc., no longer exist as cultural or national units and the proof is that not *one* modern Roman, Greek, Turk, Egyptian, Arab, "Palestinian," Chinaman, German, Frenchman, Italian, Japanese, or Spaniard SPEAKS or WRITES the language he spoke or wrote in 500 B.C. The written language of the *Jerusalem Post* (Israel, 2003) is the Biblical language written and spoken by Moses, Joshua, and Aaron more than 1,400 years before Christ. (See Zephaniah. 3:9)[15]

The first political phase of Israel's return to her land was the landmark Balfour Declaration, issued by the British government on November 2, 1917. The "original" text read as follows:

Dear Lord Rothschild,

I have much pleasure in conveying to you, on behalf of his Majesty's government, the following declaration of sympathy with the Jewish Zionist aspirations which have been submitted to and approved by the Cabinet.

His Majesty views with favor the establishment in Palestine of **the** national homeland for the Jewish people, and will use their best endeavors to facilitate the achievement of this object; it being clearly understood that nothing shall be done which may prejudice the civil and religious rights of now existing Non-Jewish communities in Palestine, or the rights and political status enjoyed by Jews in any other country. I would be grateful if you would bring this declaration to the knowledge of the Zionist Federation.

Arthur James Balfour
British Foreign Secretary

In the final version, "*the* national homeland" was altered to "*a* national homeland." This became the first of several cowardly attempts by "His Majesty's government" to appease the historic enemies of Israel. Britain's primary motive for the Balfour Declaration was to enhance her own security needs in the Suez region. However, Zionist leaders preferred to believe that the declaration was an act of gratitude for a timely Jewish contribution to Britain's war effort. During World War I, a Jew by the name of Chaim Weizmann had invented acetone by extracting it from corn harvested in Terre Haute, Indiana. The acetone was subsequently employed in the guns of the Royal Navy.

On December 11, 1917, six weeks after the Balfour Declaration was signed, General Edmund Allenby entered Jerusalem and evicted the Turks. (Over 60,000 Jews had emigrated to Palestine between 1880 and 1914.) As Psalm 2:4a states, *"He that sitteth in the heavens shall laugh,"* it just so happens that the name *Allenby*, in Arabic, means "Prophet of Allah" *(Allah-Bey)*. In the providence of God, an Englishman reared on the A.V. 1611 was able to accomplish in a single campaign what the Roman Catholic crusaders had failed to do in over two centuries of floundering—liberate "the holy city" from the "infidels."

Dr. Bob Jones, Sr., once said, "World War I prepared the land for the Jew while World War II prepared the Jew for the land." The Balfour Declaration was endorsed by the principal allied powers and later included in the British mandate over Palestine, approved by the League of Nations on July 24, 1922.

Having experienced this initial stage of restoration, the Jews encountered three immediate sources of resistance (I Corinthians 16:9): Arab terrorism, Catholic intrigue, and British betrayal. The conflict was foreshadowed in 445 B.C. when an Arabian from Ishmael offered to "help" the Jews rebuild their temple. "Geshem the Arabian" was subsequently told to "hit the pike." (Nehemiah 6:1)

Our "history book" declares that in the last days the Lord will make Jerusalem a *"**cup** of trembling unto all the people round about"* (Zechariah

12:2). In the not too distant future, the "international community" will be forced to partake of this cup:

> *For thus saith the* LORD *God of Israel unto me; Take the wine* **cup** *of this fury at my hand, and cause all the nations, to whom I send thee, to drink it.*
> *And they shall drink, and be moved, and be mad, because of the sword that I will send among them.*
> *Then took I the* **cup** *at the* LORD'S *hand, and made all nations to drink, unto whom the* LORD *had sent me.* (Jeremiah 25:15-17)

While Winston Churchill conferred with Muslim and Catholic leaders in Cairo in 1921 (no Jews were allowed to attend), throngs of threatening Arabs made their presence felt. The paranoid Prime Minister was subjected to a steady flow of placards reading, "Down With Zionism," "Palestine Is Our Country," and "Long Live The Arab Congress."

Thus, on March 27 of that year, Churchill transferred two-thirds of Israel's land allotment to a Muslim "caliph" named Abdullah. He would later brag about having "created Trans-Jordan with a stroke of a pen." Henceforth the entire area from Galilee to Edom, east of the Jordan, would be "off limits" to all Jewish settlers, property owners, and even tourists, while everything on the west side would be open for anyone and everyone, *including Muslim terrorists disguised as "Palestinian refugees."*

It was at this point that the "cup" began to "tremble." Suddenly, British authorities had more Muslim riots and terrorist attacks than they could handle. The decision to install *Haj al Amim Hussein* as the Grand Muffti of Jerusalem only exacerbated the volatile situation.

The real problem was that Churchill and his secular-minded contemporaries were "in way over their heads." Do you think that any of them could trace the Scriptural boundaries of Israel's ancient homeland? In addition to such clear passages as Genesis 15:18-21; Joshua 1:2-4; II Samuel 8:3; and I Kings 4:21, we have this further amazing truth:

> *And Solomon brought up the daughter of Pharaoh out of the city of David unto the house that he had built for her: for he said, My wife shall not dwell in the house of David king of Israel, because the places are holy, whereunto the ark of the* LORD *hath come.* (II Chronicles 8:11)

Whereas the "Holy Father" in Rome would have you believe that only *certain* sites in the "Land of Palestine" are "holy" because of

Biblical significance, the *Holy Bible* declares that *any* ground is "holy" *if the Ark of the Covenant* (called "The Holy Ark" in II Chronicles 35:3) *ever passed over that ground!* Apparently unbeknownst to Churchill, the Ark of the Covenant traveled from Pisgah on the "East Bank" clear up to the Golan Heights via Basham and Gilead, and then across Jordan to the "West Bank" plumb through the land of the Philistines and down into the Gaza Strip. (Deuteronomy 2:31-36, 3:1-6, 8-10, 12:18; and II Samuel 5)

With nothing but bloody slaughter following in its wake, the "Holy Ark" wound up in the place Jesus Christ called *"the city of the great king"* (Matthew 5:35), JERUSALEM, the *"holy city,"* the *"city of peace."* And, would you believe it came to rest on the very spot where the Mosque of Omar stands today?

Churchill's main advisor throughout the Trans-Jordan fiasco was the celebrated D. H. Lawrence ("of Arabia"). However, the Lord was not without a faithful witness. In the midst of the proceedings, Sir John Halsam, an old Puritan Bible believer, rose to his feet, and with tears running down his cheeks, read Amos 9:11-15 to his shell-shocked colleagues.[16]

But alas, it was to no avail. So the "cup" continued to "tremble." In 1927, Jews were excluded from all state and municipal jobs. Then in 1939, Lord Passfield issued his White Paper placing a strict limitation on any land that a Jew could purchase in Palestine. He did this while the Catholics, *under papal orders from "His Holiness,"* were buying up all the available land and *giving* it to Muslims.[17]

You see, on May 28, 1920, an "infallible" Pope Benedict XV issued his famous *Encyclical* presenting the "Holy See" (his personal office) as a *separate nation,* instead of a "church." It would now be known as the "Vatican *State.*" This way, "Christ's vicar on earth" could operate *politically* instead of "spiritually," *since he was trying to get control of someone else's real estate.*[18]

Consequently, a most "unholy alliance" was forged. It would now be the Vatican *State* and the Palestinian *State* versus the *State* of Israel "supposedly" backed by the United *States*. As Herod and Pilate before them (Luke 23:12), "Mary and Mohammed" tied the knot in order to destroy a common foe. An insightful photo of a Muslim youth storming Israeli security forces shows the teenaged terrorist wearing a *Notre Dame tee shirt.*[19] (Hail Mary! Holy *Jihad!* Touch Down Jesus!)

Beginning with the Jaffa Gate massacre in 1920, the ensuing years witnessed a steady escalation of Muslim atrocities against unarmed Jewish settlers. Due to a sustained British indifference, several underground Jewish militias were formed. And the "cup" continued to "tremble."

In 1939, Churchill placed the final nail in England's coffin by supporting another White Paper limiting Jewish immigration to Palestine to only 75,000 over five years. *With 6,000,000 Jews about to be slaughtered in Europe, the British Prime Minister blocked their only route of escape.* A year into the Holocaust, a shipload of Jews was sent back to Poland from a port in Bulgaria. Then the *"Patria"* was turned away from Israel to Mauritius in the Indian Ocean; it was torpedoed and two hundred Jewish refugees perished. The *Salvador* from Bulgaria was also sunk with three hundred passengers aboard. And another three hundred drowned when the *Majkura* went under en route to Israel. After successfully escaping Germany, the *Maria* was captured by the British and its passengers eventually returned to Hitler's ovens.[20] Hundreds of similar stories could be told.

So now you know why "Great" Britain was subsequently reduced to a second-rate power with the majority of her proud capital burned to the ground in the process. The nation that gave us the A.V. 1611 got flattened by Genesis 12:3.

THE PHONY PALESTINIAN PROBLEM

There is nothing so phony as the so-called "Palestinian problem." It could only be perpetrated on an American society immersed in Jerry Springer, Howard Stern and Oprah Winfrey. There are so many incongruities, I hardly know where to begin. To accuse Israel of having disenfranchised the Palestinian "nation" is ludicrous. McTernan and Koenig cite Dr. Gary Frazier accordingly:

> During the entire period of recorded history, that is more than 5,000 years, Palestinian Arabs never ruled Palestine. I want to repeat this due to the fact it is never spoken of by the media. The fact is the only constant presence in the land has been a Jewish presence since the birth of Isaac. The numbers of Jews may have been minute at times, but they have remained, regardless. In addition to the Jews, there have been the soldiers of the occupying forces.

Century after century the culture, social fabric, and identity of these inhabitants changed as the ruling powers changed. Only the Jewish presence remained consistent as the sole survivors in the land, and they alone have maintained an uninterrupted national link since Abraham and Isaac.[21]

The *historical* "Palestinians" were Jews, Greeks, Arabs, Turks, Egyptians, Frenchmen, Italians, Persians, and even some Americans. And prior to these "Palestinians" taking over the region, the "land" was occupied by Jebusites, Ammonites, Moabites, Hittites, Perizzites, Hivites, Edomites, etc. *At no time, in 3,400 years, was it ever a Muslim Church-State run by Arabs who were born in "Palestine."*[22] This is typical news media propaganda. Even the secular *World Book Encyclopedia* concedes, "Many peoples have invaded the region, and there has **never** been an independent Palestinian state."[23]

The "land of Canaan" (not Palestine) was not the united domain of a central ruler when Joshua entered the territory in 1450 B.C.; it had thirty-three kings spread over a mongrel population with no capital. (Joshua 1-9) Dr. Frazier continues:

> In the current worldwide discussion regarding the land of Israel, no one seems to mention the fact that the Jewish claim to the land goes back 4,000 years with centuries filled with vital and consistent national life supported by biblical and archeological proofs. For 3,000 years Jerusalem was the capital of the Hebrew nation. The historical and archeological evidence is irrefutable. King David legally purchased the 35-acre area known today as Temple Mount, currently said to be the center of the dispute, from Araunah the Jebusite (2 Samuel 24:21-24). This very piece of ground became the site of both the First and Second Temples in Israel; the center of Jewish life and identity 1700 years before anyone ever heard of the Dome of the Rock (687-691 A.D.), or the Al Aksa mosque.[24]

Islam's claim to Jerusalem borders on insanity. Whereas Jerusalem is mentioned more than eight hundred times in the Bible, the *Koran* does not refer to the Holy City *once!* Jews have historically prayed toward Jerusalem, while Muslims have prayed toward Mecca. Mohammed *never* entered Jerusalem for *any* reason, though in the seventeenth Sura of the "Holy" *Koran*, he did claim to have gone there on one occasion—*in a dream!* According to the filthy liar, an angel woke him up, put him on a white horse with wings, and then whisked him away to Jerusalem where he ascended up to Heaven from the temple mount. A footprint can still be "seen" in the "holy" rock. And what's more, some of the "holy hairs" from his beard have also been preserved for the faithful to view![25]

With regard to the emotionally charged "Plight of the Palestinian" refugee crisis, the official version constitutes the apex of media disinformation. Dr. Frazier continues:

> In 1947 the Arabs were offered their own state alongside the area being granted to Israel. The answer from the Muslim was, they would never live in peace with the Jews, and drive them all into the Mediterranean.
>
> On May 15, 1948, just one day after Israel's Declaration of Independence, five Arab nations attacked the infant state. Bear in mind there were only 675,000 Jews in Israel versus more than 50 million Arab Muslims. **The Muslim nations called for the Arab residents of the area to get out of the way in light of the coming invasion, promising them a quick defeat of the Jews and an opportunity to plunder Jewish property and homes following their victory.** However, the Muslim world forgot one very essential element, they were not fighting the tiny Jewish state, they were fighting God Himself who was in the process of keeping His Word spoken long ago by the ancient prophets.
>
> After eight months of fighting, a cease-fire was established and the Arabs who fled could now no longer return to their willfully vacated property. Some were driven off by the Jews during the fighting. This was the beginning of the Palestinian refugee problem, or the "Plight of the Palestinian," as so-called by the media. Following the War of Independence, Jordan took control over the region of Judea and Samaria on the West Bank of the Jordan River, which extends to Jerusalem. Egypt, likewise, controlled the Gaza Strip region as well as the Sinai Peninsula.
>
> The Palestinian Arab population, many living in their own villages and some in U.N. constructed refugee camps, were under the authority of neighboring friendly Arab Muslim countries. The irony of it was they were now in the very territory alloted to them as their state by U.N. resolution Number 181 of 1947, which had apportioned them a state next to the Jewish State. This was the very territory they had declined, preferring to have it all! It was not too late! At that time they could still have clamored for their own state but they did not. The question is why? Why did they not lay claim to the land as their state?
>
> To understand this one must understand something of the Muslim mentality . . . Islam is a non-tolerant religion and cannot peacefully coexist with any other religion. **Therefore, rather than live alongside a Jewish state in peace, the Muslim nations chose to use the Palestinian people as pawns for sympathy, political manipulation and economic gain.**

The neighboring Muslim countries elected to keep these people locked in a prison of dirty politics and abuse giving them no chance for economic gain, education, or a future with real hope. I repeat, it was the Muslim nations who did this to their own people. Using them to deceive the world and pressure Israel into compromises. I personally viewed some of these refugee camps. The filth, squalor, and overall conditions were awful to say the least. The neighboring Muslim countries could have alleviated this suffering, had they so desired.[26]

The good folks at CNN, FOX, ABC, CBS, NBC, BBC, PBS, and the EIB Network forgot to tell you that the *original* crisis was occasioned by the Muslims themselves on the eve of their 1948 invasion of Israel (i.e., the *"plight* of the Palestinians*"* being caused by the *"flight* of the Palestinians"). Then, following their ignominious defeat, the Arab League transformed a sizeable bloc of their own people into a political "soccer ball" to elicit international sympathy.

When the smoke cleared from the Six-Day War of 1967, Israel had increased her land mass from 8,000 square miles to 26,000 square miles. She was now in control of the Jordan Valley, West Bank, Old City of Jerusalem, Golan Heights, Gaza Strip, and the Sinai. The unfortunate "Palestinian pawns" in the Jordan Valley had crossed into Jordan while those in the Golan and the Sinai fled into Syria and Egypt respectively.

Another significant *fact* concerns the number of "Palestinian refugees" professing to have a legitimate claim for statehood. With only about 50,000 Palestinians fleeing in 1948, *over 2,000,000* have "returned" since 1949. And the number continues to grow.

The most obvious proof that the "poor Palestinians" are merely the political dupes of a terrorist state is the inexplicable fact that *thirty-two Muslim nations with unlimited oil reserves and a combined land mass 672 times the size of Israel have never "felt the leading of Allah" to chip in a few acres toward a new Palestinian homeland elsewhere.*

In reality, the PLO and the PA (whether you call it the Palestinian "Authority" or "Agency") is a franchise of six Muslim terrorist organizations; the Al Fatah, Fedayeen, Hamas, Hezbollah, Intifada and PLO. These religious "hit-squads" have publicly stated on *thirteen* occasions that their sole mission is a "Judenrein" Palestine (Hitlerian term for "Jew-free" or "pure from any Jews"). Having run the Jews out of Arabia, Morocco, Lebanon, Trans-Jordan, Algiers, Iraq, Iran, Syria,

Libya, Egypt, Tunisia, and Turkey, their current goal is to destroy every Jew in the land of Palestine.[27]

From a military perspective, the modern U.N. plan to create a "Palestinian State" has never been anything but a Vatican contrivance for Muslim terrorists to officially establish a "staging area" for armed troops so that a "legitimate" Arab army may be formed to drive Israel back into the Mediterranean Sea.[28] (Hitler invaded Czechoslovakia from the strategic "Auschluss;" Mao's hordes were able to clobber MacArthur via the Yula River; and the Viet Cong utilized Cambodia in a similar manner.)

For what it's worth, Yasser Arafat, the charismatic founder of the PLO, just happened to be an *Egyptian*. At the time of his death on November 10, 2004, this great "lover of peace" held six world records in terrorist activity: the largest highjacking operation; the largest number of hostages held at one time; the largest number of victims killed or wounded by boobytraps; the largest number shot in an airport; the largest ransoms demanded for hostages; and the greatest variety of targets.[29] Well did David write in Psalm 28:3, *"Draw me not away with the wicked, and with the workers of iniquity, which speak peace to their neighbours, but mischief is in their hearts."*

Another relevant observation is that Mrs. Arafat is *Roman Catholic*. Consequently, her Muslim husband had been welcomed in the Vatican *nine* times since 1994. (During televised coverage of Arafat's burial in Rammalah, FOX *News* reported that the filthy animal's widow would receive an annual pension of $2.2 million from depleted Palestinian coffers in order to maintain her "modest" Parisan lifestyle.) On February 15, 2000, the historic Vatican-Palestinian agreement was signed. The blasphemous document reads:

> An equitable solution for the issue of Jerusalem, based on international resolutions, is fundamental for a just and lasting peace in the Middle East, and that unilateral decisions and actions altering the specific character and status of Jerusalem are morally and legally unacceptable; Calling, therefore, for a special statute for Jerusalem, internationally guaranteed, which should safeguard the following:
>
> (a) Freedom of religion and conscience of all.
> (b) The equality before the law of the three monotheistic religions and their Institutions and followers in the City.
> (c) The proper identity and sacred character of the City and its universally significant, religious, and cultural heritage.

(d) The Holy Places, the freedom of access to them and of worship in them.

(e) The Regime of "Status Quo" in those Holy Places where it applies.[30]

It's hard to tell which portion of this document is the funniest—a *pope* "crusading" to allow Muslims access to the "Holy Places" in Palestine; the ludicrous connection between "freedom of religion and conscience" and *any* Muslim state; or that unscriptural rhetoric about "lasting peace" in the Middle East prior to the Second Advent.

The official Israeli response to the Vatican-Palestinian agreement reads accordingly:

> Israel expresses its great displeasure with the declaration made today in Rome by the Holy See and the PLO, which includes the issue of Jerusalem, and other issues which are subjects of the Israeli-Palestinian negotiations on permanent status. The agreement signed by these two parties constitutes a regretful intervention in the talks between Israel and the Palestinians.
>
> Furthermore, there is no denying that Israel safeguards freedom of conscience and freedom of worship for all, and provides free access to the holy places of all faiths. Similarly, there is no question that the religious and cultural character of Jerusalem is being preserved, as are the rights of all the religious communities and their institutions in the city. Consequently, Israel flatly rejects the reference to Jerusalem in the aforementioned document. Jerusalem was, is, and shall remain the capital of the State of Israel, and no agreement or declaration by these or any other parties will change this fact.[31]

Pope John Paul II grew up surrounded by six of Adolf Hitler's death camps: Sobibor, Belzec, Auschwitz, Treblinka, Thereinstadt, and Majdenak. In May 2001, the racist killer visited Syria to promote his "Mary and Mohammed" policy of genocide. The pope's remarks were recorded in the May 6, 2001, *Jerusalem Post*:

> My pilgrimage is also an ardent prayer of hope. . . . It is time to return to the principles of **international legality**: the banning of acquisition of territory by force, the right of peoples to self-determination, respect for the resolutions of the United Nations, and the Geneva Convention.[32]

The following day Syrian president Bashar el-Assad was quoted in the *Jerusalem Post* as telling the pontiff:

> We feel that in your prayers, in which you recall the suffering of Jesus Christ, you will remember that there is a people in Lebanon, the Golan [Heights], and Palestine, that is suffering from subjugation and persecution. . . . We expect you to stand by them [these people] against the oppressors [Israel] so that they can regain what was unjustly taken from them.[33]

The bottom line of John Paul's "pontifical hot air" is that it would be *illegal* and *immoral* for the Jews to be in control of their own capital: Jerusalem. Talk about a "zoned out" laity, first the Polish pope was able to get away with endorsing evolution (October, 1996); now he can call Jesus Christ a liar by rejecting His sovereign claim to the City of David! *No wonder that multi-million dollar pedophilia debacle came out of nowhere!* By the end of 2002, over 1,200 "celibate" Catholic "fathers" had been accused of sexually abusing minors nationwide! (*"And I will bless them that bless thee,* ***and curse him that curseth thee*** *. . ."* Genesis 12:3a.)

The present accommodation of Roman Catholicism by apostate evangelical Christianity (pioneered by Evangelist Billy Graham) has given the Lord yet another righteous "alibi"—this time, to wipe out believers before the Church is raptured: *"For the time is come that judgment must begin at the house of God."* (I Peter 4:17a)

With the degree of political corruption prevailing in high places, conservative Bible-believing Christians are now faced with the same predicament experienced by Rahab the harlot; *we are all trapped in a terrified city.* Because *"the love of money is the root of all evil,"* the almighty dollar will be the ultimate cause of America's sad demise. McTernan and Koening write:

> . . . oil produces large amounts of income, which produces large amounts of money for United States defense contractors, building contractors, engineering firms, and oil companies with political influence. Conversely, Arab oil producers want at least a portion of Israel's land and a section of Jerusalem. They tell their "friends" at the CFR what they want, and the CFR then influences U.S. policy at the State Department and the White House in favor of their Arab friends.[34]

The acronym CFR stands for the *Council on Foreign Relations,* America's premier think tank on the New World Order. The majority of this book will deal with the CFR and similar organizations that have been used by Satan to turn America against God.

"Slick Willie" donated $400,000,000 of American tax money to the PLO in 1998. Although eleven of the hijackers on September 11 were Saudi nationals, the Bush administration continued to spend $40 billion a year through direct aid and military personnel to Muslim nations such as Jordan, Egypt and Saudi Arabia.[35]

Since 1967, a coalition of twenty-one Arab states has prompted the U.N. to initiate over a thousand one-sided anti-Israel resolutions. Yet the same agency has never explicitly condemned any Arab terrorism against unarmed Israeli citizens.[36]

A full-page ad placed by the American Jewish Committee in the September 22, 1999, *New York Times* spoke volumes of the on-going hypocrisy. A line down the center divided the page into two halves. Atop the left column was the heading: "Countries eligible to sit on the United Nations Security Council." The names of 187 nations from *Afghanistan* to *Zimbabwe*, including the United States, were listed underneath. The adjacent heading read conversely: "Countries *not* eligible to sit on the United Nations Security Council." Would you believe only *one* nation appeared in the right column? In case you can't guess which one it was, I'll give you a hint—"*. . . lo, the people shall dwell alone, and shall **not** be reckoned among the nations*" (Numbers 23:91b). (The following year, after decades of being the only U.N. state excluded from membership in a U.N. regional group, a prerequisite for membership on the Security Council and most other bodies, Israel was granted *temporary* membership in a regional group.) To the U.N.'s "credit," a verse from the Jewish Old Testament remains prominently displayed across the street from their formidable edifice in Manhattan. (Isaiah 2:4)

Amidst our national addiction to pleasure and materialism, few have the time or interest to heed God's warning of pending judgment. (Matthew 24:37-39) Appropriately, America's death warrant was penned by a *Jew* in 60 A.D.; the "apostle to the Gentiles" admonishing the "wild olive tree":

> *Be not high-minded, but fear:*
> *For if God spared not the natural branches, take heed lest he also spare not thee.*
> *Behold therefore the goodness and severity of God: on them, which fell, severity; but toward thee, goodness, **if** thou continue in his goodness: **otherwise thou also shalt be cut off.***
> *And they also, if they abide not still in unbelief, shall be graffed in: **for God is able to graff them in again**.* (Romans 11:20b-23)

America's final judgment will not be occasioned by abortion, sodomy or witchcraft. It will come for yoking up with the Vatican State, U.N., PLO, EU, World Bank, IMF, G-8, CFR and a dozen other globalist organizations that openly reject those last nine words of Romans 11:23. *The United States will eventually crash and burn for spurning a "holy piece of dirt!"* (Genesis 12:3)

In the meantime, Christians can take comfort in their infallible "history book." While Mohammed taught that the 600-winged angel who dictated every word in the *Koran* to him later wound up in Hell (see Sura 19:19, footnote 1537), the Bible believer has *"a more sure word of prophecy."* (II Peter 2:19) Though America has begun her suicidal betrayal of Israel, Jehovah will surely pick up the slack. When 200 Syrian MiGs engaged 130 Israeli Phantom jets in 1982, the Jewish pilots destroyed 92 enemy aircraft without losing a single plane!

Our next chapter will reveal God's supernatural expansion of Japheth which resulted in the creation of America. (Genesis 9:27) The chapter following that will chronicle the role played by the Baptists in the nation's historic struggle for religious liberty, culminating in the Bill of Rights.

Jerusalem! Jerusalem!
Lift up your gates and sing,
Hosanna in the highest!
Hosanna to your King!

3

The Fourfold Enlargement of Japheth

"God shall enlarge Japheth . . ."
(Genesis 9:27a)

W HEN BILL CLINTON attended Jesuit-run Georgetown
University (1964-1968), his mentor was a Roman Catholic
instructor named Carroll Quigley. From a secular standpoint,
Quigley's academic credentials were impressive: professor of history
at the Foreign Service School of Georgetown; former faculty member
at Harvard and Princeton; lecturer on Russian history at the Industrial
College of the Armed Forces and on Africa at the Brookings Institution;
frequent speaker at the U.S. Naval College in Norfolk, Virginia; major
consultant to the Smithsonian Institution's Museum of History and
Technology; member of the editorial board of the monthly *Current
History*; and, member of the American Association for the Advancement
of Science, the American Anthropological Association, and the American
Economic Association. His three major literary contributions are *The
Anglo-American Establishment, The Evolution of Civilizations*, and the
1,300-page tome *Tragedy and Hope: A History of the World in Our Time*
(which required twenty years to complete).

During Clinton's July 16, 1992, acceptance speech for the Democratic
presidential nomination, the candidate made reference to John F. Kennedy's
inspirational "Summons to Citizenship" address. He then went on to say,
"I heard that call clarified by a professor I had named Carroll Quigley."
The New York Times added, "Quigley's . . . legacy lives on not only in
. . . President Clinton, but among hundreds of other former students and
admirers."[1] Following Clinton's election as president, James K. Fitzpatrick
wrote on the editorial page of *The Wanderer*, November 18, 1993:

Clinton told reporters in an interview that Quigley's work [*Tragedy and Hope*] centered on the existence of a permanent shadow government of powerful bankers and businessmen and government officials that controls the agenda of our political life from behind the scenes. Clinton spoke in that interview of coming to the conclusion, while still a young man, that it was necessary for him to gain access to the inner circle of this group in order to become part of the decision-making process that shapes our world.[2]

What President Clinton and Professor Quigley were referring to was the "front" of a powerful secret society, known as "the Group," emanating from England's Oxford University—more specifically, from All Soul's College. In 1870, a wealthy British socialist by the name of John Ruskin was appointed professor of fine arts at Oxford (the first to hold this position). Ruskin advocated the Hegelian principle of placing control of the state in the hands of a ruling elite (oligarchy) writing, "My continual aim has been to show the eternal superiority of some men to others, sometimes even of one man to all others."[3] (If these self-deluded fools could only wait till the Millennium.) In *Time and Tide* (1867) he wrote: "[T]he first duty of a State is to see that every child born therein shall be well housed, clothed, fed and educated. . . . But in order to the effecting this the Government must have authority over the people. . . ."[4]

The background for Ruskin's "crusade" was the poverty, ignorance and crime described by Charles Dickens and others. Quigley writes in *Tragedy and Hope*:

He hit Oxford like an earthquake . . . Ruskin spoke to the Oxford undergraduates as members of the privileged, ruling class. He told them that they were the possessors of a magnificent tradition of education, beauty, rule of law, freedom, decency, and self-discipline but that this tradition could not be saved, and did not deserve to be saved, unless it could be extended to the lower classes in England itself and to the non-English masses throughout the world. If this precious tradition were not extended to these two great majorities, the minority of upper class Englishmen would ultimately be submerged by these majorities and the tradition lost. To prevent this, the tradition must be extended to the masses and to the empire.[5]

Although this all sounds nice and compassionate, Ruskin's approach had one telling flaw—his brand of transformation was to be done *without* the Gospel of Jesus Christ! The real impact of that day was being made by spirit-filled preachers like George Mueller and William Booth. Without a single stewardship program, "Jesus First" pin, Giant

Print Bible give-away or an 800 toll-free number, Mueller prayed in $7.5 million to feed 2,000 orphans daily, not to mention distributing 111 million Gospel tracts and 300,000 Bibles while supporting 163 missionaries. The sickly General Booth planted his Salvation Army in fifty-eight countries while preaching the Gospel in thirty-four languages. The courage of his workers is legendary; for instance, while distributing tracts along the docks, Booth's "Lasses" were subjected to murderous rocket attacks at point blank range by drunken sailors.

Ruskin never viewed the King James Bible as anything more than his favorite style of prose, writing,

> From Walter Scott's novels I might easily, as I grew older, have fallen to other people's novels; and Pope might, perhaps, have led me to take Johnson's English, or Gibbon's, as types of language; but, once knowing the 32nd of Deuteronomy, the 15th of First Corinthians, the Sermon on the Mount, and most of the Apocalypse, every syllable by heart, and having always a way of thinking with myself what words meant, it was not possible for me, even in the foolishest times of youth, to write entirely superficial or formal English.[6]

Thus, as *"the natural man receiveth not the things of the Spirit of God"* (I Corinthians 2:14), John and his highbrow Oxford constituents were incapable of discerning either the cause or ultimate purpose for Britain's "Greatness"—her A.V. 1611 and the procreation of America for Israel's resuscitation and miraculous return to statehood. (And the same would apply to the Roman Catholic Quigley.)

SHEM, HAM AND JAPHETH

Our study must begin with a King James Bible, the only infallible "history" book in the Library of Congress. The Scripture declares in Genesis 9:27, *"God shall enlarge Japheth, and he shall dwell in the tents of Shem; and Canaan shall be his servant."* In this passage, the patriarch Noah rendered specific prophecies concerning the posterity of his three sons—Shem, Ham and Japheth. These utterances were provoked by a particularly lewd incident. Sometime after the flood, Noah became a husbandman and planted a vineyard. On a certain bizarre occasion, Noah became intoxicated and fell asleep, whereupon

Ham either perpetrated a homosexual act against his own father or committed incest with his mother. While Genesis 9:24 says, "And Noah awoke from his wine, and *knew what his younger son had **done** unto him,"* Leviticus 20:11 states, *"And the man that lieth with his father's wife hath uncovered his father's nakedness. . . ."* Ham has a sex problem! According to Genesis 10:19, his descendants founded the city of Sodom.

In Deuteronomy 27:20, Moses adds, *"Cursed be he that lieth with his father's wife; because he uncovereth his father's skirt.* As Ham had been previously blessed in Genesis 9:1, and because his sin was connected with his "seed," God directed Noah to place the curse on Ham's son, Canaan: *"And he said, Cursed be Canaan; a servant of servants shall he be unto his brethren."* (Genesis 9:25) Understandably, the good Lord's indiscriminate judgment on Canaan would not be in keeping with today's humanistic reasoning. The truth is, God does what He pleases, without asking anyone! Because Shem and Japheth *"took a garment, and laid it upon both their shoulders, and went backward, and covered the nakedness of their father,"* they received commensurate assurances of honor. *"And he said, Blessed be the LORD God of Shem; and Canaan shall be his servant. God shall enlarge Japheth, and he shall dwell in the tents of Shem; and Canaan shall be his servant"* (Genesis 9:26-27).

In order to appreciate the historic fulfillment of these prophecies, one must study the transmigration of Noah's descendents as revealed in the ethnological table of Genesis 10. Their movement can be illustrated from a simple game of "Connect the Dots." When a map of the Middle East is viewed, three significant coordinates appear. The ancient Tigress and Euphrates Rivers join at about three o'clock. According to Genesis 2:10-14, human life began in this vicinity. After the judgment of the flood, Noah's ark rested atop Mt. Ararat at twelve o'clock and life began anew. At the western end of the "Fertile Crescent" the Nile River empties into the Mediterranean at approximately nine o'clock. When these three dots are connected a rough triangle is formed. As discussed in the previous chapter, God promised the land within this triangle to Abraham and his descendants (through Isaac and Jacob). Everyone else (i.e., the "Gentiles") would get what was left.

When God broke up the "fellowship" at the Tower of Babel, He scattered the crowd in three directions. Japheth's descendants went off the left side of the triangle northwest into Russia and Europe. Shem went off to the right and populated the East. According to the words of David in Psalm 105:23 and 27, Ham's people went south of the triangle's base onto the continent of Africa. The renowned archeologist, Dr. Merrill F. Unger, states:

> The descendants of Ham comprise the eastern and southern people who settled originally in lower Mesopotamia and subsequently in south Arabia, Ethiopia, Egypt and Canaan (Genesis 10: 6-14). As the youngest son of Noah, Ham is regarded as the eponymous ancestor of the African peoples, as Japheth his brother is of the Indo-Europeans, and Shem of the Semites.[7]

Even the lying humanist has to come clean occasionally, as there is only so much he can hide. The 1998 edition of *World Book Encyclopedia* states, under the heading of "Noah":

> Noah's sons were Shem, Ham and Japheth. Shem became father of the Semitic peoples, including the Jews and the Arabs. Ham was the father of the Hamitic peoples. Japheth was father of Asia Minor and Europe.[8]

And under the heading "Hamites," *World Book* confirms:

> Hamites are certain African peoples who live mainly in eastern, northern, and northeastern Africa, including parts of Eritrea, Ethiopia, the Sahara, and the Sudan. Most Hamites are tall and have a narrow nose and brown skin. They are sometimes called Afro-Mediterranean peoples because of their physical characteristics and the region where they live. Because much of this region cannot be farmed, most Hamites tend herds of camels, cattle, goats and sheep.[9]

Shem's descendents continued moving *eastbound* (note the "*handfuls of purpose*" signpost in Genesis 10:30) till they crossed over the Bering Strait into North America, eventually fathering the Native American Indians. Any time you hear a man criticize the Bible's accuracy, you may rest assured that he is woefully ignorant of the historical record. Dr. C. I. Scofield wrote:

> A prophetic declaration is made that from Ham will descend an inferior and servile posterity (Genesis 9:24 and 25). A prophetic declaration is made that Shem will have a peculiar relation to Jehovah (Genesis 9:26 and 27). All divine revelation is through Semitic men, and Christ, after the flesh, descends from Shem. A prophetic declaration is made that from Japheth will descend the "enlarged" races (Genesis 9:27). Government, science,

and art, speaking broadly, are and have been Japhetic, so that history is the indisputable record of the exact fulfillment of these declarations.[10]

It is no coincidence that the world's three largest monotheistic religions—Judaism, Christianity and Islam—just happened to descend from Shem. It is also no accident that Ham's posterity has been one of continual servitude. With the Emancipation Proclamation, Fourteenth Amendment, and Civil Rights Act on the books, Ham's *predominant* contribution in twenty-first-century capitalistic America (apart from preachers and politicians) is in the sports and entertainment industries (Mike Jordan and Mike Jackson). Ham is *still* serving his brethren. (Perhaps an appropriate sequel to the racist comedy "White Men Can't Jump" would be a documentary entitled "But They *Can* Build Computers.")

As for Japheth *"the elder"* (Genesis 10:21), God declared that he would become the "enlarged race." Paul Kennedy, Dilworth Professor of History at Yale University, writes in *The Rise and Fall of the Great Powers*:

> The "impact of western man" was, in all sorts of ways, one of the most noticeable aspects of the dynamics of world power in the nineteenth century. It manifested itself not only in a variety of economic relationships—ranging from the "informal influence" of coastal traders, shippers, and consuls to the more direct controls of planters, railway builders, and mining companies—but also in the penetrations of explorers, adventurers, and missionaries, in the introduction of western diseases, and in the proselytization of western faiths. It occurred as much in the centers of continents—westward from the Missouri, southward from the Aral Sea—as it did up in the mouths of African rivers and around the coasts of Pacific archipelagoes. If it eventually had its impressive monuments in the roads, railway networks, telegraphs, harbors, and civic buildings which (for example) the British created in India, its more horrific side was the bloodshed, rapine, and plunder which attended so many of the colonial wars of the period. To be sure, the same traits of force and conquest had existed since the days of Cortez, but now the pace was accelerating. **In the year 1800, Europeans occupied or controlled 35 percent of the land surface of the world; by 1878 this figure had risen to 67 percent, and by 1914 to over 84 percent.**[11]

This would include the American Indians being evicted from their teepees to fulfill the second prophecy in Genesis 9:27, *"God shall enlarge Japheth, and he shall dwell in the tents of Shem."* Although initially subjected to many oppressive policies by the "white man's government," thousands of redeemed Indians, including the celebrated Geronimo himself, eventually made it to the *real* "Happy Hunting Grounds" because a dedicated band of Gospel-preaching missionaries (like McCoy, Posey, Jones, Brainard, Elliot and others) was able to break the spell of their satanic, peyote-smoking medicine men. *"But where sin abounded, grace did much more abound"* (Romans 5:20b).

By the end of the twentieth century, Japheth would be at the peak of his enlargement. Harvard professor Samuel P. Huntington lists fourteen categories in which "whitey" has no peers. Western nations:

- Own and operate the international banking system
- Control all hard currencies
- Are the world's principal customer
- Provide the majority of the world's finished goods
- Dominate international capital markets
- Exert considerable moral leadership within many societies
- Are capable of massive military intervention
- Control the sea lanes
- Conduct most advanced technical research and development
- Control leading edge technical education
- Dominate access to space
- Dominate the aerospace industry
- Dominate international communications
- Dominate the high-tech weapons industry[12]

THE EUROPEAN MIRACLE

According to the science of ethnology (and confirmed by the tenth chapter of Genesis), Shem fathers the "people of the East" (Genesis 10:30), Ham is the patriarch of the African continent and Japheth is the progenitor of the Caucasian race. Japheth's descendants include: the Celts, Picts, Angles, Caledonians, Saxons, Waldons, Gauls, Frisians, Franks, Aryans, and Norsemen of Northern Europe; the Circassians, Croatians, Dorians, Bulgars, Bolls, Moravians, Parsees, Scythians, Phrygians, Huns, Pisidians, Goths, Slavs, and Thracians from Russia, the Balkans and North Persia; and the Lombards, Catalans, Etruscans, Basques and Visigoths of North Spain and Italy.[13]

Dr. Scofield describes Gomer, the first of Japheth's seven sons, as "Progenitor of the ancient Cimerians and Cimbri, from whom are descended the Celtic family."[14] According to Jewish commentators and exegetes, Ashkenaz, Gomer's firstborn, settled in modern Germany.

After amassing an impressive bibliography of over 1,400 volumes in *The Rise and Fall of the Great Powers*, Professor Kennedy concedes that he and his colleagues are at a loss to explain Europe's rise to world power. Under the heading "The European Miracle," he writes:

> Why was it among the scattered and relatively unsophisticated peoples inhabiting the western parts of the Eurasian landmass that there occurred an unstoppable process of economic development and technological innovation which would steadily make it the commercial and military leader in world affairs? This is a question which has exercised scholars and other observers for centuries. . . .[15]

Perhaps he should have included an A.V. 1611 among his 1,400 sources. Without the illumination of God's Holy Word, Paul and his peers have justifiable cause for their perplexity. Ming China had a population of 100-130 million in the fifteenth century compared with only 50-55 million in Europe. About 1045, printing by movable type was invented by a Chinese man named Bi Sheng (Pi Sheng), with plenty of books and libraries bequeathed as evidence. By the end of the eleventh century, China was also producing 125,000 tons of iron per annum, a figure that even surpassed British output in the early seventeenth century.

The Chinese are also the true inventors of gunpowder with cannons being in regular use by the late fourteenth century. Paper money circulated throughout these "ancient" times as well. China's invention of the magnetic compass went along with her massive navy. Some of their junks were comparable in size to later Spanish galleons. In 1420, the Ming navy was recorded as possessing 1,350 combat vessels, including 400 large floating fortresses and 250 ships designed for long-range cruising.[16] From 1405 to 1433, Admiral Cheng Ho conducted seven voyages from Malacca and Ceylon to the Red Sea and Zanzibar, consisting of hundreds of ships and tens of thousands of men. Some of Admiral Ho's treasure ships are thought to have been around 400 feet long and displaced over 1,500 tons. Yet, to Kennedy's surprise, the nation's leadership suddenly became xenophobic.

But the Chinese expedition of 1433 was the last of the line, and three years later an imperial edict banned the construction of seagoing ships; later still, a specific order forbade the existence of ships with more than two masts. Naval personnel would henceforth be employed on smaller vessels on the Grand Canal. Cheng Ho's great warships were laid up and rotted away. **Despite all the opportunities which beckoned overseas, China had decided to turn its back on the world.**[17]

The bottom line is that *Ho* was not about to overthrow the authority of God's Holy Word. It was Japheth who was destined to do the enlarging, not Shem. Marco Polo would drop in on Kublai Khan, etc.

The Muslim states represented the most rapidly expanding force in world affairs during the sixteenth century. The Ottoman Turks and the Safavid dynasty in Persia were constantly acquiring new territories. The Ottoman Empire stretched from the Crimea and the Aegean to the Levant. Their powerful navy (like Kublai Khan in China) was specifically equipped to reduce a sea girt enemy fortress. Thus we understand the fall of mighty Constantinople in 1453. Kennedy describes the world of fourteenth-century Islam:

Its cities were large, well lit, and drained, and some of them possessed universities and libraries and stunningly beautiful mosques. In mathematics, cartography, medicine, and many other aspects of science and industry— in mills, gun casting, lighthouses, and horse breeding—the Muslims had enjoyed a lead. The Ottoman system of recruiting future janissaries [Special Forces] from Christian youth in the Balkans had produced a dedicated, uniform corps of troops. Tolerance of other races had brought many a talented Greek, Jew, and Gentile into the sultan's service—a Hungarian was Mehmet's chief gun-caster in the siege of Constantinople. Under a successful leader like Suleiman I, a strong bureaucracy supervised fourteen million subjects—this at a time when Spain had five million and England a mere two and a half million inhabitants. Constantinople in its heyday was bigger than any European city, possessing over 500,000 inhabitants in 1600.[18]

But then he relates: "Yet the Ottoman Turks, too, were to falter, to turn inward, and to lose the chance of world domination, although this became clear only a century after the strikingly similar Ming decline."[19]

He then continues:

The above remarks . . . could be made with equal or even greater force about the Mongol Empire. Despite the sheer size of the kingdom at its height and the military genius of some of its emperors, despite the brilliance of its courts and the craftsmanship of its luxury products, despite even a sophisticated banking and credit network, the system was weak at the core. . . .

The sheer rigidity of Hindu religious taboos militated against modernization: rodents and insects could not be killed, so vast amounts of food stuffs were lost; social mores about handling refuse and excreta led to permanently unsanitary conditions, a breeding ground for bubonic plagues; the caste system throttled initiative, instilled ritual, and restricted the market; and the influence wielded over Indian local rulers by the Brahman priests meant that this obscurantism was effective at the highest level.[20]

The Holy Bible predicted pagan conditions such as these. With reference to the heathen, Paul wrote in the book of Romans:

> *And changed the glory of the uncorruptible God into an image made like to corruptible man, and to birds, and fourfooted beasts, and creeping things. . . . Who changed the truth of God into a lie, and worshiped and served the creature more than the Creator, who is blessed forever. . . . For this cause God gave them up unto vile affections. . . . (Romans 1:23 and 25-26a)*

Kennedy also included Japan as a kingdom that should have made it to the "big time." After pointing out her many strengths, such as geographic insularity from overland invasion, a power structure built on clan-based futile lordships, and trade with the West resulting in imports of European armaments (especially cannons), he confirms that the land of *Nippon* folded like the rest.

In 1636, construction of oceangoing vessels was stopped and Japanese subjects were forbidden to sail the high seas. Trade with Europeans was restricted to the permitted Dutch ship calling at Deshima in Nagasaki harbor; the others were tumbled out. . . . **Like the Ming dynasty, the Tokugawa shogunate deliberately chose, with few exceptions, to cut itself off from the rest of the world.** . . .

Disdaining to engage in trade, and forbidden to travel or to display their weapons except on ceremonial occasions, the samurai warriors attached to their lords lived a life of ritual and boredom. The entire military system ossified for two centuries, so that when Commodore Perry's famous "black ships" arrived in 1853, there was little that an overawed Japanese government could do except grant the American request for coaling and other facilities.[21]

Once again, the explanation can be found in a King James Bible. While Deuteronomy 32:8 states that the Lord *"set the **bounds** of the people,"* Acts 17:26b adds that He also *"**determined the times before appointed,** and the bounds of their habitation."* Japan cut itself off from the rest of the world because God Almighty decreed it so! Commodore Perry was a descendant of Japheth.

Finally, Kennedy points to the sixteenth-century Russian kingdom of Muscovy as one more power that fizzled. After ending their vulnerability to Mongol horsemen with the acquiring of cannons, Ivan the Terrible just couldn't get the ball rolling.

EUROPE'S GEOGRAPHICAL ADVANTAGE

Although ignorant of Japheth's spiritual purpose, Professor Kennedy *was* able to discern the "evolutionary perks" unique to Western Europe.

> The one feature of Europe which immediately strikes the eye when looking at a map of the world's "power centers" in the sixteenth century is its political fragmentation. . . . **For this political diversity Europe had largely to thank its geography.** There were no enormous plains over which an empire of horsemen could impose its swift dominion; nor were there broad and fertile river zones like those around the Ganges, Nile, Tigris and Euphrates, Yellow, and Yangtze, providing the food for masses of toiling and easily conquerable peasants. Europe's landscape was much more fractured, with mountain ranges and large forests separating the scattered population centers in the valleys; and its climate altered considerably from north to south and west to east. This had a number of important consequences. For a start, it both made difficult the establishment of unified control, even by a powerful and determined warlord, and minimized the possibility that the continent could be overrun by an external force like the Mongol hordes. Conversely, this variegated landscape encouraged the growth, and the continued existence, of decentralized power, with local kingdoms and marcher lordships and highland clans and lowland town confederations making a political map of Europe drawn at any time after the fall of Rome look like a patchwork quilt. The patterns of that quilt might vary from century to century, but no single color could ever be used to denote a unified empire.[22]

King Solomon never got to be "Dilworth Professor of History at Yale," but he did have enough sense to know that it was *"[t]he great*

God that formed all things" (Proverbs 26:10). His father, David, had likewise been deprived of an Ivy League education; yet, he understood how Europe's geography was determined.

> *For the LORD is a great God, and a great King above all gods. In his hand are the deep places of the earth: the strength of the hills is his also. The sea is his and he made it: and his hands formed the dry land.* (Psalm 95:3-5)

Kennedy expands on Japheth's providential edge over Shem and Ham.

> Europe's differentiated climate led to differentiated products, suitable for exchange; and in time, as market relations developed, they were transported along the rivers or the pathways which cut through the forests between one area of settlement and the next. Probably the most important characteristic of this commerce was that it consisted primarily of bulk products—timber, grain, wine, wool, herrings, and so on, catering to the rising population of fifteenth-century Europe, rather than the luxuries carried on the oriental caravans. **Here again geography played a crucial role**, for water transport of these goods was so much more economical and Europe possessed many navigable rivers. Being surrounded by seas was a further incentive to the vital shipbuilding industry, and by the later Middle Ages a flourishing maritime commerce was being carried out between the Baltic, the North Sea, the Mediterranean, and the Black Sea. . . .
>
> In addition, because much of this trade was carried through the rougher waters of the North Sea and Bay of Biscay—and also because long-range fishing became an important source of nutrient and wealth—shipwrights were forced to build tough (if rather slow and inelegant) vessels capable of carrying large loads and finding their motive power in the winds alone.[23]

Although these North Sea "cogs" were less impressive than the lighter, more sophisticated vessels that plied the shores of the eastern Mediterranean Sea and Indian Ocean, they possessed distinct advantages in the long run. Access to the fisheries in Newfoundland tapped a surplus quantity of food, while the Atlantic Ocean supplied whale and seal oil, vital for illumination, lubrication and other purposes. Products such as sugar, indigo, tobacco, rice, furs, timber, and new plants like the potato and maize, greatly supplemented Europe's economy.

Kennedy then notes the corollary economic safeguards peculiar to the land of Japheth:

The political and social consequences of this decentralized, largely unsupervised growth of commerce and merchants and ports and markets were of the greatest significance. In the first place, there was no way in which such economic developments could be fully suppressed. This is not to say that the rise of market forces did not disturb many in authority. . . . But the basic fact was that there existed no uniform authority in Europe which could effectively halt this or that commercial development; no central government whose changes in priorities could cause the rise and fall of a particular industry; no systematic and universal plundering of businessmen and entrepreneurs by tax gatherers, which so retarded the economy of Mogul India.[24]

What this amounts to is that the Lord forced a spirit of *competition* on Japheth's descendants.

The fact was that in Europe there were always some princes and local lords willing to tolerate merchants and their ways even when others plundered and expelled them; and, as the record shows, oppressed Jewish traders, ruined Flemish textile workers, persecuted Huguenots, moved on and took their expertise with them. A Rhineland baron who overtaxed commercial travelers would find that the trade routes had gone elsewhere, and with it his revenues. A monarch who repudiated his debts would have immense difficulties raising a loan when the next war threatened and funds were quickly needed to equip his armies and fleets.[25]

Nowhere was this natural competitive pressure brought to bear any stronger than in the armaments industry. Kennedy continues:

Europe was different in that each of the rival forces was able to gain access to the new military techniques, so that no single power ever possessed the decisive edge. The services of the Swiss and other mercenaries, for example, were on offer to anyone who was able to pay for them. ["Have gun—will travel"] There was no single center for the production of crossbows, nor for that of cannon—whether of the earlier bronze guns or of the later, cheaper cast-iron artillery; instead, such armaments were being made close to the ore deposits on the Weald, in Central Europe, in Málaga, in Milan, in Liège, and later in Sweden. Similarly, the proliferation of shipbuilding skills in various ports ranging from the Baltic to the Black Sea made it extremely difficult for any one country to monopolize maritime power, which in turn helped to prevent the conquest and elimination of rival centers of armaments production lying across the sea.[26]

The author notes that Europe as a whole rose to global leadership because its individual nation states were under constant pressure to experiment with the latest military advancements.

> What it [decentralization of power] did, above all else, was to engender a primitive form of arms race among the city-states and then the larger kingdoms. To some extent, this probably had socioeconomic roots. Once the contending armies in Italy no longer consisted of feudal knights and their retainers but of pikemen, crossbowmen, and (flanking) cavalry paid for by the merchants and supervised by the magistrates of a particular city, it was almost inevitable that the latter would demand value for money— despite all the best maneuvers of *condottieri* [mercenaries] not to make themselves redundant; the cities would require, in other words, the sort of arms and tactics which might produce a swift victory, so that the expenses of war could then be reduced. Similarly, once the French monarchs of the late fifteenth century had a "national" army under their direct control and pay, they were anxious to see this force produce decisive results.[27]

The important concept to remember is that, while other powers like Ming China and the Ottomans had access to similar weapons, Europeans advanced faster as they were not subject to monopolization. Competition equaled survival. This is why Leonardo DaVinci's notebook for this era contained sketches of a machine gun, a primitive tank and a steam-powered cannon.

It was also axiomatic that "keeping up with the Joneses" militarily would lead to a commensurate rise in education and other technological advancements.

> The fairer aspect of this increasing commercial and colonial rivalry was the parallel upward spiral in knowledge—in science and technology. No doubt many of the advancements of this time were spinoffs from the arms race and the scramble for overseas trade; but the eventual benefits transcended their inglorious origins. Improved cartography, navigational tables, new instruments like the telescope, barometer, backstaff, and gimbaled compass, and better methods of shipbuilding helped to make maritime travel a less unpredictable form of travel. New crops and plants not only brought better nutrition but also were a stimulus to botany and agricultural science. Metallurgical skills, and indeed the whole iron industry, made rapid progress; deep-mining techniques did the same. Astronomy, medicine, physics, and engineering also benefited from the quickening economic pace and the enhanced value of science. The inquiring, rationalist mind was observing

more, and experimenting more; and the printing presses, apart from producing vernacular Bibles and political treatises, were spreading these findings. The cumulative effect of this explosion of knowledge was to buttress Europe's technological—and therefore military—superiority still further.[28]

Kennedy's patronizing of Bible production is too funny. Whereas the sweet psalmist of Israel declared, *"O come, let us worship and bow down: let us kneel before the LORD our maker"* (Psalm 95:6), the Yale humanist preferred to remain in the dark. He concludes:

In most cases, what was involved was not so much positive elements, but rather the reduction in the number of *hindrances* which checked economic growth and political diversity. Europe's greatest advantage was that it had fewer *dis*advantages than the other civilizations.

Although it is impossible to prove it, one suspects that these various general features related to one another, by some inner logic as it were, and that all were necessary. It was a combination of economic laissez-faire, political and military pluralism, and intellectual liberty—however rudimentary each factor was compared with later ages—which had been in constant interaction to produce the "European miracle." Since the miracle was historically unique, it seems plausible to assume that only a replication of all its component parts could have produced a similar result elsewhere. **Because that mix of critical ingredients did not exist in Ming China, or in the Muslim empires of the Middle East and Asia, or in any other of the societies examined above, they appeared to stand still while Europe advanced to the center of the world stage.**[29]

THE *TEXTUS RECEPTUS*

Now, as David wrote, *". . . thou hast magnified thy word above all thy name"* (Psalm 138:2b), we would expect the expanding enlargement of Japheth to be connected with Holy Scripture. And in this conjecture we are not disappointed. In 1517, a renegade Catholic scholar from Rotterdam by the name of Desiderius Erasmus (1469-1536) jolted the Vatican hard by producing the first printed edition of the Greek New Testament.

Although Europe received the printing press from Johannes Gutenberg in the mid-fifteenth century, the reader will recall that this technology had already appeared in eleventh-century China. The same was true for gunpowder and the magnetic compass, prompting Francis Bacon to state in 1620, "For these three have changed the whole face and state of things throughout the world."[30] However, once again it was Japheth, rather than Shem, who was destined for enlargement. The pope's shock troops were aghast, University of Cologne's Conrad of Hersbach warning,

> They have found a language called Greek, at which we must be careful to be on our guard. It is the mother of all heresies. In the hands of many persons I see a book, which they call the New Testament. It is a book full of thorns and poison.[31]

Rome's fears were justified, as her corner on the market of ignorance was about to be shattered. In 1534, a maverick monk by the name of Martin Luther used Erasmus's second edition to bestow upon his beloved Germany her first complete Bible based on the *Textus Receptus,* inspiring the Reformation adage, "Erasmus laid the egg and Luther hatched it." By way of another "coincidence," Luther posted his *95 Theses* in 1517, the very year that Erasmus produced his vanguard edition.

Other native translations followed quickly: the French versions of Lefevre and Olivetan, 1534 and 1535; Biestkens's Dutch work in 1558; the Swedish Uppsala Bible by Laurentius in 1541; a Spanish translation by Cassiodoro de Reyna in 1569; the Danish Christian III Bible in 1550; the Czech version of 1602 and the Italian translation by Diodati in 1607, to name a few. After a millennium of darkness, the light of God's Word was once again illuminating the European continent.

Luther's break with "His Holiness" over the authority of Holy Scripture divided Japheth into two opposing camps. While the Protestant powers were aligned to the north a papal confederation was deployed southward. This partition along the rulers' religious preferences was referred to as *cuius regio, eius religio.* As the Bible *"giveth understanding unto the simple"* (Psalm 119:130), we are not surprised to see the lingering effect of this geopolitical separation. With the onset of World War I, 330 out of every 1,000 Italian recruits were illiterate while the corresponding numbers for Germany was an astonishing 1/1000.[32]

THE KING JAMES BIBLE

However, as history confirms a distinctive *westbound* movement of truth (while error travels *eastbound*), the full force of Erasmus's labors was yet to be felt. Because the European continent lay within the reach of threatening papal armies, Japheth would experience a third stage of enlargement.

As the *Textus Receptus* was the indirect cause for the rise of Protestant Europe, the King James Bible would become the catalyst for the "greatness" in *Great* Britain. Of course, neither Ruskin nor Kennedy would concede, though both were born in England and educated at Oxford. The majority of "scholars" are afraid of the Bible. However, in a rare example of intellectual integrity, at least one secular historian *was* willing to "give credit where credit is due." In *A Short History of the English People,* J.R. Green acknowledged that the English Bible (from Tyndale to the A.V. 1611) was the undisputed power behind Britain's cultural transformation.

No greater moral change ever passed over a nation than passed over England during the years which parted the middle of the reign of Elizabeth from the meeting of the Long Parliament. **England became the people of a book, and that book was the Bible.** It was as yet the one English book that was familiar to every Englishman; it was read at churches and read at home, and everywhere its words, as they fell on ears which custom had not deadened to their force and beauty, kindled a startling enthusiasm . . . As a mere literary monument, the English version of the Bible remains the noblest example of the English tongue. Its perpetual use made it from the instant of its appearance the standard of our language. But for the moment its literary effect was less than its social. The power of the book over the mass of Englishmen showed itself in a thousand superficial ways, and in none more conspicuously than in the influence it exerted on ordinary speech . . . **But far greater than its effect on literature or social phrase was the effect of the Bible on the character of the people at large.** Elizabeth might silence or tune the pulpits; but it was impossible for her to silence or tune the great preachers of justice, and mercy, and truth, who spoke from the book which she had again opened for the people . . . The whole temper of the nation was changed. A new conception of life and of man superseded the old. A new moral and religious impulse spread through every class . . . **the whole nation became, in fact, a Church**.[33]

AGRICULTURAL REVOLUTION

In light of His own promise, *"Blessed is the nation whose God is the LORD . . ."* (Psalm 33:12a), Jehovah had obligated Himself to enrich any

Bible reading culture. Although the ultimate effect of this blessing would be felt in America, it was necessary that the mother country receive the initial nourishment. While Europe's benighted Roman Catholics were counting beads and lighting candles, England's enlightened citizenry was praying, *"Give us this day our daily bread"* (Matthew 6:11). Consequently, the *Agricultural Revolution* occurred in England around the first quarter of the eighteenth century. This watershed event was occasioned by three major developments: improved crop-growing methods, advances in livestock breeding, and the invention of new farm equipment.

Normal agricultural activity will cause a commensurate reduction of nutritive elements in the ground. Unless these ingredients are replaced, the soil's productive capacity will be seriously impaired. During the medieval and early modern period of European history, these nourishing ingredients were restored by the weather, providing that the land was left fallow by either one year in three, or every other year. Thus, the arable acreage would shrink by half or one third.

In the providence of God a retired English politician, Charles Townshend, began experimenting with crop rotation in the early 1700s. Through trial and error it was discovered that the dormant year could be utilized by planting a leguminous crop that would draw nitrogen from the air and channel it into the soil through the root structure.

Furthermore, prior to this amazing advancement, farmers were unable to raise adequate forage to feed their livestock through the winter. Consequently, most animals had to be slaughtered in the fall and the meat preserved with salt. However, since the miracle legume "just happened" to consist of ideal forage crops such as clover, alfalfa, sain foin and especially turnips, the Agricultural Revolution also increased the number and quality of farm animals. This not only enhanced the supply of meat and animal products for food, but also increased the fertility of the soil by augmenting the supply of animal manure for fertilization. While the words *"He that tilleth his land shall have plenty of bread"* (Proverbs 28:19) captivated a nation of grateful recipients, Charles Townshend came to be known as "Turnip" Townshend.

Another Englishman, Robert Bakewell, found that livestock could be improved by intensively breeding animals with certain desirable traits. (Jacob perfected this process when dealing with Laban in chapter 30 of Genesis.) The providential discovery enabled Bakewell to produce superior breeds of cattle, horses and sheep. His kind of sheep, called the *Leicester,* fattened so quickly it could be raised for slaughter at a negligible cost. As a result, mutton became the most popular meat in England.

A third native by the name of Jethro Tull invented the first workable seed drill. Prior to this time (about 1700), farmers still planted their seeds by sowing. Tull's breakthrough would enable Britain's farmers to conserve seeds and increase yields. As the new gizmo constituted the first successful farm machine with inner moving parts it became the ancestor of all modern machinery.

The net result of this Heaven-sent Agricultural Revolution was an increase in the *quantity* and *quality* of the nation's food supply. Also, as fewer men were needed to produce food, they were free to pursue other activities such as government, science, business, education or the ministry. Whereas the agricultural labor of twenty persons had been required to produce food for twenty-one persons in 1700, those numbers dropped to three persons supplying sustenance for twenty-one persons by 1900,[34] the difference being attributed to nine holy words— *"Blessed is the nation whose God is the LORD"* (Psalm 33:12a).

THE GREAT AWAKENING

Now, although God was pleased with the English nation as a whole, He was seriously at odds with the entrenched Anglican hierarchy. While the common man was moving toward the A.V. 1611, the clergy was heading back to Rome. Under the growing religious intolerance of a state-church relationship the Pilgrims left for Holland in 1608 and the Puritans began their migrations to America in 1629.

The Lord decided to call for an "end run." While the benefits of the Agricultural Revolution were being felt, another Bible law went into effect. Paul wrote in Romans 2:4b, *". . . knowing that the goodness of God leadeth thee to repentance."* With their food stores improved, a considerable portion of the population began responding to a pair of God-anointed preachers named George Whitefield and John Wesley. And, as an added slap at Ruskin and his intellectual pals, Whitefield and Wesley were also educated at Oxford (as were John Wycliff, William Tyndale and over a dozen of the King James translators). In fact, they had their own coterie as well, a religious society known as the *Holy Club.*

After their respective conversions, the controversial ministers were barred from preaching in any Anglican pulpit. Whitefield replied, "The churches are closed to me but, bless God, the fields are open." His first attempt at open-air preaching drew an estimated crowd of *20,000* colliers (coal miners) in Kingswood and officially launched the English phase of the "Great Awakening." Whitefield's diary reads like *Ripley's Believe It or Not,* confirming that truth *is* stranger than fiction.

> Wednesday, May 2. Preached this evening again to above **ten thousand** at Kennington Common . . . Sunday, May 6. Preached this morning in Moorfields to about **twenty thousand** people, who were very quiet and attentive . . . and at six preached at Kennington. Such a sight I never saw before. I believe there were no less than **fifty thousand** people . . . Thursday, May 10. Preached at Kennington, but it rained most of the day. There were not above **ten thousand** people, and thirty coaches . . . Sunday, May 13 . . . Went to public worship twice and preached in the evening to near **sixty thousand** people . . . Friday, June 1 . . . gave a short exhortation to a few people in a field, and preached in the evening, at a place called Mayfair, near Hyde Park Corner. The congregation, I believe, consisted of near **eighty thousand** people.[35]

In July of 1742, Whitefield addressed crowds ranging from *30,000* to *100,000* in Cambuslang, Scotland![36] The reader will note that microphones had not yet been invented. Also, the population in the British Isles in 1750 was only 10.5 million. With their stomachs full, numbers were led to the real *"bread of life."* (John 6:48)

Over the next fifty years, John and Charles Wesley organized thousands of the revival's converts into a network of religious societies. John S. Simon wrote:

> If Methodism had not come into contact with the mob it would never have reached the section of the English people which most needed salvation. . . . It was necessary that a race of heroic men should arise, who would dare to confront the wildest and most brutal men, and tell them the meaning of sin, and show them the Christ of the Cross and of the Judgement Throne.
>
> The incessant assaults of the mob on the Methodist preachers showed they had reached the masses. With a superb courage, rarely, if ever, equalled on the battlefield, the Methodist preachers went again and again, to the places from which they had been driven by violence, until their persistence wore

down the antagonism of their assailants. Then, out of the once furious crowd, men and women were gathered whose hearts the Lord had touched.[37]

INDUSTRIAL REVOLUTION

At about the same time America was preparing to "cut the umbilical cord," another major watershed hit the mother country—the *Industrial Revolution* (circa 1775). The two major areas of advancement were in the textile and iron industries.

In the 1760s a pair of new machines transformed textile production. James Hargreaves invented the *spinning jenny,* while Sir Richard Arkwright created the *water frame* or *throstle.* Both machines helped retire the antiquated spinning wheel that was limited to producing only one thread at a time. Between 1774 and 1779, a Lancashire weaver named Samuel Crompton developed the *spinning mule*, a combination of the previous two improvements. By the 1780s, England had 120 textile mills.

As with the spinning wheel, almost all weaving had been done on hand looms because no one could solve the problem of mechanical weaving. In 1733, a clock-maker, John Kay, invented the *flying shuttle.* Then, in the mid-1780s, a clergyman named Edward Cartwright perfected the first steam-powered loom. In 1830, John Horrows built an all-metal loom. By 1835, Britain had more than 120,000 power looms with most of them being used to weave cotton. Consequently, a single worker operating several power-driven looms could produce twenty times the output of a hand worker while a power-driven "mule" (or spinning machine) possessed two hundred times the capacity of a spinning wheel.

The steam engine was one of the most important inventions of this period. Building on the pioneering efforts of Thomas Savery and Thomas Newcomen, James Watt of Scotland patented his steam engine by 1776; other improvements followed. The new energy source was soon harnessed to streamline Britain's iron industry.

To make iron, the metal must be separated from the non-metallic elements in the ore. This process is known as smelting. Prior to the Industrial Revolution, smelting took place in a furnace fueled by the charcoal produced by burning hardwoods. Since lumber was also in demand for other purposes, the declining supply of timber drove iron production upward. A breakthrough occurred between 1709 and 1713 when Abraham

Darby, a Shropshire ironmaster, succeeded in using *coke* to smelt the iron. Coke is made by heating coal in an airtight oven.

Now "it just so happened" that England had large natural deposits of iron *and* coal. According to the *Survey of Energy Resources,* put out by the World Energy Conference in 1974, total world coal reserves were put at 651.7 billion tons. Whereas the United States was listed as having 200.3 billion tons, the Soviet Union was rated at 150.5 billion, with Europe (including Britain) at 139.7 billion for a total Japhetic factor of 75.3 percent, Ham's 17.2 billion tons constituted a mere 2.6 percent of the world's total coal reserves.[38] Interestingly, *Catholic* Italy was listed as possessing *zero* reserves.[39]

About 1750, Darby's son, Abraham II, developed a process that enabled coke iron to be worked as easily as charcoal iron. Thus, by the early 1800s, energy previously supplied by humans would be henceforth derived from fossil fuels and delivered through steam engines. In his book *The Unbound Prometheus: Technological Change and Industrial Development in Western Europe from 1750 to the Present,* Professor David S. Landes notes that in 1870 the United Kingdom was using 100 million tons of coal, a figure "equivalent to 800 million million Calories of energy, enough to feed a population of 850 million adult males for a year (the actual population was then about 31 million)."[40] The capacity of Britain's steam engines in 1870, some 4 million horsepower, was equal to the power which could be generated by 40 million men; but, as Landes notes, ". . . this many men would have eaten some 320 million bushels of wheat a year—more than three times the annual output of the entire United Kingdom in 1867-71."[41]

The resultant production statistics are staggering; pig iron output, a mere 68,000 tons in 1788, quadrupled to 244,000 tons in 1806 and to 325,000 tons in 1811. Kennedy comments accordingly:

> Between 1760 and 1830, the United Kingdom was responsible for around "two-thirds of Europe's industrial growth of output," and its share of world manufacturing production leaped from 1.9 to 9.5 percent; in the next thirty years, British industrial expansion pushed that figure to 19.9 percent, despite the spread of the new technology to other countries in the West. Around 1860, which was probably when the country reached its zenith in relative terms, the United Kingdom produced 53 percent of the world's iron and 50 percent of its coal and lignite, and consumed just under half of the raw cotton output of the globe. . . . Its energy consumption from modern sources (coal, lignite, oil) in 1860 was five times that of either the United

States or Prussia/Germany, six times that of France, and 155 times that of Russia! It alone was responsible for one-fifth of the world's commerce, but for two-fifths of the trade in manufactured goods. Over one-third of the world's merchant marine flew under the British flag, and that share was steadily increasing.[42]

SANITATION, TRANSPORTATION AND COMMUNICATION REVOLUTIONS

The *Sanitation Revolution* can be dated from about 1750 with the advent of vaccination, the conquest of plague and the nineteenth-century discovery of various antiseptics. This resulted in a steady decline in the death rate with a corresponding demographic explosion.

An augmented and healthier population equated to an increase in the supply of available labor. Thus, a *Transportation Revolution* occurred after 1825 with an expanding network of railroads while the *Communications Revolution* was enhanced by the use of the telegraph (after 1837) and the cable (after 1850). True to Bible prophecy in Daniel 12:4, a conquest of distance was taking place as men were beginning to "run to and fro" while "knowledge was being increased". All parts of the world were starting to come together.

FIREARMS REVOLUTION

While all these "transitions" were occurring, a most significant factor was at work that is often overlooked, especially in our modern liberal society. By 1830, democracy was spreading in America, Britain, and many parts of Europe. Next to a revival of religion, the most telling contribution for all of this societal bliss was a concurrent *Firearms Revolution!* ("God, Guns and Guts," etc.)

Throughout this period, the development of weapons had reached a level where governments were unable to procure armaments that were any more effective than those available to the private sector. Furthermore, the common man could now obtain these weapons of choice more easily due to an enhanced standard of living and because mass production enabled them to be sold inexpensively. As a result, *the various standing governments were never tempted to repress such an armed citizenry, allowing democracy to prevail accordingly.* This is precisely why our Founding Fathers gave us the Second Amendment. (See Chinese students throwing rocks at tanks in Beijing.)

Perhaps the most shocking illustration of firearm disparity occurred during the 1898 Battle of Omdurman in the Sudan. In just half-a-morning of "fighting," the Maxim machine guns and Lee Enfield carbine rifles of Lord Kitchner's forces annihilated 11,000 Dervishes (Muslims) with his troops sustaining only 40 fatalities. Similarly, in one engagement during the Matabele war (1893-94), 50 British soldiers fought off 5,000 Matabele warriors with just four Maxim guns. Kennedy then illustrates this truth in reverse order, noting: "The 1896 catastrophe at Adowa (in Abyssinia) gave Italy the awful reputation of having the only European army defeated by an African society without means of an effective response."[43]

More recently (June 1994), in Sierra Leone, a white-led, Western-equipped mercenary team of 300 South Africans (Executive Outcome) defeated an entire rebel army—the Revolutionary United Front—a force that numbered in the tens of thousands. Embarrassed by the irrefutable evidence of Japheth's superior capabilities (the uncomfortable reality of which being reinforced by throngs of cheering citizens liberated from certain genocide), the "Honorable" Kofi Annan had the EO replaced by a U.N. peace-keeping force of 18,000 blue berets. Within months of their arrival, thousands of defenseless Africans were being butchered once again.

Professor Quigley elucidates this politically incorrect reality:

> When weapons are cheap to get and so easy to use that almost anyone can use them after a short period of training, armies are generally made up of large masses of amateur soldiers. Such weapons we call "amateur weapons," and such armies we might call "mass armies of citizen-soldiers" [similar to America's colonial Minutemen]. The Age of Pericles in Classical Greece and the nineteenth century in Western Civilization were periods of amateur weapons and citizen-soldiers. But the nineteenth century was preceded (as was the Age of Pericles also) by a period in which weapons were expensive and required long training in their use. Such weapons we call "specialist" weapons. Periods of specialist weapons are generally periods of small armies of professional soldiers (usually mercenaries). In a period of specialist weapons the minority who have such weapons can usually force the majority who lack them to obey; thus a period of specialist weapons tends to give rise to a period of minority rule and authoritarian

government. But a period of amateur weapons is a period in which all men are roughly equal in military power, a majority can compel a minority to yield and majority rule or even democratic government tends to rise. The medieval period in which the best weapon was usually a mounted knight on horseback (clearly a specialist weapon) was a period of minority rule and authoritarian government. Even when the medieval knight was made obsolete (along with his stone castle) by the invention of gunpowder and the appearance of firearms, these new weapons were so expensive and so difficult to use (until 1800) that minority rule and authoritarian government continued even though that government sought to enforce its rule by shifting from mounted knights to professional pikemen and musketeers. But after 1800, guns became cheaper to obtain and easier to use. By 1840 a Colt revolver sold for $27 and a Springfield musket for not much more, and these were about as good weapons as anyone could get at that time. Thus, mass armies of citizens, equipped with these cheap and easily used weapons, began to replace armies of professional soldiers, beginning about 1800 in Europe and even earlier in America. **At the same time, democratic government began to replace authoritarian governments (but chiefly in those areas where the cheap new weapons were available and local standards of living were high enough to allow people to obtain them).**[44]

Now you can appreciate why our national leaders want to ban assault rifles; your single barrel 20-gauge shotgun is not much of a threat in the twenty-first century. Thomas Jefferson wrote in the proposed Virginia Constitution of 1776, "No free man shall ever be debarred the use of arms." And in his *Commonplace Book,* 1774-1776, Jefferson cited the following quote from criminologist Cesare Beccaria's 1764 work *On Crimes and Punishment,*

> Laws that forbid the carrying of arms . . . disarm only those who are neither inclined nor determined to commit crimes . . . Such laws make things worse for the assaulted and better for the assailants; they serve rather to encourage than to prevent homicides, for an unarmed man may be attacked with greater confidence than an armed man.[45]

An old country preacher put it this way, "Pray, read your Bible and keep your powder dry." The Son of God put it this way, *". . . he that hath no sword, let him sell his garment, and buy one."* (Luke 22:36b)

FINANCIAL REVOLUTION

Britain also benefited from a *Financial Revolution*. Whereas the cost of a sixteenth-century war could be millions of pounds, by the late seventeenth century the price tag had risen to *tens* of millions; and by the close of the Napoleonic War, expenditures by the major combatants occasionally reached a hundred million *per year*. Consequently, eighteenth-century belligerents were forced to borrow heavily in order to stay on the battlefield. By selling bonds, or better yet, negotiable long-term stock that assured an inflow of funds, ministers could authorize payments to army contractors, ship builders, provision merchants, and other appropriate agencies. Due to the great strength of Britain's industry, colonial trade and naval power, her credit rating was unsurpassed by her rivals. From 1688 to 1815, Britain's wartime expenditures totaled £2,293,483,437. With her total income at £1,622,924,377 for the same period, the balance raised by loans was £670,559,060, or 33.3 percent.[46]

Another reason for Britain's excellent credit was that her money policies were determined by a duly elected parliament. Conversely, the French had no system of public finance. The monarchy's fiscal operations were "managed" by a hodgepodge of bureaucratic publicans specializing in corruption and ineptness. Whereas British officials were answerable to their constituents, French tax collectors simply purchased their positions.

Also, extended peace and prosperity enabled Britons to invest abroad which further strengthened the nation's financial base. The £6,000,000 exported annually in the decade following Waterloo rose to over £30,000,000 a year by mid-century, and to an unprecedented £75,000,000 per annum between 1870 and 1875! The resultant income to Britain in the form of interest and dividends grew from £8,000,000 per year in the 1830s to over £50,000,000 a year by the 1870s. And most of this was immediately reinvested in an upward spiral of economic growth.[47] In his book, *Britain, Europe and the World*, Bernard Porter illustrates England's financial hegemony by depicting the island nation as ". . . the first frogspawn egg to grow legs, the first tadpole to change into a frog, [and] the first frog to hop out of the pond."[48]

Finally, not only were these seven revolutions unique to Britain but the *order* in which they occurred was also a sign of God's special favor on the people who read His Word. For instance, the Agricultural Revolution had to precede the Industrial Revolution in order to supply the food and labor requisite for the factories and industrial cities. The Sanitation Revolution arrived just in time to assuage the unhealthy living conditions that were rampant in these unprecedented urbanized communities.

This is far more significant than one might think. In non-western societies, efforts to industrialize frequently began before agricultural improvements were realized. Consequently, undernourished peasants had to suffer in order to increase profits for their tyrannical masters who contained them with superior weaponry. And the corresponding lack of sanitary advancements only insured that their suffering would end sooner than later. In his book, *The Industrial Revolution*, T. S. Ashton soberly notes:

> There are today on the plains of India and China men and women, plague-ridden and hungry, living lives little better, to outward appearance, than those of cattle that toil with them by day and share their places of sleep by night. Such Asiatic standards, and such unmechanised horrors, are the lot of those who increase their numbers without passing through an industrial revolution.[49]

Dr. Paul Lee Tan relates a peasant's description of the Russian famine from 1932 to 1933:

> We've eaten everything we could lay our hands on—cats, dogs, field-mice, birds. When it's light tomorrow you will see the trees stripped of bark . . . And the horse manure has been eaten. Sometimes there are whole grains in it.[50]

BRITANNIA RULES THE WAVES

As with the creation of Europe, there is also a major *geographic* factor to discern when considering England's special place in God's plan for the ages. In Genesis 10:25, we read, *"And unto Eber were born two sons: the name of one was Peleg* [meaning "division"]; *for in his days was the earth divided."* Unless one is an evolutionist, it would be safe to assume that sometime after the Tower of Babel fiasco, the Lord repositioned the continents according to a divine blueprint. In Deuteronomy 32:8, it appears that He divided the "sons of Adam" into twelve global regions (i.e., according to the twelve tribes of "the children of Israel"). Various lists, such as the following, have been suggested: (1) Arctica (2) Antarctica (3) North America (4) Central America (5) South America

(6) Greenland (7) England (8) Europe (9) Asia (10) India (11) Africa and (12) Australia- New Zealand.

In his work, *The Clash of Civilizations and the Remaking of World Order,* Professor Huntington cites historian Matthew Melko accordingly:

> [T]he identity of the major civilizations is not contested. "Reasonable agreement," as Melko concludes after reviewing the literature, exists on at least **twelve major civilizations**, seven of which no longer exist (Mesopotamian, Egyptian, Cretan, Classical, Byzantine, Middle American, Andean) and five which do (Chinese, Japanese, Indian, Islamic, and Western).[51]

The inhabitants of these assorted regions were generally separated from one another by impediments of "nature." This is why 75% of the planet is covered by water and why Revelation 21:1 states, with regard to the *new earth, ". . . and there was no more sea."* Moses declared that God *"set the bounds of the people"* (Deuteronomy 32:8c). This was because He knew that whenever men get together, *"this they begin to do: and now **nothing will be restrained from them, which they have imagined to do"*** (Genesis 10:6b). In the New Testament, Paul declared that God *"hath determined the times before appointed, and the bounds of their habitation; **That they should seek the Lord**, if haply they might feel after him, and find him, though he be not far from every one of us:"* (Acts 17:26b-27).

Professor Ruskin didn't have a clue as to why the future land of the King James Bible was partitioned off from the entire European landmass. *Britain became the world's greatest empire because it possessed certain advantages that the other nations lacked.* Following America's discovery, the Atlantic was deemed more important than the Mediterranean as a route of commerce and wealth. In this regard Britain was unique in two particulars. Not only did she command the westernmost longitude, but an island status as well. Thus her security would relate to a control of the seas, especially the English Channel. God chose to grant this naval superiority with the miraculous defeat of the Roman Catholic Spanish Armada in 1588. The "score" on that occasion was 17,000 killed and 80 ships sunk for the Spaniards, with only *60* killed and *zero* vessels lost for the highly outnumbered British.

Over the next three-and-a-half centuries (until the advent of modern air power) the English Channel gave Britain security and afforded her an international position unlike that of any continental force. In his work, *The Influence of Sea Power Upon History 1660-1783*, A.T. Mahan wrote:

> ... if a nation be so situated that it is neither forced to defend itself by land nor induced to seek extension of its territory by way of land, it has, by the very unity of its aim directed upon the sea, an advantage as compared with a people one of whose boundaries is continental.[52]

Kennedy adds,

> the insularity of the British Isles remained as great an advantage as ever—freeing its population from the fears of a sudden invasion by neighboring armies, allowing the emphasis upon sea power rather than land power, and giving its statesmen a much greater freedom of action over issues of war and peace than those enjoyed by the continental states.[53]

Thus, the Royal Navy literally kept the rest of the world in check with her shipbuilding superiority. In 1815, Britain possessed 214 "ships of the line" as compared with 145 for Spain, France and Russia combined; Denmark, Sweden, Italy and the United Provinces having none.[54] On the eve of WWI, Britain's warship tonnage was listed in Q. Wright's *A Study of War* as 2,714,000. The other powers were as follows: Germany-1, 305,000; United States-985,000; France-900,000; Japan-700,000; Russia-679,000; Italy-498,000; and Austria-Hungary-372,000.[55] With such maritime muscle, the armed services rarely received more than two to three percent of the Gross National Product from 1815 to 1900. In the 1860s, Britain's GNP totaled about £1 billion with less than £27 million going to defense expenditures.[56]

Along with her naval supremacy came a concomitant preeminence in merchant shipping. By the twentieth century Britain owned 39 percent of the world's oceangoing vessels (three times the number of her nearest rival).[57] Professor Quigley explains:

> Because Britain had security, it had freedom of action. That means it had a choice whether to intervene or to stay out of the various disputes which arose on the Continent of Europe or elsewhere in the world. Moreover, if it intervened, it could do so on a limited commitment, restricting its contribution of men, energy, money, and wealth to whatever amount it wished. If such a limited commitment were exhausted or lost, so long as the British fleet controlled the seas, Britain had security, and thus had freedom to choose if it would break off its intervention or increase its commitment. Moreover,

England could make even a small commitment of its resources of decisive importance by using this commitment in support of the second strongest Power on the Continent against the strongest Power, thus hampering the strongest Power and making the second Power temporarily the strongest, as long as it acted in accord with Britain's wishes. In this way, by following balance-of-power tactics, Britain was able to play a decisive role on the Continent, keep the Continent divided and embroiled in its own disputes, and do this with a limited commitment of Britain's own resources, leaving a considerable surplus of energy, manpower, and wealth available for acquiring an empire overseas. In addition, Britain's unique advantage in having security through a limited commitment of resources by control of the sea was one of the contributing factors which allowed Britain to develop its unique social structure, its parliamentary system, its wide range of civil liberties, and its great economic advance.[58]

As late as 1939, Chamberlain would curtly inform France that Britain's pledge for the Continent would be no more than two divisions. Kennedy, citing L. Dehio's work, *The Precarious Balance*, summarizes Quigley's extended comments:

> Geographical advantage and economic benefit were thus merged to enable the British brilliantly to pursue a Janus-faced strategy: "with one face turned towards the Continent to trim the balance of power and the other directed at sea to strengthen her maritime dominance."[59]

Since the European powers possessed none of these blessings, their colonial ambitions would be subordinated to matters of national security. Consequently, the old adage stated, "The sun never sets on the British Empire." (As recently as my employment in the early 1970s with British Airways, that carrier was the recognized industry leader in total air route mileage.)

THE VICTORIAN ERA

In the light of this preeminence, the Scripture makes it clear: *"For unto whomsoever much is given, of him shall be much required"* (Luke 12:48). England had not received these global advantages to increase her pride and plunder; *she was afforded this window of opportunity to get the Gospel to the heathen*. The A.V. 1611 was at the zenith of its puissance; poised and ready to strike. Lord Macaulay wrote in 1828, "The English

Bible—a book which, if everything else in our language should perish, would alone suffice to show the whole extent of its beauty and power."[60]

With so much at stake, the nation's leadership would be crucial. It has been said that the Lord always has a prepared *place* for a prepared *person*. Sometimes, though, His selection may surprise you. (Judges 4:4) As the apostle Paul wrote, *". . . how unsearchable are his judgments, and his ways past finding out!"* (Romans 11:33b). Dr. George W. Truett introduces the central political figure throughout this providential era of British history:

> When William IV of England died [June 20, 1837], there was a young girl spending the night at the palace. They awakened her and told her that she was now the Queen of England. As soon as she heard the news she dropped on her knees and asked the Heavenly Father to help and guide her through all the years that were to follow.
>
> For sixty-four years this girl, who was Queen Victoria, reigned over the British Empire. England never made greater progress than during her reign. A prince of India asked her what was the secret of England's power, and for her answer she quietly picked up a Book from the table nearby. "This is the secret," she said. The Book was God's Word, the Bible.[61]

The reason why the Bible was within arm's reach was because Queen Victoria was one of the few British monarchs who took the words of Deuteronomy 17:19 literally. With reference to a king and the Word of God, Moses wrote, *"And it shall be with him, and he shall read therein all the days of his life: that he may learn to fear the LORD his God, to keep all the words of this law and these statutes, to do them"* (Deuteronomy 17:19).

To be sure, Victoria's reign of nearly six-and-a-half decades fell short of Rome's "papal infallibility". Her lengthy administration was interrupted by many things, including nine successful pregnancies and seven unsuccessful assassination attempts. Recognized as having established the pattern for a modern monarch who "reigns but does not rule," Victoria deferred an increasing amount of governmental matters to her ministers. After the death of the Prince Consort in 1861, she delegated most of the nation's decision making to Sir Robert Pell, William Gladstone and Benjamin Disraeli. (The inevitable machinations that resulted from such a policy will be covered in chapter twelve.)

From a theological perspective, Victoria had a number of handicaps. The Scripture says, *"For we cannot but speak the things which we have seen and heard"* (Acts 4:20). Obviously, the queen was not a Baptist.

However, though the formal head of the Church of England, to her credit, Victoria preferred the simpler worship of the Scottish Presbyterians. She simply could not stand phony ministers! Elizabeth Longford writes:

> Preachers were judged according to naturalness. She could not endure mannerisms. Overemphasis, a nasal twang or heavy breathing was ruthlessly condemned.[62]

Also, as a member of the fairer sex, Victoria would have been more susceptible to the devil's subtlety. (Genesis 3:1) On her coronation day, at the tender age of eighteen, a government minister remarked:

> Poor little queen! She is at an age at which a girl can hardly be trusted to choose a bonnet for herself, yet a task is laid upon her from which an arch angel might shrink.[63]

In *Victoria the Young Queen*, Monica Charlot describes the natural spiritual differences between husbands and wives:

> Albert's attitude toward religion was also much stricter than Victoria's. The Prince had a more doctrinal view of religion than the Queen, whose faith was more tied up with ethics, morality and the law of life than with revelation.[64]

One must also consider that Victoria was a widow for two-thirds of her reign. Depression was a frequent visitor, especially after two of her children were taken in death. Christopher Hibbert claims that the grieving queen even dabbled with séances.[65] (Dr. Bob Jones, Sr., once related that he also naively attended a séance following his mother's death, and this was *after* he was saved.) Furthermore, the queen would have required wisdom to practice any faith while leading a nation of diverse beliefs. As best illustrated by our own George Washington, the historical pattern has been one of reticence in religious matters.

Whatever her faults, Victoria was smart enough to realize her need for preaching. Longford writes, "All her life she showed a highly articulate interest in sermons, from which she expected to derive the week's spiritual sustenance."[66] Responding to the light that she had, Queen Victoria was revered for two reasons; she was genuinely devoted to her family *and* her subjects.

Dr. Paul Lee Tan relates a marvelous account of God's special watch care over the one known as the "Good Queen":

The British express train raced through the night, its powerful headlamp spearing the black darkness ahead. The train was carrying Queen Victoria.

Suddenly the engineer saw a startling sight. Revealed in the beam of the engine's headlights was a weird figure in a black cloak standing in the middle of the tracks and waving its arms. The engineer grabbed for the brakes and brought the train to a grinding halt.

He and his fellow trainsmen climbed out to see what had stopped them. But they could find no trace of the strange figure. On a hunch, he walked a few yards further up the tracks. Suddenly he stopped and stared into the fog in horror. The bridge had been washed out in the middle and had toppled into a swollen stream. If he had not heeded the ghostly figure, the train would have plunged into the stream.

While the bridge and tracks were being repaired, the crew made a more intensive search for the strange flagman. But not until they got to London, did they solve the mystery.

At the base of the engine's head lamp, the engineer discovered a huge dead moth. He looked at it for a moment, then on impulse wet its wings and pasted it to the glass of the lamp.

Climbing back into his cab, he switched on the lamp and saw the "flagman" in the beam. He knew the answer now: the moth had flown into the beam, seconds before the train was due to reach the washed-out bridge. In the fog, it appeared to be a phantom figure, waving its arms.

When Queen Victoria was told of the strange happening she said, "I'm sure it was no accident. It was God's way of protecting us." [67]

One of my favorite stories has to do with Victoria's reaction to the Hallelujah Chorus at the end of a performance of Handel's *Messiah*. (Modern biographers would divert their readers' attention to the queen's impatience with either the length or tedious portions of the arrangement.) In his refreshing work *Messiah*, Dr. N. A. Woychuk cites the nineteenth-century preacher, Dr. J. Wilbur Chapman, as follows:

When Queen Victoria (1819-1901) had just ascended her throne she went, as is the custom of Royalty, to hear "The Messiah" rendered. She had been instructed as to her conduct by those who knew, and was told that she must not rise when the others stood at the singing of the Hallelujah Chorus. When that magnificent chorus was being sung and the singers were exclaiming, "Hallelujah! Hallelujah! Hallelujah! For the Lord God omnipotent reigneth," she sat with great difficulty.

It seemed as if she would rise in spite of the custom of kings and queens at that time, but finally when they came to that part of the chorus where with a shout they proclaim Him King of kings, suddenly the young queen rose and stood with bowed head, as if she would take her own crown from off her head and cast it at His feet.[68]

It has been said that one can tell a lot about an individual by studying the character of that person's enemies. Over a hundred years after her death, twenty-first-century perverts still make sardonic reference to the "Victorian Age" of sexual repression. If Victoria died without experiencing the new birth, she at least rattled the devil's cage through her "Christian" legacy. Thus, a worst-case scenario would place her alongside the Roman centurion who built a synagogue for the Jews, and Thomas Jefferson who secured religious liberty for the Baptists.

The opinions of our current AIDS-ridden society notwithstanding, the Lord must have looked with favor on Victoria's "prudish" leadership. During the queen's reign, product per capita rose two-and-a-half times. Although Albert and Victoria confessed to being totally ignorant about "the birds and the bees" on their wedding night, average real wages increased between fifteen and twenty-five percent from 1815 to 1850 and by an impressive eighty percent in the next half-century. In his book, *Victorian Economy*, F. Crouzet gives the convincing indices: "With 2 percent of the world's population and 10 percent of Europe's, the United Kingdom would seem to have had a capacity in modern industries equal to 40-45 percent of the world's potential and 55-60 percent of that in Europe."[69]

To discern the cause for Britain's unprecedented peace and prosperity, Proverbs 16:7 would be a good place to start: *"When a man's ways please the LORD, he maketh even his enemies to be at peace with him."* Not only was God pleased with England for making the A.V. 1611 her spiritual and cultural foundation but also because hundreds of selfless missionaries were willing to leave Great Britain to carry the Gospel around the world. In their day the *real* message was, "The 'Sun of Righteousness' never sets on the British Empire." (Malachi 4:2) Why else do you think England's realm expanded over 100,000 sq. miles per year from 1815 to 1865? By the turn of the century, Britain possessed the largest territory the world had ever seen—*a staggering twelve million square miles and a quarter of the globe's population!*[70]

The Cambridge Illustrated History of the British Empire lists the following territories as either ruled by Britain directly, or dominated by British influence.

Arden, Anguilla, Antigua, Ascension, Australia, Bahamas, Bahrain, Barbados, Basutoland, Bechuanaland, Bermuda, Bhutan, British Antarctic Territory, British Columbia, British Guiana, British Honduras, British Indian Ocean Territory, British Kaffraria, British New Guinea, British Somaliland, British Virgin Islands, Brunei, Burma, Canada, Canada East, Canada West, Cape Breton Island, Cape Colony, Cayman Islands, Ceylon, Cook Islands, Cyprus, Dependency of South Georgia and the South Sandwich Islands, Dominica, Egypt, Eire, Ellice Islands, Falkland Islands, Fiji, Gambia, Gibraltar, Gilbert Islands, Gold Coast, Grenada, Heligoland, Hong Kong, India, Ionian Islands, Iraq, Jamaica, Kenya, Kuwait, Labuan, Malacca, Malaya, Maldive Islands, Malta, Mauritius, Montserrat, Natal, Nepal, Nevis, New Brunswick, Newfoundland, New Hebrides, New South Wales, New Zealand, Nigeria, North Borneo, Northern Rhodesia, Nova Scotia, Nyasaland, Orange Free State, Palestine, Penang, Pitcairn Islands, Prince Edward Island, Qatar, Queensland, Rhodesia, Rupert's Land and North West, St. Christopher, St. Helena, St. Lucia, St. Vincent, Sarawak, Seychelles, Sierra Leone, Sikkim, Singapore, Solomon Islands, South Africa, South Australia, South West Africa, Straits Settlements, Sudan, Swaziland, Tanganyika, Tasmania, Tobago, Tonga, Transjordan, Transvaal, Trinidad, Tristan da Cunha, Trucial States, Turks and Caicos Islands, Uganda, Victoria, Weihaiwei, Western Australia, Zanzibar.[71]

How's *that* for an "enlargement of Japheth"?

EXPANSION OF THE ENGLISH LANGUAGE

A commensurate spread of English accompanied these colonial acquisitions, thus providing an enhanced access to the A.V. 1611. Professor Quigley notes the technical mandate for English:

> No vernacular language could have been used to teach the really valuable contributions of the West, such as science, technology, economics, agricultural science, or political science, because the necessary vocabulary was lacking in the vernaculars. When the university of the native state of Hyderabad tried to translate Western works into Urdu for teaching purposes after 1920, it was necessary to create about 40,000 new words.[72]

That English had become the world's primary language was miraculous in itself and can only be explained by the power of the King James Bible. As late as the beginning of the seventeenth century, an examination of the contents of the main Oxford library reveal that only one book out of a hundred was in English, the remainder being exclusively in classical languages. Alister McGrath writes:

> It is not generally realized that the languages of the elite in English society in the early fourteenth century were French and Latin. English was seen as the language of peasants, incapable of expressing anything other than the crudest and most basic of matters. English was just fine when dealing with spreading dung on fields. But how could such a barbaric language do justice to such sophisticated matters as philosophy or religion? To translate the Bible from its noble and ancient languages into English was seen as a pointless act of debasement.
>
> The story of the King James Bible cannot be told without an understanding of the remarkable rise of confidence in the English language in the late sixteenth century. What was once scorned as the barbarous language of plowmen became esteemed as the language of patriots and poets—a language fit for heroes on the one hand, and for the riches of the Bible on the other. Gone were any hesitations about the merits of the English language. Elizabeth's navy and armies had established England's military credentials; her poets, playwrights, and translators had propelled English into the front rank of living European languages. The King James Bible consolidated the enormous advances in the English language over the centuries, and can be seen as the symbol of a nation and language that believed that their moment had finally arrived.[73]

The "esteemed" professor of historical theology at Oxford University repeatedly explains how the A.V. 1611 impacted the English language. On page two, he writes:

> Without this Bible, the culture of the English-speaking world would have been immeasurably impoverished. The King James Bible played no small part in shaping English literary nationalism, by asserting the supremacy of the English language as a means of conveying religious truths.[74]

He states on page 257:

> One of the unintended functions of the King James Bible was to establish norms in written and spoken English. Should not the language of the Bible shape the language of the people? The growing acceptance of the King James Bible in shaping public and private religious discourse inevitably had its impact on the language as a whole.[75]

Then, on page 258, he adds:

The growing acceptance of the King James Bible must be seen as a major force in the shaping of standard English . . . The King James Bible was published within a window of opportunity, which allowed it to exercise a substantial and decisive influence over the shaping of the English language.[76]

Now, should we laugh or cry that Professor McGrath would author a book entitled *In The Beginning: The Story of The King James Bible and How It Changed a Nation, a Language and a Culture* while also being the general editor of *The NIV Thematic Study Bible*? McGrath certainly has problems stating what he really believes. While explaining on page 289 (of *In The Beginning*) how the Authorized Version surpassed the Geneva Bible, he writes, "The grounds of that triumph may partly rest in its eloquence, or in the **excellence of its translation.**"[77] Yet on the very next page, when trying to explain the enduring "uncritical adulation" of the King James Bible he says, "Perhaps familiarity dulled the senses to the **weaknesses of the translation**"[78] On page 256, the NIV exponent lets the cat out of the bag with, "More generally, the King James Bible achieves a degree of elegance that has been the envy of its successors."[79]

Then, on page 300, he finally comes clean:

Even four hundred years after the six companies of translators began their long and laborious task, their efforts continue to be a landmark for popular Christianity. Other translations will doubtless jostle for place in the nation's bookstores in the twenty-first century. Yet the King James Bible retains its place as a literary and religious classic.[80]

However, the evidence that McGrath is just another "angel of light" can be found among his book jacket endorsements. (II Corinthians 11:14) In addition to Kenneth L. Barker, executive director for the New International Version Translation Center, we have another given by "Father" Joseph A. Fitzmyer, S.J., professor emeritus, Biblical Studies, Catholic University of America, who says:

Alister McGrath has written a learned, **witty,** and fascinating **tale** about the history of the King James Bible—its place in the developing English Bible tradition and its recognition as the "noblest monument of English prose." For all readers and students of the Bible, this book will be an invaluable *vade-mecum* [manual].[81]

One day that "noble monument" will send those two straight to Hell for hustling "witty tales" about the Holy Words of the Living God!

In any event, McGrath got the part about the King James Bible and missionary activity correct.

> The expansion of British economic and military influence in the later eighteenth and nineteenth centuries was preceded and accompanied by missionary work, based on the King James Bible. Wherever English-language versions of Christianity sprang up, these would usually be nourished by this definitive translation. The impact of the King James Bible on the language and worship of Christianity in Africa and Australasia has been immense.[82]

BRITISH WORLD MISSIONS

According to the previously cited list of English colonies in *The Cambridge Illustrated History of the British Empire*, McGrath left off about 100 other fields of "impact."

At first, Britain's government and business leaders were skeptical about the concept of foreign missions. The British East India Company stated at the beginning of the nineteenth century: "The sending of Christian missionaries into our Eastern possessions is the maddest, most expensive, most unwanted project that was ever proposed by a lunatic enthusiast."[83] Yet, by the close of the same century, the English Lieutenant-Governor of Bengal acknowledged: "In my judgment, Christian missionaries have done more lasting good to the people of India than all the agencies combined."[84] Even the secular *Cambridge Illustrated History* was willing to concede, "The planting of Christianity in non-Christian areas has largely been the result of efforts by British missionaries."[85]

To render a nominal account of British missions would require a multi-volume set—a task beyond the scope of this present work. A sampling of the better known British missionaries would include:

> **William Carey**, who taught himself six languages and remained in India for forty-two years without a furlough, translating the Scriptures into forty-four languages and dialects.

James Hudson Taylor, who established 205 mission stations in China manned by 805 fellow British missionaries and 125,000 witnessing Chinese converts.

Charles "C.T." Studd, who spent forty-six years spreading the Gospel in China, India and Africa, writing, "Some wish to live within the sound of church or chapel bell; I want to run a rescue shop within a yard of Hell."

Robert Moffatt, who evangelized thousands of cannibals and witch doctors in South Africa, his most notable "trophy" being the demonic headhunter known as Africaner, chief of the Namaquas.

David Livingstone, who advanced the Gospel 1,400 miles into the heart of Africa, eventually succumbing to the debilitating effects of a dozen jungle ailments.

James Chalmers, who planted dozens of churches in New Hebrides and New Guinea before his martyrdom off the coast of Papua.

John Williams, who was killed, cooked, and eaten by cannibals in Dillons Bay, Erromanga.

John G. Patton, who so profoundly transformed the South Sea Island of Tierra del Fuego that Charles Darwin made a substantial contribution to the London Missionary Society.

James Calvert, who testified that he began his labor in the Fiji islands by burying the bones of a cannibal feast, yet lived to see those same heathen gathered around the Lord's table.

John Geddie, whose ministry at Aneityum is best summed up by the famous inscription at his mission station: "When he landed here in 1848, there were no Christians. When he left in 1872, there were no heathen."

THE "CONGO CAPTAIN"

The story of "Captain" George Grenfell (1849-1906) may be the most remarkable account of all. Born in Sancreed, near Land's End in Cornwall, England, Grenfell was converted and immersed at the Heneage Baptist Church in 1864. While employed as a teenage apprentice in a local machinery plant, he lost the sight of an eye through a work-related accident.

Grenfell came under the influence of David Livingstone and entered the Baptist College at Bristol to prepare for a mission career in Africa. After being commissioned by the Baptist Missionary Society, he reached the Cameroons in January, 1875. Early the next year he married Mary

Hakes, but had to bury her before they could celebrate their first wedding anniversary.

The Congo River enters the Atlantic Ocean six hundred miles south of the Cameroons. At 2,900 miles in length, the Congo is the world's second-largest river after the Amazon. In the wake of Stanley and Livingstone's explorations and charting of Africa's chief aquatic thoroughfare, author C.H. Patton notes in *The Lure of Africa*, ". . . the Baptists were the first to seize the great opening. . . .[86]

A hundred miles from the sea, navigation was blocked by a series of thirty waterfalls. Beyond this point, however, the Gospel could be carried to over twenty million natives via the Congo's vast system of waterways and tributaries. The task, though, would be dangerous. Africa was already known as the "white man's grave," while the Congo was called "the shortcut to Heaven." The "visitation prospects" included *demon-possessed slave merchants, witch doctors, headhunters* and *cannibals*. The Manyema were human vultures who deliberately ate dead corpses several days old without cooking them.[87] The more "civilized" cannibals did their shopping at the local butcher shop. Torday writes:

> It often happens among the Ngombe Tribes that the poor creature destined for the knife is exposed for sale in the market. He walks to and fro and epicures [connoisseurs] come to examine him. They describe the parts they prefer—one the arm, one the leg, breast, or head. The portions that are purchased are marked off with lines of colored ochre. When the entire body is sold the wretch is slain.[88]

For the record, this beats anything that was practiced in the antebellum South! Of course, our modern culture of political correctness would not recognize blacks butchering blacks as "racism."

Early in 1878, the man of God, accompanied by a new helpmeet, was on his way along the banks of the Congo. Harrison describes those first hundred miles through jungles infested with lions, leopards and snakes:

> Grenfell encountered almost insuperable difficulties. But finally, after thirteen attempts, after splashing through many swamps and tramping through grass often fifteen feet high, after frequent perilous escapes from savages and after one of his companions had been severely wounded, he passed the cataracts and reached Stanley Pool in February, 1881.[89]

Grenfell quickly discovered that a canoe ministry would be slow and dangerous. Hippopotami often upset them, after which crocodiles devoured the occupants. Thankfully, the Lord had already made provision for this need. Robert Arthington, a wealthy Christian back in England, dedicated his entire fortune to various missionary groups. On May 14, 1877, he gave the Baptist Missionary Society £1,000 for a screw steamer, a most unusual gift, writing:

> I believe the time has come when we should place a steamer on the Congo River where we can sail north-eastward into the heart of Africa for many hundreds of miles uninterruptedly and bring the glad tidings of the everlasting gospel to thousands of human beings who are now ignorant of the way of life and immortality.[90]

Grenfell promptly left his wife on the Congo, returning to London to oversee construction of the *Peace*, a vessel measuring seventy-eight feet in length and drawing twelve inches of water. Harrison relates:

> After it had been tested on the Thames, it was taken apart, put in 800 packages weighing 65 pounds each and shipped to the mouth of the Congo. It took a thousand men to carry the vessel and necessary food supplies up the river and past the rapids to Stanley Pool. Grenfell had brought with him a young missionary engineer whose special assignment was to put the vessel together and then keep it in good running order. Soon after reaching African soil, he fell sick and died. Two other engineers were promptly sent out from England, but both of them died within a few weeks.
>
> So Grenfell himself had to undertake the gigantic task of putting the ship together. This he successfully accomplished. He declared that the *Peace* was "prayed together." . . . Finally the vessel was launched, steam was up and the *Peace* began to move. "She lives, Master! She lives!" shouted the excited Africans.[91]

Captain Grenfell's maiden voyage covered twelve hundred miles. He wrote, "It was a wondrous joy to take for the first time the light of life into those regions of darkness, cruelty and death."[92] In predictable fashion, the devil was hot on his trail. At the end of one excursion, Grenfell related:

> Thank God we are safely back. It might have been otherwise, for we have encountered perils not a few. But the winds, which were sometimes simply terrific, and the rocks, which knocked three holes in the steamer when we were fleeing from cannibals, have not wrecked us. We have been attacked by natives about twenty different times; we have been stoned and shot at with arrows, and have been the mark for spears more than we can count.[93]

Having lost his first wife in the Cameroons, Grenfell would also bury four children on the banks of the mighty Congo. Harrison states: "These graves were like milestones along the river as he pushed farther and farther inland. His grave was destined to be the farthest of all."[94]

Grenfell lived to see the fruit of his labor, testifying in his twilight years: "Our services are crowded as they have never been before. God's spirit is manifestly working."[95] Concerning one place in particular, he wrote:

> Just twenty years have elapsed since I first landed at the foot of this cliff and was driven off at the point of native spears. The reception this time was very different. The teacher and a little crowd of school children stood on the beach to welcome us.[96]

What occurred at yet another site in 1905 represented the spiritual grand finale of Grenfell's missionary career.

> It was here that, twenty-one years ago, we first came into view of the burning villages of the big Arab slave-raid of 1884. This time, as we were looking for a good camping place, we suddenly heard strike up "All Hail The Power" from on board one of the big fishing canoes hidden among the reeds so that we had not observed it. What a glorious welcome! Whose heart would not be moved to hear "Crown Him Lord of All" under such circumstances? I little thought to live to see so blessed a change, and my heart went forth in praise.[97]

The Royal Geographical Society awarded Grenfell a gold medal in 1886. The "Congo Captain" went to his heavenly reward on July 1, 1906. His last words were, "Jesus is mine."

Now do you really think that Professor Ruskin and his fellow socialists at Oxford had a clue? *God almighty expanded England's sphere of influence for the sole purpose of advancing the kingdom of His dear Son.* As for Oxford's secular priorities, the King James Bible declares, *". . . that which is highly esteemed among men is abomination in the sight of God"* (Luke 16:15b).

THE FINAL ENLARGEMENT

Despite England's providential role in the A.V. 1611 and foreign missions, the nation fell woefully short in one critical area. Although James I was used to give the world the true Word of God, the *Protestant* monarch was unwilling to grant his own subjects freedom of conscience. While they could now read God's holy book for themselves, they were not always free to obey its commands. The Church of England constituted the higher authority. Though in the off-scour minority, the Baptists stood ready to *"earnestly contend for the faith"* (Jude 3). Their landmark "Confession of Faith," published in London in *1611*, read in part: "The magistrate is not to meddle with religion or matters of conscience, nor to compel men to do this or that form of religion, because Christ is King and Lawgiver of Church and conscience."[98]

On April 11, 1612, Edward Wightman, a Baptist pastor from Burton-on-Trent, was *burned alive* at Lichfield for the "crime of heresy." One of the counts in the indictment was that he declared "the use of baptism to be administered in water only to converts of sufficient age and understanding."[99]

From a human perspective, the killing of Baptists by English Christians *just a year after the King James Bible was published*, had "forced God's hand" to enlarge Japheth once again. With Baptists on the Continent being slain by papists and Protestants alike, there was literally nowhere to flee but westward. To James's "credit," Edward Wightman holds the distinction of being the *last* Baptist martyr in "Merry Old England." However, the die had been cast ideologically. Protestant Britain would go no further than Protestant Europe in the experiment of religious toleration. Both were committed to the church-state arrangement begun by Constantine the Great in 325 A.D.

Although there would be no more capital punishment over theology, Baptist dissenters would remain the most despised sect in the land. (John 15:18-25) A half century after Wightman's death the celebrated Baptist John Bunyan was committed to the loathsome Bedford "gaol" for "illegal preaching." He would spend his twelve-year sentence writing *Pilgrim's Progress* on crumpled milk bottle tops.

As late as Victoria's reign, Baptist preachers were being hampered by such indignities as the "five-mile rule" which limited their itinerant labors accordingly. Another statute prohibited Nonconformist assemblies from using the word "church" in their formal name. Hence, the Baptist pastor Charles Spurgeon delivered his Sunday sermons in the "Metropolitan Tabernacle."

Now, with such intolerance prevailing among "fellow Christians," *how could a lowly Jew expect to be treated any better?* No, the religious problems of the "Old World" could only be solved by the supernatural creation of a "New World." As early as 1783, Ezra Stiles, president of Yale University, observed:

> Heaven has provided this country, not indeed derelict, but only partially settled, and consequently open for the reception of a **new enlargement of Japheth**. Europe was settled by Japheth; America is settling from Europe; and perhaps this . . . enlargement bids fair to surpass the first.[100]

For the final enlargement of Japheth, God would use our Baptist ancestors to ensure that America was firmly established on the unprecedented doctrine of absolute religious liberty. In 1705, Valentine Wightman, *a direct descendant of Edward Wightman*, founded the first Baptist church in the colony of Connecticut. Valentine died on June 9, 1747, completing a forty-two-year ministry in Groton. Following a seven-year hiatus, the church called Valentine's son, Timothy, to be their pastor. He would lead the flock for another forty-two years before expiring on November 14, 1796. Then, in 1800, John Gano Wightman, Timothy's youngest son became the pastor and went on to serve for an incredible forty-one more years! And, as a spiritual postscript, on June 12, 1864, Palmer G. Wightman, the grandson of John Gano Wightman, was called to the Groton church and a mighty revival occurred.

Blessed are the dead which die in the Lord from
henceforth: Yea, saith the Spirit, that they may rest from
*their labours; **and their works do follow them**.*
(Revelation 14:13b)

4

Soul Liberty

"And to the angel of the church in Philadelphia
write . . . I know thy works: behold, I have set before
thee an open door, and no man can shut it."
(Revelation 3:7a, 8a)

WHEREAS JAPHETH'S INITIAL separation from his two younger brothers was followed by a "continental divide" over the *Textus Receptus*, which in turn was followed by Britain's rise to "greatness" over the A.V. 1611, America would experience the final, western extension over the doctrine of "Soul Liberty."

Though the Reformers were able to break the Vatican's power, enabling England to unleash the "Monarch of Books," little would change with regard to freedom of conscience. The *Protestant* version of Rome's church-state relationship proved an equally imposing barrier to local, New Testament assemblies.

Because the King James Bible remains the foremost authority on *any* subject of importance, including "prophetic history," the spiritual character of this age was prerecorded on the island of Patmos in 97 A.D. (Revelation 3:1-13) As a number of converted Catholics deserted their "holy mother church" under the ministries of Luther, Calvin, Zwingli and others, we are not surprised that the root word for the name *Sardis* just happens to be *remnant*. Unfortunately, much of this defection was inspired by a perceived "golden" opportunity to recapture land and estates previously pillaged by Rome. (The same is true of Rush Limbaugh's amoral, white-collar entrepreneurs who care more about private enterprise than personal righteousness.) Although the new movement was assured of *"a name"* in history (the Protestant Reformation), its spiritual progress would be retarded by compromise—"... *thou livest, and art dead"* (Revelation 3:1b).

The main error committed by the Protestant leadership was given in our Lord's indictment: *"For I have not found thy works perfect before God"* (Revelation 3:2b). As the standard Scriptural explanation for the word "perfect" has to do with possessing all of one's physical members, we can assume that the Reformers must have stopped short of a complete housecleaning. (Judges 1) Once again, the historical confirmation is striking. The rejuvenated doctrines of justification, Biblical authority and priesthood of the believer represented tremendous strides when compared to the blasphemous tenets of Romanism. However, due to political pressure from many of their superstitious constituents (especially those barons and noblemen providing muscle and financing), the Reformers "fudged" on *sole scriptura* (Scripture alone) by retaining the heresy of infant sprinkling.

They could not have made a greater mistake, as believer's baptism (by immersion) constitutes *the* Scriptural deterrent for an unregenerate church membership. (Acts 8:37) Although the first generation of any revival can ignore such a safeguard and get by with it (II Kings 20:19), the *sprinkled* "little darlings" will later develop into voting tares who eventually take over the barn. (Matthew 18:26) Only by requiring a public profession of faith upon conversion can a local assembly experience the divine perpetuity promised in Matthew 16:18. Thus, one can readily discern that Baptists are not Protestants for they trace their spiritual ancestry to the Lord Jesus Christ and not to the pope. Representing a remnant within a remnant, the faithful Anabaptists of the Sardis period were commended for having preserved their apostolic heritage. *"Thou hast a few names even in Sardis which have not defiled their garments; and they shall walk with me in white: for they are worthy"* (Revelation 3:4).

As a daughter will generally favor her mother, the Protestant denominations incorporated many other Romanist trappings such as altars, candles, sacraments, incense pots, holy days, auricular confession, and a robed priesthood. Unfortunately, when the child came of age, she also opted for her mother's unseemly profession. The student of history will note that the Roman Catholic Church, the religious system that sits on *"seven mountains"* (Revelation 17:9), is not only called *"the great whore"* (Revelation 17:1), but also *"the Mother of Harlots"* (Revelation 17:5). The Holy Ghost declared that one day the Roman prostitute would give birth to several church-state mutants like herself. And so, in the process of time, the whore of Lutheranism would replace the whore of Catholicism as the new state religion for Germany. Anglicanism would do the same in England and the Reformed whore the same in Switzerland and much of Scandinavia.

What this meant for suffering Baptists was a new wave of religious tormenters. The decree at the "Protestant" Diet of Speyer in 1529 proclaimed: "All Anabaptists and rebaptized persons, male or female, of mature age, shall be judged and brought from natural life to death, by fire, or sword or otherwise, as may befit the persons."[1]

Thus, the record confirms that any professed Christian denomination that sprinkled babies would eventually murder the "brethren" that did not, namely, the Baptists (known in Europe as Anabaptists).

For the ruthless slaughter of fellow Christians, the Protestant lands would have to be judged by the same God who pulverized Catholic Europe during the Dark Ages. The church in Sardis was given fair warning: *". . . strengthen the things which remain, that are ready to die . . ."* (Revelation 3:2a). The historical fulfillment of this prophecy was the Thirty Years' War (1618-1648). The devastation experienced by the Catholic House of Hapsburg and the Protestant powers of Germany, Sweden, Denmark, France and England was incalculable. The combined population of Germany and Austria was reduced by two-thirds. Bohemia's entire Protestant population of 1,600,000 souls was wiped off the earth. Not only were cities and towns destroyed but fields, livestock, and farming implements as well. Desolation was everywhere. (Galatians 6:7)

PILGRIMS AND PURITANS

With "Christian" Europe embroiled in this imbroglio of genocide, few noticed the departure of a creaky little vessel crowded with "religious fanatics." By year two of the Thirty Years' War, the Pilgrim Fathers had safely arrived at Plymouth Rock, over three thousand miles away. The final phase of Japheth's enlargement had begun. (Genesis 9:27)

The privation of the first winter at Plymouth Rock is legendary. The price tag for God's vindication would be high. Of the many tales of suffering, the most poignant has rarely been told. In grade school we were informed that a dozen of the original Pilgrim wives did not live to see "May flowers." What we haven't heard is why. Having spent seventy days at sea, those godly women decided that their first priority in America was to wash the clothes of their beloved husbands and children. The fact that it was November and three-quarters of a mile lay between their anchored ship and the shoreline along Cape Cod did not appear to matter. For their families' sake, they would gladly wade through the icy, waist-high water. They had not yet heard that a "woman's place is in the mall." As William Brewster had previously assured the Virginia Company that his petitioning parishioners were "not as other men," their spirited wives would likewise prove to be "not as other women." Sadly, they had not anticipated that the chilly winter temperature would prevent them from adequately drying their own drenched garments. Resigned to their fate, referring to their death shrouds as "coats of iron," most contracted pneumonia and expired before springtime. Thus, in the providence of God, a few devoted housewives became the sacred foundation deposits for the mightiest nation in history. (II Samuel 24:24) Selah!

Now although the Pilgrims were "technically" Protestants, their early exit from the Church of England and extended sojourn in Holland, coupled with the exposure of their first pastor, John Robinson, to a community of four thousand Dutch Anabaptists under exile in Norwich, brought them closer to the New Testament standard than most. They were certainly light-years removed from their Puritan cousins who established the larger Massachusetts Bay Colony in 1629. While the Pilgrims were labeled "separates" for having broken ties with their religious taskmasters, the deluded Puritans believed that they could "purify" the system from within. Not only did they fail to stem the Anglican apostasy (William Laud, etc.), but the imported consequences of their well-intentioned (Proverbs 14:12) yet hopelessly unscriptural approach (II Corinthians 6:17) threatened to corrupt "New" England as well. By the time the Puritans attempted to "give it up," they had unknowingly assimilated many of the intolerant philosophies held by their despised antagonists. Like the vermin that carried their plague-spreading fleas to Europe, the tainted leadership at Massachusetts Bay quickly established a rigid Old Testament theocracy that came to be known as Congregationalism. Henceforth, the personal spiritual convictions of individual citizens would be subject to the religious opinions of the ruling majority.

THE BAPTISTS ARRIVE IN AMERICA

Fortunately, the Lord had no intention of allowing such nonsense to interfere with His plans for America. He was not the least bit impressed with that touted "City on a Hill" in Massachusetts, as it represented *the* major ideological impediment to the eventual reinstatement of *Jerusalem* on *Mount Zion*. A small but determined number of Baptist pioneers began to appear in New England. Although John Christian writes, "The exact date of the arrival of the first Baptists in America, and their names are uncertain,"[2] the fact of their early appearance and influence was noted even by several Puritan authorities. Governor Winslow wrote of the Baptists in 1646, "We have some living among us, nay, some of our churches, of that judgment."[3] Cotton Mather adds that "many of the first settlers of Massachusetts were Baptists, and they were as holy and watchful and faithful and heavenly people as any, perhaps in the world."[4] In a discourse delivered at the dedication of The Baptist Church and Society in Warren, Rhode Island, Baptist historian J.P. Tustin declared, "Multitudes of Baptist ministers and members came from Europe, and settled in different parts of this continent, each becoming the center of an independent circle wherever they planted themselves."[5] Tustin points to Wales as one of the leading exporters of Baptist doctrine to America.

> It is a fact generally known, that many of the Baptist churches in this country derived their origin from the Baptist churches in Wales, a country which has always been a nursery for their peculiar principles. In the earlier settlements of this country, multitudes of Welsh emigrants, who left their fatherland, brought with them the seeds of Baptist principles, and their ministers and members laid the foundation of many Baptist Churches in New England, and especially in the middle states.[6]

The first Baptist church in the state of Massachusetts was formed in 1663 at the town of Swansea (Plymouth Colony) by Reverend John Myles of Wales. Other intelligent approximations for the first Baptist churches in the remaining twelve colonies are given by David Benedict as follows: Providence, Rhode Island, 1639 (though disputed by many; see next section); New York, New York, prior to 1669; Summerton, South Carolina, 1683; Coldspring, Pennsylvania, 1684; Middletown, New Jersey, 1688; New Castle, Delaware, 1703; Groton, Connecticut, 1705; Burly, Virginia, 1715; Perquimans, North Carolina, 1727; Chestnut

Hill, Maryland, 1747; Newton, New Hampshire, 1755; Kioka Creek, Georgia, 1772. (The student will notice that, in most cases, the presence of Baptist people themselves preceded by several years the above-given dates for their first churches.)

However, the same Protestant theologian who revered our Baptist ancestors as "heavenly people" referred to their doctrines as "the briars of Anabaptisme."[7] In Mather's "Holy Commonwealth," the battle lines were soon drawn over infant sprinkling. The Baptists would have none of it, referring to the unscriptural practice as "the Badge of the Whore." Not only did Baptist parents refuse to have their own infants sprinkled, but they rebelled at being forced to witness the heretical ceremony, period! While some would "turn their back at the ordinance," others would literally storm out of the meeting house only to be tackled by incensed magistrates and dragged back inside. Christopher Goodwin of Charlestown was sentenced to pay a fine of ten pounds or be given ten stripes *for having thrown the baptismal basin on the floor!* Another exasperated brother by the name of William Witter was hauled into court for having declared, "They who stayed while a childe was baptised doe worshipp the dyvill."[8]

Known Baptists could rarely vote or hold public office and were frequently subject to fines, whippings and/or imprisonment. On November 13, 1644, the General Court of Massachusetts passed a law for the suppression of Baptists, accusing them of being "incendiaries of the commonwealths, and the infectors of persons in main matters of religion, and the troublers of all churches in all places where they have been."[9] Any of the sect who would "oppose the baptizing of infants, or go about secretly to seduce others from the approbation or use thereof, or shall purposely depart the congregation at the ministration of the ordinance . . . shall be sentenced to banishment."[10] Given the unprecedented Baptist contributions to this nation, perhaps the most inane declaration of all was the prophecy uttered by a delegation of Puritan divines to the legislature in 1668. Denouncing the Baptists as "un-American subversives," they went on record as warning, "If once that party becomes numerous and prevailing, this country is undone, the work of reformation ended."[11]

ROGER WILLIAMS

The premise of this chapter is that *the Lord used local New Testament churches to procure America's unparalleled religious liberty, thereby providing a haven for Israel.* The genesis of this divine arrangement was the diminutive colony of Rhode Island. (*"For who hath despised the day of small things?"* Zechariah 4:10a.) It should come as no surprise, therefore, that Satan has obscured the true history of this period behind a veil of fabricated tradition.

Visitors to the prestigious First Baptist Church in Providence, Rhode Island, are informed that the church was planted by Roger Williams in *1638*, making it the oldest Baptist church in America. The same account is also perpetrated in the majority of Baptist schools today. However, as the available evidence will show, the official version is flawed while the true story has rarely been told.

To begin with, the so-called "official" founding date of 1638—as currently displayed on the structure's cornerstone—is itself a blatant falsehood. Dr. J. R. Graves, the renowned Baptist historian whose academic credentials, literary contributions and ministerial accomplishments occupy three pages in Cathcart's *Baptist Encyclopedia*, made a personal visit to the First Baptist Church of Providence toward the close of the nineteenth century. Upon entering the audience room he observed a commemorative tablet on the wall suggesting a different date altogether. In his book, *The First Baptist Church in America*, Dr. Graves rendered the following inscription:

> This Church was founded in **1639**, by
> Rodger Williams, its first pastor, and
> the first Asserter of Liberty of Conscience.
> It was the
> First Church in Rhode Island and
> the First Baptist Church in America.[12]

This ruse of the devil was orchestrated for a specific purpose indeed. With the Providence congregation designated the "first Baptist church in America," pedobaptists have been able to maintain a self-deluded justification to challenge the legitimacy of all subsequent Baptist growth, given the invalid polity initially employed by Williams, followed by his own abrupt resignation and life-long repudiation of organized religion in general.

Three years after Williams arrived in Providence (occasioned by his banishment from Massachusetts), the frustrated Congregationalist attempted to constitute a Baptist church in March 1639, by immersing eleven other excluded pedobaptists, having been immersed himself by one of the same (Ezekiel Holliman).

Note how Dr. Henry S. Burrage corroborates the earlier date of 1639, writing in *A History of the Baptists in New England* (published in 1894):

> The religious opinions of Williams and his associates were evidently in a transition state. The tendency of the former had been toward Baptist views for some time. Before leaving England he had been acquainted with Baptists, and was familiar with their articles of belief . . . The first sign of organization was at some time prior to **March 16, 1639,** when Mr. Williams was baptized by Ezekiel Holliman and he in turn baptized Holliman and "some ten more." [13]

However, the authority to administer baptism was conferred solely upon the local church. (Baptisms performed by individuals without church authority have been historically rejected as "alien baptisms.")

Williams also failed to produce a standard doctrinal statement. Dr. E. Brown, pastor of the First Baptist Church in Providence, acknowledged in his sermon on the church's 250th anniversary, April 28, 1889 (yet another witness to the founding date of 1639), "Our fathers founded, and the centuries have handed down to us, a church without a written creed." [14] Dr. Graves writes:

> Dr. Benedict, the venerable historian of American Baptists, confesses that in making Roger Williams the founder and first pastor of the First Baptist Church at Providence, he did not go behind the church records, but accepted them as reliable; but his testimony, before he died, was: **The more I study on this subject,** (i.e., the date of the Providence church and the statements that Roger Williams was its first pastor and it being the First Baptist Church in Rhode Island and America,) **the more I am unsettled and confused.** [15]

The candid Benedict was one of several otherwise astute Baptist historians who were beguiled on the Providence issue the same way spiritual scholars like Dr. R. A. Torrey were initially deceived by the corrupt Revised Version of 1881.

Following only four months at the helm, the unstable Williams shocked his parishioners by resigning and permanently renouncing any affiliation with the Baptist movement. Thomas Lechford, an Episcopalian, visited Providence in the years 1640-41 and recorded:

> At Providence, which is twenty miles from Newport, lives Master Williams and his company of divers opinions; most are Anabaptists; They hold there is no true visible Church in the Bay, nor in the World, nor any true Ministry.[16]

This conviction of spiritual anarchy was so strong that Williams never wavered from it during his remaining forty-three years on earth. *Thus we see that the so-called "founder of the Baptist denomination in America" was never a true Baptist for even one hour of his life!* Dr. Samuel Adlam, Rhode Island's premier historian, concludes:

> It is greatly to be regretted that it ever entered into the mind of any one to make him (a Baptist or) the founder of our denomination in Rhode Island or America. In no sense was he so . . .
> A man only four months a Baptist (and only attempting to become one at that), and then renouncing his baptism forever, to be lauded and magnified as the founder of the Baptist denomination in the New World! (Is simply absurd!) **For all he did as a statesman to aid our brethren in the, or advocacy of the, separation of church and state, I respect him; but as a Baptist I owe him nothing.**[17]

Another problem with the ecclesiastical preeminence afforded the First Baptist Church in Providence is the history of the church itself. The common claim that the existing work can be traced back to Williams's abandoned flock is a myth exposed by three historical realities.

First, the "church" that Williams jumpstarted and then abruptly deserted, went out of existence after a short while. According to the contemporary testimony of Cotton Mather, as cited by Crosby:

> At length the magistrates passed the sentence of banishment upon him [Williams], upon which he removed with a few of his own sect and settled at a place called Providence. "There they proceeded," says Mr. Mather, **"not only unto the gathering of a thing like a church**, but unto the renouncing of their infant baptism." **After this, he says, he turned** *Seeker* **and** *Familist,* **and the church came to nothing.**[18]

Dr. Adlam notes:

> Mather had the means of knowing whether that "thing like a *church*," as he called it, continued or not; and it can not be assumed that he would have written and published to the world, in almost the next town (Boston) and in the face of the church, that it was dissolved upon Williams's leaving it, if the church was then in existence, to deny the charge! Can the fact be found anywhere that any member of Williams's society, or any Baptist living in the days of Mather, ever denied this statement? Such a denial never was heard of, that I can learn.[19]

Around the year 1650 a "real" Baptist church was organized in Providence by Mr. Thomas Olney.[20] The work was soon described as a "flourishing church." However, a serious split occurred shortly thereafter over the rite of laying on of hands. John Callender states, as cited by Dr. Adlam:

> About the year 1653 or '54, there was a division in the Baptist Church at Providence, about the right of laying on of hands, which some pleaded for as essentially necessary to church communion, and the others would leave indifferent. Hereupon they walked in two churches, one under C. Brown, Wickenden, etc., the other under Thomas Olney.[21]

Historians such as Isaac Backus confirm the all-important identities of both groups:

> Thomas Olney . . . continued so to his death, over that part of the church who are called five-principle Baptists, in distinction from those who parted from their brethren, about the year 1653, under the leading of elder Wickenden, holding to the laying on of hands upon every church member.[22]

Finally, after more than sixty years of coexistence, the mother church pastored by Olney dissolved. Writing in 1738, Callender states, "This last continued till about twenty years [ago], when, becoming destitute of an elder, the members were united with other churches."[23] Morgan Edwards says that the church under Olney continued till 1715.[24]

Dr. Adlam then leaves us with the obvious inference: "From this it follows that the existing church in Providence was not founded in 1639, but in 1652; **it was not the first in the State, for it came out from an older church**."[25]

Dr. John Clarke

The Scripture says, *"Render therefore to all their dues . . . honour to whom honour"* (Romans 13:7) and *"Let another man praise thee, and not thine own mouth"* (Proverbs 27:2a). It is regrettable that the name of Roger Williams has been used to deprive another from receiving the recognition he deserves for having been the premier human vessel in God's plan for America's spiritual destiny. And to a lesser degree, it is likewise unfortunate that in the rectifying of this injustice, the legitimate *ideological* contribution of Williams can be unintentionally trashed in the process. In his opening paragraph on the life of Roger Williams, Graves writes,

> He seems providentially raised up as "a herald," "a voice," to proclaim in this, then wilderness, the eternal divorcement of Church and State, and the absolute freedom of man to worship God according to his understanding of His Word, and thus to prepare the way for the coming of His Kingdom into New England and America.[26]

The following transition by Dr. Adlam provides a worthy introduction of our noble subject:

> Williams, indeed, touched the Baptist standard, but ere he raised it his hands trembled, and it fell. It was seized by a steadier hand; at Newport it was raised, and far and near they came to it; it was carried into the heart of Massachusetts, and a work was commenced which till the last setting of the sun shall never cease; and this before we have any evidence that a church in Providence had begun to be. . . .
> There is another name, long, too long, concealed by Williams being placed before him, who will in after times be regarded with unmingled affection and respect, as the true founder of the Baptist cause in this country. That orb of purest lustre will yet shine forth, and Baptists, whether they regard his spotless character, his talents, his learning, the services he rendered, the urbanity and the modesty that distinguished him, will mention *John Clarke* as the real founder of our denomination in America. And when Baptist history is better understood than it is at present, every one, pointing to that venerable church which, on one of earth's loveliest spots, he established, will say: *"This is the mother of us all."*[27]

According to the best authorities, Dr. John Clarke was born in Suffolk, England, on October 3, 1609.[28] His parents, Thomas and Rose, were devout Puritans. John received a quality education and later became a medical doctor. He was acclaimed by his contemporaries as "scholar bred," "a man bred to learning," and "a learned physician."[29]

It is believed that his predilection for religious liberty led him to join the first church of "Particular Baptists" in London, formed in September, 1633, by Mr. John Spilsbury.[30] Professor J. C. C. Clarke, of Shurtleff College (descended from Dr. Clarke's brother, Joseph), said of his ancestor, "Dr. Clarke's connection with these Baptists is quite evident from his first day in Boston to the day of his death."[31]

When Dr. Clarke, accompanied by his wife, Elizabeth, arrived in Boston in November 1637, the intolerant city was beset by theological controversy. His biographer, Dr. Wilbur Nelson, states, "Like other suspected persons, he was disarmed."[32] In his own narrative, Clarke writes:

> I was no sooner on shore, but there appeared to me differences among them touching the covenants . . . I thought it strange that they were not able so to bear each with others in their different understandings and consciences as to live peaceably together.[33]

The following March (after an inhospitable sojourn in New Hampshire), Dr. Clarke agreed to lead an expedition of three hundred spiritual pioneers to seek out a new colony where liberty of conscience would prevail. Boston was then only seven years old and about to suffer a population reduction of thirty percent. Prior to their departure, the group drew up and signed the following compact:

> The seventh day of the first month, 1638.
>
> We whose names are underwritten do hereby solemnly in the presence of Jehovah incorporate ourselves into a Bodie Politick and, as He shall help, submit our persons, lives and estates unto our Lord Jesus Christ, the King of Kings, and Lord of Lords, and to all those perfect and most absolute laws of His given in His Holy Word of Truth, to be guided and judged thereby.
>
> Exodus 24:3 and 4
I Chron. 11:3
II Kings 11:17

William Coddington,	William Dyre,
John Clarke,	William Freeborne,
William Hutchinson, Jr.,	Philip Shearman,

John Coggeshall,

William Aspinwall,

Samuel Wilbore,

John Sanford,

Edward Hutchinson, Jr.,

Esq.,

Thomas Savage,

John Walker,

Richard Carder,

William Baulston,

Edward Hutchinson,

Sr.,

Henry Bull,

Randall Holden.[34]

It is believed that the compact was composed by Dr. Clarke, while William Coddington, whose name appears first, was chosen president and judge of that body.

After deciding against Long Island, the group migrated to an island paradise in the Narragansett Bay, known by the Indians as *Aquidneck* (meaning "Isle of Peace"). The tranquil enclave, measuring fifteen miles long by three miles wide, was subsequently purchased from the natives for the asking price of forty fathoms of white beads (less than $100), ten coats and twenty hoes; the deed bearing the date of 24 March 1638. Thus, beginning with the Mayflower's arrival in 1620 (as opposed to the debacle of esurience at Jamestown), Japheth was continuing to fulfill his part of the Noahic prophecy to *"dwell in the tents of Shem"* (Genesis 9:27).

The initial settlement was established at the north end of the island in what is now the city of Portsmouth. The words and signatures of the aforementioned compact, subsequently known as the "Portsmouth Compact," may be viewed on a bronze tablet affixed to a large pudding stone situated aside a stream that empties into a pond off Boyd's Lane, about a mile east of Mt. Hope Bridge in Portsmouth. (The tranquil site of this "Portsmouth Rock," unveiled in 1937 *and far more important to America than "Plymouth Rock,"* was appropriately called "Founders Brook," but recently renamed "Anne Hutchinson Park" by revisionists.)

In April 1639, Clarke, Coddington and several families organized a new community at Newport. The two towns united the following year on March 12 to form the colony of "Rhode Island." Dr. Nelson writes in *The Life of Dr. John Clarke:*

William Coddington was elected governor. Suitable legislation was enacted, and in March of the following year, at the General Court of Elections, a statute was adopted which declared the government to be a "democracy," the laws of which it was in the power of the freemen, by majority vote, to determine for themselves: **"That none be accounted a deliquent for doctrine"**; and that the official seal should be the figure of a sheaf of arrows bound together and marked with the motto—*"Amor Vincet Omnia"* ["Love will conquer all things"].[35]

Dr. Conrad Glover comments:

> **As far as I am able to learn, the above document was the first legislative action for personal, political and religious liberty on the American Continent.** It may be true that Roger Williams wrote more on the subject of liberty of conscience and freedom of man than did John Clarke, but Clarke did more about it by translating his views into the statutes of government and into minds and hearts of men.[36]

The modern city fathers of Portsmouth must obviously concur with this view. A prominent historical marker plainly reads, **"Portsmouth, Rhode Island—Birthplace of American Democracy."**

Although constantly busy with the affairs of state (not to mention his acclaimed medical practice), Dr. Clarke was faithful to perfect his *highest* calling. Dr. Cathcart writes in the *Baptist Encyclopedia*:

> He is spoken of by early writers as the religious teacher of the people, and as such from the beginning. **A church was gathered in 1638, probably early in the year, of which Mr. Clarke became pastor or teaching elder.** He is mentioned (in 1638) as "preacher to those of the island," as "their minister," as "elder of the church there." Mr. Lechford writes in 1640, after having made a tour through New England, that "at the island . . . there is a church where one Master Clarke is pastor." [37]

The first thirteen lines on Dr. Clarke's gravestone read as follows:

To the Memory of
DOCTOR JOHN CLARKE,
One of the original purchasers and proprieters of
this island and one of the founders of the
First Baptist Church of Newport,
its first pastor and munificent benefactor;
He was a native of Bedfordshire, England,
and a practitioner of physic in London.
He, with his associates, came to this island from Mass.,
in March, 1638, O.S., and on the 24th
of the same month obtained a deed thereof from
the Indians. He shortly after gathered
the church aforesaid and became its pastor.

Prior to visiting the First Baptist Church of Providence, Dr. Graves made a pilgrimage to the Clarke family burial plot and read the above lines, especially that insightful date of 1638. He writes:

> I sat for hours before this silent witness, sending busy recollections—of recorded events—back over the fancied scenes and transactions of the two centuries past, when these sturdy witnesses of Christ, fleeing from the persecutions of the Old World, found, in their wanderings, this haven, and cleared away the dense wilderness, and let in, for the first time, God's glorious sunlight upon this beautiful island, by the "loud resounding sea" and thanked their God for it, as their peaceful home that seemed to them but a recovered part of Paradise itself.
>
> It occurred to me that the testimony of monuments erected at, or very near, the time of the events commemorated, and by those personally conversant or *best* conversant with them, are the most reliable witnesses of the events recorded. . . .
>
> This monument was doubtless erected by the very hands that laid the loved and honored dead to rest in this lovely spot.
>
> Dr. Clarke left no child or relative to contribute this then costly mark of affection. The worn appearance of the stone testifies to its extreme age, and the language and style of the epitaph witness that it has come down to us from "former generations"—the centuries past.
>
> I unhesitatingly accepted this mural witness as unimpeachable, and studied it, examining and cross-examining it for the utmost syllable of its testimony.
>
> From it I learned [among six things listed in his full statement] . . . That this church has had a continuous existence from "1638" until the present.[38]

Dr. Graves goes on to relate the stupefaction he felt while staring at the tablet in the Providence church:

> I read again:
>
> *"This Church*
> *was founded in 1639."*
>
> A new light broke in upon my mind, making me wonder I had not seen it before—founded in 1639!! Granting the dates of constitution claimed by each contesting church to be correct, then it is undeniably true that *the Newport church is the elder by one full year.*
>
> This fact forever settles the question as to which of these churches is the First Baptist Church in Rhode Island and the First Baptist Church in America.[39]

Although Dr. Clarke's own conversion to Baptist doctrine predated his arrival in the "New World" (there being no indication of any such change occurring afterwards), his initial congregation, the first of *any* "denomination" on Aquidneck, would have necessitated a mixed multitude ripe for instruction (Acts 18:26). Any ecclesiastical gnat-strainers should also realize that Dr. Clarke was not going to a *town* to start a *church*; he was going to a *wilderness* to start a *town*. Dr. Nelson writes:

> It is evident that those to whom he ministered formed a church as early as the year 1638. Winthrop's Journal, under date of May 11, 1639, states that "they gathered a church in a very disordered way; for they took some excommunicated persons, and others who were members of the church of Boston, and not dismissed." This item refers to this church as though it had been gathered some time before, doubtless in the year 1638.
>
> There were certainly Baptists in the congregation, and Baptist sentiments were growing in the community. In another item, Winthrop states that there were "professed Anabaptists on the island." Early in 1641 he writes of troubles on the island growing out of dissension among the leaders and says that "divers of them turned professed Anabaptists." As a matter of fact, it appears that Baptist doctrines were receiving a great deal of attention in every New England colony at that time. H. M. King, in his book, *The Baptism of Roger Williams,* says, "The thoughts of the New World were all alive on Baptist questions, and its literature was saturated with their discussion. The whole atmosphere was filled with Baptist ozone. Baptist sentiments were imported with almost every ship from England." That some of these Baptists should have been among the earliest settlers or should later have joined the first settlers on the Island of Aquidneck, where the historic Baptist principle of soul liberty held full sway, was inevitable.[40]

The doctrinal dissension to which Governor Winthrop referred took place in 1641 and resulted in a number of "deeper-lifers" quitting Clarke to form the Island's first Quaker assembly. Dr. Nelson offers the following explanation:

> Just when this church became **known** as a Baptist church is uncertain . . . None of these early historians expresses a definitive opinion. What seems a reasonable explanation is that a church that was independent in character and included Baptists in its congregation was gathered in 1638, under the ministry of Dr. John Clarke. But, in view of the fact that there were people of differing religious views in the community, and only one church, this church did not assume a denominational character until after those who

differed withdrew and formed a church of their own. After that, the original church **became in name** a Baptist church. It continued its existence under the ministry of Dr. Clarke, has had an unbroken history ever since, and is now known as the United Baptist John Clarke Memorial Church of Newport.[41]

Keep in mind that this rather nebulous theory is the *worst*-case scenario. Dr. Clarke was the undisputed leader of the Newport church and was *always* known as a Baptist. The key is to differentiate between the *congregation* and the *membership*. While anyone professing a desire for truth is welcome in the *pews* of a Baptist church, the *voting* body is quite another matter, being restricted to *Baptists* in good standing.

Nelson gives the estimated population of Aquidneck in 1640 as 1,000 inhabitants. Yet he also notes that in 1648, the membership roll of the Newport church contained only fifteen names, and four of those were "Clarkes"[42] (an obvious "flop" by today's mega-church standards).

Thanks to Dr. Clarke, Rhode Island absorbed a wide range of religious practitioners who were welcome nowhere else. So, why should the good man's legacy be shortened simply because he happened to have had the only church in town at one time?

Thus we may confidently conclude that the *first church at Newport* and *not* the first church at Providence, is the *true* first Baptist church in America, and that *Dr. Clarke,* and *not* Roger Williams, was the founder and pastor of the *first Baptist church in Rhode Island and America!*

OBADIAH HOLMES

The church at Newport was destined to be honored with a second distinction as well. Obadiah Holmes was born in Preston, Lancashire, England, in 1606. He was thoroughly grounded in religion and educated at Oxford University. Yet, he chose to forsake the "faith of his fathers" for a "worldly good time."

In 1639, Holmes brought his wife and son to Salem, Massachusetts, where he established the first glass factory in America. However, when his Quaker business partner was prosecuted for a doctrinal matter, the "wayward" Holmes challenged the religious hierarchy, suffering excommunication and banishment in 1646 as a result.

He then moved to the more liberal Plymouth Colony where he had a providential encounter with Dr. Clarke around 1649. Holmes and eight fellow dissenters were subsequently baptized by Clarke. When plans for a new church were proscribed by local officials, Holmes relocated to Newport and united with Dr. Clarke's work.

In the summer of 1651 Holmes accompanied Dr. Clarke and Deacon John Crandall to Swampscott, near Lynn, Massachusetts, for the purpose of visiting Mr. William Witter, an infirm member of the Newport Church. They arrived at Mr. Witter's residence on a Saturday afternoon in July and the following day held a service there.

While Dr. Clarke was preaching from Revelation 3:10, two constables entered the private home, broke up the meeting and executed warrants for their arrest on the grounds that they were "erroneous persons, being strangers." When Dr. Clarke remonstrated in a calm manner, his antagonist replied, "Come, **shut up your book**, and go with us; we have come to apprehend you."[43] As the three "prisoners" left the house, Pastor Clarke encouraged his tearful host by making a timely application to his text (taken from the epistle to the church at Philadelphia no less), *"The hour of temptation and trial has come, but let us keep the word of His patience, and He will sustain us in the time of trouble."*[44]

As there was no jail in Lynn, the "erroneous persons" were taken to the local *ale house.* After processing and a meal, the unthinkable occurred. Because it was still the "Puritan Sabbath" (with an average service lasting four hours), the "busted Baptists" were promptly hauled from the tavern to the Congregational meeting house. Dr. C. E. Barrow writes, "The three men, whose own worship had been broken up, were now taken, without their own consent, to the meeting of the standing order."[45]

To protest their disgraceful predicament, the "visitors" refused to take off their hats, whereupon the constable removed them, "but not in the most amiable manner."[46] When Dr. Clarke tried to voice a respectful objection, he was curtly reminded that he and his companions were a "captive audience."

On Monday, the men were transferred to the jail in Boston. Among a slate of charges, the most ludicrous read: "For being taken by a constable at a private meeting on the Lord's Day" (i.e., punishing the Baptist minister because his unscrupulous arrest occurred on a Sunday). The heart of their complaint was as follows:

> for such things as shall be alleged against them concerning their seducing and drawing aside of others after their erroneous judgments and practices;

and for suspicion of having their hands in the re-baptizing of one or more among us . . .[47]

Ten days after their imprisonment, the three Baptists were found guilty and fined accordingly: Clarke, twenty pounds; Holmes, thirty pounds; and, Crandall, five pounds. The men were also curtly informed that if they could not come up with the cash (a considerable sum at that time) they were to be *well whipped*, "in Jesus's name," of course. When Holmes replied, "I bless God I am counted worthy to suffer for the name of Jesus," the "Reverend" John Wilson lost it and struck the defendant saying, "The curse of God go with thee."[48]

Dr. Clarke relates:

> None were able to turn to the law of God or man by which we were condemned. At length the Governor stepped up, and told us we had denied infant's baptism, and, being somewhat transported, told me I had **deserved death**, and said he would not have such **trash** brought into their jurisdiction.[49]

But then the haughty Endicott slipped up by saying to Clarke:

> You go up and down, and secretly insinuate into those that are weak, but you cannot maintain it before our ministers. You may try and dispute with them![50]

The next morning Dr. Clarke sent shockwaves throughout the colony by accepting the challenge to debate. While the "distinguished" theologians objected to the proposal, the kangaroo court had committed itself. Clarke was thus informed that the disputation was granted and scheduled for the next week. With a loathsome jail cell for his "study" the man of God prepared four propositions which he intended to defend.

> The testimony of *John Clarke,* a prisoner of Jesus Christ, at *Boston,* in the behalf of my Lord, and of his people, is as followeth:
>
> *First*—I testify that Jesus of *Nazareth,* whom God hath raised from the dead, is made both *Lord* and Christ. This Jesus I say is the *Christ,* in English, the *Anointed* One, (and) hath a name above every name. He is the *Anointed Priest;* none to, or with Him in point of atonement. The *Anointed Prophet;* none to Him in point of instruction; the *Anointed King,* who is gone to His Father for His glorious kingdom, and shall ere long return again; and that this Jesus Christ is also *The Lord;* none to or with Him by way of commanding and ordering (with respect to the worship of

God) the household of faith, which being purchased with His blood as Priest, instructed and nourished by His Spirit as Prophet, do wait in His appointment as He is the Lord, in hope of that glorious kingdom which shall ere long appear.

Second—I testify that Baptism, or dipping into water, is one of the commandments of this Lord Jesus Christ, and that a visible believer, or disciple of Christ (that is, one that manifesteth repentance towards God, and faith in Jesus Christ), is the only person that is to be baptized or dipped with that visible baptism, or dipping of Jesus Christ in water; and also that visible person that is to walk in the visible order of His house; and so to wait for His coming the second time in the form of a *Lord* and *King*, with His glorious kingdom according to promise; and for His sending down (in time of His absence) the Holy Ghost, or Holy Spirit of Promise; and all this according to the last will and testament of that living Lord, whose will is not to be added to or taken from.

Third—I testify, or witness, that every such believer in Christ Jesus, that waiteth for His appearing, may in point of liberty, yea, ought in point of duty, to improve that talent his Lord hath given unto him, and in the congregation may either ask for information to himself, or, if he can, may speak by way of prophecy for the edification, exhortation, and comfort of the whole; and out of the congregation at all times, upon all occasions, and in all places as far as the jurisdiction of his Lord extends, may, yea, ought to walk as a child of light, justifying wisdom with his ways, and reproving folly with the unfruitful works thereof, provided all this be shown out of a good conversation, as James speaks, with meekness of wisdom.

Fourth—I testify that no such believer or servant of Jesus Christ hath any liberty, much less authority, from his Lord, to smite his fellow-servant, nor yet with outward force, or arm of flesh, to constrain or restrain his conscience, nor yet his outward man for conscience's sake, or worship of his God, where injury is not offered to the person, name, or estate of others; every man being such as he shall appear before the judgment seat of Christ, and must give account of himself to God; and therefore ought to be fully persuaded in his own mind for what he undertakes, because he that doubteth is damned if he eat, and so also if he act, because he doth not eat or act, in faith; and what is not of faith is sin.[51]

You might say that these Bible-based tenets represented the "Old Time Religion" of our Baptist ancestors in the Philadelphia Church Age.

Our fathers, chained in prisons dark,
Were still in heart and conscience free:

> How sweet would be their children's fate,
> If they, like them, could die for thee!
> Faith of our fathers! Holy faith!
> We will be true to thee till death!

At any rate, as Dr. Clarke's reputation had preceded him, the Puritan divines "chickened out" and the debate was "indefinitely" postponed.

Clarke was then surprised to learn that he was suddenly free to go. What he didn't know was that some friends had paid the fine, securing his discharge (though this was contrary to his personal convictions). Deacon Crandall was also released upon his pledge to appear at a later session of the Court; however, his case was never called.

In the sovereign plan of God, Obadiah Holmes, Clarke's future successor at Newport (1676-1682), was ordained to become the esteemed *protomartyr* of American Baptists (the word *martyr* being understood by its ancient definition of "a *witness* for Christ"). *Brother Holmes would shed the first blood on this soil for the lovely Lord Jesus!*

When Holmes learned that the brethren had also raised the money for his fine, he graciously declined their generosity, though publicly declaring, in the spirit of the Apostle Paul at Philippi (Acts 16:37), "Having committed no crime, I will not permit my friends to pay a single farthing for me."[52]

Likewise, on the day of his ordeal (September 5, 1651), he followed his Saviour's example (Matthew 27:34) by refusing a cup of Madeira wine, stating, "No; let me so suffer that, if I am sustained, God shall have the glory."[53] With his New Testament in hand, he calmly approached the dreaded whipping post located behind the old State House. His recalcitrance surfaced yet again while being disrobed:

> "Unbutton here," said the executioner, as he gave his jacket a jerk.
>
> "No," said Holmes; "I make as much conscience of unbuttoning one button as I do of paying the sentence of thirty pounds. I will do nothing towards executing such an unjust law."
>
> Faithful to his word, he would not voluntarily assist the executioner in the least in removing his garments from his back.
>
> He was as helpless as if he were asleep, and the executioner had to handle him as though he were a statue.[54]

Having drawn a crowd (I Corinthians 4:9), the Baptist minister gave out a quick sermon:

"The Lord," said he, "having manifested His love towards me, in giving me repentance towards God and faith in Christ, and so to be baptized in water by a messenger of Jesus, in the name of the Father, Son and Holy Spirit, wherein I have fellowship with Him in His death, burial and resurrection, I am now come to be baptized in afflictions by your hands, that so I may have further fellowship with my Lord, and am not ashamed of His sufferings, for by His stripes am I healed." [55]

The executioner removed enough of his garments and having fastened him to the post, seized a three-corded whip and proceeded to apply the blows in an unmerciful manner. The victim later testified:

As the strokes fell upon me, I had such a spiritual manifestation of God's presence, as the like thereof I never had nor felt, nor can with fleshly tongue express, and the outward pain was so removed from me, that indeed I am not able to declare it to you, it was so easy to me, that I could well bear it, yea, and in a manner, felt it not, although it was grievous, as the spectators said, the man striking with all his strength (yea, spitting in his hands three times, as many affirmed) with a three corded whip, giving me therewith thirty strokes. When he had loosed me from the post, having joyfulness in my heart and cheerfulness in my countenance, as the spectators observed, I **told the magistrates, you have struck me as with roses.**[56]

Although the Lord enabled Holmes to endure the initial blows in the presence of his enemies, he later suffered extreme discomfort. (He could take no rest for weeks except as he lay upon his knees and elbows, not being able to allow any part of his body to touch the bed.) And for having embraced the bloodied minister, John Hazel and John Spur were also arrested and sentenced to pay forty shillings or be whipped. Both refused to pay the fine but were released after others bailed them out.

For what it's worth, present-day Lynn happens to be one of the most wicked cities in the state of Massachusetts. A popular motorcycle patch reads, "Lynn, Lynn, City of Sin."

THE CHARTER OF 1663

By now it should be obvious that Rhode Island's "Christian" neighbors were "a few bricks shy of a load." Between 1647 and 1692, at least twenty-three females would be executed throughout New England as witches or seditious heretics (the death of Mary Dyer being the definitive case). Consequently, the religious toleration exhibited in Rhode Island was a continual source of "irritation" (conviction) to the self-righteous Puritans of Massachusetts Bay. Every imaginable invective was heaped upon the tiny Baptist outpost from "Rogue's Island" to "The Sewer of New England."

However, although conditions appeared threatening on the home front, Dr. Clarke was wise enough to discern that the greater danger was back in England. Nelson writes:

> Massachusetts and Connecticut also had their agents in England, and pressed some of their claims with a view to disintegrating the Colony of the Providence Plantations [Rhode Island]. They proposed to make a tripartite division of her territory: that the Narragansett country should be absorbed by Connecticut and that Massachusetts should appropriate Providence and Warwick, while to Plymouth should fall the Island towns.[57]

While Roger Williams had obtained the colony's original charter from Charles I in 1644, the king's execution five years later rendered the agreement tenuous at best. The citizens of Portsmouth and Newport subsequently petitioned Dr. Clarke to go to England to monitor their affairs. He readily consented and sailed in November 1651, leaving a recovering Holmes in charge of his flock.

Although Williams also went along, being appointed by the smaller Providence colony, he returned in 1654, while Clarke continued his lobby on behalf of Rhode Island for another decade.

In his book *Fighters for Freedom*, A. K. de Blois calls Dr. Clarke "the foremost American diplomat of his age."[58] These skills were put to the test when Charles II restored the monarchy in 1660. The charter which had been granted Williams by the Earl of Warwick was promptly cancelled. The new autocrat was prejudiced against the liberal colony. Arnold writes:

> To obtain a renewal of privileges so remarkable, to secure the regard of a sovereign whose arbitrary will was an inheritance, to obtain his sanction to a system which, initiated as an experiment by a republican parliament, had come to be no longer a philosophical problem but an established fact, and which, if extended, must inevitably in time overthrow the fabric of monarchical power—these were the difficult and perhaps dangerous duties that now devolved on the agent of Rhode Island.[59]

Though confronted with insurmountable obstacles, Clarke did have two things going for him; Jehovah's plan for Israel's recovery and the promises of Holy Scripture: *"The king's heart is in the hand of the LORD, as the rivers of water: he turneth it whithersoever he will"* (Proverbs 21:1).

On July 8, 1663, Dr. Clarke obtained the signature and seal of the king on a charter so democratic, both in letter and spirit, that doubts were voiced in England as to whether the king even had a right to grant it! "The charter of Rhode Island of 1663," says Thomas Bicknell, "has been universally recognized as the most liberal state paper ever issued by the English Crown."[60]

With regard to how Charles received the Baptist preacher's bold request, John Christian writes, "The king replied benignantly, saying that he would permit the colonists to continue in the enjoyment of their liberty, and that he would not allow them to be compelled to submit themselves to the Church of England."[61]

A portion of the remarkable document reads as follows:

> That our royall will and pleasure is that noe person within the sayd colonye at any tyme hereafter shall bee in any way molested, punished or called in question for any differences in opinione in matters of religion, and doe not actually disturb the civill peace of our sayd collony; but that all and everye person or persons may from tyme to tyme and at all tymes hereafter freelye and fullye have and enjoye his and theire owne judgements and consciences in matters of religious concernment.[62]

"Christian" revisionists have done their part in the satanic conspiracy to obliterate the memory of America's Baptist founders. The much lauded *America's God and Country Encyclopedia of Quotations* (1994) by William J. Federer claims to be a "comprehensive 864-page reference tool [which] includes over 2,100 quotations from nearly 700 sources highlighting America's noble heritage."[63] Predictably, the name of Dr. John Clarke is nowhere to be found. However, Associate Justice of the United States Supreme Court Tom Campbell Clark (1899-1977) *did* make the grade for supposedly stating, "The Founding Fathers believed devoutly that there was a God and that the unalienable rights of man were rooted—not in the state, nor the legislature, nor in any other human power—but in God alone."[64] Yet, in the historic *School District of Abington Township v. Schempp, 374 U.S. 203 (1963)*—the second of two cases challenging prayer in the public schools—*Clark authored the majority opinion, which specifically outlawed Bible readings in public schools.* In fact, the first nineteen words in the above quote (constituting more than half) were used by Clark in his landmark opinion. Thus, while Federer failed to list the Baptist preacher whose myriad of religious and civic accomplishments include what some authorities believe to have been the nation's first public school (a vote being taken on August 20, 1640, "to keep a publick school for the learning youth"[65]), the Protestant justice who ultimately voted to expel God's word from America's classrooms *was* duly honored.

Although *America's God and Country Encyclopedia of Quotations* also "missed" the names of *practically every Baptist preacher listed in this chapter*, Federer *did* recognize the following "spiritual giants" (in alphabetical order): P. T. Barnum, Napolean Bonaparte, George Herbert Walker Bush, Agatha Christie, Chuck Colson, Hernando Cortez, Charles Darwin, Albert Einstein, Harry Emerson Fosdick, Anne Frank, Billy Graham, Julia Ward Howe, Queen Isabella, John F. Kennedy, Martin Luther King, Rush Limbaugh, Michelangelo, Reinhold Niebur, Richard Nixon, Edgar Allen Poe, Alexander Solzhenitsyn, Harriet Beecher Stowe, Mother Teresa and Oscar Wilde.

Also included in this widely distributed "Christian" resource are five "His Holinesses"—John Paul I, John Paul II, Leo XIII, Pius XI, Pius XII and the following inane entry (appearing on page 612):

> Constitution of the United Soviet Socialist Republic (1922-1991), stated:
> Article 124: In order to ensure to citizens freedom of conscience, the church in the U.S.S.R. is separated from the State, and the school from the church.[66]

Thus we should not be surprised to "discover" (on page 532) that the landmark "Charter of Rhode Island and Providence Plantations July 8, 1663, **was granted by King Charles II to Roger Williams.**"[67] However, the original document, kept in a fireproof safe in the office of the Secretary of State in the Rhode Island State House, tells a different story altogether. The opening lines of the charter read as follows:

> Charles the Second, by the grace of God, King of England, Scotland, etc. . . . to all to whom these presents shall come, greeting: Whereas, we have been informed by the humble petition of **our trusty and well beloved subject John Clarke,** on behalf of . . . [twenty-three names follow, with Roger Williams being the tenth].

An excerpt from the charter (originally a part of Clarke's judicious petition to Chares II), has been permanently enshrined above the main (south) entrance of the magnificent Rhode Island State House (one of the most beautiful state capitols in America, sporting one of only four marble domes in the world):

> TO HOLD FORTH A LIVELY EXPERIMENT
> THAT A MOST FLOURISHING CIVIL STATE MAY STAND
> AND BEST BE MAINTAINED WITH FULL LIBERTY
> IN RELIGIOUS CONCERNMENTS.

While James I, though remembered for the A.V. 1611, is also credited with shedding the *last* Baptist blood in *England*, it was apropos that his *grandson*, Charles II, acquiesced to the pastor of the one who shed the *first* Baptist blood in *America!*

CONGREGATION YESHUAT ISRAEL

Dr. Clarke went to Heaven on April 20, 1676. Though the average "brain-dead" Baptist of today is unaware of Clarke's significance, an array of earlier posthumous acclaim bears witness to his lifetime achievements. Cathcart called him, "one of the most eminent men of his time.[68] Bancroft says, "Never did a young commonwealth possess a more faithful friend."[69] T. W. Bicknell, "Had Dr. John Clarke of Newport no other claim to the first place among the founders of the American Colonies, the Royal Charter of 1663 would confer that honor."[70] John Callender declared that "his memory is deserving of lasting honor for his efforts toward establishing the first government in the world which gave to all equal civil and religious liberty."[71]

S. G. Arnold said,

His life was devoted to the good of others. He was a patriot, a scholar and a Christian. The purity of his character is conspicuous in many trying scenes, and his blameless, self-sacrificing life disarmed detraction and left him without an enemy.[72]

C. E. Barrows,

From its inception, Mr. Clarke was a leading spirit in the new colony. His life is so interwoven with its history that to have a correct knowledge of the one necessitates a knowledge of the other. He was almost always employed for the public good. His disciplined mind brought constant and invaluable aid to the infant colony. To no one, perhaps, was the colony under greater obligations than to him. Yet so quietly and unobtrusively did he do his work that his great merits have not been duly appreciated. But the careful student of this early period discovers in him the colony's guiding genius. The better his history is known, the more commanding is the position assigned him.[73]

The Hon. John R. Bartlett, former secretary of state of Rhode Island said, "Rhode Island owes to John Clarke a monument of granite and a statue of bronze."[74] On May 6, 2003, the Baptist History Preservation Society of Rockwell, North Carolina, placed a 5,000-pound, polished, black granite monument, measuring 7' x 4' x 10" in the Clarke burial plot on West Broadway (near the corner of Callender Avenue in Newport). The forty-ninth of fifty-three gold-lettered lines reads, "CLARKE IS KNOWN AS 'THE FATHER OF AMERICAN BAPTISTS.' " (A similar memorial honoring Obadiah Holmes was erected on the Calvary Baptist Church grounds in Middletown, Massachusetts, approximately five miles from where he lies buried on private property.)

Other testimonials add to Dr. Clarke's remarkable legacy: the trust he established on the day of his death "for the relief of the poor or the bringing up of children unto learning from time to time forever" (still functioning in the twenty-first century); the tablet at the Newport Historical Society erected in Dr. Clarke's memory by the prestigious Newport Medical Society, etc.

However, *one* tribute remains in a class by itself. The eminent Baptist historian, Isaac Backus said of Clarke, "He was a principal procurer of Rhode Island for sufferers and exiles."[75] In the spring of 1658, while Dr. Clarke was busy in England, a creaky boat-load of fifteen Jewish families arrived in Newport from the island of Barbados. (Other, less substantiated theories suggest Holland or Brazil as their point of embarkation.)[76] A contingent of twenty-three *Sephardic* Jews from Brazil had earlier emigrated to New Amsterdam (New York) in 1654, constituting the first Jewish community in the American colonies. With the capture of Brazil by the Dutch in 1631, thousands of Jews who had suffered torture and death in the Catholic nations of Mexico, Peru, Central America and the West Indies found a welcome respite in the city of Recife. When

Brazil was later subjugated by Catholic Portugal in 1654, the majority of Recife's Jewish population fled to Holland. The handful of refugees that descended on New Amsterdam in 1654 quickly learned that they were not welcome in Peter Stuyvesant's Protestant colony. Describing them as "very repugnant" and a "deceitful race," the local magistrates issued a decree ordering "that the Jews who came last year from the West Indies and now from the Fatherland must prepare to depart forthwith."[77] Although the Dutch West India Company would later grudgingly allow the Jews to remain in New Amsterdam, word was already circulating about an unprecedented climate of religious tolerance emanating from Newport, Rhode Island.

The first Jews who came to Newport in 1658 found a small village of little more than two hundred families. The houses were crude dwelling places situated on four-acre lots near the river. Having spent the majority of their tenuous existence in the shadows of dungeons and gallows, the new arrivals must have been amazed to find that the local jail was all of twelve feet by ten feet. Reverend Morris A. Gutstein (the ninth rabbi of Congregation Jeshuat Israel, Newport) wrote in his work, *The Story of the Jews of Newport:*

> Time was passed not with cards, but by reading the Bible, and chatting about happenings in the colonies, and about politics abroad.
>
> In those days people took their religion seriously and they were much happier. The meetings of the Baptists and the Quakers were well attended. No special attraction in preaching or preacher was required to have young and old devote a large part of one day a week for public worship and prayer. The services were not short, neither was the preaching. The theme of the preaching was regularly theological and doctrinal, never sensational. Freedom and liberty existed for all to do as they pleased in matters of religion. Yet, going to the meeting place for worship, whether it was in a private home as in the very early days, or, later, in the church-building, was a holiday.
>
> Among these peaceful and religious inhabitants of Newport, with their prevailing spirit of liberty and tolerance, augmented by legislation which assured to all the right to "walk as their consciences persuade them", these fifteen Jewish families that arrived in 1658, must have found a hospitable and comfortable abode. Meeting no opposition, it is said they immediately set out to organize their public worship.[78]

Rabbi Gustein described Dr. Clarke as "a familiar figure in Newport."[79] It is noteworthy that the first documentary evidence of the Jewish settlement is a deed dated February, 1678, which records that Nathaniel Dickins of Newport "sold . . . unto Mordecai Campanall and Moses Pacheckos, Jews, and to their nation, society, or friends a peice of land for a burial place."[80] Thus, within two years of Dr. Clarke's death, a Jewish cemetery was established in Newport.

Around 1693, a second wave of roughly ninety Jews arrived, this time from the West Indies island of Curaçao. Though coming from various destinations, the vanguard of American Jewery shared a common shameful experience in their recent past. To avoid the scaffold, many Jews in Spain and Portugal had made a false profession of "Christianity." Known as "Marranos" (swine), they were kept under constant surveillance by their Catholic oppressors. It is recorded that:

> In the city of Seville an Inquisitor said to the regent: "My lord, if you wish to know how the Marranos keep the Sabbath, let us ascend the tower!" When they had reached the top, the former said to the latter: "Lift up your eyes and look. That house is the home of a Marrano; there is one which belongs to another; and there are many more. You will not see smoke rising from any of them, in spite of the severe cold; for they have no fire because it is the Sabbath."[81]

Gutstein notes how such Old World paranoia followed the Jews to America:

> However, so deep was the impression of the necessity of secrecy in the observance of the Jewish religion that out of habit, some of the Jewish women who came here from the Inquisition to freedom, as they walked the streets of Newport would tell their rosaries while they repeated their Hebrew prayers. This habit had been acquired in Spain and Portugal, "for the purpose of lending the appearance of Catholic form should they be surprised at their devotion."[82]

When the Jewish community in Newport, properly, *Congregation Yeshuat Israel* ("Salvation of Israel"), constructed their synagogue in 1763, a trapdoor under the bimah was included "just in case." Although the Marranos felt comfortable enough in Newport to reclaim their cultural identities (exchanging Catholic names for Jewish ones, remarrying in the synagogue, even belated circumcision), they could never be sure just how long their measure of freedom would last.

While the Baptists had been able to plant the banner of religious liberty in Rhode Island, Parliament continued to restrict matters of citizenship, suffrage and commerce. Under a seven-fold system, Jews in Newport received the fourth classification of "Resident Aliens," which simply gave them permission to live in the settlement. Full citizenship and economic parity would have to await the Bill of Rights (another Baptist production).

We should not be surprised, therefore, to learn that many European Jews (including the Marranos) sought a measure of perceived security within the ranks of Freemasonry, *the avowed enemy of their Catholic oppressors.* Their association with the craft would continue in the New World.

However, the tiny village of Newport would have nothing to fear from the Jews. To the contrary, their Gentile benefactors were literally guaranteed a windfall return on their humanitarian investment. (Genesis 12:3) Rabbi Gutstein writes:

> **The blessing, which God gave Abraham, "And in thee shall be blessed all the families of the earth", may be applied to America in general and to Newport of the eighteenth century in particular.** The eighteenth century ushered in to Newport cultural advancement, social progress, intellectual and religious growth, and more especially economic prosperity. The seventeenth century planted the seed; the eighteenth reaped the harvest. **The success of the harvest was in no small degree due to the descendants of Abraham.**[83]

The Jews were only too glad to show their appreciation for a land void of the papal *auto-da-fé.*

> The growth of the Jewish community was characteristic of the growth of the city in general. As the city shared the profits of the enterprising Jew, so did the Jew share the profit of the progressive city. Newport was not only a beneficiary but also a benefactor in this case.[84]

After initiating an array of retail activity (dry goods, clothing shops, glassware, etc.) Jewish businessmen also made significant strides in the manufacturing end of the city's economy. In the 1740s, the Riveras established the first spermaceti candle factory in Rhode Island. The General Assembly issued a license to Moses Lopez in 1753 for the production of potash. The manufacture of Castile soap was introduced

to America in 1761 by James Lucena, a Jewish merchant in Newport.[85]
Gutstein writes:

> The community prospered in commerce and manufacture. It was aided
> to a great extent by the enterprises of the energetic Jewish "inhabitants."
> Between 1734 and 1768, one chronicler records that there were established
> in the colony of Rhode Island ten forges for making iron ore, two furnaces
> for turning the ore into pig iron and hollow ware, six spermaceti factories,
> twelve potash works, three rope-walks, and one paper mill. Besides these,
> other industries of lesser importance flourished.[86]

In their business dealings, Jewish merchants and manufacturers were
honest and punctilious. Jewish shops were closed not only on the Sabbath,
but on the Christian day of worship as well. A contemporary observer
remarked:

> The Jews and Christians who lived here side by side cultivated the
> most friendly relations, and prospered and grew rich together. . . . It is to
> the honor of our country that a zealous and conscientious Jew, and an
> equally conscientious Christian should retain for each other a boundless
> confidence and mutual respect.[87]

When Dean Berkley visited Newport in 1729, he is quoted as having
exclaimed, **"The town of Newport is the most thriving place in all
America for bigness."**[88] Yet, a full decade later the entire community
could boast only twenty-five streets and about a half-dozen lanes and
wharfs. There were seven churches in town at that time: three Baptist,
two Congregational, one Church of England and one Friends house of
worship—besides the groups that had no regular meeting place.

While the Gentile population of Newport experienced a measure of
reciprocal blessings as their Jewish neighbors worshiped in private homes,
the meter went off the scale when *Congregation Jeshuat Israel* got to
move into their own synagogue in 1763. Rabbi Gutstein relates:

> After the synagogue was built and dedicated, a period of great economic
> prosperity set in for Newport. This period has often been described as the
> "Golden Era of Newport". A contemporary has left us the following
> description of the city at this time: "Newport is a rich and pleasing sea
> and manufacturing city; it is large in circuit and the number of its houses
> runs close to two thousand. It has a beautiful and very long main street from
> which roofs one can see well the ships passing on the sea. It is a principle

inlet to America since one can come to it on the sea as well as from all neighborhoods. **One reckons Newport also among the richest cities in America".** The Jews contributed to a great extent and shared in this economic prosperity.[89]

Of the city's 150 vessels engaged in foreign trade, thirty were owned by the Jewish shipping magnate Aaron Lopez. Among the 445 letters, sailing orders, invoices, bills of lading and other trading agreements pertaining to Rhode Island commerce between 1726 and 1774 (published by the Massachusetts Historical Society), 225 are directly related to Mr. Lopez.[90] The customary shipping form of the day contained such expressions as "Shipped by the Grace of GOD," "riding at anchor in the Harbour of Newport and by GOD'S grace bound for..." and "GOD send the good (sloop) to her desired Port in Safety Amen."[91] Gutstein writes:

> That Newport was the commercial rival of New York and Boston and other ports is attested by the statement: "he was thought a bold prophet who said then, that New York might one day equal Newport." **It may sound curious today, but from this time we have a letter addressed to "New York near Newport, Rhode Island."** [92]

While the Jewish exporters in Newport had contact with numerous international ports of call, one foreign land garnered the attention of the entire Jewish community. In 1763, certain Jews residing in Palestine dispatched a letter of appeal to the Hebrew congregation in Newport. The letter, signed by four people in Hebron, recounted the suffering of the Jews in the Holy Land and the severe taxation to which they were subjected. It also stated that in order to meet the heavy tax of "25,000 Pieces of Eight" which was put on them, they had "sent forth two Brethren to collect it by Contributions."[93] An entry in the extant ledger of Daniel Gomez, dated October 3, 1770, records that twenty-five pounds and twelve shillings were received from "Road" Island for "the Holley Congregation of Hebron."[94]

Though the British occupation of Newport during the War of Independence dealt the tiny Jewish community a blow from which it was never able to recover, the God of Abraham, Isaac and Jacob had provided ample demonstration of what the entire nation could subsequently enjoy *if* she would only heed the promise of Genesis 12:3.

SUPPRESSION IN THE SOUTH

Severe as the New England persecution became under Congregationalism, the abuse endured by our Baptist forefathers in the southern colonies, particularly in Virginia, remains a story of its own. Here the tenacious foe of religious freedom was none other than the Church of England herself. History confirms that this ecclesiastical tyrant wielded a broad ax of intolerance. As early as 1661, the Virginia assembly provided that a fine of two thousand pounds of tobacco be levied on parents who refused to have their children sprinkled. The extent to which her venom had permeated the South as a whole can be gleaned from Vedder's observation that all but seven of the forty-seven Baptist churches active in America by 1734 were *north* of the Mason-Dixon line.[95] As stated earlier, the first Baptist church in Virginia was not constituted until 1715, over a century after the founding of Jamestown.

The scope of this persecution was certain to limit God's blessings on America. Applying the truth, *"When a man's ways please the LORD, he maketh even his enemies to be at peace with him"* (Proverbs 16:7), we are not surprised that the early settlers experienced a tenuous existence at best. Because the Lord is no respecter of persons, the New World was equipped with a Black Forest of its own. The question of whether or not He would clear it for Japheth's descendants rested entirely with them. A contemporary account of this threatening woodland was given as follows:

> The "American colonies" were still nothing but the sparsest fringe of seacoast settlements separated by swamps, desolation, empty beaches, and primeval forests of terrifying silence stretched out in a thin line for a thousand miles from Maine to Georgia. The innermost penetrations were rarely more than one hundred miles from where the Atlantic surf seethed up on the sand. Deeper than one hundred miles was a forested land of silence in which only stealthy shadows moved; a region as remote as the moon, as terrifying as the blackest nightmare. It was called simply, the Wilderness. The awareness of the Wilderness colored every strand of American life. The immensity of the Wilderness was an ever-present nightmare reducing human beings to insignificance."[96]

Whenever the Gospel was suppressed, the settlers would receive commensurate visits from beyond the timberline. "Drums along the Mohawk" spread terror near and far. The God who tore forty-two children to smithereens for mocking a preacher's bald head (II Kings 2:24) had plenty of bruins in reserve for a land that would afflict His servants similarly. In one of the more amazing accounts of divine retribution, a rogue who had tried to use a bomb to kill Reverend James Ireland of Culpeper, Virginia, was sleeping by a campfire between two other men when a mad wolf suddenly appeared and singled him out with a mortal bite to the nose.

Added to these everyday hardships were the "Whore's" numerous Jesuit inroads as far west as Minnesota by 1680. Authors Peter Marshall and David Manuel should be marked (Romans 16:17) as deceitful compromisers for eulogizing these Vatican hit men as "Christian soldiers . . . strong in the faith . . ." in their ecumenical fairy tale *The Light and the Glory*.[97] (I Timothy 4:1-6)

The most telltale sign of forfeited blessing was the calamitous disunity that prevailed among the colonists themselves. (Psalm 133:1) Thirteen little nations at constant odds with one another could hardly repel a major foreign invasion. And the devil had two on the calendar. The time had come for providential intervention!

GEORGE WHITEFIELD

On a balmy spring evening in 1738, a twenty-three-year-old English missionary stepped foot on American soil at Savannah, Georgia. It was fitting that the date, May 7, just happened to fall on a Sunday. The young man's name was George Whitefield. Although George Washington would be hailed as the "Father of Our Country," it would be George Whitefield's mission to ensure that a country was secured in the first place. His diary entry for May 8 states:

> I find there are many divisions amongst the inhabitants; but God, I hope, will make me an instrument of composing them. Grant this, O Lord, for Thy dear Son's sake![98]

Whitefield's strategy for attaining this unity was to "draw them by the cords of love." He would do this through the preaching of a King James Bible. Perhaps more than any person of his day, Whitefield became God's man of the hour. His initial labor in Britain had been interrupted by General Oglethorpe's Macedonian call for an orphanage in Georgia. (James1:22) However, the evangelist quickly discerned that his ultimate purpose in America would far surpass his beloved Bethesda House. As the despised Baptists lacked the political wherewithal to extricate themselves from their numerically superior oppressors, the Lord got the last laugh by infiltrating Satan's lines with a Spirit-filled renegade Anglican. (Psalm 2:4)

Whitefield's philosophy of ministry was short and to the point— "Speaking for God to an alien world." And because he strove to be "first a saint, and then a scholar," the power of God was manifested accordingly. A structure capable of accommodating his supernatural crowds could not be found on either side of the Atlantic. Whitefield, like his Master before him, was forced to preach in the open air. He said, "I thought it might be doing the service of my creator who had a mountain for his pulpit and the heavens for his sounding board, and who, when his gospel was refused by the Jews, sent his servants into the highways and hedges."[99] As noted in the previous chapter, his numbers in Great Britain were staggering: 20,000 in the Moorfields; 50,000 at Kennington Common; 80,000 near Hyde Park. In 1742, Whitefield's throngs in Cambuslang, Scotland, approached 100,000! And all of this was being accomplished without the use of a microphone. The figures he attained in the lesser-populated American colonies were not too shabby either: 6,000 in Germantown; 8,000 in New York City; 10,000 in White Clay Creek; 15,000 in Roxbury; 20,000 in Boston.

His ministerial methods were often called into question by the orthodox. Once, at the request of a condemned horse thief in New York, Whitefield accompanied him to the gallows, mounted his coffin, and promptly preached to several thousand stunned spectators.[100] When a wimpy Boston minister met him with the words, "I'm sorry to see you here, George," the man of God replied, "So is the devil," and proceeded to address a throng of 20,000 on Boston Common!

Mr. Whitefield sailed into Newport, Rhode Island, on Sunday evening, September 14, 1740, for a three-day visit. Intending to preach the Gospel, he asked Reverend James Honeyman, the minister of the Church of England, for permission to use his pulpit. Whitefield penned in his journal:

> At first he seemed a little unwilling, and wished to know "what extraordinary call I had to preach on week-days," which he said, "was disorderly?" I answered, "St. Paul exhorted Timothy to be instant in season and out of

season . . ." As to an extraordinary call, I claimed none otherwise than the Apostle's injunction, "as we have opportunity let us do good unto all men." [101]

The pastor reluctantly agreed, whereupon Mr. Whitefield sent him into shock by packing out his three thousand-seat auditorium. "God assisted me much," he wrote. "I observed numbers affected, and had great reason to believe the Word of God had been sharper than a two-edged sword in some of the hearers' souls." By Tuesday evening there was so much Holy Ghost conviction on the town that a thousand souls besieged the private home where Whitefield was being entertained. "I therefore stood upon the threshold, and spake for near an hour on these words, 'Blessed are they that hunger and thirst after righteousness, for they shall be filled.'" He observed, "It was a very solemn meeting. Glory be to God's great Name!"[102] While Mr. Whitefield would later conclude, "Rhode Island seems to be a place where much good may be done," the "hireling" Honeyman murmured in a letter to an acquaintance, "Last Sunday arrived here from South Carolina, the noisie Mr. Whitefield . . . I shall endeavor to correct his mistakes and evince a just distinction betwixt Christianity and enthusiasm,"[103] (i.e., put his members back to sleep).

Referring to Pennsylvania as the "Garden of America," Whitefield chose Philadelphia as his Capernaum. Whereas Clarke and Williams labeled Rhode Island an "*Efficacious* Experiment," William Penn described his colony as a "*Holy* Experiment." Whitefield's crowds in Philadelphia often surpassed the city's entire population of 12,000 (the largest American city at that time) owing to the fact that so many would travel from neighboring communities. On Sunday, May 11, 1740, the evangelist spoke to 15,000 in the morning and 20,000 in the evening. After measuring the area reached by his voice in one particular service, a befuddled Benjamin Franklin confirmed, "I computed that he might well be heard by more than thirty thousand."[104] Others testified that he could preach on the courthouse steps of Philadelphia and be heard on the Jersey shore, a mile away! Should we be surprised that the city of Philadelphia became Whitefield's headquarters for America's Great Awakening? After all, wasn't John's letter to the church at Sardis followed by his letter to *Philadelphia*? Whitefield himself cited the holy significance in his journal entry for November 28, 1739:

Blessed be God, for the great work begun in these parts. Oh, that what God says of the Church of Philadelphia in the *Revelation,* may be now fulfilled in the city called after her name! *"I know thy works. Behold I have set before thee an open door, and no man can shut it. Behold I will make them of the synagogue of Satan to come and worship before thy feet, and to know that I have loved thee."*[105]

As an added note of contrast between these ecclesiastical dispensations, Whitefield chided the typical Bostonian for possessing a mere "external observance of the Sabbath," while referring to the spiritual minority within the Congregationalist stronghold as *"a few names left in Sardis, which have not defiled their garments."*[106]

A statue of George Whitefield may be seen on the campus of the University of Pennsylvania as a memorial to the multitudes that came through the "Philadelphia Door." Needless to say, the average pothead student wouldn't know that Whitefield was the inspirer and original trustee for the Charity School, which later became the University of Pennsylvania. (The same could be said of Whitefield's co-laborer, William Tennent, whose Log College later developed into Princeton University.)

Although Philadelphia was noted for its Quaker-inspired religious diversity, Whitefield pointed to a Baptist preacher as the city's true spiritual leader. The Anglican evangelist acknowledged:

> I went and heard Mr. Jones, the Baptist minister, who preached the truth as it is in Jesus. **He is the only preacher that I know of in Philadelphia, who speaks feelingly and with authority.** The poor people are much refreshed by him, and I trust the Lord will bless him more and more.[107]

The esteemed pastor in question, Jenkin Jones, was born in Wales and came to America in 1710. After pastoring the Baptist church at Pennypack Creek (Township of Dublin, County of Philadelphia) from 1726-1746, Reverend Jones founded the First Baptist Church of Philadelphia in 1746 and continued in that position until his death on July 16, 1760.

BIRTH OF THE BIBLE BELT

Although the Awakening was off to a good start with respect to uniting the colonies for their coming war of independence, the South remained a spiritual wasteland. Whitefield's "crowds" in Virginia and the Carolinas were negligible to non-existent. Yet the mighty prophet was privileged, in the Spirit, to see America's "Bible Belt" before it came to pass. Note his amazing Holy Ghost perception while traveling through Virginia, the future battleground for the nation's religious liberty:

> I could not but think, that God intended, in His own time, to work a good work in these southern parts of America. At present they seem more dead to God, but far less prejudiced than in the northern parts. . . . I gave the printer leave to print my *Journals* and *Sermons*, and I trust that God Who loves to work by the meanest instruments, will be pleased to bless them to the conviction and edification of these, His people. **Visit them, O Lord, with Thy salvation.**[108]

When Whitefield passed through North Carolina he was burdened even more, declaring, "There is scarcely so much as the form of religion," and noting, "There are several dancing-masters, but scarcely one regular settled minister."[109] His diary for Sunday, December 23, 1739, reads, "Preached about noon to nearly a hundred people."[110] The site of this small service was in Bath, North Carolina, the oldest town in the state. A number of years ago, two preachers and I visited the tourist center in Bath and asked the attendant if she had ever heard of George Whitefield. In animated fashion, she pointed to a nearby bridge over the scenic Pamplico River and told us an amazing story. As the devil never gives up ground without a fight, the reason Whitefield couldn't draw flies in Bath was because the town's previous generation had grown enamored with Black Beard the Pirate, harboring the fugitive until his beheading in 1718.

The woman related how Whitefield had placed a curse on his detractors as he crossed over the bridge while making his exodus. Shaking the dust off his feet, the man of God prophesied, "This town will never grow!" She then acknowledged with all candor, "And you know what? It never has!" At the turn of the twenty-first century, the oldest incorporated town in the state had a population of only 270 people! The story of Whitefield's curse is also recounted in the center's fourteen-minute video presentation. As we exited the "packed" theater of three, our host concluded her informal tour in the spirit of Bath's Adamic ancestors. With an array of boarded up buildings and "For Sale" signs on the outside and shelves of Black Beard the Pirate paraphernalia on the inside, she proudly announced, "We like our town just the way it is!"

We then drove about thirty minutes eastward and arrived at the thriving community of New Bern (Newborn Town in *George Whitefield's Journals*). Unlike Bath (except for its proximity to the beautiful Pamplico), New Bern sported large motels, a convention center and spacious shopping areas. What is the explanation, you ask? It was here on Christmas Day, 1739, two days after the meager turnout in Bath, that Whitefield was anointed with "fresh oil" while preaching to a hungry crowd in the local courthouse. (Psalm 92:10) His diary entry reads:

> I cried mightily to the Lord in my secret devotions, and in the afternoon when I read prayers and preached, He was pleased to shew that He had heard me, for I scarcely know when we have had more visible manifestation of the Divine Presence since our coming into America. The people were uncommonly attentive, and most were melted into tears.[111]

Whitefield was stirred to believe that the South would be won for God, declaring in his journal:

> I looked upon it as an earnest of future and more plentiful effusions of God's Spirit in these parts. I believe, wherever the Gospel is preached in these parts with power, it will be remarkably blessed.[112]

The following day Whitefield uttered a remarkable prayer that would alter America's spiritual destiny. Standing in the pine thickets of North Carolina, between Newborn Town and Trent River, he cried:

> **Oh, that the Lord would send forth some who, like John the Baptist, might preach and baptise in the wilderness! I believe they would flock to him from all the country round about.**[113]

The extent to which this burden was honored can be gauged by the fact that there are more Baptist churches in the Tar Heel State today than in any other state in the Union!

What remains to be seen is the remarkable way in which the Lord brought Whitefield's "baptizing preacher" into the wilderness of North Carolina. Although he didn't know it at the time, the specific answer to his petition would be tied to yet another prayer he uttered for the spiritual welfare of his growing number of converts:

> What I mostly fear is, now there is such a general awakening, the people will not know where to go for proper food, and thereby fall into different

sects and parties. Lord Jesus, look upon them, and let not Satan divide them again; but raise them up pastors after Thy own heart. Amen and amen.[114]

Whitefield was hardly prepared for the manner in which his prayer would be answered. As Samson's parents *"knew not that it was of the LORD, that he sought an occasion against the Philistines"* (Judges 14:4a), Whitefield was likewise oblivious to God's deeper purpose for his ministry in America. When his many Protestant converts began reading their Bibles, it didn't take them long to discover that infant sprinkling was nowhere to be found. The Holy Spirit was then able to move these "New Lights" (as they were called) to either join existing Baptist churches or to start new ones altogether. Benedict, writes:

> This work began generally among the Pedobaptists, and where they opposed it, separation ensued . . . They took the Bible alone for their guide, and of course, Baptist principles soon prevailed amongst them.[115]

Apparently, for the sake of pulling off this Anglican-induced revival of Baptists, the evangelist with the ministerial credentials was not permitted to grasp what his own converts could see, encountering a "spiritual brownout" not unlike that experienced by the twelve: *"And they understood none of these things: and this saying was hid from them, neither knew they the things which were spoken"* (Luke 18:34). An incredulous Whitefield could only exclaim, **"All my chickens have turned into ducks!"**[116]

Six years after that anointed prayer meeting in North Carolina, a Congregationalist from Tolland, Connecticut, by the name of Shubal Stearns was converted under a Whitefield sermon in Boston. After six years of preaching as a New Light, Stearns was immersed by Reverend Wait Palmer, on May 20, 1751, at the Baptist church in Stonington, Connecticut, and ordained a Baptist minister. Four years later, following a brief ministry in Opekon, Virginia (corresponding today to the northeast corner of West Virginia), Whitefield's "John the Baptist" arrived in the wilderness of North Carolina. He was two months shy of his fiftieth birthday. On November 22, 1755, seven devoted couples, including Shubal's brother-in-law, Reverend Daniel Marshal (another of Whitefield's ducks), joined Pastor and Mrs. Stearns in establishing the Sandy Creek Baptist Church in Guilford County, North Carolina. (At the time, Sandy Creek lay in the heavily wooded region between Deep River and Haw River in Guilford County; now Randolph County.) Their first meeting house was a "multi-million-dollar auditorium," measuring 26' x 30'.

As to Whitefield's prayer vision that the multitudes "would flock to him from round about," we have this amazing account from Tidence Lane, a former enemy who was converted and called to preach under Stearns's ministry (as introduced by another contemporary, Morgan Edwards):

> Mr. Stearns was but a little man, but a man of good natural parts and sound judgment. Of learning he had but a small share, yet was pretty well acquainted with books. His voice was musical and strong, which he managed in such a manner as, one while, to make soft impressions on the heart, and fetch tears from the eyes in a mechanical way; and anon to shake the very nerves and throw the animal system into tumults and perturbations.
>
> All the Separate ministers copy after him in tones of voice and actions of body; and some few exceed him. His character was indisputably good, both as a man, a Christian and a preacher. In his eyes was something very penetrating, seemed to have a meaning in every glance, of which I will give one example; and the rather because it was given me by a man of good sense, I mean Tiden Lane.
>
> "When the fame of Mr. Stearns's preaching (said he) had reached the Atkin (Yadkin), where I lived, I felt a curiosity to go and hear him. Upon my arrival, I saw a venerable old man sitting under a peach-tree, with a book in his hand and the people gathering about him. He fixed his eyes upon me immediately, which made me feel in such a manner as I never had felt before. I turned to quit the place, but could not proceed far. I walked about, sometimes catching his eyes as I walked. My uneasiness increased and became intolerable. I went up to him, thinking that a salutation and shaking of hands would relieve me; but it happened otherwise. I began to think that he had an evil eye and ought to be shunned; but shunning him I could no more effect than a bird can shun the rattlesnake when it fixes its eyes upon it. **When he began to preach my perturbations increased, so that nature could no longer support them and I sank to the ground.**" [117]

The Sandy Creek Baptist Church experienced a veritable explosion of Holy Ghost power, *growing to over six hundred members in the first two years alone.* Dr. Howell, as cited by Armitage, wrote:

> The fields were white to harvest. God poured out his Holy Spirit. One universal impulse pervaded, apparently, the minds of the whole people. Evidently hungering for the bread of life, they came together in vast multitudes. Everywhere the ministry of these men was attended with the most extraordinary success. Very large numbers were baptized. Churches sprang up by scores. Among the converts were many able men, who at once

entered the ministry, and swelled continually the ranks of the messengers of salvation.[118]

At a time when only seven Baptist churches existed south of the Mason-Dixon line, Vedder gives the number of local assemblies directly started by Sandy Creek at forty-two and adds that one hundred and twenty-five ministers were sent out over a five-hundred-mile area. This statistic would appear to represent about 99 percent of the male membership! (Perhaps this is the way the congregation numbered only sixteen at Stearns's death in 1771.) The central monument at Sandy Creek, not far from the founder's grave, reads as follows:

ORIGINAL SITE SANDY CREEK CHURCH

On this site, in November-December 1755, Reverend Shubal Stearns, his wife, and those who came with him, seven other families, sixteen souls in all, built their first meeting house, where they administered the Lord's Supper. "It is a mother church, Nay, a grandmother, and a great grandmother. All the Separate Baptists spring hence: not only eastward toward the sea, but westward toward the great river Mississippi, but northward to Virginia, and southward to South Carolina and Georgia. The word went forth from this Sion, and great was the company of them who published it, in so much that her converts were as drops of morning dew."

A secondary marker affirms that by 1829, over *1,000* churches traced their origin to Sandy Creek Baptist Church! The first Baptist church in the state of Georgia, the Kiokee Baptist Church, was started in the community of Appling by Stearns's brother-in-law, Daniel Marshal. The first church of any denomination in Tennessee, the Buffalo Ridge Baptist Church in Gray, was founded by Tidence Lane out of Sandy Creek. The first Separate Baptist churches in Virginia and South Carolina were also begun by lay preachers from Sandy Creek.

At this point it is critical to observe what the "Old-Time Religion" was all about. Regarding the aforementioned satanic conspiracy to obliterate Baptist history, the main reason why students in our Baptist "colleges" are more familiar with *Protestantism* is because historic Baptist methodology is anathema to "purpose driven kingdom building." *Our Baptist forefathers believed in multiplication through division, not addition.* Furthermore, these works were not built on sham professions or cute decisions. There were no mini-bikes or other Laodicean gimmicks being distributed. And the sinners who got dunked didn't dry *up* after they dried *off*. (Acts 2:41-42) Let the record read loud and clear—America's Bible Belt began with bona fide Holy Ghost *conviction* and *conversion*. (Acts 20:21) Concerning the Gospel that was preached at Sandy Creek, David Benedict writes:

> Stearns and his party, of course, brought strange things to their ears. To be born again, appeared to them as absurd as it did to the Jewish doctor, when he asked, if he must enter the second time into his mother's womb and be born. Having always supposed that religion consisted in nothing more than the practice of its outward duties, they could not comprehend how it should be necessary to feel conviction and conversion; and to be able to ascertain the time and place of one's conversion, was, in their estimation, wonderful indeed . . . Many mocked, but the power of God attending them, many also trembled. In process of time, some of the inhabitants became converts, and bowed obedience to the Redeemer's sceptre.[119]

For an interesting postscript to this story, the student of history will note that today the Sandy Creek Baptist Church just happens to be situated in *Liberty*, North Carolina. After all, what's in a name?

PERSECUTION IN VIRGINIA

With many of these new Baptist works being planted in the fertile fields of Virginia, the inevitable backlash of Satan was swift and severe. The preachers of this period bore an enormous persecution so that you and I could one day live in a free America. Because our nation's modern history books revere the likes of Susan B. Anthony, Martin Luther King, Jr., and others, practically no one is aware of Old Dominion's "Gulag of Gaols." The "gaol" was a loathsome jail into which many a Baptist minister was committed for the "crime" of preaching the Gospel of Jesus Christ without a license from the state. Of course, it was the message itself that was so hated, Joseph Nordenhaug declaring:

> The Baptists say, and have always said, that the mercy of God and the grace of Jesus Christ are free and open to any man. They have been imprisoned for saying it, publicly whipped for saying it, driven into the wilderness, killed for saying it, and they have gone right on saying it, and they say it now: The mercy of God and the grace of Jesus Christ are free to any man. Knock and it shall be opened. God is always there Himself, waiting for each man to come in. The way is clear. You have access.[120]

To keep the way clear for others, dozens of Baptist preachers would have to hear the doors to their own cells clang somberly behind them. But then, to everyone's surprise, a most unusual phenomenon occurred. The deprived congregations started going out to the gaols to hear their Sunday sermons! As the jailed pastor would attempt to deliver his message through the prison window's iron grates, the incensed (and embarrassed) magistrates would do every imaginable thing to distract his humble flock. While some beat on drums, others would hurl snakes and hornet nests at the crowd. Still others tried to disperse the faithful by sending drunks on horseback into their midst.

The amazing story of Pastor John Weatherford of Chesterfield County represents a classic illustration of the church-state intolerance prevailing at that time. Weatherford, a father of fifteen, spent six months in the county gaol for "preaching without a license." However, his oppressors soon discovered that they had more on their hands than they had bargained for. So many locals started getting converted below the grates of Weatherford's cell that the magistrate ordered *a twelve-foot wall be erected directly in front of the preacher's window.* However, they quickly learned, to their chagrin, that out of sight was not out of range! When Weatherford's faithful congregation assembled for "church," a handkerchief on a pole would be raised as the signal that they were ready for the Sunday sermon. The man of God then proceeded to throw his voice *through* the grates, *over* the twelve-foot impediment. Such an unorthodox "worship service" was known back then as "denying the prison bounds."

Pastor Weatherford was eventually released after a lawyer by the name of *Patrick Henry* paid his fine. Today, a giant memorial bearing witness to the preacher's ordeal can be viewed less than twenty feet from the present county court house and roughly fifty feet from the site of the incarceration itself. His final resting place is not so easy to find, however. A small, worn headstone bearing the sole inscription, "J.W." stands by itself in an obscure clump of trees in the middle of a field about a mile from the road behind the Shockoe Baptist Church in Java, Virginia.

Noting her abusive similarities to "Mother Rome," someone has said that "an Episcopalian is nothing more than a Catholic who flunked Latin." One need only compare the spiritual climate at Plymouth Colony to the gold-digging debauchery at Jamestown to get the proper focus. However, "the blood of the martyrs is the seed of the church." Because these men of God were willing to rot in prison, the number of Baptist churches in Virginia experienced unprecedented growth.

RENEWED PERSECUTION IN MASSACHUSETTS

Meanwhile, back in New England, persecution was renewed along economic lines. Having granted certain dissenters toleration from obligatory church affiliation, the magistrates felt increasingly pressured to extend a similar exemption from the despised religious taxes that bankrolled the Congregational state church. Beginning in 1727, any Anglican, Quaker or Baptist who filed an annual certificate duly signed by his pastor and a committee of respectable laymen attesting to his conscientious convictions would be excluded from the roll by the parish assessors. However, when Whitefield's chickens began turning into ducks, the feathers really started to fly. Over one hundred and twenty-five new Baptist churches hit the Congregational coffers hard. Suddenly the publicans started balking at approving applications. New Light baptismal candidates were accused of "washing away their taxes." The social reproach of being a "certificate man" only added to the dissenters' standard abuse.

Fortunately, many of the Baptists began having second thoughts about the whole mess. The Holy Ghost had enlightened them to see that the certificate was a tacit acknowledgment that Caesar still controlled the conscience. (Exodus 8:28; 10:24) Consequently, they refused both the certificate and the subsequent tax. McLoughlin catalogs the resultant fallout:

> Upon refusing to pay the tax (for the same conscientious reason) these individuals were either put in prison or the constable took some item of their property and sold it at public auction to pay the tax. Many a Baptist saw his cow or horse taken from his barn by a tax collector; one man had his horse taken out from under him on the highway; another, his saddle; another, his winter's supply of beef. Carpenters had their tools taken, and women saw their pewter plates and spinning wheels sold for a few shillings' tax. There is a record of one woman in Raynham, Massachusetts, who spent thirteen months in prison for refusing to pay a tax of eight pence. And these families were fortunate compared to the ones whose breadwinner was taken off to jail for an indefinite stay while the family was left to fend for itself. Sometimes the tax collectors even sold a man's land.[121]

"The British Are Coming"

As time went on, authorities in both sections of the country started seeing political egg on their faces. A Baptist in Massachusetts declared sardonically, "These Sons of Liberty ought rather to be called Sons of Violence."[122] In Virginia, lawyers with household names such as Thomas Jefferson, Patrick Henry and James Madison began successfully representing various Baptist preachers in court. William Cathcart relates that, on one occasion, Henry "rode fifty miles to Fredericksburg to be present at the trial of John Walker, Lewis Craig and James Childs, who were indicted for the crime of 'preaching the gospel contrary to the law,' whose acquittal he speedily secured."[123] With reference to six jailed Baptists in Culpeper, Virginia, Madison wrote to a friend, "That diabolical, hell-conceived principle of persecution rages among some."[124]

Then, on March 5, 1770, the Lord got everyone's attention when five American citizens were killed by British muskets in the infamous Boston Massacre. The wake-up call occurred near the corner of Devonshire and State Streets. *Was it just another spiritual coincidence that their blood was shed only a few yards from the very spot where Obadiah Holmes was "whipped unmercifully" with thirty lashes?*

According to what we learned in school, the next most significant event in America's quest for liberty was the Boston Tea Party on December 16, 1773. However, that affair pales in comparison to a rarely told incident provoked by a band of patriotic Baptists eighteen months earlier. John Brown of Rhode Island (a brother of Nicholas Brown, after whom Brown University was named), was a devoted member of the First Baptist Church in Providence. He was also a successful merchant and owner of twenty vessels. Dr. Cathcart writes:

> **John Brown might be said to have begun the Revolution himself.**
> In 1772, a British armed schooner called the "Gaspee" came into Narragansett Bay to carry out orders from the British Commissioners of customs in Boston, with a view to prevent violations of the revenue laws. The "Gaspee" was a continual annoyance to the mariners and ship-owners, with whose business she interfered.
>
> On the 9th of June, 1772, she ran aground on Namquit, below Pawtuxet. Mr. Brown heard of it, and he immediately ordered eight boats to be placed in charge of Captain Abraham Whipple, one of his best ship-masters, and he put sixty-four armed men in them. At about 2 A.M., Mr. Brown and

his boats reached the "Gaspee;" two shots were exchanged, one of which wounded Lieutenant Duddingston. **"This was the first British blood shed in the war of Independence."**
    The crew and officers left the "Gaspee" very speedily, and Whipple blew her up. Mr. Brown was the last man on board.[125]

Thus, we conclude that while some Boston Protestants, disguised as Indians, went down in history for throwing a few crates of tea overboard, a band of freedom-loving Baptists from Rhode Island boldly blew up and sank the ship they had boarded!

The ensuing war with Great Britain gave the Baptists a golden opportunity to display their true heroics and patriotism. Within weeks of the aggression at Lexington and Concord, the Rhode Island Legislature voted to send 1,500 men to the conflict. The Baptist colony was also the first to sever formal ties with England, doing so on May 4, 1776, a full month before Virginia. Baptist troops consistently distinguished themselves on the field of battle, dying side by side with their Protestant oppressors. Christian writes, "Not a man of them proved a traitor."[126] Even the enemy understood the Baptists' contribution, British general William Howe confirming, "The Baptists were among the most strenuous supporters of liberty."[127] And to add insult to injury, Dr. John Rippon of London, in a letter written in 1784 to Dr. James Manning, president of Rhode Island College (later Brown University), declared, "I believe all our Baptist ministers in town, except two, and most of our brethren in the country were on the side of the Americans in the late dispute."[128]

Much of the credit for the army's overall performance was due to the strong spiritual leadership provided by the Baptist chaplains. Though nearly twenty different religious denominations existed in eighteenth-century colonial America, Baptist preachers filled a third of the one hundred and two chaplain positions in the Continental Army. Because of their reputation for being able to pray *and* shoot ("Bless 'em, Jesus,"—*blam*, etc.), the soldiers received a steady stream of manly, spiritual inspiration. Dr. Cathcart gives a whole new meaning to the clerical cliché "*men* of the cloth":

Elder M'Clanahan, a Baptist minister, raised a company of soldiers in Culpeper County for the Continental service, chiefly from his own denomination, to whom he ministered as a chaplain and whom he commanded as their captain. . . .

The Rev. David Barrow, a brother of spotless character, and of extensive usefulness, held in universal esteem, not only commanded patriotism to others, but when danger pressed he shouldered his musket and performed good service against the common foe, and he obtained the same reputation in the camp and in the field which he enjoyed in the happy scenes of ministerial toil elsewhere.[129]

David Jones was another "reverend" who could shoot about as well as he could pray. In April of 1775, Jones became pastor of the Baptist Church in the Great Valley, near Valley Forge. Within the year he enlisted in the army as a Baptist chaplain, serving under Colonel St. Clair, General Horatio Gates and General Anthony Wayne. He was highly respected by George Washington and preached to the suffering troops at Valley Forge. Jones's courage under fire is legendary, his defining moment occurring when he charged alone, pistol in hand, into the face of a British attack at the Battle of Brandywine. Cathcart writes:

He was never away from scenes of danger; nor from the rude couch of the sick or the wounded soldier when words of comfort were needed. He followed Gates through two campaigns, and served as a brigade chaplain under Wayne. He was in the battle of Brandywine, the slaughter of Paoli, where he escaped only by the special case of Providence, and in all the deadly conflicts in which his brigade was engaged, until the surrender of Yorktown. General Howe, learning that he was a pillar to the Revolution in and out of the army, offered a reward for his capture, and a plot was unsuccessfully laid to secure his person. Full of wit, eloquence, patriotism, and fearless courage, he was a model chaplain and a tower of strength to the cause of freedom.[130]

With reference to Richard Furman, a Baptist pastor from South Carolina (for whom Furman University was named), Lord Cornwallis was said to have remarked that he "feared the prayers of that godly youth more than the armies of Sumter and Marion."[131] Such "rebel parsons," as they were called (along with a number of spiritual Congregational chaplains), served with the understanding that, if captured, they would be killed on sight. General Washington was well aware of the priceless contribution of these men, declaring, "Baptist chaplains were among the most prominent and useful in the army."[132]

JOHN GANO

John Gano is generally recognized as the most influential chaplain of the entire war. Cathcart summarizes his outstanding testimony:

> The Rev. John Gano was born in Hopewell, New Jersey, and possessed in a large degree the patriotic spirit of the Baptists of that place, which had so many representatives engaged in the Revolution; he had great mental powers, and as a "minister he shewn like a star of the first magnitude in the American churches."
>
> His power as a minister of eminence was widely felt, and his labors extensive and successfull. From the pastorship of the First Baptist Church, of New York, he entered the army as a chaplain, and performed services which rendered him invaluable to the officers and men with whom he was associated. His love for his country's cause made the humblest soldier a brother; his genial manners and fearless daring made him the special friend of officers of all ranks: while the spirit of the Saviour so completely controlled his entire conduct that his influence over his military charge was unbounded.
>
> Headley says: "In the fierce conflict on Chatterton's Hill he was continually under fire, and his cool and quiet courage in thus fearlessly exposing himself was afterwards commented on in the most glowing terms by the officers who stood near him." He himself in speaking of it said: "**My station in time of action I knew to be among the surgeons, but in this battle I somehow got in front of the regiment;** yet I durst not quit my place for fear of dampening the spirits of the soldiers, or of bringing on myself an imputation of cowardice."
>
> He preserved his moral dignity as a Christian minister under the most trying circumstances, and by his example, spirit, and instructions, he assisted the brave patriots to endure hardships, to struggle successfully against despair, and to fight with the courage of men who were sure that God was with them, and their ultimate triumph was certain.[133]

Gano's greatest contribution to the war was the significant manner in which he impacted the venerable commander-in-chief. Washington's esteem for his favorite chaplain was evidenced on April 19, 1783, when he called on Gano to lead in prayer at the special thanksgiving service in New Windsor, New York, marking a formal end to hostilities.[134]

It was around this time and locale that the Prostetant general and the Baptist minister shared a pair of spiritual experiences too holy for the History Channel to handle. The adumbrative events would cap an intimate seven-year relationship which began at the early Battle of White Plains. While the preacher's "baptism of fire" had occurred in this engagement—the general, having watched Gano advance into the shattered and desperate firing line from his observation post on a neighboring hill—an even more compelling scene had captured Washington's soul only months before.

Upon moving his military headquarters to New York City in the spring of 1776, Washington continued his practice of frequenting the Sunday services of his denomination (the Church of England). Dr. Lemuel Call Barnes writes:

> The general requested the authorities of Trinity church and its chapel, St. Paul's, to discontinue the customary prayers for the government of England, whose battleships were then gathering in the harbor to crush the "rebellion". The rector refused to do it. But the noble general frequented his pew at St. Paul's, silently praying for this country, while the priest in the high pulpit prayed for the success of the enemies of the country.
>
> In plain sight on "Gold Hill", only two or three squares away, stood the ever-crowded meeting-house where Pastor John Gano, with his eloquent voice and heart, was preaching and praying in behalf of the colonial government and its chosen commander. Like a good soldier, Washington stood by his own church, but watched with keen interest and overflowing gratitude every sanely patriotic current in the town.[135]

Other historians cite from additional sources, indicating that Washington may have listened occasionally to portions of Gano's discourses from beneath the church window, a plausible conjecture indeed.[136] Gano had pastored the First Baptist Church of New York City since it was constituted in June, 1762. The embarrassing contrast between Washington's "cleric" and the "fighting chaplain" nurtured a growing spirit of silent nonconformity in the Protestant commander. While the humble Christian knew how to kneel in the snow at Valley Forge, he refused to do so in the Episcopal services. Rev. William White, the first bishop of the Protestant Episcopal Church in America, and rector of Christ Church where Washington was a regular attendee during his residence in Philadelphia, said of the matter, "His behavior was always serious and attentive; but . . . on the point of kneeling during service I owe it to truth to declare that I **never saw him in said attitude.**"[137]

When the first Congress assembled in Carpenters Hall, Philadelphia, September 7, 1774, White's predecessor at Christ Church, Dr. Jacob

Dusche, had the honor of opening the august meeting in prayer. While a "pious" Dusche may be seen on his knees in T. H. Matheson's famous painting "The First Prayer in Congress," Washington was not impressed. He got stuck having to employ "damage control" after the salaried Congressional chaplain later defected, wrote him an insolent letter advising that he also abandon the American cause, and then hightailed it back to religious headquarters in England.

Another manifestation of Washington's silent nonconformity was his consistent refusal to participate in the Episcopal "sacrament" of holy communion. Once again, Dr. White acknowledged, "Truth requires me to say that **General Washington never received the communion** in the Church of which I am parochial minister."[138]

The seven intense years between White Plains and New Windsor afforded Washington ample opportunity for reflection and long, quiet talks with his spiritual chaplain. There was simply no escaping reality; while his own church was overwhelmingly "Tory," the liberty-loving group to which Gano belonged was almost to the man with the colonial cause.

Washington's admiration for the Baptists was also enhanced by his firsthand knowledge of their suffering. The Lord had sown the seed of "soul liberty" in Washington's heart years earlier and in his native state of Virginia. Do you recall the well-known story about the cherry tree? One of Washington's farms was known as Ferry Farm, because it included a ferry across the Rappahannock River into the village of Fredericksburg, county seat of Spotsylvania County. A tablet there reads, "Washington's Boyhood Home." Young George spent most of his time at this place between 1739 and 1747 (ages 7 to 15). It was here, according to tradition, that he cut down the famous cherry tree. His mother lived at Ferry Farm until 1771.

Well, it "just so happened" that the docile village of "Washington's Boyhood Home" became the *first place in Virginia where Baptist ministers were imprisoned over matters of conscience.* Dr. Semple writes:

> On the 4th of June, 1768 Benjamin Waller, Lewis Craig, James Childs and others were seized by the sheriff. . . . As they were moving on from court to the prison through the streets of Fredericksburg they sang the hymn "Broad is the road that leads to death." . . . While in prison they constantly preached through the open grated windows. . . . Many heard upon whom the word was in power and demonstration.[139]

It was forty-three days before they were all released. According to Washington's diary, the thirty-two-year-old planter was in Fredericksburg from June 28 to June 30. He was no doubt one of the "many" who "heard." Eventually, his personal sympathies became more pronounced. In a later correspondence to "The United Baptist Churches of Virginia," he could say: "You doubtless remember, I have often expressed my sentiments that any man ought to be protected in worshiping the Deity according to the dictates of his own conscience."[140]

Meanwhile—back at the battlefield—following his ignominious retreat from New York, Washington made his legendary crossing of the Delaware to attack the Hessian guard at Trenton. Allow the spiritual imagery to unfold. The time of the crossing is Christmas night (1776). Gano and his prayers will accompany General Washington on his desperate maneuver. The British are so confident that the war is over, General Cornwallis has already placed his baggage on a ship bound for England. However, in the ninety-minute battle that ensued the following morning, Washington's men killed twenty-three of the enemy and captured over one thousand hung-over prisoners while suffering only four wounded! It was the first significant American victory of the conflict. *And it began with Washington and the Baptist chaplain crossing over a body of deep water.*

In 1778, the General wrote to a Virginia friend, Thomas Nelson:

> The hand of Providence has been so conspicuous in all this (the course of the war) that he must be worse than an infidel that lacks faith, and more wicked that has not gratitude to acknowledge his obligations; but it will be time enough for me to turn Preacher when my present appointment ceases.[141]

By war's end, Washington was finally able to see the "big picture." Had his army not prevailed at Yorktown, America would have remained a church state indefinitely. In a "church state" (Catholic or Protestant) one cannot become a citizen unless he has been sprinkled into the church. The unconscious infant is also "born again" in the process. According to *The Book of Common Prayer* used by Washington's denomination:

> Holy Baptism is full initiation in water and the Holy Spirit into Christ's Body the Church. **The bond which God establishes in Baptism is indissoluble.**[142]

The celebrant's prayer during the "Thanksgiving over the Water" portion of the service is just as heretical:

> We thank you, Almighty God, for the gift of water . . . We thank you, Father, for the water of Baptism. In it we are buried with Christ in his death. By it we share in his resurrection. **Through it we are reborn by the spirit.**[143]

Obadiah Holmes was given thirty lashes on his bare back for rejecting such blasphemous nonsense! Now you know why a *Baptist* pastor, Dr. Robert Lowry, penned the words:

> What can wash away my sin?
> Nothing but the blood of Jesus;
> O precious is the flow
> That makes me white as snow;
> **No other fount I know,**
> Nothing but the blood of Jesus.

From all indications, Washington's victory should have broken the Protestant curse on America. Isaac Backus explains the dilemma faced by Church of England clergy in the colonies:

> There were many others in England, that held to a lineal succession of office, who wanted to have power in America; but . . . no bishop could be ordained in England, without swearing to the king's supremacy.[144]

James Beller elaborates:

> The victory of the Revolution militarily and spiritually, forged America into a Baptist nation. This was accomplished not by establishment, but by dis-establishment. In breaking off our ties with our mother country, we broke the succession of their state-church bishopric.[145]

As the problem concerned *water*, the noble Christian general who had already delivered his nation *militarily* would now venture upon a bold and symbolic gesture in the *spiritual* realm. On July 11, 1889, the *Boston Watchman* published a letter written by General Richard M. Gano, the great-grandson of John Gano, in which he testified:

> General Washington on one occasion said to Chaplain Gano, **"I am convinced that immersion is the baptism taught in the Scriptures, and I demand baptism at your hands."**[146]

Citing *The Baptism of George Washington,* as recorded in the archives of the First Baptist Church of New York, Dr. E. Wayne Thompson writes:

> Daniel Gano, one of Gano's sons and a captain of the artillery, was present and said that he, with about forty officers and men, accompanied the chaplain down to the Hudson River where the Reverend John Gano baptized George Washington.[147]

Dr. James Norwood, a former associate pastor of Dr. J. Frank Norris, cites from *A History of the First Baptist Church in the City of New York* by I. M. Haldemann:

> While in camp at Newburgh, General Washington requested Pastor Gano to baptize him according to the Scriptures. He did so immersing him in believer's baptism, in the name of the Father, Son and Holy Ghost.[148]

With the onset of the Washington Bicentennial, a number of secular historians began to question the well-established tradition, citing an absence of "official" documentation. In an attempt to "convince the gainsayers," Dr. Lemuel Call Barnes, a respected Baptist historian, devoted *thirty-five years* to the question, "Was General George Washington baptized by Chaplain John Gano?" He notes:

> Washington said that many things about his life could be known only by tradition. He took costly pains for the preservation of his personal writings, leaving us "over 400" manuscript volumes. . . . Yet he said to a correspondent: "Notwithstanding that most of the papers, which perhaps may be deemed official, are preserved; **yet the knowledge of innumerable things of a more delicate and secret nature is confined to the perishable remembrance of some few of the present generation.**"[149]

Dr. Barnes writes (with regard to what I believe to be the crowning achievement of his unpublished, 180-page manuscript), "At my request, grandchildren of the chaplain put the certainty of their childhood teaching into affidavits."[150] After contacting several Gano descendants, I discovered that the priceless documents had been lost to the family for decades. My own investigation turned up nothing. Then, in May of 2002, my friend and colleague, Pastor James Beller, informed me that he had found the missing affidavits in the archives of the Samuel Colgate Historical Library, Rochester, New York! Two months later, I had the privilege of personally reviewing these amazing handwritten papers. Two of the notarized testimonies read as follows:

Georgetown, KY
Aug. 16, 1889

I am the grandson of Rev. John Gano, now in my eighty-third year, and the brother of Mrs. Margaret Ewing. I was raised from my fifth year to manhood by Mrs. Margaret Hubbell (nee Gano). I have heard her say that her father baptized (immersed) General Washington.

S.F. Gano, M.D.

Subscribed and sworn to in my presence this 16th day of August, 1889.

Stephen Gano Long
Notary Public
State of Kentucky[151]

To whom it may concern: I, Margaret Ewing (nee Gano) aged 90 years last May, being of sound mind and memory, make this statement: I have often heard my aunt Margaret Hubbell (nee Gano), the eldest daughter of Rev. John Gano, say that her father told her that he baptized General George Washington, at Valley Forge, to the best of my recollection. She, Mrs. Hubbell, also said that General Washington, for prudent reasons did not desire that his baptism should be made public. Rev. John Gano was a Chaplain in the Revolutionary War and an intimate personal friend of General Washington.

Margaret Ewing

Subscribed and sworn to in my presence this 16th day of August, 1889.

Steven G. Long
Notary Public
State of Kentucky[152]

That a ninety-year-old Christian widow would employ the innocent qualifier "to the best of my recollection" when suggesting *Valley Forge* as the baptismal site (as opposed to Newburg) is refreshingly disarming of suspicion.

In 1908, Rev. E. T. Sanford of Manhattan's North Church commissioned a painting of Gano baptizing Washington. The historical masterpiece was originally placed in the Baptist church at Asbury, New Jersey, where it hung until Mrs. Elizabeth Johnston, John Gano's great-granddaughter, presented it to William Jewell College, Liberty, Missouri, in 1926. (*Time* magazine named the former Baptist school as its choice for Liberal Arts College of the year in 2001.)

Dr. Barnes concludes:

> During the lifetime of George Washington he was a man of such obvious open mind and at the same time exacting conscience that honest, intelligent men, who knew him at closer range than we do, could easily think of him as walking down into an emblematic grave and being raised out of it, in order to follow with precision the example and word of the Commander-in-Chief of Christian men.[153]

This analogy of Washington submitting to his "Heavenly Commander" was reinforced many years after Dr. Barnes's death by another treasure that found its way to William Jewell College. Whereas Europeans were genuinely shocked to learn that "His Excellency" had yielded his authority back to Congress following the British surrender, a far more significant display of submission had already occurred.

In the lobby of the John Gano Chapel (underneath the painting of Washington's baptism), an encased sword is prominently featured. A commemorative plaque reads:

> The Sword
>
> In 1996, Margaret Gano Redpath, the great, great, great, great granddaughter of John Gano offered William Jewell College the family sword. George Washington had received it from the Marquis de Lafayette; in turn, he bestowed it on John Gano, the first chaplain of the Continental Army. History records George Washington gave the sword to John Gano after he baptized Washington in the Potomac.

(It was my distinct privilege to have spoken with Mrs. Redpath on more than one occasion.)

Pastor Beller renders the following profound observation in his book, *America in Crimson Red:*

> George Washington presented that battle sword, given to him by Lafayette to his Baptist chaplain, John Gano. Let us not take this gesture of kindness too lightly, for a commanding officer knows exactly the ramifications of surrendering his sword. . . . The author will leave the reader to ponder the full thrust of its meaning. However, "a word fitly spoken" is in order at this juncture of our narrative.
>
> It is the contention of this author that Washington knew the symbols he was leaving to posterity: *He was breaking the baptism of the established church-state monstrosity* by submitting to believer's baptism. He further demonstrated, to the best of his ability, his *deferment to the victor of the*

second stage of the war, the spiritual stage. This deferment was not to John Gano personally, but to the Bible and the belief system he so profoundly represented. He placed *the symbol of victory and the final break with England, and in essence, Rome,* in the hands of a Bible believing *baptized* preacher of the Gospel.

To the baptized believers, looking back through the leaves of history, the meaning of the baptism and the sword ought to be clear— America is not under the baptism of England, or Europe or Rome. America's baptism has no earthly headquarters.[154]

In other words—*"He that hath an ear, let him hear what the Spirit saith unto the churches"* (Revelation 2:7a; 3:6, 13, 22).

POSTWAR PERSECUTION

With the War of Independence behind them, many a disillusioned Baptist patriot was rewarded with even less freedom than he had known prior to Lexington and Concord. Thirteen orphans from a single Baptist family represented the epitome of this grievous injustice. Their father, "Honest John" Hart of Hopewell, New Jersey, a *signer of the Declaration of Independence,* had suffered the common fate of his fellow signatories. Following the Hessian incursion, John was separated from the bedside of his dying wife and loving children. He would never see any of them again in this life. His farm was ravaged, his timber destroyed and his livestock confiscated. His desperate children took their ailing mother to the mountains where she later died from stress. Having learned of her death while enduring his own concealment in thickets, caves and swamps, the sixty-five-year-old widower succumbed to a broken heart and joined her on May 11, 1779.

The Hart children became part of that postwar generation of Baptist refugees who were forced to continue the struggle for true independence. (John 8:36) Once again, it was the Baptists' steady growth in numbers, owing to many wartime revivals that translated into accelerated opposition from magistrates and populace alike. Because *"not many noble are called"* (I Corinthians 1:26), America's New Testament churches continued to draw from the lower echelons of society. Most New England Congregationalists believed that the arrival of Baptists lowered their real estate value and gave the community a bad reputation. In May of 1782, a mob in Hingham,

Massachusetts, broke into the house where a certain Reverend Lee was preaching to several brethren. The intruders

> seized Mr. Lee by his left arm and his collar and twitched him away with great violence, and others, taking hold of him, hauled Mr. Lee along clear out of town, cursing and swearing most terribly . . . And one of them cast soft cow dung in Mr. Lee's face. Then one Captain Theophilus Wilder took a long club over Mr. Lee's head and swore that if he ever came into that town again he would take him and tie him up and whip him thirty stripes. To which Lee replied in good pietistic style, "That is not so much as they whipt Paul." [155]

In the southern stronghold of Virginia, legislative reforms which had begun as early as 1777 had slowed considerably in the postwar years. Now that the redcoats were gone, America's first citizens fell under the delusion that they were going to enjoy their new home while continuing to antagonize their Heavenly landlord. Bad move! When the Declaration of Independence was read by Colonel John North in the courtyard of Philadelphia's State House on July 8, 1776, Samuel Adams observed, "The people seem to recognize this resolution as though it were a decree promulgated from Heaven." Having spoiled the Founding Fathers with this glorious document, the Lord of Glory decided to withhold any further political enlightenment until such time as they would come to grips with Luke 12:48b—*"For unto whomsoever much is given, of him shall be much required."*

Over the next six years, America floundered under the "wisdom" of the infamous Articles of Confederation. Fortunately, however, the nation's key patriarchs were beginning to appreciate the unique destiny of their persecuted Baptist neighbors. Patrick Henry, a devout Presbyterian, frequently went to court in their defense. Semple wrote, "The Baptists found in Patrick Henry, an unwavering friend." [156] Thomas Jefferson was another champion of religious liberty. Armitage relates how Jefferson was molded by Baptist polity:

> **Many historical writers have told us that he was in the habit of attending the business and other meetings of a Baptist Church near his residence; that he closely scrutinized its internal democratic policy and its democratic relations to its sister Churches; that he borrowed his conceptions of a free government, State and Federal, from the simplicity of Baptist Church independency and fraternity; and that, frequently, in conversation with his friends, ministers and neighbors,**

he confessed his indebtedness to their radical principles for his fixed convictions on the true methods of civil and religious liberty. If this popular tradition were entirely unsupported by contemporary testimony, his earnest and public co-operation with the Baptists in Virginia politics, and the close identity between our form of government, which he did so much to frame, and that of the Baptist Churches, must ever contribute to keep it alive; the strength of the coincidence being sufficient in itself to create such a tradition even if it did not already exist.[157]

Lemuel Barnes adds,

As a boy, Thomas Jefferson, frequently visiting in the home of his mother's sister, Mrs. Woodson, went with his aunt and uncle to their church, a "soul liberty" church. As a man, he was a close observer of such churches in his own neighborhood. As a pre-eminent citizen, he wrote: "To the Members of the Baptist church of Buck Mountain: I thank you, my friends and neighbors. . . . We have acted together from the origin to the end of a memorable revolution." **Tradition insists that he said that he acquired his clearest perceptions of democratic government from closely observing Baptist churches. It is rather more than tradition, for Mrs. James Madison said that she had a "distinct" recollection of conversations with him about it and that he was "always declaring that it was a Baptist church from where these views were gathered."** General Madison, a brother of James Madison, was a member of a church of that kind.[158]

JEFFERSON EXONERATES BAPTISTS ON C-SPAN

On July 4, 2000, C-Span featured a live call-in program with Mr. Bill Barker, one of the nation's foremost authorities on Thomas Jefferson. Barker, who even resembles his subject, has portrayed Mr. Jefferson in character for years at the Colonial Williamsburg Foundation. When I just "happened" to catch the show in progress, I immediately felt led to call and ask "Mr. Jefferson" to share his recollection of the Baptists and their contribution to religious liberty. The exchange, before millions of Americans, went as follows:

Host: Knoxville, Tennessee, go ahead . . .

Bill Grady: Yes, a question for Mr. Jefferson . . . Could you comment particularly on the role that the Baptists played in this period of persecution? I understand many of their pastors were put in the gaols (jails) and that Mr. Madison, Patrick Henry and even yourself specifically defended these pastors in courts of law, winning many of the cases, and that they were firm defenders of liberty as a sect in themselves, more so than anyone else as far as the persecution they suffered.

Thomas Jefferson: Well, you are correct, sir. You are absolutely correct that the Baptists, of course, were amongst the first dissenters from the Church of England. They refused to purchase a license in order to preach the Gospel as they saw fit. They refused to pay their tithing to the Church of England. And, therefore, they were indeed incarcerated. And you are correct that Mr. Henry and myself stood to defend them. Ah, I have always considered that, in the support of the Baptists, we supported the freedom of religious opinion. And, Mr. Henry, who stood firm on the same grounds, was wont to defend, ah, I forget the name of the Baptist preacher, but in a very famous case when the preacher was brought to trial for failure to purchase a license, Mr. Henry began the defense by saying, "Imagine, if you will, being thrown into jail for preaching the Gospel." He held but a moment and then continued, "Thrown into jail for preaching the Gospel." And he stated that comment over and over and over until the judge finally brought his gavel down and acquitted the Baptist preacher.

Therefore, sir, we should never deny that a freedom, or religious freedom, means precisely that: that we are free, not only to worship as we choose, but to preach the Gospel, or indeed, any other religious dictate or dogma or conviction as we so choose. We are free to be heard in that preaching. And, that those who desire to neglect it or not attend to it are free to do so as well. But you are absolutely correct in reference to the Baptists in their dissent from the Church of England and Mr. Henry and my support, and the support of many others, in their interest to worship as they choose.

In the process of time, Jefferson teamed up with James Madison, another champion of religious liberty, to gender legislation favorable to the Baptists. On December 17, 1785, Congress passed the Virginia Statute of Religious Liberty, disestablishing the Episcopalian harlot in the process. The landmark document read:

> Be it enacted by the General Assembly, That no man shall be compelled to frequent or support any religious worship, place or ministry whatsoever; nor shall be enforced, restrained, molested or burthened in his body or

goods, nor shall otherwise suffer on account of his religious opinions or
beliefs; but, that all men shall be free to profess and by argument to maintain
their opinions in matters of religion, and that the same shall in no wise
diminish, enlarge or affect the civil capacities.[159]

It didn't take long for the Lord to show His approval. Within a few
months, Madison was inspired to pen another significant document.
On May 25, 1787, the historic Constitutional Convention was convened
in Philadelphia's Independence Hall. Apparently, some new and improved
ideas were in the air. Yet, only God could blend them aright. After a month
of haggling, the weary delegates were on the verge of throwing in the
towel. Suddenly, an eighty-one-year-old printer took to the podium and
pointed his intellectual peers to the Lord God Almighty. Forgetting that he
was supposed to be an avowed deist, Benjamin Franklin implored:

> In this situation of this assembly, groping, as it were, in the dark to
> find political truth, and scarce able to distinguish it when presented to us,
> how has it happened, Sir, that we have not hitherto once thought of humbly
> applying to the Father of Lights to illuminate our understandings? In the
> beginning of the contest with Britain, when we were sensible of danger,
> we had daily prayers in this room for the divine protection. Our prayers,
> Sir, were heard—and they were graciously answered . . . I have lived, Sir,
> a long time; and the longer I live, the more convincing proofs I see of this
> truth, that *God governs in the affairs of men*. And if a sparrow cannot fall
> to the ground without his notice, is it probable that an empire can rise
> without his aid? We have been assured, Sir, in the sacred writings that
> "except the Lord build the house, they labor in vain that build it." I firmly
> believe this; and I also believe that, without his concurring aid, we shall
> succeed in this political building no better than the builders of Babel . . .
> [not bad for a deist].
>
> I therefore beg leave to move that, henceforth, prayers imploring the
> assistance of heaven and its blessings on our deliberations be held in this
> assembly every morning before we proceed to business, and that one or
> more of the clergy of this city be requested to officiate in that service.[160]

On September 17, 1787, forty distinguished Americans attached their
signatures to another parchment of providence. The "Father of Lights"
was pleased. For his role in paving the way for religious liberty in
Virginia, James Madison would come to be known as the "Father of
the Constitution."

JOHN LELAND

The Constitution required ratification by nine state conventions. In a truly remarkable occurrence, the Lord decreed that *a single Baptist pastor would be in the right place at the right time to literally decide the fate of Madison's venerable achievement.* Of the thirteen voting states, Virginia was by far the noblest, wealthiest and most influential. As her boundaries took in the Ohio territory, she was also the most populated, claiming one in every four Americans. Old Dominion's approval would be absolutely essential.

Patrick Henry, George Mason, and Richard Henry Lee led the opposition party (the Antifederalists) objecting that a bill of rights had not been included, the president had too much independence and the Senate was aristocratic. Henry was particularly troubled about the absence of any statutes regarding religious liberty. Agreeing that various amendments were indeed justified, Federalists Madison and Washington recommended ratifying the Constitution first and adding a bill of rights afterward. It was their conviction that a failure to approve the Constitution as initially proposed would doom the entire project.

As each county had to elect delegates to the state convention, the "Father of the Constitution" naturally *assumed* that he would be a "shoo-in" candidate in his own county of Orange. This proved to be anything *but* the case. While tarrying in Philadelphia to complete *The Federalist Papers*, Madison was unaware that opposition was forming back in Orange. After enduring decades of persecution, Baptists in all states were appalled at the lack of specific religious guarantees in the proposed Constitution. As "fate" would have it, a significant number of voters in Madison's home county "quacked." And the same ratio prevailed state-wide; Thomas Jefferson stating in his *Notes on Virginia* that two-thirds of the population had become religious dissenters (Baptists, Presbyterians, or Quakers) by the eve of the Constitution's ratification.[161] While missionary outreach at Sandy Creek had helped to establish eighteen Baptist churches in Virginia by 1770, the resultant persecution quadrupled that figure within four years! Francis L. Hawk, an Episcopalian historian, acknowledged the obvious ramifications:

> The Baptists were not slow in discovering the advantageous position in which the political troubles of the country had placed them. Their numerical strength was such as to make it important to both sides to secure their

influence. They knew this. Persecution had taught them not to love the establishment, and now they saw before them a reasonable prospect of overturning it entirely. In their Association they had calmly discussed the matter and resolved on their course; in this course they were consistent to the end.[162]

The Virginia Baptist General Committee met and agreed unanimously that the Constitution, as proposed, did not "make sufficient provision for the secure enjoyment of religious liberty." And, as they would ultimately decide who went to Richmond, you might call them the *original* "Mighty Ducks." A letter was subsequently dispatched to Madison warning him of the precarious situation. The paranoid candidate promptly battled his way back to Orange through a severe storm, arriving only days before the March 25th county election. Other notable personages such as Samuel Adams and John Jay had failed to be appointed delegates from their states. Would Madison be the most embarrassing casualty of the Convention? If he, of all statesmen was not present, who could possibly oppose the eloquent Patrick Henry, of whom Jefferson remarked, "He appeared to me to speak as Homer wrote."[163]

The man destined to be the nation's fourth chief executive had only one option. While traveling on the road from Fredericksburg to Montpelier, Madison went out of his way to call on the influential Baptist pastor, John Leland. In his acclaimed *History of Virginia* (as cited by Armitage), Robert Semple recognized the former Massachusetts native as "probably the most popular preacher who ever resided in Virginia."[164] Leland was so powerful that he pastored two thriving churches at the same time, one in Black Walnut, Orange County, and the other in Goldvine, Louisa County. Historian L. H. Butterfield pointed to Leland's "simple but graphic language, his avoidance of doctrinal refinements, his humor and his sincerity" as character traits that endeared him to his listeners. His anecdotes were legendary in the back country. From the American Antiquarian Society (citing Holland's *History of Western Massachusetts*), we read:

> A characteristic one tells how he [Leland] outdid an Episcopal clergyman in Virginia who argued in favor of state support for ministers because they have to spend so much time preparing sermons. Leland answered that he could expound the Scriptures without special preparation, and the Episcopalian challenged him to preach on a text to be provided just before beginning his sermon. Leland went into the pulpit and was handed a text which proved

to be Numbers 22:21, "And Balaam saddled his ass." Mr. Leland first commented on the account from which the text was taken, and then said he should divide his subject into three parts: 1st, Balaam, as a false prophet, represents a hireling clergy; 2nd, the saddle represents their enormous salaries, and 3rd, the dumb ass represents the people who will bare such a load.[165]

Was it just another coincidence that Leland was born in 1754, the very year that Shubal Stearns left Tolland, Connecticut, for Virginia, conducting revivals in Berkeley and Hampshire Counties on his way to Sandy Creek? Of the seven hundred souls that Leland baptized throughout his fourteen-year sojourn in Virginia (1777-1791), over three hundred of them were converted in a powerful revival in the all-important year of 1788.[166] Who, but the Lord, could set a stage like that? Some have maintained, former Massachusetts governor, the Honorable G. N. Briggs among them, that the popular preacher himself was one of the two declared anti-Constitution candidates to be nominated; Colonel Thomas Barbour being the other. The *Dictionary of American Biography* states of Leland, "He was nominated by the Baptists of Orange County as a delegate to the Virginia convention of 1788, to oppose the Constitution."[167] In any case, an extant copy of *Elder John Leland's Objections to the Federal Constitution* (as found in the Madison Papers housed in the Library of Congress) gives evidence of Leland's initial public commitment to the anti-Federalist platform. This policy statement was supplied to Mr. Barbour for use in his campaign. I was privileged to review a transcript of this document in the Archives Department of the University of Tennessee. Copies of Leland's objections were circulated throughout the state. Thus, we understand that Leland's support of the anti-Federalist platform was etched in stone on the very eve of the local election in Orange.

Despite the Leland-Madison political alliances of the past and their warm personal friendship, Mr. Madison would have his lobbying work cut out for him. Ironically, Madison was already the most outstanding proponent of religious liberty active in the political arena. (See: *Memorial and Remonstrance;* "tolerance" clause in the Virginia Declaration of Rights; etc.). According to an article in the *Annual Report of the American Historical Association* for 1901, as a teenage lad, Madison had stood alongside his father outside the Orange county jail and listened in astonishment as several Baptists preached from their cell windows.[168]

The specifics of what was said during that rendezvous with destiny will never be known this side of eternity. Obviously Madison would have given his pledge of honor to do all within his power to secure a Bill of Rights *after* the Constitution was safely in place. But the man of God would have to pray down the Spirit's leading to trust his neighbor's commitment enough to change his own well-known conviction.

Within a few days of their meeting, a throng of freedom-loving "good ol' boys" assembled near the Orange County Courthouse to literally decide the future of America. James Madison was introduced as the first speaker. After ascending a hogshead of tobacco, the 5'6" statesman promoted the Constitution for nearly two hours in a voice barely above a whisper. When he concluded his remarks, Pastor Leland took the stump and spoke for less than ten minutes. He promptly shocked the crowd by reversing his position to endorse Mr. Madison's candidacy. The preacher explained that his decision was predicated on Madison's pledge to provide a Bill of Rights after the Constitution was secure. The "brethren" took it from there! The actual tallies gave Madison 202 votes and his Federalist running mate, James Gordon, 187, while Thomas Barbour and Charles Porter received 56 and 34 votes, respectively.

With his eleventh-hour reprieve, Madison was cleared to travel on to Richmond while Barbour unpacked his suitcase in a stupor. The ensuing debate between Madison and Henry raged for two-and-a-half months. John Christian writes,

> When the Convention assembled, Patrick Henry spoke against the Constitution with a vehemence never surpassed by himself on any occasion in his whole life, and with a power that sometimes was overwhelming. Once, while this matchless orator was addressing the Convention, a wild storm broke over Richmond; the heavens were ablaze with lightning, the thunder roared, and the rain came down in torrents; at this moment Henry seemed to see the anger of heaven threatening the State, if it should consummate the guilty act of adopting the Constitution, and he invoked celestial witnesses to view and compassionate his distracted country in this grand crisis of its history. And such was the effect of his speech on the occasion, that the Convention immediately dispersed.[169]

During this time, news of Leland's defection had spread like wildfire. Consequently, a number of Henry's supporters grew more tolerant of Madison's proposal. When the final count was taken, eighty-nine delegates voted for ratification while seventy-nine voted against. The significance of Leland's paramount endorsement is evidenced by the slim margin of victory *despite Mr. Madison's weighty presence*. A mere *ten* votes had enabled Madison to prevail over Patrick "Give Me Liberty or Give Me Death" Henry, a living legend who would be reelected to five terms as Virginia's governor. *What do you suppose the final outcome would have been had the very author of the Constitution been barred from the proceedings?*

The rest is history. Madison remained true to his word. The Bill of Rights became a reality on December 15, 1791. Armitage writes,

> Thus, the contemned, spurned and hated old Baptist doctrine of soul-liberty, for which blood had been shed for centuries, was not only engrafted into the organic law of the United States, but for the first time in the formation of a great nation it was made its chief corner-stone. For the first time on that subject the quiet, pungent old truth asserted its right to immortality as expressed by Scripture: "The stone which the builders rejected is become the head-stone of the corner."[170]

THE WITNESS OF HISTORY

It was my opportunity to relate this dramatic story over a call-in program on Boston's WBZ radio station during the Southern Baptist boycott of Disney Studios (concerning Disney's decision to make the parks accessible to sodomite delegations). Nearly forty-five minutes of "Baptist bashing" had prompted me to action. After hearing what I had to say, the program host, Lovell Dyett, could only retort, "We've had Jeffersonian authors on this program many times, and we have never heard of this Leland fellah." To which I replied, "If I were you, I wouldn't laugh until you've visited the Leland-Madison Memorial Park located on Highway 20 (Route of the Constitution), four miles east of Orange, and read the plaque erected by The Sons of the American Revolution commemorating the site of the historic meeting." That "fact" ended both the call and the evening's topic of discussion. By the time I returned to my vehicle (I had phoned from a truck stop in Ohio), the new call-in subject was "Villains in the *Batman* Series." For some strange reason, no one wanted to talk about the Baptists anymore. Apparently, the "Joker" was on them.

The words on Leland's impressive marker cannot be dismissed as easily.

1754-1841
ELDER JOHN LELAND
COURAGEOUS LEADER OF
THE BAPTIST DOCTRINE
ARDENT ADVOCATE OF THE PRINCIPLES
OF DEMOCRACY
VINDICATOR OF SEPARATION
OF CHURCH AND STATE

NEAR THIS SPOT IN 1788 JOHN LELAND AND
JAMES MADISON, THE FATHER OF THE AMERICAN
CONSTITUTION, HELD A SIGNIFICANT INTERVIEW
WHICH RESULTED IN THE ADOPTION OF THE
CONSTITUTION BY VIRGINIA. THEN MADISON
A MEMBER OF CONGRESS FROM ORANGE PRESENTED
THE FIRST AMENDMENT TO THE CONSTITUTION
GUARANTEEING RELIGIOUS LIBERTY, FREE SPEECH AND
A FREE PRESS. THIS SATISFIED LELAND AND HIS BAPTIST
FOLLOWERS.
PRESENTED BY EUGENE BUCKLIN BOWEN PRESIDENT
BERKSHIRE COUNTY MASSACHUSETTS CHAPTER
SONS OF THE AMERICAN REVOLUTION

The humanist thinks he can discard this important Baptist footnote in history because neither Leland nor Madison referred to the meeting in their personal papers. However, the sensitive nature of their discussion would have warranted such reticence (the same being true with Washington's immersion—John 3:2). What would either man have gained from a disclosure? The truth of the matter is that God's people will never get their reward down here. As the songwriter asked, "Is this vile world a friend to grace to help me on to God?" Leland's gravestone marker reads simply: "Here lies the body of John Leland who labored to promote piety and to vindicate the civil and religious rights of all men." However, in the spirit of defending a man of God's reputation, I have referenced the following secular corroboration for the Leland-Madison encounter. In his definitive three-volume set, *James Madison: A Biography* (available at Montpelier), Ralph Ketcham states: ·

On his way from Fredericksburg to Orange, with the election but a few days away, Madison stopped to see the influential Baptist preacher John Leland, who had drawn a vigorous memorial protesting, among other things, the failure of the new Constitution to guarantee religious freedom. . . . In return for Leland's promise to withdraw his objections, Madison reaffirmed what he and other federalists had increasingly agreed to: they would support a bill of rights, including a firm article on religious freedom, as amendments to the Constitution *after* its ratification. . . . At the traditional court day election, the fourth Tuesday of the month (March 25), planters and tradesmen, despite a "very cold wind," gathered early, and "Colonel" Madison, Francis Taylor noted, ". . . addressed himself in a speech to the people in defense of the new Constitution, and there appeared much satisfaction."[171]

William Lee Miller, in his acclaimed *The Business of May Next* (also offered at Montpelier), picks up Madison's itinerary after leaving Mount Vernon. (Madison had visited Washington for some advice on the matter.)

Then on the way on to Orange he had a meeting with the noted Baptist preacher John Leland. Leland and many Baptists had objected to the Constitution's failure to include a protection for religious liberty, but Madison, as an old comrade-in-arms from the great Virginia struggle on that issue, was able to persuade him that the failure to ratify the Constitution would not serve religious liberty or any other good purpose . . . Madison made a speech defending the Constitution, and was an easy winner over his anti-federalist neighbor . . .[172]

From the prestigious American Antiquarian Society, we have the following comments given by L. H. Butterfield in *Elder John Leland, Jeffersonian Itinerant*:

Elder John Leland is not often mentioned in histories of the United States, even the comprehensive ones. When he is, it is invariably in connection with the gift of an enormous cheese to President Jefferson on New Year's Day in 1802 . . . But if John Leland is best known for an exploit typical of our engaging and probably harmless desire to break records, he deserves to be remembered for a better reason. **He played a substantial part in molding another American tradition that is full of meaning to all of us today—the separation of church and state in the United States.** The success of the Baptist revivalist was phenomenal in the years before the Revolution . . . On 30 January, James Madison, Sr., wrote his son that sentiment against ratification was decidedly rising in Orange County. "The Baptists are now generally opposed to it . . ." There followed a meeting between Madison and Leland that has been celebrated in local history and in Baptist annals.[173]

With reference to the Leland-Madison Park on Highway 20, Butterfield adds, "There can be no question that the monument memorializes an actual occurrence." In his address at the Bicentennial of Orange County, delivered on September 26, 1934, in the grove at Gum Spring (site of the monument), Samuel Chiles Mitchell made reference to a pair of earlier testimonies to the Leland-Madison summit. The first of these was a eulogy for James Madison that was delivered at Culpeper Courthouse on July 18, 1836, by John S. Barbour, a long-time friend and associate of Mr. Madison. Mitchell affirms that the address was published in the *National Intelligencer* of Washington, D.C., on August 2, 1836, "at the request of a committee of those who heard it, as deserving record." Concerning Madison's role in securing religious liberty, he stated:

In the accomplishment of this great object, the sect denominated Baptists took the foremost part . . . But for James Madison, we should have no constitution: I call history to be witness. He above all others, created it. He above all others, gave to it the ratification of Virginia. Without Virginia, the Union was disjointed, and was no Union, had every other state accepted, adopted and ratified the Constitution. His election to the Convention itself, in Virginia, was brought about by his sudden return to his county on the eve of the election. His soft and assuasive and lucid elocution changed two ministers of the Gospel of the Baptist church on the day preceding the election and that conversation carried him into Virginia. The celebrated John Leland was one of them. (It is thought by some that Reverend Aaron Bledsoe of Pamunkey was the other.) His mind was thrown open to the lights of reason and the power of argument. Consistency had neither pride nor trammel for his strong good sense; and I speak but the voice of faithful tradition in saying that these changes were decisive in the election."[174]

Miller's other point of evidence was a letter by the Honorable George N. Briggs, Governor of Massachusetts (1844-1851), dated, Pittsfield, Massachusetts, April 15, 1857, as found in William Sprague's nine-volume tome *Annals of the American Pulpit.* The letter's content relates to a special visit Governor and Mrs. Briggs made to the Lelands three or four years before the preacher's death when "Elder" Leland was in his early eighties. A portion of the correspondence reads:

In the course of the afternoon, I told him that I had recently seen in the public prints an extract from an Eulogy delivered by J. S. Barbour, of Virginia, upon the character of James Madison; that Barbour, had said that the credit of adopting the Constitution of the United States properly belonged to a Baptist clergyman, formerly of Virginia, by the name of Leland . . . He replied that Barbour had given him too much credit; but he supposed he knew to what he referred. He then gave this history of the matter.[175]

After giving Leland's historical-political background of the time, Briggs went on to relate the preacher's account:

On his way home from Philadelphia, Mr. Madison went some distance out of his direct road to call upon him. After the ordinary salutations, Mr. Madison began to apologize for troubling with a call at that time; but he assured Mr. M. that no apology was necessary—"I know your errand here," said he, "it is to talk to me about the Constitution. I am glad to see you, and to have an opportunity of learning your views on the subject." Mr. Madison spent half a day with him, and fully and unreservedly communicated to him his opinions upon the great matters which were then agitating the people of the State and the Confederacy.

They then separated to meet again very soon, as opposing candidates before the electors, on the stump. The day came, and they met, and with them nearly all the voters in the County of Orange, to hear their candidates respectively discuss the important questions upon which the people of Virginia were so soon to act. "Mr. Madison," said the venerable man, "first took the stump," which was a hogshead of tobacco, standing on one end. For two hours, he addressed his fellow-citizens in a calm, candid and statesman-like manner, arguing his side of the case, and fairly meeting and replying to the arguments, which had been put forth by his opponents, in the general canvass of the State. Though Mr. Madison was not particularly a pleasing or eloquent speaker, the people listened with respectful attention. He left the hogshead, and my friends called for me. I took it—and went in for Mr. Madison; and he was elected without difficulty. "This," said he, "is, I suppose, what Mr. Barbour alluded to."[176]

The Governor's remarks conclude:

A noble Christian Patriot! That single act, with the motives which prompted it, and the consequences which followed it, entitle him to the respect of mankind.[177]

Finally, 1,757 long years after God's first preachers were confronted by local authorities who *"laid hands on them, and put them in hold unto the next day"* (Acts 4:3a), the dawn of a new era had definitely arrived! Collectively ratified on December 15, 1791, the First Amendment to the Bill of Rights reads:

> Congress shall make no law respecting an establishment of religion, or prohibiting the free exercise thereof; or abridging the freedom of speech, or of the press, or the right of the people peaceably to assemble, and to petition the Government for a redress of grievances.

So there you have it—the éclat of Western civilization! No doubt "Brother Whitefield" smiled in the glory world as the door he foresaw to the Philadelphia Church Age was opened wide in the "city of Brotherly Love" by the Baptist-sponsored Bill of Rights. With the "Bloody Whore" three thousand miles away and her harlot Protestant offspring checked by the powerful First Amendment, the Baptists were liberated at long last to bring about the vindication of their holy and jealous Creator (Isaiah 42:8). Thanks to the words "freedom of speech," no American minister would be burned at the stake for street preaching. And, owing to the "free press" clause, no one would be burned for printing the Holy Bible, either. With these two safeguards in place, an army of Baptist soul winners rushed through their Philadelphia door to obey the Scriptural charge atop the Liberty Bell (also displayed in Philadelphia): *"Proclaim liberty throughout all the land unto all the inhabitants thereof"* (Leviticus 25:10).

Over the next two hundred years, the United States of America would rise to a level of prominence and prosperity unparalleled in the annals of mankind. As the Roman Empire had *"limited the Holy One of Israel"* (Psalm 78:41b), the Baptists in America had inspired a form of government that would unleash the mighty power of God. Promises such as, *"Blessed is the nation whose God is the LORD"* (Psalm 33:12a) and *"Righteousness exalteth a nation"* (Proverbs 14:34a), could now be appropriated. Whitefield's "ducks" had come a long way. The Baptist minister Samuel Smith would go on to write, "My Country, 'Tis of Thee," while another Baptist, Francis Bellamy, would author the nation's pledge of allegiance.

A TRIBUTE OF GRATITUDE

In September of 2000, the Lord enabled the Baptist History Preservation Society of Rockwell, North Carolina, to provide a fitting tribute of gratitude on behalf of Mr. Whitefield's labor in America. The "Grand Itinerant" had succumbed to asthma on Sunday, September 30, 1770, in the parsonage of Old South Presbyterian Church of Newburyport, Massachusetts. (A number of years ago, I was privileged to visit this very room.) As Whitefield was breathing his last, he asked that his body be interred under the pulpit where he had been scheduled to preach that morning. His dying plea was subsequently honored. Over two centuries later, another personal desire was granted. In the heat of the battle, Whitefield had shared an informal preference for a future tombstone inscription, the context dealing with his unwillingness to defend himself against slander. (See Volume II, *The Works of George Whitefield*, page 248). Somehow, his Protestant admirers inadvertently overlooked this.

Through the grace of God, the Baptist History Preservation Society received special permission from Old South Presbyterian Church to not only procure a memorial tablet enshrining the preacher's request, but to renovate the hallowed crypt as well. The glorious project was appropriately concluded on the 230th anniversary of Mr. Whitefield's death. The beautiful bronze plaque, which adorns the brick wall to the left of the tomb, reads:

GEORGE WHITEFIELD
1714-1770
I AM CONTENT TO WAIT TILL THE DAY OF JUDGMENT
FOR THE CLEARING UP OF MY CHARACTER: AND AFTER
I AM DEAD I DESIRE
NO OTHER EPITAPH THAN THIS, 'HERE LIES G.W. WHAT
SORT OF A MAN HE WAS
THE GREAT DAY WILL DISCOVER.'

MAZEL TOV

Thanks to Mr. Whitefield and an array of spiritual giants like Clarke, Holmes, Wightman, Stearns, Marshall, Weatherford, Brown, Hart, Jones, Gano and Leland—America was now well on her way to fulfilling the ultimate purpose for her existence. Within months of becoming the nation's first chief-executive, Washington embarked upon a tour of the colonies to promote the ratification of the Bill of Rights. He was accompanied by his secretary of state, Thomas Jefferson. In August, 1790, Washington and his entourage paid a visit to Newport, Rhode Island.

Although the new president was expected to call upon the principal cities of the fledgling republic, receiving their delegations and letters of adulation, Newport would enjoy a *special* unspoken relationship akin to his sacred baptism at the hands of John Gano. Not only was Newport the site of the first Baptist church in America, but also the home of what had formerly been the largest and most prosperous Jewish community in the nation (the other five being in New York, Philadelphia, Richmond, Savannah and Charleston).

The two had made for an explosive combination. The conviction for religious liberty was so strong in Rhode Island that two months before the Declaration of Independence was proclaimed by the General Congress in Philadelphia, the General Assembly of the colony of Rhode Island and Providence Plantations gathered in the Old State House in Providence on May 4, 1776, had passed their own Declaration of Independence from the British Crown![178] Washington understood what the modern educated fool does not—in the words of Charles Caroll, as quoted in volume one of his work *Three Centuries of Democracy*—"Rhode Island, from that moment, became, and is at this day, the oldest sovereign and independent state in the western world."[179]

On the morning of August 17 (in concert with the city's other religious leaders), President George Washington had a formal audience with a man by the name of "Moses" (Moses Seixas, that is, warden of Congregation Yeshuat Israel). The two men were well aware of the disproportionate contribution rendered to the recent War of Independence by the Jews of Newport (despite the disastrous toll it took on their personal fortunes). For instance, unbeknownst to the "professional scholar," a core of patriotic Jewish businessmen actually helped to precipitate the conflict. On October 25, 1765, in the city of Philadelphia, no less than nine Jewish merchants affixed their signatures to the volatile Non-Importation Agreement. They were Benjamin Levy, Samson Levy, Joseph Jacobs, Hyman Levy, Jr., David Franks, Mathias Bush, Michael Gratz and Moses Mordecai.[180]

More than once, Jewish money helped to save the American cause: Haym Solomon advanced to Congress for the Revolutionary War the sum of $658,007.13; Sheftal and Noah, $100,000; Isaac Moses, $15,000.[181] By October 1776, sixteen heavily armed and well-manned vessels had been dispatched from the harbor at Newport. Most were owned by Jews. (See *The Jews in the Making of America* by George Cohen.)

Many of the Jews of Newport also distinguished themselves on the battlefield. Several served as officers. One Jewish veteran by the name of Moses Isaacs had the honor of entertaining General Washington when he came to Newport on March 6, 1781, to meet with General Count de Rochambeau who was leading the French troops quartered in Newport.

However, the most remarkable manifestation of Jewish solidarity with America's war effort was in the religious realm. When the General Congress at Philadelphia ordered a Continental Fast Day to be observed throughout the United Colonies, the General Assembly of Rhode Island proclaimed July 20, 1775, as their "Public Fast Day." With the exception of the feckless Church of England, all the congregations in Newport, *including Yeshuat Israel*, conducted special services during which time the ministers preached patriotic messages. In the providence of God, a most unusual visitor just "happened" to be in town on that occasion. Rabbi Gutstein writes, citing *The Literary Diary of Ezra Stiles:*

> The Congregation Yeshuat Israel joined their non-Jewish brethren in prayer and fasting on this solemn day, conducting a special patriotic service at the synagogue during which Rabbi Samuel Cohen of Jerusalem, a visitor in town from the Holy Land since the latter part of 1772, or early 1773, preached the sermon. He chose for his text the verses in Numbers, "Phineas the son of Eleazar, the son of Aaron, the priest, hath turned My wrath away from the children of Israel, in that he was very jealous for My sake among them, so that I consumed not the Children of Israel in My jealousy. Wherefore say: Behold, I give unto him My covenant of peace."[182]

Thus we understand that only a month after the climactic Battle of Bunker Hill, a Jewish rabbi from Jerusalem, is standing behind the pulpit of the synagogue in Newport, Rhode Island, preaching a patriotic sermon from Numbers 25:11-12 on behalf of the American Revolution! (How's *that* for a Jewish conspiracy?)

Such were the sacred memories shared by the former general and the Hebrew emissary when Moses Seixas greeted President Washington and handed him the following letter:

To the President of the United States of America

Sir:

Permit the children of the stock of Abraham to approach you with the most cordial affection and esteem for your person and merits, and to join with our fellow Citizens in welcoming you to New Port.

With pleasure we reflect on those days—those days of difficulty and danger, when the God of Israel, who delivered David from the peril of the sword, —shielded your head in the day of battle:—and we rejoice to think that the same Spirit who rested in the bosom of the greatly beloved Daniel, enabling him to preside over the Provinces of the Babylonish Empire, rests, and ever will rest, upon you, enabling you to discharge the arduous duties of Chief Magistrate in these states.

Deprived as we heretofore have been of the invaluable rights of free Citizens, we now (with a deep sense of gratitude to the Almighty disposer of all events) behold a Government, erected by the Majesty of the People— a Government which to bigotry gives no sanction, to persecution no assistance—but generously affording to All liberty of conscience, and immunities of Citizenship:—deeming every one, of whatever Nation, tongue, or language, equal parts of the great governmental Machine:—**This so ample and extensive Federal Union whose basis is Philanthropy, Mutual Confidence and Publick Virtue, we cannot but acknowledge to be the work of the Great God, who ruleth in the Armies of Heaven and among the Inhabitants of the Earth, doing whatever seemeth him good.**

For all the blessings of civil and religious liberty which we enjoy under an equal and benign administration, we desire to send up our thanks to the Antient of Days, the great preserver of Men—beseeching him, that the Angel who conducted our forefathers through the wilderness into the promised land, may graciously conduct you through all the difficulties and dangers of this mortal life:—and, when like Joshua full of days and full of honour, you are gathered to your Fathers, may you be admitted into the Heavenly Paradise to partake of the water of life, and the tree of immortality.

Done and Signed by Order of the Hebrew Congregation
in Newport Rhode Island August 17th 1790

Moses Seixas, Warden

The "Father of Our Country" dictated and signed the following reply on August 18:

To the Hebrew Congregation in Newport, Rhode Island
Gentlemen.

While I receive, with much satisfaction, your Address replete with expressions of affection and esteem; I rejoice in the opportunity of assuring you, that I shall always retain a grateful remembrance of the cordial welcome I experienced in my visit to Newport, from all classes of Citizens.

The reflection of the days of difficulty and danger which are past is rendered the more sweet from a consciousness that they are succeeded by days of uncommon prosperity and security. If we have wisdom to make the best use of the advantages with which we are now favored, we cannot fail, under the just administration of a good Government, to become a great and a happy people.

The Citizens of the United States of America have a right to applaud themselves for having given to mankind examples of an enlarged and liberal policy: a policy worthy of imitation. All possess alike liberty of conscience and immunities of citizenship. It is now no more that toleration is spoken of as if it was by the indulgence of one class of people, that another enjoyed the exercise of their inherent natural rights. For happily the Government of the United States, which gives to bigotry no sanction, to persecution no assistance, requires only that they who live under its protection should demean themselves as good citizens, in giving it on all occasions their effectual support.

It would be inconsistent with the frankness of my character not to avow that I am pleased with your favorable opinion of my Administration, and fervent wishes for my felicity. **May the Children of the Stock of Abraham, who dwell in this land, continue to merit and enjoy the good will of the other Inhabitants, while every one shall sit in safety under his own vine and fig tree, and there shall be none to make him afraid.** May the father of all mercies scatter light and not darkness in our paths, and make us all in our several vocations useful here, and in his own due time and way everlastingly happy.

Go: Washington

At the time of Washington's visit, Newport's Congregation *Yeshuat Israel* had been worshiping in their own synagogue for twenty-two years. Designed by noted British architect Peter Harrison, the structure was completed in 1763 at a cost of two thousand pounds sterling. Rabbi Gutstein writes:

> The synagogue was admirable. Jewish and non-Jewish eyes looked upon it with admiration and awe.
>
> After vicissitudes of the strangest sorts, a few Marranos, having escaped the clutches of the Holy Inquisition, were at last able to walk freely in a beautiful temple of God, a miniature of the temple of Jerusalem.[183]

The extent to which Washington's pledge of safety was fulfilled is evidenced by the providential survival of the colonial synagogue down to the twenty-first century. (While the original synagogue belonging to

Congregation Shearith Israel of New York predated the synagogue in Newport, the structure was subsequently destroyed and rebuilt.) *Touro Synagogue* (named after its two primary benefactors, Abraham and Judah Touro, sons of Isaac Touro, the synagogue's *hazzan* (or "reader") from 1759 until the Revolution), is considered one of the finest examples of eighteenth-century architecture in America. In 1936, Dr. David de Sola Pool, rabbi of the Congregation Shearith Israel of New York, wrote in his introduction to Rabbi Gutstein's work, *The History of The Jews of Newport:*

> The Jew walks through Touro Street in Newport [the street connecting the synagogue with the cemetery, named after Judah Touro] quietly conscious of inheriting a tradition both of American political and religious liberty and of Jewish idealism and religious faith. The synagogue, which has stood for one and three quarter centuries and which has withstood the alarms of war and the fatalities of swiftly changing time, is a witness of Newport's liberality of spirit and reverence for the ancient Bible. . . . The quiet God's acre in which lies the dust of Newport's Jews of Colonial days speaks of the identification of the Jew with American life for well nigh three centuries since sturdy Jewish pioneers threw in their lot with their fellow Americans in wresting from the wilderness a settlement of security and refuge for those of all denominations and races seeking ampler living. The Jewish Community Center opposite the Synagogue symbolizes the vigor of the new-old Jewish life which has taken up the broken thread, and is continuing to weave on the American background the ancient pattern of the Jewish spirit.[184]

No greater tribute to Dr. Clarke can be found than the astounding fact that the *oldest existing synagogue in the United States,* erected for the *second oldest Jewish congregation in the land,* "just happens" to be located *around the corner from the first Baptist church in America!* (United Baptist Church) In fact, when one faces the front gate of Touro, the steeple of Dr. Clarke's church is conspicuously visible in the background to the left. The high-flying American flag situated on the synagogue grounds completes the solemn grandeur. And if that's not exciting enough, the nation's oldest standing *Baptist church,* the Seventh Day Baptist Meeting House—built in 1730 for the faction that departed Clarke's work in 1656 and later structurally attached to the Newport Historical Society building, constructed in 1850—is literally *right next door to Touro Synagogue! Shalom!*

J. L. M. CURRY

As an appropriate conclusion to this holy chapter, let us travel back in time to eavesdrop on a conversation at a stately dinner party in Madrid, Spain. The setting is the late 1800s. The two men who are speaking to one another are Jabez Lamar Monroe Curry, President Grover Cleveland's Minister Plenipotentiary to Spain, and the famous British philosopher, John Bright. A graduate of Harvard University in 1825, Curry's lifetime achievements required three columns of print in the renowned *Dictionary of American Biography*. Among these were included: college professor, college president, Army officer, member of Congress, and general agent of the Peabody Education Fund (a program of national aid for the removal and prevention of illiteracy among Negroes). His fame was so pronounced in his native Alabama that his bust remains one of the two representing that state in the Capitol's Statuary Hall in Washington, D.C.

However, it just so happens that J. L. M. Curry was also, in the words of Thomas Armitage, "a powerful and enthusiastic preacher of the Gospel."[185] He received the degree of D.D. in 1857 from Mercer University. His ministerial load paralleled his secular responsibilities. Dr. Curry served as president of the Alabama Baptist State Convention, the Virginia General Association and the Foreign Mission Board of the Southern Baptist Convention.

Dr. R. H. Pitts, in his November 12, 1925, address before the Baptist Journal Association, entitled "Soul Liberty—Some of Its Implications," related a profound interchange which occurred between his mentor and Mr. Bright at that Madrid dinner reception. In the course of their discussion, Bright was expounding on the many contributions England had made to the world. He then asked Dr. Curry, "What distinct contribution has America made to the science of government?" After pausing a moment, the Baptist ambassador replied, "The doctrine of Soul Freedom." Following a moment of reflection, the philosopher conceded, "A tremendous contribution indeed."[186]

5

Serpents in Paradise

*"Now the serpent was more subtil than any beast
of the field which the LORD God had made."*
(Genesis 3:1a)

HAVING ESTABLISHED THE Scriptural purpose for our
national existence and the means by which our liberties were
secured, the remainder of this volume will address its central
thesis—"How Satan Turned America Against God."

Though differing in their theological and philosophical beliefs, the
Founding Fathers concurred in their *"understanding of the times."*
Discerning which way the spiritual winds were blowing enabled them
to become God's special agents of providence for America. Armitage
writes:

> Thomas Jefferson, possibly an advanced Unitarian; Patrick Henry, a devout
> Presbyterian; and James Madison, thought to be a liberal Episcopalian,
> felt the throb of the public heart, saw that its patriotism was founded upon
> religious conviction, and, like wise men, instead of stemming the strong
> tide they gave it their leadership, under which it swept on, notwithstanding
> the opposition of English rectors and the entangling traditions of a grinding
> hierarchy.[1]

Unlike the "spinmeister" opportunists of our day, these venerable
patriarchs maintained their love of country until the very end of their
lives. Was it mere coincidence that Thomas Jefferson and John Adams
both died on July 4, 1826, *the fiftieth anniversary of the Declaration of
Independence?* As a bedridden James Madison approached his own
departure, his burden for America was heavy. Having no children of

his own, the "Father of the Constitution" determined to bequeath his national progeny a last word of paternal consolation. In the fall of 1834, the ailing statesman penned for posthumous disclosure his poignant and final "Advice to My Country."

> As this advice, if it ever see the light will not do it till I am no more, it may be considered as issuing it from the tomb, where truth alone can be respected, and the happiness of man alone consulted. It will be entitled therefore to whatever weight can be derived from good intentions, and from the experience of one who has served his country in various stations through a period of forty years, who espoused in his youth and adhered through his life to the cause of its liberty, and who has borne a part in most of the great transactions which will constitute epochs of its destiny. The advice nearest to my heart and deepest in my convictions is that the Union of the States be cherished and perpetuated. Let the open enemy to it be regarded as Pandora with her box opened; **and the disguised one, as the Serpent creeping with his deadly wiles into Paradise.**[2]

Madison's likening of America to a "paradise" was made against the backdrop of perennial European chaos. Indeed, the fledgling republic was unlike any other nation on earth. The esteemed French philosopher Alexis de Tocqueville was willing to give credit where credit was due. Following his 1831 fact-finding mission to study the U.S. prison system he wrote:

> Upon my arrival in the United States the religious aspect of the country was the first thing that struck my attention . . . In the United States the sovereign authority is religious . . . there is no other country in the world where the Christian religion retains a greater influence over the souls of men than in America.[3]

Liberal scholars who are currently rewriting American history revel in their occasional discovery of an exception to the rule. During the presidency of John Adams, a treaty was concluded with the Muslim nation of Tripoli (now Libya) in which one article began in part, "As the government of the United States of America is not, in any sense, founded on the Christian religion . . ."[4] According to Constitutional scholar John W. Whitehead, when the Constitution was adopted in 1787, the population of the United States was roughly 3.25 million, of whom at least two million were professing Christians.[5] When the Church of the Holy Trinity in New York was accused of violating a federal immigration statute for attempting to hire a clergyman from England, the United States Supreme Court ruled in 1892:

> Our laws and our institutions must necessarily be based on and embody the teachings of The Redeemer of mankind. It is impossible that it should be otherwise; and in this sense and to this extent our civilization and our institutions are emphatically Christian . . . This is a religious people. This is historically true. From the discovery of this continent to the present hour, there is a single voice making this affirmation . . . we find everywhere a clear recognition of the same truth . . . **these, and many other matters which might be noticed, add a volume of unofficial declarations to the mass of organic utterances that this is a Christian nation.**[6]

The reader will note that this official ruling by the highest court in the land was handed down nearly a century after a misguided bureaucrat attempted to placate some of Muammar Khadaffi's Islamic ancestors.

However, Madison's foreboding premonition may well have represented a degree of danger far deeper than even he was able to perceive. To comprehend the *real* peril, one must return to the theme of chapter two— God's original purpose for America. With the fall of our first parents, Adam forfeited his exalted position of being the Lord's viceroy over Creation. That God had made Adam a king, there can be no doubt, for in the day of his creation he was said to be one who was crowned *"with glory and honour"* and *"set . . . over the works of thy hands,"* and that God *"put all things in subjection under his feet"* (Hebrews 2:6-8).

As "to the victor go the spoils," Satan was ultimately permitted to become the *"god of this world"* (II Corinthians 4:4). Although this was actually a demotion for the anointed cherub (Ezekiel 28: 12-17) who had formerly ruled God's entire universe from a throne of his own (Isaiah 14: 12-15), Lucifer was "thankful" enough to have a job of any kind. Now he would appoint his own *"rulers of the darkness of this world"* (Ephesians 6:12). His greatest power over fallen humans became death itself (Hebrews 2:14)—hence, man's constant fear of the Grim Reaper. Reconciling Luke 4:6 with Romans 13:1 reveals that the Lord has allowed Satan to delegate his demonic authority to evil men of his choosing. The song "This Is My Father's World" may sound "touchy-feely," but in light of John 8:44, I wouldn't recommend it to the Body of Christ. Jesus certainly wasn't humming it before Pilate when He said, *"My kingdom is not of this world . . ."* (John 18:36). Contrary to the power of positive thinking, the Bible confirms *"The princes of this world . . . crucified the Lord of glory"* (I Corinthians 2:8).

After several generations of isolated, antediluvian witnesses and migrating Noahic descendants, the Lord suddenly appeared to Abram and promised that He would carve out a portion of Satan's domain and deed it over to his twelve great-grandsons. As previously noted, the approximate boundaries of this parcel correspond with the coordinates of the Abrahamic Covenant as given in Genesis 15:18-21.

Obviously, Satan was not about to relinquish any of his turf without a fight. Following several centuries of successful stalling maneuvers, however, he was suddenly forced to watch in horror as the walls of Jericho came tumbling down. With "the enemy" now within his territory, the devil would have to double up his diabolical efforts. To lose his earthly kingdom after being run out of Heaven would leave Hell as his only option. Then, after 459 years of persistent effort against the Hebrew incursion, Satan was able to induce "the wisest king in the world" to commit child sacrifice. (I Kings 11:7) It wouldn't be long now! Approximately 270 years later, ten of the original twelve "intruders" were evicted while the final two got the boot 136 years after that. With the returning remnant under foreign domination, all would be quiet on the eastern front for nearly four centuries.

Perhaps one can now better relate to the terror that gripped Herod "the Great" when three wise men suddenly dropped in out of nowhere in search of his replacement. It was no doubt as disconcerting as the nightmares his son, Antipas, suffered over Jesus the Nazarene. Caesar's subsequent rejection and ejection of Biblical Christianity brings us back full circle to the critical westward enlargement of Japheth and how it relates to the warning from Madison's crypt.

QUETZALCOATL

Just how significant a role *did* the Americas play in the earthly kingdom of Satan? Although *"the whole world lieth in wickedness"* (I John 5:19), did the region west of the 60th degree constitute any kind of spiritual no-man's-land of sorts? Does the location and history of the infamous Bermuda Triangle have a part in this conjecture? Despite our human inability to have full understanding of such matters, do certain historical facts exist to stimulate harmless speculation?

According to the religious history of Central and South America, Quetzalcoatl was the most important god worshiped throughout the mighty Aztec Empire. Should we be surprised that his name means "flying serpent?" (Genesis 3:14) The *Encyclopedia Americana* states that his principal form was the plumed serpent—a rattlesnake covered with beautiful green quetzal feathers. (How interesting!) When in human form, his skin was light in color. It was said that he had a strong body, broad forehead, large eyes and a flowing beard. He wore a miter on his head and usually dressed in a long, white robe. His feet were covered with a design of red crosses.[7] He was supposedly born of a virgin. His actions were full of wisdom and benevolence, except for a slight drinking problem. Actually, the story goes that Quet couldn't hold his liquor and eventually got expelled to the underworld for a number of sexual indiscretions. However, before leaving, he entrusted his teachings and the purpose of his mission to a secret "Order of Priests," who were to occupy until he was sober enough to rule once again. This is precisely why the light-skinned Hernando Cortez was greeted as the second coming of Quetzalcoatl.

As if all of this were not bizarre enough, an 1895 edition of a magazine called *Lucifer,* published by the occult *Theosophical Society,* gave a very strange insight into the origin of the word "America." Although most historians attribute the name *America* to the explorer Amerigo Vespucci, author James Pryse has a different theory altogether. The reader will recall the Scriptural principle that Satan will often produce a counterfeit for any sanctified person, place or thing. (II Corinthians 11:13-15) According to Pryse, the Aztec god Quetzalcoatl was known in Peru as *A maru,* and his domain was called—you guessed it—*Amaruca.* Pryse writes, as cited by William Still:

> From the latter comes our word *America.* Amaruca is, literally translated, "Land of the Plumed Serpent." The Priests of this God of Peace once ruled the Americas. All the Red men who have remained true to the ancient religion are still under their sway.[8]

Another prominent heathen, Manly Hall, claims that since the serpent is often a symbol of Lucifer, "it is no exaggeration to extrapolate from this that America may well mean 'Land of Lucifer.'"[9]

Whether or not any of this is true, we can be certain that Lucifer was not a happy camper when the Pilgrims came ashore at Plymouth Rock. After arranging a special welcoming committee of "Native American" Patuxet Indians (the most bloodthirsty tribe in all of New England), the devil had to watch as they were totally annihilated by a providential plague. The neighboring tribes were convinced that this had been a supernatural act. In a final act of desperation, the Powos (medicine men) spent entire days in a dark swamp to place curses on their intimidating intruders. Cotton Mather wrote, "But the devils at length acknowledged unto them, that they could not hinder those people from their becoming the owners and masters of the country."[10] The fact that Japheth would one day dwell in Shem's tents was settled way back in 2348 BC. (Genesis 9:27)

Madison warned his posterity that their liberty would be threatened by enemies seen and unseen. Among the many seeds of destruction sown in this land by Satan, three would prove banefully effective in turning America against God.

SLAVERY

The devil's first counteroffensive in America was the disastrous establishment of slavery, often referred to as the "Peculiar Institution." In today's supersensitive society, one can hardly separate the historical topic of slavery from that of current race relations. The issue of race, or more exactly "racism," is itself about as *peculiar* a subject as you can get for several reasons. First, the average brain-dead American has become so completely programmed by the liberal media that he is no longer capable of thinking for himself. Second, he has been taught to believe that no one else should be allowed to think either, much less hold or express an opinion that is considered politically incorrect (i.e., an idea that disagrees with CNN, the U.N., the NAACP, the ACLU, the NEA, Hollywood, Rome, etc.).

Remember that the major symptom of this psychotic neurosis is that facts which appear to be negative are not only completely irrelevant, but they must never be voiced in public. For instance, a television special on the subject of air disasters stated that, according to aviation statistics, passengers who fly on domestic carriers in *Africa* were *eighteen* times more likely to die in crashes than those flying elsewhere. How would the casual sharing of this *fact*, or better yet, an intelligent inquiry as to the *cause* for said fact go over during coffee and donut time at the local PTA? If somehow the subject was broached, sooner or later the right nation or nations would be found to take the blame for Africa's aerial incompetence (i.e., "Their pilots were not given the same quality training as white pilots," etc.).

As a second example, several years ago a noted Harvard University psychologist and a Bradley Fellow at the American Enterprise Institute investigated the comparative intelligence of races. Their findings were published in the prestigious *Harvard Review*. "Strangely," they evoked a storm of protest against the "researchers," as the party line for all "accredited schools" dictates that matters of race are to be approached *sentimentally* and *politically, not objectively* and *scientifically*. Without gaining prior knowledge of their results, do you suppose any community coffee clutch in America would be interested in discussing this "pig in a poke"? (See the controversial *New York Times* bestseller *The Bell Curve: Intelligence and Class Structure in American Life* by Richard J. Herrnstein and Charles Murray.)

A third reason the subject of race is so peculiar is because the widespread pressure of political correctness has pulverized the courage of America's dwindling, thinking minority. (Isaiah 10:14) More and more, people are just plain scared to tell you what they really believe. They are afraid to "speak their piece," as our grandparents used to say. *No one has the guts to tell the emperor that he's naked!*

Allow me to illustrate with the following personal observation. While visiting a local library during the Christmas season, I counted sixteen books on the subject of *Kwanzaa* (*none* of which had been checked out according to their cards). Some of the "exciting" titles included: *It's Kwanzaa Time, My First Kwanzaa Book, Kwanzaa: A Family Affair,* and *Celebrating Kwanzaa.* It is my express personal opinion as a free, thinking American that this is about as ludicrous as you can get! Now, of course this can only mean that I must hate black people, right? But maybe— just maybe—the *real* reason is that I *hate* the way many sincere black Americans are manipulated at will (i.e., see any episode of Jerry Springer, Rikki Lake or Jenny Jones)! One book declares:

> A special holiday called Kwanzaa celebrates the African culture. Blacks all over the world take part in this holiday. Kwanzaa is not religious. It does not celebrate an event. It celebrates a whole race of people.[11]

If Kwanzaa is not supposed to be a religious event, why does the "holiday" run from December 26 through January 1? According to the First Amendment, I have a God-given right to hold and state my own personal opinion. I believe Kwanzaa is an attempt to divert the attention of black Americans from Jesus Christ (*the* reason for the season) to any number of pagan African rituals that center around witchcraft and demonism. In the book, *Kwanzaa: A Family Affair*, black American families are encouraged to make traditional African masks during Kwanzaa. If Kwanzaa is not religious, why does every major encyclopedia connect such masks with spiritism? (Spiritism is a "sensitive" term for *Satanism!*) The *Academic American Encyclopedia* states:

> Masks are artificial face coverings used in ritual and primitive theater to transform the wearers into—or to identify them with the powers and properties of—animals or supernatural beings.[12]

The *World Book Encyclopedia* expands on Kwanzaa's "non-religious" agenda:

> Most of these masks not only hide the identity of the wearer but supposedly also give the masked person magic powers. Such masks represent gods or spirits . . . Ceremonial masks developed from the belief of many primitive societies that gods controlled the forces of nature. Dancers at various ceremonies wore masks that represented these gods. A mask made its wearer unrecognizable, and so he seemed to almost lose his identity and become the spirit itself. When these ceremonial dancers wore such masks, the people believed that the gods were actually present.[13] [I.e., "It's Kwanzaa time!"]

In the revival at Ephesus, the converted heathens who had formerly used "curious arts" burned their satanic garbage publicly. (Acts 19:19) Whenever Kwanzaa advocates profess to be non-religious, they're only pulling your leg. According to *Kwanzaa*, by Deborah M. Newton Chocolate:

> Africa is a big continent. Many different African tribes live in Africa and have many different customs and beliefs. But all African people know that the fruits of the earth bring life to them. The earth nourishes them, so Africans say that the earth is their mother. Africans have always celebrated planting and harvest, but even more important to Africans are the spirits of their ancestors. At harvesttime, Africans offer the first fruits of the harvest to those who have gone before them.[14]

I submit to my readers, on the authority of the King James Bible, that FAMINE is the result of worshiping an "Earthly Mother" rather than the Heavenly Father:

> *But the land, whither ye go to possess it, is a land of hills and valleys, and drinketh water of the rain of heaven: A land which the LORD thy God careth for: the eyes of the LORD thy God are always upon it, from the beginning of the year even unto the end of the year. And it shall come to pass, if ye shall hearken diligently unto my commandments which I command you this day, to love the LORD your God, and to serve him with all your heart and with all your soul, That I will give you the rain of your land in his due season, the first rain and the latter rain, that thou mayest gather in thy corn, and thy wine, and thine oil. And I will send grass in thy fields for thy cattle, that thou mayest eat and be full. Take heed to yourselves, that your heart be not deceived, and ye turn aside, and serve other gods, and worship them; And then the LORD'S wrath be kindled against you, and he shut up the heaven, that there be no rain, and that the land yield not her fruit; and lest ye perish quickly from off the good land which the LORD giveth you.* (Deuteronomy 11:11-17)

In case you haven't noticed, the "Dark Continent" is *still* a poverty-stricken Third World nightmare. Do you wonder why? Consider the following piece found in *USA Today* for April 9, 2002:

Witch doctors get paid for national soccer victory

A decade after Ivory Coast's soccer team won the African Nations Cup, the government paid witch doctors who claim to have aided in the win. The government hired witch doctors from Akradio to help the team beat Ghana. When they weren't paid, the witch doctors said they jinxed the team. It hasn't won a Nation's cup since 1992. That might change after the $2,000 payment this week.[15]

A survey of the Internet will reveal the fruit of Africa's ongoing preoccupation with Satanism. An article by Anthony C. LoBaido entitled "Child-rape Epidemic in South Africa" appeared in the December 26, 2001, *WorldNetDaily*. A few of the more revolting excerpts documenting the "social mores" practiced in the "liberated" land of Nelson Mandela and Desmond TuTu are as follows:

A bizarre belief among many African black men that sex with a virgin—even with a child or baby—can cure HIV/AIDS is fueling what is already one of the highest child sexual exploitation rates in the world.

According to the latest report by South Africa's Police Service, children are the victims of 41 percent of all rapes and attempted rates reported in the country. Over 15 percent of all reported rapes are against children under 11, and another 26 percent against children 12-17. For the year 2000, some 58 children were raped or the victims of rape attempts in South Africa every single day.

The trend is worsening. **Babies as young as only a few months old are being raped almost daily.** Many black South African men infected with AIDS erroneously believe that by having sex with a virgin—even a baby—they will be cured of AIDS or their HIV infection.

South African police statistics show that last year alone, 21,538 rapes and attempted rapes of children under the age of 18 were reported . . .

"This story has been largely ignored by the mainstream media in the United States and the Western world, in order to perpetuate the Mandela myth of the wonderful New South Africa," said former Republic of South Africa military intelligence officer Koos Ven der Merwe.[16]

So why should anyone look cross-eyed at me for trying to prevent black boys and girls from being tricked into worshiping Satan? (Ditto for any white children messing around with Dungeons and Dragons, Harry Potter, or PokeMon.) And why are America's kids also losing their grip on the English language? "Sup" (shortened version of WHASSUP, Ebonics for, "What's up?") was bad enough; but now our youngsters are being taught to say "HUJAMBO." Other "important" Kwanzaa words are as follows: KUUMBA—creativity (as in making voodoo masks, etc.); UJAMAA—using money for the good of the community; UJIMA—collective work and responsibility (street gangs); KIKOMBE CHA UMOJA—a ceremonial cup; and, BENDERA YA TAIFA—the new African American flag! (I would suggest, "MUMBO JUMBO"—"Bill Grady" for KWANZAA.)

PERSONAL TESTIMONY

Remember that the core of race-related political correctness is to equate one's perceived ability to recognize various distinctions between races ("white men can't jump," etc.) with automatic hatred. That may be how

Dan Rather thinks, but I am perfectly able to maintain my own Bible-based convictions without hating anyone. Throughout my personal ministry of over a quarter century as an ordained Baptist preacher, I have shared the Gospel with thousands of black people. When I was saved less than six months, I knelt with a black man in his living room and led his entire family to Christ while we wept and held hands together. Brother Morris went on to pastor a black Baptist church in Media, Pennsylvania. On another soul winning occasion, I picked up a black man who had run out of gas on I-95 outside of Philadelphia. At 2:00 A.M. we knelt on the highway in a mild rain while the man received Jesus Christ as his personal Saviour. Another time, in Oak Orchard, Delaware, I got to lead the wife and daughter of my wife's favorite high school teacher to Christ. They were both black.

While working my way through Bible college at the Blaw-Knox foundry in East Chicago, Indiana, I had the joy of seeing dozens of black men come to Christ. This was accomplished through personal soul winning during break times and preaching during the 3:00 A.M. nightly lunch hour service (midnight shift), which I had the privilege of overseeing with the help of several fellow students. My crane operator, Sonny D., got saved. Charlie the burner got saved. So did numerous machinists and common laborers. On one occasion, my black foreman, Bill D., got so excited he helped me fill up a church bus with fellow employees for a special Sunday morning evangelistic service honoring area blue-collar workers. Over three hundred men attended the service at First Baptist Church of Hammond with many accepting Jesus Christ as Saviour.

Another time I organized a special memorial service in the factory lunchroom for two black machinists who were killed in a motorcycle accident. Having visited the dying men in the hospital and their grieving loved ones at home I was asked to speak at the funeral. The mother of one of those young men told me that my sermon helped her more than the one delivered by her own pastor. She later began attending the First Baptist Church of Hammond and remained faithful for more than ten years.

Over 150 men attended a special Christmas service after I announced that a black Santa Claus would be in attendance. (Was I ever embarrassed when "Santa" showed up late and a tad inebriated!) About twenty souls made a public profession at the invitation following the message.

During those formative years, I also had the unique opportunity of fellowshipping with many black pastors in the Chicagoland area. Some even took me under their wings and tutored me in preaching. The braver ones turned me loose on their congregations for practice. (*"Can I get a witness?"* etc.) One of these fine men was my friend and neighbor of five years, Reverend Joe Hughes, who later pastored for a number of years in Memphis, Tennessee. Pastor Gene Dix was another. He once asked me to recruit three white ministerial students from Hyles-Anderson College to join three of his black preacher friends for a special Good Friday service at his church in Gary, Indiana. Each of us was assigned one of the seven last sayings of Jesus on which to speak. It was a wonderful day.

The Lord also led me to preach on the streets in various ghetto neighborhoods of Chicago, including the notorious hellhole, Cabrini Green. While driving through this stronghold of Satan, I came upon a block party in a vacant lot featuring blaring rock music and a half-naked dance troupe. When I noticed several parents and small children in the crowd, including some who rode our Sunday school buses, I stood up on a crate and "let 'er rip!" While the dancers just stood on the stage with their mouths open, the crowd listened respectfully and powerful conviction was felt. On another occasion, one of my converts came to the church and walked the aisle, professing Christ as his personal Saviour. He must have meant business, because he handed me a bag of heroin at the altar. I shocked my college president, Dr. Wendell Evans, by handing the white substance to him!

At that time, I was also busy distributing sermon helps to various black ministers. In fact, the Lord enabled me to sell so many copies of the *Encyclopedia of 7700 Illustrations* that I received a personal visit from Dr. Paul Lee Tan, the book's editor. I was even welcomed to set up a display at an all-black pastors'convention in Omaha, Nebraska. Apart from my three helpers, a Jewish fellow (modeling the choir robes he was selling) represented the only other white person in the crowd of over 10,000!

On the last day I went to work before leaving to accept my first full-time ministry assignment as a pastor, Reverend Daniels, a retired black minister, conducted a special farewell service in my honor. His pastoral charge was packed with power, love, and wisdom. Over the years (until the company went out of business), I had a standing invitation to reenter the plant and preach whenever I was in the area.

Owing to the fact that there weren't many blacks in neo-Nazi Northern Idaho, I rarely got the chance to witness to any during my five-year pastorate in the Coeur d'Alene area.

When I returned to Hyles-Anderson College as an instructor in 1986, I joined the jail ministry and spent the majority of my Saturdays preaching at the Westville Correctional Unit outside of Michigan City, Indiana. I would also preach at the famous Pacific Garden Rescue Mission in downtown Chicago where Billy Sunday was converted. In the course of one sermon to nearly three hundred winos (mostly black), I split the seat of my pants wide open in front of thirty Hyles-Anderson College students who were seated behind me in the choir area. A good number of these mission men were saved at the invitation. When actress Lucille Ball died in 1989, a Chicago newspaper headline read, "We Love You, Lucy— Wherever You Are." That evening the Lord impressed me to preach a message at the PGM entitled, "Where *Is* Lucy"? (With all due humility, I've been informed more than once that "the brothers" talked about that message for years.)

One of my hardworking evening college students was a fine black man who pastored a struggling storefront church in a run-down Chicago neighborhood. After receiving an invitation to preach to his Sunday morning crowd, I felt a definite prompting to speak on the theme of suffering. When I finished, "Sister Anthony" rose to her feet in tears and testified how the Lord had used the sermon to lift the burden she had been carrying since her daughter's brutal murder only two weeks before. She then went on to sing, "I'm comin' up the mountain—*on the rough side.*"

While traveling as a full-time evangelist since 1996, I have continued to witness to anyone I can, regardless of his (or her) color. On one such trip, my wife and I were privileged to lead a sweet black maid to Christ at a motel in North Carolina. For several years I have also been honored to serve on the board of International Baptist Outreach Missions in Asheville, North Carolina, founded by Dr. J. Wendell Runion. One of the more fruitful countries in which we minister is Kenya, East Africa.

During a mission trip with Dr. Runion in September, 2003, I was privileged to preach in eight Baptist churches in Kenya and Uganda. While all of the facilities were primitive, one "sanctuary" consisted of a bench and two chairs arranged under the sprawling branches of a solitary tree. In that meeting, several chickens and cows dropped by unexpectedly and caught a portion of my sermon.

Before leaving for the States, we helped officiate the graduation service for the local Bible institute. The highlight of the trip for me, personally, was the honor of laying hands on ten African pastors and praying for God's blessing on their ministries. Within a week of my return, the Lord enabled me to raise $500.00 to purchase ten bicycles for the new graduates.

Having visited over forty countries in my life, I found the Kenyan people to be some of the noblest, sweetest souls I have ever met. Unlike other African nations, which have been commandeered by Islam, Communism, or Catholicism, Kenya's cultural heritage is British; her predominant values produced by an A.V. 1611. Kenya provides a rare glimpse of Ham dwelling in docile contentment within the bounds of his habitation. (Acts 17:26) Kenya's "attitude" factor is *zero*. (Personally, I refuse to be pressured into using the racist term "African-American"; I certainly have never referred to myself as an Irish-Ukrainian-Finnish-American. However, after enjoying the company of the Kenyan people, I believe the words "American African" would be a more accurate description for the discontented element of Ham's posterity dwelling in this nation.)

Now, don't miss the subliminal message suggested by these twenty-five personal experiences, spread over as many years—*Dr. Grady is a racist! Dr. Grady hates blacks!* According to the straw-man philosophy of end-day compromisers, one cannot separate hatred from common sense. Why hasn't Martin Luther King ever been accused of racism when he preached against interracial marriage? (Ditto: Abraham Lincoln, Muhammad Ali and "Calypso Louie" Farrakhan.)

If anyone is interested, a final story will illustrate the *true* essence of racism. The incident occurred during our twenty-fifth wedding anniversary "second honeymoon" in Kauai, Hawaii. As I drove down a certain road, my wife and I spotted former NBA star Kareem Abdul Jabar jogging in what we later learned was his own neighborhood. This really amazed us as we remembered seeing him in the Los Angeles Airport twenty-five years earlier while en route to our first Hawaiian honeymoon! (*Déjà vu!*) After making an incongruous U-turn, I came upon my soul-winning prospect as he was stretching his leg against an incline. However, when I twice attempted to initiate a simple greeting, the Black Muslim made it clear that he was not about to turn around and even look at "whitey," much less talk to him. Driving away, it dawned on me that this was the same reaction I received when I approached the "Reverend" Louis Farrakhan at O'Hare Airport a year earlier. All I can figure is that they must believe in the spirit of *ujamaa* (pronounced oo-jah-mah—Kwanzaa for "discrimination"), as one of their authorities recommends, "African-Americans should set up their own businesses and patronize other African-American stores."[17]

FACTS ARE STUBBORN THINGS

According to the *World Book Encyclopedia,* the era of modern slavery began in Africa itself. (Do you recall those butcher shops along the Congo described by Captain Grenfell?) Roman Catholics from Spain and Portugal simply tapped into the lucrative market and became some of the best customers. David Brian Davis confirms: "Other African blacks helped capture most of the enslaved Africans."[18] You won't find *this* African history discussed in too many Kwanzaa books. The Dutch and other Protestant profiteers eventually joined in.

The subject of slavery in America is rarely treated in an honest and forthright manner. It is usually reported with a bias to historical facts. For instance, it is my personal opinion as a Christian American that the concept of one human being owning another human being is totally repugnant. On the other hand, I also resent how the "slavery issue" and race relations in general are continually manipulated to ensure that social agitation in America continues to escalate. To illustrate, I once had the opportunity to visit the Montpelier estate, former home to James and Dolley Madison. "A squirrel's jump from Heaven," is how President Madison described Montpelier. Yet, the average tourist receives a distinct subliminal tainting as he views the numerous exhibits to Madison's "hypocrisy" in keeping slaves on his plantation. The names of these slaves are plastered all over the walls. Now I may not be the sharpest knife in the drawer, but I'm no spoon either! I stopped counting the names of these "brutalized heathens" after eighteen: Moses, Ruth, Peter, Shaddrack, Abraham, Haana, Judah, Solomon, Paul, Sarah, Joshua, Mary, Daniel, Hannah, Jacob, Thomas, Joseph, and Simon. Isn't it rather strange how these resentful creatures chose to dump the "spirit of their ancestors" in favor of their master's Christian *imani?* (Kwanzaa for "faith.") One of the more humorous placards has a slave commenting to Mr. Madison on the damage from a Rapidan River flood: "I tell you what, Master—I think the Lord Almighty, by and large, He do most as much harm as good."

The truth of the matter is, Madison himself recognized that slavery was wrong, writing to abolitionist Francis Wright in 1825, "The magnitude of this evil among us is so deeply felt and so universally acknowledged; that no merit could be greater than that of devising a satisfactory remedy for it." The slavery issue was as complex as it was evil; it was "peculiar" in the extreme. However, for as long as it lasted, it represented one of the greatest missionary projects of all time! How else do you account for the fact that so many black folks are Baptist, especially in the South?

Phillis Wheatley represents another illustration of revisionist distortion. Born in Africa in 1753, she was placed into bondage by her own people. While still a child, she was brought to Boston and sold to Mr. John Wheatley, a tailor, as a servant for his wife. Under her "cruel taskmaster," she learned to read both English and Latin. More importantly, Phillis came to know her master's Lord and Saviour after hearing Mr. Whitefield preach. Developing a talent for poetry, she became the first black poetess in America to have her work published. The next time you visit a bookstore, ask for a copy of *Poems by Phillis Wheatley*. For one of the wildest politically incorrect—Uncle Tom hate literature at its best—examples of what *not* to read in a public gathering, try handling her most famous poem entitled *On Being Brought from Africa to America*. After all, why waste your time with kiddie-car material like *Amistad* when you can hear something that's profound?

> 'TWAS mercy brought me from my *Pagan* land,
> Taught my benighted soul to understand
> That there's a God, that there's a *Saviour* too:
> Once I redemption neither sought nor knew,
> Some view our sable race with scornful eye,
> "Their colour is a diabolic die."
> Remember, *Christians, Negroes* black as *Cain,*
> May be refin'd, and join th' angelic train.

Now while Phillis was owned by a "white guy," such was not the case for thousands of others less fortunate. As the slaves were initially sold by fellow Africans, *many of their American taskmasters turned out to be former slaves themselves!* Mr. Bill Ward, a historical researcher and author of fifty-seven works of non-fiction, comments on one of the more "politically sensitive" aspects of that *peculiar institution*:

Black slave ownership is one of the most frequently overlooked parts of the slavery story. **The U.S. Census of 1830 showed that 3,775 free Negroes owned 12,760 Negro slaves.** A fourth of the free Negro slave masters in South Carolina owned 10 or more slaves; eight owned 30 or more. Two black individuals, Justus Angel and Mistress L. Horry of Colleton District, S.C., each owned 84 slaves, which placed them in the ranks of slave magnates—those who owned 50 or more slaves.

In Charleston 125 free Negroes owned slaves, representing more than $300,000 in taxable property. In North Carolina 69 free Negroes were slave owners.

William Ellison, a freed slave who lived near Charleston, owned 63 slaves. His sons owned nine more. Ellison's wealth was greater than 90 percent of his white neighbors' and 15 times greater than the state's average for whites. In the entire state, only 5 percent owned as much real estate as Ellison, and he owned more slaves than 99 percent of the South's slaveholders.

In 1860 at least six blacks in Louisiana owned 65 or more slaves. The largest number, 152 slaves, were owned by a widow Richards and her son P. C. Richards, who owned a large sugar cane plantation. Another Negro slave magnate in Louisiana, with more than 100 slaves, was Antoine Dubuclet, a sugar planter whose estate was valued (in 1860 dollars) at $264,000. That year, the mean wealth of Southern white men was $3,978.[19]

(See also: *Dixie's Censored Subject: Black Slave Owners* by Robert M. Grooms; *Black Masters: A Free Family of Color in the Old South* by Michael P. Johnson and James L. Roak, and *Black Confederates and Afro-Yankees in Civil War Virginia* by Ervin L. Jordan Jr., a black professor at the University of Virginia.)

As space limitations and the purpose of this book do not permit more than a cursory treatment of the subject at hand, let me say next that the War Between the States was *not* fought over slavery. General William Tecumseh Sherman made the rather cryptic comment in his book, *Memoirs I,* "The truth is not always palatable and should not always be told."[20] Abraham Lincoln said, "My paramount object in this struggle is to save the Union. If I could save the Union without freeing any slaves, I would do it."[21] This is precisely why Lincoln waited so long to issue his celebrated Emancipation Proclamation, and then only as a defensive maneuver. He stated to Navy Secretary Gideon Welles on July 13, 1862, "It was a military necessity absolutely essential for the salvation of the Union, that we must free the slaves or be ourselves subdued."[22] Furthermore, the celebrated document applied only to slaves being held in *Confederate* states. Honest Abe's reprieve did not cover Yankee chattel in Kentucky, Maryland or Missouri. According to *The Gray Book,* as cited by authors James and Walter Kennedy, Union

Commander Ulysses S. Grant's excuse for not freeing his own slaves way up in "the land of Lincoln" was that "good help is so hard to come by these days."[23]

Concerning the true motive for the Civil War, Colonel Edward Mandell House, chief advisor to President Woodrow Wilson, wrote through one of his characters in *Philip Dru, Administrator,* "Cynical Europe said that the North would have it appear that a war had been fought for human freedom, whereas it was fought for money."[24] *Uncle Tom* was just the pawn that got the ball rolling. William Darrah Kelly, a liberal congressman from Philadelphia, declared rather candidly, "Yes, sneer at or doubt it as you may, the negro is the 'coming man' for whom we have waited."[25] (For added reading on the subject of slavery, see: *Myths and Realities of American Slavery: The True History of Slavery in America* by John C. Perry; *Like Men of War: Black Troops in the Civil War, 1862-1865* by Noah Andre Trudeau; *Black Confederates* by Charles Kelly Barrow, J. H. Segars and R. B. Rosenberg; *Forced Into Glory* by Lerone Bennett, executive editor for *Ebony* magazine, and any number of relevant articles by Dr. John Hope Franklin, a black professor at Duke University.)

The *real* problem underlying the slavery issue is rarely, if ever, discussed. I mentioned earlier, in reference to Madison's consternation, that an easy solution to the problem was not to be had. Remember that the theme of this material concerns *Satanic* opposition to America and the sticky wicket of slavery was one of the devil's most successful maneuvers. The issue centered around something that was obvious in America's early years: just what do you do with the slaves *after* you release them? A nation of freed slaves with minimal *kujichagulia* (Kwanzaa for "self-determination") was not up for consideration. Since blacks were perceived as being incapable of caring for themselves (see Phillis Wheatley's allusion to Genesis 4:12), the only practical solution was to send them back to Africa. But this would have crippled the treasury. Commenting on the difficult but necessary demands of emancipation *with* expatriation, Thomas Jefferson wrote: "But as it is, we have the wolf by the ears, and we can neither hold him nor safely let him go. Justice is in one scale and self-preservation in the other."[26]

Haiti, Panama, and Liberia were the leading sites under consideration by the American Colonization society for resettlement of the Negro population. Rousas J. Rushdoony summarizes:

The Emancipation Proclamation must be set in this context of colonization hopes. However illusory, they were a long-standing consideration and were legally enacted by Congress. **The Negro was to be emancipated of slavery, and, many hoped and believed, the United States was to be emancipated of the Negro.** As late as March 1865, a month before his assassination, Lincoln was considering the removal of the entire Negro population from the United States.[27]

While speaking to a delegation of free blacks at the White House, August 14, 1862, Lincoln *really* split some rails:

Your race suffers very greatly, many of them, by living among us, **while ours suffers from your presence.** In a word, we suffer on each side. If this be admitted, it affords a reason at least, why we should be separated.[28]

But how could anyone indict the "Great Emancipator" as being a *racist*? So then, why cover up "the whole story?" Did Lincoln *hate* black people because he didn't believe the races were equally endowed? In a debate with Steven Douglas at Charlestown, Illinois, on September 18, 1858, Lincoln disclosed, as cited by Richard Current:

I will say then that I am not, nor have ever been in favor of bringing about in any way the social and political equality of the white and black races . . . that I am not nor ever have been in favor of making voters or jurors of Negroes, nor of qualifying them to hold office, nor to intermarry with white people; and I will say in addition to this that **there is a physical difference between the white and black races which I believe will forever forbid the two races living together on terms of social and political equality.** And inasmuch as they cannot so live, while they do remain together there must be the position of superior and inferior, **and I as much as any man am in favor of having the superior position to the white race.**[29]

Whenever the *real* Abraham Lincoln comes into view, any number of stunned neophytes (victims of TV, America's public school system, too many video games, etc.) find themselves wondering why Abe seems to be talking as though he didn't hold to the panacean "All men are created equal" clause. Do you suppose they ever checked to see what the author of *that* abused statement believed? Weyl writes:

Jefferson opposed slavery as morally indefensible, but, he also opposed the incorporation of the Negro in the American social and

political system. He considered the Negro inferior to other races, but thought that that circumstance should not deprive him of his freedom. He was, throughout his long life, in the politically uncomfortable position of wishing the slaves emancipated, but only on the condition that they be deported *in toto* beyond the present or potential frontiers of the United States. **"Nothing is more certainly written in the book of fate,"** Jefferson wrote in his *Autobiography*, **"than that these people are to be free; nor is it less certain that the two races, equally free, cannot live in the same government."** [30]

Now here's where the rubber really meets the road. You just read one of the most remarkable prophecies in history. The issue is not whether you like it, or not; whether you agree with it or not; or whether you think it is hate literature, or not. The issue is—*Did you understand what the man wrote down in the English language; and secondly, has the prophecy come to pass?* It's only been roughly 175 years since he told you what to expect. So, was he right or was he wrong? Look at those heavy words again, "Nothing is more certainly written in the book of fate . . . than that the two races, equally free, cannot live in the same government." Has the *majority* of modern-day black Americans surpassed their emancipated ancestors in the area of self-reliance? Would a check of current welfare rolls, according to race, help to answer this question? How long does the racial tension have to go on in this country before someone is willing to admit that the man may have been right after all? You don't have to hate people in order to recognize reality. Does *realism* equal *racism*?

Nearly two centuries after he told you it wouldn't work, the poor man can't even rest in his own cemetery. Do you think that the ACLU and the Supreme Court can *force* people of different races to enjoy being in one another's company? Will Affirmative Action and "zero tolerance" policies breed *genuine* respect at the workplace? Will clamping down on racial profiling guarantee that cabbies, mail carriers and firemen do not experience a higher level of stress when entering a black neighborhood as opposed to a white one? Am I supposed to smile when Congressman John Conyers of Michigan attempts to persuade my government to grant millions of dollars in reparations to the descendants of nineteenth-century slaves alive in the twenty-first century?

Taking Ham beyond the "bounds of his habitation," and for pecuniary motives, was a colossal mistake that will never be corrected this side of the Rapture. Because of the law of sowing and reaping, we must all learn to live with the fallout. Only God can grant the needed wisdom to do so. In the meantime, don't jump every time someone cries "racism." After all, white men aren't supposed to be able to jump, remember? And, beware; the same devil that orchestrated this imbroglio is also after YOU!

ROMAN CATHOLIC IMMIGRATION

Satan's next major assault on America occurred when corrupt government officials adopted an ideological alliance with the Vatican, resulting in unprecedented waves of Roman Catholic immigrants. As discussed in the previous section on slavery, the average American knows almost nothing about the early history of this country. For instance, do you suppose the pupils in our nation's "Ritalin dens" could identify the five politically incorrect distinctives that the Founding Fathers had in common? Would it be a hate crime to inform them that they were all *white, Protestant, straight, adult males*? The television reveals who is running the country in the twenty-first century: blacks, Catholics, sodomites, children, and women. That's why our youth worship pedophiles like Michael Jackson. I once heard an old-time preacher say about Mike that, "America is the only nation on earth where a poor black boy from Gary, Indiana, can grow up to be a rich white woman in Los Angeles."

Another "Jackson" who is currently undermining what is left of America is the religious charlatan and confessed adulterer Jesse Jackson. According to "Reverend" Jackson, as quoted in *Celebrating Kwanzaa*:

> America is not like a blanket—one piece of unbroken cloth, the same color, the same texture, and the same size. America is more like a quilt—many patches, many pieces, many colors, many sizes, all woven and held together by a common thread. Even in our fractured state, all of us count and all of us fit in somewhere.[31]

It is my opinion as a free American that "Reverend" Jackson's *integrity* is in a fractured state. (See *Shakedown: Exposing the Real Jesse Jackson* by Kenneth R. Timmerman.) If Jesse wants to "fit in" where he belongs, let him start with the Cook County Jail. The "common thread" that has been holding Jackson's mongrelized quilt together is a three-fold cord (Ecclesiastes 4:12) consisting of patriots' blood, workers' taxes, and

Christians' prayers—none of which have anything to do with Rainbow Coalitions or Kwanzaa festivals!

The men who established this country, from the Pilgrim Fathers to the Founding Fathers, were trying to get away from the "Holy Fathers." Once again, this has nothing to do with hate—only literal, physical survival. Conservative estimates place the number of Christian martyrs killed in cold blood by the Roman Catholic Church at fifty million! In fact, so much blood has been shed that even Jesuit historians cannot hide it all. They can only plea-bargain their guilt. With reference to the 8,800 victims consigned to the flames by Torquemada during the infamous Spanish Inquisition, the *Catholic Encyclopedia* concedes: "These figures are highly exaggerated . . . Most historians hold . . . that the number of persons burnt from 1481 to 1504 . . . was about 2,000."[32]

After his conversion, Martin Luther addressed his former "Vicar of Christ" as the "Vicar of *Hell*." On more than one occasion, the translators of the King James Bible referred to the pope as the "Man of Sin." Within ten years of the Pilgrims' arrival at Plymouth, the first textbook of American history was begun by the colony's governor, William Bradford. *Of Plymouth Plantation* would take over twenty years to complete and now represents the primary source for information concerning our nation's earliest days. When it came to the realistic purpose for America's existence, Governor Bradford wasted no time in getting to the heart of the matter. What you are about to read constitutes the *first* sentence of the *first* page of the *first* history volume produced on American soil:

> It is well known unto the godly and judicious, how ever since the first breaking out of the light of the gospel in our honourable nation of England (which was the first of nations whom the Lord adorned therewith after the **gross darkness of popery** which had covered and overspread the Christian world), what wars and oppositions ever since, **Satan** hath raised, maintained and continued against the Saints, from time to time, in one sort or another.[33]

Bradford identified "the gross darkness of popery" as the devil's co-defendant for evil. Can you see that this has nothing to with hating anyone, but rather in trying to keep from getting "whacked," as the *Catholic* Mafia says?

Just as the first slaves to enter America had already arrived in Jamestown a year before the Pilgrims landed in 1620, the first Catholic settlements were also in place, from the Spanish at Nombre de Dios in St. Augustine, Florida, in 1535, to the French village on Ste. Croix (De Monts) Island on Maine's Scoodic River in 1604. With these beachheads established, the pope's secret service, better known as the Jesuits ("crafty" according to *Webster's Dictionary*), began infiltrating the land with pro-Vatican propaganda. This fanatical order of Roman Catholicism, officially named The Society of Jesus (How spiritual!), was begun by Ignatius de Loyola between 1534 and 1539 with the purpose of reintroducing papal authority to the "wayward" nations of Protestantism. Lamenting a resurgence of Jesuit activity, John Adams wrote to Thomas Jefferson in 1816:

> I am not happy about the rebirth of the Jesuits. Swarms of them will present themselves under more disguises ever taken by even a chief of the Bohemians, as printers, writers, publishers, school teachers, etc. If ever an association of people deserved eternal damnation, on this earth and in hell, it is this Society of Loyola.[34]

Jefferson replied, "Like you, I disapprove of the restoration of the Jesuits, for it means a step backward from light into darkness."[35]

Historical concerns such as these moved the Founding Fathers to issue one warning after another to stay clear of Catholic Europe. The thrust of President Washington's farewell address in 1796 revolved around this theme. Note the prophetic reference to Jesse Jackson's quilt:

> Why quit our own to stand on foreign ground? Why, by interweaving our destiny with that of any part of Europe, entangle our peace and prosperity in the toils of European ambition, rivalship, interest, humor or caprice? Against the insidious wiles of foreign influence—the jealousy of a free people ought to be constantly awake, since history and experience prove that foreign influence is one of the most baneful foes of republican government— 'tis our true policy to steer clear of permanent alliances, with any portion of the foreign world.[36]

Satan realized that he could eventually influence America to dump Washington's "fuddy-duddy" views on foreign alliances (U.N., NATO, SEATO, NAFTA, GATT, WEO, etc.) by importing a significant bloc of future voters. The all important half-step to achieving foreign entanglements "over there" (WWI, WWII, Korea, Viet Nam, Iraq, Kosovo, Bosnia, Grenada, Somalia, Afghanistan, East Timor) was to start by bringing foreigners "over here." A concerned Secretary of State John Quincy Adams recommended in 1817, "It may be observed that for the repose of Europe, as well as of America, the European and American political systems should be kept as separate and distinct from each other as possible."[37] The devil began his public relations campaign by attempting to convince America's business leaders that an increase in the labor pool would generate a commensurate profit margin. Foreign immigration came to be viewed as a quick fix for a greater GNP. This threatening scenario was foreseen by Thomas Jefferson who warned his nation accordingly.

"The present desire in America, (in 1781) is to produce rapid population by as great *importations of foreigners* as possible. *But is this founded in policy?* Are there no *inconveniences* to be thrown into the scale against the advantage expected from a multiplication of numbers by the importation of foreigners? It is for the happiness of those united in society to harmonize as much as possible in matters which they must of necessity transact together.

"Civil government being the sole object of forming societies, its administration must be conducted by common consent. Every species of government has its specific principles. Ours, perhaps, is more peculiar than those of any other in the universe. It is a composition of the freest principles of the English constitution, with others derived from natural right, and natural reason. To these nothing can be more opposed than the maxims of absolute monarchies. Yet, from such, we are to expect the greatest number of emigrants. *They will bring with them the principles of the governments they leave, imbibed in their early youth; or, if able to throw them off, it will be in exchange for an unbounded licentiousness,* passing, as is usual, from one extreme to another. It would be a miracle were they to stop precisely at the point of temperate liberty. These principles, with their language, they will transmit to their children. *In proportion to their numbers, they will share with us the legislation. They will infuse into it their spirit, warp and bias its directions, and render it a heterogeneous, incoherent, distracted mass.*

"I may appeal to experience, for a verification of these conjectures. But if they were not *certain in event,* are they not *possible, are they not probable?* Is it not safer to wait with patience—for the attainment of any degree of population desired or expected? May not our government be more homogenous, more peaceable, and more durable?" He asks what would be the condition of France if 20 millions of Americans were suddenly imported into that kingdom? and adds — "If it would be *more turbulent,* less happy, less strong, we may believe that the addition of *half a million of foreigners* would produce a *similar effect here.*"[38]

Having accurately predicted that Japheth and Ham would never integrate (except at the point of a bayonet), the sage of Monticello also went on record as attempting to dissuade future generations from embracing the pagan branch of Japheth's descendants, better known as "your tired, your poor, your huddled masses, etc." The built-in problem with immigration was that the arriving Europeans would never be allowed to discover *why* they were so "tired and poor." Their priests would ensure that they remained as "huddled masses" beyond the reach of soul-winning Christians. The American edition of the *Douay-Rheims Version*, the official Catholic translation of the Bible in English, was published in 1837 under the auspices of the Provincial Council of Baltimore with the attached admonition: "To prevent and remedy this **abuse**, and to guard against **error**, it was judged necessary to **forbid the reading of the Scriptures** in the vulgar language **without the advice and permission of the pastors and spiritual guides whom God has appointed to govern his Church.**"[39] What this means "in the Greek" is that "Father" O'Riley didn't want Mrs. Magillicuddy accidentally stumbling across Mark 6:1-6 and "freaking out" at the fact that the "ever-virgin" Mary had at least *six* other children *after* Jesus was born.

This is not about "Catholic bashing," but rather about bashing a system that thrives on the ignorance of its devotees. As with my track record in "black evangelism," I have also earned the right to speak out against the " pay, pray and obey" mentality of traditional Roman Catholicism. For twenty-two long years I floundered in the darkness of popery. In addition to attending twelve years of strict parochial school which included a two-year stint as an altar boy (Cardinal Francis Spellman having signed my grade-school diploma), I had the macabre experience of administering the Roman Catholic sacrament of "baptism" to my dying Lutheran mother. (When there is no time to call a priest, the Church sanctions the intermediary role of a layperson to enact the "death-bed conversion.") Although my sprinkling job should have sent her to Heaven under normal conditions, the fact that she had committed suicide led my local parish priest to recommend that I "hedge my bet" (good bingo strategy) by using my paper route money to purchase a few Mass cards on her behalf.

It is my distinct recollection of those years that the pope was constantly represented as the undisputed authority figure for all good Catholics. This was especially true since he was "infallible." The subliminal message was clear—*his* authority over a Catholic American surpassed that of the president, Congress and Constitution as well! They don't call him "numero uno" for nothing. To disregard even one of his pontifical commands was the ultimate "no-no." The August, 1868, edition of *The Catholic World* stated, "[The pope], as the head and mouthpiece of the Catholic Church, administers its discipline and issues orders to which every Catholic, *under pain of sin*, must yield obedience."[40] In his 750-page tome entitled *Rome and the Civil Power*, former Secretary of the Navy Richard Thompson wrote:

> **Nothing is plainer than that, if the principles of the Church of Rome prevail here, our Constitution would necessarily fall.** The two cannot exist together. They are in open and direct antagonism with the fundamental theory of our government and of all popular government everywhere.[41]

In the final analysis, the dictator of the Vatican State would never allow his American subjects to elevate their local officials above *his* papal authority. Consequently, President Theodore Roosevelt said:

> We should insist that if the immigrant who comes here in good faith becomes an American and assimilates himself to us, he shall be treated on an exact equality with everyone else; for it is an outrage to discriminate against any such man because of creed, birthplace or origin. **But this is predicated upon the man's becoming in every fact an American.**[42]

NATIVIST MOVEMENT

Keep in mind that the theme of this chapter centers on *deliberate* satanic aggression against the United States of America. Far from being an "accident of history," the immigration fiasco has been proven to be a major conspiracy of the Vatican. Named the "St. Leopold Foundation for the Furtherance of Catholic Missions in America," the papal plot intended to undermine America's constitutional form of government by invading her shores with excessive waves of European immigration. When the facts became known, over five hundred books and forty-five antipopery newspapers flooded the country.

The unlikely catalyst of this volatile period, known as the Nativist Movement, was the esteemed inventor Samuel F. B. Morse. While traveling through Italy in 1830 and 1831, Professor Morse, a born-again Christian and son of a Congregational minister, encountered several hostile ecclesiastics of the Church of Rome. One rather loquacious cardinal attempted to intimidate Morse by informing him that a Vatican machination under the cloak of a religious mission was about to be launched against the United States. Returning to his homeland in 1833, Professor Morse attempted to warn his endangered countrymen by authoring two books of his own: *Foreign Conspiracy Against the Liberties of the United States* and *Imminent Dangers to the Free Institutions of the United States Through Foreign Immigrants.* The inventor of the Morse code sent America the following SOS:

> We cannot be too often reminded of the *double* character of the enemy who has gained foothold upon our shores, for although Popery is a religious sect, and on this ground claims toleration side by side with other religious sects, yet Popery is also a *political*, a *despotic system*, which we must repel as altogether incompatible with the existence of freedom. I repeat it, Popery is a *political*, a *despotic system* which must be resisted by all true patriots.[43]

One such patriot was the aforementioned Richard Wigginton Thompson. His four decades of public service included stints as acting Indiana lieutenant governor, two terms in Congress, two years as circuit judge in the eighteenth district, and four years as secretary of the Navy under President Rutherford Hayes. Concerning Vatican designs on American liberties, Thompson affirmed: "The Papacy is now endeavoring, by the most active and persistent efforts, to substitute an ecclesiastical government of the people—a grand 'Holy Empire' for this free and popular republic which it has cost so much blood and treasure to establish and maintain."[44]

The reality of such a conspiracy was subsequently confirmed by a dramatic shift in the nation's census statistics. By 1830, there were only 318,000 Roman Catholics in America—compared to a total population of 12,866,020. Just fifteen years later, over 100,000 immigrants were arriving annually. Within two years' time, that figure was doubled. By 1850, the number of foreigners entering the country was 300,000 per year, and pressing half a million per annum after that. On the eve of the Civil War, the total number of American Catholics had ballooned to 3,103,000, or roughly ten percent of the nation's entire population. In just eight more years, the figure would exceed five million! Whereas a mere two hundred Catholic churches had existed in 1830, within three decades over 2,400 "Baalite temples" permeated the land of the Pilgrims' pride.

Overnight the character of America experienced a disgraceful downward spiral. Drunkenness, pauperism, immorality, lawlessness and political corruption became the staples of society. A host of new words, such as "paddy wagon," "racketeering" and "Mafia" entered the nation's vocabulary.

Roman Catholics were encouraged to fulfill the lusts of their flesh through the convenient man-made doctrine of auricular confession. The only catch was that the sinner had to perform a penance before his transgression could be removed. My penance was usually having to recite any number of "Our Fathers" or "Hail Marys." ("Don't do the crime if you can't do the time," etc.) However, in previous centuries, and especially back in the "old country," the Church offered some pretty outlandish scams to wipe the slate clean. One of the more inane examples was cited by noted historian John T. Christian in his work, *Americanism or Romanism, Which?:*

> A book of rates was published and publicly sold. In it is fixed the tax for all manner of uncleanness and debauchery. The sums for such sins as incest, perjury, murder, etc., are given. (Taxa., etc., p. 326) Espencaeus, after telling that it was openly sold, remarks: "Is it a wonder that, at this time, in this schism, such an infamous index, of such filthy and to be abhored wickedness, is not suppressed. There is neither in Germany, Switzerland, nor in any other place where there is a defection from the Roman See, a book more to their reproach. It teacheth and encourageth such wickedness as we may be afraid to hear named, and a price is set to all buyers; and yet it is not suppressed by the favors of Rome." (Tit., c.i., digr. 2, p. 479)
>
> This tariff was first established in 1316 by Pope John XXII, and first published by Pope Leo X in 1514. Many editions have been published in Latin and French. An English translation was printed in this country in 1846. I give at random a few prices:

Robbing a church	$2.25
Simony	2.25
Perjury and lying	2.00
Robbery	3.00
Burning a house	2.75
Eating meat in Lent	2.75
Killing a layman	1.75
Striking a priest	2.75
Procuring an abortion	1.50

Priest to keep a concubine 2.25
Ravishing a virgin 2.00
Murder of father, mother, brother,
sister or wife...2.50
Nun for fornication in or
out of nunnery...5.00
Marrying on a day forbidden 10.00
Adultery committed by a priest
with nuns and others....................................... 10.00
Absolution of all crimes together................... 12.00[45]

The inevitable backlash of a Baptist-Protestant Nativist coalition began in an orderly enough fashion via public forums, literature distribution and the ballot box. However, in what is undoubtedly the most concealed period of U.S history, Catholic snipers, bombings and mob violence would set the pace for thirty years of Belfast-styled religious riots in America's largest cities.

Much of the attack was centered against the King James Bible. (Should we be surprised?) In 1844, thirty-one public schools in New York City succumbed to Catholic pressure by abandoning their policy of daily Bible reading in class. And when politicians could not be bought, matches could. A Catholic priest in Carbeau, New York, shocked the nation by publicly burning a pyre of forty-two King James Bibles! Almost as deplorable was the editorial in the *Freeman's Journal,* the official publication for the Arch Diocese of New York: "To burn or otherwise destroy a spurious or corrupt copy of the Bible, whose circulators would tend to disseminate erroneous principles of faith or morals, we hold to be an act not only justifiable but praiseworthy."[46] However, the most outrageous episode of all occurred in 1850 when Archbishop John Hughes of New York City, the nation's leading Vatican spokesman, publicly acknowledged that a conspiracy to subjugate free Americans *did* exist after all! In a message delivered by Hughes in his own cathedral that November entitled "The Decline of Protestantism and its Causes," the religious gangster declared:

> There is [he said] no secret about this. The object we hope to accomplish in time, is to convert all Pagan nations, and all Protestant nations, even England with her proud Parliament and imperial sovereign. **There is no secrecy in all this.** It is the commission of God to his church, and not a human project ... Protestantism pretends to have discovered a great

secret. Protestantism startles our eastern borders occasionally on the intention of the Pope with regard to the Valley of the Mississippi and dreams that it has made a wonderful discovery. Not at all. Everybody should know it. **Everybody should know that we have our mission to convert the world—including the inhabitants of the United States,**—the people of the cities, and the people of the country, the officers of the navy and the marines, commanders of the army, the Legislatures, the Senate, the Cabinet, the President, and all![47]

Even Ray Billington, the liberal pro-Vatican author of *The Protestant Crusade*, was at a loss to explain away such a radical disclosure. In his chapter entitled, "The Catholic Church Blunders," the Harvard graduate resigns himself (and his readers) to the obvious:

Protestants who had for years disregarded the warnings of Morse and his followers as the ravings of fanatical alarmists now heard an acknowledged church leader freely admitting that a Romish plot did exist. The Pope did intend to move to the Mississippi Valley; he did seek to subjugate free America.[48]

The Catholic press went berserk! An excerpt from *Shepherd of the Valley*, the official journal of the bishop of St. Louis, declared: **"If Catholics ever gain a sufficient numerical majority in this country, religious freedom is at an end. So our enemies say, so we believe."**[49] Hughes's own paper, the *New York Freeman*, brazenly announced, **"No man has a right to choose his religion."**[50] This—my friend—is what hate literature is all about!

After Lincoln's election in 1860, conditions moved from bad to worse. Despite a declared neutrality, the "Holy See" was secretly aiding and abetting the Confederacy. The goal of Rome was to divide and conquer Christian America. The *Whore* was after the *Bride*. The degree to which the Vatican State could affect Lincoln's war measures was astounding. Catholic citizens in the North aligned with their Southern brethren by voting Democratic, dodging or defending slavery, and by opposing Lincoln on all political fronts. Irish federals deserted in droves after learning that their "Holy Father" (Pius IX) had dispatched an official communiqué of support to Jefferson Davis, formally addressing him as "The Illustrious and Honorable Jefferson Davis, President of the Confederate States of America."[51] (An English translation of the original Latin may be seen in the *Official Naval Record* under *The War of the*

Rebellion, Series IV, Vol. III, by Brigadier General Fred G. Ainsworth.) When the retreating forces from Lee's debacle at Gettysburg should have been annihilated on the banks of the swollen Potomac, Lincoln's *Catholic* commander, General George Meade "conveniently" diverted a third of his army to securing New York City during the infamous Draft Riots, perpetrated by the rampaging Irish parishioners of Archbishop Hughes. An exasperated Lincoln could only bemoan, "Our army held the war in the hollow of their hand, and they would not close it."[52] Events such as these led Lincoln to write in 1864: "If the American people could learn what I know of the fierce hatred of the priests of Rome against our institutions, our schools, our most sacred rights, and our so dearly bought liberties, they would drive them out as traitors."[53]

Only two days after Vatican hopes for a divided America were ended by Lee's surrender at Appomattox, Lincoln's life was ended by the stealth of a Jesuit plot. At least, this was the conclusion of Brigadier General Thomas M. Harris, U.S.V., one of nine appointed officers comprising the 1865 military commission that tried and condemned the conspirators in the assassination of Abraham Lincoln. These men were noted for their intellectual prowess. General Lew Wallace, for instance, would go on to author the novel *Ben Hur.* Perhaps it was the temperament of the *surgeon,* Dr. Harris, that propelled his private investigation beyond the formal trial. It was during these later years that he was able to compare his expanding notes with those of Reverend Charles Chiniquy. Although formerly a Roman Catholic priest involved in the St. Leopold conspiracy, at the time of their acquaintance, Chiniquy was a born-again Presbyterian pastor with over two thousand parishioners, who had also been a longtime friend of Lincoln's. He would later write his own book, *Fifty Years in the Church of Rome*, relating how he had repeatedly warned the president of his impending assassination. In 1897, the *patriot*, General Harris, released his own explosive volume entitled, *Rome's Responsibility for the Assassination of Abraham Lincoln*. Among other subjects discussed in this chapter, Harris concurs with Rome's infiltration through immigration[54], Reverend Chiniquy's unquestionable integrity[55], and the pope's letter to Jefferson Davis, which triggered a 72 percent desertion rate among the Irish.[56] As to the blame for the assassination itself, Harris writes:

> The *Jesuit* plans with the utmost art and cunning, unhampered by any moral restraints, and always with the utmost secrecy; and carries out his

plans in the dark. We think, however, that in this case, we have succeeded in tracing him through all the devious wanderings of his dark and slimy path, and, in fixing upon him the responsibility for the assassination of President Lincoln.[57]

After presenting his case, General Harris concludes: "Thus the history of this great crime reveals to us *Rome's responsibility for the assassination of Abraham Lincoln*, not as an individual man, however much of personal hatred on the part of the Jesuits might have led them to plan for his death, but as the head of a nation they tried to destroy."[58] In light of this heinous assassination and the Vatican's long-established track record for political intrigue, the hard-hitting General declares, "Every citizen who is loyal to the Roman Catholic Church is an enemy to our government."[59]

The material in this chapter has nothing to do with "hate." It has everything to do with *facts, reality,* and *common sense*. It is about old-time American philosophies like, "Fences make good neighbors." It is about basic survival concepts like, "Your right to swing your fist ends where my nose begins." It centers on the *rule* and not the misleading *exception*. Most importantly, it is about documented *truth* and not how one "feels" about anything. That my own great-grandfather was a Catholic immigrant from Ireland does not alter the "fact" that Catholicism has destroyed the original morality of this nation.

Whereas the spiritual foundation of America had been the Holy Bible, Jesuit agents polluted the land with Latin Masses, wafer gods, confession booths, pedophilic priests, statues, incense pots, idol worship, candles, rosaries, convents, holy days, prayers for the dead, bingo parlors, "Las Vegas nights," and numerous other "doctrines of devils." (I Timothy 4:1) With reference to the King James Bible, Andrew Jackson testified from his deathbed, "That book, Sir, is the Rock upon which our republic rests."[60] However, the newly-arrived "Christians" from Europe looked to their human/"infallible" pope for marching orders in Protestant America. Someone has said that a man's *theology* will dictate his *morality*. By 1850, the immigrants constituted only 11 percent of the population, but 50 percent of the nation's 27,000 criminals.[61] One angry patriot declared, "America has become the sewer into which the pollutions of European jails are emptied."[62] The standard Catholic vices of alcoholism, gambling, prostitution, etc., led to organized crime and general civil unrest. Billington was again forced to concede:

"All the News
That's Fit to Print"

The New York Times

Late Edition
New York: Today, cloudy, some sun late. High 59. Tonight, partly cloudy, mild. Low 50. Tomorrow, cloudy, scattered showers. High 64. Yesterday, high 56, low 48. Details, page B5.

..CXLI. No. 48,771   Copyright © 1991 The New York Times   **NEW YORK, FRIDAY, NOVEMBER 1, 1991**   50 CENTS

LAWMAKERS DEAL A CRIPPLING BLOW TO THE B-2 BOMBER

OUTLOOK DIM FOR STEALTH

Congressional Negotiators Balk at Buying Any New Planes in the New Fiscal Year

By ERIC SCHMITT
Special to The New York Times

WASHINGTON, Oct. 31 — Congressional negotiators dealt the Stealth bomber a nearly fatal blow today by effectively blocking the purchase of any new planes this fiscal year and giving its primary manufacturer, the Northrop Corporation, money only to make parts for future aircraft, planes that may never be built.

The decision leaves Northrop with the Pentagon's initial order for 15 of the radar-evading planes, known as the B-2 bomber, but little prospect for the sale of additional bombers. Each plane costs $865 million.

The Bush Administration, which as recently as last week had hoped to gain Congressional approval for a purchase of at least 35 planes, reduced from the 132 originally planned, may now have to settle for the 15 already ordered and for which money has been appropriated by Congress.

Northrop Expresses Hope

Working to complete the $291 billion Pentagon budget for the fiscal year that began on Oct. 1, a House-Senate Conference committee reached a com-

MIDEAST FOES LIST DEMANDS AND TRADE ANGRY CHARGES ACROSS CONFERENCE TABLE

BUT RIVALS LISTEN

Even Identification With P.L.O. Doesn't Bring an Israeli Walkout

By R. W. APPLE Jr.
Special to The New York Times

MADRID, Oct. 31 — In salvos of intransigent oratory, Israel and its Arab neighbors said today that they all hoped to end the bloodshed in their region, but disagreed about almost everything else — who was at fault, what to do about it, even where further peace talks should be held.

On a day when the Palestinians at last found their place at a major Middle East peace conference, the Arabs demanded that Israel stop creating settlements in occupied territories and give up territory it had taken from Arabs in 1967. The Israelis in turn demanded that the Arabs recognize Israel's right to exist.

Each accused the other of deception, brutality, treachery and aggression, exactly as they have done for most of the 43 years that they have been at each other's throats.

Photographs by Reuters
Haidar Abdel-Shafi, left, the chief Palestinian delegate, and Prime Minister Yitzhak Shamir of Israel at the Middle East peace conference.

Reporter's Notebook

Behind the Conference Babel, A Battle for the High Ground

---

antic Storm Batters the Northeast Again
cious storm battered the Northeast and mid-Atlantic states again rday, causing widespread damage. In Sea Gate, Brooklyn, emer- crews worked along a hard-hit section of beach. Page B1.

Front-page headlines of *The New York Times* for November 1, 1991.
(©*The New York Times*)

President George Bush surveys storm damage to his vacation home on Walkers Point, Kennebunkport, Maine, November 2, 1991.
(AP/Wide World Photos)

"Portrait of a Clergyman" by Guilliam De Ville, c. 1659,
believed to be Dr. John C. Clarke, founder of the first Baptist church in America.
(Redwood Library and Athenaeum, Newport, Rhode Island)

bove: Sign at city limits of Portsmouth, Rhode Island.
(uthor's collection)

ight: Royal Charter of Rhode Island, granted to
r. John Clarke by King Charles II in 1663, preserved
  fireproof, temperature regulated steel vault.
(Rhode Island State House)

elow: Replica of Portsmouth Compact, authored by
r. Clarke, displayed at Founders Brook.
(aptist History Preservation Society)

Above and left: United Baptist Church, John Clarke Memorial, Spring Street, Newport, Rhode Island, constructed in 1846. *(Author's collection)*

Below: John Clarke's grave, located in cemetery on Dr. Wheatland Boulevard, Newport. *(Author's collection)*

Touro Synagogue of Congregation Yeshuat Israel, Newport, Rhode Island, completed in 1763, oldest standing synagogue in America. Trapdoor under the bimah reflects historic tenuous existence of worldwide Jewry.
(Author's collection)

Above: Parsonage of Old South Presbyterian Church, Newburyport, Massachusetts, where George Whitefield succumbed to asthma, September 30, 1770. (*Author's collection*)

Right: Old South Presbyterian Church, constructed in 1740; Whitefield's remains interred under pulpit. (*Author's collection*)

Below: Pastor Jeff Faggart (right), founder and director of the Baptist History Preservation Society, and wife, Danielle, with author and Mrs. Linda Grady in restored Whitefield crypt.

Creek Baptist Church 1802 Meeting House, Liberty, North Carolina.
st History Preservation Society)

Grave of Shubal Stearns on Sandy Creek church grounds.
(Baptist History Preservation Society)

Left: Painting of John Gano baptizing George Washington, displayed above Washington's encased battle sword in the lobby of John Gano Chapel, William Jewel College, Liberty, Missouri.
(Author's collection)

Below: Leland-Madison Memorial Park on Highway 20 (Route of the Constitution), four miles east of Orange, Virginia.
(Baptist History Preservation Society)

This rioting and disorder naturally alarmed many Americans. Their country, long quiet and peaceful ["little house on the prairie"] now seemed teeming with violence. Mob rule was displacing the ordinary forces of law wherever the foreigners were centered.[63]

Well over a century has passed since real Americans like President Jefferson, Professor Morse, Secretary Thompson, Reverend Chiniquy and General Harris sounded their clarion calls on Roman Catholicism. Were they *right*, or were they *wrong*? A recent study revealed that there are 141 Roman Catholics seated in Congress, comprising the largest denomination in that legislative body (more than twice as many as the second-place United Methodist total of sixty-five).[64] With a dozen-plus Catholic governors added to these and several more in the Cabinet and Supreme Court, not to mention the thousands spread out throughout the FBI, CIA, BATF and Pentagon, is it any wonder that Independent Baptist churches continue to experience persecution at every level of government?

Was Jefferson *right*, or was he *wrong*, when he warned that the Catholic immigrants would flood the nation with "unbounded licentiousness?" By 1946, America's 24,402,224 Roman Catholics constituted the nation's largest denomination. For some strange reason, it has rarely dawned on the average American (even, sad to say, on the average Christian) that the traditional Mafia, Syndicate, Cosa Nostra, etc., operating in the United States has been approximately 99 percent Roman Catholic in membership! Organized crime, more than any single factor, is responsible for the dope, pornography, liquor, gambling, prostitution and political corruption that has bankrupted the moral fabric of America. Doesn't it seem just a little strange that one "church" has continued to dominate the membership rosters of the Mafia families in the United States? I mean, when was the last time you ever heard of a *Baptist* hit man? Who do you think is responsible for the adult magazines at *your* local neighborhood minimart?

Of course it would be ludicrous and unfair to imply that the majority of Roman Catholic people are tainted with these propensities. The Catholics with whom I was acquainted in my youth were some of the hardest-working people I have ever known. They were men and women of character and integrity. When the Apostle Paul testified that he had *"great heaviness and continual sorrow"* in his heart for his *"kinsmen according to the flesh,"*(Romans 9:2)—I am able to empathize with that burden. Yet, the question remains: Was Jefferson *right*, or was he *wrong*?

If you think this is just about "hate," ask the next Independent Baptist pastor you meet about his relationship with the local Planning and Zoning Commission.

In 2004, "Brother" Bush was only too happy to cooperate with the Vatican's ongoing invasion of America by recommending amnesty for eight million Roman Catholic illegal immigrants ("To continue in English, press one"). This appeal was made the same month Alabama Chief Justice Roy Moore was thrown out of office for having "taken the law into his own hands" concerning his refusal to remove his Ten Commandments monument.

SECRET SOCIETIES

Whereas slavery and immigration became two of the "open enemies" alluded to in Mr. Madison's postmortem admonition, the role of "Serpent in Paradise" would be filled by the ubiquitous secret society. A hidden foe will naturally pose a greater threat over one that can be seen. Consequently, whenever true history is examined, secret societies are inevitably linked to the ruin of civilization. In his monumental work *The Decline and Fall of the Roman Empire*, Edward Gibbon concluded that five factors destroyed the mighty nation. After listing the more obvious reasons of divorce, taxes, pleasure and despair, the historian gave as his fifth reason: "The existence of an **internal conspiracy**, working to undermine the government from within, all the time that the government was proclaiming that Rome's enemy was external."[65] Addressing the Roman Senate, Cicero said:

> A nation can survive its fools, even the ambitious. But it cannot survive treason from within.
>
> An enemy of the gates is less formidable, for he is known and carries his banner openly. But the traitor moves against those within the gate freely, his sly whispers rustling through all the alleys, heard in the very halls of government itself.
>
> For the traitor appears not a traitor; he speaks in accents familiar to his victims, and he wears their face and their arguments, he appeals to the baseness that lies deep in the hearts of all men. He rots the soul of a nation, he works secretly and unknown in the night to undermine the pillars of the city, he infects the body politic so that it can no longer resist. A murderer is less to fear.[66]

I am of the opinion that few Christians are capable of applying Scriptural principles to the study of secret societies. The majority is either totally ignorant of the conspirators or totally consumed with foiling their ineffable agenda. The rest are just apathetic. As is normally the case, a proper balance is the elusive key to understanding such matters. One must be able to weigh *"we are not ignorant of his devices"* (II Corinthians 2:11b) with *"learn not the way of the heathen"* (Jeremiah 10:2a). Those who pay the price to be properly informed will always grow in Spiritual soberness. This is the single greatest reward for plodding through so much "negativity." The Bible declares, *"he that increaseth knowledge increaseth sorrow"* (Ecclesiastes 1:18b). Our Saviour was *"a man of sorrows, and acquainted with grief"* (Isaiah 53:3b), while the greatest Christian in history confessed, *"I have great heaviness and continual sorrow in my heart"* (Romans 9:2).

The bottom line in all of this is that sober-minded Christians don't "lose their salvation" when a visitor accidentally sits in "their" pew on Sunday morning. This is why the wise man concludes, *"Sorrow is better than laughter: for by the sadness of the countenance the heart is made better"* (Ecclesiastes 7:3). Perhaps you may have noticed what the modern Charismatic filmmakers missed—that despite the Biblical truth *"A merry heart doeth good like a medicine"* (Proverbs 17:22), and despite the fact that our Saviour was perfectly balanced in His humanity (Mark 7:37), a balance that would have included, *"A time to weep, and a time to laugh"* (Ecclesiastes 3:4aq), the Holy Ghost refused to show Jesus and/or the Twelve *ever* laughing about *anything.* (See "Clownsville Revival," Pensacola, Florida.) Although we may not be able to change the downward course of future events (II Timothy 3:13), a sobering awareness of these events *can* and *will* change us!

For a Christian, "spoiled" by an infallible Bible, the study of secret societies can be nebulous, as the ultimate conspirator is both the *"author of confusion"*(I Corinthians 14:33) and the *"father of lies"* (John 8:44), whose disciples will not *"come to the light lest their deeds be reproved"* (John 3:20). However, we can be guided by some common denominators. Arthur Edward Waite, a prolific writer on secret societies, stated, "Beneath the broad tide of human history there flow the stealthy undercurrents of the secret societies, which frequently determine in the depths the changes that take place upon the surface."[67]

Secret societies in any age have constituted the devil's "local assemblies," dedicated to the spreading of evil and the suppression of God's Word. The truth of man's fallen nature and inability to redeem himself has been continually exchanged for a dogma of secular humanism; the Scriptural reality of "Paradise Lost" being discarded for the Fantasy Island "Puddle to Paradise" theory. British historian Nesta Webster writes:

> Throughout the ages the vision of a perfect world wherein the human race should enjoy an equal share in the good things in life, has haunted the imagination of dreamers. Towards this strange mirage countless bands of enthusiasts have marched untiringly, buoyed up with the hope of reaching the green oasis wherein mankind can rest, only to find themselves up against the inexorable laws that govern life on our planet.[68]

While these noble idealists were tripping over their own bootstraps in search of a morsel of bread, a few spooky strangers started hinting around that *they* were in possession of the true "Secret to Success." (See Tony Robbins's Power Pack, etc.) The secularist Webster continues:

> Now, from the earliest times groups of Initiates or "Wise Men" have existed, claiming to be in possession of esoteric doctrines known as the "Mysteries," incapable of apprehension by the vulgar, and relating to the origin and end of man, the life of the soul after death, and the nature of God or the gods. It is this exclusive attitude which constitutes the essential difference between the Initiates of the ancient world and the great Teachers of religion with whom modern occultists seek to confound them. For whilst religious leaders such as Buddha and Mohammed sought for divine knowledge in order that they might impart it to the world, the Initiates believed that sacred mysteries should not be revealed to the profane but should remain exclusively in their own keeping. So although the desire for initiation might spring from the highest aspiration, the gratification, whether real or imaginary, of this desire often led to spiritual arrogance and abominable tyranny, resulting in the fearful trials, the tortures physical and mental, ending even at times in death, to which the neophyte was subjected by his superiors."[69]

Although technically traceable to Cain and his wheelbarrow of vegetables, the majority of occultic authorities point to Egypt as the cradle of secret societies. Thus, we see that the pyramid not only figures prominently in modern spiritualist paraphernalia, but has also found its way to the Great Seal of the United States. (See dollar bill—to the left of "In God We Trust.") Appropriately enough, the serpent reigns as one of the most powerful occultic symbols of all. In his book *The Secret Teachings of All Ages,* Luciferian Manly Hall states:

> Among nearly all these ancient peoples the serpent was accepted as a symbol of wisdom . . . Serpent worship in some form has permeated nearly all parts of the earth. The serpent is the symbol and prototype of the Universal Savior, who redeems the world by giving creation the knowledge of itself and the realization of good and evil.[70]

"Sister" P.K. McCrary's Black Bible Chronicles cuts through all that hot air with her Ebonics translation of Genesis 3:1—"Now the serpent was one bad dude!"

JEWISH SECTS

There are thirty references in the King James Bible to the words *conspiracy, conspirators* and *conspired.* In every instance, the deed is perpetrated by *Jews.* The first appearance is in Genesis 37:18 where Joseph's brethren *"conspired against him to slay him"* (Joseph representing the greatest type of Christ in Scripture). The last reference is in Acts 23:13 (the sole New Testament usage) where a band of fanatical Jews swore a secret oath not to eat anything until they had murdered the Apostle Paul. While the average Christian is too "spiritual" to consider the conspiracy view of history, the Holy Ghost led Luke to write, *"And they were more than forty which had made this **conspiracy**"* (Acts 23:13). And while the four gospels make no reference to the word "conspiracy," you could say that our Saviour's public ministry was both inaugurated and concluded by a violent confrontation with "Jewish bankers." (John 2:14,15; Matthew 21:12)

With the advent of Christianity, the infant church was assailed by several Jewish secret societies. The Gnostics were the first of these aggressors. Whereas the Jewish Messiah had declared, *"I spake openly to the world . . . and in secret have I said nothing"* (John 18:20), the Gnostic whispered condescendingly, "I know something you don't know." Webster states, ". . . the role of the Gnostics was to reduce perversion to a system by binding men together into sects working under the guise of enlightenment in order to obscure all recognized ideas of morality and religion."[71] In Revelation 2:6 and15, the Apostle John referred to these false teachers as Nicolaitanes, from *niko* meaning "to conquer" and *laos* meaning "the people" or "laity." (See modern, warbly-voiced theologians telling the common folk what the original Greek and Hebrew manuscripts say.) Another Jewish sect was known as the Ebionites. The book of Galatians was written to refute their notion of salvation through Christ plus the law. The main Jewish secret society of this time was the Essenes, guardians of the sacred *Cabala*. The *Cabala* was purported to contain the mysteries Moses had learned while in Egypt. In contrast to the Talmud that relates to everyday life, the *Cabala* reveals the theosophical doctrines of Israel. Gnosticism was thus, the cabalizing of Christianity.

Now, while it is "relatively safe" to recognize what the *Bible* reveals about "Jewish conspiracies," *a great amount of wisdom and discretion is required when discussing alleged Jewish machinations beyond 70 A.D.* With the devil as the *"God of this world"* (II Corinthians 4:4), his program of disinformation and revisionism has ensured that *"truth is fallen in the street, and equity cannot enter"* (Isaiah 59:14). The documentation presented in earlier chapters would suggest the following rule of thumb: While Baptist contributions and Vatican atrocities have routinely been *concealed,* Jewish intrigues have routinely been *exaggerated.*

Bible believers possessing a decent grasp of true history are not unable to reconcile their devotion for Israel with substantiated accounts of Jewish complicity in conspiratorial matters. The Jewish Apostle Paul declared that his *"kinsmen according to the flesh"* (Romans 9:3) would never fit into Gentile culture:

> *Who both killed the Lord Jesus, and their own prophets, and have persecuted us; and they please not God, and are **contrary to all men:** Forbidding us to speak to the Gentiles that they might be saved, to fill up their sins alway: for the wrath is come upon them to the uttermost.*
> (I Thessalonians 2:15-16)

In his *Decline and Fall of the Roman Empire,* Edward Gibbons wrote of the Jews: "The sullen obstinacy with which they maintained their peculiar rites and unsocial manners seemed to mark them out a distinct species of men, who boldly professed, or who faintly disguised, their implacable hatred to the rest of humankind."[72] The Jewish-born Benjamin Disraeli, former prime minister of Britain acknowledged, "The native tendency of the Jewish race, who are justly proud of their blood, is against the doctrine of the equality of man."[73]

While the Christ-rejecting Jew is subject to the same Adamic nature as an unconverted Gentile, he is also hampered by four additional factors: his abrasive social nature, his status as a perennial exile, his legacy of suffering and victimization, and his uncanny expertise in financial affairs (a trait which facilitated his survival through the centuries). And so—with the pope's "monarchal muscle" (and to a lesser extent, the Orthodox Czars) constituting his greatest historical nemesis—*why should we be surprised that certain Jews have collaborated with any number of disgruntled Gentile revolutionaries?* While Disraeli wrote, with regard to Jewish involvement in the European revolutions of 1848, "The influence of the Jews may be traced to the last outbreak of the destructive principle in Europe," the following passage from the report of the Netherlands minister, Heir Oudendyke, in Petrograd (as forwarded to Mr. Balfour on September 17, 1918), was contained in the official Foreign Office White Paper in April 1919, concerning the subject of Bolshevism:

> The danger is now so great that I feel that it my duty to call the attention of the British and all other Governments to the fact that if an end is not put to Bolshevism in Russia at once the civilization of the whole world will be threatened. This is not an exaggeration, but a sober matter of fact. . . . I consider that the immediate suppression of Bolshevism is the greatest issue now before the world, not even excluding the war which is still raging, and unless, as stated above, Bolshevism is nipped in the bud immediately, it is bound to spread in one form or another over Europe and the whole world, as it is organized and worked by Jews who have no nationality, and whose one object is to destroy for their own ends the existing order of things. The only manner in which this danger could be averted would be collective action on the part of all the powers."[74]

Now you can better understand why Karl Marx, the Jewish founder of modern Communism would write:

> I wish to avenge myself against the One who rules above. We must war against all prevailing ideas of religion, of the state, of country, of patriotism. The idea of God is the keynote of a perverted civilization. It must be destroyed.[75]

Notwithstanding such forgeries as the *Protocols of the Elders of Zion,* some of the worst "hate literature" in history has been penned by well-known Jewish authors. James Darmester, a distinguished Jewish writer in the early twentieth century, proclaimed the end of Christianity and blasphemously described, through the eyes of Hell's minions, the descent of Jesus Christ into eternal damnation!

> And a sigh passed over that world of chaos, and Hell shuddered to the deepest fibres of its roots. And a light shone in the night from all those burning eyes . . . and I saw a spectre descending from afar off on high. He came—slowly, but without stopping or turning his head. It was Christ, the Son of Man, the Son of the Virgin! . . . Hell also knew him, and Hell's thousand legions leapt forward to welcome their approaching guest . . . And a tremendous shout burst from the throat of the pit: "So you have come at last Galilean! So here you are, stricken, just as we are; no different from ourselves! How did you fall from Heaven, Star of the Stars, Son of the Virgin? You, who used to say in your heart: I am God, world without end; I shall reign for eternity from the highest throne in Heaven, above the stars and the broken idols, and my name alone shall ring in men's ears. And now in turn your star has been cast down and broken, cedar of Lebanon, and you, the great mocker of dead gods, you too descend among the gods who live no more."
>
> Little has changed in the progress of the world. Nature is unmoved by the spectacle of this great defeat, and as always happens after events which seem to exceed the limits of tolerance assigned to her, she continues, indifferent, upon her eternal course.[76]

The protracted inspiration for this orthodox hatred of Christianity may be traced to the Talmud itself. A myriad of slander against the Jewish Messiah was inserted to further deceive a people already suffering *"blindness in part"* (Romans 11:25). This is what Jesus was alluding to with His denunciations, *"But woe unto you, scribes and Pharisees, hypocrites! for ye shut up the kingdom of heaven against men"* (Matthew 23:13) and, *"Woe unto you, lawyers! for ye have taken away the key of knowledge"* (Luke 11:52). Webster cites Barclay's comments on the earlier editions of the Talmud:

> Our Lord and Saviour is "that one," "such a one," "a fool," "the leper," "the deceiver of Israel," etc. Efforts are made to prove that He is the Son of Joseph Pandira before his marriage with Mary. His miracles are attributed to sorcery, the secret of which He brought in a slit in His flesh out of Egypt. He is said to have been first stoned and then hanged on the eve of the Passover. His disciples are called heretics and opprobrious names.

They are accused of immoral practices, and the New Testament is called a sinful book. The references to these subjects manifest the most bitter aversion and hatred.[77]

However, not only were the *Jews* kept from the *truth*, but the *Gentiles* were kept from the *lies*! As late as 1925, Webster wrote:

> One might look in vain for passages such as these in English or French translations of the Talmud, for the reason that no complete translation exists in these languages. This fact is of great significance. Whilst the sacred books of every other important religion have been rendered into our own tongue and are open to everyone to study, the book that forms the foundation of modern Judaism is closed to the general public. We can read English translations of the Koran, of the Dhammapada, of the Sutta Nipata, of the Zend Avesta, of the Shu King, of the Laws of Manu, of the Bhagavadgita, but we cannot read the Talmud.[78]

And of course, "emergency" expurgated editions of the Hebrew Talmud would keep pace with the acquiring of that ancient tongue in various Christian lands.

In the "spirit of fairness," it is just as wrong to represent the Jews, in a collective sense, as a gentle, longsuffering people, always the victims—never the perpetrators of violence—as it would be to indict all Jews for the machinations of some. *"For they are not all Israel, which are of Israel"* (Romans 9:6b) and there will always be these who *"say they are Jews, and are not, but do lie"* (Revelation 3:9b). One should never ignore *any* of the facts nor implicate *all* of the people. Christians need to rightly divide between the writings of James Darmester and the *Diary of Anne Frank*. To summarize, *"As concerning the gospel, they are enemies for your sakes: but as touching the election, they are beloved for the fathers' sakes."* (Romans 11:28).

Thus, a proper spiritual balance will enable the Christian to acknowledge that certain elements within the blinded Jewish race have mightily opposed the Gospel, while further recognizing that these rebellious sons of Abraham possess a providential "diplomatic immunity" of sorts. Though David was aware that his treacherous (Jewish) king was out to get him, he nonetheless commanded, *"Destroy him not: for who can stretch forth his hand against the LORD'S anointed, and be guiltless?"* (I Samuel 26:9). A "healthy" application of this truth will lead a Christian to *keep his negative observations to a minimum.* When the Amalekite soldier excitedly informed David that he had slain King Saul, he promptly got the shock of his life when David asked him, *"How wast thou not afraid to stretch forth thine hand to destroy the LORD's anointed?* (II Samuel 1:14). He then received an even bigger jolt from the last words he ever heard this side of eternity:

> *And David called one of the young men, and said, Go near, and fall upon him. And he smote him that he died. And David said unto him, Thy blood be upon thy head; for thy mouth hath testified against thee, saying, I have slain the LORD's anointed.* (II Samuel 1:15-16)

Even in their rejection, the *"naughtiest figs"* (Jeremiah 24:2) have served a divine purpose in effecting world affairs. As the Lord declared, *". . . neither are your ways my ways . . ."* (Isaiah 55:8b), one of His mysterious doings has been to allow a disproportionate number of Jewish bankers to *participate* in the financing of those endless military campaigns throughout the *"times of the Gentiles"* (Luke 21:24). Someone has rightly concluded, "Hell is God's judgment on the dead, while war is God's judgment on the living." Combining an aphorism of Mirabeau with one of Werner Sombart's, gives the accurate historical perspective: "War is the national industry of Prussia," and, "Wars are the Jews' harvests."[79]

However, while the Bible cautions circumspection regarding Jewish culpability, it mandates exposure of Roman Catholic corruption. (I Timothy 4:6) It was the Vatican contrived Gunpowder Plot of 1605 that nearly succeeded in blowing King James to "kingdom come"! *If the truth were known, the Jesuits would make the most notorious Jewish conspirators look like Sunday School teachers in comparison.* Yet, for some strange reason, "Jewish plots" get far more publicity than Catholic ones do. (On December 31, 2003, a spot check of the Google search engine for the topic "Roman Catholic conspiracies" revealed 8,830 entries while the topic "Jewish conspiracies" revealed over three times that number at 26,900 entries.)

Finally, the most unusual insight of all just may be the one that is most obvious. Exactly what is the worst-case scenario regarding Jewish participation in "Old World" revolutions? According to the King James Bible, the Roman Catholic Church is guilty of being *"drunken with the blood of the saints"* (Revelation 17:6). When we all get to Heaven, maybe God will show us that while the Vatican was busy murdering

Christians, the Jews were busy undermining the Catholics. At least the principle behind this theory was marvelously confirmed when Jews were finally able to live in a persecution-free environment. Can you think of any practical reasons why the Jewish immigrants at Ellis Island would begin to conspire against their Goldenah Medinah?

This is why the Israeli Cabinet declared September 12, 2001, a national day of mourning, ordering flags flown at half-staff, while Palestinians in the West Bank openly danced in the streets shouting, "God is great," and distributed candy. While grieving Jewish citizens donated blood and displayed American flags, Palestinian children flashed the victory sign while their parents honked car horns and fired automatic weapons into the air. Jerusalem's main thoroughfare, Jaffa Road, was even renamed "New York Street" for a period of thirty days.

Meanwhile, conspiracy "expert" Texe Marrs warned the Body of Christ in his January 2004, *Power of Prophecy* newsletter that Hillary Clinton, John F. Kerry, Howard Dean and Wesley Clark "are hiding the fact that they are Jewish," and that "stealth Jews have now seized control of the Democratic Party." Another issue of concern was expressed in the publication's front-page headline—"Michael Jackson's Rabbi Attacks Mel Gibson and the New Testament." According to Marrs, Orthodox Rabbi Schmuley Boteach, a recent "spiritual advisor" to Jackson (a longtime Jehovah's Witness) attacked the Roman Catholic Gibson's Hollywood movie, *The Passion of Christ.*

ISLAM

Following the development of other Gnostic sects, such as the Cainites, Carpocratians, Antitacts, Marcosians, Valentinians, Basilideans and serpent-worshiping Ophites, a number of Muslim secret societies flourished in the wake of Islam and its subsequent schisms (circa 632 A.D.). Some of the more notable Islamic cults were the Shiahs, Ismailis, Karmathites, Fatimites, Druses and Assassins. After four centuries of killing one another in the name of Allah, the "Muslim brotherhood" had to get their act together, as another religious show was coming to town—all the way from Rome.

THE KNIGHTS TEMPLAR

A major unforeseen aftermath of the bloody Crusades was the westward transfer of Eastern mysticism by way of the Knights Templar. In the year 1118, nearly two decades after the first Crusade ended with the Muslims' defeat and the capture of Jerusalem, nine French *gentilshommes* of Picardy, led by Hughes de Payens and Godefroi de Saint-Omer, formed themselves into a society, purportedly to ensure the safety of pilgrims headed for the Holy Sepulcher. One of the "perks" provided by King Baldwin II of Jerusalem was a house near the site of Solomon's Temple—hence, the acquired name of Knights Templar. The enormous donations which resulted from their initial exploits of bravery eventually led to corruption and conspiracy. First, they learned the scam of fractional banking in Alexandria, Egypt. Next, they started cutting deals with the Muslim Assassins, resulting in the defeat of other "Christian" forces. Finally, through their repeated fraternizing with the enemy, the Templars were made privy to a number of Eastern mysteries.

Deluded by these paths to greater power and wealth, the Knights Templar descended into a diabolical fraternity that centered around the worship of Baphomet (Satan). When they eventually returned to France, King Phillipe le Bel felt threatened by their mysterious and independent ways. In 1312, a royal crackdown ensued after word leaked out that initiates for this Christian organization were required to spit on a crucifix. The Grand Master of the Order, Jacques du Molay, and several of his henchmen were tried and executed.

One must understand at this point that the society itself was not extinguished, only driven into further concealment. The Chevalier de Malet writes:

> [T]hose who had escaped the storm afterwards met in obscurity so as to re-knit the ties that had united them, and in order to avoid fresh denunciations they made use of allegorical methods which indicated the basis of their association in a manner unintelligible to the eyes of the vulgar.[80]

"Christian" Europe would now become the Western repository of Eastern devil-worship. The Knights Templar constitute the vangard of Japhethic, Gentile conspirators.

THE ROSICRUCIANS

In the year 1614, an anonymous pamphlet was printed in Cassel, Germany, entitled *Fama Fraternitatis,* relating how a former monastic student, Christian Rosenkreutz, had discovered the secrets of the universe while traveling in Arab lands toward the close of the fourteenth century. Supposedly, Chris went on to establish the "hush-hush*" Fraternity of the Rose Cross* to guard these sacred mysteries before expiring in 1484 at the age of 106. Though the founder's story is probably legend, most esoteric authorities contend that the Rosicrucians themselves represent an historic reincarnation of the Knights Templar.[81]

Because *"the love of money is the root of all evil"* (I Timothy 6:10a), the most coveted mystery in any society was *alchemy*—the art of transmuting base metals into gold. The practice was also supposed to be capable of producing the so-called "philosopher's stone" through which one could gain immortality. Rosicrucians were addicted to the "spiritual" interpretation of natural science. According to one tradition, the word "rose" was not taken from the flower depicted on the Rosicrucian Cross, but rather from the Latin *res* signifying "dew," which was supposedly the most powerful solvent of gold, while *crux*, the cross, was the chemical hieroglyphic for "light."[82] They were also into child sacrificing, cherishing toads, dancing with fiends, making poisonous powders and pacts with the devil.[83]

The reader will note that we are now within chronological view of America. The pertinent question becomes—What have all these secret societies to do with the founding and latter history of the United States? William Still writes, "By the dawn of the 1700s, all along the Eastern seaboard, most of the important secret societies of Europe already had sturdy footholds in colonial America."[84] Hall adds, "The brotherhoods met in their rooms over inns and similar public buildings, practicing their ancient rituals exactly according to the fashion in Europe and England."[85] Thus, the serpents were now loose in Paradise.

THE NEW ATLANTIS

Perhaps the man most responsible, yet least recognized, for America's early colonization as well as the inception of her secret societies was none other than the renowned British statesman, Sir Francis Bacon (1561-1626). William Still, who has written for *USA Today, The Saturday Evening Post*, the *Los Angeles Times Syndicate* and *Omni Magazine*, wrote of Bacon in his book, *New World Order: The Ancient Plan of Secret Societies:*

> In the early 1600s Bacon authored a novel entitled *New Atlantis*, which laid out the idea for a utopian society across the ocean from Europe where mankind could build a new civilization based upon the principles he believed to be those of the legendary lost continent of Atlantis.[86]

One might ask how a stuffy British philosopher would be acquainted with the occultic paradise of Atlantis. Nesta Webster relates, "As we have already seen, Bacon is recognized to have been a Rosicrucian."[87] Baconian scholar and secret society enthusiast Marie Bauer Hall described Sir Francis as, "the guiding light of the Rosicrucian Order, the members of which kept the torch of true universal knowledge, the Secret Doctrine of the ages, alive during the dark night of the Middle Ages."[88] She further states:

> Bacon had been initiated into the new liberalism represented throughout Europe by Secret Societies of intellectuals dedicated to civil and religious freedom . . . Later, when the movement was propitious, he threw the weight of his literary group with the English colonization plan for America . . . cherishing as he did the dream of a great commonwealth in the New Atlantis.[89]

Still adds:

> Bacon formulated a complex and far-reaching plan to reorder the world and everything in it. As revealed in another of his books, *Instauratio Magna*, the plan would reorganize the sciences and restore man to that mastery over nature that he was conceived to have lost by the fall of Adam. Bacon envisaged knowledge as a pyramid with natural history as its base, physics as the middle, and metaphysics as the vertical point."[90]

Sir Walter Raleigh began the British colonization of America in 1585 with his gold-hunting expedition to Roanoke Island, off the coast of what is now North Carolina. The twenty-four-year-old nobleman was already a member of a secret society that would later be known as the Baconian Circle. Almost as if to tell the devil that the Tar Heel State was set apart for Shubal Stearns and the Sandy Creek Baptist Church, God allowed the local savages to completely annihilate the Roanoke settlement. In fact, all that was ever found by later rescue parties were four unintelligible letters—CROA—carved into the trunk of a nearby tree. Maybe it stood for—*Catastrophe Resembling Old Atlantis.*

Twenty-two years later, a second attempt at colonization was made at Jamestown, Virginia. Francis Bacon was one of the early members of the chartered Virginia Company. However, because these materialistic fools came for the same golden chamber pots that the Roanoke adventurers had searched for, their escapade was doomed from the start. The starving pioneers of Bacon's second *New Atlantis* were constrained to partake of cadaver stew in the rapidly expanding graveyard. And to add insult to injury, the flagship of a rescue fleet wrecked near the *Bermuda Triangle* in 1609.

As their Pilgrim cousins arrived at Plymouth in 1620 with a Scriptural agenda, we would expect to see an appreciable difference in the "blessings department." While Governor Bradford's settlers were able to say grace over their Thanksgiving feast *the first year they arrived,* that same year (the fifteenth anniversary of Jamestown), over one thousand of the twelve hundred new arrivals in Virginia starved to death.

For the record, the major difference in these colonies, apart from motives, was that the Lord gave the Pilgrim Fathers wisdom to reject the system of communalism foisted on them by the London merchants who had financed their settlement. Having assigned each family their own plot of land to work, Bradford reported in his journal, "This had very good success; for it made all hands very industrious."[91] In later years the spiritual governor would blast the welfare mentality accordingly:

> The vanity and conceit of Plato and other ancients . . . that the taking away of property, and bringing [it] in community . . . would make them happy and flourishing; as if they were wiser than God . . . [However, it] was found to breed much confusion and discontent, and retard much employment that would have been to their benefit and comfort.[92]

With this first serpent of communism temporarily removed, others more poisonous were coiling up to strike. The remainder of this volume will examine some of the deadliest secret societies to ever sink their fangs into America. But first we must answer the cynics.

6

Limbaugh's Kooks

*"Answer a fool according to his folly, lest
he be wise in his own conceit."*
(Proverbs 26:5)

THERE ARE ONLY two ways in which the events of world
history can be interpreted: the *accidental* (big bang theory,
evolution, etc.) and the *conspiratorial* position. To endorse the
latter is to be branded with the "lunatic fringe." Rousas Rushdoony wrote
in *The Nature of the American System*,

> In the eyes of most intellectuals, the hallmark of intellectual acceptability
> is to view history as the outworking of impersonal forces and factors,
> whereas the epitome of absurd, irrational and even dangerously reactionary
> thinking is to regard history as in any sense *conspiracy*. Such a view is
> primitive and naive; it is a form of belief in the devil, we are told.[1]

In his book *The West In Crisis*, James Warburg explains the accidental
view thus: "History is written more by accident than design, often by the
wholly irrational acts of madmen."[2] Another proponent of "evolutionary
history" is Zbigniew Brzezinski, former National Security Advisor for
President Jimmy Carter, who wrote, "History is much more the product of
chaos than of conspiracy . . . increasingly, policy makers are overwhelmed
by events and information."[3] To the contrary, however, Robert Welch,
founder of the John Birch Society used to say, "There are only two
schools of thought concerning views of history: those who believe in
conspiracy and those who have never studied it." Even Franklin Roosevelt
was willing to admit, "In politics, nothing happens by accident. If it

happens, it was planned that way."[4] Professor Antony Sutton notes how the so-called intellectual has missed the most obvious conspiracy of all:

> [T]he only reasonable explanation for recent history in the United States is that there exists a conspiracy to use political power for ends which are inconsistent with the Constitution. This is known by the official historians as "the devil theory of history," which again is a quick, cheap device for brushing facts under the rug. However, these critics ignore, for example, the Sherman Act, i.e., the anti-trust laws where conspiracy is the basic accepted theory. If there can be a conspiracy in the market place, then why not the political arena? Are politicians any purer than businessmen?[5]

The same would apply to the corrupting influence of organized crime on the combustible combination of gambling and professional or collegiate sports (point-shaving, dive-taking, etc.).

How could a thinking person ridicule conspiracy history if he was able to read a simple dictionary? According to the *Merriam-Webster Dictionary, Second Edition*, the word *conspiracy* is defined as follows:

> (1) "a combination of men for an evil purpose; an agreement between two or more persons to commit a crime in concert, as treason; a plot"; (2) "a combination of men for a single end; a concurrence, or general tendency, as of circumstances, to one event; harmonious action."

The prestigious *Black's Law Dictionary* adds:

> An agreement by two or more persons to commit an unlawful act; a combination for an unlawful purpose.

In 1977, my pregnant wife and I were held up at gunpoint by two doped-up "African-Americans" in a restaurant parking lot. This crime would fit Webster's definition for the word "conspiracy." Rushdoony goes on to apply this concept to what a lost man cannot comprehend:

> It is at once obvious that, in all three senses, conspiracy exists, and that, in the second sense it is present in all kinds of organizations and institutions. ... History, therefore, is not the outworking of impersonal forces but a personal conflict between the forces of God and anti-God, Christ and antichrist, with the ultimate victory assured to God and His Christ. The Bible as a whole presents a view of *history as conspiracy,* with Satan and man determined to assert their "right" to be gods, knowing or determining, good and evil for themselves (Genesis 3:5). From beginning to end, this is the

perspective of Scripture, and only a willful misreading of it can lead to any other position.[6]

According to Rushdoony, the conspiracy view of history is summarized in Psalm 2, the most frequently quoted psalm in the New Testament: "The whole world is seen as organized against the Lord in deliberate opposition to His rule, for David sees, not himself, but the Lord Messiah as the true being."[7]

In the face of these spiritual realities, a number of reasons will explain why most people, saved or lost, reject the conspiracy view of history. First and foremost is *because conspiracy history represents an extreme intrusion into one's self-contained ideological bubble of optimism.* The reason why men work so hard at making money is because they plan on eventually enjoying the fruit of their labors. Whether they believe in an afterlife or not, their focus is on the temporal present. *"Surely every man walketh in a vain shew: surely they are disquieted in vain: he heapeth up riches, and knoweth not who shall gather them"* (Psalm 39:6). In the parable of the rich young fool, Jesus put it this way:

> *The ground of a certain rich man brought forth plentifully: And he thought within himself, saying, What shall I do, because I have no room where to bestow my fruits? And he said, This will I do: I will pull down my barns, and build greater; and there will I bestow all my fruits and my goods. And I will say to my soul, Soul, thou hast much goods laid up for many years; take thine ease, eat, drink, and be merry. But God said unto him, Thou fool, this night thy soul shall be required of thee: then whose shall those things be, which thou hast provided? So is he that layeth up treasure for himself, and is not rich toward God.* (Luke 12:16b-21)

An apostate Christian in the Laodicean church age is hardly any different. ("Something good is going to happen to you," etc.) In his own mad dash for a slice of the pie, the professing born-again believer completely ignores the Bible's admonition, *"Set your affection on things above, not on things on the earth"* (Colossians 3:2). For saved and unsaved materialists alike, the message of a bona fide "conspiracy nut" is a psychological nightmare, second only to the testimony and witness of a spiritual, Bible-believing Christian. If conspiracy history is true, then the non-Christian optimist is forced to "dis" (Ebonics for "reject") the security he received from his anthropology professors in college. How could man be getting better and better and still be plotting to enslave one another in the end? (See Orwell's *1984.*) Maybe Jesus was right after all when he said, "*. . . and he that hath no sword, let him sell his garment, and buy one*" (Luke 22:36b). And getting saved sure couldn't hurt matters any!

The carnal Christian is also forced to make some "philosophical adjustments." His problem is not *physical* evolution, but rather *spiritual* evolution. In exchange for an anemic message of positivism that avoids such politically incorrect themes as mothers working outside the home, "legalistic" dress standards, interracial dating and marriage, "one, two, three, repeat after me" soul winning, dispensational salvation and conspiracy history, he has agreed to accept the post-millennial pipe dreams of any number of fundamentalist kingdom builders that national revival and world evangelism are reachable goals *this side of the Rapture!* (Matthew 24:14) The fact that an entire generation of Independent Baptist cannon fodder has burned out physically, mentally, spiritually and financially while reading such well-intentioned "classics" as *We Can Have Revival Now* and *Why Revival Tarries* means absolutely nothing to the new leaders of the old-time religion! ("Casualties are what war is all about," etc.) The irrefutable evidence for conspiracy history confirms the dispensational precept that everything man touches eventually disintegrates. Conspiracy history is unpopular because it forces man to face his failure as a "species." Thus we read in Psalm 39:5c, "*. . . verily every man at his best state is altogether vanity. Selah.*"

Therefore *any* alternative view will be readily entertained by a nervous intelligentsia. Enter political comedian extraordinaire Rush Limbaugh— a self-proclaimed "harmless little fuzzball" who utilizes his "talent on loan from God" to administrate the Limbaugh Institute for Advanced Conservative Studies. According to "El Rushbo" (as he likes to be called) he is also, "A man whom hundreds, perhaps even thousands, of American mothers hope their daughters will someday marry. (Many of these mothers no doubt harbor the same fantasy for themselves.)"[8] It is no coincidence that Rush is adored by *all* political conservatives, saved and unsaved unlike. The reason is because he gives his listeners what they all want to hear. At the conclusion of his book, *The Way Things Ought To Be,* Rush offers the following assurance to his twelve million Republican "ditto heads":

> Conservatives are an ever-growing majority. So take heart, dear reader. Don't get down. Remember how I handle them [the liberals]. **I laugh at their outrageous statements and I ridicule their latest lunacies.** So

should you. Laugh and move on. They are past. We conservatives are the future. So don't give up. Be confident. This country has not run out of opportunity. Your children can live in an America that is better, safer, more moral, and more prosperous. ["Do it again, Lord!" etc.] Those who would tear down the great traditions of this country are, in fact, losing. Don't misunderstand. They haven't lost—they won't ever be totally defeated—[Yo, Rush, try Revelation 19:11-16]—but they can be greatly deemphasized. This is a never-ending battle and if you want to follow the chronicling of their demise and learn about the people who are helping make America great again, I can think of no better way than for you to tune in to **my** radio and TV shows. I must warn you, however. Both are **highly addictive.**[9]

Through the years, however, El Rushbo's "positive" solutions have been increasingly challenged by a different breed of conservative who has insisted on discussing the *real* enemies of America. Unfortunately, though predictably, with far more important issues at stake (ratings, salary, fan adulation, etc.), the man in control of the microphone has chosen to stick with his game plan to "laugh at *their* outrageous statements" and "ridicule *their* latest lunacies." Anyone who would dare to suggest a conspiracy view of history on the *Rush Limbaugh Show* would henceforth be labeled as a "kook."

Rush has employed this technique of intimidation by ridicule in a number of ways. First, he has assured his listeners that he was once an avid reader of conspiracy material himself, but came to the conclusion that it was bunk. (Thanks for doing our thinking for us, Rush.) Another escape he has used is to point out any number of idiots who are presented as being credible conspiracy theorists. Lots of cowards use this approach by pitting the exception against the rule. Pervert Jerry Springer likes to feature "Ku Klux Klan families" with three-and four-year-olds dressed in robes and hoods sporting swastikas. A number of professing Christians like Donald McAlvany, Gary North and Jack Van Impe brought great reproach on the Body of Christ by their failed predictions concerning the Y2K "crisis." Many of these "prophets" will answer to God for the "profits" they made with their pre-Y2K sales of gold coins and survival paraphernalia. Yet, their ministries continue unabated. McAlvany even had a new book released less than two months after Chicken Little's sky refused to fall, January 1, 2000. (Deuteronomy 18:20-22)

Perhaps the most aggressive Limbaugh tactic has been a straw man approach concerning "how" the conspirators conspire their conspiracies.

According to Rush, if one believes in conspiracy history, then he must also believe in it the way Rush says he must. Thus, if you believe the races exhibit any number of noticeable differences (see 2004 NBA champion Detroit Pistons' victory mantra—"Fear the Fro!"), then you must *hate* people. He implies that a conspiracy "kook" believes that once or twice per year a secret meeting is held somewhere in the world with all of the major players in attendance. Seated before "Mr. Big" (identity unknown) are people like Alan Greenspan, Bill and Hillary Clinton, Lord Rothschild, Dan Rather, David Rockefeller, the pope, Billy Graham, Ted Turner, Walter Cronkite, Kofi Annan, the Dalai Lama, William F. Buckley, Jr., Gerhardt Schroeder, Javier Solana, Zbigniew Brzezinski, George H. W. Bush, Paul Volcker, King Juan Carlos, Jimmy Carter, Henry Kissinger, Fidel Castro, Ross Perot, Mikhail Gorbachev, Winston Lord, Ted Kennedy, Nelson Mandela, Jesse Jackson, Tony Robbins, and good ol' Newt Gingrich. And, as the scenario goes, they spend the entire meeting coordinating future assaults on the United States of America and Christianity in general.

I do not know a single conspiracy theorist who believes such a thing. Yes, there *are* secret meetings (try any of a dozen New World Order groups such as the Bohemian Grove, Bilderbergers, Club of Rome, Knights of Malta, etc.). And yes, the names I have mentioned *are* part of a conspiracy. The missing piece of the puzzle is that the conspiracy is a *satanic* conspiracy. According to I Corinthians 2:14 this is something that is beyond the comprehension of Rush Limbaugh, and for that matter, unfathomable by the best of the non-Christian conspiracy theorists themselves. Neither are many born-again believers spiritual enough to understand such things. The renowned Christian conspiracy theorist, Dr. Joe M. Boyd, told this author that women would frequently hide out in the church nursery during his "heavy, negative" messages.

The Bible's bottom line on the conspirators as a group is found in Paul's second letter to Timothy. *"This know also, that in the last days perilous times shall come. . . . But evil men and seducers shall wax worse and worse, **deceiving, and being deceived"** (II Timothy 3:1,13). These passages afford significant insight to the activities of end-day conspirators. The key thought is that such people are both deceivers *and* deceived themselves. Satan, the arch conspirator, has them all convinced that the world is theirs for the taking. As the book of Genesis reveals the precise design of an Almighty Creator, *history records the subsequent attempts by Lucifer to destroy that creation with equal calculation and* *precision.* Thus the wickedness in any generation can ultimately be ascribed to the devil's master conspiracy *". . . against the LORD, and against his anointed. . . ."* (Psalm 2:2) People like Lord Rothschild and David Rockefeller are merely satanic dupes. In the meantime, there is no way to understand how badly the minds of such men have been deceived. Some of the "lower echelon" conspirators may actually be convinced that their agenda will really make a difference in the world. (Mathew 7:21-22) There was a day when Hillary Clinton campaigned for conservative Republicans and Tipper Gore preached against rock music; *". . . yea, the time cometh, that whosoever killeth you will **think** that he doeth God service"* (John 16:2).

As for everyone sitting around a table in cooperative unity, history confirms that the devil's crowd has been at one another's throats for over six millennia. Near the end of the Tribulation, the woman gets thrown off the beast and burned with fire. (Revelation 17:16) However, though they will buck one another to acquire more "bucks," they are united in spirit. Every power broker in the world has a mindset that is totally against the Holy Word of God. In II Thessalonians 2:7, Paul called it "the mystery of iniquity." In I John 4:3, John called it "the spirit of antichrist." This willingness to unite against a common enemy was illustrated during our Saviour's passion: *"And the same day Pilate and Herod were made friends together: for before they were at enmity between themselves"* (Luke 23:12).

The main folks who have cooperated with each other throughout history have been the international bankers. It was Heinrich Heine who said, "Money is the God of our times, and Rothschild is his prophet."[10] As the bumper sticker says, "Whoever dies with the most toys wins!" The really important secret meetings are the ones that are called by the money crowd. On August 5, 1995, *The New York Times* published an article by Keith Bradsher, in which he wrote:

> In a small Swiss city sits an international organization so obscure and secretive. . . . Control of the institution, the Bank for International Settlements, lies with some of the world's most powerful and least visible men: the heads of thirty-two central banks, officials able to shift billions of dollars and alter the course of economies at the stroke of a pen.[11]

Dr. Dennis Cuddy writes,

> On June 28, 1998, *The Washington Post* published an article about the Bank for International Settlements (BIS) titled, "At Secret Meetings in Switzerland, 13 People Shape the World's Economy," which described these individuals as "this economic cabal . . . this secretive group . . . the financial barons who control the world's supply of money."[12]

After financial consultant Joan Veon sat in on the business meeting of the Bank for International Settlements in June, 1998, she wrote in her newsletter that

> the Bank for International Settlements designed the present borderless flow of monies between countries when it pushed for the deregulation (1980) of monetary laws of the major North American, European, and Asian countries. By tearing down national financial borders, they created the ability for $1.2 trillion daily to flow around the world (uncontrolled stateless money) looking for the highest interest or fastest currency play.[13]

Dr. Cuddy adds,

> On ABC television's "Nightline" (July 1, 1998), David Turecamo stated concerning certain international investors, that they can "topple politicians with the click of a mouse . . . who can move huge amounts of money into and out of markets in a nanosecond . . . Money knows no allegiance. There is no patriotism." Host Ted Koppel's response to that was, "Wouldn't you know it, when we're the last remaining superpower, it doesn't count anymore. Is that what you're saying?" And Turecamo replied, "That's it. That's exactly it."[14]

On another *Nightline* program a decade previously (September 29, 1988), Koppel, a member of the Council on Foreign Relations, referred to nationalism as a "virus."[15] What's that, you say—*you don't recall hearing any of this on the Excellence in Broadcasting Network?* Well, I for one do not know the names of the financiers who come and go at the Bank for International Settlements. However, a short list of good prospects would include men like David Rockefeller (U.S.A.), George Soros, Lord Rothschild and Lord Carrington (Great Britain), Harry Oppenheimer (South Africa), Rupert Murdoch (Australia), Prince Bernhard (The Netherlands), Giovanni Agnelli (Italy) and Heinrich von Pierer (Germany).

In a further attempt to discredit conspiracy theorists, the president of the Limbaugh Institute for Advanced Conservative Studies created and posted, on his website, the now famous *Rush Limbaugh's Kook Test*. The text of this insightful litmus test is as follows:

RUSH LIMBAUGH'S KOOK TEST

1. Do you believe that powerful Americans are behind a world conspiracy to destroy the sovereignty of the United States of America?

2. Do you believe that "The New World Order" is a secret phrase used by conspirators to identify themselves to one another in a crowd?

3. Do you believe that the Federal Reserve System exists primarily as an institution for the conspirators to enrich themselves, while at the same time destroying the United States?

4. Do you believe that the eye in the pyramid on the dollar bill is a secret code of The New World Order?

5. Do you believe that David Rockefeller, Henry Kissinger, and other famous One Worlders provide daily instructions to agents of the FBI, BATF, Interpol, and the CIA?

6. Do you believe the CFR and the Trilateral Commission serve as the front groups to train and indoctrinate future One Worlders, who seek to destroy the United States of America?

7. Do you believe that the Trilateral Commission was created because too many bright people were on to the CFR and its insidious designs?

8. Do you believe that CFR black helicopters flown by U.N. pilots have been in the sky when American citizens have been shot?

9. Do you believe that the feminist movement was the brainchild of David Rockefeller for the express purpose of having men and women at war with each other, so as to be distracted on a daily basis from the real work of the CFR, which is to destroy the sovereignty of the United States of America?

10. Do you consider Newt Gingrich to be a threat to your personal freedom?

If you have answered just one of these questions in the affirmative, not two of ten, not six of ten, not eight of ten, if you have answered just one of these questions yes, then you are a kook.

Did you catch those incredible straw men in questions two, four, and especially, number five? I mean, *really*, a "secret phrase" *to identify one another*? Tut, tut! By the way, Rush, where do *you* get off labeling Rockefeller and Kissinger as "famous One Worlders"? Is this what you *really* believe, or was it merely a Freudian slip? You're not a closet conspiracist, are you? And could we add *CIA* plots to question number eight? (By the way, who *was* piloting the helicopter that fired those murderous rounds at Waco?) Would it be okay if we isolated the phrase "destroy the *sovereignty* of the United States" from the rest of the hype in question number nine? Of course, any edition of the CFR's official publication, *Foreign Affairs,* would acknowledge that the Council's primary goal for over *eighty years* has been to foster global government, or, as you call it in question two, a "New World Order." I believe that this would have something to do with destroying the sovereignty of *all* nations. In the 1994 Fall edition of *Foreign Affairs*, Kurt Waldheim, former Nazi and secretary-general of the United Nations (and longtime personal friend of "Cawlifornia" governor Arnold Schwarzenegger), wrote, "As long as states insist that they are the supreme arbiters of their destinies—that as sovereign entities their decisions are subject to no higher authority—international organizations will never be able to guarantee the maintenance of peace."[16] Does that statement kind of clear the air, Rush? Finally, as for Newt Gingrich being a threat to my personal freedom, I think you must have gotten him confused with the content of question nine—that part about "men and women at war with each other" (although he *is* a member of the CFR, marriage problems, or not). For the record, I knew Newt was just another phony Conservative when he supported his sister's "choice" to move in with her lesbian lover. So much for good ol' Republican family values—right, Rush? (Ditto, Dick Cheney's daughter.)

I believe the time has come for Mr. Rush Limbaugh to hear from some of his better-known "kooks." His grading scale states, "If you have answered just *one* of these questions yes, then you are a kook." The first question should do fine—"Do you believe that powerful Americans are behind a world conspiracy to destroy the sovereignty of the United States of America?" (An * indicates a "Limbaugh kook" who was also a hypocrite for being part of the very conspiracy he exposed. Also, Vatican conspiracies have been included at no extra charge).

LIMBAUGH'S KOOK LIST

PRESIDENTS OF THE UNITED STATES

1. **George Washington—(1789-97)** "I have heard much of the nefarious and dangerous plan and doctrines of the Illuminati. It was not my intention to doubt that the doctrines of the Illuminati and the principles of Jacobinism had not spread in the United States. On the contrary, no one is more satisfied of this fact than I am."[17]

    "I gave it as my opinion to the confidential characters around me that if these societies [pro-Masonic, pro-Parisian Jacobins Democratic Clubs in America] were not counteracted (not by prosecutions, the ready way to make them grow stronger), or did not fall into disesteem . . . they would shake the government to its foundations."[18]

2. **John Adams—(1797-1801)** "All the perplexities, confusion and distress in America arise not from defects in the Constitution, nor from want of honor or virtue, so much as from downright ignorance of the nature of coin, credit and circulation."[19]

    "I am not happy about the rebirth of the Jesuits. . . . If ever an association of people deserved eternal damnation, on this earth and in hell, it is this Society of Loyola."[20]

3. **Thomas Jefferson—(1801-09)** "Like you [John Adams], I disapprove of the restoration of the Jesuits, for it means a step backwards from light into darkness."[21]

    "Single acts of tyranny may be ascribed to the accidental opinion of a day; but a series of oppressions, begun at a distinguished period and pursued unalterably through every change of ministers, too plainly prove a deliberate, systematical plan of reducing us to slavery."[22]

4. **John Quincy Adams—(1825-29)** "I do conscientiously and sincerely believe that the Order of Freemasonry, if not the greatest, is one of the greatest moral and political evils under which the Union is now laboring . . . [It is] a conspiracy of the few against the equal rights of the many . . . I am prepared to complete the demonstration before God and man, that the Masonic oath, obligations and penalties cannot by any possibility be reconciled to the laws of morality, of Christianity, or of the land."[23]

5. **Andrew Jackson—(1829-37)** "I was one of those who do not believe that a national bank is a national blessing, but rather a curse to a republic; inasmuch as it is calculated to raise around the administration a moneyed aristocracy dangerous to the liberties of the country."[24]

6. **Millard Fillmore—(1850-53)** "The Masonic fraternity tramples upon our rights, defeats the administration of justice, and bids defiance to every government which it cannot control."[25]

7. **Abraham Lincoln—(1861-65)** "I see in the near future a crisis approaching that unnerves me and causes me to tremble for the safety of my country; corporations have been enthroned, an era of corruption in high places will follow, and the money power of the country will endeavor to prolong its reign by working upon the prejudices of the people until the wealth is aggregated in a few hands, and the Republic destroyed."[26]

   "If the American people could learn what I know of the fierce hatred of the priests of Rome against our institutions, our schools, our most sacred rights, and our so dearly bought liberties, they would drive them out as traitors."[27]

8. **Andrew Johnson—(1865-69)** "[He had] ... no doubt that there was a conspiracy afoot among the Radicals [the Jacobins] to incite another revolution [now that the Civil War had ended], and especially to arm and exasperate the negroes."[28]

9. **Ulysses S. Grant—(1869-77)** "All secret oath-bound political parties are dangerous to any nation, no matter how pure or how patriotic the motives and principles which first bring them together."[29]

10. **James Garfield—(1881-81)** "Whoever controls the volume of money in any country [Allen Greenspan – USA] is absolute master of all industry and commerce."[30]

11. **Woodrow Wilson*—(1913-21)** "Some of the biggest men in the United States, in the field of commerce and manufacture, are afraid of something. They know that there is a power somewhere so organized, so subtle, so watchful, so interlocked, so complete, so pervasive, that they had better not speak above their breath when they speak in condemnation of it."[31]

    "The greatest monopoly in this country is the money monopoly. So long as that exists, our old variety of freedom and individual energy of development are out of the question."[32]

    "A great industrial nation is controlled by its system of credit. The growth of the nation and all our activities are concentrated in the hands of a few men. We are one of the worst ruled, one of the most completely controlled and dominated governments on earth—no longer a government of free opinion, no longer a government by conviction, and the vote of the majority, but a government by the opinion and duress of a small group of dominant men."[33]

    "I am a most unhappy man. Unwittingly, I have ruined my country."[34]

12. **Franklin Delano Roosevelt*—(1933-45)** "The real truth of the matter is, as you and I know [writing to Colonel Edward Mandell House], that a financial element in the larger centers has owned the government ever since the days of Andrew Jackson, and I am not wholly excepting the administration of W.W. (Woodrow Wilson). The country is going through a repetition of Jackson's fight with the Bank of the United States—only on a bigger and broader basis."[35]

13. **Harry S. Truman*—(1945-53)** "The United Nations represents the idea of a universal morality, superior to the interests of individual nations. . . . The men who laid down their lives for the United Nations in Korea . . . died in order that the United Nations might live."[36]

14. **Richard M. Nixon*—(1969-74)** "The nation's immediate problem is that while the common man fights America's wars, the intellectual elite sets its agenda. Today, whether the West lives or dies is in the hands of its new power elite: those who set the terms of public debate, who manipulate the symbols, who decide whether nations or leaders will be depicted on 100 million television sets as "good" or "bad". This power elite sets the limits of the possible for Presidents and Congress. It molds the impressions that move the nation, or that mire it."[37]

15. **Jimmy Carter*—(1977-81)** "The people of this country know from bitter experience that we are not going to get these chances [for new faces and ideas] merely by shifting around the same groups of insiders. . . . The insiders have had their chance and they have not delivered."[38]

"If, after the inauguration, you find a Cy Vance [CFR] as Secretary of State and Zbigniew Brzezinski [CFR] as head of National Security, then I would say we failed. And I would quit. You're going to see new faces and new ideas."[39] (Spoken by Hamilton Jordon a few weeks prior to the November election; yet, following the election Mr. Carter promptly named Cyrus Vance to be his Secretary of State and Zbigniew Brzezinski to be the head of National Security!)

16. **Ronald Reagan*—(1981-89)** "I think there is an elite in this country and they are the ones who run an elitist government. They want a government by a handful of people because they don't believe the people themselves can run their lives. . . . Are we going to have an elitist government that makes decisions for people's lives or are we going to believe as we have for so many decades, that the people can make these decisions for themselves?"[40] (By mid-1988, 313 CFR members were officiating within the Reagan-Bush administration.)

"The evidence is compelling that reconsideration of the world monetary system is overdue. Therefore, national economies need monetary coordination mechanisms and that is why an integrated world economy needs a common monetary standard, which is the best neutral inflationary coordinating device. But, no national currency will do—only a world currency will work."[41] (Spring 1983 Economic Summit, Williamsburg, VA)

17. **George Bush*—(1989-93)** "Out of these troubled times, our fifth objective—a new world order—can emerge. . . . We are now in sight of a United Nations that performs as envisioned by its founders."[42] (September 1990 televised address)

"I think that what's at stake here is the new world order. What's at stake here is whether we can have disputes peacefully resolved in the future by a reinvigorated United Nations."[43] (January 7, 1991, interview in *U.S. News and World Report*)

"[The Gulf crisis] has to do with a new world order. And that new world order is only going to be enhanced if this newly activated peacekeeping function of the United Nations proves to be effective."[44] (January 9, 1991, Press Conference)

"When we are successful, and we will be, we have a real chance at this new world order, an order in which a credible United Nations can use its peacekeeping role to fulfill the promise and vision of the U.N.'s founders."[45] (January 16, 1991, televised address)

"In the Gulf, we saw the United Nations playing the role dreamed of by its founders. . . . I hope that history will record that the Gulf crisis was the crucible of the new world order."[46] (August 1991 *National Security Strategy of the United States* issued by the White House and signed by George Bush.)

18. **Bill Clinton*—(1993-2001)** "In the twenty-first century your generation must also lead the challenge of an international financial system that has no respect for national borders."[47] (June 29, 1998, speech at Beijing University)

"We are still bedeviled by notions that our . . . religious differences are somehow more important than our common humanity."[48] (March 26, 1998, address to the Parliament of South Africa)

"What I'm trying to do is to promote a process of reorganization of the world so that human beings are organized in a way that takes advantage of the new opportunities of this era. . . . And if we can prove that you can merge integrated economies and integrated democracies, then we'll be more likely to build a global system of this kind."[49] (October 17, 1997, interview with Argentine reporters in Buenos Aries)

"As the Scripture says, our eyes have not yet seen, nor our ears heard, nor our minds imagined what we can build . . . We can do it."[50]

MEMBERS OF CONGRESS

19. **Daniel Webster (New Hampshire Representative 1813-17; Massachusetts Representative 1823-27; Massachusetts Senator 1827-41)** "It [Freemasonry] is an institution which in my judgment, is essentially wrong in the principle of its formation; that from its very nature it is liable to great abuses . . . it is in my opinion that the future administrations of all such oaths . . . should be prohibited by law . . . The supremacy of the Constitution and the laws is the very foundation stone of Republican institutions; if it be shaken or removed from its place, the whole system must inevitably totter to its fall."[51]

20. **Charles Lindbergh (Minnesota, Representative 1906-17)** "[The Federal Reserve Act] . . . established the most gigantic trust on earth. When the President signs this act, the invisible government by the money power . . . will be legitimized. The new law will create inflation whenever the trusts want inflation. From now on, depressions will be scientifically created."[52]

"The only reason that we are in danger of becoming involved in this war [WWI] is because there are powerful elements in America who desire us to take part. They seize every opportunity to push us closer to the edge. It is time for the underlying character of this country to rise and strike down these elements."[53]

21. **Carroll Reece (Tennessee Representative 1921-31; 1933-47; 1951-61)** "It has been said that the Foundations are a power second only to the Federal Government itself. Perhaps this statement should be modified because it seems to have become an affront for a congressional committee to dare subject the foundations to criticism. Perhaps the Congress now should admit that the foundations have become more powerful, in some areas at least, than the legislative branch of the government."[54]

22. **Wright Patman (Texas Representative 1928-76)** "In the United States today, we have in effect two governments. We have the duly constituted government. Then we have an independent, uncontrolled and un-coordinated government in the Federal Reserve System, operating the money powers which are reserved to Congress by the Constitution."[55]

"I am opposed to the U.S. government, which has the sovereign and exclusive power of creating money, paying private bankers for the use of its money . . . One of these days the people of this country are going to rise up in their wrath and compel the change of such an idiotic system, that compels our people to pay tribute to a few who have nothing invested and run no risk, in order to conduct the affairs of our government, and especially our national defense program."[56]

23. **Patrick McCarran (Nevada Senator 1932-54)** "In no time in our history has the United States been in such jeopardy as it is today [1954]. It is beset by enemies from within and from abroad, in greater numbers than ever before . . . until my dying day I will regret ratifying the United Nations Treaty."[57]

24. **Ushur Burdick (North Dakota Representative 1934-44; 1948-59)** "It ought to be obvious to any fair-minded person, that it is the deliberate scheme of the United Nations to destroy the Constitution of the United States, and should need no further proof."[58]

   "If this is not treason, then I do not understand the provision of the Constitution defining it."[59]

25. **Lawrence Smith (Wisconsin Representative 1941-58)** "When the mothers and fathers of our service men and women learn of the facts of those treaties (NATO and SOFT) and what they mean for American citizens, I am sure there will be general disappointment. Justice in other countries is not administered as it is in the United States, nor are the penalties the same. The Senate has removed American soldiers and sailors from the protection of the Constitution and Bill of Rights. Is this a sly and adroit move to destroy our sovereignty step by step in the direction of world government? It looks that way to me."[60]

26. **William Jenner (Indiana Senator 1944-59)** "This post-war world of crisis, convulsions and catastrophes, the world in which American taxpayers empty their pocketbooks to meet emergencies on five continents, the world in which American boys are forced to sit on powder kegs in 49 countries, is a world we never made. It was made for us, by these traitors in our own government. They monkeyed with, manipulated, and maneuvered the whole plan for the U.N. even before it was blueprinted in the State Department's top drawer."[61]

   "Today the path to total dictatorship in the United States can be laid by strictly legal means, unseen and unheard by the Congress, the President, or the people . . . Outwardly we have a Constitutional government. We have operating *within* our government and political system, *another* body representing another form of government, a bureaucratic elite which believes our Constitution is outmoded and is sure that it is on the winning side . . . All the strange developments in foreign policy agreements may be traced to this group who are going to make us over to suit their pleasure. . . . This political action group has its own local political support organizations, its own pressure groups, its own vested interests, its foothold within our government, and its own propaganda apparatus."[62]

27. **Joseph McCarthy (Wisconsin Senator 1946-57)**—*And you probably thought he was the only Congressman who saw a commie behind every bush*—"How can we account for our present situation unless we believe that men high in Government are concerting to deliver us to disaster? This must be the product of a great conspiracy, a conspiracy on a scale so immense as to dwarf any previous venture in the history of man. A conspiracy of infamy so black that, when it is finally exposed, its Principals shall be forever deserving of the maledictions of all honest men. . . ."[63]

"What can be made of this unbroken series of decisions and acts contributing to the strategy of defeat? They cannot be attributed to incompetence. . . . The laws of probability would dictate that part of . . . [the] decisions would serve this country's interest."[64]

28. **George Malone (Nevada Senator 1947-59)** "I believe—I actually believe this—that if the people of this nation suddenly fully understood what the Congress has done to them over the past 49 years, they would move on Washington, they would not wait for an election. . . . It all adds up to a preconceived plan to destroy the economic and social independence of the United States."[65]

29. **Barry Goldwater (Arizona Senator 1953-65; 1969-75)** "In my view the Trilateral Commission represents a skillful, coordinated effort to seize control and consolidate the four centers of power—political, monetary, intellectual, and ecclesiastical . . . What the Trilateralists truly intend is the creation of a worldwide economic power superior to the political governments of the nation-states involved. They believe the abundant materialism they propose to create will overwhelm existing differences. As managers and creators of the system they will rule the future."[66]

30. **Robert F. Kennedy* (New York Senator 1965-68)** "All of us will ultimately be judged on the effort we have contributed to building a New World Order."[67]

31. **Jesse Helms (North Carolina Senator 1973-2002)** "The viewpoint of the Establishment today is called globalism. Not so long ago, this viewpoint was called the "one-world" view by its critics. The phrase is no longer fashionable among sophisticates; yet, the phrase "one-world" is still apt because nothing has changed in the minds and actions of those promoting policies consistent with its fundamental tenets. Mr. President [speaking before the Senate in December 1987], in the globalist point of view, nation-states and national boundaries do not count for anything. Political philosophies and political principles seem to become simply relative. Indeed, even constitutions are irrelevant to the exercise of power. . . . In

this point of view, the activities of international financial and industrial forces should be oriented to bringing this one-world design—with a convergence of the Soviet and American systems as its center piece— into being."[68]

32. **Joseph Biden* (Delaware Senator 1973-Present)** "My answer is that the moment is upon us to define a compelling concept of a new world order to commit ourselves to it, and to lead the world to its realization. . . . The U.N. Security Council must reflect the reality of world power and the reality of world problems; it must comprise those countries with the resources—both material and human—to address the full range of global security concerns."[69]

33. **Newt Gingrich* (Georgia Representative 1979-94)** "I have an enormous personal ambition [ego]. I want to shift the entire planet. And I'm doing it." (*Washington Post*)[70]

34. **Louis McFadden (Pennsylvania Representative 1915-35)** "President Roosevelt has brought with him from Wall Street, James Warburg, the son of Paul M. Warburg. Mr. Warburg is head of the Bank of Manhattan Co. Mr. Warburg, alien born and the son of an alien who did not become naturalized here until several years after this Warburg's birth, is the son of a former partner of Kuhn, Loeb & Co., a grandson of another partner, and a nephew of a former partner, a nephew of a present partner. He holds no office in our Government but I am told that he is daily in attendance at the Treasury, and that he has private quarters there. In other words, Mr. Chairman, Kuhn, Loeb & Co. now occupy the U.S. Treasury."[71]

35. **James D. Warburg* (an International Banker from Hell)** Mr. Warburg gave the following testimony before the Senate on February 17, 1950, thirteen years after McFadden's death: "We shall have world government, whether or not we like it. The only question, is whether world government will be achieved by conquest or consent."[72]

SPECIAL HEARINGS

36. **1834 Report by Massachusetts House of Representatives, on Freemasonry** "The organization of Freemasonry, as a distinct Independent Government within our own Government, and beyond the control of the laws of the land, by means of its secrecy, and the oaths and regulations which its subjects are bound to obey, under penalties of death, have occupied much of the attention of the committee [investigating Freemasonry], in connection with the third branch of their inquiry [that Freemasonry is a *political* evil]."[73]

37. **1953 Report of The California Senate Investigating Committee on Education** "So called modern Communism is apparently the same hypocritical world conspiracy to destroy civilization that was founded by the Illuminati, and that raised its head in our colonies here at the critical period before the adoption of our Constitution."[74]

38. **Norman Dodd (Congressional Investigator)** ". . . they [the Carnegie Endowment for International Peace] must control education in this country. So they approach[ed] the Rockefeller Foundation with the suggestion that the task be divided between the two of them. The Carnegie Endowment takes on that aspect of education that has a tinge of international significance and the Rockefeller Foundation takes on that portion of education which is domestic in this relationship."[75]

PUBLIC SERVANTS

39. **Richard Wigginton Thompson (Secretary of the Navy under President Rutherford Hayes)** "The Papacy is now endeavoring, by the most active and persistent efforts, to substitute an ecclesiastical government of the people—a grand 'Holy Empire' for this free and popular republic which it has cost so much blood and treasure to establish and maintain."[76]

40. **John Hylan (New York City Mayor 1918-25)** "The real menace of our republic is this invisible government which like a giant octopus sprawls its slimy length over city, state and nation. Like the octopus of real life, it operates under cover of a self-created screen. It seizes in its long and powerful tentacles our executive officers, our legislative bodies, our schools, our courts, our newspapers, and every agency created for the public protection. It squirms in the jaws of darkness and thus is the better able to clutch the reins of government, secure enactment of the legislation favorable to corrupt business, violate the law of impunity, smother the press and reach into the courts.

   To depart from mere generalizations, let me say at the head of this octopus are the Rockefeller-Standard Oil interests and a small group of powerful banking houses generally referred to as the international bankers. The little coterie of powerful international bankers virtually run the United States government for their own selfish purposes. They practically control both political parties, write political platforms, make catspaws of party leaders, use the leading men in private organizations, and resort to every device to place in nomination for high public office only such candidates as will be amendable to the dictates of corrupt big business.

   They connive at centralization of government on the theory that a small group of handpicked, privately controlled individuals in power can be more easily handled than a larger group among whom there will most likely be men sincerely interested in public welfare. These international bankers and Rockefeller-Standard Oil interests control the majority of newspapers and magazines in this country. They use the columns of these papers to club into submission or drive out of office public officials who refuse to do the bidding of the powerful corrupt cliques which compose the invisible government."[77] (The mayor's speech was printed in *The New York Times*, March 27, 1922.)

41. **Norman Thomas* (The Socialist Party's presidential candidate in every national election from 1928-1948)** "The American people will never knowingly adopt Socialism, but under the name of Liberalism, they will adopt every fragment of the Socialist program until one day America would be a Socialist nation without knowing how it happened."[78]

42. **Felix Frankfurter* (U.S. Supreme Court Associate Justice, Founder of ACLU, attorney for NAACP, and member of CFR)** "The real rulers in Washington are invisible, and exercise power from behind the scenes."[79]

"They [Class "A" stockholders of the Federal Reserve System] are undiscoverable."[80]

43. **William O. Douglas* (U.S. Supreme Court Justice)** "Building bridges with Communist nations is the prime necessity of the day. . . . We have moved from free enterprise to a *sui generis* form of socialism. The trend toward the collective society will continue. . . . The Western and Soviet regimes may yet evolve into comparable economic systems. . . . The new [global] federalism would deal with conflicts between nations just as our own Supreme Court deals with conflicts between sovereign states"[81] (from his book *Towards a Global Federalism*).

44. **Henry Kissinger* (Member of the CFR and Trilateral Commission)** "What Congress will have before it is not a conventional trade agreement but the architecture of a new international system . . . a first step toward a new world order"[82] (written in the *Los Angeles Times*, July 18, 1993, regarding NAFTA).

45. **George F. Kennan* (Senior State Department Soviet Expert, 1960)** "There can be no greater myth than to suppose that historical myths cannot be created by design."[83]

ROOSEVELTS

46. **Elliot Roosevelt (FDR's son)** ". . . there are within our world perhaps only a dozen organizations which shape the courses of our various destinies as rigidly as the regularly constituted governments . . . this unofficial council

of the elite, the crème de la crème of global planners"[84] (from his book
The Conservators).

47. **James Roosevelt (FDR's son)** On the dust jacket of his novel entitled
A Family Affair, James Roosevelt writes, "[President] Roosevelt . . .
makes a bold secret decision—to share the results of the Manhattan
Project with the Soviet Union." The dust cover continues by informing
the reader that Roosevelt has "written a novel of spine-chilling drama
and *authenticity*."[85]

48. **Edith Kermit Roosevelt (Theodore Roosevelt's granddaughter)** "The
word 'Establishment' is a general term for the power elite in international
finance, business, the professions and government, largely from the
northeast, who wield most of the power regardless of who is in the White
House. Most people are unaware of the existence of this 'legitimate
Mafia.' Yet the power of the Establishment makes itself felt from the
professor who seeks a foundation grant, to the candidate for a cabinet
post or State Department job. It affects the nation's policies in almost
every area."[86]

"What is the Establishment's view-point? Through the Roosevelt,
Truman, Eisenhower and Kennedy administrations its ideology is constant:
That the best way to fight Communism is by a One World Socialist state
governed by 'experts' like themselves. The result has been policies
which favor the growth of the superstate, gradual surrender of United
States sovereignty to the United Nations and a steady retreat in the face
of Communist aggression."[87]

49. **Curtis Dall (FDR's son-in-law)** "For a long time I felt that FDR had
developed many thoughts and ideas that were his own to benefit this
country, the U.S.A. But, he didn't. Most of his thoughts, his political
'ammunition' as it were, were carefully manufactured for him in advance
by the CFR-One World Money group. Brilliantly, with great gusto, like
a fine piece of artillery, he exploded that prepared 'ammunition' in the
middle of an unsuspecting target, the American people—and thus paid
off and retained his internationalist political support"[88] (from his book
FDR: My Exploited Father-In-Law). "Actually, it was the calculated
'shearing' of the public by the World-Money powers triggered by the
planned sudden shortage of call money in the New York money market."[89]
(Dall, a syndicate manager for Lehman Brothers, was on the floor of the
N.Y. Stock Exchange on the day of the crash.)

MILITARY OFFICERS

50. **General William Tecumseh Sherman** ". . . the truth is not always palatable and should not always be told."[90]

51. **General Thomas M. Harris** "Every citizen . . . who is loyal to the Roman Catholic Church, is an enemy of our government."[91]

52. **General John J. "Blackjack" Pershing** "When this war is over [WWI] and should I ever become Chief of Staff, I'm going to set up an organization to check on forces that are doing things at Washington, D.C. and elsewhere that are detrimental to our Republic."[92]

53. **Admiral William F. "Bull" Halsey** "As you know [writing to Admiral Husband Kimmel, Pearl Harbor] I have always thought and have not hesitated to say on any and all occasions, that I believe you and Short were the greatest military martyrs this country has ever produced."[93]

54. **General George S. Patton** "This conference [press conference, September 22, 1945] cost me the command of the Third Army . . . I was intentionally direct, because I believed that it was then time for people to know what was going on. My language was not particular[ly] politic, but I have yet to find where politic language produces successful government. The one thing which I could not say then, and cannot yet say, is that my chief interest in establishing order in Germany was to prevent Germany from going communistic. I am afraid that our foolish and utterly stupid policy in regard to Germany will certainly cause them to join the Russians and thereby insure a communistic state throughout Western Europe."[94]

55. **General George Stratemeyer** "We had sufficient air, bombardment, fighters, [and] reconnaissance so that I could have taken out all of those supplies, those airdromes on the other side of the Yalu; I could have bombed the devils between there and Mukden, stopped the railroad operating and the people of China that were fighting could not have been supplied. . . . But we weren't permitted to do it. As a result, a lot of American blood was spilled over there in Korea."[95]

56. **General Douglas MacArthur** "I realized for the first time that I had actually been denied the use of my full military power to safeguard the lives of my soldiers and the safety of my army. To me, it clearly foreshadowed a future tragic situation in Korea, and left me with a sense of inexpressible shock."[96]

"What may well have triggered my removal [by Truman] was my recommendation, made in January shortly before my relief, that a treason trial be initiated to break up a spy ring responsible for the purloining of my top secret reports to Washington. My campaign plans, including those of the Eighth Army, were transmitted daily to Washington. General Walker complained constantly to me that the enemy was receiving prior information on his movements. We could find no leaks in Korea or Japan. Then suddenly one of my dispatches concerning the order of battle was published in a Washington paper within a few hours of its receipt. I insisted that those responsible be prosecuted in order that such subversive activity be stopped, but the case was never processed and I was shortly relieved of my command."[97]

57. **General Mark Clark** "Our country should withdraw from the United Nations which as we know after 18 years has proved a rat's nest for the promotion of World Communism and slavery and this situation has resulted in the worst crisis and danger both from within and from without in all the history of our country."[98]

58. **Rear Admiral Chester Ward** "The most powerful clique in these elitist groups have one objective in common—they want to bring about the surrender of the sovereignty and the national independence of the United States. A second clique of international members in the CFR . . . comprises the Wall Street international bankers and their key agents. Primarily, they want the world banking monopoly from whatever power ends up in the control of global government. They would probably prefer that this be an all-powerful United Nations organization; but they are also prepared to deal with and for a one-world government controlled by the Soviet Communists if U.S. sovereignty is ever surrendered to them."[99]

59. **Lieutenant Colonel James Bo Gritz (Highest decorated Green Beret in Special Forces history)** "Nine hundred tons of heroin and opium will enter the free world from Southeast Asia's 'Golden Triangle' this year [1987]. The reason is because U.S. taxpayer dollars and American equipment have been used to construct a new road that will allow narcotics to pour out of General Kuhn Sa's Shan Territories rather than trickle out by horse and mule as has been the case until the beginning of this year. . . . I am convinced that a secret combination exists today within the U.S. Government that was officially germinated during the Nixon-Vietnam years and has, through illicit drug profits, propagated itself into a self-serving righteous monster of global proportions. . . . Khun Sa has directly implicated persons within the CIA as some of his best customers. . . . I personally don't believe the Americans named by Khun Sa as conspirators in traffickings could pass an honest security check."[100] (June 30, 1987, statement before U.S. Congress, House Foreign Affairs Committee, International Narcotics Control Task Force)

60. **General Colin Powell*** "The United Nations will spearhead our efforts to manage the new conflicts [that afflict our world]. . . . Yes, the principles of the United Nations charter *are* worth our lives, our fortunes, and our sacred honor."[101]

LAW ENFORCEMENT OFFICERS

61. **François Charles de Berckheim (Special Commissioner of Police, Mayence, Germany)** "Illuminism is becoming a great and formidable power, and I fear, in my conscience, that kings and peoples will have much to suffer from it unless foresight and prudence break its frightful mechanism."[102]

62. **Scotland Yard Intelligence Report, 1921** "Martens [Ludwig C.A.K. Martens, first Soviet "ambassador" and vice president of Weinberg & Posner] is very much in the limelight. There appears to be no doubt about his connection with the Guarantee (sic) Trust Company. Although it is surprising that so large and influential an enterprise should have dealings with a Bolshevik concern."[103] (A copy of this report is in the U.S State Department Decimal File, Microcopy 316, Roll 22, Frame 656.)

63. **Dan Smoot (Special Agent for the Federal Bureau of Investigation)** ". . . I am convinced that the Council on Foreign Relations, together with a great number of other associated tax-exempt organizations, constitutes the invisible government which sets the major policies of the federal government; exercises controlling influence on governmental officials who implement the policies; and, through massive and skillful propaganda, influences Congress and the public to support the policies. I am convinced that the objective of this invisible government is to convert America into a socialist state and then make it a unit in a one-world socialist system."[104]

64. **William Colby* (Director of the Central Intelligence Agency)** "Sometimes, there are forces too powerful for us to whip them individually, in the time frame that we would like. . . . The best that we might be able to do sometimes, is to point out the truth and then step aside. That is where I think you are now. For your own personal safety and survival, step aside."[105] (Spoken to a friend a few years before his own mysterious death.)

INDUSTRIALISTS

65. **Meyer Amschel Rothschild* (Patriarch of international bankers)** "Give me the right to issue a nation's money, and then I do not care who makes its laws."[106]

66. **Walter Rathenau* (Controlled German General Electric in 1909)** "Three hundred men, all of whom know one another, direct the economic destiny of Europe and choose their successors from among themselves."[107]

67. **Mark Jones* (Financial advisor to John D. Rockefeller)** ". . . just four men, through their interlocking directorates on boards of large corporations and major banks, controlled the movements of capital and the creation of debt in America."[108]

68. **Joseph P. Kennedy* (America's premier bootlegger and election rigger)** "Fifty men have run America and that's a high figure."[109]

69. **Henry Ford*** "It is well enough that the people of the nation do not understand our banking and monetary system, for if they did, I believe there would be a revolution before tomorrow morning."[110] (A portrait of Henry Ford hung in Adolf Hitler's private office in Berlin.)

INTERNATIONAL PERSONALITIES

70. **Sir William Pitt, "the Elder" (English politican)** "There is something behind the throne greater than the king himself." [111] (Spoken before Britain's House of Lords in 1770, his words gave birth to the phrase, "power behind the throne.")

71. **Marquis de Lafayette (French statesman and officer)** "An invisible hand is guiding the populace."[112]
    "American liberty can be destroyed only by the popish clergy."[113]

72. **Prince Klemens von Metternich* (Austrian Minister of Foreign Affairs)** "Germany has long suffered from the evil which today covers the whole of Europe. . . . The sect of Illuminés . . . has never been destroyed although the same (Bavarian) government has tried to suppress it and has been obliged to inveigh against it."[114]

73. **Alexis de Tocqueville (French author and politican)** "Above this race of men stands an immense and tutelary power, which takes upon itself alone to secure their gratifications and to watch over their fate. . . . After having thus successively taken each member of the community in its powerful grasp and fashioned him at will, the supreme power then extends its arm over the whole community. . . . The will of man is not shattered, but softened, bent, and guided. . . . It does not tyrannize, but it compresses, enervates, extinguishes, and stupefies a people, till each nation is reduced to nothing better than a flock of timid and industrious animals, of which the government is the shepherd [*Animal Farm*]."[115]

74. **Benjamin Disraeli* (British Prime Minister)** "So you see ... the world is governed by very different personages from what is imagined by those who are not behind the scenes."[116]

"There is in Italy a power which we seldom mention in this House (the House of Parliament). ... I mean the secret societies. ... It is useless to deny, because it is impossible to conceal, that a great part of Europe ... to say nothing of other countries ... is covered with a network of these secret societies. ... What are their objects? They do not want constitutional government. ... They want to change the tenure of the land, to drive out the present owners of the soil and to put an end to ecclesiastical establishments."[117]

75. **Chevalier de Malet (French historian)** "The authors of the Revolution are not more French than German, Italian, English, etc. They form a particular nation which took birth and has grown in the darkness, in the midst of all civilized nations, with the object of subjecting them to its domination."[118]

76. **Reginald McKenna* (Chancellor of the Exchequer of England in 1915-1916, and Chairman of the Board of the Midlands Bank of England)** "I am afraid the ordinary citizen will not like to be told that the banks can, and do, create money. ... And they who control credit of the nation direct the policy of Governments and hold in the hollow of their hands the destiny of the people"[119] (warning to his stockholders in January 1924).

77. **Sir Winston Churchill* (British Prime Minister)** "Certainly I dispute the title of the Bolsheviks to represent Russia. ... They despise such commonplace as nationality. ... No sooner did Lenin arrive here than he began beckoning a finger here and a finger there to obscure persons in sheltered retreats in New York, in Glasgow, in Berne and other countries, and he gathered together the leading spirits of a most formidable sect, *the* most formidable sect in the world"[120] (from a speech in the House of Commons, November 5, 1944).

"This movement among the Jews is not new. From the days of Spartacus-Weishaupt to those of Karl Marx, down to Trotsky (Russia), Bela Kun (Hungary), Rosa Luxemburg (Germany), and Emma Goldman (United States), this British form of world-wide conspiracy for the overthrow of civilization and for the reconstruction of society on the basis of arrested development, of envious malevolence, and impossible equality, has been steadily growing. It played, as a modern writer, Mrs. Webster, has so ably shown, a definitely recognizable part in the tragedy of the French Revolution. It has been the mainspring of every subversive movement, during the Nineteenth Century; and now, at last, this band of extraordinary personalities from the underworld of the great cities of Europe and America have gripped the Russian people by the hair of their heads and have become practically the undisputed masters of that enormous Empire."[121]

78. **Lord Beaverbrook (English politican)** "You Americans are a strange contradiction. You spend huge sums of money fighting the fifth column in your country, but at the same time down on the East Side of New York, and partly with money given by the Rockefellers, you have erected the biggest fifth column headquarters in the world—the United Nations. It is filled with men who wish to subvert the government of the United States. Yet you pay out your good money, and Great Britain does too, to bring these people into your midst. Why a great nation like the United States bothers to belong to such a monstrous organization, why any great nation would want to join—is more than I can honestly comprehend."[122]

79. **Alexander Solzhenitsyn (Russian dissident, author, Nobel Peace Prize recipient)** "Why do we hand over to Communist totalitarianism more and more technology—complex, delicate, developed technology which it needs for armaments and for crushing its own citizens."[123]

"Our whole slave system [Gulag Archipelago] depends on your economic assistance. When they bury us alive, please do not send them shovels and the most up to date earth - moving equipment."[124]

80. **Margaret Thatcher* (British Prime Minister)** ". . . today's international policy makers' . . . short-term goal is to subordinate American and other national sovereignties to multilateral authorities; their long-term goal, one suspects, is to establish the U.N. as a kind of embryo world government"[125] (from the former Prime Minister's December 12, 1977, address at the Heritage Foundation).

81. **Mikhail Gorbachev* (Soviet President)** "We are part of the Cosmos. Cosmos is my God. Nature is my God. . . . The future society will be a totally new civilization which will synthesize the experience of Socialism and Capitalism."[126] (October 23, 1996, on *The Charlie Rose Show*)

In an article, "One World, Under Gorby" in the *San Francisco Weekly*, May 31-June 6, 1995, Jim Garrison, president of Gorbachev Foundation/USA, states: "Over the next twenty to thirty years, we are going to end up with world government. It's inevitable." (The Gorbachev Foundation/USA, now called State of the World Forum, is located at the Presidio, the former prestigious American military base in San Francisco.) In another article published in *The Washington Post*, September 24, of that same year entitled, "Global Chic: Gorby's Bash By the Bay," writer George Cothran states that "maybe challenging the powers-that-be isn't

Gorbachev's main objective. Rather than disrupting the hide-bound elites that run the world, the former Soviet president seems more intent on rejoining their exclusive club."[127]

SCHOLARS

82. **Otto Eisenshiml (Biographer of Michigan Senator Zachariah Chandler)** "The secret history of these days [Civil War] . . . concealing many startling revelations, has yet been sparingly written; it is doubtful if the veil will ever be more than slightly lifted."[128]

83. **Samual F.B. Morse (Inventor of the telegraph)** "We cannot be too often reminded of the *double* character of the enemy who has gained foothold upon our shores, for although Popery is a religious sect, and on this ground claims toleration side by side with other religious sects, yet Popery is also a political, a despotic system, which we must repel as altogether incompatible with the existence of freedom. I repeat it, Popery is a political, a despotic system, which must be resisted by all true patriots."[129]

84. **Joseph Willard (President of Harvard University)** "There is sufficient evidence that a number of societies of the Illuminati have been established in this land. They are doubtless striving to secretly undermine all our ancient institutions, civil and sacred. These societies are clearly leagued with those of the same order in Europe. The enemies of all order are seeking our ruin. Should infidelity generally prevail, our independence would fall of course. Our republican government would be annihilated."[130]

85. **Carrol Quigley (Professor at Georgetown, Harvard and Princeton Universities)** "The board of the CFR have carried ever since the marks of their origin. . . . There grew up in the 20th century a power structure between London and New York which penetrated deeply into university life, the press, and the practice of foreign policy. . . . The American branch of this 'English Establishment' exerted much of its influence through five American newspapers (*The New York Times, New York Herald Tribune, Christian Science Monitor, Washington Post,* and the late lamented *Boston Evening Transcript*)."[131]

86. **Author Edward Waite (Author of *The Real History of the Rosicrucians*)** "Beneath the broad tide of human history, there flow the stealthy undercurrents of the secret societies, which frequently determine in the depths the changes that take place upon the surface."[132]

87. **John Kenneth Galbraith* (Professor of economics at Harvard University)** "Those of us who had worked for the Kennedy election

were tolerated in the government for that reason and had a say, but foreign policy was still with the Council on Foreign Relations people."[133]
"Certainly the least predicted development under the Nixon administration was this great new thrust to socialism. One encounters people who still aren't aware of it. Others must be rubbing their eyes, for certainly the portents seemed all to the contrary. As an opponent to socialism, Mr. Nixon *seemed* steadfast."[134]

88. **Avro Manhattan (Author of over twenty major research works on the Vatican)** "Thus, whereas, the USA has a mere 250 million citizens and the Soviet Union about 300 million, the Vatican, via the Catholic Church, can influence between 800 and 1,000 million Catholics. These . . . have no frontiers whatsoever . . . and can be made to operate, independently of their own administrations, governments or regimes. A Catholic citizen, therefore . . . can and often is influenced in his social and ideological attitudes by those taken by the Vatican, acting as the political facet of the Catholic Church."[135]

ANTICHRISTS

89. **Cardinal John Hughes**** "There is no secrecy in all this. . . . Everybody should know that we have for our mission to convert the world—including the inhabitants of the United States,—the people of the cities, and the people of the country, the officers of the navy and marines, commanders of the army, the Legislatures, the Senate, the Cabinet, the President, and all!"[136] (from his sermon "The Decline of Protestantism and Its Causes, November 1850).
"No man has a right to choose his own religion."[137] (*New York Freeman*, January 26, 1852, Hughes's parish newspaper)

90. **Pope Gregory XVI**** "From this polluted fountain of 'indifference,' flows that *absurd* and *erroneous* doctrine, or rather raving, in favor and defence of *'liberty of conscience'*, for which most pestilential error, the course is opened to that entire and wild liberty of opinion, which is every where attempting the overthrow of religious and civil institutions; and which the unblushing impudence of some [John Leland, James Madison, etc.] has held forth as an advantage to religion. Hence *that pest, of all others most to be dreaded in a state, unbridled liberty of opinion,* licentiousness of speech, and a lust of novelty, which, according to the experience of all ages, portend the downfall of the most powerful and flourishing empires. Hither tends that worst and never sufficiently to be execrated and detested LIBERTY OF THE PRESS, for the diffusion of all manner of writings, which some so loudly contend for, and so actively promote"[138] (from his encyclical letter of September 1832).

91. **Pope Leo XIII**** "Freemasonry is the permanent personification of the Revolution; it constitutes a sort of society in reverse whose aim is to exercise an occult overlordship upon society as we know it, and whose raison d'être consists in waging war against God and His Church"[139] (from his encyclical of March 19, 1902).

92. **Pope Paul VI**** "Who can fail to see the need and importance of thus gradually coming to the establishment of a world authority capable of taking effective action on the juridicial and political planes? . . . Delegates to international organizations, public officials, gentlemen of the press, teachers and educators—all of you must realize that you have your part to play in the construction of a new world order"[140] (from his *Populorum Progressio* ["rope-a-dope"] of March 26, 1967, calling for "a new juridicial order").

"But nowadays, no country can keep its wealth just for itself alone. It should be normal, now, for the developed nations to help the under-developed with some agreed percentage of their additional income"[141] (written at Easter 1967).

93. **Pope John Paul II***** "As I stated at the beginning of this year in my message for the world day of peace, if men and women hope to transform society [papal pipe dream], they must begin by changing their own hearts first [another papal pipe dream, Titus 3:5]. Only with a 'new heart' can one rediscover clear-sightedness and impartiality with freedom of spirit, the sense of justice with respect to the rights of men, the sense of equality, with global solidarity between the rich and the poor, mutual trust [the ultimate pipe dream] and fraternal love. . . God bless America."[142] (Excerpt from his speech in Alaska's Fairbanks International Airport, May 2, 1984, with President Ronald Reagan at his side. For the record, both men were professional actors prior to their careers as pope and president.)

JOURNALISTS

94. *Washington Times Herald** "A relatively few people, speaking through a considerable number of microphones, can create a fictitious impression that there is a 'public demand' for policies which lack appeal to the great body of people, who have no such convenient propaganda organs to make their desires heard. . . . If misery and ruin of the Republic were the avowed objectives of these enemies within the gates, they could not have adopted doctrines and methods better calculated to achieve that disloyal purpose"[143] (an editorial written by the patriot, Colonel McCormack, January 10, 1951).

95. *Chicago Tribune** "The members of the Council are persons of much more than average influence in the community. They have used the prestige that their wealth, their social position, and their education have given them to lead their country toward bankruptcy and military debacle. They should look at their hands. There is **blood** on them"[144] (another rare patriotic editorial, December 9, 1950).

"We are not going to achieve a new world order without paying for it in **blood** as well as in words and money"[145] (CFR member Arthur Schlesinger, Jr., writing in the July-August 1995 edition of the CFR's *Foreign Affairs*).

96. *Washington Post** "If you like Conspiracy theories about secret plots to take over the world, you are going to love the administration of President-elect Jimmy Carter. At last count 13 Trilateralists had gone into top positions in the administration. This is extraordinary when you consider that the Trilateral Commission only has about 65 American members."[146]

97. **Herman Dinsmore* (Foreign editor of** *The New York Times* **from 1951-1960)** "*The New York Times* today is deliberately pitched to the so-called liberal point of view. . . . Positively and negatively, the weight of *The [New York] Times* has generally fallen on the side of the communists since the end of World War II"[147] (from his book, *All The News That Fits*, 1969).

98. **Cokie Roberts* (Cokie's mother is a former U.S. Ambassador to the Vatican)** "Global bankers are really running the world"[148] (August 28, 1994, on ABC's "This Week With David Brinkley").

99. **Walter Cronkite*** "If we are to avoid catastrophe, a system of world order—preferably a system of world government—is mandatory. The proud nations someday will . . . yield up their precious sovereignty"[149] (from his book, *A Reporter's Life*, 1996).

HYPOCRITICAL TALK SHOW HOSTS

100. **Rush Limbaugh**** (President of the EIB Network)** "You see, if you amount to anything in Washington these days, it is because you have been plucked or handpicked from an Ivy League school—Harvard, Yale, Kennedy School of Government—you've shown an aptitude to be a good Ivy League type, and so you're plucked so-to-speak, and you are assigned success. **You are assigned a certain role in government somewhere, and then your success is monitored and tracked, and you go where the pluckers and the handpickers can put you**"[150] (February 7, 1995, radio program).

"This [NAFTA] is the one issue Clinton has, other than welfare reform, where he has just flown in the face of his constituency groups. . . . **There are forces, powerful forces, outside Washington, who are steering this one.**"[151] (September 24, 1997, radio program)

Wha'd I tell ya'?—El Rushbo was just pulling your leg all along.

For what it's worth, I will leave you with a little food for thought concerning Mr. Limbaugh's hearing problems of 2000-01. A former student of mine, who was pastoring a church in Eastern Colorado at the time, drove twelve hours with his wife to hear me preach in a church in Jefferson City, Missouri. During our fellowship he related how he had distinctly heard Rush make a blasphemous statement over the air only days before ear number one went on the fritz. A typically naive Christian had called to try and explain current events in light of Bible prophecy. (He should have been cautioned by Matthew 7:6b, *"neither cast ye your pearls before swine."*) Well, after cutting him off in predictable neurotic fashion, Rush warned his vast audience that what he was about to say might very well shock many of them. He then proceeded to announce that a highly qualified theologian friend had assured him that the book of Revelation did not even belong in the inspired canon of Scripture! Unfortunately for him, the Holy Ghost disagrees! *"[T]hese words are true and faithful"* (Revelation 21:5b).

Ear number two fizzled about the time Rush went ballistic over Jerry Falwell's short-lived position that September 11, 2001, was divine retribution for America's sins.

If I were you, Rush, I'd watch that "talent on loan from God" stuff. *You* may be a "harmless little fuzz ball," but—*"He that planteth the ear, shall he not hear?"* (Psalm 94:9a) And let's not forget that brief tryout as a sports announcer followed by the rehab thing *and* that protracted criminal investigation. But then again, you *did* say that your programs were "highly addictive."

7

They Knew Too Much

". . . truth is fallen in the street . . ."
(Isaiah 59:14b)

I N ADDITION TO opposing conspiracy history with the
aforementioned tactics of misrepresentation, straw men, and public
ridicule, "ditto heads" will also confidently employ an argument
deduced from *silence*. According to this approach, if conspiracy advocates
were right, one of them would eventually stumble upon irrefutable evidence,
or better yet, a real-life defector would come forward to expose the
conspiracy. Thus, in the absence of a "smoking gun," conspiracy theorists
must resign themselves to "kook status." There are a number of things
wrong with this idiotic approach. First, plenty of hard evidence *has* been
uncovered (as the reader will discover in the following chapters) and
various credible insiders like Harvard Professor Carroll Quigley *have*
come forward with their confidential material. Quigley was naive
enough to write about Britain's Round Table Group and its American
subsidiary, the Council on Foreign Relations:

> I have no aversion to it or to most of its aims and have, for much of my
> life, been close to it and to many of its instruments. . . . In general my
> chief difference of opinion is that it wishes to remain unknown, and
> I believe its role in history is significant enough to be known.[1]

Second, though dozens of documented books have been written on
subjects such as Ruby Ridge, Waco, TWA flight 800, the Oklahoma
Bombing, etc., the media and the National Education Association (NEA)

are constantly suppressing this material. Thus, *". . . truth is fallen in the street. . . ."* (Isaiah 59:14b)

Sadly, with respect to what has been made available, the materialistic American public couldn't care less. General George Van Horne Mosley wrote, "Historians of the future will marvel most of all at the non-resistance of those who had the most to lose."[2] An appropriate adage goes, "The man in the street does not notice the devil even when the devil is holding him by the throat."

What is rarely known is the number of "Limbaugh Kooks" who were threatened, blackmailed, professionally ruined, jailed or even physically eliminated for having attempted to "blow the whistle" on various facets of conspiracy activity. (See New Jersey Congressman James Saxton, chapter seventeen.) Unfortunately, however, owing to the very nature of conspiracy, one is rarely spoiled by an abundance of pertinent information concerning a mysterious death under investigation. Whenever the government murders its own citizens it is axiomatic that the culprits just happen to be invested with the requisite power to cover their own tracks. Convenient resources such as executive privilege, executive orders, gag orders, judicial injunctions, RICO laws, wiretaps and "black helicopters" are beyond the reach of "small-time" operators like the Mafia. This is how "General Janet" was able to have two crime scenes bulldozed in eight years (e.g., Waco and Oklahoma City). Yet, two things are nearly always present at the scene of any murder—a body (or bodies) and plenty of suspicion. Therefore, I have classified the following sampling of suspicious deaths under the heading . . .

THE LIMBAUGH KOOK MEMORIAL

William Morgan: Kidnapped, killed and dumped in the Niagara River, New York, for exposing Freemasonry.

William Henry Harrison: In his inaugural speech as the nation's twelfth president (1841), Harrison cleared the air by stating:

> We admit of no government by *divine right*, believing that so far as power is concerned, the beneficent Creator has made no distinction among men; that all are upon an equality, and that the only legitimate right to govern, is upon the express grant of power from the governed.[3]

Just one month and five days later President Harrison was a corpse. The *Dictionary of American Biography* said he contracted a chill that developed into pneumonia. "Worn out by the strain of the election and by the ceaseless importunities of office seekers, he was unable to resist the disease and died on April 4, 1841."[4]

Senator Thomas Benton of Missouri disagreed, writing in his book, *Thirty Years' View*,

> There was no failure of health or strength to indicate such an event or to excite apprehension that he would not go through his term with the same vigor with which he commenced it. *His attack was sudden and evidently fatal from the beginning.*[5]

Historian Burke McCarthy adds, "He died from arsenic poisoning, administered by the tools of Rome."[6] Senator Benton also noted, regarding Harrison's family, "That the deceased President had been closely preceded and was rapidly followed by the deaths of almost all of his numerous family, sons and daughters."[7] Rare is the American who has ever read the words of a Jesuit oath:

> I do further promise and declare, that I will, when opportunity presents, make and wage relentless war, secretly or openly, against all heretics, Protestants and Liberals, as I am directed to do to extirpate and exterminate them from the face of the whole earth . . . That when the same cannot be done openly, I will secretly use the *poison cup* . . . regardless of the honor, rank, dignity or authority of the person or persons whatsoever may be their condition in life, either public or private, as I at any time may be directed so to do by any agent of the Pope or Superior of the Brotherhood of the Holy Faith of the Society of Jesus.[8]

A spurious document purporting to be a Jesuit/Knights of Columbus oath surfaced during a heated political battle in 1912 between a Quaker and a Roman Catholic in Delaware County, Pennsylvania. A copy of the entire statement was subsequently read into the Congressional Record (see House Bill 1523, contested election case of Eugene C. Bonniwell, against Thos. S. Butler, February 15, 1913, pages 3215-16). Regardless of the authenticity of this text, the wording is 100 percent consistent with the documentation of Rome's historical bloodletting. (See *Foxe's Book of Martyrs*.) The style is also in accordance with the oaths of secret societies in general and Freemasonry in particular.

Zachary Taylor: President Taylor was another target of the Vatican, McCarty writing,

> [O]n the Fourth of July, arsenic was administered to him during a celebration in Washington at which he was invited to deliver an address. He went in perfect health in the morning and was taken ill in the afternoon about five o'clock and died on the Monday following, having been sick the same number of days and with precisely the same symptoms as was his predecessor, President Harrison.[9]

James Buchanan: The fifteenth president barely survived *his* run-in with the Society of Jesus. The *New York Herald* stated, "The plot was deep and planned with skill. . . . President Buchanan was poisoned, and with great difficulty his life was saved."[10]

Abraham Lincoln: "Honest Abe" caught a bullet in his brain a year after referring to the "priests of Rome" as traitors. General Thomas Harris, one of the nine officers comprising the military tribunal, concluded,

> Thus the history of this great crime reveals to us *Rome's responsibility for the assassination of Abraham Lincoln,* not as an individual man, however much of personal hatred on the part of the Jesuits might have led them to plan for his death, but as the head of the nation they desired to destroy.[11]

If General Harris was incorrect, the next most likely candidate would be Andy Jackson's old nemesis, the prevailing international bankers who despised Lincoln for printing greenbacks during the Civil War.

Pope John Paul I: I decided to include his assassination to prove that Rome is no respecter of persons. Pope Paul VI died on August 6, 1978. When his followers' campaign for another pro-Russian Pontiff became deadlocked with a faction in league with the CIA, the stalemate was broken with the election of a neutral candidate, Cardinal Luciani, patriarch of Venice. When "Lucky" Luciani was asked in Latin, "Do you accept your election as Supreme Pontiff which has been canonically carried out?," the astute victim astonished the officiating Cardinals by replying, "May God forgive you for what you have done in my regard."[12] Only thirty-three days later, Pope John Paul I (Luciani) was "history," having died mysteriously in his sleep. The new pontiff was actually supposed to have departed sooner. A couple of weeks earlier, the Russian Orthodox

Metropolitan Nikodim, archbishop of Leningrad and Novograd, made an official visit to the Vatican. When Nikodim was invited to join Johnny for some coffee, the unfortunate Metropolitan picked up his friend's cup by mistake. One sip and he was "out of here." Avro Manhattan writes, "He clutched his chest with both hands, emitting a choking grunt, then crashed on the floor, toppling backwards, with a thud."[13] Conversely, John Paul I "passed away" in private. There was no autopsy. A team of embalmers showed up out of nowhere almost immediately after being summoned by Cardinal Villot at approximately 6:10 a.m. The corpse was a mess—bulging eyes, distorted jaw, a horrendous grimace, etc. Finally, the pope's personal "housekeeper," Sister Vincenza, the one who discovered the crime, vanished into thin air, never to be heard from again.[14]

William McKinley: A. Ralph Epperson writes, "It was now 1900 . . . President William McKinley was prosecuting the Northern Securities Company under the anti-trust laws. McKinley changed his vice-presidents for his second term, and less than a year later he was assassinated."[15]

Warren G. Harding: The nation's twenty-ninth president died on August 2, 1923. Epperson states, "There are those who believe that there were some who couldn't wait for the Teapot Dome Scandal to remove President Harding, and that he was poisoned."[16]

Louis T. McFadden: Commenting on Congressman McFadden's "heart-failure sudden death" on October 3, 1936, after a "dose" of "intestinal flu," *Pelley's Weekly* of October 14 stated:

> Now that this sterling American patriot has made the Passing, it can be revealed that not long after his public utterances against the encroaching powers, it became known among his intimates that he had suffered two attacks against his life. The first attack came in the form of two revolver shots fired at him from ambush as he was alighting from a cab in front of one of the Capital hotels. Fortunately both shots missed him, the bullets burying themselves in the structure of the cab. He became violently ill after partaking of food at a political banquet in Washington. His life was only saved from what was subsequently announced as a poisoning by the presence of a physician friend at the banquet, who at once procured a stomach pump and subjected the Congressman to emergency treatment.[17]

Frank Murphy: Epperson writes about this Supreme Court justice,

> He once had an occasion to meet with Congressman Martin Dies, the Chairman of the House Committee on Un-American Activities. Murphy told Dies, "We're doomed! The United States is doomed! The Communists have control completely. They've got control of Roosevelt and his wife as well." A few years later, in 1949, Murphy went into a Detroit hospital and died from a heart attack, just before he was scheduled to be released as recovered. Congressman Dies was convinced that he had been murdered.[18]

George Patton: General Patton was another one of these "hospital fatalities." Epperson states,

> August 8, 1945, was the day that Russia finally decided to enter the war against Japan, and this was but six days prior to that nation's surrender. It has been theorized that the reason this occurred in this sequence was to rationalize the giving of Japanese property or interests to the Russians after the war, since they were then an official enemy of Japan. One of the Americans who observed the strange behavior of the American government was General George S. Patton. He had seen enough to cause him to want to resign from the military so that he could "say what I want to" about America's "soft on Communism" stance during the war. Patton knew enough about the military that he couldn't merely retire and speak out, because military men of high rank, even though retired, are still under the control of the government. This subjection to government authority includes their ability to speak out on the main issues of the day. Should Patton resign, he would be free to speak as he saw fit. Patton had a strong dislike for what happened as the Russians acquired much of Eastern Europe, and it is said by many that he was going to speak out about this betrayal to the American people after the war was over. But, before he had a chance to resign, he was killed after an automobile accident caused him to be hospitalized.
>
> In 1979, a former undercover agent for the Office of Strategic Services, the OSS, gave an interview in which he claimed that he had been asked to kill Patton. This agent was ". . . Douglas Bazata, a veteran intelligence agent, who said he received a contract on Patton's life in 1944. According to Bazata, the order for the 'hit' came down to him from none other than the legendary Office of Strategic Services direct from [its administrator] 'Wild Bill' Donovan." When Bazata was asked why he was finally going public with this admission after so many years, he said he ". . . was in poor health and wanted the American people to know the truth." The

newspaper that carried the interview claimed that it had "a professional analyst subject Bazata's interview to the rigors of a content analysis using a Psychological Stress Evaluator (P.S.E.). His report: Bazata gives no evidence of lying." It was Bazata's contention that, although he collected more than $10,000 for the death of Patton, he was not responsible for Patton's actual death. He claimed that he knows, however, who did kill him, and that Patton was killed by a dose of cyanide in the hospital where he was taken after the automobile accident, and that it was the cyanide rather than the accident that took his life.[19]

I once had the opportunity to speak with a former OSS official residing in Pennsylvania, who was in Europe at the time of Patton's "accident." It was his opinion that the controversial general was assassinated.

James Forrestal: America's first secretary of defense was yet another "hospital victim." Like Senator Joe McCarthy, Forrestal was a member of the Roman Catholic Church who may have been more loyal to America than to the Vatican. He, too, was aware of the sinister post-war events that had troubled General Patton, stating,

> These men are not incompetent or stupid. They are crafty and brilliant. Consistency has never been a mark of stupidity. If they were merely stupid, they would occasionally make a mistake in our favor.[20]

In his book *Meeting At Potsdam*, Charles L. Mee, Jr., wrote,

> The Communists, both American and European, had good reason to hate Jim Forrestal: he hated them. He emerged from the Second War dedicated to the destruction of Communism. . . . During the war his personal files fattened alarmingly—filled with the names of journals and organizations and individuals who were "under Communist influence."[21]

President Truman insisted on Forrestal's resignation. Sensing that the secretary was under an "emotional strain," Dr. George N. Raines, chief of neuropsychiatry at the U.S. Naval Hospital in Bethesda, Maryland, decided to admit Forrestal for "observation." His personal diaries, "consisting of fifteen loose-leaf binders totaling three thousand pages, were hastily removed from his former office in the Pentagon."[22] Cornell Simpson wrote in his book *The Death of James Forrestal*,

> Before Forrestal left for Bethesda, he told a friend that he had been followed and that his telephone had been tapped. He further discussed the

impending war in Korea, a war still fifteen months from beginning. Forrestal said, "They're going to catch us unprepared. American soldiers will be dying in a year."[23]

After repeatedly being denied permission to see his own brother, Henry Forrestal telephoned the hospital to inform them that he would be arriving on May 22 (1949) to take their high profile patient for a therapeutic trip into the country. Only hours before Henry was due to board the train to Bethesda, he received news that the ex-secretary was dead. The "official" version was that Forrestal had jumped to his death from a sixteenth floor window of the hospital, the very day he was to meet his brother. His body was found sprawled grotesquely on a third floor projection of the building, with the cord of his bathrobe wound and tied tightly around his neck.

The formal report "theorized" that Forrestal had tied the other end of the bathrobe cord around a radiator and then jumped out the window to commit suicide. However, the facts betray defenestration. Forrestal left no suicide note. Furthermore, not one shred of the bathrobe cord nor a single mark on the radiator was ever found to indicate that the cord had ever been there. Also, the cord hadn't broken during the purported hanging. How could an ex-Navy man (Forrestal had also served as secretary of the Navy) have failed to tie the other end of the cord to the radiator if he had really intended to hang himself? Two years later a "gutted " version of his diary was released by the White House and published by Viking Press. Forrestal's family priest, Maurice S. Sheehy, is on record as having stated, "Many, many times in his letters to me, Jim Forrestal wrote anxiously and fearfully and bitterly of the enormous harm that had been, and was unceasingly being done, by men in high office in the United States government, who he was convinced were Communists or under the influence of Communists, and who he said were shaping the policies of the United States government to aid Soviet Russia and harm the United States."[24]

Joseph McCarthy: The number one Communist fighter in America died on May 2, 1957—in the *same* hospital where Forrestal "committed suicide." The official version of *his* passing was that he died of "acute hepatic failure." It is a matter of record that the senator suffered from infectious hepatitis. In his book *The Assassination of Joe McCarthy*, Dr. Medford Evans wrote,

A man with a history of *infectious hepatitis* could indeed succumb abruptly to *toxic hepatitis*, a deadly affair in any case. Toxic hepatitis is caused, as the name indicates, by any of several poisons, including chloroform, mercury, and snake venom, but most conveniently, perhaps, by carbon tetrachloride, the common dry-cleaning solvent. A scarcely noticeable or quickly dissipated concentration might be fatal to a man already suffering from a liver complaint [hepatitis][25]

When McCarthy was admitted into Bethesda, he was "immediately placed in an oxygen tent" which led Dr. Evans to speculate, "Do you suppose anybody could have [gotten] any carbon tetrachloride into that thing?"[26] Epperson writes,

> It is his theory that carbon tetrachloride easily could have been placed under the oxygen tent and then dissipated quickly as McCarthy was sleeping. The breathing of a poison by a man suffering from infectious hepatitis would have been fatal.[27]

Dr. Evans commented further on the senator's overall physical condition, ". . . Joe McCarthy's health was such in the Spring of 1957 as to make it incredible that he should die so swiftly of natural causes."[28] As in the case of John Paul I, no autopsy was performed on Senator McCarthy's body. Dr. Evans concludes, "A note is necessary on the relationship of the [Communist] Party—McCarthy's declared enemy, as he was theirs— to the American "establishment," which is presumably anti-Communist, and which McCarthy never attacked, but which attacked him, and was, indeed, more immediately the instrument of [his] destruction than was the Communist Party."[29]

As an interesting aside, there is also a connection between Bethesda Naval Hospital and President Richard Nixon. During the time that Nixon was preparing to resign from the White House, he was suffering from a swollen leg. He made the ominous statement that if he had gone to Bethesda to have it attended to he would have "never come out alive."[30] (And all of these cases are in addition to the 50,000 "normal" Americans who are murdered annually in our nation's hospitals according to Ralph Nader!)

John F. Kennedy: Your guess is as good as good as mine! Less than three weeks after ordering the "hit" on Ngo Dinh Diem, the first Roman Catholic president of South Viet Nam, the Catholic Kennedy got "whacked" himself. Some investigators contend it was Castro's men who pulled the trigger. Others think it may have been Sam "Momo" Giancana, as Attorney General Bobby Kennedy promptly dropped his investigations into organized crime after his brother's untimely death. The majority, however, attribute his death to the CIA or other corrupt insiders. Nineteen key witnesses to what *really* happened died under mysterious circumstances within two years! The president's brain even disappeared from the Smithsonian Institute.

J. Edgar Hoover: Harvard University graduate Dr. Leonard Horowitz, an internationally known authority in public health education, concurs with the conclusion of Anthony Summers, author of *The Secret Life of J. Edgar Hoover* that, "J. Edgar Hoover was very likely assassinated."[31] Hoover's housekeepers found his body on May 2, 1972. The time frame for *this* murder was less than two months prior to the Watergate break-in. Nixon feared that Hoover was about to expose his administration's ongoing domestic snooping ring. According to Summers,

> A year after Watergate, Mark Frazier, a young reporter working in Washington, was to pick up an intriguing lead. Three sources, he learned, had given affidavits to the Senate Watergate Committee referring to two break-in operations at Edgar's home in Rock Creek Park. They were, allegedly, "directed by Gordon Liddy." In the welter of news arising from Watergate [or possibly because of official media censorship], Frazier was unable to get the story published in a Washington paper. Instead, it ran in a university publication, *The Harvard Crimson*.[32]

Horowitz relates,

> Hoover's home, the article said, had been targeted twice for break-ins. The first operation, in "late winter of 1972," was intended to "retrieve documents that were thought to be used as potential blackmail against the White House." This attempt failed, but was followed by another which succeeded. "This time," Frazier reported, "whether through misunderstanding or design, a poison of the thiophosphate genre was placed on Hoover's personal toilet articles."
>
> Thiophosphate, a chemical commonly found in insecticides, is extremely toxic to human beings if ingested, inhaled, or absorbed through the skin. Exposure can cause fatal heart attacks, and can only be detected by an autopsy performed within hours of the lethal poisoning.[33]

Hoover's personal physician, Dr. Robert Choisser arrived on the scene. He later stated,

> Mr. Hoover had been dead for some hours. I was rather surprised by his sudden death, because he was in good health. I do not recall prescribing him medication for blood pressure or heart disease. There was nothing to lead anyone to expect him to die at that time, except for his age.[34]

Of course, we'll never know for sure as an autopsy was quite out of the question.

Carroll Quigley: Professor Quigley was another "kook" who spent the last years of his life looking over his shoulder and sitting with his back to the wall. Carroll wrote to a friend on December 9, 1975,

> Thank you for your praise of *Tragedy and Hope*, a book which has brought me headaches as it apparently says something which powerful people do not want known. My publisher stopped selling it in 1968 and told me he would reprint (but in 1971 he told my lawyer that they had destroyed the plates in 1968). The rare-book price went up to $135 and parts were reprinted in violation of copyright.[35]

In a second letter, the frustrated author stated flatly, "I am now quite sure that *Tragedy and Hope* was suppressed."[36] (What a paranoid!) On March 23, 1975, *The Washington Post* published an ominous article about Quigley titled, "The Professor Who Knew Too Much." Dr. Cuddy notes that Quigley would be dead less than two years later.[37] (For what it's worth; George Bush was director of the CIA at the time.)

"SLICK WILLY"

Many dozens of other non-related victims could be named. However, one of Professor Quigley's own students may have been responsible for producing the greatest hit list in modern history. The reprobate's name is *William Jefferson Clinton* (the man who "feels your pain"). True, some of the cases listed below may be explained away in time. But, think for a moment—have you ever known anyone who was tied to even half-a-dozen suspicious deaths? Bill Clinton has over *sixty* skeletons rattling around in his closet (not including Waco), and he's still in his prime!

The following "Body Count" of our forty-second president has been reprinted by permission from the folks at www.etherZone.com:
They write:

BODY COUNT

Here is the latest body count that we have. All of these people have been connected with the Clintons in some form or another. We have not included any deaths that could not be verified or connected to the Clinton scandals. All deaths are listed chronologically by date. This list is current and accurate to the best of our knowledge as of August 1, 2000.

Susan Coleman: Rumors were circulating in Arkansas of an affair with Bill Clinton. She was found dead with a gunshot wound to the head at 7½ months pregnant. Death was an apparent suicide.

Larry Guerrin: Was killed in February, 1987, while investigating the INSLAW case.

Kevin Ives & Don Henry: Initial cause of death was reported to be the result of falling asleep on a railroad track in Arkansas on August 23, 1987. This ruling was reported by the State medical examiner Fahmy Malak. Later it was determined that Kevin died from a crushed skull prior to being placed on the tracks. Don had been stabbed in the back. Rumors indicate that they might have stumbled upon a Mena drug operation.

Keith Coney: Keith had information on the Ives/Henry deaths. Died in a motorcycle accident in July 1988 with unconfirmed reports of a high-speed car chase.

Keith McKaskle: McKaskle had information on the Ives/Henry deaths. He was stabbed to death in November, 1988.

Gregory Collins: Greg had information on the Ives/Henry deaths. He died from a gunshot wound to the face in January, 1989.

Jeff Rhodes: He had information on the deaths of Ives, Henry & McKaskle. His burned body was found in a trash dump in April, 1989. He died of a gunshot wound to the head and there was some body mutilation, leading to the speculation that he was probably tortured prior to being killed. The state Medical examiner, Fahmy Malak, initially ruled death due to natural causes.

Richard Winters: Winters was a suspect in the death of Ives & Henry. He was killed in a "robbery" in July, 1989, which was subsequently proven to be a setup.

Jordan Kettleson: Kettleson had information on the Ives & Henry deaths. He was found shot to death in the front seat of his pickup in June, 1990.

Alan Standorf: An employee of the National Security Agency in electronic intelligence. Standorf was a source of information for Danny Casalaro who was investigating INSLAW, BCCI, etc. Standorf's body was found in the backseat of a car at Washington National Airport on January 31, 1991.

Dennis Eisman: An attorney with information on INSLAW. Eisman was found shot to death on April 5, 1991.

Danny Casalaro: Danny was a free-lance reporter and writer who was investigating the "October Surprise", INSLAW and BCCI. Danny was found dead in a bathtub in a Sheraton Hotel room in Martinsburg, West Virginia. Danny was staying at the hotel while keeping appointments in the DC area pertinent to his investigation. He was found with his wrists slashed. At least one, and possibly both of his wrists were cut 10 times. All of his research materials were missing and have never been recovered.

Victor Raiser: The National Finance Co-Chair for "Clinton for President." He died in an airplane crash on July 30, 1992.

R. Montgomery Raiser: Also involved in the Clinton presidential campaign. He died in the same plane crash as Victor.

Paul Tully: Tully was on the Democratic National Committee. He was found dead of unknown causes in his hotel room on September 24, 1992. No autopsy was ever allowed.

Ian Spiro: Spiro had supporting documentation for grand jury proceedings on the INSLAW case. His wife and 3 children were found murdered on November 1, 1992, in their home. They all died of gunshot wounds to the head. Ian's body was found several days later in a parked car in the Borego Desert. Cause of death? The ingestion of cyanide. FBI report indicated that Ian had murdered his family and then committed suicide.

Paula Gober: A Clinton speechwriter. She died in a car accident on December 9, 1992, with no known witnesses.

Jim Wilhite: Wilhite was an associate of Mack McClarty's former firm. Wilhite died in a skiing accident on December 21, 1992. He also had extensive ties to Clinton with whom he visited by telephone just hours before his death.

Steve Willis, Robert Williams, Todd McKeahan & Conway LeBleu: Died February 28, 1993 by gunfire at Waco. All four were examined by a pathologist and died from identical wounds to the left temple. All four had been bodyguards for Bill Clinton, three while campaigning for President and when he was Governor of Arkansas. They also were the ONLY 4 BATF agents killed at Waco.

Sgt. Brian Haney, Tim Sabel, Maj. William Barkley, Capt. Scott Reynolds: Died: May 19, 1993—All four men died when their helicopter crashed in the woods near Quantico, VA.—Reporters were barred from the site, and the head of the fire department responding to the crash described it by saying, "Security was tight," with "lots of Marines with guns." A videotape made by a firefighter was seized by the Marines. All four men had escorted Clinton on his flight to the carrier Roosevelt shortly before their deaths.

John Crawford: An attorney with information on INSLAW. He died from a heart attack in Tacoma in April of 1993.

John Wilson: Found dead from an apparent hanging suicide on May 18, 1993. He was a former Washington, DC council member and claimed to have info on Whitewater.

Paul Wilcher: A lawyer who was investigating drug running out of Mena, Arkansas and who also sought to expose the "October Surprise", BCCI and INSLAW. He was found in his Washington, D.C., apartment dead of unknown causes on June 22, 1993.

Vincent Foster: A White House deputy counsel and long-time personal friend of Bill and Hillary's. Found on July 20, 1993, dead of a gunshot wound to the mouth—a death ruled suicide. Many different theories on this case! Readers are encouraged to read our report in Strange Deaths.

Jon Parnell Walker: An investigator for the RTC who was looking into the linkage between the Whitewater and Madison S&L bankruptcy. Walker "fell" from the top of the Lincoln Towers Building.

Stanley Heard & Steven Dickson: They were members of the Clinton health care advisory committee. They died in a plane crash on September 10, 1993.

Jerry Luther Parks: Parks was the Chief of Security for Clinton's national campaign headquarters in Little Rock. Gunned down in his car on September 26, 1993, near the intersection of Chenal Parkway and Highway 10 west of Little Rock. Parks was shot through the rear window of his car. The assailant then pulled around to the driver's side of Parks's car and shot him three more times with a 9mm pistol. His family reported that shortly before his death, they were being followed by unknown persons, and their home had been broken into (despite a top quality alarm system). Parks had been compiling a dossier on Clinton's illicit activities. The dossier was stolen.

Ed Willey: A Clinton fundraiser. He died of a self-inflicted gunshot wound on November 30, 1993. His death came the same day his wife, Kathleen, was sexually assaulted in the White House by Bill Clinton.

Gandy Baugh: Baugh was Lasater's attorney and committed suicide on January 8, 1994. Baugh's partner committed suicide exactly one month later on February 8, 1994.

Herschell Friday: A member of the presidential campaign finance committee. He died in an airplane explosion on March 1, 1994.

Ronald Rogers: Rogers died on March 3, 1994, just prior to releasing sensitive information to a London newspaper. Cause of death? Undetermined.

Kathy Furguson: A 38-year-old hospital worker whose ex-husband is a co-defendant in the Paula Jones sexual harassment law suit. She had information supporting Paula Jones's allegations. She died of an apparent suicide on May 11, 1994, from a gunshot wound to the head.

Bill Shelton: Shelton was an Arkansas police officer and was found dead as an apparent suicide on Kathy Furguson's grave (Kathy was his girl friend), on June 12, 1994. This "suicide" was the result of a gunshot wound to the back of the head.

Stanley Huggins: Huggins, 46, was a principal in a Memphis law firm which headed a 1987 investigation into the loan practices of Madison Guaranty S&L. Stanley died in Delaware in July, 1994—reported cause of death was viral pneumonia.

Paul Olson: A Federal witness in investigations to drug money corruption in Chicago politics, Paul had just finished 2 days of FBI interviews when his plane ride home crashed, killing Paul and 130 others on September 8, 1994. The September 15, 1994, *Tempe Tribune* newspaper reported that the FBI suspected that a bomb had brought down the airplane.

Calvin Walraven: 24-year-old Walraven was a key witness against Jocelyn Elder's son's drug case. Walraven was found dead in his apartment with a gunshot wound to the head. Tim Hover, a Little Rock police spokesman says no foul play is suspected.

Alan G. Whicher: Oversaw Clinton's Secret Service detail. In October, 1994, Whicher was transferred to the Secret Service field office in the Murrah Building in Oklahoma City. Whatever warning was given to the BATF agents in that building did not reach Alan Whicher, who died in the bomb blast of April 19, 1995.

Duane Garrett: Died July 26, 1995—A lawyer and talk show host for KGO-AM in San Francisco, Duane was the campaign finance chairman for Diane Feinstein's run for the Senate, and was a friend and fundraiser for Al Gore. Garrett was under investigation for defrauding investors in Garrett's failed sports memorabilia venture. There was talk of a deal to evade prosecution. On July 26th, Garrett canceled an afternoon meeting with his lawyer because he had to meet some people at the San Francisco airport. Three hours later he was found floating in the bay under the Golden Gate Bridge.

Ron Brown: The Commerce Secretary died on April 3, 1996, in an Air Force jet carrying Brown and 34 others, including 14 business executives on a trade mission to Croatia, crashed into a mountainside. The Air Force, in a 22-volume report issued in June of 1996, confirmed its initial judgment that the crash resulted from pilot errors and faulty navigation equipment. At the time of Brown's death, Independent Counsel Daniel Pearson was seeking to determine whether Brown had engaged in several sham financial transactions with longtime business partner Nolanda Hill shortly before he became Secretary of Commerce.

Charles Meissner: died: UNK—Following Ron Brown's death, John Huang was placed on a Commerce Department contract that allowed him to retain his security clearance by Charles Meissner. Shortly thereafter, Meissner died in the crash of a small plane. He was an Assistant Secretary of Commerce for International Economic Policy.

William Colby: Retired CIA director was found dead on May 6, 1996, after his wife reported him missing on April 27, 1996. Apparently, Colby decided to go on an impromptu canoeing excursion and never returned. Colby, who had just started writing for *Strategic Investments* newsletter, worried many in the intelligence community. Colby's past history of divulging CIA secrets [was] well known. *Strategic Investments* had covered the Vince Foster suicide and had hired handwriting experts to review Foster's suicide note.

Admiral Jeremy Boorda: Died on May 16, 1996, after he went home for lunch and decided to shoot himself in the chest (by one report, twice) rather than be interviewed by *Newsweek* magazine that afternoon. Explanations for Boorda's suicide focused on a claim that he was embarrassed over two "Valor" pins he was not authorized to wear.

Lance Herndon: Herndon, a 41-year-old computer specialist and a prominent entrepreneur who received a presidential appointment in 1995, died August 10, 1996, under suspicious circumstances. He appeared to have died from a blow to the head. Police said no weapons were found at his mansion, adding that Mr. Herndon had not been shot or stabbed and there was no evidence of forced entry or theft.

Neil Moody: Died—August 25, 1996—following Vincent Foster's murder, Lisa Foster married James Moody, a judge in Arkansas, on Jan. 1, 1996. Near the time Susan McDougal first went to jail for contempt, Judge Moody's son, Neil, died in a car crash. There were other reports that Neil Moody had discovered something very unsettling among his stepmother's private papers and was threatening to go public with it just prior to the beginning of the Democratic National Convention. He was alleged to have been talking to Bob Woodward of *The Washington Post* about a blockbuster story. Witnesses said they saw Neil Moody sitting in his car arguing with another person just prior to his car suddenly speeding off out of control and hitting a brick wall.

Barbara Wise: Wise, a 14-year Commerce Department employee found dead and partially naked in her office following a long weekend. She worked in the same section as John Huang. Officially, she is said to have died of natural causes.

Doug Adams: Died January 7, 1997—A lawyer in Arkansas who got involved trying to help the people who were being swindled out of their life savings. Adams was found in his vehicle with a gunshot wound to his head in a Springfield, Missouri, hospital parking lot.

Mary C. Mahoney: 25, murdered at the Georgetown Starbuck's coffee bar over the 4th of July '97 weekend. She was a former White House intern who worked with John Huang. Apparently, she knew Monica Lewinsky and her sexual encounters with Bill Clinton. Although not verified, it has been said that Lewinsky told Linda Tripp that she did not want to end up like Mahoney.

Ronald Miller: Suddenly took ill on October 3, 1997, and steadily worsened until his death 9 days later. (This pattern fits Ricin poisoning.) Owing to the strangeness of the illness, doctors at the Integris Baptist Medical Center referred the matter to the Oklahoma State Medical Examiner's Office. The Oklahoma State Medical Examiner's Office promptly ran tests on samples of Ron Miller's blood, but has refused to release the results or even to confirm that the tests were ever completed.

Had been investigated by authorities over the sale of his company, Gage Corp., to Dynamic Energy Resources, Inc. Was the man who tape recorded Gene and Nora Lum and turned those tapes (and other records) over to Congressional oversight investigators. The Lums were sentenced to prison for campaign finance violations, using "straw donors" to conceal the size of their contributions to various candidates. Indeed, Dynamic Energy Resources, Inc. had hired Ron Brown's son, Michael, solely for the purpose of funneling $60,000 through him to the Commerce Secretary, according to Nolanda Hill's testimony.

Sandy Hume: On Sunday, February 22, 1998, Sandy Hume, the 28-year-old son of journalist Britt Hume, was reportedly found dead in his Arlington, Virginia, home. Aside from the statement that this was an "apparent" suicide, there remains in place a total media blackout on this story, possibly out of concern that the actual facts will not withstand public scrutiny. Worked for *Hill* magazine, about Congress for Congress.

Jim McDougal: Bill and Hillary Clinton friend, banker, and political ally, sent to prison for eighteen felony convictions. A key Whitewater witness, dies of a heart attack on March 8, 1998. As of this writing, allegations that he was given an injection of the diuretic Lasix has not been denied or confirmed.

Johnny Lawhon: 29, died March 29, 1998—The Arkansas transmission specialist who discovered a pile of Whitewater documents in the trunk of an abandoned car on his property and turned them over to Starr, was killed in a car wreck two weeks after the McDougal death. Details of the "accident" have been sketchy—even from the local Little Rock newspaper.

Charles Wilbourne Miller: 63, was found dead of a gunshot wound to the head on November 17, 1998 in a shallow pit about 300 yards from his ranch house near Little Rock. Police found a .410 gauge shotgun near Miller's body and a Ruger .357-caliber revolver submerged in water. Investigators concluded the Ruger was the weapon used by Miller to kill himself. Yet, two rounds in the handgun's cylinder had been spent.

He had long served as executive vice president and member of the board of directors for a company called Alltel and was deeply involved in his own software engineering company until the day he died. Alltel is the successor to Jackson Stephen's Systematics, the company that provided the software for the White House's "Big Brother" data base system and that was behind the administration's plan to develop the secret computer "Clipper" chip to bug every phone, fax and email transmission in America.

Carlos Ghigliotti: 42, was found dead in his home just outside of Washington, D.C., on April 28, 2000. There was no sign of a break-in or struggle at the firm of Infrared Technology where the badly decomposed body of Ghigliotti was found. Ghigliotti had not been seen for several weeks.

Ghigliotti, a thermal imaging analyst hired by the House Government Reform Committee to review tape of the siege [at Waco], said he determined the FBI fired shots on April 19, 1993. The FBI has explained the light bursts on infrared footage as reflections of sun rays on shards of glass or other debris that littered the scene.

"I conclude this based on the groundview videotapes taken from several different angles simultaneously and based on the overhead thermal tape," Ghigliotti told *The Washington Post* last October. "The gunfire from the ground is there, without a doubt."

Ghigliotti said the tapes also confirm the Davidians fired repeatedly at FBI agents during the assault, which ended when flames raced through the compound. About 80 Branch Davidians perished that day, some from the fire, others from gunshot wounds.

Mark Corallo, a spokesman for the congressional committee chaired by Rep. Dan Burton, R-Ind., said that police found the business card of a committee investigator in Ghigliotti's office. Corallo and Ghigliotti's work for the committee ended some time ago.

Tony Moser: 41, was killed as he crossed a street in Pine Bluff, Arkansas, on June 10, 2000. Killed 10 days after being named a columnist for the *Democrat-Gazette* newspaper and two days after penning a stinging indictment of political corruption in Little Rock.

Police have concluded that no charges will be filed against the unnamed driver of a 1995 Chevrolet pickup, which hit Moser as he was walking along in the middle of unlit Rhinehart Road about 10:10 p.m.

Police say they have ruled out foul play and will file no charges against the driver because he was not intoxicated and there was no sign of excessive speed.

"It depends on what the meaning of 'is' is."
"Wordsmith Extraordinaire" Bill Clinton
Grand Jury Investigation, August 17, 1998.

8

Freemasonry

". . . in secret have I said nothing."
(John 18:20b)

MANY OCCULTISTS CONTEND that Francis Bacon wrote a sequel to his *New Atlantis* which included comprehensive details and timetables for his celebrated Great Plan in North America. William Still, citing Hall:

> It is well known among the secret societies of Europe that the second part of the New Atlantis exists. It includes a description of . . . the crests and the coats of arms of the governors of the philosophic empire. It may be for this reason that the writings were suppressed, for these crests and arms belonged to real persons who might have been subjected to persecution, as Sir Walter Raleigh was, if their association with the secret order had been openly announced.[1]

It is also believed that this sacred document was smuggled to Jamestown, Virginia, in 1653 by Nathaniel Bacon, a descendent of the author. The legend asserts that Bacon buried his ancestor's manuscript in the capital of Williamsburg, ". . . in a great vault beneath the tower center of the first brick church in Bruton Parish."[2] The site has come to be known as the Bruton Vault and has sparked considerable investigation and conjecture. Interestingly, Nathaniel hid his secret document in 1676, exactly fifty years after Lord Bacon's death. And according to the *Academic American Encyclopedia*, it was in *May* of that same year that the "would-be whatever" began his ill-fated revolt against Virginia's governor, Sir William Berkley. Known as "Bacon's Rebellion," the colony was forcibly seized and Jamestown burned to the ground. After Nathaniel abruptly died from swamp fever in October, twenty-three of his henchmen were hanged and order was restored. Once again, as with the legends of Quetzalcoatl and Amaruca, the fact that the occultists believe them to be true is more significant than any verifiable authenticity. Long before the venerable George Washington would fire the first cannon at Yorktown, a sinister character described by a contemporary as, ". . . ominous, pensive, melancholy . . . of a most imperious and dangerous Pride of heart . . . and very ambitious and arrogant,"[3] attempted to secure Virginia for *his* god. It would appear that the precursor to the May Day World Revolution movement was led by a seventeenth-century demon-possessed Rosicrucian in search of a New Atlantis.

Now, although the average American knows more about Rosie O'Donnell than the Rosy Cross, he *has* been exposed to the modern torchbearer of all ancient societies. Since its formal inception in 1717, in London, the system of Speculative Masonry, better known as Freemasonry, has developed into the apex of mysticism and the mother of world revolution. Masonic author Manly Hall labeled it, ". . . the most powerful organization in the world."[4] Andre Tardieu, a former French premier said, "Freemasonry does not explain everything; yet, if we leave it out of account, the history of our times is unintelligible."[5] As previously cited, John Quincy Adams, the sixth president of the United States, warned in 1833: "I do conscientiously and sincerely believe that the Order of Freemasonry, if not the greatest, is one of the greatest moral and political evils under which the Union is now laboring."[6] Keep in mind, Satan's followers have no infallible authority to guide them, being *". . . turned every one to his own way . . ."* (Isaiah 53:6). This becomes readily apparent to one who would trace the "official" history of Freemasonry. According to the *Royal Masonic Cyclopedia*, no less than *twelve* theories have been advanced as to the origins of this fraternity:

(1) From the patriarchs. (2) From the mysteries of the pagans. (3) From the construction of Solomon's Temple. (4) From the Crusades. (5)From the Knights Templar. (6) From the Roman Collegia of Artificers. (7) From the operative masons of the Middle Ages. (8) From the Rosicrucians of the sixteenth century. (9) From Oliver Cromwell. (10) From Prince Charles Stuart for political purposes. (11)From Sir Christopher Wren, at the building of St. Paul's. (12) From Dr. Desaguliers and his friends in 1717.[7]

Dr. Mackey, a Masonic authority admits, ". . . the origin and source whence first sprang the institution of Freemasonry has given rise to more difference of opinion and discussion among masonic scholars than any other topic in the literature of the institution."[8] (Praise God, the humble Bible believer can sing: "On Christ the solid Rock I stand. All other ground is sinking sand.")

Prior to the 1700s, Masonry was supposedly limited to a fraternity of professional builders intent on guarding the lucrative secrets of their trade. Throughout the centuries, including the Dark Ages, the prestige of these Masonic guilds grew with the pace of their magnificent cathedrals and such. This explains the preeminence given to the compass, square and straightedge in various Masonic rituals. When modern Masons visit the greatest construction feat of antiquity, the Pyramid tombs of Egypt, they stare in amazement at the walls displaying the very signs, symbols, grips and postures, including the ceremonial apron, that were used in their own initiation. This exclusive affinity with the building trade was terminated in 1703 when the Lodge of St. Paul in London announced: ". . . the privileges of Masonry should no longer be restricted to operative Masons, but extended to men of various professions, provided they were regularly approved and initiated into the Order."[9] The establishment of the Grand Lodge of London in 1717 completed the transition from *operative* to *speculative* Masonry by providing a fresh set of rules and rituals and a new constitution. From now on, the emphasis would be on the "spooky." Nesta Webster writes:

> In reality modern Freemasonry is a dual system, a blend of two distinct traditions—of operative masonry, that is to say the actual art of building, and of speculative theory on the great truths of life and death. As a well-known Freemason, the Count Goblet d'Alviella, has expressed it: "Speculative Masonry" (that is to say, the dual system we now know as Freemasonry) "is the legitimate offspring of a fruitful union between the professional guild of mediæval Masons and a secret group of philosophical Adepts, the first having furnished the form and the second the spirit."[10]

This "group of philosophical Adepts" was probably the remnant of Bacon's Rosicrucians (theory number eight in the *Royal Masonic Cyclopedia*). While Professor Bühle emphatically states, "Freemasonry is neither more nor less than Rosicrucianism as modified by those who transplanted it into England,"[11] Webster tempers this view by concluding that the Masons "likely borrowed from the Rosicrucians a part of their system and symbols which they adapted to their own purpose."[12] (Continental Masonry will later be seen to have been influenced by a revival of Templarism.)

CAPTAIN WILLIAM MORGAN

Because the devil is so subtle, nearly everyone is in the dark concerning the true agenda of Freemasonry, including the members themselves. The fact that seventy-five percent of active Masons never advance beyond the third level—*in a system consisting of thirty-three degrees*—indicates that the ignorant majority at the base of the pyramid are consistently manipulated by the evil minority at the top. Furthermore, unlike the other degrees in the Scottish Rite, the thirty-third degree cannot be earned; it can only be bestowed upon a member by the Supreme Council. Thus the Council controls who becomes a member of the inner circle. If you look at a one-dollar bill you will note that the "all-seeing eye" in the capstone is significantly detached from the rest of the structure. (This is why John Gotti was known as the "Teflon Don.")

The powerful nineteenth-century evangelist Charles G. Finney was a Mason prior to his conversion. After the Holy Ghost led him out of the lodge, Finney authored a book entitled *The Character, Claims and Practical Workings of Freemasonry*. His opening line read, "It is high time the Church of Christ was awake to the character and tendency of Freemasonry."[13] I say, "Amen and Amen!" Finney wrote,

> [I]n taking these oaths I had been grossly deceived and imposed upon. Indeed I came to the deliberate conclusion that my oaths had been procured by fraud and misrepresentations; that the institution was in no respect what I had been informed it was; and . . . it has become more and more irresistibly plain to me that Masonry is highly dangerous to the State, and in every way injurious to the Church of Christ.[14]

The first defector from an American lodge to publish a detailed exposé of secret Masonic ritual was Captain William Morgan of Batavia, New York. (A short list of infamous Masons from Morgan's era would include Joseph Smith [1805-1844] and Brigham Young [1801-1877], founders of the Church of Latter Day Saints, and Charles Taze Russell, founder of the Jehovah's Witnesses.[15]) Morgan, a captain in the militia, was with

Andy Jackson at the battle of New Orleans in January, 1815.[16] It is noteworthy that his book *Freemasonry Exposed* was authored in 1826, the same year that Thomas Jefferson and John Adams died. It is also significant that Morgan himself would die that year, but *not* from natural causes. Morgan had written: "The bane of our civil institutions is to be found in Masonry, already powerful and daily becoming more so. I owe my country an exposure of its dangers."[17] Like that other patriot, Nathan Hale, Morgan would pay a steep price for sounding the alarm, as the cardinal survival philosophy of Masonry states: "The whole strength of Masonry lies in its discretion. Our enemies fear us all the more because we never reveal our methods of action."[18]

After a gang of Masons kidnapped Morgan in Batavia on September 11, 1826, he was subsequently drowned in the Niagara River. Now *that's* a hate crime! The story broke in early 1849 under the headline, "Confession," following the deathbed admission of Henry L. Valance that he was the man who had pushed Morgan out of the boat. Valance stated (as cited by Finney):

> Go where I would, or do what I would, it was impossible for me to throw off the consciousness of crime. If the mark of Cain was not upon me, the curse of the first murderer was—the blood-stain was upon my hands and could not be washed out.[19]

When the whole account was eventually learned, over fifteen hundred lodges went out of existence. The number of active American Masons dropped from fifty thousand to five thousand!

Just what made the Masons murder Captain Morgan in cold blood? What did he write in his book? *Morgan died for exposing the demonism that pervades the symbols, ceremonies and procedures of the Blue Lodge, comprising the first three degrees of Entered Apprentice, Fellow Craft, and Master Mason.* (Upon acquiring the third degree, a member may proceed in either, or both, of the two branches of advanced Masonry; the more popular Scottish Rite, containing twenty-nine additional degrees ranging from the fourth through the thirty third and/or the York Rite, consisting of only ten degrees.)

Morgan's step-by-step description takes his readers behind the door into the lodge to stand in the very presence of the "grand poo-bah" himself, known and addressed as WORSHIPFUL MASTER. (Matthew 23:10) The rank hypocrisy of this secret society is immediately apparent when "Worshipful" makes it clear that he doesn't want the brothers pulling any of that *secret* stuff on *him*. In one of his opening spiels he declares: "In like manner so do I, **strictly forbidding** all profane language, **private committees**, or any other disorderly conduct whereby the peace and harmony of this lodge may be interrupted while engaging in its lawful pursuits, under no less penalty than the by-laws, or such penalty as the majority of the Brethren present may see fit to inflict"[20] (i.e., throwing you into a river, etc.). Notice how he makes a connection between "private committees" and the "interruption of peace."

Former president Ulysses S. Grant wholeheartedly concurred, writing: "All secret oath-bound political parties are dangerous to any nation, no matter how pure or how patriotic the motives and principles which first bring them together."[21] Having been delivered from the clutches of Masonry, Millard Fillmore, America's thirteenth president, was more emphatic than Grant: "The *Masonic fraternity* tramples upon our rights, defeats the administration of justice, and bids defiance to every government which it cannot control."[22]

Morgan learned the hard way that Masons are serious when it comes to following through with the death threats applicable to any who would dare break their satanic security. To put the "fear of God" into rookies, candidates for the Entered Apprentice degree must affirm, among other things:

> To all of which I do most solemnly and sincerely promise and swear, without the least equivocation, mental reservation, or self evasion of mind in me whatever [i.e., crossing your fingers, etc.], binding myself under no less penalty than to have my throat cut across, my tongue torn out by the roots, and my body buried in the rough sands of the sea at low water-mark, where the tide ebbs and flows twice in twenty-four hours; so help me God, and keep me steadfast in the due performance of the same.[23]

By the way, all of this perversion goes on in the presence of an open Bible! Do you think the Holy Ghost is within a thousand miles of these blasphemous proceedings?

The candidate for the Fellow Craft degree is also threatened with life and limb, agreeing to the words: "[B]inding myself under no less penalty than to have my left breast torn open and my heart and vitals taken from thence and thrown over my left shoulder ["I left my heart in San Francisco"] and carried into the Valley of Jehosaphat, there to become prey to the wild beasts of the field, and vultures of the air, if I should prove . . ."[24] And, to "spill your guts" as a Master Mason is to insure that *your* guts will soon be spilled! "[B]inding myself under no less penalty than to have my body severed in two in the midst, and divided to the north and south, my bowels burnt to ashes in the center, and the ashes scattered before the four winds of heaven, that there might not the least track or trace of remembrance remain among men. . . ."[25] Now you know why the Masons had to hide what was left of Morgan's body in the depths of the Niagara River. (The *Mafia* brotherhood calls this "sleeping with the fish.")

INCENTIVES FOR MEMBERSHIP

At this point one may wonder why any thinking American would join such an evil organization. Once again, the reader must remember that the rank and file of the membership are never made privy to the inner core doctrine of the advanced degrees, such as open worship of the devil. In the meantime, they are used, as the anarchist Michel Bakunin used to say, for "conspiracy fodder."[26] This basic principle of a divided brotherhood is an undisputed fact that can be confirmed by consulting the book entitled *Lectures on Ancient Philosophy*, by the highly regarded Masonic author, Manly P. Hall:

> Freemasonry is a fraternity within a fraternity . . . an outer organization concealing an inner brotherhood of the elect. . . . it is necessary to establish the existence of these two separate yet interdependent orders, the one visible and the other invisible. The visible society is a splendid camaraderie of "free and accepted" men, enjoined to devote themselves to ethical, educational, fraternal, patriotic, and humanitarian concerns. The invisible society is a secret and most august fraternity whose members are dedicated to the service of a mysterious arcanum arcandrum [defined as a secret; a mystery]. These brethren who have essayed to write the history of their craft have not included in their disquisitions [a formal discourse or treatise] the story of that truly secret inner society which is to the body Freemasonic what the heart is to the body human. In each generation only a few are accepted into the inner sanctuary of the work . . . the great initiate-philosophers of Freemasonry are . . . masters of that secret doctrine which forms the invisible foundation of every great theological and rational institution.[27]

Albert Pike was even more brazen in his admission that the leaders of Freemasonry deceive their own members. With reference to the Blue Lodge, Pike wrote:

The Blue Degrees are but the outer court or portico of the Temple. Part of the symbols are displayed there to the Initiate, **but he is intentionally misled by false interpretations**. It is not intended that he shall understand them, but it is intended that he shall imagine he understands them. Their true explications are reserved for the Adepts, the Princes of Masonry.[28]

Apart from all the "Fatherhood of God and brotherhood of man" bologna, the Masons' number one recruitment technique is to dangle the carrot of greater wealth and power. That the Masons have "big bucks" is not to be denied (Luke 4:6). In 1984 the most elite Masonic fraternity, the Shriners, declared its assets to the Internal Revenue Service at $1.979 billion, making it the wealthiest "charity" in the world![29] (Masons who have reached the thirty-second degree in the Scottish Rite or the thirteenth degree in the York Rite have the option of joining the Shrine, officially known as the Ancient Arabic Order of Nobles of the Mystic Shrine.) This means that those guys with the funny hats driving their little orange go-carts in your local community parade have nearly twice the funds as the second-place finisher, the American Red Cross ($1.07 billion) and four-times as much as number three, the American Cancer Society ($446.8 million).

A cardinal perk of Masonry is the "family obligation" of pushing one another up the ladder of success. (This is known in organized crime as being a "connected guy.") Someone has said that "many a Mason has become a great man but no great man ever became a Mason." According to British Masonic expert, Stephen Knight:

> The more Masons there are in any area or profession the more important it is to be a Mason if one is not to risk losing out, as a nonmember of the club, in one's business, one's profession and one's preferment. In many fields nowadays the disadvantages of being left out of the "club" are perceived as being too serious for a great many people to contemplate, whatever they may feel personally about the morality of joining a secret society, or about the misty tenets of speculative Freemasonry.[30]

For example, folks "in the know" will tell you that in many cases a building contractor who is a Mason will have less problems getting his blueprints approved when the powers that be are brother Masons. Whenever any new business comes to town, the Masons are all over the hapless proprietor like a hog on ice. If he agrees to join (i.e., sell his soul to the devil), the lodge promises to patronize his establishment, thus giving him the edge over his non-initiated competitors. When I worked in marketing for British Airways, a fellow sales representative who was a Mason attempted to recruit me to ensure "faster promotion." I politely told him to "hit the road." Six months later I was promoted into the Gospel ministry, *hallelujah*! When I was preparing to leave for Bible College in 1976, a well-meaning, though ignorant relative offered me a full scholarship through her Eastern Star Lodge. Of course, I declined; Jesus paid my way!

Now this is where the rings and famous Masonic handshakes come in handy so one "brother" can recognize another "brother." Whenever a Mason is in trouble he may alert any fellow Mason of his need by asking, "Is there no help for the widow's son?" A brother Mason is bound to do what he can in this matter. During the Reign of Terror in France, many a condemned Mason was able to cheat the guillotine when the jailer recognized "the sign." In his acclaimed biography on the life of Confederate General Nathan Bedford Forrest, author Jack Hurst relates how a particular Union lieutenant, Mack Leaming, escaped certain death at the Fort Pillow massacre, ". . . because he was a Mason and happened to be taken [as a prisoner] by a fellow member of the order."[31] On a lighter note, a good friend of mine who had gotten a speeding ticket decided to try this "line" on the presiding judge for the fun of it. His father was a Baptist minister in California who had taken a strong and costly stand against the lodge. My friend decided to find out for himself whether his dad knew what he was talking about, or not. He told me that he got the shock of his life when the judge dismissed the charge on the spot!

A well-known saying within the cult is: "Masonry should be felt everywhere but nowhere should it be unveiled." However, sometimes the "favors" are more serious than simply "fixing" traffic tickets. A candidate for the Royal Arch degree (seventh in the York Rite and thirteenth in the Scottish) gets to drink wine out of a cup fashioned from the top half of a human skull. Agreeing "to have his skull struck off and his brains exposed to the scorching rays of a median sun" if he blows the whistle, he makes the following vow *with his hand on the Holy Bible*: "I will aid and assist a companion Royal Arch Mason when engaged in **any** difficulty, and espouse his cause so far as to extricate him from the same, if within my power, **whether he be right or wrong**."[32] Should we be surprised to learn that numerous judges and state policemen are Masons? In the *Masonic Handbook*, Masons are told what to do if they are ever selected to serve on a jury and observe that the defendant has flashed the appropriate sign:

If you're on a jury, and the defendant is a Mason, and makes the Grand Hailing sign [a secret sign that identifies one Mason to another], you must be sure not to bring the Mason guilty, for that would bring disgrace upon our order. It may be perjury, to be sure, to do this, but then you're fulfilling your obligation, and you know if you live up to your obligations you'll be free from sin.[33]

Charles Finney confirms how the "Masonic maze" was able to deflect the investigation of Captain Morgan's murder prior to Valance's deathbed confession. (After all, kidnapping and assassination would certainly fall under ". . . any difficulty . . . whether right or wrong.")

The courts of justice found themselves entirely unable to make any headway against the wide-spread conspiracy that was formed among Masons . . . It was found that they could do nothing with the courts, with the sheriffs, with the witnesses, or with the jurors.

Masons themselves . . . published two spurious editions of Morgan's book, and circulated them as the true edition which Morgan had published. These editions were designed to deceive Masons who had never seen Morgan's edition, and thus enable them to say that it was not a true revelation of Masonry.[34]

To understand how this power to conceal the truth is alive and well in the twenty-first century, just look at what the *Encyclopedia Americana* has to say about Masons. I'll give you a hint: the article was written by Alphonse Cerza—GRAND HISTORIAN, THE GRAND LODGE OF ILLINOIS! Some of the more humorous highlights are as follows:

Its chief aim is to create a universal fraternal association of people of good will . . . Although not a religion it is religious in that its precepts incorporate the fundamentals of many religions . . . **It is not a secret society, as is sometimes alleged, since it does not hide its existence, aims, or works** [On page 966 of *the New Encyclopedia Britannica*, Volume 4, Freemasonry is specifically described as "the largest world-wide secret society."] . . . Fourteen presidents have been Freemasons, from George Washington to Gerald Ford . . . Masonic lodges, grand lodges, and related organizations do a great deal of charitable work . . . In 1825 an **itinerant workman**, William Morgan, **disappeared** in Batavia, New York, and Masons were blamed. With the formation of an Anti-Masonic party, many lodges closed and members withdrew under pressure from newspapers, politicians, and clergymen. But the party met defeat in the national election of 1832 and the Anti-Masonic movement declined. Lodges resumed activity and Freemasonry, by 1840, was once again active in the United States.[35]

RECOIL AND REVIVAL

So, the itinerant worker just up and disappeared, did he? Truth is, Alphonse is a filthy liar! In 1834, a joint committee of the Massachusetts Legislature conducted a formal inquiry into Masonic activity and printed a fifty-four-page report entitled, *An Investigation into Freemasonry.* On page fourteen we read: "The organization of Freemasonry, as a distinct Independent Government within our own Government, and beyond the control of the laws of the land, by means of its secrecy, and the oaths and regulations which its subjects are bound to obey, under penalties of death, have occupied much of the attention of the Committee, in connection with the third branch of their inquiry."[36] The official conclusion of this legislative study is reflected by the three-fold division of their report: 1) Freemasonry is a moral evil. 2) Freemasonry is a pecuniary evil. 3) Freemasonry is a political evil.

With the arrival of a new generation of "conspiracy fodder," the power of the lodge was reestablished in the land. Though only ten percent of the electorate in 1872 were Masons, they constituted seventy-five percent of active government officials! John Marshall, a former chief justice of the United States, was eventually able to extricate himself from the lodge and warn his fellow Americans: "The institution of Masonry ought to be abandoned as one capable of much evil, and incapable of producing any good which might be effected by safe and open means."[37]

In his book *Freemasonry and the Vatican*, Vicomte Léon De Poncins explains why Masonry and politics can be such an explosive mixture.

> Freemasonry imposes a rigid discipline on its members, and the various Grand Lodges, at least, are strict on one point: Freemasons occupying political posts owe obedience, above all else, to the orders and directives of Masonry. The Order does not always manage to obtain this unconditional obedience, but it always insists upon it as the Mason's duty.[38]

De Poncins quotes from the official *Covenant of the Grand Orient*, to show how Masonic philosophy has been able to infiltrate and control the functions of government in his homeland:

> We do not want politicians who are Masons to adopt a dual attitude: one which they display in Parliament, and the other in the lodges. We do not want to see politicians having a foot in both camps: one in the lodge, and one in the Bishop's palace (page 48). . . .

Politicians who are Masons, and who are consequently in some degree emissaries of the Order, should remain subject to it during their term of office. As politicians, they must be guided by the work of the general Assembly, but in every circumstance of their political life they have a duty to obey those principles which govern us (page 365).

It is in our Lodges that our Brethren will acquire a philosophical spirit. Let us guard it lovingly, for it is the secret of political influence . . . We must exercise constant control; we must hear and question all those of our Brethren who, by their professions, touch on politics, the law or administration (page 442).[39]

Remember the Masonic motto: "Masonry should be felt everywhere, but nowhere should it be unveiled."

MASONIC PROPAGANDA

Whenever a God-fearing patriot discovers the darker side of Masonry, he will inevitably be puzzled at the impressive list of prominent Americans, especially among the Founding Fathers, who were purported to have been Masons. Moses Richardson, the Grand Treasurer of the Grand Encampment of Massachusetts and Rhode Island, testified at the investigation of Masonry in Rhode Island, December, 1831, through January, 1832, that all the presidents of the United States except the two Adamses were Masons.[40] The answer to this dilemma is simple, *the Masons are lying through their aprons!*

The men who established this country despised the philosophies of Masonry. Thus, while some would claim Thomas Jefferson as a member of their suppressive sect, the freethinking defender of Baptists wrote: "I know no safe depository of the ultimate powers of society but the people themselves; and if we think them not enlightened enough to exercise their control with a wholesome discretion, the remedy is not to take it from them, but to inform their discretion by education."[41] In the wake of Captain Morgan's murder, James Madison received a letter from a concerned American who inquired about his reputed Masonic connections. The "Father of the Constitution" wrote back:

Montpelier, January 24,1832

Dear Sir,

I received long ago your interesting favor of the 31st October, with the pamphlet referred to, and I owe an apology for not sooner acknowledging it. I hope it will be a satisfactory one, that the state of my health, crippled by a severe rheumatism, restricted my attention to what seemed to have immediate claims upon it; and in that light I did not view the subject of your communication; ignorant as I was of the true character of masonry, and little informed as I was on the grounds on which its extermination was contended for; and incapable as I was and am in my situation of investigating the controversy.

I never was a mason, and no one perhaps could be more a stranger to the principles, rites, and fruits of the Institution. I had never regarded it as dangerous or noxious; nor on the other hand, as deriving importance from any thing publicly known of it. From the number and character of those who now support the charges against masonry, I **cannot doubt that it is at least susceptible of abuses, out weighing any advantages promised by its patrons.** With this apologetic explanation, I tender you, sir, my respectful and cordial salutations.

James Madison[42]

When a Mason is not telling a bold-faced lie, he is usually twisting the truth. Numbers of "big name" personalities have been drafted on the spot. President Taft, General George Marshall, General Douglas MacArthur and others were made Masons "at sight," without the "bothersome formalities" of blood oaths and such.[43] (Imagine someone of Douglas MacArthur's stature committing his "heart and vitals" to a "Worshipful Master's" discretion!)

Another Masonic propaganda ploy was exposed by Joseph Ritner, former governor of the Commonwealth of Pennsylvania: "When a man of distinguished merit dies, if at any time he had been a mason, although he may have abandoned the Lodge the greater part of his life, masons immediately seize his name to add to the list of great men that belonged to the society, and ever after use it to allure new dupes to the fraternity."[44] Like many a naive youth, Benjamin Franklin entered the fraternity, but later distanced himself from their activities. In all his writings, particularly in his memoirs, not a single mention is made of his brief association with the craft. When Franklin was consulted by a relative on the advisability of his becoming a Mason, the sage of Philadelphia replied with his characteristic wit and candor, "One fool in a family is enough."[45]

GEORGE WASHINGTON

Of the numerous "commercials" for Freemasonry none is more fervently exploited than the venerable name of Washington. Did you notice how Alphonse was careful to mention our first president in his *Encyclopedia Americana* article? While staying in Charleston, South Carolina, during a preaching engagement, I received firsthand experience concerning the Masons' propensity to play the "Washington" card on unsuspecting dupes/prospects. It "just so happened" that the Lord scheduled my meeting to coincide with the 200th anniversary celebration commemorating the founding of the Supreme Council for the Scottish Rite of Freemasonry in Charleston on May 31, 1801. Over five thousand Masons were jammed into every motel in the area. But, it gets even better. To keep everything nice and cozy, the brother delegates were booked in motels according to their individual states. Having driven down from Knoxville, I was surprised to learn that my motel had 180 rooms reserved for Tennessee Masons. I suddenly felt like a blind dog in a meat factory and determined to go undercover and enjoy myself. My first contact was with a Mason and his wife in the elevator. In our brief conversation he told me they were from Gray, Tennessee. When I commented that I had been in a serious bus accident with fifty preachers in Gray, Tennessee, in May 2000, he shocked me by replying, "I remember that incident well. I'm the sheriff that supervised the response." (Was I ever glad when *that* elevator door opened!)

Among the many idiotic encounters I was privileged to enjoy, one had a particular application with regard to "Brother Washington." On the front page of a local newspaper covering the event, a cloth was featured portraying various Masonic symbols. After initiating a discussion with a pair of senior Masons from Knoxville, I naively asked them to enlighten me concerning the significance of the garment displayed in the picture. I could almost feel them winking at each other as I studied the picture in anticipation of their reply. After several dramatic seconds of careful inspection, the one casually asked the other, "Is that *Washington's* apron?" Not wanting to give myself away, I reacted with typical amazement that the Father of our country was also a great standard-bearer for the lodges, etc. They then politely excused themselves as dinner for five thousand was being served downtown. Country music icon Roy Clark and *Seinfield's* Michael Richards were slated to receive their honorary 33rd degrees as the highlight of the evening. Conversely, it was my privilege to go to a Baptist church and preach the Gospel of Jesus Christ that night!

At the request of the Pennsylvania House of Representatives, Governor Joseph Ritner presented a special address on September 8, 1837, entitled *Vindication of General Washington from the Stigma of Adherence to Secret Societies*. Several thousand copies of this message were subsequently printed, both in English and German, by Ezra Lincoln in Boston. The Governor stated in his introduction:

> That Washington was an initiate we do not doubt, as many other respectable individuals have been ... for it has been the policy of the detestable, murderous society to seduce into their ranks the most respectable members of society and then to bind them to the most shocking, anti-Christian oaths and under the still more shocking penalties of death, in various horrid forms, to keep the secrets of the institution, which chiefly consists, like a band of pirates and robbers, of the signs by which they may be known to each other! It is hardly necessary to add that of 100 initiates 99 though bound by their oaths to silence, have little more to do with the institution, although claimed as a member and "brother." Such were "brother Washington," "brother Judge Marshall" and a great number of others, who have been hypocritically brought within the pale of Freemasonry.[46]

Ritner then explained how Masons hide behind the credibility of Washington's legacy: "Each votary of the order, when pressed by the weight of reason, so easily brought to bear against him by the weakest advocate of democratic equality, answers every objection, by repeating the name of 'Grand Master Washington'."[47] Although Washington, like Benjamin Franklin, had been coaxed into the lodge as an impressionable youth, he quit the same early and stated so in print. Yet, through the years, Masons have produced a number of spurious letters from "Brother Washington" in support of their "noble fraternity." Many have been deceived by these bogus epistles, including the otherwise astute William Still, who refers to the following note supposedly sent to King David's Lodge in Newport, Rhode Island, on August 22, 1790: "Being persuaded a just application of the principles on which Free Masonry is founded, must be promotive of virtue and public prosperity, I shall always be glad to advance the interests of this Society and be considered by them a deserving brother."[48]

In his formal address before the Pennsylvania House, Governor Ritner challenged the legitimacy of these letters on the following grounds:

(1) The absence of any originals; (2) The absence of normally included dates of composition; (3) The absence of any verifiable copies in Washington's official letter file in Mount Vernon; (4) The testimony of Washington's lifelong friend and biographer, Chief Justice John Marshall (1755-1835), a former Mason himself whose professional credits claim eleven pages in the *Dictionary of American Biography*, who affirmed that he "had never heard Washington utter a syllable about any letters."[49] Of course, this would have been impossible had Washington been in charge of the lodges in North America. Incidentally, while Washington's own nineteen-page article in *the Dictionary of American Biography* includes a reference to his ". . . weekly entries of donations to . . . widows and helpless children," no such mention of any Masonic affiliations can be found.

The "rest of the story" behind Washington's supposed letter to King David's Lodge (in 1790) provides an excellent example of Masonic fabrication. Having "heard" a decade earlier that Washington was the Master Mason of America, the Newport fraternity determined to present him with an appropriate recognition when he visited their city, March 6-13, 1781 (his second trip to Newport). However, after investigating the rumor, they discovered it to be fraudulent. Governor Ritner read from the official minutes dated February 14, 1781: "The committee appointed to draft an address to our worthy Brother, His Excellency General Washington, report, **that on inquiry they find General Washington not to be Grand Master of North America, as was supposed, nor even Master of any particular Lodge.**"[50] Furthermore, with regard to the visit in 1790, while the president did receive a written greeting from King David's Lodge, Rabbi Gutstein made no reference to a reply on Washington's part. The omission is rendered conspicuous by the fact that Gutstein *did* record the full text for the other three letters in question—King David's salutation and the Touro/Washington exchange.

When Reverend Ezra Ely was rumored to be a Mason, he printed an editorial on July 23, 1830, denying the allegation. The article included an enlightening conversation between his father and Connecticut governor Jonathan Trumbull, a former aid-de-camp to Washington, in which Trumbull had solicited his general's advice on entering the Masonic Lodge. Washington replied that, ". . . masonry was a benevolent institution, which might be employed for the **best** or **worst** of purposes; but that for the most part it was merely **child's play** [what a slam!], and he **could not give him any advice on the subject.**"[51]

However, for the most incriminating evidence that the Father of our country was *never* an *active* Mason, the reader is referred to an exchange of *real* letters between Washington and the Reverend G. W. Snyder of Fredericktown, Maryland. Snyder had written to warn Washington of a new secret society intent on destroying America (the Illuminati). The minister also included a book by Professor John Robison entitled *Proofs of a Conspiracy*. Having obviously been infected by the Masons' propaganda machine, Snyder appeals in all innocence, ". . . upon serious reflection, I was led to think that it might be within your power to prevent the horrid plan from corrupting the brethren of the English Lodges **over which you preside**."[52] Washington's gracious reply puts to rest the erroneous notion that he was anyone's "Worshipful Master." Note the accompanying date of composition less than two years before his death:

Mt. Vernon, 25th Sep. 1798

The Rev. Mr. Snyder,

    Sir,—Many apologies are due to you, for my not acknowledging the receipt of your obliging favour of the 22nd ult. and for not thanking you at an earlier period, for the Book you had the goodness to send me.
    I have heard much of the nefarious, & dangerous plan, & doctrines of the Illuminati, but never saw the Book until you were pleased to send it to me.—The same causes which have prevented my acknowledging the receipt of your letter, have prevented my reading the Book hitherto;—namely—the multiplicity of matters which pressed upon me before, & the debilitated state in which I was left after, a severe fever had been removed,—and which allows me to add a little more now than thanks for your kind wishes and favourable sentiments, except to correct an error you have run into, of my presiding over the English lodges in this country. **The fact is, I preside over none, nor have I been in one more than once or twice, within the last thirty years**. I believe, notwithstanding, that none of the Lodges in this country are contaminated with the principles ascribed to the Society of the Illuminati."

With respect
I am Sir
Your Obed & H'ble servt
G. Washington

    In addition to referencing affidavits that Snyder possessed Washington's original (now part of the Sol Feinstone Collection housed in the David

Library in Washington Crossing, Pennsylvania), Governor Ritner also submitted the sworn testimony of Mr. Jared Sparks, Esq., a leading authority on correspondence legitimacy, dated November 22, 1832, that the all-important copy was found in Washington's official letter file in Mount Vernon. Conversely, Mr. Sparks also confirmed the *absence* of copies for *all five* of the non-dated copies of letters pretended by Masons to have been penned by "Brother Washington."[53]

The worst-case scenario suggested by Washington's concluding line to Snyder (written only fifteen months before his death) would place his final impression of Freemasonry somewhere between his earliest assessment of "mere child's play" and the naiveté of Mr. Madison's words, ". . . ignorant as I was of the true character of Masonry."

Finally, any doubts as to Washington's bias toward subversive movements predicated on dissemblance are dispelled by the following excerpt from his Farewell Address, September 17, 1796:

> All obstructions to the execution of the laws, all combinations and associations, under whatever plausible character, with the real design to direct, control, counteract, or awe, the regular deliberations and actions of the constitutional authorities, are destructive of this fundamental principle, and of fatal tendency.
>
> They serve to organize faction; to give it an artificial and extraordinary force; to put in the place of the delegated will of the nation, the will of the party, often a small but artful and enterprising minority of the community; and, according to the alternate triumphs of different parties, to make the public administration the mirror of the ill-concerted and incongruous projects of faction rather than the organ of consistent and wholesome plans, digested by common councils, and modified by mutual interests."[54]

The contradictory testimonies of Washington and Madison should serve as a caution when reading about the supposed Masonic affiliation of other famous Americans. And in those rare cases when the charge is valid, a number of mitigating circumstances should be reviewed. For instance, different sources have noted that conservative senators Strom Thurmond and Jesse Helms were members of the lodge. When dealing in the human arena, one may find an exception to almost any rule. It is the opinion of this author that Thurmond and Helms convinced themselves that they could use the system to further their own moral agenda. Their lifetime voting records in favor of Bible-based nationalistic legislation would make them bad Masons at best and pragmatic politicians at worst.

As the Scripture says, *"Ye shall know them by their fruits"* (Matthew 7:16a), and, *". . . if Satan cast out Satan . . . how shall then his kingdom stand?"* (Matthew 12:26). One of the last things Helms did before retiring was to blast the satanic United Nations in person when "explaining" why America was lagging behind in its dues. No one clapped when the hour-long tirade was over. Yet, the Bible is clear on the matter: *". . . to obey is better than sacrifice, and to hearken than the fat of rams"* (I Samuel 15:22b). As Dr. Bob Jones, Sr., used to say, "It's never right to do wrong to get a chance to do right." Oddly enough, in the years after Bob Senior's death, Thurmond served on the board of Bob Jones University.

This principle would also apply to a small percentage of sincere ministers who were deceived into thinking that the ends justified the means. With little understanding of the inner doctrines of Freemasonry, successful Baptist pastors such as George W. Truett and Dallas Billington elevated expediency over the Scriptures when reaching out to their communities. Sam P. Jones, a Methodist, and B. R. Lakin, a Baptist, made the same error in the field of evangelism. During our nation's early years the Baptist churches were generally united in their opposition to Freemasonry. In 1800, the Kiokee Association of Georgia received the query: "Is it lawful for a Minister of the Gospel to frequent Masonic Lodges?" The prevailing consensus of opinion was:

> We think it inconsistent both with the **Word of God** and the **Christian Character**, therefore all such are hereby admonished to withdraw from such Company, or be subject to Gospel Discipline, **as offenders of their Brethren**, whose duty it is to call them to an account of their conduct.[55]

LIBERTY EQUALITY FRATERNITY

As previously stated, the study of Freemasonry will often be attended by confusion and frustration, *"For we wrestle not against flesh and blood, but against principalities, against powers, against the rulers of the darkness of this world, against spiritual wickedness in high places"* (Ephesians 6:12). For instance, how could anyone accuse the one million Shriners of being Satan worshipers when they fund nineteen high profile children's hospitals, including three burn centers, and always treat children free of charge? After all, didn't Jesus say, *". . . Suffer little children, and forbid them not, to come unto me: for of such is the kingdom of heaven"* (Matthew 19:14)? Patriots in the American Revolution often utilized the lodge as a network of secrecy to check the intrigues of ubiquitous Torries. It is generally believed that the Boston Tea Party was the work of area Masons. Similarly, Protestant voters who belonged to the American Party during the nineteenth-century Nativist Movement were referred to as "Know-Nothings" because of their clandestine affiliation with another secret society called the Order of the Star Spangled Banner. Many of these Protestant societies were actively engaged in combating the spread of Roman Catholicism.

To better understand how Freemasonry evolved from its "Jolly Brotherhoods of the Bottle" image to a sinister force promoting world revolution, one must analyze a sequence of related events. First, a distinction should be made between the *modus operandi* of early British Masons and that which later developed on the Continent, specifically in France. As the potential "conspiracy fodder" in any nation will be affected by prevailing religious sentiments, Satan used his foothold in "Christian" England as a launching pad for more strategic conquests in "Catholic-atheistic" France. Remember that the devil is a master in leading humans to create innocent-looking organizations that he will later confiscate to the owners' destruction. (See any number of "Christian Seminaries.")

The extension of traditional British Masonry into France with its eventual wayward development, infectious transformation and fatal return to England is a study that is difficult to summarize in a few paragraphs. To begin, the Paris lodge was opened in 1725 by Charles Radcliffe, henceforth known as Lord Derwentwater, a Jacobite fugitive intent on restoring the Catholic Stuarts to British rule. One of Radcliffe's confederates was a certain Andrew Michael Ramsey, better known as Chevalier Ramsey. In the process of time, Chevalier made the acquaintance of the infamous Duc d'Orléans, who just happened to be Grand Master of the *Ordre du Temple*, a surviving (or revived) faction of ancient Templarism. Soon after his admission into the society, a major change was made in the structure of the Paris lodge. Whereas the Grand Lodge of London had limited its members to three degrees, the French Masons introduced over twenty new ones in what would come to be known as the Scottish Rite. The Templar influence can be seen by the names of such degrees as (13th) Knight of the Ninth Arch, (15th) Knight of the Sword, (17th) Knight of the East and West, (18th) Rose-Croix Knight, and (22nd)

Prince of Libanus or Knight of the Royal Axe. A Judaic tradition can also be detected in the (11th) Chief of the Twelve Tribes and (16th) Prince of Jerusalem.

The backlash of internal resistance to these changes was so violent that the government closed the Grand Lodge of France in 1767. However, this new brand of Freemasonry reappeared in 1772 as the Grand Lodge in Paris under "His Worshipful Master," the Duc de Chartres (later Philippe Égalité). Although the corrupting influence of continental Masonry would eventually move the English and American lodges from bad to worse, the French would maintain its leadership role for evil. The innocuous trilogy originally espoused in the British lodges, "Brotherly love, relief, and truth," would be henceforth overshadowed by the Parisian misnomer, "Liberty, Equality, Fraternity." Webster comments on this Communistic double-talk:

> For observe the contradiction: it is impossible to have complete liberty and equality, the two are mutually exclusive. It is possible to have a system of complete liberty in which every man is free to behave as he pleases, to do what he will with his own, to rob or murder, to live, that is to say, according to the law of the jungle, rule by the strongest, but there is no equality there. Or one may have a system of absolute equality, of cutting every one down to the same dead level, of crushing all incentive in man to rise above his fellows, but there is no liberty there. So Grand Orient Freemasonry, by coupling together two words for ever incompatible, threw into the arena an apple of discord over which the world has never ceased to quarrel from that day to this, and which has divided the revolutionary forces into two opposing camps.[56]

Still elaborates on these opposing forces of anarchy and socialism, stating:

> Perhaps the greatest difference between the two versions of the craft is that in Continental Masonry, the emphasis has been shifted towards world domination by violent revolution, whereas the more gentile Anglo/American version inspired by Lord Bacon stresses a revolution of enlightenment designed to establish their New World Order.[57]

Webster noted this distinction in 1924 when she wrote:

> Whilst Bolshevism sets out to destroy Capitalism at a blow, Socialism prefers a more gradual process. It is the difference between clubbing a man on the head and bleeding him to death—that is all.[58]

THRONES AND ALTARS

Whereas the Grand Lodge had decreed in 1717 that ". . . nothing concerning the religion or government shall ever be spoken in the lodge,"[59] the Grand Orient declared war on "thrones and alters" (i.e., on royalty and the papacy). A. Ralph Epperson notes: "No fewer than eight Popes have condemned Freemasonry on 400 occasions since it was founded in Britain in 1717."[60] However, though the "Whore's" wealth and power would bring out the worst in the beast of Freemasonry (Revelation 17:16), the *real* target was the lovely Lord Jesus. *"The kings of the earth set themselves, and the rulers take counsel together, against the LORD, and against his anointed, saying, Let us break their bands asunder, and cast away their cords from us."* (Psalm 2:2-3)

It was a comrade of Karl Marx, Freemason Pierre Joseph Proudhon (1809-1865), known as "The Father of Anarchy," who said, "Property is theft." With reference to his Creator and future Judge at the Great White Throne, Proudhon wrote:

> We reach knowledge in spite of him, we reach society in spite of him. Every step forward is a victory in which we overcome the Divine. God is stupidity and cowardice; God is hypocrisy and falsehood; God is tyranny and poverty; God is evil. Where humanity bows before an altar, humanity, the slaves of kings and priests, will be condemned . . . I swear, God, with my hand stretched out towards the heavens, that you are nothing more than the executioner of my reason, the scepter of my conscience . . . God is essentially anti-civilized, anti-liberal, anti-human.[61]

One of Pierre's disciples, "Brother Lafargue," got so shook up after hearing him speak at the International Congress in Brussels that he started shouting: "War on God! Hatred towards God! That is progress! We must shatter Heaven like a vault of paper."[62]

While the Communist Flourens wrote in 1871, "Our enemy is God. Hatred of God is the beginning of wisdom,"[63] the former Russian Commissioner of Education, Lunarcharsky, was even more articulate:

> We hate Christians and Christianity. Even the best of them must be considered our worst enemies. Christian love is an obstacle to the development of the revolution. Down with love of one's neighbor! What we want is HATE . . . Only then can we conquer the universe.[64]

Finally, the Freemason Delpech included the following blasphemy in his discourse at a Masonic banquet in 1902:

> The triumph of the Galilean has lasted twenty centuries; he is dying in his turn. . . . The illusion has lasted very long; the lying God in his turn disappears; he goes to rejoin in the dust of ages with the other divinities of India, Egypt, Greece, and Rome, who saw so many deluded creatures throw themselves at the foot of their altars. Freemasons, we are pleased to state that we are not unconcerned with this ruin of false prophets. The Roman Church, founded on the Galilean myth, began to decline rapidly on the day when the Masonic association was constituted. From the political point of view Freemasons have often varied. But in all times Freemasonry has stood firm on this principle: war on all superstitions, war on all fanaticism.[65]

Although every denunciation of "God" is an obvious reference to the triune Being revealed in the Holy Bible, upper echelon Masons are not really "atheists" in a *technical* sense. You might say they are "polytheists." On July 14, 1889, Albert Pike issued his "Instructions" to the twenty-three Supreme Councils of the world. Al's speech was recorded by A. C. De La Rive in *La Femme et L' Enfant dans la Franc—Maconnerie Universelle*:

> If Lucifer were not God, would Adonay (The God of the Christians) whose deeds prove his cruelty, perfidy, and hatred of man, barbarism and repulsion for science, could Adonay and his priests, calumniate him?
>
> **Yes, Lucifer is God**, and unfortunately Adonay is also God. For the eternal law is that there is no light without shade, no beauty without ugliness, no white without black, for the absolute can only exist as two Gods: darkness being necessary to light to serve as its foil as the pedestal is necessary to the statue, and the brake to the locomotive. . . .
>
> Thus, the doctrine of Satanism is a heresy; and the true and pure philosophic religion is the belief in Lucifer, the equal of Adonay; but Lucifer, God of Light and God of Good, is struggling for humanity against Adonay, the God of Darkness and Evil.[66]

But now, don't let all that tough rhetoric fool you; they're just "talkin' trash" (Ebonics for "using intimidation"). The truth is, they are scared to death of the Saviour! (Joshua 2:9) William Still reveals how Jesus Christ, called *"the blessed and only Potentate"* in I Timothy 6:15, has always been the Masons' worst nightmare as He alone is the *true* Worshipful Master (I Corinthians 8:4-6):

Masons don't count their years from the year of Christ's death because for a rather curious reason, they consider it a tragedy. In their initiation ceremony for the eighteenth degree, The Knight of the Rose Crucis, also known as the Rose Croix, the Red Cross, or "the Rosicrucians", Masons symbolically drape the lodge room in black and sit on the floor in silence resting their heads in their arms in mock grief around an altar above which are three crosses. They grieve not for the death of the Son of God, but, according to the French Masonic historian, Abbé Augusten de Barruel, they symbolically mourn because the day Jesus was crucified was the day Christianity was born, ever to be the antagonist of Masonry: "It is the . . . time when the veil of the temple was rent asunder, when darkness and consternation was spread over the earth, when the light was darkened, when the implements of Masonry were broke, when the flaming star disappeared, when the cubic stone was broken, when the word was lost."[67]

As the devil will often counterfeit God's work, the inspiration for these Masonic blasphemies can be traced to a major satanic "revival" that broke out in Bavaria, Germany, and later spread to the Grand Orient Lodge. Had it not been for a remarkable act of God, little would be known of this diabolical development.

9

The Illuminati

*"And no marvel; for Satan himself is transformed into an
angel of light. Therefore it is no great thing if his ministers
also be transformed as the ministers of righteousness;
whose end shall be according to their works."*
(II Corinthians 11:14-15)

O N THE AFTERNOON of July 10, 1785, a German priest by
the name of Jacob Lang (sometimes, Lanze) was struck by
lightning as he was passing through the Bavarian town of
Ratisbon (currently Regensburg). Interestingly enough, on July 2, 1505,
another German whose last name began with the same letter had his
own providential encounter with a bolt of lightning less than one hundred
and thirty miles away near the Saxon village of Stotternheim. Both charges
were fired to retard the work of Satan. However, here the similarities
end. Whereas *Luther* was *spared* to spark the German Reformation, *Lang*
was *smoked* to enable local authorities to discover the incriminating
documents that were sewn in his clothes.[1] In reality, at the time of his
"accident" the "fried friar" had been traveling incognito as a courier
for the most dangerous secret society in history!

The reader will recall President Washington's reply to Reverend
Snyder, dated September 25, 1798—"I have heard much of the nefarious
and dangerous doctrines of the Illuminati. . . ." The word *illuminati*,
Latin for "enlightened ones" (Genesis 3:7), was the name given to the
secret fraternity established by Dr. Adam Weishaupt (1748-1830),
"esteemed" professor of Canon law at the Jesuit University of Ingolstadt.
Born on February 6, 1748, Dr. Weishaupt received his own formal

training from Bavarian Jesuits but later turned on the Society of Jesus with an implacable vengeance.

The Order of the Illuminati (or, *Perfektibilisten*) was founded on the uncanny date of May 1, 1776, with *five* charter members. While America was born in 1776, May 1 became the high and holy day of her end-time nemesis, international Communism. The month that Weishaupt and his four fellow conspirators began their satanic society was also coincidental from another perspective. The twenty-first century pilot issuing a "May Day" distress call is no doubt unaware of the spiritual significance of May being the *fifth* month; *five* representing the number for *death* in Bible numerology. (See Genesis 5:5, where the first natural death on earth is announced with the words, "*and he died*;" the word "death" itself consisting of five letters, as well as the name of "*him that had the power of death*," Hebrews 2:14; the brazen altar where thousands of animals were sacrificed measuring 5 cubits x 5 cubits according to Exodus 27:1; David securing five stones to kill Goliath and his four sons, II Samuel 21:22; Christ receiving five wounds with his parted garments numbering five; a liar drops dead in the fifth verse of the fifth chapter of the fifth book of the New Testament; the deaths of Adam and Jesus being compared in Romans 5 while a lamb appears in Revelation 5, "*as it had been slain*.")

Each of the charter members chose fanciful pseudonyms, with Weishaupt's being *Spartacus*. Despite the reference in one of his letters to "[o]ur worst enemies the Jesuits,"[2] Weishaupt determined to pattern his organization after that of his former mentors. The Jesuit Barruel, quoting Mirabeau, writes that Weishaupt "admired above all those laws, that *régime* of the Jesuits, which, under one head, made men dispersed over the universe tend towards the same goal; he felt that one could imitate their methods whilst holding views diametrically opposed."[3] The Jesuit "method" of mind control was a high priority area. Once again, on the evidence of Mirabeau, de Luchet, and von Knigge, Barruel says elsewhere: "It is here that Weishaupt appears specially to have wished to assimilate the régime of the sect to that of the religious orders and, above all, that of the Jesuits, by the total abandonment of their own will and judgment which he demands of his adepts. . . ."[4] Along this line, Webster writes: "The art of secret societies has always been to seek out physical and mental degenerates and work upon their minds until they have roused them to the requisite degree of revolutionary fervor." With a more specific application to Weishaupt's order, she adds: "The art of Illuminism lay in enlisted dupes as well as adepts, and by encouraging the dreams of honest visionaries or the schemes of fanatics, by flattering the vanity of ambitious egoists, by working on unbalanced brains, or by playing on such passions as greed of gold or power, to make men of totally divergent aims serve the secret purpose of the sect."[5]

So, exactly *who* was this Adam Weishaupt and *what* havoc, if any, was caused by his Illuminati? You will generally search in vain at the local library for answers. Weishaupt's name is missing in the renowned eighteen-volume *Encyclopedia of World Biography* (as is the name Captain William Morgan)—ditto the *Encyclopedia Americana, World Book* and *Academic American Encyclopedia*. The *Encyclopedia Americana* alone contains a generic eighteen-line paragraph on the Bavarian Illuminati. Do you suppose that the history of the encyclopedia itself might shed some light on such protracted literary bias? The *Encyclopedia Americana* identifies the *Encyclopedists* as, "those men who contributed articles to the twenty-eight-volume *Encyclopédie* published in France from 1751 to 1772." (You know—those formative years leading up to the *French Revolution*.) The article states, "It contains criticisms of contemporary religious and political institutions, criticisms designed to reform society and combat persecution, superstition, intolerance, and poverty."[6] The piece concludes by reporting that the government censored the set and even stopped its publication for certain periods. Webster's volume, *Secret Societies and Subversive Movements*, acclaimed by the *New York Book Review* as "too thoroughly documented to be laughed away,"[7] tells you what the lying liberals will not:

> The *Encyclopédie* was therefore essentially a Masonic publication . . . The Masonic authorship of the *Encyclopédie* and the consequent dissemination of revolutionary doctrines has remained no matter of doubt to the Freemasons of France; on the contrary, they glory in the fact.[8]

Now you know why that deceptive *Encyclopedia Americana* article on Masonry, quoted in the previous chapter, was authored by a Mason!

Another anemic attempt to play down the revolutionary role of Adam Weishaupt can be found in the celebrated twenty-one-volume set—*Man, Myth and Magic: The Illustrated Encyclopedia of Mythology, Religion and the Unknown*. In the main article on the Illuminati we read:

It has been called a prototype secret society and accused of paving the way for the French Revolution, but nothing could be further from the truth. [How pious!] . . . If we ignore its childish mystification, it was merely a society which attracted men of progressive rather than conservative views . . . It achieved little, mainly due to the strangeness of its founder, Adam Weishaupt.[9]

The Freemason Louis Blanc (1811-1882), listed in the *Encyclopedia of World Biography* as a "French journalist, historian, and socialist politician . . . [who] greatly influenced the evolution of French socialism and modern social democracy,"[10] held a different opinion altogether. He called Weishaupt "[t]he profoundest conspirator that ever existed," and described his society as a "terrible and formidable sect."[11] This is what the Father of our country meant by "dangerous" and "nefarious."

The man who authored *Proofs of a Conspiracy* (the three-hundred-page exposé of Illuminism that accompanied Reverend Snyder's letter to Washington) was eminently qualified to assess Weishaupt's persona within the intellectual community. John Robison was a professor of natural philosophy at the University of Edinburgh, and general secretary of the prestigious Royal Society of Edinburgh. His close friend, James Watt (inventor of the steam engine), described Robison as "a man of the clearest head and the most science of anybody I have ever known."[12] Although initially deceived by the claims of Freemasonry, he was not about to be fooled twice. Concerning the aforementioned smoke screen reference to the "strangeness of its founder," Robison confirms Dr. Weishaupt's contemporary credentials accordingly: "He had acquired a high reputation in his profession, and was attended not only by those intended for the practice in the law-courts, but also by the young gentlemen at large, in their course of general education; and he brought numbers from the neighbouring states to this university, and gave a *ton* to the studies of the place."[13]

That Spartacus was indeed "the profoundest conspirator that ever existed" can be seen by the manner in which he "conned" the otherwise astute Thomas Jefferson. Having accurately predicted the permanency of racial tension and the "unbounded licentiousness" of excessive European immigration, Jefferson was beguiled by the ultimate serpent in paradise, dismissing (and defending) Weishaupt as merely "an enthusiastic philanthropist."[14] Weishaupt's skill at deception was yet another application of Jesuit methodology. A true Jesuit is the consummate embodiment of

I Timothy 4:2: "*Speaking lies in hypocrisy; having their conscience seared with a hot iron.*" The very word *Jesuitical* has entered the English dictionary as a synonym for that which is crafty or deceptive. According to Pierre Dominique in *La Politique des Jesuites* (as cited by Edmond Paris), while in training, Loyola's henchmen were taught to "hold their heads slightly down, without bending it to the left or right; they must not look up, and when they speak to someone, they are not to look them straight in the eyes so as to see them only indirectly."[15] Thus, we are not surprised to find the Jesuit-trained Weishaupt talking out of both sides of his mouth ("rope-a-dope" in Ebonics, etc.). In a letter to "Cato" (Herr von Zwack, privy councilor to the Prince von Salm), Spartacus writes: "One must speak sometimes one way and sometimes another, but so as never to contradict ourselves, and so that, with respect to our true way of thinking, we may be impenetrable."[16]

ADAM'S "AWAKENING"

Weishaupt's own descent into the world of the occult was brought about by a mysterious Jutland merchant known as Kölmer. Some believe that Kölmer was himself initiated into the Eastern mysteries by an Ismaili "holy man" during an extended sojourn in Egypt. Others contend that he was a Cabalist Jew. In any event, the rejuvenated Kölmer was soon back in Europe looking for prospects when he met and "converted" the disgruntled Bavarian professor. Webster writes: "Weishaupt, who combined the practical German brain with the cunning of Machiavelli, spent no less than five years thinking out a plan by which all these ideas should be reduced to a system . . ."[17] As the Bible declares, "*there is no new thing under the sun*" (Ecclesiastes 1:9), Weishaupt's *new system* was, in reality, nothing more than *old Satanism!* But what a powerful revival of evil it became! Webster writes in her book *Secret Societies*: "That Weishaupt was not the originator of the system he named Illuminism will be already apparent to every reader of the present work; . . . it will be evident that men aiming at the overthrow of the existing social order and of all accepted religion had existed from the earliest times. . . ."[18]

In order to get his Illuminati jump-started as quickly as possible, Weishaupt entered the Masonic Lodge Theodore at Munich in 1777. It was here that he found a band of renegade Masons who wanted more than the status quo. (Proverbs 27:20) The French Mason Mirabeau, divulged in his memoirs:

> The Lodge Theodore de Bon Conseil at Munich, where there were a few men with brains and hearts, was tired of being tossed about by the vain promises and quarrels of Masonry. The heads resolved to graft on to their branch another secret association to which they gave the name of the Order of the Illuminés. They modelled it on the Society of Jesus, whilst proposing to themselves views diametrically opposed.[19]

When we come to a review of the doctrines, philosophies and operational procedures of Weishaupt's secret order, we are indebted to the thorough investigation of the Bavarian police department following the electrocution of "Father" Lang. Local authorities raided the house of Herr von Zwack (Cato) on October 11, 1786, confiscating numerous incriminating documents, *and then some . . .*

> Here were found descriptions of a strong box for safeguarding papers which if forced open should blow up by means of an infernal machine; of a composition which should blind or kill if squirted in the face; of a method of counterfeiting seals; recipes for a particularly deadly kind of "aqua toffana", for poisonous perfumes that would fill a bedroom with pestilential vapours, and for a tea to procure abortion. A defense of atheism and materialism entitled *Better Than Horus* was also discovered . . .[20]

After getting his own sister-in-law pregnant, the pervert Weishaupt makes a veiled reference to this "abortion tea" when he states in a letter to Marius, "We have tried every method in our power to destroy the child; and I hope she is determined on everything—even d---". Professor Robison asks rhetorically, "Can this mean death?"[21] For the sake of skeptical "Ditto heads," the confiscated documents were subsequently published under the title *The Original Writings of the Order of the Illuminati* (1787). The authenticity of these papers has never been denied, not even by the embarrassed Illuminati members themselves. The publishers, moreover, were careful to state at the beginning of the first volume, "Those who might have any doubts on the authenticity of this collection may present themselves at the Secret Archives here, where, on request, the original documents will be laid before them."[22]

With reference to the sect's doctrinal base, Weishaupt's "originality" can be traced to the French philosopher Jean Jacques Rousseau (1712-1778), who fantasized that civilization was a terrible mistake and that mankind's only hope lay in a return to nature. (See: Al Gore's *Earth In the Balance*.) According to Rousseau:

> The first man who bethought himself of saying, "This is mine", and found people simple enough to believe him was the real founder of civil society. What crimes, what wars, what murders, what miseries and horrors would he have spared the human race who, snatching away the spades and filling in the ditches, had cried out to his fellows: "Beware of listening to this imposter; you are lost if you forget that the fruits of the earth belong to all and the earth to no one."[23]

Thus, in his exhortation to "Hierophants," Spartacus writes:

> With the origin of nations and peoples the world ceased to be a great family, a single kingdom: the great tie of Nature was torn. . . . Nationalism took the place of mankind. . . . Now it became a virtue to magnify one's fatherland at the expense of whoever was not enclosed within its limits, now as a means to this narrow end it was permitted to despise and outwit foreigners or indeed even to insult them. [Twenty-first century "hate crimes"] This virtue was called Patriotism. . . . So out of Patriotism arose Localism, the family spirit and finally Egoism. . . . Diminish Patriotism, then men will learn to know each other again as such, their dependence on each other will be lost, the bond of union will widen out.[24]

One's love for home and country must now be discarded ". . . to make of the human race, without any distinction of nation, condition, or profession, one good happy family."[25] According to Weishaupt, the fall of man was a fall from nature to property ownership. His nonsense continues:

> Men originally led a patriarchal life, in which every father of a family was the sole lord of his house and his property, while he himself possessed general freedom and equality. But they suffered themselves to be oppressed— gave themselves up to civil societies, and formed states. Even by this they fell; and this is the fall of man, by which they were thrust into unspeakable misery. To get out of this state, to be freed and **born again**, there is no other mean than the use of pure Reason, by which a general morality may be established, which will put man in a condition to govern himself, regain his original worth, and dispense with all political supports, and particularly with rulers. This can be done in no other way but by secret associations, which will by degrees, and in silence, possess themselves of the government of the States, and make use of those means for this purpose which the

wicked use for attaining their base ends. Princes and Priests are in particular
... the wicked, whose hands [we] must tie up by means of these associations,
if we cannot root them out all together.[26]

Self-deluded visionaries like Plato, Rousseau, Weishaupt, Marx,
Lenin, Stalin, and Chairman Mao could have saved themselves a lot of
trouble by simply observing nature, especially a dog with his bone.
Webster, citing reality:

> The inequalities they have sought to do away with they attribute to
> what they describe as "man-made laws" instead of to the laws of Nature
> whereby not only amongst human beings but in the animal kingdom the
> same inequalities are to be found. Whilst swarms of ants, like the slaves
> in ancient Egypt erecting the Pyramids, work unceasingly to construct their
> hills and bees hurry without a pause from flower to flower to collect honey
> for their hive of industry, cows and sheep loaf idly through the green meadows
> or lie in the shade beneath the trees, and in pools bordered by scented
> rushes trout move serenely through clear cool water and ducks and swans
> set out to sail lazily across its surface. ...

> [O]wnership of property ... is not peculiar to the human race. The bird has
> its nest, the dog has its bone that it will savagely defend ... [I]f everything
> were divided up today all would be unequal again tomorrow. One man
> would fritter away his share, another would double it by turning it to good
> account, the practical and energetic would soon be more prosperous than
> the idler or the wastrel. The parable of the ten talents perfectly illustrates
> the differing capacity of men to deal with money.[27]

The King James Bible declares, *"Wisdom is too high for a fool..."*
(Proverbs 24:7a). Therefore, Weishaupt was led by *his* "spiritual" father
(John 8:24) to declare war on religion, family and nationalism, stating:

> Man is not bad except as he is made so by arbitrary morality. He is bad
> because religion, the state, and bad examples pervert him. When at last
> reason becomes the religion of men, then will the problem be solved.[28]

In her book *World Revolution: The Plot Against Civilisation*, Webster
states:

> Reduced to a simple formula the aims of the Illuminati may be
> summarized in the following five points:
> 1. Abolition of Monarchy and all ordered Government.
> 2. Abolition of private property and of inheritance.

3. Abolition of patriotism.

4. Abolition of the family (*i.e.* of marriage and all morality, and the institution of the communal education of children).

5. Abolition of all religion.[29]

Sound familiar? The French historian Henri Martin summarized Adam's "elaborate system" as a humanistic pipe-dream:

> Weishaupt had made into an elaborate theory the misanthropic gibes (*boutades*) of Rousseau at the invention of property and society, and without taking into account the statement so distinctly formulated by Rousseau on the impossibility of suppressing property and society once they had been established, he proposed as the end of Illuminism the abolition of property, social authority, of nationality, and the return of the human race to the happy state in which it formed only a single family without artificial needs, without useless sciences, every father being priest and magistrate. Priest of we know not what religion, for in spite of their frequent invocations of the God of Nature, many indications lead us to conclude that Weishaupt had, like Diderot and d'Holbach, no other God than Nature herself. From his doctrine would naturally follow the German ultra-Hegelianism and the system of anarchy recently developed in France, of which the physiognomy suggests a foreign origin.[30]

RECRUITMENT AND DISCIPLESHIP

In reality, the Illuminati have had only one *real* goal that encompasses all the rest. The cult's founder declared, "Behold our secret.... If in order to destroy all Christianity, all religion, we have pretended to have the sole true religion, remember that the end justifies the means, and that the wise ought to take all the means to do good which the wicked take to do evil."[31]

To pursue his devilish agenda, Weishaupt developed an elaborate system of Jesuit-styled recruitment and training. Webster, citing Weishaupt:

> In order to give a good appearance to the Order, Weishaupt particularly indicates the necessity for enlisting esteemed and "respectable" persons, but above all young men whom he regards as the most likely subjects. "I cannot use men as they are," he observes, "but I must first form them." Youth naturally lends itself best to this process. "Seek the society of young

people," Weishaupts writes to Ajax, "watch them, and if one of them pleases you, lay your hand on him." "Seek out young and already skilful people. . . . Our people must be engaging, enterprising, intriguing, and adroit. Above all the first."[32]

Understandably, teachers, and especially writers, were viewed as the ultimate prospects. Weishaupt states:

> If a writer publishes any thing that attracts notice, and is in itself just, but does not accord with our plan, we must endeavour to win him over, or decry him. . . . In like manner we must try to obtain an influence in the military academies (this may be of mighty consequence), the printing-houses, booksellers shops, chapters, and in short all offices which have any effect, either in forming, or in managing, or even in directing the mind of man: painting and engraving are highly worth our care.[33]

The cunning Weishaupt was also interested in tapping the "Christian" community. Professor Robison quoting Spartacus:

> I have contrived an explanation which has every advantage; is inviting to Christians of every communion; gradually frees them of all religious prejudices (and) cultivates the social virtues. . . . My means are effectual, and irresistible. Our secret Association works in a way that nothing can withstand.[34]

In his private correspondence, Weishaupt mocked the foolish clergy who fell for his religious appeals:

> The most wonderful thing is that great Protestant and reformed theologians who belong to ☉ [Illuminism] still believe that the religious teaching imparted in it contains the true and genuine spirit of the Christian religion. Oh! men, of what cannot you be persuaded? I never thought that I should become the founder of a new religion.[35]

The courting and contamination of women was also essential to Weishaupt's program. (See Empress Aleksandra and Rasputin.) After all, wasn't Eve the first human to be "illuminated?" (I Timothy 2:14) Weishaupt stated:

> There is no way of influencing men so powerfully as by means of the women. These should therefore be our chief study; we should insinuate ourselves into their good opinion, give them hints of emancipation from the tyranny of public opinion, and of standing up for themselves; it will

be an immense relief to their enslaved minds to be freed from any one bond of restraint, and it will fire them the more, and cause them to work for us with zeal, without knowing that they do so; for they will only be indulging their own desire of personal admiration.[36]

Professor Robison concludes: "Nothing is more clear than that the design of the Illuminati was to abolish Christianity—and we now see how effectual this would be for the corruption of the fair sex, a purpose which they eagerly wished to gain, that they might corrupt the men."[37] (ERA—"Eve ruined Adam," etc.)

Spartacus also understood the value of good ol' "conspiracy fodder;" and the more the better!

> We must win the common people in every corner. This will be obtained chiefly by means of the schools, and by open, hearty behaviour, show, condescension, popularity, and toleration of their prejudices, which we shall at leisure root out and dispel.[38]

Weishaupt's bait for recruitment was twofold; idealism and material gain. Along with all the rhetoric about helping mankind find his way back to nature, Weishaupt knew what buttons to push:

> The pupils are convinced that the Order will rule the world. Every member therefore becomes a ruler. We all think of ourselves as qualified to rule. It is therefore an alluring thought both to good and bad men. By this lure the Order will spread.[39]

In the meantime, initates of the Illuminati (like their counterparts in Freemasonry) would have a decided edge over everyone else. Robison's work confirms: ". . . through its connections and intrigues, the conspiracy was able to place its selected members in positions of influence and power where they could enjoy all the glories of worldly success, provided they used that success to work unceasingly for the advancement of the Order."[40]

Weishaupt personally assured:

> The power of the Order must surely be turned to the advantage of its Members. All must be assisted. They must be preferred to all persons otherwise of equal merit. Money, services, honor, goods, and blood, must be expended for the fully proved Brethren, and the unfortunate must be relieved by the funds of the Society.[41]

Speaking of "funds," with world revolution for sale there would be no shortage of cold-blooded investors. As previously noted (and contrary to the views of various extremists), there have always been plenty of "Gentile" moneychangers around. In his 1937 classic *The Wealth of Nations*, Adam Smith wrote, "The bank of England is the greatest bank of circulation in Europe."[42] Other financial powers in Weishaupt's time included the Bank of the Rialto (Venice), the Bank of France, the Bank of Amsterdam, the Bank of Hamburg, and the Bank of Stockholm. However, in fairness to the historical record, it must also be noted that a bloc of Jewish bankers wielded an influence substantially disproportionate to their number. Biographer Frederic Morton concluded that the Rothschild dynasty had "conquered the world more thoroughly, more cunningly, and much more lastingly than all the Caesars before or all the Hitlers after them."[43]

With specific reference to Illuminati underwriting, Jewish author Bernard Lazare confirms, "There were Jews behind Weishaupt."[44] Edith Miller's short list of "Hebrew heavyweights" contributing to Illuminati coffers included Daniel Itzig, Friedlander, Ceerfbeer, Benjamin and Abraham Goldsmid, Moses Mocatta, and Veitel Heine Ephraim.[45] She also confirms that Moses Mendelssohn, himself the head of the *Haskalah* (Jewish Illuminati), frequently cooperated with Weishaupt's operations.

INITIATION PROCEDURES

The Illuminati functioned under the most clandestine of conditions. The initiates themselves were acquainted with none but their immediate superiors. "My circumstances necessitate that I should remain hidden from most of the members as long as I live," Spartacus wrote to Cato. "I am obliged to do everything through five or six persons."[46] Weishaupt stated elsewhere, "The slightest observation shows that nothing will so much contribute to increase the zeal of the members as secret union."[47] Hannah Arendt wrote, "Real power begins where secrecy begins . . . the only rule of which everybody in a totalitarian state may be sure."[48] Everyone was made to understand that secrecy within and secrecy without was everything! Weishaupt would repeat over and over: "The great strength of our Order lies in its concealment; let it never appear in any place in its own name, but always covered by another name, and another occupation."[49] Webster reminds her readers of André Baron's dictum: "Remember that the constant rule of the secret societies is that the authors never show themselves."[50]

Whereas rookie candidates for the Blue Lodge of Freemasonry were often scared half to death by various blood curdling oaths, Weishaupt's Illuminati was more laid back at the outset. Adepts for the probationary degree of the Order's initial level were administered the following oath:

> I ... hereby bind myself, by mine honor and good name, foreswearing all mental reservation, never to reveal, by hint, word, writing, or in any manner whatever, even to my most trusted friend, any thing that shall now be said or done to me respecting my wished-for-reception, and this whether my reception shall follow or not; I being previously assured that it shall contain nothing contrary to religion, the state, nor good manners. I promise, that I shall make no intelligible extract from any papers which shall be shewn me now or during my noviciate. All this I swear, as I am, and as I hope to continue, a Man of Honor.[51]

However, when the prospects start their gradual climb through the other twelve degrees (divided over the three stages of Nursery, Masonry and Mysteries), some of them begin to get a little nervous. Those who make it to Illuminatus Minor sign the following obligation:

> I ... protest before you, the worthy Plenipotentiary of the venerable Order into which I wish to be admitted, that I acknowledge my natural weakness and inability, and that I, with all my possessions, rank, honors, and titles which I hold in political society, am, at bottom, only a man; I can enjoy these things only through my fellow-men, and through them also I may lose them. The approbation and consideration of my fellow-men are indispensably necessary, and I must try to maintain them by all my talents. These I will never use to the prejudice of universal good, but will oppose, with all my might, the enemies of the human race, and of political society. I will embrace every opportunity of saving mankind, by improving my understanding and my affections, and by imparting all important knowledge, as the good and statutes of this Order require of me. I bind myself to perpetual silence and unshaken loyalty and submission to the Order, in the persons of my Superiors; here making a faithful and complete surrender of my private judgment, my own will, and every narrow-minded employment of my power and influence. I pledge myself to account the good of the Order as my own, and am ready to serve it with my fortune, my honor, and my blood. Should I, through omission, neglect, passion, or wickedness, behave contrary to this good of the Order, I subject myself to what reproof or punishment my Superiors shall enjoin. The friends and enemies of the Order

shall be my friends and enemies; and with respect to both I will conduct myself as directed by the Order, and am ready, in every lawful way, to devote myself to its increase and promotion, and therein to employ all my ability. All this I promise, and protest, without secret reservation, according to the intention of the Society which require from me this engagement. This I do as I am, and as I hope to continue, a Man of Honor.[52]

After ascribing to all this hot air about "saving mankind," etc., the "Man of Honor" has a sword pointed at his breast while being asked, "Will you be obedient to the commands of your Superiors?" Professor Robison states: "He is threatened with unavoidable vengeance, from which no potentate can defend him, if he should ever betray the Order."[53]

Robison then gives us a glimpse into the initiation procedure for the Regent degree:

> The candidate is presented for reception in the character of a slave; and it is demanded of him what has brought him into this most miserable of all conditions. He answers—Society—the State—Submissiveness— False Religion. A skeleton is pointed out to him, at the feet of which are laid a Crown and a Sword. He is asked, whether that is the skeleton of a King, a Nobleman, or a Beggar? As he cannot decide, the President of the meeting says to him, 'the character of being a Man is "the only one that is of importance."[54]

(The significance of this particular imagery will become apparent in chapter eleven.)

In his book *L'Apodictique Messianique* (as cited in *Light-bearers of Darkness*), encyclopedist Hoëné Wronski reproduces an oath that is taken in one of the highest degrees of Illuminism:

> In the name of the son crucified (the Pentagram, the illuminised man), swear to break the bonds which still bind you to your father, mother, brothers, sisters, wife, relatives, friends, mistresses, kings, chiefs, benefactors, and all persons to whomsoever you may have promised faith, obedience, and service. Name and curse the place where you were born, so that you may dwell in another sphere, to which you will attain only after having renounced this pestilential globe, vile refuse of the heavens! From this moment you are free from the so-called oath to country and laws: swear to reveal to the new chief, recognised by you, what you may have seen or done, intercepted, read or heard, learned or surmised, and also seek for and spy out what your eyes cannot discern. Honour and respect the *Aqua Tofana* [poison] as

a sure, prompt, and necessary means of purging the globe by death of those who seek to vilify the truth and seize it from our hands. Fly from Spain, Naples, and all accursed land; finally fly from the temptation to reveal what you may hear, for the thunder is no prompter than the knife, which awaits you in whatsoever place you may be. Live in the name of the Father, Son, and Holy Spirit. (This is the Trinity of Illuminism—Cabalistic and Gnostic. The Father—the generating fire; the Holy Spirit—the Great Mother Nature, reproducing all things; the Son—the manifestation, the vital fluid, the astral light of Illuminism. It is a perversion of Christian symbolism.)[55]

One's movement through the various degrees, from the superficial *outer* doctrines ("saving mankind," etc.) to the "true" esoteric *inner* ones, has been likened in occultic lore to the peeling back of an onion's numerous layers. Thus, whenever candidates for the higher degrees began to get a little "watery-eyed" over Weishaupt's teachings on murder, treason, revolution and Satanism, naturally, a number wanted out. Those who showed little potential were allowed to leave with a pledge of silence. However, it was too late for the others, as Weishaupt had earlier extracted incriminating written confessions of sexual indiscretions or previously hidden criminal activity in order to keep them "pealing." William Still conjectures that others may have been snared by an ancient ploy know as "communal criminality," which required candidates to participate in a common crime, thereby securing their indefinite "cooperation."[56]

INFILTRATION OF FREEMASONRY

Ever the master strategist, Weishaupt soon set his eyes on the Order's ultimate conquest. With the crossover conversion of Joseph Balsamo from Masonry to Illuminism, the Jewish "Comte de Cagliostro" became a key double agent whose self-confessed mission "was to work so as to turn Freemasonry in the direction of Weishaupt's projects."[57] Serpents like Spartacus will always be looking for new rocks they can crawl under to hide. The up-and-running network of Freemasonry (especially the Continental version) was viewed as ripe for the picking. Unaware that his secret correspondence would later be uncovered, Weishaupt told the world where he would henceforth conceal his order, writing, "None is fitter than the three lower degrees of Free Masonry; the public is accustomed to it, expects little from it, and therefore takes little notice of it."[58] After considerable political maneuvering by Balsamo, Mendelssohn, Weishaupt and others, the dreaded marriage between Freemasonry and the Order of the Illuminati was consummated on July 16, 1782, at the historic Congrès de Wilhelmsbad in the Hesse province of Germany. Webster states, "What passed at this terrible Congress will never be known to the outside world, for even those men who had been drawn unwittingly into the movement, and now heard for the first time the real designs of the leaders, were under oath to reveal nothing."[59] (See Wescott and Hort's "code of silence" employed by the Revision Committee 1871-1885.)

The Freemason Comte de Virieu, a shell-shocked member of the lodge in Lyons, could hardly conceal his alarm when questioned about the proceedings:

> I will not confide them to you. I can only tell you that all this is very much more serious than you think. **The conspiracy which is being woven is so well thought out that it will be, so to speak, impossible for the Monarchy and the Church to escape from it.**[60]

It is known that the "Jewish question" was addressed with a resolution being passed "that henceforth Jews should no longer be excluded from the lodges."[61] At the same time it was decided to move the headquarters of illuminized Freemasonry to Frankfurt, Germany, the center of Jewish finance controlled by such men as Rothschild, Oppenheimer, Wertheimer, Schuster, Speyer, Stern and others. (An insightful tale of the era relates how a certain Jew, after being told, "We don't allow any Jews in this village," replied with a twinkle in his eye—"That's why it's *still* a village!")

The timing of this historic merger was propitious for Weishaupt as it would be another three years before his courier's "Ratisbon Road" experience would expose the Order's revolutionary agenda. In the meantime, the face of Freemasonry would receive a much-needed makeover. As any Mason will tell you, the fraternity places a high regard on "spirituality." Members in the Blue Lodge look with devotion to "The Great Architect of The Universe" (or T.G.A.O.T.U. for short). Their first constitution, drawn out by Dr. Anderson in 1723, stated plainly: "A Mason is obliged, by his tenure, to obey the moral Law; and if he rightly understands the Art, he will never be a stupid Atheist, nor an irreligious Libertine. . . ."[62] By the time Spartacus and company got through with them, however, Masons in the highest degrees were making the shocking discovery that

T.G.A.O.T.U. was someone other than they thought! Albert Pike was the highest-ranking American Mason in his day. His book, *Morals and Dogma*, was published in 1871 by the Supreme Council of the Thirty-third Degree for the Southern Jurisdiction of the United States. Al wrote:

> Lucifer, the Light-bearer! Strange and mysterious name to give to the Spirit of Darkness! Lucifer, the Son of the Morning! Is it he who bears the Light, and with its splendors intolerable blinds feeble, sensual or selfish Souls? Doubt it not! for traditions are full of Divine Revelations and Inspirations: and Inspiration is not of one Age nor one Creed.[63]

The correlation between Lucifer and light is to be understood within the context of a Masonic initiation ceremony. When a candidate for the first degree is asked what he most desires, he promptly answers, "Light." As he later climbs to the second degree and beyond, the prescribed answer to this standard question is always—"More light." As noted in the previous chapter, Pike was less ambiguous in his letter to the twenty-three Supreme Councils, declaring, **"Yes, Lucifer is God . . ."**[64]

Another 33rd degree Mason, Manly Hall, wrote in his book *The Last Keys of Freemasonry*:

> When the Mason learns that the Key to the warrior on the block is the proper application of the dynamo of living power, he has learned the Mystery of his Craft. The seething energies of LUCIFER are in his hands and before he may step onward and upward, he must prove his ability to properly apply this energy.[65]

The degree to which Freemasonry had been permeated by Weishaupt's communistic dogma can be seen in the ritual of the 33rd and last degree of Antient and Accepted Scottish Rites. Paul Rosen, a Jewish Mason, gives the following account:

> For the Sovereign Grand Inspector General the 33rd is the last degree of the Rite. The Order is the Great Avenger of the assassinated Grand Master and the grand champion of humanity, for the innocent Grand Master is man, man who is Master, King of Nature, man who is born innocent and unconscious.
>
> Our innocent Grand Master was born for happiness and for the enjoyment of all rights without exception. But he has fallen under the blows of three assassins, three scoundrels have thwarted his happiness and rights and have annihilated him. The three infamous assassins are Law, Property and Religion.

Law, because it is not in harmony with the rights of the individual man
and the duties of social man in society, rights which belong to all. Duties
are but the immediate consequence of the right inherent in all, for the
enjoyment of all rights.

Property, because the earth belongs to nobody and its fruits belong to all
in proportion as they are required by each for the needs of his own well being.

Religion, because religions are but philosophies evolved by men of
genius and adopted by the people in the belief that they would increase
their well being.

Neither law, property nor religion can be imposed on man and as they
annihilate him by depriving him of his most precious rights they are assassins
on whom we have sworn to wreak vengeance, enemies against whom we
have declared war to the death and without quarter.

Of these three infamous enemies it is on religion that we must concentrate
our most deadly attacks, because no people has ever survived its religion.
Once Religion is dead, Law and Property will fall to our mercy, and we
shall be able to regenerate society by founding on the corpses of the assassins
of man, Masonic Religion, Masonic Law, and Masonic Property.[66]

Of course, should you try to "enlighten" the typical Blue Lodge
Mason in rural America that his benevolent fraternity is founded on
Satanism, he would stare at you like a calf looking at a new gate. The
truth is, the good ol' boy on the "red neck" level sold out to the same
devil of Pike and Hall's crowd by capitulating to the economic pressure
of area Masons that his business would never fly without their local
endorsement. (This is known in organizations like the Mafia and the
Rainbow Coalition as a "shakedown.") As discussed in the previous
chapter, the underlying benefit of Freemasonry is perceived to be
something between insurance and welfare. The God of Philippians 4:19
is nowhere to be found. The scary part in all this is that a line can be
crossed where a money-hungry human can unintentionally sell his soul
to the devil (Luke 4:6). Although *"[t]he secret things belong unto the
Lord our God"*(Deuteronomy 29:29), Satan is more than willing to
share a few "nuggets" with any dupes foolish enough to pay his price.
Candidates for the Entered Apprentice degree are told up front: "Masonry
possesses great and invaluable privileges to worthy men alone, voluntary
pledges of *fidelity* are required of each of its initiates."[67] Oswald Wirth,
a 33rd degree initiate of the Grand Lodge in France and the author of
several volumes on Masonry, comments on the high price of initiation:

It is a serious matter to ask for Initiation, for one has to sign a pact. . . .
At the basis of any real initiation there are certain duties contracted. Beware
then of knocking at the gate of the Temple, if you are not resolved to become
a new man. . . . It would all be nothing more than a snare and a delusion,
if you could ask to be initiated free of all obligation, without **paying with
your very soul** for your entry into brotherly communion with the builders
of this great humanitarian edifice, whose design has been traced by the
Great Architect of the Universe.[68]

Professor Robison provides an excellent illustration of the mindless
commitment required in Weishaupt's illuminized Freemasonry. He cites
one, Latocnaye, a Masonic author in the Grand Orient Lodge, as follows:

A candidate for reception into one of the highest Orders, after having
heard many threatenings denounced against all who should betray the Secrets
of the Order, was conducted to a place where he saw the dead bodies of
several who were said to have suffered for their treachery. He then saw his
own brother tied hand and foot, begging his mercy and intercession. He was
informed that this person was about to suffer the punishment due to this
offence, and that it was reserved for him (the candidate) to be the instrument
of this just vengeance, and that this gave him an opportunity of manifesting
that he was completely devoted to the Order. It being observed that his
countenance gave signs of inward horror (the person in bonds imploring
his mercy all the while) he was told, that in order to spare his feelings,
a bandage should be put over his eyes. A dagger was then put into his right
hand, and being hood-winked, his left hand was laid on the palpitating
heart of the criminal, and he was then ordered to strike. He instantly obeyed;
and when the bandage was taken from his eyes, he saw that it was a lamb
that he had stabbed. Surely such trials and such wanton cruelty are only
fit for training conspirators.[69]

WEISHAUPT'S "M.O"

To gain an *"understanding of the times . . . for such a time as this,"*
the reader would do well to acquaint himself with Weishaupt's five
major stratagems. The first of these has been the control of public
opinion. Weishaupt wrote:

We must bring our opinions into fashion by every art—spread them among
the people by the help of young writers. We must preach the warmest

concern for humanity, and make people indifferent to all other relations [i.e., relations to God, family, and country, etc.].[70]

Webster adds:

Secret societies are of importance, because they are, moreover, symptomatic, and also because, although the work actually carried out in their lodges or councils may be of a trivial character, they are able by the power of association and the collective force they generate to influence public opinion and to float ideas in the outside world which may have far-reaching consequences.[71]

Of course, ideas will always float faster through the polluted channels of a manipulated media:

With the open as with the secret forces the great method of warfare is the capture of public opinion. A hidden influence behind the press contributes powerfully to this end. . . . To-day the newspapers, no longer the echoes of public opinion but its supreme directors, throw open their columns to every form of disintegrating doctrine and close them to arguments that could effectually arrest the forces of destruction. What is the hidden influence behind the press, behind all the subversive movements going on around us? Are there several Powers at work? Or is there one Power, one invisible group directing all the rest—the circle of the *real Initiates*?"[72]

Vicomte De Poncins then highlights the obvious:

Freemasonry is practically never mentioned in the Press; history books are silent about the power and influence of the Order, and governments and parliaments never dare debate such a dangerous subject. Reports of Masonic meetings and Congresses are not available to the public; Masonic magazines and publications are not placed in the Bibliothèque Nationale or the British Museum, although the law of the land demands it.[73]

With the media under his control, Weishaupt proceeded to transmit his infectious agenda into the moral fiber of society. An old Cabalistic proverb says, "The best revolutionary is a youth devoid of morals."[74] Professor Robison said of the Illuminati:

They endeavour to destroy our religious sentiments, by first destroying our morals. They try to inflame our passions, that when the demands from this quarter become urgent, the restraints of Religion may immediately come in sight, and stand in the way.[75]

Webster wrote about her time:

> We have only to look around us in the world to-day [1924] to see everywhere the same disintegrating power at work—in art, literature, the drama, the daily press—in every sphere that can influence the mind of the public. . . . And in the realms of literature, not merely in works of fiction but in manuals for schools, in histories and books professing to be of serious educative value ["Ebonics," etc.] and receiving a skilfully organized boom throughout the press, everything is done to weaken partiotism, to shake belief in all existing institutions by the systematic perversion of both contemporary and historical facts, whilst novels and plays calculated to undermine all ideas of morality are pressed upon the public as works of genius which, in order to maintain a reputation for intellect, it is essential to admire. I do not believe that all this is accidental; I do not believe that the public asks for the anti-patriotic or demoralizing books and plays placed before it; on the contrary, it invariably responds to an appeal to patriotism and simple healthy emotions. The heart of the people is still sound, but ceaseless efforts are made to corrupt it.[76]

The word of God condemns this garbage, stating, *"Woe unto them that call evil good, and good evil; that put darkness for light, and light for darkness; that put bitter for sweet, and sweet for bitter!"* (Isaiah 5:20)

A third method of Illuminati subterfuge has been "the systematic attempt to create grievances in order to exploit them."[77] Such tactics were successfully employed throughout the French Revolution. This contrivance of "engineered agitation" is constantly at work in what is left of the United States. After thousands of females and sodomites are moved into military barracks, the press recoils in horror at reports of sexual harassment, "gay bashing" and declining morale. A crime culture created by evolution in the schools, violence in the entertainment industry and liberalism in the courts requires law-abiding citizens to surrender their Second Amendment rights.

The fourth step in Weishaupt's plan for world revolution has been to integrate the races. The French Mason, J. M. Ragon wrote:

> It is to Masonry that we owe the affiliation of all classes of society, it alone could bring about this fusion which from its midst has passed into the life of the peoples. It alone could promulgate that humanitarian law of which the rising activity, tending to a great social uniformity, leads to the fusion of races, of different classes, of morals, codes, customs, languages,

fashions, money, and measures. Its virtuous propaganda will become the humanitarian law of all consciences.[78]

In his book *Pawns In The Game*, William Guy Carr (1895-1959), a distinguished commander of the Royal Canadian Navy and author of eight works on world conspiracy, printed the lengthy transcript of a speech delivered by Rabbi Emanuel Rabinovich before a special meeting of the Emergency Council Of European Rabbis in Budapest, Hungary, January 12, 1952. A few of the rather bizarre excerpts from that discourse read as follows:

> Greetings, my children: You have been called here to recapitulate the principal steps of our new programme. . . . The goal for which we have striven so concertedly for three thousand years is at last within our reach, and because its fulfillment is so apparent, it behooves us to increase our efforts, and our caution, tenfold. I can safely promise you that before ten years have passed, our race will take its rightful place in the world, with every Jew a king, and every Gentile a slave. (Applause from the gathering) . . .
>
> Within five years, this programme will achieve its objective, the Third World War, which will surpass in destruction all previous contests. Israel, of course, will remain neutral, and when both sides [Russia and the United States] are devastated and exhausted we will arbitrate, sending our Control Commission into all wrecked countries. This war will end for all time our struggle against the Gentiles.
>
> We will openly reveal our identity with the races of Asia and Africa. I can state with assurance that the last generation of white children is now being born. Our Control Commissions will, in the interests of peace and wiping out inter-racial tensions, forbid the whites to mate with whites. The white women must cohabit with members of the dark races, the white men with black women. Thus the white race will disappear, for mixing the dark with the white means the end of the white man, and our most dangerous enemy will become only a memory. We shall embark upon an era of ten thousand years of peace and plenty, the Pax Judaica, and our race will rule undisputed over the world. Our superior intelligence will easily enable us to retain mastery over a world of dark peoples.[79]

Finally, Weishaupt's blueprint for media manipulation, moral depravity, engineered agitation and politically correct race mixing would be sustained by unmitigated fear and intimidation (more Mafia tactics). This is best illustrated by the account of the poisoning of Italian revolutionary politician and Mason, Francesco Crispi. Eventually becoming premier of the newly united Italy in 1877, Crispi's rise to power had been orchestrated by Giuseppe Mazzini, the undisputed Master Mason of Italy. For a while Crispi served his Masonic benefactors well. However, after Victor Emmanuel II was declared King of Italy in 1860, Crispi decided to switch his allegiance from Mazzini to the new monarch. Bad move, Francesco! In the process of time Mazzini's spies learned of this defection; whereupon, the "Worshipful Master" decided to surprise Crispi at a Masonic banquet in Turin. During the meal Crispi suddenly felt ill. His condition deteriorated rapidly. A fire seemed to be burning within him. Instead of offering their assistance, the other guests began to mock the dying traitor. "We have condemned you. You are poisoned. You are a dead man." In her book *Occult Theocrasy*, Edith Star Miller describes the chilling scenario:

> Crispi realized full well that he was lost. He knew there was no escape and that all the exits to the banquet hall were closed, moreover, he was too weak to fight. Without recrimination and in the throes of acute pain . . . he awaited a lingering death.
>
> The others surrounded him, watching him in silence with profound contempt. Suddenly, a door opened, a curtain was raised and a man appeared. He advanced slowly. It was Mazzini. "Poor wretch!" said he to the dying man. "I pity you." At these words, Crispi looked up. His dim eyes gleamed suddenly and he murmured feebly. "Yes, ambition made me betray . . . It is true . . . I was going to sell myself . . . But I die . . . Do not insult my agony . . . Do not mock me . . . I suffer too much!"
>
> "I do not speak to you in derision," answered the grand master. "Francesco Crispi, I forgive you . . . Drink this and you are saved. You will be reborn . . ." So saying, he forced his teeth apart and pressing a small vile to the lips of the dying man poured the counter-poison down his parched throat.
>
> After his last words, Crispi had collapsed. Some time passed. Was he still alive? He seemed a corpse. Little by little, sweat gathered on his face and hands then, slowly, his livid countenance regained some colour. For a long time he seemed inert. Then his eyelids opened and, looking around with a stunned expression of incomprehension, he asked, "Where am I?"
>
> "You have returned from the realm of the dead," murmured Mazzini gravely. "Oh! Yes, I remember now, Mercy! Mercy!" he added suddenly, recalling realities and clinging desperately to life. "I live indeed, Master. Is it not a dream?"
>
> "You live, yes, Francesco; but henceforth you are more completely enslaved than the last of the negroes for whose freedom they are fighting

over there in America . . . You live again and your ambition will be gratified
. . . You will be minister, minister of the Monarchy; You will hold in your
hands the reins of government but, without betraying us, without selling
yourself! . . .

You will part from us, not privately but publicly . . . We will denounce
you, and while denouncing you, we will push you to power. It is the monarchy
that you will betray by executing our orders, when we shall have made you
minister of the crown . . . And you will obey us in all things, even should the
orders we give you seem contradictory, even should their execution cause
you to pass for a madman in the eyes of Europe!

Yes, Francesco Crispi, from this day forward, you belong to us, for
you must never forget that, should you place us in a position where it might
be expedient to cut short your own existence a second time, no power in
the world could save you from the death, the sufferings of which you have
known today. Live then for Masonry. Fight Royalty and the Church."[80]

Miller's postscript concludes:

> This plan of action was carried out. In 1864, Crispi, on orders from
> his master, became a Royalist and duly denounced Mazzini. That is the
> explanation of his often incoherent and erratic policies in after life. Mazzini's
> promise was fulfilled and Crispi became Minister of the Interior in 1878.[81]

William Still confirms, "Crispi, Mazzini, and his compatriots went
on to do their work well, and by 1871, Italy was united under the banner
of a Masonic 'Republic.'"[82] Disraeli bemoaned in the House of Commons,
"There is in Italy a power which we seldom mention in this House . . .
I mean the secret societies."[83]

Is it any wonder, therefore, that the Order of the Illuminati was
officially suppressed by the Bavarian government in 1786? While numbers
of the society were arrested, others fled the country with bounties on
their heads—Zwack to England, Spartacus to Switzerland. Such was the
alarm that Bavarian authorities went to the trouble to forward copies
of Weishaupt's confiscated papers to every government in Europe.
However, Still reports, "Unfortunately, the rulers of Europe, possibly
out of pride, and possibly out of the unbelievability of such an extravagant
scheme, refused to take the Bavarian government's warning, or the
Illuminati, seriously."[84]

The Jesuit-trained Weishaupt had anticipated the eventual government
suppression. In fact, he had planned for such an encounter to ensure an
even greater cloak of secrecy for his future clandestine activities. In an

earlier letter to Cato he wrote, "I have considered every thing, and so prepared it, that if the Order should this day go to ruin, I shall in a year re-establish it more brilliant than ever."[85] This would be achieved in conjunction with his oft-repeated dictum, "The great strength of our Order lies in its concealment; let it never appear in any place in its own name, but always covered by another name, and another occupation."[86] Webster concludes:

> This apparent break-up of the society admirably served the purpose of the conspirators, who now diligently circulated the news that Illuminism had ceased to exist—a deception carried on ever since by interested historians anxious to suppress the truth about its subsequent activities. The truth is that not until Illuminism had been apparently extinguished in Bavaria was it able to make its formidable influence felt abroad, and public anxiety being allayed it could secretly extend its organization over the whole civilized world.[87]

A FINAL WARNING

In 1814, *twenty-eight years after the Illuminati was supposedly eradicated*, Francois Charles de Berckheim, special commissioner of police at Mayence (Bavaria), was compelled to compile an official report on the secret societies of Germany. The commissioner's complete dossier, from which the following extracts have been taken, is registered under the heading: Archives Nationales F' 6563 No. 2449, Série 2, No. 49.

> The oldest and most dangerous association is that which is generally known under the denomination of the *Illuminés* and of which the foundation goes back toward the middle of the last century. Bavaria was its cradle; it is said that it had for founders several chiefs of the Order of the Jesuits; but this opinion, advanced perhaps at random, is founded only on uncertain premises; in any case, in a short time it made rapid progress, and the Bavarian Government recognized the necessity of employing methods of repression against it and even of driving away several of the principle sectaries.
>
> *But it could not eradicate the germ of the evil.* The *Illuminés* who remained in Bavaria, obliged to wrap themselves in darkness so as to escape the eye of authority, became only the more formidable: the rigorous measures of which they were the object, adorned by the title of persecution, gained

them new proselytes, whilst the banished members went to carry the principles of the Association into other States.

Thus in a few years Illuminism multiplied its hotbeds all through the south of Germany, and as a consequence in Saxony, in Prussia, in Sweden, and even in Russia. . . .

The doctrine of Illuminism is subversive of every kind of monarchy; unlimited liberty, absolute levelling down, such is the fundamental dogma of the sect; to break the ties that bind the Sovereign to the citizen of a state, that is the object of all its efforts.

No doubt some of the principal chiefs, amongst whom are numbered men distinguished for their fortune, their birth, and the dignities with which they are invested, are not the dupes of these demagogic dreams: they hope to find in the popular emotions they stir up the means of seizing the reigns of power, or at any rate of increasing their wealth and their credit; but the crowd of adepts believe in it religiously, and, in order to reach the goal shown to them, they maintain incessantly a hostile attitude toward sovereigns. . . .

The catechism of the sect is composed of a very small number of articles which might even be reduced to this single principle: "To arm the opinion of the peoples against sovereigns and to work by every method for the fall of monarchic governments in order to found in their place systems of absolute independence." Everything that can tend towards this object is in the spirit of the Association. . . .

As the principal force of the *Illuminés* lies in the power of opinions, they have set themselves out from the beginning to make proselytes amongst the men who through their profession exercise a direct influence on minds, such as *litteratéurs*, savants, and above all professors. The latter in their chairs, the former in their writings, propagate the principles of the sect by disguising the poison that they circulate under a thousand different forms. These germs, often imperceptible to the eyes of the vulgar, are afterwards developed by the adepts of the Societies they frequent, and the most obscure wording is thus brought to the understanding of the least discerning. It is above all in the Universities that Illuminism has always found and always will find numerous recruits.[88]

In 1786, the same year as the Bavarian expulsion, Spartacus established his first lodge of the Illuminati on American soil in James Madison's Virginia. Fourteen others followed rapidly in other cities.[89] The ultimate serpent had finally slithered into paradise.

10

The Battle for Washington, D.C.

"Neither give place to the devil."
(Ephesians 4:27)

ADAM WEISHAUPT WAS only thirty-eight years old when his Order of the Illuminati was formally run out of Bavaria. The undaunted exile would spend the rest of his life (another forty-four years) laboring for the goal of world revolution.

By 1789, Weishaupt's influence was already being felt in a "new" secret society known as the German Union. Initially disguised as an anonymous literary society, the organization sought to monopolize both the press and the publishing industry. In time, the market was flooded with an array of books espousing licentiousness and civil unrest. The nation's public libraries were commandeered and transformed into repositories for anti-Christian literature. Professor Robison notes, "Many in Germany, however, ascribe the Union to Weishaupt, and say that it is the Illuminati working in another form."[1]

In 1809, the semi-dormant ancient sect of the Carbonari was jump-started in Italy with the opening of a lodge in Alta Vendita. Giuseppe Mazzini (the guy with the poison) was initiated into Carbonarism in 1827 and soon became "Boss of Bosses." Three years later, when Weishaupt was dying, the old con artist attempted to convince the world that Illuminism was no longer a threat by staging an impressive deathbed repentance and reconciliation with Rome. In reality, however, the mantle of the Illuminati had been passed to Mazzini. Two of Giuseppe's better known disciples throughout his thirty-eight-year rule were Albert Pike and Moses Mordechai Marx Levy, alias Karl Marx. While Marx wrote the *Communist Manifesto* in 1847, Pike became the undisputed head of Freemasonry in America. A committed Satanist, Al spoke sixteen ancient languages fluently.

A CATALOGUE OF CULTS

Under the "inspiration" of Weishaupt's times, dozens of secret societies were popping up everywhere, giving added emphasis to the text, *". . . the whole world lieth in wickedness"* (I John 5:19b). According to Miller's *Occult Theocrasy*, the leading spiritualist forces in the eighteenth and nineteenth centuries would include:

> The Rite of Swedenborg, Stockholm (1721); Supreme Conseil and Grand Orient de France (1725); The Convulsionaries of St. Médard, Paris (1731); The Royal Order of Scotland (1750); The Strict Observance, Saxony (1751); The Martinist Order, Paris (1754); The Illuminati of Avignon, Paris (1760); Antient And Accepted Scottish Rite, America and Atient and Accepted Rite, London (1761); The Order of the Mopse, Frankfurt (1763); The Rite of Zinnendorf, Berlin (1766); The Philaletes, Paris (1773); The Tugendbund, Berlin (1786); The Jacobins, Paris (1786); The Knights Templar of America (1790); The United Irishmen (1791); The Orange Society, Protestant and Masonic (1795); The Philadelphians, Besançon (1798); The Scottish Philosophic Rite (1799); Modern Knights Templar, England (1804); Modern Knights Templar, France (1804); Modern Knights Templar, Sweden (date unknown); Rite of Mizraim, Milan (1805); The Cerneau Rite (1808); Carbonarism, Italy (1809); The Manchester Unity of Odd Fellows, England (1810); The Hetairia of Greece, Odessa (1814); The Hung Society of China (1815); Rite of Memphis, Cairo (1815); The Calderari, Naples (1816); French Carbonarism (1820); Modern Knights Templar, Poland (1822); Brahmo Somaj, India (1830); The Mormons, U.S.A. (1830); Independent Order of B'nai B'rith, New York (1843); The Bahai Movement (1844); The Independent Order of Odd Fellows, U.S.A. (1844); Modern Spiritism, New York (1848); The Eastern Star, U.S.A. (1850); L'Alliance Israelite Universelle (1860); The International, First and Second, London (1860); Societas Rosicruciana in Anglia, London (1866); The Nihilists (1869); The Cryptic Rite, London (1871); The Sat Bhai of Prague (1872); The Ancient and Primitive Rite, England (1872); The Anarchists (1872); The Ancient and Archaeological Order of Druids (1874); The Theosophical Society, New York (1875); Primitive and Original Phremasons, Canada (1876); Société Théosophique D'Orient Et D'Occident (1882); Grand Lamaistic Order of Light (1882); The Ahmadiyyah Sect, Punjab (1882); Co-Masonry (1892); Christian Science, U.S.A. (1883); The Fabian Society, London (1883); Hermetic Society, London (1884); Order of the Golden Dawn in the Outer, London (1888); Modern Illuminism, London (1895); and the Theosophical Society of America (1895).

And, as if all these satanic clubs were not enough evil, the numerous secret societies of Roman Catholicism must be taken into account as well (i.e., in addition to the subtle Jesuits and the *visible* Vatican monstrosity). The most powerful Catholic society has been the Knights of Columbus organization, founded in 1882 in the United States by a Roman Catholic priest, "Reverend" P. McGivney of New Haven, Connecticut. Some of the other Catholic "muscle" included: The United Irishmen (1791), The Ribbon Society (1805), The St. Patrick Boys (1825), Young Ireland (1843), The Irish Republican Brotherhood (1857), Phoenix Society of Skibbereen (1858), The Clan-na-Gael (1869), The National Land League (1879), The Invincibles (1881), Gaelic Athletic Association (1884), and The Irish Socialist Republican Party (1896), (Sinn Fein would be organized in 1905 and imported to America in 1917). Dozens of these goon squads can be viewed marching down Manhattan's Fifth Avenue during the city's annual six-hour St. Patrick's Day parade, the Vatican's number one public relations coup in America. Finally, Larson's *An Encyclopedia of the Cults* adds, "Spiritualism was introduced to England and Germany in the 1850s, and in the United States mediums flourished during the years 1880-1920."[2]

It is indeed a staggering thought to realize that these numerous societies constitute but a short list of what has *really* been lurking in the dark. And because the Lord chose America to be the bastion of New Testament Christianity, the god of this world marshaled the majority of occult forces here on May 9, 1798, at Charlestown, Massachusetts. Reverend Jedediah Morse, father of the renowned inventor, Samuel F. B. Morse, preached his famous sermon on Illuminism in America from the text: *"This day is a day of trouble, and of rebuke, and of blasphemy"* (II Kings 19:3a). An excerpt from his message follows:

> Practically all of the civil and ecclesiastical establishments of Europe have already been shaken to their foundations by this terrible organization; the French Revolution itself is doubtless to be traced to its machinations; the successes of the French armies are to be explained on the same ground. The Jacobins are nothing more nor less than the open manifestation of the hidden system of the Illuminati. The Order has its branches established and its emissaries at work in America. The affiliated Jacobin Societies in America have doubtless had as the object of their establishment the propagation of the principles of the illuminated mother club in France.[3]

In July of that same year, Reverend Timothy Dwight, president of Yale University, asked in one of his sermons, "Shall our sons become the disciples of Voltaire . . . or our daughters the concubines of the Illuminati?"[4]

Of particular concern at this time was the arrival from France of Thomas Paine's blasphemous work, *The Age of Reason*. The one-time literary hero of the American Revolution (*Common Sense, The American Crisis,* etc.) had moved to France where he was elected to the National Convention in 1792. Writing from the seat of illuminized Freemasonry, Paine made a direct assault on the Holy Bible and the Lord Jesus Christ. An excerpt from *The Age Of Reason* reads:

> It is upon this plain narrative of facts, together with another case I am going to mention, that the Christian mythologists, calling themselves the Christian church, have erected their fable which, for absurdity and extravagance, is not exceeded by anything that is to be found in the mythology of the ancients. . . . Putting aside everything that might excite laughter by its absurdity, or detestation by its profaneness, and confining ourselves merely to an examination of the parts, it is impossible to conceive a story more derogatory to the Almighty, more inconsistent with his wisdom, more contradictory to his power than this story is.[5]

Keith Hardman's analysis of Paine's style fits the pattern of Weishaupt's stated agenda:

> Paine's deism and the ideas of the French Encyclopedists were, for the most part, not closely reasoned arguments for scholars. They were not designed to instruct or convince, but rather to amuse, baffle, and intrigue. They were addressed not to educated people but to the ignorant, the unthinking, and those who already were inclined to loose morals and a hatred of Christianity. The writings were directed not to the intellect but to man's weaknesses, passions, and prejudices.[6]

The distinguished Presbyterian, Dr. Ashbel Greene, characterized Paine's *Age Of Reason* as "a book in which the most contemptible ignorance, the grossest falsehood, the most vulgar buffoonery, the most unblushing impudence, and the most daring profaneness are united."[7]

When Paine visited America in 1802, the newspapers of the land teemed with fury. Note the prefigurement to Madison's analogy of a "serpent" in the wrathful versification of the *New York Evening Post* on December 8, 1802:

To Tom Paine

Detested reptile! Wherefore hast thou come
To add new evils to our groaning land?
To some wild desert let thy carcase roam,
Where naught can wither by thy blasting hand.

In the dark hour that brought thee to our shore,
The shade of Washington did awful scowl—
Hence, gloomy monster! curse mankind no more
Thy person filthy as thy soul is foul.[8]

Do you think the average Baptist preacher today has the guts to match America's early newspaper editors in telling it like it is? Truth is, they are too busy worrying about offending their worldly congregations. I have often said that the "Greek" words for compromise are "mortgage payment."

When Dr. Joseph Willard, president of Harvard University, delivered his retirement address on July 4, 1812, he warned his fellow Americans about Illuminati intrigue. His remarks were uttered on the eve of the then-looming war with Great Britain, and—*twenty-six years after Weishaupt's Order was supposedly extinguished.* Dr. Willard cautioned:

> There is sufficient evidence that a number of societies of the Illuminati have been established in this land. They are doubtless striving to secretly undermine all our ancient institutions, civil and sacred. These societies are clearly leagued with those of the same order in Europe. . . .
>
> We live in an alarming period. The Enemies of all order are seeking our ruin. Should infidelity generally prevail, our independence would fall of course. Our republican government would be annihilated . . .[9]

THE SACKING OF THE CAPITAL

On June 24, 1814, less than two years after Dr. Willard's discourse, a significant British expeditionary force came ashore and captured Washington, D.C. President Madison and the First Lady were literally forced to flee the White House dining room. Admiral Cockburn and his officers helped themselves to the abandoned fare instead. Upon entering the Capitol Building, Cockburn seated himself in the Speaker's chair and announced sarcastically, "All in favor of burning, say 'aye.'" Following a unanimous vote, every public building in the city was put to the torch. Only the patent office was saved. "The spectators stood in awful silence, the city was alight and the heavens reddened with the blaze,"[10] wrote Margaret Smith, who had witnessed the conflagration.

The victory was short-lived, however. Only three months later, the British were checked by Fort McHenry's "Star Spangled Banner" and ultimately decimated at the Battle of New Orleans on January 8, 1815. It was fitting that the Lord delivered the enemy into General Andy Jackson's hands as he later became one of the few presidents to confront and expel the international bankers from America. Two years before he died, "Old Hickory" committed his soul to the One, *"Who his own self bare our sins in his own body on the tree"* (I Peter 2:24a). Before expiring, he made a last appeal for America to build her future on the blessed Word of God, stating, "That book, Sir [pointing to the Holy Bible], is the Rock upon which our republic rests."[11]

I had often wondered why the Lord allowed the capital of our fledgling nation to be desecrated in this manner. It was so unlike our traditional (pre-9/11) perception of America's inviolability. The material presented in the remainder of this chapter will suggest a spiritual explanation for the providential catastrophe.

UNWISE EXTREMISM

If Satan has despised America for her unique relationship to the King James Bible, New Testament Christianity, world evangelism and the nation of Israel, would it not stand to reason that his wrath would focus on our capital? Although Washington, D.C., was eventually restored, the devil's unseen attacks have continued unabated. As the twenty-first century unfolds, Satan's greatest allies range from an oblivious and/or apathetic American populace to a handful of legitimate "Limbaugh Kooks" intent on throwing the baby out with the bathwater.

The salient *facts* concerning the spiritual battle for Washington, D.C., follow. While the majority of our Founding Fathers were unquestionably God-fearing, Bible-believing Christians, a number of Freemasons were professionally involved in the many construction projects of the new capital. Furthermore, as previously noted, the earliest colonial lodges were affiliated with the non-speculative *York Rite* of Great Britain ("the jolly brotherhood of the bottle," etc.), as opposed to the French-inspired,

Illuminati-infiltrated *Scottish Rite*, which didn't arrive in America until the Charleston, S.C., lodge was formed in 1801.

An exaggerated Masonic connection with the birth of our republic has led many well-intended conspiracy writers to overreact, sometimes to the brink of lunacy. One such author is Texe Marrs. After doing an excellent job of exposing America's suicidal ratification of the United Nations' Biological Diversity Treaty, Marrs goes on to indict the Founding Fathers for having inserted Article VI into the Constitution *surreptitiously*. While the article has proven to be a cancer in the otherwise venerable document, Marrs believes the ill-fated decision was a conspiratorial act. In his May 1995, *Flashpoint* newsletter Marrs wrote:

> What Washington, Franklin, Jefferson, Hancock, and other founders did was to specify in Article VI of the Constitution that *any and all treaties entered into by the U.S.A. and foreign countries have precedence and authority over every article, jot, tittle, and iota of the Constitution.* **In other words, our Masonic forefathers masterfully tricked the citizenry into believing a lie**—that the government would forever guarantee the rights of free citizens. In fact, these men made sure that dictatorial, ungodly, and savage breaches and violations could craftily be written later into law simply by the ruse of treaties.[12]

A. Ralph Epperson is another writer given to unwise extremism. With two highly documented conspiracy primers to his credit (*The Unseen Hand* and *The New World Order*), Mr. Epperson unfortunately went off the deep end with *America's Secret Destiny: The Role of Subversive Secret Societies in Shaping a Dreadful Future for America*. After announcing in the introduction, ". . . what you are about to read is perhaps the most important work ever written on the founding of this nation," Epperson shares his two key discoveries: ". . . the founding fathers were conspirators! [And] . . . the founding fathers were liars!"[13] Because article 1, Section 8, clause 17 of the U.S. Constitution appears to give Congress exclusive jurisdiction over the District of Columbia, Epperson states, "It is my opinion now that the Constitution is THE MOST OPPRESSIVE DOCUMENT EVER WRITTEN BY THE MIND OF MAN!"[14] An apropos rejoinder would be his own earlier remark, "Anyone out of touch with reality is called insane."[15] Having visited over forty countries to date, I can assure Mr. Epperson that the U.S. Constitution is anything *but* THE MOST OPPRESSIVE DOCUMENT EVER WRITTEN!

According to Epperson, the men who established this nation did so under the power of clairvoyance:

> America's "founding fathers" committed this nation to a secret destiny, and that destiny is somehow concealed in the Great Seal of the United States. . . . Those who designed the Great Seal in 1782 **knew** what they were doing: they were placing this nation on track to some "secret destiny" and they **knew they had over 200 years to create the changes needed to bring it about.** They **knew** that the American people would never approve of their "secret destiny" and that was why they kept it secret and concealed in symbols in the Great Seal of the United States. These men had an evil purpose, they made their plans in secret . . .[16]

Apparently, Mr. Epperson has never learned the fate of those original "conspirators" who affixed their signatures under the foreboding words: "And for the support of this Declaration, with a firm reliance on the protection of divine Providence, we mutually pledge to each other our Lives, our Fortunes, and our sacred Honor." John Hancock, reputed to be the richest man in all of America, had already proven his commitment by ordering a cannonade on occupied Boston, realizing that much of his own commercial property would be destroyed. In the painful years ahead, most of the signers would pay dearly for their convictions:

> Five were captured by the British and tortured before they died. Twelve had their homes ransacked and burned. Two lost their sons in the war, another had two sons captured. Nine either died from war wounds or from hardships suffered in the war. Carter Braxton of Virginia, a wealthy planter and trader, watched his ships being destroyed by the British navy. He died impoverished. Thomas McKean had to keep himself and his family in hiding, and lost all his possessions. The British destroyed the property of Francis Lewis and jailed his wife; she died a few months later.[17]

Epperson concludes his work by sinking into the quagmire of date-setting. Having rendered an accurate translation of the mysterious Latin phrase appearing on the Great Seal, he "prophesied" (in 1995):

> It is certainly a fair question to ask: if the founding fathers of America planned on giving this nation a "New World Order," why didn't they create it in 1776? And there is an answer to that question. It is because they **knew** that there was a timetable set up to do exactly that, and that this date for the creation of the New World Order was many decades ahead in the future. They **knew** that the date for the creation of this new civilization was the year 2000,

and that succeeding generations would have 224 years to create it in its entirety. That is why they "announced the birth," of this new civilization at the time with the Latin phrase ANNUIT COEPTIS rather than actually establish it.[18]

Conspiracy writers are frequently cast as born-again believers. Epperson writes, "I happen to be a Bible believing Christian."[19] However, when it comes to a clear presentation of the Gospel, he could only state, "I have attempted to induce each of you to consider the truth of the existence of God, if you are not already a believer."[20] My friend, you had better have something more than a generic belief in God! *"Thou believest that there is one God; thou doest well: the devils also believe, and tremble."* (James 2:19)

Although the majority of Epperson's works are informative (I have frequently cited them throughout this volume), the author's testimony of being a "Bible-believing Christian" should be scrutinized in light of other statements he has made. In *America's Secret Destiny*, he tacitly endorses the Roman Catholic theologian, Thomas Aquinas.[21] In his 1997 work, *Masonry: Conspiracy Against Christianity,* he writes in the concluding chapter:

> I would like to start with an examination of my views about theology [defined as: "the study of God and the relations between God and the universe"] and how I believe the Masons fit in. So I will call this chapter THEOLOGY 101, the views of Professor Ralph Epperson, instructor. . . .
>
> Like many people, I started wondering about what the purpose of life was, and what my role might be in it, about the time I was in college. So what I am about to share with you is the result of many years of thought and reflection. **I cannot guarantee that what I believe in is correct, but it is the best that I can do with all of my limited education and research**. So this is **my view** of theology. . . .
>
> It is **my belief** that each man, woman and child on this earth is being asked one simple question, and that each of us has the ability to choose an answer to that question. And so, in **my opinion**, the sole purpose of life is to make that one decision. . . .
>
> That question is recorded in the book of Matthew, Chapter 16, verse 15: "He [meaning Jesus] saith unto them [all of his disciples were with him then], BUT WHOM SAY YE THAT I AM?
>
> And the correct answer to that question is the one provided by Peter in the next verse: ". . . Thou art the Christ, the Son of the Living God."

And the **reward** for the right answer, like the one Peter gave to Jesus, is spelled out in John Chapter 3, Verse 16. . . .

So I **believe** that each man and woman has but one question to answer during their lifetime, and there is a **reward** for those who answer that question correctly . . .

They [the Masons] exist to utterly destroy Christianity so that no one will answer that question correctly. . . .

This all makes perfect **sense** to me. It **seems** to fit with everything **my mind** has told me for some 40 years. And it **seems** to fit with everything my research as an historian has shown me for over 30 years. **And I am giving you this view of my theology, not as a Christian, but as an historian** . . .

So, may I **suggest** that you find the answer to the question. Because the morning of January 1, 6000 A.L. [Masonic abbreviation for "Year of Light"] is fast approaching."[22]

With all due respect to Mr. Epperson, I thoroughly believed that Jesus was the Christ, the Son of the Living God—*while I was simultaneously praying my rosary beads in the Roman Catholic Church!* Bible words such as sin, judgment, hell, Gospel, resurrection, grace, repentance, faith and others are not to be found in THEOLOGY 101.

He then left his readers with a final "prophecy" (in 1997):

So "The New World Order" that President Bush mentioned in 1990 is coming to the world sometime after noon on December 31, 1999, A.D., meaning the afternoon and night of New Year's Eve, December 31, 5999 A∴L∴, and the morning of January 1, 2000 A.D., meaning the morning of January 1, 6000 A∴L∴.[23]

This is not an attempt to attack Mr. Epperson. Anyone who is willing to buck the system should be commended. But to confuse the bedrock tenets of orthodox Christianity is to support the conspiracy itself. On two occasions I spoke with Mr. Epperson over the telephone. He came across as courteous and sincere. However, when I shared the true Gospel with him, he didn't have a clue.

SUBLIMINAL PRO-VATICAN ABERRANCY

At the other end of the spectrum is a consortium of "super-patriot" apologists who minimize or ignore the actual Masonic perturbations of our capital's arcane development. Such writers invariably commit a second transgression by totally ignoring the numerous Baptist contributions to our government, while subtly incorporating Roman Catholicism under the banner of America's "Christian" foundation. Peter Marshall and David Manuel, co-authors of *The Light and The Glory*, sang the praises of "Father" Marquette and his band of Jesuit "missionaries" for having spread the "gospel" along the Mississippi River,[24] while David Barton and Catherine Millard have endorsed the Franciscan, Junipero Serra. In his book, *A Spiritual Heritage*, Barton features a photograph of Serra's monument in National Statuary Hall, listing him as one of "many famous Christians" in the pioneer era.[25] Dr. Millard's work, *The Rewriting of America's History* (supported by a foreward written by Dr. D. James Kennedy), presents a far more "in your face" endorsement of Roman Catholicism by devoting an entire eleven-page section to the reprobate entitled, "Junipero Serra—Man of God." Her opening line reads: "Junipero Serra, 'The Apostle to California,' as he is called, **president of the Franciscans** for many years, and first person to bring **the good news of salvation** to the West Coast of America, was a giant among men, indeed."[26]

To equate the Bible's "good news of salvation" with *any* order of the Roman Catholic Church constitutes the height of blasphemy and deceit! Should this statement startle my more sensitive or naive readers, they need only refer to three sources: a King James Bible, *Foxe's Book of Martyrs,* and the *New Catholic Encyclopedia.* The very idea!

In its article, "Serra, Junipero," the *New Catholic Encyclopedia* never once connected "Father" Serra's message with the Gospel of Jesus Christ, but pointed rather to his career-high statistics of "6,000 baptisms and 5,000 confirmations." However, the article *did* mention something that Millard "forgot" to include, "In 1752, he was appointed commissary of the Holy Office of the Inquisition!"[27] With the "Holy Office" having previously consigned tens of thousands of genuine Christians to the flames, even the *New Catholic Encyclopedia* was forced to conclude, "Judged by contemporary standards, the Inquisition, especially as it developed in Spain toward the close of the Middle Ages, can be classified only **as one of the darker chapters in the history of the church.**"[28]

Perhaps this is why one author described Serra's rapport with his parishioners accordingly: "Neophytes judged "delinquent" in their worship, labor, or personal behavior were punished by whipping them on the bare back with a rope, lariat, or flexible reed or cane . . ."[29] Given Rome's documented propensity for pedophilia and other moral perversities, the "Apostle to California" was probably a little *weird* himself: "In his austere cell, Serra kept a chain of sharp pointed iron links hanging on the wall beside [his] bed, to whip himself when sinful thoughts (including, presumably, any sexual impulses) ran through his mind in the night."[30]

After assuring her readers that Serra's primary mission was to "present the **simple** gospel plan of salvation to the lost Indians on America's West Coast,"[31] Millard makes the mistake of letting Junipero speak for himself.

> On the third Sunday after Easter, feast of the Patronage of the Holy Patriarch, St. Joseph, husband of **Mary most holy**, the second day of April in the year of our Lord, 1782, in which I, the undersigned, Fr. Junipero Serra, President of these missions of heathens, all things having been prepared in the chapel made of logs, and adorned as best as possible, **I blessed water and with it I dedicated the land to God our Lord, and afterwards a large and high cross which we adorned and adored; afterwards I celebrated the Holy Sacrifice of the Mass, the first in this land . . .**[32]

When I sent Dr. Millard an e-mail requesting an explanation for her endorsement of Serra's "Franciscan Christianity," I received the following worthless reply:

> Junipero Serra, I know, after personally researching a number of the missions he founded, based his teaching and preaching of the Gospel of Jesus Christ, Saviour, upon the Bible (his personal, well-worn **Geneva version**, 16th century Bible, is the same version used by the 1620 Pilgrims, and preserved in Carmel Mission.) see p.220. My research indicated that he preached the Gospel from this Bible, bringing many souls to Christ Jesus.[33]

However, on page 220 of her book we read, "Junipero Serra's **Latin** Bible, now in the safekeeping of the Carmel Mission, was printed at Lyons, France, in 1568."[34] (About the only thing any funnier than this is the fact that Clint Eastwood was the mayor of Carmel from 1986 to 1988.)

She also points out that, "Ronald Reagan was sworn into office as governor of California on January 2, 1967, using Serra's Bible."[35] How appropriate! At least she got one thing straight about the "land of fruits and nuts," concluding, "It has been attested that Junipero Serra's greatest legacy is California itself."[36]

People like Catherine Millard and David Barton appear to be sincere in their efforts to defend America's "Christian" heritage. However, as the Bible clearly warns that apostasy will prevail in the last days (II Timothy 4:3), it is now essential to expose the pro-Vatican elements within a growing revival of Christian patriotism. The purity of the Gospel will *always* eclipse a politically/emotionally correct neo-patriotic agenda, especially one that ignores repentance. (Jude 3)

Thus we perceive the danger of falling "into the ditch" (Matthew 15:14) when our guides for an accurate history of America's capital range from Epperson and Marrs on one side to Barton and Millard on the other. The truth is—*both extremes are wrong.* The capital's beginning and subsequent development was neither totally conspiracy-free nor disproportionately intertwined and committed to an evil, secret destiny.

While General Washington shocked Britain and Europe by meekly surrendering his power when word of the signed peace treaty arrived from Paris, Epperson has raised a number of valid points. For instance, concerning the Great Seal, he writes:

> The Great Seal of the United States has been reproduced on the back of the American dollar bill. And it is probably a certainty that nearly all of the American people have carried a dollar bill inside their purse or wallet at one time or another. The Great Seal has an eagle on one side, and a pyramid on the other. The pyramid has an eye above it, and the eagle has 32 feathers on the right wing and 33 on the left wing. The phrases are in Latin. Yet few in America know what these things mean. And therein lies the answer to a very disturbing question: why do the American people not know what these signs and symbols mean?[37]

Though I have an earned Ph.D. in history, I never once heard this subject breached in any classroom in my life. Look at one of your dollar bills. Did *you* ever learn what *Novus Ordo Seclorum* means? Would you believe—*New World Order?* Have you ever wondered what an Egyptian pyramid is doing on the back of an American dollar bill? Did you happen to notice that it has *thirteen* levels and that the capstone, with the all-seeing eye, is *above* the structure rather than *upon* it, implying that the structure has a future completion date?

Though your teachers may have been in the dark, the Masons certainly were not. Epperson cites Manly Hall (one of the most authoritative spokesmen for Freemasons) as declaring: "There is only one possible origin for these symbols, and that is the secret societies which came to this country 150 years before the Revolutionary War."[38]

One of Epperson's most insightful revelations concerns the very name of our country. Do you think there are a dozen college graduates in America who could properly spell the *original* name of their nation? Could *you?* Epperson points out that the name *as originally presented on the Declaration of Independence*, was "the thirteen *united* States of America." Somehow the name of our nation "evolved" from the "*u*nited States" to the "*U*nited States." It has been said that the American Civil War and the subsequent passage of the Fourteenth Amendment altered the geo-political structure of our nation from the United States *are* to the United States *is*.

Epperson also questions why the original phrase "*un*alienable rights" was later altered to "*in*alienable rights." According to him:

> There are Constitutional experts today who are claiming that the two words have different meanings. They claim that the word "UNalienable" means that our Rights CANNOT be separated, surrendered, or taken away, and that the word "INalienable" means that our Rights SHOULD NOT be separated, surrendered or taken away. . . .
>
> There is a difference in the two words. If there is no difference, one would still have to explain why the word has changed from the original Declaration to what is on modern copies of the document.[39]

SATAN'S SPITTOON

The old-time country preachers used to say, "The devil is always looking for a place to spit." What they were implying is that Satan will inevitably show up whenever a work for God is being attempted. This is why Paul warned the Ephesians, *"Neither give place to the devil"* (Ephesians 4:27). The Baptist songwriter, P. P. Bliss, expressed this theme with the encouraging words, "Hold the fort, for I am coming."

As previously stated, America's unique Christian purpose would have mandated Satan's wrath, especially her nascent state. Concerning the scene of our Lord's birth, Revelation 12:4 exposes a creature that is missing in the standard nativity set—*". . . and the dragon stood before the woman which was ready to be delivered, for to devour her child as soon as it was born."*

Note how John Quincy Adams connected the two "births" in a Fourth of July oration delivered in 1837. Upon asking, "Why is it that next to the birthday of the Saviour of the world, your most joyous and most venerated festival [occurs] on this day?" he answered the question himself by stating:

Is it not that in the chain of human events the birthday of the nation is indissolubly linked with the birthday of the Savior? That it forms a leading event in the progress of the Gospel dispensation? Is it not that the Declaration of Independence first organized the social compact on the foundation of the Redeemer's mission on Earth? That it laid the cornerstone of human government on the first precepts of Christianity?[40]

Applying the aforementioned frontier proverb to America's birth, you might say that our capital gained the dubious distinction of "Satan's Spittoon." How could it have been otherwise? Thanks to our Baptist forefathers, the new country would now be the only place in the world where the Gospel could be freely preached and the Bible freely printed.

Do you recall Mr. Madison's postmortem warning concerning "serpents in Paradise?" An amazing illustration depicting the spiritual battle for our nation's capital may be viewed on a wall in the Inner Courtroom of the U.S. Supreme Court building. The object to which I am referring is a marble bas-relief by Adolph Weinman entitled, "The Struggle Between Good and Evil With Good Prevailing." The sculptor has portrayed the figures on the left representing Security, Harmony, Peace, Charity and Defense of Virtue who prevail over Corruption, Slander, Deceit and Despotic Power, depicted on the right by two *serpents.*

Contrary to all the hot air put out by the ACLU and other Communist organizations, David J. Brewer, Supreme Court justice from 1890 to 1910, once gave an exhilarating lecture entitled *The United States a Christian Nation.* Unfortunately, his "sermon" is too long to reproduce in its entirety. A single excerpt reads:

> This Republic is classified among the Christian nations of the world. It was so formally declared by the Supreme Court of the United States. In the case of Holy Trinity Church vs. United States, 143 U.S. 471, that Court, after mentioning various circumstances, added, "these and many other matters which might be noticed, add a volume of unofficial declarations to the mass of organic utterances that this is a Christian nation." (Unanimous opinion, Feb. 29, 1892)[41]

It was fitting that the honorable John Jay, the Court's first chief justice, was also *president of the American Bible Society.* Incidentally, the first Bibles printed in America contained the following endorsement in the front: "The United States in Congress assembled . . . recommend this edition of the Bible to the inhabitants of the United States."[42] (They were obviously "unaware" of the sacrosanct separation of church and state mandate.) In one of his many speeches, the no-nonsense judge declared:

> By conveying the Bible to people . . . we certainly do them a most interesting act of kindness. We thereby enable them to learn that man was originally created and placed in a state of happiness, but, becoming disobedient, was subjected to the degradation and evils which he and his posterity have since experienced.
>
> The Bible will also inform them that our gracious Creator has provided for us a Redeemer in whom all the nations of the earth should be blessed— that this Redeemer has made atonement "for the sins of the whole world," and thereby reconciling the Divine justice with the Divine mercy, has opened a way for our redemption and salvation; and that these inestimable benefits are of the free gift and grace of God, not of our deserving, nor in our power to deserve.
>
> The Bible will also (encourage) them with many explicit and consoling assurances of the Divine mercy to our fallen race, and with repeated invitations to accept the offers of pardon and reconciliation. . . .[43]

Compare those words to all that mumbo jumbo from "Father" Junipero!

Another spiritual justice was Joseph Story, founder of Harvard Law School. He would have rejected the modern view of the so-called separation of church and state, having written:

> I verily believe Christianity necessary to the support of civil society, and shall ever attend to its institutions and acknowledge its precepts as the pure and natural sources of private and social happiness. The man who could subvert its influence will never receive approval from me.[44]

Concerning the Supreme Court building itself (completed in 1935), a magnificent sculpture may be viewed above the east portico, entitled "Justice, the Guardian of Liberty." Moses is shown holding the two tablets of the Ten Commandments, one in either hand. Then, as one enters the Inner Court through an impressive oak doorway, the Ten Commandments are manifested again on the lower half of each door. And finally, just inside the hallowed chamber, the Decalogue makes an incredible third appearance, this time on the bas-relief panel directly above the bench where the chief justice and eight associate justices take their seats.

Yet only thirty-eight years later, *with the sixth Commandment hanging over their heads,* seven of the nine justices legalized the bloody murder of innocent babies! (Jeremiah 20:17) By the century's end over 40,000,000 little Americans had died before their time. (Ecclesiastes 7:17) Thankfully, however, earth's loss became Heaven's gain. (Deuteronomy 1:39)

The only explanation for this contradictory, legalized genocide is a throwback to the *first* part of Weinman's sculpture, "**The Struggle Between Good And Evil** with Good Prevailing" (the truth is that *evil* prevails in the end times). Furthermore, the fact that architect Cass Gilbert designed the Supreme Court building to resemble a neo-classic Roman temple should have been a dead giveaway.

As this book was written to present a balanced, honest analysis of conspiracy related matters, an appropriate illustration of how heathens react to disinformation by professing Christians may be gleaned with regard to Millard's depiction of the Supreme Court building. Yes, Moses and the tablets are displayed; but *not* the way Millard would have you to understand. She writes:

> The sculpture over the east portico of the building is entitled: JUSTICE THE GUARDIAN OF LIBERTY. Moses is **the central figure**, holding the two tablets of THE TEN COMMANDMENTS, one in either hand, stark reminder of the origin and basis for our American legal system.[45]

Is Moses *the* central figure? Not unless the building has been given a recent face-lift. Millard "forgot" to tell you that Moses had some company. A humanist by the name of Peters took issue with her distortion, pointing out that Moses is actually depicted as one of *three* ancient lawgivers. He went so far as to quote the sculptor, Herman MacNeil, who described his original artistic intention accordingly:

> Law as an element of civilization was normally and naturally derived or inherited in this country from former civilizations. The "Eastern Pediment" of the Supreme Court Building suggests therefore the treatment of such fundamental laws and precepts as are derived from the East. **Moses, Confucius and Solon are chosen as representing three great civilizations and form the central group of this Pediment**." [46]

Peters then puts his own two cents in, stating: "Nothing in MacNeil's description, in other words, suggests any special connection between American law and the 10 Commandments. Moses is simply one of three important lawgivers from the East."[47]

And when a closer look is taken at the Inner Court, the figures are even more disproportionate. Peters writes:

The South and North wall friezes form a group that depicts a procession of 18 important lawgivers: Menes, Hammurabi, Moses, Soloman, Lycurgus, Solon, Draco, Confucius, Augustus, Justinian, Mohammed, Charlemagne, King John, St. Louis, Hugo Grotius, William Blackstone, John Marshall, and Napoleon. . . . The Moses figure is no larger or more important than any other lawgiver. . . .[48]

This just goes to prove how vital it is to *"Provide things honest in the sight of all men"* (Romans 12:17b). Anyone can make an occasional innocent mistake. However, Millard showed her need of a credibility overhaul when she tried to turn a Franciscan priest into a Bible-believing Christian!

ROMAN FOUNDATIONS

As the chief priests spat in our Saviour's face the devil has been spitting on America ever since her providential inception (Matthew 26:67). From an allegorical perspective, our nation took a step down by moving out of *Philadelphia* in the first place. Remember, it was in the "City of Brotherly Love" that the Lord opened the amazing door of religious liberty. (Revelation 3:8)

Then, as if to make matters worse, the initial ten square-mile tract ceded to Congress for the building of the new capital came from Maryland, or more precisely, *Mary's* land—*the only predominantly Roman Catholic colony in Protestant America.* (With thirteen people in the room, our Saviour had stated: *". . . Have not I chosen you twelve, and one of you is a devil?"* [John 6:70].) The District of Columbia would actually be sandwiched between Maryland and Virginia, which is also significant. Whereas the Bill of Rights was secured primarily by Virginia Baptists, Maryland became the first state to outlaw free speech under the guise of "religious tolerance." Henceforth, it would be *intolerable* for Bible-believing missionaries to tell the "heathen" in Maryland that their first Pope had a mother-in-law. (Matthew 8:14)

The history behind the land deed is also enlightening. The tract originally selected by Washington was known as Jenkins Heights. In 1663, the owner of this site was a Roman Catholic mystic named Francis Pope. While his land was already known as "Rome," the nearby river was referred to as the "Tiber." Local Catholic tradition claims that Pope had the power of "prophecy." Supposedly, he predicted that a mightier capital than ancient Rome would eventually occupy his hill. According to the *Standard History of the City of Washington from a Study of the Original Sources,* Fran foresaw that

> later generations would command a great and flourishing country in the new world. He related that he had had a dream, a vision, in which he had seen a splendid parliament house on the hill ... which he purchased and called Rome, in prophetic honor of the great city to be.[49]

This Catholic concept of a "second Rome" circulated well into the nineteenth century. The poem, "To Thomas Hume, from the City of Washington," was included in *The Poetical Works of Thomas Moore,* published in 1853. The Irishman wrote,

> Come let me lead thee o'er this second Rome ...
> This embryo capital, where Fancy sees
> Squares in morasses, obelisks in trees;
> Which second-sighted seers, ev'n now, adorn,
> With shrines unbuilt and heroes yet unborn.[50]

Indeed, this quaint tale might be dismissed with a smile *were it not supported by a long manuscript in the Maryland State Archives in Annapolis.* The deed, dated June 5, 1663, is in the name of Francis Pope and reads as follows:

> Do hereby grant unto him the sd Francis Pope, a parcell of Land called *Rome*, lying on the East side of the Anacostine River Beginning at a marked Oak, standing by the River side, the bound Tree of Robert Troop, and running North up the River for breadth Two hundred perches to a bounded Oak standing at the mouth of a Bay or Inlett called **Tiber** ...[51]

By Washington's time, most of Jenkins Heights was owned by another Roman Catholic, the celebrated "Daniel of Duddington."[52] In 1784, Dan proposed to his relative, John Carroll, that the spot would make an excellent location for the new college the latter was planning to build. Fortunately, Carroll declined the free gift and planted his Jesuit-run *Georgetown University* just a few miles down the road. While Carroll would become the first bishop of the American Catholic Church, Bill Clinton would go on to become "Father John's" most infamous alumnus.

MASONIC INFLUENCE ON THE CAPITAL

When it comes to the degree of influence exerted on the capital by Freemasonry, a number of things must be kept in mind. First and foremost is the fact that *the Masons have repeatedly shown themselves to be some of the greatest liars in the world!* For instance, in *The Temple and the Lodge* by Michael Baignet and Richard Leigh, we read that, "Washington himself at the time [1789] was Master of Alexandria Lodge No. 22, Virginia."[53] Yet, according to Washington's extant correspondence to Reverend Snyder, he had not "graced" a lodge more than two or three times in the last thirty years of his life! How could he have qualified as a member in good standing, much less a Master of a lodge when he never showed up? In the face of Washington's own handwriting, author David Ovason insists, "Some historians have maintained that after his initiation, Washington showed little interest in Masonry, **but this is completely untrue, as his surviving personal correspondence reveals.**"[54] His footnote merely refers the reader to a nebulous Masonic source (Sachse), and then lamely states, "Some correspondence in the Library of Congress, dealing with Washington, D.C., is written in such a way as to **indicate** Masonic interests."[55]

The fairy tale about Lodge 22 is a Catch-22 at best. If the Masons *could* produce a genuine Washington autograph (i.e., signed, dated, logged, analogized, and authenticated) declaring his unequivocal lifetime involvement with the lodge, then he would have been guilty of perjury regarding his other letter to Reverend Snyder; thereby discrediting the fraternity in the process.

In reality, the deceitful society merely named Washington as an "honorary" Master Mason of Lodge No. 22. At least, this is the version I was given by a Mason who worked at the Washington Monument.

This is all quite important given the added propaganda about Washington's alleged participation in the laying of the cornerstone for the Capitol. Baignet and Leigh "assure" us:

> On 18 September 1793, the cornerstone of the Capitol was officially laid. Grand Lodge of Maryland presided over the ceremony and Washington was asked to serve as Master. The affiliated lodges under Maryland's jurisdiction were in attendance, as was Washington's own lodge from Alexandria, Virginia. There was a great procession, which included

a company of artillery. Then came a band, followed by Washington himself, attended by all officers and members of the lodges in full regalia.

When he reached the trench in which the south-east cornerstone was laid, Washington was presented with a silver plate commemorating the event and inscribed with the designations of the lodges in attendance. The artillery fired a volley. Washington then descended into the trench and placed the plate on the stone. Around it, he placed containers of corn, wine and oil—standard symbolic accoutrements of Freemasonic ritual. **All present joined in prayer and Masonic chanting**, and the artillery fired another volley.

Washington and his entourage then moved to the east of the cornerstone, where the president, standing in a traditionally Masonic three-stepped rostrum, delivered an oration. **More Masonic chanting followed**, and a final volley from the artillery.[56]

The truth is, even pro-Masonic authors are forced to concede that the "historical" event is fraught with confusion. Ovason writes, "The event of the founding of the Capitol building is not without its **puzzles** or **controversies** ..."[57] As usual, we are beholden to *Masonic* authorities for the "facts," Ovason stating, "Few authentic records of the splendid event on Jenkins Heights have survived, so we have to take a guess at the time when the stone was laid."[58]

Masonic art is also passed off as a credible source of historical record. On the left valve of the Senate doors of the Capitol is a panel designed in 1868 showing George Washington in a blasphemous Masonic apron, laying the Capitol cornerstone. The demon-possessed Ovason writes:

> Undoubtedly, invisible agencies were present at the cornerstone ceremonial, but they were made visible in the apron's symbolism. The radiant eye represented the invisible presence of the Great Architect—the high Spiritual Being, who had been invited by prayer and ritual to oversee the ceremony.[59]

However, though categorizing the piece as ". . . the most famous . . . in the Capitol itself," Ovason acknowledged, "The sculptor of the panel has exercised **considerable artistic license** ..."[60] (A nice way of saying it was *bogus*.)

Along the same line, an early woodcut depicts the Father of our country marching behind the Masonic banner of Alexandria Lodge 22, dutifully wearing his apron. Though regarded as "the most famous wood engraving relating to the early days of Washington, D.C.," Ovason 'fesses up once again:

The engraving is highly imaginative—perhaps because it was cut long after the event—and while the procession of Masons **might** have been portrayed with **some** accuracy, the houses behind were **not . . . Whichever** paved street this procession of Masons marched along, it was not in the federal city, **save in the imagination of the artist.**[61]

This last statement pretty well sums up the majority of Masonic tradition— "Fantasy Island, Inc." As none of us were there, we can but speculate at best. We do know that Washington's original scheme to raise funds by selling lots fell woefully short of the goal (only 35 out of 10,000 available were sold).[62] Perhaps he was over a barrel. As a public servant, he was in no position to refuse the support, financial or otherwise, of any party, including the Freemasons. Perhaps he beat the con men at their own game.

Another problem hindering our discovery of precise Masonic involvement with the capital's foundation is an absence of essential information. Unfortunately, a history of the District's master plan and street grid cannot be determined with any degree of accuracy. Many of the official records have been lost. Furthermore, Washington and Jefferson made several changes to the original prints submitted by Pierre Charles L'Enfant (the celebrated French architect initially commissioned for the project), even though his draft was significantly altered by his American associate, Andrew Ellicott. It is also believed that L'Enfant and Ellicott were Masons, as well as two of the three building commissioners to whom they answered.[63] Ovason observes,

> This intercourse of minds means that it is very difficult for us to establish who was responsible for different aspects of the plans which lay behind the design of the federal city. . . . The design of Washington, D.C., then, though often attributed to one man, was actually the work of several, all of them geniuses in their own realms.[64]

For the sake of "affirmative action," it was necessary to include a minority in the history as well. Benjamin Banneker, described as a ". . . mathematician and astronomer of **racially mixed ancestry,**"[65] supposedly had something to do with the initial survey of Jenkins Heights. Note how Ovason tries to cover Banneker's record:

> There is little doubt that Banneker was a good mathematician, **but his reputation and ability have been greatly distorted by later writers and historians** . . . He was certainly to achieve local fame as an almanac

maker in consequence of which he was dubbed, with respect, the **"Afric-American Astronomer."** [66]

Conveniently, of course, the degree of Banneker's exact involvement with the federal project must remain unknown, as Ovason confirms once again, ". . . not a single document or contemporary record has survived this momentous event in the history of Washington, D.C."[67] (i.e., the placing of the first marker from which the District line would proceed).

Thus we can see all three of those figurative "serpents in Paradise" slithering around when our nation's capital was established: a Maryland "Pope" bequeathed the land; an "Afric-American Astronomer" assisted in the surveying; and a choir of Satan worshipers raised their voices in "Masonic chanting" before the all-seeing eye of the Great Architect of the Universe!

Seven years later, on November 22, 1800, President John Adams cleared the air by offering the following prayer in the first speech delivered in the new capital:

> May this territory [Washington, D.C.] be the residence of virtue and happiness! In this city, may that piety and virtue, that wisdom and magnanimity, that constancy and self-government which adorned the great character whose name it bears, be forever held in veneration! Here and throughout our country, may simple manners, pure morals, and true religion flourish forever![68]

As the hymn writer put it, "The *fight* is on, Oh Christian *soldier* . . ."

SIGNS IN THE STREET

Now although the order of Freemasonry has produced a legion of pathological liars, the capital's eventual design was not without arcane distinctions. How much of this *prima facie* symbology was planned or mere coincidence is impossible to discern. The pertinent fact remains, however, that the majority of colonial-era builders were members of that infernal craft, i.e., most *masons* were *Masons*. (It would be over a century before the Catholics cornered the trade.)

If the reader will take the time to secure a simple street map of Washington, D.C., an amazing discovery will be made. Remember that in Freemasonry, and the occult in general, symbols play a significant role. Occultists believe that symbols are given a supernatural power at their creation. It is also believed that this power increases to whatever degree the non-initiated remain ignorant of the sign's true meaning. According to the book *Magic Symbols* by Frederick Goodman, an occultic symbol is defined as, ". . . an image which hides an inner meaning. This meaning is usually cunningly hidden behind a form . . ."[69] Remember that popular saying within the Illuminati—"Audacity, always audacity." What you are about to see is as audacious as it gets.

One of the most potent symbols in occultism is the Pentagram. According to *Man, Magic and Myth: The Illustrated Encyclopedia of Mythology, Religion and the Unknown*, "The star with five points is traditionally a weapon of power in magic."[70] However, the all-important factor has to do with the actual *positioning* of the pentagram. "The pentagram, with one of its points projecting upwards, can be imagined as a man's body with arms and legs extended and is a symbol of the dominance of the divine spirit (the one upward point) over matter (the other four points)."[71] When the pentagram is inverted, the devil himself shows up as the *goat head of Mendes*, otherwise known as the Templars' god, *Baphomet* (or sometimes called *Mahomet).*

A reversed pentagram, with two points projecting upwards, is a symbol of evil and attracts sinister forces because it overturns the proper order of things and demonstrates the triumph of matter over spirit. The two upper points suggest the horns of the devil. "It is the goat of lust attacking the heavens with its horns," said Eliphas Levi, "a sign execrated by initiates of a superior rank."[72] [This is why the devil's followers are likened to *goats* in Mathew 25:32.]

With all of this in mind, take a look at a simple street map of the Government Center in Washington, D.C. Beginning from upper left to upper right, DuPont Circle and Logan Circle, with Scott Circle in the middle, constitute the top three points of Baphomet's goat head! Washington Circle then forms the extreme left-hand point of the goat head with Mount Vernon Square completing the extreme right-hand point. While K Street crosses perfectly from Washington Circle to Mt. Vernon Square, and Massachusetts Avenue does the same from Mt. Vernon Square back out to DuPont Circle, Rhode Island Avenue dead-ends into Connecticut Avenue after having started out of Logan Circle toward Washington Circle.

Now look at what forms the fifth, and bottom, point of Baphomet—*the White House itself!* Although Connecticut and Vermont Avenues technically end at "N" Street (across from Lafayette Square), geometrically speaking, the lines were originally angled to converge at the Executive Mansion. When inverted, the upper four points represent the four elements of the world—Fire, Water, Earth and Air—while the bottom fifth point represents the spirit of Lucifer. The "obvious" subliminal message contained in the recondite imagery is that Satan desires control of the White House. Though we must wait till we get to heaven to learn whether L'Enfant intentionally created this occultic design, or whether it was a major satanic coincidence, the fact remains that the symbol is there nonetheless.

Esoteric concepts like these grate the fire out of egotistical skeptics, especially "Christian" ones. "Suppose certain streets in Washington, D.C., *did* form an inverted pentagram . . . ?" Ralph Woodrow asks in his book *Reckless Rumors, Misinformation, Doomsday Delusions.* "Should we organize a crusade, march into Washington, D.C. with jackhammers, dig up the streets, and rearrange them?"[73] Though his point seems reasonable enough on the surface (despite the fact that it doesn't take a rocket scientist to find enough bogus claims and general buffoonery to fill up a mere 119 pages), Woodrow implies that freedom-loving Americans need not concern themselves with silly little clandestine societies. He exclaims, "Finally, if it is not the New Age Movement, the Communists, the Masons, the Jews, the Satanists, or the Illuminati that are about to do us all in, some believe the real culprit is our own United States Government!"[74] Incredibly, this statement was made in the year 2000. For some reason, Ralph did not discuss such subjects as Ruby Ridge, Waco, KAL 007, TWA 800, Clinton's body count, the Oklahoma bombing or a hundred other cases of blatant government obstruction of justice. The author finally shows his hand by tacitly opposing the "King James-only" position.[75]

The stark *fact* that most lodges openly display an inverted pentagram on their exterior walls is not the only Masonic connection to that "coincidental" street grid above the White House. Protruding from the middle top of the devil's pentagram in Goodman's magic symbol book is a lighted candle. A torch can also be seen atop Baphomet's head in the nineteenth-century drawing, *The Baphomet of Mendes,* by French magician, Eliphas Levi. Of course, "light" represents spiritual illumination. So what do you suppose will be found at 1733 16th Street, exactly *six* blocks north of Scott Circle, the center of the goat head (six being the number of man), or *thirteen* blocks north of the White House (thirteen being the number of sin and rebellion)?

As we are looking for the "light" at the top of a candle, should we really be surprised that the tenant in question is none other than the *Scottish Rite Temple which serves as the Supreme Council for the Southern Jurisdiction of American Freemasonry?* Was the Masonic architect saying that Freemasonry is the spiritual light of this goat head pentagram? The massive colonnaded structure, originally known as the "House of the Temple," was dedicated on October 18, 1915. A leading American historian of architecture called it "one of the most vital buildings erected in modern times here or in Europe."[76] The architect, John Russell Pope, based his pattern on the ancient mausoleum of King Mausolus at Halicarnassus, Turkey. A pair of Egyptian sphinxes front the pagan temple. Ovason writes, "A good viewing point is from the east, from beyond the gardens, where the 13-stepped pyramid of John Russell Pope is revealed in all its splendor."[77]

And yet there is more. The three most sacred symbols of Freemasonry—the compass, the square, and the ruler—may be seen in the street configuration connected with the capital. The circle enclosing the structure represents the top of a professional compass of that era. Pennsylvania Avenue, running from the Capitol to the White House forms one leg of the compass while Maryland Avenue, running from the Capitol to the Jefferson Memorial forms the other. One study has explained the correlation as follows:

> In this instance, you will have to lay out a ruler and draw a solid line from the Capitol to the Jefferson Memorial to get the full effect, because Maryland does not run straight through. It runs for awhile and then disappears only to reappear again further toward the Memorial. However, you can easily see the general direction runs precisely toward the Jefferson Memorial.[78]

The Freemasons' square begins at Union Square with Louisiana Avenue representing one arm and Washington Avenue the other.

> Again, you will have to draw a line down Louisiana Avenue and Washington to see the fully-formed square, because Louisiana ends at Pennsylvania and Washington ends at Maryland. The critical 90° angle of the square is pictorially missing; however, once you draw the natural continuation of Louisiana and Washington beyond their termination points you will see the square perfectly formed.[79]

Thirdly, the Freemasons' rule, or straight edge, may be seen by drawing a straight line south from the White House center to the base of the

Washington Monument and then due east to the Capitol. Thus, all these Masonic symbols are clearly visible.

While some may strain at such conjecture, the obscure figure atop the Capitol's dome is also an undisputed link to one of the most vile forms of idolatry practiced in the ancient world. Though standing nearly twenty feet high, it is rarely noticed by anyone. The "Statue of Freedom" was designed by Thomas Crawford, an American Mason, as his own rendition of the sacrosanct Statue of Liberty, itself contrived by another Mason, the Frenchman, Edward Laboulaye.

Both of these colossal structures were modeled after the Roman goddess *Libertas*. Adopted between the fifth and fourth centuries B.C., *Libertas* was worshiped as the goddess of liberty, or personal freedom. Her credo was: "If it feels good, do it." She naturally became the matron goddess of *prostitution*.

Unlike the French version, Crawford's *Libertas* was clothed in the garb of a warrior, representing a more accurate depiction of the Roman deity who would fight for the rights of her sensual devotees. As the Bible declares "*there is no new thing under the sun*" (Ecclesiastes 1:9), *Libertas* has been represented in nearly every major civilization of the past. *Isis* was her name in Egypt. In Babylon she was known as *Ishtar*. The Greeks initially called her *Astare* and then later, *Aphrodite*. The Hebrew prophets condemned her under the name of *Ashtaroth*. (I Samuel 7:3)

Crawford's creation was an enigma from the outset. His so-called "Statue of Freedom" was cast in bronze by means of slave labor and erected in the middle of the American Civil War.[80] Henceforth, with *Libertas* perched over the proceedings, an array of "liberating" legislation would eventually enslave an entire culture.

However, despite these perverse overtures, the Capitol does possess a powerful Christian tradition. An unbelievable illustration of the struggle between good and evil concerns one of the very first official acts of Congress. On December 4, 1800, that august body decided that *the Capitol building would also serve as a church building!* The Congressional Record reads as follows:

Thursday, December 4.

Another member, to wit: Samuel Goode, from Virginia, appeared and took his seat in the House. The Speaker informed the House that the Chaplains had proposed, if agreeable to the House, to hold Divine service every Sunday in their Chamber.[81]

This amazing fact has also been confirmed in the diaries of those who served in Congress at the time. While John Quincy Adams was a U.S. senator, he recorded in his diary for October 30, 1803: "Attended public service at the Capitol where Mr. Ratoon, an Episcopalian clergyman from Baltimore, preached a sermon."[82] The week before he had written: "[R]eligious service is usually performed on Sundays at the Treasury office and at the Capitol. I went both forenoon and afternoon to the Treasury."[83]

Another symbol worthy of consideration is the Washington Monument itself. How many Americans do you think can give an accurate definition for an *obelisk?* The 555 ft. high Washington Monument is an obelisk. The *Encyclopedia Americana* describes an obelisk as:

> a monument representing the sun in ancient Egyptian religions. It is a tapering monolithic shaft of stone, square in the cross section. The Egyptians were sun worshipers, regarding the great luminary as the creator of the universe, the maker of all gods above and below, and even as the author of himself.
>
> The sun as Ra (Re), the great god of the Egyptians, was represented upon monuments by the solar disc. . . . The two most striking and characteristic monuments which represented him on earth were the obelisk and the pyramid. The obelisk, symbolic of light and life, represented his daily course; the pyramid, symbolical of darkness and death, the setting sun.[84]

There are three major obelisks in the world today. The first is in St. Peter's Square in Rome, Italy. Whenever a pope serves his "bologna off the balcony," he must face the obelisk! The second is in New York City's Central Park (home to "Muggers, Inc."). The third is in Washington, D.C.

According to David Ovason, in 1800 a Congressional committee proposed that a pyramid 100 feet square at the base be constructed as a tomb for the body of George Washington. The Senate rejected the forthcoming House recommendation on May 18. (The author provides no clarifying documentation for this account.)

In 1833, former D.C. mayor and Mason, Peter Force, submitted his own plan for a pyramid, described by Ovason as, "distinctly Masonic in concept, involving a 'human' pyramid contained within a greater 'cosmic' pyramid."[85] The pyramid plan was eventually scrapped in favor of the obelisk. Consider all the trappings that were part of the original proposal. Ovason writes:

> Although the Washington Monument now has all the outer appearance of a gigantic Egyptian obelisk, this was not the original intention. The design

produced by the Freemason architect, Robert Mills, and selected by the Washington National Monument Society in 1836, was to be surrounded by a colonnaded rotunda about 250 feet in diameter and 100 feet height. Its entablature would carry statuary of four-horse chariots—the quadriga of the sun god, Helios. The driver of the chariot was to be a representation of George Washington: the Republicans who opposed kingship seemed quite prepared to equate their hero with the sun god.[86]

Other pagan symbols were initially connected with the obelisk as well. The Egyptian-revival symbol of Horus—two mighty wings supporting an image of the sun, was originally on the false lintel over the entrance to the memorial. Ovason writes, "This device, in a wide variety of subtly different forms, often appeared on doorways and *stelae* in the sacred buildings of Egypt, and was certainly involved with cosmological symbolism."[87] J. Goldsworth Bruff wanted to add a raised square surround to the base and to have its two entrances, to the east and west, guarded by pairs of sphinxes.[88]

The Washington Monument was finally completed on December 6, 1884. As if to foreshadow the modern Beltway proverb, "Compromise is the genius of politics," a thirteen-layer *pyramidion* (small pyramid) forms the top of the memorial.

Inside, the monument is hollow. The inner walls contain 193 carved memorial stones, donated by various individuals, societies, cities, states and foreign governments. Pope Pius IX even tried to get his papal toe in the door by sending over a costly marble block from the Temple of Concord in Rome. However, when news of the gift was announced, a band of incensed patriots hijacked the block and threw it into the Potomac River!

Unfortunately, such was not the case with the Masons. Ovason confirms: "Among the many memorial stones which line the inside of the shaft are no fewer than 21 from various Masonic Lodges, with lapidary inscriptions."[89] (I have personally viewed a number of these Masonic stones.)

Carl Claudy, a recognized Masonic historian, explains Freemasonry's reverential infatuation with the obelisk:

> [T]he initiate of old saw in the obelisk the very spirit of the god he worshipped . . . From the dawn of religion the pillar, monolith or built up, has played an important part in the worship of the Unseen. . . . In Egypt, the obelisk stood for the very presence of the Sun God himself . . .[90]

Albert Pike adds, "The obelisk was . . . consecrated to the Sun,"[91] while another Mason, Kenneth MacKenzie, confirms, "Sun-worship was plainly connected with the erection of obelisks . . . They were placed in front of the temples of Egypt. [They referred] to the worship of the sun."[92]

DAVID OVASON

Throughout this chapter, several quotes have been taken from an author by the name of David Ovason. In 1999, Harper Collins published a book by Ovason entitled *The Secret Architecture of Our Nation's Capital*. The foreword was written by C. Fred Kleinknecht, a Masonic "muckety-muck" with the following title: Grand Commander, The Supreme Council, 33rd Degree (Mother Council of the World), Southern Jurisdiction, U.S.A., Washington, D.C. According to the dust jacket's mini-bio:

> David Ovason has spent more than a decade researching the architecture and zodiacs of Washington, D.C. He also teaches astrology and has spent forty years studying the life and prophecies of Nostradamus. He lives in England and Washington.[93]

His previous works were listed as: *The Secrets of Nostradamus; The Zelator:A Modern Initiate Explores the Ancient Mysteries; and, The Book of the Eclipse.*

Dave is obviously a Christ-denying, Hell-bound pagan with a seared conscience. However, an appropriate saying goes— "Give the devil his due." Although he is consistently "out to lunch" in the metaphysical realm, the ol' boy has done his homework with regard to what the eye can see. His shocking discoveries, displayed in a series of sixty-four photographs, provide ample evidence of the "Battle for Washington, D.C."

Catherine Millard's company, Christian Heritage Tours, Inc., invites groups to the capital for "an exciting tour that points out the true history of our country, complete with all references to the biblical foundations of our land."[94] You can be sure that Millard's clients are never shown the "exhibits" in Ovason's book!

To begin with, Ovason has documented the location of *twenty-three satanic zodiacs in the federal district alone!* To an informed astrologist, such zodiacal density is nothing short of "astronomical." He writes:

I know of no other city in the world with a multitude of public zodiacs displayed in so small a place. In London, for example, there are presently four public zodiacs of which the Bracken House zodiac, in Cannon Street, is probably the most beautiful. In Oxford (England) there is only one—that on the Fitzjames Arch in Merton College which, by its very placing, should not really be called public. In Boston, Massachusetts, I know of three zodiacs—the two most impressive being the atrium zodiac in the floor of the Public Library, and the Egypto-Babylonian zodiac in the ceiling painting by John Singer Sargent, on the second floor. In New York, the most beautiful public zodiac is that encircling the statue of Prometheus by Paul Manship, in the Rockefeller Plaza. Even Florence—that ancient city which gave birth to the Renaissance in the 15th century—has three public zodiacs.[95]

Did you get that? An acclaimed authority on a practice that was punishable by *death* under the Mosaic code, revealed that the capital of Christian America has *twice* the number of zodiacs than the combined total displayed in London, Oxford, Florence, Boston and New York! Although *"we know that an idol is nothing in the world"* (I Corinthians 8:4b), Luke records that Paul's Ephesian converts burned their occultic paraphernalia. (Acts 19:19) This was in keeping with the spirit of the Old Testament, as evidenced by the rebuke of Isaiah:

> *Thou art wearied in the multitude of thy counsels. Let now the astrologers, the stargazers, the monthly prognosticators, stand up, and save thee from these things that shall come upon thee. Behold, they shall be as stubble; the fire shall burn them; they shall not deliver themselves from the power of the flame: there shall not be a coal to warm at, nor fire to sit before it.* (Isaiah 47:13,14)

The sad fact that Washington, D.C., "eventually turned into a city of the stars"[96] is an accurate reflection of the commensurate apostasy prevailing within the Body of Christ.

These "zodiacs in the city, and at least 1,000 zodiacal and planetary symbols"[97] entered the capital at various times of her development. They have all contributed to the "Battle for Washington, D.C." For instance, the National Academy of Sciences, constructed in 1924, features all twelve signs of the zodiac in the metal doors of the south entrance hall. A bronze statue of the atheist, Albert Einstein, stands just outside the edifice. The "genius" who said he was unable to believe in a God who was not a mathematical formula, is shown contemplating a star-spangled marble horoscope for April 22, 1979 (the day on which the statue was dedicated).

Tourists stare in wonderment as Al is seen casually resting his right foot on the stars of two cosmic giants—Boötes and Hercules. Ovason exclaims, ". . . this is probably the largest marble horoscope in the world."[98]

While some zodiacs are out in the open, others have been placed in the subtlest of locations. In the adjacent structure east of the Academy—the Federal Reserve Board Building—are two other zodiacs, fashioned by the esteemed glasscutter Steuben as decorative flanges for light bulbs. They are situated on Saturn-like rings which run in planes horizontal to the earth, around the star-studded globe of a light fixture.

The carving "America and the Federal Reserve Board," sculpted in 1937, is affixed to the rear entrance of the largest privately-owned bank in the world (called "the legitimate mafia" by Edith Kermit Roosevelt). Ovason describes the seated Lady America image as ". . . that of a female Mercury, with the Mercurial wand of office, or caduceus, derived from the ancient initiation symbol."[99] The "caduceus" is the symbolic staff of a herald with two entwined snakes and two wings at the top. It is also the official insignia of the medical profession and the U.S. Army Medical Corps. Ovason adds, "From an astrological standpoint . . . many specialists believe that the entire United States is ruled by the sign Gemini (itself ruled by Mercury . . .).[100]

Images of Mercury may be seen in various other parts of the capital as well. One of the more pronounced is on the western corner of the United States Post Office on Massachusetts Avenue NE.

Then we discover an ancient sundial in Georgetown's Montrose Park in the form of an armillary sphere with an attached zodiacal band. It marks the northernmost setting point of the sun, as viewed from the Capitol building.[101]

The *soi-disant Car of History* on display in Statuary Hall contains another significant zodiac. The statue, carved in 1819 by the Florentine sculptor, Carlo Franzoni, depicts a female figure (reported to be Clio, the Muse of History) standing in the winged chariot that is borne along by an "unseen force." Ovason writes:

The chariot wheel, designed to hold the face of a clock, rests upon a segment of the zodiac, as though to suggest that the *Car of History* stands outside the ordinary stream of time, as it is marked by the passage of the Sun through the zodiacal signs. The segment of the zodiac contains only three signs, picked out in marble relief. These . . . are Sagittarius, Capricorn and Aquarius . . .[102]

No fewer than twelve complete zodiacs, incorporated into six arcane patterns are contained in the Dirksen Building on Constitution Avenue. A total of thirty-eight zodiac images are contained on each ceiling.[103]

In 1935, Edward McCartan sculpted a naked woman with a sea horse, surrounded by dolphins, for the Interstate Commerce Commission Building on Constitution Avenue. Ovason confirms, "The detail is intended to represent the water signs of the zodiac—Cancer, Scorpio and Pisces."[104] That same year, another nude was designed by Edgar Walter for the Departmental Auditorium—a woman seated on a bull with a sheaf of corn. It also overlooks Constitution Avenue. The "artwork" was "intended to represent the earth signs of the zodiac—the other three elements also being represented in this central pediment."[105]

Finally, while another naked female was sculpted for the former Department of Labor " to represent the fire signs of the zodiac—Aries, Leo and Sagittarius,"[106] a male nude at the same location brings the "1935 Zodiacal Fair" to a close with the intention "to represent the earth signs of the zodiac—Taurus, Virgo and Capricorn."[107]

Having surveyed the nine huge structures in the crowded Federal Triangle, Ovason reveals what they contain: "I should point out that each building exhibits Virgoan, or other zodiacal symbolism, on a considerable scale."[108] These are: (1) The Mellon Foundation, (2) Federal Trade Commission, (3) National Archives, (4) Department of Justice, (5) Internal Revenue Building, (6) Old Post Office, (7) Federal Triangle Building with the Departmental Auditorium, (8) Ronald Reagan Building, (9) District Building, (10) Department of Commerce.

For the sake of time, only one will be examined—the "so-called" Department of Justice. This important edifice was dedicated at 3:00 p.m. on October 25, 1934, in the presence of President Franklin Delano Roosevelt, a 33° Mason. The Justice Department building exhibits the ultimate manifestation of Madison's imagery regarding "serpents in Paradise." Three naked men and two partially clothed women are depicted standing next to one another. The man on the viewer's extreme right *appears* to be holding a stick. Ovason explains how this arcane sculpture literally interacts with the rising of the sun:

> The esoteric element nowhere plays such an important role as in the lapidary panels on the outside of the building. Among these panels is one designed by Jennewein, carved by the John Donnelly Company, and installed in 1935 on the Constitution Avenue facade. This work is a rarity in

Washington, D.C., for it was designed to make a hermetic use of sunlight in the slow buildup toward an esoteric meaning. Given the context, this symbolism equates the sunlight with the light of justice, and deepens the significance of the Latin above the figures, *Lege atque Ordine Omnia Fiunt:* "All things are created by Law and Order."

Since the facade (and hence the panel) is oriented on the west-east line, the morning sunlight falls upon the figures fairly evenly, picking them out dramatically, as the relief is highlighted above the shadows. However, the panel has been inset in such a way that, until the whole relief is lighted, a shadow remains over the stick in the hand of the nude figure to the extreme right. As the Sun moves higher up the skies, the hand of the man is eventually picked out. The sunlight then slides slowly down the stick in his hand until the bottom symbol is revealed by its rays. This last penetration of light reveals the intent of the symbolism—a serpent, coiled in the bottom-right corner. Such a light-darkness symbolism was widely used in Egyptian architectural devices.[109]

The official explanation is that the man represents "Order" while the serpent is "the snake of Wisdom." Ovason disagrees:

> However, it is clear that whoever wrote this had not examined the statuary with any care. The serpent is not wrapped around the stick, as is the case with the majority of religious or arcane symbols, but is actually *pinned to the Earth.* A close examination reveals that the man is holding not a stick, but a spear, the point of which penetrates the body of the serpent. This is no snake of Wisdom.[110]

This subtle sculpture reveals the core doctrine of Masonic theology—and for that matter, all other religions apart from orthodox Christianity. It constitutes the fire that powers those silly little cars driven by the Shriners in local parades. It is the religion of *secular humanism.*

> The significant thing is that the man is *standing* on the speared snake, to show that he has triumphed over it. Rather than being a snake of Wisdom, it represents the overcome lower nature—the dark chthonic forces which all men and women must overcome in their search for spiritual growth . . . it clearly contains interesting Masonic symbolism of *redemption* . . . the snake remains in darkness to the last . . . The snake is the dark inner serpent which must be overcome to free the inner light.[111]

When it comes to an accurate depiction of man's standing before God, the "Justice" Department draws a *blank*. A better place to look would be in the Jefferson Memorial. Though Jefferson was an unsaved man, the following quote from his *Notes On The State Of Virginia,* as featured on the northeast wall of the Jefferson Memorial, reveals that he was certainly not a "deist" in the traditional sense of the word:

> God who gave us life, gave us liberty. Can the liberties of a nation be secure when we have removed a conviction that these liberties are the gift of God? Indeed I tremble for my country when I reflect that God is just, and that his justice cannot sleep forever.

That so potent an acknowledgement of divine holiness is currently displayed in a district overrun with zodiacs and other spiritual rubbish is a graphic illustration of the "Battle for Washington, D.C."

One of the hottest fronts in this war may be visited at the Library of Congress. Millard devotes nearly fifty pages in her book to the venerable sight. Various indications of America's Biblical heritage are noted, such as depictions of Moses and Paul on the rear Visitors' Gallery wall, the words to Micah 6:8 and Psalm 19:1 displayed in the Main Reading Room, and a myriad of sculptured angels and cherubim throughout.

Millard's basic complaint with the Library of Congress (as stated in 1991) deals with the "current disarray and confusion of this national repository for books which, only a few years ago, was considered one of the most complete and efficient in the world."[112] At the time, the library was undergoing a major renovation with a number of national treasures, sacred and secular alike, getting "misplaced" or de-emphasized in the process.

To gain a "spiritual" insight to the problem, we turn to our spiritualist guide, David Ovason. According to him, an arcane motif permeates the sacrosanct library, "which not only contains seven zodiacs, but includes two of the most beautiful in America."[113]

In 1888, an act of Congress put Brigadier General Thomas Casey, chief of Army engineers, in charge of building the Library of Congress. Casey was both a Mason and an accomplished astronomer. Ovason begins:

> The facade is the library's most exotic display ... The richly designed fountain, which shores up the stepped courtyard to the west and represents a court of the sea god Neptune surrounded by watery nereids, is Perry's masterpiece. ... In the crisp air of Washington, D.C., the god leans forward in animated contemplation of the world beyond; around him are fish-men Tritons and voluptuous nymphs riding sea horses—themselves the animals of the sea god. In the water are dolphins and turtles. ... No doubt the symbolism is there to remind us that Poseidon was ruler of the underground

watery realms of the unconscious, while the library above was designed to service the intellect of man, which flourishes in open consciousness and light. This contrast of the "lower depths" of the unconscious with the "upper sunlight" of human consciousness was a staple of esoteric symbolism in hermetic circles.[114]

The specific locations of the seven zodiacs are as follows: (1) in the Great Hall, (2) on the spandrel above the main entrance, (3) on the walls of the corridors of the east front, (4) on the window recesses of the northwest room (formerly the map room), (5) on the clock over the entrance to the Main Reading Room, (6) in a mosaic detail of astronomy in the ceiling to the east of the Great Hall, and (7) in the ceiling dome of the southeast pavilion.[115]

The huge clock in the center of the library (within the great dome of the Main Reading Room) is considered the most ornate decoration in the complex. A winged Saturn with scythe and hourglass in his hands is depicted striding over the top of the clock, accompanied by two women who are thought to represent the seasons.

The southeast pavilion is often referred to as the Pavilion of Elements since it is dominated by the four elements (fire, air, earth and water). In the center of the ceiling is an image of Apollo driving his four-horse chariot. This painting of the sun god forms the center of the zodiac.

Ovason devotes a significant amount of time to the Arts and Industry's building of the Smithsonian Institution. The founding of the Smithsonian Institution itself occurred in 1847 under President Polk. The Arts and Industry building, completed in 1881, was the Smithsonian's first separate museum. Here, the outstanding esoteric presence is the sculpture of Columbia (situated atop the structure) protecting Science and Industry. Ovason writes:

> The statuary is a tribute to the vision of architect Adolf Cluss, who commissioned it. His allegorical Columbia—patently a symbol of the District of Columbia as much as of America—stands with arms outstretched protectively over two seated figures, which represent Science and Industry. Science is intent over an open book: the owl at her feet is Athena's bird, a symbol of wisdom, which (because of man's ability to make permanent records) ranges through all history and time. Industry holds in her left hand a surveying instrument.
>
> The hem of the cloak draped over the front of Columbia's figure is decorated with stars—the symbols of timeless eternity, set in a vastness

of space. The starry hem is at an angle across Columbia's lower legs: the stars seem to point upward, from the lowest part of the statuary group, where perches the owl of wisdom, to the head of the female personification of industry. It is as though the stars irradiate Industry with the power to transform that ancient owlish wisdom into tools of advancement for the good of mankind. The statuary assures the onlookers below that science, like the mythological Prometheus, will bring down from the heavens great benefits for the future of mankind.[116]

The day after lady Columbia was hoisted into place (March 4, 1881), the cream of Washington society assembled in the museum for the inaugural ball of the new president, James Garfield. Once inside its rotunda, the sophisticated guests were confronted with a spellbinding exhibit—a giant allegorical female statue of America holding a lamp in her right hand. Their inauguration "treat" was a demonstration of the first electric lighting in Washington, D.C. To the occultist, the timing in all of this—the new museum, the new president, the new invention— was by no means a coincidence. The brightest comet seen for many decades streaked across the sky on the morning of June 22. It appeared to confirm a "prophecy" by a sixteenth-century demonic monk that "the era which had commenced in 1525, under the guidance of the planetary angel of the Moon, would come to an end in 1881."[117] According to Trithemius, an exciting direction for mankind would begin in 1881 under the rule of a new planetary angel by the name of Michael. The famed Russian occultist Madame Blavatsky drew a similar inference from the Trithemius text.[118] And so did Albert Pike, the most learned esoteric in America at that time.[119] Ovason writes:

> It was clear to everyone that electricity had opened vast vistas on a new age: it was, in the minds of many, the most important contribution made by science to the 19th century. This idea, that electricity would promote a new life for mankind, was endorsed in a thousand books and works of art.[120]

The chic term in vogue among occultists at that time was "intellectual electricity." Perhaps the Scripture most applicable to this "hocus-pocus" is Luke 10:18: *"And he said unto them, I beheld Satan as lightning fall from heaven."*

Was the year 1881 a significant turning point for America and the world? Only seventy-four days after that electric lamp went on in the Arts and Industry building, the "long-awaited" *Revised Edition* of the English New Testament was released by the Church of England. With the completion of the Old Testament in 1885, the new "Bible" would exhibit over 36,000 departures from the famed King James Bible.

Also in 1881, Lieutenant Commander Garringe of the United States Navy transported the previously mentioned obelisk from Alexandria, Egypt, to New York City. It is noteworthy that the corrupt manuscripts underlying the Revised Version have been traced to Alexandria. Consequently, after Dr. Hort wrote ". . . it cannot be wrong to desire and pray from the bottom of one's heart that the American Union may be shivered to pieces,"[121] two U.S. committees (one for each of the Testaments) were assembled in New York to serve as special reviewing bodies.

A final "highlight" of the year was the assassination of President James A. Garfield on September 19. Garfield was felled by two bullets from the revolver of a deranged lawyer, Charles J. Guiteau of Chicago. The murder occurred just a short distance from where the president had thrown that electrifying switch.

Garfield himself was a classic illustration of the epic struggle between good and evil—of the "Battle for Washington, D.C." David Barton writes:

> Garfield, according to his own account, experienced a miraculous intervention of God in his life which saved him from certain drowning in the Ohio-Pennsylvania canal. His is a wonderful story, told in his biography, *Log Cabin to White House*. Following the Providential intervention that literally saved his life, Garfield gave his heart to the Lord, committed his life to Christ, and became a minister of the Gospel.
>
> In fact, in one of his letters, he describes a revival in which he personally preached the Gospel 19 times, with 34 individuals coming to Christ and 31 of them being baptized. Although such activities are not typically associated with our Presidents today, this was part of the life of James A. Garfield, the 20th President of the United States and a minister of the Gospel of Jesus Christ![122]

Yet, on the other hand, Ovason states:

> Garfield was among the most talented 19th-century American Masons. . . . He was initiated into Masonry close to his 30th birthday, on November 22, 1861, in the Magnolia Lodge No. 20, Columbus, Ohio. His rapid progress in Masonry need not distract us here, but we should note that he was exalted to the Royal Arch Degree in Columbia Royal Arch Chapter No. 1, in Washington, D.C., on April 18, 1866.[123]

In an expanded footnote, Ovason adds:

> On May 4, 1869, he became a charter member of Pentalpha Lodge No. 23, in Washington, D.C. His Masonic degrees were worked through to the 5th Degree of the Ancient and Accepted Scottish Rite, in the Mithras Lodge of Perfection No. 2, Washington, D.C. He was initiated into the 13th Degree in the same year, **receiving this from the hand of his peer, the great Albert Pike.** He received the final degree in the Lodge of Perfection on January 2, 1872.[124]

Was this just another Masonic scam like the one perpetrated on the venerable character of our first president? Or was Garfield simply guilty of having tried to "use the system" for a perceived greater good, as have otherwise sincere men like Jesse Helms, Dallas Billington and Sam Jones? In any event, the Masons wasted no time in claiming the unfortunate victim for their trophy case. In 1887, the veterans of the Army of the Cumberland erected a bronze statue, sculpted by John Quincy Adams Ward, to Garfield's memory. Throughout his career, Garfield had excelled as a student, soldier and statesman. These phases were symbolized in the three allegorical figures seated around the pedestal upon which his statue stands. Ovason relates the anticipated arcane baggage:

> Now, above the head of the bronze scholar [the curly-haired youth wearing a short tunic and reading from a scrolled parchment to symbolize Garfield's academic achievements] is a curious cartouche which seems, even on a superficial examination, to be of Masonic design. On closer inspection, it turns out to be one of the most ingenious of the Masonic symbols in Washington, D.C. It is, indeed, one of the best-kept open secrets of the city, in that it has remained unexplained until I discovered its meaning a few years ago.
>
> The cartouche is an elaborate horoscope, the outer concentric of which is in the form of a zodiac. The horoscope is displayed in bas-relief, hanging from a swag; it is overlaid with sprays of acacia leaves and palms. At the bottom of the figure is a writing quill and a pair of Masonic compasses, no doubt symbolic of Garfield's scholarship and Masonic connections.
>
> The seven planetary spheres are encompassed by an outer concentric on which are figured tiny sgraffito images of the 12 signs of the zodiac. The spheres are represented as channels, into which have been dropped a number of small globes that represent the planets. The planet globes are located to denote a specific zodiacal position, against the 12 signs. . . .
>
> It is, like all orreries, a complex machine, intended to demonstrate the complicated motions of the planets in relation to the stars, zodiac and Earth.[125]

Ovason adds by way of a footnote, "In the archives of the architect of the Capitol, the plaque is merely described as a 'cartouche,' its astrological significance being unrecognized."[126] Remember, occultists believe that the power of their symbols increase to whatever degree the non-initiated remain ignorant of the object's true intrinsic meaning. After all, how many years did *you* carry a dollar bill around without comprehending, or even noticing, that mysterious all-seeing eye above the thirteen-tiered pyramid?

In May 1974, Joseph Biden, a liberal Roman Catholic senator from Delaware, made an official inquiry about the astrological symbols on the ceiling of the Senate Post Office and the Civil Service Committee room. An employee of what was then called the Art and Research Staff in the Capitol informed the senator's secretary that the symbols "were just decorative devices that have been in use for many years in the Capitol Hill buildings."[127] Ovason notes, "Few people who live in Washington, D.C., seem to be aware of just how much astrological imagery surrounds them, and even fewer are aware that most of these images are linked with the mysteries of Virgo."[128]

VIRGO

According to Ovason's research, the majority of astrological symbols in Washington, D.C., are related to the sign of *Virgo*. He states:

> Anyone who takes the trouble to examine the statuary and architectural details of the city cannot fail to note the extraordinary number of Virgoan images (and hints of Virgoan imagery in such symbolic details as the corn sheaf and cornucopia). It is worth pointing out that at least 50 public statues or buildings in the city are involved with the symbolism of Virgo, and each of the 23 public zodiacs emphasizes (in one way or another) this same Virgoan symbolism.[129]

Ovason adds in a footnote: "There are well over 1,000 Virgoan images in the city, if the zodiacs, corn symbols and Mercury symbols are taken into account."[130] He then concludes:

> By this means, the zodiac power of Virgo, which was called in later Masonic circles 'The Beautiful Virgin,' was able to stamp her benign influence on the building of the federal city. Was this one of the contributing

reasons why many astrologers have insisted that Washington, D.C., is ruled by zodiacal *Virgo?*[131]

As *"[t]he heavens declare the glory of God; and the firmament sheweth his handywork"* (Psalm 19:1), a number of outstanding books have already shown how the Gospel was displayed in the constellations and how pagan astrology is but a satanic distortion of God's revelation. Known as the study of *protoevangelium* (the first evangel, or first preaching of the Gospel), such works would include: *Witness of the Stars* by E. W. Bullinger, *The Gospel in the Stars* by Joseph A. Seiss, and *Many Infallible Proofs* by Henry M. Morris.

Virgo is obviously a picture of Mary, the virgin mother of Christ. (Isaiah 7:14) In her right hand she holds a branch and in her left hand some sheaves of corn or seeds of wheat. While Jesus was often typed as a "branch" in the Old Testament (Isaiah 4:2, Zechariah 3:8 and 6:12), the Saviour referred to Himself as a *"corn of wheat"* which abideth alone unless it falls into the ground and dies. (John 12:24)

Ovason provides the heathen distortion:

> Virgo has always retained some of her pagan and Christian connotations of the "Mother Goddess." She is the "nourisher" among the 12 signs, and, in Christian terms at least, a highly redemptive power: the Virgin who suckles the Christ Child is, by extension, giving suck to the whole of humanity. The Virgo of the skies is as redemptive of the human condition as the Virgin of Christianity was redemptive of the fallen Eve. The medieval mind—prone to see every material thing as a symbol—made much of the fact that when, in the biblical account, the angel Gabriel announced to the Virgin Mary that she was to have a child, he began his speech with the word '*Ave.*' This *Ave Maria,* which has reverberated through Christian churches and private prayer ever since, was recognized as the reversal of (and therefore a redemption of) the Fall set in motion by *Eva.* The reversal was not particularly subtle or arcane, but it carried a deep message of hope for millions of souls.[132]

Thus, whereas Charles Wesley had drawn inspiration from Romans 5:14 and I Corinthians 15:45 to pen the words "Second Adam from above, reinstate us in thy love," astrologists (along with the pope) would point mankind to the second coming of *Mary!*

The modern feminist movement has represented the precursor to this blasphemous concept. In his memoir, *For the Record,* former White House Chief of Staff, Donald T. Regan blew the whistle on Nancy

Reagan's dangerous pre-occupation with astrology, calling it, ". . . probably the most closely guarded domestic secret of the Reagan White House." According to him, the First Lady planned almost all presidential travel, press conferences, and even her husband's cancer surgery pursuant to the advice she received from San Francisco stargazer, Joan Quigley.

While teaching in Bible college, I heard a chapel message by Dr. Lee Roberson, in which he related an insightful conversation he once had with President Reagan. Dr. Roberson asked the president why the first family did not go to church on Sundays. Reagan's excuse was that he did not want to disturb the services with the necessary security measures, etc. When Dr. Roberson replied that he knew of several Bible-preaching Baptist churches that would love to have such a "disturbance," the onetime Hollywood actor came clean and replied, "Well, the problem is really with Nancy; *she* doesn't want to go."

Is it not strange how we have come to equate the Republican Party with traditional American values (i.e., the so-called "Religious Right")? Do you have any idea what Laura Bush told the nation during her interview on the *Today Show* for January 19, 2000 (the very eve of her husband's inauguration)? When asked for her view on reversing *Roe* v. *Wade*, the sweet little former librarian meekly replied, **"I don't think it should be reversed."**

Our modern pleasure-crazed, materialistic, Christ-denying society is now poised for its ultimate attainment—*a female chief executive*! At the time of this writing, the frontrunner for America's first "Witch in the White House" appears to be New York Senator Hillary Rodham Clinton. She certainly has all the "moral" qualifications to lead what is left of our country to its inevitable demise. (Condoleeza Rice would also be on such a short list.)

I once had the opportunity to interview a former Arkansas police officer who said that on a dozen occasions he had sat with his back to the door of room 150 at the Holiday Inn in Blytheville, Arkansas, while then-Governor Clinton entertained one, and sometimes two, local women. When I asked if he was aware of Hillary's reaction to her husband's philandering, he replied that the officers who were escorting Hillary on her *own* sexual liaisons related her only complaint as being that Bill was having more affairs than *she* was able to enjoy. (After signing a release form and supplying a photograph, the man had second thoughts and requested that his name not be used.)

According to retired FBI agent Gary Aldrich, when First Lady Hillary Clinton was in charge of the White House Christmas tree, her idea of festive ornaments included crack pipes, condoms and various sex toys.[133] And let's not forget those strange conversations she claimed to have had with that other First Lady, Eleanor Roosevelt—*in 1996!*

Unless the Lord intervenes, Hillary will one day be enthroned in our capital city as Virgo, Queen of America, thus fulfilling those 1,000 astrological tributes to her long-anticipated reign.

THE LAND OF HAM

As the "Battle for Washington, D.C." appears to be in its final stages, it does not require a college education to tell which side is winning. An early omen had occurred when a city zodiac was destroyed during the Washington, D.C., race riot of 1968 (only four years after Congress passed the panacean Civil Rights Act). This was the zodiac on the bronze Noyes armillary sphere that was designed in 1931 to emphasize the zodiacal sign of Virgo. Ovason notes that the statue "was torn down, carted away and probably broken up for scrap."[134] ("Power to the people!")

With the dawn of the new millennium, our nation's federal district holds the dubious distinction of "Crime Capital of the Planet." (As an ideological "coincidence," Washington, D.C., also boasts the strictest gun control laws in the land.) Statistically speaking, over 21,800 of the 53,500, 18 to 35-year-old males residing in the District of Columbia are in a state of perpetual motion within the city's overworked judicial system. On any given day, 42 percent of the community's young men are either in jail (7,800), on parole/probation (17,500) or awaiting trial (3,000).[135] In 1990, the city's mayor, "Hizzoner" Marion Barry, was processed through his own corrupt system after getting busted for smoking crack cocaine in an area motel. However, as "everything reproduces after its own kind," his outraged constituents returned Barry to office four years later.

The capital has come a long way since President John Adams offered that prayer of consecration in 1800. In a city where one out of every twelve residents has some kind of government job (three times the national average), absolutely *nothing* runs efficiently. While receiving 2.7 times the nation's per capita ratio of welfare and food stamps, D.C. is found to have a poverty level 50 percent higher than the rest of the country.

In 1975, the city recorded 2.3 legal abortions for every live birth. The District of Columbia School Board rakes in $5,742 per student (50 percent more than the national average) and pays its teachers the second highest salary in the land. Despite these exorbitant figures, the dropout rate is the highest in America at 44.5 percent, while SAT scores rate third from the bottom.[136]

There is some good news, however. The police are seldom charged with racial profiling and area employers are rarely embroiled in affirmative action litigation. Washington, D.C. is approximately 95 percent "African-American."

OLD GLORY

The purpose of this chapter has been to present a *balanced* account of the spiritual warfare that has engulfed our capital from its inception to the present. Despite her many faults, America remains light-years ahead of England, Europe, and the rest of the world. This unrivaled primacy can be attributed to the contributions of our spiritual forefathers, the current labors of a shrinking Bible-believing remnant, and the last vestige of a pro-Israeli foreign policy. Though our government's latent commitment to a Palestinian state within Israel's borders can only end in disaster, *don't let the devil steal your inherent sense of spiritual gratitude for being born in the good ol' U.S.A.!* When you think of America, recall her better days as pictured by the words of Numbers 23:23 (comprising the inaugural message of the newly-invented electric telegraph)—*"What hath God wrought!"* A concluding look at our illustrious flag will illustrate the importance of savoring what is left of America's spiritual heritage.

Francis Scott Key, a born-again Christian, penned the words to the *Star Spangled Banner* on September 14, 1814, only three months after Washington, D.C., was burned. An act to make his poem the national anthem of the United States was passed on March 3, 1931, by both houses of Congress. "Old Glory" has since stood for all that is good about the "land of the free and the home of the brave."

Consequently, given the fact that Freemasonry is as vile as the Hell that spawned it, we should not be surprised to learn that many within the fraternity actually despise the flag despite a projected aura of patriotism. Consider the following excerpt from Ovason:

Perhaps it was of little public importance that Edwin Eugene Aldrin, who was one of two men to step onto the Moon on July 20, 1969, was a Mason. However, it was public knowledge that he and his companion in the Apollo 11 spacecraft carried the Stars and Stripes. The photograph of Aldrin standing on the lunar surface, his globular visor reflecting the landed spacecraft, and the American flag set on a vertical pole in front of him, is probably one of the most famous in history.

What is not widely known is that alongside the national flag, Aldrin also carried a Masonic banner. This had been embroidered especially for this strange journey by the librarian of the Masonic House of the Temple, in Washington, D.C.[137]

The banner in question was that of the Scottish Rite (Supreme Council, Southern Jurisdiction, USA) and is housed in the Grand Master's room in the former temple, Washington, D.C. An autographed photograph of Aldrin on the moonwalk is also on display.[138] (Temple records confirm that Aldrin is a 32nd Degree.[139])

In the interest of forthrightness, it should be noted that many of the Apollo astronauts carried an assortment of items to the moon for their obvious subsequent historical value. As a fitting illustration of the battle between good and evil, astronaut Jim Irwin took an Israeli flag to the moon on Apollo 15 and later presented it to Golda Meir. (David R. Scott, the mission commander also left a "small Bible" behind in the lunar rover vehicle.) Conversely, while Texe Marrs "exposes" Aldrin for having taken the Masonic flag to the moon (*Conspiracies, Deceptions, and Mysteries of the U.S. Space Program*, two-tape series), he simultaneously advertises other "products" that question whether we ever went to the moon in the first place (see his *Leviathan in Space* video).

Ovason then attempts to tie our national flag to astrology:

> The popular name of the national flag of the United States leaves one in no doubt that there were stars upon it. These stars were five-pointed—and exactly like the secret star on the Masonic banner.
>
> What is the mystery of this star which can be at once so public, yet so esoteric?[140]

Without going into all of the author's conjecture, Ovason implies that the five-pointed star on the American flag is actually a replica of *Spica,* the most important star in the constellation Virgo. According to him, ". . . it seems to have been the source of the five-pointed star adopted for the American flag.[141]

Another "cause for alarm" is the fact that John Philip Sousa, the celebrated composer of *The Stars and Stripes Forever* (later adopted as the national march of the United States), was also a Mason, affiliated with Hiram Lodge No. 10, Washington, D.C.[142]

However, according to the longstanding version of the flag's origin (as given at the historic Betsy Ross House in Philadelphia), the number of points for the star was determined according to *sewing expediency* rather than *conspiratorial intrigue*. A three-man secret committee from the Continental Congress had authorized Betsy Ross to make the first American flag in 1776. As head of the commission, George Washington's original desire was to have a *six*-pointed star. However, after Betsy demonstrated how much simpler it was to snip a *five*-pointed star, the august committee unanimously acquiesced to the pragmatism of a widowed seamstress.

Perhaps the greatest picture of God's unique relationship to America can be taken from the flag itself. When "Old Glory" is examined in her final composition, a number of spiritual "coincidences" appear. You might call it a *Holy Ghost conspiracy*.

For instance, does that *blue* field adorned with *stars* make you think of a place you'd like to go when you die? However, you cannot get to Heaven without the full payment for your sins being met; this is why the rest of the flag consists of *stripes*. Does that word ring a bell? (Try looking in your concordance.)

But notice how many stripes are on the flag. Did you know that *thirteen* just happens to be the Biblical number for *sin* and *rebellion?* The first time the word *sinner* shows up in the King James Bible, it does so in Genesis 13:13. (Guess how many words are in the verse.) The sin being dealt with in the context is homosexuality. (Guess how many letters are in the word.)

Yet it gets even better! Did you notice how the thirteen stripes are divided between *seven* red and *six* white, rather than the other way around? This way, you cannot get into the *white* without passing through the *red*. As Revelation 7:14b says of the Tribulation saints—*"These are they which came out of great Tribulation, and have washed their robes, and made them **white** in the **blood** of the Lamb."* And, with seven being the number of God and six being the number of man, you'd "almost" think that the esoteric message contained in Old Glory concerned a God/man who bore our stripes in His own body—you know, *". . . by whose stripes ye were healed"* (I Peter 2:24b).

Then we have the fact that our flag has *fifty* stars. Would you believe that according to Biblical numerology the number fifty stands for *liberty?* Under the law of Moses all debt was forgiven every *fifty* years. Thus we read in Leviticus 25:10, *"And ye shall hallow the fiftieth year, and proclaim liberty throughout all the land unto all the inhabitants thereof: it shall be a jubilee unto you; and ye shall return every man unto his possession, and ye shall return every man unto his family."* How appropriate that the abbreviated text, *"Proclaim liberty throughout all the land unto all the inhabitants thereof,"* may be viewed on the *Liberty Bell* not far from where Betsy Ross sewed our first flag. (And let's not forget about that door God Himself opened in Philadelphia as prophesied in Revelation 3:8.)

With regard to the stars themselves, Daniel 12:3 reads, "And they that be wise shall shine as the brightness of the firmament; and they that turn many to righteousness as the stars for ever and ever." Applying this Old Testament verse to the Church Age in a practical sense, you might say that we have a "soul winning Christian" as a type of our individual states. Although this is poor exegesis, the truth remains that America's door of liberty could only stay open if her Bible-believing inhabitants continued to proclaim the very Gospel that opened the door in the first place.

Finally, a subtle picture that the "Battle for Washington, D.C." has been lost is the fact that our flag's traditional colors of red, white and blue are now enclosed by a yellow-gold braid. Many researchers believe that the current flag is similar to what was known in the nineteenth century as an *"Admiral's flag."* When American ships passed into international waters, the gold-braided flag was a reminder that the Admiral was now the sovereign authority onboard. He could marry you or make you walk the plank, etc.

While the Internet contains much misinformation (as well as *dis*information) on this nebulous subject, two things are readily apparent: The only colors my generation ever knew were red, white and blue; and, the gold fringe *does* have a distinct military heritage. According to chapter 1, paragraph 6 of Army Regulation 840-10, dated 1 November 1998:

> [F]lags designed primarily for indoor and parade display will normally be made of banner rayon or heavyweight nylon **with rayon fringe**. Those designed primarily for outside display will be made of nylon-wool or heavyweight nylon **without fringe**.

Although there are no tangible legal ramifications, the historical typology is clear; the present gold-braided flags found in every court in the land constitute an unspoken message that our beloved Constitution is no longer worth the paper it is printed on.

It is just about time for that Heavenly door to open. (Revelation 4:1) Are you ready to go? (I Thessalonians 4:16) Have you placed your trust in the One who took your stripes? (John 3:16) Like Sousa said, it is "The Stars and Stripes *Forever.*" How will *you* spend eternity—smoking or non-smoking?

"And the smoke of their torment ascendeth
up for ever and ever . . ."
(Revelation 14:11a)

11

Skull and Bones

"... he that getteth riches, and not by right, shall
leave them in the midst of his days, and
at his end shall be a fool."
(Jeremiah 17:11b)

THE BAVARIAN COMMISSIONER of police had warned that Weishaupt would be specifically targeting colleges and universities. An infiltration of any faculty would naturally lead to a control of that student body. The Illuminati itself was spawned at the University of Ingolstadt. This strategy would also extend to authors and publishers. (If "readers are leaders," then *writers* are *leaders of leaders.*) It was Martin Luther's astute observation that the first time Satan shows up in the Bible he's sitting under the tree of knowledge—and, he hasn't moved since. In the devil's plan, two world-class universities would take the lead in preparing mankind for the rule of Antichrist. The remainder of this chapter will give a brief outline of the first school while the second will be surveyed in the following chapter.

In 1832, only two years after Weishaupt's death (and just three before James Madison's), a Yale University junior by the name of William Huntington Russell of Middletown, Connecticut, returned to New Haven after a brief period of study in Germany. Somewhere in the "Land of Illuminism" Russell had been initiated into a secret society and given a commission to establish an American chapter at Yale. Assisted by fellow student Alphonso Taft (father of President William Howard Taft), Russell organized "Chapter 322" of The Order of Skull and Bones the following year. For legal purposes, "The Order" was formally incorporated as the "Russell Trust

Association" in 1856. Furthermore, by a special act of the state legislature in 1943, its trustees are exempt from the normal requirement of filing corporate reports with the Connecticut secretary of state.

Previously known as "The Brotherhood of Death," Skull and Bones constitutes a most unusual collegiate entity. To begin with, The Order is not your typical Greek-letter college fraternity, nor is it to be confused with the highbrow centers of snobbery scattered about the Ivy League in general. Princeton University sports the "eating clubs," especially Ivy Club and Cottage Club. At Harvard the blue bloods hang out at the Porcellian (also known as the "Porc" Club). While Teddy Roosevelt bragged to the German Kaiser of his membership in that club, Franklin Roosevelt belonged to the slightly "lower" Fly Club.

Chapter 322 is a *secret* organization whose members are sworn to silence. Also, it is a senior-year society and exists only at Yale. The fifteen juniors who receive and accept the coveted annual "tap" of induction will spend less than a year frequenting the Bones' Temple, an eerie three-story windowless structure, appropriately called "The Tomb." This implies that the society is geared to the postgraduate outside world. Having undergone a ceremonial name change to *Knight* "So-and-So" at initiation, Skull and Bones alumni are henceforth known as *Patriarchs*. The Order's annual "retreat" is held on Deer Iland (spelled Iland after the request of patriarch G.D. Miller), located just a few miles northeast of Alexander Bay on the St. Lawrence River in New York. Outsiders, known as *Gentiles* and *Vandals*, are not welcome for obvious reasons.

Senior-year societies, in themselves, are also unique to Yale. In addition to Skull and Bones (the most prestigious), roughly half a dozen others can be found at New Haven, but none elsewhere. Collectively, they comprise less than ten percent of the senior class.[1] Elitist "wannabes" who fail to make the first team are usually absorbed by Scroll and Key, Wolf's Head, Book and Snake, Spade and Grave or Berzelius. Power brokers Dean Acheson and Cyrus Vance were members of Scroll and Key, as were Benjamin Spock, Paul Mellon, Cole Porter, Garry Trudeau, Calvin Trillin, Harvey Cushing and A. Bartlett Giamatti. *Scribner's* magazine noted in 1897:

> Except for the curriculum itself, no force in the college is to be compared with the senior societies. The bond among their members lasts through life, and so close is it that even the college world knows nothing of their proceedings, and can only conjecture their purpose.[2]

The common denominator for all of these societies is the promise of power and financial reward. However, to achieve these objectives, the candidate must be willing to "sell out." (Have we heard this one before?) Stanford University professor Antony C. Sutton writes:

> In selection emphasis is placed on athletic ability—the ability to play on a team. The most unlikely potential member of The Order is a loner, an iconoclast, an individualist, the man who goes his own way in the world. The most likely potential member is from a Bones family, who is energetic, resourceful, political and probably an amoral team player. A man who understands that **to get along you have to go along**. A man who will sacrifice himself for the good of the team. A moment's reflection illustrates why this is so. In real life the thrust of The Order is to bring about certain objectives. **Honors and financial rewards are guaranteed by the power of The Order.** But the price of these honors and rewards is sacrifice to the common goal, the goal of The Order.[3]

In 1952, George Pierson described Yale's unique emphasis on being a "team player" as follows:

> Yale conformed. There was no doubt about it. A true Yale man was not at Yale just for what he could get out of it. He was not even being educated to rely on himself or to pit his judgment against popular opinion. At some of the institutions of the newer West everything old was automatically suspect. At Cambridge, as a Harvard editor confessed, the Harvard man was apt to be such a law unto himself that team play and concerted effort were often impossible. **But at Yale, individualism was not encouraged.** Campus sentiment was against it, and traditions stood in the way. A man's classmates valued his cooperation far more than his criticism. Originality of ideas was suspect and, outside of a tolerated range, eccentricity of dress or conduct was frowned on. To succeed at Yale one must avoid queerness, make friends, do something. And, whatever the activity or however calculated the underlying motive, the assumption was always the same. To "go out" and do something was to work for the welfare of the College.[4]

Of course, this lofty emphasis on conformity has always been fueled by greed. Pierson continues:

> A considerable element had come to college to learn not from books but from each other—not how to be scholars but how to succeed. Success was really their goal, not Veritas. What they were surely preparing for in their competition was the struggle of making a living. . . . The undergraduates

knew that, provided they first learned the rules of the game, they were destined for great prizes, sure to make fortunes, and bound for the managing posts in society.[5]

However, while all these "team players" were learning from and helping out one another, they *never* lost sight of the fact that the ultimate Yale experience was a "tap" for Skull and Bones at the end of their junior year.

> He who became a big man in his class and was tapped by Bones or Keys seemed already made. His would be the pick of the job opportunities. For him the big law firms would be waiting and the doors of the Wall Street houses would swing open.[6]

Thus, while engaged in outward conformity, the underclassman who aspired to a senior society was always sure to keep two things in mind. The first had to do with mastering the gutless art of groveling. As the *Yale Daily News* explained in 1878:

> Now is the time of year when the Junior creeps into his hold and remains there, keeping as much out of sight as possible, and spending his time in waiting and praying, if perchance fortune may so smile upon him as to grant him the boon of a Senior election. . . . Now he is circumspect as to his bows, and bows low and obsequious or lofty and condescending, according to the great or little influence possessed by the party. . . . fearful lest he may not bow according to the aforesaid gentleman's pleasure, and by so doing, diminish his so considered sure chances. . . .[7]

The second law of the jungle was to never get caught socializing with a *loser*. William Lyon Phelps, an 1887 Yale graduate wrote:

> Anyone who has watched how carefully the candidates begin to choose their companions in Sophomore year, how skillfully the Sunday afternoon walks on Whitney Avenue are manipulated, and how every precaution is taken **to avoid being seen with "chumps"** understands how undemocratic that life is. And this influence extends even long after graduation; for at all class gatherings society men unconsciously cohere.[8]

So, now you know why *rowing* is *the* extracurricular activity at Yale—everyone pulling in the same direction, etc. And for a Bonesman, *keeping your mouth shut* is the most important "stroke" to master. The power of the patriarchs to keep us Vandals and Gentiles in the dark can be seen by the prevailing media blackout of Skull and Bones activity. In the first one hundred and fifty years of The Order's existence, a total of only *three* published articles have drawn attention to the society.

On October 13, 1873, a frustrated student at Yale published a critical exposé of The Order entitled *The Iconoclast*. With reference to the official college paper, *Courant and Record*, he wrote: "We speak through a new publication, because the college press is closed to those who dare to openly mention 'Bones'."[9] Three years later, an anonymous satirical essay entitled "The Fall of Skull and Bones" was circulated, following a break-in at the Bones Temple by other disgruntled students. An entire century would pass before the next article would appear. In the September 1977 edition of *Esquire* magazine, Ron Rosenbaum, a 1968 Yale graduate, wrote a mild-mannered piece entitled "The Last Secrets of Skull and Bones." Apart from a rash of frivolous articles in 1991 concerning The Order's hotly debated decision to end its policy of excluding women from membership, the media lid has remained in tact. An excerpt from *The Iconoclast* states:

> For more than forty years a secret society called Skull and Bones has existed in Yale College. It receives a certain number of men from each class. These are chosen nominally by the members of the class . . . although it is understood that a prominent man's influence avails for his friends and relatives through several years after his graduation. By observing the men elected from year to year, we find that they are chosen with a distinct end in view, namely, that of obtaining for the society the most honors. Some of these honors are given to literary, some to wealthy men. This, then, is the case. Men receive marks of distinction from Yale College or from their entire class, because of which they are taken into this secret society. **Since Yale honors men, this fraternity professes to honor them also.**[10]

This humanistic philosophy is diametrically opposed to the words of Jesus Christ, *"How can ye believe, which receive honour one of another, and seek not the honour that cometh from God only?"* (John 5:44) It is also opposed to Yale's original charter, which called for the training of youth, "for Publick employment, both in Church and Civil State." The early presidents of Yale were men of exemplary piety and moral courage. Dr. Naphtali Dagget (1766-1777) refused to run when an army of redcoats under General Tryon marched on New Haven, July 5, 1779. The aged minister climbed to the top of a hill with fowling piece in hand to singlehandily reconnoiter the enemy. After firing several rounds at the invaders, Dr. Dagget was captured and later died in captivity. In the earlier months of the war, one of Dr. Dagget's former students at Yale scaled a significant mound of his own. While the critical battle on Breed's Hill was raging, Chaplain David Avery, a convert of Mr. Whitefield's, was interceding for America from atop the adjacent heights of Bunker Hill. A line from Reverend Avery's diary reads, ". . . but amid the terror of the dread encounter, the Lord was our rock and our fortress." (Now you know why the two locations get confused with one another; while the *fighting* took place on *Breed's* Hill the *victory* was won on *Bunker* Hill!) The great Revolutionary War hero and fervent Christian, Nathan Hale, was another graduate of Yale. A statue of Hale adorns the Old Campus at Yale.

Reverend Ezra Stiles, president of Yale from 1778 to 1795, emphasized the Christian destiny of America by stating, with regard to the "enlargement of Japheth," "May we not see that we are the object which the Holy Ghost had in view four thousand years ago, when he inspired the venerable patriarch with the visions respecting his posterity?"[11]

Reverend Timothy Dwight served as the eighth president of Yale from 1795 to 1817. A grandson of Jonathan Edwards, Dwight was a precocious child who mastered the entire alphabet in one sitting and was able to read the Bible at age four. He was also a valued chaplain to George Washington. Under his presidency, succeeding revivals broke loose on campus in 1802, 1808, 1813 and 1815. Among the many converts was tutor Benjamin Silliman who wrote to his mother, "Yale College is a little temple, prayer and praise seem to be the delight of the greater part of the students, while those who are still unfeeling are awed into respectful silence."[12]

Looking back on his days at Yale, Lyman Beecher (1775-1863) said of Dwight,

> They [the students] thought the Faculty were afraid of free discussion. But when they handed Dr. Dwight a list of subjects for class disputation, to their surprise he selected this: "Is the Bible the word of God?" and told them to do their best.
>
> He heard all they had to say, answered them, and there was an end. He preached incessantly for six months on the subject, and all infidelity skulked and hid its head.
>
> He elaborated his theological system in a series of forenoon sermons in the chapel. . . . To a mind appreciative like mine, his preaching was

a continual course of education and a continual feast. He was copious and polished in style, though disciplined and logical.

There was a pith and power of doctrine there that has not been since surpassed, if equaled. . . . He was universally revered and loved. I never knew but one student undertake to frustrate his wishes.[13]

But all of this was prior to 1832. The "pith and power of doctrine there" left when Skull and Bones arrived. Although his father was converted under Dwight's preaching, Benjamin Silliman, Jr., chose to hook his wagon to Skull and Bones in 1837. The *Iconoclast* article confirms that The Order literally captured Yale University for the devil.

Out of every class Skull and Bones takes its men. They have gone out into the world and have become, in many instances, leaders in society. They have obtained control of Yale. Its business is performed by them. Money paid to the college must pass into their hands, and be subject to their will.[14]

Many appropriate statistics could be cited. Every Yale secretary from 1869 to 1921 was chosen from Skull and Bones. Between 1862 and 1910, forty-three of the forty-eight university treasurers were Bonesmen. So were eighty percent of the university's professors between 1865 and 1916. From 1886 to 1985, the president of Yale was an alumnus of Bones, Scroll and Key or Wolf's Head for sixty-eight of ninety-nine years.[15]

In 1986, Professor Sutton wrote a book entitled *America's Secret Establishment: An Introduction to The Order of Skull and Bones*. Sutton's secular credentials are more than impressive: educated at the universities of London, Gottingen and California; former economics professor at California State University; research Fellow at the Hoover Institution, Stanford University, from 1968 to 1973; author of sixteen books, including: *Western Technology and Soviet Economic Development; Wall Street and The Rise of Hitler; Energy, the Created Crisis; The War on Gold; Technological Treason; Gold versus Paper; Wall Street and the Bolshevik Revolution and National Suicide: Military Aid to the Soviet Union in 1973*. Professor Sutton wrote:

Above all, The Order is powerful, unbelievably powerful. If the reader will persist and examine the evidence to be presented—which is overwhelming—there is no doubt his view of the world will suddenly come sharply into focus, with almost frightening clarity.[16]

Rosenbaum concurs, ". . . the people who have shaped America's national character since it ceased being an undergraduate power had *their* undergraduate character shaped in that crypt over there" (i.e., the "temple" on the Yale Campus).[17] As if to picture the wealth that awaits them, tradition states that each inductee receives an expensive grandfather clock and a fifteen thousand-dollar check just for accepting the "tap". But, remember, they have to sell their soul for the power. (Luke 4:6)

GUESS WHO?

On an April evening in 1947, a junior by the name of *George* rapped on the massive triple-padlocked Temple door to join the other "tappees" for The Order's annual initiation ceremony. His father had also stood there thirty years previous. With reference to the candidates as a whole, Rosenbaum states, "Tonight he will die to the world and be **born again** into The Order."[18] Rosenbaum was able to procure a dossier describing the procedure for the same service in 1940. Assuming that the format has been one of routine, a bone with George's full name on it was tossed onto a bone heap at the start of the "program." Following orders, the young man proceeded to strip off his clothes and climb into a coffin. He was then carried to a red velvet room by several patriarchs dressed in skeleton suits where he was "chanted over and **reborn** into society."[19] After climbing out of the casket he plunged into a mud pile to wrestle with the other fourteen naked initiates. The new knight was then given a special robe with several mysterious symbols.

Later in the year, George was also required to spill his guts about his personal sexual history. The reader will recall how Adam Weishaupt pioneered this procrustean safeguard against patriarchs spilling the beans in the future. The rule for the procedure, known as "Continual Bliss," mandated explicit and intimate details. Rosenbaum notes: "Some women have discovered that their lovers take their vows to Bones more solemnly than their commitments to women."[20] In George's case, the patriarchs would have leaned on him a little harder than the others as he was married (and for only twenty-seven months). However, given the fact that his fifteen thousand-dollar check cashed, he probably dumped the whole truckload.

As a patriarch his star was destined to rise. In 1971, President Nixon appointed him U.S. ambassador to the United Nations. During his brief tenure, Taiwan was replaced by the communist People's Republic of China (PRC). In 1974, President Ford asked him to head the American liaison office in Beijing, the capital of Red China. A year later he became director of the Central Intelligence Agency. And finally, after two stints as second in command, "Poppy" (as he is affectionately known) became the forty-first president of the United States of America in 1988. Not a bad return for only one night in a sarcophagus! The *full* name on that bone was George Herbert Walker Bush.

AMBITIOUS ACTIVISM

In the process of his investigative report for *Esquire*, Rosenbaum was able to get a few folks to talk, including an anonymous Bonesman or two. One man warned,

> They don't like people tampering and prying. The power of Bones is incredible. They've got their hands on every level of power in the country. You'll see—it's like trying to investigate the Mafia. Remember, they're a secret society, too.[21]

Professor Sutton acknowledged his own additional source of information:

> After 16 books and 25 years in basic research I thought I'd heard it all . . . the world was a confused mess, probably beyond understanding and certainly beyond salvation—and there was little I could do about it. . . .
>
> Then a year or so ago I received an eight-inch batch of documents— nothing less than the membership lists of an American secret society. Glancing through the sheets it was more than obvious—this was no ordinary group. The names spelled Power, with a capital P. As I probed each individual, a pattern emerged . . . and a formerly fuzzy world became crystal clear . . .
>
> How did this material make its way into outside hands? It is possible that one or more members, although bound by oath, would not be dismayed if the story became public knowledge. That's all we will say. . . .
>
> The core of the research for this book is the "Addresses" books. With these we can construct a picture of motives, objectives and operations. The

actions of individual members are already recorded in open history and archives.

By determining when members enter a scene, what they did, what they argued, who they appointed and when they faded out, we can assemble patterns and deduce objectives.[22]

When the research of Sutton and Rosenbaum is added to the *Iconoclast* article and the revelations from "Yale-gate" (the successful 1873 break-in of the Bones' Temple), the following *modus operandi* begins to unfold. Since 1832, over twenty-five hundred graduates of Yale have been formally inducted into The Order of Skull and Bones. At any one time, about five-to-six hundred patriarchs are alive and working. Roughly one quarter of these take an active role in furthering The Order's sinister agenda; the others simply lose interest or recant their original views. However, with their "sex confessions" on file, rare is the defector who is willing to talk. Sutton explains the development of The Order's powerful nucleus:

> During the 150-year interval since 1833, active membership has evolved into a core group of perhaps 20-30 families; it seems that active members have enough influence to push their sons and relatives into The Order, and there is significant inter-marriage among the families. These families fall into two major groups.
>
> First we find old line American families who arrived on the East coast in the 1600s, e.g., Whitney, Lord, Phelps, Wadsworth, Allen, Bundy, Adams and so on.
>
> Second, we find families who acquired wealth in the last 100 years, sent their sons to Yale and in time became almost old line families, e.g., Harriman, Rockefeller, Payne, Davison.
>
> Some families, like the Whitneys, were Connecticut Yankees and acquired wealth in the nineteenth century.
>
> In the last 150 years a few families in The Order have gained enormous influence in society and the world.[23]

The following list of estates belonging to Bonesman William Collins Whitney (1841-1904) illustrates the wealth of such inner-core families:

> a city residence in New York, a Venetian palace and 5,000 acres in Wheatley Hills, near Jamaica, L.I.; a Sheepshead Bay house, with a private track covering 300 acres; a mansion at Berkshire Hills, Mass., with 700 acres of land; October Mountain house, with a large tract of land; Stony Ford Farm, New York, used as an auxiliary to his Kentucky Stock Farm; an

Adirondack game preserve of 16,000 acres; a lodge at Blue Mountain Lake with a fine golf course, a Blue Grass farm of 3,000 acres in Kentucky; and an estate at Aiken, S.C., comprising a mansion, race course, and 2,000 acres of hunting land.[24]

Given its origin in nineteenth-century Germany, the philosophical foundation for Skull and Bones has remained the dialectical system espoused by Georg Wilhelm Friedrich Hegel (1770-1831) which taught that the state was absolute (i.e., "Ask not what your country can do for you; but rather ask what you can do for your country," etc.). This means that a good Bonesman is committed to *"AMBITIOUS ACTIVISM TOWARDS A NEW WORLD ORDER GOAL."*[25] Sutton writes:

> Our whole way of life is based on the assumption that the individual is superior to the State. That the individual is the ultimate holder of sovereignty. That the State is the servant of the people. It's deeply engrained within us.
>
> The Order holds the opposite—that the State is superior, that the common man (the peasant) can find freedom only by obedience to the State.
>
> Now, of course, the State is a fiction. So who or what controls the State? Obviously, The Order.[26]

ANGLOPHILIA

At this point, a most important distinction must be made with respect to the hidden core beliefs of Skull and Bones. Although grounded on German philosophy while promoting a pro-U.S.A. super-patriot image, The Order is actually committed to an *Anglophilic oligarchy*. What this translates into is a reverence for British tradition and a goal to eventually return America to the fold. (Some refer to Bonesmen as *Atlanticists* due to their rigid opposition to isolationism.)

By the time Russell began Skull and Bones in 1833, Britain had already lost two shooting wars in an attempt to subdue her upstart colonies. Throughout both crises, American security was constantly at risk by the treachery of British loyalists known as Torries. The Russell family of Middletown, Connecticut, was extremely wealthy and a bastion for Tory intrigue. Russell's "kinfolk" were allied through marriage with several other prominent pro-British families; notably, the Pierpont, Edwards, Burr,

Griswold, Day, Aslop and Hubbard clans. In 1815, the Connecticut Tory lobby went so far as to host the infamous Hartford Convention for secession.

Another fact to consider is the source of the family wealth. Samuel Russell, second cousin to Bones founder William H., established Russell and Company in 1823. The main "product" of this operation was opium. After acquiring the dope from Turkey, it was then smuggled into China via the British East India Company. Massachusetts Torries like the Coolidge, Sturgis, Forbes, and Delano families also got in on the action. By the 1830s, Russell and Company was the largest narcotics exporter in America. While 4,244 chests of opium were smuggled into China from 1820 to 1821, a staggering 40,200 chests valued at over $12 million entered the country illegally from 1838 to 1839. A single chest cost two dollars wholesale and was retailed for ten. By the early 1800s, close to one-third of the Chinese population was addicted to the drug. With everyone's hand in the till, Britain and China eventually came to blows in the Opium War of 1839 to 1842.

Most of the men who get tapped for Skull and Bones are already closet Anglophiles, having been indoctrinated at any number of New England prep schools. To add insult to injury, Prescott Bush (the father of George Herbert Walker Bush) attended the Episcopalian St. George's School in Newport, Rhode Island. Do you recall how the Church of England was the only congregation in Newport that declined to support the national day of prayer and fasting during the War of Independence? (Though not a member of Skull and Bones, former Vermont governor Howard Dean also graduated from St. George's and Yale.) Two of the more notorious institutions are Groton and Andover. Averell Harriman attended Groton where baseball was out and cricket was in. Walter Isaacson and Evan Thomas write in *The Wise Men*:

> The rest of Groton's curriculum included large doses of Latin and Greek, ancient history, and European studies with a particular emphasis on England. **American history was generally snubbed**: Roland Harriman [Averell's brother] noted that history teachers "made us learn all the names and dates of the French and English kings while neglecting to tell us that one hundred years before the Pilgrim fathers landed in Massachusetts, the Spaniards were in California."[27]

Franklin Delano Roosevelt, grandson to one of Russell's key "pushers," Warren Delano, Jr., entered Groton in 1896 at the age of fourteen.

Phillips Academy in Andover, Massachusetts, was specifically targeted by Skull and Bones' "missionaries" in the 1870s. Satanic secret societies were subsequently established for teenagers. In his official bicentennial history of Andover, a retired faculty member revealed:

> [A] major concern of the membership was the initiation ceremony. In K.O.A. [the oldest of the societies] the ceremony involved visiting one of the local cemeteries at midnight, various kinds of tortures, running the gauntlet—though the novice was apparently punched rather then paddled, being baptized in a water tank, being hoisted in the air by a pulley, and finally **being placed in a coffin**, where he was cross-examined by the members.[28]

Former president George H. W. Bush graduated from Andover in the class of 1942. He belonged to the school's second-oldest cult, A.U.V., which stands for *Auctoritas, Unitas, Veritas* (Authority, Unity and Truth). Part of "Poppy's" weeklong initiation ceremony required him to be in the local *cemetery* every night from 12:30 a.m. to 5:00 a.m.[29] The A.U.V. seal displays the number 321 to confirm it's proud affiliation with The Order's Chapter 322. (The Anglophile connection at Skull and Bones will become even more apparent when we examine Oxford's secret society in the following chapter.)

PENETRATION PROPAGATION PERPETUATION

From the outset, Skull and Bones has rigorously pursued a three-fold attack on the key components of American culture. After *penetrating* (or in some cases, *pioneering*) a particular segment of society, The Order's agenda would be *propagated* without while being *perpetuated* within. Sutton writes:

> The Order has either set up or penetrated just about every significant research, policy, and opinion-making organization in the United States in addition to the Church, business, law, government and politics. Not all at the same time, but persistently and consistently enough to dominate the direction of American society. The evolution of American society is not, and has not been for a century, a voluntary development reflecting individual opinion, ideas and decisions at the grass roots. On the contrary, the broad direction has been created artificially and stimulated by The Order.[30]

A review of the society's membership rolls confirms that Bonesmen have infiltrated such areas as law, education, business, finance, industry, medicine, commerce, politics, foundations, religion, publishing, history, psychology and the media. And in many cases, a patriarch got in on the ground level. (When asked for the secret to his many cavalry victories, the legendary semi-literate Confederate General Nathan Bedford Forrest was reported to have replied, "I just gets there *firstest* with the *mostest.*")

Speaking of history, Bonesman Andrew Dickson White (1953), the *first* president of Cornell University was also the *first* president of the *American Historical Association.* Now you know why The Order is never mentioned in our public school history books. Having gotten there "firstest," White got to set the agenda and handpicked his successor, who would handpick his successor, who would . . . etc.

Henry Elmer Barnes wrote in *The Struggle Against the Historical Blackout:*

> It may be said, with great restraint, that, never since the Dark and Middle Ages, have there been so many powerful forces organized and alerted against the assertion and acceptance of historical truth as are active today to prevent the facts about the responsibility for the second World War and its results from being made generally accessible to the American public. Even the great Rockefeller Foundation frankly admits (*Annual Report*, 1946, p.188) the subsidizing of a corps of historians to anticipate and frustrate the development of any neo-Revisionism in our time. And the only difference between this Foundation and several others is that it has been more candid and forthright about its politics.[31]

The degree to which The Order has controlled the field of public education is truly astounding. Among other dubious attainments, the celebrated Horace Mann is credited with forcing the "Look-Say" system of reading for the deaf on the hearing students in Massachusetts. After five years of unpopular experimentation, *Mother's Primer* was ejected by the state board of education in 1840. However, as president of the Unitarian Antioch College of Yellow Springs, Ohio, Horace continued to do the bidding of Skull and Bones. Alphonso Taft, co-founder of The Order, just happened to be the most powerful Trustee at Antioch—how convenient!

Bonesman Daniel Coit Gilman (1852) was the *first* president of Johns Hopkins University, the *first* American university for graduate education established along German lines. In 1898, he invited Fabian Socialists Beatrice and Sidney Webb to address the faculty at Johns Hopkins. William Welch (1870) was appointed dean of the prestigious medical school and president of the Rockefeller Institute for Medical Research.

He also became a trustee for the Carnegie Institution from 1906 onward. The founder of the *American Chemical Society* pioneered a chemical based medicine that induced the medical community to sever its ties with the conservative element of naturopathy. Current cancer statistics reveal "the rest of the story."

Under Gilman's direction, Richard Ely was invited to take the Chair of Political Economy at Johns Hopkins. Hegel's doctrine of the supremacy of the state would now be applied to economics. Capitalism and free trade were subsequently projected in a negative light while state economic planning would be seen as the panacea for man's future survival. Ely also became the founder and *first* secretary of the *American Economics Association*. Sutton writes, "An economic association is also of significance because it conditions how people who are not economists think about the relative merits of free enterprise and state planning."[32] Ely later went on to head the department of economics at the liberal University of Wisconsin. Gilman also appointed G. Stanley Hall to the Chair of Philosophy and Pedagogy. Hall was promptly given a psychological laboratory with a thousand dollars a year for equipment. He then went on to establish the *American Journal of Psychology*. Hall would eventually concede, "The psychology I taught was almost entirely experimental and covered for the most part the material that Wundt had set forth in the later and larger edition of *Physiological Psychology*."[33]

Hall was the *first* American to receive a doctorate in Germany from the renowned Hegelian physiologist, Wilhelm Maximilian Wundt (1832-1920). It is at this juncture that things get more than a little interesting! To begin with, Wundt was professor of philosophy at the University of Leipzig. His grandfather, Kirchenrat Karl Kasimir Wundt (1744-84), was a professor of history and geography at Heidelberg University. *He was also known as "Raphael" in Weishaupt's Order of the Illuminati!*

In 1875, Wundt established the work's *first* laboratory in experimental psychology to measure an individual's response to stimuli. Sutton writes:

> Wundt believed that man is only the summation of his experience, i.e., the stimuli that bear upon him. It follows from this that, for Wundt, man has no self will, no self determination. Man is in effect only the captive of his experiences, a pawn needing guidance.
>
> Students from Europe and the United States came to Leipzig to learn from Wundt the new science of experimental psychology. These students

returned to their homelands to found schools of education or departments of psychology, and trained hundreds of Ph.D.s in the new field of psychology.[34]

Wilhelm was himself a product of another Germa, Johann Friedrich Herbart (1776-1841), professor of philosophy and pedagogy at Göttingen. Three of Herbart's leading mentors were Johann Heinrich Pestalozzi (1746-1827), Johann Wolfgang Goethe (1749-1832) and Johann Gottried Herder (1744-1803), *known respectively in the Order of the Illuminati as "Alfred," "Abaris" and "Damascus pontifex"!*

Well, we certainly expected to find a direct connection to Adam Weishaupt sooner or later! In fact, one of the more enlightening discoveries from "Yale-gate" was a German slogan painted "on the arched walls above the vault" in room 322 which reads, *"Wer war der Thor, wer Weiser, Bettler oder Kaiser? Ob Arm, ob Reich, im Tode gleich."* Do you recall the initiation ceremony for the Regent degree of Illuminism where the candidate has a skeleton pointed out to him, at the feet of which are laid a crown and a sword? When the initiate is unable to answer the question "whether that is the skeleton of a king, nobleman, or beggar," the president of the lodge replies, "The character of a man is all that is of importance." Well, it just so happens that the German slogan in the Bones Temple translates accordingly: "Who was the fool, who was the wise man, beggar or king? Whether poor or rich, all's the same in death."[35]

During Hall's tenure at Johns Hopkins, 149 doctorates were awarded in the field of experimental psychology. Wundt's other American protégés were no less industrious in spreading Illuminati philosophy: J. McKeen Cattell, Columbia University, 344 doctorates; E.W. Scripture, Yale University, 138 doctorates; H. Gale, Minnesota University, 123 doctorates; G.T.W. Patrick, Iowa University, 269 doctorates and C.H. Judd, University of Chicago, 196 doctorates.[36] This collective influence came to be known among psychologists as "The Americanization of Wundt."

While Hall was spewing out his intellectual poison, a twenty-three-year-old doctoral student was listening attentively. He was also being molded by the Hegelian philosopher, George Sylvester Morris. In 1884, John Dewey received one of the *first* doctorates under Gilman's presidency. He then went on to serve as professor of philosophy at the University of Michigan where he authored *Psychology*, a blend of Hegelian philosophy applied to Wundtian experimental psychology. Dewey moved to the University of Chicago in 1894 where he became president of the *American Psychological Association*. Eight years later he was appointed director of the newly founded, Rockefeller-financed, School of Education. The rest is history. An article in the *Encyclopedia Americana* states, "Without a doubt, Dewey was the best known American educator of all time, both at home and abroad."[37]

Dewey left Chicago in 1904 to become a professor of philosophy at Columbia University. In 1915, he became the founder and *first* president of the *American Association of University Professors*. In 1920, he helped to organize the communist American Civil Liberties Union. However, the brunt of his influence would be felt in the Teachers College at Columbia. *More than any single person, Dewey would ensure that Weishaupt's "global gospel" would be faithfully proclaimed throughout the schools of the land.* In his work, *My Pedagogic Creed*, Dewey wrote:

> **The school is primarily a social institution.** Education being a social process, the school is simply that form of community life in which all those agencies are concentrated that will be most effective in bringing the child to **share** in the inherited resources of the race, and to use his own powers for social ends. **Education, therefore, is a process of living and not a preparation for future living.**[38]

Note Dewey's affinity with Hegel who wrote, "The State is the absolute reality and the individual himself has objective existence, truth and morality only in his capacity as a member of the State."[39] Current educational priorities are not *child*-centered but rather *state*-centered.

William B. Stanley, assistant professor of the Department of Curriculum and Instruction at Louisiana State University, expressed these satanic philosophies accordingly in the May 1982 *Educational Leadership*: "An attempt should be made to redress the present overemphasis on individualism in current programs . . . students need to develop a sense of community and collective identity."[40] In a program for the 1976 Bicentennial entitled *A Declaration of Interdependence: Education for a Global Community*, the National Education Association proclaimed: "We are committed to the idea of Education for Global Community. You are invited to help turn the commitment into action and mobilizing world education for development of a world community."[41] "Spartacus" could not be any "happier." Former Assemblyman John Vasconcellos of California, who has also been chairman of the Joint Committee on the Master Plan for Higher Education and the Education Goals Committee for the California State Assembly, wrote:

It is now time for a new vision of ourselves, of man, of human nature and of human potential, and a new theory of politics and institutions premised upon that vision. What is that vision of Man? That the natural, whole, organismic human being is loving . . . that man's basic thrust is towards community.[42]

Unlike Dewey, Vasconcellos was an elected official who took an oath to uphold the Constitution. Dewey's garbage has literally covered the nation. In his book *Self Knowledge and Social Action*, Obadiah Silas Harris, associate professor of Educational Management and Development at New Mexico State University, Las Cruces, New Mexico, fantasized:

When community educators say that community education takes into consideration the total individual and his total environment, they mean precisely this: the field of community education includes the individual in his total psycho-physical structure and his entire ecological climate with all its ramifications—social, political, economical, cultural, spiritual, etc. It seeks to integrate the individual within himself (sic) and within his community until the individual becomes a cosmic soul and the community the world.[43]

He then goes on to state:

The Cosmic soul . . . the whole human race is going to evolve an effective soul of its own—the cosmic soul of the race. That is the future of human evolution. As a result of the emergence of the universal soul, there will be a great unification of the entire human race, ushering into existence a new era, a new dawn of unique world power.[44]

These are the crazy people who are running America's schools. So now you know *why* "Johnny can't read!" The Order of Skull and Bones has a more important agenda for our children.

The Order has permeated numbers of other American institutions as well. William Howard Taft (1878) was the only man to be both president *and* chief justice of the United States. Potter Stewart (1936) was also a chief justice of the U.S. Supreme Court from 1958 to 1981. Members in the U.S. Senate have included John Heinz (1931); Jonathan Bingham (1936); David Boren (1963); and John Chaffee (1947). Pierre Jay (1892) became the *first* chairman of the New York Federal Reserve Bank. Other notable financiers would include: Harold Stanley (1908), founder of Morgan Stanley; Henry P. Davison, Jr. (1920), senior partner Morgan Guaranty Trust; Artemus Gates (1918), president of New York Trust

Co.; and Dean Witter, Jr. (1944), investment banker. Among hundreds of corporate CEOs that could be cited, Frederick W. Smith (1966) became the founder of Federal Express.

The most prominent law firms in New York are saturated with members of The Order. Together with his father, Daniel Lord (another Yale graduate), Bonesman George DeForest Lord (1854) established the New York office of Lord, Day and Lord. Among its present-day clients are *The New York Times* and the Rubin Foundation. C.E. Lord (1949) has been Comptroller of the Currency. Winston Lord (1959) has been chairman of the CFR, ambassador to China and assistant secretary of state in the Clinton administration. Other powerful names in the New York legal community are Simpson, Thacher and Bartlett; David, Polk, Wardwell and Debevoise, Plimpton, the Rockefeller family law firm. Bonesman J. Richardson Dilworth (1938) served as the Rockefeller Family Associates' chief financial and administrative officer.

Percy Rockefeller climbed into the "magic coffin" in 1900. The so-called conservative editor of *National Review*, William F. Buckley, did the same in 1950. So did Henry Luce (1920), founder of *Time-Life*; Richard Ely Danielson (1907) of *Atlantic Monthly*; Alfred Cowles, *Des Moines Register* and the *Minneapolis Star*; and Russell Wheeler Davenport (1923) of *Fortune* who also established the *Fortune 500* list. Amory Howe Bradford (1934) became general manager of *The New York Times*. The most prestigious award in the field of journalism is a Nieman Fellowship at Harvard University. Between the years 1937 and 1968, over three hundred scholarships were awarded. The *first* director of the Nieman Fund was Bonesman Archibald McLeash (1915).

The Order has also infiltrated and manipulated some of the most powerful trusts and foundations in America. Daniel Coit Gilman became the *first* president of the Carnegie Institution. Gilman was also on the scene for the organizing of the Peabody, Slater, and Russell Sage Foundations. James Jeremiah Wadsworth (1927) founded the Peace Research Institute in 1963, which later became the Institute for Policy Studies. Bonesman McGeorge Bundy (1940) was president of the Ford Foundation from 1966 to 1979. In fact, The Order so abused the Ford wealth that two Fords resigned from the board of their own foundation!

The *first* chairman of the *American Society for the Judicial Settlement of International Disputes* was William Howard Taft (1878). This organization was the forerunner of the League to Enforce the Peace which later evolved into the League of Nations and finally into the infamous United

Nations. Professor Sutton identified Archibald McLeash as "... the brains behind the constitution of the UNESCO organization."[45]

Last, but not least, we find that The Order has even dabbled with "Christianity." With respect to Yale Divinity School itself, the culprit was none other than Timothy Dwight "the younger" (1828-1916), grandson of the previously mentioned Timothy Dwight (1725-1817). Unlike his spiritual namesake, this Congregational minister was a loyal member of Skull and Bones, being initiated in 1849. After returning from post-graduate studies (programming) at the Universities of Berlin and Bonn from 1856 to 1858, Dwight was appointed assistant professor of sacred literature, becoming a full professor in 1861, the year of his ordination.

The *Dictionary of American Biography* says, "During his professorship the Divinity School was practically refounded." This is quite the understatement. The article also notes that Dwight was "of much service to the American committee on the revision of the Bible, of which he was a member from 1873 to 1885."[46] The chairman of this blasphemous committee was the German apostate, Dr. Phillip Schaff, of New York's Union Theological Seminary. In May 1881, the New Testament portion of Westcott's and Hort's corrupt *Revised Version* was released, with the Old Testament following in 1885. Schaff's cronies were finally able to market their version of the British product in 1901, copyrighted as the *American Standard Version* (or, ASV for short). Both of these perversions exhibited nearly 36,000 departures from the text of the venerable A.V. 1611.

In 1886, "Reverend" Dwight also became the *first* Bonesman to capture the presidency of his own Alma Mater. It was during his administration that Yale "College" made its prestigious transition to Yale "University," earning him the title, "Father of the University." Arthur Twining Hadley, who followed Dwight as Yale's thirteenth president from 1899 to 1921, was also a member of The Order. And so was Charles Seymour, the school's fifteenth president, from 1937 to 1950. Professor Sutton concludes, "Every President of Yale since Timothy Dwight has either been a member of The Order or has family connections to The Order."[47]

An even greater perspective of Skull and Bones influence on American society can be gained by simply comparing the number of active patriarchs with the market of "normal" college graduates. Sutton elaborates:

> A tribute to the success of The Order has been an ability to implement one of its principles. This principle is: "That only he who wears upon his breast, Their emblem, he for every post shall be considered best."

The practice of absolute preferment for members of The Order has worked to perpetuate its influence over time in a remarkable manner. . . . The Order has only initiated about 2500 members in its history in the United States. Each year 15 new members are initiated, no more, no less. On the other hand, between 800,000 and 1 million persons receive college degrees each year from an institute of higher learning, including about 30,000 doctorates.

When you follow the chain of influence . . . hold in mind that out of 30-40 million degree holders, a few hundred men . . . are presumed to be the only ones fit to occupy top posts in government. No one else is even seriously considered. We are asked to believe that only a few hundred members of The Order are capable of guiding the United States.[48]

Even the official Yale history concurs with this disproportionate extension of power. On page five of *Yale College 1871-1922*, we read:

The power of the place remain(s) unmistakable. Yale was organized. Yale inspired a loyalty in its sons that was conspicuous and impressive. Yale men in after life made such records that the suspicion was that even there they were working for each other. In short, Yale was exasperatingly and **mysteriously** successful. To rival institutions and to academic reformers there was something irritating and **disquieting** about Old Yale College.[49]

THE WISE MEN

This success became a thorn in the side of Yale's chief competitor—Harvard University. In 1892, a Harvard instructor, George Santanyana, went so far as to visit the New Haven campus to personally investigate the "disturbing legend" of Yale power. Santanyana later quoted a Harvard alumnus who intended to send his son to Yale, because in real life, "all the Harvard men are working for Yale men."[50]

The perfect illustration that "Yale was [and is] exasperatingly and **mysteriously** successful" and that "all the Harvard men are working for Yale men," is contained in the insightful book by Walter Isaacson and Evan Thomas entitled *The Wise Men*. The authors concur with Sutton's observation that Skull and Bones alumni obtained positions of power which were highly disproportionate to their number, writing, "Not everyone was Ivy League, by any means, but **Yale's secret societies were better represented in the inner councils than any state university.**"[51]

The volume covers the lives of six political figures whose careers peaked during the Truman era. They were: W. Averell Harriman (multiplied positions, including governor of New York, ambassador to the Soviet Union and top level diplomatic negotiator for five presidents; Robert Lovett (under secretary of state and later secretary of defense and founder of the Central Intelligence Agency); Dean Acheson (secretary of state); John McCloy (high commissioner to Germany); George Kennan (State Department advisor and ambassador to the Soviet Union); and Charles Bohlen (State Department advisor). The book labels these men the "architects of the American century" who "left a legacy that dominates American policy to this day."[52]

Who were these power brokers credited with "providing the education of Harry Truman?" Harriman was the most influential "wise man" of the six. Isaacson and Thomas say that Harriman spent more time with Joseph Stalin than any other American. A naked Averell climbed out of the coffin in 1912. Robert Abercrombie Lovett climbed out of his in 1918. Dean Acheson was a 1915 initiate of Yale's Scroll and Key society. McCloy and Bohlen were Harvard men while Kennan went to Princeton. As for Harvard men working for Yale men, McCloy's career motto was to "run with the swift." Acknowledging his desire "to work with people who were better than I,"[53] the Harvard grad confessed of his Yale mentors,

> They were Skull and Bones, Groton, that sort of thing. That was the elite. Lovett, Harvey Bundy, Acheson, they called on a tradition, a high tradition. They ran with the swift. I always had in mind, even to this day, that I was not really a part of that.[54]

Referring to McCloy, who would handle Rockefeller's legal affairs and go on to be president of the World Bank, and Dean Rusk, who would become President Kennedy's secretary of state, the authors write, "Just as they sought admission to what they considered a special elite, the group sought to groom them and others for inclusion in its tradition of high-minded service."[55]

When "wise man" George Kennan was eighty-one years of age, he acknowledged that he, like McCloy and Bohlen, had also been willing to "go along" in order to "get along," stating, "To the extent that I was accepted among those in the Establishment, it was in the role they decided to cast for me, rather than because of who I really was."[56]

With reference to the men from Yale, Isaacson and Thomas wrote, "The values they embodied were nurtured in prep schools, at college clubs, in the boardrooms of Wall Street, and at dinner parties in Washington."[57] The liberal authors were honest enough to confirm in print, "To be tapped by Bones in that era was akin to canonization, and its prestige was enhanced by its secrecy."[58] They were also willing to confirm their Illuminati-Skull and Bones mindset, "But by breeding and training, this handful of men and a few of their close colleagues knew that America would have to assume the burden of a global role."[59] And again, "As internationalists who respected the manners and traditions of Europe they waged a common struggle against the persuasive isolationism of their time."[60] And finally, such delusions of grandeur became manifest in their elitist detachment from the American people and our constitutional republic, "For it is another defining characteristic of their group that they were decidedly nonpopulist, serving in the executive branch while remaining proudly aloof from the pressures of public opinion and its expression in Congress."[61]

PARANOIA IN THE TOMB

In 1999, a letter was dispatched to The Order's alumni from Skull and Bones headquarters. The disconcerting memo read in part:

> In view of the political happenings in the barbarian world, I feel compelled to remind all of the tradition of privacy and confidentiality essential to the well-being of our Order and strongly urge stout resistance to the seductions and blandishments of the Fourth Estate.[62]

Apparently, something was about to really "rattle their bones." After enjoying a century-and-a-half of convenient anonymity, The Order's mystique had been abruptly violated by Mr. Rosenbaum's *Esquire* article in 1977. When Bush lost the 1980 Republican presidential nomination to Reagan, the weary candidate confided to a friend, Fay Vincent:

> Fay, let me tell you something. If you ever decide to run for office, don't forget that coming from Andover, Yale, Skull and Bones and the Trilateral Commission is a big handicap. People don't know what they are, so they don't know where you're coming from. It's really a big, big problem.[63]

The problem grew in 1986 when Sutton released his scholarly exposé. In 1988, the *Washington Post* reported on charges that Prescott Bush had robbed the grave of Geronimo at Ft. Sill, Oklahoma. Then, the Internet decided to get in on the action. Suddenly, a growing number of America's rank and file were discovering that an elitist cabal was attempting to micromanage their destinies. The EIB Network began experiencing a resurgence of "kook calls."

In the 1992 race for the Republican presidential nomination, Pat Buchanan (a conservative Roman Catholic) accused President Bush of running "a Skull and Bones presidency."[64] The following year, during Jeb Bush's Florida gubernatorial campaign, one of his constituents asked him, "You're familiar with the Skull and Crossbones Society?" Jeb's response, "Yeah, I've heard about it," to which the man replied, "Isn't your aim to take control of the United States?"[65]

The final blow came in 2000 when Hollywood decided it was time to cash in on the unprecedented "consumer awareness." The aforementioned Skull and Bones memorandum was occasioned by the soon-to-be-released Universal Pictures film, *The Skulls*. Now it would be "G. W.'s" turn to dodge those bothersome questions. When asked about The Order by ABC News, he smugly replied, "Does it still exist? The thing is so secret that I'm not even sure it still exists."[66]

In 2001, with the pressure continuing to mount, President Bush released his much awaited autobiography, *A Charge to Keep*. He skillfully relegated the controversial topic to a mere two sentences:

> My senior year [at Yale] I joined Skull and Bones, **a secret society, so secret I can't say anything more**. It was a chance to make fourteen new friends [i.e., "mud wrestlers"].[67]

The lid had now opened for the world to discover just how deeply the Bush family was entrenched in The Order of Skull and Bones: Senator Prescott Bush of Connecticut; followed in the coffin by sons, President George Herbert Walker Bush and financier Jonathan Bush; then by his grandson, President George W. Bush.

That same year the History Channel and A&E aired programs dealing with The Order. After maintaining the standard skeptical attitude, the narrator for the History Channel special, *History's Mysteries—Secret Societies*, suddenly exclaimed with regard to Skull and Bones:

> It would all be rather funny if it weren't for the fact that among the former Bonesmen are three presidents; William Howard Taft, George H. W. Bush, George W. Bush; numerous senators and ambassadors; industrialists

like William Whitney; CIA agents; State Department officials and publishing magnate Henry Luce.

Things were bound to get worse. In the April 2001 edition of the *New York Observer*, Ron Rosenbaum published an account of what he believed was a Skull and Bones initiation ceremony. On Saturday evening, April 14, Rosenbaum's commandos had scaled the Tomb's walls and used a high-tech night-vision camera to videotape a portion of the secluded ritual occurring in the inner courtyard. The brief clip portraying scenes of throat cutting and sodomy is simply too perverse to recount here. However, the news media had a field day. Peter Jennings of *ABC Nightly News* introduced Rosenbaum's tape with the words:

> Finally this evening, getting under the skin of the Ivy League. Those eight, old, definitely distinguished colleges that are known for their ivy-covered buildings and their sometimes superior attitudes to other colleges and universities, which often gets under the skin of people who went elsewhere. Yale University is three hundred years old this year and were you to visit its campus you would see that it still has exotic club houses which look like tombs, where Yale's legendary secret societies meet. Their prestige and importance have largely evaporated [Yeah, right, Pete!], but the rituals are still a secret. And so when we heard that some enterprising characters had managed to spy on the famous Skull and Bones Society, **well, we couldn't resist.**[68]

ROBBINS TO THE RESCUE

It just so happened that I caught Peter Jennings's broadcast that evening and discerned a subliminal effort to make light of Skull and Bones as well as Rosenbaum's effort to expose them. Then the following year it seemed the unthinkable occurred. A Skull and Bones apologist came riding over the hill posing as a combination pseudo-intellectual/investigative journalist. The author's name is Alexandra Robbins and her book is entitled *Secrets of the Tomb: Skull and Bones, The Ivy League, and The Hidden Paths of Power*. According to the dust jacket:

> Now, in *Secrets of the Tomb*, acclaimed journalist Alexandra Robbins accomplishes what no one before her ever has. She has managed to get scores of Bonesmen to talk about what really happens inside the Tomb

and exactly what influence the organization truly wields. . . . Robbins takes us inside the Tomb and onto Skull and Bones' private island. She exposes the organization's secret initiation rites and dissects their true impact on world affairs.

A spectacular feat of investigative reporting, *Secrets of the Tomb* is more than the definitive book on the most secret society in the world. It is also a provocative exploration of our collective obsession with conspiracy and connection.[69]

One of the dead giveaways that Robbins is nothing more than a manipulated hireling is the jacket endorsement by Seymour Hersh. When the powers that be needed a "definitive" work to cover up the murder of 269 innocent people, including a sitting U.S. congressman (KAL Flight 007), the Pulitzer Prize-winning Hersh was their man.

Another telltale sign was provided by Robbins herself:

> This vow of silence remains the society's most important rule. Bonesmen have been exceedingly careful not to break this code of secrecy, and have kept specific details about the organization out of the press. . . .
>
> But they have already spoken to me. When? Over the past three years. Why? Perhaps because I am a member of one of Skull and Bones' kindred Yale secret societies. . . . **What follows, then, is the truth about Skull and Bones.**[70]

Sure, Alexandra, sure!

The outstanding impression I received from dissecting *Secrets of the Tomb* was the author's consummate skill at talking out of both sides of her mouth. But first, it was necessary to draw the reader in with a few dramatic revelations. Robbins claims that she received some ominous calls from Bonesmen before and after writing an earlier story about The Order in *Atlantic Monthly*. According to her, "an older Bonesman" threatened, "If it's not portrayed positively, I'm sending a couple of my friends after you."[71] (*Whoa*—Dude!) Following the article's publication another negative conversation supposedly occurred:

> "I have just gotten off the phone with our people."
>
> "Your *people*?" I snickered.
>
> "Yes. Our people." He told me that the society demanded to know where I got my information . . .

Then he got angry. He screamed at me for a while about how
dishonorable I was for writing the article. "A lot of people are very
despondent over this!" he yelled. . . .
"There are a lot of us at newspapers and at political journalism
institutions," he coldly hissed. "Good luck with your career"—and he
slammed down the phone.[72]

Wow—that's some freaky stuff! Once the reader believes Robbins
is willing to risk life and limb in pursuit of the truth, he lowers his
guard only to run through a minefield of disinformation and double speak.
For instance, in one place she remarks: "It is **astonishing** that so many
people continue to believe, even in twenty-first-century America, that
a **tiny college club** wields such an enormous amount of influence on the
world's only superpower."[73] But then she flip-flops over to Professor
Sutton's documented analysis, conceding:

> The list of prominent members of Skull and Bones is **staggering**, particularly
> given that, with only fifteen new members initiated each year, there are
> only approximately eight hundred living members at any one time. It would
> seem to be no small coincidence that a **tiny college club** has somehow
> managed to spawn three presidents of the United States.[74]

Elsewhere, she states:

> Certainly, a relatively large number of Bonesmen have achieved
> influential positions that control foreign policy; several members have
> served on the Council on Foreign Relations, including Winston Lord, its
> president from 1977 to 1985.[75]

One of Robbins's main objectives is to extricate the modern Bonesman
from the embarrassing stigma of his Order's reputation. This vital sleight
of hand assignment is attempted by relegating the worst-case scenarios
to the past while labeling them somewhere between legend and juvenile
shenanigans. Once again, this can only be done by allusion and
contradiction. She writes:

> As the first page of a Skull and Bones booklet titled "Continuation of the
> History of Our Order for the Century Celebration," dated June 17, 1933,
> reads, "I hereby confess: That there is no History of the Bones. How could
> that be? **It is the very essence of our traditions that there is no change.**[76]

After quoting this clear statement from a Skull and Bones publication, Robbins summarily dismisses practically all of the objectionable baggage dug up by Rosenbaum, Sutton and others as outdated nonsense.

> It is possible, that in its **early days**, Skull and Bones directed odd rituals in coffins and the kind of sexual braggadocio typical of adolescent boys. **Today**, however, there is no coffin in the ceremony, and any sordid sexual activity is not part of the regular program, but rather the unsurprising exploits of a coed group of college kids, or even a member sneaking a significant other into the building.[77]

She then assures us that the infamous Skull and Bones initiation is nothing more than harmless fun:

> The initiation itself is a cross between an amusement park haunted house and a human pinball game, with the blind dizziness of a trip through a sandstorm—"something like a Harry Potter novel," described a patriarch who is now an engineer. "It consisted of all kinds of **goofy stuff**. It was one of the most exciting things ever. It was this incredible fantasy created just for you."[78]

Compare that warm and fuzzy appraisal with the following excerpts from *The Old Brown Jug* as printed in the *Iconoclast*, October 13, 1873. With reference to the Tomb, the author wrote:

> "A sound of revelry by night,"
> A sound that seems to tell
> That **demons wild** instead of men
> Within its portals dwell.
>
> And often as the dark midnight,
> When earth is draped in gloom,
> The **beings weird** are seen emerge,
> From out their living tomb.
>
> They step so proud, they look so loud,
> Their bearing is so high,
> That common folk are fain to shrink,
> Whenever they pass nigh.
>
> Like **spirits from another world**,
> Down, deeper down than ours,
> They seem to come all furnished
> With **dark and deadly powers**.

And on their breasts they wear a sign
That tells their race and name;
It is the **ghastly badge of death**,
And from his kingdom came.

The **son of Satan, son of Sin,**
The enemy of man,
Still claims these worthies as his own
And counts them in his clan . . .[79]

While attempting to diminish The Order's tradition of blood and gore, Robbins repeatedly documents the same.

But the tomb seems like more of a shrine to those who do not survive: **death imagery is everywhere**. One Latin phrase engraved in the tomb is *"Tempus fugit"* ("Time flies"). Dozens of skeletons and skulls, both human and animal—elk, buffalo—grip the walls. A mummy lies prone on a mantel in the upstairs hall. The death's-head logo stamps everything from crockery to painted borders on the wall to glittering Exit signs printed with letters composed of tiny skulls. In the kitchen, each piece of silverware bears the mark S.B.T. (for Skull and Bones Tomb or Skull and Bones Treat). Cups and mugs of all sizes are skull-shaped. In the dining room, dim and intimate, light shines through the gaping eyeholes of fixtures in the shape of skulls. . . .

The walls celebrate death as if it were a victory, or at least some measure of glory, with artistic adornments such as a variety of framed pictures of skulls as well as *The Signing of the Death Sentence of Lady Jane Grey* and *The Earl of Strafford Going to Execution. . . .*

In the main foyer lies a tablet inscribed *"Memento mori"* ("Remember that you must die") dedicated "to the departed Bones."[80]

With such a ubiquitous death motif, *why should anyone be surprised that The Order's initiates would have to spend some time in a coffin (including "Brother" Bush)?* In fact, by the time a student is tapped for Skull and Bones, he is certainly familiar with the proceedings. In *Four Years at Yale* (1871), Lyman Bagg recounts a typical initiation ceremony for one of Yale's *freshman* societies:

He is officiously told to rest himself in a chair, the seat of which lets him into a pail of water, beneath, though a large sponge probably saves him from an actual wetting; his head and hands are thrust through a pillory, and he is reviled in that awkward position; he is rolled in an exaggerated squirrel wheel; a noose is thrown around his neck, and he is dragged beneath the guillotine, when the bandage is pulled from his eyes, and he glares upon the glittering knife of block-tin, which falls within a foot of his throat, and cannot possibly go further. Being thus executed, he is thrust into a coffin, which is hammered upon with such energy that he is at length recalled to live, pulled out again, and made to wear his coat with the inside outwards.[81]

In reality, the whole "coffin thing" is a blasphemous attack upon the Biblical doctrine of regeneration (John 3:3-8, Titus 3:5). Expressions such as "recalled to life" or "reborn into society" are familiar ones within The Order's glossary of terms. The length of the initiate's *gestation* period was just another "coincidence" (transcending the mere length of a normal school year). Elting Morison, a biographer of Bonesman Henry L. Stimson, who was secretary of war during World War II, wrote, ". . . how in **nine months**, in weekly meetings, in secret places, whole lives were changed, is past all discovery."[82] Robbins writes:

> There is reason to everything Skull and Bones does; its headquarters, program, and rituals have all been carefully calibrated to cultivate its power by essentially training its members. The presence of the tomb is only the first step toward breeding new knights. It is introduced to the second-semester juniors as their own private space, which they quickly learn can serve as hideout, library, office, lounge, and café. It is hardly uncommon for new knights to spend practically the entire week after initiation in the tomb, where they explore the artifacts, raid the kitchen, write term papers, and marvel at their exclusive access to this large property—a new alternative to the usual dorm room/common room/restaurant/bar options. . . . Each serves as a factor that sets the Bonesmen apart in their exclusive, elusive, illusory little world.[83]

Robbins's book is all about damage control. In chapter four she makes a valiant effort to reproduce a typical modern initiation ceremony. A few of the highlights reveal how *"fools make a mock at sin"* (Proverbs 14:9).

> When an initiate approaches the front door of the **tomb**, the door creaks open and Bonesmen immediately cover his head with a bag, hood, or, in the nineteenth century, a "bladder." . . . he hears rushing water, which supports the rumor of an in-house swimming pool, but the Bonesmen are actually just **flushing the toilets** over and over again; the initiate is told, "This is where **the Bones whore** lives," as the patriarchs hide their smiles.
> In the Inner Temple . . . Uncle Toby [the knight conducting the proceedings] wears a distinctive robe; the knight in the role of the **Little**

Devil, clad in a **devil's** costume, lies in wait; the four brawniest knights serve as shakers, while in earlier times may have worn only **jock straps** and sneakers; . . . a senior dressed as the **Pope** sits in the chair to the left of the fireplace with one foot, covered in a white slipper monogrammed "SBT," perched on a **stone skull** . . . a crew of extras in **skeleton costumes** and carrying noisemakers, scatter about the room in specified spots. Everyone in the room wears a **mask**. ["Kwanzaa Time!"]

The stage is set: The **oath of secrecy**, retrieved from its resting place in a drawer of the **card table**, waits on the table. The Yorick, a **skull** container named for the owner of the **skull** the **gravedigger** throws in *Hamlet*, is filled with "**blood**"—"if it's not Kool-Aid, it's Gatorade," a Bonesman admitted to me—and rests at the foot of the **Madame** [an encased **skeleton** purported to be "Madame de Pompadour, the fashionable socialite mistress of King Louis XV"[84]] . . . the shakers fire the junior toward a picture of a woman that Bonesmen call "Connubial Bliss." The crowd cries, "Connubial Bliss! Connubial Bliss! Connubial Bliss!" . . . The shakers whisk the neophyte to a picture of **Judas Iscariot**, whose name the crowd screams three times.

The shakers push the initiate to his knees in front of the Yorick and force his head toward the pool of "**blood**." To the neophyte's dismay, the crowd implores him to "Drink it! Drink it! Drink it!," which he must. The shakers hurry the initiate to the **Pope**, but not before the **Devil** whips him in the face with his tail. The initiate bends to kiss the **Pope's slippered toe** on the **skull**. When the initiate is brought to Don Quixote, who stands just in front of the fireplace with a **sword** in his right hand, he is pushed once again to his knees, but this time for **glory** as the crowd falls silent once again. Quixote taps the junior on the left shoulder and says, "By order of our order, I dub thee Knight of Eulogia." [The Order's goddess of eloquence]. The **skeleton** nearest the tocsin in the room strikes it three times, then two times, then twice again, and the crowd shouts, "**Bones!**"[85]

One of the few "legends" Robbins appears to have endorsed concerns the ritual before "Connubial Bliss."

At this point during the first meeting in the fall, all knights participate in the "vacation experiences" discussion, which is something like an oral "What I Did on My Summer Vacation." Beginning with the next meeting, each knight spends a Sunday session standing in front of the painting of a woman that Bones calls "Connubial Bliss," **where he delivers his sexual history**. . . . The speeches can take several hours . . . It is an activity that some members dread and some await with delicious anticipation—a knight named Yorick of the club of 1917 wrote to a friend that the CB was "a wonderful sensation." Another Bonesman said to me that the CB "could be in as comic or sincere a fashion as you wanted it to be. It was entirely up to you how much you revealed about yourself." And the reason that "people really unloaded," a patriarch has said, was that "the one thing we all agreed on was that whatever was said in that room would never leave that room."[86]

Like First Lady Laura Bush told Jay Leno during a Spring 2004 appearance on his show, "What happens in Vegas—stays in Vegas!"

GEORGE W. BUSH

This is what President Bush meant when he wrote, "My senior year I joined Skull and Bones, a secret society, **so secret I can't say anything more.**"[87] The only problem with that statement is that it was made by the leader of the free world who *also* took an oath to uphold the United States Constitution.

However, in a major conflict of interest, globalists like the Bush dynasty privately view the Constitution as a reproachful parchment to be circumvented at will. Grandpa Prescott, the "honorable" senator from Connecticut and the first Bush to lay in a coffin at Yale (1917), found himself at the center of a major banking scandal in 1942. On October 20 of that year, the U.S. government ordered the seizure of Nazi German financial operations in New York City under the authority of the "Trading with the Enemy Act." (See: Alien Property Custodian Vesting Order No. 248.) Robbins acknowledges, ". . . Hitler's financier stowed $3 million in the Union Banking Corporation, a bank that counted among its seven directors Prescott Bush."[88] (In 1941, the *New York Herald-Tribune* had featured a front-page story headlined "Hitler's Angel Has $3 Million in U.S. Bank," the "angel" being a reference to German steel baron, Fritz Thyssen.)

In 1976, 1981, and 1985, "G.W.'s" daddy was sworn in as director of the CIA and as vice president by fellow Bonesman Supreme Court Justice Potter Stewart, who frequently attended Bush family barbecues.[89] Then, following his election to the highest office in the land, "President Poppy" declared in his *first* State of the Union address:

What is at stake is more than one small country. It is a big idea. A **new world order**, where diverse nations are drawn together in common cause to achieve universal aspirations of mankind—peace and security, freedom and the rule of law. Out of these troubled times, our fifth objective, a **new**

world order can emerge. Now we can see a **new world** coming into being, a world in which there is the very real prospect of a **new world order**.[90]

So "Dubya" certainly knows where *his* bread is buttered. Robbins wrote, "Of Bush's initiation, a patriarch participant told me, 'All I will say about it is that he caught on pretty quickly and I was pleased with his response.'"[91] She also confirmed:

> At least fifty-eight Bonesmen—four from George Bush's 1948 club, six from George W. Bush's 1968 club, and seven from William F. Buckley's 1950 club—contributed at least $57,972 to Bush's presidential bid, though many of them tried to circumvent campaign finance rules and donate more than the legal limit.[92]

Upon attaining the prize, the payoffs began. Robbins writes:

> Also like his father, George W. Bush has used his presidential power to reward his fellow Bonesmen. One of the first social gatherings (possibly the first gathering) George W. held at the White House after his inauguration was a reunion of his Skull and Bones clubmates. Some of his Bones cohorts would receive much more than a White House meeting, however. In November 2001, Bush appointed Edward McNally (Bones 1979) general counsel of the new federal Office of Homeland Security and a senior associate counsel to the president for national security.
>
> Frederick W. Smith (Bones 1966) was reportedly George W.'s top choice for secretary of defense until he withdrew from the running because of a heart problem. One of President Bush's first appointments was 1968 Bones clubmate Robert D. McCallum, Jr., to the $125,700-per-year position of assistant attorney general, civil division, the largest litigation component in the Justice Department. The division represents the federal government in significant domestic and foreign policy cases such as fraud, international trade, patents, bankruptcies, and foreign litigation, which can involve billions of dollars.... His administration appointed Evan G. Galbraith (Bones 1950) as the secretary of defense's representative in Europe and as the defense advisor to the U.S. mission to NATO.[93]

About this time the inevitable question arises, "But isn't President Bush a born-again Christian?" As this is his stated profession, the reader is referred to the subject's "personal testimony" as recorded in his own autobiography:

My family had attended the First Presbyterian Church in Midland; with the move to Houston we began attending the Episcopal church, the denomination my dad was raised in. I served communion at the eight A.M. service at St. Martin's. I loved the formality, the ritual, the candles, and there, I felt the first stirrings of a faith that would be years in the shaping.[94]

The president relates that his "faith" was stirred for the first time amidst the *formality, ritual and candles of an Episcopalian Church*. Does Mr. Bush know that the Episcopal Church is the most liberal Bible-denying denomination in Protestantism? (Someone has said that "an Episcopalian is a Catholic who flunked Latin.") America sank to a new low in 2003 with the election of a divorced, openly sodomite priest as bishop of New Hampshire's Episcopal diocese. The "Rev." V. Gene Robinson announced that he plans to be "a good bishop, not a gay bishop."

Mr. Bush seems to date his "salvation experience" to a personal contact with evangelist Billy Graham at Kennebunkport (six years before the Perfect Storm came through). Pay close attention to the following watered down account:

Actually, the seeds of my decision had been planted the year before, by the Reverend Billy Graham. **He** visited my family for a summer weekend in Maine. I saw **him** preach at the small summer church, St. Ann's by the Sea. We all had lunch on the patio overlooking the ocean. One evening my dad asked Billy to answer questions from a big group of family gathered for the weekend. **He** sat by the fire and talked. And what **he** said sparked a change in my heart. I don't remember the exact words. It was more the power of **his** example. The Lord was so clearly reflected in **his** gentle and loving demeanor. The next day we walked and talked at Walker's Point, and I knew I was in the presence of a great man. **He** was like a magnet; I felt drawn to seek something different.[95]

Now, get ready; here it comes!

He didn't lecture or admonish; he shared warmth and concern. Billy Graham didn't make you feel guilty; he made you feel loved.[96]

Do you think Mr. Bush has ever read John 3:36? *". . . and he that believeth not the Son shall not see life; **but the wrath of God abideth on him**."* Do you think Mr. Bush ever heard the words to *Amazing Grace*? "'Twas grace that taught my heart to **fear**, And grace my **fear** relieved." Do you think Mr. Bush had ever learned that the most famous sermon in the history of America was entitled, "Sinners In the Hands of An **Angry** God?" Do you think Mr. Bush is familiar with the views of Job and David on the matter? While the former testified, *"Therefore am I troubled at his presence: when I consider, I am **afraid** of him"* (Job 23:15), the latter stated, *"My flesh trembleth for **fear** of thee; and I am **afraid** of thy judgments.* " (Psalm 119:120)

He then concludes his politically correct remarks by stating:

> Over the course of that weekend, Reverend Graham planted a mustard seed in my soul, a seed that grew over the next year. He led me to the path, and I began walking. And it was the beginning of a change in my life. I had always been a religious person, had regularly attended church, even taught Sunday school and served as an altar boy. But that weekend my faith took on new meaning. It was the beginning of a new walk where I would **recommit my heart to Jesus Christ**.
>
> I was humbled to learn that God sent His Son to die for a sinner like me. I was comforted to know that through the Son, I could find God's amazing grace, a grace that crosses every border, every barrier and is open to everyone. Through the love of Christ's life, I could understand the life-changing powers of faith.[97]

No one has ever gotten saved by recommitting his or her life to Jesus; you get saved when God the Holy Ghost convicts you that you will fry in Hell like a Jimmy Dean sausage unless you repent and put your faith in Jesus Christ as Lord and Saviour! Mr. Bush messed up by taking Graham's word over Jesus's. "Billy" told *Time* magazine on November 15, 1993, what he had often stated before:

> The only thing I could say for sure is that hell means separation from God. We are separated from his light, from his fellowship. That is going to be hell. **When it comes to a literal fire, I don't preach it because I'm not sure about it.** When the Scripture uses fire concerning hell, that is possibly an illustration of how terrible it's going to be—not fire but something worse, a thirst for God that cannot be quenched.[98]

President Bush should have placed his faith in what Jesus had to say about the matter:

> *"And if thy hand offend thee, cut it off: it is better for thee to enter into life maimed, than having two hands to go into hell, **into the fire that never shall be quenched**. Where their worm dieth not, and the fire is not quenched. "* (Mark 9:43-44)

The president's entire testimony was as anemic as the solitary verse of "Scripture" which he quoted from a worthless modern translation: "Now it is required that those who have been given a trust must prove faithful." (I Corinthians 4:2) George W. Bush is about as spiritual as the "minister" who arranged his Inaugural Prayer Luncheon on January 19, 2001, a Washington event that drew over 1,700 public officials, ministers, and conservative activists. The toastmaster on this "holy" occasion was none other than the "Reverend" Sun Myung Moon, the same guru who paid former president George H. W. Bush $900,000 for nine speeches during 1995 and 1996.[99] (See *Reuters*, November 25, 1996, "Bush Praises Sun Myung Moon as 'Man of Vision.'")

A month before the 2000 election, Larry King asked Governor Bush if he would have any problem appointing sodomites in his administration. With my own ears I heard "Brother" Bush reply, "No. My religious convictions do not allow me to make judgments like that!" *What do "religious convictions" have to do with knowing that a man is not supposed to kiss another man?*

However, the president's greatest problem continues to be his inability (or unwillingness) to recognize Jesus Christ as *"the true God and eternal life"* (I John 5:20b). The Bible leaves no room for compromise on this bedrock doctrine: *"Whosoever trangresseth, and abideth not in the doctrine of Christ, hath not God"* (II John 9a). On November 20, 2003, President Bush participated in a joint press conference with Tony Blair in London. A reporter asked Bush the following question:

> Mr. President, when you talk about peace in the Middle East, you've often said that freedom is granted by the Almighty. Some people who share your beliefs don't believe that Muslims worship the same Almighty. I wonder about your views on that.

"Brother" Bush, the great standard-bearer for the Church of Jesus Christ responded:

> I do say that freedom is the Almighty's gift to every person. I also condition it by saying freedom is not America's gift to the world. It's much greater than that, of course. **And I believe we worship the same God.**[100]

Of course, this ecumenical garbage is nothing new. On February 18, 2002, our "Christian" president entered the ornate Shinto Temple erected to house the spirits of the late Emperor Meiji. With the prime minister of Japan left sitting in the car—forbidden from entering the shrine by a postwar constitution written by the U.S. proscribing government officials from practicing emperor worship—"Dubya" clapped once and bowed reverently, following the common etiquette of worship at such pagan hellholes. Dr. Robert Morery, author of over forty books dealing with cults and false religion in general commented, "So the Prime Minister stayed in the limo while Bush and his wife went into the temple and clapped to awaken the demon and then bowed in worship and signed the book of worship."[101]

Although there is no guarantee when the Church Age will end, Christians need to familiarize themselves with a dangerous precedent that was established by Jimmy Carter in 1974. Carter, a liberal Southern Baptist, became the first modern chief executive to popularize the phrase "born-again." That one line forged an immediate bond between Carter and evangelical Christians.

The Dark Ages began when the majority of professing believers in the fourth century accepted the phony conversion testimony of Emperor "Constantine The Great;" a man who was so "spiritual," he secured his throne by murdering eighteen family members, including his oldest son! *Could you think of a better way for history to repeat itself than for a generation of "boob-tube believers" to follow another Constantine into the darkness?* As they say—"The only lesson a man ever learns from history is that man *never* learns from history."

THE WIZARD OF OZ

Having exonerated The Order from the stigma of myth, embellishment and calumny, Robbins concludes her book with a rather profound hypothesis. Yet her Bonesmen beneficiaries are actually caught in a no-win situation to whatever degree her theory proves valid. Robbins got the bright idea that the best way to account for The Order's morbid baggage was to simply claim that it was all a big smoke screen perpetuated by the patriarchs themselves. She writes:

> In truth, Skull and Bones itself is like a hall of mirrors. The society has become so difficult to pin down for nearly two centuries because of the countless contradictory reflections—ricocheting from Bonesmen, patriarchs, Yale, and barbarians—that bounce against each other. But the reflections

begin from within. "It really is a place that is full of itself," a Bonesman said to me. "It loves its own hype. They *love* perpetuating the mystique." Inside the tomb, the seniors desperately want to believe that they are part of something larger than themselves.[102]

Thus, while none would be "caught dead" crawling in and out of coffins, etc., they certainly wouldn't mind if *you* became mesmerized at the prospect of such activity. Robbins continues:

> As soon as freshmen arrive at the New Haven campus for the start of "Camp Yale," those few days after registration ends and before classes begin, they hear stories about the university's infamous secret-society system. Often wide-eyed, sometimes afraid, and always curious, they can't help but wonder—when they see tight-lipped, black-hooded students silently single-filing into a windowless building, when they hear about the seniors who never show up in the dining hall on Thursdays and Sundays, when they encounter the strange insignias stamped menacingly on campus—what goes on in these organizations.[103]

Though Skull and Bones apologists have consistently sugarcoated the society's eccentricities, others were willing to tell it like it was. In a letter from the 1870s, Yale professor Thomas Thacher blasted The Order for its subliminal effect on the campus:

> I should be glad if the whole system of petty *perpetuata* societies in this college should perish. . . . But I feel bound to add that it is not their *secrecy* which makes them an evil. Almost all the evil which they cause here, except the waste of time and money, would cease, if every one of them should become really secret, if their places and times of meeting, the names of their members and even the names of the societies and their very existence were absolutely unknown except to the members. **It is what is known about these societies, not their secrets not their secret doings, which works evil among us.**[104]

No doubt, Professor Thacher knew of what he spoke. Both his son and grandson were members of Skull and Bones.

Another missive was sent through a 1933 editorial published in Yale's *Harkness Hoot*:

> These campus Elks, Masons, secret what-you-wills, that undertake to select men on a basis of personality and accomplishment, seem so hideously out-dated, so out of step with the very ideals of university life, that it is

hard for us to believe in their existence today. **It is hard for us to believe in them because fundamentally they and their impositions are unreal.** The standards they set up create an artificial distinction between individuals. That a man can be kept by any obligations from talking to an intimate friend after a meeting is of course farcical; but in a more general sense the silent shrouding of secrecy about Societies is unreal because it is unbelievable that any one should not be entirely free to examine into and question all that he meets. We believe it definitely harmful for any one to grow into habits of unthinking acceptance. The importance of Senior Societies is accepted at Yale today; but there is no reason why that importance should go on forever. When the organizations have become a burden and a repressive force, it is time to end the play.[105]

Robbins then offered the following astute observations:

> Yale's *Harkness Hoot* published this editorial in 1933, surely without even fathoming that the societies would still thrive nearly three-quarters of a century later, and the piece remains noteworthy not only because it reflects a still-enduring attitude that the secret societies manage to thwart, but also because it has a concept backwards. "It is hard for us to believe in them," it states, "because fundamentally they and their impositions are unreal." **In fact, it is precisely because these secret societies project such unreal impositions that we believe in them in the first place. . . .**
>
> The society has always demanded invisibility while simultaneously publicizing its supremacy. It is a paradox that dichotomizes swagger and silence . . .[106]

Someone has rightly observed—"A hit dog yells." After reading *Secrets of the Tomb*, one can sense The Order's rabid indignation that their secrecy has been violated. The author records more than one four-letter word addressed to Mr. Rosenbaum.[107]

But now, watch these elitist power mongers shoot themselves in the foot. All you need is a simple English dictionary to discover what Skull and Bones is about. Robbins writes:

> The rumors and conspiracy theories about Skull and Bones, as described in the Introduction, are widespread and deep-rooted. **Probably the most fascinating thing that I learned through my interviews with members of Skull and Bones is that the majority of those rumors were carefully planted by the Bonesmen themselves.** The patriarchs are the publicists, leaking gossip to the columnists; they are the politicians, spinning stories as distractions; they are the magicians, directing patter to enhance the

sleight of hand. By spreading rumors about their society, they create a cloak of mystery that both protects the privacy surrounding what they truly do and makes them feel as if they belong to something transcendent and omnipotent, when in truth the society is less than the sum of its parts.[108]

Her anonymous sources were quick to concur:

As one Bonesman said, "It's essential to have a certain amount of confusion and uncertainty about just what goes on because it actually protects what goes on inside. It's an effective smokescreen to protect privacy." A Bonesman from the late 1950s was more blunt: "Rumors, true or untrue, heighten the mystery."[109]

She then draws an amazing parallel between Skull and Bones and the Wizard of Oz:

The patriarchs blow up smokescreens that allow the barbarians outside to see within the mist whatever it is that they want their imagination to find. **They lay the foundation for broad speculative postulations and then they encourage the conspiracy theories.** And why wouldn't they? If people believe in something strongly enough, it becomes the truth to them. **Skull and Bones is, at its core, equivalent to the Wizard of Oz, the puny but cunning man hidden behind a curtain of mystique, projecting images that inspire awe and terror in order to expand himself into something great and terrible.** This is not to downplay the remarkable power of the Bones network or the impact that the network has had. But many of the secrets of Skull and Bones—the initiation ceremony, the membership rolls, the tomb's artifacts—may simply serve as skulduggery to mask the society's biggest mystery, or lack thereof.[110]

Robbins concludes her cute theory with the words:

If the Wizard of Oz can represent Skull and Bones, then one must point out that, for a while, Oz *needed* its Wizard to provide balance and a constant current of reassurance. Likewise, the power of organizations such as Yale and its secret societies is similarly found in the facades in which people leap to believe. It is hardly revelatory to note that the United States places appearance on a pedestal, or that this devotion expands progressively with technological advance. It is also worth mentioning that Oz was not without his power. He had used his smarts to his advantage, and if much of his strength came from a facade, that facade came from him. Connections are power. . . .

Lord Chesterfield wrote, "A proper secrecy is the only mystery of able men; mystery is the only secrecy of weak and cunning ones." The assertion that Skull and Bones both boasts a proper secrecy and skulks behind mystery is not a matter of trying to have it both ways. Skull and Bones surely has its secrets. But these are the secrets of an organization that traffics in intangibles. . . .

Whether the legend of Skull and Bones reflects a sinister veracity or a prismatic distortion depends almost entirely on one's desired perception.[111]

This is so funny I don't know where to begin. In their haste to discredit students of conspiracy history, The Order dropped its guard completely. They didn't count on the fact that a standard English dictionary could expose them. Now, how did that quote go, Alexandra? "Probably the most fascinating thing that I learned through my interviews with members of Skull and Bones is that **the majority of those rumors were carefully planted by the Bonesmen themselves.**"[112]

You would think that Robbins and her satanic cohorts could *read* a simple dictionary. With all the time they spend using four-letter words to lampoon conspiracy theorists, do you suppose that any of them even know what the word "conspiracy" means? According to the 1996 *Webster's New Universal Unabridged Dictionary* (as we have already seen in chapter five), the word is defined as:

1. The act of conspiring.
2. An evil, unlawful, treacherous or surreptitious plan formulated in secret by two or more persons; plot.
3. A combination of persons for a secret, unlawful or evil purpose.[113]

Would the glaring concession that "the majority of these rumors were carefully planted by the Bonesmen themselves" fit somewhere in the above definition? Not even the Wizard of Oz could be labeled a conspirator, as he acted alone. The truth is, Robbins knew all along that she was covering up one of the most vile conspiracies in United States history. She just waited until the second to the last sentence of her apologia to say so!

The great **conspiracy** surrounding the society is one of half-truths and our own willing complicity. And its secret, great and terrible, is that Skull and Bones, unreal, has mastered both.[114]

At worst, The Order of Skull and Bones is a secret society of macabre conspirators espousing a globalist agenda; at best, you may substitute the word *lying* for macabre.

VICTOR ASHE

On a providential summer afternoon in 2000, the Lord gave me a unique opportunity to observe this "elitist detachment" under ideal laboratory conditions. While enjoying a rare day at home, the telephone suddenly disturbed my tranquility. The recorded message informed me that I was being invited to attend a "Meet the Mayor Night" to be held at a local elementary school the following week. Two things arrested my attention. First, it just so happened that I was scheduled to be in town on the day of the meeting. And second, that very week I had been scanning a list of prominent Skull and Bones alumni when a most unusual name popped up: You guessed it—Victor Ashe (1967), mayor of Knoxville, Tennessee! The Holy Ghost immediately pressed my spirit, "Why not take the mayor up on his invitation?" I didn't need a second prompting.

When I arrived at the designated location a bit early, there was only one other person ahead of me. By the time the meeting began, the number had grown to forty. The format was announced as an informal "one-on-one" with the mayor who would be seated at a table off to the side.

I wore my bright orange University of Tennessee Volunteer shirt and used my title of "Dr." Grady (something I rarely do) to gain a window of perhaps ninety seconds. When my name was called we traded the typical "politician meets voter" pleasantries. I then initiated the following exchange: "Mayor, while doing research for a current book project, I came across your name on a most unusual Internet site."

"Oh," he replied with a serious demeanor, "and what was that?"

Picking up the pace, I continued, "You were listed as a member of The Order of Skull and Bones; everything I have ever read about that organization has been negative, anti-American and internationalist. But, I believe in separating fact from fiction. Can you help me in this regard?"

While his face turned white as snow, he crossed his hands in mid-air and snapped in a most irritated tone, "I'm not going to discuss that!" When I looked him eyeball-to-eyeball, he added, "All I will say is that there are a lot of myths out there." So I innocently replied, "Like what?"

For some strange reason, the loquacious politician had suddenly been struck with lockjaw. "I'm not going to discuss that!" he reiterated. My response was logical enough. "Well, Mayor, if a Skull and Bones alumnus will not dispel the myths, who will?" By this time, he was becoming quite agitated. "I'm not going to discuss that; I'll just say there are a lot of myths out there!"

At that point, a still, small voice whispered, "Ask him about the coffin." Just when "his honor" thought he had intimidated his nosey constituent, I blurted out, *"Would you classify lying naked in a casket as a myth?"* Boy, did *that* ever do it! This time he *really* got loud. "I'M NOT GOING TO DISCUSS THAT!" The others waiting their turn were beginning to wonder why the mayor was so shook up. I attempted to defuse the situation by assuring him that I had intended to keep my questions private (giving him the benefit of the doubt). He then replied, "If we were in my office behind closed doors, I would not discuss this subject!"

My only alternative was to answer, "Well, Mayor, whenever I write or speak I always prefer to document my material!" At that he stood to his feet, extended his palm for the parting handshake ("Here's your hat; what's your hurry?") and said, "Well, you can inform your readers that you received a polite turn down!" With that, the Lord seemed to say, "Time's up!"

Shortly afterward, President Bush announced the appointment of Victor Ashe to the board of directors of the Federal National Mortgage Association (Fannie Mae), the country's largest source of welfare financing for home mortgages. Our girl from Yale confirms:

> Prior to Ashe's appointment, a mayor had never been named to the board of directors, a position that is accompanied by a hefty compensation package including stock options (four thousand shares per year at the trading price on the first day of the appointment), $1,000 for each of the seven annual meetings, and reimbursement for travel expenses.[115]

And then, appointed by President Bush and confirmed by the U.S. Senate, Ashe was sworn in as Ambassador Extraordinary and Plenipotentiary of the United States of America to the Republic of Poland on June 23, 2004.

Dzien Dobri!

12

The Group

*". . . for my determination is to gather the nations,
that I may assemble the kingdoms, to pour upon them
mine indignation, even all my fierce anger: for all the
earth shall be devoured with the fire of my jealousy."*
(Zephaniah 3:8)

ONE OF THE devil's key stratagems in turning America against God was to get to the Mother Country first, and then employ her in our demise. An applicable cultural trait of the last days is "without natural affection." (II Timothy 3:3) Can anyone calculate the degree of permanent damage inflicted upon the morals of my generation by *Sir* Paul McCartney, *Sir* Mick Jagger and other satanic participants of the so-called "British Invasion"? (The same would apply to later waves led by the likes of *Sir* Elton John, etc.)

As noted in the previous chapter, Yale's Order of Skull and Bones was established by Torries and Anglophiles. The present material will examine Britain's fall from grace, the subsequent rise of her ultimate secret society, and the means it has used to undermine the United States.

The Bible warns, *"Pride goeth before destruction . . ."* (Proverbs 16:18a). At the midpoint of the nineteenth century, England's Prime Minister, Sir Robert Peel, contrived an idea to commemorate the nation's technological advances from the Industrial Revolution. The celebration would be known as the Great Exhibition of 1851. To accommodate the more than 100,000 displays that were expected, Prince Albert contracted Joseph Paxton to design an enormous glass structure encompassing nineteen acres called the Crystal Palace. The world's first international trade fair opened on May 1 and continued through October 11 as six million awe-struck visitors passed under the sprawling canopy measuring 1,848 feet long by 408 feet wide.

Alfred Lord Tennyson captured the mood of gratitude in the air, writing:

> Uplift a thousand voices full and swell,
> In this wide hall with earth's inventions stored,
> And praise the invisible Lord,
> Who lets once more in peace the nations meet,
> Where Science, Art, and Labor have outpour'd
> Their myriad horns of plenty at our feet.[1]

And sing they did! On one occasion, with Victoria and Albert in attendance, a choir sang the "Hallelujah Chorus" and the voices literally shook the glass panels of the structure.[2]

However, note the type of comment that would eventually provoke Britain's jealous God. (Deuteronomy 32:16) Charles Kingsley, vicar of Eversley—a Bible rejecting social reformer—exclaimed through "flowing tears of joy":

> The spinning jenny and the railroad, Cunard's liners and the electric telegraph, are to me . . . signs that we are, on some points at least, in harmony with the universe; that there is a mighty spirit working among us . . . the Ordering and Creating God.[3]

Unfortunately, the "spirit" that was beginning to work was the spirit of *pride*. The British neo-classical economist, W.S. Jevons, described England in 1865 as the "trading center of the Universe." (Better watch out! Does anybody remember a king by the name of Nebuchadnezzar?) Jevons boasted:

> The plains of North America and Russia are our spaces; Chicago and Odessa our granaries; Canada and the Baltic are our timber forests; Australasia contains our sheep farms, and in Argentina and on the western prairies of North America are our herds of oxen; Peru sends her silver, and the gold of South Africa and Australia flows to London; the Hindus and the Chinese grow tea for us, and our coffee, sugar and spice plantations are all in the Indies. Spain and France are our vineyards and the Mediterranean our fruit garden; and our cotton grounds, which for long have occupied the Southern United States, are now being extended everywhere in the warm regions of the earth.[4]

Six years after the Great Exhibition closed, the Lord fired a warning salvo over the English Channel. On May 1, 1857, sepoys of the Bengal army shot their British officers and marched on Delhi to restore the aged Mughal emperor, Bahadur Shah to power. The ensuing Indian mutiny spread down the Ganges Valley to Agra, Cawnpore, Luchnow and into central India, encouraging a widespread civil revolt against the institutions of British rule. With India comprising seventy-five percent of the Empire's inhabitants, Parliament was in shock! Yet, the problem could be traced to that aforementioned spirit of pride. As we shall see later, *offering* the Gospel to a pagan nation is one thing; *forcing* them to change their heathen ways is quite another. The cause for the mutiny lay in attempts to inculcate British-style army discipline into Indian warrior traditions—the celebrated issue of rifle cartridges greased with animal fat being symptomatic of wider problems.

By late September, Sir Colin Campbell's army had yet to reoccupy the key strategic points along the Ganges. The nation decided it was time to repent. A "Fast-Day Service" was scheduled for October 2 at the vacant Crystal Palace. The official announcement read:

> Being the Day appointed by Proclamation for a solemn fast, **humiliation**, and prayer before Almighty God: **in order to obtain pardon of our sins**, and for imploring His blessing and assistance on our arms for the restoration of tranquility in India.[5]

When it came to selecting the preacher for this somber occasion, the choice was never in doubt. Anglicans were all right if you wanted a religious nap; however, if you intended to "git aholt of *God*," you had better find a *Baptist*. The nod went to Charles Haddon Spurgeon, the minister known as the "Prince of Preachers."

In volume one of his *Autobiography*, Spurgeon relates a miraculous incident that occurred just a few days prior to the service:

> The Lord set His seal upon the effort even before the great crowd gathered, though I did not know of that instance of blessing until long afterwards. It was arranged that I should use the Surrey Gardens pulpit, so, a day or two before preaching at the Palace, I went to decide where it should be fixed; and, in order to test the acoustic properties of the building, cried in a loud voice, "Behold the Lamb of God, which taketh away the sin of the world." In one of the galleries, a workman, who knew nothing of what was being done, heard the words, and they came like a message

from Heaven to his soul. He was smitten with conviction on account of sin, put down his tools, went home, and there, after a season of spiritual struggling, found peace and life by beholding the Lamb of God. Years after, he told this story to one who visited him on his death-bed.[6]

On Wednesday, October 7, 1857, nearly 24,000 earnest souls from all stations of society crowded into the center transept of London's glittery Crystal Palace. The preacher they had thronged to hear was only twenty-three years of age, saved for only seven, married for less than two and formally educated—zero! However, because the power of the Holy Ghost was upon him, nearly 7,000 parishioners were already attending his weekly Sunday sermons at the Music Hall of the Royal Surrey Gardens (while plans were being drawn for the massive Metropolitan Tabernacle).

Spurgeon ascended the pulpit. The man of God chose Micah 6:9b for his text, *". . . hear ye the rod, and who hath appointed it."* As the printed sermon fills seven pages, we are limited to just a few of the hard-hitting highlights. Compare the following missive to America's post-9/11 unrepentant rhetoric typified by her "Power of Pride" bumper stickers, etc.

> **I feel persuaded that there are such things as national judgments, national chastisements for national sins—great blows from the rod of God, which every wise man must acknowledge to be, either a punishment of sin committed, or an admonition to warn us to a sense of the consequences of sins, leading us by God's grace to humiliate ourselves, and repent of our sin.**
>
> O, my friends, what a rod is that which has just fallen on our country! My poor words will fall infinitely short of the fearful tale of misery and woe which must be told before you can know how smartly God hath smitten, and how sternly he hath chidden us. . . .
>
> First, there are the sins in the community that never ought to have been allowed. O Britain, weep for deeds which thy governors have not yet strength of mind to stop. . . . If there be a crime for which God will visit England, it is the sin of allowing infamy to walk before our eyes thus publicly. . . . It is a most fearful thing that those who are honest and moral cannot walk the streets, without being insulted by sin in the robes of the harlot. . . .
>
> Look ye too, men and brethren, at some of the amusements of yours, in which ye are wont to indulge . . . when we know that lords and ladies of the land, have sat in playhouses, and listened to plays that were a long way from decent, it is time that some voice should be lifted up against them. These are glaring sins . . .

But, my friends, I am inclined to think that our *class sins* are the most grievous. Behold this day the sins of the rich. How are the poor oppressed! How are the needy down-trodden! In many a place the average wage of men is far below their value to their masters. In this age there is many a great man who looks upon his fellows as only stepping-stones to wealth. . . .

Mark, again, the sins of merchants. Was there ever an age when the merchants of England had more fallen from their integrity? . . . Ye heap up your companies, and ye delude your myriads; ye gather the money of fools; ye scatter it to the winds of heaven, and when the poor call upon you ye tell them it is gone: but where? O England, Thou wast once true, upright, honest . . . but now, O Britain, alas! for thee! . . .

[Having blasted the rank and file to smithereens, Spurgeon turned his guns on the professing Christians with a special emphasis on the "nasal twang" crowd.]

And now, "Hear ye the rod." O church of God, the rod has fallen, and *the church* ought to hear it. . . . *We*, I believe, have been remiss in our duty; for many and many a year pulpits never condescended to men of low estate. Our ministers were great and haughty; they understood the polish of rhetoric, they had all the grandeur of logic; to the people they were blind guides and dumb dogs, for the people knew not what they said, neither did they regard them. The churches themselves slumbered; they wrapped themselves in a shroud of orthodoxy, and they slept right on . . . whilst Satan was devouring the world, and taking his prey, the church sat still, and said, "Who is my neighbor?" and did not arouse herself to serve her God. . . . O church of God! awake! awake! awake! for verily the rod has fallen for thy sake.

[Spurgeon then extended a hope for deliverance and a plea to the unregenerate to trust Christ as Saviour.]

How many of you have been awakened, convinced of sin, of righteousness, and of judgment! How many times have you vowed you would repent! How many times have you declared that you did hear the rod, and that you would turn to God! And yet you have been liars to the Almighty; you have defrauded the Most High; and whilst the bill is due it still stands dishonoured. Tremble!

God may smite you yet; and if to-day you are despisers of Christ, remember, you have no guarantee that you will be in this world another hour. You may before this sun is set stand before your Maker's bar. What then? what then? what then? To perish forever is no light matter; to be cast into the flames of hell is no little consideration. "Turn ye, turn ye, turn ye; why will ye die, O house of Israel!" Repent! "The times of your ignorance God winked at, but now commandeth all men everywhere to repent." And remember that when he gives repentance and faith he has appended the blessing to them. "Jesus Christ of the seed of David" was nailed to a cross; he died that we might not die, and to every believer heaven's gate is open, to every penitent the path to paradise is free.

Sinner! dost thou believe? If so, Christ hath blotted out thy sin. Be happy! Soul! dost thou repent? Thou art safe. God hath helped thee to repent, and inasmuch as he hath done that, he hath proved that he loves thee. . . .

I have done my sermon.[7]

A collection of £700 was received at the end of the meeting for the Indian Relief Fund. After retiring that evening, Spurgeon was so exhausted he slept till Friday morning.

Unfortunately, the devil was wide awake! Although the Lord honored the service by restoring order in India after six weeks, a far deadlier revolt was well under way. Four years prior to the Indian uprising a conspiracy was hatched against the King James Bible that would eventually dismantle the mighty British Empire.

THE REVISED VERSION

In 1853, Cambridge alumni, Drs. Brooke Westcott and Fenton Hort, began a covert project to alter the *Textus Receptus* Greek text (underlying the A.V. 1611) in over 5,000 particulars. As their private translation based on the corrupt *Vaticanus* and *Sinaiticus* manuscripts was nearing its completion, they began to lobby the Anglican hierarchy for a formal revision of the Authorized Version. Unaware of the new Greek text, numerous scholars were drawn into the project on the pretext of merely assisting with cosmetic improvements in the English. On the dates of February 10 and May 3 and 5, the Southern Convocation of the Church of England passed formal resolutions limiting revision activity to "Plain and Clear Errors." So long "Great" Britain—it was nice knowing you!

A special inaugural Communion service was held on June 22 in Henry VII's chapel. One of the participants was Dr. Vance Smith, pastor of St. Stephen's Gate *Unitarian* Church. The Christ-rejecter partook of the elements but refused to recite the Apostles' Creed to avoid "compromise of his principles as a Unitarian."[8] Although several thousand Anglican divines affixed their signatures to a solemn protest, the pervert was allowed to remain on the committee.

With the Eucharist fiasco ended, the initial session was convened. After taking a solemn oath of silence regarding any and all forthcoming procedures and pronouncements, the hundred-plus revisers were issued copies of the new Westcott and Hort Greek Testament. Dr. Benjamin G. Wilkinson writes:

> When the English New Testament Committee met, it was immediately apparent what was going to happen. Though for ten long years the iron rule of silence kept the public ignorant of what was going on behind closed doors.[9]

Most of the revisers resigned in disgust. Dean John William Burgon, the outstanding A.V. 1611 exponent within the Church of England, confirmed, "The average attendance was not so many as sixteen."[10] For the record, Burgon was excluded from the project from the outset. Slimeballs like Westcott, Hort, Ellicott, and Smith introduced one corrupted alteration after another into the text. Even Queen Victoria managed to get offended, Stanley Weintraub writing:

> Later in 1870, for example, when affairs in France and Prussia were dominating newspapers, conversations and the Queen's dispatch boxes, she seemed at least as concerned with the impropriety of the genealogical lines in the revised St. Matthew Gospel, where the indirection of the words "David begat Solomon of her of Uriah" was clarified from Authorized Version to revised text, to read, "David begat Solomon of the wife of Uriah." "This" Victoria complained, "suggested Solomon's illegitimacy, although his parents, David and Bathsheba, had married after Bathsheba became a widow." "The Queen," Colonel Ponsonby wrote for her to Dean Stanley, "is rather scandalized by the proposed alteration." "This, I believe" he added, "is nearly the only subject we have had much discourse on for the last three weeks, except the war, which entirely absorbs our . . . faculties."[11]

Solomon was not the only bastard created by the Revision Committee. Remember Dr. Smith? Whereas I Timothy 3:16 in the King James Bible reads, *"God was manifest in the flesh,"* Smith led in the alteration to *"who* was manifest in the flesh," writing:

> The old reading is pronounced untenable by the Revisers, as it has long been known to be by all careful students of the New Testament. . . . It is in truth another example of the facility with which ancient copiers could introduce the word God into their manuscripts,—a reading which was the natural result of the growing tendency in early Christian times . . . to look

upon the humble Teacher as the incarnate Word, and therefore as "God manifest in the flesh." [12]

On May 17, 1881, the long-awaited Revised Version of the English New Testament was released amidst much fanfare upon a gullible nation. The Old Testament was published in 1885. Together they altered the King James Bible in over 36,000 instances.

With reference to codices *Vaticanus* and *Sinaiticus*, Dean Burgon prophesied, "Those two documents are caused to cast their sombre shadows a long way ahead and to darken all our future."[13] Queen Victoria was able to see the handwriting on the wall. In a letter to her daughter concerning the rise of Weishaupt's German socialism, she warned:

> These socialist atheists are awful! Believe me, when there is no respect for God—no belief in futurity—there can be no respect or loyalty to the highest in the land. Authority of some kind does come from Above, and if that is trampled under foot and if the clergy—narrow-minded though they be—are ridiculed and abused, everything will go down! Philosophy without religion will bring the nation down . . . do remember that.[14]

So, do you happen to recall the year that England formally elected to get rid of her ancient spiritual foundation? Were these revision resolutions passed in 1870 by chance? In *The Lion's Share: A Short History of British Imperialism*, one of Paul Kennedy's 1,400 bibliography sources, author Benjamin Porter writes:

> **From 1870 to 1970 the history of Britain was one of steady and almost unbroken decline, economically, militarily and politically, relative to other nations, from the peak of prosperity and power which her industrial revolution had achieved for her in the middle of the nineteenth century.**[15]

Note how Professor Quigley concurs with these dates:

> The unification of Germany in the decade before 1871 ended a balance of power in Europe which had existed for 250 or even 300 years. During this long period, covering almost ten generations, Britain had been relatively secure and of growing power. She had found this power challenged only by the states of western Europe. . . . The unification of Germany by Bismarck destroyed this situation politically, **while the rapid economic growth of that country after 1871 modified the situation economically.**[16]

Well, my, my, my—the Bible *must* be true after all! And in just another "coincidence," 1870 was the year Pio Nono (Pope Pius IX) proclaimed the doctrine of papal infallibility.

Britain's subjects would pay dearly for the sins of their "spiritual" leaders. And soon, they would suffer even more over Parliament's repudiation of the Balfour Declaration. In the process of time, English culture devolved from the A.V. 1611 to the tabloid. According to the *London Times*, June 24, 2004, the latest Bible version to hit the market, titled *Good as New*, received a major endorsement from the 104th archbishop of Canterbury, Dr. Rowan Williams, leader of the Church of England. With the baton of Westcott and Hort firmly in hand, Dr. Williams lauded the perverse translation of fellow heretic and former Baptist minister John Henson as a book of "extraordinary power." A solitary comparison between Henson's rendering of I Corinthians 7:1-2 and that of the King James translators, will suffice:

KJV: *Now concerning the things whereof ye wrote unto me: It is good for a man not to touch a woman. Nevertheless, to avoid fornication, let every man have his own wife, and let every woman have her own husband.*

New: Some of you think the best way to cope with sex is for men and women to keep right away from each other. That is more likely to lead to sexual offences. My advise is for everyone to have a regular partner.

In a January 2, 2005, *Telegraph* interview on the Asian tsunami, Williams stated, "The question 'How can you believe in a God who permits suffering on this scale?' is therefore very much around at the moment, and it would be surprising if it weren't—**indeed it would be wrong if it weren't.**"

With the King James Bible dethroned by the Revised Version of 1881, a diabolical secret society was able to perpetrate numerous conspiratorial acts against Great Britain and, eventually, the United States as well.

CECIL RHODES

Among Professor Ruskin's most devoted followers at Oxford was a circle of intimate friends, which included Alfred (later, Lord) Milner, Arthur Glazebrook, George (later, Sir) Parkin, Philip Lyttelton Gell, Henry (later, Sir) Birchenough, and Arnold Toynbee. A similar coterie of Cambridge men included Reginald Baliol Brett (Lord Esher), Sir John B. Seeley, Albert (Lord) Gray, and Edmund Garrett. These Englishmen were so captivated by Ruskin that they devoted the remainder of their lives to fulfilling his humanistic pipe dreams. For the record, most of John's disciples "converted" to Christian Science (i.e., "You just *think* you're sick").[17] In fact, the editor of the *Christian Science Monitor* eventually became the chief American correspondent for Ruskin's gospel of Anglophilia.

Arnold Toynbee (1852-1883) became the undisputed intellectual-philosophical leader among the early "Ruskinites," forming what came to be known as "The Toynbee Group" at Oxford's Balliol College about 1873 (three years into the Revised Version project). Toynbee's main protégé was Alfred Milner who related twenty-one years after his first meeting with Arnold, "I fell at once under his spell and have always remained under it." (I John 4:1)[18]

Toynbee's "three-point outline" for a do-it-yourself post-millenial Kingdom Age was as follows:

(a) a conviction that the history of the British Empire represents the unfolding of a great moral idea—the idea of freedom—and that the unity of the Empire could best be preserved by the cement of this idea

(b) a conviction that the first call on the attention of any man should be a sense of duty and obligation to serve the state ["Ask not what your country can do for you . . ."]

(c) a feeling of the necessity to do social service work (especially educational work) among the working classes of English society.[19]

Following Arnold's early death in 1883, Toynbee Hall was established in London as a settlement house in his honor. His globalistic views (and those of Ruskin's) were passed down to our generation by his nephew, Arnold Joseph Toynbee (1889-1975), who "prophesied" in his book, *Surviving the Future* (published in 1971),

I expect that the World is going to be united politically in the teeth of nationalistic resistance. . . . The people of each local sovereign state will have to renounce their state's sovereignty and subordinate it to the paramount sovereignty of a literally world-wide world government. . . . **I want to see a world government established.**[20]

The movement's most influential disciple was another visionary named Cecil Rhodes (1853-1902). When Ruskin gave his inaugural lecture at Oxford, Rhodes copied the message in longhand and kept it with him for over thirty years. With financial aid from Lord Rothschild and Alfred Beit, Cecil was able to monopolize the diamond fields of South Africa under the name De Beers Consolidated Mines. The trust deed from this company granted extraordinary powers to acquire lands and rule them, thus extending the British Empire in the process. Rhodes repeated the process with the gold mines as Consolidated Gold Fields. In 1888, Cecil's agents secured mining concessions from Lobengula, King of the Ndebele, which by an exaggerated interpretation handed Rhodes a claim to what later became Rhodesia. The following year Albert Grey, the future Earl Grey and a member of the Toynbee-Milner group (1880-1884), helped Rhodes secure a royal charter for his British South Africa Company which, in 1890, put white settlers into Lobengula's territories, establishing Salisbury and numerous other towns in the process.

By the mid-1890s Rhodes had a personal income of at least a million pounds sterling per annum (then, about five million dollars). Aided by his personal war chest, Rhodes became the prime minister of Cape Colony (1890-1896). His power continued to grow as he contributed to various political parties and gained parliamentary seats in both England and South Africa. With Ruskin's manuscript at his breast, Rhodes committed his vast fortune to advancing the socialistic agenda of his Oxford mentor.

Rhodes was, first and foremost, an impassioned exponent of the coming New World Order. According to biographer Sara Millin, "The government of the world was Rhodes' simple desire."[21] Professor Quigley sets the foreboding scene:

> One wintry afternoon in February 1891, three men were engaged in earnest conversation in London. From that conversation were to flow consequences of the greatest importance to the British Empire and to the world as a whole. For these men were organizing a secret society that was, for more than fifty years, to be one of the most important forces in the formulation and execution of British imperial and foreign policy.[22]

The trio Quigley was referring to were Cecil Rhodes, the wealthiest and most powerful man in South Africa; William T. Stead, the best-known and probably most sensational journalist of his day; and Reginald Baliol Brett, later known as Lord Esher, friend and confidant of Queen Victoria, and later, the key adviser to King Edward VII and King George V.

Rhodes had been planning his secret society, known as the Group, for over sixteen years. In the autumn of 1890, he wrote his newspaper friend Stead:

> The key of my idea discussed with you is a Society, copied from the Jesuits [here we go again folks] as to organization . . . an idea which ultimately (leads) to the cessation of all wars and one language throughout the world. . . . The only thing feasible to carry this idea out is a secret one (society) gradually absorbing the wealth of the world to be devoted to such an object. . . . Fancy the charm to young America . . . to share in a scheme to take the government of the whole world![23]

PROFESSOR QUIGLEY

Professor Carrol Quigley, a giant in the academic community, made the *faux pas* of the century by letting the cat out of the bag concerning Rhodes and his network of conspirators. After writing *The Anglo-American Establishment* in 1949, he could not find a mainline publishing house for his manuscript. Quigley's volume was eventually accepted by *Books in Focus, Inc.* and published posthumously in 1981. Under the heading "Publisher's Note," Stephen A. Zarlenga wrote:

> On very rare occasions a book appears which forever changes the way in which we perceive the world around us. Within a short while it becomes hard to understand how we could have functioned without the knowledge gained from it. *The Anglo-American Establishment* is such a book. In it Professor Carroll Quigley presents certain "keys" crucial to the understanding of 20th century political, economic and military events—events of the past, present, and future. . . . The fact that Carroll Quigley, a highly respected professor at Georgetown University and an instructor at Princeton and Harvard, could not find a publisher for this work, is in itself significant.[24]

After some difficulty I was able to secure a used copy of *The Anglo-American Establishment* from a source in Australia; the cost was $100 USD!!

In 1965, Quigley did the unthinkable; he wrote *another* research work, this time candidly discussing the reality of a powerful international cabal! On page 950 of *Tragedy and Hope*, he acknowledged:

There does exist, and has existed for a generation, an international Anglophile network which operates, to some extent, in the way the radical Right believes the Communists act. In fact, this network, which we may identify as the Round Table Groups, has no aversion to cooperating with the Communists, or any other groups, and frequently does so. I know of the operations of this network because I have studied it for twenty years and was permitted for two years, in the early 1960s, to examine its papers and secret records. I have no aversion to it or most of its aims and have, for most of my life, been close to it and to many of its instruments. . . . [I]n general my chief difference of opinion is that it wishes to remain unknown, and I believe its role in history is significant enough to be known.[25]

Once again, the naive professor would pay a price for trying to force his ideological comrades out of their closets. As certain right-wing organizations became aware of Quigley's disclosures, an increased demand for *Tragedy and Hope* triggered a conspiracy of its own. In a personal letter dated December 9, 1975, Quigley replied to a reader:

Thank you for your praise of *Tragedy and Hope*, a book which has brought me headaches as it apparently says something which powerful people do not want known. My publisher stopped selling it in 1968 and told me he would reprint (but in 1971 he told my lawyer that they had destroyed the plates in 1968). The rare-book price went up to $135 and parts were reprinted in violation of copyright.[26]

In another personal letter expressing frustration with his publisher, Quigley wrote:

They lied to me for six years, telling me they would reprint when they got 2,000 orders, which could never happen because they told anyone who asked that it was out of print and would not be reprinted.

They denied this to me until I sent them Xerox copies of such replies in libraries, at which they told me it was a clerk's error. In other words, they lied to me but prevented me from regaining publication rights. . . . **I am now quite sure that *Tragedy and Hope* was suppressed.**[27]

Although a dupe himself, the professor remains the definitive source for a proverbial peek behind the curtain. In *The Anglo-American Establishment*, Quigley explained the Group's operational structure:

The plan of organization provided for an inner circle, to be known as "The Society of the Elect," and an outer circle, to be known as "The Association of Helpers." Within The Society of the Elect, the real power was to be exercised by the leader, and a "Junta of Three." The leader was to be Rhodes, and the Junta was to be Stead, Brett, and Alfred Milner. In accordance with this decision, Milner was added to the society by Stead shortly after the meeting we have described.[28]

There are thirty-three power brokers listed in *The Anglo-American Establishment* as belonging to "The Society of the Elect," or "The Inner Circle" of the Group. A few household names would include Nathan Rothschild—Baron Rothschild, Arthur James Balfour (Balfour Declaration of 1917), Waldorf Astor—Viscount Astor (Waldorf Astoria in New York City), Nancy Astor—Lady Astor, Sir Abe Bailey, Lionel Curtis, and Robert Henry Brand—Baron Brand, Leopold Amery, Geoffrey Dawson, and Sir Thomas Brassey—Lord Brassey, the wealthy naval enthusiast whose name is preserved in *Brassey's Naval Annual.*

Quigley then explains the need to differentiate between the "inner" and "outer" aspects of Rhodes's monster. (Remember how the Masons and the Illuminati do it?)

[There is] an inner core of intimate associates, who unquestionably knew that they were members of a group devoted to a common purpose; and an outer circle of a larger number on whom the inner circle acted by personal persuasion, patronage distribution, and social pressure. It is probable that most members of the outer circle were not conscious that they were being used by a secret society.[29]

There are seventy-two names listed under "The Association of Helpers." Some of the more powerful would be: Arnold Toynbee, William L Hichens, Edward Grigg (Baron Altrincham), James S. Metson (Baron Metson), Lord Robert Cecil (Viscount Cecil of Chelwood), Sir Reginald Coupland, Harry Vincent Hodson, Sir Alfred Zimmern, Sir James Arthur Salter, William G. A. Ormsby-Gore (Baron Harlech), John A. Simon (Viscount Simon), Samuel J. G. Hoare (Viscount Templewood), John W. Wheeler-Bennett, and the celebrated Edward Frederick Lindley Wood (First Earl of Halifax), better known as Lord Halifax.

For an insightful illustration as to how a secret society can pull the needed strings in government, consider the following passage from the *Journals and Letters of Reginald, Viscount Esher* (4 vols., London, 1938) under the date of November 21, 1892. Keep in mind that Quigley labeled

Reggie as "one of the most influential and one of the least-known men in British politics in the last two generations."[30]

> I went to London on Friday and called on Rhodes. He had asked me to do so. . . . Rhodes asked for the Government carriage of his telegraph poles and 200 Sikhs at Blantyre. Then he will make the telegraph. He would like a gunboat on Tanganyika. I stayed there to lunch. Then saw Rosebery. He was in good spirits.[31]

Clinton's "prof" then applies this "inner-outer core" principle to the intrigue of international finance.

> It must not be felt that these heads of the world's chief central banks [Alan Greenspan, etc.] were themselves substantive powers in world finance. They were not. Rather, they were the technicians and agents of the dominant investment bankers of their own countries, who had raised them up and were perfectly capable of throwing them down. The substantive financial powers of the world were in the hands of these investment bankers (also called "international" or "merchant" bankers) who remained largely behind the scenes in their own unincorporated private banks. These formed a system of international cooperation and national dominance which was more private, more powerful, and more secret than that of their agents in the central banks.[32]

THE REPATRIATION OF AMERICA

Rhodes mentioned his secret society in the first five of his seven wills, leaving no question as to the Group's ongoing sinister objectives. In his first will in 1877 (seven years into the R.V. project), composed after surviving a serious heart attack at age twenty-four, he wrote of his desire for,

> The extension of British rule throughout the world, the perfecting of a system of emigration from the United Kingdom and of colonization by British subjects of all lands wherein the means of livelihood are attainable by energy, labour and enterprise, . . . and **the ultimate recovery of the United States of America as an integral part of the British Empire**, the consolidation of the whole Empire, the inauguration of a system of Colonial Representation in the Imperial Parliament which may tend to weld together the disjointed members of the Empire, and finally the foundation of so

great a power as to hereafter render wars impossible and promote the best interests of humanity.[33]

Did you get that part about " the ultimate recovery of the United States of America as an integral part of the British Empire?" I wasn't aware that America was in need of being recovered—were you?

At this point the careful student will note that the invisible baton, passed from Germany's Adam Weishaupt to Italy's Guiseppe Mazzini, had now found its way into the hands of England's Cecil Rhodes. You say, "Dr. Grady, this is getting a little confusing to follow." Now you're getting the idea. (I Corinthians 14:33) Note the devil's familiar *modus operandi* for recruitment as contained in Cecil's "Confession of Faith," written in 1875. Remember, *"there is no new thing under the sun"* (Ecclesiastes 1:9b). Rhodes wanted:

> Men of ability and enthusiasm who find no suitable way to serve their country under the current political system; able youth recruited from the schools and universities; men of wealth with no aim in life; younger sons with high thoughts and great aspirations but without opportunity; rich men whose careers are blighted by some great disappointment. All must be men of ability and character. . . . a group of the ablest and the best, bound together by common unselfish ideals of service to . . . the greatest cause in the world. There is no mention of material rewards. This is to be a kind of religious brotherhood like the Jesuits, "a church for the extension of the British Empire."[34]

By the time we come to Rhodes's sixth and seventh wills, however, a significant change has occurred. The Group is no longer mentioned, with the attention being deflected to an educational institution that will award lucrative scholarships in order to propagate Rhodes's ideals. In 1894, Stead talked with Rhodes about how the academic arm would function and then wrote about their meeting after the latter's decease. Again, note the unmistakable Illuminati format:

> We also discussed together various projects for propaganda, the formation of libraries, the creation of lectureships, the dispatch of emissaries on missions of propaganda throughout the Empire, and the steps to be taken to pave the way for the foundation and the acquisition of a newspaper which was to be devoted to the cause.[35]

Dr. Adam Weishaupt
1748-1830

Graves of Adam Weishaupt and son in Gotha, Germany.
(*Courtesy Regional Museum of History and Folklore, Gotha*)

The Scottish Rite Temple (formerly the House of the Temple) of the Supreme Council (Southern Jurisdiction), located on 16th Street NW in Washington, D.C.
(Author's collection)

Embroidered silk flag taken to the moon aboard Apollo 11 by Mason-astronaut Edwin Eugene Aldrin.
(Author's collection)

ove: The *Law and Order* limestone relief on Constitution Avenue facade of the Department of Justice
ilding. This sculpture employs the movement of sunlight to convey an arcane message. Impaled
pent to extreme right is the last figure to emerge from the shadows as the sun moves southeast.
thor's collection)

ow: The twelve signs of the zodiac set in marble in the Great Hall of the Library of Congress.
thor's collection)

Missionaries John Birch and Oscar Wells
shortly after arrival in China, c. 1940.
*(Courtesy Heritage Collection,
Arlington Baptist College)*

General Claire Lee
Chennault pins Legion
of Merit on
Captain John Birch.
(U.S.A.F.)

Oscar, Myrtle and baby
Shannon back in America
following their release
from a Japanese prison camp.
*(Courtesy Heritage Collection,
Arlington Baptist College)*

中共同仁共同協力爭取了今日的勝利特留影紀念
"VICTORY THROUGH SINO AMERICAN COOPERATION"
Hsieh Wan, Anhwei, China, 17 August 1945

Above: Captain Birch on immediate left of Chinese officer two days after Japanese surrender and eight days before his murder by Communist cadre. (*Courtesy George C. Pappas*)

Right: Robert Birch at his brother's memorial, Warner Robins Air Force Base Museum, Warner Robins, Georgia. (*Author's collection*)

Below: ". . . killed by stray bullets." (*Courtesy George C. Pappas*)

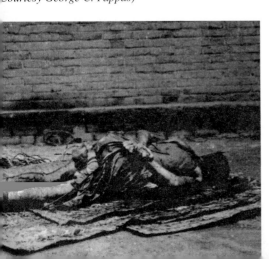

Flying Tigers/AVG triple ace Brigadier General David Lee "Tex" Hill, U.S.A.F (Ret.), displaying the Distinguished Service Cross he received over a half-century after destroying "at least" 18 Japanese aircraft.

Author interviewing AVG legend Brigadier General Robert L. Scott, U.S.A.F. (Ret.), described by General Chennault as a "one-man Air Force."

Above, left: Congressman Lawrence Patton McDonald, 1935-1983.
(Courtesy The Larry McDonald Memorial Foundation, Inc.)

Above, right: Mr. Tommy Toles, longtime friend and press secretary to the slain congressman. *(Author's collection)*

Left: Dr. McDonald's wife, Kathryn, and son, Trygvi, at Washington memorial service. *(Bettman/Corbis)*

Left: Floating debris from military aircraft recovered north of Moneron Island by Japanese Maritime Safety Agency within three days of KAL 007's disappearance. Item at top of photograph is a pilot's ejection seat, whose propulsive charges appear to have been fired, indicating ejection seat was used. *(Kimura)*

Below: Michel Brun, author of *Incident at Sakhalin,* exhibits a piece of titanium wing retrieved from the bottom of the Sea of Okhost by a Japanese fishing boat in 1990. Fragment i from a high-tech aircraft, possibly one of the casualties during the aerial battle of Sakhalin. *(Yoshida)*

As with Toynbee Hall, most middle class Americans have at least heard of the prestigious Rhodes Scholars. Unfortunately, the great majority of these nerds have repudiated our constitutional republic while laboring for world government. Therefore, to cover their tracks, Dr. Frank Aydelotte, the leading American authority on Rhodes's wills, claims that Rhodes made no reference to the secret society in his last two, having abandoned the idea. In the first chapter of his book, *The American Rhodes Scholarships,* Frank reiterates that between 1891 and 1893 Rhodes underwent a great change in his attitude and in his sixth will ". . . he abandons forever his youthful idea of a secret society."[36] (This ploy is almost as slick as the account of Adam Weishaupt's death bed renouncing of the Illuminati.)

Having studied the Group's private papers for two years, Professor Quigley rejected this smoke screen, writing:

[W]hen Rhodes talked with Stead, in January 1895, about the scholarships at Oxford, he did not abandon the society but continued to speak of it as the real power behind the scholarships. It is perfectly clear that Rhodes omitted mentioning the secret society in his last two wills because he knew that by that time he was so famous that the one way to keep a society from being secret would be to mention it in his will. [DUH!] Obviously, if Rhodes wanted the secret society after 1893, he would have made no mention of it in his will but would have left his money in trust for a legitimate public purpose [Rhodes Scholarships] and arranged for the creation of the secret society by a private understanding with his trustees. This is clearly what happened, because the secret society was established, and Milner used Rhodes's money to finance it, just as Rhodes had intended.[37]

As Frank Aydelotte was the first American secretary to the Rhodes Trustees, who ever heard of turning your back on the fox who was guarding the hen house? In his book on the history of Rhodes's wills, Stead wrote:

Mr. Rhodes was more than the founder of a dynasty. He aspired to be the creator of one of those vast semi-religious, quasi-political associations which, like the Society of Jesus [the Jesuits], have played so large a part in the history of the world. To be more strictly accurate, he wished to found an Order as the instrument of the will of the Dynasty, and while he lived he dreamed of being its Caesar and its Loyola. It was this far-reaching, world-wide aspiration of the man which rendered, to those who knew him, so absurdly inane the speculations of his critics as to his real motives.[38]

Then, sixty pages later, he stated:

> The question that now arises is whether in the English-speaking world there are to be found men of faith adequate to furnish forth materials for the Society of which Mr. Rhodes dreamed.[39]

In an 1891 letter to Stead concerning the prospect of a federal union with the United States, Rhodes confided, "The only feasible (way) to carry this idea out is a secret one (society) gradually absorbing the wealth of the world to be devoted to such an object."[40] Should there be any doubt that Dr. Aydelotte is nothing more than an urbane prevaricator, consider the postscript Stead attached at the end of the letter when he published it in 1902:

> Mr. Rhodes has never to my knowledge said a word nor has he ever written a syllable, that justifies the suggestion that he surrendered the aspirations which were expressed in this letter of 1891. So far from this being the case, in the long discussions which took place between us in the last years of his life, he reaffirmed as emphatically as at first his unshaken conviction as to the dream—if you like to call it so—a vision, which had ever been the guiding star of his life.[41]

THE JAMESON RAID

Cecil expired in Muizenburg, South Africa, on March 26, 1902, at the relatively young age of forty-eight. His health had been in steady decline after being caught in a four-month siege of the town of Kimberly at the outbreak of the Anglo-Boer War (1899-1902). No doubt the Dutch Afrikaners viewed this as poetic justice due to an earlier outrage perpetrated against them by Rhodes in 1895. Like all egotistical do-gooders, Rhodes believed that his views were so superior they should even, if necessary, be forced upon the ignorant masses. (Remember those Indian cartridges greased with animal fat?) Of course, they would eventually see the light.

Rhodes decided he would begin his roughshod evangelism in the South African Republic known as Transvaal by secretly instigating an armed rebellion by the mostly British "outlanders" (Uitlanders) against the legal residents known as Boers, or Afrikaners (descendants of the Dutch colonists who had made the first European settlements in the seventeenth century). *The fact that Rhodes was the prime minister of Cape Colony at the time did not seem to matter.* He intended to absorb the Transvaal into a British South African federation.

To make a long story short, the revolt blew up in Cecil's face. A "spontaneous" uprising by the outlanders in Johannesburg did not go off as scheduled. Meanwhile, nobody told Leander Starr Jameson (later Sir Starr), the fall guy who was supposed to save the day. On December 29, 1895, Rhodes's personal physician and closest friend came galloping into the Transvaal "on cue" at the head of 500 Rhodesian police to *liberate the downtrodden masses.* When Jameson determined that the "masses" preferred to take their chances with the Dutch president, Paul Kruger, over Rhodes and company, he surrendered to republican commandos near Krugersdorp on January 2, 1896. The fiasco has been known ever since as the Jameson Raid. Rhodes was forced to resign as prime minister in the aftermath.

ALFRED MILNER

As the end drew near, Rhodes made it known that Alfred Milner was his chosen successor. In 1898, he made the bellicose statement to Stead,

> You will support Milner in any measure that he may take short of war. I make no such limitation. I support Milner absolutely without reserve. If he says peace, I say peace; if he says war, I say war. Whatever happens, I say ditto to Milner.[42]

Rhodes felt a philosophical bond with the youthful Milner based on years of observation. Quigley writes:

> Both sought to unite the world, and above all the English-speaking world, in a federal structure around Britain. Both felt that this goal could best be achieved by a secret band of men united to one another by devotion to the common cause and by personal loyalty to one another. Both felt that this band should pursue its goal by secret political and economical influence behind the scenes and by the control of journalistic, educational, and propaganda agencies.[43]

Milner's strategy was to become the hub of three divergent spokes of influence: creed, cash and contacts. As previously noted, the "Toynbee group" provided his ideological foundation. Concerning the movement's need for funding, Quigley relates, "Milner was the only really active trustee and he controlled the bureaucracy which handled the [Rhodes] trust."[44] With regard to the adage, "It's not *what* you know, but *who* you know" (or, the generic equivalent, "Joe sent me"), Milner's consolidation of power would require perspicacity, patience and timing.

At the time of Rhodes's death, a nexus of political and social power known as the "Cecil Bloc" revolved around the person of Robert Arthur Talbot Gascoyne-Cecil, Viscount Cranborne and third Marquess of Salisbury (1830-1903). Lord Salisbury was one of the most influential men of his day. He was prime minister for fourteen years (between 1885 and 1902), a fellow of All Souls (from 1853), chancellor of Oxford University (1869-1903), and was a leading contributor to *The Quarterly Review*. Milner would later incorporate the methods perfected by the Cecil Bloc, which can be summarized under three headings:

> (a) a triple-front penetration in politics, education, and journalism; (b) the recruitment of men of ability (chiefly from All Souls) and the linking of these men to the Cecil Bloc by matrimonial alliances and by gratitude for titles and positions of power; and (c) the influencing of public policy by placing members of the Cecil Bloc in positions of power shielded as much as possible from public attention.[45]

If you think this sounds like a rehash of the Jesuits, Illuminati, Masons, and Skull and Bones—you're right! Remember, they are all working for the same arch-conspirator.

When Lord Salisbury died in 1903, his nephew, Arthur J. Balfour, attempted to guide the network, but lacked the requisite qualities of ambition and determination. Milner was able to fill this leadership vacuum and eventually absorbed a significant portion of the Cecil Bloc into his own clandestine empire.

Another man who brought Milner into contact with Britain's power brokers was George J. (later Lord) Goschen. He was both a member of Parliament and director of the Bank of England. In the space of three years (1880-1883) he declined the posts of viceroy of India, secretary of state for war and speaker of the House of Commons. Milner served as Goschen's private secretary for one year (1884-1885).

Lord Salisbury's third son (of five), Lord Robert Cecil (Viscount Cecil of Chelwood), became a productive member of the Group's Outer Circle. His posts included member of Parliament (1906-1923), parliamentary under secretary for foreign affairs (1915-1916), minister of blockade (1916-1918), Lord Privy Seal (1923-1924) and chancellor of the Duchy of Lancaster (1924-1927). He was also one of the original drafters of the Covenant of the League of Nations.

Rather than sort through a myriad of names and titles that came into the Milner orbit, consider the following foreboding analysis of Limbaugh "Kook" Carroll Quigley:

> No country that values its safety should allow what the Milner Group accomplished in Britain—that is, that a small number of men should be able to wield such power in administration and politics, should be given almost complete control over the publication of the documents relating to their actions, should be able to exercise such influence over the avenues of information that create public opinion, and should be able to monopolize so completely the writing and the teaching of the history of their own period.[46]

OXFORD UNIVERSITY

Through their money and political clout the Milner Group was able to gain control of several strategic centers of power. As The Order gleaned its patriarchs from Yale University, the Group did the same at Oxford, specifically All Souls, Balliol and New Colleges. Quigley described All Souls as "the most peculiar of Oxford Colleges." The reason for this is because the institution admits only postgraduate members who are generally not in pursuit of a higher degree. The roster is filled by twenty to thirty "fellows" who are paid out of the school's substantial endowment to study. There are also eleven fellowships without emolument to be held by the incumbents of various chairs at Oxford. Other "opportunities" include: ten Distinguished Persons fellowships without emolument, to be held for seven years by those who have distinguished themselves in law, humanities, science or public affairs; a varying number of research and teaching fellowships, for five to seven years with annual emoluments of £300-600; twelve seven-year fellowships with annual emoluments of £50 for past Fellows; and six fellowships to be held by incumbents of various college or university offices.[47]

In his biography, *Viscount Halifax*, A. C. Johnson mirrors the Skull and Bones mystic:

It is safe to assert that the Fellow of All Souls is a man marked out for a position of authority in public life, and there is no surprise if he reaches the summit of power, but only disappointment if he falls short of the opportunities that are set out before him.[48]

During Lord Salisbury's fourteen years as Prime Minister, he filled many positions throughout the empire with Fellows from All Souls. Quigley confirms,

In the twentieth century, the Milner Group has recruited from and influenced All Souls. . . . [I]t has also been important in contributing to the general direction and policy of the college. . . . [I]t is the chief, if not the controlling, influence in it, especially in recent years.[49]

From All Souls, Milner was able to infiltrate Balliol and New Colleges. Of the eighteen Fellows listed at Balliol for the first half of the twentieth century, nine were members of the Milner Group. Another eight Milner Fellows were listed at New College. Quigley writes,

It is clear from these lists that almost every important member of the Milner Group was a fellow of one of the three colleges—Balliol, New College, or All Souls. Indeed, these three formed a close relationship, the first two on the undergraduate level and the last in its own unique position. The three were largely dominated by the Milner Group, and they, in turn, largely dominated the intellectual life of Oxford in the fields of law, history, and public affairs. They came close to dominating the university itself in administrative matters. The relationships among the three can be demonstrated by the proportions of All Souls Fellows who came from these two colleges, in relation to the numbers which came from the other eighteen colleges at Oxford or from the outside world. Of the one hundred forty-nine Fellows at All Souls in the twentieth century, forty-eight came from Balliol and thirty from New College, in spite of the fact that Christ Church was larger than these and Trinity, Magdalen, Brasenose, St. John's, and University colleges were almost as large. Only thirty-two came from these other five large colleges, while at least fifteen were educated outside Oxford.[50]

These figures are similar to the disparity at Yale where fifteen Skull and Bones patriarchs outbid the other 1,000,000 annual graduates for high-profile positions in government and business. Practically all of the presidents of Oxford during the twentieth century were part of the Milner Group. Alfred himself was president in 1925!

The Milner power at Oxford also enabled them to gain control of the prestigious *Dictionary of National Biography* (displayed in any moderate-sized library). Henry W. C. Davis, a member of the Outer Circle, became the editor of the publication in 1921, continuing in that capacity until his death in 1928, when another Milner flunky, J. R. H. Weaver, took the helm. Quigley remarks, "This control of the *Dictionary of National Biography* will explain how the Milner Group controlled the writing of the biographies of its own members so completely in that valuable work."[51]

Following Milner's successful coup d'etat at Britain's most important university, the Rhodes Scholarships were established to provide $1,000 annually to qualified applicants. According to Cecil's will, such would exhibit "good literary attainments, a taste for outdoor sports and qualities of leadership from every self-governing British colony, the United States and Germany, so that they might appreciate the advantage of imperial unity and the union of the English-speaking world." (The reader will note that Adam Weishaupt's homeland was included in this Anglophilic consortium; Milner was also born in Germany.) Seen through "English eyes," Quigley relates, "Oxford tended to become an international university."[52]

After their arrival at Oxford, the aspiring scholars would imbibe a steady indoctrination of Milner's views: the development of the British Empire into an Imperial Federation, with an eventual absorption of the remaining countries into a league of nations. As these students were destined to become the leading authors, educators and statesmen of tomorrow, the Group's agenda was certain to be perpetuated.

THE TIMES

The next major target for Milner and company was *The Times* of London. The publication had been controlled by the Cecil Bloc since 1884. The Milner group was able to take over by 1912 through patient infiltration. The Group's linchpin for transition was George E. Buckle (1854-1935), a graduate of New College in 1876, member of All Souls since 1877, and editor of *The Times* from 1884 to 1912. Other Milner plants included

Leopold Amery, Lord Esher, Sir Edward Grigg, B. K. Long, William Monypeny, Geoffrey Dawson, and Basil Williams.

Milner's control was solidified when Lord Astor and his brother became the chief proprietors of *The Times* by buying out the Harmsworth interest in 1922.[53] Astor would become one of the most important figures in the Group after Milner's death. Flora Shaw was the head of the Colonial Department of *The Times* in 1890. She was also an impassioned disciple of Ruskin and Rhodes.

Quigley illustrates how *The Times* could be manipulated to fashion public opinion; in reference to the Boer War fiasco, he writes:

> It was *The Times* that published as an exclusive feature the famous (and fraudulent) 'Women and Children' letter, dated 20 December 1895, which pretended to be an appeal for help from the persecuted British in the Transvaal to Dr. Jameson's waiting forces, but which had really been concocted by Dr. Jameson himself on 20 November and sent to Miss Shaw a month later. This letter was published by *The Times* as soon as news of the Jameson Raid was known, as a justification of the act.[54]

Although *The Times* had a limited circulation (only about 35,000 at the beginning of the century; 50,000 at the outbreak of the First World War; and 187,000 in 1936), it was considered the most influential paper in England because of its exclusive readership. Quigley writes:

> This influence was not exercised by acting directly on public opinion, since the Milner Group never intended to influence events by acting through any instruments of mass propaganda, but rather hoped to work on the opinions of the small group of "important people," who in turn could influence wider and wider circles of persons. This was the basis on which the Milner Group itself was constructed.[55]

As with their acquisition of the *Dictionary of National Biography* through Oxford, the Group also gained control of the acclaimed *Encyclopedia Britannica* through *The Times*.[56]

ROUND TABLE GROUPS

With Oxford and *The Times* in tow, Milner set about to create the Group's fanciful Imperial Federation of English-speaking nations. He had already gained much experience while serving as governor general and high commissioner of South Africa from 1897 to 1905. (The union of South Africa was later achieved in 1910.) There, his network, known as "Milner's Kindergarten," worked at forming local groups of influential men to agitate for imperial federation while staying in touch with one another through personal correspondence and a quarterly periodical.

Milner formed his Round Table to reproduce the South African model throughout the British Empire. The majority of his henchmen stayed on board. Phillip Kerr was appointed secretary of the London circle while Lionel Curtis became the organizing secretary for the whole movement empire-wide. After London, the chief Round Table groups were formed in South Africa, Canada, New Zealand, Australia, India and the United States. Their motto was reminiscent of the Three Musketeers'—"The Government of Each by Each and All by All." Abe Bailey financed a quarterly journal called *The Round Table*.

The tenets of Milner's "New World Order" can be summed up in his own words spoken on the occasion of his 1905 exodus from South Africa:

> What I pray for hardest is, that those with whom I have worked in a great struggle and who may attach some weight to my words should remain faithful, faithful above all in the period of reaction, to the great idea of Imperial Unity. Shall we live to see its fulfillment? Whether we do or not, whether we succeed or fail, I shall always be steadfast in that faith, though I should prefer to work quietly and in the background, in the formation of opinion rather than in the exercise of power. . . .
>
> When we who call ourselves Imperialists talk of the British Empire, we think of a group of states, all independent in their local concerns, but all united for the defense of their own common interests and the development of a common civilization; united, not in an alliance—for alliances can be made and unmade, and are never more than nominally lasting—but in a permanent organic union. Of such a union the dominions as they exist today, are, we fully admit, only the raw material. Our ideal is still distant but we deny that it is either visionary or unattainable. . . .
>
> The road is long, the obstacles are many, the goal may not be reached in my lifetime—perhaps not in that of any man in this room. You cannot hasten the slow growth of a great idea like that by any forcing process. But what you can do is to keep it steadily in view, to lose no opportunity to work for it, to resist like grim death any policy which leads away from it.
>
> I know that the service of that idea requires the rarest combination of qualities, a combination of ceaseless effort with infinite patience. But then think on the other hand of the greatness of the reward; the immense privilege

of being allowed to contribute in any way to the fulfillment of one of the noblest conceptions which has ever dawned on the political imagination of mankind.[57]

Milner was correct in at least one prediction—that part about the goal not being reached. The locals throughout the Empire were not impressed with the fine print. In Asia and Africa, England's civilizing mission was to be carried out by force, if necessary, as "the function of force is to give moral ideas time to take root."[58] Note the blatant Hegelianism in some of Milner's other rantings.

> The end of the State is to make men, and its strength is measured not in terms of defensive armaments [gun-control] or economic prosperity [capitalism] but by the moral personality of its citizens [humanism]. . . . The function of the State is positive and ethical, to secure for its individual members that they shall not merely live but live well. . . . A life of satisfaction depends not on higher wages or lower prices or on leisure for recreation, but on work that calls into play the higher capacities of man's nature. . . .
>
> The cry of the masses should be not for wages or comforts or even liberty, but for opportunities for enterprise and responsibility. A policy for closer union in the Empire is full of significance in relation to this demand.[59]

Milner's grand Imperial Federation crashed and burned on the runway in the period from 1910 to 1917. He never could generate the needed backing at home or abroad. In his 1917 *Letter to the People of India,* Curtis wrote, "The people of the Dominions rightly aspire to control their own foreign affairs and yet retain their status as British citizens."[60]

According to Quigley, the main "sticking points" were: the varied character of the British imperial possessions; the backwardness of many of the native peoples involved; the independence of many of the white colonists overseas; and, the growing international tension which culminated in the First World War.[61] As usual, Africa was a total mess, the "Land of Kwanzaa" being in perpetual desiccation. Quigley writes:

> [A]gricultural practices were so deplorable that water shortages and erosion grew with frightening rapidity, and rivers which had flowed steadily in 1880 largely disappeared by 1950. As lands became too dry to farm, they were turned to grazing, especially under the spur of high wool prices during the two great wars, but the soil continued to drift away as dust. . . . The basic problem was lack of labor, not so much the lack of hands but the low level of productivity of those hands.[62]

Though citing Lionel Curtis elsewhere, "The task of preparing for freedom the races which cannot as yet govern themselves is the supreme duty of those who can,"[63] the politically correct professor tries to blame Africa's problems on "the color bar which refused to allow native labor to become skilled."[64]

The Biblical prophecy in Genesis 4:12 concerning Cain and his posterity is far more up-to-date, *"When thou tillest the ground, it shall not henceforth yield unto thee her strength; a fugitive and a vagabond shalt thou be in the earth."* (See the phrase "Negroes, black as Cain" from the poem, *On being brought from AFRICA to AMERICA*, by converted slave Phyllis Wheatley.)

As noted in chapter three, India's problem can also be understood in the light of Romans 1:22-25. Quigley unknowingly concurs, writing:

> The diversity of social groups and beliefs was naturally reflected in an extraordinarily wide range of social behavior from the most degraded and bestial activities based on crude superstitions to even more astounding levels of exalted spiritual self-sacrifice and cooperation. Although the British refrained from interfering with religious practices, in the course of the nineteenth century they abolished or greatly reduced the practice of thuggism (in which a secret caste strangled strangers in honor of the goddess Kali), suttee (in which the widow of a deceased Hindu was expected to destroy herself on his funeral pyre), infanticide, temple prostitution, and child marriages.
>
> At the other extreme, most Hindus abstained from all violence; many had such a respect for life that they would eat no meat, not even eggs, while a few carried this belief so far that they would not molest a cobra about to strike, a mosquito about to sting, or even walk about at night, lest they unknowingly step on an ant or worms. Hindus, who considered cows so sacred that the worse crime would be to cause the death of one (even by accident), who allowed millions of these beasts to have free run of the country to the great detriment of cleanliness or standards of living, who would not wear shoes of leather, and would rather die than taste beef, ate pork and associated daily with Muslims who ate beef but considered pigs to be polluting.
>
> In general, most Indians lived in abject poverty and want; only about one in a hundred could read in 1858, while considerably less could understand the English language.[65]

Milner and his reformers could have saved themselves a lot of trouble if they had paid attention to the words of John Adams concerning the

U.S. Constitution: "Our constitution was made only for a moral and religious people. It is wholly inadequate for the government of any other."[66]

After noting Milner's initial Skull and Bones dictum of "trust" as stated in his work *The Problems of a Commonwealth* (1916), ". . . if political power is granted to groups before they are fit they will tend to rise to the need,"[67] Quigley concludes that the Group wasn't that trusting after all: "To be sure, it [an Imperial Federation] was an undemocratic kind of socialism, which was willing to make many sacrifices to the well-being of the masses of people but reluctant to share with these masses political power that might allow them to seek their own well-being."[68]

Consequently, Milner was forced to drop back and punt. If the targeted nations could not be forced into a legal federation, then they would have to be held together by a common ideology until a more propitious season. Thus, the concept of an Imperial Federation slowly (and painfully) gave way to a Commonwealth of Nations.

One of the key players at this time was Lionel Curtis, described by a member of the Order as the *fons et origo* (source and origin). His writings, however, have the stench of a cesspool. Here we go again . . .

> States, whether autocracies or commonwealths, ultimately rest on duty, not on self-interest or force. . . . The quickening principle of a state is a sense of devotion, an adequate recognition somewhere in the minds of its subjects [sure, Lionel] that their own interests are subordinate to those of the state. The bond which unites them and constitutes them collectively as a state is, to use the words of Lincoln, in the nature of *dedication*. Its validity, like that of the marriage tie, is at root not contractual but sacramental. Its foundation is not self-interest, but rather some sense of obligation, however conceived, which is strong enough to over-master self-interest.[69]

Lionel's basic problem (like Ruskin, Rhodes, Milner and everyone else) was that he rejected what the Bible says about man's total depravity. Yet he knew how to *use* the Scriptures to add pathos to his secular humanism (see Isaiah 2:4 on the United Nations wall). Observe his views on the "new birth." Quigley writes:

> To Curtis, the Empire was to be absorbed into a world organization. This second idea was fundamentally mystical. Curtis believed: [Get this!] **"Die and ye shall be born again."** He sincerely felt that if the British Empire died in the proper way (by spreading liberty, brotherhood, and justice), it would be born again in a higher level of existence—as a world community, or, as he called it, a "Commonwealth of Nations." It is not yet

clear whether the resurrection envisaged by Curtis and his associates will occur, or whether they merely assisted at the crucifixion of the British Empire.[70]

Sadly, both Curtis and Quigley are aware by now that they should have paid more attention to the death, burial and resurrection of Jesus Christ. By trading his birthright for a bowl of pottage, Lionel received a measure of unquestionable power from his association with the Group. In 1916, he authored a book entitled *The Commonwealth of Nations* in which he specifically advocated that the name of His Majesty's Dominions should be changed from "British Empire" to "Commonwealth of Nations." This was officially done in 1948.

ARTHUR JAMES BALFOUR

From a Biblical perspective, the Group's machinations regarding Israel are of paramount concern. The name Arthur James Balfour, first Earl of Balfour and Viscount Traprain (1848-1930), was previously listed as one of the original thirty-three initiates comprising The Society of the Elect. The Milner-controlled *Dictionary of National Biography* devotes sixteen pages to the renowned philosopher-statesman.

Although Balfour was prime minister of Great Britain (1902-05), he is more readily known to history for a single policy statement given in 1917 during his tenure as foreign secretary. The reader will recall the monumental significance of the propitious *Balfour Declaration*, originally issued in the form of a letter to Zionist leader, Nathan Rothschild (another original initiate of the Group), advocating "the establishment in Palestine of a national home for the Jewish people."

Thus, we are confronted by a disconcerting paradox, given the stated thesis of this book in relation to Genesis 12:3. Why would the world's leading conspirators befriend God's covenant people? A superficial analysis could easily conclude that Baron Rothschild was a "double agent" working for Jehovah.

Professor Quigley reconciles the apparent contradiction by revealing the Group's hidden agenda for a Jewish presence in Palestine. He begins by identifying Milner as the real author of the paper.

This declaration, which is always known as the Balfour Declaration, should rather be called "The Milner Declaration," since Milner was the actual draftsman and was, apparently, its chief supporter in the War Cabinet. This fact was not made public until 21 July 1937. At that time Ormsby-Gore, speaking for the government in Commons, said, "The draft as originally put up by Lord Balfour was not the final draft approved by the War Cabinet. The particular draft assented to by the War Cabinet and afterwards by the Allied Governments and by the United States . . . and finally embodied in the Mandate, happens to have been drafted by Lord Milner. The actual final draft had to be issued in the name of the Foreign Secretary, but the actual draftsman was Lord Milner." Milner had referred to this fact in a typically indirect and modest fashion in the House of Lords on 27 June 1923, when he said, "I was a party to the Balfour Declaration." [71]

The Bible states, *"For God is not the author of confusion . . ."* (I Corinthians 14:33a). Quigley opines accordingly, "Probably no document of the wartime period, except Wilson's Fourteen Points has given rise to more disputes than this brief statement of less than eleven lines." [72] In chapter two it was pointed out that the phrase "*the* national homeland" was altered to "*a* national homeland" in the final draft of the text. Quigley elaborates:

> It is to be noted that this was neither an agreement nor a promise but merely a unilateral declaration, that it did not promise a Jewish state in Palestine or even Palestine as a home for the Jews, but merely proposed such a home *in* Palestine, and that it reserved certain rights for the existing groups in the area. [73]

While British Jewery interpreted the Balfour Declaration as a mandate for statehood, Milner concealed his private interpretation behind a cloak of ambiguity. In a speech to the House of Lords on June 27, 1923, he acknowledged that the real purpose for importing Jews into Palestine was motivated by "filthy lucre." (I Timothy 6:10)

> I am not speaking of the policy which is advocated by the extreme Zionists, which is a totally different thing. . . . I believe that we have only to go on steadily with the policy of the Balfour Declaration **as we have ourselves interpreted it in order to see great material progress in Palestine . . .** [74]

Milner's vision of a British-based commonwealth of nations would have to include a league of Arab states beholden to the Group.

I believe in the independence of the Arab countries, which they owe to us and they can only maintain with our help. I look forward to an Arab Federation.[75]

The problem with Milner's plan was the politically incorrect reality that the Arab population, as a whole, was characterized by rank indolence. At least this was the firsthand observation of Colonel Richard Meinertzhagen, author of *Middle East Diary*, a detailed chronicle of the inner workings of English, Arabic, Jewish, and Vatican politics from the time of the Balfour Declaration to the War of Independence. (Colonel Meinertzhagen was originally transferred to Egypt in 1912 to take charge of General Allenby's intelligence service.) He wrote:

> A prosperous Israel would strengthen the British Empire in the Middle East. . . . The Jews are virile and brave, determined and intelligent. The Arabs are decadent, stupid, dishonest, and have produced little beyond eccentricities, influenced by the romance and silence of the desert. The Arab is a poor fighter, although adept at looting, sabotage, and assassinations.[76]

Little has changed in nearly a century. Apart from oil (a raw material), the Middle East exports virtually nothing else of significance to the global economy. The value of U.S. imports of goods manufactured in Hong Kong alone is twice that of imports from the entire Arab league! In 2004 the Middle East accounted for a "whopping" three percent of world-wide exports.

The Group believed that a proportioned influx of Jewish initiative and business acumen would invigorate Palestine, thereby offering the Arab world an appealing "front door" to western ideas. John Dove, editor of *The Round Table,* wrote:

> If the Arab belongs to the Mediterranean, as T.E. Lawrence insists, we should do nothing to stop him getting back to it. Why our own nostrum for the ills of mankind everywhere is Western Civilization, and, if it is a sound one, what would be the good of forcing a people who want direct contact with us to slink in and out of their country by a back door which, like the Persian Gulf, opens only on the East? It would certainly check development, if it did not actually warp it.[77]

Dove viewed the industrious Jew as the economic savior of the land:

> Personally, I don't see the slightest harm in Jews coming to Palestine under **reasonable conditions**. They are the Arabs' cousins as much as the

Phoenicians, **and if Zionism brings capital and labour which will enable industries to start, it will add to the strength of the larger unit which some day is going to include Palestine.** But they must be content to be part of such a potential unit. They need have no fear of absorption, for they have everything to gain from an Arab Federation. It would mean a far larger field for their activities.[78]

Milner echoed these sentiments in his speech before the House of Lords:

There is plenty of room in that country for a considerable immigrant population without injuring in any way the resident Arab population, and, indeed, **in many ways it would tend to their extreme benefit.**[79]

This pecuniary policy is described in the world's only inspired "history" book, Daniel having prophesied in 534 B.C. that the coming Antichrist would *"divide the land for gain"* (Daniel 11:39b).

However, though the Jew would be used to stabilize the region, independence was entirely out of the question. Quigley notes:

He [Milner] then went on to say that he felt that Palestine would require a **permanent mandate** and under that condition could become a National Home for the Jews, could take as many Jewish immigrants as the country could economically support, but **"must never become a Jewish state."** [80]

According to Quigley, Milner's grand scheme failed because of four reasons: the obstructionism of the Arabs; the intention of the Zionists to have political control of their National Home, if they got one; the pressure on Jew and Arab alike following the world depression of 1929; and the need for a refuge for European Jews after 1933.[81]

By 1937, the Group was ready to throw in the towel. Consequently, Sir Reginald Coupland (a member of Milner's inner circle since 1914) prepared a scholarly study for the Peel Commission, rehearsing the deplorable conditions in Palestine. Quigley writes:

For the first time in any government document, the aspirations of Jews and Arabs in Palestine were declared to be irreconcilable and the existing mandate unworkable. Accordingly, the report recommended the partition of Palestine into a Jewish state, an Arab state, and a neutral enclave containing the Holy Places. This suggestion was accepted by the British government in a White Paper (Cmd. 5513) issued through Ormsby-Gore. [William G. A. Ormsby-

Gore, Baron Harlech, a member of the Outer Circle in The Association of Helpers.][82]

To implement the policy of partition, the government appointed a new commission of four members in March 1938. Known as the Woodhead Commission, the body contained no members from either the Milner Group or the Cecil Bloc. Because the proposal represented a "Catch-22" to Arab pride (i.e., a divided economy would permit the cream to rise to the top), mounting pressure led the politicians to reject the measure as "impractical on the grounds that any acceptable method of partition into two states would give a Jewish state with an annual financial surplus and an Arab state with an annual financial deficit."[83]

This conclusion was accepted by the government in another White Paper (Cmd 5983 of 1938). An alternative proposal called for a Round Table conference of Jews and Arabs in Palestine, including representatives from Arab states outside of Palestine. True to his nature, "Ishmael" went ballistic with bloody rioting quickly escalating to open civil war. (Genesis 16:12) The Arab delegation included leaders who had to be released from prison in order to attend; and *then* they refused to be seated if Jews were allowed to participate.

After the conference disintegrated, the government issued a new statement of policy (Cmd 6019 of May 1939). The Christian nation that produced the King James Bible would now join forces with Islam against the seed of Abraham! Quigley notes:

It was a drastic reversal of previous statements and was obviously a turn in favor of the Arabs. It fixed Jewish immigration into Palestine at 75,000 for the whole of the next five years (including illegal immigration) and gave the Arabs a veto on any Jewish immigration after the five-year period was finished. As a matter of principle, it shifted the basis for Jewish immigration from the older criterion of the economic absorptive capacity of Palestine to the political absorptive capacity. This was really an invitation to the Arabs to intensify their agitation and constituted a vital blow at the Jews, since it was generally conceded that Jewish immigration increased the economic absorptive capacity for both Jews and Arabs.[84]

With their natural route of escape blocked by this cowardly pro-Arab embargo of humanity, 6,000,000 European Jews would be consigned to Hitler's ovens. And yet, the ensuing international outcry over the Holocaust became the very catalyst that led to Jewish statehood in

May 1948. As the Scripture says, *"Surely the wrath of man shall praise thee . . ."* (Psalm 76:10a).

ROYAL INSTITUTE OF INTERNATIONAL AFFAIRS

Curtis was also commissioned to establish the Group's most powerful network of all—the Royal Institute of International Affairs. When the United States Congress rejected President Wilson's fourteen-point League of Nations peace proposal, Milner and Curtis rightly concluded that America would not abandon her sovereignty unless something was done to create a different "climate of opinion." The new organization was to be a visible arm of the covert Round Table groups. Quigley writes:

> At the end of the war of 1914, it became clear that the organization of this system [Round Table Groups] had to be greatly extended. Once again the task was entrusted to Lionel Curtis who established, in England and each dominion, a front organization to the existing local Round Table Group. This front organization, called the Royal Institute of International Affairs, had as its nucleus in each area the submerged Round Table Group.[85]

In 1923, Curtis so intrigued Canadian Colonel R. W. Leonard with his vision that he purchased Lord Kinnard's house at 10 St. James Square and donated it to the Institute. Since William Pitt (Earl of Chatham) had once lived in the building, "Chatham House" became the name for the Institute's formal headquarters. (The designation "Chatham House" has generally been applied to the Institute as well.)

With their varied propaganda devices in place, the Group became a powerful conspiracy indeed. Quigley summarizes how the various parts interacted to impact life in Great Britain. (Are you listening, Rush?)

> *The Times* was influential, but the degree of its influence would never be realized by anyone who examined only the paper itself. The greater part of its influence arose from its position as one of several branches of a single group, the Milner Group. By the interaction of these various branches on one another, under the pretense that each branch was an autonomous power, the influence of each branch was increased through a process of mutual reinforcement. The unanimity among the various branches was believed by the outside world to be the result of the influence of a single Truth, while really it was the result of the existence of a single group.

Thus, a statesman (a member of the Group) announces a policy. About the same time, the Royal Institute of International Affairs publishes a study on the subject, and an Oxford don, a Fellow from All Souls (and a member of the Group) also publishes a volume on the subject (probably through a publishing house, like G. Bell and Sons or Faber and Faber, allied to the Group).

The statesman's policy is subjected to critical analysis and final approval in a "leader" in *The Times*, while the two books are reviewed (in a single review) in *The Times Literary Supplement*. Both the "leader" and the review are anonymous but are written by members of the Group. And finally, at about the same time, an anonymous article in *The Round Table* strongly advocates the same policy.

The cumulative effect of such tactics as this, even if each tactical move influences only a small number of important people, is bound to be great . . . [and] an analogous procedure in reverse could be used for policies or books which the Group did not approve.[86]

COUNCIL ON FOREIGN RELATIONS

Now, here is where Milner's British-based conspiracy really hits home. You know those Round Table extensions around the English-speaking world? Do you recall Rhodes's original goal for the "ultimate recovery of the United States as an integral part of the British Empire?" During the Institute's formative meeting at a dinner party held at the Majestic Hotel in Paris on May 30, 1919, it was resolved that the new front organization would have *two* central branches—one in Great Britain and the other in the United States. Professor Carroll Quigley confirms, "In New York it was known as the Council on Foreign Relations, and was a front for J. P. Morgan and Company in association with the very small American Round Table Group."[87]

Headquartered in the elegant Pratt House (donated by the Rockefeller family) at 58 East 68th Street in New York City, the CFR was incorporated in 1921 and released the following statement of purpose a year later:

The Council on Foreign Relations aims to provide a continuous conference on the international aspects of America's political, economic and financial problems. . . . It is *simply* a group of men concerned in spreading a knowledge of international relations, and, in particular, *in developing a reasoned American foreign policy.*[88]

Former FBI agent Dan Smoot cut through this elitist jargon by declaring:

> The purpose of the Council on Foreign Relations was to create (and condition the American people to accept) what House [Mandell House, corrupt advisor to President Wilson] called a "positive" foreign policy for America—to replace the traditional "negative" foreign policy which had kept America out of the endless turmoil of old-world politics and had permitted the American people to develop their great nation in freedom and independence from the rest of the world.[89]

Many others have agreed with Smoot's appraisal. Arthur Schlessinger, Jr., described the CFR as a "front organization" for the "heart of the American Establishment."[90] In his work, *The Best and the Brightest,* David Halberstam labeled it, "the Establishment's unofficial club."[91] Yet, the CFR is rarely assailed by investigative reporters as its ranks include top executives from *The New York Times,* the *Washington Post,* the *Los Angeles Times,* the Knight newspaper chain, NBC, CBS, *Time, Life, Fortune, Business Week, U.S. News and World Report* and numerous others [171 organizations and associations according to John F. McManus].[92]

The cardinal doctrine espoused by CFR devotees is the pressing need for a one world government. (Sound familiar?) Although the Council claims to be pluralistic, even the liberal *New York Times* conceded that the organization has a "uniform direction."[93] This predominant focus on globalism can be easily seen by examining the back issues of their official publication, *Foreign Affairs,* called by *Time* magazine, "the most influential periodical in print."[94] An article in just their second issue in December 1922, declared:

> Obviously there is going to be no peace or prosperity for mankind so long as it remains divided into fifty or sixty independent states . . . Equally obviously there is going to be no steady progress in civilization or self-government among the more backward peoples until some kind of international system is created which will put an end to the diplomatic struggles incident to the attempt of every nation to make itself secure . . . The real problem today is that of world government.[95]

A 1944 CFR publication, *American Public Opinion and Postwar Security Commitments,* acknowledged that the traditional American in "Mayberry RFD" was still opposed to a globalistic society:

> The sovereignty fetish is still so strong in the public mind, that there would appear to be little chance of winning popular assent to American membership in anything approaching a super-state organization. Much will depend on the kind of approach which is used in further popular education.[96]

In 1959, the Council issued a position paper entitled *Study No. 7, Basic Aims of U.S. Foreign Policy* "proposing" that the United States "build a new international order." The recommended steps were as follows:

1. Search for an international order in which the freedom of nations is recognized as interdependent and in which many policies are jointly undertaken by free world states with differing political, economic, and social systems, and including states labeling themselves as "socialist."
2. Safeguard U.S. security through preserving a system of bilateral agreements and regional arrangements.
3. Maintain and gradually increase the authority of the U.N.
4. Make more effective use of the International Court of Justice, jurisdiction of which should be increased by withdrawal of reservations by member nations on matters judged to be domestic.[97]

However, the most dangerous aspect of the CFR is that it furnishes the personnel for most of the upper echelon positions within the United States government. Pulitzer Prize recipient Theodore White wrote that the Council's "roster of members has for a generation, under Republican and Democratic administrations alike, been the chief recruiting ground for cabinet-level officials in Washington."[98] *All six of Isaacson's "wise men" were members.* Dozens of other Bonesmen have joined as well.

Calling the Council a "school for statesmen," Joseph Craft parallels White's statement in a July 1958 *Harpers Bazaar* article, "It has been the seat of . . . basic government decisions, has set the context for many more, and has repeatedly served as a recruiting ground for ranking officials."[99]

Isaacson and Thomas said that Dean Acheson (Scroll and Key) was "more responsible for Truman Doctrine than President Truman and more responsible for the Marshall Plan than General Marshall."[100] David Halberstam concludes sardonically, "They walk in one door as acquisitive businessmen and come out the other door as statesmen-figures."[101]

In 1971, a rare article about the CFR appeared in the November 21 edition of *Time* magazine. Written by Anthony Lukas, it acknowledged:

> Everyone knows how fraternity brothers can help other brothers climb the ladder of life. If you want to make foreign policy, there's no better fraternity to belong to than the Council.
>
> When Henry Stimson—the group's quintessential member [Skull and Bones, 88]—went to Washington in 1940 as Secretary of War, he took with him John McCloy ["Harvard men work for Yale men"], who was to become Assistant Secretary in charge of personnel. McCloy has recalled: "Whenever we needed a man we thumbed through the roll of the Council members and put through a call to New York."
>
> And over the years, the men McCloy called in turn called other Council members.[102]

Literally hundreds of elected and appointed government officials have been "recruited" from the 3,000-plus membership roll of the Council on Foreign Relations. Former John F. Kennedy aide Arthur Schlesinger, Jr., pretty well summed things up by saying:

> The New York financial and legal community was the heart of the American Establishment. Its household deities were Henry L. Stimson [Skull and Bones, '88] and Elihu Root [Whitney's attorney]; its present leaders, Robert A. Lovett [Skull and Bones, '18] and John J. McCloy; its front organizations, the Rockefeller, Ford and Carnegie Foundations [infiltrated by The Order] and the Council on Foreign Relations [initiated by the Group].[103]

RHODES SCHOLARS

In addition to these various Round Table organizations, Milner determined to alter America's "climate of opinion" through an army of elitist intellectuals known as *Rhodes Scholars*. Cecil's will had directed that his Trust underwrite the prestigious Rhodes Scholarships so as to perpetuate the English ruling class tradition throughout the world. Adam Weishaupt's "commitment to education" would henceforth be honored at Oxford like it has been at Yale. Professor Quigley wrote in *The Anglo-American Establishment,* "The (Rhodes) Scholarships were merely a facade to conceal the secret society, or, more accurately, they were to be one of the instruments by which members of the secret society could carry out Rhodes' purpose."[104] Sir Francis Wiley, first Oxford secretary to the Rhodes Trust, revealed in an article in the January 1945 edition of *The American Oxonian* that a Rhodes Scholarship "is not an educational endowment as ordinarily understood . . . but to encourage in the rising generation of English-speaking people a particular outlook on the problems of the world—to give them, in fact, a political bias."[105]

Dr. Dennis Cuddy provides a penetrating analysis in his volume, *Secret Records Revealed:*

> The Group's basic objective was to penetrate and control the areas of politics, economics, education, and journalism [exactly like The Order]. And a key criterion for anyone being accepted for participation in their plan was that the individual (e.g., Rhodes Scholar) must believe that the first duty of any man is to serve society and the State.
>
> The way the idea would work would be that after three or four decades, enough individuals would be in positions of influence so that a conspiracy would no longer be necessary. Rather, these individuals with a one-world elitist outlook would simply open doors to positions of prominence for other like-minded globalists, who in turn would do likewise for others. It would operate like the old political adage that "personnel is policy." [106]

Consider this incredible piece. In *Cowboys Into Gentlemen: Rhodes Scholars, Oxford, and the Creation of an American Elite* (1998), authors Thomas and Kathleen Schaeper write:

> [Frank] Aydelotte (American Secretary to the Rhodes Trustees) also became known as a sort of "king maker" of college presidents. He believed that the best way to promote academic excellence was to appoint Rhodes Scholars to every vacancy for college presidencies or deanships. Whenever he heard that a university was seeking a new executive or dean, he worked his private networks to ensure that Rhodes Scholars received serious consideration. Though no selection committee would ever admit it, it was widely believed that dozens of college presidents and deans owed their new jobs to his cloakroom lobbying.[107]

For the record, Walter Isaacson, co-author of *The Wise Men* with Evan Thomas, is both a Rhodes Scholar *and* a member of the CFR. Isaacson, like numerous other Rhodes Scholars, is continuing to fulfill the will of Adam Weishaupt with regard to societal mind control. In the July 22, 1951, edition of the *Chicago Tribune*, staff writer William Fulton noted:

> [T]he American Rhodes Scholars network in the United States—is completed and glued together by their numbers in the field of molding public opinion. ... Rhodes Scholars in the public opinion field constitute a faithful clique for their colleagues in the government, primarily in the State Department which they dominate. ... With this tie-in, they're attempting to bring about the fulfillment of the lifelong ambitions held by their educational benefactor, Cecil John Rhodes.[108]

Like the gold pin on a Bonesman's lapel, the power of a Rhodes scholarship is a ticket to the top, in *any* area of professional endeavor. The Schaepers write:

> Nearly every field in the world of business has, at one time or another, had a Rhodes Scholar at or near its pinnacle. ... The huge investment banking firm of Goldman Sachs has included dozens of [Rhodes] scholars over the past half century, but never as many as in the 1990s, when at any given moment at least a half dozen have been partners. ... Many [Rhodes] scholars agree that there is one area in which a strong Oxford network does ... operate: government.[109]

Do you think Mr. Rhodes got a decent return on his investment? Should Rush find a different day job? Another article in the *Chicago Tribune* that month stated:

> Today many American Rhodes scholars are working assiduously to make the dream of their imperial patron come true. ... More than a third of the 1,185 living American scholars are in the educational field. ... Rhodes scholars also command posts in the United Nations and economic cooperation administration. The returning savants are active in the field of opinion molding with a large sprinkling among the eastern internationalist press, magazines, and radio.[110]

The following survey of these opinion-molding "savants" will serve as a fitting conclusion to our chapter and hopefully enhance your *"understanding of the times . . . for such a time as this."*

Bernadette Schmitt was a Rhodes Scholar in 1905 and went on to be president of the American Historical Association. (Do you recall who founded the AHA?) That same year, A. E. Rollins was awarded a scholarship and became the managing editor for *Compton's Encyclopedia*, while Frank Aydelotte was made a trustee of the Carnegie Foundation. After receiving his scholarship in 1906, Arthur Chenoweth became president of the Miss America Pageant. Edwin Hubble was a Rhodes

Scholar in 1910. He helped convince Albert Einstein in 1931 that a "big bang" made more sense than Genesis 1:1. NASA even named a telescope after the reprobate. Brand Blanshard, a major signer of the *Humanist Manifesto*, received his scholarship in 1913. Henry Allen Moe was a Rhodes Scholar in 1919 and later became president of the renowned Guggenheim Foundation. Stanley Hornbeck, a 1920 recipient, became a special consultant to Skull and Bones Secretary of War Henry Stimson. He later acknowledged under oath that he knew about the subversive connections of Soviet spy Alger Hiss for seven years without telling anyone. John M. Harlan was another 1920 Rhodes Scholar who eventually became a U.S. Supreme Court justice (1955-1971). Joseph Brandt, a 1921 Scholar, took over the presses of Princeton University and the University of Chicago, later becoming president of Henry Holt and Company publishers. Charles Saltzman, a Rhodes Scholar in 1925, became vice president of the New York Stock Exchange. John K. Fairbanks, a recipient in 1929, became another Rhodes Scholar to be appointed president of the American Historical Association. The liberal, John M. Templeton, was a Rhodes Scholar in 1934 and went on to establish the satanic Templeton Prize for Progress in Religion.

Rhodes Scholars in the field of higher education are legion. A smattering would include: CFR member Neil Rudenstine (R.S., 1956) became president of Harvard University; James Hester (R.S., 1947), president of New York University; O. C. Carmichael (R.S., 1913), chancellor, Vanderbilt University; Robert Porter (R.S., 1947), dean, Yale University; Robert Marston (R.S., 1947), president, University of Florida; Frederick Houde (R.S., 1929), president, Purdue University; David Frohnmayer (R.S., 1962), president, University of Oregon; Jon Wrestling (R.S., 1964), executive vice president and provost, Boston University; John Wilson (R.S., 1953), president, Washington and Lee University; Guido Calabresi (R.S., 1953) dean, Yale Law School; Lee Badgett (R.S., 1961), provost and dean of faculty, Virginia Military Institute; Howard Burnett (R.S., 1952), president, Washington and Jefferson College; Jane Stromseth (R.S., 1978), associate professor, Georgetown University Law Center; Thomas Bartlett (R.S., 1951), president, Colgate University; Michael Cannon (R.S., 1973), vice chancellor, Washington University; Kermit Gordon (R.S., 1938), president, Brookings Institution; Dr. Robert Ebert (R.S., 1936), dean, Harvard University Medical School; Bernard Rodgers (R.S., 1947), commandant, U.S. Military Academy; Stevens Muller (R.S., 1949), president emeritus,

Johns Hopkins University; Wesley Posvar (R.S., 1948), president emeritus, University of Pittsburgh; Edgar Shannon, Jr. (R.S., 1947), president emeritus, University of Virginia; Thomas Mendenhall (R.S., 1933), president emeritus, Smith College; R.W. MacVicar (R.S., 1939), president emeritus, Oregon State University; Leigh Gerdine (R.S., 1938), president emeritus, Webster University; and John Nason (R.S., 1928), president emeritus, Carleton College.

Richard Goodwin became a Rhodes Scholar in 1934 and later taught economics at Harvard University. However, Goodwin was denied tenure after fellow Rhodes Scholar Daniel Boorstin gave testimony before the U.S. House of Un-American Activities Committee that Rich was a Communist. Crane Brinton, a Rhodes Scholar in 1919, became Carroll Quigley's tutor at Harvard. He would be yet another Group/Order editor of the American Historical Association.

Other areas of the educational field were penetrated as well. Phillip Kaiser (R.S., 1936) served as chairman of *Encyclopedia Britannica International LTD* from 1969 to 1975. Daniel Boorstin (R.S., 1934) became the Librarian of Congress, later passing the baton to CFR member James Billington (R.S., 1950). In his comical book *Fire In the Minds of Men*, Jim wrote, "What is new is the belief that a perfect secular order will emerge from the forcible overthrow of traditional authority."

A number of Rhodes's eggheads went on to promote their coming New World Order (or, *"Novus Ordo Seclorum"*). Robert Lee Humber (R.S., 1918) declared in his book, *The Declaration of the Federation of the World*, ". . . all peoples of the earth should now be united in a commonwealth of nations." (Have we heard *that* buzz word before?) Harland Cleveland (R.S., 1938, and CFR affiliate) became a board member of the World Future Society. Amos Jordan (R.S., 1947) and CFR "Wiseman" Paul Nitze contributed to William Frye's *A United Nations Police Force,* published in 1957 under the auspices of the Carnegie Endowment for International Peace. Robert Lee Humber (R.S., 1947) became another early vice-president of the United World Federalists. Stringfellow Barr (R.S., 1917) co-authored the 1948 *Preliminary Draft of a World Constitution.* Other "Fantasy Island" publications included: *Federation: The Coming World Structure of Government*, released in 1944, by William Maddox (R.S., 1922); *The World Must Be Governed* in 1949, by Vernon Nash (R.S., 1916); *The Ugly American* in 1959, by Eugene Burdeck, (R.S., 1948); and *America's Unwritten Constitution* in 1983, by Donald R. Price (R.S., 1954).

The United States in the World Aren, by Walt Rostow (R.S., 1936) was published in 1960. The CFR pinko wrote:

> It is a legitimate American national objective to see removed from all nations—including the United States—the right to use substantial military force to pursue their own interest. Since this residual right is the root of national sovereignty and the basis for the existence of an international arena of power, it is, therefore, an American interest to see an end to nationhood as it has been historically defined.[111]

International Government by Clyde Eagleton (R.S., 1914) was published in 1932. In the 1948 second edition, Clyde added:

> I am concerned with . . . the slowly evolving constitutional law and organization of the community of nations, developing toward international, or world, government. . . . The following arguments have been offered in favor of regionalism: (1) Development should be attempted gradually, rather than in one jump toward world government. Such a world system could be better built upon the solid foundation of regional systems. . . .[112]

As Professor Cuddy has already provided over two hundred pages of testimony from Rhodes's scholars and their confederates, I will relate only two others. In July 1948, *Foreign Affairs* published "A New World Takes Shape," by Sir Harold Butler (the Group), in which he asked:

> How far can the life of nations, which for centuries have thought of themselves as distinct and unique, be merged with the life of other nations? How far are they prepared to sacrifice a part of their sovereignty without which there can be no effective economic or political union? . . . Out of the prevailing confusion a new world is taking shape . . . which may point the way toward the new order.[113]

Then, we have *The New World Order,* by Samuel Zane Batten, issued in 1919 by, of all sources, the American Baptist Publication Society! With over 30 million casualties sustained during the previous five years, unwitting Baptist contributors enabled Sam to share his personal hallucinations accordingly:

> The old order passes from view; the new world rises upon our vision. . . . We have vindicated the right of social control. . . . There must be developed a national spirit of service. . . . Society must break the stranglehold of capitalism. . . . The natural resources of the nation must be socialized. . . . The

state must socialize every group. . . . Men must learn to have world patriotism. World patriotism must be a faith. . . . There is no more justice for the claim of absolute sovereignty on the part of a nation than on the part of an individual. . . . The only alternative is *World Federation* . . . with a world parliament, an international court, and an international police force. . . . Men must have an international mind before there can be a world federation. They must see and affirm that above the nation is humanity. Internationalism must first be a religion before it can be a reality and a system.[114]

To facilitate the propagation of this "gospel of globalism," dozens of Rhodes Scholars in the media have been keeping the American public hopelessly in the dark. James Fallows (R.S., 1970) became the editor of *US News and World Report.* Edward Pelz (R.S., 1939) was made an executive with *The New York Times.* Also employed by the *Times* were Douglas Jehl (R.S., 1984) and Donald Bruckner (R.S., 1955). Jason McManus (R.S., 1958) became editor-in-chief of *Time Warner, Inc.* While Russ Hamachek (R.S., 1964) was appointed vice president of planning for The Washington Post Co., Boisefeuillet Jones, Jr. (R.S., 1968) became vice president of planning for *The Washington Post*, with Barton Gellman (R.S., 1982) joining the same as a columnist. The nation's "smaller" newspapers were similarly infected.

A string of corrupt politicians rounded things off by telling the people whatever they wanted to hear. The gamut has run from U.S. Supreme Court Justice David Souter (R.S., 1961) all the way down to the "African-American" sex pervert, Congressman Mel Reynolds (R.S., 1975), who was busted in 1992 for the statutory rape of a sixteen-year-old girl. And let's not forget New York Knicks legend Bill Bradley (R.S., 1965). In his *Life on the Run* (1976), the "born-again" New Jersey Senator and former presidential contender wrote, "At Oxford . . . I questioned my religious faith and sought workable moral values instead of simply rules. I became more playful and rebellious, responding to events in a way that discipline and obligation had outlawed before. . . . Specific studies were neglected without guilt."[115]

Then, to ensure that the American people lost their power to think, numbers of Rhodes Scholars invaded the entertainment industry as well. Did you know that Kris Kristofferson was a Rhodes Scholar in 1958? His popular albums, "Jesus Was a Capricorn" and "Shake Hands with the devil," were released in 1972 and 1979 respectively. The degenerate testified that his song writing was "influenced in one way or another by the freedom I was exposed to at Oxford. It was at such a liberating time of my life."[116]

After serving as president of Warner Brothers in Hollywood, Frank Wells (R.S., 1953) became president and chief operating officer of the Disney Corporation to ensure that the nation's children are nipped in the bud. Now you know why throngs of Aids-spreading, pedophilic sodomites are warmly embraced at Disneyland and Disney World. (Ironically, on the eve of *Operation Iraqi Freedom* in March 2003, President Bush created special no-fly zones over the "family-oriented/homosexual-friendly" theme parks. Wait 'til they try that in the Tribulation Period!)

Dennis Stanfill (R.S., 1950) became chairman and CEO of Twentieth Century Fox as well as chairman of Metro-Goldwyn-Mayer. Darrell Walker (R.S., 1976) became senior vice president of Columbia Pictures, Columbia Studios. And to better manage the homosexually dominated world of classical music, Frank Taplin (R.S., 1937) became president and CEO of the Metropolitan Opera, while Stephen Stamas (R.S., 1953) became chairman of the New York Philharmonic.

Finally, to destroy America's wives and mothers, Naomi Wolf (R.S., 1984) published her feminist missive, *Fire With Fire: The New Female Power and How It Will Change the 21st Century,* in 1993. Naomi promotes "power feminism" to enable women to "become goddesses of disobedience".[117] Do you remember how Adam Weishaupt approached the fairer sex? Have his methods faded away?

BILL CLINTON

As a fitting conclusion to this chapter, can anyone deny the fact that an Arkansas hayseed by the name of William Jefferson Clinton was able to tap the awesome power of this Oxford nexus? After that ill-fated handshake with America's first Catholic president culminated in Clinton's education at Georgetown (like Weishaupt's years at Ingolstadt), the liberal Southern Baptist set his sights for the lights! Do you happen to recall where the young profligate was when he "didn't inhale?" Can we say "Oxford University?"

Following two years of doping, fornicating, protesting and "studying" as a Rhodes Scholar, Clinton returned to the United States in 1970 to round off his internationalist training at Yale University's Law School. There he met and lived with Hillary Rodham until their marriage in

1975. From Yale, Bill went back to Arkansas where he promptly won election as attorney general and then governor.

In 1988, he was tapped for membership in the CFR and only one year later welcomed into David Rockefeller's other global society, the Trilateral Commission. Then, in 1991, he traveled to Baden-Baden, Germany, to attend the secret annual meeting of the Bilderbergers, a one-world group formed by Rockefeller and Prince Bernhard of the Netherlands, at the Hotel de Bilderberg in Oosterbeek, Holland, in 1954. (Some contend that Clinton is a Freemason as well.)[118]

The following year, Bill Clinton became the forty-second president of this nation. For the record, "CFR/the Group" Clinton was able to prevail over "CFR/the Order" Bush because "CFR" Perot was sent in from the bench by "the *real* powers that be!" In fact, the following blurb was seen on the front page of the *Wall Street Journal* on May 29, 1992, only six months after the "election."

> Friend in need: Perot's candidacy for the prestigious Council on Foreign Relations several years ago was seconded by . . . George Bush. A Perot aide says Bush's letter was "lovely" but there aren't any plans to release the text.[119]

Although America's new commander-in-chief was denied the standard presidential national security clearance, being required to have a chaperone (due to his rap sheet of "weed" smoking and draft dodging), Bill was determined to have a good time and help a few of the boys up the ol' ladder in the process.

With a Rhodes man in the White House, Dr. Cuddy exposes the philosophical nepotism that prevailed:

> Some of the Rhodes Scholars appointed by President Clinton are: Robert Reich (Secretary of Labor), Michael Warren (special assistant to the Chief-of-Staff and Secretary of Labor), Thomas Williamson (Department of Labor chief council), James Woolsey (CIA Director), George Stephanopoulos (Communications Director) . . . Ira Magaziner (Senior Advisor for Policy Development) . . . Strobe Talbott (Ambassador-at-large and Special Advisor to the Secretary of State on the New Independent States and Russia), Stephen Oxman (Assistant Secretary of State for European Affairs), Walter Slocombe (Deputy Undersecretary of Defense for Policy), Sarah Sewall (Deputy Assistant Secretary of Defense for Peacekeeping/ Peacemaking Policy), Ashton Carter (Assistant Secretary of Defense for Program Analysis and Evaluation), Susan Rice (National Security Council), Joseph Nye (head of the National Intelligence Council), Richard Gardner (Ambassador to Spain),

Jack Davison (Ambassador to Niger), Bonnie St. John Deane (Director of the National Economic Council), W. Bowman Cutter (National Economic Council deputy assistant), Sylvia Matthews (an aide to the National Economic Council who will be White House Deputy Chief-of-Staff), Bruce Reed (Domestic Policy Council deputy assistant) . . . Kevin Thurm (HHS chief-of-staff), Daniel Porterfield (an HHS speechwriter), Atul Gawande (HHS), and Renee Stone (EPA).[120]

Cuddy adds, "Of the aforementioned, Thomas Williamson, James Woolsey, George Stephanopoulos, Strobe Talbott, Stephen Oxman, Walter Slocombe, Sarah Sewall, Ashton Carter, Joseph Nye, Richard Gardner, and W. Bowman Cutter are CFR members, with Nye (Rhodes Scholar 1958-60) and Gardner also being Trilateralists."[121]

Some of the more discerning leaders on Capitol Hill grew "alarmed" as Clinton continued stacking the deck. *New York Times* correspondent Douglas Jehl gave evidence of this concern in his March 21, 1993, article entitled, *Rhodes to Rhodes: On the Inside Looking In*: "They seem to be everywhere," said Senator John H. Chaffee, the Rhode Island Republican, who at a recent confirmation hearing found himself staring down at a witness table lined with nothing but Rhodes Scholars."[122] (Incidentally, you might say that Jehl was qualified to write his piece, having been a Rhodes man himself in 1984.) And just where do you think Johnny went to school? Talk about "the pot calling the kettle black," would you believe that "the Honorable Gentleman from Rhode Island" spent time in a coffin at Yale?

As to the new president's "moral" fiber, John McManus writes in *The Insiders:*

> Character, patriotism, religious values, personal integrity, family loyalty, honesty, and virtually all else that Americans hope to find in a chief executive count for nothing with Insiders. Those who know Mr. Clinton best know that he exhibits none of these important traits. Those who publish the only statewide newspaper in his home state, the *Arkansas Democrat Gazette,* know it, too. Their blistering editorial refusing to support him for President stated, "It is not the compromises he has made that trouble so much as the unavoidable suspicion that he has no great principles to compromise." [123]

By the time "Monica-gate" was ready to hit the fan, thirty-nine separate, significant Clinton scandals had already been identified; a list that was eventually obtained by the House Oversight Committee.[124] Two of the more disturbing exposés of the Clinton presidency are: *Unlimited Access,* by retired FBI agent Gary Aldrich, assigned to the White House to perform background checks on White House personnel; and *Dereliction of Duty,* by Lt. Col. Robert "Buzz" Patterson, USAF (Ret.), custodian of the suitcase containing the nation's sensitive launch codes, known as the "nuclear football."

While the president is never to be separated from his Secret Service detachment, much less from the nuclear button, Aldrich confirms that Clinton *frequently snuck out of the White House,* hiding under a blanket in the back seat of a sedan driven by longtime friend and staffer Bruce Lindsey, *to rendevous with hookers* at the Marriott Hotel in downtown Washington.[125]

Colonel Patterson's experience was even more unbelievable. After issuing Clinton his new set of nuclear "go codes" (known as "the biscuit") during their first security conference (the code sequence being updated annually), Colonel Patterson and a military aide nearly went into shock when their commander-in-chief blurted out that he was unable to produce (locate) the old set! He wrote:

> One of the most important symbols of military power in the history of man had just exchanged hands. . . . President Clinton looked up sheepishly and confessed, "I don't have mine on me. I'll track it down, guys, and get it back to you."
>
> We were dumbfounded—*the president losing his nuclear codes.* He is required to have the codes on him at all times. President Clinton normally kept the world's most sensitive document rubber-banded to his credit cards in his pants pocket. . . .
>
> As we left, we couldn't help wondering how long the codes had been missing.
>
> We immediately alerted the Joint Staff in the Pentagon. "What do you mean? How could this happen? You've got to find it ASAP!" They were incredulous.
>
> For days, we turned over everything in the White House. We talked to the ushers and valets, and asked them to search the president's clothes and furniture in the residence. We asked the senior staff, specifically John Podesta and Bruce Lindsey, for help.
>
> The president finally threw up his hands and said casually, "I just can't find it . . . don't know where it is." As far as he was concerned, that was the end of the story.[126]

With honor and virtue thrown to the wind, Dr. Cuddy highlights the traits that *really* count when dealing with the Group:

[A]ccording to Rhodes biographer Sarah Millin, Rhodes told Stead that the scholars should have the following characteristics: "smugness, brutality, unctuous rectitude, and tact." In the future, President Clinton will be described as smug and brutal. Also, concerning "unctuous rectitude," *Webster's Dictionary* defines "unctuous" as "oily in speech or manner; plastic; moldable; characterized by a smug, smooth pretense of spiritual feeling, fervor, or earnestness, as in seeking to persuade" ["I did not have sex with that woman," etc.]. This will fit the nickname given to Bill Clinton.[127]

In the December 7, 1992, *Christian Science Monitor* (which is influenced by the Group), Robert Rotberg (R.S., 1957) wrote in his article entitled, "A Rhodes Scholar Reaches the Top":

Rhodes was a man of unparalleled vision. . . . Mr. Clinton's accession to the American presidency fulfills Rhodes' deepest aspiration. . . . Rhodes believed that he had discovered an idea that could lead "to the cessation of all wars and one language throughout the world." Rhodes also specified fairly clearly the kinds of men who should receive the opportunity to go to Oxford. He had Clinton in mind. . . . They were to "esteem the performance of public duties" as their highest aim [Monica Lewinsky?]. Rhodes wanted the best men for "the World's fight." . . . "In the ninety years of scholarships, only Clinton has taken Rhodes' dreams to the top."[128]

You say, "Dr. Grady—how has all this evil been allowed to permeate our land? How is it that we have gone from an 'honest Abe' to a 'slick Willie'; from 'I cannot tell a lie' to 'I didn't inhale?' " The answer is a sick one; sick, but accurate. With reference to the up-and-coming careers of the "Wisemen," Rhodes Scholar Walter Isaacson observed, "As World War II drew to a close, most of their fellow citizens wanted nothing more than to turn inward and, in Harriman's words, 'go to the movies and drink coke.' "[129]

And, as the twenty-first century unfolds, we can only anticipate that this satanic symbiosis of societal escapism and conspiratorial intrigue will continue to escalate. In 2003 the world caught a glimpse of things to come when the coalesced power of Yale and Oxford reached it's zenith in the jingoistic alliance of George Bush and Tony Blair. After Bush (Skull and Bones, 1968) and Blair (St. John's College, Oxford, 1975) led their three-nation "coalition" against Saddam Hussein—*in the first preemptive war in United States history*—the "dynamic duo" spent the rest of the year dodging questions about those elusive weapons of mass destruction. Few of the deluded citizens in either nation were capable of discerning the historical significance of the "Bush-Blair Damage Control Summit" held in Britain during November 18-20, 2003. With the torchbearer for Cecil Rhodes hosting the ideological descendant of William Russell and Alphonso Taft, something "special" would be necessary to commemorate the occasion. Whereas other American presidents had visited Britain and stayed as guests of the monarch, their trips had never been designated by Buckingham Palace as *state* visits. *USA Today* reported that the Bush excursion to Britain constituted "the first state visit of a U.S. leader." It was during this meeting that "Brother" Bush made the fateful blooper (quoted in the previous chapter) that Allah and Jehovah are one and the same.

Having been a pastor myself, I wrote the following chapter as a special benefit for God's men.

13

Attitude Check

*"Keep thy heart with all diligence; for out
of it are the issues of life."*
(Proverbs 4:23)

TO BE SUDDENLY confronted by over one hundred and fifty
years of previously unknown conspiratorial intrigue would be
a disconcerting experience for any normal American. Daniel
Webster once said, "There is nothing so powerful as truth and often
nothing so strange." Thus, it would behoove my readers to take the
following "attitude check" before advancing to the heavier material in
the chapters to follow. Though certain of these principles have already
been discussed, their content is worthy of review, as repetition is the
key to learning.

Satan never intended for you to read this book. He is all too familiar
with the maxim of George Washington that, "Truth will ultimately prevail
when there are pains taken to bring it to light." Therefore, as he can no
longer keep you in the dark, his only option is to blind you with the
light by leading you to react to your discovery in an unscriptural manner.
It's been said that if the devil can't get you to do a wrong thing, he'll
get you to do a right thing in a wrong way. There are at least eight ways
that a Christian can be harmed by the study of conspiracy history:

1. **Denial**: This is certainly the convenient "out" for many. Like the
pretty woman who replied to the ugly man's request for a date, "Are you
doing anything Friday evening?" with, "I've *got* to be doing *some*thing,"
some people will refuse to embrace a conspiracy view of history no matter
how many facts they are shown. There just *has* to be another explanation.
The Holy Ghost warned that a "moral majority" of gutless wonders

would usher in the Laodicean apostasy. Paul wrote in II Timothy 4:3a, *"For the time will come when they will not endure sound doctrine."* An unprecedented temptation of materialism will constitute *the* root cause for this recalcitrant denial. (II Timothy 4:1-6; Revelation 3:7) Like the typical Christian teenager who prefers a "post-marriage Rapture," his worldly parents can't possibly believe that the world could be coming to an end when they have so much "stuff" to acquire.

Having embraced the "something good is going to happen to you" philosophy rather than the Biblical forecast, *". . . in the last days perilous times shall come"* (II Timothy 3:1a), Christians who might have made a difference will forfeit the spiritual benefits of conspiracy history in their quest to "call America back to God." Approximately ninety-nine percent of these self-deluded crusaders will eventually burn out for Jesus in the "killing fields" of fundamentalist kingdom builders.

2. **Panic**: For the otherwise sincere believer who might be spiritually immature when he first discovers the conspirators' trail, the initial shock may prove to be more than he can handle. Without the requisite wisdom to properly digest conspiracy history, one may successfully overtake his foe, like Asahel did with Abner, only to be smitten to the ground in the process. (II Samuel 2:18-23) If a Christian is not *prepared* for the true lessons of history he will most assuredly be *perplexed* by them. (Proverbs 27:12) Furthermore, this state of stupefaction will retard his spiritual production, the Bible warning, *"He that observeth the wind shall not sow; and he that regardeth the clouds shall not reap"* (Ecclesiastes 11:4). The only way to avoid being stampeded by reality is to obey the charge of Job 22:21a, *"Acquaint now thyself with him, and be at peace."* Christians must remind themselves that *"He that sitteth in the heavens shall laugh: the Lord shall have them in derision"* (Psalm 2:4). Another comforting admonition is, *"Fret not thyself because of evildoers, neither be thou envious against the workers of iniquity. For they shall soon be cut down like the grass, and wither as the green herb"* (Psalm 37:1-2). In the meantime, *"Trust in the LORD, and do good; so shalt thou dwell in the land, and verily thou shalt be fed"* (Psalm 37:3). Paul summed it up with the words, *"For God hath not given us the spirit of fear; but of power, and of love, and of a sound mind"* (II Timothy 1:7).

3. **Imbalance**: Christians who forget that the earth is the Lord's footstool (Isaiah 66:1) often recoil from their former ignorance of secret societies to the opposite extreme of hyper, anti-conspiracy activity. What goes on in the White House suddenly becomes more important

than what goes on in the church house. Bus captains quit their routes to become precinct captains. Door-to-door visitation is replaced by political canvassing. Exposing the bankers becomes a higher priority than exegeting the Bible. Going off the deep end will cause a believer to lose his spiritual equilibrium. The Scripture says of our Saviour, *". . . He hath done all things well"* (Mark 7:37b).

4. **Depression**: Whenever a disproportionate amount of time is diverted to the study of conspiracy history, the Christian will eventually lose his spiritual strength, which is *"the joy of the LORD"* (Nehemiah 8:10). His face will often reflect this imbalance. Jesus rebuked the Pharisees of His day, saying, *". . . be not, as the hypocrites, of a sad countenance: for they disfigure their faces, that they may appear unto men to fast"* (Matthew 6:16a). There is a fine line between melancholia and Biblical soberness. The typical "conspiracy expert" will repulse more people than he will enlighten.

A second cause for depression is the inevitable exasperation that occurs when an idealistic conspiracy fighter realizes that his efforts are not even making a dent in a system that is destined to *"wax worse and worse"* (II Timothy 3:13a). *Rare is the Christian who can handle such negative reality.* A moral deterioration of over two hundred and twenty-five years has occurred between that first generation of colonial minutemen and our present-day militia volunteers. While the clerical president of Harvard University, Dr. Samuel Langdon, organized a midnight prayer meeting atop Bunker Hill on the eve of the immortal battle, David Koresh was the presiding "minister" at Waco. Although some of America's modern patriots may sport bumper stickers that read "Guns, Guts and God," a significant portion would not profess to be "religiously inclined." While distancing themselves from abject atheism, such God-fearing "good ol' boys" would also be quick to point out that they can worship God in the woods as easily as they can in a church. The sad reality is that Lexington and Concord marked the birth of America while Waco and Ruby Ridge constitute the nation's death knell. (Psalm 9:17) This is why a "Declaration of INTERdependence" was issued in 1976 by the National Education Association (NEA) and the World Affairs Council of Philadelphia. The blasphemous document proclaimed, "Two centuries ago our forefathers brought forth a new nation; now we must join with others to bring forth a new world order." [1]

5. **Pride**: This is perhaps the most dangerous reaction of all as the Bible declares, *"Pride goeth before destruction and an haughty spirit before a fall."* (Proverbs 16:18) Because *"[k]nowledge puffeth up"* (I Corinthians 8:1b), conspiracy neophytes are subject to great temptation. As the devil is nobody's fool, he can get the anti-conspiracy zealot so preoccupied with his research that he will eventually assimilate the very character of the enemy. After discovering and recognizing the potential for evil inherent in any *secret* society, the puffed up repository of truth will then proceed to tantalize his intellectual inferiors with an "I know something you don't know" attitude. Now that *he* has learned the "mysteries" (about secret orders, etc.), *they* must come to *him* for enlightenment. This is precisely what the Puritans did in America when, after fleeing the religious persecution in England, they erected their own intolerant system in Massachusetts Bay.

The "conspiracy geek" is the guy who likes to drop names around the common folk. His "turn on" occurs when "Brother So-and-So" exhibits a puzzled reaction after hearing of such strange things as the Group, the CFR or the Trilateral Commission. Beware of the Nicolaitanes who live to conquer the laity. (Revelation 2:6,15)

6. **Obnoxiousness**: Conspiracy advocates who major on knowledge while minoring on wisdom are often used by Satan to sow discord in the local New Testament assembly. The average overworked pastor is usually more concerned about budget pressures and backslidden church members than he is with the Federal Reserve System or The Order of Skull and Bones, etc. This is not to say that he is disinterested in such important subjects. He just doesn't need some belligerent, insecure "coconut" stirring up his flock. (Remember Y2K?) If a spiritual pastor is held up in prayer by his congregation, God will lead him to the truth eventually. In the meantime, well-intentioned conspiracy crusaders would profit from recalling the former days of their own ignorance. Remember, *"God resisteth the proud, but giveth grace unto the humble"* (James 4:6b).

While I was conducting a Bible conference in the Detroit area (March 2004), Constance Cumbey, acclaimed authority on the New Age movement, visited one of the services. The pastor informed me that she wanted to meet with us afterward to discuss her research that posited Javier Solana as a leading candidate for the Antichrist.

However, she became visibly agitated from the beginning of the service. As I developed my sermon (Baptist history in America), she spent most of the time staring at her Bible, her body turned away from the pulpit.

Although she still wanted to meet with us (despite the "ordeal"), I politely declined, stating that her bizarre attitude had seriously hampered the meeting. "Sister Cumbey" then proceded to tell me a thing or two— I was inflammatory, I made too big a deal about immersion and I spoke to smaller audiences than she did. I somehow got the impression that the crowd she runs with would try to assassinate the Antichrist if given the opportunity.

7. **Presumptuousness**: Not only can a prideful conspiracy advocate abuse his own fellow church members through obnoxiousness, but he may also antagonize and alienate any number of misguided dupes of the conspiracy itself by exhibiting a spirit of presumptuousness. Very few Masons believe that they are worshiping Lucifer. Most public school teachers are unaware of the NEA's agenda. The local bank teller doesn't have a clue about the Federal Reserve System. The typical Roman Catholic does not equate his "Holy Father" with a "Bloody Whore." Yet, half-cocked Christians will accuse these types of people of being agents of the Illuminati, etc. This is why con artists like Rush Limbaugh have a market for "kook tests." The Bible says that the conspirators themselves will be *"deceiving and being deceived"* (II Timothy 3:13b). Satan has everybody conned. (See former CBS anchor Dan Rather and his "investigative" reporting on President Bush's National Guard record.) One of the scarier prophecies is found in John 16:2b, *"yea, the time cometh, that whosoever killeth you will think that he doeth God service."* No doubt this is part of that incredulous crowd who will be crying out at the Great White Throne, *"Lord, Lord, have we not . . . in thy name done many wonderful works?"* (Matthew 7:22). It is our responsibility to take the Word of God and attempt to deprogram some of these poor souls.

When I was a professor at Hyles-Anderson College, one of my Church history students asked me if I believed that Jesuits had ever infiltrated the college faculty. I told him that in the first place, no Jesuit could destroy a Bible college nearly as well as the average egotistical, apostate Baptist of today could. In the second place, I replied that Rome wasn't really that intimidated by Hyles-Anderson College, or any other modern Bible school for that matter. I then proceeded to list some of the "local" competition within a few hundred miles of the college (situated in Crown Point, Indiana): Loyola University, DePaul University, Marquette University, and Notre Dame University. I informed him that Notre Dame's library alone is fourteen floors high and open until midnight. Why would the Vatican be worried about *us* when *Billy Graham* spoke at Notre Dame in 1977 and *Jerry Falwell* did the same in 1986? The conspirators are definitely out there, but they are not hiding under every rock or behind every bush. Once, after preaching in the Washington, D.C., area, I spoke with a church member who informed me that he worked at the U.S. Department of Justice. When we discussed the subject of conspiracy, he expressed the rather candid opinion that the normal day-to-day operation at the Justice Department was probably too chaotic for the average conspirator to manipulate. On the other hand, Janet "Nero" has certainly done the bidding of the powers that be.

On another occasion, I happened to be in New York City during the same week that the Council on Foreign Relations was convening for a major conference. As the Lord would have it, I arrived at the Council's Manhattan headquarters at 68th Street and Park Avenue at the very time the delegates were coming out for a break. The dozen or so that I observed were all dressed to kill and sporting impressive looking nametags. Most of them were chatting away on their cell phones.

Using all the tact and discretion I could muster, I was able to speak briefly with an economics professor from Northwestern University and a "distinguished" member of the International Monetary Fund. After getting the inevitable brush-off, I concluded that I wouldn't trust either man as far as I could throw him. On the other hand, I did notice a percentage of delegates who appeared to represent the organization's necessary "conspiracy fodder." For them, membership in the prestigious CFR was probably more of an ego/career booster than a conscious opportunity to undermine America.

8. **Impetuousness**: The average student of conspiracy history will generally learn just enough material to be dangerous. Unaware of the breadth and complexity of the conspiracy as a whole, neophytes tend to formulate premature conclusions that are based on their initial limited discoveries. They are usually too shocked to realize that their find is but a small part of a much larger operation. Thus, one novice may believe that Freemasonry runs the world, while another may have cut his teeth on the CFR or the Trilateral Commission. While a converted Protestant may view the Jewish bankers as Satan's pandemic for evil, ex-Catholics will instinctively conclude that the pope is the one who calls the shots. The sick truth is that no *one* satanic group has a monopoly on conspiracy. Professor Sutton concurs, "All these groups have cooperative and

competitive features. But to argue that all the world's ills can be ascribed to any *one* of these groups is false." [2]

In a similar vein, Nesta Webster cautions against a legalistic pursuit of Adam Weishaupt's original movement.

> Illuminism in reality is less an Order than a principle, and a principle which can work better under cover of something else. Weishaupt himself had laid down the precept that the work of Illuminism could but be conducted "under other names and other occupations," and henceforth we shall always find it carried on by this skilful system of camouflage.[3]

Yet conversely, Texe Marrs assured his readers in 1995 (before he went off the deep end regarding Israel), "Cloaked in mystery and shrouded in secrecy, ten ruthless men comprise the 'Inner Circle' of the Illuminati conspiracy"[4] (insinuating that he knows who they are).

The Bible points to a multifaceted coalition of conspirators collectively inspired by the devil himself. In Psalm 2:2, it is "kings" and "rulers" who have gathered against the Lord and against His anointed. In Ephesians 6:12, Paul warned that the Christian must wrestle against *"principalities"* (plural), *"powers"* (plural), and *"the rulers of the darkness of this world"* (plural). And in II Timothy 3:13, he wrote, *"But evil men and seducers shall wax worse and worse, deceiving, and being deceived."* John gives us the final two scenarios as *"kings of the earth"* in Revelation 19:19 and a *"number of whom is as the sand of the sea"* in Revelation 20:8.

If a student will not patiently probe beyond his initial discoveries he will become like Ahimaaz of old and take off with only part of the message. It was Cushi who waited until he had the complete picture. (II Samuel 18:29-32)

An excellent illustration of how first impressions can lead to sweeping generalizations is the poem *Blind Men and An Elephant* by American poet John Godfrey Saxe (1816-1887). Mr. Saxe based his poem on a fable that was told in India many years ago. The story relates how six sightless men formed their impression of what an elephant looks like based on the particular body part they encountered first. The closing line reads, "Though each was partly in the right, And all were in the wrong."

If a Christian can study conspiracy history without succumbing to denial, panic, imbalance, depression, pride, obnoxiousness, presumption, or impetuousness, he may then glean the major spiritual benefit from such material. As stated in an earlier chapter, though we may be powerless to change the present course of evil events (II Timothy 3:13), we can allow the awareness of these developments to work a change in us! *"For in much wisdom is much grief: and he that increaseth knowledge increaseth sorrow"* (Ecclesiastes 1:18). A church member who understands what The Order of Skull and Bones is all about will not get bent out of shape if a visitor "accidentally" sits in his seat during the Sunday morning service. Knowing what is just around the corner will produce that spiritual quality of soberness required in I Peter 5:8.

In the midst of this mandated negativism, author William Still provides a beautifully balanced, positive perspective for God's children:

> Although the eventual ascendency of the Antichrist to a position of global power is inevitable, the ascendency of Communism is certainly not. Every day that Communism's march toward global hegemony is retarded is, in Christian terms, another day to rescue a few more souls from Satan's grasp and in political terms, another day to live in that uniquely gentle form of freedom found only in America.[5]

And the Psalmist concurs:

> *Fret not thyself because of evildoers, neither be thou envious against the workers of iniquity. For they shall soon be cut down like the grass, and wither as the green herb. Trust in the* LORD, *and do good; so shalt thou dwell in the land, and verily thou shalt be fed.* (Psalm 37:1-3)

The following two chapters serve a unique purpose in this book. They document a pair of unmistakable warnings that the Lord sent America— warnings that went tragically unheeded.

14

Bey Shang We

*"Precious in the sight of the LORD is
the death of his saints."*
(Psalm 116:15)

THROUGHOUT MY SEVEN years of ministerial training at two Christian colleges and a Bible institute, I cannot recall that a single professor ever once mentioned the name of John Morrison Birch. How much have *you* heard about him?

John Birch was born May 28, 1918, near Landaur, India, within sight of the snowcapped Himalayas. His parents, George and Ethel, were Bible-believing Presbyterian missionaries. A descendant of John Alden, "Buffalo Bill" Cody and Calvin Coolidge, John appeared destined from infancy to fulfill his own unique calling in life. His mother wrote:

> When John was very small I used to take him in his little bassinet when I went house to house with my Hindustani Bible to women in the villages round about the Agricultural Division of the Ewing Christian College at Allahabad, India, where Mr. Birch was teaching. The women and children would flock to see the little "padre sahib" (preacher-boy) as they called him. Actually, he unknowingly was used in a special way for the Lord, as the people out there would listen to the good news of salvation through the shed blood of Jesus Christ better since I was the mother of a son.
>
> John learned to talk very young. When he was about a year old, he would astonish the Hindustanis who crowded the streets of the marketplace as in his high childish treble voice he would cry out, "hut, bhago, gari ati hai," ("look out the carriage is coming"), as we drove along in our two wheeled tong (cart).[1]

When health problems forced the family to return stateside, they settled near Ethel's relatives in Vineland, New Jersey. Denominational apostasy eventually moved George to visit the West Baptist Church where he and his wife became convinced of their need for immersion. At the age of seven, John came under conviction, trusted Christ as his personal Saviour and was baptized himself. He surrendered to foreign missions at age eleven.

John was endowed with a prodigious intellect. Although only two-and-a-half years old when he left India, the little "padre sahib" was already fluent in Hindustani. His mother taught him English during their six-week voyage to America. By the time John was five he was reading better than most adults. A sample of his regular material (apart from the Bible) included *Pilgrim's Progress*, *Hurlburt's Story of the Bible*, *National Geographic* and the *Saturday Evening Post*. His budding precocity was later confirmed after receiving a personal examination by Dr. Edgar Doll, director of the Psychological Laboratory of the Training School at Vineland. According to the prestigious Simon Binet Measuring Scale of Intelligence, John possessed the mental faculties of a sixteen-year-old. His startled teachers promptly decided that he should skip grades five and six.

A job opportunity during the Depression led George to relocate his family, now numbering eight, to his native central Georgia. Pursuing his call to the ministry, John enrolled at Mercer University where he continued to excel in academics. He would establish the highest scholastic average in the school's history while graduating *magna cum laude*. In his junior year, John was selected by a faculty committee as Mercer's nominee for a Rhodes Scholarship.

While pastoring the Benevolence Baptist Church in Zenith during his final year at Mercer, John attended a local church revival meeting and heard the controversial J. Frank Norris preach from II Kings, chapter 18. When the speaker made an impassioned appeal for lost souls in China, John committed his life to that field. As Dr. Norris was exposing the liberalism of Southern Baptist schools in Texas and elsewhere (including Mercer), John enrolled the following September in the preacher's newly-formed Fundamentalist Baptist Bible Institute in Fort Worth, Texas. In May of 1940, John joined Oscar Wells and Ralph Van Northwick to comprise the school's first graduating class.

Within weeks, John, barely twenty-two, and Oscar, only two years older, boarded a Japanese freighter, the *SS Teaimariau*, in Seattle and headed for mainland China. This took great courage as a third of the country was already occupied by the Japanese who had been at war with China since 1937. Mr. Robert Birch, second to the youngest of John's six siblings (five of whom were still alive at this writing), informed me that John's middle name was taken from an ancestor, Robert Morrison, considered by some to have been the first Protestant missionary to China.

Shortly after arriving, they began attending a language school in Shanghai. As the complex Chinese alphabet consists of numerous pictures and symbols, John's near-photographic memory enabled him to carry on a simple street conversation after just six weeks of study.[2] Oscar met and married a missionary's daughter by the name of Myrtle Huizenga. The couple was blessed with a beautiful girl whom they named Shannon. Their inaugural evangelistic labors were suddenly interrupted, however, by the Japanese attack on Pearl Harbor. It would now be "open season" on all Americans, sacred or secular. While John was able to escape, being away when the political climate reversed, Oscar, Myrtle, and six-week-old baby Shannon were captured by the Japanese and imprisoned for nearly two years before the U.S. State Department was able to secure their release and return to America. Reverend Wells would spend the rest of his life sending sermon tapes, Gospel literature and Bibles into China.

RESCUE OF JIMMY DOOLITTLE

As a red-blooded American, John felt that he should do his part for the war effort and decided to request a chaplain's position. While his application was being considered, the patriotic missionary had a most unusual encounter of historical proportions. During a preaching tour in Chekiang Province in late April, John was approached in a restaurant by a cautious Chinese stranger who led him to an enclosed sampan (small riverboat) laying low in the water. The nervous little man rolled his eyes toward the door of the boat and whispered in broken English, "Americans." In their book, *The Secret File on John Birch*, authors James and Marti Hefly write:

> He walked over to the door and knocked softly. "Are any Americans
> in there?" he asked in his soft Georgia drawl. Silence. Then a muffled
> voice saying, "No Japanese could make up an accent like that!" The door
> swung open and John entered the dark hold. He blinked a moment,
> adjusting his eyes to the faint light given off by a lantern that swung from

the low ceiling. Then he shook his head, finding it hard to believe what he saw: five overgrown American flyers stuffed into the little hold, all grinning at him. "Wha—what . . . Who . . . How" he stammered. The commanding officer gave him a little mock salute and introduced himself. "Colonel James H. Doolittle, United States Army Air Force. The boys and I just delivered a little present to Tojo, and we're having a bit of trouble getting back home." [3]

By the grace of God, John was able to lead Colonel Doolittle and his men to safety through Japanese-occupied territory. For some "strange" reason, the typical World War II historian has neglected to mention the Baptist missionary when chronicling Doolittle's rescue. However, Doolittle acknowledged in his autobiography:

> Birch was as delighted to see us as we were to see him. He obviously knew his way around and could speak the language. I briefed him on our predicament and he agreed to join us, translate for us, and help us on our way to Chuchow.[4]

In 2004, Leo Loving, president of Loving Images, released a documentary on John's life entitled *Who is John Birch?* Through God's providence, Mr. Loving was able to locate two of the Doolittle Raiders rescued by Bey Shang We, Lieutenant Colonel Richard Cole (co-pilot) and Colonel Hank Potter (navigator). Sixty years after the fact, Col. Potter recalled an impromptu exchange that exemplified John's genuine love for his fellow man. Profoundly startled at the sudden appearance of an American in Chinese attire, speaking English with a Georgia drawl—and at 6:00 a.m., no less—Airman Paul Leonard blurted out the personal name of our Saviour; whereupon, John replied, "That's a very good name, but I'm not Him."

THE FLYING TIGERS

Doolittle was so impressed with his rescuer that he recommended him to another WWII legend, General Claire Lee Chennault, founder of the famed Flying Tigers. The "Big Tiger," as Chennault was called by the Chinese, persuaded John to assist him in developing a critically needed espionage network. In his personal memoirs, *Way of a Fighter*, Chennault also set the record straight regarding Doolittle's rescue. "Captain John

Birch, a Georgia Baptist, had been a missionary in Hangchow and was led into our fold by Jimmy Doolittle after Birch had guided Jimmy and his raiders out of East China."[5] The crusty general readily agreed to the missionary's only stipulation—that he be permitted to preach in the village churches along the way. His actual response was, "John, I don't care if you preach to the devil, so long as you do your job."[6] Born in 1890 and reared in northeast Louisiana, Chennault made reference to his own spiritual background, saying, "I became interested in religion at an early age, largely because of the historical interest that I found in the Bible, and was baptized and received in the Baptist Church when I was eleven years old."[7]

Prior to the bombing of Pearl Harbor the Flying Tigers had constituted a civilian mercenary unit named the American Volunteer Group (A.V.G.) that aided Generalissimo Chiang Kai-Shek against Japanese aggression. With America's formal declaration of war against Japan making Nationalist China an official ally, Chennault was directed to continue rendering assistance but under the auspices of the 14th Air Force Command. It was fitting that John was inducted as a 2nd Lieutenant into the China Air Task Force of the U.S. Army on *July 4*, 1942. Henceforth, every Japanese soldier that Chennault, Birch and the Generalissimo could contain would be one less enemy to threaten American boys in the Pacific theater.

Over the next four years, missionary John Birch rose to the rank of captain as he successfully spearheaded a major intelligence-gathering operation deep behind enemy lines. Chennault wrote:

> John Birch was the pioneer of our field-intelligence net. Until the Doolittle raiders began dropping out of the dark China night, Birch was organizing a new chain of missions in Chekiang Province to replace those lost when the Japanese interned Americans in Hangchow. By the time Birch was rounding up the Doolittle raiders, the Japanese were burning his new mission, so John laid aside his Bible and took up the sword for the duration. For three years he worked steadily in the field with only brief respites for medical treatment. He refused all leave or temporary duty in the United States with the comment, "I'll leave China when the last Jap is gone."[8]

John's first mission was to target unsuspecting Japanese ships for air strikes by recruiting and training a network of Chinese short-wave radio operators strategically perched above the shores of the South China Sea. He would use the secret call letters "DOG-SUGAR-EIGHT." His next assignment was even more dangerous, requiring personal reconnaissance to pinpoint Japanese bases, mark their location (with white strips of cloth on the ground) and then remain in harm's way to radio in the strafing P-40s. In his "spare time" the Baptist preacher rescued numbers of downed U.S airmen and stranded missionaries. Chennault recalled a sortie where John's contribution was typical.

> While on the Yangtze, Birch discovered the Japanese were much more dependent on the Shihweiyao iron mines and smelter than we had suspected. He sent us detailed information that enabled us to cripple the blast furnaces and docks by bombing. On this same mission Chinese guerrillas told Birch of a small city near Hankow that the Japanese were using to conceal a big munitions dump and garrison from our air attacks on Hankow. When bombers were unable to locate the target, Birch filtered back through the lines and rode in the nose of the lead B-25 to pin-point the target for the bombardier. The seemingly deserted town erupted into a volcano of smoke and fire when the first bombs hit, as the munitions exploded. Birch's guerilla friends, watching from a nearby hill, were impressed with his performance. They later told him thirty trucks had been required to carry away the dead Japanese, and the dump was completely destroyed.[9]

John's exploits were becoming legendary. He worked twenty hours a day for weeks at a time. Once he rode a Mongolian pony sixty miles through a snowstorm over rough terrain in a single day. He cheerfully endured his share of endemic maladies such as typhus and malaria. The Chinese greatly admired their missionary-soldier, calling him in Mandarin, *Bey Shang We* (literally, "Birch Captain"). By his Christ-like spirit he was able to inspire them to accomplish unbelievable feats. On more than one occasion they constructed airstrips together—by hand! Perhaps the most amazing story of all occurred when a P-40 crashed about ten miles from Linchuan after developing a leak in the gas line. Fortunately, the pilot was able to parachute to safety. About a week later, a throng of coolies marched into the backyard of John's residence in Linchuan. When the preacher went out to investigate, their commander announced proudly, "Here's your plane," and with a tremendous crash they dropped it in the courtyard! One hundred and twenty of them had lifted the tangled wreckage out of the earth and physically carried it across country to Bey Shang We.[10]

WORDS OF COMMENDATION

John's admirers were legion. They readily fulfilled their part of the Scriptural formula, *"Let another man praise thee, and not thine own mouth"* (Proverbs 27:2a). The Nationalist General Marshal Hsueh Yo said, "Give me fifty men like Lieutenant Birch and I'll whip the whole dwarf army with one hand tied behind my back."[11] Captain James Hart called him "the bravest man I knew."[12] Arthur Hopkins, a Yale graduate and fellow intelligence officer, called John "the most brilliant, the finest, the most able, and the bravest officer I ever met."[13] Lieutenant Edwin James said, "I've only worshiped one man in my life. That was Captain John Birch."[14] He would point John out to fellow officers and remark, "There goes the most important *one* man in our China operations."[15] Colonel Wilfred Smith called John "the eyes of the 14th Airforce," stating:

I have recommended John for the Silver Star. He deserved every bit of it. He was the pioneer of our intelligence operations in China and more loyal to his God and his friends than any young man I ever knew.[16]

One of his closest colleagues, Lieutenant Bill Miller, recalled:

During my stay with John, I came to know him as a dedicated man of God ... Although John was a Baptist minister and he knew me to be a Roman Catholic, we had nothing but the most congenial discussions about religion as we lay on our bunks and talked far into the unbelievably quiet night. In spite of his profoundly religious beliefs, John lived among men of conflicting faiths without causing friction of any sort, and by his exemplary Christian living did more to influence Chinese and American agnostics than any amount of preaching could have accomplished.[17]

Though John was willing to exercise wisdom when needed, he readily shared the Gospel with anyone who would listen. He firmly believed that Christ was the true panacea for Adam's fallen race. In one of the many letters to his family, he wrote:

There is only one real problem in the world with all its complicated evils, and there is only one answer, amidst the maze of futile plans. Here is the problem and the answer: *"The wages of sin is death, but the gift of God is eternal life through Jesus Christ our Lord"* (Romans 6:23).[18]

Appraising John as "more than just a very good officer," Chennault sent him the following letter of commendation which was typical of many others he received:

1. Your recent secret mission in relation to intelligence matters, which led you extremely close to enemy territory, has been invaluable to the China Air Task Force. The successful accomplishment of this hazardous mission required fortitude, courage, and devotion to duty. The excellent manner in which you have carried out this difficult duty is highly commended.

2. A copy of this letter will be placed in your 201 file.

> C.L. Chennault
> Brigadier General,
> A.U.S. Commanding[19]

Chennault personally pinned the Legion of Merit medal on John's chest, July 17, 1944, "for exceptionally meritorious conduct in performance of outstanding service."[20]

Another career officer who had a personal relationship with John was fellow Macon resident Brigadier General Robert L. Scott, Jr., USAF (Ret.). When the A.V.G. became the 23rd Fighter Group of the China Air Task Force, Chennault appointed the then-Colonel Scott as his group commander. With twenty-two confirmed kills, Scott was known by his men as a "one-man Air Force." Tokyo Rose labeled him a war criminal, announcing over Shanghai Radio that the Japanese government had placed a price on his head.

In a two-part article in the *Orlando Sentinel* on August 20 and 27, 1961, Scott stated:

> I saw him many times and came to know the quiet, efficient man very well. I'll never forget him. Not for anything I saw him do, because of necessity John Birch had to go it mostly alone—he was a legal spy. His job was 10 times tougher than any other combat job out there in China and remember they were all pretty tough then. He jumped out of airplanes behind enemy lines and hadn't even been trained in the parachute school. He put on Chinese clothing and simply walked through the villages eastward to the enemy and then walked back with information for Chennault. . . .
>
> One day I heard Chennault explaining to John Birch while they stood in front of a Chinese map and pointed far behind the enemy positions that he needed information about targets and weather. Later the same day John disappeared in a jeep. Chennault didn't tell me any more until three

days later when his radio man ran in with the news that the frequency he'd been guarding constantly had come to life. We three hurried to the communications cave and I heard John Birch making his report from behind Japanese lines, sitting somewhere on a mountaintop from which he informed Chennault the number of enemy aircraft on a certain field, the state of the weather, where the fuel dump was and the ammo. After that it was my business to escort 12 bombers with seven P-40s and knock them off. And I got a medal. But I'd have been scared to death if I'd had to do what John Birch did in his calm way . . . I even heard he stood in one enemy-occupied city and gave the searching U.S. bombers a steer with his portable radio transmitter when the weather closed in over Changsha— enabling them to home on the target in spite of the weather having closed-in. Of course, such action made Birch part of that target, the very center part, but such things didn't seem to matter much to the Baptist missionary-soldier. I call it the utmost in courage and so did Chennault.[21]

General Scott is the author of sixteen books on military aviation, including the best-seller, *God is My Co-Pilot*, which was later released as a feature-length film by Warner Brothers. I had the opportunity to interview General Scott at the Aviation Museum of Robins Air Force Base in Warner Robins, Georgia. When I asked him to share his personal recollections of John, he replied,

He was one of the greatest guys I ever met in my life. He was very necessary to General Chennault. We didn't know much about him, because his work was all secret, but I knew he was out there doing things for us. I didn't have a lot of time to speak with him because he was always on the run. And yet, I felt closer to him than I was because we were both from the town of Macon.[22]

I was also privileged to interview General Chennault's premier fighter pilot, Brigadier General David Lee "Tex" Hill, USAF (Ret.). A major at the time, Hill was assigned to Hengyang as one of Scott's four squadron commanders. After a half century of stonewalling by the military establishment, the maverick triple ace received his long overdue Distinguished Service Cross in May 2002 for having destroyed "at least" eighteen enemy aircraft. It was Hill's character that actor John Wayne portrayed in the Hollywood film *The Flying Tigers*. As his own father, Dr. "P. B." Hill, had served as a Presbyterian minister, missionary to Korea and highly regarded chaplain of the Texas Rangers, Hill esteemed

Chennault's unique missionary-soldier with equal admiration. The general recalled:

> John Birch did a [expletive] of a job over there [China]. He spoke so many dialects. John Birch was so invaluable to us; because what would happen is that he would go way behind the lines . . . [You] see, the Japanese only controlled certain lines of communication. We'd take off and he would be up on a high point where he could look around and see troop movements and things. And we'd check in with him on the radio and he'd say, "A bunch of cavalry people just pulled some horses in a compound over here," and describe the location. We couldn't see the horses, but we'd see the compound and so we'd go in there and attack it.[23]

What made John Birch so unusual was his ability to wage war on two fronts simultaneously. General Chennault's well-intentioned remark about John "laying his Bible aside and taking up the sword" was not an accurate assessment. Captain Birch never ceased enduring "*hardness, as a good soldier of Jesus Christ*" (II Timothy 2:3). He was the ultimate embodiment of Nehemiah's ambidextrous men on the wall, "*. . . every one with one of his hands wrought in the work, and with the other hand held a weapon*" (Nehemiah 4:17b). In a letter John received from Fort Worth, "General" Norris reported that he had asked Secretary of State Cordell Hull to instruct consular officials in Shanghai to keep a check on his welfare. He then offered his spiritual soldier the following words of "encouragement": "I know you're in a dangerous position, but you're serving the Lord where the battle is hottest. I have no pity for you whatsoever."[24]

John was discerning enough to read between the lines. He thanked his pastor for looking after him and then gave a full report of recent missionary journeys including the growth of the church in Hangchow.

> One man, who walked sixteen miles into Hangchow to be baptized last fall, has since led six other men to a saving knowledge of Jesus Christ; another, recently saved, is thus reported by his neighbors to have "gone crazy." They say all he can do is "talk about this Jesus Christ and that book." God grant that many more may likewise "go crazy!"
>
> You are dead right, sir, when you say you feel no pity for my position. Why, I'm having the time of my life![25]

John was also careful to maintain his burden for souls in America. He once received a tender letter from a boy he had taught in Sunday

School. "Do you like it over there?" he asked. With bullets flying around his head every other day, John replied,

Dear Bob:

Yes sir! I do like it over here! There is war, starvation, disease, sin, idolatry, superstition, suffering, and death on every side, but our wonderful Savior keeps saving souls, answering prayers, and giving joy in the midst of sorrow.

Two questions for you: First, has Jesus Christ saved you? Second, if he has, is he now using you to save other sinners? I trust the answer is "yes" both times.

Yours in His love,
John M.Birch[26]

CIVIL WAR

As the end of the war drew near, John's hatred for Communism was reaching the boiling point. "John knew better perhaps than any other American about Communist activities in the region where we worked," Lieutenant Miller recalled. "He talked about communism by the hour."[27] After risking his life for three years to save the Chinese people from *Japanese* aggression, John watched as Mao Tse-Tung's forces turned on their *own* nation. *The man with a nearly photographic memory was making plenty of notes.*

Just as the Russian Revolution "happened" to break out at the end of World War I, the overthrow of mainland China began in the closing chaos of World War II. It was John's observation that Communist guerillas had abandoned Nationalist forces to the Japanese on numerous occasions. The Hefleys write, "He had long believed that the Chinese Communists were more interested in fighting their own Nationalist countrymen than the Japs and would try to take over once the Allies had won the war.[28]

John was also aware that the Communists were moving into positions abandoned by the retreating Japanese. He warned Captain James Hart, "The Commies are dodging around now so that when peace comes they'll be able to kill their brothers who are loyal to the Generalissimo."[29] General Albert Wedemeyer was one of the few officers in the Eastern theater who concurred, noting that the Communist forces had never fought a single battle of consequence against the Japanese, but instead "played the role of jackal or hyena against the wounded and suffering Chinese elephant who would not submit to his enemy."[30] Thousands of innocent peasants died as a result of subsequent Communist treachery. Lieutenant Miller wrote:

> As house guest in my tiny walled compound John and I discussed the serious Communist forces breaching the dykes farther up the river in order to flood areas of the Yellow River bend held by Nationalist guerillas. The aftermath of this ruthless action was all too apparent to us. The fertile countryside between Fouyang and John's station some 55 miles away having been transformed into an enormous lake 10 feet deep with only the old Pagodas and occasional village hammocks and walled towns protruding above the swirling yellow waters. This flooding was the tragic climax of one of the greatest crop years in the memory of living Chinese in the plains of the Yellow River delta.[31]

From John's Christian perspective, the deteriorating scene was all the more tragic given the fact that Chiang Kai-Shek was a pro-American, born-again Methodist with a preacher for a father-in-law. John was righteously indignant that the Bible-believing Chiang was being maligned in the American press while the bloody murderer Mao was being heralded as a "noble agrarian reformer." The source of this treasonous propaganda was the Communist-controlled U.S. State Department. In his book, *While You Slept*, John T. Flynn reviewed twenty-two pro-Communist books published between 1943 and 1949. Flynn notes that these books received "glowing approval" in the literary reviews of the *New York Times, The Herald Tribune*, and other left-wing publications.[32] It was not until 1971 that the Senate Committee on the Judiciary issued a twenty-eight page document entitled "The Human Cost of Communism In China," concluding that Mao and Chou were "responsible for the deaths of as many as 64 million people."[33] (This figure is over ten times the number of Jews who perished in Hitler's death camps.) Yet, despite this horrendous revelation of genocide, David Rockefeller viewed the carnage as a successful "social experiment."[34]

In the meantime "Chou and Mao" could not afford to let expert witnesses like Captain Birch spill the beans on their murderous designs. John was well aware of the danger around him, writing to his parents, May 1, 1944, "If my hour to depart should strike, I am ready to go, thanks to the merit of our Saviour, the Lord Jesus Christ."[35] On August 13,

1945, John wrote his brother George, "I have tried, as wholeheartedly as I could, to serve the flag that had protected me all my life."[36] The following day John wrote his parents, "The word has just come over the radio that Japan has unconditionally surrendered! Praise God from whom all blessings flow. . . . Liberty is worth its price."[37] Now Captain Birch would have to make it home alive. In what was perhaps his last letter, John wrote prophetically to his intelligence colleague, Lieutenant Bill Drummond, August 20, 1945: "They [the Communists] are getting ready to start the real war. After China they'll go for Korea. . . . Sooner or later we'll have to fight them."[38]

THE FINAL MISSION

Unfortunately for John, the fight would come sooner rather than later. By 1944, Major General William "Wild Bill" Donovan had extended his corrupt European-based Office of Strategic Services to General Chennault's turf. The OSS had many Bolsheviks in its units under the misguided assumption that the USSR was a true and staunch ally. During the closing months of the war, John was officially "on loan" to Donovan and his infiltrated staff. In a particular moment of consternation, Captain Birch radioed his mentor Chennault, "When do I return to Air Force stop Would rather be a private in the 14th than colonel in OSS."[39] (Chennault himself would be forced into retirement within weeks of the war's end.)

With the emperor's public capitulation, John was ordered northward to Suchow to arrange terms of surrender for the Imperial Japanese High Command and to assure the safety of Allied POWs. His team was comprised of three additional Americans, two Koreans and seven Chinese. On August 24, the men set out from Kweiteh by train, arriving at Lichwang in the dark where the Japanese put them up for the night. The following morning John was advised that further travel by locomotive was impossible as Mao's insurgents were reportedly destroying sections of rails up ahead. Undaunted, Captain Birch commandeered a handcar and continued his mission.

After proceeding only a short distance, however, he encountered a force of three hundred armed Communist guerrillas. John and his Chinese adjutant, 1st Lieutenant Tung Chin-Sheng, attempted to negotiate. In his sworn testimony recorded on October 3, 1945, Lieutenant Tung stated:

> Captain Birch went forward to the first group, spoke with them a while, gave them some watermelon and we were permitted to pass. At this time I noticed that Captain Birch's attitude toward the communists was a little severe and I thought it particularly dangerous in our present position.[40]

In the aftermath of the tragedy, State Department apologists and liberal members of the press keyed in on Tung's appraisal of John's "lack of diplomacy." Their articles tainted his heroic sacrifice with such negative adjectives as "stubborn, rash, braggadocio, zealous, angry and rigidly right wing." They never did present John's side of the situation. There was a definite reason *why* the American officer, in full uniform, was adamantly unwilling to be intimidated or disarmed by supposed allies. Tung's affidavit continues:

> I mentioned this to Captain Birch who replied, "Never mind, I want to see how the communists treat Americans. I don't mind if they kill me, for America will then stop the communist movement with atomic bombs." [41]

John knew that his countrymen were being deceived by the media regarding the true nature of Mao's "agrarian reform movement." He just happened to be brave enough to lay his life on the line to alert them.

Tung was able to secure John's concession that he do the talking in any further encounters. They also decided that Tung would leave his weapon with John during such times. As they proceeded, Tung successfully negotiated with two other groups of soldiers who were engaged in destroying tracks and telephone lines.

At approximately 2 p.m., John and his unit were halted on the outskirts of the tiny Lunghai Railroad station at Hwang Kao. Observing that a cadre of Communist guerillas had surrounded them and were evidently in control of the town, John sent Tung to mediate. He wanted clearance to pass through the garrison which the Japanese had recently abandoned to Nationalist troops who in turn had been attacked and driven out by superior Communist forces. Tung relates the full picture of what occurred next:

> I went forward to a group of communist soldiers in the station and asked to see the officer in charge and noted at that time that they had a belligerent attitude. I was taken to an officer and I stated that our group was from the 14th Air Force but we had been ordered to go to Suchow. I overheard men whispering: "Here comes more spies—we had better disarm them first—wait till we find out the truth before we give them

back their guns; otherwise kill them all." Someone else said: "Lock him up", pointing to me, "and surround and disarm them", indicating the rest of the group. I replied: "The war is over and we have no more enemies. The Americans have helped us a lot. Captain Birch's party is going to Suchow under orders to inspect the air field. If you want to disarm the Americans then you may cause a serious misunderstanding between communist China and America." The communist officer then said: "We will send one man to go along with you", and to a subordinate he said: "Bring your gun along. If anything happens, kill this man first and then kill the rest of the Americans." I then asked the officer his name, to which he said: "You don't have to ask my name; by the time you get there you will find out." After a pause he added proudly, "My surname is 'Mao'."

Then I returned with the subordinate to Captain Birch and, in a low voice, told him what I had overheard. At the receipt of this information Captain Birch faced the subordinate and taking a hands-on-hips stance said; "Well! So you want to disarm us!" An angry conversation upon the four Americans followed and Captain Birch continued: "At present the Americans have liberated the whole world, and you want to stop us and disarm us! Are you bandits? Are you the responsible man? Do we have to give our guns to you?" At this time our party was surrounded by 60 or 70 soldiers armed with rifles and one automatic rifle. The communist subordinate replied, "No, I am not responsible." Captain Birch then asked to be taken to the responsible man, and at this moment a second officer approached wearing a Sam Brown belt. He answered "No" to Captain Birch's questions as to whether he was the responsible man, and added: "Since you are not willing to be disarmed, you may proceed," and in a threatening manner he added: "If anything happens to you, we are not liable."

Captain Birch refused to be satisfied with this and stated: "No, I must find out what division these men belong to and who is the commanding officer. I want to talk to him." The communist officer replied, "If you want to see him, all right. Come with me." At this time and at the urging of General Peng of the Chinese Army who was accompanying the group, I suggested to Captain Birch that he be more tactful, but he replied: "Never mind, you don't know what my feelings are. I want to find out how they intend to treat Americans. I don't mind if they kill me. If they do they will be finished, for America will punish them with atomic bombs."

Soon we reached a house and went in while the second officer began to whisper to other men, we were told to sit down on a bed and wait. At that point Captain Birch said aloud, and in an angry voice: "After all, who is the chief? Will you or won't you let me see him? You have already delayed us for more than half an hour." The second officer replied: "You sit a while. We have to report in order of rank." At this, I said: "Please hurry as we are on an official mission. After we see him we can proceed." The second officer answered "All right, we will send a man along with you to the third garrison." When we arrived there I noticed it was the same house to which I had been taken when I was alone. There were no officers there and we were taken to the north gate where no one was found.[42]

In a sermon preached to the Christians in Wai Chang on January 18, 1941, John had chosen as his text, *"For unto you it is given in the behalf of Christ, not only to believe on him, but also to suffer for his sake"* (Philippians 1:29). Two years later, in a letter to his parents dated January 30, 1943, the missionary-soldier wrote, "The eternal Word, the sword of the Spirit, is even now more important than the thunder of guns and the crash of bombs."[43] With Scriptures such as *"Be not afraid of their faces . . ."* (Jeremiah 1:8a) steadying his nerve in the presence of *twenty gun-toting atheists*, Captain John Morrison Birch (Serial No. AC, 0-889028) made a conscious decision to push the envelope in a heroic display of contrived brinkmanship on behalf of "freedom and justice for all." Lieutenant Tung concludes his report:

When the Communist soldier who accompanied us started to lead us back to the place from which he had just come, Captain Birch became very angry and stopped the man by grabbing him at the back of his collar, saying, "After all, what are you people? If I say bandits you don't have the appearance of bandits. You are worse than bandits."

I had become increasingly alarmed about Captain Birch's attitude and, because there were about 20 other communist soldiers walking with us, I tried to sooth [sic] the situation by saying: "Don't take him seriously; he is only joking."

A short distance further someone said: "Come over here, here is our leader." At this time we went over and saw that it was the second officer again. I saluted but he did not return it. This officer was addressed as "instructor" (Tze Tao Yuan) by one of the enlisted men. I do not believe that this officer was advised of the rough handling which Captain Birch had given the soldier who accompanied us.

This officer then ordered, in a swearing manner: "Load your guns and disarm him first." He referred to Captain Birch because I was not armed. I then said: "Wait a minute, please. If you want to disarm him, I will get the gun for you, otherwise a serious misunderstanding may develop." The officer who was standing about 15 feet from us then ordered: "Shoot him first." An enlisted man who was standing about 10 feet to our right then raised his weapon and hesitated until the officer uttered a curse and again ordered him to fire. I was hit by the shot and after a second shot was fired, heard Captain Birch say: "I'm hit on the leg—I can't walk." Later I heard a third shot fired and I think that was the one which killed Captain Birch.

I became unconscious at that point and next heard someone say: "This man is not dead yet", and immediately someone struck me across the bridge of the nose with a rifle butt. A voice repeated "He is not dead yet." Another voice said "Though he is not dead yet, this had been sufficient to finish him." Another voice added: "We cannot leave the bodies here."

Two men then picked me up by the arms and legs and carried me over to some kind of hole in the ground where I felt Captain Birch's body next to mine. My face was opposite the middle portion of his body, and I was unable to see his face. While I was in this dugout, all of my clothes were taken from me.

Later some farmers approached and said: "We cannot leave the bodies here in open air—we will be afraid at night. We had better bury them." At that I opened my eyes and said: "I am not dead yet. Please rescue me. If you can't, kill me. Don't leave me like this." The farmer answered: "The communists are still here. We cannot move you right now. Wait until they go and we will remove you. The other man is already dead."

That night the farmers came and took me to a locomotive dugout where I was placed on a board. That night some Japanese soldiers with an interpreter came and questioned me, seemed disgruntled and went away.

The next morning more Japanese came from Lichwang and recognized me as having been the one who had stayed with them overnight in the railroad station. They took care of me and gave me treatment and seemed to be very concerned about the events that had taken place. They placed me in the Japanese infirmary at the Hwang Kao railroad station which the communists had meanwhile abandoned. The next day they left me at the station instead of taking me to Suchow as they had promised, and on the next day Chinese troops arrived and took me to the Suchow hospital.

Captain Birch was in full uniform with insignia and sidearms at the time of his death. I had no insignia on, but wore an army cap, shirt and shorts. The communists may have thought I was merely an interpreter for Captain Birch.

It is my opinion that if Captain Birch had been calm, nothing would have happened. I was afraid that there would be shooting if Captain Birch continued his manner. He would have become violent if any communists tried to disarm him. At no time, however, did Birch or I draw our weapons and the only movement approaching the drawing of weapons was the time when Captain Birch placed his hand on his hips.

The only communists I can identify are the first officer, the officer who ordered Captain Birch and me shot, and the bugler who took us for the first time to see the officer who finally ordered us shot.

I certify that this has been read to me by an interpreter and that it is a correct statement of all that happened.

> Tung Chin-Sheng
> 1st Lt, A.G.
> Int. Act.
> Hqs., 10th War Zone[44]

AUTOPSY, FUNERAL & REPORTS

After being abandoned in a garbage strewn trench, John's corpse was initially rolled in a mat and buried in a shallow grave by superstitious farmers (the same men who had rescued Tung). The next day Japanese troops arrived and took charge of the body. It was then turned over to a special investigator, Colonel Ma Cheng-Chao of the 4th Section, A.O.D. Headquarters, 6th Route Chinese Army (Puppet) who immediately ordered that a series of photographs be taken. Just as his adjutant, John had been shot with an *outlawed* dum-dum bullet, but in the left thigh instead. His feet were then bound together at the ankles and his hands tied from behind. He had, no doubt, been forced to kneel in the traditional posture of Communist executions as a second bullet, the one Tung recalled, passed through his skull from back to front. Colonel Ma reported that bits of brain matter and flesh were found at the site of the murder.

But there was something else. On August 28, John's remains were transferred to the Chinese military hospital in Suchow where Lieutenant Tung was battling for his own life with a fever of 106 degrees. Following a formal autopsy, the attending civilian doctor confirmed that "the flesh on the face and neck had been removed by slashes with a knife or bayonet, that teeth had been knocked out and that the nose was missing."[45] Positive identification was made through the victim's missing dental bridge.

The next day Lieutenant Bill Miller arrived in Suchow aboard a Japanese armored train to assist with the mopping up operations. Hefley writes:

> The stationmaster invited him to have a cup of tea, and while they were exchanging polite amenities his host casually asked if Miller had heard

about the murder of an American army captain by Communists. "I understand it was a very brutal murder," he added. A cold shiver ran up Miller's spine as he thought, "That could have been John." "The Captain's Chinese name was 'Bey Shang We,' " the stationmaster continued. "Did you know him?" Miller's ashen face and shocked expression answered the question even before he muttered numbly, "He was my good friend. My very good friend. We talked every day on the radio." [46]

After rushing to interview Lieutenant Tung at the hospital, Miller proceeded to the morgue where he viewed the mutilated corpse of the heroic patriot-martyr. He then began funeral arrangements with a local *Jesuit priest* (the devil's way of adding insult to injury). As two American pilots had just died in crash landings at the Suchow Airport, the decision was made to incorporate their funerals with John's.

At the appointed hour the entire Japanese high command in Suchow, twenty high-ranking officers, Chinese officials, and other leading citizens marched solemnly with Lieutenant Miller into the towering Catholic cathedral for a requiem high mass.

Following the mass, a mournful Japanese military band led a procession through the streets of the city. Twenty-four Chinese coolies carried the flag-draped coffins to the burial site on a wooded slope of the Hung-lung Mountain overlooking the south side of Suchow.

The three American officers were to be interred in side-by-side crypts, with John in the center. At the graveside a Chinese Protestant minister performed the final rites, followed by Latin prayers from the priests. As the coffins were eased into their final resting places, a Japanese drummer beat a sad farewell while the crowd of dignitaries, Confucianists, Buddhists, Shintoists, Catholics, and a few Protestants stood in respectful silence. Then at the command of a Japanese officer, three rifle salutes were sounded and the masons began cementing the stones in place. After the crypts were secured, the workmen stenciled vital statistics at the front of each vault, adding below John's name and date of death, HE DIED FOR THE CAUSE OF RIGHTEOUSNESS.[47]

In an attempt to head future critics off at the pass, Lieutenant Miller concluded his own official report accordingly:

In the case of the murder of Captain John Birch, 14th Air Force by members of the Eighth Route Army, the facts of which having been reported to General Wedemeyer, it is my sincere hope that his death will not go unhonored. I have known Captain Birch for many months in Anhwei

Province and feel that his intense devotion to duty and invaluable contributions in the line of intelligence should not be overlooked. He went to his death fearlessly in the cause he knew was righteous.[48]

In a much later correspondence to a friend dated 28 March 1992 (a copy of which I received from Mr. Robert Birch), Lieutenant Miller was given to self-abasement. Stating, "[I]would like to get some of my personal adventures recorded before I, too, start shoveling coal in the Hereafter," he then confessed,

> John was—like me—an ideological nut who thought that Communism was bad for China; the opinion of the State Department types to the contrary notwithstanding. Only John was willing to die for his beliefs while I chickened out after locking horns with the Liberal establishment in Washington. (After all, I still thought I might have an Army career at that point in time.)[49]

As for the other eleven men in John's detachment, they were subsequently disarmed, bound and led away at bayonet point. Although all were eventually released, it would be two months before the three Americans were permitted to fly back to Chungking. On November 7, 1945, an eleven-page report was issued by the three—Albert C. Grimes (a civilian), Lieutenant Laird M. Ogle and Sergeant Albert C. Meyers, in which they confirmed:

> There followed a strong statement of the Communist cause [by their captors] and a threat that the Communists would brook no interference in the pursuit of their aims. The Kuomintang [Chiang's government] was violently attacked, and the US personnel involved were accused of being their agents.[50]

On September 15, 1945, the Communist General Chu Teh, commander-in-chief 18th Army Group, responded to General Wedemeyer's formal inquiry of August 31 with the following predictable fabrication:

> In this tense period, two sentries of the rear guard under the deputy battalion commander Chang—Chang Chuensheng and Tu-Li-min—discovered two armed persons, a foreigner and a Chinese coming from the enemy direction towards them. They were immediately challenged by the sentries to halt and be recognized, but they did not obey the order, pulled out their arms, and dashed forward to the place where deputy battalion commander Chang was. They cursed while they were advancing. Commander Chang then

ordered two couriers to bring them to the Regiment Headquarters. The
two persons argued and struggled, cursing: "You people are traitors, bandits."
Their attitude was very aggressive and at the same time they pointed their
pistols at Commander Chang. **At this critical moment the couriers, for
self-defence, opened fire killing both of them.** At first we did not know
what nationality the foreigner belonged, but the three Americans coming
later identified that the foreigner must have been Captain Birch of the U.S.
Army. These are the details of the unfortunate death of Captain Birch at
Huang Ko.[51]

A better word for "details" would be "lies." Many American officers
were convinced that John's murder was anything but a chance encounter.
Author C.O. Lamp cites Colonel Richard H. Wise of the 14th Air Force
as stating:

During the last few days of the war I tried repeatedly to get him out of
that area. I knew the minute the war was over the Communists would kill
him, but I couldn't reach him. Captain Birch worked with us but he was
never under my command. He didn't work *for* me. . . .
   Once the war with Japan ended civil war would resume. Only a fool
would think otherwise. John knew all their agents. They couldn't have
a man running around who could identify all the operators. He had too
much influence with the peasants. He could speak with them, eat with
them, live with them. And there was the religion thing. There was no way
the Communists were going to let him live.[52]

"STRAY BULLETS"

On the morning of September 12, 1945, a delivery vehicle for Western
Union approached a small, two-story white clapboard house just off
State Highway 87 in Macon, Georgia. When the car honked, Ethel Birch
was busy in the yard. "Telegram for Mrs. George Birch," the courier
announced. "Please sign here." Her mother's heart fluttered; with four
sons in the military and the war finally over she wondered who would
be the first to wire his arrival details. Since John had been in the longest
she assumed that the message was his. Whatever the news, though, it
would be hers to receive alone as her husband was away on a work
assignment for the Georgia Health Department. Her hands trembled as she
opened the yellow envelope. Strange, it was from the War Department.

Why—*their* wartime telegrams were usually about . . . She read with foreboding attentiveness,

> THE SECRETARY OF WAR HAS ASKED ME TO EXPRESS HIS DEEP REGRET THAT YOUR SON CAPT BIRCH JOHN M WAS KILLED IN CHINA 25 AUG 45 CONFIRMING LETTER FOLLOWS.
>
> EDWARD F WITSELL
> ACTING ADJUTANT GENERAL OF THE ARMY[53]

Her first reaction was understandably one of denial. How could John have been "killed" ten days *after* the war ended? Had not the Lord preserved her boy through one dangerous mission after another? Surely the telegram was a terrible mistake. The next two days were a fog. Upon learning the news, Mr. Birch was incredulous as well. The follow-up letter from Major General Witsell arrived on the fourteenth.

> It is with deep regret that I confirm the telegram of recent date informing you of the death of you son, Captain John M. Birch, 0889028, Air Corps.
> The official casualty report states that your son was killed on 25 August 1945 on route to Suchow, China on the Lunghai Railway, **as the result of stray bullets**. . . .
> I sincerely regret that this message must carry so much sorrow into your home and I hope that in time you may find sustaining comfort in knowing that he served his country honorably.[54]

Their worst fears were confirmed when a package arrived containing John's few earthly belongings. Among the items were a *Cruden's Concordance* and a well-marked *Scofield Bible*. Though stricken with grief, they were also forced to question the stated cause of their son's untimely death—"as a result of *stray* bullets." Thus, according to the War Department, one of the sharpest intelligence officers in the eastern theater was killed by *stray* bullets *ten* days after the cessation of hostilities. What could all of this mean? John's biographers continue the sequence of events:

> A week later an Army jeep pulled into the drive. She was alone again. A young officer, carrying a clipboard, came to the door. "I'm from the Chaplain's office at Warner Robbins," he informed her. "What information have you had concerning your son's death?" Stoically, Mother Birch handed him the telegram from the War Department and the letter from

General Witsell. The young man laid his clipboard on the dining table and turned aside to read the official communications.

While he was diverted, Mother Birch glanced at a photostat on top of the sheaf of papers on the clipboard. She caught the name "Captain John Birch" and moved closer. "Oh, my," she gasped, "this says he was killed by Communists!" The officer whirled and snatched up the clipboard. "You ought not to have seen that, Ma'am." "Why not? He's *my* son," Mother Birch protested in growing shock. "You ought to know that a photostat is more likely to be correct than a typed telegram." "No, uh, well, yes," the white-faced soldier sputtered. "Ma'am, I made a terrible mistake. I was very careless. You weren't supposed to see this. Why, I could be court-martialed." "But I want to know. He's my son!" she pleaded. "Please. Please let me read it."

"Okay," he sighed. "Read it. But I beg you, don't say anything for at least three weeks. I'll be discharged by then." He passed the clipboard to her. "Captain Birch was killed by Chinese Communists on the Lunghai Railroad, August 25, 1945."

"I've got to go, Ma'am. Please don't say anything for three weeks. I could be court-martialed for this." Mother Birch promised. The officer left. She never heard from him again.[55]

George and Ethel were now more perplexed than ever. If John had been killed by Communists, why did their letter employ the nebulous phrase, "stray bullets"? On October 30, the following letter arrived from General Chennault:

Dear Mr. Birch:

I have only just been advised of John's death. This news has indeed been as much of a blow to me as it must have been to you and Mrs. Birch— I have always felt that John was more than just a very good officer in my command, in fact I have always felt towards him as a father might feel toward a son.

Although it is poor consolation at this time, I would like very much to tell you that John did a magnificent job with me. I always felt that he would always be depended on to see things through. His loyalty to me personally and his devotion to duty was beyond anything that was expected of him. I cannot praise his work sufficiently.

I know and realize how hard it must be for you and Mrs. Birch to accept this great loss, that he died for his country doing a splendid job is not always enough compensation for the loss you are called upon to accept, but I want you to know that my deepest sympathy is with you and Mrs. Birch.

John is being recommended for the Distinguished Service Cross—I cannot think of anyone of my officers who deserved it more.

If there is anything I can do for you at any time, please do not hesitate to call upon me.

> Please convey my deepest sympathy to Mrs. Birch.
>
> With kindest personal regards, I am,
> Most sincerely yours,
> C. L. Chennault.

Chennault had left China only a short time before the war ended. In reality he was forced out for his politically incorrect views ("guts"). Yet, as John's former commander why hadn't he heard about the murder for over two months?

George then learned that the general was scheduled to speak in Atlanta on December 10. After contacting Chennault's office in Washington, D.C., they obtained an appointment to see him at the Henry Grady Hotel. Ethel recorded everything that was said on a portable typewriter.

> "Tell us how he died," the Birches requested. "Was he killed by stray bullets or Communists?" "Communists!" the old war eagle snorted. "That's what friends have told me, although the War Department classified his file 'top secret.' His party was stopped on their mission by Communists. Being the officer in charge, John went to talk to them. . . . They knew who he was. He walked straight toward them, and they killed him. They murdered one of the most loyal men I ever had." [56]

In his memoirs, Chennault added, ". . . if I had still been in China, there would have been a squadron of B-25's blasting that Communist position with no further questions asked."[57]

George and Ethel were determined to get to the bottom of their son's death. Climbing into the family's 1940 Chrysler, they drove all the way to the War Department itself. However, the unexpected treatment they received in the nation's capital only added to their grief. For some "strange" reason, no one was willing to discuss John's death by "stray bullets." The convenient bottom line was that the file on Captain John M. Birch was classified "Top Secret." This was the end of their heart-broken investigation.

During my interview with General Hill, the Flying Tiger ace concurred with Chennault's assessment of John's cold-blooded execution.

First report was that he was killed by a stray bullet walking along the Lunghai Railway. But that wasn't it at all. He had a confrontation with the Chinese Communists and they killed him—shot him in the leg and then they mutilated his body.[58]

And in answer to my follow-up question, "Is it true that the government covered up his murder?" General Hill replied,

Yeah, it was covered up. It really was. They gave a bad report on the thing and they never told the true story of it and that was because—it's the State Department. **They're the guys that get us into all this trouble.**[59]

General Scott agreed. When I asked him about John's murder and subsequent cover-up, he replied, "It was one of the most significant tragedies of the entire war. It was terrible; just terrible."[60]

I then solicited his opinion on the perennial corruption within the State Department.

I think there is something peculiar about the State Department like there is with the CIA. Spies seem to be able to operate from within for years and years without being detected. **They ought to be shot!** That's the way I look at it.[61]

As for the tragic aftermath of John's murder and the abandonment of Chiang Kai-Shek in favor of Mao—Scott noted insightfully:

We have the greatest country in the world. We have the greatest military. **The problem is, when we win the war, the State Department seems to go in and lose the peace.** With the greatest force on earth, we win the wars and lose the peace. That's what I worry about.[62]

Some believe that General Scott's career was hindered by his outspoken remarks concerning John's murder and about Communism as a whole. With such a rare connection to the past seated before me, I couldn't help seizing the moment by asking,

Looking back over your long military career, it appears that you were always in the thick of controversy for bucking the system. You would commandeer unauthorized vehicles if your mission was in danger. Once, you threatened to shoot the Communist union leader John L. Lewis. On another occasion, you even warned General Bissell that you might shoot him if he didn't quit harassing General Chennault. Yet, you were able to retire as a Brigadier General. If you had it to do over again, would you do anything different?

Scott replied:

> The problem in the Pentagon has always been the "yes boys." I never did operate like that. I got to work for a wonderful general named Chennault, and he simply told it like it was. And that's what I believe in doing.[63]

I then remarked, "It seems that Chennault ruined you in the right sense." To which the 94-year-old retired Brigadier General concluded, with fire in his eyes:

> Exactly. I got away with murder! **And if I had it to do over, I'd do it again—and harder!**[64]

Had John's execution at the hands of Chinese Communists been made known to the American public, the fall of China could have been averted. As we shall see in volume three of this work, China's betrayal would lead to the bloody debacles in Korea, Cambodia and Vietnam.

THE JOHN BIRCH SOCIETY

Following another five years of frustration, Mrs. Birch caught the attention of California Senator William Knowland. After listening to her story he requisitioned the top-secret file. The senator could hardly believe what he was reading in the fifty-five-page report. On September 5, 1950, while more than 35,000 other "John Birches" were being slaughtered in the Korean "police action" (many by Chinese bullets), Knowland stomped onto the Senate floor and "dumped the entire truckload!" In his concluding remarks, he said:

> If the Members of Congress had had this information in August or September of 1945, is there any person here who feels that they would have tolerated the subsequent activity of the State Department in trying to force a coalition between the government of the Republic of China and

the same Communists represented by the man who shot Captain Birch in cold blood?

Is there any person here who does not believe that this simple story of a lone American officer, who was willing to sacrifice his life so that this nation might find out whether these Communists were friends or enemies, would not have warned us in time that these Chinese Communists were the same ruthless killers that Communists are the world over?

Does any person here think that if the story of Captain Birch had been known to the American Congress or the American people, that any American would have been taken in by the theory of fellow travelers that Chinese Communists were also agrarian liberals? . . . Mr. President, if the Secretary of State and the President of the United States have not read the eyewitness account of the death of Captain Birch, I think it is unfortunate that it was not called to their attention as soon as it was available in 1945. If they have read it, I do not see how they could have approved the policies we followed in China subsequent to 1945.[65]

One of many who heard about Knowland's speech was Robert Welch, a conservative political analyst, sporting high academic credentials. At the age of *two* he had already learned to read; by age *seven* he had finished all nine volumes of Ridpath's *History of the World*; at *twelve* he was a freshman at the University of North Carolina. His post-graduate work covered two years at Harvard and two years at the U.S. Naval Academy where he ranked fourth in a class of nearly one thousand cadets.

Welch published a biography of John Birch in 1954 that caused an immediate sensation in the public arena. *The Saturday Evening Post* was even pressed to acknowledge in an editorial, January 22, 1955:

Amazingly, there were in Washington responsible officials who were willing to suppress news of the murder of an American officer, apparently to prevent the American people from rising in their wrath and vetoing further appeasement of communism. Not a great deal can be said for the judgment, discretion and reliability of those responsible for suppressing the tragic and revealing story of Captain John Birch.[66]

Although some might conclude that John's life was taken in vain, the patriotic missionary had a spiritual premonition of an extended influence beyond the grave. He confided to his sister Betty in a letter dated March 22, 1945, "Often in these days I feel that these barren years are my apprenticeship, God-given, and that a message is being formed, by him, within me that will one day burn its way out and across man's barriers, into the souls of many."[67]

In 1958, the year following Senator McCarthy's "death," Welch formed an anti-Communist society to acquaint his fellow Americans with the steady erosion of their constitutional liberties. After securing permission from John's parents, Welch named his new organization *The John Birch Society* in honor of their son's martyrdom. As "a hit dog yells," the insiders sought to discredit Welch and his associates from the outset. Wesley McCune, then director of Group-Research, Inc., a Washington-based organization which monitored the activities of political conservatives, went so far as to publish an article in the *Washington Post* entitled "John Birch: Did He Seek Death?" The "conservative" columnist, William F. Buckley, was also among the Society's literary detractors. Even the nation's PTA clubs were deceived into smearing John's memory.

The Kremlin was responsible for much of this activity. On July 11, 1961, Mr. Edward Hunter appeared before the Senate Sub-Committee of the Eighty-seventh Congress, First Session to report that an emergency meeting of international Communists had convened in Moscow in November, 1960. According to Hunter's sworn testimony, ". . . a Manifesto was issued on 5 December 1960 calling for a destruction of the spontaneous grass-roots, anti-communist movement in the U.S.A., and elsewhere."[68]

Of the many reproaches John's family was forced to endure, the account of his missing medals proved especially painful. As previously stated, John received the Legion of Merit for the Changteh campaign in 1943. After his death, his father accepted an Oak Leaf Cluster for which John had been recommended in 1945 while posted in Anhwei Province. However, given the horrific conditions of his ultimate sacrifice, Captain Birch was also recommended for several posthumous awards. They were: Distinguished Service Cross, recommended by General Charles B. Stone, who succeeded General Chennault in the China War Theater; the Silver Star, recommended by Colonel Wilfred Smith, John's immediate supervisor in the 14th Air Force; and the Congressional Medal of Honor, recommended by Captain James H. Hart, who was associated with John in Anhwei Province. In 1967, Ethel Birch sadly confirmed, "None of the posthumous awards were ever given."[69] She then went on to relate the following bizarre exchange that she had with Major General Edward F. Witsell (the one who had sent her the letter containing the phrase "stray bullets").

One thing I had earlier seen the General about was the awards John had been recommended for. So at that interview, I brought up the point that the facts showed that John was first shot in the leg, and (according to Lieutenant Thompson's account) then said to the Communists when they ordered him to walk, that he couldn't walk anymore. That showed that he was wounded before they bayonetted him to death. But when I insisted we should be given the Purple Heart, General Witsell said that *the Chinese Communists were our allies* and the Purple Heart was given only when one was wounded by the enemy![70]

John's only immediate recognition came from the national government of the Republic of China. On November 3, 1945, Bey Shang We was posthumously awarded the DECORATION OF BREAST ORDER OF CLOUD, with Certificate, by a grateful (though soon-to-be abandoned) ally.

Though the government would later recant concerning the Purple Heart (even throwing in a Bronze Star for good measure), the other three medals remained unaccounted for, a frustrating postscript to the tragedy.

In the course of his research, Mr. Loving was able to obtain a copy of John's file through the Freedom of Information Act. While all previous inquiries had proven futile, according to the National Personnel Records Center in St. Louis, Missouri, John's "Decorations and Awards" should have included the Distinguished Service Cross. On December 9, 2002, Loving wrote to Mr. Andrew H. Card, Jr., chief of staff for President Bush, informing him of the travesty. Among other things, he asked:

> Would it not be a wonderful vindication for a tragic oversight, that this award be bestowed posthumously, to the memory of this truly heroic United States military officer? . . . Is the awarding of this medal something that President Bush may wish to become involved with? Is it too late to award this medal?[71]

Mr. Loving is to be commended for his initiative. However, as of July 2004, Robert Birch informed me that the matter had been dropped.

Yet, despite this miscarriage of justice, John's family can always rejoice in the countless testimonials to the lives he impacted. Miss Adeline Gray, a newspaperwoman who knew John in China, wrote Mrs. Birch the following comforting lines in November 1945:

> He extended a profound effect upon the thousands of people who came in contact with him. The American GIs he met were influenced to a better life, and higher ideals and better modes of personal behaviour by your son's

own noble example. Tens of thousands of Chinese loved him as dearly as though he were their own brother. Your son was truly one of the finest men it has ever been my fortune to meet. His loss is a great loss to not only China, but America and the world. He loved China and the Chinese people dearly, and planned to stay in China all his life.[72]

In my own case, I cannot escape the spiritual "coincidence" that John was killed on August 25, *the very day I would receive Jesus Christ as my personal Saviour in 1974!*

Perhaps the family's most precious keepsake of all is John's original handwritten poem displayed at the Warner Robins museum. When he turned sixteen in 1934, John's grandmother died leaving his father and two aunts a 500-acre farm in Macon. Though the call to China removed him from his cherished Birchwood, a love for the simple life had been sown in his heart. This vision was no doubt a source of comfort through many dark times. In one letter he wrote, "Never let your mind be too busy, or too sensed or dulled to find pleasure in the beauty of nature and God's handiwork." John sent his parents the following lines just four months before his death.

War-Weary Farmer

I should like to find the existence of what my father called,
"Plain living and high thinking."

I want some fields and hills, woodlands and streams I can call my own.
I want to spend my strength in making the fields green, and the cattle fat,
so that I may give sustenance to my loved ones, and aid to those
neighbors who suffer misfortune.
I do not want a life of monotonous paper-shuffling or of trafficking
with money-mad traders.

I only want enough of science to enable a fruitful husbandry of the land
with simple tools, a time for leisure, and the guarding of my family's
health. I do not care to be absorbed in the endless examinings of force
and space and matter, which, I believe can only slowly lead to God.

I do not want a hectic hurrying from place to place on whizzing machines
or busy streets. I do not want an elbowing through crowds of impatient
strangers who have time neither to think their own thoughts
nor to know real friendship.
I want to live slowly, to relax with my family before a glowing fireplace,

to welcome the visits of my neighbors, to worship God, to enjoy a book, to lie on a shaded grassy bank and watch the clouds sail across the blue.

I want to love a wife who prefers rural peace to urban excitement, one who would rather climb a hilltop to watch a sunset with me than to take a taxi to any Broadway play. I want a woman who is not afraid of bearing children, and who is able to rear them with a love for home and the soil, and the fear of God.

I want of Government only protection against the violence and injustices of evil or selfish men.

I want to reach the sunset of life sound in body and mind, flanked by strong sons and grandsons, enjoying the friendship and respect of my neighbors, surrounded by fertile fields and sleek cattle, and retaining my boyhood faith in Him who promised a life to come.

Where can I find this world? Would its anachronism doom it to ridicule or loneliness? Is there yet a place for such simple ways in my own America? Or must I seek a vale in Turkestan where peaceful flocks still graze on quiet hills."

15

KAL 007

". . . but no man knoweth of his sepulchre
unto this day."
(Deuteronomy 34:6b)

A S MR. WELCH entered his senior years he passed the reigns of leadership to Dr. Lawrence Patton McDonald, a U.S. congressman from Georgia's seventh congressional district. Prior to his foray into politics, Dr. McDonald had distinguished himself as a urological surgeon in Atlanta.

Larry became acquainted with the spread of Communism while he was a Naval surgeon in Iceland and physician to diplomatic personnel at the American Embassy in Reykjavik. His older brother, Dr. Harold McDonald, Jr., recalled:

> He went to the commanding officer in Iceland when he thought the U.S. Embassy appeared to be doing things advantageous to the Communists, who were very influential in the country. He was told something that rang in his ears: "You don't understand the big picture." He began to think, "Maybe I do."[1]

Larry possessed a strong intellect and disciplined study habits. Completing high school and pre-med in four years had enabled him to enroll in Emory University Medical School at seventeen. He then began devouring books on political history and foreign affairs. After joining the John Birch Society in 1967, he was elected to the House of Representatives seven years later. While typical politicians can be influenced by the "buck," Larry's level of devotion was evidenced by the six-figure income he relinquished when he left the medical profession.

Like his distant cousin, General George C. Patton, the six foot-two inch freshman congressman became an immediate force to be reckoned with. Illinois Republican Phil Crane said of the Georgia Democrat, "I regard Larry as one of the most staunch conservatives here in Congress."[2] Throughout his four-plus terms in the House, Larry accumulated a perfect 100 percent score on "The Conservative Index," then compiled by *The Review of The News*.

However, Larry's greatest service to his nation was in continuing the legacy of Bey Shang We. Unlike his agnostic predecessor, the new chairman of the John Birch Society was a committed evangelical Christian. I once heard a tape of the spirited Free Methodist congressman addressing a throng of 3,000 shouting Independent Baptists at Dr. Sammy Allen's Faith Baptist Camp in Resaca, Georgia. Speaking for over an hour (without notes) on the theme "America's Spiritual Heritage," McDonald declared:

> It states in our founding documents that we as Americans hold strongly and clearly to the view that, as free men, we receive our basic rights, not from government, not from the Constitution, but from God on high . . . In the United States of America the function of the government is to protect God-given rights. Our Founding Fathers knew that if we ever accept the view that it is the government that gives us our rights, our freedoms would be limited. The day would come when what the government said they gave us, the government would come and take away.[3]

As he labored in the political arena, Larry often drew a Scriptural analogy to the watchman on the wall in Ezekiel 3:17-21, stating:

> If evil, villainy, or war comes, and if the Watchman does not sound the trumpet, then the blood is on his hands. Any of the blood that is shed is on the hands of the Watchman who goes to sleep. But if the Watchman sounds the trumpet and the people are too lethargic, too busy enjoying the good life to care, then the blood and responsibility is on the hands of the people.[4]

Larry and his "Congressional trumpet" were inseparable, James Perloff stating, "McDonald was Washington's most outspoken critic of trade and technology transfer to the USSR."[5] In his forward to Gary Allen's book *The Rockefeller File*, Larry condemned "the drive of the Rockefellers and their allies to create a one-world government, combining super-capitalism and Communism under the same tent."[6] He also had denounced President Reagan's lifting of the embargo on pipe-laying technology to the Soviets for the construction of a mammoth trans-Siberian natural gas pipeline to be constructed by slave labor. Sensing that history was about to repeat itself, the "Watchman" warned:

> Many government officials are enthusiastically promoting trade with the greatest tyranny the world has ever known: the Soviet and Chinese dictatorships. One imagines that they would have been leading the parade to trade with Hitler in the mid-to-late 1930s, apparently unwilling to accept the reality of tyranny and the Nazi's desire for world domination. Today the names have changed. No longer is it Hitler, but rather Andropov and Teng. But the goal is the same: destruction of the West.[7]

As with John Birch before him, Larry was also endowed by his Creator with a mastery for debate. A friend, Dr. Daniel Jordan, recalled:

> His personal magnetism allowed him to swing a number of voters to his side who didn't always agree with him . . . Opponents knew that taking on Larry in a head-to-head confrontation meant being destroyed. His political enemies in the news media in Atlanta and Georgia's regular Democratic organization feared him less for his views than his effectiveness, his charismatic personality, his intelligence, and his overwhelming knowledge. This infuriated the Atlanta media, because no one was supposed to know things as well as they did. And when he could overcome their knowledge, it was infuriating because he was on the other side; they could have tolerated him if he had been one of them.[8]

While his hireling peers hoped that he would go away, a grass roots constituency began to form on the horizon. There was talk of a run for the Senate, and eventually perhaps, for the White House itself. The congressman's foreign affairs advisor, Hilaire du Berrier, stated:

> Larry was a comer. All the things which he had said and for which the American press had sneered at him were proving valid. He was the most handsome, personable, and most articulate man in the House of Representatives. . . . Among the qualities that make for greatness, he had the rare gift of inspiring confidence in the hearts of those in his presence and he had an indefinable ring of verity in his voice. **Above all, he was honest and a patriot.**[9]

However, though McDonald's stock was rising among red-blooded Americans, he was regularly being vilified by *Pravda, Tass* and Radio Moscow. Warren Mass wrote, ". . . Larry McDonald had become the most dangerous enemy the Communists had."[10] Harold McDonald confirmed that his brother had taken to wearing a bulletproof vest following several threats on his life.[11] Larry was well aware of the potential cost for sustaining liberty in America, stating:

> We must realize that we as United States citizens and as heirs to Western civilization should put our priorities in order and know that we are in a fight for our lives. . . . [I]t's a matter of whether this entire civilization is prepared to fight the Communist plague or be destroyed. This is not something that our children or grandchildren will face. This is something that we shall have to face.[12]

OFF TO SOUTH KOREA

Shortly before midnight on August 31, 1983, Larry boarded KAL 007 at New York's JFK Airport en route to Seoul, Korea, with a refueling stop in Anchorage, Alaska. Senator Jesse Helms of North Carolina had been asked to lead a delegation of six conservative legislators to Seoul for the thirtieth anniversary of the signing of the United States-South Korea Mutual Defense Treaty. Garrett N. Scalera, president of the Tokyo Institute of Policy Studies, one of the principle sponsors of the conference and its overall coordinator, rightly surmised that the meeting was a slap in Yuri Andropov's face, stating:

> The Soviets saw the conference as a threat to their long-range plans to terrorize and eventually dominate free Asian nations. The purpose of the conference, as well as an earlier one in Tokyo, was to begin laying the groundwork for a northeast Asia security framework.[13]

Twenty minutes before Larry landed in Anchorage, KAL 007's Seoul-bound sister flight KAL 015 arrived from Los Angeles carrying Helms, Senator Steve Symms of Idaho and Congressman Carroll Hubbard of Kentucky. (Senators Orrin Hatch of Utah and Ed Zorinski of Nebraska had elected to travel the following day.) While most of the passengers aboard both planes disembarked to stretch their legs in the terminal, Larry chose to catch up on his sleep.

Senator Helms noticed a young family from KAL 007. The mother was reading Bible stories to their two small daughters. When she finished, he went over and introduced himself. Neil J. Grenfell and his wife Carol Ann were originally from Australia. Grenfell was the marketing director for the Eastman Kodak Company in South Korea and was returning from a visit with his wife's parents in Rochester, New York. As any grandparent would understand, Senator Helms was very interested in meeting five-year-old Nolie Ann and her three-year-old sister, Stacy Marie. He would later sadly recall:

> If I live to be one thousand, I will never forget those little girls. They played on my lap, giggling and kissing my cheeks. And when they went to get on that plane they waved bye-bye and blew kisses at me. That's why I'll never forget those two little girls. They had a right to live.[14]

KAL 007 took off from Anchorage on runway 32 at 5:00 a.m. local time or 1300 GMT (Greenwich Mean Time, also called UTC for universal time coordinated, or Z time); KAL 015 followed fourteen minutes later. The next eight hours should have been an enjoyable, though uneventful, travel experience. (Such is my own recollection, having flown KAL to Seoul for a speaking engagement in 2000.) After ninety minutes in flight, Korean Air procedure called for stewardesses to change into their native dress—long skirts known as *chima* and flared blouses called *chogori*. Following a light meal a film would have been shown.

The 269 people aboard constituted fifteen different nationalities: 105 Koreans (including the 29 crew members), 61 Americans, 28 Japanese, 23 Taiwanese, 15 Filipinos, 12 residents of Hong Kong, 9 Canadians, 6 Thais, 4 Australians, 1 Swede, 1 Indian, 1 Briton, 1 Dominican, 1 Vietnamese, and 1 Malaysian.[15] At least 115 were females and 29 were children. A dozen were over sixty, the oldest being eighty.

Congressman McDonald was assigned aisle seat 2A in first class. According to the passenger manifest, the Grenfells were seated only five rows behind in coach. Did he hear the same innocent laughter that had so delighted Senator Helms? Perhaps he was mulling over the speech he was scheduled to deliver during the conference. Larry was planning to expose KGB collusion with the North Korean agents south of the 38th parallel. "I believe that in a number of cases," one part of the speech read, "we can detect probable 'active measures' on behalf of the North Korean regime in Pyongyang carried out by that regime's agents and on their behalf by the Soviet KGB."[16]

Only a few air miles away, Senator Symms was experiencing a disconcerting anxiety aboard KAL 015. (At this time it just so happened that Symms was my senator, as I was pastoring a Baptist church in Coeur d'Alene, Idaho.) In a later interview with Jeffrey St. John, author of *Day of the Cobra: The True Story of KAL Flight 007,* Symms acknowledged:

> I had really a very uneasy feeling during the flight. Usually when traveling on airplanes I am the easiest flyer in the world. I just don't worry about anything. But I was very restless during the flight and was glad to get to Seoul. . . .
>
> I don't know whether it was ESP or not; but in the middle of the flight out of Anchorage, I guess it must have been about four hours out, after dinner and looking at the inflight movie, Fran was asleep and so were most of the first class passengers. I got up to go to the bathroom and on my way out I stopped and looked out the window in the rear of the plane. The moon was out and it was a clear night. I distinctly remember this crazy thought: "We are close to Russian territory; wouldn't it be just like the Soviets to look on this airplane as a fat duck flying so near they might think of shooting it down!" I then remember thinking, "What am I doing up here with Helms? It would be just like the Soviets to shoot the plane down because he's riding on it." It was just a crazy passing thought and I didn't dwell on it until later, and I was amazed at what I thought at the time.[17]

Larry's wife Kathryn experienced a similar intuitive caution. St. John writes,

> Kathryn McDonald recalled later that in the last telephone conversation she had with her husband, she pleaded with him to cancel his trip to Seoul because she had an uneasy feeling and was concerned that McDonald was exhausted from his heavy workload. "I have to go," Mrs. McDonald quoted her husband as saying. "I have given my word and as much as I would like to come home for a rest with you and the children, the South Koreans are counting on my being there."[18]

When I listened to the congressman's impassioned message at Sammy Allen's tabernacle, I marveled that it was delivered on Wednesday, November 24, 1982. How was he to know that the following day would be his last Thanksgiving on earth (or at least his last in America)? While KAL 015 went on to land at Kimpo International Airport as scheduled, KAL 007 disappeared in the darkness, the victim of foul play.

"THE TARGET IS DESTROYED"

By midmorning of September 1, the world had yet to receive an official report about the fate of KAL 007. Then at 10:45 a.m. EST, the American secretary of state, George Shultz, held a news conference in which he stated:

> At 1400 hours Greenwich Mean Time (GMT) yesterday, a Korean Air Lines Boeing 747, en route from New York to Seoul, Korea, departed Anchorage, Alaska. Two hundred and sixty-nine passengers and crew were on board, including Congressman Lawrence P. McDonald [D.-Ga.].
>
> At approximately 1600 hours Greenwich Mean Time, the aircraft came to the attention of Soviet radar. It was tracked constantly by the Soviets from that time.
>
> The aircraft strayed into Soviet airspace over the Kamchatka Peninsula and over the Sea of Okhotsk and over the Sakhalin Island. The Soviets tracked the commercial airliner for some 2½ hours.
>
> A Soviet pilot reported visual contact with the aircraft at 1812 hours. The Soviet plane was, we know, in constant contact with its ground control.
>
> At 1821 hours, the Korean aircraft was reported by the Soviet pilot at 10,000 meters. At 1826 hours, the Soviet pilot reported that he fired a missile, and **the target was destroyed**.
>
> At 1830 hours, the Korean aircraft was reported by radar at 5,000 meters. At 1838 hours, the Korean plane disappeared from the radar screen.
>
> We know that at least eight Soviet fighters reacted at one time or another to the airliner. The pilot who shot the aircraft down reported after the attack that he had, in fact, fired a missile, that he had **destroyed the target**, and that he was breaking away.
>
> About an hour later, Soviet controllers ordered a number of their search aircraft to conduct search-and-rescue activity in the vicinity of the last position of the Korean airliner reflected by Soviet tracking. One of these aircraft reported finding kerosene on the surface of the seas in that area.

Shultz went on to say, "The Soviets offered no information"; "grave concern" was expressed to the Soviet chargé d'affaires in Washington "over the shooting down of an unarmed civilian plane carrying passengers of a number of nationalities"; the State Department "demanded an explanation from the Soviet Union"; "The United States reacts with revulsion to this attack"; and, "Loss of life appears to be heavy" (note the word *heavy*).

During the ensuing question and answer session, the reporters wanted to know if the Soviet pilot had clearly identified the target as a commercial aircraft.

Q. "Did the Soviet Union give any warning to this aircraft and request it to land or try to force it down before it shot it down?"

A. "We have no evidence of that. There was apparently no ability to communicate between the two aircraft. But as the statement says, the Soviet plane that shot down the commercial airliner moved itself into position where it had visual contact with the aircraft, so that with the eye you could inspect the aircraft and see what it was you were looking at."

Q. "Do we know whether the Soviets sought to force the KAL plane down without using missiles?"

A. "We have no information about that. And as I said, as far as we can see, there was no communication between the two aircraft except that they did track this aircraft for 2½ hours; at least eight fighters at one time or another were around in the vicinity; and the aircraft that shot the plane down was close enough for visual inspection of the aircraft."

The material presented in the remainder of this chapter will expose the preceding remarks as a collection of distortion and disinformation. For the record, the secretary of state didn't get two words out of his mouth before his audience was already being misled. KAL 007 did *not* depart from Anchorage at 1400 hours GMT. The correct time was 1300 GMT. This seemingly insignificant error, constituting the first two words of his official statement, was an omen of what would follow over the next twenty-plus years!

While Shultz was attempting to convince his listeners that the Soviet pilot had indeed gained enough visual contact with the "target" to have positively identified it as a commercial Boeing 747, he dramatically waved a document, supposedly containing sensitive intelligence discourses, corroborating his account. The paper was later confirmed to have been a prop.[19] The truth is, a thorough examination of all intercepted Soviet transmissions reveal that, at no time did any of their pilots believe they were pursuing anything other than an intruding military aircraft of undetermined national origin (though it was presumed to be American).

THE ACTOR-PRESIDENT

Meanwhile, "back at the ranch" (literally), the leader of the free world was eating breakfast with Nancy out in Santa Barbara. And it just so happened that the president's four top advisors, Edwin Meese, William Clark, Howard Baker, and Michael Deaver, were also out of town at that critical moment. Understandably, the White House went into shock when Reagan informed them he had no intention of cutting his vacation short over the "mere" slaughter of sixty-one Americans, including a sitting United States congressman. In fact, Senior Advisor Mike Deaver told fellow staffer Stuart Spencer that the president was "in concrete" over his decision to run things from California.[20] However, the cement "cracked" that evening during the *CBS Evening News*. With the nation, Congress, and most of the world in turmoil over the apparent Soviet atrocity, cameras stationed three miles away were able to show Ron and Nancy casually enjoying their usual afternoon horseback ride at the ranch.

Reagan promptly decided to "ride" back to Washington the following day, calling the CBS clip a "cheap shot." Standing on the airport tarmac at Point Mugu Naval Air Station in California shortly after noon local time, the president made his first public statement concerning the shootdown. Whereas Shultz had shown his hand after only two words, Reagan did the same with his opening statement:

> First, let me say that Nancy and I were deeply saddened last night to hear of the death of **Senator Henry Jackson**. He was a friend, a colleague, a true patriot, and a devoted servant of the people. He will be sorely missed, and we both extend our deepest sympathy to his family.
>
> And now, in the wake of the barbaric act committed yesterday by the Soviet regime against a commercial jet liner . . . [blah, blah, blah] . . .

Did you catch it? No, it was *not* a misprint. The president simply chose to begin his remarks by consoling the family of a moderate senator who had died from natural causes while totally ignoring the wife and children of a conservative representative who had been murdered by a foreign government (the first such assassination in the history of our country). The remainder of his brief statement constituted a line of predictable anti-Soviet rhetoric.

After again failing to mention Larry's death during his radio address on September 3, the president dropped a subliminal bomb during his formal speech to the nation on September 5.

> My fellow Americans, I am coming before you tonight about the Korean airline massacre—the attack by the Soviet Union against 269 innocent men, women and children aboard an unarmed Korean passenger plane. This crime against humanity must never be forgotten, here or throughout the world.
>
> Our prayers tonight are with the victims and their families in their time of terrible grief. Our hearts go out to them—to brave people like Kathryn McDonald, **the wife of the Congressman**, whose composure and eloquence on the day of **her husband's** death moved us all. **He** will be sorely missed by all of us here in government.

Then followed Act III of Reagan's dramatic post-September 1 sideshow—"The Soviet's are barbarians," etc. But what about those unbelievable subliminal suggestions? Did you discern the three times that Reagan adamantly refused to mention the slain government official by name—"Kathryn McDonald, **the wife of the Congressman**," ". . . on the day of **her husband's** death," and "**He** will be sorely missed. . . ." And if you think I've over-exaggerated the point, notice how midway through his remarks Reagan returns to his convenient hiding place:

> **Senator Henry Jackson**, a wise and revered statesman and one who probably understood the Soviets as well as any American in history, warned us, "the greatest threat the United States now faces is posed by Soviet Union." But **Senator Jackson** said, "If America maintains a strong deterrent—and only if it does—this nation will continue to be a leader in the crucial quest for enduring peace among nations." The late senator made those statements in July on the Senate floor, speaking in behalf of the MX missile program he considered vital to restore America's strategic parity with the Soviets.

In a message supposedly commemorating the victims of KAL 007, President Reagan referred to "the late senator" Jackson by name twice, yet failed to mention Larry altogether. Howard Phillips, chairman of the Conservative Caucus noted, "Frankly, I was rather shocked that the president failed to mention Representative McDonald in any of his statements."[21]

The White House snub continued when Reagan not only declined Kathy McDonald's personal invitation to speak at Larry's special memorial service, but refused to attend as well. He also failed to send an official representative in his place. The four thousand mourners who packed Washington's Constitution Hall for the Sunday affair were righteously indignant. St. John described them as "representatives of the fundamentalist Christian political right, who, like McDonald, scorn politics without principles and persist in the increasingly unpopular belief that the Kremlin leadership is a satanic force that cannot be fought without religious faith."[22] Even the Mormon, Orrin Hatch, got hot under the collar, stating:

> Larry was a decent and honorable, honest, hard-nosed man. He stood up to his own liberal party and had primary opponents from within his own party dominated by liberals because of his fight against communism. He was a courageous and honest man who deserved a more lasting memorial than a few mentions in the *Congressional Record*.[23]

So, why was Ronald Reagan so intimidated by the name "Larry McDonald"? The reason is simple. Reagan merely *professed* to be what McDonald *was* in reality! Larry was willing to take on the issues everyone else feared. His wife called him "the total gladiator for the right cause," stating that "he was never afraid to do the unpopular . . . and unaccepted."[24] Republican Congressman Newt Gingrich eulogized his fellow Georgian as a loner, "who refused to vote for the Speaker of his own party, a strong conservative who marched to the beat of a drum that others did not hear. Many people thought he was strange; almost everyone knew he was not typical."[25]

What Gingrich saw as a "drumbeat" was probably the inner leading of the Holy Ghost. Larry opposed a national holiday for the communist "Michael" Luther King. (His name was never legally changed to Martin.) He resisted the nomination of Andrew Young as President Carter's ambassador to the United Nations. And for that matter, he had absolutely no use for the perverted organization itself, declaring:

> Under the auspices of the United Nations we have seen bloody wars in Korea and Vietnam, the subjugation of Eastern Europe and the mass slaughter of tens of millions of people in China. We have witnessed the Soviet invasions of Hungary and Czechoslovakia. We are witnessing today the genocide in Cambodia. In all of these instances, the United Nations did nothing. . . . I think we should admit reality. The U.N. has become

a smokescreen for dilution of American sovereignty, for the diverting of American purpose, and the whittling down of our potential for world leadership. It is also now and has been a cover for world wide Communist aggression.[26]

However, the thing that probably irked Reagan most was that Larry "had his number." A year before his death, the congressman confided to St. John:

> The fundamental problem with President Reagan is that he is not a hardball player when it comes to politics. He's very persuasive. But I have come to the conclusion he's the type of person who likes to sit around a table for a friendly chat, work out any disagreements and try to resolve them within an hour and a half, work out an agreement, reach a general compromise, everybody smiles, shakes hands, and then he says, let's go to dinner.[27]

James Mann adds in *Rise of the Vulcans:*

> In their memoirs, both Powell and Shultz admitted their considerable embarrassment when, at the beginning of Reagan's Washington summit with Gorbachev, the Soviet leader gave a detailed presentation on arms control and the American president could offer only a joke about a cabdriver.[28]

What people fail to remember is that *Ronald Reagan was a successful professional Hollywood actor before he entered politics.* From all his saber rattling you would think he was the communists' worst nightmare. However, a simple look at how the United States responded to the Soviet Union tells a different story altogether. Reagan began the charade by demanding that: the Soviets apologize; reparations be paid to the victims' families; and promises be made that such a bad thing would never happen again. The predictable Soviet reaction was—*"Nyet! Nyet! Nyet!"*

Despite such a brash refusal, Reagan insisted that his diplomats continue to press the Soviets for a "meaningful" disarmament accord. The president had no intention of deviating from the "positive" game plan he announced during his televised address, "We know it will be hard to make a nation that rules its own people through force to cease using force against the rest of the world. But we must try." A White House reporter received no reply when he asked, "Mr. President, if you say they are barbarians, how can we negotiate?"[29] Unfortunately, the man with the answers was gone. Less than six months before this hypocritical press conference, Larry had accurately prophesied: "Reality counts for little and illusion is frequently king, but in the struggle for the survival of Western civilization, it will be the real world, not illusions or delusions, that will determine which way the future will go."[30]

It was now time for Congress to follow Reagan's lead. Senator Percy of Illinois "lashed out" at the Russians by recommending passage of Joint House Resolution 353 which constituted a mere formal censure without any proscribed penalties. Realizing that the craven measure was less than a slap on the wrist, Jesse Helms led a hard core of conservative senators to propose a slate of eight amendments "with teeth." Among other modalities, Helms called for a tightening of technology exports, a moratorium on imports produced by slave labor, and the recall of our ambassador to the U.S.S.R. Needless to say, the "extremist" proposal was defeated by a landslide. Senator Edward Kennedy exonerated the murderous Soviet regime by attributing the unfortunate shootdown to "a single moment of international madness."[31]

Thus, when all the smoke finally cleared, the sum total of America's formal diplomatic reprisals against the U.S.S.R. for the destruction of KAL 007 was as follows: 1) the closure of Aeroflot Airline offices in the U.S.; 2) suspension of plans to open a consulate in Kiev; and 3) cancellation of several cultural exchange programs. St. John noted, ". . . the observation made the rounds in Washington that Mr. Reagan demonstrated more toughness when the air traffic controllers went on an illegal labor strike than he did with the Soviets over KAL 007."[32]

The explanation for all of this is that Mr. Reagan was just a puppet being manipulated by the *real* powers that be. The Bible says, *"For the love of money is the root of all evil . . ."* (I Timothy 6:10a). On the very day of KAL 007's destruction, the Soviets purchased 900,000 metric tons of wheat and corn from the U.S.[33] And the cash register would continue to ring *after* September 1 as well! William Safire, a columnist for *The New York Times* wrote, ". . . when it comes to 'the transfer of valuable free world technology' that will *strategically* benefit the Soviet Union, it was during the Reagan Administration that the floodgates were opened."[34]

Two days after the shootdown, with Larry's empty seat as a portent, Senator Hatch told his South Korean audience at the Skulla Hotel in Seoul, " I know from conversations with the State Department that many of (the president's) advisors plan to urge business as usual with the Russians."[35] Two weeks later, on September 17, Reagan attempted to counter the senator's negative prognostication by declaring, "History will say that this tragedy was a major turning point because this time the world did not go back to business as usual."[36] The reader is invited to decide for himself. St. John writes:

> A moral amnesia set in only three weeks after the 007 massacre. One hundred top American agricultural and high-technology company representatives, apparently taking their cue from Washington, announced on September 23, 1983, that they would go ahead with plans to attend an agricultural trade exhibit sponsored by the USSR Trade and Economic Council and the Chamber of Commerce and Industry in Moscow. Ralston Purina, Occidental Petroleum, Monsanto Chemical, Archer Daniels Midland, and **Coca-Cola** made it known they would go to Moscow for the trade fair despite the midair massacre.[37]

Less than a week after Reagan's milquetoast assurance, it *was* "business as usual" for greedy corporate America! As Bonesman A. L. Harriman noted, America's post-WWII generation wanted nothing more than to "go to the movies and drink **Coke**." By 1986, Kathy McDonald was so incensed at the way her husband's martyrdom had been eclipsed by filthy lucre that she and a lady friend went to see Reagan at the White House. She didn't get far, however. Reagan was Reagan; back slapping—"Well, we're glad to see you; we really are sorry about what happened to your husband; we're doing our best to create a good nation; we appreciate people like you . . . yada, yada, yada."

Too emotionally robbed to say anything, Kathy cut the appointment short. As the two women were leaving the White House, the grieving widow was subjected to yet another callous indignity. ABC News correspondent Sam Donaldson accosted her with the question, "Mrs. McDonald, are you going to be taking a Korean Airlines flight back to Georgia?"[38] She maintained her dignity by ignoring the filthy animal.

A MURDER WITHOUT A BODY

Within days of the shootdown hundreds of ships from the Soviet Union, Japan and America were literally jostling alongside one another in a frantic race to locate the wreckage of KAL 007. The frenzied search was occurring in the international waters off Moneron Island, situated in the Tatar Gulf to the west of Sakhalin Island. W.T. Piotti, Jr., commander of the U.S. Seventh Fleet Task Force 71, assessed the enormity of his job, stating, "Not since the search for the hydrogen bomb lost off Palmares, Spain has the U.S. Navy undertaken a search effort of the magnitude or import of the search for the wreckage of KAL Flight 007."[39] But alas, all was in vain. Apparently no rescue team could find KAL 007 in waters that were only 525 feet deep (barely twice the length of a Boeing 747). By November 10, the "show" was just about over. However, a Russian-American who spent twenty years in U.S. Army Intelligence, informed me that the Soviets had found what they were looking for within weeks, but had kept their trawlers out for nearly six months, at considerable expense, to prolong the ruse before U.S. satellites.

Now the point is, two months after the tragedy, the victims' grieving survivors were *still* in the dark. Without a wreckage site, the all-important black boxes could not tell the world what had *really* happened to KAL 007. The strangest mystery of all, however, was the unprecedented absence of all 269 bodies, as well as any portion of a debris field!

On June 23, 1985, an Air India Boeing 747 with 329 persons aboard suddenly exploded from what is believed to have been a terrorist bomb. After the crippled jetliner plunged from an altitude of 31,000 feet into the North Atlantic Ocean (southwest of Ireland), 132 bodies were recovered, 123 of them on the same day. Practically all of the bodies were later identified as well. Moreover, several thousand pieces of wreckage, including the black boxes were retrieved from a depth of 6,700 feet! Luggage from this crash was reported still floating on the surface of the Irish Sea a month after the crash.

By contrast, though the Soviets "claimed" to have recovered about 800 pieces of KAL 007, they only released about ten percent; and, forty-five percent of these fragments could not be positively identified as part of the missing Boeing 747. The pathos in the words of Congressman McDonald's widow was shared by thousands of other heartbroken family members and friends:

> All the debris that the Soviet Union boxed up and turned over to us contained, as far as I know, nothing of Larry's. But I want something physical, something concrete. The clerk of the House of Representatives wanted me to know that the House pays for a headstone and funeral expenses. But where can we put it? We don't have anything that proves to us that Larry is no more! It's as if he packed his bags, went into the elevator,

blew me a kiss as the door closed, and got on that airplane and flew off. That's it! It's a problem that few have to face; it's a death without the victim, **a murder without a body.**[40]

The fact that Larry's body has never been recovered is even more sobering in light of a disclosure made by Reverend Joseph C. Morecraft III, a friend and spiritual advisor to the late congressman:

> In the last speech Larry McDonald delivered, the Saturday before his death, he said if we are going to win this war before us, we must give ourselves selflessly and relentlessly to the advancement of the causes of God, of righteousness, and of truth until one of two things happens—we win or we are laid in our graves.[41]

So What *Did* Happen?

Since day one the public has been told that KAL 007 was shot down by a Soviet interceptor after it strayed off course and entered Russian airspace. Such is considered to be the politically correct, non-conspiratorial position. Seymour M. Hersh wrote the definitive work espousing this view entitled *The Target Is Destroyed.* James Oberg, a space engineer in Houston (considered by some to be an expert in Soviet aerospace secrets), is another proponent of the safe, or "non-lunatic fringe," position. His circle of like-minded professionals have been referred to as "the Truth Squad."[42]

Whenever a person makes his first contact with an alternative theory, it is easy to see why the so-called "traditional view" appears to require less faith from its proponents. Also, he is not about to flunk the Limbaugh Kook Test. However, to endorse the official position requires one to believe that the *most* experienced commercial airline pilot in South Korea, utilizing the *most* sophisticated navigational equipment available, *inadvertently* veered 300 miles off course over the *most* militarily sensitive region of the *largest* country in the world while carrying the *most* anti-Communist member of the United States Congress on board!

The pilot in command of KAL 007 was Captain Chun Byung-In, age forty-five. Chun joined KAL in 1972 after a distinguished ten-year career with the South Korean Air Force. His combined total flying experience exceeded 20,000 hours—6,618 aboard 747s. He had flown the route between Anchorage and Seoul (R-20) for five years. Such was his attention to detail that, according to his wife, if a picture on the wall was out of place as much as a nail's width, he would rehang it.[43] In 1982, he received a citation for his accident-free record. He was so respected, that when the president of South Korea—the target of several assassination threats—visited the United States in February 1981, Chun was specifically chosen to be the pilot.

Now this is the caliber of the man *supposedly* responsible for one of the worst navigational errors in modern history! A study of the Internal Navigation System (INS) conducted shortly before the KAL disaster found it to be almost error free; only about one flight in ten thousand was found to stray some fifty miles off course and that was usually attributed to pilot error. Chun's flight "wandered" more than 300 miles from R-20.[44] The INS has even been used by American astronauts to guide the Shuttle's pinpoint landings. St. John states, "Don Walters, a spokesman for Litton Industries, which manufactures the INS, maintained that the system is nearly 'fail safe' and has a possible margin of error of two miles for every hour of aircraft flight."[45] Brad Dunbar of the National Transportation Safety Board noted that in all the years the agency has investigated air crashes, "We've never had an accident investigation involving an INS failure on an airliner."[46]

A civil court in Washington, D.C., later ruled that Korean Airlines was guilty of willful misconduct in that the cockpit crew of KAL 007 *had* to have known that they were dangerously off course.[47] Does the court's decision imply that the pilot was following a *different* flight plan altogether?

To explain the mysterious contradiction, Seymour Hersh employed the expertise of aviation "expert" Harold Ewing. However, the pipe dream posited by Ewing was so fraught with improbable conjecture that even Hersh was constrained to label it "highly speculative."[48] He also noted that Harold himself "acknowledged that his scenario calls for a leap of faith."[49] Keep in mind—these are the same intellectual heavyweights who thrive on intimidating any who dare to question the politically correct account.

Another relevant piece of the puzzle involves the precise territory that was "accidentally" violated by KAL 007. Although it is certainly true that "the best of men are but men at best," R-20 was the *last* flight path where Captain Chun should have "goofed." To begin with, any route that skirted the Soviet border was potentially threatening due to established technological machinations by the Russians. Jack Anderson wrote in the *Washington Post,* September 20, 1983:

> The Soviets routinely try to lure U.S. military and intelligence aircraft into Soviet airspace so they can "legally" shoot them down. This is done by a jamming technique, called "meaconning," which confuses pilots trying to follow radio signals from the ground.[50]

A similar revelation was made in the January 1984 *Readers Digest* article entitled "What *Really* Happened to KAL Flight 007?"[51] Stanford University Professor Alexander Dallin, another apologist for the traditional view, labels such a hypothesis as "fanciful and at best farfetched."[52] However, the airline industry is in sharp disagreement with the West Coast egghead on this matter. Mr. Cho Choong Hoon, president of Korean Airlines, believed that a jamming technique *was* responsible for the navigational problems encountered by KAL 007, stating, "The possibility is high that the Soviet Union has developed a system to cause planes to lose their direction."[53] Mr. Chang Chi Ryang, former air marshal of the South Korean Air Force, also believed that a jamming device was used on KAL 007.[54]

On the FAA navigational maps for R-20, two warnings are posted in bold type in the left-hand corner. The first states that aircraft may be fired on without warning if they stray from their course. The second caution flag is highly significant, given the topic at hand: "Warning: Unlisted Radio Emissions from This Area May Constitute a Navigation Hazard or Result in Border Over Flight Unless Unusual Precaution Is Exercised."[55]

Captain Chun was also aware that another Korean airliner, KAL 902, had previously been attacked by Soviet interceptors on April 20, 1978, while en route from Paris to Seoul. The damaged aircraft was forced to land on a frozen lake near the White Sea fishing port of Kem. Two passengers were killed while thirteen others were wounded by shrapnel. Fortunately, the pilot, Kim Chang Kyu, was able to issue a Mayday call, alerting the world to what had occurred. Their Soviet captors subsequently freed the 108 survivors. The crew testified after their release that "an electrical shock paralyzed the navigation system" just prior to their veering into Soviet airspace.[56] However, the instruments were never examined as the Soviets chose to keep the crippled Boeing 707 as a souvenir.

It is axiomatic that many conservatives formed the immediate conclusion that the controversial John Birch Society chairman had been slain according to a cold-blooded Communist plot. How could it *possibly* have been a coincidence? Garrett N. Scalera, one of the principal sponsors of the Seoul conference, told St. John: "Some of the toughest and most militant anti-Communists in Congress were slated to attend, and wiping out important and vocal conservative anti-Communists like Senator Jesse Helms (R–N.C.) would have set back the work we were doing to form a security framework for northeast Asia."[57] St. John adds:

> Lilly Fediay, staff member of the Washington-based Institute of American Relations and cosponsor of the conference, said that she gave the Korean embassy in Washington a **complete list of the names and airline schedules for the U.S. congressional delegation traveling to Seoul.** U.S. intelligence experts maintain that the Soviets routinely monitor Telex and cable traffic from foreign embassies in Washington.[58]

Senator Symms believed that his colleague was definitely the victim of a premeditated act, though the language he attributes to Larry betrays his ignorance of spiritual matters:

> I will always believe that Larry McDonald knew he had been shot down by the Russians. He was smart enough and his instincts were such that he looked out and saw the wing on fire; and I just feel that he probably thought to himself, "Those dirty [expletive] finally got me."[59]

Larry's former press secretary and friend, Mr. Tommy Toles, holds to a scenario involving a planted hijacker who was later double-crossed by the Soviets.

> My understanding is that on most KAL flights back then, the cabin door was not locked. If that was the case, it would have been extremely easy for a hijacker to go in, and as you know, at that time it would have been easy to smuggle in anything, especially if you were a member of the crew. I think a hijacker could explain the lack of communications of a Mayday call.
> I think there's a possibility—I've thought this over in my mind—I know there are a lot of suicidal terrorists like those that flew into the World Trade Center. And the North Koreans—many of them being very fanatical, as has been demonstrated lately—it could be that a hijacker was told, "Okay, you're going to bring it down and you're going to be shot down," but I think maybe that's too complicated. I think an agent might

have been told, "What we want you to do is to force the plane down, perhaps in North Korea," and at that point, perhaps they were going to plant some kind of equipment on the plane after a period of time.

When the other Korean plane was forced down in 1978, it took a while to get the passengers back and all this sort of thing; it doesn't happen overnight. It would have been relatively easy for them—if it was to be landed in North Korea, or even on Sakhalin Island for that matter—to plant alleged spy equipment on the plane, like a throw down knife at a crime scene. I think it would have been easy to tell a hijacker, "We want you to force the plane down," and perhaps, unbeknownst to the hijacker, it was going to be shot down.

I think that is more plausible than trying to coordinate a lone hijacker who is told that he will be shot out of the air. This would also explain the absence of a distress call.[60]

Yet, the longer one studies the entire picture, the more it appears that something else may have been afoot that night. For instance, why did Chun's wayward route just happen to make the right zigs and zags to place it over the two most militarily sensitive areas in the entire U.S.S.R.? According to the relevant data, KAL 007 supposedly deviated from R-20 and overflew both the Kamchatka Peninsula and Sakhalin Island. The Soviet specialist Dallin writes:

> Precisely Kamchatka Peninsula, Sakhalin Island, and Vladivostok—the three "targets" on the presumed track of KAL 007, as the Soviets claimed it—are the most important and perhaps most sensitive Soviet areas in this connection. Something like ninety nuclear-powered submarines are based at Petropavlovsk-on-Kamchatka, including apparently twenty-nine missile-carrying submarines. The Chukotka Peninsula, to the north, has been identified as the site for Soviet mobile missiles, which (some experts allege) could hit the United States. Kamchatka is also the impact area for Soviet ICBMs test-fired from the central part of the USSR. Sakhalin has at least six important airbases and a naval base.[61]

What a place to show up unannounced!

TOP SECRET/CODEWORD

With the passage of years it seemed as though fate had consigned the mystery of KAL 007 to oblivion. Not a single body or suitcase had ever been recovered. Andropov was dead. Reagan was retired. Yet a myriad of vital questions remained unanswered. Closure was unfairly eluding the victims' families. And then it happened!

In late October, 1992, South Korean legislator Son Se Il, a member of the opposition Democratic party, shocked the world by announcing that he was in possession of a "Top Secret/Codeword" report postulating an entirely new account of KAL 007's fate. According to the seventy-eight page CIA dossier, the probability was high that Captain Chun had been able to orchestrate an emergency landing at sea, resulting in many lives being saved. Although Son refused to disclose his source, *Reuters News Service* obtained their own copy and published the salient portions on October 26. The public was now being told that the Boeing aircraft "probably ditched successfully, there may have been survivors, the Soviets have been lying massively, and diplomatic efforts need to be made to return the possible survivors."[62]

I have personally read every word of this report. There is a cover sheet with a rubber stamp giving the seal of the CIA, name and address of the CIA's Office of Congressional Affairs and a box with "To:" followed by a blank. The title page carries the line, "Sensitive Restricted Access." To say its contents are unsettling would be a gross understatement. The opening paragraph reads as follows:

> This intensive study has found, on the basis of the aggregation and analysis of extensive evidence, that KAL-007 probably attempted to "ditch at sea." The evidence and analysis suggests further that KAL-007 may have successfully ditched at sea. If KAL-007 successfully ditched at sea, the evidence suggests that there may have been some survivors.[63]

Under the heading "Summary," that all-too-familiar sticky-wicket appears:

> The principal mystery of the 1983 Soviet shoot-down of Korean Airlines Flight KAL-007 over international waters is the confirmed failure by the U.S. Navy search and salvage ships, and the apparent failure or the Soviet naval search and salvage ships, to recover any identifiable bodies, luggage, "black boxes," or any significant wreckage from KAL-007.[64]

The background and origin of this report is most intriguing. It begins with a man by the name of Avraham Shifrin. Although unfamiliar to most Americans, Mr. Shifrin was considered to be the world's foremost authority on the Soviet system of prisons and slave labor camps.

Born October 8, 1923, in Minsk, Byelorussia, Shifrin was reared and educated in Moscow. In 1938, his father was arrested and sent to the gulag during one of Stalin's political purges. After being drafted into the Soviet army in 1941, Shifrin later altered his identity and rose to the rank of major, receiving numerous decorations for valor and a battlefield commission.

Following the war, Shifrin earned a law degree and became a legal advisor to the Soviet Ministry of Defense. However, in 1952, he was arrested during Stalin's final reign of terror, spending the next decade in prison.

The Jewish Shifrin emigrated to Israel in 1970 where he established the Research Centre for Prisons, Psychprisons and Forced Labor Concentration Camps of the USSR. In February, 1973, Shifrin was invited to testify before the U.S. Senate Internal Subcommittee concerning Soviet suppression of religious freedom and widespread anti-Semitism in particular. His extensive research was published in 1980 as *The First Guidebook to Prisons and Concentration Camps of the Soviet Union.*

In 1989, the Research Centre began its own investigation into the mystery of KAL 007. By 1990, Shifrin was convinced through his various underground channels in the U.S.S.R. that the Korean Boeing 747 did not crash into the sea after being hit by two Soviet rockets, but rather had landed safely in shallow water in the vicinity of Moneron Island near Sakhalin. He was also led to believe that many of the passengers, *including Congressman McDonald*, survived landing and were transferred to the mainland by Soviet Coast Guard personnel.

JESSE HELMS'S INVESTIGATION

The following year, Shifrin was able to establish contact with Senator Jesse Helms, ranking minority member of the Senate Committee on Foreign Relations, advising him of his findings. In January 1991, Helms sent staff member David Sullivan to Jerusalem to meet with Shifrin in person. Sullivan returned in May with Dr. James P. Lucier, minority staff director for the committee and Victor Fedei, a senior defense intelligence analyst. Shifrin states that they received access to all details of our investigation, debriefed our witnesses who had arrived from the USSR, registered their testimonies, and were completely convinced that there were compelling reasons for insisting that Korean Boeing 747, Flight KAL 007 had not crashed and that its passengers were alive and safe after the water landing.[65]

Shifrin later confirmed,

In June 1991, we were informed by Mr. D. Sullivan, one of the Senator's three aides, that our investigative materials had been given to the CIA and to the Pentagon for evaluation and that the response was that, indeed, our information had proved authentic.[66]

It is believed by many that the core portion of this mysterious CIA report was prepared by Helms's senior advisors. Apparently, a concerted effort was made to purge the document of any internal evidence betraying its origin. However, a curious remark appears on page 43, which also happens to be the only page without the rubber-stamped heading "TOP SECRET/CODEWORD." The last sentence of the next-to-the-last paragraph reads as follows: "This June, 1991 National Security Agency re-analysis was requested for use in this Republican Staff Study."[67]

The degree to which Senator Helms was swayed by this voluminous report is evidenced by the following amazing letter he sent to Boris Yeltsin six months later:

United States Senate
Committee on Foreign Relations
Washington, D.C. 20510-6225
December 10, 1991

His Excellency
Boris Yeltsin
The President of the
Russian Republic
The Kremlin,
Moscow, U.S.S.R.

Dear Mr. President:

One of the greatest tragedies of the Cold War was the shoot-down of the Korean Airlines flight KAL-007 by the Armed Forces of what was then the Soviet Union on September 1, 1983.

This event had elements of a personal catastrophe for me, since I was on the parallel flight that night of KAL-015, which departed Anchorage,

Alaska about fifteen minutes after KAL-007. Both flights stopped in Anchorage for refueling. I shall never forget mingling with the doomed passengers of KAL-007 in the transit lounge, including two sweet young girls who waved goodbye to me when they were called to return to their fatal flight.

The KAL-007 tragedy was one of the most tense incidents of the entire Cold War. However, now that relations between our two nations have improved substantially, I believe that it is time to resolve the mysteries surrounding this event. Clearing the air on this issue could help further to improve relations.

Accordingly, I respectfully request that the government of the Russian Republic gain access to the files of the former KGB and of the Ministry of Defense in order to resolve the attached questions. I hope that you will personally intervene with the relevant authorities of the former Soviet Union in order to provide answers to these questions.

The American people, indeed, the families of all passengers on KAL-007, will be deeply grateful for your efforts.

Sincerely,
[signature]

Jesse Helms: jl

QUESTIONS ON KOREAN AIR LINES FLIGHT KAL-007

   I. KAL-007 Landing
     1. **Please provide depositions or accounts from eye witnesses who saw KAL-007's landing.**
     2. **Please provide the geographical coordinates of the location of where KAL-007 landed.**

   II. Eye Witness Accounts from Soviet Military Radar Tracking Stations
     1. Please provide depositions or accounts from eye witnesses from Soviet military tracking stations, who saw the track of KAL-007's descent.
     2. Please provide the exact locations of these military radar tracking stations, and a map showing their disposition.
     3. What was the ground and air tracking range of these military tracking stations?
     4. How far away from the KAL-007 landing site were these tracking stations and their command posts?

III. Soviet and Japanese Radio Transmissions Related to KAL-007
1. Please provide transcripts of all available Soviet civil and military radio transmissions related to the entire flight of KAL-007.
2. Please provide transcripts of all available Soviet intercepts of non-Soviet radio transmissions related to the flight of KAL-007.

IV. KAL-007 Passengers and Crew
1. From Soviet reports on the incident, please provide:
   a. **A list of the names of any living passengers and crew members removed from the airplane;**
   b. A list of missing passengers and crew;
   c. A list of dead passengers and crew;
   d. A list and explanation of what happened to the bodies of any dead passengers and crew;
   e. A list of items of luggage and other items removed from the plane;
   f. A list and description of the disposition of the luggage recovered and any other recovered items, and where such material is now kept;
   g. A description and disposition of any other recovered cargo.

V. Soviet Search and Rescue Efforts. Please provide a copy of the reports of all Soviet search and rescue operations, and the military and KGB "after action" reports.

VI. Information on Congressman Larry McDonald
1. **Please provide detailed information on the fate of U.S. Congressman Larry McDonald.**

VII. KAL-007 Passengers and Crew
1. **How many KAL-007 family members and crew are being held in Soviet camps?**
2. **Please provide a detailed list of the camps containing live passengers and crew, together with a map showing their location.**[68]

Initial Reports

The substance of the "Top Secret/Codeword" report that prompted the above correspondence includes several convincing particulars. In addition to the telltale problem of the missing bodies, they are as follows:

The ETA for KAL-007 at Kimpo International Airport was 6:00 a.m. After the flight failed to arrive, KAL-015 landed at 6:20 a.m. It was not until 7:20 a.m. that Korean Airline officials informed the anxious crowd that the overdue aircraft had encountered unexpected difficulties, though there was nothing to worry about, etc. A news flash was subsequently broadcast over KBC, the Korean television station, acknowledging that KAL-007 was reported missing. For some strange reason, a similar story had been aired by ABC in America a half hour earlier.[69]

Finally, at precisely 10:00 a.m., the South Korean minister of foreign affairs announced that he had received confirmation from the CIA that **"the plane had landed at Sakhalin. The crew and passengers are safe."**[70] The throng went wild at the news! A similar message was issued in Tokyo by the Japanese government. Senator Helms was notified at his hotel that his colleague's flight **"was on the ground at Sakhalin and all the passengers are safe."**[71]

At 10:47 a.m., Charley Cho, vice president of Korean Air Lines, appeared in person to reassure the families, stating, "I can't tell you how it happened, but that's unimportant as long as the passengers are all alright."[72] He did remark, however, "In my opinion the plane was forced from its route."[73] Just then a staff member handed him a note and Cho excitedly reaffirmed the earlier pronouncement: **"It has now been confirmed. The minister of foreign affairs has been informed by the United States CIA that the plane is down on Sakhalin and the passengers are safe."**[74]

A few minutes after making this statement, Cho took off for Tokyo onboard a company DC-10 to organize repatriation of the passengers and crew. His parting words were, "In less than twenty-four hours the problem will be straightened out, and I promise to bring them back to you."[75] Hersh confirms, "The report circulated in time for CBS-TV to insert it, attributed to United Press International, in its delayed West Coast edition of the evening news."[76]

Amidst widespread media coverage on September 1, the front-page headline of the *Rocky Mountain News*, Colorado's largest newspaper, read, **"Congressman's Flight Reportedly Forced to Soviet Isle."** A portion of the accompanying UPI story appeared as follows:

> A Korean Air Lines jumbo jet flying from New York to Seoul Wednesday with 269 people aboard, including a U.S. Congressman, **was forced to land on Sakhalin, a Soviet-occupied island north of Japan,**

the government-run television said. "The passengers were reported safe. Among them was Rep. Larry McDonald, D-Ga., John Birch Society chairman, whose spokesman said in Washington that American officials believed the jet was forced down by Soviet or North Korean fighter planes. A report on the Korean Broadcasting System said Thursday the CIA had informed the Seoul government of the landing on the Soviet-occupied island about 850 miles north of Tokyo.[77]

In the opinion of this author, the explanation suggested by Hersh to account for this "obvious error" was just another "leap of faith" on his part. The gist of his complex conjecture attributes the erroneous announcement to an informal remark made to the Japanese press by Dennis H. Wilham, the Federal Aviation Administration's representative in Asia. As his phone began ringing off the hook, Wilham supposedly told the reporters of several airports in the Kuriles where Flight 007 *could* have landed.

"I was determined to get the panic level down. We were all running around. I'm probably responsible," Wilham sadly acknowledged during an interview in Tokyo, "for the stories about the airliner being 'down in Sakhalin.'"[78]

Hersh then attempts to explain the CIA connection with an even greater leap of faith. According to Seymour, Mr. Jangnai Sohn, the Washington, D.C.-based undercover station chief for the Korean CIA, was distraught over the fate of his wife's sister who was aboard KAL 007.

CIA officials were aware of his personal interest in the flight, and one of Sohn's close friends in the agency was telephoning him at home periodically during the night to keep him up-to-date. Sohn naturally considered the information, which he knew came from the CIA's Operations Center, to be reliable, and was in turn relaying what he learned by telephone to his intelligence colleagues in Seoul. His CIA ally telephoned as soon as the first press reports were filed from Japan indicating that the airliner may have landed on Sakhalin. Sohn promptly passed along the good news to the Korean CIA, apparently communicating in the process the fact that his information had come from the CIA. By the time he was told, a few hours later, that the airliner had definitely been shot down, word of the airliner's safe landing had been passed from Korean intelligence to the Foreign Ministry. It went from there to officials of Korean Airlines, who made the information and its source public.[79]

The Pulitzer prize-winning author would thus have his readers believe that the critical chain of events had the Korean and Japanese governments ultimately gaining their false reports from an American Central Intelligence agent who got his information from the Japanese "boob tube," which in turn got it from the early morning speculation of a well-meaning employee of the American FAA. The part Hersh "forgot" to tell his fans was that the initial Japanese press reports of a Sakhalin landing were traced to details involving *radar data* and not Wilham's misguided optimism. The September 1 afternoon edition of the *Mainichi Shimbun* contained the following pertinent details:

> The Korean plane suddenly veered from its route and overflew the Chishima archipelago in the Kuril Islands; crossing the Sea of Okhotsk, it violated the airspace over Sakhalin, where fighters intercepted it. Radar facilities at Wakkanai in northern Japan observed a group of three interceptors flying parallel to the Korean plane in the vicinity of Yuzhno-Sakhalinsk on three occasions. The first occurred at 03:20, the second at 03:32, and the third at 03:53. **These observations confirmed that the fighters pursued the plane for more than a half hour above Sakhalin and forced the Korean plane to land.**[80]

On the basis of reciprocity agreements, Japanese intelligence agencies relayed this information to their American counterparts, the CIA, who in turn released it to the Korean government. Retired Air Force Colonel L. Fletcher Prouty, who served in the Pentagon from 1955 to 1964, wrote:

> In diplomatic channels, all messages contain an authenticated source code on the message form. In this case, the Koreans had received a message with the U.S.-CIA identifier on it. They are all too familiar with the system. That CIA message with its official authentication therefore could not have been created by the Soviets.[81]

The Japanese news story is consistent with the first reports received by Mr. Toles. Michel Brun writes:

> Also at 11:00 A.M. Tokyo time, which was 10:00 P.M. Eastern Daylight Time, Orville Brockman, the duty officer at FAA headquarters in Washington, reached Tommy Toles by telephone at his home in Georgia. . . . Brockman told Toles that he had learned from Mr. Takano of the Japanese Ministry of Transport that **Japanese radar had followed the Korean airliner to a landing on Sakhalin**. At 10:50 P.M. EDT this information was "confirmed" to Toles by Reed Clark of the State Department, who added that **KAL 007 had landed safely**.[82]

Shifrin provides the following exact account of Brockman's message that indicts Wilham and his "innocent blooper" theory.

> We have just received information from our FAA representative, Mr. Dennis Wilhelm [sic] in Tokyo, as follows: He has been advised by the Japanese Civil Aviation Bureau headquarters, Air Traffic Division, Mr. Takano . . . who is his counterpart in Japanese aviation as follows: **Japanese Self Defense Force confirms that the Hokaido [sic] radar followed Air Korea to a landing in Soviet territory on the island of Sakhalinska** . . . and it is confirmed by the manifest that Congressman McDonald is on board.[83]

THE TOLES TAPES

I had the opportunity to interview Tommy Toles on April 3, 2003. (At the time he was the managing editor of four newspapers in his native state of Georgia.) Mr. Toles had had the presence of mind to tape-record nearly every telephone conversation he received or initiated during the long night of KAL 007's "disappearance." In the privacy of his personal office, Mr. Toles graciously played every recording for my benefit. For nearly two hours I was transported back in time as I listened, mesmerized by the dramatic dialogue between him and various officials of KAL, the FAA, CIA, Congress, Pentagon and State Department.

With my own ears I heard Orville Brockman read every word in the critical pronouncement attributed to him by Shifrin. In my opinion, as Brockman clearly attributes the communiqué to Dennis Wilham, this one recording seriously undermines the credibility of both Wilham and Seymour Hersh. Why would Dennis conspire with Seymour to blame the initial Sakhalin landing story on his own unguarded remarks, *while knowing all along that he had advised Brockman of Takano's radar report?* Isn't it strange that the Pulitzer Prizewinning journalist failed to include Brockman's statement in his "definitive" account?

Another conundrum is the fact that Wilham never mentioned Sakhalin by name. To the contrary, Hersh claims he "told the reporters of the many airports in the **Kuriles** where Flight 007 could have landed."[84] Yet, Sakhalin Island was the *only* landing site Tommy Toles heard anything about during one high level conversation after another.

At 10:50 p.m., Mr. Reed Clark called from the State Department. Referring to his meticulous notes (as this was one of the few unrecorded conversations), Mr. Toles quoted Clark as stating: "KAL 007 had safely landed on Sakhalin and that the Soviets had confirmed it. All aboard were safe."[85] The September 1, 1983, *New York Times* corroborates this non-recorded message, quoting Larry's brother, Dr. Harold P. McDonald, as stating, "We've heard from the State Department that the plane is down and apparently the passengers are safe. We're just going to wait and pray."[86] Mr. Frank Rogers, Tokyo correspondent for Mutual Radio, also called around this time to report, "KAL 007 had landed safely on Sakhalin Island."[87]

Colonel Tom Roundtree called from the Pentagon between 11:30 p.m. and midnight, stating:

> Korean television is now broadcasting that the aircraft has landed with all 240 passengers safe on Sakhalin Island. And that is as good information as we have and we believe it to be a true report.[88]

Mr. Cliff Cernick, public affairs officer for the FAA in Anchorage, said in another call:

> I'm looking at a message that we received from Tokyo that says, "Understand Korean Air 007 intercepted; left at Sakhalin." But this has not been confirmed, nor do I have any information at all that confirms that the aircraft did indeed land safely on Sakhalin; and I have that it was intercepted by Russian military aircraft. However, I have a feeling that this was the case and that the aircraft is safe, and the passengers are safe . . . I have nothing more . . . It looks good. I hope I'm not wrong.[89]

Mr. C. K. Suh, regional manager for KAL in Los Angeles, informed Toles:

> I just called Korean Airlines in Seoul head office. According to the information I got from them, the U.S. embassy in Korea informed the Korean government, Minister of Foreign Affairs, that the plane has landed in Sakhalin . . . And our Minister of Foreign Affairs gave us the information at Korean Airlines and the Korean Broadcasting Company.[90]

After a while, however, the spirit of the calls began to change with regard to the "Sakhalin connection." Around 12:30 a.m. Mr. Richard Burt, assistant secretary of European affairs at the State Department, contradicted Clark's earlier report by quoting the Soviets as stating, "We cannot confirm that [a Sakhalin landing] at this time."[91] A follow-up call by David Lambert, also of the State Department, affirmed, "Our strong supposition is that at this point it is in the water . . . there is an American search-and-rescue aircraft that is virtually over the scene by now."[92] (No such rescue craft had been dispatched.)

Of the many officials who spoke with Mr. Toles, Commodore Brickell, deputy director of operations at the National Military Command Center at the Pentagon, impressed me the most for his genuine concern and obvious frustration that something was amiss. He said:

> The Korean government is saying on television that everyone is on the ground and safe, and that was the same word that the airline was saying. . . . We went back to the FAA and asked them to confirm what their sources were and we had a **fuzzy** answer. It is very unusual for that kind of plane with sophistication—with that much communication capability—not to say something to someone. That's what was concerning me. We certainly would have picked up anything that they sent to anybody. I can guarantee you that. We have no communications on that airplane.[93]

Conversely, Mr. Dale Peterson of the Central Intelligence Agency came across as the least concerned and least credible of all the officials I heard. How's this for his opening two lines?

> **We don't know anything, to be honest and truthful. I know there are reports indicating that the CIA somehow played a role in the whole thing—and, uh—not true!**[94]

Talk about being on the defensive! He then continued the charade:

> **We do not have any information about what happened to the plane.** If I hear anything I will call you right back. . . . The director of Central Intelligence and his deputy are aware of this, but haven't heard anything to this point. **I'll let them know of your interest.**[95]

An irritated Tommy Toles interjected:

> **It's a little bit more than interest!** We expect some contact or something prior to—you know—the normal opening of business at 8:00 a.m. or 7:30 a.m., or whatever.[96]

Commodore Brickell called back at 3:45 a.m. with the following sober report:

Another agency is talking in terms of 90% that the plane is lost. . . .
One of the things that the CIA did confirm was that the Russians are saying
that there is no plane on Sakhalin Island and they have no indication of
the location. The latest news I am getting all points to the fact that the
plane was lost.[97]

Following this shattering news, the burdened press secretary for
a missing U.S. congressman (and liaison for his anxious wife and children)
had to endure another hollow update from Agent Peterson:

> **We do not have any information at this time on what happened.
> Both Korea and Japan maintain that the CIA informed the South
> Korean government about the plane; not true! We did not make that
> statement to the South Koreans.[98]**

DISTURBING EVIDENCE

One of the main strengths of the "ditched landing" hypothesis is the
indisputable fact that the aircraft *identified* as KAL 007 stayed aloft
for at least *twelve* minutes after the Soviet interceptor pilot announced,
"Target is destroyed." The reader is reminded of Secretary Shultz's
first press conference in which he stated: "At **1826** hours, the Soviet
pilot reported that he fired a missile and the target was destroyed. . . .
At **1838** hours the Korean plane disappeared from the radar screen."
The CIA report corroborates this account:

> In sum, special intelligence shows that Soviet radars tracked KAL-
> 007 for at least 12 minutes after it was hit. . . . KAL-007 seemed to have
> quickly descended to a marginally safe breathing altitude of 16,400 feet in
> a very fast, 5 minute spiral, as if following standard airline flight procedures
> in case of rapid decompression, and thereafter it slowed its descent.
>
> Because it then seemed to reduce its rate of descent, while continuing
> to descend, this indicated that the pilots probably were in some degree of
> control. It then proceeded toward the area in Soviet territorial waters near
> Moneron Island. All this occurred during the 12 minutes after it was hit.[99]

The report adds, "Moreover, KAL-007 possibly could have flown
longer than 12 minutes after being hit, at a very low altitude beneath
the reported 1,000 foot radar detection threshold, before ditching or

crashing."[100] Remember that KAL 902 had stayed aloft for ninety minutes after being struck by Soviet fire. Shifrin writes:

> After the attack, flight KAL 007 was seen on several Soviet radar screens; particularly, we have at our disposal the evidence given by Captain of Soviet air defense troops V.V. Rishkov who personally watched flight KAL 007 on his radar and photographed its movement from his air defense post in military unit 1845 located in Zavet Ilyicha settlement.[101]

Another relevant point has been made from the results of flight simulation tests. At thirty-five thousand feet (the confirmed altitude for KAL 007 at the time of the attack) a free-falling B-747 would have crashed into the ocean in approximately two-and-a-half minutes.[102]

The evidence contained in Shifrin's files and the "Top Secret/Codeword" report goes into many additional areas as well. At least eight Russian coast guard vessels were dispatched to the waters off Moneron Island.[103] Within four hours, intercepted conversations between Soviet pilots confirmed that American citizens had been aboard the "destroyed intruder."[104] How could Soviet pilots have detected this so quickly from the air if KAL 007 had slammed into the ocean in the middle of the night?

Soviet officials severely hampered U.S. rescue efforts at the "crash site." Bogus search area coordinates, decoy pingers and displaced reference point markers kept the American vessels away from what the Russians were hiding.[105]

However, the most startling news of all concerned the possibility that some of the passengers and crew of KAL 007 might still be alive! Shifrin had indeed received such reports from Soviet émigrés to Israel. He writes:

> The Soviet coast guard under command of KGB General Romanenko alerted all its vessels along the coastal line as soon as it received information that a plane has been shot down. Therefore, the Soviet patrol vessels approached the plane almost immediately upon its water landing and received on board all the plane people (the passengers). By order of Gen. Romanenko all the passengers and crew were transported to a coast guard base. By his order too, the passengers' luggage was unloaded and also transported to the coast guard base.
>
> Gen. Romanenko reported on the incident and his consequent actions to the Far Eastern District Army Commander Gen. Tretyak and the latter transferred it further to Andropov that flight KAL 007 had not crashed. As a result, Gen. Romanenko received Marshal Ogarkov's order to tow

the plane from the shoal to deeper waters and sink it. It was also ordered to transfer the passengers to a KGB guarded camp on the mainland (Soviet Gavan), while **Congressman McDonald was to be sent, strictly guarded and incognito, to Moscow**. General Romanenko was ordered in the future to keep strictly secret, whatever concerns the fate of the plane and its crew and passengers and to insist that the plane had crashed into the sea killing all on board. At the same time the Soviet Union released an official TASS statement asserting the crash of the plane and the death of everybody on board.

Gen. Romanenko fulfilled exactly the order that originated from Andropov himself who personally followed all the developments: the passengers, crew members and **Congressman McDonald disappeared in the KGB hiding places**. In view of the above, it is extremely interesting to note that some time later Gen. Romanenko disappeared too: his name has been erased from the KGB computers and such a man seems never to have existed at all.

Our investigation (incomplete as yet) has brought us on the tracks of the kidnapped people. We know, for instance, that **Congressman McDonald has gone through a number of prisons in Moscow, among them the Central Lubyanka, Lefortovo, a "special dacha" of the KGB in a suburb of Moscow**. As far as his present whereabouts are concerned, the investigation is underway, and the information available at the moment cannot be disclosed. We partially know the camps where the passengers were and, with a high degree of probability, are kept now. As for the children from the plane, they where separated from their parents and safely hidden in the orphan houses of one of the Soviet Middle Asian republics.[106]

Are such startling reports fact, fraud or fantasy? Have Noelle and Stacy Grenfell been reared in a Siberian orphanage? Could Congressman McDonald still be alive? The prospects defy closure while fostering a cruel spirit of ambivalence.

Though we may never know the truth in this life, one thing is certain—Shifrin's information caused a considerable stir. Toward the end of 1990 the Soviet newspaper *Izvestiya* began a long series of articles on the KAL 007 affair. In the spirit of *glasnost*, Andrej Illesh, the lead reporter and the series editor, made a number of explosive concessions. Following years of Soviet denials, the wreckage of KAL 007 apparently *had* been located after all! On January 29 and 30, 1991, *Izvestiya* printed an interview with divers from the *Mikhail Mirchinko* who supposedly had spent most of October investigating the site at 46° 32′ N, 141° 20′ E (north of Moneron Island). The men revealed:

It took us two or three days to find our way around the wreck. . . . The plane was filled with all kinds of stuff, **but there were no bodies**. . . . In some places the debris was one and a half meters [5 feet] thick. **We didn't see any bodies on either the first or the second day**. . . . We managed to find our way around the aircraft. **Later, I saw a hand with a black glove on it.** I participated in all the dives. I remember it very clearly: the plane was filled with all sorts of stuff, **but there was absolutely no sign of any bodies. Why? I didn't see any human remains. There was no luggage, not even a handbag.** . . . On the other hand there were lots of things you wouldn't expect to find on a passenger plane . . . **reels**, for example.[107]

The "reels" were purported to be "several miles of tape" related to computers and recording devices. Thus, if we are to take their testimony at face value, "the divers recovered two hundred one-and-a-half-by-two-meter (five-by-seven-foot) baskets, filled with documents and electronic equipment, from this one wreck."[108] This was obviously not your average "commercial aircraft."

With regard to a credible theory concerning the missing bodies, Soviet authorities could only speculate, "The crabs ate them."[109] These must have been extremely hungry little critters as they apparently devoured the *skeletons, clothing, luggage and life vests* as well!

In light of such bizarre developments a letter demanding an explanation was addressed to President Gorbachev in June 1991 signed by Senators Bill Bradley, Edward Kennedy, Carl Levin and Sam Nunn. Unfortunately, Mikhail was overthrown before he could reply; which brings us full circle to Jesse Helms's letter to Boris Yeltsin dated December 10, 1991.

On March 21, 1992, Russia 1 TV finally confirmed that the Soviet Defense Ministry *did* have the "missing" black boxes belonging to KAL 007. Following a six-month drunk, Boris himself "'fessed up" to the nation. Then he went and did it! During a state visit to South Korea on December 19, Yeltsin shocked President Roh Tai Woo by handing over the cockpit voice recorder (CVR) and flight data recorder (FDR) purportedly belonging to KAL 007. According to an *Agence France-Presse* dispatch, Yeltsin was promptly awarded a commendatory "laurel" by the South Korean government for releasing the long-held transcript of the painful international incident.

His fame was short-lived, however. On November 30, a Seoul transport ministry spokesman reported that one of the black boxes (supposedly containing the FDR tapes) was empty while the other black box contained only copies of four CVR tapes. Two of the latter had been recorded backwards while one of the others was practically unintelligible due to background interference.

By the following month, the Montreal-based United Nations agency, the International Civil Aviation Organization (ICAO), succumbed to mounting pressure and reluctantly agreed to reopen the investigation.

However, just when things were starting to happen, a disconcerting shake-up occurred within the D.C. offices of Senator Jesse Helms. Dr. Lucier was abruptly replaced by Admiral Bud Nance as minority staff director. Sullivan would later be dismissed as well. On February 11, 1992, Nance wrote to Shifrin at the behest of Senator Helms. Among other things, he stated:

> The CIA found your information to be very interesting, and consistent with some of their information. **Unfortunately, however, CIA was not able to either confirm or deny the balance of it.** Both CIA and the Committee will keep your information confidential.[110]

Apparently, something happened that caused Senator Helms to drop the matter entirely. All efforts to continue the investigation were nixed. Mr. Fedei died in 1992. Neither Lucier nor Sullivan will discuss the subject in public. On March 5, 1998, Shifrin passed away in Jerusalem at the age of 74. Then Helms retired in 2002. Upon pursuing the matter further, I received a communiqué from a spokesman for an organization dedicated to the rescue of KAL 007 survivors. A portion of his remarks reads:

2/5/03

Dear Dr. Grady,

In response to your note of February 4 concerning the dropping of the investigation into KAL 007 by Senator Helms and his staff, this is a puzzling incident about which we have very little concrete information. Mr. Lucier refuses to discuss KAL 007. It is almost as if he has been sworn to secrecy. The general understanding that we have is that Admiral Bud Nance was brought in to "clean house" and that both Lucier and Sullivan were fired. . . .

The conclusion that we are led to is that some very strong high-level pressure was exerted on Helms and his people to drop the subject. Helms did send us a message in February, 2002, commending us on our efforts but he has not been more forthcoming than that.

While we may never learn the reason for the discontinued probe, we do know that there are no free lunches in this life. Senator Helms is a professing Christian and a dedicated patriot. Unfortunately (as discussed in chapter eight), he is also a practicing Mason. No one, including Helms, can ultimately defy a system he has willingly utilized without the threat of eventual repercussions. (Captain William Morgan, George "Bugsy" Segal, etc.)

MICHEL BRUN

Unless and until Senator Helms and/or his former staffers are willing to clear the air, freedom-loving Americans will be forced to draw their own conclusions. One theory for the terminated probe is that Helms stumbled upon the preliminary findings of yet another independent investigation, suggesting an entirely new and far more sinister scenario.

Michel Brun is a French aviation expert who has piloted multi-engine aircraft on long overwater flights. He has served as an aircraft accident investigator as well as the CEO of an airline based in Tahiti. He has also been a captain in the Merchant Marines. As a youth, Brun was commended by Charles de Gaulle for leading raids on German army camps in North Africa during World War II. In addition to his native French, Brun is fluent in Japanese, English, Spanish and Polynesian.

Soon after the KAL 007 tragedy, Brun realized that the early statements of Japanese Air Self-Defense Force and intelligence offices simply could not be reconciled with the single-intrusion, single-interception, single-shootdown account insisted on by the U.S. State Department. In 1985, he began his own private investigation of the affair. By May of 1991, *Izvestiya* was already discussing his research. While a number of his suppositions were rejected, others were acknowledged to be correct. However, in an effort to discredit Brun via ridicule (Limbaugh Kook Test, etc.), the *Izvestiya* editor let an important cat out of the bag. Illesh wrote, "I will not give this expert's complete version for two reasons—because it is **so large** and because it is such a fantasy."[111] This was a candid admission that the Frenchman had done his homework. Andrej added "Although, we must mention it because it was finally presented to very important American groups."[112]

It would be four more years before Brun's disquisition was published under the title *Incident at Sakhalin: The True Mission of KAL Flight 007*. The strength of this decade-long project is the author's ability to detect and reconcile a myriad of contradictions and disinformation endorsed by the governments of Japan, Russia and the United States. Brun states in his introduction:

> What is certain is that the destruction of KAL 007 gave rise to one of the greatest propaganda campaigns that either side of the Iron Curtain had known. The truth about the events that occurred in the sky over Sakhalin on the night of August 31-September1 has been carefully concealed beneath a barrage of contradictory accounts. **It has taken ten years to sort it out.**[113]

As Illesh's assessment of Brun's work was painfully accurate, I can barely do it justice as the mere conclusion of a chapter. A decent survey of the aforementioned contradictions would fill a chapter by itself. For instance, according to the Japanese military, KAL 007 "disappeared from the radar screens a few minutes later, at 03:29."[114] Yet American officials have never varied from Shultz's original statement, "At 1838 hours [GMT] the Korean plane disappeared from the radar screen." Brun writes:

> The difference between the two versions was not lost on the Japanese press. It emphasized the "mysterious" difference of nine minutes between the two given for the destruction of the airliner—03:29 in the Japanese version, 03:38 in the American. When on September 2 the Pentagon claimed that the Soviet fighter that had shot down the Korean airliner was not a MiG-23, as Secretary Shultz had said, but an SU-15, the Japanese press was quick to point out the discrepancy between the two versions of the story coming from Washington.[115]

A September 3 news release from *Tass* in Moscow claimed that warning shots had been fired at the intruder. The following day a UPI story from Washington contradicted the Soviet account:

> According to information from NATO, the SU-15 was armed with two missiles but did not have any guns. As a result it could not have fired any warning shots to draw the pilot's attention.[116]

Brun notes:

> The American government initially denied that any warning had been given. Changing the type of interceptor involved may have been intended

to lend credence to the American version of events. On September 11 the American government reversed itself on this point, however, because the pilot's remark about firing cannon bursts could clearly be heard on the tape it had released to the United Nations on September 7.[117]

Rear Admiral Isamu Imamura of the Japanese Maritime Safety Agency (JMSA) testified that he was eventually given *three* different crash sites to investigate. "Official" radar reports initially sent him to 46° 30′ N, 141° 30′ E, northeast of Moneron. The airplane that disappeared at this spot was believed to have exploded in flight at an altitude of 33,000 feet. However, after only a few hours, Imamura was given a second position about 1,500 meters east-southeast of a point 46° 35′ N, 141° 16′ E. Japanese fishermen aboard the *Chidori Maru* observed *this* aircraft explode just above the surface of the water. A distance of twelve miles separated the first two locations.[118] The admiral was then given "authoritative" information about a third impact site, situated far from the other two. Vladimir Pavlov, Russia's ambassador to Japan, informed the Japanese government that Soviet radar had tracked an airplane as it crashed into the water west of Moneron Island.[119] A distance of *thirty* miles now separated the first and third crash sites. (Of course, while all of this was going on, Soviet ships were combing two completely different areas approximately twelve miles to the east.[120])

The substance of what was found at these locations (as well as what was *not*) has also been kept from the general public. Stanford's Professor Dallin comments sardonically, "Conspiracy buffs continued to comb the debris of information for new clues and hypotheses that would explain it all."[121] I doubt whether Dallin would brand Admiral Imamura a "conspiracy buff." On September 3, Imamura held a press conference at JMSA headquarters in Wakkanai in which he stated that "if no debris from the Korean airliner is found in the next few hours, we must accept the evidence and conclude that the plane did not crash in this area."[122]

Dallin's wisecrack about conspiracy buffs combing through the debris is too funny. *There wouldn't be a KAL 007 conspiracy had there been a legitimate debris field to investigate in the first place.* However, this is *not* to imply that the numerous crash sites were lacking in debris. There was plenty of "general debris" around, just *NOTHING* from KAL 007! This is what Imamura was referring to. It would be *nine* days before the first clearly identifiable KAL 007 debris would be spotted off Moneron Island.

Finally, the ludicrous accounts supplied by the divers were prefaced by Illesh's warning: "This is the most confusing part of the 007 incident—the search for the Boeing's wreckage."[123] In his article on January 28, 1991, Illesh printed the testimony of Captain Nikolai Sergeievich Antonov describing the oceanographic conditions at 46° 35′ N, 141° 45′ E.:

> I arrived in the search area five or six days after the Boeing was destroyed [oh, say, September 5-6]. . . . **There was a thick layer of mud on the bottom** and the nets broke frequently. The seafloor was dead, **there was no sign of aquatic life.** No one had ever caught any fish in the area. Finally the fishermen hooked the Boeing.[124]

However, only four days later, on February 1, Illesh allowed Captain Ivan Varfolomeievich Shaydurov to present an entirely different scene. According to the JMSA situation maps, *this* "discovery" took place in the area 16NM (nautical miles) northwest of Moneron. Ivan states:

> More than a month had passed since the shootdown when we got to the spot. In fact, almost two months. We found the airplane on the seventeenth or eighteenth of October. We spent the following days working on the bottom, **which was crawling with crabs and all kinds of shrimp and fish. There were even some octopus.**[125]

The water in *this* locale was far from muddy. Vladimir Kov, a diver, recalled:

> **The water was so clear** you could see everything very distinctly. You could see 50 meters (165 feet) in front of you. **You could make out the individual grains of sand.** It was breathtakingly beautiful. But it was cold.[126]

Then we have the problem of conflicting testimony concerning the condition of the wreckage itself. The aircraft discovered in the muddy water was described by chief mate Zhan Aleschenko as follows:

> The wreckage from the plane was severely damaged. **It had been reduced to pieces.** The largest pieces we saw were the pivot support structures, which are extremely solid. These were between four and six feet long, and twenty to twenty-four inches wide. **Everything else was in small pieces.**[127]

However, it appears from statements given by the divers in the clear water that a large part of the plane's fuselage remained intact.

> We managed to find our way around **the aircraft** ... **the plane** was filled with all sorts of stuff, **but there was absolutely no sign of any bodies** ... [128]

INCIDENT AT SAKHALIN

Prior to the publication of Brun's exhaustive treatise, a number of precursors had been written suggesting that KAL 007 was involved in an ill-fated espionage mission for the American CIA. Three of the leading works in this regard are: *KAL-007: The Cover-up* by David E Pearson; *Shootdown: Flight 007 and the American Connection* by R. W. Johnson; and *KAL 007: The Hidden Story* by Oliver Clubb. In the October 1993 *American Spectator*, James Oberg classified these authors as "conspiracy nuts" and ridiculed their conclusions under the heading, "Useful Idiots: An Honor Roll."[129] For the record, Clubb is a graduate of Syracuse University; Pearson submitted *KAL-007: The Cover-up* as his Ph.D. thesis at Yale; and Johnson was a political science don at Oxford's Magdalen College for twenty-six years. Even Dallin acknowledged, "There is little doubt that United States agencies have on earlier occasions used civilian planes for intelligence purposes—presumably for data gathering, as "ferrets," or (less relevantly) for purposes of transportation."[130]

Although the general public rarely discovers how and when the CIA has engaged in cloak-and-dagger brinkmanship, occasionally a credible exposé makes its way to the market. *War Scare* by Dr. Peter Vincent Pry was published in 1997. Dr. Pry served as senior military analyst with the CIA from 1985-1995, whereupon he became a permanent staff member of the House National Security Committee. Following a heavy advertising campaign utilizing such venues as *The New York Times Book Review*, *Washington Post Book World*, *Publishers Weekly*, C-Span and National Public Radio's *Talk of the Nation*, a number of Americans were made privy to some pretty heavy news. According to Pry, the world literally stood on the brink of nuclear apocalypse on August 19, 1991; May 20, 1992; October 4, 1993 and January 25, 1995.[131] (II Peter 3:10) He then "reassures" his readers:

Today, in 1996, when the President of the United States [the guy who can't find his nuclear "go codes"] tells us that Russian missiles no longer target U.S. cities, and Moscow and Washington are routinely referred to as "strategic partners," many intelligence professionals and strategic warning analysts maintain private contingency plans to evacuate their families in the event of a Russian nuclear strike. While nuclear civil defense is virtually non-existent for the average American, some intelligence officers have recently built private nuclear fallout shelters.[132]

This is analogous to a commercial airline pilot heading toward the rear of the plane with a parachute on his back while telling the passengers that everything is just fine. Although Pry follows the party line about KAL 007, he did state, "The KAL 007 incident illustrates the hair trigger mindset of the Soviet military, born of their fear that World War III was imminent."[133]

During my visit to Seoul, I had the opportunity to interview a retired KAL captain who was flying B-747s in 1983. Although he was not willing to endorse the previously cited opinion of KAL President Cho Choong Hoon (intentional electronic navigational interference), my acquaintance did recall a distinct Soviet paranoia at the time. He related this atmosphere to a serious territorial intrusion by the U.S. Pacific fleet which occurred on April 4, 1983. On that date, a group of at least six Navy aircraft from the *Midway* and the *Enterprise* violated Soviet borders by overflying the island of Zeleny in the Kurile archipelago. Two days later a formal diplomatic note of complaint (known as a demarche) was delivered to the American Embassy in Moscow. The official U.S. response was something like, "Tough toenails!" Dallin placed this serious encroachment within the context of Reagan's drive to deploy Pershing II missiles throughout Europe, and Moscow's determination to resist:

> Meanwhile, the tension tended to be expressed increasingly in terms of what might be labeled superpower body language: a partially unadvertised complex of activities including not only muscle-flexing by symbolic movement of naval vessels, paratroop units, marine detachments, and nuclear submarines, but also extensive mutual monitoring of missile tests, military communications, and troop movements, satellite photography of significant installations and deployments, shadowing of naval vessels by adversary submarines, and virtually incessant air patrol by reconnaissance aircraft of each side. This, plus the increasingly bitter rhetoric, added to the nervousness everywhere, compounded by the jitters generated by growing attempts—

especially in Western Europe—to dramatize the potential devastation of a nuclear exchange.[134]

After ridiculing "conspiracy buffs" and walking a tightrope of noncommitment throughout his scholarly study, the hypocritical Dallin bites the bullet himself by conceding that some "hanky-panky" may have transpired on that mysterious night after all. With reference to a suggested scenario—"a mission undertaken by some of the members of the flight crew of KAL 007, presumably on behalf of an American (and/or South Korean) government agency"—Dallin concludes, "In fact, it must be acknowledged that with the passage of time this argument, unlike all others, looms stronger than before."[135] While noting that *Black Box* "is extensively annotated and benefits from Dallin's experience as a Soviet scholar," a jilted Seymour Hersh whines that Al arrived at his controversial conclusion "on the basis of no evidence."[136]

As Dallin went on record in 1985 concerning the possibility of new evidence arriving "with the passage of time," Michel Brun was just getting started. His decade-long odyssey would include a study of: the intercepted transmissions of Soviet pilots over Sakhalin; the FAA and Japanese Ministry of Transportation tapes of air-traffic control communications between Anchorage and Tokyo on the one hand, and KAL 007 with its sister ship, KAL 015, on the other; the archives of the Japanese press in the Diet Library in Tokyo, as well as the relevant proceedings of the Diet; Japanese Maritime Safety Agency situation maps showing the successive positions of American, Japanese, and Soviet ships during the naval search off Sakhalin; the after-action report of the U.S Navy task force participating in the search; the sixty-plus articles *Izvestiya* printed on the shootdown; the documents Boris Yeltsin released in 1992; the 1983 and 1993 ICAO reports; and, perhaps most importantly—the hundreds of hours that he personally invested combing the beaches of Japan in search of the elusive KAL debris.

Now, the author's hypothesis is so utterly fantastic you might as well get it straight from the inside dust jacket flap.

> Here, as a result of more than ten years of research, Michel Brun reveals the truth, which at least four governments have colluded to conceal. *Incident at Sakhalin* not only demolishes the official story of a lone civilian airliner flying innocently off course. It does much more. The book establishes that **as the Korean Boeing 747 approached the Russian island of Sakhalin, so too did a number of U.S. military and reconnaissance**

aircraft in an ill-conceived intelligence and provocation operation that turned into a two-hour battle in which thirty or more U.S. Air Force and Navy personnel were killed and ten or more U.S. aircraft were shot down.

Contrary to "official" reports from the United States and the International Civil Aviation Organization, KAL 007 was not shot down over Sakhalin but was destroyed off Honshu, the main Japanese island, nearly an hour later than the reports claimed and by means and for reasons still not clear.

Incident at Sakhalin is an astonishing chronicle of a Cold War catastrophe that raises questions about a democracy and its relationship to its military and intelligence agencies.[137]

"Whew . . .!" you say—"Dr. Grady, that's about as *far out* as you can get!" My answer is—"Not really"; the high profile endorsement on the back cover is even *wilder*:

This book has importance far beyond its sensational and dramatic revelations of a Cold War intelligence ploy that turned into a military engagement—an aerial battle that could easily have escalated into World War III.

That importance concerns the covenant that exists in a democracy between the government and its people regarding the matter of honesty. A democracy depends on an informed electorate, and it ceases to be a democracy when its agents conspire to deny the people the truth.

Democracy is no democracy when it is conducted in the dark. When the people are forced by its own misdeeds to distrust their government, the nation is weakened and the democracy itself is imperiled. As harsh as may be the truth here exposed, it can be hoped that these revelations will inspire a greater responsibility in government and thus justify the people's confidence in it.[138]

You'd better brace yourself for this one, folks! (Don't say I didn't warn you.) The person who gave this endorsement was none other than— Walter Cronkite! Surely such a wild-eyed pronouncement would make the "dean of twentieth-century journalism" eligible for an "honorary doctorate" from the Limbaugh Institute for Advanced Conservative Studies! However, not even a notorious Reagan-basher like Cronkite would jeopardize his reputation and lifetime career accomplishments for an unsubstantiated, crackpot theory. An "insider" himself, Walt may have been privy to some of the confidential shenanigans uncovered by Brun's persistence. Even *Izvestiya's* Tokyo correspondent, Sergei

Agafonov, was willing to relate the following candid admission by a senior Soviet official. Brun writes:

> When President Gorbachev visited Japan in April 1991, Sergei Agafonov traveled to Khabarovsk ahead of the president to cover the event. There he met people in the president's entourage, including a "high-ranking and powerful general who was a member of the government." Agafonov asked the general his opinion of my investigation. The general said, "Michel Brun has discovered part of the truth. The real story is more complicated than the official version of the event." The general told Agafonov that the wreckage at Moneron was "from military aircraft and there were three of them." It may have been the general's comments that prompted *Izvestiya* to mention my investigation, even though the editors tried to minimize its implications.[139]

Should a skeptic raise his eyebrow at Brun's use of an anonymous source, he would do well to read Seymour's convenient smoke screen concession:

> Most of the material was provided during interviews with men and women who processed or analyzed the communications intelligence stemming from the shootdown of Flight 007. Of course they cannot be named. Other officials who served in the White House, State Department, and Pentagon agreed to be interviewed on the condition that they not be named.[140]

The Lord impressed me to ask a couple of my Christian friends who have government experience to review Brun's book. One is a major in the Air Force with eighteen years in Intelligence (referred to in the Introduction) while the other is employed by the CIA in the field of communications. The major acknowledged that Brun's impeccable research forced him to personally question the official shootdown account, while my other contact remarked, "The book rings true."

The documentation Brun presents for his dogfight thesis is nearly overwhelming. It certainly is, in the words of Andrej Illesh, "so large." Brun contends that the U.S. naval provocation in April was far more threatening than any American citizen realized:

> In the spring of 1983, a U.S. three-carrier battle group, accompanied by B-52 bombers, AWACs, F-15 fighters, submarines, and submarine-patrol aircraft, were for the first time put into the normal patrol area of the Soviet submarine fleet. USS *Midway*, blacked out, on radio silence, and with all other monitorable electrical systems shut down, was put into Soviet territorial waters (twelve-mile limit) near Petropavlovsk. . . . There is evidence that

multiple and sustained overflights by U.S. carrier aircraft again took place in June in the same general area. We cannot be sure what lessons the United States may have drawn from these incidents and the lack of Soviet response. Perhaps they thought that there would be no response to the greater provocation of August 31.[141]

One of Brun's many interviews was conducted with a reserve officer in the Soviet Armed Forces by the name of Colonel Privalov. At the time of the KAL 007 affair, Privalov was on Kamchatka, serving with his friend, the commanding general of the entire military region. According to Privalov, the general stated that Soviet intelligence viewed the April intrusion as a "rehearsal for a massive invasion."[142]

At a special briefing on September 3 with congressional leaders, the unsettling fact was disclosed that an American RC-135 intelligence plane, the Cobra Ball, had indeed been airborne on the night of August 31-September 1 and had even been tracked within a few moments' flying time of KAL 007.[143]

Although the "solitary" RC-135 was reported to have hightailed it home long before violating Soviet air space, a serious discrepancy in the 1993 ICAO report tells a different story altogether. The Sukoi SU-15 Flagon-F interceptor that supposedly destroyed KAL 007 has been identified as Aircraft #805 in its audio communications with Sokol Airbase Command Post Fighter Controller (Deputat). According to official audio transcripts (as contained in the ICAO report which I have personally scrutinized), the Soviet pilot made the following four statements:

18:10   (interference) it is flying with **flashing lights**
18:18   The air navigation light is on, the **flashing light** is on.
18:21   The target has a **flashing light**. I already approached it to a distance of somewhere like 2 kilometres.
18:26   The target is destroyed.[144]

Yet, in this same ICAO report we read, under the heading **"Aircraft lighting,"** 1.13.4.1—**"Aircraft HL7442 [KAL 007] was not equipped with white strobe anti-collision lights."**[145] Colonel Prouty concludes, "Therefore when he saw strobe lights flashing, he was not seeing KE 007. He was seeing a U.S. Air Force RC-135."[146]

Also, it just so happened, that on the same evening, a highly secretive Soviet missile test had been scheduled to take place. An SS-X-25 was to be fired from Plesetsk (near the White Sea) across Siberia to Northern

Kamchatka. The normally noncommittal Dallin was even forced to speculate: "It would be natural for U.S. intelligence to seek to use all possible resources to monitor the test. Perhaps KAL 007 was to have had a role in this effort: this would explain many strange coincidences."[147]

A decade after these words were written, Michel Brun produced the following "explanations" for the host of "strange coincidences": While debris confirmed to be from KAL 007 was not found near the designated crash site for nine days, Brun points to the immediate recovery of numerous fragments belonging to *military* aircraft. According to a JMSA report dated September 5, 1983, fifty-four pieces of debris were collected by JMSA patrol vessels north of Moneron, though none (with the possible exception of one) were identified as being part of the Korean airliner.[148]

Brun was able to secure copies of official government photographs validating the existence of these highly classified, controversial objects. One picture displays a bulkhead made of carbon fiber that appears to have come from an SR-71, a U.S. high-speed, high-altitude reconnaissance aircraft known as a Blackbird.[149] Another shows what looks like the wing flap of an EF-111,[150] as well as the shell for a McDonnell Douglas ACES II Zero Zero ejection seat (its propulsion charges appeared to have been fired, suggesting that the ejection seat was used.)[151] In another amazing picture, the author is holding the fragment of a titanium wing recovered by chance from the ocean floor of the Sea of Okhotsk in 1990 by a Japanese fishing boat.[152] Included in the sizable inventory of non-commercial aircraft fragments is another spent ejection seat and several small life rafts, clearly military.[153]

Brun then takes two entire chapters to reconcile the conflicting testimony regarding the so-called official crash site coordinates. The net result is a grid that accurately substantiates *nine* different wreckage locations![154]

His chapter entitled "The Air Battle of Sakhalin" is perhaps the most provocative section of the entire book. As the pages unfold, Brun unravels and reconciles a myriad of previously unintelligible radar data and contradictory statements between the Soviet pilots and their ground commanders. All I can do at this point is to, hopefully, whet your appetite with a single paragraph of the author's action-packed commentary.

> I will review these sightings to give the reader an idea of the picture Soviet commanders on Sakhalin were looking at. They saw six intruder aircraft coming at them virtually simultaneously. At 05:05, a first intruder

had entered Sakhalin airspace. At 05:07, a second intruder was spotted 340 kilometers to the ENE of Plantatsia, tracking 200 degrees. Four minutes later, at 05:11, a third intruder, looking like a TU-95, was sighted. Its altitude and behavior made Soviet observers worry that it might be a Soviet aircraft. They checked Soviet flights and found that it could not be one of theirs. It was south of Terpeniya, tracking 240 degrees, straight toward Makarov 100 kilometers away from it, where it was feared it might bomb but didn't. At the same time, a fourth intruder was observed on a bearing of 45 degrees and at a distance of 110 kilometers from Smirnykh. Still at the same time, a fifth intruder was observed crossing the Kurils. And at 05:12, the Japanese radars spotted a sixth intruder, some 150 kilometers south of Makarov and 420 kilometers south of the target observed by Plantatsia.[155]

Confirming that Moscow military (standard) time is three hours later than Greenwich time (not four hours later as the ICAO would have it), Brun recreates an air battle that lasted close to two hours.[156] On one tape segment from Narita Airport a pilot can be heard yelling, "Repeat conditions . . ." and "Gonna be a blood bath . . . real bad."[157] Even the *Izvestiya* article has a Soviet pilot exclaiming, "I see the air battle"![158]

At this point a novice might wonder how so many government personnel could be lost without loved ones asking questions. A sad, yet simplistic, answer is that standard intelligence operatives are so much expendable fodder. The truth is probably a lot closer to Hollywood than any of us realize. Dallin notes that twenty-five U.S. aircraft engaged in electronic surveillance were attacked or destroyed, mostly in the 1950s and '60s.[159] Apart from Gary Powers (one of the "lucky" ones who lived to tell about his experience), how many of the other unfortunate victims have you ever heard about?

A case in point is the intriguing picture of a young Asian girl displayed on the front dust jacket of *Incident at Sakhalin*. Through a providential chain of events, Brun was shown a copy of the photograph in 1993. The original and the leather wallet in which it was initially discovered had lain in storage as part of the KGB's secret collection of un-returned "KAL 007" paraphernalia. Brun was able to persuade the Japanese television station TBS to broadcast the little girl's picture on its evening news program during prime time. It was also shown in Seoul. Brun writes:

> That evening, somebody telephoned the Seoul television station and identified the girl and her father. The girl was working as a secretary in Seoul. Her father, a military man, had disappeared in 1983. When TBS heard of the

development, they immediately tried to learn more but were prevented from going further. They were stonewalled everywhere. Rumors surfaced that the father of the little girl had not been a passenger aboard KAL 007. He had been an officer with the South Korean Army, working with the intelligence service, the KCIA. He disappeared at the same time as the Korean airliner and had never been heard of since.[160]

This is particularly interesting as the author notes that a cockpit transmission was recorded between KAL 007 and an unidentified, non-commercial aircraft. The individual piloting the ghost plane was conversing in Korean. Brun had the tape analyzed by Dr. K. Tsuboi, director of the Iwatsu Electric Company's laboratory in Kaguyama, near Tokyo. Brun confirms, "None of the speakers was KAL 015, the voice prints of whose pilot and copilot Dr. Tsuboi had previously identified."[161]

KAL 007'S END

As indicated by the previously quoted jacket flap material, the author's most dramatic revelation about KAL 007 concerns the location where it went down. Brun believes the Korean airliner met its fate off Honshu, the main Japanese Island—*nearly four hundred miles southward and an hour later than previously supposed.* This view is consistent with the original *Tass* statement, read without comment on the Soviet evening news, September 1, 1983: "The intruder plane did not react to the signals and warnings from the Soviet fighters and **continued its flight in the direction of the Sea of Japan.**[162]

Were the "bad guys" telling the truth all along? The discrepant crash-site theory was based on two important finds. The first involved debris. Brun spent several months of his research personally combing the beaches along certain stretches of Japanese coastline. It didn't take long before he made his first discovery of KAL 007 fragments near Sai in the extreme north of Honshu. It was a piece of weatherworn aluminum known as honeycomb. In aircraft engineering, glass-reinforced honeycomb materials are mainly used in aircraft exterior structures (i.e., nose fairing of a fuselage and a wing, wing and tail unit panels, high-lift devices, as well as in sound-absorbing structures of the engine, floor panels, etc.).

However, to his amazement the amount of debris he recovered increased the further *south* he traveled. This was highly significant because of the current flow in that region. The Tsushima Shio is the powerful *north*flowing current that dominates the eastern side of the Sea of Japan. Brun was finding KAL 007 debris hundreds of miles to the *south* of where the airliner was thought to have crashed. Yet it was theoretically impossible for any object to drift from Moneron *down* to the Japanese coast!

With the last debris discovered north of Nigata on Honshu, Brun arrived at the following hypothesis:

> First, KAL 007 had not been shot down over Sakhalin but had crashed in the Sea of Japan some four hundred miles south of the official search area. The facts that the current flowed north and that debris from the airliner did not show up in the official search area for more than a week indicated this.
>
> Second, the debris found on the day of the disaster in several distinctly different areas near Moneron showed that several military aircraft, at least some of them American, had been shot down.[163]

The other indication that KAL 007 crashed north of Nigata, Honshu, came from a cockpit transmission recorded by Tokyo's Narita airport at 04:12 hours—*forty-six minutes after the airliner was supposedly destroyed!* Throughout the night KAL 007 "appeared" to be having radio trouble. When KAL 050 (a third KAL airliner) entered the Tokyo control zone at 04:08, an air traffic controller asked the pilot to attempt radio contact with Captain Chun. KAL 050 followed through with the request accordingly:

04:08:30 (KE 050):	Ah Tokyo, Ah Korean air zero zero seven, this is Korean air zero five zero.
04:09:15 (KE 050):	Ah, Korean air zero zero seven, Korean air zero five zero, on one one eight niner [VHF 118.9].
04:09:34 (KE 050):	Korean air zero zero seven, this is Korean air zero five zero on one two one decimal five, how do you read?
04:09:51 (KE 007):	**Zero five . . . seven.**
04:09:54 (KE 050):	Ah, Roger, Ah, Tokyo Center advises you to contact Ah, one one eight decimal niner, over.
04:10:04 (KE 007):	**(transmission in Korean)**
04:10:10 (KE 050):	(transmission in Korean)[164]

Dr. Tsuboi at the Iwatsu Laboratory has confirmed that the voice in the above transmissions ascribed to KAL 007 is that of the copilot, Son Dong-Hwin.[165] Even Andrei Illesh conceded this important point, stating in his *Izvestiya* article:

> This is no fantasy either. The radio conversations of the Korean pilots were recorded by both Japanese and Americans. . . . These conversations occurred long after Lieutenant Colonel Osipovich shot down an aircraft. Correspondents from Asahi Television in Moscow showed me the results of the analysis of these conversations (independently conducted in the U.S. and Japan), which prove that the voice belongs to the pilot of KAL 007.[166]

A stickler for detail, Brun corrects Illesh in a footnote that the voice print and spectrographic analysis were conducted in Japan only.

BRUN'S THEORY

One reason that *Incident at Sakhalin* is so thought-provoking is because of Brun's genuine humility. When the author feels certain about a point, he says so; and when not, he's secure enough to acknowledge the same.

Brun contends that KAL 015 collaborated with KAL 007 in an espionage mission that "went south." He notes that Park and Chun were old friends who had also served in the Korean Air Force together.[167] According to John Keppel (the retired Foreign Service officer who wrote Brun's introduction), U.S. Attorney Charles Herrmann played the Narita excerpt—"must have been a bloodbath . . . real bad"—for Kim Ok-hee, Captain Chun's widow, who affirmed that the "bloodbath" phrase was in her husband's voice.[168]

A synopsis of Brun's conjecture is as follows:

> How could a U.S. action of that degree of folly have been conceived, planned, and set in motion? Its genesis may have been much more normal than the final product. It seems likely to have started with the U.S. military's wish to utilize its . . . new capabilities in space to improve intelligence gathering and communications networking. They were looking for a way to send information from reconnaissance satellites directly to cruise missiles and strategic bombers approaching the Soviet Union.
>
> Previously, information from reconnaissance satellites had to be dropped by canister and parachute over Hawaii and Big Pine in Australia, recovered, and analyzed. Only then could it be transmitted to the user. But by August 1983 the United States could for the first time process global battlefield intelligence in real time. On the night in question two Ferret satellites were in position to collect information on Soviet air-defense activities and communications and could send it on via Tracking Data and Relay Satellite No.1 (TDRS One) and military communications satellites in elliptical

orbit high over the pole. The Shuttle STS-8 (*Challenger*), also in orbit at the time, may or may not have had a role in the exercise that was planned.

Something, however, was needed to turn on the Soviet air defenses and communications. Satellites were predictable, and if all that was going on was that one was passing overhead, the Soviets could leave their aircraft on the ground and their radars switched off. We have no hard evidence on the point, but it seems likely that Casey told the National Security Council that, in conjunction with Clark and a few others of the NSC staff, he would take care of any planning and execution that were needed to get Soviet air defenses to operate in a big way. The planning of the operation may thus have started with a relatively normal military wish to develop new capabilities. But with Casey, Clark, and some other hard-liners involved, the broader (and supremely unwise) strategic provocation objectives seem to have taken over.[169]

While the CIA may have intended to limit their initial incursion to what is known in Soviet doctrine as a *profasila*—a move forward until there is a reaction, followed by a tactical withdrawal—Brun implies that even a fatal mission would be a "win-win" for the U.S. while a "lose-lose" for the Russians:

Regardless of the operation's goals, it went terribly wrong in execution, leading in the eyes of the Reagan administration to the need for immediate remedial action. As a result of emergency work done by CIA during the evening and night of August 31, when it had a chance to review the intelligence information on the disaster, the U.S. government was able to transform what threatened to be a major political setback into a global propaganda success. The transformed account of events discredited the Soviet Union, contributed to the subsequent passage of the U.S. military budget (which had been in some trouble) through Congress in maximal form, overcame objections to the emplacement of Pershing II and cruise missiles in Europe, and did much to break the back of the peace movement in Europe and the United States. All this, based on the blunder of the operation and the big lie of the cover-up.[170]

Colonel Prouty concurred with this analysis:

In the games nations play, the biggest game of them all is that which was created for the Super-Powers after World War II, called "DEFENSE." Since that time the military-industrial complex of the world has consumed no less than **seven trillion dollars** as a result of the East-West confrontation. This is so massive an effort on the part of all contestants, and so extremely profitable, that the major powers skillfully create situations, many of which are illusions and deliberately false . . . known in the trade as "disinformation" and "deception" . . . in order to enhance the appearance of rivalry among them and the threat of a supremely dangerous, bi-polar confrontation.

Such incidents serve to keep the pot boiling and to raise the stakes on both sides. Many of these incidents, at the time considered to be grave and frightening, are found later to have been untrue and to have been contrived . . . by either side, sometimes both.

The loss of Korean Air Lines Boeing 747, Flight KE 007, on the night of Aug. 31-Sept. 1, 1983, in the far Pacific, is an example of one of these events. As the record clearly shows, the stakes—in terms of Defense dollars—were raised by **hundreds of billions** shortly after that event. These new **hundreds of billions** will be added to the **seven trillion dollars** that have been consumed.[171]

The reader will note that the man who made this sober statement held a security clearance that placed him in the top 54 of 32,000 Pentagon employees (reserved for those attending the early morning briefings).

With regard to the ultimate fate of KAL 007, Brun leaves his readers with three possibilities, the first and second being occasioned by the aerial commotion over Sakhalin. An appropriate adage for determining a worst-case scenario of his incredible theory would be, "Where there's smoke, there's fire." Maybe Brun was "way off" in the main theme of his book. Perhaps only "five or six" planes were "winged" in a "thirty-minute skirmish." Like the Soviet general said, "Michel Brun has discovered **part** of the truth." Is there any doubt that *something* out of the ordinary occurred that night? A compilation of all the available cockpit transmissions shows that at least two interceptors came from Postovaya, a Soviet Air Force base across the Tatar Gulf in Siberia, and two Soviet AWACs were sent from Vanino, also on the mainland. Brun writes:

> Some twenty air bases were on Sakhalin with fighters and interceptors in sufficient numbers to repel any likely intrusion, let alone one by a single off-course civilian airliner. The call for reinforcements from the mainland illustrates the seriousness of the situation in the eyes of the Soviet command.[172]

By the time Captain Chun made his way toward Tokyo, the Japanese Air Force had been put on high alert, DEFCON 3, one step below general mobilization. Brun notes, "Seventy-two fighters, half the active fighters in the Japanese Air Force, had been assembled at Chitose air base."[173] American interceptors were also close by on the U.S. bases of Yokota and Misawa. Thus, the author was compelled to speculate:

> What happened to KAL 007 between 19:12 and 19:30 GMT? The plane was out of range of Soviet interceptors, so a shootdown by the Soviets north of Niigata seems unlikely. Catastrophe as a delayed result of damage sustained at Soviet hands farther north also seems unlikely. KAL 007 had been communicating, normally if ambiguously, with other KAL planes long after it left Sakhalin. It never sent a distress message and never signaled any problem. It vanished suddenly, minutes before reaching Niigata, without any apparent reason.
>
> Among the several things that could have happened to it, two are suggested by analogy and by facts that came to my attention in my investigation. One, the airliner was shot down by the Americans under the mistaken impression it was a Soviet aircraft bent on retaliation for what had happened up north. Or, it was shot down by the Japanese under the mistaken impression it was a Soviet aircraft threatening Japan in a widening conflict.[174]

As an example, Brun cites the accidental destruction of an Iranian Airbus with 293 passengers aboard by the confused crew of the USS *Vincennes* on July 3, 1988.

For his third suggestion, Brun notes:

> It is technically feasible for the airliner to have been destroyed by a radio-activated bomb. On its route south from La Pérouse Strait, KAL 007 was continuously within line-of-sight radio range of U.S. installations at Wakkanai and Misawa.[175]

Citing a letter in *Armed Forces Journal International*, January 1990, Brun writes, "Col. Fletcher Prouty, a retired U.S. Air Force intelligence officer of wide experience, has said that **the United States intentionally destroyed KAL 007 by activating a previously planted explosive charge.**"[176] Though Prouty believed KAL 007 sank into the Kurile Oceanic Trench in the North Pacific Ocean (an opinion expressed a decade before Brun's findings were published), his initial view was that "it was destroyed by an explosive device that had been placed on board."[177]

Colonel Prouty's service record speaks for itself. The last nine years of his twenty-three-year military career were spent in the Pentagon (1955-1964); two years with the secretary of defense, two years with the Joint Chiefs of Staff and five years with Headquarters U.S. Air

Force. In 1955, he was appointed the first "Focal Point" officer between the CIA and the Air Force for Clandestine Operations per National Security Directive 5412. He served as briefing officer for the secretary of defense from 1960 to 1961. He was also assigned to attend MKULTRA meetings. He retired as a colonel from the U.S. Air Force in 1964 and was awarded one of the first three Joint Chiefs of Staff Commendation Medals by General Maxwell Taylor, chairman of the Joint Chiefs of Staff.

Among a slate of civilian endeavors pursued upon retirement, Prouty became vice president of International Operations for General Aircraft Corporation, a company created by MIT and Harvard engineers that designed and manufactured aircraft for the CIA and Army special forces. At the request of Oliver Stone, Prouty worked as creative advisor (1990-1991) on production of his film "JFK."

With his exposure to the inner workings of the CIA, Colonel Prouty became privy to a veritable cesspool of corruption. As a secular patriot, he made the inevitable transition to the variegated ranks of "right-wing extremism." One website concludes, "Prouty is pretty clearly a full blown nut case" (i.e., "Limbaugh Kook"). Other fallible pro-American "nut cases" would include: President Thomas Jefferson (agnosticism); General George C. Patton (reincarnation); Senator Joseph McCarthy (Catholicism); Colonel "Bo" Gritz (Mormonism); and Senator Jesse Helms (Freemasonry).

Dallin challenged "unverified claims that a Boeing 747 without markings had been spotted at Andrews Air Force Base, Maryland, weeks before the fatal flight."[178] Illesh took the "rumor" more seriously, however, writing in *Izvestiya*:

> A South Korean passenger aircraft, tail number NL-7442, was located at Andrews Air Base in Washington D.C. for three days, from the 11th to the 14th of August 1983 in an area not designated for passenger aircraft. This was the very same "Boeing-747", which three weeks later was shot down over Sakhalin. What was it doing at Andrews, at the hanger[sic] of a company, which specializes in installation of special electronic equipment?[179]

The problem continues to be an unwillingness by both the American and Soviet governments to "come clean" on this reprehensible international travesty. A high-ranking Russian naval officer who was assigned to the Pacific Ocean Fleet in the autumn of 1983 told Illesh in a private interview:

They say that you want to learn the truth about the Boeing? Well then, answer one question. Why did the Americans suddenly stop spending all their time on this problem in the press? Maybe it was not desirable for them to have everything brought to light? Even my colleagues have raised such a possibility. Yes, the Soviet navy managed to find the "black box." Experts managed to decipher its data. But this text did not favor the Americans . . . And this is what happened next. The Soviet and American sides (unfortunately I don't know at what level) simply reached an agreement . . . And they tried to bury this mutually inconvenient mystery a little further and a little deeper.[180]

Although the esteemed Soviet commander "forgot" to specify *which* of the ten or more black boxes he was referring to, the gist of his statement was "right on."

In the immediate aftermath of KAL 007, the U.S. State Department put the "kabosh" on the NTSB's jurisdictional mandate to investigate *any* crash involving the loss of American lives. Though promising to conduct it's own investigation, the State Department never did. Yet, one extant transmission at 14:34:01 GMT has an unidentified military controller at Elmendorf Air Force Base alerting his FAA counterpart at Anchorage, Kenneth DeGarmo: "Okay, you guys got someone bumping into the Russians' air defenses over here," with the latter responding, "Oh, you're kidding. A person should warn him."[181] The FAA promptly extricated itself by erasing the originals and providing unintelligible copies. The 1993 ICAO report confirms:

> The representatives of the United States reported that the original Anchorage ATC tapes were no longer available, but provided certified authentic copy tapes of the recordings . . . The representatives of the United States also made available a copy tape that contained a segment of the Anchorage ARTCC recording at 14:34 hours. This segment of the tape contained nearly inaudible and unintelligible words that had been alleged in 1985 to be the phrase "persons should warn them." This segment had been analyzed by the laboratory of the Federal Bureau of Investigagion (FBI) of the United States in 1985 and a copy of the report was made available. The FBI report concluded that "an aural examination of the designated portion of channel 4 . . . revealed that no decision can be made as to the words spoken, due to the very low recording level." The report also concluded that simultaneous crosstalk from channel 3 to channel 4 occurred ten seconds later.[182]

On the legal front, following hundreds of lawsuits, a measure of compensation from Korean Air Lines was eventually awarded. However, any litigation against the primary suspect responsible for the deaths of those aboard—namely, the United States of America—was conveniently dismissed in the courts. Brun writes, "In the key case in the U.S., that in the District Court in Washington, D.C., Judge Robinson made it clear he would hear no evidence concerning the U.S. military."[183]

There was one "positive" development, however. On June 17, 1992, Russian President Boris Yeltsin assured a joint session of the U.S. Congress (*minus Representative Lawrence Patton McDonald*): "There will be no more lies—ever. The same applies to biological weapons experiments, and the facts that have been revealed about American prisoners of war, KAL 007, and many other things."[184] Apart from the politically correct standing ovation he received, the only thing any funnier is the fact that the words, *"And ye shall know the truth, and the truth shall make you free"* (John 8:32), are prominently inscribed at the CIA headquarters in Langley, Virginia. Near the end of his book, the Frenchman asks in genuine consternation:

> How in countries where there is supposed to be freedom of information can such egregious contradictions be passed by in silence for so many years? It is important for their citizens to know. Acceptance of official lying breaks down the fabric of responsible government.[185]

Unfortunately, the lying started a lot earlier than KAL 007. Keppel writes in his preface to *Incident at Sakalin*:

> As a member of an interagency working group in Washington after Francis Gary Powers's U-2 went down over Sverdlovsk on May 1, 1960, I had taken part myself in official lying. Not realizing that the Soviets had the U-2's cameras virtually intact and Powers himself alive, we (the members of the working group) very stupidly recommended that President Eisenhower stick to the cover story that the U-2 was a weather plane that had inadvertently strayed off course. It is hard to realize today that when Eisenhower got caught in the lie we thrust upon him, it was the first time many Americans realized that a U.S. president would lie to them on an important subject. We had made our contribution to the erosion of truth-telling, on which democracy in large measure depends.[186]

(In 2002, while on my second trip to Moscow, I received permission to visit the KGB museum at the infamous Lubyanka prison. Aside from running his mouth about having recently hosted actor Robert DeNiro, my KGB guide spent the greater part of our tour gloating over the Gary Powers exhibit.)

LINE OF NO RETURN

Pending the unlikely eventuality of a full disclosure, surviving family and friends of KAL 007 victims (along with a shrinking remnant of incensed American patriots) must remain victims themselves, consigned to supposition and conjecture, especially with regard to the bodies. Emotions are freshly traumatized with each new guess by the "experts." While *Izvestiya* suggested that the remains were eaten by crabs, an article in *U.S. News and World Report*, January 14, 1991, professing to represent an advance report on a pending *Izvestiya* release (which turned out not to be so), recklessly stated: "Moscow then ordered the bodies of the 269 victims destroyed in a local crematorium."[187] A particularly sad illustration with which I am familiar concerns a woman who has a recurrent nightmare that her dead husband is sleeping between her and her new husband.

During my interview with Mr. Toles, the former press secretary for Congressman McDonald expressed an understandable irritation at the lingering speculation by some that his best friend might still be "alive" and rotting in a Soviet gulag. No doubt, after twenty long years, annoyance is preferable to anxiety; finality to endless ambivalence.

As to my own opinion, I believe that Mr. Brun's exhaustive documentation will explain Walter Cronkite's weighty endorsement. *Incident at Sakhalin* reconciles far too many contradictions for it to be lightly dismissed. Some "target" was undoubtedly "destroyed" in mid-air, while another no doubt landed on Sakhalin. While one aircraft was seen crashing into the ocean, another was viewed safely ditching in the same. Soviet coast guard vessels probably pulled someone (or several someones) out of those recovered military lifeboats. Could they have been the pilots who fired those two recovered ejection seats?

KAL 007's initial intrusion may have served as a diversionary tactic, or even as a human shield for one or more American reconnaissance aircraft snuggled closely alongside in a single radar blur.[188] An example of this very scenario was given in the 1983 ICAO report. With reference to KAL 007 it stated, "At 1601 hours the blip of a second aircraft came close to the RC-135 [Cobra Ball] and their blips merged for about ten minutes."[189]

Yet much of the data actually suggests that Captain Chun may have faked an intrusion and avoided Soviet airspace altogether. Perhaps the most startling revelation contained in the Toles recordings concerns a report that was given by FAA Duty Officer Orville Brockman while attempting to relay a call from Mr. Steve Gradick, a McDonald staffer, to the previously mentioned Cliff Cernick, FAA public affairs officer in Anchorage, Alaska. While Steve was waiting for Mr. Cernick to come to the phone, the official attempted to fill in the time by stating:

> While you're waiting, Mr. Gradick, we just got a cablegram from the American embassy in Seoul; it doesn't have anything new to offer except, they gave us the last known position of it . . . at 03:30 Korean time their position was 147° 28′ East, 42° 43′ North, which placed them southeast of Hokkaido Island. This was the last communication they had with them and that was two hours and twenty-three minutes before their ETA for Seoul, which was at 05:53 Korean time.[190]

This is most significant as a map of the area will show. At the precise time KAL 007 was supposed to have crashed off Sakhalin Island, an American embassy communiqué positioned the aircraft on its prescribed R-20 flight path 350 NM to the southwest. The September 1, 1983, *New York Times* gave 007's last stated location as "113 miles south of Nemuro, on the eastern end of the Japanese Island of Hokkaido."[191] Hersh relates that CBS had the Korean Boeing 747 even closer to home, stating: "CBS subsequently reported on its West Coast edition of *The CBS Evening News with Dan Rather* that Flight 007's last radioed position had been off the northwest coast of Japan in the North Pacific."[192]

Acting on a hunch, I enlisted the services of a personal friend who is a seasoned corporate pilot. I gave him the pertinent data for KAL 007 listed in the ICAO report (departure time, altitude, speed, fuel load, etc.) and asked him to calculate whether the flight path would have matched the time and coordinates contained in the embassy cablegram. According to his onboard computer, 147° 28′ East, 42° 43′ North is *exactly* where Captain Chun should have been at 03:30 Korean time. However, in a heavy conspiratorial coincidence, the very same data would also have allowed KAL 007 to be over the official crash site at the prescribed time had the flight "strayed" from R-20. (Something was *really* "rotten in Denmark.")

The official explanation for this obvious contradiction is that the report emanated from the wayward aircraft itself. Because R-20 was beyond radar range of the FAA in Anchorage, procedure required the pilots to periodically call in their own positional settings. The 1983 ICAO report states: "Since the aircraft's flight progress was routinely reported by the flight crew as if it were proceeding along the assigned route and since no transmissions from the aircraft were received in Anchorage and Tokyo other than routine reports and requests for a change in cruising level, there was no indication that the pilot knew or suspected that the aircraft was off track."[193] This would mean that Korea's number one pilot not only inadvertently strayed 350 NM off course, but dispatched *seven* incorrect waypoint confirmations at NABIE, NUKKS, NEEVA, NINNO, NIPPI, NYTIM, and NOKKA, as well. The ICAO report reaffirms, "The possibility of a failure of all three INS must be regarded as **extremely remote**."[194]

An overlooked piece of evidence negating the possibility that the crew of KAL 007 could have strayed off course unwittingly involves the proximity of the accompanying topography. For one thing, while R-20 is exclusively over water until it crosses Honshu Island, Captain Chun supposedly flew directly over Soviet territory for nearly three hours. Then we have Hersh shooting himself in the foot when he quotes Wilham as stating: "The thing about this particular route in these days is— it's so boring, so [expletive] boring. The only thing that's happening is the (Kurile) Islands going by."[195] Had 007 flown where Hersh claims it did, I assure you that the flight would have been anything *but* boring— *with that 600-mile long island chain passing by on the wrong side of the aircraft!* And remember, Senator Symms had described the atmospheric conditions that evening as affording high visibility—"The moon was out and it was a clear night."

While doing research for this chapter, I solicited the expertise of a senior pilot with American Airlines who had formerly served as a navigator with the Royal Air Force (R.A.F.). Speaking from his own experience, the veteran flyer expanded on Wilham's comment, stating that occasional landmarks encountered during long over-water flights did more than merely break the boredom; they served as a welcome assurance that the flight was still on course.

After reading Brun's book and studying the ICAO reports, my acquaintance assured me that something was surely amiss. It was his professional opinion that KAL 007 could not *possibly* have strayed off course for so long—regardless of the visibility—given the sophisticated navigation system onboard. Colonel Prouty described this equipment accordingly:

> It had two Bendix RDF-IF weather units with a 200 mile range capability. They are excellent for long-range, over-water navigation purposes. They can be used much as anyone would use two strong flashlights on a dark night. With them, the crew can see islands and shorelines as well as with eyes . . . better than eyes . . . in weather and at night. It had 2 VOR/ILS receivers that are used by all military and commercial air crews for tuning on fixed stations to obtain automatic navigation and landing data.[196]

After noting that they also had two Distance Measuring Equipment (DME) units, two Automatic Direction Finders (ADF) and two compasses, Prouty concludes, "The allegation that KE 007 had strayed over Soviet territory is absurd."[197]

Yet, while acknowledging that, "Its use would have indicated to the flight crew of KE007 that the flight was straying to the right of R-20," the 1993 ICAO report forces one more incredulous scenario upon its readers: "It was concluded that the radar either was not functioning properly or that the ground mapping capability was not used."[198] Brun notes the unspeakable inference:

> If the Korean airliner, which seems likely not to have overflown any Soviet territory, had not been destroyed in the south and that fact had not been suppressed, the Soviets could not have been accused of an atrocity. And the search for military debris in the north could not have been presented as a search for the Korean airliner. The ugly facts of the military overflights and the air battle of Sakhalin would have come out. The alternative to the accidental destruction of the airliner is, of course, its intentional destruction as the first step in the cover-up.[199]

While the absence of a Mayday call (similar to the one that saved KAL 905 in 1978) mitigates the ditched landing theory, a bomb blast would negate the possibility of a distress signal being transmitted. The fate which Tommy Toles ascribes to a betrayed hijacker may have befallen Captain Chun instead.

However, all things being considered, we appear to be right back where we started. *What happened to the bodies?* Though Brun contends that KAL 007 "was out of range of Soviet interceptors, so a shootdown by the Soviets north of Niigata seems unlikely,"[200] he reports elsewhere, ". . . on September 13, 1983, less than two weeks after the destruction of KAL 007, a squad of Japanese fighters intercepted four Soviet planes, including two reconnaissance planes, there [i.e., at the Niigata site, known as KADPO]." He then asks, "Did they have information about where KAL 007 had actually crashed?"[201]

Thus the question remains—Where *are* "the remains"? At the height of my own frustration with the elusive mystery I suddenly dropped to my knees and prayed for any kind of a clue. Within just a few minutes, the Holy Ghost directed my attention to seven enlightening words in *Day of the Cobra.*

As previously stated, the easiest (and most desirable) theory for sincere conservatives to harbor is that the effective anti-Communist JBS chairman was gunned down by a premeditated act. After all, the Soviets did have access to his travel plans; Chun and Park's collaboration may or may not have been arranged; and the B-747 was rumored to have been sabotaged at Andrews AFB. But then St. John informs us, regarding the itinerary of several other American officials also traveling to the Seoul conference (Ron Mann, Robert McCormick, William Scheider, Jr. and Dr. Donald Stims): "At the last minute they decided to take a flight from New York on Sunday, August 28, **which Congressman McDonald missed by only minutes.**"[202] Even the *Izvestiya* article caught the "quirk of fate," stating: "Among the passengers [on KAL 007] was a member of the U.S. House of Representatives. He had missed the previous flight because the plane . . . which he was . . . to take from Atlanta, Georgia, to New York was forced to land in Baltimore because of bad weather."[203]

Mr. Toles shared his personal recollection of that last day with his best friend. (Note that Larry experienced the same misgivings expressed by his wife and Senator Symms.):

> Larry and I had been in the north end of the district, northwest Georgia, and I was taking him to the airport to fly to New York to catch the KAL flight. We were coming down US 27 through a little town community called Armuchee. Usually Larry loved going on trips like that. But coming down the highway, he said, "You know, I really don't want to go on this trip." I said, "You're the boss; you don't have to go. If you don't

want to go, don't go . . ." He had never, ever said before he did not want to go on a trip. To my knowledge this was the first time he just really did not want to go. He finally decided that he had made an obligation; he said he would go, so therefore he *had* to go, even though he really didn't want to. So I took him to the airport.

The next morning he called me and it was a surprise to me. I said, "Where are you?", 'cause I thought he was on the way to Korea on the plane. He said, "I'm still in New York." I said, "What happened; why are you still in New York?" He said that a massive thunderstorm had struck New York at the time his plane was supposed to arrive from Atlanta. The plane had circled over and over and was finally diverted to Baltimore, and then went back to New York. Once it got back to New York, everything was flooded, especially the baggage area. He told me it took him a while to get his bag and everything and he was racing to the counter and **got there basically as the flight was taking off that he was supposed to have been on**. Anyway, he was telling me all this and we were going over just other things relating to the district and the family; generally chewing the fat about things. I said, "When are you going to leave?" He said, "Well, I'll be leaving on this flight . . ."; he didn't tell me what KAL flight it was, but he did tell me the time it was supposed to be departing. And I said, "Well, I guess it worked out okay if you get there on time." He said, "Yeah, I'm supposed to be there on time and there shouldn't be any problems." And then we talked about other things we were planning to do in the district once he got back. Then he said, "Well, anything else?" I said, "No, I guess that's about it." Then he says, "Well, I'll be seeing you." "Yeah, I'll see you when you get back."

And then, after I had talked to him that day, at 7:15 p.m. I was watching NBC news when it came up that his plane was missing. And that's when I called a couple of places to confirm that it was him and his flight; although, I somehow inside knew it was. Everything started from that point.[204]

Larry missed the plane on which he was originally scheduled by "only minutes!" Had the Soviets been coordinating an intricate "assassination plot" via his original flight reservation, we cannot assume that his last-minute absence was automatically detected. Contrary to popular opinion, Russian "spies" are woefully incompetent. We do know, however, that the Korean airliner he was supposed to be on arrived in Seoul without incident. And, to whatever degree Brun "has discovered part of the truth," it is untenable that so complex a plot could have been planned for August 29 and then completely restructured in only three days.

The providential timing of Congressman McDonald's death can be illustrated by examining a Soviet Air Force term—the "line of no return." Because Communism was such a "wonderful" system, Iron Curtains and Berlin Walls had to be erected to keep its "contented" citizens from escaping. To minimize expensive and politically embarrassing defections by Soviet fighter pilots, units began filling their aircraft with just enough fuel so that a pilot would have no chance of reaching the nearest foreign airport. Thus, the "line of no return" represented the furthest point in any mission where a U-turn was mandatory to ensure a safe landing at the home base.

The spiritual application to Larry's death is sobering. According to Romans 8:28, there are no "accidents" for the Christian. Larry's Heavenly Father approved the weather conditions that forced him to miss the earlier flight. *It was simply his time to go.* However, the significant point is the *reason* for his homegoing. I believe the way in which Larry's warnings about Communism went unheeded by his congressional peers merely reflected how their constituents as a nation had passed *God's* "line of no return." The exhausted legislator was well aware of the ignorance and apathy engulfing his beloved country. Only two months before his death, Larry told St. John:

> **In the final analysis, the problem is in the living rooms of America. We have lost an informed electorate.** Which leads me to the most powerful branch of government. The national news media now have the power to drum up interest in any issue and present it as "news." They, along with Congress and the judiciary, have contributed to using government as an instrument for social engineering that has led to a conflict-ridden society, as various groups compete for a piece of the federal pie. The news media play an important role in creating conflict and destroying the Constitution by editorializing in the news and creating the *appearance* that mass support exists for various social programs.[205]

In his Thanksgiving Eve message at Resaca, Larry invoked a special warning by Thomas Jefferson: "Yes, we did produce a near-perfect republic. But will they keep it, or will they, in the enjoyment of plenty, lose the memory of freedom?"[206] From a spiritual perspective, it appears that the Lord would not allow his servant to cast any more pearls before swine. Rather, a last-minute schedule change would ensure that the congressman's tragic murder became a powerful object lesson to a giddy people, *". . . so that they are without excuse"* (Romans 1:20b).

Larry's House colleague, Carroll Hubbard of Kentucky (Democrat), articulated this principle accordingly:

> By his death Larry McDonald causes many more people to be aware of the brutal, cruel attitude of the Soviet Union's leadership and military than he ever did by his words on the floor of the U.S. House of Representatives. In other words, Larry McDonald tried to convince us during his lifetime that the Soviet Union regarded their airspace to be of a higher priority than human lives, even those inside the Soviet Union. Now that Larry McDonald is dead, we know he was right.[207]

While Congressman Austin Murphy of Pennsylvania (Democrat) told the House, "I am angry that American technology sold to the Soviets was the basis for the guidance system, the radar, and the computers used by the Soviet plane," Dr. Miles Costick, president of the Washington-based Institute on Strategic Trade relates a chilling illustration of how Western technology provides enhancement of Soviet military power:

> The missiles used to destroy the Korean airliner were direct duplications of the U.S. Sidewinder, including the electronic circuitry produced by U.S. firms and sold to West Germany, which the Soviets either bought or gained by industrial espionage. We have now been able to establish that the 269 innocent people aboard KAL 007 were sent to their deaths by a Sidewinder type of air-to-air missile fired by that Soviet fighter over Sakhalin Island.[208]

TWO OLIVE TREES

The Bible declares, *"The secret things belong unto the LORD our God . . ."* (Deuteronomy 29:29a). Regardless of how KAL 007 met its end, the Lord surely called His servant home according to a divine timetable. And the picture becomes even more profound when Larry's experience is compared with that of John Birch.

The two were similar in many ways. They were *both* professing Christians; *both* were "Georgia boys" (the Birch household being located in Larry's seventh congressional district); *both,* men of intense character and integrity. *Both* were willing to pull double-duty to fulfill the will of God for their lives; John—the missionary/soldier, Larry—the surgeon/statesman. *Both* were also devoted patriots who were willing to pay the ultimate price for their country. As such, their resting places would reflect the magnitude of their sacrifice. In John's case, perhaps only the Lord knows exactly where his grave may be found (if at all). Although his mutilated remains were originally entombed in a brick vault situated on a hillside overlooking the city of Suchow, his murderers later took over the turf. And as for Larry, the available choices remain—*camps, crabs, crematorium,* or *other.*

John and Larry were like God's two witnesses in Revelation, chapter 11. They appear to have played a significant role in the final days of the Church Age. John spoke out against the evils of *Chinese* Communism, while Larry warned his nation about *Russian* Communism. *Both* were murdered for their convictions, after which their own government conspired to conceal the atrocity. While Captain John Birch was heralded as the first causality of World War III, the chairman of his namesake organization, Congressman Larry McDonald, gained the ignominious distinction of being the first elected American official to be slain by a foreign power.

Though their final burial sites remain unknown, one thing is absolutely certain—*the Lord they served was not about to let Christian America get away with such despicable treachery!* In the same hour that God calls Moses and Elijah home in the midst of the Tribulation period, there will be *"a great earthquake, and the tenth part of the city [will fall], and in the earthquake [will be] slain of men seven thousand"* (Revelation 11:13a).

The fact that *both* men were abandoned by their own government is a sure sign of pending judgment according to a little known principle in the book of Acts. After the Jews crucified their Messiah, Jehovah graciously attributed the deed to ignorance (Acts 3:17) and offered them a second opportunity to repent (Acts 2:22-41). Had the nation responded, many Bible teachers believe that the Tribulation period would have begun, followed by the Second Advent. Though such speculation is rendered moot by the actual events as they unfolded, the Scripture clearly dates the beginning of God's transition away *from* Israel *to* the New Testament Church with the stoning of Stephen. The critical part of the story is that his execution was sanctioned by the ruling leaders. (Acts 6:12, 15; 7:58)

In a similar vein, the Lord is now turning away from an apostate Church and preparing to renew his relationship with Israel. (Romans 11:23; Esther 1:12) The accompanying widespread corruption in our government is an important fulfillment of prophecy in this regard. (II Timothy 3:5)

One of the most underrated occurrences of this time was the reproachful treatment afforded Kathy McDonald and her children at Larry's memorial service in Washington, D.C. It did not go unnoticed in Heaven, however. With eighty-three Bible verses mentioning "widows" and forty-three references to "the fatherless," Reagan's presidential boycott just might have been the spiritual catalyst for America's final judgment. As the Scripture plainly warns, *"Ye shall not afflict any widow, or fatherless child"* (Exodus 22:22), that inexplicable three-fold snub may one day be understood in the light of a popular cliché from our pleasure-crazed culture—"Three strikes and you're out!" While a debilitated Ronald Reagan was suffering the effects of Deuteronomy 27:19a— *"Cursed be he that perverteth the judgment of the stranger, fatherless, and widow,"* the rest of the nation experienced its own horrific object lesson. The date of Larry's special memorial service "just happened" to be—*September 11!* And as the Bible mandates a four-fold retribution for sin (II Samuel 12:6), you might say that it was *four* planes for *one!*

> What happens to people who lose the knowledge of their foundation? In Isaiah 5:13 and Hosea 4:6 we find two Old Testament prophets lamenting the fact that their people, at separate times, were led off to captivity because their people had lacked knowledge and had deserted the laws of their God.
>
> And we in this century, as Americans—not in the next century, in *your* lifetime—not in the lifetime of your grandchildren or your children, in *your* lifetime—stand a very real chance, if we do not change our ways, of losing the heritage and the liberties that our Founding Fathers gave us, because we have lost sight of the fundamentals that our Founding Fathers understood so well . . . Fellow Christians, this is the challenge we face tonight.

> Congressman Lawrence P. McDonald
> November 24, 1982
> Faith Baptist Camp
> Resaca, Georgia

16

Clash Equals Cash

"For the love of money is the root of all evil . . ."
(I Timothy 6:10a)

ITH THE VIOLENT deaths of John Birch and Larry McDonald providing the Lord with a pair of fresh alibis, America set a course for her cataclysmic denouement. While the State of Israel was born less than three years after John's murder, the "perfect storm" would flatten Kennebunkport only eight years after KAL 007 went down. The current chapter examines the fatal European philosophy that will lead to America's eventual demise; the remaining material will illustrate this declension by three contemporary events.

In his book *Histoire des Jacobins,* Lombard de Langres describes the sinister methods employed by various leaders of the French Revolution.

> Mirabeau [a Freemason and Illuminatus], in the exuberance of an orgy, cried one day: "That *canaille* [Fr. for pack of dogs, rabble, common people] well deserves to have us for legislators!" These professions of faith, as we see, are not at all democratic; the sect uses the populace as revolution fodder . . . as prime material for brigandage, after which it seizes the gold and abandons generations to torture. **It is veritably the code of Hell.**[1]

This depiction of conspiracy activity as "the code of Hell" was far more accurate than Langres could have ever imagined. For one thing, it gives Satan the credit he deserves. The devil's minions rarely understand how they are manipulated. (II Timothy 3:13) The Bible clearly teaches that

Satan is able to inspire the evil deeds of deluded men. (John 13:2, Acts 5:3) Jesus prophesied, *"the time cometh, that whosoever killeth you will think that he doeth God service"* (John 16:2b). Consequently, many will go into shock at the Great White Throne Judgment. (Matthew 7:21-23)

A balanced Scriptural approach to conspiracy history precludes the preferred scenario that a hidden nucleus of international powerbrokers fulfill the *recognized* agenda of Satan through an *equally* enlightened coalition of bankers, politicians, educators, clerics, entertainers and media personnel. Such sensational conjecture offends thinking people as it allows a simplistic thesis to negate complex realities. The devil has a much better plan.

One aspect of the "code of Hell" is to allow unregenerate man to "follow his heart" (i.e., *"we have turned every one to his own way"* (Isaiah 53:6b); *"every man did that which was right in his own eyes"* (Judges 21:25b); *"There is a way that seemeth right unto a man, but the end thereof are the ways of death"* (Proverbs 16:25). As *"the love of money is the root of all evil"* (I Timothy 6:10a), we would expect Satan to offer the appropriate incentives. The worldly-wise Benjamin Franklin observed,

> There are two passions which have a powerful influence on the affairs of men. These are . . . love of power and love of money. . . . When united . . . they have the most violent effects.[2]

The German author, Heinrich Heine (1797-1856), once remarked in Paris, "Money is the God of our times, and Rothschild is his prophet."[3] Along this line, it doesn't take a rocket scientist to recognize that war is big business. For centuries, bankers and arms dealers have been padding their pockets by following a simple three-point outline: 1) Arm the potential belligerents; 2) Supply both sides throughout the war; 3) Loan the necessary funds for clean up (e.g., $50,000,000,000 Marshall Plan). Major General Smedly Butler of the United States Marine Corps said, "War was largely a matter of money. Bankers lend money to foreign countries and when they cannot repay, the President sends Marines to get it."[4]

In addition to the love of money and power, other carnal attributes which coalesce in the man Satan uses include *pride, egoism, vanity, elitism, naiveté, optimism* and *Darwinism*. For instance, in the early years of WWII, American ambassador William Standley actually attempted to befriend the Russians by distributing Walt Disney Films.[5]

With regard to the disastrous concessions made at Yalta, one could justifiably suspect the "coincidence" that Roosevelt and Churchill were 33rd degree Masons. However, other factors should be penciled in as well. In his book, *I Was There,* Eliott Roosevelt reported that 1,800 quarts of liquor were consumed at the conference.[6] On numerous occasions, FDR boasted that he had the personality to charm "Uncle Joe" into doing things his way. Even Isaacson and Thomas acknowledged that Roosevelt "harbored the conceit that he could conduct foreign policy out of his hip pocket."[7] William Still relates that Martin Dies, chairman of a special House committee on un-American activities, testified before Congress that Roosevelt told him, "I do not believe in communism any more than you do, but there is nothing wrong with the communists in this country. Several of the best friends I have are communists."[8] And then we have that other 33rd degree Masonic president, Harry S. Truman, who wrote in his diary: "I'm not afraid of Russia. They've always been our friends and I can't see any reason why they shouldn't always be."[9]

In more recent times, President George W. Bush assured the American people in November 2001 that he and Russian President Putin had worked out a two-thirds nuclear reduction by way of a "gentlemen's agreement" (i.e., without a formal treaty).

While the devil has often used those who were bent on destroying our nation (Adam Weishaupt, Alger Hiss, Giuseppe Mazzini, Dexter Elliot White, etc.), he has also utilized men who were their own worst enemies. (II Timothy 2:25) Most of America's twentieth-century leaders were far too "evolved" to embrace the "primitive" Biblical views of the Founding Fathers concerning man's sinfulness. (Psalm 39:5) James Madison wrote, "The truth was that all men having power ought to be distrusted to a certain degree."[10] In answer to his own question, "Why has government been instituted at all?" Alexander Hamilton stated, "Because the passions of men will not conform to the dictates of reason and justice without constraint."[11] Although Thomas Jefferson was not a Christian, he was certainly in agreement with the Scriptural position on human depravity, writing, "In questions of power, then, let no more be heard of confidence in man, but bind him down from mischief with the chains of the Constitution."[12] Thomas Hooker put it simply, "The law is not subject to passion."[13]

Conversely, on the eve of his appointment as ambassador to Russia in August 1943, Bonesman A. L. Harriman wrote President Roosevelt, "As you know, I am a confirmed optimist in our relations with Russia because of my conviction that Stalin wants, if obtainable, a firm understanding with you and America."[14] With only days to live, however, a dejected Roosevelt banged his fists on his wheelchair and conceded, "We can't do business with the Soviets."[15] Harriman later recalled: "I think he was thoroughly alive to the fact they hadn't kept their agreements and he was quite bitter about it. I felt his Dutch jaw was out and he wasn't going to be pushed around by Stalin anymore."[16]

This is what the Bible means by end-day power mongers *"deceiving, and being deceived"* (II Timothy 3:13). Unfortunately, FDR "saw the light" *after* he consigned Eastern Europe to an Iron Curtain existence. Upon learning of a proposal to fund a State Department code-breaking agency in 1929, Secretary of War Henry Stimson replied, "Gentlemen do not read other people's mail."[17] Twenty years later, when Stimson was attempting to persuade President Truman to embrace the Soviet Union in an atomic arms "covenant," he employed his favorite Bonesman maxim, "The chief lesson I have learned in a long life is that the only way you can make a man trustworthy is to trust him."[18] Whereupon, "Give 'em Hades Harry" replied, "We must take Russia into our confidence."[19] (By this time, roughly *fifty million* human beings had died at the hands of "Uncle Joe.")

Thus, we conclude that in addition to utilizing a bona fide cabal of international bankers, the devil has achieved a significant portion of his end-day agenda by manipulating an array of *self-deluded, money hungry, Bible-rejecting, globalistic, Darwinian narcissists* who care more about their "place in history" than they do about matters of national security. As King Hezekiah selfishly reasoned, *"Is it not good, if peace and truth be in my days?"* (II Kings 20:19b). Believe it or not, CFR-controlled *Time* magazine actually voted Adolph Hitler "Man of the Year" for 1938! Incidentally, Henry Robinson Luce, founder and editor-in-chief of *Time* (as well as *Life, Fortune* and *Sports Illustrated*), climbed out of *his* coffin at Yale in 1919.

Again, as *"the love of money is the root of all evil,"* a love of *power* would have to enter the picture eventually, as the two are interrelated. Money buys power and power has the potential to produce more money, etc. Samuel Adams wrote, ". . . ambition and lust for power . . . are predominant passions in the breasts of most men."[20] Pearl Buck, a longtime admirer of the Kennedy family, wrote in her book, *The Kennedy Women,* "Rose Kennedy (the wife of Joseph Kennedy) knew that the man she loved loved a power beyond the power of money. He wanted the power of government, and he would have it."[21] Throughout the centuries, Satan has pursued his never-ending quest to subvert planet earth by enabling his ubiquitous moneychangers to underwrite the treachery of one aspiring dictator after another. An old Prussian proverb says, **"In case of rain, the war will be held in the auditorium."** Remember that not even the devil knows when the trumpet will blow. Consequently, he could never be sure who the Antichrist would be. This would have necessitated that he always have a qualified tyrant waiting in the wings of every generation.

Concerning methodology, Satan is a stickler for detail. While he may be the "author of confusion" when it comes to destroying the lives of others (I Corinthians 14:33), he is wise enough to follow God's principle of orderliness (I Corinthians 14:40) when pursuing his own program (Ephesians 6:12). Sadly, his offspring are generally more devoted than the Christians, prompting Jesus to declare in Luke 16:8, *". . . the children of this world are in their generation wiser than the children of light."* (This is why perverts like Michael Jackson and Marilyn Manson will practice for hours, while the typical unprepared singing group in a Baptist church will try to hide their laziness behind such platitudes as, "Y'all pray for us; we haven't practiced since Shep was a pup," etc.) Make no mistake about it—Satan goes by the book! Western civilization is currently winding down via the *"code of Hell"*!

G. W. F. HEGEL

When the sad demise of Christian America is considered, a noteworthy method of Satan's "code" comes into view. The Apostle Paul warned God's people to avoid philosophy. (Colossians 2:8) Whereas Greek philosophers assailed the infant church (Acts 17:18), the German school would administer the *coup de grâce* in the last days. As mentioned in chapter eleven, the teachings of G. W. F. Hegel constituted the philosophical foundation for The Order of Skull and Bones. Hegel had a profound influence on the tumultuous twentieth century, especially with respect to America's two-fold disastrous involvement with ancient European and Asiatic rivalries.

Although the Bible scorns philosophy as a never-ending "babble-thon" about nothing (John 18:38; Acts 17:21; II Timothy 3:7), the heathen are nonetheless captivated by such deception. Of particular note is Hegel's personal theory of history known as the *dialectic*. The German argued that each significant historical development was the natural result of a clash between two opposing forces. In philosophical jargon, the *thesis* is confronted by the *antithesis,* which in turn produces the *synthesis,* a supposed resolution of the two antagonists. Hegel viewed the debilitating aftermath of any war as "progress," as the individual would be weaker while the state would be stronger. John Dewey, the Hegelian pioneer of the modern education system, wrote in *German Philosophy and Politics,* "War is the most effective preacher of the vanity of all merely finite interests, it puts an end to that selfish egoism of the individual by which he would claim his life and his property as his own or as his family's."[22]

The *Gentile* "House of Rockefeller" built its financial empire on Hegel's dialectic. David Rockefeller stated in *The New York Times,* August 10, 1973:

> **Whatever the price** of the Chinese Revolution, it has obviously succeeded not only in producing more efficient and dedicated administration, but also in fostering high morale and community of purpose. The **social experiment** in China under Chairman Mao's leadership is one of the most important and successful in human history.[23]

The price of Chairman Mao's "social experiment" was about *sixty million human lives* (and it didn't have a thing to do with "leadership.")

Applying Hegel's *dialectic* to World War II casts the Allies as the *thesis,* the Axis powers as the *antithesis* and the United Nations as the *synthesis.* The identical match-up occurred in the First World War between the Central and Entente powers to produce the infamous League of Nations. Thus conflict between opposing factions brings about a synthesis or a "new and better historical situation." It also spells profit for bankers and arms dealers as "clash equals cash."

Of course, Christians know that Hegel's dialectic is a false hypothesis. A positive charge added to a negative charge will *always* equal a negative charge. One does not "catch" *good* health. Such is the basis for the Scriptural doctrine of separation. (II Corinthians 6:14-17: Ephesians 5:11)

This is precisely why George Washington warned his countrymen about making foreign alliances. It was also the reason Thomas Jefferson opposed European immigration. An understanding of the Hegelian dialectic process will dispel much of the confusion concerning American politics.

NOT A DIME'S WORTH OF DIFFERENCE

That the Council on Foreign Relations is philosophically committed to a globalistic society can be easily confirmed by reviewing various articles in that organization's monthly publication, *Foreign Affairs*. Through 1988, 14 secretaries of state, 14 treasury secretaries, 11 defense secretaries and scores of congressmen and other federal department heads have been members of the CFR. It was Alabama governor George Wallace who put Hegel's dialectic "waist high over the plate" by remarking, **"When you get to the top of the political pyramid, there isn't a dime's worth of difference between the Democratic and Republican parties."** On one occasion, when "Wise Man" John McCloy (assistant to Henry Stimson) was visiting the White House, Roosevelt took a phone call and began talking unguardedly about campaign strategies. "Mr. President, remember I'm a Republican," McCloy interjected with feigned embarrassment, whereupon FDR replied, "[expletive] it, I always forget."[24] The elephants just act more righteous than the donkeys do. A Democratic administration will dismember you with a chain saw while the Republicans will send you to the same morgue via a gas leak in your sleep.

Every four years Americans "get to choose" between one-world *Democrats* and one-world *Republicans*. In 1952 and 1956, CFR Adlai Stevenson opposed CFR Dwight Eisenhower. As late as the fall of 1951, President Harry Truman unquestionably viewed Dwight Eisenhower as a loyal member of the Democratic party.[25] However, in 1952, Ike abruptly professed his loyalty to the GOP. Henry Cabot Lodge rounded out the charade by announcing that Dwight had been a lifelong Republican.[26] (Rhodes Scholar General Wesley Clarke, a lifetime Republican, suddenly became a Democrat in his failed 2004 bid for the White House.) In 1960, it was CFR Kennedy versus CFR Nixon. When the conservative wing of the GOP nominated Barry Goldwater in 1964 over the ultimate Council member, Nelson Rockefeller, the CFR press took care of Barry in no time. In 1968, CFR Nixon was pitted against CFR Humphrey. The

1972 "contest" featured CFR Nixon against CFR McGovern. CFR Ford opposed TC (Trilateral Commission) Jimmy Carter in 1976. (Carter would eventually join the CFR.) Four years later, "smiling" Jimmy was unseated by Ronald Reagan. Although not a member of the CFR, Reagan more than compensated for his "conspiratorial shortcomings" by choosing for his running mate, Bonesman George H. W. Bush, a former director for *both* the Council *and* the Trilateral Commission. The president's transition team included 18 CFR "agents." By mid-1988, *313* CFR members were officiating within the Reagan-Bush administration.[27] In 1988, George "New World Order" Bush defeated CFR Dukakis only to be ousted by CFR Bill Clinton in 1992. America's professional politicians are about as genuine as professional wrestlers!

And don't forget that the *secretive* Order of Skull and Bones is more dangerous than the *high profile* CFR. Consequently, I was utterly amazed to read the following admission by Rhodes Scholar Walter Isaacson (as cited in the chapter eleven) concerning The Order's disproportionate influence throughout the Cold War years in foreign affairs: **"Not everyone was Ivy League, by any means, but Yale's secret societies were better represented in the inner councils than any state university."**[28]

Antony Sutton explains how Skull and Bones has applied the Hegelian dialectic to our "former" two-party system:

> The Order is neither "left" nor "right." "Left" and "right" are artificial devices to bring about change, and the extremes of political left and political right are vital elements in a process of controlled change.[29]

As the American people have continued to reject God, their leaders have been more than happy to follow suit. Our nation's moral stench has reached its apex at the top of the political pyramid. The will of the individual citizen no longer counts. As William Penn warned, "If we will not be governed by God, then we will be ruled by tyrants." Sutton continues with his sober analysis:

> What then is the function of a Parliament or a Congress for Hegelians? These institutions are merely to allow individuals to feel that their opinions have some value and to allow a government to take advantage of whatever wisdom the "peasant" may accidentally demonstrate. As Hegel puts it: "By virtue of this participation, subjective liberty and conceit, with their general opinion, (individuals) can show themselves palpably efficacious and enjoy the satisfaction of feeling themselves to count for something."[30]

Do you see how it works? Rush Limbaugh and the FOX *News* team are there to make you "feel" that your opinions have some value. Yet even Rush knows that the two-party system is a myth, acknowledging in *The Way Things Ought To Be:*

> For most American voters, politics has become a four-letter word . . . That's not surprising. The current political system has erected a curtain around the Washington Beltway that insulates everyone inside from the views of the average person. Our institutions are failing. **Both major parties are failing.** There is no one, neither Democrat or Republican, who is providing real leadership.[31]

In his chapter entitled "The Imperial Congress," Limbaugh cites the banking scandal in the House of Representatives (early '90s) when 355 members of Congress wrote 20,000 hot checks over a three-year period. According to the General Accounting Office (GAO), ninety-nine Representatives bounced checks in excess of $11 million! Professor Quigley writes:

> [T]he chief problem of American political life for a long time has been how to make the two Congressional parties more national and international. The argument that the two parties should represent opposed ideals and policies, one, perhaps, of the Right and the other of the Left, is a foolish idea. . . . Instead, the two parties should be almost identical, so that the American people can "throw the rascal out" at any election without leading to any profound or extensive shifts in policy.[32]

Despite the fact that the majority of Americans opposed NAFTA and GATT, the bills received enthusiastic support from both President Bush (Republican) *and* President Clinton (Democrat) and were eventually passed by Congress. With regard to the role of transnational corporations in the passage of NAFTA and GATT, Quigley notes how the ability of vested interests to nullify our two-party system substantially predates the Reagan/Limbaugh era. The tycoons who dominated market conditions in the nineteenth century were guided by the Hegelian maxim—"clash equals cash."

> [T]hey expected that they would be able to control both political parties equally. Indeed, some of them intended to contribute to both and to allow an alternation of the two parties in public office in order to conceal their own

influence, inhibit any exhibition of independence by politicians, and allow the electorate to believe that they were exercising their own free choice.[33]

Lewis Carroll's characters, "Tweedledee" and "Tweedledum," illustrate the corruption that has permeated our government. Quigley gives a specific illustration from the career of J. P. Morgan:

> The associations between Wall Street and the Left, of which Mike Straight is a fair example, are really survivals of the associations between the Morgan Bank and the Left. To Morgan all political parties were simply organizations to be used, and the firm always was careful to keep a foot in all camps. Morgan himself, Dwight Morrow, and other partners were allied with the Republicans; Russell C. Leffingwell was allied with the Democrats; Grayson Murphy was allied with the extreme Right; and Thomas W. Lamont was allied with the Left. Like the Morgan interest in libraries, museums, and art, its inability to distinguish between loyalty to the United States and loyalty to England, its recognition of the need for social work among the poor, the multipartisan political views of the Morgan firm in domestic politics went back to the original founder of the firm, George Peabody (1795-1869). To this same seminal figure may be attributed the use of tax-exempt foundations for controlling these activities, as may be observed in many parts of America to this day, in the use of Peabody foundations to support Peabody libraries and museums. **Unfortunately, we do not have space here for this great and untold story, but it must be remembered that what we do say is part of a much larger picture.**[34]

Although Morgan was not a member of The Order, a number of his partners were (i.e., Henry P. Davidson, Thomas Cochran, etc.). In fact, after Morgan's death the firm became Morgan, Stanley and Co. The "Stanley" was Harold Stanley (Skull and Bones, 1908).

By now the reader will have recognized the similarity between Hegel's dialectic of *managed conflict* and the *engineered agitation* espoused by that other German, Adam Weishaupt. These pagan philosophies have been at the core of America's demise for over a century. The first executive order issued by President Bill Clinton was "Don't ask— Don't tell." The *thesis* here was the heterosexual soldier, the *antithesis* was the sodomite, and the resulting *synthesis* was a serious decline in morale. Responsible gun owners represent another *thesis* while gun-control advocates constitute the *antithesis*. A loss of Second Amendment rights with a corresponding increase in crime becomes the "positive" *synthesis.* The predominantly white student body in the nation's suburban public schools in the early 1960s was the *thesis.* Busloads of blacks from the ghetto became the *antithesis.* The *synthesis* was the noticeable "improvement" in student life when the caliber of everyday classroom infractions "evolved" from talking, chewing gum, making noise, running in the halls, getting out of turn in line and not putting paper in the waste baskets to *rape, robbery, assault, burglary, arson, bombings, murder, suicide, absenteeism, vandalism, extortion, drug abuse, alcohol abuse, gang warfare, teen pregnancies, abortions* and *venereal diseases!*

If conflict creates change, Professor Sutton postulates that one's ability to control conflict would result in a commensurate power to direct the very flow of history!

The operational history of The Order can only be understood within a framework of the *Hegelian dialectic* process. **Quite simply this is the notion that *conflict creates history.***

From this axiom it follows that *controlled* conflict can *create* a predetermined history. For example: When the Trilateral Commission discusses "managed conflict," as it does extensively in its literature, the Commission implies the managed use of conflict for long run predetermined ends—not for the mere random exercise of manipulative control to solve a problem.

The dialectic takes this Trilateral "managed conflict" process one step further. In Hegelian terms, an existing force (the thesis) generates a counterforce (the antithesis). Conflict between the two forces results in the forming of a synthesis. Then the process starts all over again: Thesis vs. antithesis results in synthesis.

The synthesis sought by the Establishment is called the New World Order. Without controlled conflict this New World Order will not come about. Random individual actions of persons in society would not lead to this synthesis, it's artificial, therefore it has to be created. And this is being done with the calculated, managed, use of conflict. And all the while this synthesis is being sought, there is no profit in playing the involved parties against one another. This explains why the International bankers backed the Nazis, the Soviet Union, North Korea, North Vietnam, ad nauseum, against the United States. The "conflict" builds profits while pushing the world ever closer to One World Government. The process continues today.[35]

Appearing on the *Charlie Rose Show,* October 23, 1996, Mikhail Gorbachev stated, "We are part of the Cosmos. Cosmos is my God.

Nature is my God. . . . The future society will be a totally new civilization which will **synthesize** the experience of Socialism and Capitalism."[36] In retrospect, is Tweedledee Gorby's "New Civilization" that much different from Tweedledum Bush's "New World Order"?

TREATY OF VERSAILLES

World Wars I and II generated the greatest "cash flow" of the twentieth century with the infamous Treaty of Versailles constituting the historical linkage between the two. Many historians have concluded that the Treaty, officially ending World War I, was one of the most iniquitous documents ever signed by the representatives of so-called civilized nations. To attain this perspective, one must first understand the circumstances that surrounded the signing of the initial armistice on November 11, 1918. The German High Command did not request the cease-fire because they feared imminent disaster; contrary to the views of some, the German armies had never suffered a *decisive* military defeat on the field of battle. The First World War can be described by a single word—*stalemate.*

The real motivation for the armistice was a growing fear within the German High Command of Communist gains in the Fatherland. According to a French government document, Raymond Robins (a Wall Street agent for New York Federal Reserve president William Thompson) was involved in this affair. The paper reads, "It appeared that Colonel Robins . . . was able to send a subversive mission of Russian bolsheviks to Germany to start a revolution there."[37] This mission resulted in the abortive German Spartacist revolt of 1918. Rosa Luxemberg and her *Spartacus Bund* were attempting to duplicate Lenin's revolution in Germany. By early 1918, many of her agents had infiltrated the German High Seas fleet and were spreading rumors of a planned suicide invasion of Great Britain. German sailors were unnerved by "reports" that a secret chemical weapon developed by British scientists could envelope their landing craft in a sea of flames and noxious gases. The petrified lads mutinied on November 3, 1918. Four days later a large body of marines also deserted while on their way to the Western front. Communist cells had informed them that they would be the cannon fodder to spearhead the invasion.[38]

In the meantime, strikes and riots nearly shut down German industry. Rosa's rumormongers held the nation by the throat. Finally, on November 9, the Kaiser abdicated. Two days later, the Armistice was signed, primarily to enable the German High Command to devote their effort to preventing a full-scale Communist revolution.

Therefore, it is of the utmost importance to understand that the Armistice was agreed upon only as a prelude to a *negotiated* peace. It was anything but an unconditional surrender. However, as another world war, to be followed by another revolution was already on the schedule, Germany would be double-crossed by the diabolical descendents of Adam Weishaupt's Illuminati. As British Foreign Secretary Lord Curzon would later declare after reviewing the incendiary treaty: "This is no peace; this is only a truce for twenty years."[39] Curzon, who felt that the terms would set the stage for a second world war, correctly predicted the year it would begin—1939!

The celebrated Paris Peace Conference was literally overrun with international bankers. Mr. Paul Warburg, who drafted the Federal Reserve System in the United States, arrived in January 1919 to lead the American delegation. His banker-brother Max (you know—*Tweedledum*) arrived to "represent" the German delegation. Quigley confirms that the financiers "dominated the British delegation to the Peace Conference of 1919; [and] it had a great deal to do with the formation and management of the League of Nations and of the system of mandates."[40] Alfred Milner was one of the signers of the League of Nations.

While a smoke screen "Inter-Allied Conference" was supposed to be drawing up preliminary terms for Germany's consideration, the moneychangers were in the back room hammering out a surprise ultimatum. Quigley confirms,

> On one level, in the full glare of publicity, the Inter-Allied Conference became the Plenary Peace Conference, and, with considerable fanfare, did nothing. On the other level, the Great Powers worked out their peace terms in secret and, when they were ready, imposed them simultaneously on the conference and on the Germans.[41]

For the most part, the "Great Powers" consisted of President Wilson of the U.S.A., British Prime Minister David Lloyd George, French Premier Georges Clemenceau and Vittorio Emmanuele Orlando, prime minister of Italy. These men (with Orlando frequently absent) conducted over two hundred sessions in a period of thirteen weeks (March 27 to June 28). However, Quigley notes how the bankers called the shots:

> At all of these meetings, as at the Peace Conference itself, the political leaders were assisted by groups of experts and interested persons, sometimes self-appointed. Many of these "experts" were members or associates of the international-banking fraternity. At the Paris Peace Conference the experts numbered thousands and were organized into official staffs by most countries, even before the war ended. These experts were of the greatest importance. They were formed into committees at Paris and given problem after problem, especially boundary problems, usually without any indication as to what principles should guide their decisions. The importance of these committees of experts can be seen in the fact that in every case but one where a committee of experts submitted a unanimous report, the Supreme Council accepted its recommendation and incorporated it in the treaty.[42]

Although Wilson may have appeared to be the predominant personality, the American president knew where his bread was buttered. Comte de St. Aulaire wrote, "Those who look for the truth elsewhere than in the official documents know that President Wilson, whose election had been financed by the Great Bank of New York (Kuhn-Loeb & Co.), rendered almost complete obedience to its beck and call."[43] William Carr notes one of the more outrageous examples of this traitorous relationship:

> The power of the international bankers is well illustrated by an incident that happened during the preliminary conferences held in Paris in 1919. The negotiations tended to stray away from the policy set by the international bankers. Thereupon, Jacob Schiff, of New York, sent President Wilson, who was attending the Paris conferences, a two thousand word cable. He "instructed" the president of the United States what to do in regard to the Palestine Mandate, German Reparations, Upper Silesia, The Sarre, The Danzing Corridor, and Fiume. The cablegram was dated May 28th, 1919. Schiff sent it in the name of the Association of the League of Free Nations. Upon receipt of the cablegram President Wilson immediately changed the direction of the negotiations.[44]

As soon as the Great Powers had been "persuaded" to make Palestine a British Protectorate (as dictated in Schiff's cable), the various "experts" were instructed to make the reparations in the Treaty so severe that the German people would never be able to tolerate them.

Whereas Lloyd George was in tune with the British electorate who were hysterical with hatred of Germany, Quigley informs us that the Milner Group was now beginning "to think in terms of balance of power and of the need to reconstruct Germany against the dangers of 'bolshevism' on one hand and of 'French militarism' on the other, and they felt that if Germany were made democratic and treated in a friendly fashion she could be incorporated into the British world system as well as the Cape Boers had been."[45] This was in keeping with the policy Britain had followed since 1500 of supporting the second-strongest power on the Continent against the strongest power to prevent the latter from attaining Continental supremacy.

The completed Treaty of Versailles was formally presented to a shocked German delegation on May 7, 1919, with the further insulting news that they would have only five days to sign. After reviewing the document, Foreign Minister Count Ulrich von Brockdorff-Rantzau made a long speech bitterly protesting the lack of negotiation and the violation of prearmistice commitments. As an intentional insult to his listeners, the foreign minister spoke from a seated position.[46]

The terms were outrageous! Germany was "billed" *269 billion* gold marks to be paid in forty-two annual installments.[47] Perloff states that the vanquished nation was even being required to pay the pensions of allied soldiers.[48] In fact, Quigley notes that "Article 322 was concerned with the reparations obligation, listing ten categories of damages of which the tenth, concerned with pensions and inserted by General Smuts, represented a liability larger than the aggregate of the preceding nine categories together."[49] This was far too much for even John Maynard Keynes, the liberal economist, who prophesied, "The peace is outrageous and impossible and can bring nothing but misfortune behind it."[50]

The German delegation returned home immediately and recommended that their government refuse to sign. The Cabinet resigned rather than agree to the travesty. A new Cabinet consisting of Catholics and Socialists was hastily convened. There was no alternative as Rosa Luxemberg had already forced the new Socialist government to demobilize the armed forces.

On June 28, 1919, exactly five years after the assassination of Archduke Ferdinand at Sarajevo, the Treaty of Versailles was formally signed in the Hall of Mirrors by all the delegations except the Chinese. Within four short years, the Reichsbank was issuing millions of German marks per day into the inflation-ravaged economy. The heavy gold reparations were taking their devastating toll. By November 15, 1923, the Reichsbank had already issued the incredible sum of *92,800,000,000,000,000,000* (quintillion) paper marks.[51] The German mark fell from a value of twenty to one English pound to an unbelievable *20,000,000,000* to the pound by December 1923, practically destroying trade relations between the two countries. The German people suffered accordingly. The price of a single pound of butter soared from 3.00 marks in 1918 to *6,000,000,000,000* marks in 1923. Even 100 million marks was not enough to buy a box of matches. Conditions such as these paved the way for Adolf Hitler to appear with his promises of relief and revenge.

LEAGUE OF NATIONS

There was, believe it or not, one "positive" development from the otherwise negative Paris Peace Conference. President Wilson had also been instructed to create a "League of Nations" to afford "mutual guarantees of political independence and territorial integrity to great and small states alike." Assuming that he would get to be the first "president of the world," Wilson eagerly signed the new League's charter on behalf of the United States on January 10, 1920. However, recalling the warning of George Washington, the Senate promptly rejected the treaty.

With America's refusal to sign, the Milner Group grew increasingly hostile toward the League. Theoretically, Wilson's brainchild was supposed to limit military aggression among cooperating members by requiring a three-month moratorium for discussing and resolving any crisis. There was no provision for collective power to enforce any potential injunctions. Quigley writes, "The Milner Group never intended that the League should be used as an instrument of collective security or that sanctions should be used as an instrument by the League."[52] Britain sought only two things from the League; that it might be used as a center for international administration in nonpolitical matters, and that it become a hub for dialogue in political areas. As we shall see momentarily, this was intended to advance the Group's long-range agenda.

The problem came when the French, paranoid over the prospect of a revived Germany, insisted on putting teeth in the League's covenant. The British were "horrified" when the French delegation at the Paris

Peace Conference demanded that the new organization be a "Super-State" with its own army and power. Milner's people insisted on nonmilitary cooperation only. Robert Cecil gave a speech at Birmingham on November 12, 1918, stating,

> The most important step we can now take is to devise machinery which, in case of international dispute, will, at the least, delay the outbreak of war, and secure full and open discussion of the causes of the quarrel. For that purpose . . . all that would be necessary would be a treaty binding the signatories never to wage war themselves or permit others to wage war till a formal conference of nations had been held to enquire into, and, if possible, decide the dispute. It is probably true, at least in theory, that decisions would be difficult to obtain, for the decisions of such a conference, like all other international proceedings, would have to be unanimous to be binding. But since the important thing is to secure delay and open discussion, that is to say, time to enable public opinion to act and information to instruct it, this is not a serious objection to the proposal. Indeed, from one point of view, it is an advantage, since it avoids any interference with national sovereignty except the interposition of a delay in seeking redress by force of arms. This is the essential thing. . . . To that extent, and to that extent only, international coercion would be necessary.[53]

In light of such remarks, one might conclude that the Group was not so "globalistic" after all. However, this would be a faulty deduction. Milner's real problem with the League was that someone *else* would get to be "top banana." It was perfectly all right for the League to come under the Group, but he wasn't about to surrender *his* sovereignty to *them*. (When two boys were on the playground and one suggested, "Let's play Zorro," the other replied, "Great idea, *I'll* be Zorro!" Milner is the second lad.) Quigley explains:

> The Group's own statement on this subject appeared in the December 1918 issue of *The Round Table* in an article called "Windows of Freedom," written by Curtis. He pointed out that British seapower had twice saved civilization and any proposal that it should be used in the future only at the request of the League of Nations must be emphatically rejected. The League would consist of fallible human beings, and England could never yield her decision to them. He continued: "Her own existence and that of the world's freedom are inseparably connected. . . . To yield it without a blow is to yield the whole citadel in which the forces that make for human freedom are entrenched; to covenant to yield it is to bargain a betrayal

of the world in advance. . . . (The League must not be a world government.) If the burden of a world government is placed on it it will fall with a crash." He pointed out it could be a world government only if it represented peoples and not states, and if it had the power to tax those peoples. It should simply be an interstate conference of the world.

[He concludes,] "Such a conference [the Paris Peace Conference] cannot itself govern the world, still less those portions of mankind who cannot yet govern themselves. But it can act as a symbol and organ of the human conscience, however imperfect, to which real governments of existing states can be made answerable for facts which concern the world at large." [54]

Milner was also frustrated by the fact that the Dominions were now more committed to the League than they were to Great Britain. The March 1920 issue of *The Round Table* protested that the Covenant

gave the Dominions the grounds, or rather the excuse, to avoid closer union with the United Kingdom. . . . In other words, they mortgaged their freedom of action to a league of foreign States in order to avoid the possibility of mortgaging it to the British Government. . . . Canada, Australia, South Africa, and New Zealand are, in fact, bound by stronger written obligations to Poland and Czechoslovakia, then to the British Isles.[55]

Yet, in reality, Milner had ensured that England's legal commitment was mitigated by certain defeasible clauses throughout the document. Quigley confirms that the only objection Milner had to world government was in *timing.*

The ability of the Milner Group to mobilize public opinion in regard to the League of Nations is almost beyond belief. It was not a simple task, since they were simultaneously trying to do two things: on the one hand, seeking to build up popular opinion in favor of the League so that its work could be done more effectively; and, at the same time, seeking to prevent influential people from using the League as an instrument of world government before popular opinion was ready for a world government.[56]

In the interim, Milner was *more* than willing to manipulate the League to further the Group's objectives. With reference to America's unwillingness to join, the March issue of *The Round Table* "let the cat out of the bag" (Quigley's expression).

The League has failed to secure the adhesion of one of its most important members, The United States, and is very unlikely to secure it. . . . This situation presents a very serious problem for the British Empire. We have not only undertaken great obligations under the League which we must now both in honesty and in self-regard revise, but we have looked to the League to provide us with the machinery for United British action in foreign affairs.[57]

1917 MASONIC CONFERENCE

While the Group grew increasingly opposed to the League, the Masons were there to pick up the slack! (Remember, according to II Timothy 3:13, the dual experience of evil men in the last days is *"deceiving, and being deceived."*) The treachery employed throughout the Paris Peace Conference was acutely outlined at an earlier gathering in the "City of Light." According to the French historian Vicomte Léon de Poncins, a special Masonic Congress had convened at the Grand Orient Lodge in the Rue Cadet, Paris, from June 28 to 30, 1917. The minutes (from their previous meeting, January 14 and 15) announced: "The object of this Congress will be to investigate the means of elaborating the Constitution of the League of Nations, so as to prevent the recurrence of a catastrophe similar to the one at present raging which has plunged the civilised world into mourning."[58]

This wartime conference was attended by representatives of the leading lodges of allied and neutral countries such as Italy, Switzerland, Belgium, Serbia, Spain, Portugal, Argentina, Brazil and the United States.[59] The official minutes of the meeting (which came to light in 1936) continue:

> It is the duty of Freemasonry at the close of the cruel drama now being played out, to make its great and humanitarian voice heard, and to guide the nations towards a general organisation which will become their safeguard. It would be wanting in its duty, and false to its great principles, were it to remain silent.[60]

In his opening speech "Brother" Corneau (president of the Grand Orient of France) proclaimed,

> This Masonic Congress of the Allied and neutral Nations has come at the right time. We all know the disasters of the past; now we must build the happy city of the future. It is to undertake this truly Masonic work that

we have invited you here. . . . What are we faced with? This war, which was unleashed by the military autocracies, has become a formidable quarrel in which the democracies have organised themselves against the despotic military powers. . . . **Thus it is absolutely indispensable to create a supranational authority, whose aim will be not to suppress the causes of conflicts, but peacefully to resolve the differences between nations.**

Freemasonry, which labours for peace, intends to study this new organism, the League of Nations. **Freemasonry will be the propaganda agent for this conception of universal peace and happiness.** That, my Most Illustrious Brethren, is our work. Let us set to it.[61]

After two days of deliberations, the following motion was adopted:

This Congress sends to Mr. Wilson, President of the United States, the homage of its admiration and the tribute of its recognition of the great services he has rendered Humanity.

Declares that it is happy to collaborate with President Wilson in this work of international justice and democratic fraternity, which is Freemasonry's own ideal,

And affirms that the eternal principles of Freemasonry are completely in harmony with those proclaimed by President Wilson for the defence of civilisation and the liberty of peoples.[62]

And finally, in their third motion, the Congress

Declares that faithful to their traditions, and like their glorious ancestors, the Freemasons today are still the devoted labourers of the emancipation of the human race,

Warmly appeals to all the Brethren for their support in the task of bringing into being the League of Nations, which alone can guarantee the future and the liberty of peoples, and international justice and law.[63]

It sure does sound like this "Christian" organization has a handle on the teachings of the King James Bible!

CASUS BELLI

The saying goes, "If at first you don't succeed, try, try again." While an earlier generation of wiser Americans had rejected the League of Nations, a second world war, with a couple of atomic bombs thrown in for good measure, not only "induced" our government to embrace the League's ideological successor, the newly-formed United Nations, but to headquarter the satanic organization in her largest city as well.

Although the U.N. was ostensibly created to prevent the outbreak of war, everyone knows that "too much peace is bad for business." The "code of Hell" followed by the "merchants of death" in every age has been the Hegelian maxim—"clash equals cash." Following our gutless betrayal of Chiang Kai-Shek and the Republic of China (1945-1949), millions of dollars were made in the U.N. "police action" in Korea. The humiliating stalemate cost the lives of *55,000* Americans.

In the period between the close of the highly profitable Vietnam debacle and the first Persian Gulf War, the "cash" was able to flow from the mere *potential* for "clash" (i.e., "deterrents equal dividends"). The only thing that any good Republican administration had to do (the Reagan presidency, for instance) was to look the other way while corporate America kept our enemies propped up with enough Western technology to justify our massive defense budget allocations. (See volume two in this series.)

While the pillaging of our coffers has been bad enough, Satan's *ultimate* goal for America extends beyond mere bankruptcy. As no economy can be drained indefinitely (see Social Security fund), "the end of the cash will equal the lash"; bondage is the devil's forte. In his documented work, *9-11: Descent into Tyranny,* Alex Jones writes:

> *War*—Empires are built and maintained by it. Populations rally during times of war. Nothing on earth centralizes power like war. Throughout history, leaders have used this unifying force to control populations. Humans instinctively shift into mindless "group think" when faced by an outside threat—whether real or manufactured. Now, in the twenty-first century the system of control continues, but with more sophistication. If there isn't an enemy to fight, one has to be manufactured.[64]

If you doubt that the minds of the American people have devolved into mush since 9/11, just look at what they are watching on the "boob tube." Ozzie and Harriet have been replaced by the Osbournes while Rosie O'Donnell has become the modern equivalent of Donna Reed. "Queen for a Day" has been eclipsed by Bravo's "Queer Eye for the Straight Guy." Ellen Degeneres is the new Lucy Ricardo. "Car 54" has been traded in for "NYPD Blue," while "The Sopranos" have become more popular than "The Untouchables." Our children have gone from watching "Looneytoons" to Japanimation; from "The Flintstones" to "The Simpsons." Shows about snakes, crocs and other dangerous predators are in, while "Lassie," "Rin Tin Tin" and "Fury" are out. The nation's music has shifted from "Lawrence Welk" and "Sing Along with Mitch" to MTV, BET and gangster rap.

The American voter appears to have lost his ability to differentiate between qualified leaders and media celebrities. While former professional wrestler Jesse Ventura vacated the governor's mansion in Minnesota, former Cincinnati mayor Jerry Springer is contemplating a return to "public service." After falling behind in the initial weeks of the campaign, a desperate Senator John Kerry successfully revived his bid for the 2004 Democratic nomination for president by donning a black leather jacket and roaring down the aisle of *The Tonight Show with Jay Leno*. Fellow Democratic hopeful Howard Dean was featured on the cover of the January 16, 2004, issue of *Rolling Stone* magazine.

The "Reverend" Al Sharpton endeavored to improve his own shot at the White House by hosting an episode of *Saturday Night Live* in December 2003. His skits ranged from doing a James Brown dance number to perching on a camel as one of the Three Wise Men. (Can you imagine George Washington, Thomas Jefferson or James Madison in such an inane performance?) Within a month of the camel ride, CNN reported that Sharpton's war chest was missing a little "gold, frankincense and myrrh." When asked about the allegations, "Brother" Al replied that he was an activist, not a bookkeeper. (Of course, he would have nothing to worry about, as the media only spent about a week and-a-half reporting the details of "Reverend" Jesse Jackson's affair.)

Though not running for office (at least, not at the moment) former Secretary of State Colin Powell closed out the annual ASEAN Regional Forum (Asia's largest security meeting) held in Jakarta, July 1-2, 2004, by leading five other U.S. officials in an asinine rendition of the Village People's disco classic "YMCA." As part of the after-dinner entertainment traditionally provided by the diplomats themselves, Powell performed his "sodomite stomp" while wearing a hard hat and tool belt.

Ironically, one of the few celebrities who *should* have entered the political arena refused to be drafted by his admirers. Chicago Bears legend Mike Ditka, affectionately known as "Da Coach," cited business commitments in his decision to consign Illinois' vacant Senate seat to Democratic challenger, Barack Obama. Meanwhile, out on the West coast, "The Governor" is being heralded as America's last hope for honest government; that is, if the Constitution can be circumvented to allow a naturalized citizen to become president. *("Even so, come, Lord Jesus.")*

Now if the right prearranged "clash" can replace a nation's "cash" with a "lash," then the key would be staging the right *pretext* to precipitate the "clash." History confirms that most wars are jump-started on the basis of a *contrived pretense* (the same being true for totalitarian "reforms" within democratic societies). In diplomatic jargon, such a catalyst is known as a *casus belli* (or, "justification for war").

In 64 A.D., the Roman emperor Nero was able to launch the first government persecution of Christians after blaming them for the fire that he started. On February 15, 1898, the *Maine* was blown up by American sailors as a pretext for war with Spain. Though German officials had posted warnings in *The New York Times* that the *Lusitania* was carrying an undisclosed cargo of armaments, the ship was sunk and American doughboys eventually found themselves "over there." After Hitler solidified his dictatorship by torching the Reichstag and then blaming it on the Communists, he later invaded Poland "in retaliation" for their having attacked a German radio station in Gleiwicz (an "attack" staged by Reinhard Heyrich's stormtroopers dressed in Polish uniforms). It was Hitler who said, "What good fortune for governments that the people do not think." While President Roosevelt was able to galvanize a naive country with those dramatic words, "December 7, 1941—a date which will live in infamy," we now know that the old scoundrel had plenty of advance knowledge concerning the so-called "sneak attack." (See *Honolulu Advertiser* front-page headline for November 30, 1941: "Japanese May Strike Over Weekend!") In *Day of Deceit: The Truth About FDR and Pearl Harbor,* author Robert B. Stinett includes a memo by Lieutenant A. H. McCollum of naval intelligence recommending an eight-step plan for Roosevelt to follow that would provoke the Japanese to attack America. Letter F states: "KEEP THE MAIN STRENGTH OF THE U.S. FLEET NOW IN THE PACIFIC IN THE VICINITY OF THE HAWAIIAN ISLANDS." McCollum concludes, "If by these means Japan could be led to commit an overt act of war, so much the better."[65]

With regard to another Roosevelt scam, attorney Anthony D'Amato filed a federal lawsuit in Washington, D.C., July 29, 2002, on behalf of hundreds of former U.S. prisoners of war who claim the wartime administration deliberately used them as pawns to incite domestic support for a war against Japan. Marcia Fee Achenbach, a former prisoner, claims to have uncovered papers in the U.S. National Archives that prove the government restricted the travel of 7,000 American citizens from the Philippines. The deserted Americans were subsequently captured by the Japanese and thrown into the notorious Philippine POW camps where hundreds perished as a result of starvation and disease.[66]

British Prime Minister Margaret Thatcher was another politician acquainted with the "power of pretext." In a meeting in Colorado with President Bush on August 2, 1990 (the day the Iraqis invaded Kuwait), the "Iron Lady" had attempted to stiffen his resolve to commit U.S. forces by stating, "George, now don't be wobbly." However, former governor John Connelly alleged in his autobiography that her most persuasive advice was bluntly political: "George," he has her saying, "I was about to be defeated in England [in 1982] when the Falkland conflict happened. I stayed in office for eight years after that."[67]

OPERATION NORTHWOODS

Although most incriminating documents rarely see the light of day, occasionally a nugget is uncovered that represents but the tip of the iceberg. One such revelation appeared in James Bamford's 2001 blockbuster *Body of Secrets: Anatomy of the Ultra-Secret National Security Agency from the Cold War Through the Dawn of a New Century.* According to *The New York Times Book Review*: "There have been glimpses inside the NSA before, but until now no one has published a comprehensive and detailed report on the agency . . . Mr. Bamford has emerged with everything except the combination to the director's safe."[68] In a chapter dealing with the botched Bay of Pigs invasion, Bamford writes:

> According to secret and long-hidden documents obtained for *Body of Secrets*, the Joint Chiefs of Staff drew up and approved plans for what may be the most corrupt plan ever created by the U.S. government. In the name of anticommunism, they proposed launching a secret and bloody war of terrorism against their own country in order to trick the American public into supporting an ill-conceived war they intended to launch against Cuba.
>
> Codenamed Operation Northwoods, the plan, which had the written approval of the Chairman and every member of the Joint Chiefs of Staff, called for innocent people to be shot on American streets; for boats carrying refugees fleeing Cuba to be sunk on the high seas; for a wave of violent terrorism to be launched in Washington, D.C., Miami, and elsewhere. People

would be framed for bombings they did not commit; planes would be hijacked. Using phony evidence, all of it would be blamed on Castro, thus giving Lemnitzer [Chairman of the Joint Chiefs] and his cabal the excuse, as well as the public and international backing, they needed to launch this war.[69]

Bamford indicates that President Eisenhower may have initiated the outlandish proposal near the end of his second term in office.

The idea may actually have originated with President Eisenhower in the last days of his administration. With the Cold War hotter than ever and the recent U-2 scandal fresh in the public's memory, the old general wanted to go out with a win. He wanted desperately to invade Cuba in the weeks leading up to Kennedy's inauguration; indeed, on January 3 he told Lemnitzer and other aides in his Cabinet Room that he would move against Castro before the inauguration if only the Cubans gave him a really good excuse. Then, with time growing short, Eisenhower floated an idea. If Castro failed to provide that excuse, perhaps, he said, the United States **"could think of manufacturing something that would be generally acceptable."** What he was suggesting was a **pretext**—a bombing, an attack, and an act of sabotage—carried out secretly against the United States *by* the United States. Its purpose would be to justify the launching of a war. It was a dangerous suggestion by a desperate president.[70]

I have in my possession a copy of the twelve-page Northwoods document. The words—TOP SECRET SPECIAL HANDLING NOFORN—appear in big bold letters across the top of the Joint Chiefs of Staff stationery. The text of the cover letter is as follows:

13 March 1962

MEMORANDUM FOR THE SECRETARY OF DEFENSE
Subject: Justification for US Military Intervention
in Cuba (TS)

1. The Joint Chiefs of Staff have considered the attached Memorandum for the Chief of Operations, Cuba Project, which responds to a request of that office for brief but precise description of **pretexts which would provide justification for US military intervention in Cuba.**
2. The Joint Chiefs of Staff recommend that the proposed memorandum be forwarded as a preliminary submission suitable for planning purposes. It is assumed that there will be similar submissions from other agencies and that these inputs will be used as a basis for developing

a time-phased plan. Individual projects can then be considered on a case-by-case basis.

3. Further, it is assumed that a single agency will be given the primary responsibility for developing military and para-military aspects of the basic plan. **It is recommended that this responsibility for both overt and covert military operations be assigned [to] the Joint Chiefs of Staff.**

For the Joint Chiefs of Staff:
L. L. LEMNITZER
Chairman
Joint Chiefs of Staff[71]

In the APPENDIX TO ENCLOSURE A, on page five, we read:

3. This plan, incorporating projects selected from the attached suggestions, or from other sources, should be developed to focus all efforts on a specific ultimate objective which would provide adequate justification for US military intervention. **Such a plan would enable a logical build-up of incidents to be combined with other seemingly unrelated events to camouflage the ultimate objective and create the necessary impression of Cuban rashness and irresponsibility on a large scale, directed at other countries as well as the United States.** The plan would also properly integrate and time phase the courses of action to be pursued. **The desired resultant from the execution of this plan would be to place the United States in the apparent position of suffering defensible grievances from a rash and irresponsible government of Cuba and to develop an international image of a Cuban threat to peace in the Western Hemisphere.**[72]

On page seven, General Lemnitzer advocates a military assault on the U.S. Naval base at Guantanamo Bay, Cuba, by "friendly Cubans" dressed in Cuban military uniforms. (Is this the same way World War II was started?)

2. **A series of well coordinated incidents will be planned to take place in and around Guantanamo to give [the] genuine appearance of being done by hostile Cuban forces.**

    a. Incidents to establish a credible attack (not in chronological order):

        (1) Start rumors (many). Use clandestine radio.

        (2) Land friendly Cubans in uniform "over-the-fence" to stage attack on base.

        (3) Capture Cuban (friendly) saboteurs inside the base.

(4) Start riots near the main gate (friendly Cubans).
(5) Blow up ammunition inside the base; start fires.
(6) Burn aircraft on air base (sabotage).
(7) Lob mortar shells from outside of base into base. Some damage to installations.
(8) Capture assault teams approaching from the sea or vicinity of Guantanamo City.
(9) Capture militia group which storms the base.
(10) Sabotage ship in harbor; large fires—napthalene.
(11) Sink ships near harbor entrance. Conduct funerals for mock-victims (may be lieu of (10)).
b. United States would respond by executing offensive operations to secure water and power supplies, destroying artillery and mortar emplacements which threaten the base.
c. Commence large scale United States military operations.[73]

Do you remember "Remember the Maine"? The General's lunatic scenario continues:

3. **A "Remember the Maine" incident could be arranged in several forms:**
   a. **We could blow up a US ship in Guantanamo Bay and blame Cuba.**[74]

There were 266 U.S. sailors killed when the Maine was blown up in 1898. He then recommends a wave of terrorist attacks against U.S. cities!

4. **We could develop a Communist Cuban terror campaign in the Miami area, in other Florida cities and even Washington.** The terror campaign could be pointed at Cuban refugees seeking haven in the United States. **We could sink a boatload of Cubans enroute to Florida (real or simulated).** We could foster attempts on lives of Cuban refugees in the United States even to the extent of wounding in instances to be widely publicized. Exploding a few plastic bombs in carefully chosen spots, the arrest of Cuban agents and the release of prepared documents substantiating Cuban involvement also would be helpful in projecting the idea of irresponsible government.[75]

To his credit, President Kennedy was not amused with Operation Northwoods. Three days after Lemnitzer submitted his grand scheme to Defense Secretary Robert McNamara, Kennedy told the general that there was virtually no possibility that the U.S. would ever use overt military force in Cuba. Within months, Lemnitzer was denied a second term as JCS chairman and transferred to Europe as head of NATO. Several observations are in order at this time. First, the Northwoods document was not the product of a single deranged individual, but constituted *the collective genius of the highest ranking members of each branch of the U.S. military.* "Operation Northwoods called for a war in which many patriotic Americans and innocent Cubans would die senseless deaths," Bamford wrote, "all to satisfy the egos of twisted generals back in Washington, safe in their tax-payer-financed homes and limousines."[76] Following Lemnitzer's transfer to Europe his fellow conspirators kept up the struggle. One of their plans was to create a war between Cuba and any number of her Latin neighbors. This would provide the U.S. with an excuse to come to the aid of an ally. Bamford writes,

> Among the nations they suggested that the United States secretly attack were Jamaica and Trinidad-Tobago. Both were members of the British Commonwealth; thus, by secretly attacking them and then falsely blaming Cuba, the United States could lure England into the war against Castro.[77]

Then we are confronted with the disturbing reality that General Lemnitzer and his fellow crazies were allowed to remain in the system, often in positions of considerable influence. Lemnitzer was Supreme Allied Commander in Europe from 1963 to 1969. Who knows *what* he got away with during those years! *Do you suppose the fact that he was a loyal member of the Council on Foreign Relations had anything to do with his immunity?* (More than half of the JCS chairmen have been members of the CFR.) While Lemnitzer took his secrets to the grave in 1988, his old boss was still around after Bamford's book came out. When the *Baltimore Sun* cornered McNamara in April 2001 about the Northwoods documents, the CFR member replied with a straight face, "I never heard of it."

Perhaps Lemnitzer's plan for invading Cuba was scrapped because there were bigger moneymaking opportunities on the horizon. After Kennedy got "whacked," McNamara stayed on to "guide" Lyndon Johnson through the Vietnam imbroglio. Bamford writes:

> Lemnitzer was a dangerous—perhaps even unbalanced—right-wing extremist in an extraordinarily sensitive position during a critical period. But Operation Northwoods also had the support of every single member of the Joint Chiefs of Staff, and even senior Pentagon official Paul Nitze

argued in favor of provoking a phony war with Cuba. The fact that the most senior members of all the services and the Pentagon could be so out of touch with reality and the meaning of democracy would be hidden for four decades.

In retrospect, the documents offer new insight into the thinking of the military's star-studded leadership. Although they never succeeded in launching America into a phony war with Cuba, they may have done so with Vietnam. More than 50,000 Americans and more than 2 million Vietnamese were eventually killed in that war.

It has long been suspected that the 1964 Gulf of Tonkin incident— the spark that led to America's long war in Vietnam—was largely staged or provoked by U.S. officials in order to build up congressional and public support for American involvement. Over the years, serious questions have been raised about the alleged attack by North Vietnamese patrol boats on two American destroyers in the Gulf. But defenders of the Pentagon have always denied such charges, arguing that senior officials would never engage in such deceit.

Now, however, in light of the Operation Northwoods documents, it is clear that deceiving the public and trumping up wars for Americans to fight and die in was standard, approved policy at the highest levels of the Pentagon. In fact, the Gulf of Tonkin seems right out of the Operation Northwoods playbook: "We could blow up a U.S. ship in Guantanamo Bay and blame Cuba . . . casualty lists in U.S. newspapers would cause a helpful wave of indignation." One need only replace "Guantanamo Bay" with "Tonkin Gulf," and "Cuba" with "North Vietnam." The Gulf of Tonkin incident may or may not have been stage-managed, but the senior Pentagon leadership at the time was clearly capable of such deceit.[78]

Now although Bamford's revelation was insightful, his motives must remain suspect, given his leftist career associations. The former investigative producer for ABC's *World News Tonight with Peter Jennings* spent enough time harping on Lemnitzer's "right-wing extremism" and Robert Welch's "propaganda" to expose his own liberal ideology. He is also woefully inconsistent when he makes a tacit connection between Eisenhower and Welch by stating, "Eisenhower looked on Lemnitzer as his protégé," and "Lemnitzer's regard for Eisenhower 'bordered on reverence.' "[79] Mr. Welch single-handedly (and knowingly) splintered his own anti-communist organization by writing *The Politician*, a highly controversial, documented exposé of Ike's coadunation with Soviet Russia's anti-American agenda. Bamford's subliminal approach would indict Senator Joseph McCarthy for the fact that "Lemnitzer and the Joint Chiefs had quietly slipped over the edge."[80]

Anytime you find a book supporting conspiracy history, authored by a former associate of Peter Jennings (the guy who sneered at Ron Rosenbaum's footage of the Skull and Bones initiation), published by *Doubleday* and praised by *The New York Times Book Review*, you can be *sure* that the underlying motivation is "clash equals cash." The dust jacket tells it all:

> *Body of Secrets* is must-reading for people fascinated by the intrigues of a shadowy underworld. As one of the most important works of investigative journalism to come out of Washington in years, it should be read by everyone concerned about the inevitability of Orwell's Big Brother.[81]

If *The New York Times really* believed the premise of Bamford's book, their recommendation would go beyond people who were "fascinated by the intrigues of a shadowy underworld" and "concerned about the inevitability of Orwell's Big Brother." So, in the meantime, "*Sell as many books to the conspiracy suckers as possible.*"

Therefore, the question arises—If 100 percent of the military's top brass could be so corrupt when America was watching Jack Benny, should we expect less conspiracy activity half-a-century later in the era of Howard Stern? Now you know why the theory of evolution is the most popular drug in America.

17

Oklahoma City Bombing

"None calleth for justice, nor any pleadeth for truth:
they trust in vanity, and speak lies; they conceive
mischief, and bring forth iniquity."
(Isaiah 59:4)

O N APRIL 19, 1995, a total of 168 men, women and children
were killed when multiple explosions tore through the Alfred P.
Murrah Federal Building in downtown Oklahoma City. Federal
authorities called it the single largest terrorist attack in United States
history. According to "Waco veterans" Bill Clinton and Janet Reno, the
massive structure was demolished by a single truck bomb detonated by
the late Timothy McVeigh, the so-called "lone gunman." (See: Lee Harvey
Oswald and the single bullet theory, 1963.) However, the first reports
from the scene confirm that several bombs had been in place within the
Murrah Building that morning. Oklahoma City's NBC affiliate, KFOR,
in a live broadcast immediately after the bombing, reported:

> The first bomb that was in the Federal Building did go off. It did the
> damage that you see right there. The second explosive was found and
> defused. The third explosive that was found—and they are working on
> right now as we speak, I understand—both the second and the third
> explosives—if you can imagine this—were larger than the first.[1]

At the same time, a CNN anchorman reported:

> "The Justice Department is reporting that a second explosive device has
> been found in the A. P. Murrah Building in downtown Oklahoma City.
> Mike, you're still with us aren't you?"

Mike Arnett, an attorney in downtown Oklahoma City, on phone with CNN: "Yes, and in addition to that, what we were told at the scene a few minutes ago was that in fact two different explosive devices were found in addition to the one that went off, for a total of three."[2]

A reporter for Oklahoma City CBS affiliate, KWTV, then announced: "It has now been confirmed through federal authorities that a second bomb has been found inside that federal building in Oklahoma City."[3] Oklahoma Governor Frank Keating related the same development to reporters over the telephone, stating: "The report that I have is that one device was deactivated. Apparently there is another device, and obviously whatever did the damage to the Murrah Building was a tremendous, very sophisticated explosive device."[4]

Yet the "official version" quickly became the single Ryder truck bomb account.

OKLAHOMA BOMBING INVESTIGATION COMMITTEE

At the time of the bombing Charles Key was serving his fifth term in the Oklahoma legislature as a state representative. Within days, survivors and relatives of victims began contacting him to express concerns they had about the manner in which the federal government was conducting the investigation. They implored him in his capacity as an elected official to pursue the case more thoroughly. This grassroots petition resulted in the formation of the Oklahoma Bombing Investigation Committee (OBIC), funded solely through the private sector.

For six long years Representative Key and his small group of dedicated citizens (V. Z. Lawton, Dale Phillips and George B. Wallace) endured a barrage of criticism, intimidation and stonewalling from federal authorities within the Clinton administration. Having compiled volumes of evidence, eyewitness interviews, court transcripts, and reports of scientific experts, the OBIC published its findings in a 576-page exposé entitled *Final Report on the Bombing of the Alfred P. Murrah Federal Building April 19, 1995.* Mr. Key writes in the preface:

> Our one common goal has been, from the beginning, to arrive at the truth. . . . Over the past six years since the bombing, much of the evidence we have accumulated has been ignored or derided by the mainstream media. We are not the enemy. We are not antigovernment. It is because we love our country that we demand and have the right to expect the best

possible government. . . . We serve no political agenda. We did not do this for personal gain or glory. We did this in order to preserve our country and to make our world safer for future generations.[5]

It was my privilege to discuss the investigation with Mr. Key personally. Among a wide range of chapter titles such as "The Eyewitnesses," "Prior Knowledge," "The Search for John Does and Others Unknown" and "Government Improprieties," I was particularly impressed with the array of professional testimonials contained in chapter five, "Damage To The Alfred P. Murrah Federal Building." How's *this* for a list of bona fide "Limbaugh Kooks"?

Dr. Ernest B. Paxson has over forty years' experience as an aerospace engineer in the field of structural mechanics and dynamics. A portion of that time was devoted to the topography of failed structural systems and structural components. At Fort Leonard Wood, Missouri, U.S. Army Corps of Engineers, he was also trained in the use of explosives to destroy various types of structures. In a letter to Charles Key, November 5, 1999, Dr. Paxson wrote:

> A 4800 lb ANFO [ammonium nitrate and fuel oil] truck bomb is an extremely inefficient way to bring down a reinforced concrete structure. It might blow a hole in the curtain wall closest to the truck, but it would hardly affect the massive supporting columns of the building. . . . To be assured of destroying any structure, one would have to place a sufficient amount of explosive charge in intimate contact with the pertinent supporting members.[6]

Roger Raubach holds a Ph.D. in physical chemistry which deals with rates of chemical reaction and the heat-energy relations involved in reactions. (The evaluation of explosives and their properties falls within the realm of the physical chemist.) Dr. Raubach stated in a letter to Key, dated June 28, 1995:

> The possibility of an ammonium nitrate fertilizer bomb, regardless of size, demolishing a reinforced concrete structure at a twenty or thirty foot standoff not only strains the limit of credibility but exceeds it by a considerable margin. . . . Ammonium nitrate . . . [is] not "fast" enough to shatter concrete and break steel reinforcing rods.[7]

Alvin V. Norberg has been a licensed professional engineer in the state of California, having earned a B.S. degree from the University of California, Berkley, December 1939. He is the electrical engineer of record of over 5,000 building construction projects and has served as an "expert witness" in 150 fire and accident investigations and testified in Superior Court on a number of cases. In a letter to Key, dated November 1, 1999, Mr. Norberg affirmed:

> You have requested my professional opinion which I offer as follows: . . . the damage to the Murrah Building on April 19, 1995 *cannot* be ascribed to a *single* truck bomb containing 4800 lbs of ANFO.[8]

C. Frederick Hansen earned his doctorate in aeronautical engineering in 1982 from Nagoya University, Japan. He spent thirty years with NASA as a research scientist, and chief of the Physical Gasdynamics Branch at the Ames Research Laboratory, Moffett Field, California. He has lectured at San Jose State, Stanford, MIT, the University of Oregon, the University of Nagoya, Japan, the Indian Institute of Science, Bangalore, India and the Chung King National University, Tainan, Taiwan. Dr. Hansen wrote in his letter to Key, dated August 20, 1997:

> The main reason I have supported your Grand Jury inquiry into the Oklahoma City bombing is that I feel certain truth has been deliberately obscured. . . . Part of my specialty with NASA was on shock waves and detonation waves, and I know how quickly a blast wave attenuates as it travels through air. I am absolutely certain that the explosion in front of the building could not have sheared the columns of the building. Most likely a high explosive like RDX was placed on those columns, perhaps to detonate upon arrival of the blast wave.[9]

Brigadier General Benton K. Partin (Retired) spent twenty-five of his thirty-one years with the U.S. Air Force in research design, development, test and management of weapons development. His professional training includes the chemistry of explosives, warheads, explosive train design, terminal ballistics fuses, wave shaping, propellants, and numerous other weapons, rocket and aerodynamic disciplines. General Partin holds a B.S. in Chemical Engineering, an M.S. in Aeronautical Engineering, and completed the academic requirements for a Ph.D. in Statistics with a minor in Operations Research. Key writes:

> About two weeks after the 19 April 1995 bombing of the Murrah Building in Oklahoma City, Partin did a bomb damage analysis and concluded that the building could not possibly have been collapsed the way it was by 4,800 pounds of ANFO as claimed by the FBI. . . . Partin then prepared a six-

page technical analysis based on information available in the media. This report indicated that the FBI's single-truck-bomb theory was "beyond credulity". . . . Partin's analysis determined that "the damage pattern on the reinforced concrete superstructure could not possibly have been attained from the single truck bomb," and that supplemental demolition charges were used to bring the building down.[10]

Perhaps the most distinguished professional to challenge the government cover-up is Sam Cohen. Mr. Cohen is retired after a forty-year career in nuclear weaponry. He was assigned to the Manhattan Project at Los Alamos, New Mexico, during World War II. He later joined the RAND Corporation as a nuclear weapons analyst. In 1958, Cohen developed the technical slant military concept of the Neutron Bomb and consulted with the Los Alamos and Livermore Nuclear Weapons Laboratory, U.S. Air Force and Office of the Secretary of Defense. He issued a written statement to the OBIC, dated June 29, 1995, categorically rejecting the ammonium nitrate bomb theory:

I believe that the demolitions charges in the building were placed inside at certain key concrete columns (and) did the primary damage to the Murrah Federal Building. It would have been absolutely impossible and against the laws of nature for a truck full of fertilizer and fuel oil—no matter how much was used—to bring the building down.[11]

The official single-truck-bomb theory was so incredible that an army officer from British International Security (MI5) resorted to dark humor in a letter to Stephen Jones, lead defense counsel for Timothy McVeigh and Terry Nichols: "If your clients are guilty, Mr. Jones, I hope, before your government executes them, that you will make them available to the rest of us so we can find out how they did it."[12]

Seismographic equipment in Oklahoma City and Norman recorded the explosion(s) that occurred at the Murrah Building. The Oklahoma City reading, taken at the Omniplex Science Museum, shows two separate events while the Norman seismograph, located sixteen miles from ground zero, registered three events. Many experts contend that the first activity resulted from internal charges, while the second, larger spike occurring 4.2 seconds later came from the Ryder truck blast, with the third reading constituting the partial structural collapse that ensued.

Robert D. Vernon is president of Microlithic Technologies, a firm that specializes in computer-based image analysis and data-visualization services for Cultural Resource Management firms (contract archaeology) and provides consulting engineering to high-tech companies. Vernon is a chemist with over thirty-five years' experience in failure analysis, engineering and troubleshooting in microelectronics and process control industries. At the request of the OBIC, Mr. Vernon performed an in-depth analysis of photographic, seismic, and blast/brisance data connected with the bombing at the Murrah Building. Concerning the seismographic data, Vernon writes:

> Seismic records from the Omniplex . . . show approximately four (4) seconds of small-amplitude earth motion ("first motion") *preceding* a much larger signal. . . .
> The small first motion observed on 19 April is totally *inconsistent with* the high-amplitude impulse first motion seismic signature typically produced by an above ground explosion of a single large device.
> Two audio recordings from 19 April both ostensibly exhibit a sharp "crack" impulse 4.2 seconds prior to the sound of a large explosion (or "boom"). High detonation-velocity charges produce a "crack," not a "boom". . .
> Disintegrated concrete with smooth fracture-termination signatures typical of localized high-brisance damage were documented on critical structural members.[13]

Although the seismograms have been widely discussed and debated by geophysical scientists, multiple survivor testimonies of earthquake-like shaking prior to the large blast are a matter of record. Mr. Vernon states, "At least six survivors reported that the building shook, and they had time to think an earthquake had occurred, and to seek cover—before the truck bomb blast blew in the windows and lifted the floors beneath their feet."[14]

Charles Watts is an attorney who was in the Federal Courthouse immediately across the street from the Murrah Building. He is also a Vietnam veteran who has experienced the effects of being within one hundred feet of B-52 air strikes. Mr. Watts stated:

> I was up on the ninth floor . . . with nothing between the two buildings. We were on the south side, in the foyer, outside the courtroom. It was 9:00 or just very, very shortly thereafter. Several lawyers were standing there talking and there was a large explosion. It threw several of the people close to me to the floor. I don't think it threw me to the floor, but it did move me significantly, and I threw myself to the floor, and got down, and

about that time, a huge blast, unlike anything I've ever experienced, hit. . . .
A second blast. There were two explosions. The second blast made me
think that the whole building was coming in.[15]

Joe Harp is a retired CIA operative who now resides in Texas. On
the day of the bombing he was in the Murrah Building at about 11:00 a.m.
attempting to locate a friend who was thought to be among the victims.
In a sworn affidavit presented to the OBIC, Mr. Harp related:

> I knew right away that the explosive device that had caused the building
> damage was not an ANFO (ammonium nitrate fuel oil) bomb for two reasons:
> 1) There was a strong sulfur smell in the air that was very reminiscent of
> the gas-enhanced "Daisy cutter" bombs I am familiar with from my tours
> of duty in Vietnam, as well as other military experience. It was not an ANFO
> smell. 2) I could see right away from the bomb signature—the damage to
> the structure of the building—that there must have been explosive charges
> inside the building. The truck bomb could not have done that damage from
> out on the street.
>
> . . . While I was up in the building, the police and fire department started
> evacuating people from the area because of the discovery of additional
> explosive devices. . . . I observed members of the fire department EOD
> removing two devices and placing them in the bomb disposal unit. The
> devices were military olive drab in color, and the size of round five-gallon
> drums, with black lettering designating the contents as fulminated mercury,
> a high-grade explosive. I was also close enough to see what looked to me
> like mercury switches on the devices, which I presumed were for detonation
> purposes. I have had significant experience with these materials in the
> military and so readily recognized them.
>
> . . . I took residue samples from the bomb site and scrapings from
> another building across the street from the Murrah Building to a laboratory
> for chemical analysis. That analysis showed that there was fulminated
> mercury residue, along with other chemicals, in the sample.
>
> I affirm that the above statements are true.[16]

For the record, *Firehouse* magazine, in their September 1995 issue,
listed four bomb scare evacuations occurring at the Murrah Building at
10:00 a.m., 10:22 a.m., 10:45 a.m., and 13:51 (1:51 p.m.).[17]

The repercussions caused by so many high-profile personalities
challenging the official account resulted in the expedient dismantling of
the crime scene. On May 23, 1995, the Murrah Building was demolished
without ever having been officially investigated by demolition or explosives

agents. The ruins were subsequently buried in cement, under guard at a private landfill. Robert Vernon asks: "What was the *real* reason for the rush to demolish and bury the building—before it could be independently examined and analyzed? Who—at all levels—was involved in, and responsible for, approving the demolition?"[18]

General Partin hand-delivered copies of his amplified bomb-damage analysis to the offices of all 535 senators and congressmen. In the cover letter, he stated: "No government law enforcement agency should be permitted to demolish, smash and bury evidence of a counter-terrorism sting operation, sabotage or terrorist attack without a thorough examination by an independent, technically competent agency."[19]

You would think that an organization called the Federal Bureau of Investigation would appreciate the need to preserve pertinent evidence. Yet this was merely a repeat performance of that which occurred in the aftermath of Waco. Incidentally, the Murrah Building was bombed on the two-year anniversary of the Branch Davidian conflagration.

THE THIRD TERRORIST

Having surreptitiously eradicated the crime scene, Janet Reno perpetrated a second flagrant abuse of her power by confiscating over a dozen surveillance tapes and satellite photographs citing "matters of national security," etc. They included footage from the Regency Tower Apartment Building, the Southwestern Bell Telephone Building, the Journal Record Building and numerous other sites in the downtown Oklahoma City area. Now that the federal cases against McVeigh and Nichols are completed, *why are these tapes still unavailable to the public?* Supreme Court Justice Warren Burger once stated, "People in an open society do not demand infallibility from their institutions, but it is difficult for them to accept what they are prohibited from observing."

On April 13, 2004, during the 9/11 hearings, Commissioner Lehman asked former FBI director Louis Freeh about the allegations contained in a recently published book entitled *The Third Terrorist* by Jayna Davis. Known for his computer illiteracy, Freeh was able to dodge the question by smugly replying that he hadn't read the book.

The truth is, Louie was lying. ("F.I.B.", etc.) *Everyone* in the bureau's upper echelon was aware of Jayna Davis. *They only spent about nine years trying to suppress her research into the Oklahoma City bombing!* R. James Woosley, director of Central Intelligence from 1993 to 1995, stated on the dust jacket:

> This fascinating product of Jayna Davis's near-decade of brave, thorough, and dogged investigative reporting effectively shifts the burden of proof to those who would still contend that McVeigh and Nichols executed the 1995 Oklahoma City bombing without the support of a group or groups from the Middle East.

David P. Schippers wrote the foreword for *The Third Terrorist.* Mr. Schippers's distinguished legal career has run the gamut from shutting down the Chicago Mob as lead prosecutor for Attorney General Robert Kennedy's Organized Crime and Racketeering Unit to successfully impeaching Bill Clinton as former Chief Investigative Counsel of the House Judiciary Committee. He wrote, "I predict that *The Third Terrorist* will drop like a missile on the federal bureaucracy."[20] The reason why everyone is so nervous about Davis's book is because it reveals what appears on those confiscated surveillance tapes. Schippers writes, "If you are a citizen who is seriously concerned over your own security and that of the United States, it is critical that you read this book cover to cover."[21]

Whereas the most significant revelation of the OBIC was the impressive expert testimony confirming the use of "multiple charges," Jayna Davis focused her research on the fact of "multiple culprits." In reality, one fails to exist without the other.

Within hours of the bombing, dozens of witnesses began notifying law enforcement officials that suspicious-acting Middle Eastern individuals had been seen in the vicinity of the Murrah Building that morning. The following FBI all-points bulletin (APB) was subsequently dispatched the same day:

> Be on the lookout for a late model, almost new, Chevrolet, full-size pickup. It will be brown in color with tinted windows, smoke-colored bug deflector on the front of pickup . . . Middle-Eastern male, 25 to 28 years of age, six feet tall, athletic build, dark hair and a beard. . . . Driver of the vehicle was not identified. Subjects were last seen heading north on Walker at a high rate of speed. . . . Authorization FBI.[22]

Following Timothy McVeigh's bizarre apprehension that day (for driving a vehicle minus a license plate) and later arrest for the bombing, his unidentified Middle Eastern accomplice would come to be known as "John Doe 2." Although not in Oklahoma City on April 19, Terry Nichols would also be indicted for the crime. In a preliminary hearing eight days after the bombing, the federal government filed an affidavit to show probable cause naming not only McVeigh and Nichols, but also "Others Unknown." A police sketch of an Arab male had already been distributed throughout the media.

Such was the immediate consensus of several other authoritative voices. "This is the work of Hamas," Israeli Prime Minister Yitzhak Rabin emphatically decreed across international airwaves.[23] In an interview with USA Today, William Webster, the former director of both the CIA and the FBI, noted that the bombing had all the hallmarks of Mideast terror.[24] "I think what we've got here is a bona fide terrorist attack," Oliver "Buck" Revell informed the Baltimore Sun. The former FBI assistant director and counterterrorism expert spoke from years of experience. "I think it's most likely a Middle East terrorist. I think the modus operandi is similar. They have used this approach."[25] The Dallas Morning News released the contents of an FBI internal communiqué circulating within hours of the bombing which suggested "the attack was made in retaliation for the prosecution of Muslim fundamentalists in the bombing of the World Trade Center in February 1993 . . . [and] we are currently inclined to suspect the Islamic Jihad as the likely group."[26]

Yet within weeks of the bombing, Janet Reno and Louie Freeh suddenly chose not to pursue "John Doe 2," determining that no other accomplice existed. Directives were then issued to FBI field offices to hold all searches for "Others Unknown" in abeyance. Thus began the amazing odyssey of Jayna Davis and her husband, Drew.

At the time of the bombing, Davis was employed as an investigative reporter at KFOR, an Oklahoma City television station. She and her news crew had arrived at the Murrah Building approximately thirteen minutes into the carnage. As with Representative Key and his constituents, Davis became alarmed at the government's abrupt and unexplained abandonment of the manhunt for John Doe 2. Stonewalled by federal officials, she pursued her own painstaking investigation. The substance of her completed manuscript is threefold: an incredible compilation of eyewitness affidavits, implicating several Islamic terrorists; a full-blown, ongoing cover-up by the FBI; and the personal cost of her commitment, which included having to fight two lawsuits simultaneously, one filed by John Doe 2 himself, and the other initiated by her former employer (KFOR having been purchased by *The New York Times*).

As *The Third Terrorist* consists of 355 electrifying pages, a survey of the pertinent content can hardly be accommodated. In her introduction entitled, "Cast of Characters," Davis gives a biographical summary of thirty-eight witnesses and the twelve Middle Eastern suspects that they implicated. (Many of these individuals were also listed in *Final Report*.) All of the witnesses have signed sworn affidavits attesting to the veracity of their accounts.

While some of the suspects were seen on the day of the attack, both before and after the blast, other testimony concerns their local whereabouts prior to April 19. A firm consensus has identified Hussain Hashem Al-Hussaini, a former Iraqi soldier, as Timothy McVeigh's mysterious accomplice. The other reprobates served as cohorts in the crime.

A chronological survey of these critical sightings begins at the "Cactus Motel" (a pseudonym chosen by Davis to protect the proprietor from possible terrorist reprisals). No less than seven witnesses placed McVeigh in the company of Al-Hussaini and other Middle Eastern collaborators. These individuals are: the motel owner, the manager and his wife, a maintenance man and his wife, a second maintenance man and a customer.[27] On the evening of April 15, 1995, McVeigh was seen drinking beer with Hussaini at an Oklahoma City nightclub. The men were identified by a bartender and a male patron.[28]

An Oklahoma City gas station attendant stated that he sold one hundred gallons of diesel fuel to Al-Hussaini after the Iraqi pulled up to the pump in a large Ryder moving van on April 18, 1995.[29]

Several people saw McVeigh's accomplices on the morning of the bombing. An Oklahoma County official and two local business executives independently observed Hussaini racing on foot from the vicinity of the Murrah Building in the early hours of April 19, 1995. (It is believed he was timing his planned getaway.)[30]

A salesman at Johnny's Tire Shop testified that he gave McVeigh directions to Fifth and Harvey streets approximately thirty minutes before detonation. The witness identified Al-Hussaini as accompanying McVeigh in the passenger seat of the Ryder truck. A co-worker corroborated the same.[31]

A downtown employee viewed McVeigh conversing with a disheveled, shabbily dressed pedestrian at the rear of the Ryder truck. The vehicle was parked only a couple of dozen yards south of the Murrah Building. Al-Hussaini was seated in the cab. The time was approximately 8:45 a.m.[32]

Only moments before the explosion, bombing victim Daina Bradley was inside the Murrah Building on the first floor at the Social Security Office accompanied by her mother, two children, and sister. She was there to change her son's social security card. The blast killed her mother and children, while severely injuring her and her sister. Having been pinned in the rubble for twelve hours, she was finally extricated, but only after having her right leg amputated.

Daina was the only victim who lived to place Hussain Hashem Al-Hussaini at the scene of the crime. Davis relates her interview with the traumatized survivor:

"What did you see?"

"I was standing in the building, and I was looking out the window of the Social Security office. I saw the Ryder truck, and I saw the man get out of the Ryder truck"

"Can you describe him?"

"He had an olive complexion, and he had black, curly hair. He was wearing a baseball cap, but his curls were sticking out from his head. It was short in the back, but you could still see the curls in his hair."

"Was he American?"

"No, he was not American," she stressed. "He was foreign. You could tell by his skin and his face, the way his face was." Daina then recounted the suspect's erratic behavior as he crossed the sidewalk and walked behind the Ryder truck.

"He was acting very paranoid. His head moved around very fast. He was looking around like somebody was after him."

I motioned the photographer who was recording our interview to capture a wide angle shot of Daina as she perused the photo lineup of the Middle Eastern men [arranged by KFOR-TV]. "Please take your time as you look over these pictures," I instructed.

Her hands trembled slightly as she flipped the pages. After several interminable minutes of quiet concentration, the witness froze. Terror flooded her expressive ebony eyes.

"It was him," Daina proclaimed as she traced her finger around the face of Hussain Al-Hussaini. "The man I saw get out of the truck looked like him."

The enormity of the moment shook me. "Can you describe the similarities?" I asked.

"He has the same olive complexion and same curly black hair. And the same features on his face," Daina quivered.

"Would you testify to that under oath before a grand jury?"
"Yes, I would."[33]

Four witnesses observed various stages of the getaway. A printing press operator for *The Journal Record* was nearly run over by a speeding Mercury Marquis being driven by McVeigh with a "swarthy companion by his side."[34] An Oklahoma City attorney identified one of Al-Hussaini's Iraqi associates in the driver's seat of a pale yellow sedan as it sped away from the Murrah Building.[35] A migrant worker and a local computer programmer testified that they were nearly struck (in separate instances) by a brown, late model Chevrolet pickup being driven by two Middle Eastern males.[36]

An Oklahoma City resident identified a Middle Eastern cohort of Hussaini's as the man she witnessed sitting in the driver's seat of a yellow pickup that was abandoned at her apartment complex on April 27, 1995. Her husband asserted further that the FBI had informed him that the abandoned vehicle was, in fact, the subject of the official all-points bulletin the bureau had issued targeting foreign suspects.[37] (The change in paint color was an obvious attempt to avoid detection.)

Finally, the former girlfriend of another Al-Hussaini associate, Majid Ajaj, testified in an affidavit that Ajaj confessed to involvement in the Oklahoma City bombing and also inferred complicity in the attack on September 11, 2001.[38]

THE NEO-NAZI CONNECTION

Representative Key and the OBIC uncovered an added dimension to the plot that explains why McVeigh and Nichols had conspired with Middle East terrorists to bomb the Murrah Building. The public was told that the pair were right-wing fanatics who had attacked the government facility in retaliation for the debacles at Waco and Ruby Ridge. What they weren't told was that the FBI had plenty of prior information that tied the two "militia types" to an array of neo-Nazi extremist organizations in Arizona, Michigan, Elohim City, Oklahoma and to German, Russian, Japanese and Middle Eastern terrorists. In a "quirk of fate," the Murrah Building was bombed on the very day that Richard Snell, a prominent member of "The Covenant, the Sword and the Arm of the Lord" (a violent, anti-government movement), was executed for the murder of a pawn broker. Snell had predicted that there would be catastrophic events on that day.[39] Key comments on this neo-Nazi-Middle East coalescence:

> It seems confusing and preposterous to assume that all these elements came together to plan and carry out the bombing of the Murrah Federal Building—until one realizes that cooperation between these groups takes place on a frequent basis. The question arises: With all that separates these groups, including political ideology, cultural and ethnic differences, an innate distrust of one another and often opposing agendas, why would they cooperate on any joint venture? **Because, they have two things in common—a hatred for the U.S. Government and a hatred for the Jews.**[40]

Key notes that the Stockholm Revisionist Historian Conference held in Sweden in November 1992, constitutes an example of these diverse groups coming together for a common cause.

> Organized by Ahmed Rami, formerly of "Radio Islam," the Conference was attended by numerous Nazi and neo-Nazi figures as well as by members of Hezbollah and Hamas (Arab extremist groups), Japanese extremists, and Pamjat (a Russian extremist group).[41]

He adds:

> The U.S. involvement with defending Israel during the Gulf War generated high levels of neo-Nazi hostility, which have not dissipated since the Gulf War. The U.S. support of Israel during the Palestinian violence makes the U.S. a continued object of neo-Nazi/Middle Eastern displeasure.[42]

After the Gulf War, President Bush began a foolish program of resettlement of Iraqi prisoners to the U.S. This policy was continued and expanded under Clinton. Scores of Middle-Eastern students are now attending colleges and universities across America with the University of Oklahoma having one of the largest Arab populations. While many are law-abiding citizens and visitors, Key relates that "many also are likely 'plants' from government-sanctioned extremist organizations in their respective countries of origin, here at the ready to participate in any terrorist actions their organizations desire."[43]

Terry Nichols expanded his effectiveness as a neo-Nazi terrorist by taking bomb-making courses in the Philippines. Nichols's first trip to the islands, ostensibly to marry Marife Torres, a seventeen-year-old mail-order bride, occurred in 1990. Davis asserts that he returned to the Philippines dozens of times, frequently without his wife. His alibi was that he was looking for business opportunities.

Ramzi Yousef, the Iraqi terrorist who was indicted for masterminding the 1993 attack on the World Trade Center, operated a major terrorist cell in Manila. It is strongly believed that Nichols met with Yousef during his trip to the Philippines in 1994. An FBI 302 report cites that a neighbor of Marife's parents said Marife's father told him he saw Nichols with a book on building bombs. When questioned by the Philippine National Police, Marife's father affirmed that it was true.[44]

Even the skeptical Richard Clarke gave credence to the possibility of a Nichols-Yousef connection, writing in his 2004 blockbuster, *Against All Enemies:*

> Another conspiracy theory intrigued me because I could never disprove it. The theory seemed unlikely on its face: Ramzi Yousef or Khalid Sheik Muhammad had taught Terry Nichols how to blow up the Oklahoma Federal Building. [Muhammed would serve as the chief architect of the September 11, 2001, attacks.] The problem was that, upon investigation, we established that both Ramzi Yousef and Nichols had been in the city of Cebu on the same days. I had been to Cebu years earlier; it is on an island in the central Philippines. It was a town in which word could have spread that a local girl was bringing her American boy friend home and that the American hated the U.S. government.
>
> Yousef and Khalid Sheik Muhammad had gone there to help create an al Qaeda spinoff, a Philippine affiliate chapter, named after a hero of the Afghan war against the Soviets, Abu Sayaff. Could the al Qaeda explosives expert have been introduced to the angry American who proclaimed his hatred for the U.S. Government? We do not know, despite some FBI investigation. We do know that Nichols's bombs did not work before his Philippine stay and were deadly when he returned. We also know that Nichols continued to call Cebu long after his wife returned to the United States. The final coincidence is that several al Qaeda operatives had attended a radical Islamic conference a few years earlier in, of all places, Oklahoma City.[45]

In any event Yousef, Nichols and McVeigh would eventually become "neighbors," occupying 8'x10'x12' cells in solitary confinement at the United States Penitentiary Administrative Maximum Facility (ADX), Florence, Colorado, America's toughest prison, known as the Alcatraz of the Rockies.

The evidence of so many anomalies can only foster suspicion in the minds of thinking people. Key writes:

The speculation occurs because our Government has so little faith in its people that it thinks it has to keep unpleasantness from us for our own protection and peace of mind—the "What you don't know can't hurt you" mentality—except that this time it did hurt us—to the tune of 168 people dead.[46]

Thus, at this point, the conscientious citizen is left with three areas of consideration: coincidence, conjecture and certainty. With regard to the first, Alex Jones writes:

Martin Keating, Governor Frank Keating's brother, wrote a novel entitled *The Final Jihad*. In the book, a Tom McVeigh masterminds the bombing of an Oklahoma City federal building. Keating's brother dedicated the book to the Knights of the Secret Circle, a term used by members of the Illuminati when they talk about their organization. Martin Keating wrote the book *two years* before the bombing.

KFOR's Linda Cavanaugh made this report, which pertains to this novel: "The NewsChannel has learned of another strange development. Apparently before the bombing, Governor Frank Keating's brother, Martin, had been working on a novel about a terrorist bombing in Oklahoma City. Stranger still, one of the characters in the novel was named Thomas McVeigh."[47]

Another "coincidence" has to do with the "fact" that *none* of the seventeen ATF agents with offices in the Murrah Building were at their desks when the blast occurred. (The OBIC discredits the ATF fable regarding two agents who supposedly got caught in a free-falling elevator, but escaped with their lives;[48] as well as the agent who mysteriously appeared on the ninth floor.) This leads to the conjecture of whether the government had prior knowledge of the attack. "Were agents forewarned about a bomb in Oklahoma City?" asks Linda Cavanaugh, a co-worker of Jayna Davis at KFOR. "Did they know the Murrah Building was a target?"[49] For instance, hotel receipts confirm that Danny Culson, the FBI's top counterterrorism agent, checked into an Oklahoma City motel nine hours before the blast occurred.[50] Enough documentation exists pointing to the prospect of prior knowledge that Key's committee could devote an entire chapter to the uncomfortable subject. He writes:

Katherine E. Mallette, an Emergency Medical Technician, Intermediate, with EMSA responded to the explosion at the Murrah Federal Building between 10:30 and 11:00 a.m. As her ambulance was waiting to transport victims to area hospitals, two ATF agents walked by her ambulance, and she heard one of the agents say to the other, "Is that why we got the page not to come in today?" (Source: Signed affidavit of Katherine Mallette).[51]

Bruce Shaw, whose wife worked in the Murrah Building at the Federal Credit Union, also signed an affidavit testifying that an ATF agent informed him that "agents were tipped on their pagers not to come into the office that morning."[52] *It is unfortunate that the day care center was not given the same notice!*

While the question of "prior knowledge" may be difficult for most Americans to swallow, the issue of a massive, ongoing cover-up is an airtight reality. Several startling revelations of FBI complicity appear in Davis's book. After having compiled a litany of testimony identifying Al-Hussaini as the original John Doe 2, the author confirms that:

> Eleni Kalisch, the FBI's section chief for governmental relations, impudently conceded that Hussain Al-Hussaini had never been interviewed. . . . The FBI . . . had corralled hundreds of John Doe look-alikes while pursuing additional conspirators, but it refused to even speak to a man whom a plethora of witness affidavits named as Tim McVeigh's principal accomplice. This decision . . . left the FBI on the record and without excuse.[53]

If "comedians" like Geraldo Rivera ever got around to pressing Louie Freeh for an explanation, the plot would only thicken. Technically speaking, the FBI has a pretty good alibi for not having interrogated Al-Hussaini. When Davis tried to give the FBI her findings, she got the shock of her life:

> In the fall of 1997, upon the advice of my lawyer, I set an appointment with an FBI agent to surrender all twenty-two witness statements and hundreds of pages of corroborative documentation. Upon arriving at the Oklahoma City field office accompanied by notary public, Pam Nance, I was rebuffed. **The FBI brazenly refused to take receipt of the investigative file.**
>
> When I demanded an explanation for such an absurdity, one of the lead prosecutors for Terry Nichols's approaching federal trial informed my attorney, Tim McCoy, that the Justice Department did not want any more "documents for discovery" to turn over to the defense teams. . . .
>
> I was dumbfounded. The federal government's capital investment in resources and manpower to track down the killers in the Oklahoma bombing was historically unparalleled. But the FBI slammed the door on a reporter from the mainstream media who desired to share credible information that needed to be investigated.[54]

In a lame attempt to cover his tracks, the prosecutor issued the following ludicrous statement: "The United States (DOJ) has not made any investigative demands for any knowledge Jayna Davis may or may not have."[55]

However, the story does not end there. In January 1999, a courageous FBI agent, Dan Vogel, agreed to take custody of Davis's evidence. Jayna writes:

> In October 2001, the legal drama reached a crescendo when retired FBI Agent Dan Vogel was subpoenaed to testify in Nichols's Oklahoma pre-trial proceeding. . . . In a court proffer, the defendant's lawyers told Oklahoma State District Judge Ray Dean Linder that Agent Vogel readily admitted "he received twenty-two affidavits from reporter Jayna Davis in January 1999," **but after he turned the materials over to the FBI legal department in the Oklahoma City field office, the sworn declarations disappeared.**[56]

So—do you see how it works? How could Lou be held responsible for evidence he never saw? When Jayna asked another trusted federal agent, "Why would the FBI deep-six twenty-two witness affidavits which I gave the Bureau in the presence of my attorney?" he replied:

> Jayna, if the FBI does not possess your investigative file, agents can swear under oath the documentation never existed. Therefore, the Bureau is under no legal obligation to open a national security investigation into the Middle Eastern connection.[57]

They would then be free to make up their own fantasy as to what occurred at the crime scene.

Dr. Fredrick Whitehurst, a forensic scientist with the FBI crime lab, became so outraged at the Bureau's ongoing corruption that he prepared a paper critical of procedures and criminal investigation results within the FBI lab. Citing numerous instances of sloppy, deceptive, and even falsified forensic test results, he spoke of the "pressures continually applied upon these scientists to 'interpret' their data in the 'appropriate' manner."[58] A resulting report by the inspector general "blasted the world-renowned lab for flawed scientific work and inaccurate, pro-prosecution testimony in major cases including the Oklahoma City and World Trade Center bombings."[59]

YOSSEF BODANSKY

Perhaps the most intriguing part of the entire affair is that the Lord placed a *Jew* in the perfect place to warn America that an attack was on the way. Yossef Bodansky is an internationally renowned military and threat analyst. In the past he has served as director of research for the International Strategic Studies Association, senior editor for the Defense and Foreign Affairs group of publications, National Security Fellow of the American Security Council Foundation, a visiting scholar in the Security Studies Program of Johns Hopkins University, and a consultant to the U.S. Departments of Defense and State. He is the author of eight books on international terrorism and global crisis. In 1999, Bodansky published the definitive study of the world's rising archterrorist, *Bin Laden: The Man Who Declared War on America,* a *New York Times* No. 1 bestseller.

At the time of the Oklahoma City bombing, Mr. Bodansky was the chairman of the Congressional Task Force on Terrorism. On February 27, 1995, his committee issued a formal warning which stated that there would be an "Iran-sponsored Islamic attack" on U.S. soil.[60] The primary targets at this time were understood to be in Washington, D.C., specifically Congress and the White House. The warning was immediately disseminated to the FBI and other federal intelligence agencies.

Jayna Davis contacted Mr. Bodansky in April 1996 and found the veteran terrorism analyst sympathetic to her plight. She writes:

> During the ensuing weeks, I learned that cultivating such an esteemed source would be tantamount to navigating a minefield. As director of the Task Force, Bodansky maintained a fierce commitment to federal laws which sealed matters of national security—rules he had sworn to uphold. It was unfathomable for him to open up his files and invite me to pull up a chair. However, Bodansky also exuded a passionate loyalty to the truth. When I inquired about the plausibility of eyewitness accounts that implicated Arab men in the Murrah Building bombing, he pondered his rejoinder with discernable caution.
>
> "How shall I put it? You're scratching the tip of the iceberg. However, you're scratching the right place in the right direction," he said encouragingly.[61]

According to Davis, Mr. Bodansky went on to name the very suspects implicated in her voluminous research, stating:

Yossef Bodansky confided in a personal meeting in May 1996 that he had independently targeted the same foreign conspirators in the initial stages of the investigation he conducted on behalf of the Congressional Task Force. Through rare circumstances, I was privileged to corroborate this assertion.[62]

As the thesis of Arab complicity in the Oklahoma City bombing is conspicuously absent from Bodansky's published works, I chose to contact him myself to verify Davis's assertions, assuming that a professional conflict of interest on his part would explain the omission. In the course of our telephone conversation he assured me that Jayna Davis had quoted him correctly.

On March 3, 1995, a series of new discoveries led the Task Force to update its warning. The Middle Eastern terrorists now planned to strike at "the heart of the U.S."[63] Bodansky writes, "Other Iranian sources confirmed Tehran's desire and determination to strike inside the U.S. against an object symbolizing the American government . . ."[64]

Bodansky also explained the role that McVeigh and Nichols played in the Middle Eastern plot. In a letter to Davis, he wrote:

> As for the warnings: (1) The Israeli warning [received by Bodansky] was actually that it will be an Islamist operation but will be carried out by non-Arabs. (2) One of the main reasons the Task Force narrowed down the warnings in the spring of 1995 to the heartland were indications—not absolute proof—that Lily Whites would be activated for the forthcoming operation. This meant that Oklahoma City should have been on the short list of objectives because of the known prominence of the local Islamist networks.[65]

Representative Key confirms that the FBI was well aware of the Muslim threat in Oklahoma City:

> The FBI had a secret eavesdropping operation underway in Oklahoma City before the bombing. A prior raid on a mosque in Oklahoma City may have been the catalyst for the operation. Arabic linguists from the U.S. Army were loaned to the FBI with approval from the Secretary of the Army to listen to and interpret wiretap tapes.[66]

On the evening of the bombing, John McWethy of ABC's *World News Tonight* confirmed: "Sources say the FBI has been watching dozens of suspicious Islamic groups throughout the American Southwest and several right in Oklahoma City."[67]

With regard to Bodansky's allusion to an "Israeli warning," Davis writes:

> But while the tentacles of investigative leads stretched worldwide, the Middle Eastern mercenaries of death were believed to be hiding in plain view. On April 20, the *Associated Press* dispatched to newsrooms nationwide the startling comment of Yigal Carmon, a counterterrorism advisor to former Israeli Prime Minister Yitzhak Shamir. The news report claimed Mr. Carmon asserted that "Islamic militants have set up a well-funded infrastructure throughout the United States, and stated further that he knew of fundraising efforts in Oklahoma City."[68]

That the Oklahoma City bombing was indeed a premeditated Middle Eastern conspiracy was confirmed within hours of the blast, via a high profile international telephone conversation. The call was placed by a Saudi major general, responsible for protecting the royal family, to the private residence of former CIA counterterrorism chief Vince Cannistraro. The two men had known each other for over fifteen years. Without delay, Cannistraro passed the delicate information to FBI Special Agent Kevin Foust, the Bureau's top investigator in charge of apprehending and prosecuting international terrorists. Agent Foust noted the following facts in an FBI interview report which is officially catalogued as a "302":

> The Saudi official told CANNISTRARO that he (the source) had information that there was a "squad" of people currently in the United States, very possibly Iraqis, who have been tasked with carrying out terrorist attacks against the United States. The Saudi claimed that he had seen a list of "targets," and that the first on the list was the federal building in Oklahoma City, Oklahoma. The second target was identified as the INS office in Houston, Texas, and the third target was the FBI office in Los Angeles, California.[69]

The fact that these various reports alternate between Iranian and Iraqi complicity is consistent with Bodansky's profile on Bin Laden's ability to promote Jihad. With regard to these two former enemies, Bodansky confirms that "strategic coordination and de facto cooperation had existed among these countries for a long time . . ."[70] The main breakthrough in the "all-Islamic revival" occurred when the Shiites and the Sunni majority agreed to bury the hatchet—in the skull of "Uncle Sam." The new message was simple: "Given the duality of the threat—the American presence and influence—the various national Islamist movements should combine their efforts against their common enemy."[71]

Unfortunately, however, the House Republicans, to whom Bodansky reported, summarily dismissed his findings and warnings of future attacks on American soil as "Zionist propaganda."[72] On the evening of July 17, 1996, TWA 800 exploded off the Long Island coast killing all 230 passengers aboard. Bodansky attributed the "accident" to HizbAllah International with Osama bin Laden officiating in a senior position.[73] His book on bin Laden (written in 1999) contained the following "positive" forecast:

> Throughout the Muslim world, from the Philippines to Morocco and in numerous Muslim émigré communities from Western Europe to the United States, Islamist terrorist and subversive cells are getting ready to strike out. As of late 1998, with the confrontation escalating between the United States and the Islamist international terrorist system as represented in the person of Osama bin Laden, the terrorists have become increasingly ready with redundant and resilient networks, weapons of mass destruction, and powerful bombs, as well as zeal and readiness for martyrdom—all for what they perceive to be the noble cause of bringing the United States suffering and pain.[74]

Among a variety of Islamic threats, he mentioned the specific warning by the London-based al-Muhajiroun Movement, led by Sheikh Omar Bakri that "the Americans will be buried under the rubble . . ."[75]

PRELUDE TO 9/11

The manner in which our government refused to pursue the Islamic conspirators emboldened Hussain Al-Hussaini to sue Jayna Davis for libel. However, his arrogant abuse of the American civil justice system backfired profoundly. On November 17, 1999, U.S. District Judge Timothy Leonard delivered sweeping vindication for Davis, dismissing the case in a ruling which upheld as "undisputed" *all fifty statements of fact and opinion that KFOR-TV asserted implicating Al-Hussaini in the bombing!*[76]

Unfortunately, in this case, the mass-murderer had been the plaintiff while the one described by David Schippers as "a true patriot and a courageous young woman" had been the defendant. Al-Hussaini was able to rejoin his comrades in terror.

Timothy McVeigh's execution by lethal injection on June 11, 2001, brought a measure of closure for many naive Americans. Two months later, the OBIC *Final Report* was released. An eerie prophecy appeared at the end of the preface:

> It is our belief that the bombing in Oklahoma City will not be the last terrorist attack on U.S. soil. Since all of the perpetrators have not been caught, they are still free to continue their work. **This will happen again.**[77]

In the aftermath of 9/11, many others would concur with Key's deadly analysis. Special Agent Dan Vogel unburdened himself in a rare interview with *Indianapolis Star* columnist James Patterson, April 20, 2002:

> We may have been in a position to start a massive investigation deep down in the Oklahoma City office based on the information that Jayna Davis had come up with on this Middle Eastern connection. Whether or not there was a connection didn't really matter. What really mattered was the fact that there was something very sinister going on with these individuals just because of the information that Jayna had gathered. . . .
>
> Jayna Davis was giving us a warning back as early as 1997 and we didn't do anything with it. We just refused to take the documents. And I don't know to this day what happened to the documents.[78]

Robert Wright is another FBI agent who chose to blow the whistle on the Bureau's reprehensible cover-up. Bodansky's Israeli counterparts had also advised him that two Islamic militants from Oklahoma City had traveled to Chicago in the summer of 1993 to attend a Hamas terrorist training camp.[79] As Special Agent Wright of the FBI's Chicago office attempted to close in on Mohammed Salah, the Arab-American who ran the terrorist cell, his efforts were squelched by his superiors.

When David Schippers discovered that the Oklahoma City terrorists had fine-tuned their bomb-making skills in his own city, the veteran attorney who had successfully prosecuted the likes of Sam "Mo Mo" Giancana, Sam "Teets" Battaglia, and Bill "Slick Willy" Clinton was understandably outraged. A review of Davis's material in March 2001 put him over the edge.

> "I want a meeting with General Ashcroft," David Schippers demanded in a June 2001 phone conversation with a high ranking deputy attorney general in Washington, D.C. "I have in my office volumes of credible evidence indicating Middle Eastern involvement in the Oklahoma City bombing, and

quite frankly, it scares the [expletive] out of me. If nothing is done, I'm afraid these terrorists are going to blow up Lower Manhattan."

"Well, sir, we don't normally start our meetings at the top," the DOJ official cautioned as he delivered the bureaucratic brush-off. "But I'll see what I can do and get back to you!"

That call never came.[80]

Schippers would go on to represent "ex-Agent" Wright in his subsequent battles with the Bureau over his courageous revelations. During an interview on ABC's news magazine show, *Primetime Live*, December 19, 2002, an incensed Wright asserted:

> September 11 is a direct result of the incompetence of the FBI's International Terrorism Unit. . . . No doubt about that. No doubt about that.[81]

In his foreword to *The Third Terrorist*, Schippers expressed the same conviction:

> It is my honest opinion that if the Department of Justice and the federal investigative agencies had not ignored Jayna Davis and instead accepted the mass of creditable evidence compiled by her, indicating direct Middle Eastern involvement in the bombing, the course of future events may have been altered. **Had those investigators taken their duty seriously and followed up on the investigation of that information, it is entirely likely that the Twin Towers would still be standing.**[82]

There are a number of particulars that link the Oklahoma City bombing suspects at large to the later tragedy on September 11, 2001. Upon Al-Hussaini's August 1994 arrival in Boston from the Middle East, he resided with two brothers, Abu and Marwan Mahmud. The "demonic duo" were veterans of Saddam's military and had fought against American forces during the 1991 Gulf War.

As the November 1994 Thanksgiving holiday approached, Abu took Al-Hussaini to Oklahoma City to "start a new life." After helping him settle in, Abu returned to Boston and resumed his employment at Boston Logan International Airport. *Is it mere coincidence that two of the four ill-fated flights on 9/11 had originated from this very airport?* Federal investigators theorized food suppliers had secretly planted the box cutters that the hijackers used to overpower the flight crews and passengers. Would you like to guess *where* Abu worked at Logan? Can we say—*in food catering services for the commercial airlines?*

A final story remains to be told. According to "Randy Christian" (Davis's pseudonym for the owner of the "Cactus Motel"), *three of the 9/11 hijackers visited his establishment a month before the attacks!* (Christian made this startling discovery after seeing the hijackers' pictures on the news.) Davis writes:

> Just four days after the World Trade Center disintegrated on live television, Randy recounted his fantastic story. The self-styled ringleader Mohammed Atta, his dutiful sidekick Marwan Al-Shehhi, and the surviving would-be hijacker Zacarias Moussaoui entered the Cactus Motel lobby in early August of 2001. The trio inquired about renting a room with a kitchenette, but the owner cordially explained there were no vacancies.
>
> Acting as the group's decision maker, Atta sauntered across the room, standing an arm's length from the owner. "We're going to be attending flight school in Norman and would really like to stay at your motel **because we have heard such good things about it,"** the slight framed man insisted as he broke into a broad smile.
>
> Randy considered Atta's persistence quite peculiar given the ample availability of discount motels that provided convenient proximity to the Norman aviation schools.
>
> "Our motel is at least a thirty mile drive, one-way. I'm sure you will have no problem renting a room at a reasonable rate much closer," Randy graciously suggested. But Atta, conspicuously clad in a heavy leather flight jacket on a blistering hot summer day, was not dissuaded. **He gushed with compliments about the "outstanding" reputation of Randy's motel.** In hindsight, the men appointed to die in a few short weeks, intended to deliver yet another humiliating slap in the face to American law enforcement by signing their names to the register at the very motel that served as the staging grounds for their Middle Eastern predecessors, as if to say, "Ignore us at your own peril."[83]

In an interview with *LA Weekly* reporter Jim Crogan, Special Agent Dan Vogel summarized the dreadful consequences of the FBI's refusal to pursue *The Third Terrorist*:

> What they (FBI) did was unconscionable. . . . The American people deserved the truth and the Bureau needed to look into this Middle East network here in Oklahoma City. If they had, maybe they would have come upon the network behind the September 11 attacks. But I guess that now, we'll never know.[84]

"THEY WILL DESTROY ME"

As a fitting conclusion to this chapter, I will recount the content of a most enlightening e-mail I received from Jayna Davis on May 22, 2004. With *The Third Terrorist* making its debut on *The New York Times* bestseller list, Mrs. Davis found herself receiving more than enough press coverage. However, for some reason, the GOP appeared about as willing to acknowledge her findings as the FBI had been. She wrote:

> To give you a true picture of the political pressure under which Mr. Bodansky was working, I must relate the disturbing revelations gleaned from my recent journey inside the Washington beltway.
>
> I am saddened and utterly shocked to learn that while many in Washington know firsthand that the evidence presented in *The Third Terrorist* rises to the level of proven fact, they have justified not dredging up the past for the sake of the Republican Party. After all, if the outcome of such a re-opening of the OKC case proved to be messy then the Republicans would be blamed for not investigating my research in 1997 when the U.S. Task Force on Terrorism and Unconventional Warfare took custody of the investigative materials.
>
> That said, I am even more grieved by the candid conversation I had with a high ranking career congressman at the Capitol Hill Club on Wednesday evening. He sorrowfully confessed that he was well aware of my investigative work as far back as 1996 and did nothing because **"they will destroy me."** When asked to define "they" he nodded his head and shrugged his shoulders. When asked who was ultimately responsible to investigate my evidence on an Iraqi John Doe who went on to work at Boston Logan, he proclaimed, "I was."
>
> What do I do now? I, too, fear that Americans must face the very real possibility these fundamentalist extremists will once again commit wholesale mass murder.
>
> I felt as if you and your friends deserve to know the truth. I am prepared to name the Congressman and suggest you write him a letter or contact him personally to explain his reprehensible actions that might have contributed, in part, to the massive intel failure of 9-11.

In a follow-up correspondence, Mrs. Davis identified the party in question as Republican Congressman *James Saxton* who formerly served as the co-chair of the Congressional Task Force. She then added:

Please let me know what he says. If he tries to deny the statements, remember there were several witnesses at the table.

On May 26, 2004, I mailed Congressman Saxton a six-page missive confronting him with Mrs. Davis's allegations. As this book was going to press, the "'honorable' gentleman from New Jersey" had yet to reply.

A FITTING MEMORIAL

The Journal Record Building stands directly across the street from the site where the Alfred P. Murrah Federal Building once existed. Originally constructed as a Masonic temple, it now serves as the Oklahoma City National Memorial. A heartfelt message was left on the facade by a courageous band of rescuers. Visitors are confronted by the convicting text:

Team 5
4-19-95

We Search For the truth
We seek Justice.
The Courts Require it.
The Victims Cry for it.
And GOD Demands it!

18

9/11 – An Overview

"For he bringeth down them that dwell on high . . ."
(Isaiah 26:5a)

ECH. SGT. JEREMY Powell's heart was pounding heavily as he raised his hand and started waving it vigorously to get attention. James Bamford writes:

> He sat in a quiet pool of emerald light, staring at a matrix of slowly moving white dots, cryptic flashing letter-number combinations, lines going in all directions, and green circles that would form at the center and then expand outward, like a ripple from a stone tossed in a morning pond. Represented by every dot was a small cross-section of humanity, packed in an aluminum tube and traveling in the air near the speed of sound. Jeremy Powell was sitting in front of a glowing radar screen, scanning the skies over America's East Coast for any indication of attack, invasion, or airborne drug dealers.
>
> This green room, like a leprechaun's lair, was the Operations Command Center of "Huntress Control"—the Air National Guard's Northeast Air Defense Sector. . . .
>
> A moment earlier, Powell had taken a call from Boston Center. "Watch supervisor, I have a possible hijack of American 11 heavy," a Boston military liaison with the Federal Aviation Administration (FAA) told him. "Recommend notifying NORAD." . . . It was 8:40 a.m.[1]

Unbeknownst to Powell, over twenty-five minutes earlier, the "small cross-section of humanity" aboard American Airlines 11 had already been reduced by five—two first-class flight attendants, a business-class passenger and both pilots being slashed to death by Mohamed Atta and his band of terrorists. As the blood-soaked "aluminum tube" careened southward toward New York City (having diverted from its original flight path to Los Angeles), two courageous stewardesses huddled out of sight, using crew telephones to relay critical details in real time to American Airlines ground manager Michael Woodward at Boston's Logan Airport. One of the women, Betty Ong, repeatedly interjected, "Pray for us."[2]

Unfortunately, her prayers would go unanswered (with the hundreds of generic "Oh my God's!" exclaimed throughout the crisis moving Heaven even less), the God of our Founding Fathers having decided that the wayward nation was in serious need of a 9-1-1 call. The fate of the passengers and crew would henceforth be in the hands of four religious fanatics. Having passed their final days in strip clubs and adult bookstores, the "backslidden" Muslims were undoubtedly anticipating their promised upgrade to "heavenly virgins" as they crashed Flight 11 into the North Tower of the World Trade Center at 8:46 a.m., shouting, "Allah be praised!"

With the force of three additional hijackings yet to be felt, the single darkest day in American history was well underway. When Pakistani Ambassador Maleeha Lodhi reacted to Richard Armitage's post-9/11 pressure to side with the United States by attempting to explain the background to Pakistan's relationship with the Taliban, the deputy secretary of state cut him short: "History starts today," he said.[3] However, at the time of this writing (nearly forty months later), while most Americans have been induced to put the tragedy behind them—in order to focus on the so-called "War on Terror"—a cloud of ambiguity continues to vex a discerning minority.

To gain *any* insight as to what *really* happened on 9/11, the following resources must be employed: Holy Scripture, demonstrable facts, historical precedent, and reasonable conjecture.

With all due respect to the 9/11 Commission, the first five verses of Isaiah 26 shed more light on *why* the World Trade Center and Pentagon were attacked than all five hundred pages of the official published report. Verse one states: *"In that day shall this song be sung in the land of Judah; We have a strong city; salvation will God appoint for walls and bulwarks."* While technically a Kingdom Age passage, the truth of God's willingness to protect any nation that honors His Word was appropriated by Great Britain and the United States on numerous occasions. From the defeat of the Spanish Armada through the evacuation at Dunkirk to the victorious Battle of Midway, the Lord has manifested His ability to protect whom He will.

Through the centuries, any nation desiring to move within the walls and bulwarks of this strong city had to agree to only one condition; verse two states, *"Open ye the gates, that the righteous nation which keepeth the truth may enter in."* You could say that *righteousness* is the sole *rent* God requires nations to pay. If a tenant will fulfill *his* part of the lease, the Landlord will certainly do the same; verses three and four state, *"Thou wilt keep him in perfect peace, whose mind is stayed on thee: because he trusteth in thee. Trust ye in the LORD for ever: for in the LORD JEHOVAH is everlasting strength."*

Thus, the only question that pertains to 9/11 is whether or not our nation's rent was current. The answer should be painfully and frightfully obvious. America's sins are too many and too vile to examine here. Suffice it to say, *witchcraft, sodomy,* and *abortion* were hardly the cultural staples that inspired hymns like *America the Beautiful, My Country 'Tis of Thee* and *God Bless America.*

Would the Landlord then be within His rights to send out a late notice or two? Would President Clinton's impeachment proceedings, Y2K and the 2000 election crisis qualify as such? And should the problem persist, would He have the right to initiate eviction proceedings? Would He possess the needed *alibi* to move America's furniture out on the curb? Verse five explains how JEHOVAH handles deadbeats: *"For he bringeth down them that dwell on high; the lofty city, he layeth it low; he layeth it low, even to the ground; he bringeth it even to the dust."* Since America's Christians have rejected the King James Bible, perhaps an appropriate paraphrase of Isaiah 26:5 would be, "For he bringeth down the Twin Towers; the Big Apple, he layeth it low; he layeth it low, even to the Ground Zero; he bringeth it even to the dust."

While Psalm 33:12a states, *"Blessed is the nation whose God is the LORD,"* David also wrote, *"The wicked shall be turned into hell, and all the nations that forget God"* (Psalm 9:17). Note the twenty-first-century application of this text in the radio transmission of NYPD helicopter pilot Timothy Hayes, as related by Bamford:

"Unable to land on roof. . . . Captain, this is impossible. This is undoable. I can't see the roof." He later added, **"The smoke had covered 90 percent of the entire roof,** so I couldn't even see the roof to make an evaluation of where we could go. **We were looking at probably fifteen to twenty stories burning simultaneously. Probably well over a thousand degrees, you know, if not more.** I never felt so helpless and guilty in my life.

When you get there with these millions of dollars of equipment . . . and there was absolutely nothing we could do. There was nothing. We couldn't get on that roof, we couldn't get people out of that building." . . .

As he pulled away, the hundreds or thousands still trapped on the upper floors of the towers saw their last hope disappear. . . . **The towers had now become sky-high chimneys.**[4]

For those with spiritual discernment, the very location where Jeremy Powell made his first radar observation of AA11 was not without symbolic relevance. The site is *Rome*, New York. Historically, the American flag first flew in the face of battle, during the American Revolution at Fort Stanwix, situated in what is now the center of the city of Rome. Unfortunately, however, less than a year into our nation's post-9/11 "revival of patriotism," the U.S. Circuit Court of Appeals for the Ninth Circuit ruled in *Newdow* v. *U.S. Congress* that the phrase "under God" in the Pledge of Allegiance violates the Establishment Clause of the First Amendment of the Constitution. So, as "fate" would have it, Francis Bellamy, the Baptist minister who authored the original version of the Pledge (the phrase "under God" being added in 1954) "just happens" to be buried in the local cemetery!

00001

While I realize many of the victims of 9/11 were probably hardworking men and women of character, and that their untimely deaths caused immeasurable grief for their families and friends—*the Bible remains true nonetheless.* God *will* judge *any* nation that repudiates His infallible Word! (And the last time I checked, nations were comprised of *people*.) *"Hear, O earth: behold, I will bring evil upon this people, even the fruit of their thoughts* [Howard Stern, Jerry Springer, Hugh Hefner, Michael Jackson, Harry Potter, etc.], *because they have not hearkened unto my words, nor to my law, but rejected it"* (Jeremiah 6:19). Consequently, a fitting depiction of Ground Zero could be Job 40:11-13: *"Cast abroad the rage of thy wrath . . . Look on every one that is proud, and bring him low; and tread down the wicked in their place. Hide them in the dust together . . . "* The sad truth is, had the unsaved victims of 9/11 heard a clear presentation of the Gospel on 9/10, probably most, if not all, would have rejected Jesus Christ as personal Lord and Saviour. (Matthew 7:13-14)

And the same would apply to those who survived the attacks, along with the grieving family members of those who did not. Shockingly, the vast majority of 9/11 funerals were conducted by a Bible-rejecting denomination, governed by thousands of dress-wearing child molesters! (*"Am I therefore become your enemy, because I tell you the truth?"* Galatians 4:16)

The theme of "divine retribution" has represented the most politically incorrect message in history. (The 2004 killer tsunami that wiped out a considerable portion of Indonesia *undoubtedly* put a damper on the bloody persecution of Christians by that nation's 85 percent Muslim population.) It constitutes the *last* sermon rebellious men will ever receive. Thus, in Acts 7:52a, Stephen boldly asked the council, *"Which of the prophets have not your fathers persecuted?"* This is why Jerry Falwell recanted after his "conservative" media pals threatened to stone *him* for having suffered a momentary flashback to the convictions of his youth.

Though not a social masochist by nature (while working for British Airways in my unconverted days, I could down Scotch with the best of them at the corporate Speedbird Club on Manhattan's Park Avenue), I am perfectly willing to suffer reproach for proclaiming the truth about America's sin and God's judgment. I don't know if you listen to *your* boss; I can only pay attention to *mine*: *"Cry aloud, spare not, lift up thy voice like a trumpet, and shew my people their transgression . . ."* (Isaiah 58:1a).

Accordingly, I would ask of my own detractors—*Do you know what the word "duh" means?* In case you are unaware, may I tell you who the first casualty was on 9/11? As the man of God states in Job 21:3b, *". . . after that I have spoken, mock on"*—let the record show that victim No. 00001 at Ground Zero "just happened" to be a *sodomite* Roman Catholic priest with the last name of *Judge*, as in *"He shall judge among the heathen, he shall fill the places with the dead bodies . . ."* (Psalm 110:6a). Describing "'Father' Mike" (Matthew 23:9) as "a devout, gay, recovering-alcoholic Catholic priest," the *New York Metro* dubbed him "the first and most famous victim of the World Trade Center attack."[5]

Mychal Judge was one of five chaplains assigned to the FDNY. He was also a member of the Catholic sodomite activist group "Dignity." In March 2000, Judge marched in an alternative sodomite St. Patrick's Day Parade in Queens. Fire Commissioner Thomas Von Essen stated, "I had no problem with it. I actually knew about his homosexuality when I was in the Uniformed Firefighters Association."[6] Former FDNY officer Steven McDonald called the filthy pervert "a living example of Jesus Christ."[7] At his funeral, the "Reverend" Michael Duffy said that Judge had to be the first casualty of the World Trade Center because God required his services! "There were too many dying firemen for him to bless while still living," he fantasized. "Judge had to greet them on the other side, with his arms outstretched."[8] In their sugar-coated take on the "tragedy," the bridge-building, ecumenical publication *Christianity Today* quoted Mayor Giuliani as stating, "He was a saint, a wonderful man."[9] Indeed, a worldwide movement is currently underway to have the dead Franciscan canonized a saint. Meanwhile, a Hudson River ferry and a stretch of W. 31st Street have been named in his honor. Most recently, Pope John Paul II formally accepted Mike's helmet from a visiting FDNY delegation.

Finally, in their rush to appease Rome, the apostates at *Christianity Today* helped to perpetuate a popular myth as to *how* the sodomite died. They write, "Before Judge administered last rites to an injured firefighter, he removed his helmet. Falling debris from the tower hit by American Flight 11 killed him."[10] I don't *think* so! According to Numbers 16:29, when the Lord wants to make a point, he will occasionally cause men to die an "*uncommon* death." How's *this* for uncommon? The *New York Metro* reports:

> Bill Cosgrove, a lieutenant in the Manhattan Traffic Task Force, was in a car on West Broadway when he heard on his radio about the first plane hitting the World Trade Center. He raced to Tower One to help guide rescuers in and out of the area. Later, inside the building, he found a group of firemen including Christian Waugh, clustered around a granite desk at the tower's emergency command post. "I was just about to tell them which way to drive," says Cosgrove. "That's when the whole building shook. The lights went out. And there was this giant vacuum sound." Waugh dropped to the ground. Others, including Cosgrove, ducked into the nearby stairwell. "We thought it was our building that was collapsing," says Cosgrove. "It wasn't." He's now pretty sure it was Tower Two. "The pressure was sucking the windows out of Tower One."
>
> The men waited in total darkness. Abruptly, they were enveloped in plumes of smoke, fireproofing, and pulverized cement. "You couldn't breathe," says Cosgrove. "You couldn't see. It was totally dark. Someone shouted, 'Everybody hold hands!'" Gasping, their eyes stinging, the men reached out for one another and started a slow, awkward march out of the stairwell and back through the lobby. They had proceeded no more than

twenty paces when it happened. Cosgrove tripped over something. A body. Everyone stopped. One of the firefighters aimed his flashlight low across the ground. A halo of light framed a man's face. Everyone saw it. "Oh, my God," they began to shout. "It's Father Mike."

He wasn't buried under much rubble; his body, even his face, was still perfectly intact. They took his pulse. Nothing. "I took an arm" says Cosgrove. "Someone else took an arm. Two other guys took his ankles." Waugh grabbed him by the waist, and together the men carried him out of the building. They found a bunch of broken chairs on an outdoor plaza and nestled Judge into one of them, so that they could carry him down a staircase to the street.[11]

Thus, we understand that the first official victim of 9/11 died in the *North* Tower from the collapse of the *South* Tower. (The dead priest was subsequently given the last rites of his denomination as his body lay at the intersection of Church and Vesey streets—a most significant location, as we shall later discover.)

About this time I can hear shouts of protest: "Dr. Grady, how could you be so insensitive, etc.?" In reply I would point my critics to about 100,000 males who were sodomized in their youth by "Father" Mike's celibate colleagues. Can someone tell me what difference there is between the sexual "proclivities" of Mychal Judge and those of Michael Jackson? Quite frankly, having marched with my Irish father in the New York St. Patrick's Day parade in the early 1960s, I am at a loss as to why a sodomite priest would suddenly be held in high esteem by one of the most macho professions in America. And why should I, as a *Baptist* minister, have to do the pope's "dirty work" for him? The Biblical mandate for *true* shepherds is blunt and to the point—*"Them that sin rebuke before all, that others also may fear"* (I Timothy 5:20). Furthermore, you'd think this would be especially relevant in the midst of a "Church"-wide pedophilia epidemic that makes Jim Bakker and Jimmy Swaggart look like Salvation Army bellringers.

WHAT'S WRONG WITH THIS PICTURE?

Richard Clarke, national coordinator for security, infrastructure protection, and counterterrorism under Presidents Bill Clinton and George W. Bush, began his opening statement before the 9/11 Commission by personally apologizing to the American people for having failed to protect them. A similar confession was made by David Kay, former head of the Iraqi Survey Group who told the Senate Armed Services Committee on January 28, 2004, "We were almost all wrong, and I certainly include myself." He stated that 85 percent of the work was done and he did not expect to find WMD stockpiles in Iraq. "It is going to take an outside inquiry," he said, to investigate the intelligence failure on WMD. He argued that it was "important to acknowledge failure" . . .[12] The long-anticipated final report of the Commission boiled down to the following two conclusions: *Everyone* was guilty of "failing" *somewhere* and *somehow* the "failures" would have to figure out a way to prevent future "failures."

However, although the "esteemed" Commission was correct in many respects, absolutely *no one* in Washington has the guts to acknowledge *why* the failures persist. Because America has rejected its Judeo-Christian heritage, the Bible is now irrelevant. The reason our nation is currently headed toward inevitable denouement was given by Jesus Christ two thousand years ago—*". . . for without me ye can do nothing"* (John 15:5c).

While a good deal of the bad things happening in America are conspiracy related, a significant number of our problems continue to be *self*-inflicted. The first of twenty end-day character flaws prophesied in II Timothy 3:2-5 reads, *"For men shall be lovers of their own selves."* When our country revered the Word of God, Christian patriots like Nathan Hale were the norm. Facing the gallows, the humble school teacher issued his noble remark, "I regret that I have but one life to give for my country." How does *that* caliber of selfless devotion compare to the internecine warfare that rages within the federal bureaucracy? In his book *Against All Enemies*, Clarke pretty well summed up the basic reason why the FBI and CIA would rather let America go to Hell than cooperate with each other—"Turf is a powerful thing in Washington."[13] Senator Bob Graham, former chairman of the Senate Select Committee on Intelligence, concurs, adding in his own book, *Intelligence Matters:*

> Ultimately, I would reach the conclusion that September 11 was the culmination of a long trail of American intelligence failures both at home and abroad—an almost bewildering array of mistakes, missteps, and missed opportunities caused by warring governmental cultures, bureaucratic incompetence and neglect, lack of imagination, and perhaps, most tragic of all, a failure of leadership at the highest levels of government.[14]

Graham's disturbing exposé documents *twelve* fateful instances where the tragedy of 9/11 might have been averted—but for a "web of complicity." The fourth of these missed opportunities is just plain unbelievable! "The FBI had an informant who was extremely close to two of the September 11 hijackers, and actually housed one of them, yet the existence of this informant and the scope of his contacts with the hijackers were covered up."[15]

The first time man started getting bigger than his britches, the Holy Trinity declared, *"Go to, let us go down, and there confound their language, that they may not understand one another's speech"* (Genesis 11:7). Contrary to what deists believe, the Lord has always been willing to throw in the proverbial monkey wrench when needed. This is why police, fire and ambulance personnel were unable to adequately communicate with one another on 9/11, thus experiencing a higher number of fatalities. The owner of a New Jersey telecommunications firm who had tried unsuccessfully to convince the city of New York to upgrade its inept system told me that the real problem stemmed from a standard communications breakdown within the corrupt bureaucracy itself. Air Force Lt. Gen. Michael Hayden, director of the ultra-secret National Security Agency, has acknowledged that our intelligence gathering modalities have fallen woefully behind the surge within the telecommunications industry. Bamford writes:

> According to Hayden, "NSA downsized about one-third of its manpower and about the same proportion of its budget in the decade of the 1990s [while President Clinton was wandering around with those nuclear launch codes rubberbanded to his credit cards]. That is the same decade when packetized communications (the e-communications we have all become familiar with) surpassed traditional communications. That is the same decade when mobile cell phones increased from 16 million to 741 million—an increase of nearly 50 times. That is the same decade when Internet users went from about 4 million to 361 million—an increase of over 90 times. Half as many landlines were laid in the last six years of the 1990s as in the whole previous history of the world. In that same decade of the 1990s, international telephone traffic went from 38 billion minutes to over 100 billion. (By 2002) the world's population will spend over 180 billion minutes on the phone in international calls alone."
>
> Looking back, said Hayden, no one would have predicted such enormous growth [the general should have read Daniel 12:4]. "Forty years ago, there were 5,000 stand alone computers, no fax machines, and not one

cellular phone. Today, there are over 180 million computers—most of them networked. There are roughly 14 million fax machines . . . and those numbers continue to grow. The telecommunications industry is making a $1 trillion investment to encircle the world in millions of miles of high-bandwidth fiber-optic cable. They are aggressively investing in the future."

Simply sending an internal e-mail, Hayden discovered, was a major problem. It takes "an act of God," he said, to send an e-mail message to all of the agency's 38,000 employees because of NSA's sixty-eight separate e-mail systems. Nor could the three computers on his desk communicate with one another.[16]

So how can our various intelligence agencies be expected to "communicate with one another" when they can't even get their own computers to cooperate internally? Now you know why former FBI director Louie Freeh was "indicted" for computer illiteracy. In January 2005, FBI officials conceded that their long anticipated $170 million computer overhaul project, known as the Virtual Case File, was *another* colossal failure. Senator Patrick Leahy described it as "a train wreck in slow motion." But— "Don't worry, be happy"—*these are only the folks in charge of keeping us safe!*

The extent of America's growing ineptness was illustrated on August 20, 1998, when President Clinton ordered a cruise missile attack on a bin Laden camp at Zhawar Kili (eastern Afghanistan) in retaliation for the bombings of our embassies in East Africa. The "attack" was a joke! When the smoke cleared following the impact of sixty-five U.S. Tomahawk cruise missiles, *costing $750,000 each*, there were about twenty-one people dead, with scores of others wounded. Osama and his cronies were nowhere to be found. (A second strike sent thirteen additional missiles streaking across the Indian Ocean to "take out" an *aspirin factory* in the Sudanese capital of Khartoum.)

With all that hot air about the high cost of Clinton's impeachment proceedings (which "just happened" to be cresting at the time of the "attack"), the president's *failed* hit on Osama cost the U.S. taxpayers about $2,321,428 per unintended victim. As an added irony, the White House press corps, accompanying the president to Martha's Vineyard on August 20 (three days after his televised "apology" for "Monicagate") actually passed the time prior to his impromptu national security announcement about the missile strikes—watching the film *Wag the Dog* (in which a president fabricates a phony war with Albania to distract the public from a breaking sex scandal).[17]

However, a stronger indication of our nation's growing weakness was the *fact* of the "attack" itself. Though most Americans were too preoccupied with television and video games to have noticed, *President Clinton fired sixty-five cruise missiles at an individual; a man without a country.* The title of Yossef Bodansky's 1999 *New York Times* No. 1 bestseller is *Bin Laden: The Man Who Declared War on America.* As the twenty-first century unfolds, the mightiest nation in the history of mankind, and the world's preeminent nuclear power, appears to be at war with *a solitary, stick-toting, towel-headed troglodyte who seems to be holding his own to boot!*

The very idea was too preposterous for Michael Moore to accept. Relating his comments to various news reports that allege bin Laden is suffering from kidney problems, the pagan writes:

> How could a guy sitting in a cave in Afghanistan, hooked up to dialysis, have directed and overseen the actions of nineteen terrorists for two years in the United States and then plotted so perfectly the hijacking of four planes and then guaranteed that three of them would end up precisely on their targets? How did Osama do this? I mean, I can't get this computer to stop crashing every time I type the word "gingivitis." I can't get a cell signal from here to Queens! And he's supposed to have pulled off all of September 11 from his little cave, 10,000 miles away? What was he doing, then, when we started the bombing over there? Was he running from cave to cave in Afghanistan with his tubes and dialysis machine trailing behind him? Or, um, maybe there was a dialysis machine in every third cave in Afghanistan. Yeah, that's it! A real modern country, Afghanistan! It has about fifteen miles of railroad track. And lots of dialysis machines, I guess.[18]

Well, gee, Mike, *maybe God is not as mad at Osama as he presently is at America.* At least this is the Biblical precedent—but how could *you* understand such matters? (*"Wisdom is too high for a fool . . ."* Proverbs 24:7a.) The Lord commissioned Jeremiah to deliver the following "patriotic" message to Zedekiah, king of Judah, with regard to Nebuchadnezzar's siege of Jerusalem:

> *Thus saith the LORD God of Israel; Behold, I will turn back the weapons of war that are in your hands, wherewith ye fight against the king of Babylon, and against the Chaldeans, which besiege you without the walls, and I will assemble them into the midst of this city.*

And I myself will fight against you with an outstretched hand and with a strong arm, even in anger, and in fury, and in great wrath.

And I will smite the inhabitants of this city, both man and beast: they shall die of a great pestilence. . . .

For I have set my face against this city for evil, and not for good, saith the LORD: it shall be given into the hand of the king of Babylon, and he shall burn it with fire. (Jeremiah 21:4-6,10)

There has been no shortage of telltale signs that our country is on a slippery slope with God. These indicators connect the dots between America's brash provocations and the Lord's swift retaliation. Remember, because our national leaders are a product of Dewey's corrupt secular universities, they are incapable of considering such warnings as, *"Beware of him, and obey his voice, provoke him not . . ."* (Exodus 23:21). A mere five days after President Clinton was sworn into office, Mir Amal Kasi parked his pickup truck near the entrance to CIA Headquarters in Langley, Virginia, and exited the vehicle with an AK-47 assault rifle. At the height of morning rush hour, the Muslim "redneck" began methodically firing at several cars stopped at a traffic light, waiting to turn down the agency's access road. When he finally ran out of ammo, he calmly climbed back into the truck and returned to his local apartment. The carnage on that bitter cold morning of January 25, 1993, claimed two lives with another three seriously wounded. The next day Kasi boarded a plane to Pakistan. He would later remark, "I decided to do the shooting at the CIA or the Israeli embassy but decided to shoot at the CIA because it was easier because CIA officials are not armed."[19] A month later, an Iranian-sponsored Islamist terrorist cell in the New York/New Jersey area detonated a huge car bomb in the underground parking lot of the World Trade Center.

Of the countless ways President Clinton provoked the Lord, his appointment of Madeleine Albright as secretary of state was a classic no-win situation for American foreign policy in the Middle East. While she was definitely on the same pro-Palestinian page as her boss, the fact that she was both a woman *and* a Jew constituted a major insult and an insurmountable barrier to her diplomatic counterparts in the land of Allah.

Her "on again-off again" relationship with Yasser Arafat bordered on the lunatic fringe. "What are you doing to our Arafat?" she would ask the Israelis whenever he went into one of his frequent "mood swings."[20] Yasser definitely had his problems; Bodansky relates, "Arafat had markedly raised the number of armed guards around him, and he never moved without his 'emergency button'—an electronic buzzer that activated an elaborate security system." According to one of those present at a meeting between Israeli and Palestinian officials, "When Arafat was momentarily separated from his emergency button, he went crazy."[21]

On another occasion, the PLO leader went berserk at 30,000 feet when Israeli Prime Minister Ehud Barak directed his Air Force commander to prevent Arafat's plane from landing at Gaza Airport. Bodansky writes, "Having been informed of these instructions, Arafat rushed to the cockpit, grabbed a microphone and started cursing anybody who might be listening."[22] According to Israeli officials, the spectacle lasted about an hour and a half, until Arafat was able to convince Egyptian President Hosni Mubarak to intercede with Barak, whereupon the plane was finally allowed to land.

My favorite "Kodak moment" of Madame Albright and Yasser Arafat occurred in the U.S. Embassy in Paris on October 3, 2000. Having apparently suffered another "anxiety attack," Arafat abruptly stormed out of a meeting with the secretary of state. Bodansky confirms, "Albright literally ran after him, shouting to the Marine guards, 'Shut the gates!'"[23] Effectively detained in the Embassy compound, Yasser returned to the room but refused to cooperate. (It is not known whether or not he set off his "emergency buzzer.") Comparing this nutty scene with that august encounter between our first secretary of state and Moses Seixas will help you to see how far America has come.

Not to be outdone in the "politically correct" department, President-elect George W. Bush stacked *his* cabinet and key administration posts with women and minorities. Of his first nineteen appointments, only *eight* were white males. As previously noted, God elected Japheth as the progenitor of Western civilization. And yes, the Bible *does* teach that the male gender has the higher *economic* value in most areas (see Leviticus 27). While the Lord has been known to allow an occasional exception to His own rule (Deborah, Queen Victoria, Kim Phuc, etc.), you sure wouldn't want to try forcing any of that affirmative action nonsense in *His* face. For instance, if you were to put, say, a Hamite male in charge of foreign policy and a non-married, Hamite female in charge of national security—*your nation just might experience its greatest breach of national security in history perpetrated by foreign terrorists, and all before nine months had passed!* From a cultural perspective, the ultimate confrontation of the 9/11 Commission hearings occurred when New York City native Attorney Richard Ben-Veniste literally had to force "Dr. Rice" to reveal the title of the then-classified Presidential Daily Brief (PDB) for August 6, 2001. It was too funny watching the evasive Rice, who almost got away with not appearing before the Commission at all, use her facial expressions and body language to reply nonchalantly, "I believe it was 'Bin Laden Determined to Attack *Inside* the United States.'"

The sad fact that America is no longer as sharp as she used to be was evidenced by various events preceding 9/11, as well as by those which occurred on the day of the tragedy itself. As the expression goes, "What's wrong with this picture?" For instance, when President Bush read the critical PDB on August 6, he was relaxing at his Crawford ranch, dressed in what the press calls his "Crawford casual" ensemble—jeans with a big belt buckle, a short-sleeved button-down shirt, and cowboy boots.[24] Bush had decided to spend more than a couple of days there— he was going to kick back at Crawford for the entire month of August, purportedly to take walks and fish for bass. The president defended his long vacation. "I just want to remind you all I love to go walking out there, seeing the cows," he said. "Occasionally, they talk to me, being the good listener that I am."[25] Craig Unger writes:

> But the press didn't like it. "By the time President Bush returns to Washington on Labor Day after the longest presidential vacation in 32 years, he will have spent all or part of 54 days since the inauguration at his parched but beloved ranch," the *Washington Post* observed. "That's almost a quarter of his presidency. . . . Throw in four days last month at his parents' seaside estate in Kennebunkport, Maine, and 38 full or partial days at the presidential retreat at Camp David, and Bush will have spent 42 percent of his presidency at vacation spots or en route."[26]

(Dr. Jack Hyles, the late pastor of the giant First Baptist Church of Hammond, Indiana, took *his* charge so seriously that he worked over thirty years without taking a *single* day off; i.e., how one can run the entire nation while taking month-long vacations at a time remains a mystery to me.)

After the August 6 meeting was concluded, Condoleezza Rice showed up to assure the president that there was nothing to worry about. Unger writes, "According to Rice, the memo [PDB] was merely analytical and historical, discussing the practices al Qaeda had used in the past."[27] (This was the same bologna she stated during her televised appearance at the 9/11 Commission hearings.) Thus, with Condi's reassurance, "Bush placed a white cowboy hat on his head and drove off in his truck to the canyons. He spent the rest of the day fishing for bass in his pond."[28] Over the next thirty days, the president would have no further meetings about terrorism.

Apparently President Bush took his cows more seriously than the highly classified warnings of Richard Clarke and the CIA. Excerpts from the two-page August 6 PDB follow:

> **Clandestine, foreign government, and media reports indicate Bin Laden since 1997 has wanted to conduct terrorist attacks in the US.** Bin Laden implied in US television interviews in 1997 and 1998 that his followers would follow the example of World Trade Center bomber Ramzi Yousef and "bring the fighting to America."
>
> After US missile strikes on his base in Afghanistan in 1998, Bin Laden told followers he wanted to retaliate in Washington, according to a (foreign intelligence) service. . . .
>
> **Al-Qa'ida members—including some who are US citizens—have resided in or traveled to the US for years, and the group apparently maintains a support structure that could aid attacks.** Two al-Qa'ida members found guilty in the conspiracy to bomb our Embassies in East Africa were US citizens, and a senior EIJ member lived in California in the mid 1990s. . . .
>
> FBI information . . . indicates patterns of suspicious activity in this country consistent with preparations for hijackings or other types of attacks, including recent surveillance of federal buildings in New York.
>
> The FBI is conducting approximately 70 full field investigations throughout the US that it considers Bin Laden-related. CIA and the FBI are investigating a call to our Embassy in the UAE in May saying that a group of Bin Laden supporters was in the US planning attacks with explosives.[29]

The problem with George and Condi was that neither was the best "man" for their respective jobs. While campaigning in 2000, Bush remarked, "Nobody needs to tell me what to believe. But I *do* need somebody to tell me where Kosovo is."[30] Pulling another campaign gaffe, Bush drew a blank when a writer for *Glamour* magazine asked him to identify the Taliban. The embarrassed writer had to drop a hint. "Repression of women in Afghanistan?" he offered. "Oh, I thought you said some band," Bush replied. "The Taliban in Afghanistan. Absolutely. Repressive."[31] (Prior to his inauguration the would-be leader of the free world had only been out of the United States on *three* occasions.)

And Dr. Rice isn't that "swift" either. Richard Clarke wrote in *Against All Enemies*, "As I briefed Rice on al Qaeda, her facial expression gave me the impression that she had never heard the expression before." He then relates how he suddenly felt the need to give the national security advisor an emergency précis: "Most people think of it as Usama bin Laden's group, but it's much more than that. It's a network of affiliated terrorist organizations with cells in over fifty countries, including the U.S."[32]

Bush spent the afternoon of August 7 hitting golf balls at the Ridgewood Country Club in Waco (the town where his predecessor incinerated 174 Americans in 1993). By now the intelligence community was beside itself. "Throughout the summer of 2001," said NSA Director Michael V. Hayden, "we had more than thirty warnings that something was imminent."[33] Many seasoned officials called the heightened activity "unprecedented."[34] Congressman Porter J. Goss, chairman of the House Intelligence Committee said, "The chatter level went way off the charts."[35]

Mohamed Atta, the reputed ringleader of the 9/11 attacks, had already been allowed to re-enter the United States on three occasions in 2001, despite the fact that he had violated his visa by taking flying lessons and had let it expire in 2000, was known to have terrorist connections, and was under FBI surveillance.[36]

In April, Atta was cited for a traffic violation in Broward County, Florida; then, three months later, stopped in the same county for speeding. Also in April, Nawaf al-Hazmi, one of the four terrorists who hijacked AA77, was ticketed along Interstate 40 in western Oklahoma, driving 85 miles per hour in a 70-mile-per-hour zone. He had a valid California driver's license and an address in San Diego. Believe it or not, the reprobate actually mailed in his ticket and the $138 fine in money orders! And then on September 9, only two days before the hijacking, Ziad Jarrah, who is believed to have been at the controls of United Flight 93 when it crashed in Pennsylvania, was pulled over by a Maryland state trooper on I-95 going 90 miles per hour in a 65-mile-per-hour zone. The trooper determined that Ziad's license and registration were in order. The ticket was later found in the glove box of the rental car at Newark airport.[37]

Clarke writes, "By late June, Tenet and I were convinced that a major series of attacks was about to come. 'It's my sixth sense, but I feel it coming. This is going to be the big one,' Tenet told me."[38]

Yet the president continued to putter around in Crawford, population 705. On August 23, Bush visited the local elementary school where the children showered him with questions. He then shared his afternoon schedule: following a meeting with Dr. Rice, he would call the president of Argentina; have lunch with the first lady; spend time with the family pets; make a call to his personnel office; and last, but not least, take a tree lesson. "We've got a horticulturist coming out from Texas A&M to help us identify the hardwood trees on our beautiful place," he said.[39]

While Bush was taking time for pets and trees, a small coterie of Middle Eastern men unobtrusively checked into the eighty-room Valencia Motel in Laurel, Maryland, just a few miles from the NSA's front gate. Khalid Almihdhar and his confederates would begin the final preparations for their assault on the Pentagon in room 343, a small living room-kitchenette suite. Despite the fact that a specialized CIA unit designed to track al-Qaeda operatives (code-named Alec Station) was aware from January 2000 that Almihdhar had attended a terrorist conference in Kuala Lumpur carrying a multi-entry visa to enter the United States, Bamford notes:

> Never disguising their presence, they checked in using their real names, paid the weekly rent of $308 with a credit card, ate at a local pizza parlor, **visited an adult bookstore**, shopped at the Giant supermarket, washed their clothes at the Sunshine Laundry, and bought weekly memberships at Gold's Gym in nearby Greenbelt. Team member Hani Hanjour, who had a pilot's license, went up with instructors several times at the nearby Freeway Airport in Bowie, and both Mohamed Atta and Ziad Jarrah, the student from war-torn Beirut came to visit.
>
> As millions of intercepted communications from around the world funneled into the agency's giant satellite dishes, **Almihdhar was communicating with Atta and Khalid Shaikh Mohammed back in Afghanistan at the local Kinko's, a few miles away, through simple Internet chat groups**. None of the hijackers had their own computers.[40]

On September 4, 2001, the Principals Committee dealing with al-Qaeda (that Richard Clarke had urgently requested on January 25) finally met. He writes:

> In preparation for that meeting I urged Condi Rice to see the issue cleanly, the Administration could decide that al Qaeda was just a nuisance, a cost of doing business for a superpower (as Reagan and the first President Bush had apparently decided about Hezbollah and Libya when these groups had killed hundreds of Americans), and act accordingly, as it had been doing. Or it could decide that the al Qaeda terrorist group and its affiliates posed an existential threat to the American way of life, in which case we

should do everything that might be required to eliminate the threat. There was no in-between. **I concluded by noting that before choosing from these alternatives, it would be well for Rice to put herself in her own shoes when in the very near future al Qaeda had killed hundreds of Americans: "What will you wish then that you had already done?"**[41]

Though attended by Condoleezza Rice, Colin Powell, Donald Rumsfeld and George Tenet, Clarke would later write that it "was largely a nonevent" as "Rice ended the discussion without a solution."[42] She did pat him on the head by requesting that he finalize a National Security Presidential Directive on al-Qaeda and send it to her for presidential signature.

BODIES FALLING FROM THE SKY

The morning of September 11, 2001, could only be described as surreal. The blessings of God were nowhere in sight. While Timothy Hayes and his NYPD helicopter were circling helplessly above the Twin Towers, Port Authority police officers reported the horrific scene unfolding before them at street level:

> "There's body parts all over the place," said one officer. "So much—bodies blew out of the building. . . . There's got to be hundreds of people killed in there. There's body parts like five blocks away." Another reported, "I've got dozens of bodies, people just jumping from the top of the building onto . . . in front of One World Trade . . . **bodies are just coming from out of the sky.**"[43]

Some dazed pedestrians were literally killed by falling bodies. By 9:09 a.m., people were also beginning to throw themselves out of Tower Two. *At this very moment, America's commander-in-chief was seated in a small, second-grade chair in an elementary school in Sarasota, Florida, listening to seven-year-olds read a book about a goat!* While American citizens were hurling themselves out of the Twin Towers, preferring a quick death to burning alive or suffocating from smoke, the president was smiling as Sandra Kay Daniels's second-graders read, "The-Pet-Goat. A-girl-got-a-pet-goat. But-the-goat-did-some-things-that-made-the-girl's-dad-mad."[44] Ever the "good listener," Bush made a joke, saying: "Really good readers, whew! These must be sixth graders."[45]

Despite the fact that Andrew Card, Bush's chief-of-staff, had whispered to him at 9:06: "A second plane hit the second tower. America is under attack,"[46] the president appeared to be in no hurry. When the lesson was over, he said,

> Hoo! These are great readers. Very impressive! Thank you all so much for showing me your reading skills. I bet they practice too. Don't you? Reading more than they watch TV? Anybody do that? Read more than you watch TV? (Hands go up) Oh that's great! Very good. Very important to practice! Thanks for having me. Very impressive.[47]

Had Bush made this pep talk under normal conditions it would have been hypocritical enough given his own reputation for academic "advancement." Concerning the president's request that the number of pages in his daily PDB be shortened, Bamford writes, "It was prepared, said one former senior intelligence official, with the understanding that Bush was a 'multimodality learner who processes information better through questions and answers while reading along.' In other words, he wasn't much of a reader."[48]

However, during this particular photo shoot the United States of America was under violent attack. Lorie van Auken, whose husband perished on 9/11, reacted with dismay after seeing a video of Bush entertaining the children, stating "I couldn't stop watching the president sitting there, listening to second graders, while my husband was burning in a building."[49] She also questioned how Bush could make a joke.

According to *Washington Times* correspondent, Bill Sammon, the president finally meandered out of the classroom at 9:16 "as if he didn't have a care in the world" and "in the most relaxed manner imaginable."[50]

Meanwhile, several other anomalies were occurring. Because NORAD was "apparently" suffering a massive systemic failure, Major Mike Snyder telling the *Boston Globe* on September 15 that *no* fighters were scrambled until *after* the Pentagon was hit—an hour and eighteen minutes after Flight 11 was known to be hijacked,[51] three F-16s from the 121st Fighter Squadron of the D.C. National Guard were sent instead. (Within a few days, NORAD would reverse Major Snyder's statement by taking the untenable position that *supersonic* aircraft had indeed been scrambled, but had arrived too late.)

As to "what's wrong with this picture"—Can you believe that the three F-16s took off after their targets *without any weapons*? Bamford states, "All, however, were prepared to likely sacrifice their lives **by using their aircraft to ram the hijacked plane**."[52] Lt. Col. Marc H. Sasseville, director of operations for the 113th Air National Guard Wing, later said, "If I played it right, I'd be able to bail out. One hand on the stick and one hand on the ejection handle, trying to ram my airplane into the aft side of the (airliner's) wing."[53] (Such primitive tactics were actually employed by Soviet pilots during World War II.)

Bamford states with bone-chilling frankness, **"On September 11, 2001, the entire United States mainland was protected by just fourteen planes spread out over seven bases."**[54] Back at NORAD's Battle Cab in Rome, New York, Col. Robert Marr concurred with the reality of this assessment, stating after he witnessed Tower Two collapse on television, "I have determined, of course, that with only four aircraft, we cannot defend the whole northeastern United States."[55]

Another incredible "failure" was the apparent inability of several key officials to even learn that the attack was underway. For instance, on the morning of 9/11, George Tenet was having a leisurely breakfast with an old friend, David Boren, in the luxurious atmosphere of Washington's St. Regis Hotel. Bamford writes:

> At their table next to a window overlooking K Street, Tenet was completely unaware of the first plane hitting the World Trade Center, or of the hijackings, or of the "battle stations" alerts. It was not until sometime after the second plane hit Tower Two, after much of the country knew of the terrorism, that the Director of Central Intelligence received a phone call. "Mr. Director, there's a serious problem," an aide told him. Officials in the blue-carpeted CIA Operations Center on the seventh floor of the agency had learned of the attack from CNN. It would be after 9:30 when the Director was back in his office at CIA headquarters.[56]

Air Force Lt. Gen. Michael Hayden was in the middle of a meeting at his NSA office at the time of the attack. His executive assistant, Cindy Farkus, walked in and informed him that a plane had struck the World Trade Center. "The immediate image I had was a light plane, off course, bad flying," he recalled in a January 2004 interview in his office. Bamford continues the sequence of events:

> Shortly after nine at NSA, Cindy Farkus again broke into Lieutenant General Hayden's meeting, but this time she was almost running. Another plane had hit the second tower, she said. "One plane's an accident, two planes is

an attack," said Hayden, who immediately adjourned his meeting and asked Farkus to quickly summon the agency's top security officials to his office.

That was not the way it was supposed to be. NSA was not supposed to find out about an airborne attack on America from CNN, after millions of other Americans had already witnessed it. It was supposed to find out first, from its own ultrasecret warning center, and then pass the information on to the White House and the strategic military forces.[57]

The U.S. military command also seems to have been in the dark on the morning of 9/11. With the chairman of the Joint Chiefs of Staff, Army General Henry Shelton, somewhere over the Atlantic en route to Europe, his deputy, Air Force General Richard Myers, was in charge of the nation's armed forces. Incredibly, he would remain out of the loop during the entire series of attacks. Bamford writes:

> Myers was on Capitol Hill waiting to meet with Georgia Senator Max Cleland about his upcoming confirmation hearings to become the new Joint Chiefs chairman. While in Cleland's outer office, he watched live television reports following the first crash into the World Trade Center and then went into Cleland's office for his routine meeting. There he would remain for the next forty-five minutes, self-promoting his talents to lead the military as the rest of the targets were attacked and the country succumbed to enormous death and destruction.
>
> Through it all, the general in charge of the country's military was completely ignorant of the fact that the United States was under its worst attack in nearly two centuries. Nor did he know that about forty minutes earlier, the President had decided to declare war. "It was initially pretty confusing," Myers later said. "You hate to admit it, but we hadn't thought about this."[58]

Bamford elaborates on Myers's painful concession by stating, with regard to NORAD's massive Operations Center (spread over 4½ acres deep within the bored-out heart of Colorado's Cheyenne Mountain), "Every day, technicians track more than 8,000 objects in near-Earth orbit, most of which is 'space junk.' But since its start, the early-warning system has always been focused on what was coming in, not on what was already present in the country."[59] And so, "Once sealed inside and surrounded by billions of dollars' worth of the most sophisticated intelligence and early-warning equipment, tied into advanced spy satellites and building-size surveillance antennas, the nation's guardians were left to watch the country undergo its worst attack in nearly two centuries on $300 television sets tuned in to CNN."[60]

Some of the more embarrassing images of the day were the panicked evacuations out of New York City and Washington, D.C. While thousands of proud New Yorkers were seen racing across the Brooklyn Bridge, America's growing image of a decadent paper tiger was only amplified by scenes of "bedlam in the Beltway." Describing the mass exodus at our nation's capital as an episode out of *Monty Python's Flying Circus*, Bamford writes:

> "A plane is heading for the Capitol!" said a reporter excitedly. Suddenly senators, members of Congress, staff, and visitors all began charging down hallways, pushing through doors, crowding onto elevators, and running down stairwells in a mad effort to escape the building. "Get off the sidewalks," yelled a Capitol police officer. "Moving everybody back. Moving everybody back."
>
> "The scene was total chaos," said [Tom] Daschle.[61]

To serve as a form of poetic justice, the shameful proceedings unfolded beneath the watchful eye of "Lady Libertas" herself. With Washington no longer the capital of a Bible-believing republic, Secret Service Agent Pete McCauley—his back pressed against the wall of the White House as two F-15 Eagles screeched across the South Lawn at three hundred feet—could only exclaim "Holy Mary, Mother of God."[62] Pete's elevated mediatrix would prove about as useful on 9/11 as those nineteen satanic zodiacs scattered throughout the city.

As everything rises and falls on leadership, America's commander-in-chief set the pace by skedaddling himself. While Tower Two began its implosion, the presidential motorcade pulled onto the tarmac of Sarasota's Bradenton International Airport. Just off to the side was Jones Aviation, where less than a year earlier Mohamed Atta and Marwan Al-Shehhi had taken their flying lessons.

Moments later, as the president's limousine came to a stop at the foot of the portable stairway, Bush made a mad dash for the doorway of Air Force One. "The President, famous for his courtesy, hurried past the local officials who had gathered to see him off," said surprised Florida Republican Congressman Dan Miller, who had earlier been invited to fly back to Washington with Bush.[63]

Safe inside, Bush made his first call to Dick Cheney—the *real* President of the United States! John Dean, a veteran conspirator himself, states in his book *Worse Than Watergate:* "By March 2001, three months into the new presidency, Beltway insiders appreciated that Cheney was doing what he did best, operating out of sight but running the White House."[64] During his early years as Don Rumsfeld's deputy in the Ford administration, Cheney was assigned a codename by the Secret Service that would perfectly fit his disposition: "Backseat." "Bush (is) the nation's chairman of the board, Cheney (is) America's chief executive," the *Washington Post* proclaimed."[65] Susan Page, a columnist for *USA Today*, was more blunt as she described the inner workings at the Bush White House: "You name it, (Cheney) runs it." He "quietly has become prime minister, the go-to guy on everything from appointments to budget to congressional relations."[66] (Now you know how Bush can spend so much time fishing at Crawford.) Dean adds, "Cynics say that if anything happened to Cheney, Bush would become president."[67]

Cheney took Bush's call in the White House presidential bunker (where else?). Though the Secret Service had continually urged him to leave by helicopter for the undisclosed relocation headquarters on the Maryland-Pennsylvania border (known as Site R), Dick had stubbornly refused to budge. Condi Rice was also hunkered down in the command bunker. *They* would call the shots while "Dubya" did what he does best—*listen.*

The Pentagon had also been struck by this time. Initially, Bush and his entourage were *sent* to Barksdale Air Force Base in Shreveport, Louisiana. Like everyone else that day, the president stayed abreast of breaking developments by watching CNN; only in his case, the television signal aboard Air Force One was haphazard (i.e., *literally*, "What's wrong with this picture?"). "Everyone is watching the monitors, trying to get snippets of visual information, and the reception keeps going in and out," recalled Eric Draper, President Bush's personal photographer. "It was like a bad dream," he said. Thus, information, as well as rumors, were passed throughout the plane the old-fashioned way, by word of mouth. "This is like a Tom Clancey novel," Congressman Miller kept thinking. "It can't be happening."[68] Bamford concludes, "As a result, the President and those around him on the plane continually knew less than millions on the ground below them."[69]

Air Force One landed at Barksdale at 11:45 a.m. Bush was immediately taken to Building 245, the headquarters of the Eighth Air Force, where he videotaped an anemic two-minute address—a mere 219 words—to be aired later that day.

> "He looked nervous," said *The New York Times* reporters David E. Sanger and Don Van Natta, Jr. *The Washington Post* reporters Dan Balz and Bob Woodward agreed. "When Bush finally appeared on television from the base conference room," they wrote, "it was not a reassuring picture. He spoke haltingly, mispronouncing several words as he looked down at his notes." Judy Keen of *USA Today* noted that Bush "looked grim. His eyes were red-rimmed." An administration official later admitted, "It was not our best moment."[70]

By then many in the press were beginning to question why the commander-in-chief hadn't gone back to Washington to personally manage the crisis. Yet, rather than return, the decision was made to move even further in the opposite direction. At 2:50 Eastern time, Air Force One, accompanied by two F-16 jet fighters, touched down at Offutt Air Force Base, near Omaha, Nebraska, home of the United States Strategic Command—STRATCOM—the successor to the Cold War Strategic Air Command, SAC. Within minutes, Bush went "down the bunny hole" into the cinder block command structure, several stories underground. Bamford notes, "It was like a scene from *Dr. Strangelove,* or *Seven Days in May.*"[71]

As the president was sweating things out in his secret hideout, many back in Washington were dumbfounded by his absence:

> "I am stunned that he has not come home," said one Bush fund-raiser. "It looks like he is running. This looks bad." William J. Bennett, a former education secretary under President Ronald Reagan . . . said that it was important for Bush to return to the White House as soon as possible. "This is not 1812," he said. "It cannot look as if the President has been run off, or it will look like we can't defend our most important institutions."[72]

Of course, as previously noted, the "real" president had *not* been run out of town.

Bush finally returned later that evening and gave his second speech to a shell-shocked nation. Like the earlier-taped address, it was brief and unimpressive. *The New York Times* reported, "Republican advisors to the administration said the speech fell flat, that it failed to meet either the magnitude of the day's events or the nature of the task ahead."[73]

Before going to bed, Bush wrote in his personal diary: "The Pearl Harbor of the 21st century took place today. We think it's Osama bin Laden."[74] As he turned out the light, the commander-in-chief must have been one tired little puppy. Being chased halfway across his own country by a Middle East boogey man had also been a humiliating experience. However, the president would soon regain that macho Texas *image* we've all come to admire. Indeed, that very evening, following his bellicose address from the Oval Office, Bush nearly bit Rumsfeld's head off when the secretary cautioned that international law allowed the use of force only as a defensive measure and not for retribution: "No," the president yelled across the narrow conference room, "I don't care what the international lawyers say, we are going to kick some [expletive]."[75] At a private conference with Italian Prime Minister Silvio Berlusconi on January 30, 2003, a fully recovered George Bush boasted, "We have put together a lethal military, and we will kick his [expletive]."[76] While such rhetoric might have shocked Bush's guest, it was the kind of talk Colin Powell admired. In a 1995 interview with "African-American" scholar Henry Louis Gates, Jr., Colin summarized his views on the use of force by employing an Ebonics rendition of Bush's words: "I believe in the bully's way of going to war. 'I'm on the street corner, I got my gun, I got my blade, *I'ma kick yo' [expletive]*' "[77]

Unfortunately, there was only one problem with the president's pledge to Berlusconi; the guy he was threatening to "whoop" for having engineered the 9/11 attacks was *not* the Arab he originally accused in his diary—he was the *Persian,* Saddam Hussein.

"OUTRAGEOUS CONSPIRACY THEORIES"

Many additional indicators of divine disfavor would continue to be seen in the aftermath of 9/11. For instance, we certainly didn't win any points with the Lord by having a Muslim "cleric" open in prayer at the ecumenical memorial service held in Washington Cathedral.

At home, America's shaky air travelers started feeling the recoil from all the "socio-stupidity" they had previously tolerated. Thanks to Affirmative Action, the nation's airports were staffed primarily by minorities, including the passenger screeners and other security personnel (though reality prevailed in the cockpit with "Japheth" piloting nearly all of the flights).

While that would all have to be changed in light of 9/11, other social doctrines would persist. Because of racial profiling, "random" checks of passengers had to be conducted with sensitivity. It didn't matter if the ninth person in line was a skittish Middle Eastern male with a patch on his eye and a turban on his head—an eighty-year-old granny would be frisked, as the regulation called for every *tenth* passenger—period! (On the second anniversary of 9/11, I was actually seated on a British Airways jet at the Nairobi Airport, listening to an intercom request that a passenger by the name of *Hussein* make his presence known.)

With "good ol' Yankee ingenuity" traceable to our Judeo-Christian heritage (John 15:5c), modern America's growing ineptness would manifest itself overseas as well. While an entire section in the next chapter will cover this subject, suffice it to say that the Taliban chief, Mullah Omar, was able to escape from his city hideout on a simple moped—in a country (Afghanistan) that was under the control of Western allies.[78]

However, sooner or later the uncomfortable prospect of government complicity in the 9/11 tragedy must be addressed. And yet, as previously noted, it's not like we would be the only ones caught with our fingers in the cookie jar, manipulating catastrophic events for political advantage.

Following the attacks on September 11, 2001, Russian President Vladimir Putin held a special news conference in which he expressed his sympathy to the American people, condemned the incidents as a "terrorist act" and called upon the international community to "unite in the struggle against terrorism . . . a blatant challenge to humanity." Putin then traveled to Shanghai on October 21 to personally encourage his "good friend," George Bush. In an act of unprecedented post-Cold War solidarity, the two world leaders issued a "Joint Statement on Counterterrorism," resolving "to advance cooperation in combating new terrorist threats."

Vladimir, of all people, could empathize with the American president, as his own capital had been rocked by a series of terrorist attacks in September 1999. Over 300 Russian civilians were killed in three separate apartment house bombings, believed to be the work of Chechen Muslims. At the time, the former KGB chief was President Yeltsin's prime minister. The only "good" that resulted from the carnage was the timely mandate Putin received for an immediate invasion of the breakaway province, a move which would catapult him to the presidency in a wave of patriotic euphoria the following March.

President Putin would also be able to help his American comrade deal with the "pain" caused by those who would question whether he had prior knowledge of 9/11. On September 22, 1999, an alert resident at an apartment house in the city of Ryazan prevented a fourth bombing by alerting local police after a trio of suspicious individuals were seen fleeing from the basement. An explosive charge was subsequently discovered and defused by a bomb disposal team. In the ensuing investigation the three men were apprehended and interrogated. Would you believe the "Chechen terrorists" turned out to be undercover agents for the Federal Security Service (FSV), the successor to the Soviet KGB? *(The New York Times*, March 6, 2002, "A film clip, and charges of a Moscow Plot.") However, Nikolai Patrushev, head of the FSV in Moscow, promptly assured everyone that the incident in Ryazan had been nothing more than a "training exercise" staged by the FSV to test local vigilance. He also confirmed that the bomb was not a *real* bomb, but only a package of "harmless sugar." In Russia, Hegel's universal dialectic is known as "rumbles equal rubles."

Mr. Putin—nicknamed "Pootie-Poot" by President Bush[79]—would also claim to be one of several government leaders who had warned the United States of an imminent terrorist attack. According to MSNBC on September 15, 2001, as cited by Griffin:

> Russian President Putin later stated that in August, "I ordered my intelligence to warn President Bush in the strongest terms that 25 terrorists were getting ready to attack the US, including important government buildings like the Pentagon." The head of Russian intelligence also said: "We had warned them" on several occasions, but they "did not pay the necessary attention."[80]

While the Bush administration might have second-guessed the Russians, there could be no excuse for having ignored a timely alert from the Israelis. *Telegraph Group Limited* ran a story on September 16, 2001, entitled "Israeli security issued urgent warnings to CIA of large-scale terror attacks." According to the article written by David Wastell in Washington and Phillip Jacobson in Jerusalem:

> Israeli intelligence officials say that they warned their counterparts in the United States last month that large-scale terrorist attacks on highly visible targets on the American mainland were imminent. . . .
> The Telegraph has learnt that two senior experts with Mossad, the Israeli military intelligence service, were sent to Washington in August to

Above, left: Skull and Bones Temple at Yale University, known as "The Tomb."
(Author's collection)

Above, right: Author standing at front door of "The Tomb."

Left: Former JCS chairman, General Lyman L. Lemnitzer, architect of infamous "Operation Northwoods" proposal.
(Library of Congress)

Below: Pratt House, 58 East 68th Street, New York City, headquarters of the Council on Foreign Relations.
(Author's collection)

The Alfred P. Murrah Federal Building, Oklahoma City, Oklahoma, following terrorist bombing, April 19, 1995. "It would have been absolutely impossi[ble] and against the laws of nature for a truc[k] full of fertilizer and fuel oil – no matter how much was used – to bring the buil[ding] down." Mr. Sam Cohen, "Father of the Neutron Bomb."
(Courtesy City of Oklahoma City)

"Cactus Motel" where Timothy McVeigh and Iraqi national spent the night of April 18, 1995, in room 105.
(Author's collection)

Team 5
4-19-95
We Search for the truth
We Seek Justice
[T]he Courts Require it.
Victims Cry for it.
[An]d GOD Demands it!

Author with former Oklahoma state representative Charles Key, chairman of the Oklahoma Bombing Investigat[ion] Committee, at south wall of the old Journal Record Building, now the Oklahoma City Memorial Museum.

Above: Pope John Paul II receiving President Bush
in the Vatican library, June 4, 2004.
(AP/Wide World Photos)

Left: Bush holding hands with Saudi Crown Prince
Abdullah bin Abdul Aziz at the Hotel Royal in the
French resort Evian, June 1, 2003.
(Luke Frazza/AFP/Getty)

Below: Prince Bandar and the president relaxing at
Crawford ranch, August 2002.
(Eric Draper/White House/Sipa)

". . . bodies are just coming from out of the sky,"
North Tower, September 11, 2001.
(AP/Wide World Photos/Richard Drew)

Pentagon's west facade moments after
portion of Ring E collapsed.
(Anonymous)

Mychal Judge, victim 00001 on 9/11,
killed in lobby of WTC 1 by implosion of WTC 2.
(REUTERS/Shannon Stapleton)

Above and left: Historic St. Paul's Chapel, located at 55 Church Street, lower Manhattan.
(Author's collection)

Below: An exhausted rescue worker sleeps on pew in St. Paul's as police officers sit in background during recovery operations at Ground Zero.
(AP/Wide World Photos/Kathy Willens)

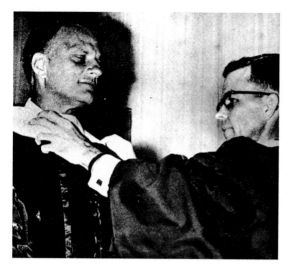

Above: Evangelist Billy Graham receiving honorary doctorate from Roman Catholic Belmont Abbey College, November 21, 1967.
(Gastonia Gazette/Paul Smith)

Above, right: Reverend Graham, accompanied by wife Ruth, kneeling before his star on Hollywood Walk of Fame, October 15, 1989.
(Wire Image/Ron Galella)

Below: George and Laura Bush confer with Billy and Franklin Graham in Jacksonville, Florida, during 2000 election crisis.
(REUTERS/Rick Wilking)

THE WHITE HOUSE

WASHINGTON

October 14, 2003

I send greetings to the members of Metropolitan Community Church
Los Angeles as you celebrate your 35th anniversary.

Faith plays an important role in the lives of many Americans, offering
strength and guidance for the challenges of each new day. By encouraging
the celebration of faith and sharing the message of God's love and boundless
mercy, churches like yours put hope in people's hearts and a sense of purpose
in their lives.

This milestone provides an opportunity to reflect on your years of service
and to rejoice in God's faithfulness to your congregation. In the days ahead,
may your community continue to grow in faith and friendship.

Laura joins me in sending our best wishes for a memorable celebration.

George Bush

Presidential letter of congratulations sent to Metropolitan Community Church
during Bush-endorsed, anti-sodomite "Marriage Protection Week."

Above, left: President Bush kisses Condoleezza Rice after announcing her nomination for secretary of state. *(AP/Wide World Photos/Pablo Martinez Monsivais)*

Above, right: Ozzy Osbourne at White House Correspondents' Association dinner, May 4, 2002. *(Paul J. Richards/AFP/Getty Images)*

Left: Senator John Kerry bites into a Philly cheese steak at Pat's King of Steaks during campaign stop in South Philadelphia. *(AP/Wide World Photos/Jacqueline Larma)*

Right: American astronaut Dr. S. Lucid giving an interview from the core module of the Russian space station Mir, August 22, 1996. *(AP/Wide World Photos/NASA TV)*

alert the CIA and FBI to the existence of a cell of as many as 200 terrorists said to be preparing a big operation.[81]

Must we accept at face value *whatever* the government tells us concerning the tragic events of 9/11? Bamford's earlier book, *Body of Secrets*, was released in the Spring of 2001, only months before the World Trade Center attack. On his opening page, the author quotes from an October 2000 U.S. Senate Report entitled *Secrecy in International and Domestic Policy Making: The Case for More Sunshine*, citing Senators Daniel Patrick Moynihan and Rob Wyden: "Behind closed doors, there is no guarantee that the most basic of individual freedoms will be preserved. And as we enter the 21st Century, the great fear we have for our democracy is the enveloping culture of government secrecy and the corresponding distrust of government that follows." If veteran senators were cautioning Americans to sleep with one eye open *before* 9/11, should we be less vigilant *afterward*?

Should President Bush have his way, books like mine would never be allowed on the shelf. In a speech at the satanic United Nations, broadcast on CNN, November 10, 2001, the "born-again Bonesman" told his listeners not to tolerate anyone who would *dare* to think for themselves: **"Let us never tolerate outrageous conspiracy theories concerning the attacks of September 11, malicious lies that attempt to shift the blame away from the terrorists themselves, away from the guilty."**[82]

According to our own president it is now un-American to investigate the facts. And yet, to the contrary, even Lieutenant General Kenneth A. Minihan (U.S.A.F.), former director of the National Security Agency, was forthright enough to state in the June 1997 *NSA Newsletter,* **"The public has a duty to watch its Government closely and keep it on the right track."**[83] In a carefully crafted address at the Pentagon Memorial, Bush himself appears to qualify as a bona fide "Limbaugh Kook." What you are about to read is *not* a Freudian slip.

> The hijackers were instruments of **evil** who died in vain. **Behind them is a dark cult of evil who seeks to harm the innocent and thrives on human suffering.** Theirs is the worst kind of cruelty—the cruelty that is fed, not weakened, by tears. Theirs is the worst kind of violence! Pure malice while daring to claim the authority of God. We cannot fully understand the designs and power of **evil**. It is enough to know that evil—like goodness—exists. And in the terrorists **evil** has found a willing servant.[84]

Richard Clarke is another loyal member of the establishment (yin-yang) who believes in conspiracy theory, but only if attributed to the "bad guys": "Al Qaeda is a worldwide political conspiracy masquerading as a religious sect."[85] Like former CIA director Richard Helms once said, "The nation must, to a degree, take it on faith that we . . . are honorable men devoted to her service."[86] *Sure*, Dick!

So why did President Bush just *have* to make that eerie reference to *Pearl Harbor* in his diary entry on 9/11? Would that not have been a red flag to any student of history? I mean, it's not like we haven't read the diary entries of that *other* Bonesman, Secretary of War Henry Stimson, regarding the war-making exploitation that was engineered by the *real* Pearl Harbor attack: "We face the delicate question of the diplomatic fencing to be done so as to be sure Japan is put into the wrong and makes the first bad move—overt move," and "The question was how we should maneuver them (the Japanese) into firing the first shot."[87]

The problem for President Bush is that a spectacular surprise attack like 9/11 cannot help appearing like a major conflict of interest. An article in *U.S. News and World Report* stated, "Then came 9/11. Worldwide revulsion and the shared sense of threat handed Washington a once-in-a-generation chance to shake up international politics."[88]

At a meeting broadcast on C-Span, September 14, 2001, Gary Hart, co-chair of the U.S. Commission on National Security in the 21st Century, stated: "There is a chance for the president of the United States to use this disaster to carry out what his father [wanted]—a phrase his father only used once, and it hasn't been used since—and that is a New World Order."[89]

The watershed events of 9/11 and the prevailing fear of renewed terrorist attacks were foreshadowed in the 1998 book, *The Grand Chessboard,* by Zbigniew Brzezinski, former national security advisor to President Jimmy Carter. Brzezinski is a member of the Council on Foreign Relations and co-founder of the Trilateral Commission with David Rockefeller. He writes: "Moreover, as America becomes an increasingly multicultural society, it may find it more difficult to fashion a consensus on foreign policy issues, except in the circumstance of a truly massive and widely perceived direct external threat."[90] Reminding his readers that the public supported America's engagement in World War II, "largely because of the shock effect of the Japanese attack on Pearl Harbor," he gloats that America will ultimately be attacked by Middle Eastern terrorists.[91]

Uncomfortable Coincidences
and Unresolved Anomalies

When the inevitable subject of potential government complicity on 9/11 is considered (those politically incorrect, "outlandish conspiracy theories"), the following three questions should be asked: 1) Did the Bush administration have a hidden agenda that stood to gain from the attacks?; 2) Is there a consistent historical precedent for the use of pretext and exploitation?; and 3) Does the Bible teach that such activity would intensify in the last days? By now, the answers to these questions should be painfully obvious.

Of the many books that deal with government complicity on 9/11, *The New Pearl Harbor* by David Ray Griffin offers a highly documented treatise on the subject (though falling short of papal infallibility). While the EIB network would "deep-six" his thesis, the author is not without intellectual patronage. In his foreword to *The New Pearl Harbor*, Richard Falk, Professor Emeritus at Princeton University, touted Griffin's work as "[a]n extraordinary book," one that has "potential to become a force of history."[92] One of the publisher's eleven endorsements is given by acclaimed trial lawyer Gerry Spence, author of *How to Argue and Win Every Time.* He writes:

> This book is as full of research and authoritative notes as a field full of springtime daisies. The author raises frightening questions, and the questions beg for answers. One thing we can conclude for certain. The events surrounding 9/11, both before and after, cannot be simply swept under the rug of conventional wisdom.... **This book gives us a foundation to discover the truth, one that we may not want to hear.**[93]

Colleen Kelly, sister of Bill Kelly, Jr., who was killed in the North Tower, stated simply, "It will be painful, and disturbing, to turn the pages of this thoughtful and meticulously researched book. But turn we must. For we owe the truth to those who died, and nothing less."[94]

Griffin offers eight possible views on the question of "official complicity," and lists them in ascending order of seriousness (meaning the seriousness of the charge against the Bush administration that the view would imply):

1. *Construction of a False Account:* One possible view is that although US officials played no role in facilitating the attacks and did not even expect them, they constructed a false account of what really happened—whether to protect National Security, to cover up potentially embarrassing facts, to exploit the attacks to enact their agenda, or for some other reason. Although this would be the least serious charge, it would be sufficiently serious for impeachment—especially if the president had lied about 9/11 for personal gain or to advance some pre-established agenda, such as attacking Afghanistan and Iraq.

2. *Something Expected by Intelligence Agencies:* A second possible view is that although they had no specific information about the attacks in advance, some US intelligence agencies—such as the FBI, the CIA, and some intelligence agencies of the US military—expected some sort of attacks to occur. Although they played no role in planning the attacks, they perhaps played a role in facilitating them in the sense of deliberately not taking steps to prevent them. Then, having done this without White House knowledge, they persuaded the White House after 9/11 not only to cover up their guilt, by constructing a false account, but also to carry out the agenda for which the attacks were intended to gain support.

3. *Specific Events Expected by Intelligence Agencies:* A third possible view is that intelligence agencies (but not the White House) had specific information about the timing of the attacks.

4. *Intelligence Agencies Involved in Planning:* A fourth possible view is that intelligence agencies (but not the White House) actively participated in planning the attacks.

5. *Pentagon Involved in Planning:* A fifth possible view is that the Pentagon (but not the White House) actively participated in the attacks.

6. *Something Expected by White House:* A sixth possible view is that although the White House had no specific knowledge of the attacks in advance, it expected some sort of attacks to occur and was a party to facilitating them, at least in the sense of not ordering that they be prevented. This view allows the possibility that the White House might have been shocked by the amount of death and destruction caused by the attacks that were actually carried out.

7. *Specific Advance Knowledge by White House:* A seventh possible view is that the White House had specific foreknowledge of the targets and the timing of the attacks.

8. *White House Involved in Planning:* An eighth possible view is that the White House was a party to planning the attacks.[95]

The author states, "as these possibilities show, a charge that 9/11 involved 'complicity' or 'conspiracy' on the part of US officials can be understood in many ways, several of which do not involve active involvement in this planning."[96]

Retired Marine General Anthony Zinni, who headed the U.S. Central Command from 1997 to 2000, notes the thread of conspiracy connecting "Operation Northwoods" and the Gulf of Tonkin incident with our preemptive strike on Iraq. The general laments that:

> [Iraq] reminds me of Vietnam. Here we have some strategic thinkers who have long wanted to invade Iraq. They saw an opportunity, and they used the imminence of the threat and the association with terrorism and the 9/11 emotions as a catalyst and a justification. It's another Gulf of Tonkin.[97]

While genuinely patriotic Americans would prefer to give their government the benefit of the doubt, especially in the midst of a shooting war, an array of uncomfortable coincidences and unresolved anomalies continue to foster apprehension, suspicion and distrust.

For instance, why did the 9/11 attacks just *have* to occur exactly ten years to the day that President George H. W. Bush uttered his infamous pronouncement about the New World Order? Why did Marvin Bush, the brother of President G. W. Bush, *have* to serve as a director and major shareholder of a company, Securacom (now Stratesec), which handled security for three clients that figured prominently in the attack—United Airlines; Dulles Airport, from which American Airlines Flight 77 was hijacked; and the World Trade Center itself?[98] (Marvin conveniently left the board on the eve of 9/11.) Why did the *Boston Globe* for October 27, 2001, *have* to report that certain government officials were incensed because information pertinent to the 9/11 investigation was being destroyed by the National Security Agency?[99] Why must we read reports that governmental agencies had nearly all 300,000 tons of steel from the Twin Towers sold to local scrap dealers and exported to places like China and Korea without any criminal investigation?[100] (Why would this make me think of those other violated crime scenes at Waco and Oklahoma City?) And, as alluded to previously, how come NORAD and the FAA could get a fighter escort to golfer Payne Stewart in twenty minutes but required an hour and fifteen minutes to scramble fighters on 9/11?

The sticky wicket questions appear to be endless. If "clash equals cash," should we expect to uncover evidence of "insider trading" just prior to 9/11? While the major networks were concentrating on Martha

Stewart, they failed to tell you that certain "folks in the know" were even able to profit by betting on the doomed airlines. Jones writes:

> Also in early September, between September 5 and 10, 4,744 record put options (a highly risky form of speculation where you bet against a stock that it will go down) were purchased against United Airlines' stock, compared to only 396 call options (speculation that a stock will go up in value). This was a highly abnormal level of put options that were purchased, and not against airline stocks in general, but against United Airlines.
>
> Many of United Airlines' put options were bought through Deusche Bank/AB Brown, a firm managed until 1988 by the current executive director of the CIA, A. B. "Buzzy" Kronguard (Sources: *London Independent, The New York Times, Wall Street Journal*).
>
> On September 10, 2001, a record 4,516 put options were placed against American Airlines compared to just 748 call options (Source: *London Independent*, October 14, 2001, "Mystery of Terror," "Insider Dealers"). Continuing the pattern, the put options were purchased only against American Airlines and United Airlines, not against airline stocks in general. The put options purchased on both airlines were six hundred percent over normal. All of this activity took place at a time when airline stocks were doing well compared to other sectors (*Reuters Business,* September 10, 2001, "Airline Stocks May be Poised to Take off").[101]

Then we have the problem of the president's own testimony concerning *how* and *when* he came to learn of the attacks. Bamford writes:

> Disturbingly, the story George W. Bush often tells of his learning of the attacks cannot possibly be true. "I was sitting outside the classroom waiting to go in," he told an audience in Florida on December 4, 2001, "and I saw an airplane hit the tower—the TV was obviously on, and I used to fly myself, and I said, 'There's one terrible pilot.' And I said, 'It must have been a horrible accident.' " He repeated the story a month later, on January 5, 2002, to another audience in California. It is the version that is on the White House Web page. "When we walked into the classroom, I had seen this plane fly into the first building. There was a TV set on. And you know, I thought it was pilot error and I was amazed that anybody could make such a terrible mistake."
> **The problem with the account is that there was no video of the first plane hitting the World Trade Center until later that day.** The only video was of the second plane hitting the World Trade Center at 9:02:54.[102]

This obvious contradiction prompted the *Boston Herald* to write:

> Think about that. Bush's remark implies he saw the first plane hit the tower. But we all know that video of the first plane hitting did not surface until the next day. Could Bush have meant he saw the second plane hit—which many Americans witnessed? No, because he said that he was in the classroom when Card whispered in his ear that a second plane hit.[103]

Bamford reveals that the Bush fantasy is a "Catch-22" at best:

> It's possible that he saw those images on live television when he ducked into an empty room set up so he could talk with Condoleezza Rice at the White House. He reportedly did not enter the class until 9:04, more than a minute after the United Flight 175 smashed into Tower Two. Thus, he may have learned of the second plane even before he went in to address the seven-year-olds. That would raise a serious question of judgment: How could a president ignore what to millions of people was an obvious terrorist attack and just go about a political photo op as if nothing had happened?
>
> If he had not seen the second attack and could not have seen the first attack, then how could he make the later claims? Few people can ever forget the moment they just learned of the events of 9/11, especially if the person happens to be the President of the United States.[104]

WHISTLEBLOWERS AND LITIGANTS

The government's complicity is so blatant that San Francisco attorney Stanley Hilton filed a $7 billion lawsuit on behalf of four hundred family members of victims who died at the World Trade Center, Pentagon and Pennsylvania crash sites. He filed his suit in U.S. District Court against President Bush and key members of his administration for allowing the terrorist attacks to occur. Also named in the suit were Vice President Richard Cheney, National Security Advisor Condoleezza Rice, Secretary of Defense Donald Rumsfeld and Transportation Secretary Norman Mineta. Hilton, a former top aide for Senate Majority Leader Bob Dole was interviewed by Alex Jones on his radio talk show program.

> Stanley Hilton told the listeners of my radio broadcast that he has proof from dozens of high-level officers in every branch of the armed services, especially the Air Force and Space Command based in NORAD,

that Bush ordered the fighter aircraft to stand down on September 11 and that Bush conspired to create the September 11 attacks for his own political gain.... He says that he also has sources in the CIA, FBI, NSA, and naval intelligence who can confirm the allegations made in the lawsuit.[105]

In a follow-up interview with Jones (as reported by Thomas Buyea of *Rense.com*, September 17, 2004) the high profile Hilton announced that a major break-in had occurred at his law office. "Files were stolen," he said. "Files dealing with this particular case and particularly with the documents I had regarding the fact that . . . some of these hijackers, at least some of them were on the payroll of the U.S. government as undercover FBI, CIA, double agents." He also stated that the FBI had been seriously harassing his staff.

As this book was going to press, a long overdue exposé of the so-called "Stand Down Conspiracy" was being initiated by Senator Mark Dayton (D-Minnesota), who told leaders of the 9/11 Commission on July 30, 2004, that a NORAD chronology made public a week after the attacks was grossly misleading. Dayton charged that NORAD officials "lied to the American people, they lied to Congress and they lied to your 9/11 commission to create a false impression of competence, communication and protection of the American people."[106]

On May 30, 2002, Judicial Watch, the public interest law firm best known for its part in the impeachment of President Clinton held a press conference at the National Press Club featuring FBI Special Agent Robert Wright. Standing over six feet in height, the veteran FBI agent began to cry as he shared his remarkable story. Jones writes:

> He said that he had been threatened that he would be arrested on national security violations if he told the press what he knew about government prior knowledge.
>
> Representing Agent Wright, David Schippers, former lead council in Bill Clinton's impeachment in the House Judiciary Committee, stated that the agents that he represented could not divulge the majority of their information on government prior knowledge. He said that there are many other agents from around the country who wanted to come forward and tell how they had been prevented from stopping al-Qaeda. They were unable to do so because of similar threats. Schippers himself had received a letter from the Justice Department the day before the press conference threatening all those coming forward with arrest.[107]

According to a July 26, 2001, article in *CBCNEWS* entitled "Ashcroft Flying High," in the weeks prior to September 11, the Justice Department secretary was "traveling exclusively by leased jet aircraft instead of commercial airlines." The cabinet head who was threatening Mr. Schippers claimed he had avoided commercial travel because of a "threat assessment" by the FBI.[108]

Agents like Robert Wright have complained that the Bush administration repeatedly impeded their investigation of al-Qaeda and other terrorist groups. Several FBI personnel have filed lawsuits as a result. (See *Judicial Watch*, November 14, 2001, "Active Special Agent Files Complaint Concerning Obstructed FBI Anti-Terrorist Investigations"; *The Times of India*, November 8, 2001, "Bush took FBI Agents off Laden family trail"; *AFP*, November 7, 2001, "Bush Thwarted FBI probe against bin Ladens"; *The Guardian*, November 7, 2001, "FBI and Spy Agents Say Bush Spiked bin Laden Probes before 11 September; *Ananova*, November 7, 2001, "U.S. Agents told to back off bin Ladens.")[109] Richard Clarke summarizes:

> Somewhere in [the] FBI there was information that strange things had been going on at flight schools in the United States. . . . They had specific information about individual terrorists from which one could have deduced what was about to happen. None of that information got to me or the White House.[110]

While the "Religious Right" has made a lot of noise about "Slick Willy" having been only the second president in U.S. history to be impeached, they are strangely silent with regard to "Brother" Bush's claim to fame— *the nation's first chief executive to be sued in Federal Court under the RICO (Racketeer Influenced and Corrupt Organizations) Act!* On November 26, 2003, attorney Philip J. Berg held a news conference in Philadelphia to announce that Ellen Mariani, whose husband was on United Airlines Flight 175, had taken the action against Bush (and several of his "mobster" cohorts—Ashcroft, Cheney, Rice, Rumsfeld and Tenet) "for 'failing to act and prevent' the murder of Plaintiff's husband, Louis Neil Mariani, for financial and political reasons" and that they "have 'obstructed justice' in the aftermath of said criminal acts and omissions."[111]

> Defendant GWB "owed a duty" not only to Plaintiff, but the American People to protect and defend against the preventable attacks based upon substantial intelligence known to Defendant GWB prior to "911" which

resulted in the death of Plaintiff's husband and thousands of other innocent victims of "911." . . .

Defendant GWB has not been forthright and honest with regard to his administration's pre-knowledge of the potential of the "911" attacks and Plaintiff seeks to compel Defendant GWB to justify why her husband Louis Neil Mariani died on "911." . . . (T)he compelling evidence that will be presented in this case through discovery, subpoena power by this Court and testimony at trial will lead to one undisputed fact, Defendant GWB failed to act and prevent "911" knowing the attacks would lead to our nation having to engage in an "International War on Terror (IWOT)" which would benefit Defendants both financially and for political reasons. . . .

Plaintiff believes, Defendant GWB et al, allowed the attacks to take place to compel public anger and outcry to engage our nation and our military men and women in a preventable "IWOT" for personal gains and agendas. . . .[112]

Unfortunately, while the RICO Act has proven tough enough to send scores of Mafia dons to the slammer, it never made a dent in the "Bush crime family." Richard Clarke writes: "As one Republican columnist told me, 'These guys are more inbred, secretive, and vindictive than the Mafia.' "[113]

As things began to heat up, the president had Cheney call six Congressional committees and threaten them with repercussions if they asked too many questions. On March 1, 2002, the *Washington Post* ran an article entitled "Bush Seeks To Restrict Hill Probes of September 11." The piece quotes Cheney as stating that "a review of what happened on September 11 would take resources and personnel away from the war on terrorism."[114] Senate Majority Leader Tom Daschle told reporters, "I think the American people are entitled to know what happened and why."[115] Larry Klayman, the chairman of Judicial Watch, would later conclude: "This (Bush-Cheney) administration is the most secretive of our lifetime, even more secretive than the Nixon administration. They don't believe the American people or Congress have any right to information."[116]

The ultimate challenge to the government's ongoing cover-up was occasioned by the most knowledgeable specialist on terrorism within the FBI itself. In their book *Forbidden Truth: U.S.-Taliban Secret Oil Diplomacy and the Failed Hunt For Osama Bin Laden,* French co-authors Jean-Charles Brisard and Guillaume Dasquié recount the interview they conducted in late July 2001 with John P. O'Neill, former chief of the FBI's National Security Division in New York. The meeting took place at the Plaza Hotel in Manhattan.

Sitting in the China Club at the top of a building overlooking Manhattan, John O'Neill recounted the heated exchange with the American ambassador, his disappointment in the State Department's impotence—feigned or not—and above all the threat of Osama bin Laden. For him, everything originated in Saudi Arabia, and everything could be explained and solved through this prism. **"All the answers, all of the clues allowing us to dismantle Osama bin Laden's organization, can be found in Saudi Arabia,"** he told me, emphasizing "the inability of American diplomacy to get everything out of King Fahd" concerning terrorist networks. The reason? There was only one: corporate oil interests. Could this single explanation keep the United States from investigating one of the principle terrorist networks in the world? Yes—for the simple reason that the American administration had refrained from using the investigation as a means of putting pressure on its Saudi friends.[117]

Do you suppose this professional assessment by the FBI's top counter-terrorism expert would explain why Osama bin Laden and *fifteen* of his nineteen 9/11 hijackers were *Saudi* nationals while *none* were from Iraq? The negative connotation was certainly understood by Prince Bandar (Saudi ambassador to America), who stated afterward, "I felt as if the Twin Towers had just fallen on my head."[118] Now you know why President Bush refused to declassify those *twenty-eight* pages of the July 2003 Congressional report that implicated Saudi Arabia in the 9/11 attacks! Even *Time* reported that the blacked-out pages produced "the smell of a cover-up of complicity in the worst terrorist attack in U.S. history."[119] Robert Baer, a former CIA operative, adds: "As if Americans needed more evidence, perhaps two-thirds of al Qaeda prisoners being held in the Camp Delta prison facility at the Guantanamo Naval Base in Cuba—'the worst of the worst,' according to Secretary of Defense Donald Rumsfeld—were said to be Saudi nationals."[120] When Saudi dissident Mohammed Khileri defected to the U.S. with 14,000 documents implicating Saudi citizens in financing terrorism, the FBI refused to examine them.[121] (Sound familiar?)

As with the suit filed by Stan Hilton, the case for conspiracy is made manifest by the extent of serious protracted litigation. Unger writes:

Allegations that specific members of the royal family, or members of the Saudi merchant elite, had prior knowledge of 9/11 or knowingly financed Al Qaeda are grave charges indeed, and should not be made unless they can be backed up by strong evidence. Some of these questions may be answered by the **$1-trillion civil suit** brought by families of victims of 9/11 against hundreds of individuals and entities, many of whom are prominent Saudis.[122]

In predictable fashion, the Saudi royal family, including Prince Bandar's father, Prince Sultan, were represented by Baker Botts, the law firm of Carlyle partner and lifetime Bush crony, James A. Baker.

Described as the government's "most committed tracker of Osama bin Laden and his al-Qaeda network of terrorists,"[123] O'Neill quit the Bureau on August 22, 2001, citing "repeated obstruction of his investigations into al-Qaeda."[124] (These charges were later acknowledged on CNN's *American Morning with Paula Zahn*, January 8, 2002.[125]) On the evening of September 10, he reportedly told a colleague, "We're due for something big. I don't like the way things are lining up in Afghanistan."[126]

In another one of those "uncomfortable coincidences," the forty-nine-year-old former FBI chief became head of security at the World Trade Center. Unfortunately, his first day at his new office on the thirty-fourth floor of the South Tower was also his last. Clarke writes, "We were told that parts of my FBI friend, John O'Neill, had been found in the rubble in New York . . ."[127] The outspoken "G-man" had literally taken his secrets to the grave. With regard to his claim that his "probe of Mr. bin Laden and Al-Qa'ida in Afghanistan had been blocked by the U.S. oil lobby," the *London Independent* reported on May 25, 2002, "John O'Neill was right but he paid for his judgment with his life."[128]

Like General George Patton, had O'Neill survived, he would undoubtedly have become the government's "worst nightmare." Unbeknownst to the general public, America's oil executives spent the decade following the break-up of the Soviet Union pursuing a pipeline across Afghanistan. Just beyond the Afghan mountains to the north lie the rich subsoils of Turkmenistan, Uzbekistan, and Kazakhstan. The one sticking point in the deal was the prevailing anarchy in Afghanistan. Marty F. Miller, vice president of Unocal, told the *Washington Post* that his firm had plans to build "two mammoth pipelines across Afghanistan to carry oil and gas from Turkmenistan to Pakistan" but all potential sources of financing "have consistently advised us that there will have to be a single entity governing Afghanistan that has international recognition" before they will invest any money.[129]

As the Taliban (meaning "pupils" or "students") became the "single entity" of choice, charges of terrorist ties to Osama bin Laden would have to be denied (beginning with the first international arrest warrant made by a state against Osama bin Laden, issued by Libya for murder and illegal possession of firearms, released by Interpol, April 15, 1998). The obvious problem was that any meaningful investigation of bin Laden would implicate the Taliban and "rupture" the pipeline. Thus, we find Barnett Rubin, an Afghanistan specialist at the Council on Foreign Relations, stating in October 1996: "The Taliban do not have any links to Islam's international radicals. [*"Sure, Barn!"*] In fact, they hate them."[130] Consequently, when O'Neill and his team (derided as "Rambos" by the local authorities) attempted to enter Yemen to investigate the *Cole* bombing, the American ambassador, Barbara Bodine, forbade them from doing so. "This despite the fact that, according to O'Neill, the FBI had in hand all the evidence needed to implicate Osama bin Laden's terrorist network in the attack,"[131] write Brisard and Dasquié. The facts are enough to indict both the Clinton *and* Bush administrations for treason. The authors continue:

> February 1996. Three months after the attack against the National Guard building in Riyadh that claimed five American lives, the United States intelligence services were intensifying their investigations into the network of the man who had already been identified as the ringleader: Osama bin Laden.
>
> From that day onward, bin Laden, who until that time had simply been observed from a distance, now became a major target for investigators. Everything was set in motion to identify his network and destroy its operational structures. . . .
>
> For the United States, these measures did not seem to contradict the dialogue with the Taliban and the unconditional support given to Saudi Arabia. The superpower believed that it could conduct two distinct policies leading to two different objectives, which in reality were intimately tied: the political stabilization of the Taliban regime and the war against Al Qaeda, which had availed itself of Afghanistan that May.
>
> As the investigation advanced, these two objectives turned out to be incompatible and irreconcilable, since the United States could not accommodate itself with the Taliban and at the same time let the FBI point a finger at the warlords and the support they gave to terrorism.
>
> **In the face of this contradiction, the United States made the historic choice to favor diplomacy over security.** It persuaded itself that bin Laden was a lesser evil, "under control" in a country that was offering him temporary refuge. . . .
>
> The United States turned to its allies in the European intelligence community and spun a similar story: that bin Laden was a renegade from the Saudi kingdom, that he was isolated, that he had no relations with his family or that he had little support from them, especially in the heart of the

Arab world. The idea that the Arab world would be indifferent to bin Laden's message was a dangerous one and, as we know, ultimately fatal.[132]

With this treasonous policy about to blow sky high (and the Unocal pipeline on hold since 1997), U.S. officials threatened the Taliban in July 2001, "Either you accept our offer of a carpet of gold or we bury you under a carpet of bombs."[133]

OSAMA'S KIN FOLK AND THE CARLYLE CONNECTION

As John O'Neill was being buried under the rubble at the intersection of Liberty and Greenwich at Ground Zero, a brother of Osama bin Laden was being honored at the Ritz-Carlton hotel in Washington, D.C. The occasion was the annual international investor conference of the Carlyle Group, a powerful merchant bank specializing in the timely purchase and resale of floundering companies, especially defense-related industries. (Such entities are typically bought with a mix of capital and debt, somewhat mitigating the risk of the buyer; hence, known as the leveraged buyout, or LBO.) Named after the extravagant Carlyle Hotel in Manhattan (located on 76th Street and Madison Avenue), the company was jumpstarted in 1987 through the Great Eskimo Tax Scam—a tax loophole exploited by co-founders Stephen Norris and David Rubenstein. "Merchants of death" like the Carlyle Group obviously make their greatest "killings" in times of war. As of 2003, the Washington-based firm had "over $13 billion under management and more political connections than the White House switchboard."[134]

Well it "just so happens" that the Saudi Binladin Group, a $5 billion construction conglomerate, pioneered by family patriarch Mohammed bin Laden (primarily from Saudi government projects) was one of the most esteemed clients in the Carlyle portfolio. (The Saudi ambassador, Prince Bandar, was another royal client.) However, the plot *really* thickens when one discovers how the Carlyle Group has been able to "cash in" by knowing the right people in Washington. *If the truth were known, Bush and Cheney would make Nixon and Agnew look like Paul and Silas!* Unger writes:

> Before Carlyle came along, the so-called revolving door in Washington worked something like this: As every new administration moved into

Washington, a coterie of powerful Beltway politicians would move out from the public sector into the private sector, where they cashed in by renting their access to power for $500,000 a year or so as lawyers or lobbyists at huge law firms like Williams & Connolly or Akin Gump Strauss Hauer & Feld, and PR firms like Hill & Knowlton. Everyone did it—Democrats and Republicans alike.

But after laboring over multibillion-dollar defense contracts, certain politicians began to realize that they could do rather better than a mere half million dollars or so a year. Much better. In an era of *trillion*-dollar federal budgets, half a *million* was chump change, proverbial shoe-shine money. How come the guys on Wall Street were Masters of the Universe when the men on Capitol Hill managed so much more money?

As a result, through Carlyle, the most powerful figures of the Reagan-Bush era decided not just to rent their access to the White House, to the Pentagon, to the regulatory agencies, but to transform it into corporate assets—real equity in publicly held corporations—stocks worth hundreds of millions of dollars. Carlyle was on its way to perfecting the art of what might be called "access capitalism."[135]

Putting aside the president's requested moratorium against tolerating "outrageous conspiracy theories," could the "Skull and Bones" Bush Dynasty (assisted by CFR Cheney) have profited from the costly aftermath of September 11? (i.e., Would an *indefinite* "War against Terrorism" have an *indefinite* price tag, and *who* would stand to gain?) Perhaps a story that appeared in the *Wall Street Journal* on September 27, 2001, can provide an answer to the disturbing question. (Ecclesiastes 1:18) The article is entitled, "Bin Laden Family Is Tied To U.S. Group." A few of the highlights follow:

> If the U.S. boosts defense spending in its quest to stop Osama bin Laden's alleged terrorist activities, there may be one unexpected beneficiary: Mr. bin Laden's family.
>
> Among its far-flung business interests, the well-heeled Saudi Arabian clan—which says it is estranged from Osama—is an investor in a fund established by *Carlyle Group*, a well-connected Washington merchant bank specializing in buyouts of defense and aerospace companies.
>
> Through this investment and its ties to Saudi royalty, the bin Laden family has become acquainted with some of the biggest names in the Republican Party. **In recent years, former President Bush, ex-Secretary of State James Baker and ex-Secretary of Defense Frank Carlucci have made the pilgrimage to the bin Laden family's headquarters in Jeddah,**

Saudi Arabia. Mr. Bush makes speeches on behalf of Carlyle Group and is senior advisor to its Asian Partners fund, while Mr. Baker is its senior counselor. Mr. Carlucci is the group's chairman. . . .

A U.S. inquiry into bin Laden family business dealings could brush against some big names associated with the U.S. government.[136]

Alex Jones adds:

The Carlyle Group is the biggest defense contractor on the planet. The majority owners of the Carlyle Group are the Bush family and the bin Laden family. They are profiting in the hundreds of billions off this new war (*Judicial Watch*, September 28, 2001, "Bush Sr. in Business with Bin Laden Family Conglomerate Through Carlyle Group"; *The Village Voice*, October 11, 2001, "Bush Sr. Could Profit from War"; BBC News, December 4, 1997, "Taleban in Texas for talks on gas pipeline").

While almost every sector of the market has been steadily declining, defense and security stocks have been increasing or holding their value. The Carlyle Group, before September 11 was listed as one of the top five defense contractors in the world. **Since the attacks of September 11, it has taken the lead as the largest defense contractor in the world thanks to special treatment by senior shareholder George W. Bush.** . . .[137]

In 1990, George W. Bush became Carlyle's first significant personnel acquisition, joining the board of Caterair, a recently purchased airline catering firm destined for bankruptcy. Though "G. W." left the sinking ship three years later, the resultant political contacts cultivated therein were deemed more valuable to Carlyle than the stinging financial losses. Unger notes, "Carlyle has what everyone wants: the luxury of being able to make decisions—multibillion-dollar decisions, at that—with a reasonable certainty that it knows the outcome of its decisions in advance."[138] (For the record, Carlyle holds to the Hegelian dialectic, employing prominent Democrats as well, such as former Speaker of the House Tom Foley, and Arthur Levitt, former head of both the Securities and Exchange Commission and the American Stock Exchange.)

Meanwhile, just a few miles from the Pentagon, the Carlyle delegates at the Ritz-Carlton hotel were glued to TV monitors showing the WTC attacks in progress. In his 2003 book *The Iron Triangle: Inside the Secret World of the Carlyle Group,* award-winning business journalist Dan Briody writes:

That same morning, in the plush setting of the Ritz-Carlton hotel in Washington, DC, the Carlyle Group was holding its annual international investor conference. Frank Carlucci, James Baker III, David Rubenstein, William Conway, and Dan D'Aniello were together, along with a host of former world leaders, former defense experts, wealthy Arabs from the Middle East, and major international investors as the terror played out on television. There with them, looking after the investments of his family was Shafiq bin Laden, Osama bin Laden's estranged half-brother. **George Bush Sr. was also at the conference, but Carlyle's spokesperson says the former president left before the terror attacks, and was on an airplane over the Midwest when flights across the country were grounded on the morning of September 11.** In any circumstance, a confluence of such politically complex and globally connected people would have been curious, even newsworthy. But in the context of the terrorist attacks being waged against the United States by a group of Saudi nationals led by Osama bin Laden, the group assembled at the Ritz-Carlton that day was a disconcerting and freakish coincidence.[139]

Shafiq knew exactly what Bandar meant by his comment about the Twin Towers falling on his head. Unger writes: "According to one source, after the second plane hit, Shafig bin Laden removed his name tag. He and James Baker, the source added, left shortly thereafter in separate cars."[140]

Briody then proceeds to the historic truth that "clash equals cash":

> It is impossible to say whether during the darkest day in America's history, it dawned on the partners at the Carlyle Group that what was to come, as a direct result of this attack, would serve their financial interests. . . . Regardless, there was little doubt by the third day after the attacks that Carlyle was in for some heady times. Congress overwhelmingly approved $40 billion in emergency funds, about half of which was earmarked for the armed services. Also in the works was a massive increase in the Pentagon budget, $33 billion, in time for the Department of Defense's 2002 fiscal year, beginning October 1, 2001.[141]

On September 26, just two weeks after the attacks, the Army signed a $665 million contract with United Defense (owned by the Carlyle Group) for the next phase of the *Crusader's* development (the most advanced artillery system the U.S. Army had ever conceived).[142] Briody writes:

> The defense landscape had changed so dramatically, and so thoroughly, after September 11 that Carlyle quickly and wisely decided it was time to take United Defense public weeks after the attacks on America. On October 22,

2001, the company filed an S-1 registration with the Securities and Exchange Commission, planning an initial public offering before the end of the year. . . .

William Conway [co-founder of Carlyle] would later go on the record as saying "No one wants to be a beneficiary of September 11," in a report in *The Nation* entitled "Crony Capitalism Goes Global." Neverless, Carlyle took United Defense public on December 14, the day after Congress passed the defense authorization bill allowing for full funding of Crusader program going forward. On that single day, Carlyle took profits of $237 million. On paper, the company had made three times that amount.[143]

However, as already noted, charges that Carlyle had profited from the tragedy of 9/11 was only *half* the problem. Bush senior hadn't snuck out of the Ritz-Carlton early for nothing. Briody adds:

> In the meantime, Carlyle was dealing with yet another public relations crisis, and this one dwarfed all that came before it. Carlyle had been doing business with dozens of families and businesses throughout the Middle East since the early 1990s. And they had been extremely successful in the region. So successful that they had garnered a reputation for having a tremendous amount of influence over the deal flow in the area. . . . In a sense, Carlyle had become the gatekeeper to foreign investing in Saudi Arabia.
>
> **The article in the *Wall Street Journal* pointed out the most stunning and atrocious irony of Carlyle's history: through Carlyle, the bin Laden family was in a position to make millions from the war being waged against their own brother.** The news that George Bush Sr., James Baker III, and Frank Carlucci had visited the bin Ladens in recent years also stunned the American public. It was, in fact, the Carlyle Partners II fund in which the bin Laden family was invested. The same fund that held United Defense, as well as a host of other defense holdings.
>
> Carlyle told the press that the bin Ladens were only in for $2 million, a relatively small amount of money considering the whole fund was worth $1.3 billion. But one bin Laden family financial representative says the number was much larger. And Al Rahim says that earlier in his time with Carlyle, which ended in 1997, the bin Laden family had several times that amount invested in the company. Regardless of the actual amount, the irony ultimately proved too much for Carlyle, and by the end of October, they severed ties to the family, liquidating their holdings.[144]

Upon leaving the White House in 1961, Dwight D. Eisenhower warned future generations about the dangers of a "military-industrial complex," and the "grave implications" of the "conjunction of an immense military establishment and a large arms industry." He went on to presciently say:

> In the councils of government, we must guard against the acquisition of unwarranted influence, whether sought or unsought, by the military industrial complex. The potential for the disastrous rise of misplaced power exists and will persist. We must never let the weight of this combination endanger our liberties or democratic process.[145]

An insider himself, Ike would qualify as one of those "Limbaugh kooks" with an asterisk after his name. Craig Unger, an Establishment author who has written for *Esquire, Vanity Fair,* and the *New Yorker*, reveals a fact that is *too* heavy for Bill O'Reilly:

> The **Bohemian Grove** has held secret meetings for a global elite since 1873 in a redwood forest of northern California [outside San Francisco]. In addition to Republican presidents **Eisenhower, Nixon, Reagan,** and **George H. W. Bush**, members have included **James Baker, Richard Cheney, Donald Rumsfeld,** David Rockefeller, William Casey, and Henry Kissinger. **Each year, the members don red, black, and silver robes and conduct a ritual in which they worship a giant stone owl.**[146]

Saudi Airlift

Another "unresolved anomaly" concerns the exclusive airlift of nearly 140 Saudi nationals—most of whom were related to the Saud and bin Laden families—that began on September 13, 2001. Regardless of a vehement denial by the Bush administration and harsh reviews of the Michael Moore film *Fahrenheit 9/11*, the evacuation *did* occur with many of the initial flights taking place while U.S. air traffic was all but shut down. Although some *commercial* flights were permitted to resume service on September 13, an FAA restriction on *private* aviation was still in effect. Unger notes that three private planes violating the ban that day in Maryland, West Virginia, and Texas were promptly forced down by jet fighters.[147]

Now despite the fact that it was *our* country going through the greatest crisis of its history, and that "most of the killers were Saudi,"[148] Unger relates:

Bandar [the Saudi ambassador] set up a hotline at the Saudi embassy in Washington for all Saudi nationals in the United States. For the forty-eight hours after the attacks he stayed in constant contact with Secretary of State Colin Powell and National Security Advisor Condoleezza Rice.[149]

The government's effort to distance itself from the growing controversy evolved to the ludicrous position that the massive Saudi airlift had never even happened! (They must have been "phantom" flights, etc.) With regard to a ten-passenger Lear jet that flew three young Saudi men from Tampa to Lexington on Thursday, September 13 (as later confirmed by Senator Graham[150]), Chris White, a spokesman for the FAA, told the *Tampa Tribune*, "It's not in our logs. . . . It didn't occur."[151] Secretary of State Powell approached the matter more sanely, acknowledging in a September 7, 2003, appearance on *Meet the Press*, "I don't know the details of what happened. . . . But my understanding is that there was no sneaking out of the country; that the flights were well-known, and it was coordinated within the government."[152] However, Prince Bandar was more than willing to give credit where credit was due. "With coordination with the FBI," he said on CNN, "we got them all out."[153]

With at least seven planes involved, the airlift occurred in three phases: on September 13 and 14 the passengers were assembled at various staging areas in cities such as Tampa, Orlando, Lexington, Los Angeles, Las Vegas, Cleveland, Houston, Washington, D.C., Boston, Newark and New York;[154] the first flights bound for Riyadh (via Europe) departed September 16 through 19, while the last batch left September 22 through 24. The "evacuees" were mostly young professionals and students attending high school and college. Abdullah bin Laden, a younger brother of Osama's, was a 1994 graduate of Harvard Law School and had offices in Cambridge, Massachusetts. Wafah bin Laden, a twenty-six-year-old graduate of Columbia Law School, lived in a $6,000-a-month rented loft in New York's fashionable SoHo and was considering a career in show business.[155]

That so many relatives of Osama bin Laden were whisked out of the country—only days after the attacks, without being properly questioned by the FBI—simply defies explanation. One story, in particular, graphically illustrates the shock experienced by those affected by the fiasco. According to a source close to the evacuation,

[A] young female member of the bin Laden family was the sole passenger on the first leg of the flight, from Los Angeles to Orlando [September 14].

In the immediate aftermath of 9/11, boarding any airplane was cause for anxiety. But now that the name Osama bin Laden had become synonymous with mass murder, boarding a plane with his family members was another story entirely. To avoid unnecessary dramas, the flight's operators made certain that the cockpit crew was briefed about who the passengers were—the bin Ladens—and the highly sensitive nature of their mission.

However, they neglected to brief the flight attendants.

On the flight from Los Angeles, the bin Laden girl began talking to an attendant about the horrid events of 9/11. "I feel so bad about it," she said.

"Well, it's not your fault," replied the attendant, who had no idea who the passenger really was.

"Yeah," said the passenger. "But he was my brother."

"The flight attendant just lost it," the source said.[156]

"BANDAR BUSH"

Now, while this couldn't *possibly* have anything to do with *who* authorized the mystery airlift, it "just so happens" that earlier on that very day (September 13) President Bush and Prince Bandar were literally kicked back at the White House smoking Cohiba cigars on the Truman Balcony, a casual, yet private outdoor spot behind the pillars of the South Portico. (The "timing" was not missed by Senator Graham who wrote in his own exposé of the airlift, "Neither the President nor Prince Bandar has disclosed what was discussed in that meeting. But later that day, something strange began to happen."[157]

While it might surprise some that a foreigner could have such an informal audience with the president of the United States—a mere two days after the horror of 9/11—the White House door has *always* been open to the Saudi ambassador. And for that matter, *so has every other important door in the country.* Colin Powell once complained that the Saudi plutocrat functioned on the level of a cabinet officer within the Bush administration. Unger notes "Between 1984 and 1987, he met or talked to Defense Secretary Caspar Weinberger at least sixty-four times."[158]

Truth is, he was probably a little pampered given all those billions he's been able to dish out. A devoted fan of the Dallas Cowboys, Bandar often stirred up controversy when his friend, team owner Jerry Jones, allowed him to stroll along the sidelines during games. The fact that his thirty bodyguards also got to accompany him didn't mitigate the problem any, especially with regard to the growing consternation of Cowboys' coach, Jimmy Johnson. After Dallas fumbled the ball in a game against the Chicago Bears in December 1992, Johnson looked up to see Bandar and his entourage standing nearby. Unger writes, "Enraged by the distraction, Johnson marched up to the owner's box and erupted at Jones for allowing the Saudi prince to intrude on his turf."[159]

Things only got worse when Bandar started visiting the Cowboys' locker room as well. Despite the fact that he had won two consecutive championships, Johnson was forced to resign. Unger states, "Jerry Jones repeatedly denied that his friendship with Bandar had been a factor, but it was widely reported as a major irritant between the two men."[160]

Yet, how does one compare a Jerry Jones to a connection with the *Bush* family? While the flamboyant playboy-prince has been widely known as the "Arab Gatsby," with his trimmed goatee and tailor-made double-breasted suits, the president's mama had a much more personal sobriquet for him. Unger writes:

> When George and Barbara Bush visited American troops in Saudi Arabia during the Thanksgiving holiday in 1990, the *New Yorker* reported, Bush called Bandar, who was in the country at the time. The Bushes were staying in the royal palace, and when Bandar arrived at their quarters, the president told him how much his recently divorced daughter, Dorothy, appreciated the friendship of Bandar's family. Dorothy had been alone at the White House with her children when Princess Haifa, Bandar's wife, invited her and the rest of the family over for Thanksgiving. The gesture so deeply touched the president that he was moved to tears. The first lady began to call him Bandar Bush.[161]

You might say that Bandar became one of the family. In the summer of 1998, just prior to the East African embassy attacks, the Saudi ambassador stopped by to see George and Barbara at Kennebunkport. Unger relates, "For former first lady Barbara Bush, the visit was an unexpected but delightful surprise, with Bandar cooking up a storm in the kitchen."[162] (What a buzzword in light of the *Perfect Storm*.)

Incidentally, according to a story in the *Washington Post*, Prince Bandar is not the only foreign wacko to appeal to the pro-choice "Queen Mum" of America. When British rocker Ozzy Osbourne attended the White House Correspondents' Dinner on May 4, 2002 (eight months after 9/11), "Brother" Bush acknowledged the demon-possessed drug addict from the podium, stating, "Ozzy, Mom loves your stuff" (the "stuff" cited being: "Facing Hell," "Bloodbath in Paradise," "Sabbath Bloody Sabbath," "Black Skies," and "Party with the Animals") to which Ozzy responded by standing on a table, saluting and throwing kisses.[163]

Then there was the time Bandar extended a little of his own Arab hospitality to the elder Bush as he "sweated out" the election of his son. On November 14, 2000, Bush arrived in England accompanied by General Norman Schwarzkopf, commander of U.S. forces during the Persian Gulf War. After joining up with former national security advisor Brent Scowcroft, the party headed out to Prince Bandar's enormous estate in Wychwood, England, for a little game hunting. In olden days the site had been a royal hunting ground used by Norman and Plantagenet kings.[164]

One can even make the case that "Dubya" could never have won the election in the first place without the Muslim vote. Early on, Bush campaign strategist Grover Norquist recognized the great, untapped potential of a Muslim-American electoral bloc. Consequently, despite the risk of negative publicity, the GOP decided that even anti-Semitic Muslim terrorists could be incorporated under the banner of "compassionate conservatism."

On March 12, 2000, Bush and his wife Laura met with Muslim leaders at a local mosque in Tampa, Florida. Among them was Sami Al-Arian, a Kuwaiti-born Palestinian who was an associate professor of engineering at the University of South Florida. The Bushes had their photo taken with Al-Arian and his wife Nahla at the Florida Strawberry Festival. Laura dutifully complimented Nahla's traditional head scarf, whereupon, she returned the gesture by remarking, "The Muslim people support you."[165]

Unfortunately, Al had a number of terrorist friends as well! Unger notes:

> Since 1995, as the founder and chairman of the board of World and Islam Enterprise (WISE), a Muslim think tank, Al-Arian had been under investigation by the FBI for his associations with Islamic Jihad, the Palestinian terrorist group. . . .
>
> In addition, *Newsweek* reported that Al-Arian had ties to the 1993 attack on the World Trade Center. Among his claims to fame, the magazine said, Al-Arian had "made many phone calls to two New York-area Arabs who figured in the World Trade Center bombing investigation."
>
> There were also Al-Arian's own statements. In 1998, he appeared as a guest speaker before the American Muslim Council. According to conservative author Kenneth Timmerman, Al-Arian referred to Jews as "monkeys and pigs" and added, "Jihad is our path. Victory to Islam.

Death to Israel. Revolution! Revolution! Until victory! Rolling, rolling to Jerusalem! . . ."

When he appeared at a fund-raising event, Timmerman says, he "begged for $500 to kill a jew."[166]

The "rag head" would eventually be arrested in Florida in February 2003 on dozens of charges including conspiracy to finance terrorist attacks in which over a hundred victims would die.[167] Nevertheless, Norquist continued to lobby Allah's people on behalf of the Bush campaign.

The Republican National Convention was convened in Philadelphia on the last day of July 2000. Whereas the Lord had opened a door of unprecedented liberty in America because the church of Philadelphia had kept His word, "Brother" Bush chose to blaspheme the proceedings by inviting a Muslim "cleric" to lead in "prayer." As a portent of things to come, Talat Othman offered up a *duaa* (Islamic benediction) on behalf of the Republican Party. (The only thing any wilder than this is my previous reference to "Reverend" Moon having sponsored "Dubya's" inaugural prayer luncheon in January 2000.) Unger writes: "When the convention ended on August 3, after George W. Bush had formally been nominated for president, between his family's extended personal and financial ties to the House of Saud and his campaign's ties to Islamists, it could be said that he was truly the Arabian Candidate."[168]

When push came to shove in the ultimate battleground state of Florida, there is no question that the Muslims handed Bush the White House. Unger states:

> In the end, the outcome of the election would be decided by Florida's electoral college votes. And in Florida the result was so close, and so riddled with irregularities, that a recount was necessary. . . .
>
> But in the thousands of postmortems about the election, one factor was largely overlooked. According to an exit poll of Muslims in Florida conducted by the American Muslim Alliance, 91 percent voted for Bush, 8 percent for Ralph Nader, and only 1 percent for Al Gore. Likewise, the Tampa Bay Islamic Center estimated that fifty-five thousand Muslims in Florida voted and that 88 percent of them favored Bush. All of which meant that the margin of victory for Bush among Florida Muslims was many, many times greater than his tiny statewide margin of victory of 537 votes.
>
> With the Bush restoration in full swing, GOP partisans eagerly claimed whatever credit they might reasonably take for the Bush victory, and Grover Norquist was no exception. "George W. Bush was elected President of the

United States of America because of the Muslim vote," he wrote in the right-wing *American Spectator*. "That's right," he added, "the Muslim vote."

Like every other group that contributed to Bush's victory, the Islamists realized that the tiny margin of victory in Florida had increased their leverage. Agha Saeed, the AMPCC chairman, said, "It won't be long before political analysts realize that Muslim voters have played a historic role." . . .

In other words, without the mobilization of the Saudi-funded Islamic groups, George W. Bush would not be president today.[169]

So, now you know why "Bandar Bush" has the run of the "joint," i.e., America! Unger summarizes the little known historical linkage between the House of Bush and the House of Saud.

The two men were scions of the most powerful dynasties in the world. The Bush family and its close associates—the House of Bush, if you will—included two presidents of the United States; former secretary of state James Baker, who had been a powerful figure in four presidential administrations; key figures in the oil and defense industries, the Carlyle Group, and the Republican Party; and much, much more. As for Bandar, his family effectively *was* the government of Saudi Arabia, the most powerful country in the Arab world. They had hundreds of billions of dollars and the biggest oil reserves in the world. The relationship was unprecedented. Never before had a president of the United States—much less, two presidents from the same family—had such close personal and financial ties to the ruling family of another foreign power.

Yet few Americans realized that these two dynasties, the Bush family and the House of Saud, had a history dating back more than twenty years. Not just business partners and personal friends, the Bushes and the Saudis had pulled off elaborate covert operations and gone to war together. They had shared secrets that involved unimaginable personal wealth, spectacular military might, the richest energy resources in the world, and the most odious crimes imaginable.

They had been involved in the Iron-curtain scandal, and in secret U.S. aid in the Afghanistan War that gave birth to Osama bin Laden. Along with then Vice President Bush, the Saudis had joined the United States in supporting the brutal Iraqi dictator Saddam Hussein for seven full years after knowing that he used weapons of mass destruction. . . . In the 1991 Gulf War, the Saudis and the elder Bush had fought side by side. And now there was the repatriation of the bin Ladens, which could not have taken place without approval at the highest levels of the executive branch of President George W. Bush's administration.

Only Bush and Bandar know what transpired that day on the Truman Balcony.[170]

Although the original purpose for their meeting supposedly concerned the Palestinian-Israeli issue, the two men could have chatted about any number of "relevant" subjects as they blew smoke rings in the air. Bandar probably conveyed the view of his countrymen that the 9/11 attacks were orchestrated by "Zionists."[171] He would later protest media reports that referred to the 9/11 terrorists as "Saudis," stating: "We in the kingdom, the government and the people of Saudi Arabia, refuse to have any person affiliated with terrorism to be connected to our country."[172] A full year later, the powerful minister of the Interior, Prince Nayef Ibn Abd-Al-Aziz, maintained his belief in a Jewish conspiracy, asking, "Is it possible that nineteen youths, including fifteen Saudis, carried out the operation of September 11?"[173] *Of course, having received over $13 million from Arab Americans for his 2000 election campaign, Bush would have been nodding in agreement.*[174]

The prince may have asked Bush for his opinion regarding any fallout his Saudi colleagues might encounter in the marketplace. Among other Western icons, the bin Ladens did business with Disney, Snapple, Porsche and the Hard Rock Cafe.[175] (As previously noted, Carlyle would dump the Saudi Binladin Group by November.)

According to "official" statements, the topic of discussion centered on how the two men would work together in the war on terror. One "leak" stated that the United States would hand over to the Saudis any al-Qaeda operatives who failed to cooperate; the unmistakable implication being that the Saudi interrogators could employ any means necessary—including torture—to get the prisoners to talk.

However, moving beyond this humorous musing, the obvious priorities on the docket would have been Bandar's request for the "emergency" airlift and the president's willingness to authorize the same—for a "fee," that is. Being a good Arab, the prince undoubtedly engaged in heavy negotiation. After all, at least $1.476 billion had previously found its way from Saudi coffers to the massive network of companies and institutions comprising the House of Bush.[176] (See detailed breakdown of Saudi investments to companies, foundations, and charities owned by the Bushes and their associates in Appendix C of Unger's book *House of Bush, House of Saud*.) But then again, the Carlyle Group had done a lot for Bandar's country, especially the $163 million "make-over" of the Saudi

National Guard (a Middle Eastern version of ancient Rome's Praetorian Guard, ensuring that King Fahd got to wake up on a regular basis, etc.).[177]

In any event, the two titans eventually settled on a final figure. Unger writes:

> On Friday, September 14, a dozen ambassadors from Arab nations—Syria, the Palestinian Authority, Algeria, Lebanon, Saudi Arabia, Egypt, Jordan, and the Persian Gulf states—met at Prince Bandar's home in McLean, Virginia, to discuss how they would respond to Bush's new policies. Bandar himself had pledged his support for the war on terror and, perhaps most important, vowed that Saudi Arabia would help stabilize the world oil markets. In a breathtaking display of their command over the oil markets, the Saudis dispatched 9 million barrels of oil to the United States. As a consequence, the price instantly dropped from $28 to $22 per barrel.[178]

The prince also pledged to help his friend get reelected, Woodward writing, "According to Prince Bandar, the Saudis hoped to fine-tune oil prices over 10 months to prime the economy for 2004. What was key, Bandar knew, were the economic conditions before a presidential election, not at the moment of the election."[179]

THE ALMOST TRIPLE CROWN

The unbelievable story of Prince Ahmed bin Salman bid Abdul Aziz represents a classic illustration of the abject corruption behind the Bush-Saud alliance. It also reveals the caliber of suspect that was permitted to leave a crime scene without undergoing even minimal interrogation. On September 16, 2001, Prince Ahmed boarded a flight in Lexington, Kentucky, en route to London. (A copy of the passenger manifest drawn up by the Saudi embassy, displaying the name Prince Ahmed bin Salman at the top, may be viewed in Unger's book.) The owner of many legendary race horses, Ahmed spent a lot of time "hanging out" in Lexington. He was considered one of the most Westernized members of the royal family.

Six months after Ahmed's escape, the CIA captured terrorist Abu Zubaydah in the suburbs of Faisalabad in western Pakistan. The thirty-year-old Zubaydah was the al-Qaeda operations chief who had personally supervised the USS *Cole* bombing. His arrest constituted the highest-ranking al-Qaeda operative ever to be taken into custody. White House spokesman Ari Fleischer said: " This represents a very significant blow to al Qaeda," calling Zubaydah "a key terrorist recruiter, an operational planner and a member of Osama bin Laden's inner circle."[180]

His interrogation began on Sunday, March 31, three days after the raid. The definitive source for this episode is Gerald Posner's *Why America Slept*. According to Posner, the CIA attempted to trick Zubaydah by using two teams of debriefers as a variation of the good cop-bad cop routine. While the first crew was made up of Americans, bound by the Geneva Convention, etc., the second consisted of Arab-Americans, disguised as Saudi security agents, feared for their methods of brutality. The logic was that Zubaydah would much rather talk to the Americans than be turned over to the Saudis.

However, the exact opposite occurred. While barely speaking to his American captors, Zubaydah "suddenly started talking animatedly" when confronted by the Saudi team. Unger writes, citing Posner:

> "He was happy to see them, he said, because he feared the Americans would torture and then kill him. Zubaydah asked his interrogators to call a senior member of the ruling Saudi family. He then provided a private home number and cell phone number from memory. 'He will tell you what to do,' Zubaydah promised them."
>
> The name Zubaydah gave came as a complete surprise to the CIA. It was Prince Ahmed bin Salman bin Abdul Aziz. . . .
>
> He said that several years earlier the royal family had made a deal with Al Qaeda in which the House of Saud would aid the Taliban so long as Al Qaeda kept terrorism out of Saudi Arabia. Zubaydah added that as part of this arrangement, he dealt with Prince Ahmed and two other members of the House of Saud as intermediaries, Prince Sultan bin Faisal bin Turki al-Saud, a nephew of King Fahd's and Prince Fahd bin Turki bin Saud al-Kabir, a twenty-five-year-old distant relative of the king's. Again, he furnished phone numbers by memory.[181]

The faux Saudi interrogators responded by telling Zubaydah that 9/11 had changed everything; the House of Saud would never stand behind him after that. The prisoner then dropped the "mother of all bombs."

> "Zubaydah said that 9/11 changed nothing because Ahmed . . . knew beforehand that an attack was scheduled for American soil that day," Posner writes. "They just didn't know what it would be, nor did they want to know more than that. The information had been passed to them, said Zubaydah, because bin Laden knew they could not stop it without knowing the specifics,

but later they would be hard-pressed to turn on him if he could disclose their foreknowledge."[182]

After being moved to an undisclosed location two weeks later, Zubaydah discovered the ruse, recanted his entire tale, and tried to strangle himself.

Now if you think the Bush administration blew it by letting Ahmed out of the country, what possible excuse could they offer for allowing him to return—to attend a horse race, no less—and then letting him slip away a *second* time? As the Saudi government had "assured" CIA officials that Prince Ahmed was not an al-Qaeda contact, etc., Unger notes that the Bush administration was left "with nowhere to go—unless it wanted to create an international incident."[183] The State Department was subsequently instructed to issue Ahmed's visa.

And so, on May 7, 2002, Prince Ahmed's War Emblem entered the Kentucky Derby, as a 20-1 shot. It was a gorgeous day at Churchill Downs racetrack in Louisville. Eight months after 9/11, however, America was still in mourning, and at 5:15 p.m., about fifty minutes before the race, a trumpet played taps, and the crowd of 145,000 attending the country's premier horse racing event fell silent. Firefighters from New York City's Ladder Company 3 on East Twenty-ninth Street were the guests of honor, standing at attention in front of the winners' circle. Twelve members of the company had lost their lives in the World Trade Center attack. . . .

War Emblem broke cleanly at the gate and took the lead in front of Proud Citizen. And that was it. He pulled away at midstretch, holding the lead wire to wire, winning by four lengths.

A few people jeered as Prince Ahmed made his way to the winners' circle, but that did not seem to bother him. "Everyone respects me here," he said. "Everybody actually makes me feel so good, sometimes I'm embarrassed. The American public treats me better than in Saudi Arabia."

"It's a great achievement," he added. "This was important for me and it's an honor to be the first Arab to win the Kentucky Derby."

Columnist Jimmy Breslin, covering the Derby for *Newsday*, did not fail to notice Prince Ahmed's self-satisfaction. "Prince Ahmed bin Salman of Saudi Arabia held up the winner's cup and gloated with the thought of the million and more he made with the win, and did this in the presence of firefighters from Ladder 3," Breslin wrote. ". . . I wondered right away if Prince Ahmed had done anything to let us know he was sorry and could he do anything to assist after what bin Laden and other homegrown degenerates did to this city. . . . But the guy did nothing. What are you bothering me for, the prince said in Louisville, I am in horse racing, not politics."[184]

Two weeks later, War Emblem won the Preakness Stakes in Baltimore. Prince Ahmed's colt now had a chance at being the first Triple Crown winner since Seattle Slew in 1977. When asked by a reporter how much he wanted to win the triple, he replied, "As badly as I want my son and daughter to get married. . . . To win the Triple Crown would really knock me out."[185]

However, on June 8, Prince Ahmed was a surprising "no show" at the Belmont Stakes, the third leg of the Triple Crown. "I'm disappointed the prince wasn't here," said trainer Bob Baffert.[186] According to an unnamed associate, Ahmed was said to be "tending to family obligations in Riyadh" (though the nature of such "obligations" was unknown).[187] In any event, War Emblem stumbled as he came out of the gate and finished eighth. The dismal showing must have proved quite a shock to Ahmed; about six weeks later, on July 22, the ol' boy was *dead*! (i.e., He *really* got "knocked out.") News reports said the forty-three-year-old nephew of King Fahd had died in his sleep due to a heart attack. Unger provides "the rest of the story":

> As Gerald Posner has reported, Ahmed was not the only person named by Zubaydah to suffer ill. The next day, July 23, Ahmed's cousin, Prince Sultan bin Faisal bin Turki al-Saud, was killed in a one-car crash while en route to Ahmed's funeral. A week later, on July 30, Prince Fahd bin Turki bin Saud al-Kabir, a third member of the royal family who had been named by Zubaydah, was found in the desert, having apparently died of thirst.[188]

In its brief mention of the Saudi evacuation, The *9/11 Commission Report* blandly states: "Our own independent review of the Saudi nationals involved confirms that no one with known links to terrorism departed on these flights."[189] The Satan-worshipping Muslims were less hypocritical. On September 4, 2003, nearly two years after the controversial airlift, Saudi embassy spokesman Nail al-Jubeir appeared on CNN and was asked by newscaster Paula Zahn, "Can you tell us unequivocally tonight that no one on board had anything to do with either the planning or the execution of the September 11 plot?" "There are only two things that I'm sure about," al-Jubeir replied. "That there is the existence of God and then we will die at the end of the world. Everything else, we don't know."[190]

THE TWIN IMPLOSIONS

According to the "official account," the Twin Towers of the World Trade Center collapsed as a result of two factors: the impact of the airliners plus the intense heat produced by the resulting fires. On May 20, 2002, the Federal Emergency Management Agency (FEMA) issued its formal report on the collapse. In the history of high-rise fires, not one incident had ever resulted in a building collapse. Thus, even FEMA was forced to thrice concede:

> The collapse of the towers astonished most observers, including knowledgeable structural engineers . . . The collapse of these structures is particularly significant in that, prior to these events, no protected steel-frame structure, the most common form of large commercial construction in the United States, had ever experienced a fire-induced collapse . . . Prior to September 11, 2001, there was little, if any, record of fire-induced collapse of large fire-protected steel buildings.[191]

As to *why* the Twin Towers collapsed, well, even FEMA couldn't come up with a straight answer, concluding, "the sequence of events leading to the collapse of each tower could not be definitively determined."[192] ("Duh!") Griffin notes that many professionals challenged the government's position from the outset.

> It was rejected already in January of 2002 in an article by Bill Manning entitled "$elling Out the Investigation," which was published in *Fire Engineering*, a trade magazine with ties to the New York Fire Department. Manning reported that a growing number of fire protection engineers had suggested that "the structural damage from the planes and the explosive ignition of jet fuel in themselves were not enough to bring down the towers." In the meantime, many more objections to the official theory have been raised.[193]

Initially it was believed that the Twin Towers collapsed when the heat of the fires, fed by the jet fuel, melted the structure's steel columns. That view has now been generally discarded. To melt steel requires a temperature of approximately 2,770°F (1,500°C). According to Thomas Eagar, professor of materials engineering and engineering systems at MIT, the maximum possible temperature for an open fire fueled by hydrocarbons (refined kerosene, which is what jet fuel is) would be 1,600 to 1,700°F.[194]

Eagar estimates that since the WTC fires were fuel-rich fires, as seen by the fact that they produced a high amount of black smoke, they were only mild hydrocarbon fires, "probably only 1,200 or 1,300°F."[195]

While the "melted steel" theory has been rejected, the "weakened steel" view has become the explanation of choice. Because the steel used in the Towers was able to sustain five times its load, theoretically, a collapse could have occurred if the steel columns were heated to the point that they lost eighty percent of their strength. This scenario would have only required a temperature of about 1,300°F. However, Griffin contends that this was highly unlikely:

> To evaluate this issue we must acknowledge the distinction, emphasized by Eagar himself, between temperature and heat (or energy). Something, such as a burning match or light bulb, can have a very high temperature but not generate much heat (energy), because it is so small. A burning match would never bring a steel beam up to its temperature. A 1,300°F fire would bring a huge steel beam up to this temperature only if it were a very big fire, so that it had lots of energy.
>
> There is one more condition: The big fire would have to be applied to the steel beam for a considerable period of time.
>
> For the official theory to be credible, therefore, the fires in the towers must have been moderately hot; they must have been large fires, spreading throughout the buildings; and they must have burned for a considerable length of time. All the available evidence, however, suggests that the opposite was the case. . . .
>
> Photographs of the North Tower provide no evidence of any fire that could have weakened its steel significantly. . . .
>
> The South Tower had a far bigger fireball because it was hit near a corner, so more fuel was spilled outside. These fireballs generated a great amount of heat. But it was momentary, because the fuel was quickly burned up. . . .
>
> The facts about the fire, therefore, seem to rule out any version of the official account according to which each tower had hot, widespread, long-lasting fires. Insofar as there were hot fires, they were localized and of short duration. Such fires, even if they were 1,300°F, could not have brought much if any steel up to that temperature.[196]

Another fact that mitigates against the fire theory is that the South Tower collapsed first. Griffin expands on the significance of this reverse order anomaly:

As we saw, it would take considerable time for fire to heat steel up to its own temperature. All other things being equal, then, the tower that was struck first should have collapsed first. And yet, although the South Tower was struck 17 minutes later than the North Tower, it collapsed 29 minutes earlier. This surprising fact would perhaps not create a problem if the fire in the South Tower had been much bigger. As we have seen, however, the fire in the South Tower was actually smaller. Upon hearing that one tower took almost twice as long as the other one, therefore, one would assume that that was the South Tower. And yet the opposite was the case. This complete reversal of expectations suggests that the collapse of these buildings was caused by something other than the fires.[197]

The "weakened steel" theory becomes the basis for the so-called "pancake type" collapse theory; "As the joists on one or two of the most heavily burned floors gave way and the outer box columns began to bow outward, the floors above them also fell."[198] There are a number of serious problems with this view. Each of the towers was approximately 1,300 feet high. To stabilize these immense structures (the tallest buildings in New York City) 47 steel columns were positioned in the central core of each tower with another 240 steel columns placed around the perimeter. Also, the columns had a greater thickness at the bottom than at the top. Eric Hufschmid points out in his book *Painful Questions,* "In order for a floor to fall, hundreds of joints had to break almost simultaneously on 236 exterior columns and 47 core columns."[199]

Next, if each floor produced even a minimal amount of initial resistance—no more than half-a-second per floor—the collapse of all floors involved would have taken forty to forty-seven seconds, or four times as long as what actually occurred.

The biggest objection to the "pancake" theory is the fact that the collapse of the Twin Towers was a *total* collapse, resulting in a mountain of fine dust. What happened to the lower parts of the massive support columns? If the official version is true—that the damage resulted from the impacts and fires which occurred only in the upper floors, and that the floors proceeded to pancake—the steel support columns in the central core for at least the lowest twenty to thirty floors should have remained standing.[200] While no credible explanation has been given for the disintegration of these massive columns, the phenomena *does* explain how the 1,300 foot building was able to "pancake" to ground level in roughly ten seconds. Like Emeril says—"BAM!"

Thus, many contend the preceding observations leave no other alternative but to consider the inevitable "controlled demolition" theory. Common folk like myself must wrestle with such repulsive speculation because of what we have witnessed with our own eyes. While conspiracy theorists are frequently ridiculed for being non-scientific, I would posit that the laboratory conditions relevant to the Twin Towers collapse are beyond the intellectual prowess of the average "ditto head." How's *this* for an elementary lesson in common sense? Most of us have witnessed more than one controlled demolition of some hotel or other large structure. As they all look alike, the process is a no-brainer to our memory banks. On the other hand, *none* of us have ever seen a protected steel-frame structure collapse on its own, *as such an incident has never occurred in the history of mankind.* As a 1991 FEMA report related about a fire in a large Philadelphia building that year—the fire was so energetic that "[b]eams and girders sagged and twisted," but "[d]espite this extraordinary exposure, the columns continued to support their loads without obvious damage."[201] When FEMA said that "the collapse of the towers astonished most observers," the FDNY was probably at the top of the list. Why do you think so many were willing to rush into the towers with reckless abandon? While they possessed plenty of raw courage, the partial collapse of even one tower would have come as a total shock. Even the official *9/11 Commission Report* was willing to acknowledge:

> They [FDNY chiefs] also received advice from senior FDNY chiefs that while the building [North Tower] might eventually suffer a partial collapse on upper floors, such structural failure was not imminent. No one anticipated the possibility of a total collapse.[202]

Consequently, when we viewed the "collapse" of the North and South towers on 9/11—well, we simply couldn't help ourselves; we already knew what a controlled demolition looked like. I mean—we didn't want to become "Limbaugh Kooks," but we were stuck in reality. The fact that *both* 1,300-foot towers imploded in perfect symmetrical fashion didn't help matters much. At least a hundred websites can show you hours and hours of footage providing various angles and clips you didn't see on the major networks. (The unedited coverage supplied by various European sources is among the most insightful and unnerving.) Granted, some of these sites espouse any number of unscriptural ideologies (e.g., anti-Semitism), but the video footage of the Twin Towers can't hurt you. (John 8:32)

One site displays the implosion of a hotel on the left side of the screen with the implosion of the North Tower on the right. Both showed the same puffs of smoke (demolition squibs) shooting out of the building at various levels in advance of the collapse. The action is literally spellbinding. Hufschmid estimates, "Perhaps 100,000 tons of concrete in each tower was pulverized to a powder. This required a lot of energy.[203] Griffin notes: "The powder was ejected horizontally from the buildings with such force that the buildings were surrounded by enormous dust clouds that were perhaps three times the width of the buildings themselves. . . . What other than explosives could turn concrete into powder and then eject it horizontally 150 feet or more?"[204]

A seventy-minute color documentary entitled *911 In Plane Site* contains some very disturbing footage, much of which was broadcast during live news coverage. However, as in the case of the initial Oklahoma City bombing reports, the controversial clips were never seen again. Numerous snippets by FOX *News* and CNN reporters describe explosions going off at the World Trade Center after the planes had struck. An unidentified female announcer for CNN is heard stating in an excited voice: "The entire top of the building just blew up." Aaron Brown of CNN is shown having made three separate announcements concerning explosions. "There's a second explosion." Later, "There's another explosion." Then, while he's talking, the words **"Third Explosion Shatters World Trade Center in New York"** *appear clearly across the bottom of the screen.* He is later shown giving yet another update, "We have a report now of a fourth explosion at the Trade Center." When the South Tower collapses, Brown remarks, "It almost looks like one of those implosions of buildings that you see. . . ."

Several similar statements are made near Ground Zero. An unidentified male reporter for FOX *News* says, "There was a very loud blast—explosion. It's not clear now why this explosion took place." Another FOX reporter asks a policeman, "Do you know if it was an explosion or a building collapse?" The officer replies, "To me it sounded like an explosion." Another voice is heard saying, "It was a huge explosion." The FOX reporter then points to some debris thought to be from one of the hijacked planes and states: "The FBI is here as you can see. They have roped this area off. They were taking photographs and securing this area just prior to that huge explosion that we all heard and felt."

Dramatic evidence of this "huge explosion" was accidentally shown by CNN during a live interview with author Tom Clancey (how appropriate). The time is about 9:30 a.m. Both towers are still standing. The camera is looking from west to east. The smoke from the WTC is being blown toward Brooklyn, away from the camera toward the southeast. Thus there is a very clear view of the north side of the Twin Towers. When you look toward the base of the left tower a huge plume of white smoke can be seen rising almost 60 stories high! Dave vonKleist, the narrator of *911 In Plane Site*, asks, "How could this plume of smoke be rising from the base of the towers if neither one of the towers had collapsed?" A close-up photograph of the giant smoke cloud taken at ground level is included for good measure.

There were many eyewitness testimonials regarding explosions at Ground Zero. However, these stories have been suppressed by the mainline media. Like the Tom Clancey piece, they remain off-limits to public scrutiny. Ask yourself—How much of this was discussed during the 9/11 Commission investigation? Griffin continues:

> Kim White, an employee on the 80th floor, said: "All of a sudden the building **shook**, then it started to sway. We didn't know what was going on. . . . We got down as far as the 74th floor. . . . (T)hen there was another **explosion**." . . .
>
> Construction worker Phillip Morelli reported that while he was in the fourth subbasement of the North Tower, he was thrown to the floor twice. Whereas the first of these experiences apparently occurred at the time of the plane crash, the second one involved a more powerful **blast**, which blew out walls. . . .
>
> Stationary engineer Mike Pecoraro, who was working in the sixth subbasement of the North Tower, reported that after feeling and hearing an **explosion**, he and his co-worker found the parking garage and the machine shop, including a 50-ton hydraulic press, reduced to rubble. They also found a 300-pound steel and concrete fire door wrinkled up "like a piece of aluminum foil." These effects were, he said, like the effects of the terrorist bombing of 1993.[205]

A poignant scene of a final conversation between a husband and wife overshadows a piece of evidence that unintentionally exacerbates the tragedy. Bamford writes:

By now [Beverly] Eckert knew there was little hope left. "Sean," she said with great sadness, "it doesn't seem to me that they are going to be able to get to you in time. [He was trapped on the 105th floor of the North Tower.] I think we need to say good-bye." For the next few minutes, the two talked about their love and the happy years they had spent together. Eckert said she wished she were there with him. [He] asked her to give his love to everyone. "I love you," he said. . . .

Over the phone, Eckert suddenly heard **an enormous explosion followed by a crack and then a roaring sound**. "The floor fell out from underneath him," she said. "It sounded like Niagara Falls. I knew without seeing that he was gone." With the phone cradled next to her heart, she walked into another room and on the television she could see Tower Two collapsing—the first tower to go down.[206]

Many firemen also witnessed the effects of what appeared to be a controlled demolition. Three members of the FDNY appear in Mr. vonKleist's documentary and relate, with great animation, what they observed as they were literally running for their lives: ". . . we started running. . . . Floor by floor it started popping out. . . . **It was like they had detonated it—*boom, boom, boom, boom, boom*—like it was planned to take down a building**. I was watching it and running. . . ." On 9/11, Louie Cacchioli was a twenty-year veteran firefighter assigned to Engine 47 in Harlem. His personal testimony appeared in the on-line edition of *People* magazine, September 12, 2001 (and later in the newsstand format on September 24).

We were the first ones in the second tower after the plane struck. I was taking firefighters up in the elevator to the 24th floor to get in position to evacuate workers. **On the last trip up a bomb went off. We think there were bombs set in the building.**[207]

Eyewitness disclosures like Mr. Cacchioli's will soon be as inaccessible as those initial Oklahoma City newscasts and confiscated surveillance tapes. A judgment by the New York State Supreme Court on January 8, 2004, denied nine family members of persons who died in the World Trade Center access to portions of 9-1-1 tapes and recorded departmental interviews containing the firefighters' "personal expressions of feelings, opinions and recommendations" (i.e., "We *think* there were bombs set in the building").

A former New Jersey fireman with several close friends in the FDNY told me that many of the men grapple with a sense of betrayal and anger. He said, "It is hard to get them to talk and if they open up at all, it is usually after a few beers at the neighborhood bar." For some, the lingering bitterness concerns matters like the failed radios that resulted in so many needless deaths. However, for others it is a topic of far greater implications. My contact told me in the strictest confidence, "A captain I know who lost a dozen men in the Towers, was particularly disturbed by the serious structural damage he personally observed between the twentieth and thirtieth floors."

Seismograph readings taken at Columbia University's Lamont-Doherty Earth Observatory in Palisades, New York (twenty-one miles north of the WTC) tend to corroborate a controlled demolition scenario. With regard to the fireballs caused by the impacts of the two planes hitting the Twin Towers, Arthur Lerner-Lam wrote in the November 20 issue of *Eos* (published by the American Geographical Union), "The energy contained in the amount of fuel combusted was the equivalent to the energy released by 240 tons of TNT."[208] The official seismograph report for the two aircraft impacts registered local magnitude (ML) 0.9 and 0.7. However, the Towers' subsequent collapse registered magnitudes of 2.1 and 2.3. Huge seismic "spikes" marked the moment the greatest energy went into the ground. The Palisades seismic record confirms that the strongest jolts were registered at the beginning of the collapses, well before the falling debris struck the earth. Lerner-Lam confirms, "During the collapse, most of the energy of the falling debris was absorbed by the towers and the neighboring structures, converting them into rubble and dust or causing other damage—but not causing significant ground shaking."[209] Griffin adds:

> Still more support is provided by seismic evidence that a moderately powerful earthquake was recorded as each tower was collapsing. The seismographs . . . recorded a 2.1 magnitude earthquake beginning at 9:59:04, then a 2.3 quake beginning at 10:28:31. In each case, "the shocks increased during the first 5 seconds then dropped abruptly to a lower level for about 3 seconds, and then slowly tapered off." This pattern, Hufschmid suggests, reflects the fact that the first explosives detonated were those near the tops of the towers, where the steel columns were the thinnest. The shocks get stronger as the detonation pattern, controlled by a computer program, worked its way down.

The final explosions at the base of the tower and in the basement had to break joints on columns made from 100 mm thick steel, so they were powerful explosives. The seismic data peaked when the explosives in the basement were detonated. Then the explosions stopped and the rubble continued to fall for another couple of seconds, resulting in small seismic tremors.[210]

You say—"Dr. Grady, these scenarios are totally insane!" I agree (though a more *accurate* word would be "perilous"). But have you taken a good look at the alternatives? After all, it was our own secretary of defense, Mr. Rumsfeld (nicknamed "Rumstud" by President Bush after *People* magazine listed him as one of the world's sexiest men[211]), who warned us about the "great unknown":

> As we know, there are known knowns; there are things we know we know. We also know there are known unknowns, that is to say, we know there are some things we do not know. But there are also unknown unknowns—the ones we don't know we don't know. If one looks throughout the history of our country and other free countries, it is the latter category that tends to be the difficult ones.[212]

While it goes against the grain of the average American to even *think* that his government could be capable of compromising his security, the truth is, he could be in the final stages of denial. As Mike Moore answers his own question concerning why President Bush does not "stop prohibiting the truth from coming out,"

> Perhaps it's because George & Co. have a lot more to hide beyond why they didn't scramble the fighter jets fast enough on the morning of September 11. **And maybe we, the people, are afraid to know the whole truth because it could take us down roads where we don't want to go.**[213]

Like the *Koran's* version of our perverted "Don't ask; don't tell" policy puts it—"Ask not about things which, if made plain to you, may cause you trouble."[214]

Thus, it might behoove all of us to heed the warning uttered by Dick Armey in his farewell address at the National Press Club following his long career in Congress. The former House majority leader cautioned his fellow countrymen about

> [the] awful dangerous seduction of sacrificing our freedoms for safety against this insidious threat (of terrorism) that comes right into our neighborhoods. . . .

We the people had better keep an eye on . . . our government. Not out of contempt or lack of appreciation or disrespect, but out of a sense of guardianship.[215]

At the very least you might want to talk with a few native New Yorkers about the possibility of government complicity in the 9/11 attacks. From a secular standpoint, residents of New York City are some of the sharpest people in the world. While naive Baptists continue to circulate the bogus tale about a microphone that supposedly was lowered down a deep mine shaft, recording the cries of the damned in Hell, the Italians in my old Manhattan neighborhood would have asked, "How come da heat didn't boin da wires?" The same would apply to politics. On August 30, 2004, the Republican National Convention opened in Madison Square Garden with former New York mayor Rudy Giuliani as the keynote speaker. This time it was the Muslim Iman Izak-El Mu-eed Pasha who got the ball rolling with a quote from the "holy" *Koran*, ". . . whoever obeys God and his messenger will indeed achieve a mighty success," followed by the "prayers" of Church of Christ minister and author Max Lucado, evangelical speaker Joni Eareckson Tada and Mormon publisher Sheri Dew. While Christians have always endorsed "Brother" Bush, on the opening day of the convention Zogby International released the findings of a poll they conducted in New York that week focusing on the question of whether some government leaders had foreknowledge of the 9/11 attacks. An article on the Zogby news page stated:

> On the eve of a Republican National Convention invoking 9/11 symbols, sound bytes and imagery, half (49.3%) of New York City residents and 41% of New York citizens overall say that some of our leaders "knew in advance that attacks were planned on or around September 11, 2001, and that they consciously failed to act," according to the poll . . . conducted from Tuesday August 24 through Thursday August 26, 2004. Overall results have a margin of sampling error of +/-3.5.
>
> The poll is the first of its kind conducted in America that surveys attitudes regarding US government complicity in the 9/11 tragedy. Despite the acute legal and political implications of this accusation, nearly 30% of registered Republicans and over 38% of those who described themselves as "very conservative" supported the claim. . . .
>
> Less than two in five (36%) believe that the 9/11 Commission had "answered all the important questions about what actually happened on September 11th . . ."[216]

What this translates to is the ugly *fact* that one out of every two New Yorkers who came in contact with a visiting delegate that week *wouldn't trust President Bush as far as they could throw him*—one out of every two taxi drivers; one out of every two hotel maids; one out of every two waiters; one out of every two hot dog vendors; one out of every two . . . As the third anniversary of 9/11 neared, a Greek immigrant who worked as a janitor on the second shift at the Twin Towers told an acquaintance of mine, in broken English, "Terrorists no bring down this building; Americans bring down this building!"

While MSNBC reported on September 3, 2004, that Britney Spears's used chewing gum was selling for $14,000 on E-bay, the Zogby poll reveals that there are at least a few folks left in this country who can still think and chew their *own* gum at the same time. As the saying goes— "You can fool *all* of the people *some* of the time, *some* of the people *all* of the time, but you can't fool *all* of the people *all* of the time."

WORLD TRADE CENTER 7

At 5:20 on the afternoon of 9/11, with the City of New York in utter chaos and the president supposedly on his way back to Washington— the strangest incident of that infamous day occurred. Yet, the one event that should have become the *most* investigated "smoking gun" of the entire "terrorist onslaught," sadly, has been relegated to the *least* known episode of all! (Remember, when you put something past a New Yorker, "You're good, Baby, good!" *Bada Bing, Bada Boom!*) In the Zogby poll, question number four (of six) dealt with "the inexplicable and largely unreported collapse of the third WTC skyscraper on 9/11—what was its number?" *A staggering 72 percent did not know the answer!*[217] Yo!— Do *you*?

On the eve of the third anniversary of 9/11, three out of every four of those cabbies, maids, waiters and hotdog vendors could not identify the forty-seven-story skyscraper that mysteriously imploded in their own backyard!

The structure to which I am referring is the Solomon Brothers Building, known as WTC 7, in the World Trade Center complex. If I may speak frankly, the implosion of WTC 7 is a matter of historical record. As it collapsed, former CBS News anchor Dan Rather exclaimed, "It's amazing, amazing, incredible—pick your words. For the third time today, it's reminiscent of those pictures we've all seen too much on television before, a building was deliberately destroyed by well-placed dynamite to knock it down."

Well there goes *another* one of those "Limbaugh Kooks" (with an asterisk after his name) passing along his subliminal suggestion about *another* one of those optical illusions visible to the naked eye—how a building gets "deliberately destroyed by well-placed dynamite," etc. However, we are getting ahead of ourselves here.

While Dan was correct about connecting the *implosion* of WTC 7 with that of WTC 1 and 2, the demise of the Solomon Brothers Building is in a category all by itself. (Believe me, it doesn't get any heavier than this!) While the government is barely holding its own when it blames the collapse of the Twin Towers on the "twin effects" of aircraft-induced structural damage and jet fuel-ignited fires—*neither of those hypothetical causes can be applied to WTC 7!* Did-you-get-that?

Despite the fact that both Towers imploded in perfect symmetrical fashion (the *9/11 Commission Report* specifically stating with regard to Tower Two, "The building collapsed into itself . . ."[218]), a "substantial" amount of falling debris supposedly ignited a number of "serious" fires in WTC 7, situated a full block away (across Vesey Street), or about 355 feet from the North Tower. The official story goes that as the occupants of WTC 7 had self-evacuated, the FDNY decided to let the building burn rather than risk any more loss of life.

Yeah, I know all about that, but exactly what made the forty-seven-story skyscraper "collapse" at 5:20 p.m.? In case you are an honest, conscientious, patriotic citizen who would rather go through proper channels than feed off wacko conspiracy websites and chat rooms—well, good luck to ya. But at least let me save you some time. Here is what you will find on the official FEMA website: "The specifics of the fires in WTC 7 and how they caused the building to collapse remain unknown at this time."[219]

With regard to the leading theory that the collapse resulted from a fire induced by diesel fuel stored on the ground floor, FEMA states, "Although the total diesel fuel on the premises contained massive potential energy, the best hypothesis has only a low probability of occurrence."[220] To FEMA's "credit," they do point out that the building's sophisticated sprinkler systems *failed* (though no reason was offered for this, either). And don't bother wasting your time reading the report issued by the House Science Committee. Griffin states that it "also provided no explanation."[221]

So, take a guess how much space the *9/11 Commission Report* devoted to explaining the mysterious implosion of WTC 7. The "collapse" is not even mentioned, much less discussed. In an essay entitled "WTC-7: The Improbable Collapse," Scott Loughrey states in abject consternation:

> FEMA's nonchalance about WTC-7's collapse is stunning. Structural failures of this magnitude do not normally take place. . . . (Do) we now live in an era when tall steel buildings can collapse in large cities without any significant discussion of why?[222]

To use the Wizard of Oz as a rather sick analogy, as far as our government is concerned—WTC 7 is "that man behind the curtain!"

In 2003, I happened upon an amazing discovery that appeared to unravel the mystery of WTC 7. A number of radio talk show hosts who promote the conspiracy view of history began informing their listeners about a PBS documentary entitled *America Rebuilds,* which aired on the one-year anniversary of 9/11. When the subject of WTC 7 was discussed, Larry Silverstein, the owner of the World Trade Center complex, made the following candid admission:

> I remember getting a call from the fire department commander, telling me that they were not sure they were gonna be able to contain the fire, and I said, "We've had such terrible loss of life, maybe the smartest thing to do is to pull it." And they made the decision to pull and we watched the building collapse.[223]

As anyone familiar with the demolition industry can affirm, the expression "*pull* a building" means to bring the structure down, usually with explosive charges. (In an earlier segment of the documentary, engineers discuss the care they employed while later "pulling" Building 6 with cables and bulldozers.) For the record, Silverstein purchased the WTC in early 2001 and promptly took out a record $7 billion insurance policy. In February 2002, Silverstein Properties won an initial settlement of $861 million from Industrial Risk Insurers to rebuild on the original site of WTC 7. With the estimated investment in WTC 7 at $386 million, the decision to "pull the building" resulted in a quick profit of about $500 million![224]

Developments like this remind some of that old story about the three tycoons who were sitting around a pool discussing recent insurance settlements. After the first two disclosed how they had each received $50,000 for *fire* related claims, the third man remarked that he had just won over $1 million in compensation for a *flood*; whereupon, the startled pair replied, "How do you start a *flood*?"

Such a stark "confession" made on nationwide television seemed too good to be true. Dramatic footage of WTC 7's implosion resonates on the screen during Silverstein's last statement, "And they made the decision to pull and we watched it collapse." It certainly *appeared* as though the billionaire owner of the World Trade Center had shot himself in the foot with a colossal "Freudian slip"; the obvious problem being that under normal conditions, several days of meticulous efforts would have been needed to properly set the necessary demolition charges for a building the size of WTC 7. In this case, however, after the fires "broke out" sometime after the collapse of WTC 1, the forty-seven-story skyscraper crashed to the ground in 3.2 seconds at approximately 5:30 p.m.! Do you *really* suppose that a qualified demolition team could have been assembled on the spur of the moment, amidst the greatest chaos the nation had ever experienced, and then, with explosives in hand, rush into an "inferno," set the charges with the required precision, and then make their way out—all in less than three to four hours (depending on when Silverstein got his supposed phone call)?

However, while conspiracy theorists were in the throes of jubilation over the apparent "Silverstein disclosure," the Holy Spirit prompted me to do a little investigating. Like Peter Jennings said, "If you hear a rumor your mother loves you—*check it out!*"

I began by placing a call to Silverstein Properties, Inc. on May 18, 2004. When I asked to speak with someone in public relations, I was put in touch with a Mr. Dara McQuillan. He informed me that when Mr. Silverstein used the word "pull," he was referring to an "evacuation" of the building. As I naturally *assumed* he meant an evacuation of the "tenants," the plot seemed to thicken as I couldn't imagine how anyone would still be in WTC 7 after the Twin Towers had collapsed.

I then sent an e-mail to Deputy Commissioner Frank Gribbon of the New York Fire Department (FDNY), asking him to confirm if an evacuation of WTC 7's occupants had occurred on 9/11. He affirmed the obvious, stating in his reply, ". . . the vast majority (if not all) persons in WTC #7 had self evacuated. . . . No mass evacuation took place, as there was no need."

This prompted me to send Mr. Gribbon a second e-mail requesting any clarification he could offer for the apparent contradiction between Silverstein's public statement, McQuillan's interpretation of that statement and the FDNY's own statement. With the possibility that Mr. McQuillan misspoke (intentionally or otherwise) I asked Mr. Gribbon rather bluntly, "Did a Fire Commander make a decision to 'demolish' WTC 7?"

In his response, the deputy commissioner wrote, "There was no decision to 'demolish' the building." He also acknowledged, "I am unable to locate any chief officer with whom he spoke. (Many chiefs have since retired, so it is quite possible he spoke with someone, but they are no longer on staff.)"

He then made a statement that arrested my spirit. "In terms of decisions by our chief officers that day with respect to WTC 7, I can only tell you the following: they determined we could not fight the fire, and therefore evacuated all FDNY members." So—while there was no evacuation of "tenants," there *was* an evacuation of "firefighters." Very interesting!

As Scripture declares, *"God is not the author of confusion,"* I believe at this point the Holy Spirit showed me that Satan had devised a most ingenious snare to discredit well-intentioned conspiracy advocates. When describing *his* enemies in Psalm 64:5, David wrote, *"They encourage themselves in an evil matter: they commune of laying snares privily; they say, Who shall see them?"*

Talk about deception—anyone who viewed the PBS documentary would have witnessed the same four things: 1) In an earlier segment, when engineers are seen discussing how they used bulldozers and cables (as opposed to dynamite) to bring down the charred shell of WTC 6 in late October, they twice employed the term "pull," i.e., "we're getting ready to *pull* building 6," and, "when you *pull* a building you have to be careful how it falls . . ."; 2) Silverstein says, ". . . maybe the smartest thing to do is to pull *it*,"—"it," not "them," as in a *thing* (the structure) rather than *humans* (whether occupants or firefighters). He obviously did *not* employ language that would have more accurately conveyed the purported intent of his statement—"maybe the smartest thing to do is to *evacuate the firemen,"* or even, ". . . to *pull* the *firefighting attempt,"* or, ". . . to *pull* the *firefighters";* 3) Mr. Silverstein uses unmistakable body language (shrugging his shoulders, looking away with an expression of resignation, etc.) as he tacitly announces his decision to "sacrifice" his building in order to save more lives; 4) The nonchalant transition from Silverstein's concluding remark and body language to the breathtaking footage of WTC 7's perfect implosion leaves the viewer with the indelible subliminal message that the implosion was *caused* (i.e., by the landlord) rather than *experienced* and *endured*.

Thus, while this, the third skyscraper to implode on 9/11 (and in all of history as well), requires the greatest scrutiny (as it was neither struck by an airliner nor subject to burning jet fuel), should Larry Silverstein be charged with conspiracy to commit fraud for inadvertently acknowledging the contrived demolition of his own building—be assured he would only claim that "it" referred to *FDNY's attempt to save his building.* To employ the incomparable casuistry of William Jefferson Clinton—"It depends on what the meaning of *'it'* is."

About this time, typical "ditto heads" will be found shooting off their mouths that a simple tactful letter to Mr. Silverstein would put the controversy to rest. Well, ya know, I tried that novel idea back on August 4, 2004, and have yet to receive a reply—*not* that I was expecting one. (And yes, I secured a delivery confirmation.) But why would a billionaire real estate magnate mess with a two-bit "conspiracy kook" when he can indulge in a little diversionary myth-making, Skull and Bones style? Then again, he might have been too preoccupied by that multi-billion-dollar lawsuit filed by attorney David Warby on behalf of roughly 800 people who worked on the World Trade Center cleanup without proper protection from dust, asbestos and other toxins. (I guess this is the sort of thing that happens when you tidy up a crime scene too fast.)

You see, the problem is, while self-righteous "conservatives" like Bill O'Reilly and Rush Limbaugh maintain their ratings by ridiculing any form of conspiracy history (no matter how much documentation is afforded), the nation's *real* patriots who are willing to ask the *really* tough questions can't get the folks with the answers to talk! A final illustration and I rest my case.

In an e-mail dated September 2, 2004, I asked Mr. Gribbon four questions concerning 9/11. Question number three read as follows:

> The FEMA report is extremely inconclusive concerning the cause of WTC 7's collapse. They state, "The specifics of the fires in WTC 7 and how they caused the building to collapse remain unknown at this time"; and with regard to connecting the collapse to the diesel fuel on site, ". . . the best hypothesis has only a low probability of occurrence." One author has

asked in frustration, "Do we now live in an era when tall steel buildings can collapse in large cities without any significant discussion of why?" **Given the fact that WTC 7 was neither struck by an aircraft nor exposed to abnormally intense heat from airline fuel, can you improve on FEMA's anemic explanation?**

On September 3, 2004, the deputy commissioner for the New York Fire Department answered my inquiry as follows: "I **cannot** comment on #3." *Here we go again, folks!* If he had *only* said, "I cannot comment on #3 *because* it is out of my area of expertise," etc., or "contact 'so-and-so'" or "read 'such-and-such.'" But *no*—he *had* to say, "I **cannot** comment on #3"—PERIOD! Even a generic rehash of FEMA's "rope-a-dope" would have been preferable to "I **cannot** comment on #3."

Gribbon's five-word reply fostered an ambivalent reaction in my spirit. A part of me recognized the same evasiveness used by President Bush in his classic one-liner, "My senior year, I joined Skull and Bones, a secret society, so secret I **can't** say anything more." On the other hand, a side of me wants to give Deputy Commissioner Gribbon the benefit of the doubt. Was I supposed to have read something into his truncated answer? Was his reply similar to that scene where the woman being held at gunpoint by an intruder hiding behind the door rolls her eyes at an unsuspecting neighbor who happened to drop by?

Until someone is willing to talk, the doubts and suspicions must remain. I mean, can you *really* blame the "conspiracy kooks" for being a tad paranoid when several floors of office space in WTC 7 were occupied by the U.S. Secret Service, the Central Intelligence Agency (CIA), the Department of Defense (DoD), the Office of Emergency Management (OEM), and the Internal Revenue Service (IRS)?

MAINTAINING CREDIBILITY

After years of analyzing current events in the light of conspiracy theory, I have come to see a practical correlation to the doctrine of the Second Advent with regard to dogmatism. While a Christian may be certain that the Lord will come again, he must not engage in date-setting, though he may encourage himself by discerning signs of the times.

Similarly, while we may also be certain that a satanic conspiracy will eventually envelope America, dogmatism with regard to *particular* incidents can be unwise. Christians are commanded to *"Provide things honest in the sight of all men"* (Romans 12:17b). Some areas of government complicity are irrefutable, as evidenced by the Operation Northwoods document. The photo depicting the mutilated corpse of Captain John Birch, *hands tied behind his back*, is a glaring denunciation of General Witsell's letter to John's parents stating that he was "killed by stray bullets." The shootdown of TWA 800 was validated by the verbal testimony of 188 eyewitnesses. That the Alfred P. Murrah Building was an "inside job" is substantiated by a host of highly qualified experts, led by the scientist who invented the neutron bomb.

However, other charges of conspiracy activity may require further investigation to confirm their veracity beyond a reasonable doubt, or they may turn out to be fallacious, to the detriment of that particular advocate's credibility. As witnessed by Mr. Silverstein's gaffe to "pull *it*" (as in, "your *leg*"), the devil has plenty of other traps along the way. For example, just when frustrated Americans like myself thought we'd seen it all regarding government complicity on 9/11, something new bursts on the scene demanding a hearing. Once again, the trouble stems from what the eye can see and communicate to the brain. Like they say, "A picture is worth a thousand words." In his controversial documentary, Mr. vonKleist explains how he purchased the CNN DVD *America Remembers* and then played it in slow motion to examine the footage frame by frame. What he reveals is startling! First, something resembling a "pod" is clearly attached to the underbelly of the aircraft that struck the South Tower. (Pods are normally affixed to military aircraft and are utilized in the firing of warheads.)

Then, less than a split second before UA Flight 175 crashes into the tower, a distinct flash of light can be seen by the naked eye. To refute charges that it was merely a trick of sunlight or a reflection, the same flash is shown from four different angles from as many cameras.

An identical flash can also be viewed on the sole footage of AA Flight 11 striking the North Tower, taken by French filmmakers Jules and Gédéon Naudet (the clip President Bush saw in his dreams). To refute charges that the flash occurred when the fuselage made contact with the building, vonKleist points out that the flash appears to the right of the aircraft (i.e., ahead of same) and that the flash was reflected on the fuselage *prior* to impact. He believes that the incendiary was designed to act as a match to ignite the enormous amount of jet fuel about to be dispersed. Whether the flash was a missile or a controlled detonation, vonKleist makes the case that the terrorists were not limited to box cutters.

I immediately called General Benton K. Partin (U.S.A.F., Ret.) and asked him about the phenomenon. As stated in the previous chapter, General Partin's expertise is in the area of weapons development, the chemistry of explosives, explosive train design, warheads, terminal ballistic fuses, wave shaping, propellants, etc. While he provided some of the most sophisticated scientific evidence supporting a government cover-up in the TWA 800, Waco and Oklahoma City bombing debacles, the general has never been one to jump on every conspiracy bandwagon to come down the pike. He informed me that when fast-moving objects are filmed by standard videography, the leading edge, or forward image (in this instance, the aircraft's nose), will have an exposure time approaching zero, compared to an image, say, ten feet back. Like in an old episode of *Twilight Zone*, it's as if you can see an image before the event takes place. According to General Partin, a flash is produced when aluminum hits steel, converting kinetic energy to thermal energy which then turns to vapor. Thus, while the celebrated flash of light on the 9/11 footage could have been caused by an incendiary blast, more than likely (though far less sensational) it was merely an unintended optical illusion.

Another theory that has fostered significant debate contends that the "hijacked" aircraft on 9/11 were flown by remote control technology. According to an article in the *London Economist*, September 20, 2001, former British Airways CEO Robert Ayling is alleged to have affirmed that an aircraft could be commandeered from the ground or air and then flown by remote control.[225]

Global Hawk technology, developed by the Defense Department, has been around since 1997 and enables an airplane to virtually fly itself from take-off to landing. According to one report, "the US had on several occasions flown an unarmed aircraft, similar in size to a Boeing 737, across the Pacific from Edwards Air Force base in California to South Australia . . . on a pre-programmed flight path under the control of a pilot in an outside station."[226] Such a thesis would compliment the consensus of professional airline pilots that a band of high-strung amateurs were incapable of soloing their Boeings with the finesse attributed to them by our government. For instance, consider the irregular flight path of AA77. Not one line in the 567-page *9/11 Commission Report* attempts to explain how a strung-out "camel jockey" could have executed this difficult maneuver. In his book, *The War on Freedom: How and Why America Was Attacked September 11, 2001,* Ahmed Nafeez Mosaddeq cites military expert Stan Goff's consternation at the ridiculous proposal:

> A pilot they want us to believe was trained at a Florida puddle-jumper school for Piper Cubs and Cessnas conducts a well-controlled downward spiral, descending the last 7,000 feet in two-and-a-half minutes, brings the plane in so low and flat that it clips the electrical wires across the street from the Pentagon, and flies it with pinpoint accuracy into the side of a building at 460 nauts. . . . When the theory about learning to fly this well at a puddle-jumper school began to lose ground, it was added that they received further training on a flight simulator. This is like saying you prepared your teenager for her first drive on I-40 at rush hour by buying her a video driving game.[227]

Goff's remonstrance is reinforced by the fact that the Saudi terrorist who was *supposed* to be the pilot, Hani Hanjour, was reportedly not only a novice, but a sorry one at that. (One look at his mug shot is sufficient.) According to a story in *The New York Times:*

> Staff members characterized Mr. Hanjour as polite, meek and very quiet. But most of all, (a) former employee said, they considered him a very bad pilot. "I'm still to this day amazed that he could have flown into the Pentagon," the former employee said. "He could not fly at all."[228]

A report on CBS News corroborated this ineptness:

> Months before Hani Hanjour is believed to have flown an American Airlines jet into the Pentagon, managers at an Arizona flight school reported him at least five times to the FAA. They reported him not because they feared he was a terrorist, but because his English and flying skills were so bad. . . . [T]hey didn't think he should keep his pilot's license. "I couldn't believe he had a commercial license of any kind with the skills that he had," said Peggy Chevrette, Airzona flight school manager.[229]

Hani's backup "pilots" were not much better. In May 2000, Nawaf al-Hazmi and Khalid al-Mihdhar began aviation training at Sorbi's Flying Club in San Diego. After a half-dozen lessons it was clear that the pair would never get their wings. Instructor Rick Garza eventually gave up, describing his inept pupils as "like Dumb and Dumber."[230]

Furthermore, why would the terrorists have struck the *west* wing of the Pentagon in the first place? Griffin writes:

Assuming that terrorists in control of a Boeing 757 would want to be certain of hitting their target, why would they aim at one of the facades, which are only 80 feet high, when they could have simply dived into the roof, which covers 29 acres? More important, one would assume that they would have wanted to cause as much damage to the Pentagon and kill as many of its employees as possible, and these aims would have made the roof the logical target. . . .

The force of this question is increased by the fact that according to the reported radar data, the aircraft, given its trajectory, was able to hit the west wing only by executing a very difficult downward spiral. In other words, it was actually *technically difficult* to do as little damage to the Pentagon as was done.[231]

COLONEL DONN DE GRAND PRÉ

In May 2003, a Portuguese newspaper reported that a marathon seminar of veteran U.S. pilots, held in Washington, D.C., September 16 to 19, 2001, concluded that "the flight crews of the four passenger airlines involved in the September 11th tragedy had no control over their aircraft." The incredible story was never carried by the American press.

On February 25, 2004, radio talk show host Alex Jones interviewed the man who organized the high-profile symposium, Colonel Donn de Grand Pré (U.S. Army, Ret.). While still in his teens, de Grand Pré was transferred to the OSS in the closing days of World War II. (Interestingly, as his OSS assignment included a tour in Kunming, China, de Grand Pré was an historical contemporary of John Birch.) During the Ford and Carter administrations, he was considered the top U.S. arms dealer to the Middle East.

His take on 9/11 is unsettling: "These planes were being piloted by remote control," he said, "probably an AWAC aircraft taking over that airplane or airplanes; or drones, unmanned drones. And flying them at 5 and 8 G-force, *that* no pilot could withstand."

Describing his gathering of anonymous participants as a "wonderful mix of commercial, military and civilian pilots," Colonel de Grand Pré confirms that the controversial conclusions "were unanimous." He then claims to have submitted a twenty-four-page report to the then vice-chairman of the Joint Chiefs of Staff, Richard Myers, who in turn circulated over five hundred copies of the document throughout the government and military, including one to the commander-in-chief himself.[232]

The bottom line technical argument is that two of the "hijacked" aircraft exceeded their software limits on 9/11. An unnamed source cited by de Grand Pré states:

> The Boeing 757 and 767 are equipped with fully autonomous flight capability, they are the only two Boeing commuter aircraft capable of fully autonomous flight. They can be programmed to take off, fly to a destination and land, completely without a pilot at the controls.
>
> They are intelligent planes, and have software limits pre set so that pilot error cannot cause passenger injury. Though they are physically capable of high g maneuvers, the software in their flight control systems prevents high g maneuvers from being performed via the cockpit controls. They are limited to approximately 1.5 g's, I repeat, one and one half g's. This is so that a pilot mistake cannot end up breaking grandma's neck.
>
> No matter what the pilot wants, he cannot override this feature.
>
> The plane that hit the Pentagon approached or reached its actual physical limits, military personnel have calculated that the Pentagon plane pulled between five and seven g's in its final turn.[233]

One of de Grand Pré's staunchest supporters is Kent Hill, an American Airlines captain assigned to the European route. Hill was a lifelong friend of Charles "Chic" Burlingame, the captain of AA flight 77 that crashed into the Pentagon. They were both graduates of the Naval Academy and flew F-4 Phantoms in Vietnam. The *Portuguese News* article states:

> During the press conference Captain Hill maintained that the four airliners must have been choreographed by an Airborne Warning and Control System (AWACS). This system can engage several aircraft simultaneously by knocking out their on-board flight controls. He said that all the evidence points to the fact that the pilots and their crews had not taken any evasive action to resist the supposed hijackers. They had not attempted any sudden changes in flight path or nose-dive procedures—which led him to believe that they had no control over their aircraft.[234]

In his book *The Viper's Venom* de Grand Pré quotes Captain Hill as stating: "Even if I had a gun at my head, I'd never fly a plane into a building. I'd try to put it anywhere—a field or a river—and I'd be scaring the [expletive] out of them (the hijackers) by flying upside down first."[235] Another pilot he quotes gives a similar testimony: "On hearing a major scuffle in the cabin, the pilot should have inverted the aircraft and the hijackers end up with broken necks."[236]

Now although this scenario offers a sophistication that appeals to many, the alert reader will note a stark contrast in the testimony of its proponents. While one "expert" affirms that the aircraft's software limitations were designed to prevent a pilot error from "breaking grandma's neck," another believes the right evasive maneuvers would have caused "the hijackers [to] end up with broken necks."

However, such contradictions notwithstanding, the feasibility of remote control technology having been established, a core of conspiracy theorists made their natural transition to the next level. During his interview, Colonel de Grand Pré issued a dramatic declaration: "Those aircraft carrying crew and passengers went over the Atlantic and that was all she wrote." Jones fills in the blank, "Yeah, you remote control the original planes out, then your loaded drones attack." In answer to a caller's question about what hit the Pentagon, the colonel replied, "It was a cruise missile. It could have been a Global Hawk. It was not a commercial aircraft."

While the fact that the cell phone commentary of Betty Ong (AA 11) and Peter Hanson (UA 175) continued to within a few minutes of the Towers being struck would appear to mitigate against duplicate aircraft theories (though Barbara Olson's call aboard AA 77 was "cut off" as much as twenty minutes before the Pentagon was hit), devil's advocates reared on Darwinism have a right to expect that twenty-first-century conspirators exhibit a higher level of sophistication than their ancestors did in the more primitive "Lemnitzer Period." This is why in the months following 9/11, Hollywood writers and producers were invited to the Pentagon to suggest ingenious terrorist scenarios. It just seems that more "cloak and dagger" stuff should be available to the "X-Files" generation than was to the "Howdy Doody" era. In any event, even if the planes were not switched, they still could have been piloted by remote control technology.

Remember, no matter how outlandish some of these ideas may sound, generally, "where there's smoke, there's fire." Consider the following exchange that aired live on FOX *News* after the North Tower was hit, as featured in *911 In Plane Site:*

"Mark Burnback, a FOX employee, is on the phone with us. Mark witnessed this from what we understand. Mark, were you close enough to be able to see any markings on the airplane? . . ."

"Yeah, there was definitely a blue logo, like a circular logo on the front of the plane. **It definitely did not look like a commercial plane. I didn't see any windows on the side. . . .**"

"Mark, if what you say is true, those could be cargo planes or something like that. You said you didn't see any windows in the side?"

"I didn't see any windows in the sides. I saw the plane flying low. I was probably like a block away from the subway in Brooklyn and that plane came down very low. **And again it was not any normal flight that I'd ever seen at an airport.** It was a plane that had a blue logo on the front. It did not look like it belonged in this area, to speak frankly about it, I mean, that's not an accident."

Try reading between the lines of this loaded statement in the *9/11 Commission Report*:

> Within minutes, New York City's 911 system was flooded with eyewitness accounts of the event. Most callers correctly identified the target of the attack. **Some** identified the plane as a commercial airliner.[237]

After including another clip of a female eyewitness frantically yelling—"That wasn't an American airplane that hit the building," vonKleist points out that the Air Force "just happens" to have a windowless B-757 fuel tanker. However, it is when we examine the theory that a missile hit the Pentagon that our eyes *really* begin to play tricks on us.

FLIGHT 77 AND "THE BLACK HOLE"

The Pentagon attack has developed into a major mystery of its own. Once again, average patriotic Americans like myself must be troubled with questions that concern the identity of exactly what *did* strike the Pentagon. Griffin writes:

> Although later that day the aircraft that struck the Pentagon was said to be Flight 77, which was a Boeing 757, this equation was evidently not immediately obvious. Danielle O'Brien, one of the air traffic controllers at Dulles who reported seeing the aircraft at 9:25, said: **"The speed, the maneuverability, the way that he turned, we all thought in the radar room, all of us experienced air traffic controllers, that that was a military plane."** Another witness, seeing the plane from a 14th floor apartment in Pentagon City, said that it "seemed to be able to hold eight or twelve

persons" and "made a shrill noise like a fighter plane." Lon Rains, editor at *Space News*, said: **"I was convinced it was a missile. It came in so fast it sounded nothing like an airplane."** Still another witness, who saw it from his automobile, was reported as saying that it **"was like a cruise missile with wings."** The official account, however, would be that it was a much bigger aircraft, a Boeing 757—indeed, Flight 77 itself.[238]

Photographs taken at the Pentagon moments after the impact reveal a scene that simply boggles the imagination. (I would sit down for *this* one if I were you.) *How does a plane 125 feet wide and 155 feet long fit into a hole only 15 to 18 feet wide?* And why is there *no* serious wreckage or crater from "Flight 77" on the manicured lawn of the crash site? Griffin writes:

> Most important is the evidence provided by photographs that were taken immediately after the crash. . . . [one] photo taken at this time shows that the hole in the facade was between 15 and 18 feet in diameter. . . . This photo also shows no damage above the hole or on either side of it. And neither photo shows any sign of an airplane—no fuselage, no tail, no wings, no engines—or any evidence that the lawn had been scraped. Whatever struck the Pentagon made a clean hit from the air and went completely inside. . . .
>
> [Another] photo shows that the inside wall of the third of the Pentagon's five rings, known as the C-ring, was penetrated, resulting in a hole about seven feet in diameter. This means that the aircraft had the power to penetrate six reinforced walls.
>
> This photographic evidence creates enormous problems for the official account, according to which the damage was caused by an aircraft as large as a Boeing 757. The most obvious problem is that since the aircraft penetrated only the first three rings of the Pentagon, only the *nose* of a Boeing 757 would have gone inside. . . . The rest of the airplane would have remained outside. . . .
>
> But not the slightest sign of a burnt-out wreck is shown in . . . any of the other photographs.
>
> The official story, to be sure, takes account of this problem by saying that not simply the nose but the entire airplane went inside the Pentagon. This is why it does not appear in the photographs. Other features of the photographic evidence, however, create insuperable difficulties for this theory. One of these features is the fact that the orifice created by the impact, as mentioned above, was at most 18 feet in diameter. **Is it not absurd to suggest that a Boeing 757 created and then disappeared into such**

a small hole? As Meyssan points out, the hole was big enough for the passenger cabin, which is less than twelve feet in width. But the plane's wings give it a breadth of 125 feet. **Can anyone seriously believe that a 125-foot-wide airplane created and then went inside a hole less than 20-feet wide?**[239]

As to vertical damage, *whatever* entered the Pentagon, took out only the first two floors of the five-story structure. The earliest photos show that the facade above the opening is clearly intact and unmarked. A partial collapse of the upper floors did not occur until 9:57 a.m., twenty minutes after the initial impact. Thus, when the editors of the *9/11 Commission Report* included a photo of the official "crash site" they were slick enough to employ a later one exhibiting the building in its collapsed condition. The misleading caption underneath reads, "The Pentagon, after being struck by American Airlines Flight 77."[240]

I can still recall my utter bewilderment when a man with aircraft maintenance experience tried to tell me with a straight face that *both* wings simply compressed backward against the fuselage while the forty-foot high tail section crunched downward with *no* portions of these three massive sections detaching at the point of impact!

A swirl of controversy also surrounds what was found on the other side of the hole—or I should say—what was *not* found. Although an aluminum Boeing can be highly flammable, once again it appears that the official version is pushing the envelope of credulity. Griffin relates:

> At a Pentagon briefing on the day after 9/11, Ed Plaugher, the county fire chief who was in charge of putting out the fire in the Pentagon, was asked whether anything was left of the airplane. He said there were "some small pieces . . . but not large sections. . . . (T)here's no fuselage sections and that sort of thing." According to Plaugher's eyewitness testimony the day after the fire, therefore, there was no fuselage or any other large pieces, such as jet engines.[241]

We are thus forced to believe, Griffin postulates, that the metal (including engines made from tempered steel) "not only melted but was vaporized."[242] However, according to at least one version of the official story (*Washington Post*, November 21, 2001, and *Mercury*, January 11, 2002), authorities claim to have identified crash victims by their fingerprints. Griffin concludes, "To provide support for the official account, therefore, the fire would have to be hot enough to vaporize aluminum and steel and cool enough to leave human flesh intact."[243]

Whatever struck the Pentagon, it appears that the FBI experienced a serious "anxiety attack" at a local gas station. According to the *Richmond Times Dispatch,* as cited by Paul Thompson:

> [A]n employee at a gas station across the street from the Pentagon that services only military personnel says the gas station's security cameras should have recorded the moment of impact. However, he says, "I've never seen what the pictures looked like. The FBI was here within minutes and took the film."[244]

Maybe Geraldo Rivera should ask Donald Rumsfeld to tell us what *he* knows. Griffin writes:

> At 8:44, Secretary of Defense Rumsfeld was in the Pentagon talking about terrorism with Representative Christopher Cox. "Let me tell ya," the Associated Press quoted Rumsfeld as saying, "I've been around the block a few times. There will be another event. There will be another event." And, if he in fact said this, he was right. Two minutes later, at 8:46, Flight 11 crashed into the WTC's North Tower.[245]

And then, citing an article in *Parade* magazine, Griffin adds,

> An interesting footnote to this chapter: While correcting page proofs, I learned of an interview with Secretary of Defense Rumsfeld in the Pentagon on October 12, 2001, in which he, in speaking of the various kinds of weapons used by the terrorists, referred to "the **missile** (used) to damage this building." Was this a revealing slip?[246]

In July 2004, I had the opportunity to interview one of Secretary Rumsfeld's employees—a man who has spent nearly thirty years working for the federal government, the last fifteen at the Pentagon. At the time the Pentagon was struck, he was less than a mile away at another government facility. Following our discussion, I asked him to summarize his impressions in an e-mail. (For obvious reasons his name will remain anonymous; as an added bonus, he happens to be a born-again, King James Bible-believing, Independent Baptist.) To ensure historical accuracy, he took time to personally interview a former subordinate, an Army staff sergeant duty driver, who was waiting for a major general who was inside the Pentagon. He was parked "at the end of the Pentagon's Mall/River

Entrance Parking Lot (the area of the parking lot directly next to the wall of the Pentagon that was impacted by the 'aircraft')." As to Secretary Rumsfeld's "Freudian slip/missile theory," perhaps the following eyewitness observations may provide some technical corroboration.

(1) When the impact and subsequent explosion of the aircraft occurred, the front end of the government vehicle (Dodge Caravan) he was sitting in, was lifted up off the ground from the blast of the explosion.

(2) [SSG----] temporarily had lost his ability to hear because he had a terrible ringing in his ears, caused by the explosion's blast noise.

(3) Almost immediately, [SSG----] observed small birds dropping out of the sky and falling to the ground, dead; the area these birds were falling were on the immediate ground area of the parking lot he was parked at, which was near the impact zone.

(4) In addition to birds falling dead out of the sky, other debris was falling to the ground also, such as jagged metal that looked like sheet metal, other large pieces of metal parts, and noticeably, something that looked like a section of a window from an airline. That piece of debris that looked like an airline window section had the windows in tact.

A final observation is in order concerning the more outlandish appearing theories that question the identities of the airborne objects involved on 9/11: Mr. Burnback's description of the plane that struck Tower Two; the various eyewitness accounts of the aircraft that hit the Pentagon; and the staff sergeant's testimony about "something that looked like a section of a window from an airplane." To speculate as to the government's capacity for deceiving its own citizens, specifically with regard to aeronautical shenanigans, we might want to take another look at General Lemnitzer's infamous Operation Northwoods document, circa 1962. Bamford writes in *Body of Secrets:*

> Among the most elaborate schemes was to "create an incident which will demonstrate convincingly that a Cuban aircraft has attacked and shot down a chartered civil airliner en route from the United States to Jamaica, Guatemala, Panama or Venezuela. The destination would be chosen only to cause the flight plan to cross Cuba. The passengers could be a group of college students off on a holiday, or any grouping of persons with a common interest to support chartering a non-scheduled flight."
>
> Lemnitzer and the Joint Chiefs worked out a complex deception:
>
> An aircraft at Elgin AFB would be painted and numbered as an exact duplicate for a civil registered aircraft belonging to a CIA

proprietary organization in the Miami area. At a designated time the duplicate would be substituted for the actual civil aircraft and would be loaded with the selected passengers, all boarded under carefully prepared aliases. The actual registered aircraft would be converted to a drone (a remotely controlled unmanned aircraft). Take off times of the drone aircraft and the actual aircraft will be scheduled to allow a rendezvous south of Florida.

From the rendezvous point the passenger-carrying aircraft will descend to minimum altitude and go directly into an auxiliary field at Elgin AFB where arrangements will have been made to evacuate the passengers and return the aircraft to its original status. The drone aircraft meanwhile will continue to fly the filed flight plan. When over Cuba the drone will be transmitting on the international distress frequency a "May Day" message stating he is under attack by Cuban MIG aircraft. The transmission will be interrupted by destruction of the aircraft, which will be triggered by radio signal. This will allow ICAO (International Civil Aviation Organization) radio stations in the Western Hemisphere to tell the U.S. what has happened to the aircraft instead of the U.S. trying to "sell" the incident.[247]

DNA EVIDENCE

As I pondered the overwhelming perplexity of this phase of the 9/11 tragedy, once again, the Lord graciously intervened by specifically prompting me to pursue the results of DNA testing of victim remains. Gene Codes Corporation of Ann Arbor, Michigan, is the creator of Sequencher, the dominant commercial program in the market for DNA sequencing software. Sequencher is a groundbreaking, computational technology for taking bits of genetic material and arranging them in proper order. Following the events of September 11, Gene Codes Corporation was asked by the Office of Chief Medical Examiner (OCME) for the City of New York to assist in the process of victim identification at the World Trade Center. The result of this work has come to be known as the Mass-Fatality Identification System on M-FISys (pronounced "emphasis").

I called Mr. Howard Cash, President, CEO, and founder of Gene Codes Corporation and asked him to confirm the obvious. He assured me that the total 9/11 victim count identified through DNA reference specimens included most of the passengers and crewmembers from the World Trade Center and Pentagon crash sites. He then referred me to the Armed Forces

Institute of Pathology (AFIP) in Rockville, Maryland, to obtain more specific data concerning victim identification at the Pentagon. After I was able to talk with Mr. Christopher Kelly, director of public affairs at AFIP, he was kind enough to send me the following e-mail:

Dr. Grady:

189 people died in the September 11, 2001 terrorist attack on the Pentagon.

64 were passengers and crew on American Airlines flight #77, including the terrorists, and 125 were in the Pentagon at the time [of] the plane crash.

Of these 189 individuals, one died later at a local hospital, leaving search and recovery crews at the Pentagon to recover the remains of 188 individuals. These remains were transported to the Dover Air Force Base Port Mortuary in Dover, Delaware.

At the same time DNA reference specimens were collected from families in order to help make a positive identification on all the deceased. This specimen collection resulted in 183 reference specimens collected.

At Dover, staff from the Office of the Armed Forces Medical Examiner, including DNA scientists, worked to make positive identifications of the deceased. Our staff also generated 183 unique DNA profiles from the victims.

Of these 183 unique profiles, 178 of them matched the reference specimens collected. Using DNA, dental and fingerprint records, we positively identified 178 of the victims. 5 other sets of remains yielded a DNA profile that did not match collected reference specimen—these belonged to the terrorists, and those remains were segregated and turned over to the FBI as evidence.

We were unable to make a positive identification on 5 other victims for whom we had a reference specimen. Because of the intense fire at the Pentagon no biological material was available for these 5 victims and they were later declared legally dead in a court of law.

So, let's review:

189 total deaths in Pentagon terrorist attack

American Airlines Flight #77:
59   passenger/crew (victim) deaths
5   terrorist deaths.

64   total

Pentagon:
125   victims
− 1   victim who later died at a local hospital (not an OAFME case)

---

124 victims

OAFME staff positively identified 178 of the 183 VICTIMS in this case using a combination of DNA, dental and fingerprint modalities. 70 of the victims were identified using DNA alone. Our scientists generated 5 unique DNA profiles that did not match family reference specimens—these belonged to the terrorists. We had no biologic material available to identify 5 other VICTIMS—they were later declared legally dead in a court of law.

I hope this clarifies your questions and responds to your concerns.

I also spoke with Elaine Mar, director of the World Trade Center DNA Identification Unit in the OCME who verified that a number of victim remains taken from Ground Zero were identified as crew members and passengers from flights AA11 and UA175. I then received the following letter of confirmation from Grace Drugess on behalf of Ellen Borakove, director of public affairs:

Dr. Grady:

In response to our recent conversation, the number of WTC disaster Flt AA11 and Flt UA175 are as follows:

FLT AA11	Identified	Not Identified
Crew	8	3
Passengers	47	29
FLT UA175		
Crew	4	7
Passengers	21	28

If you need any further information, feel free to contact us.

Thank you.

Grace Brugess

Rather than face reality, diehard conspiracy buffs would *have* to conclude that the DNA reports were also part of the conspiracy and/or cover-ups, etc. My personal instincts disagree, however, as the likelihood of any suspicious act being a bona fide "conspiracy" will always lessen as the number of necessary "conspirators" increases—the classic case in point being the insane claim that we never went to the moon! Such a hoax would have required the complicity and ongoing silence of literally hundreds of rank and file professionals.

But let me assure you, it is far more suspenseful to detect a *satanic* conspiracy than any mere *human* one. For instance, if the DNA reports are true (and I believe they are), the question remains—How *does* a plane 125 feet wide and 155 feet long fit into a hole which is only 16 to 18 feet wide? Confused? *Now* you're getting the idea! *"For **God** is not the author of confusion . . ."* (I Corinthians 14:33a).

You see, it's really no big deal for the devil to make an airplane disappear (Bermuda Triangle, David Copperfield, etc.). When it comes to conspiracy related "set-ups," Satan remains *the* undisputed master illusionist. Thus, Griffin *appears* to make a valid point when he states, "Neither photo [of the Pentagon] shows any sign of an airplane—no fuselage, no tail, no wings, no engines—or any evidence that the lawn had been scraped." However, what if you discovered that over half the plane *was* there but you just couldn't see it?

In November 2004, I called Dr. Paul K. Carlton, Jr., Lt. General, (U.S.A.F., Ret.) and received the most fantastic perspective to date. Dr. Carlton is a fellow and former Air Force governor of the American College of Surgeons as well as the former surgeon general for the Air Force. He is also a professing evangelical Christian. Dr. Carlton played a vital role in the Pentagon rescue effort on 9/11, personally leading the first response team into the inner courtyard only five minutes after the attack!

According to him, as the Boeing 757 hit the Pentagon with an estimated weight of 181,520 pounds (including 5,300 gallons of fuel) at a speed of 460 knots (about 100 knots above red line), only the fuselage and a minimal section of the wings entered the building; everything else disintegrated into thousands of irregular shards averaging 1 to 2 inches in size. Frank Probst, a West Point graduate, decorated Vietnam veteran and retired Army lieutenant colonel, was near the Pentagon heliport when the crash occurred and recalls that fine pieces of wing debris floated down around him.[248] Much of this debris *can* be seen in a photo taken near the northern portion of the impact area, which appears in the *Pentagon Building Performance Report*, published by the American Society of Civil Engineers. The photographic evidence confirms that although the breadth of entry was significantly wider than Griffith believed, the greater part of both wings failed to penetrate. The *Pentagon Building Performance Report* states:

> Along the path of the movement of aircraft debris through the building, the most severe damage was confined to a region that can be represented approximately by a triangle centered on the trajectory of the aircraft . . . with a base width at the aircraft entry point of approximately 90 ft and a length along the aircraft path of approximately 230 ft. . . .

An examination of the area encompassed by extending the line of travel of the aircraft to the face of the building shows that there are no discrete marks on the building corresponding to the positions of the outer third of the right wing. The size and position of the actual opening in the facade of the building (from column line 8 to column line 18) indicate that no portion of the outer two-thirds of the right wing and no portion of the outer one-third of the left wing actually entered the building.[249]

In a follow-up e-mail, Dr. Carlton stated that he distinctly observed the detached landing gear of AA Flight 77 nearly three hundred feet into the structure.

I was next to the landing gear in the AE ring. That is an alley between the B and C rings of the Pentagon. The landing gear is the largest piece, structurally, of the airplane and you would expect it to travel the furthest after an impact. It did, and ended up punching a hole through the E, D, and C rings of the Pentagon before bouncing off the B ring outer wall and coming to rest in the alley.

The staff sergeant duty driver, who was questioned by my anonymous Pentagon source, specifically mentioned having encountered large pieces of aircraft debris:

Well, once [SSG---] began to get relief from the terrible ringing in his ears (caused by the original explosion at the Pentagon) he got on his cell phone and called the OTJAG Executive Officer, and inquired about whether he should stay and wait for [MG---], or try to leave (because he feared another attack might be imminent) to get back to our OTJAG Executive Office in Rosslyn . . . he was told "wait for the general!" So he did what he was told, and waited for the general.

After a wait of about ten minutes, [MG---] returned back to [SSG---] in the waiting Dodge Caravan. Remember, there was lots of debris that had fallen to the ground where he was parked, so when the general got into the minivan, [SSG---] asked [MG---], "Sir, should I try to drive around the debris? **Some of those [expletive] debris pieces are huge!**" [MG---] advised, "No [expletive, expletive]; drive right on through it. Just get the [expletive] out of here." [SSG---] drove through the debris field in the Pentagon's Mall/River Entrance Parking Lot and made it safely back to the OTJAG's Executive Offices in Rosslyn, a half mile away.

GIVING THE DEVIL HIS DUE

At this point, I suggest we "give the devil his due." I mean, who would have imagined that so many eerie coincidences could have coalesced on the same day—that Larry Silverstein had a *genuine* alibi after all; that the ominous flash of light was merely an *optical illusion*; that three flight school dunces *could* successfully pilot commercial airliners to precise, predetermined targets under intensely chaotic conditions; and, that AA Flight 77 *was* there all the time. And, who knows—Maybe WTC 1, 2, and 7 *were* the first three skyscrapers in history to implode in perfect symmetrical fashion *without* the use of internal demolition charges. My brother-in-law, who has been a structural designer for over thirty years, told me that the consensus among structural engineers who have studied the WTC data, is that the Twin Towers *did* implode as a result of natural causes without evidence of foul play. At my request he sent me the following e-mail:

> The primary vertical supporting elements of a structure are columns, which transfer the dead loads (the constant weight of the structure) and vertical live loads (transient loads from such things as number of occupants, furnishings, mechanical equipment, snow on roofs, etc.) from each floor and roof levels to the foundation below. Columns are also designed to resist variable horizontal forces such as wind and earthquake either by a bracing system, or massive moment connections, or a combination of both. The twin towers of the World Trade Center were also designed to resist the impact of an errant aircraft. Such an event has happened to other structures before. However, they were not designed to resist the impact of two closely timed and deliberately targeted widebody commercial jets with nearly full capacities of aviation fuel. Such an event would have been considered highly unlikely. The construction cost would have been prohibitive. In theory, a structure can be built to resist any earthly catastrophic event imaginable, supposing the wealth of the world is made available and that there is a general consensus to do so. It would be like designing the perfectly safe automobile.
>
> Aviation fuel burns with an extremely intense heat. This heat would be sufficient to alter the microscopic granular structure of steel, causing reduction in load-bearing capacity measured in kips (1,000 pounds in English units) per square inch. This would cause the initial collapse of the several upper floors at the point of impact. This would in turn cause the collapse of

each successive floor below as the added weight and acceleration of falling debris accumulated, creating a "pancaking" effect.

Maximum destruction of life and property would have been achieved if the towers were to topple sideways instead of straight down, wreaking havoc over most of southern Manhattan Island. The towers were very slender structures having high aspect ratios as determined by their heights compared to their areas at the base. The greater this aspect ratio becomes increases the engineering requirements to achieve a controlled structural failure. Each tower was designed to collapse upon itself in order to reduce the amount of collateral damage to adjacent structures and loss of life. To bring down structures of such heights and sophisticated design as the World Trade Center towers in any other manner than was intended in the design of these structures brought about by some unfortunate catastrophic event is inconceivable.

Some conspiracy theorists suggest that demolition charges were placed at the base of the towers by terrorists. Several months of study of building plans and placement of explosive charges are required to cause a building to collapse upon itself. It is highly unlikely a terrorist cell would have the logistical mean to access building plans or have sufficient access to secured buildings in order to place charges. It would require teams of people working constantly, carrying highly suspicious materials about and making quite a din in placing explosive devices. Charges would have to be placed at virtually every floor and would have to be timed to detonate within seconds of each other along a predetermined time line. The technical knowledge to collapse such structures with such precision belongs to relatively few engineers and explosives experts.

Having disappointed a number of conspiracy buffs in these particulars, I *will* say that in the final analysis, the rarely discussed "crash" of AA Flight 93 appears to offer the strongest case for government complicity on 9/11—*that the commercial airliner was likely destroyed by an F-16 fighter.* The relevant press coverage for this theory would include: *Pittsburgh Post Gazette*, September 13, 2001, confirming that debris and human remains were discovered over *six* miles from the main crater at Shanksville; the *Boston Herald* article two days later, in which Deputy Secretary of Defense Paul Wolfowitz reportedly said, "[T]he Air Force was tracking the hijacked plane that crashed in Pennsylvania . . . and had been in a position to bring it down if necessary"; the *Washington Post* story, January 27, 2002, stating that Vice President Cheney gave *three* separate go-aheads for the fighter engagement of Flight 93; and the December 28, 2004, *CNN* account of Donald Rumsfeld's Christmas Eve address to U.S. troops in

Baghdad, in which the defense secretary states that "the people who attacked the United States in New York, **shot down the plane over Pennsylvania.**" Another Bible believer I know (who must *also* remain anonymous) works for a company that was contracted by the Pentagon to do cleanup at the crash site. He shared a remarkable private conversation he had with a former Pentagon employee:

> One most incredible story that was relayed to me was by a lady who worked as a secretary for a 3 star general. She told me that flight 93 was actually shot down by our jets over Pa. She said that the news media would never get this from them, and that the plan was to go with the story of the passengers' attempted takeover (which she says did happen, but was unsuccessful) and the plane crashing into the ground.

Like I said, when it comes to "sleight of hand," Satan wrote the book on disinformation, half-truths, misrepresentation, rumor mongering, etc. His methodology is proven and predictable: choose a sensational thesis; reinforce it with an aura of legitimacy and unassailability; then expose it at the most opportune moment. This enables him to discredit those who take the bait ("Pull it"; "Hunt the Boeing," etc.) while drawing attention away from his *real* agenda: deceiving the Body of Christ; betraying the State of Israel; destroying the morals of our nation; war profiteering at the cost of American lives; and, undermining the U.S. Constitution.

The main lesson in all of this is that no single conspiracy theorist can have all the answers, or be right 100 percent of the time. We are like the four blind men who bumped into the elephant. (In retrospect, the fact that David Ray Griffith has been, for thirty years, Professor of Philosophy of Religion at the Clairmont School of Theology in California—*a notoriously liberal United Methodist school*—would not have increased *his* chances of being guided by *"the Spirit of truth . . . into all truth"*–John 16:13a.) However, it could have something to do with the fact that mere mortals (and, in most cases, unconverted mortals) are attempting to investigate and indict the most intelligent creature in the universe. Truth is, it's probably a miracle if we ever get so much as a glimpse into his well-oiled, diabolical operation. James Melton writes in his excellent work, *Satan's New World Order:*

> The only sensible (or safe) position for the Christian is to assume that Satan is alive and active in world affairs and that his system is well organized and well guarded at the highest levels. After all, he isn't called "the god

of this world" for no reason. We can safely assume that the Prince of Darkness has a fair number of his loyal subjects in the high offices of this world. How else could his kingdom have endured the past 6,000 years of human history? Obviously, it couldn't have survived without the use of conspiracies. They are in the Bible, and it is foolish to think that they do not exist today.[250]

While I cannot endorse every conspiracy view discussed in this chapter (and anyone who quotes me as such would be lying—my personal conjecture, as taken from Griffin's chart, being a combination of numbers 4, 5, and 6, with 1 a bare minimum), nor presume to speak for the many gracious individuals whom I have interviewed and/or quoted, I *can* ensure that my readers are dutifully acquainted with the breadth of contemporary conspiracy theory (both the sane and the insane); the plethora of loose ends, discrepancies, contradictions, irregularities, ambiguities, anomalies and sophistry that pervade many accessible government documents; the voluminous testimony of history beginning with Cicero's famous line regarding "enemies within the gates" on through the Founding Fathers' admonition concerning the Illuminati and Freemasonry, culminating with the twentieth-century treatises of Antony Sutton and Carroll Quigley exposing Skull and Bones and the CFR; the many high-profile personalities from our present time who have openly or tacitly endorsed various segments of the conspiracy, such as Sam Cohen, Admiral Thomas Moore, Commander William Donaldson, General Benton K. Partin, Colonel Fletcher Prouty, Special Agent John O'Neill, Attorney Stanley Hilton, Attorney David Shippers, and Attorney Gerry Spence (not to mention sacrosanct insiders like Walter Cronkite); the numerous statements by leaders within our own government warning us not to turn our back on *them*; and finally, the wealth of Scripture that told end-day believers to expect these very conditions.

Thus, while it may require prudence to discern *individual* acts of conspiracy, one can rest assured that the federal government is guilty of perpetual complicity in the *aggregate*, based on a preponderance of evidence (both factual and circumstantial) and a sustained unwillingness to be investigated by a *credible* entity.

My Christian contact in the Pentagon gave an accurate assessment of reality in the closing remarks of his e-mail:

> I've read everything that you can find about this subject matter. . . . Brother Grady, I honestly don't know what to tell you about these conspiracy theories. To be honest with you, it all makes my stomach turn upside down [my own sentiments, exactly]. . . .

My background is in communications and intelligence. I know things that the average American doesn't know about. Some things I've been exposed to as a government employee with "need to know" clearance, I can never speak about (for fear of being arrested for divulging classified information of a sensitive "national security" nature). . . .

I've worked for the United States government for nearly 30 years, and with the security clearances I've had over these years I've been privy to incidents and actions by our government that have NEVER been reported on the nightly news or in the print media. There are too many secrets! . . .

Brother Grady, I'm a patriot, to the bone! I'm "red, white, and blue" in my blood. I believe in the "grand ole' flag" and what it stands for—FREEDOM. I'm an AMERICAN through and through! But as much as I love my country, and the Constitution of the United States and all of the rights and privileges it is "supposed" to enable us with—I'm disenchanted! . . .

I work at the Pentagon (a.k.a. "The Puzzle Palace"). That name is indicative of the fact that things aren't always as they seem! Being a Bible believer, I understand that things must get worse and worse in order for the end times prophecy to come to pass. **[Are] our current, and past, governments guilty of hiding the truth of things behind incidents like the shootdown of KAL 007, the crash of TWA Flight 800, the Ruby Ridge, Idaho, debacle, the FBI's Waco, Texas, charade, the Oklahoma City bombing cover-up, and the September 11th, 2001, attacks of the World Trade Center Twin Towers, and the Pentagon? As much as I regret it, I'm afraid the answer my friend is a profound, "Yes!"**

Am I frustrated? My answer is not just, "Yes," but pardon me, **"Heck, yes"!** . . .

The government is getting very selective of who works for them, and the more you are willing to show a desire to risk and show an ability to keep secrets, the more desirable you are as a prospective employee. . . .

I think I'm better informed about what really is happening in government circles than the average American citizen who only gets their news from the corrupt and controlled news media. I don't know who originated this saying, but for whatever its worth, it is a truth that "power corrupts and absolute power corrupts absolutely." Brother Grady, I have seen power in government used in corrupt ways, all the way down to my levels in the military establishment. There is an extreme measure of selfishness and "what's in it for me" attitude that permeates all levels of the government and military establishment. It is enough to make a Bible believing Christian beg to see the Rapture happen.

As to who *ultimately* gave the order to "pull" the World Trade Center on 9/11, you might want to review the first chapter of the oldest book in the Bible. For a perfectly controlled implosion that resulted in a number of intended fatalities, try reading Job 1:19—*"And, behold, there came a great wind from the wilderness, and smote the four corners of the house, and it fell upon the young men, and they are dead . . ."* And if you want to see a *real* "Hebrew code," just reverse the numbers in the Scripture address. *Selah.*

GOD'S *CASUS BELLI* FOR 9/11

Now, although various facets of conspiratorial intrigue are beyond the range of human understanding, the Bible-believer may resort to a privileged standard of absolute truth. While we may never know the *many* "hows" of 9/11, we can be certain of the *one* essential "why." The infallible lynchpin of current events remains, *"And I will bless them that bless thee, and curse him that curseth thee"* (Genesis 12:3a).

The problem with Colonel Donn de Grand Pré and most conspiracy theorists is their abject hatred of the Jews. De Grand Pré recently published a trilogy of impressive-looking hardback volumes entitled *Barbarians Inside the Gates*. The books are literally teeming with anti-Semitic paranoia. A sample of the chapter titles include: "Nazi-Zionist Secret Alliance" (subtitled "Adolf Hitler: Co-Founder of Israel"), "Israeli Acts of Terror," "Ultimate Jewish Triumph," "The Jewish Peril," and "Understanding the Hoax of the Holocaust."

A biographical note on page 602 of *The Rattler's Revenge* informs the reader: "Donn de Grand Pré quit the Pentagon and has devoted his life to following Jesus Christ." Truth is, however, the author's idea of "Christianity" is the Jew-hating, bloody Whore of Rome! The back dust jacket of *The Viper's Venom* features a photograph of Mrs. Ursella de Grand Pré posing with the couple's infant daughter, Marguerite, "after Easter Sunday High Mass at St. Agnes Church, Arlington, Virginia, 1963."

Colonel de Grand Pré's pro-Vatican, anti-Semitic views would relegate his overall credibility to "worthless" at best. During a brief telephone interview in September 2004, de Grand Pré told me rather emphatically that "the presidential election would *not* take place as Bush's 'neo-cons' would engineer a national crisis to trigger martial law." (I *almost* called him back on November 3.) Although the *scenario* he predicted is certainly within the realm of possibility (perhaps sooner than you think), once again, the name of the *devil's* game is "playing the fool" via date-setting. *"When a prophet speaketh in the name of the LORD, if the thing follow not, nor come to pass, that is the thing which the LORD hath not spoken, but the prophet hath spoken it presumptuously: thou shalt not be afraid of him"* (Deuteronomy 18:22).

However, Donn's greatest "revelation" is found in an e-mail to a Mr. Craig Brooks, June 16, 2004:

> As to who carried out the attacks on 9/11, consider that the preliminary scientific conversions of the commercial aircraft were probably done by the Israelis. It is also conceivable that the overall planning for the event (9/11) was also carried out by the Israelis.
>
> My friends, ask not about the theories of the New World Order; just ask once and for all which ethnic grouping has actually planned for world dominion for lo these many centuries.

Because a mob of cold-blooded *Italians* in Rome (with an occasional "Polack" thrown in for good measure) has been the *main* "ethnic grouping" that has spent the last fifteen centuries aspiring for "world domination," Donn and his fellow Catholics have been *"turned unto fables"* (II Timothy 4:6). As to *why* the buildings came down on 9/11, the answer remains— *"I will . . . curse him that curseth thee"* (Genesis 12:3b), for *"the curse causeless shall not come"* (Proverbs 26:2b).

On August 23, 2001, Crown Prince Abdullah saw President Bush make a statement on television that sent him into a rage. According to one Saudi official, he "just went bananas." Unger relates the rarely heard sequence of events that puts the tragedy of 9/11 in a Biblical context:

> From the comfort of his luxurious Riyadh palace, Abdullah listened to President Bush hold forth on the recent violence in the Middle East. "The Israelis will not negotiate under terrorist threat, simple as that," Bush said. "And if the Palestinians are interested in a dialogue, then I strongly urge Mr. Arafat to put one hundred percent effort into . . . stopping the terrorist activity. And I believe he can do a better job of doing that."
>
> In the seven months or so that Bush had been president, high-level Saudis had not been terribly impressed by him. One used the word *goofy* to describe him. Some thought of him as a lightweight who had not mastered foreign policy. Bandar thought Condoleezza Rice's lack of familiarity with the Middle East was partially to blame.

What they especially didn't like was that Bush, pushed in part by neoconservatives in his administration who were close to Israel's Likud party, was blaming all the violence on the Palestinians. Two months earlier Bush senior had assured Abdullah that his son would toe the line. But now, those words appeared to be hollow promises. To the Saudis, it was as if the president of the United States had again become nothing more than a mouthpiece for Israeli prime minister Ariel Sharon.

Prince Bandar happened to be watching the same news conference at his $36-million Rocky Mountain retreat in Aspen, Colorado, when the phone rang. It was Abdullah, directing him to confront the White House. **He knew well that the United States still relied on the Saudis for vast amounts of oil, as it had for decades. And the United States still hoped for strategic support from the Saudis in other Middle East regional issues even though their shared interests were less clear than they had been a decade earlier. It was time to use that leverage to the fullest.** Less than a year earlier, Bandar had gone hunting on his English estate with Bush senior, his close friend of two decades. Now he was going to draw a line in the sand with Bush's son—and push the Bush-Saudi relationship to the brink.

On August 27, with Bush still in Crawford, Bandar met with Condoleezza Rice in her White House office. "This is the hardest message I've had to deliver between our two countries since I started working in this country in 1983," Bandar said, using a twenty-five-page document from Abdullah as his script. As related by a senior Saudi official, the message said, "We believe there has been a strategic decision by the United States that its national interest in the Middle East is 100 percent based on Israeli prime minister Ariel Sharon." . . .

The message made clear that the Saudis had concluded that Bush was a lost cause. "Starting from today, you're from Uruguay, as they say. You Americans, go your way; I, Saudi Arabia, go my way. From now on, we will protect our national interests, regardless of where America's interests lie in the region."

And Bandar left no room for compromise. Now was the time to "get busy rearranging our lives in the Middle East," he said. He was instructed not to have any further discussions with the United States. Could it be that the two countries' sixty-year alliance was finally coming to an end?

Shocked by this ultimatum, Rice told Bandar that there had been no change in U.S. policy. She agreed to take the message to the president.

For his part, Bush still had no intention of getting involved in the sticky Middle East peace process. **Nevertheless, Bush was so stunned by the Saudi threat that he immediately did an about-face. Within thirty-six** hours, **Bandar returned to Riyadh with a groundbreaking personal message written by the president to mollify Abdullah.** "I am troubled and feel deeply the suffering of ordinary Palestinians in their day to day life and I want such tragedies and sufferings to end," Bush wrote. **"I firmly believe that the Palestinian people have a right to self-determination and to live peacefully and securely in their own state in their own homeland."**

Bush was not just getting involved. For the first time, he was publicly supporting a Palestinian state—and he had done it in writing. He also addressed the Saudi moral concerns, saying he believed the blood of all innocent people was the same—whether they be Israeli or Palestinian, Jewish, Christian, or Muslim.

Abdullah had played the game well. He had banged his fist and the United States had jumped. He was so thrilled with his victory, the *Post* reported, that he proudly showed off his correspondence—Bush's two-page letter and the long message he had given Bandar—as trophies to Arab leaders in Syria, Egypt, and Jordan.

At Abdullah's invitation, Yasir Arafat came all the way from South Africa to Riyadh especially to read it. Then Abdullah sent Bandar back to Washington to help transform the words into deeds—and to convince the president to make public that he was calling for a Palestinian state.

On Friday, September 7, three days after Richard Clarke's attempt to lobby his proposal to fight Al Qaeda through the administration, Bandar met with Condoleezza Rice, Dick Cheney, Colin Powell, and President Bush in Washington and told them how happy he was to discover that he had misinterpreted the White House's policy toward the Middle East. **The administration reiterated its desire to pursue new peace initiatives immediately.**

Many questions were unresolved about how to pursue such initiatives, but suddenly there was enough goodwill that discussions continued between the two countries over the weekend of September 8 and 9. At issue was whether Colin Powell or President Bush should make the speech announcing the new plans. **Bush was even willing to meet with Arafat at the United Nations—a prospect that pleased the Saudis immensely.** And lest anyone doubt that Bush would follow through this time, he had invited Bandar to the White House the following Thursday to pursue these matters.

And so, on that Monday night, Prince Bandar bin Sultan bin Abdul Aziz was, in his own words, "the happiest man in the world." As he told the *Washington Post*, he decided to relax in the indoor swimming pool of his lavish McLean residence, smoking a cigar. He had been back and forth between Saudi Arabia and Washington with the Bush response and then the Saudi response. He had worked through the entire weekend, until three or four o'clock in the morning, and then he had worked all day Monday. He deserved a rest, so he called his office. **He told them he was taking Tuesday off—Tuesday, September 11, 2001.**[251]

On Friday, September 14, President George Bush spoke at Ground Zero, appropriately enough, through a *bull* horn. Dispersed throughout the sixteen-acre cemetery before him lay the remains of over 2,700 Americans, including those of John P. O'Neill. In the skies above, members of the bin Laden and Saud families continued their homeland journeys. However, the most powerful imagery of all was positioned just off to the president's side. It was truly a scene that only *God* could have arranged. While the "mighty" Twin Towers had lasted a mere three decades, the ancient edifice at 55 Church Street has stood *literally* for centuries. Though utilized in a myriad of practical ways in the immediate aftermath of 9/11, this structure had a far more significant purpose for having survived the ravages of time. For one thing, "Father" Mychal Judge—the nation's foremost sodomite Catholic priest—was given the last rites of his "church" on a sidewalk just a few feet away.

However, the central message conveyed by the proximity of this place with the presidential "bull" session "just happens" to involve another chief executive, and with the same first name, no less. While our *forty-third* president was *outside* announcing his *public* war on *terror*, some weary rescue worker *inside* St. Paul's Chapel was undoubtedly resting on the very pew where our *first* chief executive initiated his *private* war on *tyranny*!

19

"Bring It On!"

*"Pride goeth before destruction, and
an haughty spirit before a fall."*
(Proverbs 16:18)

ACCORDING TO SCRIPTURE, the rapture of the church will be ushered in by three related conditions: widespread apostasy, an acceleration of evil, and worldwide deception. (II Timothy 3:1-13) While the general public may grow increasingly alarmed over Mr. Rumsfeld's "unknowns" (both *known* and *unknown*), humble Bible believers have the assurance that *"the secret things belong unto the LORD our God"* (Deuteronomy 29:29a). As Christians are commanded to be *"wise as servants"* (Matthew 10:16), this chapter was written to expose the many falsehoods propagated by the Bush administration in the days following 9/11, and to posit an explanation for such treachery.

"MISSION ACCOMPLISHED"

Realizing that the movie *Top Gun* had been a major box office hit, chief White House "choreographer" Karl Rove had President Bush stage his memorable landing on the USS *Abraham Lincoln*. (The May 1 date should have been a *dead* giveaway.) Dean writes:

> Bush did nothing to dispel the illusion that he had piloted the plane to the deck; in fact, he was a passenger in a pilot's costume. Then, after changing clothes and at a perfect moment of twilight (timed to the minute, with the great ship making lazy circles so the cameras would have an ideal setting),

he delivered his speech announcing the end of hostilities in Iraq, a banner over his shoulder reading, MISSION ACCOMPLISHED (which, contrary to Bush's later claim, had been purchased and placed there by his staff, not the ship's crew).[1]

The acclaimed American playwright Arthur Miller, whose enlightening essay "On Politics and the Art of Acting" was published shortly before 9/11, stated in an e-mail to Dean, "The crowning moment of his pretension was his having emerged from an airplane that he did not land, in a pilot's get-up with the helmet gallantly under one arm, as if he had passed through heavy enemy fire. . . . I'm afraid the yahoos may have fallen for it."[2] (Based on Miller's statement, I'm afraid the majority of my preacher brethren have *also* shown themselves to be "yahoos" in this regard.)

President Bush was able to get away with his strut on the *Abraham Lincoln* because Americans are far more familiar with Tom Cruise than they are with the carrier's namesake. In his Proclamation for a National Day of Fasting, Humiliation and Prayer, delivered at the height of the War Between the States, President Lincoln confessed:

> We have been the recipients of the choicest bounties of heaven. We have been preserved, these many years, in peace and prosperity. We have grown in numbers, wealth and power, as no other nation has ever grown. **But we have forgotten God.**
>
> We have forgotten the gracious hand which preserved us in peace and multiplied and enriched and strengthened us; and we have vainly imagined, in the deceitfulness of our hearts, that all these blessings were produced by some superior wisdom and virtue of our own.
>
> Intoxicated with unbroken success, we have become too self-sufficient to feel the necessity of redeeming and preserving grace, too proud to pray to the God that made us!
>
> **It behooves us, then to humble ourselves before the offended Power, to confess our national sins, and to pray for clemency and forgiveness.**[3]

Can anyone really picture "Honest Abe" (with *all* of his faults) yelling "Bring it on!" or boasting about "kicking Bobbie Lee's (expletive)"?

As the Bible "Brother" Bush professes to believe states that *"Pride goeth before destruction, and an haughty spirit before a fall"* (Proverbs 16:18), we are not surprised that the Hollywood stunt would come back to haunt him on many occasions; the MISSION in Iraq being anything *but* ACCOMPLISHED! Thus, by late November, it was time for another illusion; accordingly, Dean writes, "Later his producers came up with a better photo-op, sending the commander in chief to Baghdad for Thanksgiving with pictures of him carrying a large tray with a turkey (that turned out to be fake) to supposedly serve the troops (who had all been prescreened and transported to the airport site).[4]

That presidential blooper aboard the *Abraham Lincoln* represents a profound fulfillment of II Timothy 3:13 with regard to end-day conditions, which states, *"But evil men and seducers shall way worse and worse, deceiving, and being deceived."* Obviously, President Bush deceived the nation by declaring that the MISSION in Iraq was ACCOMPLISHED. *But who deceived him into thinking this was so?* The answer might have something to do with that dazed look on Bush's face after Andrew Card whispered into his ear that the second tower had been struck. However, we are getting ahead of ourselves once again (but keep in mind that *somebody* wanted to trick the American people into thinking that Bush had piloted a plane, *which he had not*).

As we are all aware by now, this was not the first time that President Bush was caught *"deceiving, and being deceived."* While Bill Clinton was impeached for testifying, "I did not have sexual relations with that woman, Miss Lewinsky," George Bush was reelected, having convinced the American people that "He [Saddam Hussein] has weapons of mass destruction—the world's deadliest weapons—which pose a direct threat to the United States, our citizens and our friends and allies." After all, hadn't George Tenet, the activist CIA director assured him, "It's a slam dunk case"?[5] Another lie attempted to blame the 9/11 attacks on Saddam as well. Yet another gave the impression that a simple regime change would transform the country into a bastion of democracy.

Arguments such as these enabled President Bush to lead our nation into its first preemptive war in history. Like I said, since when do the American people know anything about their heritage? In a letter to William H. Herndon, February 15, 1848, Representative Abraham Lincoln wrote:

> Allow the President to invade a neighboring nation, whenever he shall deem it necessary to repel an invasion, and you allow him to do so, whenever he may choose to say he deems it necessary for such a purpose— and you allow him to make war at pleasure. . . .
>
> If, today, he should choose to say he thinks it necessary to invade Canada, to prevent the British from invading us, how could you stop

him? You might say to him, "I see no probability of the British invading us" but he will say to you, "Be silent; I see it, if you don't."[6]

Now we all know that "Slick Willy" was a bum, but do you have any idea how many full-length books have been published on the sole subject of "Brother" Bush's lies? A sample would include Al Franken's *Lies: And the Lying Liars Who Tell Them—A Fair and Balanced Look at the Right*, Jim Hightower's *Thieves in High Places*, Joe Conason's *Big Lies*, Molly Ivins and Lou Dubose's *Bushwhacked: Life in George Bush's America*, Michael Moore's *Dude, Where's My Country?*, Lakshmi Chaudhry, Christopher Scheer, and Robert Scheer's *The Five Biggest Lies Bush Told Us About Iraq* and David Corn's *The Lies of George Bush.*[7]

I realize most of these authors are liberals and atheists, but gee whiz, do you think that George Washington's detractors had a tenth of this material to use in their critique of *his* presidency?

"THE HANDWRITING ON THE WALL"

On September 17, 2004, CNN *Headline News* aired footage of a New Jersey mother being led away in handcuffs after she had attempted to interrupt a speech by First Lady Laura Bush. The woman's tee shirt read "President Bush—You Killed My Son." (One of the very next stories showed the president's cheesy daughters bragging about the fact that their father had given up cheesecake for the campaign.) The following week in Arizona, a different mother suffered an aneurysm and collapsed in her kitchen after returning home from viewing the remains of her son who was also slain in Iraq. "She died of a broken heart," a friend told the *Tucson Citizen* newspaper. In the funeral procession to the cemetery, mother's hearse followed son's.

These mothers, along with thousands of other grief-stricken parents, were initially led to believe that their children were risking life and limb in order to bring liberation and democracy to an enslaved people. "An explosion of joy will greet our soldiers," said Deputy Defense Secretary Paul Wolfowitz.[8] However, as the months went by following the "fall" of Baghdad—as the statues were toppled, as Uday and Qusay were blown away, and as the old man himself was "caught" hiding in a hole, etc.—reports began to trickle in to the effect that the masses were not all that grateful about our having "liberated" them after all.

Whereas the G.I.s who liberated Paris in World War II were greeted by cheering throngs, the troops of Operation Iraqi Freedom encountered a different "welcoming committee" altogether; *their* "kisses" and "flowers" were bombs and demonstrations. Yossef Bodansky writes in *The Secret History of the Iraq War:*

> By early June [2003], the frequency of attacks on American forces was growing rapidly. On average, at least one attack a day resulted in casualties for the United States; the ambushes, firefights, and grenade assaults that failed to inflict American casualties were too numerous to count. Some of these ignored incidents were of strategic importance. For example, U.S. planes and helicopters regularly came under fire while attempting to land or take off all over Iraq—particularly in Baghdad, Mosul, and Tikrit. U.S. officials acknowledged that "Baghdad International Airport will remain closed to commercial flights as long as the shooting on the planes continues." American troops were besieged on a daily basis with pelted stones, waved fists, and shouted insults; the tires on their vehicles were burned regularly. Graffiti were beginning to pop up on walls in Baghdad and elsewhere, ranging from the broad—"Long live President Saddam Hussein!"—to the highly specific—"We swear to Allah that we will cut all the hands that waved to the American soldiers stained with the blood of our heroic martyrs." Such hostile activities reflected an increasingly despondent and hostile Iraqi population.[9]

In another place he writes:

> The Bush administration's profound misunderstanding of the realities in Iraq—particularly the country's convoluted ethnic and religious dynamics, which breed the armed resistance and terrorism—has only been aggravated by **America's inexplicable refusal to literally see the handwriting on the wall—that is, the graffiti adorning walls throughout Baghdad and other Iraqi cities.** . . . In central Baghdad, the transformation of anti-Americanism was flagrantly there for the administration to see—if they only cared to look.[10]

In another one of these "coincidences," the expression "handwriting on the wall" is taken from the King James Bible where the phenomenon occurred in the presence of King Belshazzar—in *Iraq*! (Daniel 5)

As the commander-in-chief chose to see "progress" through such generic venues as a concert tour by an Iraqi orchestra,[11] the "grunts" in harm's way continued to observe what was being kept from the folks back home. Thousands shouting anti-American slogans celebrated Saddam's sixty-sixth birthday on April 28, 2003, in a wild demonstration in the city of Tikrit.[12] Throngs of Iraqi citizens, including women and children, frequently gathered and danced around the wreckage of disabled American vehicles. Following a particular Friday "prayer" service in the fiercely nationalist Abu-Ghraib western district of Baghdad, a thousand "worshippers" gathered near the mosque and began shouting pro-Saddam, anti-American rhetoric; Abrams tanks, Bradley combat vehicles and helicopter gunships pronounced the benediction.[13] About the only "positive" slogan ever encountered was "Saddam was bad; America is worse; Yankee go home!" A Fallujah-based mujahedin commander named "Jamal" told mark Franchetti of the London *Telegraph:*

> Our message to the Americans is clear. You are our enemies. We do not want Saddam back but we want you to go home. You are the enemies of Islam and you must leave Iraq or be killed. Leave now, before it's too late.[14]

By late July, the pace and lethality of attacks on U.S. forces stood at twenty-five per day.[15] These were mostly ambushes with small arms, RPG's and roadside bombs. American units were suffering two soldiers killed daily and close to a dozen wounded.

Another drain on the soldiers' morale was their constant exposure to civilian casualties, especially the unfortunate victims of collateral damage. In one heartrending story, a boy lost both his arms *and* his parents when a U.S. missile struck their home. With tears streaming down his cheek, he begged nearby reporters to help him find his arms.[16]

The Iraqi police and others employed by the Americans (including their relatives) were being killed on a daily basis. In a typical scene on June 6, 2003, a local mob gathered around the main police station in Fallujah and began demolishing the three-story building with hammers and axes. On August 29, an "apostate" Shiite cleric, Imam Baqir, was killed when two highly sophisticated car bombs were detonated simultaneously on both sides of the gate to the Imam Ali Mosque in Najaf. Unfortunately, approximately two hundred worshippers were also "wiped out" and another thousand wounded in the Muslim "hit."

While Rumsfeld and Powell continued to give their smug elitist takes on the growing quagmire in Iraq, American GIs were being subjected to the worst psychological warfare in U.S. military history. Not only were they being ordered—"Go into that building over there," but they had to do so knowing that some religious fanatic was inside "praying" that his suicide bomb would not let him down! The ferocious house-to-house fighting in the Battle of Stalingrad during World War II produced over one million casualties *without* the added phenomenon of suicide bombings. While Japanese *kamikaze* pilots were the exception (hitting their peak near the war's end), Iraqi suicide squads were the norm.

The carnage of a suicide bombing is beyond our comprehension. When the American Embassy in Dar-es-Salaam was severely damaged by a truck bomb on August 7, 1998, *the top half of the driver's body hit the building still clutching the steering wheel!* [17] Frank Presley, a communications manager who survived the bombing of our embassy in Nairobi, described *his* ordeal as follows:

> All of a sudden I was flying. . . . I think for a few seconds I kind of lost things. I hit a wall. . . . I noticed a ceiling had gone. I tried to stand up. It was difficult. I stood up and I just could not believe what I saw. I looked around and I saw like chunks of blood or red kind of meat on the walls. . . . I lost part of my jaw. I lost a large section of my shoulder . . . I looked down and I saw bone sticking out of my shirt . . . I saw some legs, a pair of just man's legs with pants on. [18]

As if to mock Western technology employed by Coalition forces, insurgents fired rockets at targets in downtown Baghdad from missile launchers concealed in commonly used donkey carts equipped with sophisticated timers and left parked in preselected areas. On October 26, a barrage of ten rockets struck the al Rashid Hotel just as Paul Wolfowitz (remember that name), the deputy defense minister most associated with the American invasion, was preparing for his morning slate of meetings. An American colonel was killed and a score of military and civilian officials were wounded in the surprise attack.

Early on, the Bush administration had insisted that all the ruckus was being caused by a small rabble of Islamic insurgents (Muslim wackos, etc.), while the majority of Iraqis were solidly behind the Coalition. This has proven to be the *biggest* lie of all!

The day before Mr. Wolfowitz barely escaped with his life, over 10,000 Muslims held an "ecumenical" rally at the Abu-Hanifa Mosque, sporting banners that read "Pull out tanks, don't provoke people," and, "No to Shiism, no to Sunnism—Yes to Islamic unity." Bodansky notes, "American authorities should have been alarmed by these sentiments, because if the population of one of Baghdad's most Westernized and urbane districts aspired to erect an Islamic republic, the slums and countryside were sure to be far more radicalized."[19]

One of the greatest demonstrations of anti-American sentiment took place barely a month after Operation Iraqi Freedom was launched. If you want a good idea of what our men and women are up against, get a load of *this* "million man march," held on April 22, Ashura Day, the holiest day in Shiite Islam. Bodansky writes:

> Over the previous few days, **millions of devotees** carrying Shiite flags, chanting slogans, and bloodying themselves with chains and swords started marching toward Najaf and Qarbalah from all over Iraq. As fervor overtook them, the marchers became hysterical by the time they reached their destination. . . . **Millions of others** joined in from nearby communities and villages. . . . **"Yes, yes to Islam, no to America, no to Israel, no to colonialism, no to occupation,"** chanted the Shiite throngs in Qarbalah. "We are against colonization and occupation. We have just finished with one oppressive regime and we don't want another," explained a young Shiite covered in his own blood, in reference to the possibility of an imposed regime.[20]

The only thing any wilder than the actual scene itself, was the recurring political slogan being voiced by the mass of humanity. (*Trust* me—you are *not* going to believe *this* one!) Can you imagine if the average American ever put down his video games long enough to learn that the very ploy Mr. Bush used to justify his ongoing, multi-billion-dollar occupation of Iraq—*the gift of a Western-styled democracy*—is the absolute *last* thing we are prepared to unleash on those maniacs. Bodansky reveals this unbelievable and generally unknown imbroglio:

> The Shiites began advocating swift elections—chanting "one man, one vote," **the same rallying cry used by Gore supporters during the uproar surrounding the 2000 presidential elections**—to determine the style of government and basic character of the new Iraq, knowing full well that an overwhelming majority would support a Shiite-style government. U.S. declarations that it would not permit the establishment of an Islamic republic in the Iranian mode made a mockery of the administration's oft-repeated commitment to bringing democracy and freedom to Iraq.[21]

Though the majority of Muslims are *Sunnis*, the *Shiites* represent two thirds of Iraq's population, while also forming the predominant power in neighboring Iran (the only distinctively Shiite state in the Muslim world). Yet despite their numerical advantage, Shiite Muslims were consistently suppressed by the Ba'athist regime of Saddam Hussein. (A nationalist/secularist ideology, Ba'athism emerged in the 1930s urging the use of modernization as the primary instrument for establishing Arab power.)

Thus, when the Shiites figured out that Bush was going to do *them* like he did Gore, they went even further off the deep end:

> The Hawza, the main Shiite seminary of Najaf, now became the unofficial seat of power in predominantly Shiite Iraq. "Ninety-eight per cent of the people are Muslims. . . ." The Hawza elite committed to methodical progress at the national level, having resolved to ultimately establish an Islamic state even if the Shiite community had to fight the United States.[22]

No matter *what* the news media is telling you, the Muslim nation of Iraq will *never* have a working democracy. John Adams wrote, "Our constitution was made only for a moral and religious people. It is wholly inadequate for the government of any other."[23] Bodansky summarizes the ideological dilemma:

> In mid-November, Washington had announced that the United States would withdraw from Iraq by July 1, 2004, by which time there would be, in the words of President Bush, a "free and democratic society" in Iraq, serving as "a model for the rest of the Middle East." Officials hastened to clarify that the American commitment to a speedy withdrawal did not include the American military presence, which they expected to continue for several years. To divert attention from, and reduce the power of the Governing Council, the United States committed to "prompt elections," which would in turn increase the legitimacy of any interim authority in Baghdad.
>
> But Iraq's demographic reality—the Shiite majority—had to be addressed. Hence, explained a senior British official in Baghdad, the United States decided on "the initial ballot (that) is not likely to meet the one-man-one-vote criterion in order to ensure that Iraq's Shia majority cannot dictate the new constitution." In response, the most conservative Shiite clerics, led by Ayatollah Ali Hussein al-Sistani, issued a series of fatwas demanding that the prospective constitution adhere to the principles of one-man-one-vote. "But the United States, along with more liberal members of the (Governing Council), fears that such an election so soon would produce a body dominated by the majority of the Shia, which would draw up a theocratic constitution," explained the British official. A tense political

impasse emerged in response, in which the entire Shiite community—two thirds of Iraq's population—saw itself, not without reason, prevented from assuming political power.[24]

As in the case when the defeated Confederate States of America were forced back into the Union only to be disenfranchised from the ballot during Reconstruction, the Shiites would be dragged into a democracy that denied *them* a vote. But in the meantime, keep sending *your* children to Iraq to "help spread democracy," etc.

You say, "Dr. Grady, this looks like a major quagmire!" You got *that* right!! Martin Fletcher of the London *Times* wrote:

> What is striking to a newcomer to Baghdad is the depth of hostility to the Americans, not just among the tiny minority who attack U.S. troops, but also among the millions of ordinary Iraqis who do not. It is astonishing how, in the space of six months, the image of the U.S. military has changed from that of welcome liberator to hated occupier.[25]

Do you suppose our image was enhanced by the inflammatory photos from Abu Ghraib Prison depicting female American guards abusing male Iraqi prisoners? Did that unforgettable rash of grisly, televised beheadings begin in the aftermath of the scandal? Could part of the problem involve the fact that the military police commander at Abu Ghraib was a brigadier general named *Janis*? Would the Lord have gotten a good laugh out of this one in light of Proverbs 1:26?

On November 10, the CIA station chief in Baghdad sent a top secret report to the inner sanctum of the Bush administration warning them of the no-win situation in Iraq. An intelligence source in Washington informed Julian Borger of the *Guardian* that the report was a "bleak assessment that the resistance is broad, strong and getting stronger," despite all the cosmetic efforts of the U.S. authorities.[26] Douglas Jehl of *The New York Times* reported that the CIA had concluded, "[T]he situation in Iraq is approaching a crucial turning point, with ordinary Iraqis losing faith in American-led occupation forces and in the United States-appointed Iraqi Governing Council."[27] Jehl wrote that the CIA was increasingly worried about "the danger that Iraqi Shiite Muslims, who represent a majority of the country's population, could soon join minority Sunni Muslims in carrying out armed attacks against American forces."[28] ("Get your tee shirts—three for ten dollars!")

Returning to the "failure" theme of the previous chapter, Bodansky states:

> Before the war, Washington was convinced that the Shiites would be largely grateful to the Americans and the British for liberating them from the oppressive regime of Saddam Hussein and, once provided with a legitimate leader, would closely cooperate with the coalition authorities. Thus Washington **failed** to recognize both the Shiites' uncompromising refusal to accept any non-Muslim rule, no matter how supportive, and the extent of Iran's influence over the Iraqi Shiite population.[29]

Richard J. Kerr, former deputy director of the CIA who investigated the agency's prewar analysis of Iraq, told the *Los Angeles Times*, "It is very hard to see (the prewar analysis on Iraq) as anything but a **failure** in terms of the specifics that (the CIA) provided."[30] A May 1 editorial in the Jedda *Arab News*, the most important English-language newspaper in Saudi Arabia, wholeheartedly concurs with the pessimistic conclusion: "In truth, the American behavior in Iraq could not have been more inept or more disastrous if George Bush had handed the planning of the occupation to Saddam Hussein himself. . . . **The Americans have done pretty well everything wrong**."[31]

However, while the handcuffed mothers of our slain soldier-boys bear heavy hearts beneath their pathetic tee shirts, the "rag heads" could not be happier with the "inept" policies of America's commander-in-chief. "George Bush may go down in the annals of history as the best thing that ever happened to the Muslim *Ummah*" [the universal Muslim state], noted one Western Islamist activist. "With the invasion and rapid occupation of Iraq, it has become abundantly clear to the whole world that America intends to control all of the oil-rich Arab countries, and furthermore, it believes this can be easily accomplished."[32] Bodansky elaborates, "In other words, he continued, most Arab countries, no matter how pro-Western, had now realized that they surely were somewhere in the American list of targets for attack and occupation."[33] Thus, whatever fragile relationship they may have had with the West would now be eclipsed by the lure of their massive oil reserves.

With all those "prayers" Bush continually solicits from Muslim clerics, we are not surprised that Osama bin Laden saw the disastrous American occupation of Iraq as the providential intervention of Allah! Stressing the historic symbolism inherent in the fact that the climactic clash was being fought in and for Baghdad, Osama declared:

God sent (President Bush) to Baghdad, the seat of the Caliphate, the homeland of people who prefer death to honey. So they (the Iraqis) turned his profits into losses, his joy into sadness, and now he is merely looking for a way back home. **Thanks be to God Almighty who has exposed the lies of George Bush and made his term as president a term of continual catastrophe.**[34]

In an article in the London *Al-Hayah* of July 19, 2003, Ghassan Sharbil notes how the occupation can only enhance the Islamist agenda:

> It can be said here that George Bush has fulfilled Osama bin Laden's wish. The al-Qaeda leader's aim from the New York and Washington attack was to draw the U.S. (military) machine into a war on an Islamic land where it is difficult to win it by air forces alone. The current Iraqi situation provides it superbly: a confrontation on the Arab-Islamic land and in an inflammable region. The more the U.S. Army retaliates against the ambushes, the more profound its clashes with the population become.[35]

BIBLE STUDY TIME

In a meeting with Polish president Aleksander Kwasniewski on January 14, 2003, President Bush told his Catholic guest, "We believe that Islam like Christianity can grow in a free and democratic manner."[36] Now if Mr. Bush *is* a Christian, then he ought to dump hirelings like Jerry Falwell and Billy Graham and find some *real* men of God who can show him what the King James Bible says about the potential for democracy and economic stability in *Islamic* Iraq.

> *The word that the LORD spake against Babylon and against the land of the Chaldeans by Jeremiah the prophet. . . . A sword is upon the Chaldeans, saith the LORD, and upon the inhabitants of Babylon, and upon her princes, and upon her wise men. . . . Therefore the wild beasts of the desert with the wild beasts of the islands shall dwell there, and the owls shall dwell therein: **and it shall be no more inhabited for ever; neither shall it be dwelt in from generation to generation.** (Jeremiah 50:1,35,39)*

Fourteen years before his ignominious capture in a hole in the ground, Saddam Hussein crowned himself Nebuchadnezzar II in a formal ceremony on the ruins of Babylon. While a *literal* interpretation of the passage that would mandate "zero" inhabitants for the entire area comprising the territorial boundaries of ancient Babylonia (i.e., *"the land of the Chaldeans"*) may await a Kingdom Age fulfillment—the Lord's *drift* with regard to the interim should be adequate. *"Therefore thus saith the LORD of hosts, the God of Israel; Behold, I will punish the king of Babylon and his land . . ."* (Jeremiah 50:18).

"Brother" Bush might also want to have a little Bible study with his cabinet concerning their nonstop optimism about the future Palestinian State:

> The burden of the word of the LORD to Israel by Malachi. I have loved you, saith the LORD. Yet ye say, Wherein hast thou loved us? Was not Esau Jacob's brother? saith the LORD: yet I loved Jacob, **And I hated Esau**, and laid his mountains **and his heritage** waste for the dragons of the wilderness. Whereas Edom saith, We are impoverished, but we will return and build the desolate places; thus saith the LORD of hosts, **They shall build, but I will throw down;** and they shall call them, The border of wickedness, and, **The people against whom the LORD hath indignation for ever.** And your eyes shall see, and ye shall say, The LORD will be magnified from the border of Israel. (Malachi 1:1-5)

As I have stated throughout this volume, America is not about to survive the expanding turmoil in the Middle East because her humanistic leaders refuse to acknowledge what the Bible says about the situation. The problem is that the Author is *beyond* "politically incorrect," especially with regard to "hate" and "intolerance." The federal head of the Palestinian people was a "nut job," plain and simple, and the majority of his descendants are chips off the old block! *"And he [Ishmael] will be a wild man; his hand will be against every man, and every man's hand against him; and he shall dwell in the presence of all his brethren"* (Genesis 16:12). And the Lord is no less intolerant with Mubarak and Arafat's people, *"But against any of the children of Israel shall not a dog move his tongue, against man or beast: that ye may know how that the LORD doth put a difference between the Egyptians and Israel"* (Exodus 11:7).

Praise the Lord for a remnant of Muslim converts won to Christ by dedicated missionaries; but the regional population as a whole is unfortunately consigned to eternal indignation (while verses such as Isaiah 19:23-25 and Zechariah 14:18-21 indicate that conditions will vary in the Millenium, especially with regard to Egypt).

A third "nugget" of Bible truth would show our "born-again" president that his so-called War on Terror is in perilous conflict with God's current judgment on America. You see, "terror" happens to be a major tool the Lord uses on wicked people. For instance, Job 18:5a and 11a state, *"Yea, the light of the wicked shall be put out . . . Terrors shall make him afraid on every side . . ."* In Psalm 73:19, we read, *"How are they brought into desolation, as in a moment! they are utterly consumed with terrors."*

Conversely, the spiritual believer can cry out like Jeremiah of old: *"Be not a terror unto me: thou art my hope in the day of evil"* (Jeremiah 17:17). As the Apostle Paul wrote, *"For God hath not given us the spirit of fear; but of power, and of love, and of a sound mind"* (II Timothy 1:7). While it may come as a shock to the religious world, a terrorized society is actually one of the many signs of our Saviour's return—*"Men's hearts failing them for fear . . ."* (Luke 21:26a).

Thus, as previously noted with regard to the providential role played by Nebuchadnezzar in Israel's judgment, it would not be inconsistent to discern a similar relationship between Osama bin Laden and wayward America. And talk about a guy who knows his "terror"! In *The Quranic Concept of War,* Pakistani author S. K. Malik argues that *terrorism* is the quintessence of Islamic military strategy:

> Terror struck into the hearts of the enemies is not only a means, it is the end in itself. Once a condition of terror into the opponent's heart is obtained hardly anything is left to be achieved. It is the point where the means and the end meet and merge. Terror is not a means of imposing decision upon the enemy; it is the decision we wish to impose upon him.[37]

"UNKNOWN UNKNOWNS"

At the outset of Operation Iraqi Freedom, the American-led "coalition of the willing" included such "military powers" as Palau (a group of North Pacific islands with roughly twenty thousand inhabitants), Eritrea, Micronesia, Ethiopia, Iceland, Afghanistan, the Marshall Islands, Latvia, Costa Rica, Macedonia, Azerbaijan, Bulgaria, Estonia, Poland, Hungary, Uzbekistan, Italy, the Solomon Islands, Albania (Wag the dog), and last but not least, Morocco. (Although Morocco was unable to donate any troops, as was the case with most of the above, they did offer to send two thousand monkeys to help detonate land mines in Iraq.)[38] As this book was going to press, the shell-shocked remnants of the original invasion force were being opposed by a *billion* suicide bombers led by a *billionaire* cave dweller. (How's *that* for "truth being stranger than fiction"?) Back on August 29, 1998, the Egyptian Islamist organization al-Jamaah al-Islamiyah issued a stinging denunciation of America (following President Clinton's foiled missile attacks), affirming that the might of Allah was unstoppable, for "one billion Muslims are capable of turning their bodies into bombs which are equal in force to all the weapons of extermination and mass destruction possessed by the Americans." Bodansky comments, "The message of al-Jamaah al-Islamiyah left no doubt about Islamist commitment to a prolonged, lethal terrorism campaign."[39]

So, how did we get into this mess in the first place? Could it be that our "Christian" president has kept us in the dark with regard to a number of relevant particulars? Should we view them as some of Mr. Rumsfeld's "unknown unknowns"?

As the world of Islam has increased its intense loathing of America at several significant milestones, one cannot grasp the current debacle without an understanding of those salient developments. To "begin at the beginning," as they say, Bodansky writes:

> The crisis in the Muslim world intensified as isolation turned to subjugation when the West penetrated the Hub of Islam—the area between Morocco and India, where Muslims not only constitute the overwhelming majority of the population but also determine the sociopolitical and civilizational way of life. The process began with Napoleon's arrival in Egypt in 1789. Then came the Russian wars with Turkey and the conquest of Central Asia in the nineteenth century, followed by the Turkish Empire's collapse and occupation by Britain in World War I and the ensuing artificial redrawing of the Middle East's map by the imperialist powers. The experience has been a trauma from which the Muslim world, particularly the Hub of Islam, has yet to emerge.[40]

With respect to Iraq's specific creation in the twentieth century, he continues:

> Iraq has never been a real country, and neither the American incursion into Baghdad nor the political declarations from the administration could

change this reality. From its inception, Iraq has remained an amalgam of hostile ethnic, national, and religious entities glued together in the early 1920s to further Britain's colonial, strategic, and economic interests. Winston S. Churchill acknowledged this phenomenon on the eve of the war: "It was my grandfather, Winston Churchill, who invented Iraq and laid the foundation for much of the modern Middle East. In 1921, as British colonial secretary, Churchill was responsible for creating Jordan and Iraq and for placing the Hashemite rulers, Adbullah and Feisal, on their respective thrones in Amman and Baghdad." Now, the assault on Iraq and the removal of Saddam Hussein and the Baath regime discredited and effectively destroyed the only mechanism holding these mutually hostile entities together.[41]

Thus we see that the "problem" in Iraq is merely a symptom of an underlying powder keg that permeates the entire Middle East. Muslims hold a fanatical commitment to a doctrine called *Ummah* ("The Nation"), a term used to denote all disciples of Islam wherever they are (i.e., "the Body of Mohammed"). With the dismemberment of the Ottoman Empire following World War I, the massive Muslim kingdom, known as the "Hub of Islam," was subdivided in the image of its Western conquerors. Whereas *Ummah* mandates a giant Muslim state, Churchill and Wilson created a network of independent secular states. For over eighty years the prevailing mindset of the suppressed *Ummah* has been analogous to that stubborn little schoolboy who, when scolded by his teacher to "Sit *down*," says to himself, "I may be sitting down, but I'm standing up in my heart." *This* is the spirit that breeds a culture of suicide bombers!

The British learned this lesson the hard way in their failed attempt to build a modern democratic state in Iraq during the eighteen-year period between 1914 and 1932. Their debacle, as a prime historical precedent, *should* have enabled America to avoid a similar fate, but why study history when you can watch television? Toby Dodge, an associate fellow at the Royal Institute of International Affairs (The Group) writes in his book *Inventing Iraq:*

> If one were able to pick up Iraq like a good piece of china and turn it over, it would bear the legend: "Made in Whitehall, 1920." Britain's failed attempt, during the 1920s and 1930s, to build a liberal state in Iraq forms the historical backdrop against which the removal of Saddam Hussein in 2003 and its aftermath should be understood. . . . How the British understood Iraq made it impossible for them to accomplish what they had initially set out to do: build a liberal, modern, sustainable state capable of reshaping for

the better the lives of the Iraqi people and the system of international order their newly founded autonomy was supposed to safeguard and promote. The British did not mean to undermine the nascent Iraqi state. But, hobbled by an ideologically distorted view of Iraqi society and facing financial and political limits, they did. The United States in Iraq today must understand that it is both living with the consequences of that failure and in danger of repeating it.[42]

The parallels between their experience and ours are truly remarkable. While Britain and the League were busy trying to overthrow God's Word by insisting that Shem could replicate the autonomy and economic prosperity of Japheth, Dodd confirms that "British public opinion, loudly expressed in the media and in Parliament, continued to denounce the extended commitment of resources to Iraq."[43] As the Bible declares, *"[T]here is no new thing under the sun"* (Ecclesiastes 1:9c), Bonar Law reflected public sentiment during his successful election campaign of November 1922 when he assailed Lloyd George with the words, "[W]e cannot alone act as the policeman of the world."[44] Britain's use of lethal, high-tech Western military technology in the form of the newly invented warplane became the sole means of holding the natives in check.

> When order broke down, as it routinely did, the British turned to the airplane. This was Winston Churchill's lasting contribution to the British enterprise in Iraq: the concerted use of air power—of what would in a later context be called "shock and awe"—to terrorize and subdue dissident factions of the Iraqi people.[45]

As reality settled in, political corruption became the accepted norm. Sir Henry Dobbs wrote in December 1929:

> My hope is that, even without our advice, Iraq may now be so well established, that she may be able to rub along in a corrupt, inefficient, oriental sort of way, something better than she was under Turkish rule . . . If this is the result, even though it be not a very splendid one, we shall have built better than we knew.[46]

Of course, no sooner did the "training wheels" come off, than the A.V. 1611 was vindicated. Dodd writes:

> Iraq, one of the first postcolonial states, exhibited from the beginning the instability that would come to haunt international relations in the aftermath of decolonization. After entry into the League of Nations in 1932, formal

state commitments to liberal democracy were quickly dispensed with and the polity was rocked by a series of bloody coups, culminating in the Baath Party's seizure of power in 1968. In the 1970s, oil wealth and the growth of a rentier economy allowed the government of Saddam Hussein to gain unprecedented autonomy from, and power to rule over, Iraqi society.[47]

With the British exodus from Iraq serving as a model, other Muslim nations were inspired to resist their colonial taskmasters as well. More recently, an *Ummah*-wide, "Allah-sent" revival resulted in the faithful ratcheting up their "hit lists" to include any number of fellow Muslims participating in the halls of their puppet-sponsored governments. Bodansky writes:

> All Muslims must fulfill their obligation of jihad both in global causes—such as Afghanistan—and in the defense of their oppressed Muslim brothers and sisters by fighting the un-Islamic regimes (meaning Muslim leaders who rule secular states) of their homelands. Both types of jihad were components of a greater drive—namely, establishing Allah's rule on earth. Islamists call the unified pan-Islamic state that rules the entire Hub of Islam, and ultimately the entire Muslim world, the Khilafah (Caliphate).[48]

The assassination of Egyptian President Anwar Sadat caused many other "presidents" of Middle Eastern "nations" to sleep with one eye open.

With regard to the feckless efforts of the Coalition Provisional Authority (CPA), Dodge writes:

> The sense of incoherence and political division at the heart of American attempts to rebuild Iraq has been seriously exacerbated by the CPA's inability to establish meaningful communications with Iraqi society. Short of Arabic speakers and devoid of any Iraqi expertise themselves, the coalition has been forced to rely on the Iraqi political parties formed in exile to act as their intermediaries. In fact, the nature of these organizations has increased the divide between U.S. forces and Iraqis. Despite setting up numerous offices around Baghdad, publishing party newspapers, and spending large sums of money, the two main exiled groups, the Iraqi National Congress and Iraqi National Accord, have failed to mobilize significant support. All the Iraqis I met—rich or poor, religious or secular—showed at best indifference and more often outright hostility to the returned exiles. This was especially the case with the INC and INA, whose avowed secular outlook identifies them with external manipulation.[49]

So, *now* do you realize why our troops have received such a *negative* welcome? The majority of Iraqis simply don't give a *rip* about *our* wonderful values—no matter *how* much the Bush administration tells us they do. Bodansky states:

> The goals of the first phase of the war accurately addressed America's security concerns, and, accordingly, what's good for America. But the framers of the new American Internationalism also sought to unilaterally determine what's good for the vanquished. Washington hoped that Iraq could become the first Arab democracy once "liberated" by U.S. forces. Noble as this objective is, it completely ignores the endemic problems of the Muslim world and Islam's millennia of bitter struggle against the encroachment of Westernization and modernity, and herein lie America's dangerous arrogance of power—the messianic belief that deep down everybody around the world wants to be like us, and that it is America's destiny and in its self-interest to make this happen. Moreover, the conviction of the devotees of the new American Internationalism was so strong that they failed to adequately prepare for the possibility that most Iraqis would consider themselves occupied and reject the lure of democratization. But this is exactly what happened, and the disparity between America's noble intentions and the grim reality in Iraq now threatens to reverse the great achievements of the American march on Baghdad, not only in Iraq but throughout the Muslim world.[50]

Harvard professor Samuel P. Huntington writes in *The Clash of Civilizations and the Remaking of World Order:*

> Some Westerners, including President Bill Clinton, have argued that the West does not have problems with Islam but only with violent Islamist extremists. Fourteen hundred years of history demonstrate otherwise. . . .
> The underlying problem for the West is not Islamic fundamentalism. It is Islam, a different civilization whose people are convinced of the superiority of their culture and are obsessed with the inferiority of their power. The problem for Islam is not the CIA or the U.S. Department of Defense. It is the West, a different civilization whose people are convinced of the universality of their culture and believe that their superior, if declining, power imposes on them the obligation to extend that culture throughout the world. These are the basic ingredients that fuel conflict between Islam and the West.[51]

Yet, despite these historical realities, President Bush dutifully conformed to Ecclesiastes 1:11, telling the press on March 21, 2002, "We understand history has called us into action; and we're not going to miss this opportunity to make the world more peaceful and more free."[52] Personally, I'll go with the wisdom of Marine General Anthony Zinni (Ret.), head of U.S. Central Command from 1997 to 2000, who stated six months later:

> If we think there is a fast solution to changing the governance of Iraq, then we don't understand history, the nature of the country, the divisions, or the underneath suppressed passions that could rise up. God help us if we think this transition will occur easily. The attempts I've seen to install democracy in short periods of time where there is no history and no roots have failed. Take it back to Somalia.[53]

Over two decades before the horror of 9/11, historian Fernand Braudel presciently warned the West that ignoring the fault lines and reemerging cultural identities of ancient civilizations could result in the most tragic consequences:

> [A]s far as anyone interested in the contemporary world is concerned, . . . and even more so with regard to anyone wishing to act within it, it "pays" to know how to make out, on a map of the world, which civilizations exist today, to be able to define their borders, their centers and peripheries, their provinces and the air one breathes there, the general and particular "forms" existing and associating within them. **Otherwise, what catastrophic blunders of perspective could ensue!**[54]

VALENTINE'S DAY, 1945

Another major cause for Islamic hatred of the West is the sixty-year love affair between America and Saudi Arabia over oil. Standard Oil Company of California was the first to obtain a concession to explore the black gold, initially in Bahrain in 1932, then in Arabia in May 1933. To exploit this concession (a sixty-year agreement), the American company created California Arabian Standard Oil Company. (In 1944, the company would change its name to Aramco, the Arabian American Oil Company.)

The first exploitable quantities of Saudi crude were taken from Damman Well Number Seven near Dhahran in September 1939 (the same month Hitler invaded Poland). Following the historic Yalta conference, President Franklin Roosevelt steamed to the Great Bitter

Lake in the Suez Canal. On February 14, 1945, Ibn Sa'ud, king of Saudi Arabia, came aboard the USS *Quincy* for a series of talks with Roosevelt. In his book *Sleeping With the Devil*, former CIA case director Robert Baer writes:

> Contemporary historians and other commentators tended to treat the meeting as an aside, and even modern historians are apt to give it short shrift. Yalta is where the action was. The war was winding down. Europe needed to be rebuilt; Germany and Japan, to be shaped into pacifist nations. But it was on the *Quincy*, not at Yalta, that the energy cornerstone of America's postwar industrial machine was laid.[55]

The Quincy Accords marked the beginning of the monopoly granted to the United States for the exploitation of Saudi oil. The British had missed the boat. Brisard and Dasquié write:

> Soon the Americans would install a military base in Dhahran—a close flight to any of the Gulf emirates—and become the privileged partners of Saudi Arabia and its king, who, thanks to the royalties he received from the oil exploitation, soon became one of the richest men in the world. The "heroes of liberty," the new world superpower combating Soviet totalitarianism in Europe, had just invented, under the Tropic of Cancer, a petro-monarchy— a mix of political and religious absolutism with a new universal currency, the dollar. With this new foul-smelling liquid, the East Coast and the Persian Gulf—including the oil port of Damman and Dhahran, and awaiting the hotels in Al Khobar—became the materialist counterpart of the West Coast, symbol of Islamic spiritualism and home of the minarets of Mecca, Medina, and Jeddah, where (according to legend) Eve's tomb lies, next to the Red Sea.[56]

As the Saudi-U.S. relationship blossomed, Saudi oil production grew from 21.3 million barrels extracted in 1945 to 142.9 million in 1948 and over 300 million by 1952. *Only a sovereign God could have known how the demand for oil in a modernized society would coincide with Laodicean apostasy and the eventual end of civilization.* As late as the mid 1920s, the vast interior of the Arabian peninsula existed, as Baer describes, "in almost total isolation from the rest of the world—a place characterized not by oil and its riches but by poverty, religious xenophobia and fanaticism, and, at its heart, an almost impenetrable desert culture."[57] Oil would be the means used to fulfill Zechariah 12:2a—*"Behold, I will make Jerusalem a cup of trembling unto all the people round about . . ."* (It is fitting that the substance was a literal by-product of the flood—*"As it was in the days of Noah . . .")* Less than six months later, Captain John Birch would be murdered.

The Saudi-American alliance was destined to be a "lose-lose" affair for both parties. Muslims despised America as a land preoccupied with the adulation of money. Majid Anaraki, an Iranian who lived for several years in southern California, described the United States as "a collection of casinos, supermarkets, and whore-houses linked together by endless highways passing through nowhere."[58] The oil boom would now infect the land of Allah as well—only Saudi Arabia is not your average Muslim country—it is the venerated custodian of Islam's two "holiest" shrines, Mecca and Medina. The arrival of Western capitalism was cause for great alarm as it forced a fanatically religious culture to indulge in daily compromise. The sin became known as *"gharbzadegi"* or "Westoxication" of Muslim societies. Bodansky writes:

> The Islamists were determined to ensure that this malaise that had already "destroyed" Christendom did not penetrate and similarly corrupt and destroy the Muslim world. All means, including the use of violence and terrorism, were justified to prevent such corruption. But the Islamists could not separate their world—the Hub of Islam—from the West. The development of their oil resources required Western technology, and so did their medical system. Muslims drove cars made in the West, used phones installed by Western contractors, and ate imported food while watching imported TVs. Meanwhile their leaders protected their dictatorial regimes using weapons purchased abroad.[59]

Various consumer items were banned from entering Saudi Arabia and the Middle East as a whole. (The American idol, Barbie, was excluded from Iran.) The technology most hated was electronic media, from satellite TV to the Internet.

In a major "theological" development, Unger notes how the House of Saud was viewed as committing adultery with America.

> More specifically, the House of Saud's political legitimacy was based on its allegiance to the sect of Sunni Islam known as Wahhabism and dated back three hundred years. It was at the core of the kingdom's existence. Since many Wahhabis saw the United States as the Great Satan, that meant the Saudis had vital relationships essential to their survival—a double marriage of sorts—with partners who were mortal enemies.[60]

With corruption rampant throughout the royal family (consisting of over thirty thousand members by 2002) and increasing numbers of Saudis traveling abroad, the *Ummah* found itself at a historical crossroads. "The world as it is today is how others (that is, non-Muslims) shaped it," the leading Iraqi Shiite scholar Ayatollah Muhammad Baqir al-Sadr explained. "We have two choices: either to accept it with submission, which means letting Islam die, or to destroy it, so that we can construct the world as Islam requires."[61]

Meanwhile, on the other side of the bed, "Christian" America would be doomed for embarrassing a partner whose national flag reads, "There is no God but Allah and Muhamad is his prophet." (Of course, Coalition forces were quick to remove the inscription *Allah hu Akbar* from the Iraqi flag.) When the volume of America's imported oil nearly doubled from 3.2 million barrels a day in 1970 to 6.2 million a day in 1973 (due to the emergence of an elaborate suburban car culture), Saudi Arabia's share of world exports skyrocketed from 13 percent in 1970 to 21 percent in 1972. Flooded with petro dollars, the Saudis invested a staggering $860 billion in American companies over the next twenty-five years (an average of more than $10 million a person). Craig Unger writes, "They took the United States by storm, selling crude, buying banks, building skyscrapers, buying weapons, investing everywhere."[62]

Overnight, nearly every politician in America was for sale. "In Washington, to bring up the 'revolving door' between government and business is like discussing incest in the family," Baer wrote. "What has made the Saudi money so effective is that it is well targeted, and in Washington especially, the Saudis have hooked up with a culture that seems willing to do almost anything to get it."[63] (Is anyone thinking about "Bandar Bush" and his friends at the Carlyle Group?) With the Saudis holding over a trillion dollars in the U.S. stock market, Baer writes:

> Prince Bandar, Saudi Arabia's longtime ambassador to the United States, once told an associate that he is careful to look after American government officials when they return to private life. "If the reputation then builds that the Saudis take care of friends when they leave office, you'd be surprised how much better friends you have who are just coming into office," Bandar observed, according to a *Washington Post* source. When you're rich and arrogant enough, you can buy the luxury of candor.[64]

In a PBS *Frontline* interview, Bandar acknowledged that his family had misappropriated tens of billions of dollars. "If you tell me that building this whole country . . . we misused or got corrupted with fifty billion, I'll tell you, 'Yes.' . . . So what? We did not invent corruption, nor did those dissidents, who are so genius, discover it."[65]

As Muslims were forced to look the other way when importing Western technology, American officials have had to do likewise with regard to the endless civil rights violations of their billionaire benefactors. Having invaded Iraq to rescue the population from violence and abuse, the Bush administration appears to have given Saudi Arabia a special dispensation to commit similar atrocities. In March 2002, for example, at least fourteen students at a girls' public intermediate school in Mecca died in a fire. Unger notes that according to *Human Rights News*, "[S]everal members of the Committee for the Promotion of Virtue and the Prevention of Vice obstructed rescue attempts because the fleeing students were not wearing the obligatory public attire (long black cloaks and head coverings) for Saudi girls and women."[66] While Saddam had been known to blow up his victims by remote control, the House of Saud is not far behind. Saudi Arabia leads the world in public beheadings. The most popular venue for the grisly practice is a Riyadh plaza known as Chop-Chop Square. And do I have to tell you that no one in the kingdom, national or visitor, can practice any religion but Islam?

Although the *Ummah* remains aghast at the Saudi-American affair, there is a certain degree of smugness in seeing the once-strong Christian nation begging for Allah's oil. Professor Huntington writes:

> The Islamic revival, it has been argued, was also "a product of the West's declining power and prestige. . . . As the West relinquished total ascendance, its ideals and institutions lost luster." More specifically, the Resurgence was stimulated and fueled by the oil boom of the 1970s, which greatly increased the wealth and power of many Muslim nations and enabled them to reverse the relations of domination and subordination that had existed with the West. As John B. Kelly observed at the time, "For the Saudis, there is undoubtedly a double satisfaction to be gained from the infliction of humiliating punishments upon Westerners; for not only are they an expression of the power and independence of Saudi Arabia but they also demonstrate, as they are intended to demonstrate, contempt for Christianity and the pre-eminence of Islam." The actions of the oil-rich Muslim states "if placed in their historical, religious, racial and cultural setting, amount to nothing less than a bold attempt to lay the Christian West under tribute to the Muslim East." The Saudi, Libyan, and other governments used their oil riches to stimulate and finance the Muslim

revival, and Muslim wealth led Muslims to swing from fascination with Western culture to deep involvement in their own and willingness to assert the place and importance of Islam in non-Islamic societies. Just as Western wealth had previously been seen as the evidence of the superiority of Western culture, oil wealth was seen as evidence of the superiority of Islam.[67]

AL-NAQBA

Another major cause for the seething hatred of Islam is the sustained existence of the tiny state of Israel. Muslims refer to Israel's establishment in 1948 as *al Naqba*—"the Holocaust." While the American public is constantly focused on Iraq, the historic Arab-Israeli conflict over the land of "Palestine" is *the* key to the entire regional crisis. Bodansky writes:

> At the core of the conflict, irrespective of the political and ideological formulations at any given time, is the clash between Islam and the West's forward post in the Hub of Islam. In current Islamist terms, it is the confrontation between Islam and "the illegitimate offspring of the Great Satan" over the control of Palestine and the holy mosques of Jerusalem. In other words, in contrast to the prevailing myths espoused in the Western media, it is less that the Arabs and Islamists hate the United States for supporting Israel than that they hate Israel because it furthers, by its very existence, the interests of the hated U.S.-led West. The failure of the West—particularly Washington and, at some crucial points, also Jerusalem—to recognize this fact is the basis of the current disaster.[68]

From a geographical perspective (another monkey wrench of providence), the very location of Israel makes a bona fide *Khilafah* (caliphate) a virtual impossibility, thus eliciting further rage from the *Ummah*. Bodansky explains:

> Ever since Israel consolidated its control over the Negev in 1949, it has constituted a Jewish wedge between Egypt and the rest of the Mashriq. The repeated efforts by Egypt's President Gamal Abd-al-Nasser to establish Arab unity, including a short-lived formal union with Syria in the 1950's known as the United Arab Republic, failed, and Egyptian intellectuals attributed this failure to the lack of territorial unity. "Part of the Arab World is in Asia and the other part in Africa," Mohamed Heikal wrote in 1975, "and Israel separates them. This is an impossible situation, both

historically and geographically, for a Nation insisting that it is a Single Nation."[69]

In the summer of 1964, Yasser Arafat founded the Palestinian Liberation Organization (PLO) for the sole purpose expressed by its name (i.e., the liberation of Palestine). The first article of the Palestinian Covenant stated, "Palestine is part of the Arab World and the Palestinian people are part of the Arab Nation, and their struggle is part of its struggle."[70] The central objective of the PLO, according to their own founding charter, was the destruction of Israel by force of arms, with all Arabs being invited to participate.

After Israel captured the West Bank and Jerusalem in the Six-Day War of 1967, the Muslim world went into virtual shock. They had lost the Dome of the Rock, the third "holiest" shrine in Islam. Suddenly, a renewed hatred for Israel (and her American sponsor) became the rallying cry for Muslim unity. Bodansky notes that "the lowest common denominator holding the Arab world together was the commitment to the destruction of Israel."[71]

Then, following Israel's victory in the 1973 Yom Kippur War, a significant change occurred in PLO strategy. A team of North Vietnamese communists convinced Arafat to adopt a program that would be more appealing to the International Community. Bodansky writes:

> Especially in dealing with the United States, the Vietnamese explained, one must "sacrifice the unimportant if only in order to preserve the essential." They emphasized that while the PLO must remain committed to its ultimate objective—namely, "the establishment of a unified democratic state in the entire Palestine"—in the near term it would be politically advantageous to accept transient phases and even interim solutions. The Vietnamese suggested that accepting "the division of the land between two independent states," without making it clear that this was only an interim phase, would neutralize the PLO's opponents in the West.[72]

The result of this advice was the Phases Program/Phased Plan adopted as the resolution of the Twelfth Palestinian National Council in Cairo on June 19, 1974. The new approach called for the establishment of a Palestinian *state* on any part of the disputed territory that becomes available, whether through war or through a negotiated peace. Bodansky notes the critical fine print of this Palestinian *conspiracy:* "In adopting this policy, the PLO leadership stressed that accepting any part of Palestine was legitimate as long as the entity established there would serve as the basis for the liberation of the rest of the country—that is, the ultimate destruction of Israel."[73]

This is not the opinion of Mr. Bodansky. The "man with the buzzer" had expressed this stratagem on numerous occasions. In an interview with Oriana Fallaci, Arafat stated: "Peace for us means the destruction of Israel and nothing else."[74] In 1994, he wrote:

> In order to obtain the goal of returning to Palestine, all of us sometimes have to grit our teeth. But it is forbidden that this harm the continued struggle against the Zionist enemy. . . . Only a state like that can then continue the struggle to remove the enemy from all Palestinian lands.[75]

On January 30, 1996, Arafat waxed eloquently in a session with Arab diplomats in the Spiegal Salon at the Grand Hotel in Stockholm. His inflammatory address was entitled "The Impending Collapse of Israel."

> "We will take over everything, including all of Jerusalem," he stated repeatedly. . . .
> "Within five years we will have six to seven million Arabs living on the West Bank and in Jerusalem. All Palestinian Arabs will be welcomed back by us," he declared. "You understand that we plan to eliminate the State of Israel and establish a purely Palestinian State. We will make life unbearable for Jews by psychological warfare and population explosion; Jews will not want to live among us Arabs!"[76]

As the Islamic revival continued to grow, Arafat came under increased pressure over his plan to create a secular state, Palestinian or otherwise. The central sticking point remained that *all* of Palestine was a *waqf*—land that belongs to the Muslim *Ummah*—and therefore cannot be ceded to non-Muslims. The ultimate angle Arafat came up with was truly ingenious. Bodansky cites from a speech made by Yasser at a Khartoum summit in early January 1993:

> Significantly, he justified his involvement in the peace process by comparing it with the Prophet Muhammad's Treaty of Hudaibiya, signed with the Jewish tribe of Quraysh in A.D. 628. In that treaty, the Prophet, under duress, promised his enemies peace for ten years. However, he violated the treaty two years later, ostensibly in reaction to a provocation, but in reality as soon as his armies were ready; he then conquered Mecca and slaughtered all the Quraysh. "Negotiations with the enemy are no less vicious than any military operation carried out by our mujahideen and

revolutionaries," Arafat declared. "We have not closed any of our options, which include jihad."[77]

The following year he reiterated the conspiracy during a message in a mosque in Johannesburg, South Africa. Concerning recent accords he had signed with Israel, Arafat stated, "I regard this agreement as no more than the agreement signed between our prophet Muhammad and the Quraysh in Mecca." He then went on to say, "As the Prophet Muhammad accepted it (the Treaty of Hudaibiya), . . . we now accept the peace agreement (with Israel), but in order to continue on the way to Jerusalem." After telling his listeners that the PLO needed them "as Muslims and as mujahedin," he concluded by chanting, "Until victory, until Jerusalem, until Jerusalem, until Jerusalem."[78]

As Yasser fine-tuned his amazing con game, he used a Bill Clinton approach when comparing the word "state" to the word "homeland." The former denotes a *transient* entity; thus, a *state* might be temporarily established in whatever part of Palestine Israel withdraws from. However, the latter denotes *sacred* land; the homeland is Palestine in its entirety and no compromise over it is permissible or possible.

So I ask—Do you think that President Bush and his illustrious cabinet were aware of Mr. Arafat's blatant conspiracy? *Have they not been capable of reading the same documented sources I have quoted for you?* I have a lot of preacher friends who'd better get their heads out of the clouds. According to *Reuters*, November 4, 2004, when reacting to a disputed report of Arafat's death, our "Christian" president told a news conference: "My first reaction is, 'God bless his soul.'" "Brother" Bush is a co-conspirator with the spirit of a dead man for continuing to push the Land for Peace scam with its ultimate goal of a Palestinian State. The "Roadmap to Peace" is a "Roadmap to *Perdition.*"

"ISLAMIC FRANKENSTEIN"

During the closing days of 1979, the Soviet Union invaded Afghanistan. The following year, Iraq declared war on Iran. The United States would play a decisive role in both conflicts.

In 1983 and 1988, Donald Rumsfeld served as presidential envoy to Saddam Hussein's Iraq. Unger writes, "He [Rumsfeld] privately assured Iraqi leaders that even though the United States was publicly protesting Iraq's use of chemical weapons, America's goal of improving relations with Iraq remained undiminished."[79] Although the Coalition forces were unable to discover any WMD, the Bush administration had good reason to believe Saddam had them—*as the United States had previously sent the Iraqi dictator all the germs he could handle.* (See Dr. David Satcher's letter to Senator Donald Reigle, Jr.) Unger writes:

> Beginning in 1984, the Centers for Disease Control began providing Saddam's Iraq with biological materials—including viruses, retroviruses, bacteria, fungi, and even tissue that was infected with bubonic plague. Among the materials that were sent were several types of West Nile virus and plague-infected mouse tissue smears. . . .
>
> "We were freely exchanging pathogenic materials with a country that we knew had an active biological warfare program," said James Tuite, a former Senate investigator. "The consequences should have been foreseen."[80]

To add insult to injury, Unger further notes with regard to the March 1988 chemical attack on Halabja, an Iraqi town in Iranian-held territory in which 5,000 Iraqi Kurds were killed—"U.S. intelligence sources told the *Los Angeles Times* that the poison gas was sprayed on the Kurds from U.S. helicopters, which had been sold to Iraq for crop dusting."[81]

On June 9, 1992, the deadpan Ted Koppel opened his ABC News *Nightline* program with the statement: "It is becoming increasingly clear that George Bush, operating largely behind the scenes through the 1980s, initiated and supported much of the financing, intelligence and military help that built Sadam's Iraq into the aggressive power that the United States ultimately had to destroy."[82]

Even Al Gore, of all people, was able to get in a few jabs. In September, the Democratic vice presidential candidate made the astute observation that, "George Bush wants the American people to see him as the hero who put out a raging fire. But new evidence now shows that he is the one who set the fire."[83]

However, this is not to say that all the "bad guys" were discriminated against; when it comes to "tolerance" and "diversity" no group is more "sensitive" than the merchants of death! How's *this* for "clash equals cash" Hegelianism at its best? Philips writes:

James Adams, defense correspondent of the *Sunday Times* of London, reported "an extraordinary feeding frenzy by the sharks of the arms business. Fifty countries sold arms to the protagonists in the war. Of these fifty, four countries sold only to Iraq, eighteen to Iran and twenty-eight, including

France, China, Italy, South Africa, Britain, the United States and West Germany, sold weapons to both sides.

Swollen by Iraqi and Iranian war demand, the Persian Gulf nations accounted for 30 percent of all arms deliveries to the third world in 1984-1988, according to the Stockholm International Peace Research Institute. The Middle East in its entirety took 48 percent.[84]

Our involvement in the Soviet-Afghan war was even more outrageous. Osama bin Laden was one of the first Arabs to volunteer for military service in Afghanistan after the Soviet invasion. "I was enraged and went there at once," he told an Arab journalist.[85] Bin Laden would spend the rest of the decade raising funds and manpower for the resistance. "One day in Afghanistan was like one thousand days of praying in an ordinary mosque," he was often heard to say.[86] The various *mujahedin* (Islam's "holy" warriors) who responded to Osama's call were trained in different camps in Pakistan, primarily Peshawar. They came to be known as "Afghans" and later constituted the core group for *al-Qaeda* (commonly translated as "the base" or "the foundation").

Unbeknownst to the average American, President Reagan came up with the "bright idea" of building up Osama's gang in order to weaken the Soviet Union. Over the course of the 1980s, $3 billion was funneled to the Afghan resistance through the corrupt Pakistani Intelligence Agency (ISI). Because part of the money was also being used to finance Pakistani mujahideen in Kashmir and the Punjab, the CIA was kept at arm's length. A steady flow of Islamic militants passed through Pakistan during the decade-long war. Between 16,000 to 20,000 arrived from twenty different nations in the final year alone. While most of these "Afghans" were Arab Islamists, their diversity ranged from Malaysia to Bosnia.

The fighting between Iran and Iraq came to an end July 20, 1988, with the Soviet withdrawal from Afghanistan occurring the final year. By September 1991, the demise of the U.S.S.R. was "official." The menacing Berlin Wall that I saw as a teenager came crumbling down. President Reagan received the credit. However, not as readily perceived is the fact that the Twin Towers *also* came crumbling down through the efforts of the *same* terrorist Mr. Reagan had created to bleed the Soviets. *"Then said Hezekiah unto Isaiah. . . . Is it not good, if peace . . . be in my days?"* (II Kings 20:19). In his introduction to *Forbidden Truth*, Joseph Trento (author of *The Secret History of the CIA*) labels *al-Qaeda* an "Islamic Frankenstein" that "turned against its creators with effectiveness and vengeance." He then adds, "A serious investigation would demonstrate that George Bush's father was the midwife to the birth of this monster."[87]

OPERATION DESERT STORM

On February 28, 1991, Operation Desert Storm was launched in the Persian Gulf. The subsequent flash of indignation that reverberated throughout the *Ummah* constitutes another "unknown unknown" with regard to the underlying causes of 9/11 and the growing quagmire in Iraq.

As the Scripture says, *"The thing that hath been, it is that which shall be . . ."* (Ecclesiastes 1:9a), the invasion would *have* to be occasioned by a *pretext.* In the movie *Wag the Dog,* a professional actress is made up to look like a girl from Albania. The "terrorized" child is then filmed fleeing with a dog in her arms through a studio set resembling a village. The clip was subsequently shown to the American people when the president was making his case for a war with Albania.

When making *his* case for a war with *Iraq,* President G. H. W. Bush said, "The fight isn't about oil. . . . The fight is about naked aggression that will not stand."[88] (The fact that we had been equipping the Iraqi dictator for years did not enter the equation.) What Bush needed was a *girl* from *Kuwait* to convince the nation that an invasion was indeed justified.

On August 11, just nine days after the Iraqi incursion, Hill & Knowlton (the world's largest public relations firm) agreed to represent Citizens for a Free Kuwait, a front group funded almost exclusively by the corrupt Kuwaiti government. Then, on October 10, the company was granted a forum to present its "evidence" against Saddam Hussein before the Congressional Human Rights Caucus. The chief witness was—get a load of this—*a fifteen-year-old Kuwaiti girl* who supposedly had firsthand knowledge of Iraqi atrocities! She went only by her first name—Nayirah, as her last name was being withheld, presumably to avoid reprisals against her family. Unger writes:

> As recounted in *Second Front,* Nayirah cried as she testified about her time as a volunteer at the al-Addan hospital. "While I was there, I saw the Iraqi soldier come into the hospital with guns and go into the room where fifteen babies were in incubators," she said. "They took the babies

out of the incubators, took the incubators, and left the babies on the cold floor to die."

After the hearing, Congressman Tom Lantos said that "we have never had the degree of ghoulish and nightmarish horror stories coming from totally credible witnesses that we have at this time." President Bush said that he was happy that the atrocities in Kuwait had been highlighted on CNN. Bush referred to the incubator story at least five more times during the next five weeks. Amnesty International published the story with only a minor qualification, saying that over three hundred premature babies had been left to die. Repeated again and again, it spread quickly across the globe.[89]

Over the next three months the "baby killer" story was carried everywhere—*The New York Times* and the *Sunday Times* of London, on CBS and CNN, in *Time*, in countless newspapers from the *Los Angeles Times* to the *St. Louis Dispatch*. Calling the alleged incidents "outrageous acts of barbarism," President Bush went so far as to say, "I don't think that Adolf Hitler ever participated in anything of that nature."[90]

As to the story's veracity—I believe the expression goes, "A lie can travel around the world three times while truth is putting its boots on." Middle East Watch, a New York-based human rights organization, did a thorough investigation of the story and found it to be totally bogus! Amnesty International, the highly respected human rights organization was forced to make an embarrassing retraction conceding that its team had "found no reliable evidence that the Iraqi forces had caused the death of babies by removing them or ordering them removed from incubators." (While some infants had died during the turmoil, Dr. Fayeza Youssef, chief of obstetrics, confirmed that their deaths were caused by a shortage of nursing staff.[91]

Oh, there's just one more thing—that part about the Kuwaiti girl's last name. Turns out there was a different reason altogether for keeping it a secret. Would you believe the traumatized little thing was *the daughter of the Kuwaiti ambassador to the United States, Saud al-Sabah?* Unger notes, "It is worth adding that Nayirah was not just the ambassador's daughter, but as such was a member of the ruling family of Kuwait, the *same* family that had granted oil concessions to George H. W. Bush's Zapata Off-Shore company thirty years earlier."[92]

But who cares, anyone can mess up occasionally—right? Besides, by the time the "mistake" was caught, the war was already over! So what's the big deal, etc.? *Get over it!*

That Bush would blame the deaths of fifteen infants on Saddam Hussein as a pretext for the Gulf War is also the height of hypocrisy, given the 600,000 Iraqi children who succumbed to more than a decade of corrupt international sanctions. The brutal U.N. mandate was just another cause for rising Muslim hatred, Osama bin Laden declaring, "Killing those Iraqi children is a crusade against Islam."[93]

Saving Private Lynch

When George "Top Gun" Bush would need a good public relations face to keep the home fires burning during *his* romp in the Gulf—Private Jessica Lynch was his gal! In their April 3, 2003, *Washington Post* article entitled "Lynch kept firing until she ran out of ammo," Susan Schmidt and Vernon Loeb wrote:

> Pfc. Jessica Lynch, rescued Tuesday from an Iraqi hospital, fought fiercely and shot several enemy soldiers after Iraqi forces ambushed the Army's 507th Ordnance Maintenance Company, firing her weapon until she ran out of ammunition, U.S. officials said yesterday.
> Lynch, a 19-year-old supply clerk, continued firing at the Iraqis even after she sustained multiple gunshot wounds and watched several other soldiers in her unit die around her in fighting 11 days ago, one official said. . . .
> "She was fighting to the death," the official said. "She did not want to be taken alive." Lynch was also stabbed when Iraqi forces closed in on her position . . . [94]

And of course, her rescue was no less dramatic:

> Lynch's rescue at midnight local time Tuesday was a classic Special Operations raid, with U.S. commandos in Blackhawk helicopters engaging Iraqi forces on their way in and out of the medical compound, defense officials said.
> Acting on information from CIA operatives, they said, a Special Operations force of Navy SEALS, Army Rangers and Air Force combat controllers touched down in blacked-out conditions. An AC-130 gunship, able to fire 1,800 rounds a minute from its 25mm cannon, circled overhead,

as did a reconnaissance aircraft providing real-time overhead video imagery of the operation as it unfolded.

"There was shooting going in, there was some shooting going out," said one military officer briefed on the operation.[95]

Now, although "Saving Private *Lynch*" was less dramatic than "Saving Private *Ryan*," it did provide the nation with a few welcome goose bumps at the time. Unfortunately, it has proven to be just another Hollywood stunt of the Bush administration. A May 15, 2003, *BBC News* article by John Kampfner stated:

> Private Jessica Lynch became an icon of the war, and the story of her capture by the Iraqis and her rescue by US special forces became one of the great patriotic moments of the conflict. **But her story is one of the most stunning pieces of news management ever conceived.** . . .
>
> They were said to have come under fire from inside and outside the building, but they made it to Lynch and whisked her away by helicopter.
>
> Reports claimed that she had stab and bullet wounds. . . . "I examined her, I saw she had a broken arm, a broken thigh and a dislocated ankle," said Dr. Harith a-Houssona, who looked after her. "There was no [sign of] shooting, no bullet inside her body, no stab wound—only [evidence of a] road traffic accident. . . ."
>
> Witnesses told us that the special forces knew that the Iraqi military had fled a day before they swooped on the hospital. "We were surprised. Why do this? There was no military, there were no soldiers in the hospital," said Dr. Anmar Uday, who worked at the hospital.
>
> "It was like a Hollywood film. They cried 'go, go, go,' with guns and blanks without bullets, blanks and the sound of explosions. They made a show for the American attack on the hospital–action movies like Sylvester Stallone or Jackie Chan."
>
> There was one more twist. Two days before the snatch squad arrived, Harith had arranged to deliver Jessica to the Americans in an ambulance. But as the ambulance, with Private Lynch inside, approached a checkpoint American troops opened fire, forcing it to flee back to the hospital. The Americans had almost killed their prize catch.[96]

Thankfully, for *her* sake, doctors confirm that Jessica has no recollection of the whole episode and probably never will.

THE UNCAGED LION

If the truth were known, *Saddam Hussein* was the one with a valid *casus belli* for invasion. It seems as if the greedy Kuwaitis had been using sophisticated drilling equipment to siphon off $2.5 billion in oil from the Rumaila field (which the two countries shared).[97]

However, the most pertinent "unknown unknown" from Operation Desert Storm was the way in which it set Osama bin Laden on a collision course with the West, especially the United States. The problem modern Americans have when trying to understand chaotic conditions in the Middle East is based on the fact that we have become a secular, materialistic culture while Muslims remain fanatically religious. In other words, the typical, spoiled, unregenerate, hell-bound existentialist in this country cannot relate to a person who would rather blow himself up than compromise his religious convictions, no matter how unorthodox they may be and no matter how much filthy lucre you wave under his nose. An Islamic communiqué on November 21, 1995, stated, "These innocent people, despite their weakness, possess what America and all governments subservient to it do not possess—faith in Almighty Allah and love of death for His sake."[98]

The single most important concept to grasp with regard to our emerging culture of terror concerns the moral outrage experienced by bin Laden when Crown Prince Abdullah informed him that the Saudis had chosen the "Great Satan" as their source of deliverance rather than his proven Muslim Afghans. *This point cannot be over-emphasized.* Unger writes:

> For all their anti-Americanism, even the most militant Islamists agreed that something had to be done about Saddam Hussein, a secular ruler who was seen as bent on destroying Islam. Immediately after Iraq invaded Kuwait in August, one of their leaders went to Riyadh to meet Defense Minister Prince Sultan and to present him with an alternative way of going after Saddam without having to rely on the U.S. military. That militant leader was Osama bin Laden.
>
> By this time a battle-hardened thirty-three-year-old, bin Laden told Sultan that the kingdom did not have to allow American infidels on Saudi soil to fight Saddam's troops. Fresh from driving the Soviets out of Afghanistan, Osama was ready to take on another superpower. . . . Thanks in part to U.S. support for the Afghanistan campaign, bin Laden already had a global network of Islamic warriors ready to bolster Saudi forces. If the Islamic forces could defeat a true superpower like the Soviet Union, he argued, they could certainly take on Saddam Hussein. . . .

Stunned by bin Laden's proposal, Prince Sultan warned Osama that Saddam had four thousand tanks. . . . "We (will) fight him with faith," bin Laden replied. He said he could lead the fight himself and promised to put together one hundred thousand former warriors from the Afghanistan War. . . .

According to one report . . . bin Laden left his meeting with Prince Sultan thinking that the House of Saud agreed with him and was going to accept his offer. But soon, he received the news that would transform his life: King Fahd was going to allow U.S. forces into the kingdom.

To bin Laden, this development was "a backbreaking calamity." For decades, the secretive House of Saud had maintained its two different realities. In the West, it proudly paraded its alliance with the United States as evidence of its security and the Saudi entry into the modern world. But within Saudi Arabia, the House of Saud had downplayed any ties to the United States so as not to provoke militant Islamists. Now, however, the double marriage between the two mortal enemies was out in the open.[99]

Bodansky adds, "It was the House of al-Saud that earned the wrath of the Islamists by choosing the Americans over the Saudi Islamist."[100]

When King Fahd asked the *Ullma*—the country's senior religious leaders—to sanction the deployment of Coalition forces, his request was categorically denied. However, following Dick Cheney's assurance that, "After the danger is over, our forces will go home . . . they will not stay in Saudi Arabia a minute longer than they are needed," the king persuaded a meeting of 350 *Ullma* clerics at Mecca to reluctantly agree to a temporary, emergency presence—but only until after the crisis passed. *(Suckers!)* Bodansky states:

> For the Muslim world, it was a traumatic experience in which the sacred all-Muslim unity was so shattered that Arab-Muslim states joined ranks with the hated West to fight and defeat another Arab-Muslim state. Not surprisingly, the Islamists call this period *al-Azma*—"the Crisis"—a calamity for Islam and its believers second only to *al-Naqba*—"the Holocaust"— the establishment of the state of Israel.[101]

As we all know by now, that promise was never kept; U.S. forces have stayed in Saudi Arabia ever since, providing Osama bin Laden with his *own* casus belli for invasion! Citing Rahimullah Yusufzai, Bodansky writes:

"In an Islamic world desperately short of genuine heroes, Osama bin Laden has emerged as a new cult figure." He symbolized the defiance and hostility toward the United States the Muslim world aspires to. Since *Osama* means "lion" in Arabic, many speakers in mass rallies declared that "Osama the Lion had come out of his cage to devour the enemies of Islam." This popular support and adulation created an expectation among the Islamists that they had to live up to the popular sentiments. . . . And there should be no doubt that the Islamists will soon satisfy their supporters.[102]

Soon afterwards, a series of deadly bombings were orchestrated by a consortium of terrorist organizations with bin Laden serving as the catalyst. In addition to Americans, the targets included various governments perceived to be surrogates of the West. Among the bloodiest were: the two attacks in Buenos Aires in 1992 and 1994; the Aden and Golden Moor hotels in Aden, Yemen, December 29, 1992; the initial strike at the World Trade Center in 1993; the "Black Hawk Down" fiasco, October 3-4, 1993; the December 11, 1994, downing of a Philippine airline; Oklahoma City, April 1995; the National Guard building, a joint Saudi-U.S. facility in Riyadh, November 13, 1995; the truck bomb attack on the Egyptian embassy in Islamabad, November 20, 1995; the June 25, 1996, detonation outside the Khobar Towers military complex in Dhahran; the "fuel tank" explosion aboard TWA 800, July 17, 1996; the gruesome 1997 torture-slaying of fifty-four Western tourists in Luxor; the dual embassy strikes in Nairobi and Dar-es-Salaam, August 7, 1998; and the infamous attack on the USS *Cole*, October 12, 2000. (Several others were foiled, such as the attempted assassinations on Egyptian president Hosni Mubarak and Pope John Paul II, as well as the attacks that were planned to occur during the Millennium rollover.)

Osama's philosophy was short and to the point: "You cannot defeat heretics with this book [the Koran] alone, you have to show them the fist!"[103] While America's politicians and corporate CEO's were putting oil ahead of national security, the *Ummah* was preparing for a global *jihad* against the West. In November 1994, a terrorist summit convened in Larnaca, Cyprus. Among the participants were key intelligence officials from Iran, Sudan, and Syria, as well as senior commanders from various Islamic organizations—the Islamic Action Front (Jordan), the Popular Front for the Liberation of Palestine-General Command, HAMAS (the Palestinian Islamist terrorist organization operating in Israel and the territories), HizbAllah, Jordanian "Afghans" from Pakistan and the Islamic Liberation Party Jordan. Bodansky writes:

> The Larnaca conference decided on a twin-track approach to the future terrorist offensive in the United States—the creation of "an environment of terror" and a series of "spectacular operations." ... The key to the success of this campaign would lie in the aggregate impact on the American people, which in turn would build popular pressure on the U.S. government to change policies in order to stop it.[104]

What this ultimately translates to is our State Department applying pressure on Israel (which leads to incoherent weather patterns and other climatic perturbations in America, etc.).

In August 1996, the "Lion" issued his first lengthy and detailed *bayan* (a doctrinal manifesto, or policy statement) which constituted his first formal "declaration of war" known as *jihad*. "Waging jihad against *Yahood-u-Nasaara* [Jews and Christians]," bin Laden said, "has become the religious obligation of the Muslims throughout the globe, and if they displayed lethargy in the fulfillment of this obligation they would be held accountable and would have to face the anguish of Almighty on the day of Judgment."[105]

The critical point in all of this is that, unbeknownst to the American public, the U.S.-led Coalition is actually at war with the entire Middle East—minus Israel! From the outset, Iranian-controlled Shiite "militias" began emerging in the Shiite slums of Baghdad, all of them well armed, well organized, and well funded.[106] With war imminent, thousands of militants—Arabs, Pakistanis, Afghans and Chechens—answered Saddam's call for help and began their trek toward Iraq. Iran and Syria allowed them to pass through their territories without the usual documentation. Many of their passports had Iraqi visas listing "jihadi" as the reason for visiting Iraq.[107] By April 7, 2003, Jordanian officials estimated that more than 5,600 volunteers had crossed into Iraq via Jordan alone.[108] Still others arrived from Algeria, Tunisia, Egypt, Syria, Yemen, Jordan, and Morocco (minus any monkeys). Bodansky summarizes:

> "The 'foreign legion' stunned British troops with their skills and fanaticism," the *Times* reported. The actual number of Islamist volunteers is not clear, but according to Amir Hamza, a central leader of the Jamaat-ud-Daawa, "40,000 Arab mujahedin had reached Iraq."[109]

And so, would you like to guess *how* this coalition of "ragtag rag heads" was able to arm itself to the teeth? Phillips writes:

> In 1990, after Saddam Hussein's partially U.S.-equipped forces invaded Kuwait, George H. W. Bush successfully organized a coalition to expel him, which further enlarged the U.S. military presence in the Persian Gulf— and with it the regional arms build up. Although the cost of the first Gulf War in 1991 was mostly borne by allied nations, the United States quickly thereafter sold the member states of the Gulf Cooperation Council (GCC)— Bahrain, Kuwait, Oman, Qatar, Saudi Arabia, and the United Arab Emirates—the advanced weaponry and basing facilities needed to support any follow-up rapid U.S. deployment. **"Between 1990 and 1997 alone," noted one expert, "the United States provided these countries with arms and ammunition worth over $42 billion—the largest and most costly transfer to any region in the world by any single supplier in recent history."**
>
> From a military standpoint, the strategy of arming the Gulf Cooperation Council worked well enough into 2003. But the larger effects of a four-decade influx of U.S. weaponry, money, support personnel, and covert operations could not be ignored: **The Middle East and southern Eurasia were turning into an Islamic Dodge City. This was the core of what Chalmers Johnson called "blowback"—"the unintended consequences of policies that were kept secret from the American people."**[110]

With the 2004 election looming on the horizon, President Bush continued to assert that the Iraqi resistance was "small and dying." Of course, the exact opposite was true. In reality, time was on the side of the "insurgents." Whatever percentage of "undecided" or nominally pro-democratic Iraqis may have existed at the outset of the occupation, their numbers dropped significantly the longer they witnessed American setbacks, the sustained destruction of their infrastructure and the murder of their friends and relatives (i.e., "Bush *who*?"). Bodansky writes:

> However, the cardinal error of the Bush administration—an error that might ultimately determine the fate of the American endeavor in Iraq—is Washington's abject failure to address and comprehend the profound transformation the Iraqi populace, in its entire ethnic and national tapestry, has undergone since American forces entered Baghdad. The enduring failure of the occupation authorities to normalize life in Iraq has bolstered the grassroots withdrawal into religious and ethnic social frameworks that are inherently and uncompromisingly anti-American. And this profound transformation of society breeds the growing popular support for and

empowerment of the escalating guerrilla warfare. Fixated as it is with the struggle against the remnants of Saddam's regime, the Bush administration is missing this crucial development.[111]

Mr. Bodansky pretty well sums up the situation in Iraq with the statement: "America fought the war in English, in a region that marches to Arabic drums."[112]

ISRAEL SACRIFICED FOR COALITION

As the Lord drew Pharaoh into the Red Sea by deploying the children of Israel to an untenable position (Exodus 14:3), He is currently using the irresistible allurement of *oil* to gather all nations to Armageddon. Those who survive the Tribulation will then be brought into the Valley of Jehoshaphat to be judged by Jesus Christ Himself solely on the basis of their treatment of the Jews. (Joel 3:2,12; Matthew 25:31-46) Of the many "unknown unknowns" behind America's growing quagmire in Iraq, once again, the paramount issue concerns our relationship with Israel.

From its inception, the PLO has fostered a campaign of unmitigated hatred against *Yahood-u-Nasaara*. On May 15, the Arab world remembers Nakba Day (*nakba*, as previously mentioned, being Arabic for catastrophe, calamity or holocaust). The PA media broadcast a major speech by Yasser Arafat on May 15, 2001. You might call him another "Limbaugh Kook"; less than four months before 9/11, he stated:

> On this day, the day we commemorate the Nakba that befell our people on 15 May 1948, our entire people—men, women, elders, young, cubs and flowers, the people of exceeding strength—rise to announce to the world the word of truth, justice, and history. They will say that our people, the Palestinian people, faced injustice which is unprecedented in history. They will also say that this noble people who were dispersed by the **grand conspiracy** and whose homeland was usurped with the force of arms and aggression would not accept this black destiny that was concocted by the **grand conspiracy** against their existence. . . . With their deep-rooted faith, our people remain committed to their principles in the face of the **grand conspiracy** with an unrelenting willpower. They will not bow their heads or give in. Generation after generation has been offering sacrifices and martyrdom . . . for the homeland, freedom, glory, and for rejuvenating the struggle against the **fierce conspiracy**.

> [The] masses of our steadfast Palestinian people, who are mujahedin
> in a heroic manner, blind force will not hold for long in the face of justice,
> truth, and historical authenticity.[113]

Arafat's constituents had remained in a state of heightened frenzy
after rampaging through the Arab Quarter of the Old City, December 8,
2000, igniting two "days of rage" in the aftermath. The route of the riot
was along the Via Dolorosa. It ended near the Lions Gate with the Israeli
police station being torched. Bodansky writes:

> The police tried to disperse the Shabab with rubber-coated bullets, but
> the rioting mob overwhelmed them; twenty-one policemen were wounded
> by rocks, and some ten Palestinians were wounded by bullets and/or rocks.
> **Rather than render first aid, the rioters covered their hands and faces
> with the blood of their wounded friends and stormed the bewildered
> security forces. Others wrote jihadist slogans and made handprints
> with blood on nearby walls.** The orgy of hatred startled even the most
> experienced observers.[114]

The benchmark illustration of prevailing anti-American sentiment in
the Middle East was manifested in the days following 9/11. According
to a Saudi intelligence survey of educated Saudis between the ages of
twenty-five and forty-one, taken in mid-October, *95 percent of those
surveyed "supported bin Laden's cause."* Prince Nawwaf attributed the
shocking figure to "the feelings of the people against the United States"
stemming from the Americans' "unflinching support of Israel against
the Palestinians."[115] Bodansky renders a sober glimpse into the barbaric
Palestinian mindset:

> In Gaza, the Islamist weekly *Al-Risala* published an open letter, "To
> America," by Atallah Abu al-Subh. "America, oh sword of oppression,
> arrogance and sin; do you remember how you crushed the humanity of
> man?" Abu al-Subh asked. "America, have you ever tasted the taste of
> horror, sorrow, and pain? This is the taste that has been our lot for so
> long." Abu al-Subh called the strikes in answer to the Arabs' prayers. "We
> stand in line and beg Allah to give you to drink from the cup of humiliation—
> and behold, heaven has answered. . . . Allah has answered our prayers;
> the sword of vengeance has reached America and will strike again!" The
> Islamist attacks, Abu al-Subh argued, were the obvious reaction to U.S.
> policies worldwide—not just in the Middle East. **"America, you planted
> in the hearts of all men and animals the seedling of hatred of you!
> You never considered that the day would come when the saplings would**

grow and put out your eyes, even if those eyes were placed at the top of the World Trade Center, among the clouds." The strikes also generated hope for change among the Arabs. "America, it transpires that you are weaker than the weak, and that you are as wretched as any refugee that you forced to flee with his children, his wife, and the clothes on his back from a village that was once on the coast of Palestine." Abu al-Subh concluded with a harsh warning: "There is no doubt that this is a deed unprecedented in ancient and modern history. You cannot but realize that the perpetrator will strike again and again if you continue with your corruption."[116]

While preparing for the War in Iraq, Vice President Cheney visited ten Middle Eastern countries in March 2002 and was bombarded with the identical theme. Woodward writes:

> The trip was something of a wake-up call for the vice president. The leaders pounded on him not about Iraq, or the threat of Saddam Hussein, or terrorism, but about the Middle East peace process. He kept hearing that the president had better get involved and throw his weight around to set the region on some process to resolve the Israeli-Palestinian conflict.[117]

The resultant policy decision affecting Israel's role in the approaching invasion would spell disaster for our sole ally in the region. (And don't even *think* about mentioning Turkey.) Bodansky states, "The Bush administration specifically urged Jerusalem to look the other way as Washington tried to get such countries as Syria and Iran to "join the coalition."[118] Not only were the Israelis the sole nation excluded from the so-called "coalition of the willing," but they were also informed that they would not be allowed to strike back if attacked.

Maj. Gen. (Res.) Amos Yaron, the director general of Israel's Ministry of Defense, was summoned to Washington for a conference, October 1, 2002. Bodansky writes, "Senior administration officials stressed to Yaron that the United States expected Israel not to become involved in any military campaign to topple Saddam, virtually regardless of any sort of attack on Israel."[119] On March 7, 2003, CIA Director George Tenet arrived in Jerusalem for a meeting with Ariel Sharon and his senior defense and intelligence officials. According to Bodansky, "Tenet demanded Israeli restraint regarding the Palestinians and Iraq and declared America's right to veto Israeli massive retaliation if Israel were attacked."[120] "The Americans have asked us to keep a low profile, and we accept that," an Israeli official told *USA Today*.[121] (Less than two weeks after threatening

Israel, Tenet would lose his own top informant, Rokan, in the failed assassination attempt of Saddam Hussein at Dora Farms.)

What this translated to was that Washington would be doing a little "looking the other way" itself. *For the sake of mollifying Allah, the PLO would be allowed to terrorize Israeli citizens at will.* Bodansky writes:

> Because Arafat and HAMAS were not likely to comply with U.S. demands, the only way to prevent such an eruption was by pressuring Israel into not reacting to cycles of terrorism and civilian casualties. Obsessed with getting Riyadh to spearhead yet another confrontation with Iraq, or at the very least to permit the use of Saudi bases and facilities, the Bush White House no longer had the slightest interest in the particulars of the Palestinian terrorist strikes in Israel—that is, the reason for Jerusalem's desire to conduct military operations. The "peace process" and "mutual restraint" rhetoric had become simply a fig leaf for the administration's real objectives. Therefore, in insisting that the Americans address the PA's responsibility for acts of terrorism against Israeli civilians, Jerusalem was repeatedly forcing them to confront reality—reminding them of their choices and priorities. Hence, the Bush White House increasingly considered the Sharon government to be a major source of irritation.[122]

The abandonment of Israel was particularly despicable given the history of Palestinian terrorism in the area. On March 26, 2001, a Tanzim sniper, using a U.S.-made rifle and scope provided by the CIA, shot a ten-month-old baby girl in the head as she lay in her crib in Hebron.[123] Two fourteen-year-old boys (one of them a U.S. citizen) who had taken a shortcut in a settlement south of Jerusalem on the night of May 14, were set upon by a group of local Arabs, dragged into a cave, and slowly murdered with extreme cruelty; the attackers finished their mission by mutilating the bodies.[124] During the late hours of June 1, a lone young man entered the Dolphinarium discotheque in Tel Aviv and promptly blew himself up in a crowd of several hundred teenagers, killing more than twenty and wounding close to a hundred. (An autopsy later revealed that the martyr-bomber was infected with a highly contagious strain of hepatitis B, constituting the horrific milestone of biological warfare against Israeli youth.[125]

In early July, Arafat instructed his senior commanders to "kill a settler every day" and to "shoot at settlers everywhere." "Woe to you," he admonished his commanders, "if you let them reach their homes in peace or travel in the roads peacefully."[126] In an interview with BBC radio,

Prime Minister Peres noted the mounting consternation with sustained Palestinian violence. "Israel," he said, "did not have a single day without funerals, without ambulances, without sirens."[127]

On Passover Eve—the night of March 27-28, 2002—a suicide bomber entered a hotel in Netanya and blew himself up in the midst of a Seder gathering, killing some thirty and wounding hundreds. Ironically, among the victims were relatives of those who died in the Dolphinarium attack, invited for a communal Seder to help mitigate their grief.[128] The following day, a sixteen-year-old Palestinian girl blew herself up in a West Jerusalem supermarket, killing an Israeli girl and wounding scores.[129]

In May, a martyr-bomber blew himself up in an ice cream parlor near Tel Aviv killing a fifty-six-year-old woman and her eighteen-month-old granddaughter. Among the thirty wounded were ten young children and babies.[130]

On June 18, a Palestinian male blew himself up on a city bus in southern Jerusalem, killing nineteen and wounding several others. The very next day another disciple of Allah pulled the cord at a crowded bus stop in northern Jerusalem, killing five—including another grandmother and the infant granddaughter she was coddling in her arms—and injuring over twenty five.[131]

Secretary of State Colin Powell arrived at Ben Gurion Airport on the evening of April 11, 2002, for a series of talks with Peres and Arafat. Earlier that morning, a martyr-bomber had blown himself up on a bus from Haifa, killing eight and wounding twenty. The blast lifted the bus over a yard into the air. While motorcading down Highway 1 with Prime Minister Peres, Powell nearly got his *own* "expletive" kicked but for the timely intervention of an alert Israeli security detachment. An ambulance transporting the remains of a Palestinian official to burial services in Gaza was intercepted and searched when it made a "wrong turn" and headed toward Highway 1. A huge bomb was subsequently discovered under the corpse. The plan had been to park the ambulance near a bend in the road where Powell's convoy was bound to slow down, and then *boom!*[132]

Undaunted, Yasser made a second attempt to assassinate Powell before he left the country. As the secretary was heading for an Air Force helicopter, a suicide bomber blew herself up less than a few hundred yards away in the Mahne Yehuda market in Jerusalem, killing six and injuring more than sixty. Moments after hearing the explosion and witnessing the smoke rising, Powell and his entourage over-flew the blast site. Bodansky notes, "Seeing the carnage below at first hand, Powell was shocked. Still, he remained adamant on resurrecting the negotiations."[133] (For "some reason," Colin was a no-show at the filthy animal's funeral.)

While terrorist attacks on American soil are relatively new, and few and far between, they have been a part of daily life in Israel since 1948, exacting a major psychological toll on her people. On August 12, 2001, a suicide bomber blew himself up in a Haifa café. Bodansky's insightful account reveals that only two classes of citizens exist in Israel—the "quick" and the dead:

> This bombing was less successful than the Sbarro one [a restaurant in western Jerusalem where eighteen people were killed and over a hundred wounded three days earlier] . . . because of the quick action of the café's owner. The would-be martyr said "goodbye" to a waitress as he walked in. She screamed, and the owner reacted swiftly, throwing a chair at him. Hence the bomb exploded in the doorway, causing only a few casualties.[134]

Predictably, the violence doubled after Israel was pressured to practice restraint on behalf of the Coalition, etc. Early in the morning on November 21, 2002, a HAMAS martyr-bomber blew up a bus in the Kiryat Menahem neighborhood of Jerusalem, killing eleven and wounding fifty. This incident was uniquely horrific in that the bus was packed with children on their way to school. Bodansky writes, "When Israeli officials pointed out the intentional killing and maiming of schoolchildren, the White House unleashed tremendous pressure on Jerusalem not to do anything that might interfere with the ongoing preparations for the war on Iraq."[135]

On May 18, 2003, another bus was blown up in Jerusalem killing seven and wounding twenty-four. The next day a female suicide bomber blew herself up in a shopping mall in Afula, leaving three dead and over seventy injured.[136] On July 8, a suicide bomber killed an elderly woman and wounded her three grandchildren in a village inside Israel's coastal plains.[137]

Yet another wired Muslim boarded a bus in Jerusalem near the Wailing Wall on the evening of August 19. Some twenty minutes later he blew himself up, killing twenty and wounding over 130; most of the casualties were women and children. Bodansky notes, "The operation was so horrific because the martyr bomber—himself the father of two small children—stood in the bus for up to twenty minutes, patiently waiting for the bus to fill with children before detonating his bombs."[138]

While the American public cannot relate to such callousness, Yasser Arafat's version of "Camp Granada" is one of the most bizarre "unknown unknowns" of all. Bodansky writes:

> In the summer camps for boys organized by the PA's education department, the children were divided into groups named after Israeli cities— Haifa, Acre, Safed, Jaffa, Tiberias, Deir Yassin. They wore T-shirts showing a unified Palestine in which Israel did not exist. Young children were taught how to use assault rifles. Yelling "Commando!" and "Jihad!" they jumped through a ring of fire. The songs taught in these camps included "We'll Throw Them into the Sea," "Revolution Until Victory," and "My Children—in the Suicide Squads." . . .
>
> The Children's Club TV show features a primary school classroom with posters of Mickey Mouse and Donald Duck on one wall and a smiling, fatherly Arafat on another. Several of the festively dressed 6–8-year-old children on one program announced their intention of becoming suicide bombers, to the applause of their teachers. "And when I shall wander into the entrance of Jerusalem," announced one girl, "I will turn into a suicide warrior." On another program, one boy explained what should be done with the Jews: "We will throw them into the sea. The day is near when we will settle our account with stones and bullets." Not a single utterance throughout these activities for children suggested coexistence, let alone peace, with a legitimate Israel.[139]

On April 9, 2002, one such ten-year-old came running down an alley with his school bag toward a detachment of Israeli security forces in the Qandahar refugee camp near Jenin. As the soldiers called to him to clear the way, the boy kept running and when he got close enough, he activated trip wires and blew himself up. Subsequent explosions brought the surrounding structures down on the dumbfounded IDF men.[140]

Those who live to their teenage years are exposed to an even more intense agenda. John F. Burns wrote in *The New York Times*, August 8, 2000:

> It is summer camp time for 25,000 Palestinian teenagers, and strikingly unusual camps they are, too. . . . As run by the men who handle psychological warfare for Yasir Arafat, the Palestinian leader, they allow no horsing around in the dorm, no fun-in-the-sun by a cool clear lake, no rousing sing-alongs beside a roaring campfire. Instead, there is the chance to stage a mock kidnapping of an Israeli leader by masked Palestinian commandos, ending with the Israeli's bodyguards sprawled dead on the ground. Next, there is

the mock attack on an Israeli military post, ending with a sentry being grabbed by the neck and fatally stabbed. Finally, there is the opportunity to excel in stripping and reassembling a real Kalashnikov rifle.[141]

It cannot be emphasized enough that the main reason America will continue her suicidal betrayal of Israel by insisting on a Palestinian state can be summed up in one word—*oil* ("Texas tea"). Phillips writes:

> The geography of world oil production (and U.S. oil import dependence) was shifting decisively. By 1980, the United States produced under 20 percent of world petroleum output and had to import 30 percent of its needs. By 2000, the U.S. share of production had shrunk further and 50 percent of U.S. consumption had to be imported. For all that scientists talked about new fuel sources, notably hydrogen, few policymakers expected a real alternative to oil before 2020, or more likely 2030. The crunch would come between 2000 and 2020, when world oil consumption was predicted to increase by 50 percent, spurred by development in Asia—a virtual doubling of demand by China, India, and the Middle East.
>
> By this point, the oil industry was lopsidedly Republican—or, more precisely, the GOP White House was now filled with oilmen—and the new Bush-Cheney regime made concern about the United States' losing further ground in the global oil competition a top priority. Within months of George W. Bush's 2001 inauguration, Cheney's energy task force predicted that domestic oil production would decline 12 percent by 2020, compelling the United States to import fully two-thirds of its oil. Leverage would continue to swing to the Middle East, with Gulf producers alone expected to provide 54 to 67 percent of world oil exports in 2020. Next to Saudi Arabia's 262 billion barrels of proven reserves, Iraq was second with 120 billion—and possible but unproven Iraqi reserves could carry the total a lot higher. **A careful listener could almost hear the war drums.**[142]

It is rather fitting that Kevin Phillips, a professional journalist, would sardonically describe former Attorney General John Ashcroft as a "lay activist in the Pentecostal Assemblies of God, pious enough that before being sworn in he had himself anointed with cooking oil in the biblical manner of King David."[143] (For the record, "Brother" Ashcroft was so "pious" that within three months of replacing Janet Reno, he would end a sixteen-year tax dispute between the IRS and the Indianapolis Baptist Temple, by approving an armed takeover of the church property, a first in American history.)

Roadmap for Peace

At a special 10 a.m. Rose Garden ceremony on Friday, March 14, 2003, President Bush announced agreement on a "roadmap for peace" in the Middle East. The move was an obvious effort to placate Arab opposition to America's occupation of Iraq by "helping" the "poor Palestinians," etc. The White House also discerned that addressing PA grievances would win back support from Western Europe, which had always viewed saving Arafat as the highest policy priority in the area. This, in turn, would alleviate the political pressure on Tony Blair. "Bush had to choose between Arik (Sharon) and Tony (Blair), and he chose Tony," explained a White House insider in May.[144]

The Israelis viewed the roadmap as a major stab in the back by "Brother" Bush. Bodansky writes:

> Israel felt shocked and betrayed in view of its tremendous support for the United States during the war. From the very beginning of the conflict, Sharon had instructed the entire Israeli defense and intelligence establishments to give the Americans all possible assistance, and wanting not to unnecessarily complicate Washington's tenuous relations with the Arab world, Jerusalem agreed that their cooperation would go without public recognition or thanks. Several Israeli experts were in Iraq throughout the war, sharing their expertise and unique experience as well as risking their lives to help their American allies. Israeli intelligence played a major role in helping the CIA and other American intelligence agencies overcome some of their initial setbacks by providing access to unique sources and material. . . .
>
> Israel also provided the American military with specialized systems for urban warfare and special operations—many of which were taken from operational units of the Israeli Defense Forces. . . .
>
> As the major war was drawing to a close and the guerrilla warfare was taking shape, Israel was content to continue aiding Washington without any public recognition. However, Jerusalem did expect the Bush administration to take the Israeli contribution to the war effort into account when defining the postwar Middle East. Therefore, the formulation of a decidedly pro-Palestinian policy so soon after the war came as a total shock to the Knesset. The Road Map (a document including, for the first time, a defined set of chronological milestones leading to the establishment of a Palestinian state in 2005) was officially handed to Israel on April 30, after Abu-Mazen was sworn in as prime minister of the Palestinian Authority. The next day a British al-Qaeda martyr-bomber working on behalf of

HAMAS bombed the Tel Aviv pub Mike's Place (a bar near the U.S. embassy), a fitting reaction to the new policy. Three civilians were killed and over twenty were wounded in the bombing.[145]

WEAPONS OF MASS DESTRUCTION

The United States is destined to pay a steep price for its deceitful dealings with Israel. The political fallout Bush experienced over his bogus claim connecting Saddam Hussein to uranium from Niger was a portent of things to come. In his State of the Union address on January 27, 2003, the president uttered sixteen words that would come back to haunt him: "The British government has learned that Saddam Hussein recently sought significant quantities of uranium from Africa." The basis for this allegation was a packet of dubious documents uncovered by Italy's Military Intelligence and Security Service (SISMI) purporting that Wissam Al-Zahawiah, Iraq's ambassador to the Holy See, had visited Niamey, Niger, in 1999 to secretly arrange a large shipment of uranium to Iraq in 2000. Included among the papers was a July 30, 1999, message requesting an "answer on the uranium supply," and a confidential memo dated three days earlier referring to the deal—No. 381-NI 2000—for the "supply of 500 tonnes of uranium."[146]

The entire incident was eventually debunked as an elaborate forgery. Bamford devotes ten pages to the hoax in *A Pretext For War* (pp. 298-307). Once again, the hapless Bush administration was constrained to plead *nolo contendere,* while the public will never know if their leader was in on the scam. The truth is probably somewhere between that series of books on the lies of George Bush and the text *"deceiving and being deceived"* (II Timothy 3:13).

However, the so-called "rest of the story" would prove even more embarrassing to President Bush should it ever become widely known. On the night of September 13, 2002, Israeli Special Forces captured a three-man team attempting to cross the Jordan River and enter the Palestinian territories on their way to Arafat's Ramallah compound. Their subsequent interrogation revealed that they were highly skilled members of the Baghdad-based Arab Liberation Front (ALF) sent to launch terrorist attacks under the sponsorship of Arafat's Fatah. Bodansky writes:

The Israeli interrogators were most interested in what the three had to say about their training: During the summer, they had been trained along with other squads of ALF terrorists at Salman Pak—a major base near Baghdad—by members of Unit 999 of Iraqi military intelligence. They recounted that in an adjacent part of the camp, other teams of Unit 999 were preparing a select group of Islamist terrorists specifically identified as members of al-Qaeda. Although the training was separate, and individuals used code names exclusively, they were able to learn a great deal about the missions of their Islamist colleagues.

The three ALF terrorists told the Israelis that in addition to the myriad special operations techniques taught at Salman Pak, the Islamists also received elaborate training with chemical weapons and poisons, specifically ricin. Moreover, on their way to their operational deployment zones, the Islamists were taken to a derelict complex of houses near Halabja, in Kurdistan, where they conducted experiments with chemical weapons and poisons. The area where the training took place was nominally under the control of Ansar-al-Islam, Osama bin Laden's Kurdish offshoot.[147]

The captives further recounted that from there, Islamist detachments were dispatched to Turkey where they were to strike American bases with chemical weapons at the outbreak of war. Other units were sent to Pakinsy Gore in northern Georgia (on the border with Chechnya) to assist Chechen terrorists in their strikes against Russia. Bodansky continues:

> Within a week of the capture of the ALF trio, a delegation of senior Israeli military intelligence officers traveled to Washington to brief the White House about their findings. By then, there had already been independent corroborations of the Israeli reports: Turkish security forces, acting on tips provided by Israel, arrested two al-Qaeda operatives studying plans to attack the U.S. air base in Incerlick with chemical weapons, and American intelligence also learned from its own sources about the activities of foreign mujahedin in Georgia's Pakinsy Gore. Then, on October 23, a group of Chechen and Arab terrorists captured a Moscow theater in the middle of a performance, taking over seven hundred people hostage, rigging the theater with bombs, and threatening to kill everyone inside the building.[148]

While nearly two hundred hostages died in the classic "rescue" operation that ensued, the mere occurrence of a spectacular strike in the heart of Moscow confirmed the accuracy of the information supplied by the captured ALF agents. When Israel passed the warning along to various European governments, the subsequent disruption and capture of several Arab and Chechen terrorist networks in Paris, London, and Manchester, along with support networks in Spain and Italy, further substantiated the Israeli reports.[149]

However, in one of the biggest mistakes of his career, President Bush declined to publicize this demonstrable evidence because it revealed Israel's major contribution to the war on terrorism while implicating Arafat in the same. Bodansky relates:

> Yet in the first of several indecisive and self-contradicting political maneuvers, the Bush administration preferred to accommodate Blair's pressure to keep Israel at arm's length, not implicate Arafat, and placate Blair's fellow West European leaders rather than go public with the findings of the investigation. . . .
>
> Having to choose between further alienating the Western Europeans who insisted on keeping Arafat out of the war, and bolstering its case against Iraq by providing concrete Israeli evidence, the White House decided to go with the Europeans. On February 5, 2003, during his presentation at the UN, Secretary of State Colin Powell showed an aerial shot of the Ansar-al-Islam facility, which he called a "poison and explosive training center." When foreign journalists pointed to the derelict status, Washington remained mum rather than hint at evidence that would confirm Powell's claims but also prove Arafat's involvement with Iraqi terrorism and WMD and point to Israel's contribution to the effort to disarm Iraq.[150]

Thus, while WMD *were* a part of Saddam's arsenal, the Lord judged Bush for slighting Israel in favor of the Niger fairytale.

As to what eventually happened to Saddam's cache of WMD, you'd think the Bush administration would have asked the man who led the Congressional Task Force on Terrorism and Unconventional Warfare for more than a decade. After all, with seven major works on the subject of global terrorism, including the number one *New York Times* bestseller *Bin Laden: The Man Who Declared War on America,* Yossef Bodansky is not your typical "Beltway bureaucrat." But then again, the fact that he is *Jewish* (with plenty of connections in the Mossad, IDF and Knesset) would cause *his* information to be "dissed" as well by the pro-oil "House of Bush."

To begin with, the reason Hans Blix and his team of U.N. inspectors failed to locate WMD in Iraq was because they were hidden in several sophisticated underground storage facilities—their whereabouts known only to Saddam and a small number of confidants.

In the mid-1990s, after much internal debate, Saddam brought in North Korean and Chinese experts and construction teams to build a whole new system of underground facilities for himself, his inner circle, and the underground parallel party's fighting units. To ensure complete secrecy, the new system of underground facilities—bunkers, command centers, and communication storage sites—was built from scratch by North Korean workers. Since no Iraqi labor was involved, very few Iraqis knew about the existence, let alone the location, of these facilities. Furthermore, the North Koreans were able to render the facilities virtually impervious to detection by American surveillance. Their methods included digging a relatively small hole in a shaded mountainside, then expanding the underground spaces through laborious tunneling and carving from the inside. The dirt was evacuated through the hole during the night and dumped into nearby waterways, so that no visible traces of the excavation remained. Some of the key facilities were dug under nearby lakes, to further reduce the likelihood of detection by U.S. national technical means. . . .

Among the concealed bunkers built under Chinese supervision was a network of special long-term storage sites for strategic stockpiles of weapons and ammunition, including weapons of mass destruction, for times of extreme national emergency. A former Iraqi colonel with a Ph.D. in engineering, who escaped in 1999 and is now hiding in Australia, reported that he personally knows of five such secret storage bunkers that were built near Baghdad, Basra, and Tikrit. Other such bunkers were constructed in the deep desert of western Iraq. . . . **The colonel reported that the three such bunkers he visited in the late 1990s were stocked with large quantities of conventional weapons and ammunition, artillery shells, and 122mm GRAD rockets armed with chemical warheads, as well as drums with chemical agents.**[151]

The largest underground complex is in al-Qaim, an area in Iraq's northwestern desert extending between al-Qaim and Lake Qadissiyah to the east. A second key facility extends from the Ramadi area and Lake Habbaniyah to the south, while a third is spread in the triangle of Tikrit, Samarra, and the mountain lakes on the Jabal Hamarin range to the east of both cities. After the invasion began, many WMD were relocated to Syria and northeastern Lebanon.

Once American forces started advancing toward al-Qaim [April 11], intense activities were observed in the thick foliage along the Euphrates. Under cover of darkness, numerous large objects, tanks, and containers were moved from their hiding place and taken across the nearby border with Syria.[152]

A similar nocturnal evacuation of WMD occurred the previous week.

While heavy artillery fire resumed that night [April 5] on the airport compound, the anticipated Iraqi ground offensive failed to materialize. Russian intelligence sources reported, however, that a group from the Republican Guard and other units of the regular army from the Tikrit area made their way to Syria in a daring operation including three hundred tanks, one hundred GRAD multiple-barrel rocket launchers (MBRLs), **many of which had chemical warheads**, and many other weapon systems, including Iraq's entire WMD arsenal. Lebanese sources with access to eastern Syria confirmed the arrival of the column.[153]

The Russian intelligence was flawed, only as it reported that the April 5 incident comprised the "Iraqis' entire WMD arsenal." As late as November, further shipments of WMD were moving to Syria.

Toward this end, the Iraqi stockpiles then stored near Kamishli were now moved to permanent storage sites in central Syria and northeastern Lebanon. **The moving and concealment of the Iraqi WMD were conducted under the command of General Zou al-Himma al-Shaleesh**, a veteran of Syrian-Iraqi strategic cooperation and smuggling. Assaf Shawqat, Bashar's brother-in-law and deputy chief of Syrian military intelligence, personally supervised the undertaking. **The first specific account of this action to transfer and hide the Iraqi WMD was provided by Syrian opposition journalist Nizar Nayyouf**, on the basis of detailed maps and notes he had received from "a Syrian senior officer who'd become a dissident." **Several Lebanese, Syrian, and other Arab security and/or intelligence sources subsequently confirmed Nayyouf's reports, and provided additional details about the whereabouts of Iraq's WMD.**

First to be moved were the large tanks containing chemical materials. They were put on flatbed trucks and moved to areas of northeastern Lebanon under Syrian military control where they were buried in pits near Hermel and in the northern Bekaa. . . .

Iraqi chemical warheads, ballistic missiles, and missile components (mainly engines and guidance kits) **were concealed in North Korean-built tunnels in Al-Baida**, about 2 kilometers from Misyaf near Hama, the site of Syria's main SCUD and warheads factories. . . . **Vital parts of Iraq's WMD munitions were stored in a Syrian Air Force munitions factory near the village of Tal Sinan,** between the towns of Hama and Salamiyyah. This factory produces aerial munitions and tanks for the Syrian Air Force.[154]

At this point I was at a loss to explain *why* Saddam had failed to use his WMD against either Israel or the American-led Coalition forces. Indeed, as Bodansky notes, "According to a wide variety of sources, ranging from Arab intelligence officials and Iraqi defectors to Western technical intelligence, Saddam also prepared a 'chemical defensive belt' around Baghdad with the weapons concealed in underground shelters, ready to be used once American forces crossed a specific 'red line' on their way to Baghdad."[155] Consequently, I sent Mr. Bodansky an e-mail on July 25, 2004, requesting his thoughts on the matter. Among other questions, I asked, "Given the established barbarity of his character (i.e., as evidenced by his previous use of WMD against the Kurds), why would he take the trouble to amass such weapons and then allow himself to be forced out of power without ever using even one?" Later that same day, he replied:

> A few weeks before the outbreak of hostilities—around March 1, 2003—Saddam decided suddenly on the adoption of defenseive strategy. I still don't have a good explanation as to "why" he made this decision. In any case, this decision resulted in unilaterally abandoning the option to attack Israel.
>
> There are indications that Saddam DID order the use of chemical weapons against the advancing US forces—the broadcast of the world "Damm" (blood) as described in p. 217 [of *The Secret History of the Iraq War*]. After the war, a couple of Iraqi senior officers claimed that having realized that the war was already lost, they ignored the order. Saddam's people transferred most of the WMD munitions to Syria and concealed the rest in North Korean-built bunkers for eventual use in the guerrilla war against the U.S.

When I read this analysis, the Holy Spirit brought Habakkuk 3:2c to mind—*"in wrath remember mercy."* No doubt, a number of praying mothers got through.

The same would apply to what should have been a protracted and bloody siege of Baghdad, population five million! During a high-level briefing with President Bush, August 5, 2002, General Tommy Franks warned that Saddam might fold quickly and pull back to Baghdad with his Republican Guard to "circle the wagons."[156] On October 15, Secretary Rumsfeld sent the president a three-page Top Secret memo stating, "Fortress Baghdad could prove to be long and unpleasant for all."[157] Everyone agreed the prospect represented the supreme "known unknown."

The Iraqis were aware of this tactical advantage. After the war, a Mukhabarat officer recalled "Baghdad was like a castle. The Americans could never come close—we were sure of it."[158] Yet, as we all remember, the "resistance" appeared to collapse overnight. Bodansky notes "Key units retreated away from American concentrations. No explanation was given for these developments, and no central communications or discernable instructions were detected by American or other intelligence sources."[159] When I asked Mr. Bodansky if he thought Saddam actually may have intended that his capital fall so quickly to replicate an Iraqi version of Napoleon's "disastrous victory" at Moscow, he answered, "No, Saddam planned on defending Baghdad in a prolonged and bloody urban warfare. He was genuinely surprised by the speed the defense around the city collapsed."

Bodansky attributes the sudden collapse of Baghdad to four factors: Qusay Hussein's antagonistic attitude and repeated berating of senior officers;[160] his inept, costly military decisions;[161] the inevitable defections;[162] and the loss of Saddam International Airport.[163]

Ultimately—while an initial token of mercy may be attributed to the prayers of God's people—the U.S. military will have to pay for the sins of its leaders, especially with regard to our perfidious treatment of Israel. In fulfillment of Powell's calculated caveat—"You break it; you buy it"—the August 23, 2004, headline for *USA Today* read, "Insurgents showing no sign of letting up: U.S. officers say **attacks may continue for years**." The accompanying article reported that "attacks against U.S. and allied forces have averaged forty-nine a day since the handover of sovereignty June 28 . . ."

Furthermore, amidst all the hoopla over the "fall of Baghdad," somehow we missed the fact that our unexpected *victory over* the Republican Guard did not include the *surrender of* the Republican Guard. (*Duh!*) Bodansky describes what appears to be a Muslim version of the Rapture:

> But by the afternoon of April 4, a new quandary had emerged. Some 70,000 Republican and Special Republican Guard troops who were expected to defend Baghdad's southern approaches simply vanished. . . . There was

no logical reason for their disappearance and no clue to their whereabouts or that of their weapons—including tanks, artillery, and combat vehicles.[164]

Like the old saying goes—"They ran away to fight another day." Bodansky then relates how Saddam's loyalists were subsequently "converted" to Islamic *mujahedin.*[165]

Of course, the American people would also have to suffer back in the homeland. For instance, after the Bush administration spent most of August and September 2004 pressuring Israel to evict Jewish residents from "unauthorized" settlements in Gaza, Judea and Samaria, *the state of Florida was rocked by four deadly hurricanes in five weeks.* Beginning with Charlie—the same week President Bush and Senator Kerry went through Pensacola on simultaneous campaign stops—Frances, Ivan and Jeanne followed in ominous succession. The last time a single state was hit by that many hurricanes in one season was back in 1886! With three storms yet to arrive, the president's brother, Governor Jeb Bush, bemoaned on August 7, "Our worst fears have come true."

When it was all over, more than seventy people were dead with at least $12 billion in insured damage. Significantly, while many of the Israelis who face eviction from twenty-three West Bank settlements live in mobile homes, a total of twenty-five Florida counties were declared disaster areas, with mobile homes comprising a substantial number of the affected dwellings, Polk County alone reporting 3,663 mobile homes sustaining major damage with 6,365 receiving minor damage.

The September 28 *USA Today* headline read, "After four storms: 'We're just tired'; Weary Floridians yearn to get back to normal." (For what it's worth, a byline directly to the left announced, "Mount St. Helens might erupt again," while the picture of a Roman Catholic bishop indicted for child molestation appeared in the lower right corner; a "non-related" story on page 9A reported that recent **"suicide bombings in Israel killed 16 people."**) While "normalcy" is an understandable goal for residents of the sunshine state given their new life cycle of: watch the news; prepare to evacuate; evacuate, or stay; wait for the hurricane to pass; clean up; survive; rewind—it could be a while in coming, given our current faithless policies with Israel. On CNN *Headline News,* September 17 (the same day the New Jersey mother was featured in handcuffs), a blip across the bottom of the screen read, "After four storms in five weeks, a scientific study concludes that such conditions can be expected over the next thirty years."

"The Bills Are Coming"

Having surveyed a myriad of "unknown unknowns" relating to conditions in Iraq and the historic events that coalesced to produce them, we will now examine some of the equally unknown *motives* behind the war itself—the "method to the madness."

An old expression goes, "If it doesn't make sense, there's probably a buck in it." On April 24, 2002, General Franks met with his combat commanders in Doha, Qatar, to discuss a number of preparatory tasks that appeared endless. Woodward writes:

> Bush clearly had given him extraordinary authority, declaring that the cost would be whatever it was.
>
> Franks told his commanders to inform him as to what they needed, because henceforth they would no longer make financial requests to Washington. So if they needed to do work on a combat vehicle ramp in Kuwait that would cost several million, just do it. Same with extending a runway in Oman. Or pouring concrete in Jordan. Do it.
>
> Later Franks reported to Rumsfeld: **The bills are coming.** The Pentagon comptroller had the money, Rumsfeld said, so let's go ahead.[166]

In a follow-up meeting between Franks and Rumsfeld on July 17, start-up costs were being put at $700 million.[167] One of the more bizarre "budget items" involved the heavy bribes being paid by the CIA to Iraqi informants. In one operation alone, two brothers were receiving $1 million a month for "intelligence." Woodward writes:

> Tim [an undercover CIA agent] was also doling out millions to the PUK [Patriotic Union of Kurdistan] to keep them happy and for the intelligence and security they provided. One day the PUK leader, Jalal Talabani, came to see him.
>
> "Tim, I will need if you can bring me ones and fives and tens because now everything in Sulaymaniyah costs $100." The $100 bills had caused extreme inflation. It seemed even a cup of coffee was going for $100 because no one could make small change.
>
> Tim promised he would try. A million dollars in $100 bills weighed about 44 pounds, so in all tens it would be hundreds of pounds, and in dollar bills thousands of pounds. . . .
>
> Once the shooting started, the teams might need enough money for two or three months or more. Saul [the mission supervisor] decided to give Tim and the other team a big money dump—$35 million in cash. That

was nearly one ton of $100 bills. It was a pain to smuggle it in, hiding it under MREs (Meals Ready-to-Eat) and other supplies. It took three border crossings to get the $35 million into northern Iraq.[168]

As we are all painfully aware of by now, war is big business—"clash equals cash." By November 2003—six months after Bush's triumphal strut on the USS *Abraham Lincoln*—an occupation force of 130,000 American troops was costing the U.S. taxpayer *$4 billion per month* with another *$70 billion* earmarked for further military operations and reconstruction projects.[169] Like the president told General Franks— "the cost would be **whatever** it was." Dean relates, "The Center for Public Integrity, a nonpartisan organization, has reported that so far some seventy American companies and individuals who were substantial contributors to the Bush-Cheney campaign have been awarded billions of dollars in contracts in Iraq, all with secrecy clauses prohibiting the companies from disclosing their profits, and the White House has direct (if not exclusive) oversight of this activity."[170]

Because the American people have lost their ability to think, they are incapable of discerning the true identity of their political leaders. Does anybody really believe that former Arkansas First Lady Hillary Clinton understands the needs of the people who live in New York? Mr. Bloomberg spent $75 million of his own money to become the mayor of New York City. Would you trust him as far as you could throw him?

The men who hold the highest offices in the federal government generally have three things in common: they are nearly always members of the Council on Foreign Relations (as well as any number of other New World Order groups, such as the Trilateral Commission, Bilderbegers, Bohemian Grove, Club of Rome, etc.); they remain connected to the system for decades, shifting from one powerful position to another in various administrations; and, they are heavily involved in global financial interests affected by U.S. foreign policy.

This means our so-called "public servants" are really "private investors" who use their government positions to increase their wealth. In a sick sort of way, you might be able to trust a Jesse Ventura or even an Arnold Schwarzenegger more than a Dick Cheney or George Bush (i.e., what *professional* politician in his right mind would degrade his opponents as "girly men"?)

For instance, the previously cited *Wall Street Journal* piece revealed, "In recent years, former President Bush, ex-Secretary of State James Baker and ex-Secretary of Defense Frank Carlucci have made the pilgrimage to the bin Laden family headquarters in Jeddah, Saudi Arabia."[171] Casper Weinberger, secretary of defense during the Reagan administration and now chairman of Forbes, Inc., met with the bin Laden family twice, according to the *Journal*. Former Treasury Secretary Nicholas Brady was previously a prominent attorney with the Wall Street firm of Dillon Reed and later a board member of the Amerda Hess oil company. Don Evans, a close friend of George W. Bush, who served as commerce secretary under his first administration, spent the majority of his career in the oil sector (as CEO of Tom Brown), as did former Energy Secretary Spencer Abraham. Kathleen Cooper, undersecretary for economic affairs, had been the chief economist for Exxon.[172]

Condoleezza Rice left the "court" of "George I" in 1991 (having served as a "specialist" in Soviet relations) to join the board of Chevron Corporation, formerly Standard Oil Company of California. Three years prior to her arrival, Chevron sold its remaining shares of Aramco stock to Saudi Arabia. If the U.N.'s "favorite" Scripture is Isaiah 2:4 and the CIA's—John 8:32, then a wrenched interpretation of Psalm 93:10 would be the perfect text for America's greedy oil executives: *"I shall be anointed with fresh oil."*

Starting in 1991, Chevron joined the mad dash for oil in the former Soviet republics of Kazakhstan, Turkmenistan and Kyrgyzstan. Located north of Afghanistan, Kazakhstan has been nicknamed the "New Kuwait" by experts in oil procurement. The Kazakh subsoil has fifteen million proven barrels of oil and sixty-five million estimated. Chevron is a major participant in this market via the Tengizchevroil consortium it controls. Brisard and Dasquié state that "from 1991 to 2000, Rice was a director of the Chevron group—one of the leading oil companies in the world—in which she notably dealt with questions related to developments in Kazakhstan."[173] Condi was so well-liked, the company even named an oil tanker after her—"a red-hulled, 129,000-ton, Bahamas-registered Suezmax behemoth."[174] With the restoration of the Bush dynasty under "George II," Condi changed hats to become head of the newly created National Security Agency and later, secretary of state. (The vessel was discretely renamed *Altair Voyager*.)

"THE GODFATHER"

The degree to which Dick Cheney has been able to profit from Hegel's dialectic is a mind-boggling odyssey in itself, surpassed only by the extent to which he has been able to conduct his piracy out in the open. As secretary of defense under George H. W. Bush (1988-1992), Cheney played a major role in the first war against Iraq. In 1992, he hired Brown and Root Services, a division of the Dallas-based Halliburton Corporation, to conduct a feasibility study detailing how private companies—Brown and Root prominently among them—could render logistics for U.S. military forces in potential war zones around the world. That very year, Brown and Root (having since become Kellogg, Brown and Root) received the first non-bid, five-year logistics contract from the U.S. Army to support American troops in such hell-holes as Zaire, Haiti, Somalia, the Balkans, and Saudi Arabia.[175] Kevin Phillips writes in *American Dynasty:*

> According to a survey by the Center for Public Integrity and the International Consortium of Investigative Journalists, Halliburton is first and foremost among the two dozen or so U.S. firms that fit the new category of "private military companies" (PMCs) —primarily service providers of high-tech warfare, including communications and intelligence, logistical support, and battlefield training and planning. Since 1994, the Defense Department has entered into just over 3,000 contracts with PMCs, valued at more than $300 billion; 2,700 of them were held by just two companies: Kellogg, Brown and Root, the Halliburton subsidiary, and the Virginia-based management and technology consulting firm Booz, Allen and Hamilton. . . .
>
> The employees of PMCs ran a considerable gamut, from cooks and bottle washers to retired generals, with wide variations in their duties and proximity to combat. At least one PMC, Oregon-based ICI, had no restriction about using weapons in combat situations. . . . Privatizing military functions circumvented accountability to Congress, while effectively militarizing confrontations in which the Pentagon might otherwise be reluctant to send uniformed troops. In addition, by using for-profit "soldiers," the executive branch could evade Congressional limitations on troop strength.[176]

Thus, with the stroke of a pen, the Bush-Cheney coalition replaced John Wayne and the "Fighting Seabees" with a privatized military mutation—just in time for the present imperceptible "War on Terrorism."

Reminiscent of Senator William Proxmire's "Golden Fleece Award," the main problem with the DoD-Halliburton relationship is how the contract is put together. Dan Briody, an award-winning journalist whose book *The Iron Triangle: Inside the Secret World of the Carlyle Group* was cited in the previous chapter, writes in his 2004 national bestseller *The Halliburton Agenda:*

> The contract is structured as a *cost-plus* contract, or in contract legalese, a *cost-reimbursement, indefinite-delivery/indefinite-quantity* contract. Even a layman can tell that means good things for the contractor. In cases where the government and its contractor will have difficulty estimating the resources needed in fulfillment of a particular contract, cost-plus provides the flexibility to continually add on "task orders," or additional services to the contract on an ongoing basis. Basically, it's a blank check from the government. The contractor makes its money from a built-in profit percentage, anywhere from 1 percent to 9 percent, depending on various incentive clauses. . . . When your profit is a percentage of the cost, the more you spend, the more you make.[177]

Another abuse is the fact that most of the government contracts with Halliburton have been "awarded" without the built-in safeguard of competitive bidding. The standard explanation offered by Halliburton has been that *they* were often the only firm capable of fulfilling the specifications of the contracts in question, especially under emergency conditions. Such a ridiculous suggestion flies in the face of America's proven free enterprise system. Truth is, due to Halliburton's fine-tuned political connections, they were frequently privy to proprietary knowledge and often allotted the unfair advantage of designing the contract itself. Briody writes, "The company was in the unique and highly coveted position of drawing up contracts that only it could win."[178]

As the contractor of choice, Halliburton made a cool $109.7 million in Somalia. In August 1994, they collected $6.3 million from Operation Support Hope in Rwanda. The following month, Operation Uphold Democracy in Haiti netted the company $150 million and in October 1994, Operation Vigilant Warrior earned them another $5 million.[179]

In 1995, while President Clinton was distracting the nation with a labyrinth of corruption and immorality, Dick Cheney—"private citizen"— quietly became the CEO of Halliburton, remaining in that position until becoming vice president to George W. Bush in 2000. Now why do you suppose one of the largest corporations in the world would hire a man with zero business experience, and to become their CEO, no less? [Can we say—*Duh!*?] Phillips relates the obvious:

> Awarded contract dollars rose in the late nineties after Cheney became chief executive officer. . . . Federal government contracts with Halliburton and its subsidiaries also expanded, jumping from roughly $300 million in 1995 to $800 million in 1999 and higher under Bush after 2000. During Cheney's five years as CEO the total awarded was $2.3 billion, up from $1.2 billion for the five preceding years.[180]

While Cheney worked at Halliburton, the company went from seventy-third to eighteenth on the Pentagon's list of top contractors (a growth of 91 percent).[181] Obviously, Dick was hired for his Rolodex.

On July 13, 2002, an article appeared in *The New York Times* entitled "In Tough Times, a Company Finds Profits in Terror War." How's *this* for a timely illustration of "clash equals cash"?

> From building cells for detainees at Guantanamo Bay in Cuba to feeding troops in Uzbekistan, the Pentagon is increasingly relying on a unit of Halliburton called KBR, sometimes referred to as Kellogg, Brown and Root. **Although the unit has been building projects all over the world for the federal government for decades, the attacks of Sept. 11 have led to significant additional business.** KBR is the exclusive logistics supplier for both the Navy and the Army, providing services like cooking, construction, power generation and fuel transportation. The contract recently won with the Army is for **ten years and has no lid on costs, the only logistical arrangement by the Army without an estimated cost.**[182]

Phillips adds:

> Revealingly, the contract [awarded in 2001] also provided that KBR would "provide for the continuity of operations of the Iraqi oil infrastructure," which included "operation of facilities and distribution of products." By early May [2003], the company was pumping 125,000 barrels of oil per day, a circumstance that one Democratic congressman found "at odds with the administration's repeated assurances that the Iraqi oil belongs to the Iraqi people."[183]

We are therefore confronted by the bizarre scenario that CEO Cheney used the very apparatus he created (PMCs) to help *rebuild* the country he had previously helped *destroy* as secretary of defense. He then went on to help destroy it a *second* time as vice president, leaving his "former" company to clean up the mess once again. Now you know why Dick has been so hard to find since 9/11. Odds are he has spent more time in the smoke-filled boardroom at Halliburton Corporation than he has in any of those funky FEMA command bunkers! (See "Site R.")

While Cheney told Tim Russert on *Meet the Press*, September 14, 2003, "Since I've left Halliburton to become George Bush's vice president, I've severed all my ties with the company, gotten rid of all my financial interests,"[184] Briody writes:

> Cheney is still in touch with the executives at Halliburton. One financial analyst that covers the company but declined to be identified said "Cheney is very loved within Halliburton. He's seen as almost like the Godfather. Executives have told me, '[Y]es, I still have contact with Dick Cheney. He calls me up once in a while just to see how things are going and to find out what's going on in the energy business.'"[185]

Dick was *really* fibbing about the severed financial ties bit:

> The Congressional Research Service, a nonpartisan agency that investigates political issues at the request of elected officials, says otherwise. Cheney has been receiving a deferred salary from Halliburton in the years since he left the company. In 2001, he received $205,298. In 2002, he took in $162,392. He is scheduled to receive similar payments through 2005 and has an insurance policy in place to protect the payments in the event that Halliburton should fold. In addition, Cheney still holds 433,333 unexercised stock options in Halliburton, the profits from which he has agreed to donate to charity.[186]

In a humorous statement issued in 2002, the company asserted that Cheney had "steadfastly refused" to market Halliburton/Kellogg, Brown and Root services to the U.S. government during his five years as chief executive.[187] After word leaked out that the firm was adding insult to injury by bilking the Coalition in its fuel sales (to the tune of sixty million dollars), Halliburton was rewarded with another $1.2 billion contract in January 2004. When a subsequent CNN clip featured Cheney responding to allegations of impropriety, I watched in astonishment as the grizzled corporate titan meekly replied, "I wouldn't know *how* to fix those contracts if I *wanted* to." That same month, Justice Antonin Scalia had accompanied Cheney aboard Air Force II on a duck-hunting trip to southern Louisiana (at taxpayers' expense)—only three weeks after the Supreme Court had agreed to take the vice president's case concerning his refusal to release certain energy task force records. While Scalia declined to recuse himself, Dick "ducked" the matter entirely as the documents in question would severely implicate the Bush dynasty in the Enron collapse (not to mention the fact that the accounting firm Halliburton used was Arthur Andersen, the same company that went down with Enron[188]).

Since the television has unplugged the minds of the American people, simple one-and-two-syllable words like "graft" and "kickback" can no longer be processed by the brain. Rather than seriously investigate these gross acts of malfeasance, the major networks opted to center their attention on the circus atmosphere surrounding the Michael Jackson child molestation trial. Although a major story *did* "break" on October 28, 2004, about an FBI probe into Halliburton policies, the Cheney-Bush team was returned to power five days later. As this book was going to press, Halliburton was under investigation by no fewer than four federal agencies, including the Department of Defense, the SEC, the Department of Justice, and the General Accounting Office, with the investigations spanning four different countries (Afghanistan, Bosnia, Iraq and Nigeria).[189]

While the aforementioned material is bad enough, or to quote General William Nash (the former American commander in Bosnia and the U.N. administrator in Kosovo)—"Personally, I think that these rebuilding contracts smell to high heaven,"[190] Briody writes:

> Understanding a company like Brown & Root and Halliburton is nearly impossible without historical context. All of the confusing talk of no-bid, cost-plus contracts in Iraq and the relationship of Dick Cheney to Halliburton make little sense when viewed as an isolated event. It might even seem excusable to the casual observer. Taken with the company's history, particularly its long relationship with Lyndon Johnson and other prominent politicians, an undeniable pattern emerges, one that is far less likely to be overlooked. The abuse of political influence is endemic to Brown & Root, a pathology that repeats itself decade after decade. And the story rarely changes.[191]

Obviously, space constraints permit only a thumbnail sketch of this history. Erle P. Halliburton founded his oil well cementing business in 1919. Fellow Texan and contemporary Herman Brown began his career in roadbuilding, then later branched out into the construction industry with his younger brother, George. (In gratitude for a timely loan from

his brother-in-law, Dan Root, Herman named the company Brown & Root.)
The two firms merged in 1962 with Halliburton as the parent company.

The key to understanding the present relationship between Halliburton
and the Bush White House is to uncover the corrupt track record of
Brown & Root that began with the company's lucrative alliance with
Lyndon B. Johnson. Briody writes:

> From the time that Johnson became a congressman in 1937, through
> his successful Senate run in 1948, he collected hundreds of thousands of
> dollars, maybe millions, from the Browns and their friends. While the
> extent of the relationship was apparent to some close observers in and
> around Texas, the rest of the country had no idea how deep the ties between
> Johnson and the Browns went. With so much money at stake at every
> stroke of a pen in Washington, the Browns' investments in Johnson were well
> worth it. Johnson would eventually become part of the most powerful
> circles of influence in all of the nation, the Suite 8F crowd. This group of
> Houston businessmen and politicians met regularly at Herman Brown's
> suite in the Lamar Hotel in downtown Houston. Ideas were exchanged,
> plans were hatched, and money changed hands. . . . It was accepted as the
> way business was done. Mostly though, Texans just wanted to get in on
> the action. Other politicians in the state came to know that Lyndon Johnson
> was the man to see to get some of Herman Brown's money. Businessmen
> in the state knew that the way to get political influence was through Herman
> Brown. If anything was getting done in 1940s Texas, it was going to have to
> go through either Johnson or Brown, the most powerful team in the state.[192]

The Brown-LBJ pact strengthened significantly when President
Roosevelt got in on the action. Briody writes:

> In addition to the money that Herman Brown contributed to Johnson
> for his congressional reelection, Brown donated heavily to Johnson's allies
> throughout the country. In October 1940, after a whirlwind month of arm-
> twisting and political back-scratching, Lyndon Johnson won an informal
> role advising the Democratic Congressional Campaign Committee. The
> position gave Johnson a new national profile, and put him in a position to
> help Democratic candidates for Congress all over the country. He immediately
> called on Brown & Root. . . .
> The money began to pour in just five days after Johnson had secured
> his post on the Committee. . . . Letters poured in from desperate Democrats
> locked in mortal battle with their GOP opponents. Johnson made sure to
> let each of the lucky candidates know that it was he, not the Committee, who
> was responsible for their good fortune. Suddenly, dozens of congressional

hopefuls found themselves owing Lyndon Johnson, and indirectly Brown & Root, favors. Herman Brown knew that the more powerful Lyndon Johnson became, the more powerful he would be as well.

The 1940 election was an overwhelming success for the Democrats. Dozens of congressmen owed their seat in the House to Johnson, and President Roosevelt himself was eternally grateful for the role Johnson had played in securing a Roosevelt-friendly House. Those elections vaulted Johnson into a new role of national power, with Herman Brown lurking in the shadows behind him. As Caro bluntly puts it, "(Johnson's) power base wasn't his congressional district, it was Herman Brown's bank account."[193]

With the assassination of President Kennedy over three decades later, Brown's "fair-haired boy" had finally arrived. While researching the historical linkage between the Browns and Lyndon Johnson, I contacted one of my "better connected" friends who owns a 4,000-acre ranch in southeast Texas. He sent me the following anecdote:

> Yes, I knew a lot about the B&R folks. They were the company that built a lot of military bases and other mega projects around the world. George Brown was in thick with all the politicians and LBJ was the closest. He had a big home in San Antonio and it is still inhabited by his heirs, I think.
>
> I met him one time on a bird hunting trip I gave for B&R. He had his main man, Herbert Frensley, John Connally and LBJ with him. George, Herbert, and John were decked out in hunting garb and showing off for everyone—the best guns, the best clothes, the best knives, on and on. The president finally, after about 15 minutes, got out of his limo dressed in street shoes, slacks and a banlon shirt with a Scotch in one hand. He shook my hand warmly and then went on to the others standing around. When he was done, he came back to me and asked where I got my name, and I told him. I then asked him what type of gun he was going to shoot today, and he said, "Oh, [expletive], whatever they give me!"
>
> We had a lot of little Mexican kids there bringing everyone drinks, more ammo, and they would go and fetch the birds as they fell. Mr. Brown always traveled with his black porter, Henderson. On this occasion he loaned him to LBJ to assure the best treatment for the president during the hunt. At one point, Henderson flagged me down while I was driving around checking on everyone. He wanted to know where the president's limo was. I asked him if LBJ was getting any hunting done. He said, with a straight face, "Well, suh, de only ting dis president is huntin' is de missing bottle of Scotch."

The president's drinking problem grew noticeably worse during the bloody Vietnam imbroglio. However, while Lyndon was taking all the heat, the "merchants of death" at Brown & Root couldn't be happier; the coffers were overflowing. Briody confirms:

> As part of the single most lucrative contract the company had ever entered into, Brown & Root was in Vietnam from 1965 to 1972 pulling down $380 million in revenue in the process. . . .
> **They did 97 percent of the construction work in the country during the seven years they operated there**. The remaining 3 percent went to local Vietnamese contractors.
> They were moving enough dirt to dig the Suez Canal and paving enough roads to surface the Jersey Turnpike every 30 days. They had a small army of their own in the country, 51,000 at the height of operations in 1967, the largest employer in Vietnam. . . .
> **In 1947, Brown & Root was the forty-seventh largest construction company in the country. By 1965, they were number two, and by 1969, number one, with sales of $1.6 billion.** Most of the momentum took place while Johnson was president, a coincidence not lost on the competition.[194]

Briody concludes, "As striking as the similarities between modern-day Kellogg Brown & Root (KBR) and the company's distant past are, there is no escaping the fact that history is indeed repeating itself when we look at the role the company played during the Vietnam War and compare it to KBR's work in Iraq today."[195] Apparently, given the 2004 election returns, over half the population has yet to realize that our last three wars were started by Texans, with the lion's share of the profits going to the same Texas firm each time!

Now I ask you—Are these men and women dedicated American patriots in the tradition of Washington, Jefferson and Madison, or greedy New World Order conspirators in the shadows of Weishaupt, Pike and Rhodes? I mean, *really*—the president of the United States of America being sued under RICO?; his vice president, Dick "Back Seat" Cheney, described as "The Godfather" at Halliburton? And let's not forget "Dubya's" other co-conspirators—George "Slam Dunk" Tenet, Condoleezza "Super Tanker" Rice, Donald "Rumstud" Rumsfeld, and, last but not least, John "The Crisco Kid" Ashcroft.

What can we expect in the future? Will things get better or worse? Is a national revival *really* around the corner? If this is so, *like the majority of our Christian leaders proclaim*, why did Paul describe the last days as a time when *"evil men and seducers shall wax worse and worse"*? (II Timothy 3:13a) Could it be that the so-called "big-name preachers" who continually shield their tithing members from the negative reality of America's final days are, in reality, even greater enemies of the truth than the Kissingers, Brzezinskis and Rockefellers? While it is one thing for "Reverend" Pat Robertson, the *Yale*-educated Charismatic charlatan who speaks "ex-cathedra" for the "Religious Right," to create and promote the modern Constantines, Independent Baptists should hold their leaders to a standard that is *Biblically* correct rather than *politically* or *emotionally* correct. Despite the fact that "Brother" Bush can fellowship with Moonies, Muslims and rockers, harbor a network of domestic terrorists and profiteers within the exclusive confines of an ever-expanding shadow government, and labor for the establishment of a Palestinian state within the present borders of Israel, *Newsweek* magazine could state on March 10, 2003, "Bible-believing Christians are Bush's strongest backers."

WHAT THE "CRAZIES" *REALLY* BELIEVE

While the war in Iraq generated plenty of profits for the merchants of death and their political cronies, the Bush administration was also motivated by a perceived opportunity to realize its elitist agenda. The background for the comparison of 9/11 to Pearl Harbor and its becoming the "convenient" pretext for our multi-billion dollar quagmire in Iraq can be traced to the globalistic philosophies espoused by Dick Cheney and Paul Wolfowitz in 1992. With the breakup of the former Soviet Union and the end of the Cold War, America was suddenly recognized as the world's only superpower. Given the propensity of fallen man to usurp the role of his Creator, visionaries like Cheney and Wolfowitz decided to seize the moment. They—not Jesus—would finally bring peace on earth and good will to mankind! Dean writes:

> In late 1991, recognizing that the United States' military needs had changed with the end of the Cold War, [Defense Secretary] Cheney formed a group at the Department of Defense to develop "forward leaning" military plans for the future. No secretary of defense had ever done more for the care and feeding of the military-industrial complex than Cheney, and his forward-looking plans would follow that pattern. Paul Wolfowitz, a mathematician-turned-political-scientist (Ph.D., University of Chicago, 1972), then serving

as Cheney's undersecretary of defense for policy (with some seven hundred policy wonks at his command), took charge of the study.[196]

When the newly completed Defense Policy Guidance plan was being circulated for review in the spring of 1992, it was leaked to *The New York Times* by a Pentagon official "who believe[d] this . . . strategy debate should be carried out in the public domain." Public debate, however, quickly derailed Cheney's plans for the United States' "ruling the world," as one commentator described it. The most offensive plank in the radical strategy was Cheney's doctrine "to take military steps to prevent the development of weapons of mass destruction [by] pre-empting (such) an impending attack."[197]

With Bush I denied a second term, Cheney would have to wait out the Clinton years to implement his global agenda under Bush II. In the meantime, Dick and Paul were not about to let any grass grow under their feet. In 1996, three of their henchmen traveled to Israel for a clandestine meeting with Prime Minister Benjamin Netanyahu. Richard Perle, Douglas Feith and David Wurmser would later serve in the Bush administration as his leading national security advisors. The centerpiece of their proposal was the removal of Saddam Hussein as the first step in transforming the Middle East into a region friendly to Israel and the West. Bamford writes:

> This would be done, they recommended to Netanyahu, "by reestablishing the principle of preemption" and by "rolling back" its Arab neighbors. From then on, the principle would be to strike first and expand, a dangerous and provocative change in philosophy. They recommended launching a major unprovoked regional war in the Middle East, attacking Lebanon and Syria and ousting Iraq's Saddam Hussein. **Then, to gain the support of the American government and public, a phony pretext would be used as the reason for the original invasion.**
>
> The recommendation of Feith, Perle, and Wurmser was for Israel to once again invade Lebanon with air strikes. **But this time, to counter potentially hostile reactions from the American government and public, they suggested using a pretext.** They would claim that the purpose of the invasion was to halt "Syria's drug-money and counterfeiting infrastructure" located there. They were subjects in which Israel had virtually no interest, but they were the ones, they said, "with which America can sympathize."
>
> Another way to win American support for a preemptive war against Syria, they suggested, was by "drawing attention to its weapons of mass

destruction program." The claim would be that Israel's war was really all about protecting Americans from drugs, counterfeit bills, and WMD— nuclear, chemical, and biological weapons.[198]

Does this sound like Operation Northwoods revisited? "It was rather extraordinary for a trio of former, and potentially future, high-ranking American government officials to become advisors to a foreign government," Bamford adds. "More unsettling still was the fact that they were recommending acts of war in which Americans could be killed, and also ways to masquerade the true purpose of the attacks from the American public."[199]

While Netanyahu was aware that his nation had resorted to preemption in the past (e.g., Six-Day War), to his credit, he rejected the task force's plan.

By Spring 1997, the Cheney-Wolfowitz cabal had created the Project for the New American Century—a well-funded "non-profit, educational organization" to promote their goal of global peace *vis à vis* military intervention. Unger lists Florida governor Jeb Bush among its key members.[200] The following year, eighteen prominent members of the New American Century wrote President Clinton, urging him to remove Saddam Hussein. While Cheney did not sign the letter, a slate of his future underlings did, including Paul Wolfowitz, Don Rumsfeld, Richard Perle, R. James Woosley and Richard Armitage.

On the eve of the 2000 election, Cheney's "Dream Team" released an amazing seventy-seven page "Pipe Dream" entitled *Rebuilding America's Defenses: Strategy, Forces and Resources For a New Century; A Report of The Project for the New American Century, September 2000.* Mr. Wolfowitz was listed as one of the twenty-seven project participants. The introduction states:

> As the 20th century draws to a close, the United States stands as the world's most preeminent power. Having led the West to victory in the Cold War, America faces an opportunity and a challenge: Does the United States have the vision to build upon the achievement of past decades? Does the United States have the resolve to **shape** a new century favorable to American principles and interests?
>
> (What we require is) a military that is strong and ready to meet both present and future challenges; a foreign policy that boldly and purposefully promotes American principles abroad; and national leadership that accepts the United States' global **responsibilities**.

Of course, the United States must be prudent in how it exercises its power. But we cannot safely avoid the **responsibilities** of global leadership of the **costs** that are associated with its exercise. America has a vital role in maintaining peace and security in Europe, Asia, and the **Middle East**. If we shrink from our **responsibilities**, we invite challenges to our fundamental interests. The history of the 20th century should have taught us that it is important to shape circumstances **before** crises emerge, and to meet threats **before** they become dire. The history of the past century should have taught us to embrace the cause of American leadership.[201]

In an article entitled "Promoting the National Interest" that appeared in *Foreign Affairs*, January-February 2000, Condoleezza Rice argued that the United States should avoid becoming bogged down in nation-building enterprises. Within months of 9/11 she would make the incredible remark that America should not use its military as "the world's 911."[202] To assess her words as constituting the height of hypocrisy would be the nadir of understatement. Condi knew, better than anyone else, where America was heading. James Mann writes in *Rise of the Vulcans*:

> During the campaign Bush's foreign policy advisors came up with a nickname to describe themselves. **They dubbed their team the Vulcans, in honor of the Roman god of fire, the forge and metalwork.** Rice, who was serving as foreign policy coordinator for the Bush campaign, had been raised in Birmingham, Alabama, where a mammoth fifty-six-foot statue of Vulcan on a hill overlooking downtown paid homage to the city's steel industry. The name had started as a joke, but it caught on, and the campaign began to use it in public. That word, *Vulcans*, captured perfectly the image the Bush foreign policy team sought to convey, a sense of power, toughness, resilience and durability.[203]

While it is unknown whether "Mr. Spock's" race was named after the same Roman deity, the *Vulcan* moniker would certainly fit the political leadership of a pagan culture that currently features a *Klingon* translation of the Holy Scriptures (see: "JoH'a' 'oH wIj DevwI' jIH DIchDaq Hutlh pagh"—an actual rendition of Psalm 23:1 for spaced-out "Trekkies"). Mann unwittingly concurs, adding, "Ironically, Birmingham's statue of Vulcan was taken down for repairs in 1999 because it was beginning to fall apart, a detail that the Bush team understandably did not emphasize when it began employing the metaphor."[204]

Three of the core missions for the U.S. military forces, advocated in the New American Century report are: 1) defend the American homeland;

2) fight and decisively win multiple, simultaneous major theater wars; and, 3) perform the "constabulary" duties associated with shaping the security environment in critical regions.[205] Thus, if the Vulcans have their way, America's future will fluctuate somewhere between fighting "multiple simultaneous large-scale wars" and "long-term, independent constabulary operations."[206] (Get the report and read it for yourself.)

The name Thomas P. M. Barnett appears as one of the twenty-seven project participants for the September 2000 New American Century report. Barnett is a senior strategic researcher and professor at the U.S. Naval War College. His academic credentials include a Ph.D. in political science from Harvard. In December 2002, *Esquire* named him "The Strategist" for a special edition entitled "The Best and the Brightest."

While Texas Representative Mac Thornberry (a Republican) called Barnett ". . . one of our most provocative and cutting-edge thinkers about national security issues," John Petersen, president of The Arlington Institute, labeled him ". . . one of the most thoughtful and original thinkers that this generation of national security analysts has produced.[207] With regard to his 2004 blockbuster, *The Pentagon's New Map*, former CTO of AOL Time Warner, William J. Raduchel, Ph.D., writes, "If you are an investor, an executive, or a citizen—meaning everyone—you need to understand this worldview."[208] *Esquire* states succinctly, "Barnett puts the world in context."[209]

So what does this tome, predicted to be "one of the most talked-about books of 2004—and beyond," have to say about what the "crazies *really* believe?" His work is basically a detailed commentary on the September 2000 report by the New American Century. He writes:

> To me, 9/11 was an amazing gift—as twisted and cruel as that sounds. It was an invitation from history, albeit one with a horrific price tag. . . .
>
> On that morning, America was forced to wake up from the dreamlike nineties.[210]

Barnett is another incorrigible optimist who believes that mankind is now on the brink of universal peace.

> But 9/11 the world-historical event must ultimately yield far more hope than fear, far more love than hatred, and—most important—far more understanding than pain. But that will happen only if America *chooses* to see it for what it was: feedback from a world in significant stress.[211]

The only problem with Barnett's positive thinking is that *your* grandchildren and *mine* are the ones destined to become the new "constables" in charge of alleviating the global "stress." His thesis is extremely dangerous because it is an easy one to pitch. In theory, the Cold War was the time when a climate of nuclear parity kept the two global powers engaged in a protracted, nail-biting standoff. With the dismemberment of the Soviet Union (the "bad" global power) a door of unprecedented opportunity opened for the United States (the guys in the white hats) to usher in the Kingdom Age. He writes, "America has basically arrived at a point in world history where—if we really want to— we can render organized mass violence of all sorts essentially obsolete."[212] According to him, this could now be done simply by absorbing the world's disconnected states into the global market after eliminating whatever dictators or transnational terrorists stand in the way.

Of course, eliminating *all* the villains could take a while. In a January 16, 2005, *AOL News* article entitled "No Rush to Bring Troops Home From Iraq," AP reporter Nedra Pickler states: "The president would not commit to significantly reduce troops **by the end of his second term in 2009**."[213] In case you'd like to know how long the so-called "War on Terrorism" will last, Dr. Barnett is only too happy to give you that information. The Pentagon's premier military strategist stated the following:

> And here's where I get to my final point about this Administration—and every one that follows—getting level with the American public: **we are never leaving the Gap** [the world's disconnected states] and **we are never "bringing our boys home."** There is no exiting the Gap, only shrinking the Gap, and if there is no exiting the Gap, then we'd better stop kidding ourselves about "exit strategies." *No exit means no exit strategy.*[214]

In another place he gives a similar "encouraging" scenario:

> Understanding globalization's most crucial strands of connectivity (the flows of people, energy, money, security) helps us understand the nature of the grand historical struggle we now face. It puts this war on terrorism within the context of everything else. **It helps us understand why our loved ones won't be coming home anytime soon.** It helps us realize the balance of life all around us and why America's continued role as security Leviathan across the Gap is necessary not only for keeping the violence *over there*, but for making sure that globalization makes it *over there*.[215]

Being a good Roman Catholic, Barnett wouldn't know that the forty-first chapter of Job casts *Leviathan* as a major Bible type of the *devil*. (Is this why the Islamic world calls America the "Great Satan"?)

Barnett's cloud of perpetual "constabulary responsibilities" has at least one silver lining—it should improve the nation's unemployment rate; "Boots on the Ground, Inc." will eventually hire more Americans than Wal-Mart.

> There are many different ways a superpower like the United States goes about making other states feel more secure. . . .
> **That is exporting security.** It consists of America giving the world something we have in abundance: a belief in the future. It is a wonderful gift, and frankly, only the United States has either the wherewithal or the generosity to actually provide it. It is one of the best things we can provide the planet, and it has changed the course of human history for the better.[216]

It is therefore axiomatic that a "9/11" caliber disaster would afford a most convenient *pretext* for launching Dr. Barnett's global peace crusade. Should we, then, be concerned at the following statement in the *New American Century* report of September 2000? "Further, the process of transformation, even if it brings revolutionary change, is likely to be a long one, **absent some catastrophic and catalyzing event—like a new Pearl Harbor.**"[217] *And Rush Limbaugh wonders why some Americans would question the integrity of their present government?*

Like the legion of New World Order advocates directing our nation's destiny, Dr. Barnett believes that 9/11 was *the* clarion call for change.

> Today, America and the world stand at a crossroads similar to the one we faced following World War II. The terrorist attacks of 9/11 have provided us all a glimpse of the new form of international crisis that will define our age. As such, I believe it is absolutely essential that this country lead the global war on terrorism, because I fear what will happen to our world if the forces of disconnectedness [Osama bin Laden, et. al] are allowed to prevail—to perturb the system at will. . . .
> Globalization will remain out of balance so long as America herself remains out of balance, and America will remain out of balance until we achieve new understanding of what constitutes real crisis in our age.[218]

Barnett's liberal agenda can be summed up in a single phrase: "In short, *we the people* needs to become *we the planet*."[219] Tom's Catholic roots would disqualify him from being able to appreciate the fruit of

America's Judeo-Christian heritage—a *proper* separation of church and state, functioning within a democratic republic and stabilized by a code of written law. Rather ironically, Barnett "just happens" to live within a few miles of a sign that reads: *Portsmouth—Birthplace of American Democracy.*

"SHOCK AND AWE"

Through the years, "Limbaugh Kooks" have been ridiculed for warning that American foreign policy was being geared to stretch our military so far across the world that we would eventually have to import U.N. troops in the event of an "unforeseen" domestic crisis. Unlike the EIB network, the gurus of globalism have long concurred with this portentous forecast. Zbigniew's mentor, Dr. Henry Kissinger, stated in 1991 at a Bilderberger Conference in Evians, France:

> Today, America would be outraged if U.N. troops entered Los Angeles to restore order. Tomorrow they will be grateful! This is especially true if they were told that there were an outside threat from beyond, whether real or promulgated, that threatened our very existence. It is then that all peoples of the world will plead to deliver them from this evil. The one thing every man fears is the unknown. When presented with this scenario, individual rights will be willingly relinquished for the guarantee of their well-being granted to them by the World Government.[220]

It came as no surprise, therefore, when a group of Democratic congressmen sent "The Honorable Kofi Annan" an urgent letter on July 1, 2004, requesting that the U.N. dispatch election observers to monitor the November 2, 2004, election. Texas Representative Eddie Bernice Johnson spearheaded the unconscionable petition in response to the plea of Florida Rep. Corrine Brown. According to David de Sola on CNN.com for August 8, 2004, "The Organization for Security and Cooperation in Europe was invited to monitor the election by the State Department. The observers will come from the OSCE's Office for Democratic Institutions and Human Rights." Thus, a treasonous letter occasioned by a pair of unmarried "African-American" female legislators to the African Secretary General of the United Nations resulted in our "African-American" Secretary of State inviting Roman Catholic Europeans to monitor our election. *It's enough to make the Founding Fathers roll over in their graves!*

On election day, ninety-two observers from thirty-four countries, including fifty-six parliamentarians, stuck their foreign noses into America's business in several states, including Florida, California, Nevada, Ohio, Maryland, North Carolina, Illinois, New Jersey, Minnesota and New Mexico. According to Undur Gunnarsdottir and other reprobates from the OSCE, the U.S. election was "mostly fair." I would strongly recommend that Undur take her people over to New York City and monitor "Kofi and Kojo." (One of Kofi's more "important" projects for 2005 is called "The Three Amigos"—a series of twenty animated T.V. ads to stop the spread of aids featuring multi-color cartoon condoms named "[expletive]," "[expletive]," and "[expletive].")[221]

Since the "Shock and Awe" of 9/11, the American people appear to be groping in a fog of instability and trepidation, ready to sell their souls to *anyone* with a viable plan to shield them from future acts of violence (i.e., War on Terror; Patriot Act; Department of Homeland Security).

But let us return for the moment to that portentous presidential diary entry on the evening of 9/11—"The Pearl Harbor of the twenty-first century took place today. We think it's Osama bin Laden." Indeed, President Bush had received flawless intelligence that implicated al-Qaeda in the 9/11 attacks. Bamford writes:

> Shortly after the devastating explosion caused when American Airlines Flight 77 slammed into the Pentagon, Rumsfeld and other officials evacuated to the bombproof War Room—the National Military Command Center—in the Pentagon's basement. Then, at five minutes past noon, CIA Director George Tenet passed him the information intercepted by NSA at 9:53 that morning, only minutes after the crash.
>
> A bin Laden operative in Afghanistan, Tenet related, had telephoned a number in the former Soviet republic of Georgia and asked if he had "heard good news." At the same time, he had indicated that at least one more target was yet to be hit. Ten minutes later, United Flight 93 crashed in Pennsylvania en route to a fourth target in Washington.[222]

Now here comes the kicker. (Are you listening, Rush?) Bamford continues:

> Yet despite the implications that a member of bin Laden's team appeared to have foreknowledge of one of the attacks, Rumsfeld dismissed the intelligence as "vague," that it "might not mean something," and there

was "no good basis for hanging hat." The clear evidence aside, it was not the Afghan cave dweller that Rumsfeld was interested in.

At 2:40 that afternoon, an aide to the Defense Secretary jotted notes of Rumsfeld's conversations. Written deep in the War Room, the notes describe the Pentagon chief as wanting **"best info fast; judge whether good enough hit S.H. (Saddam Hussein) at same time. Not only U.B.L. (Osama bin Laden)." "Go massive,"** he noted. **"Sweep it all up. Things related, and not."**

From the notes it was clear that the attacks would be used as a pretext for war against Saddam Hussein. Despite the fact that there was absolutely no evidence implicating the Iraqi leader, Rumsfeld wanted to "hit S.H. at the same time." The idea was to "sweep" him up, whether "related" to 9/11 or "not." Wolfowitz had the same idea and quickly began talking up an Iraqi connection in conference calls with other officials, including Cheney.[223]

Twelve hours later, around 2:00 a.m. on September 12, Counterterrorism Coordinator Richard Clarke headed back to the White House for a series of meetings. He had left the building less than two hours earlier to take a shower and change clothes. "I expected to go back to a round of meetings examining what the next attacks should be," he recalled, "what our vulnerabilities were, what we could do about them in the short term." Clark writes:

> Instead, I walked into a series of discussions about Iraq. At first I was incredulous that we were talking about something other than getting Al Qaeda. **Then I realized with almost a sharp physical pain that Rumsfeld and Wolfowitz were going to try to take advantage of this national tragedy to promote their agenda about Iraq.** Since the beginning of the administration, indeed well before, they had been pressing for a war with Iraq. My friends in the Pentagon had been telling me that the word was we would be invading Iraq sometime in 2002. On the morning of the 12th DOD's focus was already beginning to shift from Al Qaeda.
>
> By the afternoon on Wednesday, Secretary Rumsfeld was talking about broadening the objectives of our response and "getting Iraq" . . . I vented. **"Having been attacked by Al Qaeda, for us now to go bombing Iraq in response would be like our invading Mexico after the Japanese attacked us at Pearl Harbor."** . . . Later in the day, Secretary Rumsfeld complained that there were no decent targets for bombing in Afghanistan and that we should consider bombing Iraq, which, he said, had better targets. At first I thought Rumsfeld was joking. But he was serious and the President did not reject out of hand the idea of attacking Iraq. Instead,

he noted that what we needed to do with Iraq was to change the government, not just hit it with more cruise missiles, as Rumsfeld had implied.[224]

As the day progressed, Bush's morbid focus on Hussein intensified. Clarke continues:

> Later, on the evening of the 12th, I left the Video Conferencing Center and there, wandering alone around the Situation Room, was the President. He looked like he wanted something to do. He grabbed a few of us and closed the door to the conference room. **"Look," he told us, "I know you have a lot to do and all . . . but I want you, as soon as you can, to go back over everything, everything. See if Saddam did this. See if he's linked in any way . . ."**
> I was once again taken aback, incredulous, and it showed. "But, Mr. President, al Qaeda did this."
> **"I know, I know, but . . . see if Saddam was involved. Just look. I want to know any shred . . ."**
> "Absolutely, we will look . . . again." I was trying to be more respectful, more responsive. "But, you know, we have looked several times for state sponsorship of al Qaeda and not found any real linkages to Iraq. Iran plays a little, as does Pakistan, and Saudi Arabia, Yemen."
> **"Look into Iraq, Saddam," the President said testily and left us.**[225]

Bamford adds, "A few days later at Camp David, Wolfowitz would tell Bush that the terrorist attacks created an opportunity to strike Iraq."[226]

The reason President Bush reacted "testily" to Mr. Clarke's realistic assessment was because his counterterrorism coordinator was messing with his *prearranged agenda*. The first meeting of the Bush national security team was convened shortly after 3:30 p.m. on Tuesday, January 30, 2001. Mr. Bush had been president for ten days. Bamford transports us to the pivotal conference:

> As the ten brown leather chairs around the table filled, place cards identified each of the players. On one side of Bush, who occupied the seat at the head of the table, was Vice President Dick Cheney, and on the other side sat Secretary of State Colin Powell. Opposite the President at the other end, National Security Advisor Condoleezza Rice acted as state manager. **"Condi will run these meetings,"** said Bush. "I'll be seeing all of you regularly, but I want you to debate things out here and then Condi will report to me."[227]

Of course, Richard Clarke was conspicuously absent from the meeting. The fact that Osama bin Laden had put out a contract on the American Terrorism Czar never entered the equation.[228] Bush had a different method of evaluating the relevant strengths of his advisors. "They [President Bush and Condoleezza Rice] bonded at Kennebunkport," said Coit Blacker, a Stanford colleague who was Rice's oldest and closest friend in academia. "She is a sports fanatic, and he's a sports fanatic too. . . . Condi has told me that one of the things she found most endearing about George W. is that he used sports metaphors, and Condi does too."[229] (For another "endearing thing," see the presidential kiss planted on Condi's cheek at the formal announcement of her appointment as secretary of state.) Bamford continues:

> Then Bush addressed the sole items on the agenda for his first high-level national security meeting. The topics were not terrorism—a subject he barely mentioned during the campaign—or nervousness over China or Russia, but Israel and Iraq. From the very first moment, the Bush foreign policy would focus on three key objectives: Get rid of Saddam Hussein, end American involvement in the Israeli-Palestinian peace process, and rearrange the dominoes in the Middle East. A key to the policy shift would be the concept of "preemption."[230]

Less than two weeks into his administration and a full eight months before 9/11, Bush had his sights fixed squarely on Saddam Hussein. When the conference began, the immediate focus was on the substance of the previously cited meeting between Richard Perle, Douglas Feith, David Wurmser, and Israeli Prime Minister Benjamin Netanyahu.

> Condoleezza Rice led off the discussion. But rather than mention anything about threats to the United States or weapons of mass destruction, she noted only "that Iraq might be the key to reshaping the entire region." The words were practically lifted from the "Clean Break" report, which had the rather imperial-sounding subtitle: "A New Strategy for Securing the Realm."
> Then Rice turned the meeting over to CIA Director George Tenet, who offered a grainy overhead picture of a factory that he said "might" be a plant "that produced either chemical or biological materials for weapons manufacture." There were no missiles or weapons of any kind, just some railroad tracks going to a building; truck activity; and a water tower—things that can be found in virtually any city in the United States. Nor

were there any human intelligence or signals intelligence reports. "There was no confirming intelligence," Tenet said.

It was little more than a shell game. Other photos and charts showed U.S. air activity over the "no-fly zone," but Tenet offered no more intelligence. Nevertheless, in a matter of minutes the talk switched from a discussion about very speculative intelligence to which targets to begin bombing in Iraq.

By the time the meeting was over, Treasury Secretary O'Neill was convinced that "getting Hussein was now the administration's focus, that much was already clear."[231]

Bamford concludes his analysis with an uncomfortable reference to that all too familiar theme of conspiracy history:

> In the weeks and months following the NSC meeting, Perle, Feith, and Wurmser began taking their places in the Bush administration. Perle became chairman of the reinvigorated and powerful Defense Policy Board, packing it with like-minded neoconservative super-hawks anxious for battle. Feith was appointed to the highest policy position in the Pentagon, Undersecretary of Defense for Policy. And Wurmser moved into a top policy position in the State Department before later becoming Cheney's top Middle East expert.
>
> With the Pentagon now under Secretary of Defense Donald Rumsfeld and his deputy, Paul Wolfowitz—both of whom had also believed that Saddam Hussein should have been toppled during the first Gulf War— the war planners were given free rein. **What was needed, however, was a pretext—perhaps a major crisis. "Crises can be opportunities," wrote Wurmser in his paper calling for an American-Israeli preemptive war throughout the Middle East.**[232]

Thus, the attacks on the World Trade Center and the Pentagon provided the New World Order with its ultimate pretext for military invasion. While Clinton's guests had viewed *Wag the Dog* just prior to his missile launch announcement, Bush spent the evening before *his* March 17, 2003, invasion speech aboard Air Force One with his staff watching Mel Gibson's film *Conspiracy Theory*. Woodward relates, "Bush loudly summarized the plot, and during the rest of the movie made fun of it as fairly predictable."[233]

The 9/11 affair has also proved to be the most sophisticated conspiracy to date. While the architects of America's "War on Terrorism" have been applying Hegel's "clash equals cash" dialectic on an ever-expanding list of international targets, they have also been closing in on the most dangerous threat of all. Though Saddam Hussein was the celebrated "Ace of Spades" in the popular "Most Wanted Iraqis" deck of cards, the nebulous "Joker"—my friend—is YOU!

IF THIS WERE A DICTATORSHIP,
IT'D BE A HECK OF A LOT EASIER,
JUST SO LONG AS I'M THE DICTATOR.[234]

George W. Bush
18 December 2000
CNN

I SAY TO THE AMERICAN PEOPLE WE WILL CONTINUE
TO CONDUCT MARTYRDOM OPERATIONS INSIDE AND
OUTSIDE THE UNITED STATES UNTIL YOU DEPART
FROM YOUR OPPRESSIVE COURSE AND ABANDON
YOUR FOLLIES AND REIGN IN YOUR FOOLS.

Osama bin Ladin
19 October 2003
Al-Jazeera[235]

20

Why America is Finished

"For men shall be lovers of their own selves . . ."
(II Timothy 3:2a)

AS OUR MODERN culture is predicated on a "positive mental attitude," the title of this chapter would be rejected by heathens and Christians alike. Such a fatal aversion to "negative truth" was foreshadowed in the words of Ahab as recorded in I Kings 22:8: *"And the king of Israel said unto Jehoshaphat, There is yet one man, Micaiah the son of Imlah, by whom we may enquire of the LORD: but I hate him; for he doth not prophesy good concerning me, but evil."* The end day complicity of America's hireling clergy can be found in verse 13: *"And the messenger that was gone to call Micaiah spake unto him, saying, Behold now, the words of the prophets declare good unto the king with one mouth: let thy word, I pray thee, be like the word of one of them, and speak that which is good."* Rare is the twenty-first-century minister depicted in verse 14: *"And Micaiah said, As the LORD liveth, what the LORD saith unto me, that will I speak."*

Yet the prospect of America's imminent demise has at least one built-in advantage that is, shall we say, "out of this world." For instance, is there anything this side of eternity more "negative" than *death*? This is why the rapture of believers is referred to as the *"blessed hope."* (Titus 2:13) But, according to II Thessalonians 2:3a, the trumpet cannot sound until the Church goes into apostasy: *"Let no man deceive you by any means: for that day shall not come, except there come a falling away first . . ."* For instance, the *Yellow Pages* for Knoxville, Tennessee (population 300,000), lists 190 Baptist churches *along with 153 escort services!* America is dying because her Christian nucleus is terminally ill. Thus, the prospect of a national revival will only increase the odds that you wind up at the cemetery with your relatives. Each degenerating facet of the prevailing apostasy points to a single encouraging truth—"The trumpet is out of the case!"

It has been stated throughout this volume that *deception* is a major characteristic of the end times. The devil certainly had a banner year in 2004, mocking the anemic Body of Christ. Heaven only knows how many believers were exposed to Janet Jackson's breast during their foolish Super Bowl Sunday "services." On a Liberty University infomercial aired the following month, some of Dr. Falwell's "champions for Christ" can be seen being tossed around in a mosh pit during a campus "Christian" rock concert.

Then, in March, I listened in astonishment as Jack Van Impe assured his television audience that their *pets* would accompany them at the Rapture! The startling "revelation" was the theme of Jack's latest video offer—"Animals in Heaven." As he waved a copy before the camera he announced that over ten thousand copies had been sold in the first two weeks alone!

Later that summer I had the bizarre experience of running into Chuck Ohman, Van Impe's "spooky" announcer, in the men's room of a Knoxville McDonald's restaurant. As he was momentarily trapped like a rat, I asked him point blank—"You don't really believe all that stuff about dogs and cats going up at the Rapture, do you?" Whereupon, he darted his eyes to the side, stared at the floor for a second or two and then dodged the question entirely, replying, "Jack has compiled a number of statements on the subject by various theologians."

At this point, I injected a little humor into our tense bathroom dialogue, stating, "Dogs, maybe; cats, *no way*—they go to the *other* place." Well, this got Chuck laughing so hard that he leaned over and put his hand on my shoulder. His guard down once again, I quickly asked if the "Walking Bible" had included Ecclesiastes 3:21 in his video: *"Who knoweth the spirit of man that goeth upward, and the spirit of the beast that goeth downward to the earth?"* With that he made a beeline for the door, stating that Jesus was coming soon and would clear everything up at that time. He then blew out of the parking lot in a shiny black Lexus.

However, the unsettling manner in which King James Bible-believing Baptist ministers endorsed Mel Gibson's R-rated movie, "The Passion," constitutes the zenith of spiritual naiveté. The film made Gibson over a half-billion dollars. That so many genuine Christians could be led to believe that the Holy Ghost intended to use a Hell-bound, Roman Catholic, Hollywood director to spark a national revival is *beyond* my comprehension! (Apparently, not all the meatballs are in the spaghetti sauce.)

BUSH VS. KERRY

The 2004 presidential race served as a fitting conclusion to the year. By election eve, the ultimate conspiracy scenario was about to break upon a gullible nation. You could call it the "Perfect Storm" of conspiracy history. In the final analysis it wouldn't have mattered who won—business was destined to continue as usual. In this landmark contest, American voters were "privileged" to exercise their constitutional rights by choosing between Republican incumbent George W. Bush—a member of Skull and Bones, and the Democratic challenger John F. Kerry—a member of Skull and Bones! (Kerry's brother-in-law from his first marriage, David Throne, was also Bones, as was the late husband of Kerry's current wife, Teresa Heinz Kerry.)

Thus we see that beginning in 1988 with the presidency of George H. W. Bush—the man who initiated the "land for peace" fiasco—the White House will have been occupied by either a member of "The Order" or "The Group" through at least 2008. *This is what the United States gets for abandoning Israel to the Vatican-backed Palestinian Authority.*

Both "candidates" were (and remain) consummate chameleons—establishment elitists out of touch with reality and the common man. During his 2003 campaign stop in the "City of Brotherly Love," Kerry attempted to demonstrate his affinity for the "Rocky Balboas" of this land by "doing lunch" at the well-known "Pat's King of Steaks." In what may go down as the greatest *faux pas* in history, the senator promptly sent shock waves through the joint by asking if his Philly cheese steak could be made with *Swiss* cheese! (While Rush Limbaugh predicted that he probably lost the election with that gaffe, I personally believe his demise was caused by the one night he let Teresa out of her cage to address the Democratic National Convention!)

Now, although Senator Kerry was the senior "vampire" (having climbed out of *his* coffin in 1966, two years before his opponent did the same), Bush had the decided edge in political makeovers, having learned from his father's unsuccessful foray into Lone Star politics in 1964. Kevin

Phillips notes, "Biographers have recounted episodes such as how he was laughed at for wearing Bermuda shorts in Baptist West Texas and the advertising in one early campaign that featured him walking with a poodle straining at the leash."[1] Incumbent Democratic senator Ralph Yarborough was able to easily overcome Bush's challenge in 1964 by mocking him as a "Connecticut carpetbagger." "Dubya's" need to reinvent himself was exacerbated when his father was turned out of office by "Beelzebubba" in the 1992 election. Among the leading theories advanced for his ignominious defeat, political pundits focused on a lingering "Wimp Factor." Phillips describes the subsequent metamorphosis of "George II":

> Bush still relied on the four mainstays of his father's establishment: finance, oil and energy, the military-industrial complex, and the national security–intelligence community. These power bases were quite compatible with the increasingly southern base and the conservative ideological evolution of the Republican Party. What was different was Bush's nonelite demeanor: the cow country accent, the rumpled clothing, the chewing tobacco, the style of religiosity, the moral fundamentalism, the outsider language, the disdain for the Harvards and Yales, the six-gun geopolitics and not least the garb of a sinner rescued from drink and brought to God by none other than evangelist Billy Graham.[2]

Texas author Michael Lind described Bush as "The gun-toting, Bible-thumping Anglo-Celtic Texan in former Mexican and Indian territories, with his admiration for the Hebrew patriarchs and professed devotion to the Ten Commandments . . ."[3] The anticipated effectiveness of personality on the decisive swing voters was evidenced by one election year poll in which a significant number of committed Kerry supporters admitted that given the same choices as to who they'd rather "hang with" at the neighborhood barbecue—Bush was the obvious choice. In contemporary political strategy, fantasy has become the new bottom line. "When you're talking about Clinton fatigue, part of it is that we loved Ozzie and Harriett," explained Ron Kaufman, George H. W. Bush's former political director. "We really did. People want *Little House on the Prairie* to be real, and the Bushes represent that."[4]

Some of the biggest suckers in the national electorate are "militant" fundamentalists and apostate evangelical Christians. For instance, during the 2004 campaign, Bush attempted to avert the numerous policy disasters of his first term by focusing on a constitutional amendment defining the marriage relationship as existing between one man and one woman.

Naturally, the "Religious Right" rallied behind their "Christian" standard-bearer. "Spiritual giants" such as Pat Robertson, James Dobson, James Kennedy and Jerry Falwell praised "Brother" Bush for being the only candidate with enough moral backbone to oppose the sodomite agenda of same-sex marriage, etc.

Do you believe the president was motivated by genuine spiritual conviction or mere political expediency? (Hopefully, the answer to this question will shock a few of the brethren back into reality.) The Metropolitan Community "Church" in Los Angeles constitutes the most influential sodomite congregation in America, performing over six thousand same-sex marriages annually. On October 14, 2003, President Bush sent this assembly the following letter of congratulations on behalf of their thirty-fifth anniversary:

THE WHITE HOUSE
WASHINGTON

October 14, 2003

I send greetings to the members of Metropolitan Community Church Los Angeles as you celebrate your 35th anniversary.

Faith plays an important role in the lives of many Americans, offering strength and guidance for the challenges of each new day. By encouraging the celebration of faith and sharing the message of God's love and boundless mercy, churches like yours put hope in people's hearts and a sense of purpose in their lives.

This milestone provides an opportunity to reflect on your years of service and to rejoice in God's faithfulness to your congregation. In the days ahead, may your community continue to grow in faith and friendship.

Laura joins me in sending our best wishes for a memorable celebration.

George Bush

A photo on the "church's" website features MCC founder "Reverend" Elder Troy Perry and current "pastor" Neil Thomas (complete with earring and wedding band) proudly posing with the president's letter. (The perverts declined my request to print the picture.)

Now, in case you're wondering, that sick feeling in the pit of your stomach may have something to do with Ecclesiastes 1:18b—". . . *he that increaseth knowledge increaseth sorrow.*" Thus, we understand that in addition to Moonies, Muslims, and rock stars, the president's ever-widening circle of fellowship would now include sodomites as well.

AMERICA REPUDIATES HER HERITAGE

There is a specific underlying reason why George W. Bush has been able to deceive so many people, including a considerable percentage within the Body of Christ. Karl Rove, the president's chief White House political advisor, is widely regarded as a "Machiavelli aficionado."[5] (The late Lee Atwater, a key strategist to the senior Bush, reread Machiavelli yearly.) Niccolò Machiavelli (1469-1527) is considered to be the foremost political theorist of the Italian Renaissance. His definitive volume, *The Prince*, was dedicated to Lorenzo dé Medici, the duke of Urbino. It covered various methods, from fraud to religion, by which the ascendant rulers could maintain their control of the masses. Phillips writes:

> Rove was a great reader of Machiavelli, who was quoted as follows: "The great majority of mankind is satisfied with appearances, as though they were realities." . . . [He advised that] **"A prince must take great care that nothing goes out of his mouth which is not full of . . . five qualities . . . mercy, faith, integrity, humanity and religion.** Machiavelli's underlying advice, however, is to practice deceit, because the most successful princes— he names Casare Borgia and Pope Alexander VI—have been relentless deceivers. **"However, it is necessary to be able to disguise this character well, and to be a great feigner and dissembler; and men are so simple and so ready to obey present necessities that one who deceives will always find those who allow themselves to be deceived."** In short, **"the experience of our times shows those princes to have done good things who have had little regard for good faith, and have been able by astuteness to confuse men's brains."** Still another chronicler has pointed out Machiavelli's tribute to fraud in *The Discourses*, book 2, chapter 13: "Machiavelli's writings contain numerous discussions of the indispensable role of fraud in political affairs, ranging from analyses of deceptions and stratagems in war to the breaking of treaties to the varied types of fraud met with daily in civil life. . . . He generalizes that **'from mean to great fortune, people rise rather by fraud than by force.'** "[6]

If it was true in Machiavelli's day that "the great majority of mankind is satisfied with appearances, as though they were realities," how much more would the principle apply in our modern television culture? ("People want *Little House on the Prairie.*") In their 2003 book, *Bush's Brain: How Karl Rove Made George Bush Presidential*, co-authors Wayne Slater and James Moore gave credit to Rove for one of the guiding principles of the Bush platform: namely, that "perception is reality."[7]

The fact that the American people are currently being deceived by a political strategy spawned in Catholic Europe is not without significance. Having rejected the *Revised Standard Version* of the Bible in 1952, evangelical Christians enthusiastically embraced the *New American Standard Version* published by the Lockman Foundation in 1971. The pertinent manuscript evidence confirms that the NASV was translated from the same Greek text underlying the various English translations of the Roman Catholic Church. While the King James Bible—the historical standard-bearer for the Philadelphia Church Age and Christian America— was translated from the *Textus Receptus*, the NASV and nearly all subsequent "improvements" (the New International Version of 1973 being the most popular) were rendered from the corrupt Westcott and Hort text centered on *Codex Vaticanus.* Rome's connection to the NASV is so blatant that the official stamp of the Catholic Church—the "Chi-Rho," resembling an X with a P in the center—was once displayed on the front flap of the jacket of their New Testament (second edition). This is the very sign affixed to the robes worn by bishops when saying Mass in the Vatican. It also happens to be the sign Constantine claims to have seen in the sky on the eve of his historic battle and subsequent "conversion" to Christianity.

For the record (i.e., "to clear the air"), had it not been for the prescient and unique ministry of Dr. Peter S. Ruckman, the current remnant of King James Bible-believing Independent Baptists would have never divorced themselves from the misguided recommendations of well-intentioned men such as Dr. John R. Rice and others. On page 383 of *Our God Breathed Book—The Bible*, published in 1969, Dr. Rice wrote:

> Now there is available the *New American Standard Bible* New Testament, published by Moody Press. The *American Standard Version* of 1901, widely acclaimed for its word-for-word fidelity to the Greek, has been painstakingly revised by the Lockman Foundation in the light of the latest textual advances. Dr. Wilbur M. Smith says, "Certainly the most accurate and most revealing translation of the New Testament that we now have."[8]

Thus, while the late founder of the *Sword of the Lord* can still be commended for his writings on the home, Dr. Ruckman should be recognized for his timely defense of the King James Bible (especially in light of I Timothy 5:17). Of course, most of the brethren are far too insecure and intimidated by their own "popes" to give credit where credit is due. In fact, in the evolution of spinelessness, "Ruckman bashing" is now in vogue among the great host of "Johnny-come-lately" A.V. 1611 apologists. Among other subjects mentioned on the back cover of *Touch Not the Unclean Thing* (2001), author David H. Sorenson states that his book "[d]ocuments the basic error of Peter Ruckman."[9] And while the fiery Presbyterian Ian Paisley possessed the courage to publicly confront the pope by holding up a red sign with the words "John Paul II ANTICHRIST" painted in black (the incident occurring on October 11, 1988, at the European Parliament Building in Strasbourg, France, at which time he was beaten and unceremoniously carried out), the "popes" in Greenville, South Carolina, have proven a bit more intimidating. In his 1997 book, *My Plea For the Old Sword* (published only a month *after* Dr. Bob Jones, Jr., died), Dr. Paisley also takes a slap at the man who has labored over half a century in defense of the Sword in question. He even goes so far as to suggest that Dr. Ruckman is guilty of promoting a Roman Catholic heresy. "This new doctrine called Dual Inspiration which affirms that the process extends to the Authorised Version is known as Ruckmanism, after Dr. Peter Ruckman who popularised this doctrine, had its beginnings in Rome."[10]

Strange, though Dr. Ruckman was perceived as a threat worthy of exposure, the same man who was arrested in Vatican Square for distributing copies of the King James Bible couldn't bring himself to excoriate Dr. Stewart Custer and the other apostate prima donnas on the faculty of Bob Jones University. Incidentally, with regard to the specific charge of "Dual Inspiration," in a sermon before the World Congress of Fundamentalists at Bob Jones University, August 1993, Dr. Paisley said, "Now the question is asked, 'Have I got God's inspired Word in my hand?' I want to answer it. 'YES, I HAVE GOD'S INSPIRED WORD IN MY HAND.' "[11] How quickly they forget! *Christian* revisionists will have a lot to answer for at the Judgment Seat of Christ. (Philippians 1:18)

Now it "just so happens" that in 1960—the very year the NASV debuted through its vanguard publication of the Gospel of John (the entire New Testament coming out in 1963, with the Old Testament being released in 1971)—the nation's *first* Roman Catholic president was elected! Having chosen a chief executive whose professed religious creed mandated that his first allegiance be to a foreign power (the Vatican *State*), America set her course for an eventual alliance with the Beast against the nation of Israel. In the meantime, our political culture would continue to incorporate characteristics of old-world European monarchies; *Japheth was going backward*. In 1993, Lewis Lapham, the editor of *Harper's* wrote:

> The wish for kings is an old and familiar wish, as well known in medieval Europe and in ancient Mesopotamia, but its recent and cringing appearance in late twentieth-century America, in a country presumably dedicated to the opposite premise, coincided with the alarms and excursions of the Cold War, with the presidency of John F. Kennedy, and with the emergence of the theatre of celebrity.[12]

The Kennedy White House would come to be known as Camelot. While the Founding Fathers recoiled at the prospect of hereditary rulers, Jack was scarcely in power before he "dubbed" his brother Robert as U.S. attorney general and managed to bequeath his Massachusetts senate seat to his youngest brother, Edward, who barely met the age requirement. Less than five years after the president was slain, Bobby tried to recapture the "throne," but was also felled by an assassin's bullet. When John F. Kennedy, Jr., died in a plane crash in 1999, the media insisted on eulogizing him as "America's first crown prince."

A number of books have been written that implicate Lyndon Johnson in the Kennedy assassination. Should this hypothesis ever be proven, it would make Johnson the first "ruler" in American history to have gained the "kingdom" by employing the standard Vatican technique of *political assassination*. (Don't forget *where* Kennedy was killed.) In any event, LBJ would allow his Catholic secretary of defense, Robert McNamara (Operation Northwoods), to escalate the fighting in Southeast Asia, an untenable situation that began when the Roman Catholic prime minister of South Vietnam, Ngo Dinh Diem (assisted by his two brothers, Archbishop Ngo Dinh Thuc and Ngo Dinh Nhu, chief of the secret police), initiated a volatile policy of religious repression against the fourteen million Buddhists comprising 93% of the nation's population. Johnson's "positive" legacy became the infamous Civil Rights Act of 1964, another cause for rejoicing in Vatican City.

With no male heir to succeed him, Johnson was followed by "King Richard" (a.k.a. "Tricky Dicky"). John Dean writes, "Nixon's White House was so secretive that the Joint Chiefs of Staff believed it necessary (for military preparedness and national security) to plant a spy in the National Security Council, who literally pilfered information from Henry Kissinger's briefcase, made copies, and sent relevant documents to the Joint Chiefs."[13] President Nixon, a member of the CFR, will always be remembered as the first chief executive to "abdicate the throne." However, few Americans are aware of just how close the nation came to anarchy during the final days of the Watergate crisis. While Johnson may have secured the presidency by assassination, his psychotic successor tried to save *his* seat of power by resorting to *another* Vatican technique—*a military coup!* On October 26, 1973, syndicated columnist Carl Rowan broke the story that President Nixon may well have been planning a military takeover of the government! In a column in the *Washington Star* entitled "Has President Nixon Gone Crazy?," Rowan wrote: "Those who wonder about the President's emotional balance have now begun to suspect that even in the face of a vote to impeach he might try, as 'commander-in-chief,' to use the military forces to keep him in power."[14]

In a story on August 27, 1974, entitled "Military Coup Fears Denied," the *Washington Post* reported that Secretary of Defense James Schlesinger had taken special measures to protect the military chain of command should any illegal orders come from President Nixon:

> Defense Secretary James Schlesinger requested a tight watch in the military chain of command to ensure that no extraordinary orders went out from the White House during the period of uncertainty. . . .
>
> Department officials have confirmed that Schlesinger and Gen. George S. Brown, chairman of the Joint Chiefs of Staff, discussed among themselves how they should be aware of any illegal orders being issued to military units outside the formal chain of command structure.[15]

William Still, whose articles have appeared in *USA Today, The Saturday Evening Post* and the *Los Angeles Times* syndicate, wrote in his book *New World Order*: "Secretary of Defense Schlesinger investigated how quickly the Army's 82nd Airborne Division could be brought to Washington, D.C. from Fort Bragg, North Carolina to counterbalance Marine contingents loyal to Nixon."[16]

An article in the August 1983 edition of the *Atlantic Monthly* confirmed:

> Schlesinger began to investigate what forces could be assembled at his order as a counterweight to the Marines, if Nixon—in a crisis—chose to

subvert the Constitution. The notion that Nixon could at any time resort to extraordinary steps to preserve his presidency was far more widespread in the government than the public perceived in the early days of Watergate or perceives today.[17]

Gerald Ford, a Shriner and CFR member, had the dubious distinction of replacing Spiro Agnew as vice president and then going on to replace Nixon himself! Between beaning people with golf balls and hiding Betty's boozing, the hapless stand-in found time to pardon his former boss from any further prosecution.

Jimmy Carter, a member of both the CFR and the Rockefeller-created Tri Lateral Commission (TLC), became the first chief executive to call himself a "born-again" Christian. With plenty of positive things to say about the demon-possessed pope, the Democratic president laid the groundwork for Jerry Falwell's ecumenical Moral Majority. John Paul II was also pleased when Jimmy gave our canal to Catholic Panama so they could turn it over to Communist China.

The 1980 presidential election was a classic in European cloak-and-dagger intrigue. Although Reagan had initially balked at the prospect of George Bush being his running mate, the "Gipper" quickly grew to appreciate the advantage of having a former CIA director on the ticket. (Of course, this is not to say that Ron wouldn't be sleeping with one eye open after the *Houston Post* ran a story on March 31, 1981, stating: "Scott Hinckley, the brother of John Hinckley, Jr., who is charged with shooting President Reagan and three others, was to have been a dinner guest Tuesday night at the home of Neil Bush, son of Vice President George Bush the *Houston Post* has learned."[18])

As events unfolded, "Poppy" proved to be especially adept in covert campaigning. William Casey, a former intelligence agent with the Office of Strategic Services (OSS) during World War II, and a member of the CFR, was recruited to become Reagan's campaign manager. (In 1981 he would be promoted to CIA director.) Also, many of the over eight hundred disgruntled CIA operatives abruptly dismissed by the Carter administration in 1977 gladly volunteered their "services" for the Reagan ticket. In an interview nine years later, Richard Allen, Reagan's foreign policy chief who went on to serve briefly as White House national security advisor, recalled that in 1980 "a plane-load of former CIA officers" came to the Reagan-Bush campaign headquarters in Arlington, Virginia, where they were "playing cops and robbers." He added that the antics of these "nutballs" caused him "to work [primarily] out of his own downtown Washington office."[19]

By April 1980, the fate of the fifty-four American hostages being held in Iran was looming as the decisive factor in Jimmy Carter's bid for reelection. When a rescue team of eight helicopters was dispatched from the aircraft carrier USS *Nimitz* on April 28, the mission was quickly aborted after three of the choppers developed "mechanical" problems and a fourth crashed in the desert. Three of the major planners of the scrubbed mission (inauspiciously named Operation Eagle Claw) were Major General Richard Secord, Major (soon to be Lieutenant Colonel) Oliver North, and Albert Hakkim. Phillips writes, "All would emerge as prominent Bush operatives by the mid-1980s."[20] (On a personal note, the Lord allowed me the privilege of seeing one of the Special Forces snipers involved in a support phase of this operation walk the aisle and trust Christ as his personal Saviour in a special evangelistic service I conducted in Tifton, Georgia, on the one-year anniversary of 9/11.)

With Carter's Iranian albatross dragging on into the summer, Beltway pundits renewed their traditional anticipation of the so-called "October surprise." (In 2004, it would be a tape by Osama bin Laden.) Everyone knew that Carter had only two options for getting reelected in November; either he could mount a second, successful rescue, or he could cut a deal with the Ayatollah to have the hostages returned before the polls closed. As events unfolded, the "man from Plains" was no match for Reagan's spy-studded campaign team. According to the book *October Surprise: America's Hostages in Iran and the Election of Ronald Reagan* by former Navy captain Gary Sick, Casey met with Iranian representatives in Spain during late July and simply outbid the feckless Carter camp. Kevin Phillips, citing Sick, gives the following synopsis:

> Iran would not release any hostages before Reagan became president in January 1981. As a quid pro quo, the Reagan administration on taking office would release a large portion of the $12 billion in blocked Iranian assets held in the United States and provide further covert arms shipments. Meanwhile, Casey would see to the September or October delivery to Iran of needed U.S. armaments and vital spare parts for existing Iranian aircraft . . .[21]

Mansur Rafizadeh, former chief of SAVAK (the Iranian secret police) under the Shah, stated during an interview for a U.S. public radio documentary that when he had checked with "powerful" sources in Iran to inquire how the U.S. government was pressing for release of the hostages, he was informed, "You are wrong. American government doesn't want the hostages released, or possibly there's a government inside of the government."[22]

But why are we entertaining such "outrageous conspiracy theories"? October passed without a hitch; the American hostages were *still* behind bars when Carter crashed and burned at the polls, losing by a margin of ten percentage points. And how ironic that election day fell on November 4, 1979, the one-year anniversary of the hostage crisis. Thankfully, however, the captives were all eventually released. In fact, talk about "coincidences," the plane that airlifted them home literally took off from Iran while Ronald Reagan was being sworn in as our fortieth president. (Should we have expected anything less dramatic from the nation's first Hollywood actor turned chief executive?)

While Reagan was completing his second term in office, Jimmy Carter was *still* eating sour grapes over the CIA-orchestrated "Reagan-Khomeini alliance." Exposing himself as a bona fide "Limbaugh Kook," Carter publicly recalled that "former Iranian president Bani-Sadr gave several interviews stating that such an agreement *was* made involving Bud McFarlane, George Bush and perhaps Bill Casey."[23] (So now you know how "George I" got his foot in the door at the White House.)

The eight-year reign of Ron and Nancy would transform the capital into a mini-"Tinseltown." Frank "The Chairman of the Board" Sinatra— a "good" Roman Catholic with more Mafia contacts than Carter has "liver" pills and one of Hollywood's all-time leading fornicators—helped America's First Family get the show on the road by coordinating their "modest" inaugural ball. The message was clear: *peanuts* were out, *glitz* was in. Phillips writes:

> Their arrival in Washington began with inauguration festivities costing a record **$16 million**, an outlay that critics found redolent of both Edwardian England (it featured the dated formality of a morning "stroller suit") and Versailles (the lavish thoughtlessness of the affair). **Following the inaugural hubbub, Ronald and Nancy Reagan became patrons of what one cultural historian described as an "aristocratic movement" spanning the worlds of White House, communications media, fashion, department store, and museum.** The Reagans and their California friends embraced a series of exhibitions and dinners organized under the aegis of *Vogue* and *Harper's Bazaar,* the Metropolitan Museum of Art, Bloomingdale's, and Neiman Marcus and in honor of designers like Yves Saint Laurent, Pierre Cardin, Oscar de la Renta and Ralph Lauren.[24]

Phillips also notes the psychological relation between the aristocratic Reagan White House and the most-watched television series in the United States (and for a while, the world)—*Dynasty*. He cites the following observation made in the mid-1980s by California cultural historian Debora Silverman:

> There is a mutually reinforcing connection between popular opulent fashion and the dual roles of White House Nancy Reagan on one hand and the television fantasy of "Dynasty's" Krystle Carrington on the other. In the weekly evening show, Krystle is the devoted wife of a rich and loving "entrepreneur" and her sartorial splendor, like Mrs. Reagan's, is presumed to be the natural physical expression of her husband's competitive success in the marketplace. "Dynasty" began programming during the week of the first Reagan inaugural in 1981, and exploited the confusion between fantasy and reality by occasionally featuring recognizable political figures, such as Henry Kissinger and Gerald Ford, as guests at some of the extraordinarily lavish parties attended by the Carrington clan. "Dynasty" has been complemented by a new popular show, "Lifestyles of the Rich and Famous," which purports to tell true stories of the rich. "Dynasty" fashions, along with perfume, jewels, accessories, and lingerie, are now marketed as department store signature items and advertised to consumers as a way to "share the luxury," "share the treasures," and "share the magic" of the Carrington characters' staggering riches by buying their imprint.[25]

Whereas President Kennedy inaugurated the age of "boob-tube politics" by capitalizing on a superior makeup job to defeat Nixon in their first televised debate, Ronald "Death Valley Days" Reagan would kick the new era into high gear. The former president of the Screen Actor's Guild was able to convince a bunch of naive Christians that he was God's agent of providence to restore traditional morality to America, despite the fact that he had been married to two Hollywood actresses (one of whom being a fanatical astrologist). Phillips writes, "In an age of celebrity, image was more than a match for fact."[26]

President Reagan also possessed enough charisma to become the first president to persuade Congress to ratify the U.N. Genocide Treaty, originally adopted by a vote of 55-0 at a meeting of the U.N. General Assembly in Paris on December 9, 1948. Thanks to our cowardly ratification of this satanic international treaty and the subsequent wave of domestic hate-crime legislation, "Polack jokes" are now illegal though "Christian bashing" is still an accepted norm.

As for Reagan's macho performance against the "former" Soviet Union ("Take down that wall," etc.), you will have to wait for my second volume to discover how Congress has allowed corporate America to literally create and sustain the evil empire of Soviet communism. (See any number of relevant works on this subject by the late Professor Antony Sutton, Hoover Institute of War and Peace, Stanford University.)

On December 14, 1981, Reagan picked up the White House telephone and conducted a ten-minute conversation with Pope John Paul II. "His Holiness" repaid the courtesy by granting the American president a special audience in the Vatican library on June 7, 1982. The two "former" actors talked in private for about fifty minutes. In a *Time* magazine article, February 24, 1992, entitled "The Holy Alliance," reporter Carl Bernstein quotes Reagan's first national security advisor Richard Allen, a Roman Catholic, as stating, "This was one of the great secret alliances of all time."[27]

While the Nazi Holocaust provided the ideal smoke screen for the numerous assaults on free speech hidden throughout the voluminous Genocide Treaty, the threat of Soviet communism would more than justify a rapprochement with the "Bloody Whore" of Revelation. Consequently, in April 1984 (an election year), Reagan appointed a Roman Catholic proselyte, William S. Wilson, official United States ambassador to the "Holy See." With the Vatican's reciprocity, the formal exchange of envoys revived an unholy alliance that had been dead for over a century. Avro Manhattan, author of more than twenty books on Roman Catholicism, acknowledged, "But the exchange was an equally important event in the Catholicization of the U.S. making the Catholic Church a special religious-diplomatic-political entity operating in the very heart of the U.S."[28]

After faithfully serving in the Reagan court for two terms, "George I" came to the throne in 1988. Phillips writes:

> Early biographies of George H. W. Bush stressed the seventeenth-century New England roots on both the Bush and Walker sides of the family, alleging that Senator Prescott Bush and his family descended from English king Henry III. Then, after George H. W. had won the 1988 presidential election, London-based *Burke's Peerage*, the world's authority on royal lineage, all but bowed.
>
> Harold Brooks-Baker, publishing director of *Burke's*, allowed that some other U.S. presidents had royal connections, "but none as royal as George Bush." Rather than to Henry III, he traced Bush's family history

to Mary, the sister of King Henry VIII, who became part of the Bush family tree by wedding the duke of Suffolk. Queen Elizabeth, Brooks-Baker pronounced, was thus the president's distant cousin.[29]

Bush became the first American "monarch" to duplicate the ultimate European debacle known as the Crusades. Bodansky writes:

> Officials throughout the region explained this rapprochement among the Muslim and Arab states in terms that anticipated fateful events. Very significant was the frequent invocation by Arab leaders of the Muslim defeat of the Crusaders as a metaphor to describe the challenges currently facing the Arabs in their confrontation with Israel. . . .
>
> Islamist leaders were even more explicit in comparing current circumstances in the Middle East with those in the days of the Crusaders, when the entire Muslim world united behind a single (non-Arab) leader— Saladin—in order to defeat and evict the Crusaders and liberate al-Quds.[30]

As the "Christians" defeated the infidels in the First Crusade, "George I" was likewise victorious in Operation Desert Storm. However, the Europeans would get their plows cleaned over the next seven crusades. ("Tee shirts, tee shirts—get your tee shirts.")

Although G. H. W. Bush would be turned out of office by Bill Clinton— a graduate of the largest Jesuit university in America and the first Rhodes Scholar to become president—he would become the first chief executive to have his regal power restored by an heir. (The two Adamses were separated by over a quarter century with John Quincy put in office by a different political party from his father.) In the November 10, 2002, "Week in Review" section of *The New York Times*, a half-page color picture of Air Force One was displayed with the heading: "Defying Expectations, a Bush Dynasty Begins to Look Real."[31]

"George II" became the first president since 1888 who had not won at least a plurality of the popular vote. After losing to Al Gore by more than half-a-million ballots, he was selected by a four-vote margin in the electoral college, courtesy of a five-to-four decision in the U.S. Supreme Court. And let's not forget that "Prince Jeb" presided over the "Kingdom of Hanging Chad." (You might want to keep an eye on the soft-spoken Florida governor; that January 2005 "trial balloon" mission on which he was sent with outgoing Secretary of State Powell to tsunami-ravaged Southeast Asia looked *real* presidential. Jeb's Latino in-laws must have been ecstatic when he told the nation on FOX *News* that he *prayed the rosary* after seeing the devastation.)

But why quibble about trivial matters? America had become infatuated with the glitter of Roman Catholic culture and the new Bush was even more aristocratic than his father (despite the nasty fact that he "chewed.") Phillips writes:

> Perhaps the ultimate insinuation of U.S. aristophilia and de facto monarchism came from the London publishers of *Burke's Peerage*. On the day before the 2000 presidential election, they predicted that George W. Bush would win because he had more royal blood than his opponent—and because the candidate with the most royal blood always won U.S. presidential contests. George W. Bush was even more "royal" in ancestry than his father because his mother's royal connections included French Bourbon and several Scandinavian monarchs, as well as members of the Russian, Spanish, and German monarchies.[32]

Of the 535 members of the 107th Congress elected in 2000, some 77 were relatives of senators, representatives, governors, judges, state legislators, or local officials. The most "illustrious" freshman senator could even boast of being married to a former chief executive! The only scenario any scarier than Hillary restoring the Clinton dynasty in 2008 would be to factor Bill into the equation as Kofi Annan's replacement. (See *WorldNetDaily*, February 19, 2003, "Bill Clinton: Next U.N. Chief?") On January 4, 2005, Bill O'Reilly, host of the highest-rated program on FOX *News* channel, endorsed Slick Willy to replace Kofi as secretary-general of the United Nations. In an interview with Richard Holbrooke, former U.S. ambassador to the United Nations, O'Reilly was asked by the guest what he would like to see happen. Just weeks after his "kinky phone sex" lawsuit with Andrea Mackris was "discreetly" settled out of court, the "conservative giant" answered:

> I'd like to see Annan out of there. I'd like to see Bill Clinton take the job. The world loves him. He'd do a good job. It would be good for the United States. Hillary would love it."[33]

Should applicable regulations be amended at the U.N., the Church Age could end with a reincarnation of Ahab and Jezebel ruling the world! Remember—truth *is* stranger than fiction; *whatever* God has planned for *His* finale, you can be assured that He will leave amateurs like Stevie Spielberg in the dust.

The strongest indication that America is finished was evidenced in the 2004 presidential campaign by the total lack of opposition to Senator Kerry being a Roman Catholic. When the *real* JFK ran in 1960, voter resistance was so intense that Kennedy was forced to go on the defensive, repeatedly assuring the nation that his "religious convictions" (i.e., his required allegiance to a foreign power—the Vatican *State*) would never interfere with his oath to uphold the U.S. Constitution. Less than fifty years later, the only challenge to Kerry's Catholicism came from his own "Church" over his support for abortion.

"SECOND TERM, OZZY!"

As previously stated, "The Osbournes" were among the 2,700 honored guests at the May 4, 2002, White House Correspondents' Association dinner. Even with all the dope in his brain, Ozzy knew he didn't rate an invitation, much less the personal recognition he received from President Bush. According to *WorldNetDaily*, he sputtered, "It's [expletive] blowing my mind!" with wife Sharon adding, "What can you say? It's the most incredible thing that he would even mention Ozzy. It's a bit overwhelming."[34]

The man who promised to clean up the White House after eight years of Bill Clinton, apparently doesn't mind socializing with a demon-possessed psychotic whose biographical highlights include: a decade of performing with the premier heavy-metal rock band Black Sabbath; getting arrested, clad in a woman's dress, for urinating on the Alamo; biting off the head of a bat during a concert in Des Moines, Iowa; and appearing in Howard Stern's R-rated movie "Body Parts."

Joseph Farah, editor of *WorldNetDaily*, described the pervert in a May 12, 2002, article accordingly:

> Satanic lyrics, evil worldview, disgusting mouth, no musical ability, drug abuse. This is Osbourne. He is a depraved moral terrorist, seducing young kids who don't know any better into deadly lifestyles.[35]

In his May 6, 2002, *Washington Post* story entitled "Great and Powerful Ozz," David Montgomery wrote:

The hotel lobby was thronged with famous people in tuxedos and party dresses. Oh, Drew Carey! Ah, Raquel Welch! Soon there would be generals, Cabinet secretaries and, of course, the president himself.

But who cared? There was someone else everyone *really* wanted to see. Tourists stood to one side, eyes riveted on the lobby doors, disposable cameras ready. Press photographers elbowed for position on the other side. Everyone waited. When would he arrive? What would he wear? Would his wife accompany him? What would he say? If he said anything, would anyone understand?

Suddenly a Gothic profusion of black and magenta and pink and blue—the clothes, the hair, the shades, the tattoos—rushes through the doors. Himself had arrived—and he brought the missus. Ozzy and Sharon Osbourne made their debut with official Washington Saturday night at the White House Correspondents' Association dinner, and in spite of itself, this segment of capital society went as crazy as the rest of the country over the stars of MTV's new reality hit, "The Osbournes."

The tourists in the lobby shouted "Ozzy," the professional photographers shouted "Ozzy," and the Osbournes disappeared into a tsunami of reporters and fans, including reporters who *were* fans. "Ozzy, what do you want to tell the president?" a reporter called out. The man whose mumbly British dialogue is frequently unintelligible on television—with lots of words bleeped out, as in "I hate (bleeping) Christmas!"—must find the rest of the world equally unintelligible, for his first quote for official Washington was: "I beg your pardon?" The question was repeated. And he replied, "I hengh heenth hunh president denngh hmmhmme heng! . . .

Then they did meet, the commander in chief and the one-time satanic-singing, bat-chewing television anti-dad. Bush was seated at the head table, when Ozzy, at Table 168, saw his chance. He made his way forward until he was separated from Bush by only the 10-foot security no man's land: men commanding two kinds of power, face to face, silently taking each other's measure.

Ozzy put his hands together in an almost prayerful acknowledgment, paying respects. The president nodded. Then Ozzy grabbed a fistful of his stringy brown-and-pink hair and shouted: "You should wear your hair like mine!"

Bush did not reply immediately. He turned a little red, then got that wiseguy grin of his. He leaned forward and shouted back: **"Second term, Ozzy!"**[36]

Thanks to the "Religious Right"—a voting bloc far more deluded than the *eight million* voyeurs who "merely" monitor the Osbournes on a weekly basis—America's "Christian" president was returned to office and will subsequently do what he pleases. Approriately enough, *Time* magazine, founded by Skull and Bones member Henry Luce, declared President Bush "Man of the Year." (But, did you happen to notice how many Cabinet members flew the coop within days of Bush's reelection? Do *they* know something *we* don't know?)

In order for a president to "sport a different hair style" in his second term, certain preparations must be made in the first. For instance, only two months before the "Ozzy and Dubya" show, a story appeared in the March 1, 2002, *Washington Post* entitled "Shadow Government Is at Work in Secret." The article states:

> President Bush has dispatched a shadow government of about 100 senior civilian managers to live and work secretly outside Washington, activating for the first time long-standing plans to ensure survival of federal rule after catastrophic attack on the nation's capital. . . .
>
> Deployed "on the fly" in the first hours of turmoil on Sept. 11, one participant said, the shadow government has evolved into an **indefinite precaution**. . . .
>
> Known internally as the COG, for "continuity of government," the administration-in-waiting is an unannounced complement to the acknowledged absence of Vice President Cheney from Washington for much of the past five months. . . .
>
> According to officials with firsthand knowledge, the Bush administration conceived the move that morning [Sept. 11] as a temporary precaution, likely to last only a few days. But further assessment of terrorist risks persuaded the White House to remake the program as a **permanent feature** of "the new reality, based on what the threat looks like," a senior decisionmaker said.[37]

Did you catch that scary stuff about the president's shadow government evolving into an "**indefinite** precaution"? You see, "Brother" Bush was just utilizing the excellent training he received in that crypt at New Haven. Jones states, "For the first time in history, FEMA command bunkers are brimming with National Security Agency personnel."[38] John Dean adds in *Worse Than Watergate:*

> From the outset of the administration, Cheney focused on national security. . . . To support his national security work, rather than relying on the National Security Council (NSC)—a statutory creation, which is part of the Executive Office of the President (and where Condi Rice as national

security advisor to Bush was cutting back on staff)—Cheney formed what is, in effect, a shadow NSC. Indeed it was actually Bush's NSC staff who first called Cheney's operation a "shadow" government. This shadow operation, while informally integrated, actually has its own agenda as well as the power to realize it through the vice president's clout. **It is a secret government— beyond the reach of Congress, and everyone else as well.**[39]

And "thank heavens," the *microchip* has finally arrived to reinforce the unprecedented "Patriot Act." In a report by Diane Sawyer on "Good Morning America," we learned that a paranoid Florida family became our nation's first guinea pigs for the *mark of the beast!* (Revelation 13:17)

> Diane Sawyer: We have a Florida family who are really pioneers in a brave new world. They have volunteered to be the first ever to have microchip identification devices implanted into their bodies.
>
> Woman: After 9/11 I was really concerned with the security of my family....[40]

You gotta hand it to George Orwell—*he was only off by eighteen years*!

With all the autocratic shenanigans that have occurred during the reign of "George II," conservative apologists like Limbaugh, O'Reilly, Hannity and Coulter can only be viewed as court jesters for consistently failing to recognize and expose the abuse. And yes, as I have repeatedly stated, the liberal Democrats are admittedly worse—*on paper*. The problem is that America is now so morally polluted and primed to dump Israel at the first sign of renewed terrorist attacks here that the law of sowing and reaping mandates we no longer have a clear choice between good and evil; it is between *yin* and *yang*. While Republicans project the higher moral image, the party has long since sold its soul to corporate America. Conversely, Democrats feign compassion for the so-called "little guy"—in the *material* realm—while consigning his soul to Hell in the *spiritual*. John Adams was absolutely right when he said, "Our constitution was made only for a moral and religious people. It is wholly inadequate for the government of any other."[41] Whereas Kerry represented the haymaker, Bush was the sucker punch; John and Teresa represented the chain saw, George and Laura will deliver the slow gas leak.

The sin of the "Religious Right" was *not* in voting for Bush as a *political* candidate, it was their enthusiastic endorsement of his flagrantly compromised brand of "Christianity." One of the main reasons why believers remain so deceived in this regard is because they surmise "their" candidate to be the target of the Left (the same bunch that "Brother" Bush will fellowship with in private—Ozzy, Metropolitan Community "Church," etc.).

But don't forget friends, a vote for Bush was more than just a vote *against* Kerry—it was also a vote *for* Dick Cheney! How's this for a timely illustration of America's return to a monarchical mindset? Dean writes in *Worse Than Watergate*:

> With Bush and Cheney, not only is Cheney the senior partner, he is prime minister *sub silentio*. Cheney's enveloping influence on Bush and national security policy has been noted within the Beltway, even if it is largely unnoticed beyond. For example, by the end of the third year of the Bush-Cheney administration, the *American Conservative* (Feb. 2, 2004) declared Cheney the American Richelieu, "the hand behind the throne." In describing the Bush II White House, Washington-based journalist Georgie Anne Geyer has written that Cheney is "the most important vice president in history—some say the most influential man in America." She reported that "George W. (Bush) most resembles the many French dauphins come suddenly to the throne—the young, inexperienced prince, with a defensive chief who has definite Napoleonic tendencies, and a flowing group of courtiers with their own agendas and loyalties, some to foreign countries and some to secret societies outside the realm. With this court, Dick Cheney has become George Bush's Cardinal Richelieu." The comparison is, indeed, fitting.[42]

The *American Conservative* also noted the precise historical precedent:

> You do remember Cardinal Richelieu? It was the time of the religious wars in Europe in the 16th century and the era of a weak king, Louis XIII. In 1585, Armand-Jean du Plessis, Cardinal and Duke de Richelieu, was born to a minor noble family and became a priest, a bishop, a cardinal, then France's Secretary of State for foreign affairs in 1616, and, finally, the prime minister of France in 1624. He would go down in history as a man obsessed with bringing order to France under royal authority, and he believed in the divine right of the king and the obedience of the people. Yet, even as he believed in the "light of natural reason," still he remained always the pessimist with regard to human nature and believed fully that the ends justified the means.[43]

The article further pointed out Richelieu's "horrible overspending for France on war he fostered" as he "committed war expenditure with little regard for the difficulties of raising revenue and he was given to economic improvisation that was often unsound."[44] But why encourage the Body of Christ to waste their time reading history? Such a phenomenon would negate the infallibility of Holy Scripture as Ecclesiastes 1:11a declares, *"There is no remembrance of former things"* ("no remembrance" *means* "no remembrance").

As a culture grows increasingly enamored with royalty, the power of its "parliament" must decrease commensurately. For example, unbeknownst to most Americans, the vice president dealt a serious blow to our traditional system of checks and balances by provoking, then prevailing in the historic federal lawsuit *Walker* v. *Cheney*. The problem began in April 2001 when Beltway buzz had it that Cheney's newly formed and highly secretive National Energy Policy Development Group was awash in corruption. At the prompting of Congressman Henry Waxman (D-Calif.), ranking member of the Committee on Government Reform, and John Dingel (D-Mich.), ranking member of the Energy and Commerce Committee, David Walker, head of the General Accounting Office (GAO), the investigative and auditing arm of Congress, made a simple request for information about the composition of Cheney's energy group and its activities in developing a national energy policy.

David Addington, counsel to the vice president, adamantly refused to cooperate with Walker's request, stating that it was an attempt "to intrude into the heart of Executive deliberations, including deliberations among the President, the Vice President, members of the President's Cabinet, and the President's immediate assistants, which the law protects to ensure the candor in Executive deliberation necessary to effective government."[45]

After nine months of being stonewalled by Cheney's office, Walker informed Congress, the president and the vice president that the GAO was going to court. Dean notes:

> For the first time since it was created in 1920, the GAO was required to "file suit to enforce (its) access rights against a federal official," because of Cheney's action. . . . **If the GAO could not get the information it requested, then there was a black hole in the federal firmament— a no-man's-land where a president and vice president could go free from congressional oversight."**[46]

To make a long story short, U.S. District Court Judge John Bates (a rookie Bush appointee) tossed the GAO's case out of federal court.

Basically, the judge claimed that the GAO had provided no evidence that Congress had been injured by Cheney's failure to cooperate. Dean summarizes:

> This was an absurd reading of the law. Comptroller Walker had filed his lawsuit pursuant to a 1980 statute that expressly authorized him to bring such an action. But Judge Bates effectively told Congress that it could not give the comptroller general standing (or authority) to act on its behalf, thereby gutting the enforcement authority of the General Accounting Office's statutory mandate. . . .
>
> Despite the GAO's extraordinarily cautious approach, lawyers at the Congressional Research Service (CRS) at the Library of Congress are concerned that *Walker* v. *Cheney* has serious implications for congressional oversight. **It greatly diminishes the GAO's investigative powers, particularly against a president and vice president**. The GAO has lost not only standing to file a lawsuit but the leverage of the threat of filing such a lawsuit, should an executive department or agency stonewall the way Cheney did. The GAO must now simply take what the White House (and its many appendages, such as the National Security Council, National Economic Council, Domestic Policy Council, Office of the Vice President, Office of the First Lady, White House Communications Agency, White House Transportation Agency, White House Military Office, to mention a few) volunteers. This has never before been the case. **Even if the GAO knows that a crucial document is missing or that the information provided is incomplete to the point of being inaccurate, it can do nothing. It will see only what Bush and Cheney want it to see and no more.**[47]

As to the previously mentioned suit brought against Cheney by Judicial Watch, the Supreme Court decided to kick the case back down to the U.S. District Court of Appeals for the District of Columbia Circuit (*after* Dick's duck hunting trip with Antonin).

The great statesman Patrick Henry once warned, "The liberties of the people never were nor ever will be secure when the transactions of their rulers may be concealed from them."[48] Thomas Jefferson concurred with a similar note of caution: "When the government fears the people, there is liberty; when the people fear the government, there is tyranny."[49] Thus, in a veiled rebuke to the Bush administration, Judge Damon J. Keith of the U.S. Court of Appeals for the Sixth Circuit declared, "Democracies die behind closed doors."[50]

"YE SHALL BE AS GODS"

It is no coincidence that the most popular American president since World War II "just happened" to be a professional actor from Hollywood. The words "In my heart I believe that man is good" can be found on a curved wall at the tomb of Ronald Reagan. However, the King James Bible would strongly disagree with this optimistic assessment of humanity. While David declared in the Old Testament, *"verily every man at his best state is altogether vanity"* (Psalm 39:5c), Paul wrote in the New Testament, *"there is none that doeth good, no, not one"* (Romans 3:12b).

Ronald Reagan was loved by his fellow men because he told them exactly what they wanted to hear. And who could ask for a higher earthly authority than a former movie star turned president?

Along this line, a major correlation exists between "Ronnie's" Hollywood haunts and our current, irredeemable Hell-bound society. When America's Christians traded their infallible Bible for the corrupt text of a dress-wearing, *self*-professed infallible *man*, they did far more than facilitate the return of our political ideology to a *man*-centered European monarchy—as opposed to a *constitution*-centered democratic republic—*they ensured that our entire culture would eventually grow addicted to the phenomena of "man worship" better known as "show biz."* Apart from our national passivity concerning the ongoing dismemberment of Israel, the rise of the professional entertainment industry constitutes the greatest blight in our land.

In Isaiah 42:8, the God of the universe declares, *"I am the LORD: that is my name: and my glory will I not give to another."* The first commandment reads: *"I am the LORD thy God, which have brought thee out of the land of Egypt, out of the house of bondage. Thou shalt have no other gods before me"* (Exodus 20:2-3). When the devil tempted Eve in the Garden of Eden, he knew exactly what buttons to push: *"For God doth know that in the day ye eat thereof, then your eyes shall be opened, and ye shall be as gods, knowing good and evil"* (Genesis 3:5). Our first parents were promptly expelled from God's presence for the identical reason Satan was thrown out of Heaven. (Isaiah 14:14)

By Noah's day, the sin of "man worship" had reached epidemic proportions. Most Bible teachers believe that the "sons of God" in Genesis six were fallen angels (Job 1:6; 2:1; and 38:7) that cohabited with women. (The position that angels "cannot reproduce" is arrived at by altering the reading in Matthew 22:30 to omit the words "in heaven" and then by further maligning the truth by teaching that angels are "sexless.")

In any event, the mutant offspring, described as *"mighty men which were of old, men of renown,"* (Genesis 6:4c) became the catalyst for the decadent conditions described in the following verse: *"And GOD saw that the wickedness of man was great in the earth, and that every imagination of the thoughts of his heart was only evil continually* (Genesis 6:5).

While some of the more "cultured" brethren find such a view repulsive, I would remind them that *whatever* took place "back yonder," *it made God mad enough that he wiped out the entire world (save eight).* The subject of "gods," though ignored in any standard Bible college, is mentioned rather frequently throughout Scripture. (See Psalm 82:1, 6; Jeremiah 10:11; John 10:34; Acts 12:22, 14:11; I Corinthians 8:5; and I John 5:20.) As noted in Alexander Hislop's *Two Babylons*, it has also formed a significant part of secular history. (See Ulysses, Apollos, Venus, Aphrodite, Tammuz, Semiramis, Bacchus, Mary, Ashtoreth, Baal, Diana, Jove, Wotan, Jupiter, Thor, Zeus, Marduk, the Minator, Theseus, Atlas, Mercury, Medusa, the Lorelei, etc.[51])

The reason this topic is so relevant is because the Lord stated in Matthew 24:37, *"But as the days of Noe were, so shall also the coming of the Son of man be."* Thus, according to the word of God, one of the major end-day signs to look for would be *"mighty men . . . men of renown"*—enter *Hollywood*, located (get this) in the "City of *Angels*"— *the world's foremost manufacturer of "human gods," appropriately known as "stars."*

In the words of the ancient Lycaonians, *"The gods are come down to us in the likeness of men"* (Acts 14:11). If you doubt whether Hollywood celebrities are filled with the power of Satan, just watch what happens when "mere mortals" come into their presence. Have *you* ever gotten to meet a real live "star"? What was *your* first reaction? In his *Washington Post* article, David Montgomery wrote:

> Finally the doors open and the Osbournes hold court at Table 168. Hundreds clamor for autographs and pictures with Ozzy.
>
> Why, here's Rep. Dennis J. Kucinich (D-Ohio) with pad and pen. "My sister Beth Ann loves Ozzy," Kucinich says. Oh, so the autograph is for his *sister*. Hmm. In a shaky scrawl, Osbourne writes, "To Beth Ann, much love, Ozzy Osbourne." Kucinich threads back out of the crowd,

pondering the question of why on earth Ozzy is such a star here, among this slice of Washington.[52]

Cyber journalist, Matt Drudge observed: "When Karl Rove arrived, hardly anyone noticed. When Ozzy Osbourne came in, the sea parted. This is the state of the city in 2002."[53] And let's not forget how the president himself yelled out to his guest of honor—"Mom loves your stuff, Ozzy!"

Heathen Drew Carey told the audience how the two biggest celebrities in the room actually had a few things in common:

> First of all, they both love their families. They both partied a little too hard when they were younger. Half the time you can't understand a word either of them is saying. And neither one of them can make a move without their wife's approval.[54]

The shocking bottom line regarding the satanic entertainment industry is that a select group of mortals get to spend their entire lives receiving worship that belongs to God alone. The Apostle Paul makes reference to this abomination in Romans 1:25: *"Who changed the truth of God into a lie, and worshipped and served the creature more than the Creator, who is blessed forever. Amen."* Just imagine how hot *their* Hell will be!

But yet, there is more. Because the devil knows that only a handful of aspirants will make it to the "big time," he fixed things so that just about anyone can get in on the action. Can we say—*karaoke?* When you know what to look for, it's amazing to see the myriad of opportunities our society affords everyday nobodies to achieve their so-called "fifteen minutes of fame." From telling everything they know on the local call-in talk shows to running stark naked across a sports stadium, any number of venues can be found for hard up humans to attain a measure of desperately needed attention. While some are content to merely hold a sign in front of the NBC *Today Show* cameras, others more daring would rather be seen on *Real TV* spitting out their teeth after a dramatic skateboard crash. And who can forget that idiot in the "land of fruits and nuts" who stole an army tank and wiped out several city blocks before being shot to death by police? If you're too stupid for *Jeopardy*, too pretty for *The Swan,* or lack the talent for *American Idol*, there's always the *Jerry Springer Show.* If your spouse is unfaithful, tell the world all about it on *Cheaters*; the rest of your dirty laundry can be aired before *Judge Judy.* In this marvelous land of opportunity even winos and street people can get a piece of the pie by consenting to be physically assaulted on various "reality" television shows. And, if all else fails, you might have a pet that could make you famous via Animal Planet's *Pet Stars!*

Apart from the traditional status symbols of loaded cars and luxurious houses, some of the more popular contemporary "insecurity indicators" would include (moving from the simple to the bizarre): bumper stickers; personalized tee shirts and ball caps; multiple cell phone ringer tones, wireless laptops and MP3 players; customized horn sounds, wheel spinners and hydraulic suspensions; exorbitant fashion and jewelry expenditures; visits to spas, tanning beds, nail salons, make-over clinics and an inordinate affection for health clubs; and, finally, tattoos and body piercings, especially facial metal.

Could the Bible have been any more accurate with its prediction that men would be *"lovers of their own selves"* (II Timothy 3:2a)? And we haven't even discussed the world of professional sports (Ham's primary public relations platform) with its trickle-down effect extending all the way to the local Little Leagues. From steroids to soccer moms, our modern culture stands convicted of being *"lovers of pleasure more than lovers of God"* (II Timothy 3:4).

Having considered these applications, a major truth about the end times comes into focus; it is *the* key to why America is truly finished. One of the most profound, and least understood, reasons why a *national* revival is utterly impossible is because *the great majority of prospects have rendered themselves unreachable by their willful addiction to the cult of god-making.* For instance, why should the average sinner in this country waste any time listening to you or me tell him about some invisible God (with a whole lot of intolerance "hang-ups" to boot) when he is already infatuated with a pantheon of visible "deities"? While there was a day when unsaved people could be reached by telling them that Jesus Christ was *"the resurrection, and the life"* (John 11:25a); *"the way, the truth, and the life"* (John 14:6a), and, thereby, the One who *"giveth life"* (John 6:33b)—the *silver* screen would now project mere humans as *"bigger"* than life." With "silver" portrayed in Scripture as a major type of *redemption,* "stars" such as Rudolph Valentino, Douglas Fairbanks, Jr., Clark Gable, John Wayne, Rock Hudson, Sean Connery, Clint Eastwood, Robert DeNiro, Brad Pitt, and Vin Diesel would become America's new saviors! But, then again, depending on where the sinner sees himself in the "god-wannabe" pecking order, he's probably expecting a little worship himself. (For what it's worth, I believe that a subconscious correlation exists between our nationwide preoccupation with human "gods" and the near-addictive usage of the buzz phrase "Oh, my God!" for just about every situation from a genuine crisis to a winning lottery ticket.)

Tragically, such a deluded mindset will blind a poor human from seeing one of the richest truths in all the universe—*God had to become a man because man wanted to become a god.* The Apostle Paul put it this way: *"For ye know the grace of our Lord Jesus Christ, that, though he was rich, yet for your sakes he became poor, that ye through his poverty might become rich"* (II Corinthians 8:9).

Yet, the very time of the year that our nation has traditionally allotted to the glorious incarnation has become our latest mile-marker on the way to perdition. Because America has become so preoccupied with the *season,* she no longer has any interest in the *reason.* Thus, like Nazareth of old, the good ol' U.S.A. has also chosen to say—*"No room in the inn for Jesus."* As this book was nearing completion (December 2004), the festive season was abuzz over yet another unthinkable challenge to our Judeo-Christian heritage. First, little school children were told they could not recite the Pledge of Allegiance; then a state Supreme Court chief justice was told that he could not keep his Ten Commandments monument in his own courthouse; and now, a pastor has been told that his congregation could not participate in their city's seasonal parade because they intended to sing traditional yuletide hymns and display a banner reading "Merry Christmas" (as opposed to the politically correct "Happy Holidays.")

Denver Mayor John Hickenlooper reacted to the huge backlash resulting from his controversial action against Pastor George Morrison and his flock in Arvada, Colorado, saying, "I apologize to anyone who may have been offended or mistakenly felt I was being anti-Christmas. Hickenlooper might have two O's, but I am not Scrooge."[55] In his own defense, parade spokesman Michael Krikorian made the incredible statement that: "We want to avoid that specific religious message out of respect for other religions in the region. It could be construed as disrespectful to other people who enjoy a parade each year."[56] The mayor was not a total party pooper, however, as the Parade of Lights *did* include a variety of floats representing (in addition to Santa): Belly Dance Concepts, Colorado Clowns, Mestizo Dancers, Kung Fu Artisans, Taiko Drummers, T.E.V. Edelweiss Schuhplattlers, and the Two Spirit Society of Denver, which honors homosexual and lesbian American Indians as "holy people." The program also included performers from the Lion Dance, a Chinese New Year tradition "meant to chase away evil spirits and welcome good luck and good fortune for the year."[57]

In "fairness" to Mayor Hickenlooper, although the Parade of Lights technically takes place at the height of the Christmas season, it was never intended to be construed as a "Christmas" parade. According to an article in *BP News*,

> The Parade of Lights, a two-day event which began in 1974 and drew an estimated 375,000 people this December, is sponsored by a group of businesses called the Downtown Denver Partnership. Jim Basey, the partnership's president, told The New York Times the parade was meant to be "cutesy" for kids as a way to get bodies downtown.[58]

Thus, when it comes to being "cutesy" for kids during a Christmas parade in present-day America, the "Little Drummer Boy" is *out* while "Taiko Drummers" are *in*! As George Bush would say—"God Bless America!"

Now, despite such insane conditions, the prospect of an imminent national revival remains the drug of choice being pushed on our "doped-up" congregations. If you have the kind of syrupy-talking, "positive-minded" CEO/pastor who knows more about palm pilots than right division, you could be in serious trouble with regard to an *"understanding of the times."* The young people in any generation represent an accurate gauge of what to expect in the future. When the *NASV* Gospel of John showed up in 1960, America's youth were being stereotyped by such innocuous characters as Wally Cleaver and Dobie Gillis. While Elvis certainly did some damage, to his "credit" he never urinated on the Alamo or sunk his teeth into a bat! If you want to see a generation that's *totally* "all shook up," take a gander at the teenagers of the twenty-first century. A policeman in Milton, Florida, told me that the latest craze among teens is getting surgical implants to distort their features, especially in the forehead area; devil's horns and alien ridges are two of the more popular styles. (Have we come a long way from the "Okie from Muskogee," or what?)

If you think such pitiful creatures will be shown a better way by our "Christian" president, think again. While "Granny Bush" is an "Ozz freak," the Bush twins chose pervert Kid Rock to headline their gala inaugural youth concert, January 18, 2005. "Our first job is to provide a quality experience for our attendees," said Gordon C. James, a deputy director of inaugural events, expected to cost in excess of $40 million.[59] In a January 3, 2005, *New York Times* story entitled " 'Pony Up' and Then 'Party On,' Inaugural Officials Say," Elisabeth Bumiller wrote, "The Kid, as he is called, notably said at a party during the Republican National Convention that if he were president he would never be caught having sex in the Oval Office but would instead install cameras in the Lincoln Bedroom."[60] During the same gig, attended by 2,000 young Republicans, including the First Twins, the slimeball also said, "If I was president I would do the State of the Union address while smokin' a joint on Air Force One."[61]

Kid Rock's "professional" résumé is just the kind you'd expect to see associated with "Brother" Bush's genre of Machiavellian "Christianity": former porn star; voted "sluttiest male celebrity" by MTV; boyfriend of former *Playboy* playmate Pamela Anderson, etc. His main "contribution" to Western culture is merging rap with rock. According to an article on *patridiots.com* entitled "Moral Values My (Expletive)," some of the "Kid's" greatest hits would include "Pimp of the Nation," "Wax the (Expletive)" and "(Expletive) You Blind." As Jen and Barb's rap sheet will readily attest, "Dubya's" wilder days—captured in the lyrics of "Killin' Brain Cells"—are *obviously* worth emulating today:

> So [expletive] college and a good education
> All we need to learn is how to hold hands
> Then we could live in peace in my homeland
> God [expletive] the way my pain swells
> I spend all my time killin' brain cells
> The light shed on me was a dim gleam
> So I live life in a bottle of Jim Beam
> Droppin' dots or sniffin' that blow back,
> I go to sleep at night watchin' Kojak
> [Expletive] hoes cuz I'm no big fag
> Roll with zig zags like to read skin mags [62]

However, following a storm of protest led by *WorldNetDaily*, the Kid was summarily *dumped* at the eleventh hour. "Rumor" had it that Barbara Bush pulled the plug after discovering that she had been "dissed" in one of the rapper's tunes! (Just "Kid"ding!)

> Pimp of the Nation, I could be it
> As a matter of fact, I foresee it
> But only pimpin' hoes with the big [*expletive*]
> While you be left pimpin Barbara *Bush* [63]

The story does have a "happy" ending, however. As things played out, the young Republicans did not go away disappointed in the filth department, having heard the "F" word at least once. In his *VH1.com* article entitled "Fuel Singer Shouts Obscenity At President's Bash," Gil Kaufman writes:

> Tuesday night's youth-oriented inauguration bash for President Bush took an unexpected turn when Fuel singer Brett Scallions shouted an obscenity during his band's set. "Welcome to the greatest [expletive] country in the world!" Scallions yelled at the youth-oriented show in the D.C. Armory, according to *The Associated Press*. Scallions then sheepishly added, "Oops. I wasn't supposed to say that."[64]

Finally, though forced to back down on "Kid Pervert," the president wasted no time avenging his daughters' "honor." In an interview aboard Air Force One on January 14, "Brother" Bush blew a little smoke of his own. According to the *Washington Post*, "For the first time, Bush said he will not press senators to pass a constitutional amendment banning same-sex marriage, the top priority for many social conservative groups."[65] A follow-up article related the inevitable "duh": "Social conservatives who helped stoke record turnout for Bush in the 2004 election expressed concern that he is dropping the issue he passionately touted during the campaign now that he has been reelected."[66] For further study on the "Bush position," see the August 8, 2004, *USA Today* article, "Cheney says he opposes marriage amendment"[67]—"double duh!"

All I can say is—Praise the dear Lord *Kerry* didn't win! ("Second term, Ozzy!")

It's Not About *You*

While "Dubya's" crowd was downing their martinis and kicking up their heels on inauguration night, a nineteen-year-old girl who had just clocked out from her cashier's job at a Tyler, Texas, Wal-Mart was being abducted at gunpoint in the store parking lot by an "African-American" marine.

The following morning the teen's murdered corpse was discovered lying on a roadside in West Texas over four hundred miles away.

Now, of course, anytime the unsaved start growing more wicked, you can be sure that the salt has begun to lose its savor. (II Timothy 3:13; Matthew 5:13) If you want to have a *serious* "religious experience," just open your eyes and begin noting the many ways *believers* have unconsciously succumbed to this gross sin of man worship. Like the heathen, God's people have their *own* deified celebrities and pecking order to pursue. Can you think of any "camps" that have lost it when it comes to exalting men beyond the prescribed boundaries of legitimate affection? (Acts 8:10, 14:12-15, 20:37; I Thessalonians 5:13; I Peter 5:3; III John 9) For instance, could you see the Apostle Paul naming a college after himself? Would he have wanted a life-size statue erected in his memory? When John the Baptist was slain, the Bible simply states that *"his disciples came, and took up the body, and buried it, and went and told Jesus"* (Matthew 14:12). There was no mention of mourners leaving Reese's Peanut Butter Cups, Diet Dr. Peppers, or notes of affection at any "shrine." Is the entire Independent Baptist movement being sapped of its strength by an abuse originally attributed to a single carnal assembly? (I Corinthians 3:4)

How long has it been since you heard a sermon that did *not* revolve around the speaker? Paul wrote, *"For we preach not ourselves, but Christ Jesus the Lord . . ."* (II Corinthians 4:5a). When was the last time you heard a preacher *genuinely* deflect credit away from his ministry's accomplishments? Again, the Apostle wrote, *"But God forbid that I should glory, save in the cross of our Lord Jesus Christ, by whom the world is crucified unto me, and I unto the world"* (Galatians 6:14). And my, how we *love* to confer honorary degrees on one another. Job wrote, *"Let me not, I pray you, accept any man's person, neither let me give flattering titles unto man. For I know not to give flattering titles; in so doing my maker would soon take me away."* (Job 32:21, 22)

While the Charismatic crowd is about as worldly as it gets ("Christian" tattoo parlors, "Charlton Heston Presents The Bible," Gospel "artists," Dove Awards, Bill Gaither's "Homecomings," etc.), Independent Baptists are not far behind. Ask the old-time preachers how they feel about clapping for singers after a special. Could you see Paul and Silas harmonizing under the lights to a soundtrack? I wonder how many Bibles our Baptist ancestors ever signed. Evan Roberts was used to spark the mighty Welsh

Revival, one of the greatest movements of the Holy Spirit in history. Have you ever seen a photo of this mighty preacher? Odds are you haven't as he steadfastly refused to have his picture taken for fear of losing the power of God! As for "Christian drama," the only "show" I'd recommend is the sobering reenactment of the Waldensean persecution, conducted annually in Valdese, North Carolina. And, can you *even* wait to see which "big name" preacher in "our circle" becomes the first "spirit-filled" pulpiteer to don the ubiquitous wireless headset microphone?

Preachers in the Laodicean Age who rely on the power of their persona must resort to any number of props and gimmicks to sustain *their* movements. One "Madison Avenue" promoter of whom I am thinking has used an ad for his annual conference that reads, "Win Cash: $3,000-$2,000-$1,000—Call church for details." Can you picture the Ephesian elders receiving such a flyer from the Apostle Paul for *his* "soul winning clinic" in Miletus? Other camps employ different enticements; "Christian" cruises are especially popular (see Acts 27). What does *your* pastor use to draw a crowd apart from the Holy Ghost of God? *Does the truth hurt?* A former student of mine who pastors in New York state, cancelled me for a meeting when I informed him that the *real* "Pentecost Sunday" was *one* Jewish fisherman reaching *three thousand* of his *own* people *on the spot*, without giving them *anything* but an ultimatum, and then seeing *all* of them back in church the following Sunday (Acts 2:41,42); not *2,000* college students beating the bushes for *several weeks* in every *Hamite* neighborhood within driving distance, only to see their "converts" *disappear* after "making church history" ("eclipsing the old record held by the First Baptist Church of Jerusalem," etc.), hauling their mini-bikes, furniture coupons and other prizes away with them. (Now before some of the weaker brethren "freak out" over such needed frankness—just because a preacher blows it in one area does not imply that his lifetime of consecrated service should be slighted; it simply means that the next generation can learn from his mistake.)

Another of my former students, who pastors a fine church in Kentucky, has gotten a better handle on the issue of "power" vs. "promo." The struggle this preacher has been going through began at a meeting we had in 2000 when the Holy Ghost *actually* showed up. Eight adults walked the aisle for salvation after the Sunday morning service; four more came forward that evening; another ten or so did the same by Wednesday night. Neither one of us knew what to do but stand back and watch.

In a candid moment, the man of God confessed, "If I could get one notion out of my head, it would be that 'numbers equal success.' " (I Timothy 6:5)

I'll never forget how his eyes opened wide when I gave him the following solution: The biggest hang-up American pastors have stems from their failure to realize a single enlightening truth—while they think, and therefore, act like *Japheth* ("enlargement," the name literally meaning "extension"), their boss is a *Shemite*. (See bumper sticker: "I work for a Jewish carpenter from Nazareth.") While *Japheth* is pragmatic and will do *anything* to grow a ministry (e.g., the satanic "Purpose Driven Church"), Shem will shut down a mighty revival so the evangelist can visit a solitary Hamite in the desert. (Acts 8:26-39) Japheth is committed to growth at any price; Shem is committed to truth. (Isaiah 66:1-2)

One of the great keys to pastoring in the West is learning to accept that a certain amount of "waste" will often be factored into our well-intended efforts to "do something for God," etc. When our alabaster box breaks and the precious ointment falls to the ground, it's *never* in vain *if* it first trickles down our lovely Saviour's brow. *"And Jesus said, Let her alone; why trouble ye her? she hath wrought a good work **on me**"* (Mark 14:6). Thus, our waste becomes His cologne—*if* we let Him have it with the right spirit. (II Corinthians 9:7) E. Margaret Clarkson wrote:

> So send I you to leave your life's ambition,
> To die to dear desire, self-will resign,
> To labor long, and love where men revile you—
> So send I you to lose your life in Mine.

But, alas, most "preachers" in twenty-first century America would rather sell their souls to the devil than be deprived of homage from their worthless peers. When it comes to pure asininity, Jerry Falwell continues to lead the pack! If you need proof that God messes with the minds of those who mess with "The Book," just read the following ad that appeared on the Publisher's Page of the November 2004 *National Liberty Journal:*

Put Jerry on Your Desk

The Flames Club, Liberty University's sports booster club that sponsors athletic scholarships to the university, has come up with an interesting new fundraising tool—the Jerry Falwell Bobblehead. National Liberty Journal and Liberty Update are joining with the Flames Club to help in this school effort.

The Falwell bobbleheads are available for a cost of only $20 (which includes shipping and handling fees). What's more, Dr. Falwell will autograph and personalize dolls for donations of $50. (Dr. Falwell signs the dolls on the back in a gold pen. Because of size limitations, a typical two-line signature reads: "To John and Mary, Jerry Falwell.") The dolls are packaged in bubble wrap and sent out in sturdy boxes to those making orders.

Alumni who purchased the bobbleheads during homecoming weekend found them to be great reminders of their days at Liberty.[68]

The bobblehead has Jerry holding *a* "Bible" in his right hand. On my one, and only, visit to Liberty University (in the late 1990s) the manager of the campus bookstore was unable to show me a single King James Bible, although a variety of perverted translations were prominently displayed. Thus, we have a bobblehead of a bobblehead holding a bobble-Bible being shipped in bubble wrap to any number of bubble brains who would shell out $20 for the keepsake!

In a *National Liberty Journal* news release the previous month, Jerry's affinity for *the* "Church" behind the modern "Bible" movement was reaffirmed for the umpteenth time. The article states, "Dr. Falwell credits four conservative giants that preserved freedom and truth in the last decades of the 20th century—Ronald Reagan, Margaret Thatcher, **Pope John Paul II** and Jesse Helms."[69]

Getting back to reality, can you think of any other areas to guard against? The temptation usually lies in an opportunity to promote ourselves. The use of our personal testimony can be an effective tool in witnessing (Acts 9:1-16, 22:1-16, 26:9-18); on the other hand, it can also lead to self-aggrandizement. (Romans 12:3) Throw in a website, some prayer cards and a few color brochures, and the danger level increases. Incidentally, don't think I am any less tempted than you are; who do you think wrote the "About the Author" section in my first two books? (Hint: Probably the president of Grady Publications, Inc.) And, yes, one of my five degrees *is* an "honorary" doctorate. (Confession is good for the soul.)

Most people talk far more than they should and frequently give their opinions about anything and everything (whether solicited or not). The wisest man who ever lived wrote, *"Even a fool, when he holdeth his peace, is counted wise: and he that shutteth his lips is esteemed a man of understanding"* (Proverbs 17:28). The word "study" is used only three times in the entire Bible; Paul exhorted the Thessalonians, *"And that ye study to be quiet"* (I Thessalonians 4:11a).

Brethren, the message is really quite simple—it's not about *you* and it's not about *me*; it's *all* about the lovely Lord Jesus Christ—*period*! Someone has said that the last three letters in the word "Christian" stand for "I am *nothing*." When the priests and Levites from Jerusalem asked John the Baptist, *"Who art thou?"* and *"What sayest thou of thyself?"* (John 1:19,22), the man of God could only reply, *"I am the voice of one crying in the wilderness, Make straight the way of the Lord, as said the prophet Esaias"* (John 1:23). He then fades out of the picture with the words that mark his spiritual legacy: *"He must increase, but I must decrease"* (John 3:30). As to how the Saviour recognizes those who refuse *"honour one of another,"* preferring *"the honour that cometh from God only"* (John 5:44), Jesus would later say, *"Among them that are born of women there hath not risen a greater than John the Baptist"* (Matthew 11:11a).

AMERICA'S PREACHER

On October 15, 1989, America received the greatest picture of Laodicean apostasy imaginable. If you go to 6901 Hollywood Boulevard you will find a star in the cement commemorating the life of a man who has been listed in Gallup's "Ten Most Admired Men in the World" poll over forty consecutive years! (John 15:19) Of the over twenty-two hundred "gods" enshrined along the historic crossroads at Hollywood and Vine, *one* stands out for its uniqueness, a local reporter describing the unlikely recipient as "the first of his profession to be so honored." Drum roll please: Star number nineteen hundred was awarded to none other than America's foremost hireling and the Vatican's greatest undercover agent— "your friend and mine"—*Evangelist Dr. Billy Graham!* Some of Billy's fellow "cement mates" include: Hugh Hefner, Alice Cooper, Frank Sinatra, Michael Jackson, George Burns, Jimi Hendrix, Johnny Carson, David Copperfield, Little Richard, Arnold Schwarzenegger, Liberace, The Beatles, Ronald Reagan, Britney Spears, Marilyn Monroe, Jane Mansfield, Mae West, Lassie, Mickey Mouse, and, last but not least, *God*zilla. (Were John the Baptist alive today, they would *bury* him in the cement!)

The only award any more revealing of Billy's "commitment" to truth was the honorary Doctor of Humane Letters (D.H.L.) he received on November 21, 1967, from the Roman Catholic Belmont Abbey College in Belmont, North Carolina. Paul Smith of the *Gastonia Gazette* quoted the proud honoree as stating he "knew of no greater honor a North Carolina preacher, reared just a few miles from here (Charlotte), could have than to be presented with this degree. I'm not sure but what this could start me being called 'Father Graham,' he facetiously added."[70] Uttering such blasphemy in the shadow of Sandy Creek Baptist Church, Billy went on to say, "The gospel that built this school and the gospel that brings me here tonight is still the way to salvation."[71] As his worldwide ministry had been jumpstarted by the Catholic newspaper magnate, William Randolph Hurst, Billy couldn't help becoming a pawn of Rome.

After a half-century of kissing the pope's toe, basking in the glory of Hollywood and reigning as the most admired man in the world, Billy finally came clean during a January 2, 2000, interview with FOX *News* commentator Tony Snow. When it came to a basic understanding of the Gospel, the most famous preacher on the planet didn't have a clue!

> Snow: When you get to Heaven, who's going to speak first, you or God?
>
> Graham: When I get there, I'm sure that Jesus is going to say that he will welcome me. But I think that he's going to say: "Well done, our good and faithful servant." **Or he may say, "You're in the wrong place."**
>
> Snow: You really worry that you may be told you're in the wrong place?
>
> Graham: **Yes**, because I have not—**I'm not a righteous man.** People put me up on a pedestal that I don't belong in my personal life. And they think that I am better than I am. I'm not the good man that people think I am. Newspapers and magazines and television have made me out to be a saint. I'm not. **I'm not a Mother Teresa.** And I feel that very much.[72]

Thus, the more you donate to the various tsunami relief agencies, the better your chances for getting into Heaven, etc. When I called the Billy Graham Evangelistic Association in Minneapolis and demanded an explanation for this unconscionable travesty, I was politely informed that "this was simply Dr. Graham's way of being humble."

With one foot on a banana peel and the other in the grave, Billy got blindsided in 2002 by the release of a thirty-year-old tape on which he was heard telling President Richard Nixon that the Jews had a "stranglehold" on the American media which had "to be broken or the country's going down the drain."[73] He later mentions that he has friends in the media who are Jewish, saying, "They swarm around me and are friendly to me"; he then goes on to confide in "Tricky Dicky" (as the tape continues to roll), "They don't know how I really feel about what they're doing to this country."[74] After Nixon relates that eleven of the twelve writers for *Rowan and Martin's Laugh-In* are Jewish, Billy reacts with surprise, "That right?" In the 1960s, *Laugh-In* was *the* cutting edge program for risqué dialogue and plenty of flesh.

Having denied rumors of anti-Semitism for decades, Billy was now forced to make an official apology. But why should anyone be surprised that a chameleon with a doctorate from Rome would harbor animosity for Jews? In his formal statement, Billy covered himself by stating that he "did not recall" making the insensitive remarks, etc.

Now before you go and rush to judgment about Billy being the president's spiritual mentor and all that, there's something you ought to know. When Dr. Graham appeared on *Larry King Live*, December 21, 2000, King specifically asked him about the life-changing encounter Bush claimed to have had with him at Kennebunkport in 1985. Billy replied, "I don't remember that particular one."[75] But never fear, Bush apologist Dr. Stephen Mansfield has already covered "Dubya's" (expletive) by offering a much better "conversion" account that antedates the "Billy Mustard Seed" story by a full year. On pages 64-65 in his 2003 "classic," *The Faith of George W. Bush*, Stevie gives the "Religious Right" exactly what they need—a *perfectly* worded, "one-two-three, repeat-after-me" sinner's prayer. This time, the "mighty evangelist" who brought Bush to God was none other than Arthur Blessitt, a long-haired, Charismatic wacko who walks around the world carrying a wooden cross on his shoulder! According to "Brother" Art's website, he has now made the pilgrimage to 303 nations, having covered 36,651 miles since Jesus first "told" him to go in September 1969. Appropriately, the "man of God" launched his worldwide trek from *Hollywood* on Christmas Day. Though failing to capture the White House in 1976, Blessitt did earn a slot in the *Guinness Book of Records* for the "World's Longest Walk." And if all goes well, his high-mileage cross is scheduled to blast off into outer space aboard a special satellite on January 26, 2005, five days after his famous "convert" is inaugurated for a second term.

In a follow-up article by *MSNBC* entitled "Bush—born again, or not?," Alex Johnson pointed out the obvious contradiction, stating, "Any discussion of President Bush's presumed evangelicalism is complicated." After noting that the president's autobiography failed to mention Blessitt's version, the secular journalist rightly concludes: "George Bush has not said directly that he was ever born again. He has often said he was pointed on the path to God after a discussion with evangelist Billy Graham in 1985."[76]

Oh well, to quote Chuck Ohman, "Jesus is coming back soon and will straighten out everything then." Boy—will He *ever*! For the record, even Dr. Mansfield left himself a little "wiggle room," conceding in his final chapter, "On many issues, Bush is less doctrinaire than his faith would make him appear, and this too is part of the mystery of George W. Bush."[77]

THE MASTER RACE

About this time, some paranoid conspiracy addict like Texe Marrs would attempt to discredit the thesis of my book, pointing out that Jews *do* run the media, Hollywood, the ACLU and many other key facets of the nation's economic and cultural infrastructure. In an address to a Jewish pro-life group gathered at Catholic University on November 12, 1998, Ben Stein, a television personality, as well as a man of letters, revealed:

> The head of every major Hollywood studio is Jewish. The heads of all the networks are Jewish. The heads of two out of the four national newspapers are Jewish. The heads of every Ivy League university are Jewish.[78]

It is also noteworthy that Jews pioneered and dominated the precursor to motion pictures—the Broadway musical. Legends such as Florenz Ziegfeld, Irving Berlin, George Gershwin, Richard Rodgers, Oscar Hammerstein, Artie Shaw, Jerome Kern, Al Jolson, Eddie Cantor, Sophie Tucker, and Fanny Brice ensured that the name "Broadway" lived up to its Biblical type—*"for wide is the gate, and **broad** is the **way**, that leadeth to destruction, and many there be which go in thereat"* (Matthew 7:13b).

And yes, their collective impact on the moral deterioration of America is without question. (See smut purveyors Howard Stern and Jerry Springer.) However, there is a Biblical explanation for this enigma that is beyond the reach of unbalanced folk like Marrs.

While Jewish people have the same capacity for civility as anyone else, they are frequently the most contentious people on earth. The Bible agrees, declaring in I Thessalonians 2:15b, *"and they please not God, and are contrary to all men."* When David Ben-Gurion visited the White House in 1948, President Truman remarked that it must be wonderful being prime minister of the new State of Israel; whereupon, Ben-Gurion replied: "Mr. President, I am prime minister of 500,000 prime ministers!"

The underlying cause for this air of superiority will utterly astound you. While coon hunting one evening I asked my guide the following question: "How in the world does a *human* teach a *dog* how to chase a *raccoon* up a tree? The man replied in the most nonchalant manner— "You don't; *it's in their genes.*"

According to the Word of God, the city of Jerusalem is destined to become the literal capital of the entire universe. The prophet Zechariah wrote:

> *Thus saith the LORD of hosts; It shall yet come to pass, that there shall come people, and the inhabitants of many cities: And the inhabitants of one city shall go to another, saying, Let us go speedily to pray before the LORD, and to seek the LORD of hosts: I will go also. Yea, many people and strong nations shall come to seek the LORD of hosts in Jerusalem, and to pray before the LORD. Thus saith the LORD of hosts; In those days it shall come to pass, that ten men shall take hold out of all languages of the nations, even shall take hold of the skirt of him that is a Jew, saying, We will go with you: for we have heard that God is with you.* (Zechariah 8:20-23)

Thus, the reason why Jews can be so antagonistic and, often downright arrogant, is because *it is in their genes to run the world!* Hitler was right in his belief about a master race; he just picked the wrong race! The problem is that *"blindness in part is happened to Israel, until the fulness of the Gentiles be come in"* (Romans 11:25b). Because the Jews have rejected their national Messiah— *"when Moses is read, the vail is upon their heart"* (II Corinthians 3:15b).

Consequently, while a Jew is "wired to rule," he exists in a world of intense frustration because he cannot see that his unbelief has technically consigned him to the wrong dispensation. Though the Bible declares, *"And so all Israel shall be saved"* (Romans 11:26a), the Jews—as an unconverted race—have always posed a threat to whatever nation would accommodate them. The problem is simple—*they can't help being endowed with superior capabilities*—which fact has inevitably led to their persecution and/or banishment. And as previously discussed, the ubiquitous pogrom led many Jews to resist through various secret societies, especially in Roman Catholic lands.

Dr. Oscar Levy was a Jewish intellectual of immense stature both in England and America. In response to a request from his Gentile colleague, Professor George Pitt-Rivers of Worcester College, Oxford, for a review of his manuscript entitled *The World Significance of the Russian Revolution*, Dr. Levy wrote in 1920:

> **There is no race in the world more enigmatic, more fatal, and therefore more interesting than the Jews.**
>
> Every writer, who, like yourself, is oppressed by the aspect of the present and embarrassed by his anxiety for the future, must try to elucidate the Jewish Question and its bearing upon our Age.
>
> For the question of the Jews and their influence on the world, past and present, cuts to the root of all things, and should be discussed by every honest thinker, however bristling with difficulties it is, however complex the subject as well as the individuals of this race may be. . . .
>
> **There is no doubt that the Jews regularly go one better or worse than the Gentile in whatever they do, there is no further doubt that their influence today justifies a very careful scrutiny, and cannot possibly be viewed without serious alarm.** The great question, however, is whether the Jews are conscious or unconscious malefactors. I myself am firmly convinced that they are unconscious ones, but please do not think that I wish to exonerate them on that account. . . . A conscious evildoer has my respect, for he knows at least what is good; an unconscious one—well, he needs the charity of Christ—a charity which is not mine—to be forgiven for not knowing what he is doing; **But there is in my firm conviction not the slightest doubt that these revolutionary Jews do not know what they are doing; that they are more unconscious sinners than voluntary evildoers. . . . You have noticed with alarm that the Jewish elements provide the driving forces for both Communism and Capitalism, for the material as well as the spiritual ruin of this world. . . .** [79]

I have often been told that older Jewish men tend to suffer serious bouts of depression for not having made a greater mark on their world, such aspirations having been instilled by the local rabbi in their youth. As Dr. Levy continues, note how he shares this very burden on behalf of Jews everywhere:

> I confess it you, openly and sincerely, and with a sorrow, whose depth and pain an ancient Psalmist, and only he, could moan into this burning universe of ours. . . . **We who have posed as the saviors of the world, we have even boasted of having given it "the" Savior, we are today nothing else but the world's seducers, its destroyers, its incendiaries,**

its executioners. . . . We have promised to lead you to a new Heaven, we have finally succeeded in landing you into a new Hell. . . . There has been no progress, least of all moral progress. . . . And it is just our Morality, which has prohibited all real progress, and—what is worse—which even stands in the way of every future and natural reconstruction in this ruined world of ours. . . . I look at this world, and I shudder at its ghastliness; I shudder all the more as I know the spiritual authors of all this ghastliness.[80]

While Dr. Levy blamed the world's ills on the failed morality of *his* race, such an appraisal, though a noble one, is inconsistent with the teaching of Scripture. The great unwritten *spiritual* history of America has been a confluence of three powerful forces: political, economic and moral. As previously discussed, our nation's unique separation of church and state, occasioned by the First Amendment, afforded a providential haven for persecuted Jewry. With Genesis 12:3 provided as the earnest of our potential for prosperity (i.e., "the sky's the limit"), the Jew was able to enter the free enterprise system with his decided edge in turning a profit. Having grown up in Manhattan, my aged father told me that the Jewish owner of a local jewelry store would shoo him away from lingering in front of his shop. "Stay 'avay' from my 'vindow,' he would say. "Let the sun shine in on my diamonds." Over six decades after my father heard those eccentric words, the chairman of the board at the Federal Reserve is a Jew by the name of Alan Greenspan!

What Dr. Levy did not, and could not, understand is that America's first line of defense in the *morality* department, has always been the responsibility of Christians, not Jews. The Saviour enjoined His disciples, *"Ye are the salt of the earth: but if the salt have lost his savour, wherewith shall it be salted? it is thenceforth good for nothing, but to be cast out, and to be trodden under foot of men"* (Matthew 5:13). Our nation was born in the Philadelphia Church Age when the average believer had a testimony strong enough to keep the sin of his unsaved neighbors *relatively* in check. This is why the visiting Alexis de Tocqueville would write in the early part of the nineteenth century, "Upon my arrival in America the religious aspect of the country was the first thing that struck my attention . . ."[81] When the "Old Time Religion" was more than just a song, our forefathers had the "strange" idea that a correlation existed between the morals of a country and its belief in the doctrine of a literal Hell. While sinners in modern America can find refuge in any number of compromising, Hell-denying "churches" (i.e., the "Dubya-Billy" rapport), such was not the case in our nation's earliest days. When an unsaved person visited the Baptist church in town, he was certain to hear, "If you don't get 'borned ag'in,' you'll split Hell wide open!" Petrified, he would run out of the building and flee into the First Presbyterian Church next door. Because the minister appeared more reserved, the sinner was prone to lower his guard. This time, the shocking message was, *"If you're not one of the elect*, you'll split Hell wide open, and there's nothing you can do about it either!" Having staggered out the back door and across the street into the last church in town, the poor wretch is last seen jumping out the window with the Methodist preacher screaming at the top of his lungs, "Even if you *are* born again, you can still lose it and split Hell wide open anyway!"

In fact, eighteenth-century America was *so* far to the Right that Christmas celebrations were actually banned, as many felt the holiday was based more on paganism than Scripture. The Pilgrims had set the pace back in 1620 by spending *their* first Christmas in the New World initiating construction on the colony's first building for common usage.

Thus, the crux of the matter may be summarized by a combination of the following observations. First, while Jews have the same unregenerate flesh as Gentiles (I Corinthians 15:39), they have a greater propensity for money and material things. The cause for this unique racial trait is twofold: Their *genes* tell them they are destined to "inherit the earth"; their *history* teaches that their very survival depends on cunning. The psalmist wrote, *"If I forget thee, O Jerusalem, let my right hand forget her cunning"* (Psalm 137:5). As I stated in chapter two, old habits are hard to break. One Jewish writer has captured the essence of Jacob's instinct for resourcefulness with an amusing anecdote:

> It was a terrible discovery. Some scientists had conducted an investigation and determined, to their horror, that the polar icecaps had begun melting at such a rate that in six months most of the inhabited world would be under 500 feet of water. The calculations were checked and rechecked by other scientists. There was no doubt that Judgment Day was at hand. Panic set in and religious leaders around the world began preparing their flocks for the great beyond. Billy Graham, the Archbishop of Canterbury and all the other Protestant ministers implored their minions to repent, repent, repent, and prepare to meet their Maker. From Rome the Pope put forth a proclamation ordering all Catholics to Mass every hour on the hour to confess and beg forgiveness. In Israel, however, it was a bit different. The

Chief Rabbi of Jerusalem issued an injunction: "Jews of the world. You have six months in which to learn living under 500 feet of water."[82]

Second, not only is a Jew more disposed to filthy lucre as a proven means to his survival, but as previously noted, he is also endowed with the ability to fulfill this inherent drive. Someone has said that the main reason Gentiles hate Jews is because Gentiles love money and Jews know how to make it! An old expression among Jewish merchants goes, "Jesus saves, but Moses invests."

Finally, when the heavy waves of Jewish immigration began arriving at Ellis Island in the late nineteenth century, the nation as a whole was still under the restraining moral influence of the Philadelphia Church Age (the devil's major strongholds being the emerging metropolitan centers with their decidedly Catholic populations). Consequently, the majority of money-making opportunities in early *Goldenah Medinah* were limited to the recognized professions of medicine, law, business and finance.

However, this would all begin to change with the onset of Laodicean apostasy occasioned by the modern Bible movement. While the *Revised Version* of 1881 and the *American Standard Version* of 1901 set the deterioration in motion, the bottom fell out after the arrival of the *New American Standard Version*. And so, as Christians began to lower *their* standards the rest of the population took advantage, following the dictates of their Adamic nature. (II Samuel 12:14a) With less and less preaching against the "picture show" and the local high school dance, suddenly the market for sin began to expand.

Now can you see where the Jew fits in? The profound truth of the matter is that *the Body of Christ determines how many potential customers the merchants of smut will have.* For instance, don't blame the Jews for taking control of the lucrative pornography industry (pioneered by *Gentiles* such as Hugh Hefner, Larry Flynt and Bob Guccione); it would be against their *nature* to turn away patrons with cash in hand. Not even a Jew can market sin without clients, and clients are produced by apostate Christians. If you're looking for the *real* "conspirators" responsible for the destruction of America, try any number of Bible correctors like Rick Warren, best-selling author of the sacrosanct *Purpose Driven* series, as well as the faculties of Bob Jones University, Liberty University, Tennessee Temple University, Baptist Bible College, Detroit Baptist Seminary, Northland Baptist Bible College, Piedmont Baptist College, and Maranatha Baptist Bible College. And don't trust any of those tuition-hungry schools that merely pay lip service to the King James Bible. *You ought to know who I'm talking about by now!* They usually want to project an "intellectual defense" of the King James version, a path that inevitably leads to promoting the *Textus Receptus* as the higher authority.

In 1998, following a five-year resurgence of the A.V. 1611—described in the October 23, 1995, edition of *Christianity Today* as "a grassroots backlash against contemporary English-language Bibles"—Pensacola Christian College attempted to cash in on the momentum by releasing a three-part video series affirming their *own* "militant" stand on the issue. Dr. Del Johnson, the effeminate-sounding "girly-man" professor who conducted the seminar, ended his remarks by ridiculing my own work on the subject, a 400-page, hardback volume entitled *Final Authority: A Christian's Guide to the King James Bible.* By the time PCC had decided to jump on the KJV bandwagon, *Final Authority* was already in its ninth printing, being used as a textbook in over two hundred Bible institutes, colleges and seminaries. After a host of unsavory comments in which he misrepresented my position, criticized other KJV advocates, and blatantly contradicted himself, the former PCC instructor labeled me an "extremist." Having included 1,026 endnotes, 183 bibliography entries, a twelve-page index, a glossary of terms, and a glossary of proper names—I can only assume that Del was referring to my *research*.

In summary, like the manacled prisoner being guarded by the sheriff near the campfire, that aspiring Jewish entrepreneur cannot hurt America *unless* the Church falls asleep on the job.

Silly Women

As anemic twenty-first century Laodiceans grow *more* addicted to "the *box*" and *less* acquainted with "the *Book*," America's females (saved and lost alike) will continue to imbibe the deadliest poison of all. In his prophetic passage to Timothy, the Apostle Paul described a scenario where evil men would be able to creep into the houses of sin-laden silly women, leading them away to captivity through divers lusts. (II Timothy 3:6) Can you think of an easier way for Satan to fulfill this ancient prophecy than through television? (See: the *Lifetime* channel.) Has more than one generation of evil men (known as Hollywood executives) sent a legion of "creeps" into our very living rooms via the "boob tube"? You tell me—

Is a demon-possessed, billionaire, Hamite, New Ager by the name of Oprah Winfrey the reigning guru for the white women of this nation? Could a steady diet of corrupt televangelists like Benny Hinn, Rod Parsley, T. D. Jakes, Jesse Duplantis, Oral and Richard Roberts, Paul Crouch, Creflo Dollar, John Hagee, Joel Osteen, Robert Tilton and Kenneth Copeland have anything to do with an increase of Charismatic activity in our Baptist churches? How many demons do you think are afflicting the "weaker vessels" of this land as they watch such "women preachers" as Paula White, Joyce Meyers, Marilyn Hickey, Gloria Copeland and Jan "Baby Doll Dresses" Crouch? (And we thought Tammy Bakker was bad!)

As for primetime viewing, it is easy to see where the concept of "reality" television comes from. Just try to find "reality" in the slate of "normal" programs; *feminism and affirmative action agendas rule the airwaves!* Typically, shows that really put Japheth in his place revolve around criminal investigation, courtroom drama and hospital emergencies. The *subliminal* script is hilarious: white woman detective drops bad guy with powerful roundhouse kick; black woman FBI agent grills nervous white male suspect; white female prosecutor consistently defeats white male counterpart; black doctor bails out white subordinate; yada, yada, yada. (For a dose of *real "reality," see patrol car footage of white female police officer getting the snot beaten out of her by black male traffic violator.*)

Like her prototype in the Garden, the "last Eve" is about as mixed up as "Hogan's goat." While visiting a library in North Carolina, I overheard a conversation that perfectly illustrates "why America is finished." A woman patron approached the desk and asked, "Do you have any more of those *Left Behind* books?" When the librarian replied, "No," the woman then inquired, "Do you have any *Harry Potter* ones?" (So much for Timmy LaHaye and his money-making "Christian" fantasy series.)

"A PICTURE OF THE CITY"

If I may now turn your attention back to that infamous debacle in Denver; just what kind of a "church" do you suppose Mayor Hickenlooper encountered? Well, guess what—While plenty of end-day apostates instinctively distance themselves from the reproachful tag of "Baptist," Reverend George's congregation took the pragmatism a step further.

Come to find out, according to their website, they're not even a "church" after all, their official name being listed as "Faith Bible *Chapel—A Family of Faith.*"

After a brief telephone call to the "chapel," I was able to confirm what I had already surmised—Faith Bible Chapel is a non-denominational, Charismatic assembly that specializes in music and drama. The 4,000-member operation is overseen by a staff of twenty-five "ministry leaders." Among other "extras," the "chapel" features an atrium café, dinner theater, a dance troupe, and informal monthly communion services. The receptionist with whom I spoke told me that their people were so hopped-up about Mel Gibson's *Passion* that they rented a local theater for an entire week! Conversely, the "preaching" is so "edifying" that the Sunday evening services have been cancelled.

As to Scripture preference, Faith "Bible" utilizes the *New King James Version* in their Sunday mega-services. For the record, the NKJV made over 100,000 changes to the text of the Authorized Version. In I Corinthians 1:21b, *"the foolishness of preaching"* is altered to "the foolishness of the message preached." The occultic Mobius symbol (serpent noad) on the spine should have been a dead giveaway. Popularized by Satanist Aleister Crowley (circa 1900), this ancient depiction of 666 was also featured on the cover of Led Zeppelin's rock album *The Presence*, as well as New Age author Marilyn Ferguson's *The Aquarian Conspiracy.*

By the way, in case you're wondering what type of "Christian" witness the Faith Bible Chapel had intended to display, Jean Torkelson of the *Rocky Mountain News* cites the pastor accordingly: "I was thinking of a float, a little choir, some musicians and a cross-cultural band," that would include Hispanic and black Christians, he said. "A picture of the city."[83] (A likeminded congregation in my own city conducted a Sunday morning Christmas "service" in 2004 featuring a Gospel-preaching, ice-skating ballerina!)

Do you understand how things work now? A sorry bunch of Charismatic tongues-speakers plan a "Christian" version of "We Are The World," and a dupe of the Jewish-dominated ACLU gets to proscribe the entry and then mock the rejects as well! How's *this* for adding insult to injury? According to an article in *Free Republic*:

> The Allied Jewish Federation of Colorado has announced that Denver Mayor John Hickenlooper will once again light the community Menorah on the first night of Chanukah. . . .

"I look forward to joining the Denver Jewish community in lighting the community Menorah again this year," said Mayor John Hickenlooper, who will make his second consecutive appearance at the Federation's ceremony. "Chanukah brings communities across Colorado and the world together in celebration of light, freedom and peace." . . .

"We are honored that Mayor Hickenlooper will once again be taking part in our community Menorah lighting ceremony," stated Doug Seserman, President and CEO of Federation. "The Mayor's presence represents Denver's support and observance of this important Jewish holiday and we appreciate his participation," Seserman continued.[84]

It is not without significance that the greatest concentration of Laodicean apostasy in America "just happens" to be located less than an hour to the south of Mayor Hickenlooper's parade route. The city of Colorado Springs is home to over a hundred para-church organizations, with Dr. James Dobson reigning as the local "godfather."

OY VEY!

Concerning the "Boss of Bosses," do you recall how Billy Graham showed surprise when President Nixon informed him that eleven of the twelve writers for *Rowan and Martin's Laugh-In* were Jewish? His exact response was, "That right?" As both men were well aware that *Laugh-In* pushed the envelope of morality on a weekly basis, the "preacher" had to show the greater revulsion, especially given the fact that Jews were to blame, etc. Personally, I find this rather amusing. Having watched the filthy show religiously as a lost Catholic teenager, even after all these years I can *still* remember when "Reverend" Graham graced the broadcast with his presence. (*Oy Vey!*) If I'm not mistaken, I believe his classic one-liner was—"The family that *laughs* together *stays* together."

AL, BOB, ED, SAM AND HYMAN

On a more *positive* note, we can all rejoice that such perversion cannot go on much longer. Our Saviour's return must surely be close at hand. Praise God, we will not have to experience the reign of the greatest usurper of all time. (Revelation 13:8) When the Lord gets through with this planet after the Tribulation period, the desolation will make the 2004 tsunami look like a Sunday School picnic! (Matthew 24:21; Revelation 8:8, 9) According to Revelation, chapters 16-18, Jack Van Impe's "buddy" is going to be in a world of hurt! John wrote, *"And the great city was divided into three parts, and the cities of the nations fell: and great Babylon came in remembrance before God, to give unto her the cup of the wine of the fierceness of his wrath"* (Revelation 16:19).

With the United States crippled by the Rapture, the most likely scenario to follow would have the leader of spiritual Babylon (a.k.a. "El Papa") providing the "moral" *casus belli* at the U.N. for the secular European federation of Antichrist to break its treaty with Israel in the midst of Daniel's seventieth week. (Daniel 9:27) Consequently, the Lord gave *"His* people" a specific warning in Revelation 18:4a: *"And I heard another voice from heaven, saying, Come out of her,* **my people**, *that ye be not partakers of her sins."* That Israel is the subject is confirmed by the cross reference in Jeremiah 51:6: *"Flee out of the midst of Babylon, and deliver every man his soul: be not cut off in her iniquity; for this is the time of the LORD'S vengeance; he will render unto her a recompence."* With regard to the necessary preliminaries, which have drawn our military forces into the region of historical Babylon, you might want to read verse eleven: *"Make bright the arrows; gather the shields:* **the LORD hath raised up the spirit of the kings of the Medes**: *for his device is against Babylon, to destroy it; because it is the vengeance of the LORD, the vengeance of his temple"* (Jeremiah 51:11). Would you say that the "spirit" of the *Medes* has been stirred up enough to allow a prophecy by Zephaniah to begin unfolding before our very eyes? *"Therefore wait ye upon me, saith the LORD, until the day that I rise up to the prey: for my determination is to gather the nations, that I may assemble the kingdoms, to pour upon them mine indignation, even all my fierce anger: for all the earth shall be devoured with the fire of my jealousy"* (Zephaniah 3:8).

From the looks of Revelation 17:16, 18:8-10 and 17-19, the EU just might nuke "His Holiness!" (This would not be the first time Satan's capital was "bombed." On the day before Easter Sunday 1991, Evangelist Bill Eubanks "banked" a Cessna 172 over the pope's obelisk at about 800 feet while his petite helpmeet Janet *dumped a payload of 85,000 Italian-language Chick tracts on the startled "pilgrims" below!* See *13 Minutes Over the Vatican* by Brother Eubanks.) With a weekly church attendance of 3 percent across the Continent, roughly 97 percent of indigenous

Europeans are Catholic in name only. However, in a most intriguing passage, the Lord appears to instruct "His people" to take the Vatican out. *"Reward her even as she rewarded you, and double unto her double according to her works: in the cup which she hath filled fill to her double"* (Revelation 18:6).

Though neither a prophet, nor the son of a prophet (Amos 7:14), I believe I can discern at least one way in which the efforts of certain Jews may have *indirectly* paved the way for the eventual destruction of *"that great city which reigneth over the kings of the earth"* (Revelation 17:18). To begin with, while the Lord assured Noah that He would never destroy the world again with *water*, He didn't say anything about "nukes." Looking into the future, a Jewish fisherman wrote in 60 A.D.:

> *"But the day of the Lord will come as a thief in the night; in the which the heavens shall pass away with a great noise, and the elements shall melt with fervent heat, the earth also and the works that are therein shall be burned up. . . . Looking for and hasting unto the coming of the day of God, wherein the heavens being on fire shall be dissolved, and the elements shall melt with fervent heat . . . "* (II Peter 3:10,12)

Now, remember our little study that revolved around "coon dogs?" Well, if a *Jewish* king is going to *melt the elements* in the not-too-distant future, should we be surprised to learn that His brethren have a similar propensity to things nuclear? (i.e., "It's in the genes.") How's *this* for a "Jewish conspiracy": Albert *Einstein*, Father of the Atomic Age; Robert J. *Oppenheimer*, Father of the Atom Bomb; Edward *Teller*, Father of the Hydrogen Bomb; Sam *Cohen*, Father of the Neutron Bomb; Hyman *Rickover*, Father of the Nuclear Submarine. Now try *real* hard to guess what these five men have in common! (I'll give you a hint: "Stay 'avay' from my 'vindow.'")

As of this writing (December 2004), Mr. Cohen is still alive and will be eighty-four years old in January. It has been my privilege to have had over two dozen interviews with this esteemed physicist, our initial discussions being occasioned by his participation in the Oklahoma bombing investigation. While the Lord has opened many doors for me since I began this volume in January 1999, the connection with Mr. Cohen has been unlike all the rest. For reasons known only to God, He allowed our professional relationship to develop into a warm friendship. (Matthew 11:19) In his personal memoirs entitled *Shame: Confessions of the Father of the Neutron Bomb*, the author professes to be an atheist, a common ideology among Jewish scientists. (Obviously, he would strongly disagree with most of the ideological views expressed in this book.) Yet, the Holy Spirit has afforded me several opportunities to give Mr. Cohen the Gospel, and I continue to pray for his soul. (Perhaps you could join me in claiming II Corinthians 3:16 in his behalf?)

Of the many historical nuggets I have gleaned from our talks, one bears a particular significance to my thesis regarding God's plan for the Jews to exact revenge on the "Great Whore." The custodian of this momentous link to the past was born on a kitchen table in Brooklyn, New York, in 1921. At the age of twenty-two, he was assigned to the Manhattan Project in Los Alamos, New Mexico, to work on "Fat Man," the atomic bomb that was later dropped on Nagasaki. In his memoirs, Mr. Cohen acknowledges, "I will say that regarding nuclear weapons, Jews, by far and away, have had a disproportionate effect on their development and the policies for their use."[85] Already beyond the four-score mark, the retired scientist has no use for computers and never even learned how to use a pocket calculator. Talk about natural endowments—he made his original calculations for the neutron bomb on a simple slide rule his father gave him for his fifteenth birthday.[86] As only a Jew could, he makes a joke about nuclear weapons, stating: "Thank God the Fathers, at least the ones I know of, of all these bombs have been Jewish; can you imagine how much more insidious these weapons, especially the neutron bomb, would have been were they parented by Jewish mothers?"[87]

Thus, without further adieu, you might call the following eyewitness account given by the Father of the Neutron Bomb an unintentional commentary on Revelation 18:6. (Keep in mind that nearly all of Hitler's henchmen, including the Fuehrer himself, were members of the Roman Catholic "Church"; see *Hitler's Pope: The Secret History of Pius II* by award-winning journalist John Cornwell.) Mr. Cohen writes with regard to his work at Los Alamos:

> Going from the lowest (symbolized by yours truly) to the highest at the lab, there was the matter of its director, J. Robert Oppenheimer. . . . He was a real sadist, but also one of the greatest Americans of our time. . . . before he left Los Alamos there was [an] episode involving Oppenheimer deservant of the most special mention here. . . .
>
> Rarely, when some of us at the lab discussed our project and its meaning did we dwell very much on the profound moral aspects of what we were

doing. This is not to imply that many of us did not do so privately (I never did). However, when two or more of us got together we never doubted openly that we were doing the right thing for a righteous cause. We were Americans whose country was at war with detestable enemies.

This was particularly true for most Jewish scientists, and there were a lot of them, including Oppenheimer. Many of them were refugees from Hitler, whose friends and relatives had suffered hideously at his hands, and who harbored precious little affection for the Nazis. They had a vindictive and even barbaric compulsion to complete the project in time to bomb Germany. . . .

Undoubtedly nuclear bombing Germany would have made many scientists at Los Alamos, especially the Jews, including myself, deliriously happy. How sweet it would have been, but it would have been the sweetness of revenge, not necessarily of victory. . . .

One August afternoon in 1945, a familiar voice came out over the laboratory intercom. It was the voice of a young lady who usually was paging somebody who somebody else wanted to talk to. . . . This time, however, nobody was being paged. Instead the young lady announced that one of our "units" had been dropped over Japan and that evening Dr. Oppenheimer would address the scientific staff on the matter.

So much for the rest of the day's occupation. The place went into a frenzy of excitement and anticipation of what Oppenheimer was going to say. Long before the time Oppenheimer was supposed to show up, the staff had collected in one of two motion picture theaters at Los Alamos which were used not only for showing movies, but social events like community dances (with a live band that would have given Benny Goodman an instant coronary). . . .

The custom for these colloquia was that Oppenheimer, a very punctual guy, would walk out on stage from one of the wings, make a few general remarks in his own quiet way, and then introduce the speaker. Not this time. He arrived very late and entered the theater from the rear, strode down the aisle while all of us rose and cheered him, stomped our feet and in general behaved like a pack of bloodthirsty savages welcoming back their conquering warriors, who were displaying the heads or genitals, or both, of the conquered.

When Oppenheimer was able to finally quiet down the mob, he set about telling us what little was known about the results of the bombing. There was one thing he knew for sure: the "Japs" (not Japanese) didn't like it. More howling, foot stomping, and the like. **Then he got to the nub of the matter: While we apparently had been successful, and his chest was practically bursting with pride, he did have one deep regret,**

that we hadn't completed the Bomb in time to use against the Germans. That really brought down the house.

This had to be the most fascinating, to say nothing about being the most historic, speech I've ever heard. Apart from those who were there that night, I don't recall ever meeting anyone who had ever heard of it. . . .

Needless to say, when the war was over, there were innumerable articles, books, movies, etc., on the development of the Bomb and its use on Japan. However, none of these even alluded to Oppenheimer's speech on Hiroshima eve. . . . To the best of my knowledge no one ever taped it or took notes, even though it was one of the most momentous and meaningful speeches of our time. . . . I'm afraid . . . that with each passing year, as the ranks of those in attendance that evening grow thinner and thinner, the probability that this historic occasion will be explored in detail by historians grows smaller and smaller.[88]

"Lights, Camera, *Action!*"

As I said earlier, Hallelujah for the Rapture, *"For God hath not appointed us to wrath, but to obtain salvation by our Lord Jesus Christ"* (I Thessalonians 5:9). Yet, let us never forget that our soon departure will leave unconverted family and friends behind. And if I were you, I wouldn't waste any time, for that trumpet is surely out of the case by now!

In fact, one of the most profound eschatological truths in all of Scripture sits unnoticed in the Genesis account of the Flood. Remember that Jesus specifically stated, *"But as the days of Noe were, so shall also the coming of the Son of man be"* (Matthew 24:37).

Well, it "just so happens" that Thomas A. Edison began his laborious research on motion picture technology in 1887 (two years after the *Revised Version* was finished), completing his Kinetograph camera and Kinetoscope viewing apparatus in 1891. The world's first motion picture studio was built two years later. Known as the "Black Maria," it was situated on a turntable so that it could be moved to keep the light of the sun from coming through the roof. The Edison Kinetoscope was a "peep-show" device, housed in a cabinet with an eye-piece on the top. Only one customer at a time could view the show. The first flick was only fifty feet long, with forty-eight pictures being shown per second. The entire movie lasted all of *thirteen* seconds (thirteen being the Biblical number for sin and rebellion). Public exhibition of the Kinetoscope in New York City in 1894 was greeted with wild acclaim.

Following a number of meaningless films shown in conjunction with vaudeville shows, the first movie with an actual story debuted in 1903. Comprising only eight hundred feet of film, "The Great Train Robbery" was an instantaneous phenomenon. Thus, the multi-trillion-dollar entertainment industry was off and running with patrons paying five cents for admission at the local *nickelodeon*. By the eve of World War I, over 10,000,000 Americans were going to the movies daily. The "gods" had finally come down *"in the likeness of men"* (Acts 14:11b).

You say, "Dr. Grady, what does the history of motion pictures have to do with the Second Advent?" Do you recall what our longsuffering God said when those *first* stars began showing up in 2353 B.C.? *"And the LORD said, My spirit shall not always strive with man, for that he also is flesh: yet his days shall be an hundred and twenty years"* (Genesis 6:3). Do the math!

You cannot choose the land of your birth.
You can choose the land you love.

www.amendforarnold.com
November 2004

21

The Little Bitty Baby

"He that sitteth in the heavens shall laugh . . ."
(Psalm 2:4a)

A S THE RAPTURE of the church draws near, world events will grow more chaotic. Only God knows how the quagmire in Iraq will proceed. After several conversations with Mr. Cohen, I am convinced that the great majority of our mounting casualties could have been avoided had the Bush administration employed the neutron bomb. One technical article has described this unique weapon as follows:

> This was a small nuclear weapon designed to do its work, killing enemy military forces, without destroying a country's infrastructure. The idea was to design a fission-fusion bomb in which the number of high-energy neutrons released, the dominant killing mechanism, was maximized while the physical damage-producing mechanism, the fission component, was minimized. Only that minimal amount of plutonium, the fission component, needed to ignite or "burn" a capsule containing a deuterium-tritium mixture, would be used. This deuterium-tritium mixture produced the killing mechanism, a sudden burst of high-energy neutrons, while the fission blast was minimized.[1]

What this essentially means in layman's terms is that a neutron bomb can wipe out an entire neighborhood of "insurgents" without wiping out the neighborhood! The benefits should be readily apparent. First, and foremost, our boys would be spared from having to root out the "rag heads" in precarious urban warfare. Second, the local population would have less reason to hate our guts when they could return to their homes at an appointed time.

Even the Vatican was forced to concede that the neutron bomb, though nuclear in "name," was a far more merciful weapon than generally understood. In 1979, Pope John Paul II awarded Mr. Cohen a peace medal for his invention. The recipient writes:

> Over the first several centuries of Christianity, efforts were made by Catholic scholars to formulate a code of morally acceptable warfare (excuse the oxymoron). Out of this came the theory of Just War, that theoretically still prevails. The most important tenets of Just War theory include all the items that decent Americans of any religious denomination should accept: the right to defend against unwarranted aggression; the desire to keep the battle to the battlefield; the necessity to protect non-combatants and their societal fabric through discriminate means; the requirement to keep the response to aggression as proportionate to the level of aggression as possible; and other obviously decent objectives.[2]

But, of course, such conventional wisdom would have to be rejected as it not only threatened to eliminate the "President Bush—You Killed My Son" tee shirt industry, but the lucrative destroy-rebuild-destroy cycle of Halliburton, Carlyle and other merchants of death as well. Yet, in reality, the debate over employing neutron bombs in Iraq is moot, as we no longer *have* any neutron bombs to employ!

Prior to the 1980 presidential campaign, Mr. Cohen was asked to personally brief Governor Reagan on the tactical advantages of his controversial weapon. As the candidate responded by incorporating Sam's recommendations into his slate of election-year promises, several hundred *hybrid* neutron bomb warheads were subsequently produced and stockpiled during Reagan's two terms in office (known as enhanced radiation reduced blast warheads, consisting of three kilotons of neutrons and three kilotons of fusion). However, they were all destroyed under the reign of "George I." Mr. Cohen informed me that the decision was based primarily on the vigorous remonstrance of then-General Colin Powell following the first Persian Gulf War. Powell alludes to this incident in his biography, *My American Journey:* "I had ordered the Joint Staff to do a study on the usefulness of tactical nuclear weapons. The staff's recommendation was to get rid of the small, artillery-fired nukes because they were trouble-prone, expensive to modernize, and irrelevant in the present world of highly accurate conventional weapons."[3]

The practical justification for scrapping the neutron bomb was because many believed the use of such a device would only make nuclear war more likely. The neutron bomb was "banned because it destroyed the sharp distinction between conventional and nuclear weapons by minimizing the fission blast and radiation by-products."[4] Mr. Cohen's objection follows:

> Needless to say, since Just War theory was accepted by allegedly Christian nations, rarely has it been practiced to any respectable degree. To the contrary, and this goes for the United States as well as any other nation, the history of conventional warfare has been mainly a gross violation of the theory, and this includes the recent war in the Persian Gulf where despite claims of the Bush administration our forces were adhering to its tenets, we broke nearly every one of them. (I'm glad we did, even though the hypocrisy considerably bothered me; for otherwise the war might have gone on much longer with many U.S. casualties.) However, I would point out that if instead of building up a force of a half million soldiers, hundreds of fighter and bomber aircraft, and all the ships at sea, we had quickly dispatched, say, a hundred neutron bombs (a fraction of our arsenal of these weapons), and let our Arab allies do the ground fighting, we could have gotten the Iraqis out of Kuwait in short order, sparing Kuwait of much of the horror it went through, and driven to Baghdad, while erasing the Iraqi army, and done away with Saddam Hussein and his cronies. To say nothing of saving the tens of billion dollars the war cost and using the money, if we were so inclined (which I doubt) to improve the lot of enormous numbers of human beings.[5]

Thus, the record stands accordingly—When the United States was facing one of its greatest decisions in the realm of national defense, our leaders chose to follow an "African-American" from the Bronx over a "Jewish American" from Brooklyn; a *Hamite* with a preference for switchblades over the *Shemite* Father of the *Neutron Bomb*! (Ecclesiastes 9:13-18)

Obviously, the neutron bomb remained dormant under the Clinton administration. As we have already seen, the commander in chief could not even handle the nukes that *were* at his disposal. However, to Bill's "credit," in 1994 the U.S.A.F.'s Wright Laboratory in Dayton, Ohio, came mighty close to inventing the world's first "S" Bomb, the "S" standing for *sodomite*. According to declassified documents, scientists had planned for the chemical weapon to "spur homosexual activity among enemy troops."[6] ("Make love, not war," etc.)

Now this is not to say that other foreign powers—*like Osama bin Laden*—would have a problem using a nuke or two on *us*. Yossef Bodansky (another Jew) warned in 1999:

A new generation of mujahideen is being prepared in the numerous training camps, especially in eastern Afghanistan and Pakistan. A recent Arab visitor to Afghanistan identified in one cluster of camps some 5,000 trainees, between sixteen and twenty-five years old, who have come from virtually all corners of the world. The most promising of them are assigned to the Martyrdom (suicide) Battalions of the (Armed) Islamic International. **They call themselves human bombs and are trained and molded to carry out spectacular operations worldwide in the name of all-Islamic causes.** "They are there to wage a global war of Jihad and are poised to fight on all fronts wherever they are needed," the visitor observed. **The next time these martyrs strike, they might be carrying weapons of mass destruction.**[7]

Bodansky then relates a most unnerving scenario:

With bin Laden's limitless financial resources and the economic crisis in the former Soviet Union nearly out of control, a sale of nuclear suitcase bombs could ultimately be arranged by the Chechen Mafia. After all, General Aleksandr Ivanovich Lebed, the former security czar of Russia, acknowledged back in 1997 that several nuclear suitcase bombs had disappeared from Russia's arsenal.

A senior Arab intelligence official asserted in early October 1998 that "Osama bin Laden has acquired tactical nuclear weapons from the Islamic republics of Central Asia established after the collapse of the Soviet Union." This overall assessment is shared by Russian intelligence and several Arab intelligence services based on recent evidence of bin Laden's quest for nuclear weapons. **Although there is debate over the precise quantities of weapons purchased, there is no longer much doubt that bin Laden has finally succeeded in his quest for nuclear suitcase bombs.** Bin Laden's emissaries paid the Chechens $30 million in cash and gave them two tons of Afghan heroin worth about $70 million in Afghanistan and at least ten times that on the streets of Western Europe and the United States.

Evidence of the number of nuclear weapons purchased by the Chechens for bin Laden varies between "a few" (Russian intelligence) to "more than twenty" (conservative Arab intelligence services). Most of the weapons were purchased in four former Soviet states—Ukraine, Kazakhstan, Turkmenistan, and Russia. These weapons are a mix of suitcase bombs and tactical warheads/bombs. An Arab nuclear scientist, a Western-educated expert who worked for Saddam Hussein's nuclear program before he became Islamist, supervised the acquisition process for bin Laden and now runs the program for him. He is assisted by five Muslim Turkoman nuclear experts and a team of engineers and technicians, all of them Central Asian Muslims, whom they brought with them. For security reasons they condition these weapons for operational use in two clusters of facilities—one in the deep tunnels in the Khowst area and the other in the deep caves in the Qandahar area. . . .

Leaders of the Chechen Mafia are known to have approached Ukranian and Baltic mercenaries in Shali, Chechnya, on behalf of bin Laden, asking for veterans of the Soviet SPETSNAZ (Special Forces) trained in using the suitcase bombs. . . .

If bin Laden succeeds in finding a nuclear-qualified former SPETSNAZ trooper, he will have overcome the greatest hurdle to carrying out a nuclear terrorist strike in the West—specifically in the United States. According to former GRU (Soviet military intelligence) colonel Stanislav Lunev, who defected to the United States in March 1992, GRU and SPETSNAZ teams during the Cold War had already selected sites for potential use of these suitcase bombs near the main cities of the United States—sites and a mode of operation that can now be taught to bin Laden's terrorists by the former SPETSNAZ personnel he has recruited. Colonel Boris Alekseyev, chief of the Russian Federation Ministry of Defense Ecological Center, noted that once authorized by a coded radio transmission from Moscow, a single SPETSNAZ trooper can prepare a suitcase bomb for explosion within half an hour. **It is not inconceivable that bin Laden's nuclear experts would be able to "hot-wire" a suitcase bomb so that the coded transmission is no longer required to activate the bomb. Then only a single would-be martyr could activate it.**[8]

Bodansky's apocalyptic scenario becomes even more surreal when we factor in the rumored existence of "red mercury." Mr. Cohen elaborates:

> **There is, however, another class of nuclear explosives that from a terrorist standpoint may be far more insidious . . . because of its extremely small size and practically unlimited availability of the nuclear fuel.** Specifically at issue here is an extremely small pure-fusion mini-neutron bomb, roughly the size of a baseball, which in all probability the Soviets developed years ago and with the knowledge of Boris Yeltsin and the Russian Mafia and what used to be called the KGB have been smuggling the technology and perhaps even the bombs themselves to known terrorist states and others who feel a need for them—at a price, a big one.
>
> By pure-fusion what is meant here is a nuclear explosive totally devoid of fissionable nuclear materials—plutonium, used in the Nagasaki bomb and uranium-235, used in the Hiroshima bomb, both these materials used in warheads developed after the war. The particular device of concern here uses an equal mixture of the two heavy forms of hydrogen—deuterium and tritium. If non-nuclear means can be developed to compress and heat

but a fraction of a gram of this mixture to a degree where fusion of these hydrogen nuclei takes place at an efficient level, what is at hand is a mini-neutron bomb whose yield can be as low as a thousandth or even lower of the fission-fusion neutron bombs developed and stockpiled (and then later destroyed) by the U.S.; in other words on the order of a *ton* or *tons* (not a kiloton or kilotons) or even less of high explosive equivalent. . . .

The triggering material, known as red mercury, is a remarkable non-exploding high explosive which technically is one of a very special class of so-called "ballotechnic" explosives which apparently Los Alamos has been investigating (at the classified level) in nuclear weapon research. **Red mercury produces vastly more energy per pound than conventional explosives but does not explode in the conventional sense—emitting a cloud of smoke and producing a blast wave in the surrounding medium while blowing apart. Instead, upon being detonated, it becomes very hot, extremely hot, which allows pressures and temperatures to be built up that are capable of igniting the heavy hydrogen and producing a pure-fusion mini-neutron bomb.**

Red mercury, in its fusion explosive form is the product (one might say the ultimate product) of an industrial high compression material development which began in the 1960s in the U.S. and the then Soviet Union. Originally it was an oxide using mercury and antimony. Today, at least in Russia, it is almost a mystical alchemical substance produced by mixing special nuclear materials in very small amounts into the ordinary compound and then inserting the mixture into a nuclear reactor or bombarding it with a particle accelerator beam. When this process has been completed, the new substance, in which the mercury and antimony now act as one atom, is highly compressed and ready for forming into a trigger for the fusion explosive. (Most of this comes from secret interviews by a British investigative team with top level Russian nuclear scientists who have become deeply concerned with the issue and willing to talk, with no small amount of danger to their personal safety, to the investigators—one of whom is a former British nuclear weapons scientist, Frank Barnaby who became conscience stricken and decades back left his weapons lab and became a leading, very powerful, member of the international anti-nuclear movement.)[9]

Sam Cohen is not your typical "Zionist conspirator" out to destroy America, etc. In fact, you might call him Texe Marrs's worst nightmare. Reared by an atheist father, Sam found his "religious" calling in unabashed patriotic fervor. "I've never, in my unabiding and rigid way, held to any particular political spiritual dogma," he wrote. "The only true belief I've ever had was a total dedication to my country's military security, which while sorely tested over the years, when I was in the nuclear weapons business, has stayed with me."[10] He found it quite remarkable when I told him about the *other* Sam Cohen who officiated at the prayer and fasting service at Touro Synagogue in 1775. Like those first Jewish settlers in Newport, Sam has been grateful for a refuge in America, writing, "[I]t's been pretty good to me, allowing me to have an interesting and sometimes fascinating life."[11]

Having inaugurated his lifetime commitment to our national defense in 1943, over a half-century later he leaves us with a sober warning:

> **Using an explosive of, say, 10 tons yield, whose lethal radiation radius would reach out six or seven hundred yards, detonated inconspicuously in Lafayette Park across the street from the White House could effectively do away with the administration in one fell swoop. . . . Or how about doing in the whole government by detonating one of these devices near the Capitol Building while the President is giving his State of the Union address?** . . .
>
> The blast damage, say for a White House attack, would be minimal; the windows of the Oval Office might be shattered but there would be no serious physical damage inside, or to the rest of the building for that matter. **The human carnage would be horrendous.** Most of the occupants would have received lethal doses with no realistic hope of effective treatment. There would be significant radioactive fallout in the vicinity of the burst, but not of the kind associated with fission explosives. . . .
>
> For the above-mentioned reasons we should be far more concerned about nuclear terrorism than we are now. **We should be terrified!**[12]

KEEP YOUR EYE ON "POOTIE-POOT"

While Mr. Cohen has supported the election of several Republican presidential candidates, he has been outspoken in his contempt and distrust of the Bush dynasty. (And it has little to do with "religion"; I "preach" to Mr. Cohen all the time and our bond only seems to grow stronger.) In addition to the ongoing, bungling deathtrap in Iraq, Mr. Cohen has a serious problem with the prevailing positive attitude toward the "former" Soviet Union. "Pootie-Poot" may be "Dubya's" pal, but the Father of the Neutron Bomb doesn't trust the former KGB chief as far as he can throw him. You might call this negative assessment a holdover view of the "old school." He asks, "Are the new Russians all that different from the old ones—deceitful, deceptive, liars, misinformers, disinformers, and other such traits Russians have had over the centuries?"[13]

Less than two weeks after President Bush was reelected, his Russian counterpart began to engage in a little nuclear saber rattling. On November 17, 2004, *CNN* stated in an article entitled "Russia tests new missile systems":

> Russian President Vladimir Putin announced Wednesday that his country's armed forces will soon have access to advanced nuclear systems unavailable in any other country. "We are conducting research and are testing the most up-to-date nuclear missile systems, which, I'm sure, will be supplied to the armed forces in the near future," Putin told a conference of high-ranking military officials, according to a translation from Russia's Interfax New Agency. **"What is even more important, these systems will have no analogues in the other nuclear powers during the next few years."**
>
> The Bush administration said the developments in Russia's nuclear program are consistent with the Moscow treaty signed between President Bush and Putin in May 2002. "We are confident that Russia's plans are not threatening and are consistent with its obligations, and I think are indicative of a new strategic relationship between the United States and Russia that is focused on reducing threats and increasing confidence," deputy State Department spokesman Adam Ereli told reporters.
>
> The treaty, which required both sides to reduce their deployed strategic nuclear warheads to between 1,700 and 2,200 by 2012, was designed to establish a new strategic relationship between the two nations based on partnership and cooperation. But State Department officials told CNN on conditions of anonymity that although they don't think Putin's comments are anything to worry about, they will be seeking further clarification from the Russians about the specific modernization in Moscow's program. **"As far as we can tell there is nothing to be concerned about, but Putin did not give a lot of detail," one official said. "We are trying to figure out what he meant. Did he mean what we think he means or is this something that is not covered by the treaty?"**[14]

As far as our ability to *really* know what the Soviets are up to, Sam is rather skeptical:

> If you're planning for a nuclear war, it follows logically that you have to have an identifiable enemy. In the early days that was easy enough, *the* enemy was the Soviet Union. Fine, but to do good planning you have to

know something about the enemy—namely, you have to have good intelligence. In the nuclear area we never had, and despite the apparent opening up of what used to be the USSR, when we're given guided tours of their nuclear facilities and shown missiles being carried off for destruction, **I'm suspicious we still don't.**[15]

And yet, truth is, if we *had* better intelligence we *still* wouldn't know what to do! After noting the massive amounts of disinformation fed to the American people at the height of the arms race, Mr. Cohen states:

> **There's a profound lesson to be learned about the great H-bomb debate; that it was a farce.** I'm sure (or am I?) that many scholars now understand how farcical it was, but you'd never know it from their writings. However, whether generals, admirals, congressmen, and Presidents have grasped this, I wonder. In fact, I don't wonder too much, for as I observe the passing scene with arguments on the Stealth bomber, the MX missile, and all that nuclear business that is supposed to mean so much for our survival, I don't think they've learned a thing. **They still carry on in the same way, fighting over expensive nuclear weapon systems they don't understand, to be used in a war we don't know how to fight.**[16]

The president's unwavering public relations theme of a growing Russian-American alliance in the so-called "War on Terror" is just one more example of his blatant disregard for basic Bible knowledge. With spiritual mentors ranging from a longhaired, cross-carrying Charismatic to a longhaired, Hell-denying, pro-Vatican, bona fide Hollywood celebrity, how could "Brother" Bush know anything about Ezekiel 38 and 39? And besides, with the panacean "Road Map" prepared to bring in the Kingdom, why worry over some apocalyptic scenario about a *"great company"* descending *"out of the north parts"* upon *"the mountains of Israel"* in *"the latter days"* (Ezekiel 38:8, 15, 16)?

Countdown to Armageddon

As to how much time we have left, only the Lord knows for sure. However, from a purely economic perspective, there appear to be two significant indicators that it can't be much longer. First, if oil is the end-day commodity that will draw all nations to Armageddon, that window is destined to close in the near future. Barnett writes:

A Middle East that seeks to survive in the future solely on the slim connectivity offered by its energy exports to the Core will have no future whatsoever in globalization's advance. As the Core progressively decarbonizes its energy profile, moving off oil and into hydrogen to power vehicles, the Middle East's security deficit becomes a cross not even the United States will long be willing to bear. **That clock is ticking right now.** Once that tipping point is reached, it will be a slippery slope ride to the same sort of depths we have witnessed in Central Africa over the past decade. If we are lucky, we will end up with nothing more than a giant Taliban-like "paradise" that keeps the West out, the women down, and our narcotics flowing.[17]

While Christians may be too dense to realize the clock is ticking, Revelation 12:12b states, *"Woe to the inhabiters of the earth and of the sea! for the devil is come down unto you, having great wrath, **because he knoweth that he hath but a short time.**"*

The second market indicator has to do with China's expanding role in the global economy. Samuel Huntington writes in *The Clash of Civilizations and the Remaking of World Order:*

According to most estimates, the Chinese economy will become the world's largest early in the twenty-first century. With the second and third largest economies in the world in the 1990s, Asia is likely to have four of the five largest and seven of the ten largest economies by 2020. By that date, Asian societies are likely to account for over 40 percent of the global economic product. Most of the more competitive economies will also probably be Asian.[18]

The Apostle John knew all about this over nineteen centuries ago when he wrote in Revelation 16:12: *"And the sixth angel poured out his vial upon the great river **Euphrates**; and the water thereof was dried up, that the way of the **kings of the east** might be prepared."* Note the use of the plural *kings.*

It was Napoleon who said, "When China awakens the world will tremble." Professor Huntington continues:

Analysts compare the emergence of China to the rise of Wilhelmine Germany as the dominant power in Europe in the late nineteenth century. The emergence of new great powers is always highly destabilizing, and if it occurs, China's emergence as a major power will dwarf any comparable phenomena during the last half of the second millennium. "The size of China's displacement of the world," Lee Kuan Yew observed in 1994, "is such that the world must find a new balance in 30 or 40 years. **It's not possible to pretend that this is just another big player. This is the biggest player in the history of man.**" If Chinese economic development continues for another decade, as seems possible, and if China maintains its unity during the succession period, as seems probable, East Asian countries and the world will have to respond to the increasingly assertive role of this biggest player in human history.[19]

With regard to Beijing's lingering military threat, Mr. Cohen writes, "China, which still is Red, has been in the nuclear weapons business for some 30 or so years and short of all-out nuclear war poses similar nightmares [as posed by Russia]."[20] Huntington concurs, emphasizing China's role in the WMD market, particularly in the Middle East:

> Weapons proliferation is where the Confucian-Islamic connection has been most extensive and most concrete, with China playing the central role in the transfer of both conventional and nonconventional weapons to many Muslim states. These transfers include: construction of a secret, heavily defended nuclear reactor in the Algerian desert, ostensibly for research but widely believed by Western experts to be capable of producing plutonium; the sale of chemical weapons materials to Libya; the provision of CSS-2 medium range missiles to Saudi Arabia; the supply of nuclear technology or materials to Iraq, Libya, Syria, and North Korea; and the transfer of large numbers of conventional weapons to Iraq. Supplementing China's transfers, in the early 1990s North Korea supplied Syria with Scud-C missiles, delivered via Iran, and then the mobile chassis from which to launch them.[21]

However, akin to the Wal-Mart imbroglio, China's projected energy demands will ensure that the last days of the oil era will do more to heighten international tensions than "mere" nuclear capabilities. Barnett gives the following sobering analysis:

> But of course, the Middle East's slender connection to the global economy is an important one. In 2001 the planet burned just over 400 quadrillion (Quad) Btu of energy (e.g., oil, gas, coal, renewables), and almost 40 percent of that total was supplied by oil. Of the oil used last year by the world, just over 70 percent of it was imported from a foreign source. The Persian Gulf itself accounted for only about a quarter of that global trade, or 17 million barrels per day (mbd) out of a total of 56 mbd. But the Middle East accounts for just over half the known global reserves of oil. So as the world proceeds into the future and continues to increase its

consumption of oil, the Persian Gulf will account for roughly half of that increase. Naturally, growth in oil consumption around the world will vary in the next couple of decades, and this is where things get interesting.

North America has been the global demand center of energy markets for so long we cannot imagine a future that does not place America at the head of that line. But that future is coming. North America burned 116 Quad Btu in 2001, with Asia right on our heels at 113 Quad. But while we'll burn only about 50 percent more energy by 2025, Asia's demand will come close to doubling, meaning those nations will be looking for a lot more energy from the planet than we will—roughly 40 quadrillion Btu more. A good rule of thumb for calculating Quad Btu is to divide that number by 2, with the result representing how many millions of barrels of oil you would need to burn each day to achieve that energy. So 40 Quad would equal about 20 million barrels of oil per day—roughly what the U.S. consumed in oil last year, importing more than half.

By 2005, Asia will burn 211 Quad Btu, according to the latest Department of Energy projection. Right now, DOE estimates that that need will be met with 39 percent coal, 37 percent oil, 13 percent natural gas, and 11 percent renewables (e.g., wind, solar, hydro, nuclear). The 37 percent oil share (38 mbd) will be devoted largely to transportation needs, which are expected to grow dramatically by 2025—basically a fivefold increase in the number of cars. Of course, if all those cars are gas-guzzling SUVs, then the millions of barrels of oil per day that Asia would need to burn would be pushed up quite a bit. On the other hand, if hybrids and/or fuel-cell cars capture a large share of that growing market, then the barrel number could be lightened quite a bit. (There is a lot of give in these projections, or what the Pentagon likes to call "swag.")

Either way, Asia produces very little oil for itself today, and by 2025 the region as a whole will import more than 90 percent of its oil requirements, or 35 out of 38 mbd. That is roughly twice as much as Asia imports today (18 mbd).

Six OPEC members located in the Persian Gulf—Iran, Iraq, Kuwait, Qatar, Saudi Arabia, and the United Arab Emirates—control two-thirds of the proven, "conventional" oil reserves and over 90 percent of the excess productive capacity in the system.

Of the 18 mbd Asia imports today, just over half comes from the Persian Gulf, but of the 35 mbd Asia will import in 2025, 22 mbd—60 percent—will come from the Gulf. Meanwhile, the Persian Gulf's share of North America's oil imports will decline slightly from 22 percent today to 20 percent then. The Gulf will boost production for export from 17 mbd today to 36 mbd by 2005, and 11 of those extra 19 mbd will go to Asia, while just under 3 will go to North America. **That means the Persian Gulf will be the main source of oil to accommodate Asia's rising economic prominence within the global economy.**[22]

So now you know why China has a vested interest in marketing WMD to the oil-exporting *Ummah*. Huntington notes:

> In addition, China's increasing needs for oil are likely to impel it to expand its relations with Iran, Iraq, and Saudi Arabia as well as Kazakhstan and Azerbaijan. Such an informal arms-for-oil axis, one energy expert observed in 1994, "won't have to take orders from London, Paris or Washington anymore.[23]

Ironically, prone to being deceived through greed like any other pagan nation, China's aggressive nuclear exports may very well contribute to the spark that ignites the march to Meggido. If you think the "War on Terrorism" is exploitable at present, "you ain't seen nothin' yet." Barnett warns:

> So let's say that in 2025 some evil mastermind decides to cripple the Gulf's exporting of oil. In that scenario, North America would have to go find 6 mbd somewhere else in a global marketplace with a capacity of roughly 60 mbd, while Asia would be shopping around for three and a half times that amount. North America would be facing the loss of roughly 7 percent of its total energy requirement, whereas Asia would be trying to replace almost 20 percent of its Quad Btu.[24]

Robert Baer served as a case officer in the Directorate of Operations for the Central Intelligence Agency from 1976 to 1997. His overseas assignments have included stints in such outposts as Northern Iraq, Dushanbe, Rabat, Paris, Beirut, Khartoum, New Delhi and elsewhere. He has overseen agents who have infiltrated Hizballah, PFLP-GC, PSF, Libyan intelligence, Fatah-Hawari, and al Qaeda. In his 2003 bestseller, *Sleeping With The Devil: How Washington Sold Our Soul For Saudi Crude,* Baer presents the following "Doomsday Scenario" with respect to the gargantuan oil processing facilities at Abqaiq, Saudi Arabia:

> The white Ford pickup rolled quietly to a stop below Tower Number Seven, one of ten large cylindrical structures at Abqaiq that are used to remove sulfur from petroleum, or turn it from "sour" to "sweet," in oil-patch jargon. A dirty tarp covered the cargo bed; extra-heavy shocks kept the bed from sagging onto the axle. To the east, across the Saudi desert,

a hint of the morning sun peeked over the horizon. The truck driver, one of thousands of Shi'a Muslims who work the Saudi oil fields, cut the engine, checked his watch one last time, and began reciting verses from the Qur'an, memorized long ago. The lights of the world's largest oil-producing facility twinkled all around him.

Three hours earlier, a fishing boat equipped with twin two-hundred-fifty-horsepower Evinrude engines had set out from Deyyer, on the southern coast of Iran. By dark, the boat had sprinted across the Persian Gulf to the Saudi port at al Jubayl. From there, the Iranian pilot had crept south, hugging the coastline, until he came in sight of the Sea Island oil-loading platform at Ras Tanura, forty-five miles to the northeast of Abqaiq. Now, with the water beginning to glow pink, he pointed the bow at Platform Four and slammed the throttle to full.

Just inland from Ras Tanura, at Qatif Junction, an Egyptian engineer—a Muslim Brother who had made the grand tour of militant Islam, from Cairo to Tehran—flicked on his flashlight and admired his handiwork. The Semtex was expertly crammed into and around every manifold, every valve, every last pipe junction. It was art, really, lacing it all together in a single charge: a work of beauty, of Allah's great creation.

West of Abqaiq, in the foothills of the al Aramah Mountains at a small Bedouin encampment, a Saudi in his mid-twenties bent over a 120-mm Russian-made mortar for what seemed the hundredth time. A Wahhabi, descended from the religious zealots who brought the House of Sa'ud to power, he had been trained in munitions in Afghanistan by a man who was taught by the Central Intelligence Agency. Below him, at the base of the foothills, sat Pump Station One, the first stop on the oil pipeline that carried nearly a million barrels of extra-light crude daily from Abqaiq across the peninsula to the Red Sea port at Yanbu.

A pager vibrated lightly against his chest and went dead. It was time. The Al Sa'ud were coming down. The oil that fed their whoring and corruption would flow no more. Islam would be purified; the American devils, crippled; and their Israeli protectorate, cut free to die on its own. The world would have to take notice, and for the simplest of reasons: The global economy was [expletive].[25]

As the Russian General Staff concluded at a major conference in Moscow, July 2001: "[T]he most unexpected things take place in the Orient—**sometimes at the very last minute**."[26] (I Thessalonians 5:3)

Thus, the final "bottom line" in this book constitutes the "mother of *all* bottom lines"—*an increase in the demand for Middle East oil will foster a commensurate increase in the demand for a Middle East peace.* And

we certainly know what "land for peace" is all about by now—*don't we?*
Barnett summarizes the growing consensus of the international community:

> **The clock is running on the Middle East and on any hope we may have of someday integrating it into the Core.** The bin Ladens of the Muslim world know they're in a race. They know they have only so much time to successfully turn back the clock on most Middle Eastern societies, and they will fight more desperately with each passing year.
>
> That will only make our race with destiny all the more difficult to sustain, because as these forces of disconnectedness strain to kill us in new and more diabolical ways, we'll need to push ahead with efforts to ensure just the opposite outcome of greater connectivity. How hard will it be to spare a billion-plus Muslims from a future of diminishing expectations? I'm guessing more agony than ecstasy ["Get your tee shirts—3 for $20!"], but it is indisputably the right thing to do. And it simply cannot happen on its own.
>
> **It will be a cross we will bear for years. And, yes, we will need to turn the other cheek time and time again.** But there will never be peace in the Middle East until the region joins the world. If we surrender the region to the bin Ladens of disconnectedness, we will end up losing far more than access to cheap oil. **We will be surrendering globalization's promise of eternal peace.**[27]

When it comes to discerning the future of our planet, a cartoon that appeared in *Mad* magazine would be hard to beat. The scene depicted a frantic bomber pilot clutching the controls of his devastated aircraft. Smoke was billowing from the cockpit. Bullet holes were everywhere. Turning to his bleeding copilot, he says, "If you think *this* is bad, *just wait 'til we get out of the hangar!*"

"HE'S GOT THE WHOLE WORLD IN HIS HANDS"

As a young boy growing up in New York City during the 1950s, I was totally cut off from any semblance of Bible-believing Christianity. My religious life was dominated by the likes of Pope John XXIII, Francis Cardinal Spellman, "Father" Duffy, "Mother Superior" Benedict, "Sister" Kevin, St. Patty's Day, "The Bells of St. Mary's," "Angels with Dirty Faces," etc. There was, however, an occasional glimpse of light from the outside world. For instance, once a year I was exposed to Salvation

Army bellringers. Because my mother was a Lutheran, I was naturally more tolerant of "Protestants" than were my peers. Though even deprived of what was supposed to be our *own* "Bible"—the corrupt *Douay* version—the escalating arms race (with those never-to-be-forgotten classroom air-raid drills—"Under the desks, *now!*") actually fostered whispered speculation among some of us as to the mysterious content of the last book in the Bible. At St. Stephens of Hungary Elementary School, rumor had it that the "yellow race" would one day rule the world.

In the midst of such unsettling times, the junk we sang at daily Mass, like "Ave Marie" and "Long Live The Pope," did little to encourage my troubled heart. And then I heard it—my *first* non-Catholic hymn; a message that really spoke to my soul. It would be another decade before I would graduate to such standards as "Amazing Grace," "The Old Rugged Cross" and "How Great Thou Art"; but for now, it was the stirring theme conveyed by a black Gospel singer named Mahalia Jackson. (And some folks think I'm a racist!) If you want to know whether there's a God in Heaven, just picture a little Irish Roman Catholic kid on the Upper East Side of Manhattan (circa 1962) being ministered to by the words:

> He's got the whole world, in His hands,
> He's got the whole wide world, in His hands,
> He's got the whole world, in His hands,
> He's got the whole world in His hands!

Over four decades later, the profound truth in this simple hymn still resonates within my being. The God I serve isn't worried about *anything*! From *Osama* to *Obama*, He's got *everything* under control—"He's got the whole wide world in His hands."

Now I believe this would include "Pootie-Poot" as well—*would it not?* Such being the case, do you think the author of Ezekiel 38 and 39 is the least bit intimidated by Russia's nuclear arsenal? Truth is, whatever "international crisis" may be occurring as you read these lines, rest assured that it's being aired on *Heaven's* comedy channel! While the Bible never shows our Saviour laughing down on earth, Psalm 2:4 reveals, *"He that sitteth in the heavens shall laugh: the Lord shall have them in derision."*

For instance, if and when "Brother" Art ever gets his cross into orbit, don't you think God will laugh as that Charismatic creation passes through

His special domain? Psalm 115:16 says, *"The heaven, even the heavens, are the LORD'S: but the earth hath he given to the children of men."*

Well, getting back to Vladimir's crowd, I will end my tome with a closing illustration that I trust will lift your spirit in these uncertain times. It also has to do with one of these unauthorized missions into God's space. This book could have been dedicated to the memory of John Birch and Larry McDonald. As both men were ultimately murdered by Moscow (with John's death occurring at the hands of Stalin's emerging Asian surrogate), the Lord prepared a most unusual postscript to serve as a reminder that the great "Russian Bear" will shortly be turned into "birdseed"! (Ezekiel 39:4; Revelation 19:17)

Our story took place in 1996 and gave the Lord a good laugh for six months. From March to September, the Russian Space Station Mir orbited the earth in a major public relations coup for the murderous regime that made Kathy McDonald a widow.

However, on this particular mission there was a slight complication; one that only God could have arranged. The two Russian cosmonauts, Commander Yuriy I. Onufriyenko and Flight Engineer Yuriy V. Usachov, had a special guest researcher on board from the United States. But this was not your run-of-the-mill guest researcher. From an ego standpoint, the "Yuriy brothers" would have been more than a little intimidated by their American counterpart. In the academic arena, Dr. Lucid earned a bachelor of science degree in chemistry from the University of Oklahoma in 1963, and master and doctor of philosophy degrees in biochemistry from the same institution in 1970 and 1973, respectively.

Dr. Lucid's professional résumé was equally intimidating. A veteran of four shuttle missions, the NASA legend flew on STS 51-G in 1985, STS-34 in 1989, STS-43 in 1991, and STS-58 in 1993. At the conclusion of the Mir flight—covering 75.2 million miles in 188 days at an average speed of 17,500 miles per hour—Dr. Lucid would hold the American record for most flight hours in orbit at 5,354 or 233 days in space.

But then there was the ultimate cause for alarm in the "ego" department. The prestigious American guest researcher "just happened" to be a *woman*. Dr. Shannon Lucid, former chief scientist at NASA Headquarters in Washington, D.C. (February 2002 to September 2003), is also a happily married wife, mother of three and grandmother of two!

Can you imagine how much laughter all of this caused in the glory world? And then to really rub it in, the God who determines when an exception to His own rule may occur for some greater purpose, allowed this record-breaking woman astronaut to be a consecrated Christian as well! An Associated Press article in September 1999 described her as "a shy, religious woman."[28]

Dr. Lucid is the daughter of an ordained minister who is now with the Lord. I once had the opportunity to interview a longtime friend of the family, Evangelist Harold Boyd, who shared a number of personal memories about Shannon and her father. He told me that she would personally fly them to various out-of-the-way mission stations in the Caribbean and South America. While the two preachers conducted services for the teenagers and adults, Shannon would minister to the children.

Having laid it on pretty "thick" concerning Dr. Lucid and the "commie cosmonauts," in all fairness to Commander Onufriyenko and Flight Engineer Usachov—apart from their celebrity status in Russian society— they are probably just two more Hell-bound dupes of the devil who believe they are making the world a better place, etc. (The very name of their space station means "world peace.") Over such a long flight, Shannon would have developed a natural burden for the men, prayed for their souls, displayed the love of Christ and worked in a Gospel witness or two whenever she was "off the clock." A retired pastor, who was saved under her father's ministry, told me her dad related that she gave the cosmonauts Bibles at mission's end.

However, be that as it may, the politically incorrect spiritual imagery is much too powerful to overlook. Like I said, John Birch and Larry McDonald lost their lives because of Russian communism *and the lauded breakup of the Soviet Union hasn't changed a thing*—least of all, chapters 38 and 39 of Ezekiel!

Should the unheeded clarion call of Sam Cohen represent America's final warning, we could be in for some "perilous times" after all. But fear not—

> He's got you and me brother, in His hands,
> He's got you and me sister, in His hands,
> He's got you and me brother, in His hands,
> He's got the whole world in His hands!

To help us "hang in there" till the Rapture, our Heavenly Father orchestrated a spectacular object lesson of His ability to preserve the saints. It all has to do with Dr. Lucid's earliest weeks on earth.

As each rotation of Mir's orbit afforded the Lord a fresh chuckle (Proverbs 1:26) over Gog's future destruction (Ezekiel 39:11; Revelation 20:8-9), one of Shannon's daily vantage points would serve as a special altar of praise and thanksgiving. (II Samuel 7:8) Somewhere, approximately 250 miles straight down, lay an insignificant tract of earth where over a half-century earlier, baby Shannon had been tenderly carried on her father's shoulders through several restless nights.

Though oblivious to her abnormal surroundings at the time, "daddy's little girl" was being walked on a floor of dirt. In fact, her "nursery" was ringed with barbwire and the "attendants" all carried rifles with long bayonets.

So, have you been able to guess the identity of Shannon Lucid by now? Would it help if I told you that her father's name was—*Oscar Wells*?

As the uncertain finale of the turbulent Laodicean Age approaches, it would behoove us all to dwell upon the concluding statement of this volume—The same God who could transport a six-week-old infant girl from an unsanitary World War II Japanese P.O.W. camp into the record books of NASA can *also* take care of *you and me*!

> He's got the Little Bitty Baby, in His hands,
> He's got the Little Bitty Baby, in His hands,
> He's got the Little Bitty Baby, in His hands,
> He's got the whole world in His hands!

> *"And call upon me in the day of trouble: I will deliver*
> *thee, and thou shalt glorify me.*
> (Psalm 50:15)

Epilogue

I N 1984, JOHN KELLEY became pastor of the Curtis Corner Baptist Church in Wakefield, Rhode Island, located about twenty miles from Newport. John and I were classmates in Bible college during the late 1970s.

On February 6, 2004, he and six other American preachers flew to Iraq to ordain a native pastor and to help start the Bible Baptist Church of Baghdad. While riding in a taxi with three of the men on February 14, John was shot and killed when a sedan full of Muslim terrorists, firing Russian-made Kalashnikov assault rifles, overtook their van around 4:30 p.m. local time, near the village of Mahmodia thirty minutes south of Baghdad.

At approximately the same hour John was going to Heaven, a member of Curtis Corner Baptist Church was doing the pastor's bidding by surprising Mrs. Jane Kelley with a dozen red roses for Valentine's Day.

The following morning, two very different women would pursue their spiritual schedules in the state that inspired American democracy. The first one is a *total* blank. In an interview with *Booknotes* host, Brian Lamb, May 30, 2004, Portsmouth resident, Thomas P. M. Barnett (". . . we are never 'bringing our boys home' "), actually admitted that his Catholic wife, Vonne—a card-carrying member of the ACLU—*made* him take her maiden name Moisley, which he subsequently incorporated as a second middle initial ("P" standing for Patrick).

Meanwhile, over at Wakefield, a grieving widow played the accompaniment to "Count Your Blessings" and "Nothing But The Blood" for her departed husband's Sunday morning congregation. Brother Kelley will also be sorely missed by his four heartbroken children—Julie 23, James 21, Jason 17 and Jenny 15.

One parishioner said, "Pastor Kelley was willing to give his life so that people would hear the message that Jesus had." Robert Lewis, the man who led the team to Iraq, eulogized the fallen Rhode Island Baptist, stating:

> My grief is without description. John Kelley was a great man. He served in the U.S. Marines, pastored for more than twenty-five years, and was a pillar of Christian manhood. He has certainly been a blessing to all with whom he has had contact.

Despite intense persecution from Muslims and Catholics alike, the Bible Baptist Church of Baghdad held its first service on Easter Sunday, 2004, with fifty Iraqis in attendance.

Pastor John Kelley was the epitome of a *Christian* soldier who was faithful unto death. Let us all profit from his courageous legacy as we likewise strive to

Keep On The Firing Line

If you're in the battle for the Lord and right,
Keep on the firing line;
If you win, my brother, surely you must fight,
Keep on the firing line;
There are many dangers that we all must face,
If we die still fighting it is no disgrace;
A coward in the service, he will find no place,
So keep on the firing line.

Refrain:
Oh, you must fight, be brave against all evil,
Never run, nor even lag behind;
If you would win for God and the right,
Just keep on the firing line.

God will only use the soldier He can trust,
Keep on the firing line;
If you'll wear a crown then bear the cross you must,
Keep on the firing line.
Life is but to labor for the Master dear,
Help to banish evil and to spread good cheer;
Great you'll be rewarded for your service here,
So keep on the firing line.

When we get to heaven, brother, we'll be glad,
Keep on the firing line;
How we'll praise the Savior for the call we had,
Keep on the firing line;
When we see the souls that we have helped to win,
Leading them to Jesus, from the paths of sin,
With a shout of welcome, we will all march in,
So keep on the firing line.

"Thou therefore endure hardness, as a good
soldier of Jesus Christ"
(II Timothy 2:3)

Afterword

HEAVEN ONLY KNOWS why an unbelieving Jewish scientist in Los Angeles would be recommending a 1,000-page opus written by a Baptist minister in Corryton, Tennessee (though we both hail from New York City). My reasons for doing so follow. First, I consider Bill Grady to be one of the most unusual friends I have known in my eighty-four years.

Second, though unable to relate to the spiritual content of this book, I concur wholeheartedly with the author's exceptional grasp of America's current disastrous foreign policy, as well as our growing vulnerability in matters of national security. Having been immersed in the "system" for over four decades (my endless protests resulting only in an early retirement), I can assure you that Bill hardly scratched the surface with regard to perfidy and corruption prevailing in our government. In nearly every instance, the underlying motive has been avarice, *especially* at the Defense Department. Albert Einstein was right when he stated (concerning the atomic age), "Everything has changed but human nature."

Most Americans are totally oblivious to their precarious surroundings. Several years ago, my longtime friend and colleague Joe Douglass authored a book (*America the Vulnerable: The Threat of Chemical and Biological Warfare*) whose preface contained the following statement:

> While the United States debates the development of a massive defense effort against nuclear attack. . . . the fact remains that this nation is almost entirely defenseless against chemical, biological, and toxin weapons of mass destruction. Some of these weapons may already be secreted within our borders; others could be synthesized by our enemies within a matter of hours, or days at the most. Indeed it is doubtful that most biological attacks would even be recognized for what they are. Even if it could be proven with certainty that the outbreak of a particular disease was not a natural

occurrence and instead was deliberately instigated, it would be almost impossible to pinpoint the exact source.

However, the most compelling reason for my incidental part in this book (a part, by the way, which I *volunteered* to contribute) concerns the caliber of Bill's constituents. As a lifetime political conservative, I have associated with numerous evangelical Christians and found them to be highly patriotic and decent human beings, especially the Baptists. Unfortunately, I cannot say the same for many of their leaders—charlatans like Pat Robertson and Jerry Falwell, for instance—who are governed by little more than self-aggrandizement. *I believe the single greatest weakness among the ranks of the Religious Right is gross naiveté.* Apparently, few have the necessary *chutzpa* to ask the obvious questions.

Along this line of thought I will conclude my remarks by sharing a *Jewish* version of that timeless fable—"The Emperor's New Clothes." The wisest utterance I've ever heard came from a rabbi who lived his life in the last century, in a small village in Lithuania, the land of my ancestors who also lived in small villages (my grandfather was a village blacksmith, his father a peasant tilling soil from dawn to dusk). The rabbi, venerated by everyone in the village for his wisdom, grew old and older and one day he lay dying in his bedroom. In the room were his immediate family, including his loving wife. In the adjoining room were his closest relatives. Outside the house were more distant relatives and friends and all the nice Jewish people of the village who so loved and respected him, who formed a long line going down the street.

All of them wanted to be kept up to date on the rabbi's condition. One of them at the end of the line, the village idiot, wanted to know whether the rabbi had passed on any last words. So he tapped the person in front of him on the shoulder and asked that the word get off to the rabbi's wife as to what his last words were. The query worked its way down the line and into the bedroom to the wife, who realized there weren't any last words. This was unacceptable. By now the rabbi had slipped into a coma. However, so insistent was everyone on getting an answer that the poor rabbi had to be shaken violently out of his coma. He came to. His wife looked into his eyes and said, "Dearest, what are your last words?" The rabbi pondered a moment and replied, "Life is a cup of tea." And slipped back into a coma.

His last words now worked their way out of the bedroom, into the adjoining room, out of the house and down the street to the village idiot at the end of the line. The village idiot pondered the rabbi's utterance for a while. Then he tapped the shoulder of the person in front of him and asked, "Why is life like a cup of tea?" This was very disconcerting. The person felt obliged to repeat the question to the person in front of him, and so on all the way up to the rabbi's wife. She too found this question disconcerting and decided an explanation was in order.

Again the poor rabbi was shaken into consciousness and asked the village idiot's question. Again the rabbi pondered, this time a lot longer because he knew how all important his answer would be for the villagers. Finally, he spread his arms, looked up at his wife, and replied, "All right, so life is *not* a cup of tea." With that he expired.

If you are *really* burdened about the future of America, then apply what you can from this unusual *book* written by my unusual *friend*.

Sam Cohen
Father of the Neutron Bomb
Brentwood
February 2005

Acknowledgments

THIS BOOK CAME together over a six-year period while I was traveling in full-time evangelism. The pace was nothing short of surreal. With the first page being written on a stone table at a highway rest area in southwest Florida, portions of other chapters were subsequently penned in airports, motels, prophet's chambers, libraries, restaurants, parking lots, and a variety of other locations spanning twelve countries on four continents.

Throughout this incredible odyssey, the Lord raised up a number of key secular contacts and a host of consecrated believers who labored with me to make this volume a reality. Without their collective assistance, *How Satan Turned America Against God* would have never seen the light of day. As the Scripture says, *"[A]nd what hast thou that thou didst not receive? now if thou didst receive it, why dost thou glory, as if thou hadst not received it?"* (I Corinthians 4:7).

Apart from the lovely Lord Jesus, my precious wife Linda was the single greatest asset to the project. A registered nurse when we married, she willingly submitted to several "career changes" in the decades following my conversion: pastor's wife, homeschool mom, professor's wife, evangelist's wife, bookkeeper, office manager, and finally, editor and proofreader. She helped me to make literally thousands of editorial decisions in this tome. *"The heart of her husband doth safely trust in her . . ."* (Proverbs 31:11).

I should next like to thank my three married children and their families for the patience and understanding afforded me during this protracted time. Eight of my ten "crowns" came into this world (with *Sammi* going to Heaven) while Grandpa was writing his book. (Proverbs 17:6)

My research was greatly facilitated by Nick Cultrara, Jack Minor and Mitch Canupp.

A highly qualified team of professionals worked behind the scenes in the technical arena: Tammy Butler rendered an enormous degree of thoroughness in typesetting and text design; Nadine Pilato did a major share of the proofreading; the many photographs were screened and arranged by Jason Fraker of Graphic Creations, Inc.; Tommy and Lori Ray designed the dust jacket with the incredible artwork done by Chris Ellison; Eric Rishell, Tammy Nickle, Carol Woods and Nikki Williams of R. R. Donnelley & Sons rendered both professional and personal service during the printing phase.

In the spiritual realm, Linda and I have been blessed with a dedicated pastor and first lady, Dr. David and Ann Reagan, and a warm fellowship of believers at the Antioch Baptist Church.

Many prayer warriors across this nation faithfully travailed over the book you have just completed. A mighty army of over four hundred widows comprised the core group. (I Timothy 5:5) In addition to these, Evangelist Walter Ziglar, Dr. Randy Gibson, Dr. Don Green, Gary Sifford, and my special friends—Hugh Anderson, *Toan, Kim, Tung and Nu*—deserve particular mention.

As Peter and John stated in Acts 4:20, *"we cannot but speak the things which we have seen and heard,"* the Lord used a number of human instruments to point me in the right direction. Nearly twenty years ago, my good friend Dr. Mark Rasmussen introduced me to the study of conspiracy history. In 1988, my eyes were opened for the first time to the final authority of the A.V. 1611 through the book *Manuscript Evidence* by Dr. Peter S. Ruckman. (John 9:25) The thesis for my own book, as developed in chapter two (Goldenah Medinah), was inspired by *Israel: A Deadly Piece of Dirt,* also by Dr. Ruckman.

Over the past six years the devil attempted to hinder this project on several occasions. (I Thessalonians 2:18) Thankfully, a number of "holy brethren" were in the right place at the right time to refresh my spirit. (II Timothy 1:16) A short list would include Pastor Jeff Faggart, Evangelist Chris Stansell, Dr. Jack Patterson, Dr. James West, Dr. Wendell Runion, Dr. Doug Stauffer, Dr. Lou Guagdano, Pastor Randy Dignan, Pastor Tom Benson, Pastor Mike Watkins, Pastor Bill Waugh, and my two pals from the "Big Apple," Pastor Joe Costa and Brother Bill Whitelaw.

The Lord checked my pride further by ensuring that I would need additional helpers in a variety of areas. While some were used to bring pertinent information to my attention, others were in position to arrange many of the high-profile interviews I was privileged to conduct. A number provided unsolicited financial support at critical times. Still others fulfilled unspoken needs. Their providential participation greatly enhanced the content of this book. You might call them charter members of the 7000 Club (I Kings 19:18):

Dr. Sammy Allen, Pastor Jim Alter, Pastor Ken Anderson, Pastor Charlie Andrews, Mrs. Ina Ashley, Pastor Marion Atkinson, Pastor Leonard Ballinger, Pastor Dan Barnes, Evangelist Ricky Bell, Pastor Jim Beller, Reverend David Beyea, Pastor Dennis Black, Dr. Bill Boruff, Dr. Joe Boyd, Pastor Larry Branham, Pastor Randy Brannon, Pastor Eric Brazelton, Austin and Nana Brown, Keith Brown, Pastor Steve Brown, Mrs. Vicki Bryant, Reverend Phil Buckner, John Campbell, Pastor Gene Carpenter, Pastor William Carter, Pastor Clint Caviness, Pastor Jesse Chambers, Missionary Phil Clayton, Pastor Steve Clayton, Evangelist Craig Cobb, Evangelist Boyd Collins, Pastor Bill Coppenger, Terry and Debbie Coy, Pastor Steve Crane, Reverend Terry Cruise, Lance and Nancy Crivellone, Pastor Jay Cubbison, Pastor Ed Decker, Greg and Renee Deitsch, Pastor Larry Delli, Dennis Denneau, Dr. Greg Estep, John Evans, Ron Forte, Dr. James Gardner, Pastor Jerry Garner, Reverend Helmut Getto, Dan Grady, Reverend Paul Grady, Dr. Tim Green, Pastor Thomas Gresham, Missionary Jim Griggers, Dr. Ernest Groce, Lou Guagdano, Jr., Reverend Pete Guagdano, Pastor Richard Hack, Pastor Jeff Harris, Pastor Larry Hickam, Pastor Dennis Hicks, Pastor Tommy Holbrooks, Pastor Mickey Hollers, Pastor Jimmy Hood, Reverend Noah Hutchins, Forrest James, Pastor French Jenkins, Reverend Allen Johnson, Nick Johnson, Pastor Clayton Jones, Reverend Ellis Jones, Reggie Jones, Pastor Jim Keeling, Mrs. Jane Kelley, Pastor Mike Kent, Pastor Jim Koffman, Pastor Arthur Lands, Paul Lester, Pastor Greg Little, Pastor John Liviner, Charles Lloyd, Jr., Karl Lohman, Leo Loving, Pastor Daniel Major, Pastor Dave Malucci, Pastor Phil Manning, Rick Marmon, Pastor Dave Martin, Pastor Mike Martin, Reverend Mike Martin, Jr., Pastor Vince Massa, Pastor Randy McAllister, Pastor James McCarroll, Pastor Ray Meir, Pastor James Melton, Reverend Robert Mellitello, Pastor Jerry Monday, Pastor Ernie Moore, Breck Moreland, Nathaniel Morris, Pastor David Morrissey, Pastor Bill Murdock, Pastor Bob Nogalski, Pastor James Odom, Chris Olson, Dr. John Paisley, Pastor Craig Peak, Shep Phillips, Pastor Mike Poole, Pastor Todd Poynter, Pastor Tony Price, Pastor Ricky Prophet, Gary Reed, Pastor Rusty Riggs, Dr. Jimmy Robbins, Dave and Louise Roberts, Pastor Dolton Robertson III, Dr. Jerry Rockwell, Pastor Chris Sadler, Pastor Steve

Sanders, Reverend Phil Schipper, Alan Scholl, Dr. Walt Schuler, Walt F. "Poke" Schuler IV, Pastor Jerry Siler, Pastor Ted Smarzynski, Dr. Bob Smith, Dr. Rick Sowell, Evangelist Charles Spurgeon, Pastor Chris Staub, Pastor Lonnie Taylor, Pastor Willard Thomas, Darren Tischnor, Pastor Roger Tripplet, Gerald Tyson, Dave Underkofler, Richard and Lynn Vanberschot, Pastor Ronnie Vice, Jim Villanti, Pastor Matt Walters, Missionary Warren Webster, Doug Williams, Mickey Winters, Pastor Philip Wishon, Kim and Amy Wittingham, Pastor David Wood, Pastor Tony Wood, and Pastor Bill Wright. (I Samuel 30:24)

Having begun this book when Bill Clinton was president, I fear the possibility exists that some worthy contributor may have been overlooked; but the Lord knows.

Finally, a word of gratitude is in order for the numerous individuals who were either interviewed or quoted for this volume. As many would not ascribe to the general tenor of the book, their gracious willingness to share firsthand knowledge of the truth for the sake of history is to be commended. My *special* thanks to George R. Bonnewell, Robert Birch, V. Z. Lawton, Dale Phillips, George B. Wallace, Charles Key, Tommy Toles, Yossef Bodansky, and *Sam*.

Appendices

A) John Leland's Ten Objections to the Constitution
(Library of Congress)

House, the more parties, the more they are divided, & where the Wisdom is scattered, sometimes one house may prevent the Error of another & the same holds true of twenty Houses) But the Question is, whether they do more good than harm the Business is certainly thereby retarded & the Expence enhanced.

7th. We are not informed whether Votes in all cases in the lower house are to be by Members or by States,— I question whether any one can find out the Riddle but by plowing with Sampsons Heifers, if each Member is not to have a Vote why are they to be chosen according to the Numbers of Inhabitants, & why should Virginia be at ten times the Expence of Delaware for the same Powers, if the Votes are always to be by States, why is it not Expressed as in the choice of a President, in certain Cases, if each member is to have a Vote why is it Expressed concerning Senators, & not Concerning Representatives, this Blank appears to me, to be designed, to encourage the Small States with hopes of Equality, & the Large States with hopes of Superiority —

8. We have no assurance that the Liberty of the press will be allowed under this **Constitution** —

9th. We have been always taught that it was dangerous mixing the Legislative & Executive Powers together in the same body of People but in this Constitution, we are taught better or worse ————

10th. What is clearest of all — Religious Liberty, is not Sufficiently Secured, No Religious test is required as a Qualification to fill any office under the United States, but if a Majority of Congress with the President favour one System more than another, they may oblige all others to pay to the Support of their System as much as they please, & if Oppression does not ensue, it will be owing, to the Mildness of Administration & not to any Constitutional defence, & if the Manners of People are so far Corrupted, that they cannot live by republican principles, it is very dangerous leaving Religious Liberty at their Mercy ——

Revd. John Leland's, Objections to the Federal Constitution Sent to Col. Thos Barbee by his Request, a Copy taken by Jos. Spencer, entended for the Consideration of Cap Jo. Walker Culpeper.

B) James Madison's "Advice to My Country"
(Library of Congress)

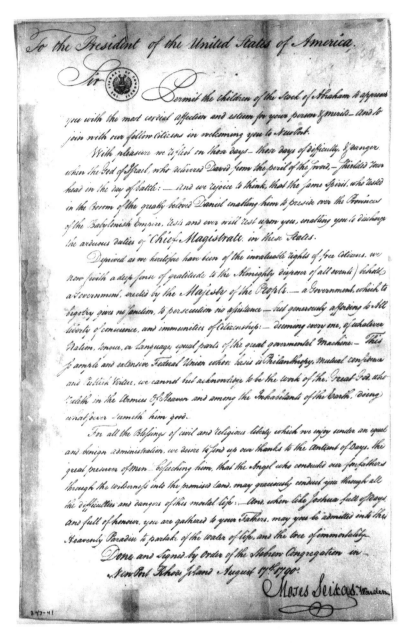

C) Touro Synagogue's Letter to George Washington
(Library of Congress)

To the Hebrew Congregation in Newport
Rhode Island.

Gentlemen.

While I receive, with much satisfaction,
your Address replete with expressions of affection
and esteem; I rejoice in the opportunity of assuring
you, that I shall always retain a grateful remem:
brance of the cordial welcome I experienced in
my visit to Newport, from all classes of Citizens.

The reflection on the days of difficulty and
danger which are past is rendered the more sweet,
from a consciousness that they are succeeded by days
of uncommon prosperity and security. If we have
wisdom to make the best use of the advantages with
which we are now favored, we cannot fail, under the
just administration of a good Government, to become
a great and a happy people.

The Citizens of the United States of America
have a right to applaud themselves for having given
to mankind examples of an enlarged and liberal
policy: a policy worthy of imitation. All possess
alike liberty of conscience and immunities of
citizenship. It is now no more that toleration is
spoken of, as if it was by the indulgence of one
class of people, that another enjoyed the exercise
of their inherent natural rights. For happily
the

D) Washington's Reply to Touro Synagogue
*(Courtesy of B'nai B'rith Klutznick National Jewish Museum,
on loan from the Morgenstern Foundation)*

the Government of the United States, which gives to
bigotry no sanction, to persecution no assistance
requires only that they who live under its protection
should demean themselves as good citizens, in giving
it on all occasions their effectual support.

It would be inconsistent with the frankness
of my character not to avow that I am pleased with
your favorable opinion of my administration, and
fervent wishes for my felicity. May the children of
the Stock of Abraham, who dwell in this land, continue
to merit and enjoy the good will of the other Inhabitants;
while every one shall sit in safety under his own
vine and figtree, and there shall be none to make
him afraid. May the father of all mercies scatter
light and not darkness in our paths, and make
us all in our several vocations here, and in his
own due time and way everlastingly happy.

G. Washington

Mount Vernon 25. Sep. 1798

Sir,

Many apologies are due to you, for my not acknowledging the receipt of your obliging favour of the 22d Ult; and for not thanking you, at an earlier period, for the Book you had the goodness to send me.

I have heard much of the nefarious, & dangerous plan, & doctrines of the Illuminati, but never saw the Book until you were pleased to send it to me. — The same causes which have prevented my acknowledging the receipt of your letter, have prevented my reading the Book, hitherto, — namely — The multiplicity of matters which pressed upon me before, & the debilitated state in which I was left after, a severe fever had been removed. — And which allows me to add little more now, than thanks for your kind wishes and

favourable

E) Washington's Letter to Reverend G. W. Snyder
(Sol Feinstone Collection, David Library of the American Revolution,
on deposit at the American Philosophical Society)

favorable sentiments, except to correct an error you have run into, of my
presiding over the English lodges in
this Country. — The fact is, I preside over
none, nor have I been in one more than
once or twice, within the last thirty years —
— I believe notwithstanding, that
none of the Lodges in this Country are
contaminated with the principles ascribed to the Society of the Illuminati

With respect
I am Sir
Your Obad't H'ble Serv't
G. Washington

The Rev'd
M'r Snyder.

79.

Georgetown Ky
Aug 16th 1889

I am the grandson of Rev John Gano now in my eighty third year and the brother of Mrs Margaret Ewing I was raised from my fifth year to manhood by Mrs. Margaret Hubbell (nee Gano) I have heard her say that her father baptised (immersed) General Washington.   S. F. Gano M.D.

Subscribed and sworn to in my presence this 16th day of August 1889
    Stephen Gano Long.
    Notary Public.
    State of Kentucky.

F) Affidavit of S. F. Gano, M.D.
(American Baptist Historical Society, American Baptist—Samuel Colgate Library)

Georgetown Ky
Aug 16ᵗʰ 1889

To whom it may concern

I, Margaret Ewing. (nee Gano) aged 90 years last may, being of sound mind and memory, make this statement. I have often heard my aunt Margaret Hubbell (nee Gano) the eldest daughter of Rev. John Gano, saying that her father told her that he baptized General George Washington, at Valley Forge to the best of my recollection. She, Mrs Hubbell, also said that General Washington, for prudent reasons, did not desire that his baptism should be made public. Rev. John Gano was a chaplain in the Revolutionary war, and an intimate personal friend of Gen. Washington

Margaret Ewing

G) Affidavit of Margaret Ewing
(American Baptist Historical Society, American Baptist—Samuel Colgate Library)

Subscribed and sworn to
in my presence this 16th
day of August 1889.
            Stephen G. Long
            Notary Public
                State of Kentucky

(a) All right, title and interest, arising under the laws of the United States, of every kind or nature whatsoever, of the owners thereof in, to and under the copyrights described in Exhibit A attached hereto and made a part hereof, including but not limited to all accrued royalties, all rights to receive royalties, all damages and profits recoverable at law or in equity from any or all persons, firms, corporations or governments for past infringement thereof, and all rights of renewal subject to be exercised by or through such owners.

(b) All right, title and interest, arising under the laws of the United States, of every kind or nature whatsoever, of the authors of the publications described in Exhibit A attached hereto and made a part hereof in, to and under the copyrights described in said Exhibit A, including but not limited to all accrued royalties, all rights to receive royalties, all damages and profits recoverable at law or in equity from any or all persons, firms, corporations or governments for past infringement thereof and all rights of renewal subject to be exercised by such authors or by their widows, children, executors or next of kin.

Such property and any or all of the proceeds thereof shall be held in a special account pending further determination of the Alien Property Custodian.

This shall not be deemed to limit the powers of the Alien Property Custodian to return such property or the proceeds thereof, or to indicate that compensation will not be paid in lieu thereof, if and when it should be determined that such return should be made or such compensation should be paid.

Any person, except a national of a designated enemy country, asserting any claim arising as a result of this order may file with the Alien Property Custodian a notice of his claim, together with a request for a hearing thereon, on Form APC-1, within one year from the date hereof, or within such further time as may be allowed by the Alien Property Custodian. Nothing herein contained shall be deemed to constitute an admission of the existence, validity or right to allowance of any such claim.

The terms "national" and "designated enemy country" as used herein shall have the meanings prescribed in section 10 of said executive order.

Executed at Washington, D. C., on October 19, 1942.

[SEAL] LEO T. CROWLEY,
Alien Property Custodian.

and determining that to the extent that any or all of such nationals are persons not within a designated enemy country, the national interest of the United States requires that such persons be treated as nationals of the aforesaid designated enemy country or countries (Germany and/or Hungary), and having made all determinations and taken all action, after appropriate consultation and certification, required by said executive order or Act or otherwise, and deeming it necessary in the national interest, hereby vests such property in the Alien Property Custodian, to be held, used, administered, liquidated, sold or otherwise dealt with in the interest of and for the benefit of the United States.

Such property and any or all of the proceeds thereof shall be held in a special account pending further determination of the Alien Property Custodian. This shall not be deemed to limit the powers of the Alien Property Custodian to return such property or the proceeds thereof, or to indicate that compensation will not be paid in lieu thereof, if and when it should be determined that such return should be made or such compensation should be paid.

Any person, except a national of a designated enemy country, asserting any claim arising as a result of this order may file with the Alien Property Custodian a notice of his claim, together with a request for a hearing thereon, on Form APC-1, within one year from the date hereof, or within such further time as may be allowed by the Alien Property Custodian. Nothing herein contained shall be deemed to constitute an admission of the existence, validity or right to allowance of any such claim.

The terms "national", "designated enemy country" and "business enterprise within the United States" as used herein shall have the meanings prescribed in section 10 of said executive order.

Executed at Washington, D. C., on October 20, 1942.

[SEAL] LEO T. CROWLEY,
Alien Property Custodian.

[F. R. Doc. 42–11568; Filed, November 6, 1942; 11:31 a. m.]

EXHIBIT A

Copyright No.	Nature of work	Titles of works	Copyright owners	Authors
E35717....	Musical composition...	Essential finger exercises.	Rozsavolgyi & Co., Budapest, Hungary.	E. von Dohnanyi, a national of Hungary.
E9095....	Musical composition...	Essential finger exercises.	Rozsavolgyi & Co., Budapest, Hungary.	E von Dohnanyi, a national of Hungary.
E6351....	Musical composition...	Waltz from the Ballet Nails.	Rozsavolgyi & Co., Budapest, Hungary.	E von Dohnanyi, a national of Hungary.
E566706...	Musical composition...	Capriccio; in Klavier F. Moll.	Rozsavolgyi & Co., Budapest, Hungary.	E von Dohnanyi, a national of Hungary.
A45434...	Book..............	Magnesium und seine Legierungen.	Julius Springer, Berlin, Germany.	Adolph Beck, H. Altwicker and others, nationals of Germany.

[F. R. Doc. 42–11567; Filed, November 6, 1942; 11:33 a. m.]

[Vesting Order Number 248]

ALL OF THE CAPITAL STOCK OF UNION BANKING CORPORATION AND CERTAIN INDEBTEDNESS OWING BY IT

Under the authority of the Trading with the enemy Act, as amended, and Executive Order No. 9095, as amended,[1] and pursuant to law, the undersigned, after investigation, finding:

(a) That the property described as follows:

All of the capital stock of Union Banking Corporation, a New York corporation, New York, New York, which is a business enterprise within the United States, consisting of 4,000 shares of $100 par value common capital stock, the names of the registered owners of which, and the number of shares owned by which respectively, are as follows:

Names	Number of shares
E. Roland Harriman..................	3,991
Cornelius Lievense..................	4
Harold D. Pennington..................	1
Ray Morris..................	1
Prescott S. Bush..................	1
H. J. Kouwenhoven..................	1
Johann G. Groeninger..................	1
Total..................	4,000

[1] 7 F.R. 5205.

all of which shares are held for the benefit of Bank voor Handel en Scheepvaart, N. V., Rotterdam, The Netherlands, which bank is owned or controlled by members of the Thyssen family, nationals of Germany and/or Hungary,

is property of nationals, and represents ownership of said business enterprise which is a national, of a designated enemy country or countries (Germany and/or Hungary);

(b) That the property described as follows:

All right, title, interest and claim of any name or nature whatsoever of the aforesaid Bank voor Handel en Scheepvaart, and August Thyssen-Bank, Berlin, Germany, and each of them, in and to all indebtedness, contingent or otherwise and whether or not matured, owing to them, or each of them, by said Union Banking Corporation, including but not limited to all security rights in and to any and all collateral for any or all of such indebtedness and the right to sue for and collect such indebtedness,

is an interest in the aforesaid business enterprise held by nationals of an enemy country or countries, and also is property within the United States owned or controlled by nationals of a designated enemy country or countries (Germany and/or Hungary);

[Vesting Order Number 250]

CERTAIN PERSONAL PROPERTY OF ALOIS SCHLICK

Under the authority of the Trading with the enemy Act, as amended, and Executive Order No. 9095, as amended[1] and pursuant to law, the undersigned, after investigation, finding that the property described as follows:

One Schlick Universal High Speed full width Beaming Machine, stored with Robert Reiner, Incorporated, 556 Gregory Avenue, Weehawken, New Jersey, and belonging to Alois Schlick, a citizen of Germany whose last known address was represented to the undersigned as being Hohenstein-Ernsthal, Saxony, Germany,

is property within the United States owned or controlled by a national of a designated enemy country (Germany),

H) Vesting Order No. 248
(Library of Congress/Law Department)

ALREADY IN THE THEATER OF OPERATIONS.
F. A CONSIDERABLE DUTCH NAVAL FORCE IS IN THE
ORIENT THAT WOULD BE OF VALUE IF ALLIED TO U.S.

8.   A CONSIDERATION OF THE FOREGOING LEADS TO THE
CONCLUSION THAT PROMPT AGGRESSIVE NAVAL ACTION AGAINST JAPAN BY
THE UNITED STATES WOULD RENDER JAPAN INCAPABLE OF AFFORDING ANY
HELP TO GERMANY AND ITALY IN THEIR ATTACK ON ENGLAND AND THAT
JAPAN ITSELF WOULD BE FACED WITH A SITUATION IN WHICH HER NAVY
COULD BE FORCED TO FIGHT ON MOST UNFAVORABLE TERMS OR ACCEPT
FAIRLY EARLY COLLAPSE OF THE COUNTRY THROUGH THE FORCE OF BLOCKADE.
A PROMPT AND EARLY DECLARATION OF WAR AFTER ENTERING INTO SUIT-
ABLE ARRANGEMENTS WITH ENGLAND AND HOLLAND, WOULD BE MOST EFFECTIVE
IN BRINGING ABOUT THE EARLY COLLAPSE OF JAPAN AND THUS ELEIMINATING
OUR ENEMY IN THE PACIFIC BEFORE GERMANY AND ITALY COULD STRIKE
AT US EFFECTIVELY.   FURTHERMORE, ELIMINATION OF JAPAN MUST SURELY
STRENGTHEN BRITAIN'S POSITION AGAINST GERMANY AND ITALY AND, IN
ADDITION, SUCH ACTION WOULD INCREASE THE CONFIDENCE AND SUPPORT
OF ALL NATIONS WHO TEND TO BE FRIENDLY TOWARDS US.

9.   IT IS NOT BELIEVED THAT IN THE PRESENT STATE OF
POLITICAL OPINION THE UNITED STATES GOVERNMENT IS CAPABLE OF
DECLARING WAR AGAINST JAPAN WITHOUT MORE ADO; AND IT IS BARELY
POSSIBLE THAT VIGOROUS ACTION ON OUR PART MIGHT LEAD THE
JAPANESE TO MODIFY THEIR ATTITUDE. THEREFORE, THE FOLLOWING
COURSE OF ACTION IS SUGGESTED:

A. MAKE AN ARRANGEMENT WITH BRITAIN FOR THE USE OF
   BRITISH BASES IN THE PACIFIC, PARTICULARLY
   SINGAPORE.
B. MAKE AN ARRANGEMENT WITH HOLLAND FOR THE USE OF
   BASE FACILITIES AND ACQUISITION OF SUPPLIES
   IN THE DUTCH EAST INDIES.
C. GIVE ALL POSSIBLE AID TO THE CHINESE GOVERNMENT
   OF CHIANG-KAI-SHEK.
D. SEND A DIVISION OF LONG RANGE HEAVY CRUISERS TO
   THE ORIENT, PHILIPPINES, OR SINGAPORE.
E. SEND TWO DIVISIONS OF SUBMARINES TO THE ORIENT.
F. KEEP THE MAIN STRENGTH OF THE U.S.FLEET NOW IN
   THE PACIFIC IN THE VICINITY OF THE HAWAIIAN ISLANDS.
G. INSIST THAT THE DUTCH REFUSE TO GRANT JAPANESE
   DEMANDS FOR UNDUE ECONOMIC CONCESSIONS, PARTI-
   CULARLY OIL.
H. COMPLETELY EMBARGO ALL U.S. TRADE WITH JAPAN,
   IN COLLABORATION WITH A SIMILAR EMBARGO IMPOSED
   BY THE BRITISH EMPIRE.

10.   IF BY THESE MEANS JAPAN COULD BE LED TO COMMIT AN
OVERT ACT OF WAR, SO MUCH THE BETTER. AT ALL EVENTS WE MUST BE FULLY
PREPARED TO ACCEPT THE THREAT OF WAR.

A.H. McCOLLUM ✓

CC-OP-16
OP-16-F
FILE

I) Lt. Commander Arthur McCollum's Memorandum
*(Discovered by Robert B. Stinnett in Box 6 of a
special U.S. Navy collection in RG 38 in the Military
Reference Branch of Archives II, January 24, 1995)*

J) *The Honolulu Advertiser* Front Page, November 30, 1941
(Courtesy of The Honolulu Advertiser)

China – April, 1945

War-Weary Farmer —

I should like to find the existence of what my father called, "Plain living and high thinking".

I want some fields and hills, woodlands and streams I can call my own. I want to spend my strength in making the fields green, and the cattle fat, so that I may give sustenance to my loved ones, and aid to those neighbors who suffer misfortune. I do not want a life of monotonous paper-shuffling or of trafficking with money-mad traders.

I want only enough of science to enable a fruitful husbandry of the land with simple tools, a time for leisure, and the guarding of my family's health. I do not care to be absorbed in the endless examinings of force and space and matter, which, I believe can only slowly lead to God.

I do not want a hectic hurrying from place to place on whizzing machines or busy streets. I do not want an elbowing through crowds of impatient strangers who have time neither to think their own thoughts nor to know real friendship. I want to live slowly, to relax with my family before a glowing fireplace, to welcome the visits of my neighbors, to worship

K) *War-Weary Farmer* by John Birch
(Courtesy of Robert Birch)

God, to enjoy a book, to lie on a shaded grassy bank and watch the clouds sail across the blue.

I want to love a wife who prefers rural peace to urban excitement, one who would rather climb a hilltop to watch a sunset with me than to take a taxi to any Broadway play. I want a woman who is not afraid of bearing children, and who is able to rear them with a love for home and the soil, and the fear of God.

I want of Government only protection against the violence and injustices of evil or selfish men.

I want to reach the sunset of life sound in body and mind, flanked by strong sons and grandsons, enjoying the friendship and respect of my neighbors, surrounded by fertile fields and sleek cattle, and retaining my boyhood faith in Him who promised a life to come.

Where can I find this world? Would its anacivonism doom it to ridicule or loneliness? Is there yet a place, for such simple ways in my own America? Or must I seek a vale in Turkestan where beautiful flocks still graze on quiet hills. JMB

AG 201 Birch, John M.   WASHINGTON 25, D. C.
PC-0 251009

                                         12 September 1945

        Mrs. George Birch
        R. F. D. #1
        Macon, Georgia

Dear Mrs. Birch:

        It is with deep regret that I confirm the telegram of
recent date informing you of the death of your son, Captain John M.
Birch, 0689028, Air Corps.

        The official casualty report states that your son was
killed on 25 August 1945 enroute to Suchow, China on the Lunghai
Railway, as the result of stray bullets.

        In order that families may receive as much information
as possible, provisions have been made for the unit commander or
chaplain to send a letter containing further information to the
emergency addressee or next of kin of each person who dies overseas
in the service of our country. It is not known just when the
letter can be expected, but it is hoped that it will not be
long delayed.

        I sincerely regret that this message must carry so much
sorrow into your home and I hope that in time you may find sustaining comfort in knowing that he served his country honorably.

        My deepest sympathy is extended to you in your bereavement.

                              Sincerely yours,

                              Edward F. Witsell

                              EDWARD F. WITSELL
                              Major General
                              Acting The Adjutant General of the Army

1 Inclosure
WD Pamphlet No. 20-15

L) General Witsell's Letter to Mrs. George Birch
(Courtesy of Robert Birch)

This Government has been informed that a Jewish
state has been proclaimed in Palestine, and recognition
has been requested by the *provisional* Government thereof.

The United States recognizes the provisional government as the de facto authority of the new *State of* Jewish
state. *ISRAEL*

Harry Truman

Approved,
May 14, 1948.

6.11

B File

M) President Truman's Press Release, May 14, 1948
*(The Harry S. Truman Presidential Museum
and Library, Charlie Ross Papers)*

TOP SECRET SPECIAL HANDLING NOFORN

THE JOINT CHIEFS OF STAFF
WASHINGTON 25, D.C.

UNCLASSIFIED   13 March 1962

MEMORANDUM FOR THE SECRETARY OF DEFENSE

Subject: Justification for US Military Intervention
          in Cuba (TS)

     1. The Joint Chiefs of Staff have considered the attached
Memorandum for the Chief of Operations, Cuba Project, which
responds to a request of that office for brief but precise
description of pretexts which would provide justification
for US military intervention in Cuba.

     2. The Joint Chiefs of Staff recommend that the
proposed memorandum be forwarded as a preliminary submission
suitable for planning purposes. It is assumed that there
will be similar submissions from other agencies and that
these inputs will be used as a basis for developing a
time-phased plan. Individual projects can then be
considered on a case-by-case basis.

     3. Further, it is assumed that a single agency will be
given the primary responsibility for developing military
and para-military aspects of the basic plan. It is
recommended that this responsibility for both overt and
covert military operations be assigned the Joint Chiefs of
Staff.

                          For the Joint Chiefs of Staff:

SYSTEMATICALLY REVIEWED
BY JCS ON ___21 May 84___
CLASSIFICATION CONTINUED

                          L. L. LEMNITZER
                             Chairman
                       Joint Chiefs of Staff

1 Enclosure
  Memo for Chief of Operations, Cuba Project   EXCLUDED FROM GDS

                              ┌─────────────────────────────┐
                              │ EXCLUDED FROM AUTOMATIC   │
                              │ REGRADING; DOD DIR 5200.10 │
                              │   DOES NOT APPLY   │
                              └─────────────────────────────┘

TOP SECRET SPECIAL HANDLING NOFORN

N) "Operation Northwoods" Document (selected pages)
(Originally obtained for, and cited by,
James Bamford in Body of Secrets)

SECRET SPECIAL HANDLING NOFORN

ANNEX TO APPENDIX TO ENCLOSURE A

PRETEXTS TO JUSTIFY US MILITARY INTERVENTION IN CUBA

(Note: The courses of action which follow are a preliminary
submission suitable only for planning purposes. They are
arranged neither chronologically nor in ascending order.
Together with similar inputs from other agencies, they are
intended to provide a point of departure for the development
of a single, integrated, time-phased plan. Such a plan would
permit the evaluation of individual projects within the context
of cumulative, correlated actions designed to lead inexorably
to the objective of adequate justification for US military
intervention in Cuba).

1. Since it would seem desirable to use legitimate
provocation as the basis for US military intervention in Cuba
a cover and deception plan, to include requisite preliminary
actions such as has been developed in response to Task 33 c,
could be executed as an initial effort to provoke Cuban
reactions. Harassment plus deceptive actions to convince the
Cubans of imminent invasion would be emphasized. Our military
posture throughout execution of the plan will allow a rapid
change from exercise to intervention if Cuban response justifies.

2. A series of well coordinated incidents will be planned
to take place in and around Guantanamo to give genuine
appearance of being done by hostile Cuban forces.

   a. Incidents to establish a credible attack (not in
   chronological order):

      (1) Start rumors (many). Use clandestine radio.

      (2) Land friendly Cubans in uniform "over-the-fence"
      to stage attack on base.

      (3) Capture Cuban (friendly) saboteurs inside the
      base.

      (4) Start riots near the base main gate (friendly
      Cubans).

UNCLASSIFIED

TOP SECRET SPECIAL HANDLING NOFORN

(5) Blow up ammunition inside the base; start fires.

(6) Burn aircraft on air base (sabotage).

(7) Lob mortar shells from outside of base into base.
Some damage to installations.

(8) Capture assault teams approaching from the sea
or vicinity of Guantanamo City.

(9) Capture militia group which storms the base.

(10) Sabotage ship in harbor; large fires -- napthalene.

(11) Sink ship near harbor entrance. Conduct funerals
for mock-victims (may be lieu of (10)).

b. United States would respond by executing offensive
operations to secure water and power supplies, destroying
artillery and mortar emplacements which threaten the base.

c. Commence large scale United States military operations.

3. A "Remember the Maine" incident could be arranged in
several forms:

a. We could blow up a US ship in Guantanamo Bay and
blame Cuba.

b. We could blow up a drone (unmanned) vessel anywhere
in the Cuban waters. We could arrange to cause such incident
in the vicinity of Havana or Santiago as a spectacular result
of Cuban attack from the air or sea, or both. The presence
of Cuban planes or ships merely investigating the intent of
the vessel could be fairly compelling evidence that the ship
was taken under attack. The nearness to Havana or Santiago
would add credibility especially to those people that might
have heard the blast or have seen the fire. The US could
follow up with an air/sea rescue operation covered by US
fighters to "evacuate" remaining members of the non-existent
crew. Casualty lists in US newspapers would cause a helpful
wave of national indignation.

4. We could develop a Communist Cuban terror campaign in
the Miami area, in other Florida cities and even in Washington.

8   Annex to Appendix
                                    to Enclosure A

The terror campaign could be pointed at Cuban refugees seeking haven in the United States. We could sink a boatload of Cubans enroute to Florida (real or simulated). We could foster attempts on lives of Cuban refugees in the United States even to the extent of wounding in instances to be widely publicized. Exploding a few plastic bombs in carefully chosen spots, the arrest of Cuban agents and the release of prepared documents substantiating Cuban involvement also would be helpful in projecting the idea of an irresponsible government.

5. A "Cuban-based, Castro-supported" filibuster could be simulated against a neighboring Caribbean nation (in the vein of the 14th of June invasion of the Dominican Republic). We know that Castro is backing subversive efforts clandestinely against Haiti, Dominican Republic, Guatemala, and Nicaragua at present and possible others. These efforts can be magnified and additional ones contrived for exposure. For example, advantage can be taken of the sensitivity of the Dominican Air Force to intrusions within their national air space. "Cuban" B-26 or C-46 type aircraft could make cane-burning raids at night. Soviet Bloc incendiaries could be found. This could be coupled with "Cuban" messages to the Communist underground in the Dominican Republic and "Cuban" shipments of arms which would be found, or intercepted, on the beach.

6. Use of MIG type aircraft by US pilots could provide additional provocation. Harassment of civil air, attacks on surface shipping and destruction of US military drone aircraft by MIG type planes would be useful as complementary actions. An F-86 properly painted would convince air passengers that they saw a Cuban MIG, especially if the pilot of the transport were to announce such fact. The primary drawback to this suggestion appears to be the security risk inherent in obtaining or modifying an aircraft. However, reasonable copies of the MIG could be produced from US resources in about three months.

Annex to Appendix
to Enclosure A

UNCLASS...

7. Hijacking attempts against civil air and surface craft
should appear to continue as harassing measures condoned by the
government of Cuba. Concurrently, genuine defections of Cuban
civil and military air and surface craft should be encouraged.

8. It is possible to create an incident which will demonstrate
convincingly that a Cuban aircraft has attacked and shot down
a chartered civil airliner enroute from the United States to
Jamaica, Guatemala, Panama or Venezuela. The destination would
be chosen only to cause the flight plan   route to cross Cuba.
The passengers could be a group of college students off on a
holiday or any grouping of persons with a common interest to
support chartering a non-scheduled flight.

    a. An aircraft at Eglin AFB would be painted and
    numbered as an exact duplicate for a civil registered
    aircraft belonging to a CIA proprietary organization in the
    Miami area. At a designated time the duplicate would be
    substituted for the actual civil aircraft and would be
    loaded with the selected passengers, all boarded under
    carefully prepared aliases. The actual registered
    aircraft would be converted to a drone.

    b. Take off times of the drone aircraft and the actual
    aircraft will be scheduled to allow a rendezvous south of
    Florida. From the rendezvous point the passenger-carrying
    aircraft will descend to minimum altitude and go directly
    into an auxiliary field at Eglin AFB where arrangements will
    have been made to evacuate the passengers and return the
    aircraft to its original status. The drone aircraft
    meanwhile will continue to fly the filed flight plan. When
    over Cuba the drone will being transmitting on the inter-
    national distress frequency a "MAY DAY" message stating he
    is under attack by Cuban MIG aircraft. The transmission
    will be interrupted by destruction of the aircraft which will
    be triggered by radio signal. This will allow ICAO radio

10

Annex to Appendix
to Enclosure A

UNCLASSIFIED

stations in the Western Hemisphere to tell the US what
has happened to the aircraft instead of the US trying to
"sell" the incident.

9. It is possible to create an incident which will make it
appear that Communist Cuban MIGs have destroyed a USAF aircraft
over international waters in an unprovoked attack.

a. Approximately 4 or 5 F-101 aircraft will be dispatched
in trail from Homestead AFB, Florida, to the vicinity of Cuba.
Their mission will be to reverse course and simulate fakir
aircraft for an air defense exercise in southern Florida.
These aircraft would conduct variations of these flights at
frequent intervals. Crews would be briefed to remain at
least 12 miles off the Cuban coast; however, they would be
required to carry live ammunition in the event that hostile
actions were taken by the Cuban MIGs.

b. On one such flight, a pre-briefed pilot would fly
tail-end Charley at considerable interval between aircraft.
While near the Cuban Island this pilot would broadcast that
he had been jumped by MIGs and was going down. No other
calls would be made. The pilot would then fly directly
west at extremely low altitude and land at a secure base, an
Eglin auxiliary. The aircraft would be met by the proper
people, quickly stored and given a new tail number. The
pilot who had performed the mission under an alias, would
resume his proper identity and return to his normal place
of business. The pilot and aircraft would then have
disappeared.

c. At precisely the same time that the aircraft was
presumably shot down a submarine or small surface craft
would disburse F-101 parts, parachute, etc., at approximately
15 to 20 miles off the Cuban coast and depart. The pilots
returning to Homestead would have a true story as far as
they knew. Search ships and aircraft could be dispatched
and parts of aircraft found.

11

TOP SECRET SPECIAL HANDLING NOFORN

Rocky Mountain News

Weather
Beautiful
page 171

125th year, No. 132 | Denver, Colo. | **Thursday** | September 1, 1983 | 25¢

RTD axes executive director

By JOE GARNER
Rocky Mountain News Staff Writer

L.A. Kimball, executive director of the Regional Transportation District for two years, was fired by the district board of directors Wednesday night.

After meeting for more than 2½ hours in a closed session, the board voted 9-5 to fire Kimball, effective immediately.

After the vote was taken in a reconvened public session, Kimball stalked out of the meeting room, pushing his way past a knot of reporters and members of the audience who had stayed until 11 p.m. to see the outcome of the vote. He looked straight ahead, ignoring questions, as he got into an elevator alone. The door closed behind him.

Kimball had appeared cool as he returned to the meeting room when the public session reconvened, giving the impression he didn't realize that he would be ousted from the $71,5000-a-year post.

Under the terms of Kimball's contract, he is to receive six months' severance pay plus an additional 60 days' pay because he was fired without notice, said William Johnson, chairman of the RTD board. Kimball will receive about $48,000.

Johnson said the consensus of the board was that Kimball 54 should be fired "in the best interests of the district. Nothing else will be said. This is a very sensitive issue to a fine gentle-

See KIMBALL, page 41

MARINE OFFICER in combat gear salutes at coffin of 2nd Marine Lt. Donald Losey, slain in Lebanon, under tail of C-141 transport which returned the body to Dover Air Force Base, Delaware. At right Air Force chaplain reads prayer. SEE STORY, PAGE 3

Congressman's flight reportedly forced to Soviet isle

SEOUL, South Korea (UPI) — A Korean Air Lines jumbo jet flying from New York to Seoul Wednesday with 269 people aboard, including a U.S. congressman, was forced to land on Sakhalin, a Soviet-occupied island north of Japan, the government-run television said.

The passengers were reported safe. Among them was Rep. Larry McDonald, D-Ga., John Birch Society chairman, a diplomat spokesman said in Washington that

American officials believed the jet was forced down by Soviet or North Korean fighters planes.

A report on the Korean Broadcasting System said Thursday the CIA had informed the Seoul government of the landing on the Soviet-occupied island about 650 miles north of Tokyo.

In Tokyo, the Japanese foreign ministry said the Soviet foreign ministry had denied the plane was on Sakhalin in a message conveyed to the Japanese embassy in Moscow. Soviet officials in Moscow re-

fused comment and the South Korean foreign ministry said it had no confirmation of the reports.

The situation was complicated because South Korea does not have diplomatic relations with Moscow. Soviet news agency Tass did not report the incident.

The Boeing 747 jetliner was reported missing Wednesday and officials originally feared the plane may have been hijacked.

The plane, KAL Flight 7, which originated in

See JET, page 34

O) *Rocky Mountain News* Front Page, September 1, 1983
(Reprinted by permission of Rocky Mountain News)

- 21 -

1.13.2.2 A KAL flight release sheet was prepared by the flight operations officer on duty. It contained the following information:

a) general data: flight number (KE 007) aircraft registration (HL7442), estimated time of departure and estimated time of arrival;

b) mass and balance calculation;

c) take-off data;

d) fuel calculations including reserve fuel for diversion to alternate airport (Kimhae - 40 minutes), holding (30 minutes) and contingencies (10 per cent);

e) weather information; and

f) copies of NOTAMs regarding airport maintenance work at Seoul/Kimpo International Airport and the closing of runway 09/27 at Osan Airport. The pilot-in-command was informed that the Anchorage VOR/DME was out of service.

1.13.2.3 The flight release sheet was signed by the pilot-in-command. He also approved the mass and balance calculations which showed that the mass and balance of the aircraft were within limits for take-off and for the landing in Seoul.

1.13.3 Use of headset/speaker

1.13.3.1 The use of headsets during climb and approach was a company requirement. At cruising altitude, the use of either headsets or speakers was at the discretion of the pilot-in-command.

1.13.4 Aircraft lighting

1.13.4.1 Aircraft HL7442 was not equipped with white strobe anti-collision lights. The red anti-collision rotating beacons and the navigation lights were on when KE 007 left Anchorage. The KAL logo light on the vertical fin was normally illuminated but its use was at the discretion of the pilot-in-command. It was common practice for many airlines, including KAL, to fly at night with window shades lowered.

1.13.4.2 The lighting of the flight deck during cruise (dimmed or fully illuminated) was at the discretion of the pilot-in-command.

1.13.5 Radio communication

1.13.5.1 Company procedures required the distress frequency 121.5 MHz to be monitored throughout flight. The procedure with the VHF radios was for 121.5 MHz to be set on VHF 1, leaving VHF 2 to be used for ATC while VHF 3 was on standby and was normally used for company communications and ATIS. The DFDR radio transmission keying parameters showed that KE 007 used VHF 2 for communications with ATC and VHF 3 for company communications including communications with KE 015. As VHF 1 was to be tuned to 121.5 MHz no transmissions were

P) ICAO Report, 1993 (selected pages)
(International Civil Aviation Organization)

- 69 -

Time	Station: From - To	Track 1	Track 4	Track 6	Track 7
	805 - Deputat			Yes, approaching it, approaching closer.	
	Deputat - 805			Roger.	
	805 - Deputat			The target has a flashing light. I already approached it to a distance of somewhere like 2 kilometres.	
	Deputat - 805			Is the target descending?	
	805 - Deputat			The target? No, at ten thousand.	
	Deputat - 805			Roger.	
	163 - Deputat			163, contact with both, range 10-15 kilometres.	
	805 - Deputat			805, my instructions.	
	163 - Deputat			Roger.	
	805 - Deputat			The target is reducing speed.	
	CPO - RCA				So, RCA, do you have contact with 163 from Smirnykh's airbase?
	RCA - CPO				I see 805.
	CPO - RCA				Roger. Monitor 805, 163 and 121 is approaching.
	RCA - CPO				Into this area?
	CPO - RCA				All in a close area.
	RCA - CPO				I monitor all of them.
	Deputat - 805			Roger, 805.	
	805 - Deputat			I...am already moving out in front of the target.	
6.22	Deputat - 805			Increase speed, 805.	

- 72 -

Time	Station: From - To	Track 1	Track 4	Track 6	Track 7
	805 - Deputat			Already switched on.	
	121 - Deputat			121, on heading 30.	
6.25.31	805 - Deputat			Launch.	
6.25	805 - Deputat			Executed launch.	
6.26.01	805 - Deputat			The target is destroyed.	
	Deputat - 805			Break off attack, to the right, heading 360.	
	805 - Deputat			Breaking off attack.	
	163 - Karnaval			For 163 instructions.	
	163 - Karnaval			Karnaval, 163.	
	Karnaval - 163			Remainder.	
	163 - Karnaval			My wing tanks indicators lit up. The remainder differs by 600 litres for now.	
	Deputat - 805			805 remainder.	
	805 - Deputat			Remainder 1500.	
	Deputat - 805			Roger, turn to the right, heading 60 degrees, to homing, altitude 8.	
	805 - Deputat			Wilco, request distance to the base.	
	Deputat - 805			Your distance 125.	
	805 - Deputat			Roger.	
	Karnaval - 163			For 163, "that's all".	
6.27	163 - Karnaval			Karnaval, 163.	
	Deputat - 163			163, Deputat, Deputat, controlling you and contact with you, controlling, turn to the left, to heading 180.	

United States Senate
COMMITTEE ON FOREIGN RELATIONS
WASHINGTON, DC 20510-6225

December 10, 1991

His Excellency
Boris Yeltsin
The President of the
Russian Republic
The Kremlin
Moscow, U.S.S.R.

Dear Mr. President:

One of the greatest tragedies of the Cold War was the shoot-down of the Korean Airlines flight KAL-007 by the Armed Forces of what was then the Soviet Union on September 1, 1983.

This event had elements of a personal catastrophe for me, since I was on the parallel flight that night of KAL-015, which departed Anchorage, Alaska about fifteen minutes after KAL-007. Both flights stopped in Anchorage for refueling. I shall never forget mingling with the doomed passengers of KAL-007 in the transit lounge, including two sweet young girls who waved goodby to me when they were called to return to their fatal flight.

The KAL-007 tragedy was one of the most tense incidents of the entire Cold War. However, now that relations between our two nations have improved substantially, I believe that it is time to resolve the mysteries surrounding this event. Clearing the air on this issue could help further to improve relations.

Accordingly, I respectfully request that the government of the Russian Republic gain access to the files of the former KGB and of the Ministry of Defense in order to resolve the attached questions. I hope that you will personally intervene with the relevant authorities of the former Soviet Union in order to provide answers to these questions.

The American people, indeed, the families of all passengers on KAL-007, will be deeply grateful for your efforts.

Sincerely,

Jesse Helms

JESSE HELMS:jl

Q) Senator Jesse Helms's Letter to Boris Yeltsin
*(The International Committee for the Rescue
of KAL 007 Survivors, Inc.)*

United States Senate

COMMITTEE ON FOREIGN RELATIONS

WASHINGTON, DC 20510-6225

February 11, 1992

Mr. Avraham Shifrin
Executive Director
Research Centre for USSR Prisons
P.O. Box 23678
Ramot 91235
Jerusalem, Israel

Dear Avraham:

Senator Helms has asked me to respond to your recent letter to him of January 26, 1992. His health is quite good, and he sends you and Elena his best regards.

There has been a major re-structuring and re-organization of Senator Helms' staff of the Senate Committee on Foreign Relations, and he has named me to be his new Staff Director for the Minority. Dr. Lucier is no longer on the staff, but David Sullivan has been retained.

The information which you conveyed to them last year is safe and fully protected. As David told you, a copy of it was given to the U.S. Central Intelligence Agency for possible corroboration. The CIA found your information to be very interesting, and consistent with some of their information. Unfortunately, however, CIA was not able to either confirm or deny the balance of it. Both CIA and the Committee will keep your information confidential.

Enclosed are copies of two letters to Russian President Boris Yeltsin which Senator Helms sent in December. You can see that the letter inquiring about the fate of KAL-007 is a direct result of your information. Senator Helms has not yet had replies from Yeltsin, but we expect to get them. I will certainly let you know what Yeltsin's response is.

Senator Helms appreciates very much the extensive work which you have done on the KAL-007 incident, and I hope that you will continue to keep us informed of your research as it progresses.

Sincerely,

Bud Nance

Bud Nance
Rear Admiral (U.S. Navy, retired)
Minority Staff Director

R) Rear Admiral Nance's Letter to Avraham Shifrin
(The International Committee for the Rescue of KAL 007 Survivors, Inc.)

CENTRAL INTELLIGENCE AGENCY
Office of Congressional Affairs
Washington, D.C.20505
Telephone: 482–6136

TO:

S) CIA Top Secret/Codeword
(John Campbell/John Birch Society)

TOP SECRET/CODEWORD

SENSITIVE RESTRICTED ACCESS

UNITED STATES

DID KAL-007 SUCCESSFULLY DITCH AT SEA AND WERE THERE SURVIVORS?

HOW THE SOVIET MILITARY'S COVER-UP OF THEIR MANY MISTAKES IN THEIR 1983 SHOOTING DOWN OF KOREAN AIRLINES FLIGHT-007 LED TO THE SOVIET "SPY PLANE" DECEPTION COVER-STORY, WHICH IS NOW FINALLY UNRAVELLING

TOP SECRET/CODEWORD

DEPARTMENT OF HEALTH & HUMAN SERVICES   Public Health Service

Centers for Disease Control
and Prevention (CDC)
Atlanta GA 30333

JUN 21 1995

The Honorable Donald W. Riegle, Jr.
United States Senate
Washington, D.C. 20510-2201

Dear Senator Riegle:

In 1993, at your request, the Centers for Disease Control and
Prevention (CDC) forwarded to your office a listing of all
biological materials, including viruses, retroviruses, bacteria,
and fungi, which CDC provided to the government of Iraq from
October 1, 1984, through October 13, 1993. Recently, in the
course of reviewing our shipping records for a Freedom of
Information Act (FOIA) request from a private citizen, we
identified an additional shipment, on May 21, 1985, that was not
included on the list that was provided to your office. Following
this discovery, we conducted a thorough review of all of our
shipping records and are confident that we have now included a
listing of all shipments. A corrected list is enclosed (Note:
the new information is italicized).

These additional materials were hand-carried by Dr. Mohammad
Mahmud to Iraq after he had spent three months training in a CDC
laboratory. Most of the materials were non-infectious diagnostic
reagents for detecting evidence of infections to mosquito-borne
viruses. Only two of the materials are on the Commodity Control
List, i.e., Yersinia pestis (the agent of plague) and dengue
virus. (The strain of plague bacillus was non-virulent, and CDC
is currently petitioning the Department of Commerce to remove
this particular variant from the list of controlled materials).

We regret that our earlier list was incomplete and appreciate
your understanding.

                                 Sincerely,

                                 David Satcher, M.D., Ph.D.
                                 Director

Enclosure

        CDC SHIPMENTS TO IRAQ OCTOBER 1, 1984 THROUGH PRESENT

4/26/85   8 vials antigen and antisera   Minister of Health
           (R. rickettsii and R. typhi)   Ministry   of   Health

           to diagnose rickettsial infections Baghdad, Iraq
           (non-infectious)

           Etiologic Agents
5/21/85   lyophilized arbovirus seed   Dr.   Mohammad   Imad

                                               Al-Deen M. Mahmud
           West Nile Fever Virus   Dept. of Microbiology
           Lyophilized cultures of avirulent   College of Medicine
             Yersinia pestis and   University of Basrah
           Y. pseudotuberculosis (strain T)   Basrah, Iraq
           0.5 ml Bhanja Virus (Ig 690)
           0.5 ml Dengue Virus Type 2 (New Guinea C)
           0.5 ml Dengue Virus Type 3 (H-87)
           0.5 ml Hazara Virus (Pak IC 280)
           0.5 ml Kemerovo Virus (Rio)
           0.5 ml Langat Virus (TP 21)
           0.5 ml Sandfly Fever/Naples Virus (original)
           0.5 ml Sandfly Fever/Sicilian Virus (original)
           0.5 ml Sindbis Virus (EgAr 339)
           0.5 ml Tahyna Virus (Bardos 92)
           0.5 ml Thoyoto Virus (II A)

T) Dr. David Satcher's Letter to Senator Donald Riegle, Jr.
(Business Week)

Diagnostic Reagents and Associated Materials
2 vials each Y. pestis FA (+ & -)
  conjugates
2 vials Y. pestis Fraction 1 antigen
10 vials Y. pestis bacteriophage impregnated paper strips
5 plague-infected mouse tissue smears (fixed)
Various protocols for diagnostic bacteriology tests
23 X 0.5 ml Bhanja (Ig 690) antigen
22 X 0.5 ml Dengue Type 2 (New Guinea C) antigen
22 X 0.5 ml Dengue Type 3 (H-87) antigen
22 X 0.5 ml Hazara (Pak IC 280) antigen
23 X 0.5 ml Kemerovo (Rio) antigen
21 X 0.5 ml Langat (TP 21) antigen
24 X 0.5 ml Sandfly Fever/Naples (original) antigen
24 X 0.5 ml Sandfly Fever/Sicilian (original) antigen
23 X 0.5 ml Sindbis (EgAr 339) antigen
23 X 0.5 ml Tahyna (Bardos 92) antigen
20 X 0.5 ml Thogoto (IL A) antigen
23 X 0.5 ml Bhanja (Ig 690) antigen
21 X 0.5 ml West Nile (Eg 101) antigen
20 X 1.0 ml Normal SMB antigen
10 X 0.5 ml Normal SML antigen
5 X 1.0 ml Bhanja (Ig 690) antibody
5 X 1.0 ml Dengue Type 2 (New Guinea C) antibody
5 X 1.0 ml Dengue Type 3 (H-87) antibody
5 X 1.0 ml Hazara (Pak IC 280) antibody
5 X 1.0 ml Kemerovo (Rio) antibody
5 X 2.0 ml Langat (TP 21) antibody
5 X 1.0 ml Sandfly Fever/Naples (original) antibody
5 X 2.0 ml Sandfly Fever/Sicilian (original) antibody
5 X 1.0 ml Sindbis (EgAr 339) antibody
5 X 1.0 ml Tahyna (Bardos 92) antibody

5 X 1.0 ml Thogoto (IL A) antibody
5 X 1.0 ml West Nile (Eg 101) antibody
3 X 1.0 ml Normal MHIAF (SMB) antibody
3 X 1.0 ml Normal MHIAF (SML) antibody
1.0 ml A polyvalent grouping fluid
1.0 ml AIYA, etc. polyvalent grouping fluid
1.0 ml B polyvalent grouping fluid
1.0 ml BUN polyvalent grouping fluid
1.0 ml BWA polyvalent grouping fluid
1.0 ml C-1 polyvalent grouping fluid
1.0 ml C-2 polyvalent grouping fluid
1.0 ml CAL polyvalent grouping fluid
1.0 ml CAP polyvalent grouping fluid
1.0 ml CON polyvalent grouping fluid
1.0 ml GMA polyvalent grouping fluid
1.0 ml KEM polyvalent grouping fluid
1.0 ml PAL polyvalent grouping fluid
1.0 ml PAT polyvalent grouping fluid
1.0 ml PHL polyvalent grouping fluid
1.0 ml QRF polyvalent grouping fluid
1.0 ml Rabies, etc. polyvalent grouping fluid
1.0 ml SIM polyvalent grouping fluid
1.0 ml TCR polyvalent grouping fluid
1.0 ml VSV polyvalent grouping fluid
1.0 ml polyvalent 1
1.0 ml polyvalent 2
1.0 ml polyvalent 3
1.0 ml polyvalent 4
1.0 ml polyvalent 5
1.0 ml polyvalent 6
1.0 ml polyvalent 7
1.0 ml polyvalent 8
1.0 ml polyvalent 9
1.0 ml polyvalent 10
1.0 ml polyvalent 12
1.0 ml Group B1 reagent
1.0 ml Bluetongue reagent
4 x 0.5 ml Dengue 1-4 set monoclonal antibodies
1.0 ml St. Louis Enc. (MSI-7) monoclonal antibody
1.0 ml Western Eq. Enc. (McMillan) monoclonal antibody

6/26/85	3 yeast cultures Candida sp. (etiologic) College of Medicine	Dr. Mohammed S. Khider University of Baghdad Department of Microbiology Baghdad, Iraq
3/10/86	1 vial Botulinum Toxoid # A-2 (non-infectious)	Dr. Rowil Shawil Georgis M.B.CH.B.D.F.H. Officers City Al-Muthanna Quartret 710 Street 13, Close 69, House 28/I Baghdad, Iraq
4/21/86	1 vial Botulinum Toxoid (non-infectious)	M.B.CH.B.D.F.H. Officers City Al-Muthanna Quartret 710 Street 13, Close 69, House 28/I Baghdad, Iraq
7/21/86	teaching supplies (non-infectious) CDC procedure manuals Zikak 54, House 97	Dr. Faqid Alfarhood Mehela 887 Hay Aljihad Kerk, Baghdad, Iraq
7/27/86	teaching supplies (non-infectious) CDC procedure manuals Zikak 54, House 97	Dr. Faqid Alfarhood Mehela 887 Hay Aljihad Kurk, Baghdad, Iraq
11/25/89	5.0 mls Enterococcus faecalis 5.0 mls Enterococcus faecium 5.0 mls Enterococcus avium 5.0 mls Enterococcus raffinosus 5.0 mls Enterococcus gallinarum 5.0 mls Enterococcus durans 5.0 mls Enterococcus hirae 5.0 mls Streptococcus bovis (etiologic)	Dr. Nadeel T. Al Madithi University of Basrah College of Science Department of Biology Basrah, Iraq

BIN LADEN Usama
A-268/5-1998

PRESENT FAMILY NAME: BIN LADEN

FORENAME: Usama   SEX: M

DATE AND PLACE OF BIRTH: 1957 - Jeddah, Saudi Arabia

FATHER'S FORENAMES: Abdulrahamn 'Awadh

IDENTITY CONFIRMED - NATIONALITY: SAUDI ARABIAN (CONFIRMED)

LANGUAGE SPOKEN: Arabic.

ACCOMPLICES:

AL-'ALWAN Faraj Mikhaïl Abdul-Fadeel Jibril, born in 1969, subject of red notice File No. 199 Control No. A-270/5-1998;

AL-WARFALI Faez Abu Zeid Muftah, born in 1968, subject of red notice File No. 1998/20223, Control No. A-271/5-1998;

AL-CHALABI Faraj, born in 1966, subject of red notice File No. 1998/20230, Control No. A-269/5-1998.

SUMMARY OF FACTS OF THE CASE: LIBYA: On 10th March 1994, BIN LADEN, AL-CHALABI, AL-'ALWAN and AL-WARFALI killed two German nationals near Surt.

REASON FOR NOTICE: Wanted on arrest warrant No. 1.27.288/1998, issued on 16th March 1998 by the judicial authorities in Tripoli, Libya, for murder and illegal possession of firearms.

EXTRADITION WILL BE REQUESTED FROM ANY COUNTRY EXCEPT ISRAEL.

If found in a country from which extradition will be requested, please detain; if found elsewhere, please keep a watch on his movements and activities. In either case, immediately inform INTERPOL TRIPOLI (Reference 6.27.8497.352 of 15th April 1998) and the ICPO-Interpol General Secretariat.

File No. 1998/20232   Control No. A-268/5-1998

CONFIDENTIAL INTENDED ONLY FOR POLICE AND JUDICIAL AUTHORITIES

U) Interpol Arrest Warrant for Osama bin Laden
(Jean-Charles Brisard and Guillaume Dasquié)

"All the News That's Fit to Print"

The New York Times

Late Edition

New York: Today, hazy sunshine, hot and humid with light winds. High 92. Tonight, hazy, warm. Low 73. Tomorrow, hazy, hot. High 96. Yesterday, high 91, low 69. Details are on page C4.

VOL.CXLI .. No. 49,070   Copyright © 1992 The New York Times   NEW YORK, WEDNESDAY, AUGUST 26, 1992   50 CENTS

Bush's Gains From Convention Nearly Evaporate in Latest Poll

Public Wants Talk on Economy and Health Care

By ADAM CLYMER
Special to The New York Times

WASHINGTON, Aug. 25 — President Bush's gains from four days in the spotlight at the Republican National Convention have almost completely evaporated, as the President failed to convince the public that he is committed to change and to reviving the economy, the latest New York Times/CBS News Poll shows.

Gov. Bill Clinton of Arkansas re-established a strong lead, holding a 51 percent to 36 percent edge in the poll, which was taken Sunday and Monday. That is about the same margin he held before last week's convention.

The poll showed the public had far more interest in hearing about Mr. Clinton's favorite issues, the economy and health care, than in topics featured at the convention, like family values and homosexuality.

The survey of 903 registered voters also provided fresh evidence of the loose allegiances of voters this year, showing that large numbers of men, young people, the poor and the financially comfortable all shifted back and forth in the last two weeks.

Turnaround Among Men

Men, for example, had supported President Bush by 47 percent to 40 percent in a Times/CBS News Poll taken last Thursday as the convention ended. By the time of this poll, they supported Mr. Clinton by 51 percent to 38 percent. Their shift accounted for most of the change between the two polls, as the earlier one favored Mr. Clinton, but only by 45 to 42 percent overall.

Robert M. Teeter, chairman of the President's re-election campaign and a leading Republican poll taker for a quarter century, said he thought the

results were more favorable to Mr. Clinton than was actually true. He said the Bush campaign had done no fresh polling since the convention but added, "Usually you will not lose what you gained" from a convention.

"My view is the race is about 50 to 48," he said.

Stan Greenberg, Mr. Clinton's poll taker, said his latest data did indicate a double-digit Clinton lead that "re-

Continued on Page A19, Column 1

Clinton Confronts Draft Record In a Frank Address to Veterans

ISRAEL OFFERS PLAN FOR ARABS TO RULE IN OCCUPIED LANDS

ELECTIONS FOR A COUNCIL

Move, Consistent With Accord at Camp David, Falls Short of Palestinian Objective

By ROBERT PEAR
Special to The New York Times

WASHINGTON, Aug. 25 — Israel gave Palestinian negotiators a detailed set of proposals today for Palestinian self-rule in the occupied West Bank and the Gaza Strip.

On the second day of the latest round of Middle East peace talks, the Israelis, representing the new Labor-dominated Government, said the proposals would allow the Palestinians to run many aspects of daily life through an elected "administrative council." Elections could be held in April or May of next year, the Israelis said.

There have been widespread expectations that the Labor coalition would push harder for some breakthrough in the talks with the Palestinians, demonstrating its willingness to go further than the preceding Likud Government of Prime Minister Yitzhak Shamir, which resisted giving much in the way of autonomy to the Palestinians.

Camp David Outline

The proposals, which are consistent with the principles of the Palestinian autonomy plan approved in 1978 by Egyptian, Israeli and American negotiators at Camp David, Md., but never put into effect, specify areas of activity in which the Palestinians would have complete discretion and other areas in which they would be required to coordinate their activities with Israel.

Under one Israeli proposal, for example, Palestinian authorities could collect taxes from Palestinians in the occupied territories, but they would be expected to consult Israeli authorities

Thousands Homeless in Florida Storm

Miami residents turned out to get safe drinking water after the hurricane left many areas without service.

Down to the Basics: Hunting For Food, Water and Shelter

By LARRY ROHTER
Special to The New York Times

MIAMI, Aug. 25 — Amid mounting public impatience, widespread confusion and rising estimates of the hurricane damage inflicted on South Florida, the authorities are struggling to restore water, electricity and other basic services.

Throughout today hundreds of thousands of people ignored warnings to stay off the streets. Instead they roamed metropolitan Miami in cars or on foot to search for ice, canned foods, gasoline, batteries and charcoal for

supply. "I drove all the way to Broward County — 42 miles up and 42 miles back — to get gas and go to a grocery store," said Patricia A. Thomas, a Pine Lakes resident who is a data processor with a credit card company.

"They are saying on the radio that you should boil all your water," she said as she waited for hours for two 1.5 liter bottles of purified water that could barely tide her family through the night. "But what am I supposed to boil

Louisiana Is Hit by High Wind and Water

By JAMES BARRON

One of the century's most powerful hurricanes barreled across the Gulf of Mexico and slammed into the Louisiana coast last night, carrying torrential rains and gale force winds into coastal Mississippi and Texas, as the storm's toll in lives and property climbed in South Florida.

Gov. Lawton Chiles of Florida said the number of people killed had

---

V) *The New York Times* Front Page, August 26, 1992
(©*The New York Times*)

Endnotes

INTRODUCTION

1 Admiral Thomas H. Moorer, open letter to all Americans, *Accuracy in Media*, in author's personal files.
2 Commander William S. Donaldson, *Interim Report on the Crash of TWA 800 and the Actions of the NTSB and the FBI* (Washington, D.C.: U.S. House of Representatives, 1998), 39.
3 *Ibid.*, 121-24.
4 "Warning not passed down, 9/11 Inquiry Says," *USA Today*, 19 September 2002, 9-A.
5 Donaldson, *Interim Report*, 121.
6 Texe Marrs, "Zionism and Israel," *Conspiracyworld.com*, 20 August 2003 (http://www.conspiracyworld.com).

CHAPTER 1
Land For Peace

1 John McTernan and Bill Koenig, *Israel: The Blessing or The Curse* (Oklahoma City, Okla.: Hearthstone Publishing, 2002), 61.
2 *Ibid.*, 61-62.
3 *Ibid.*, 63.
4 Tom Raum, "Bush surveys storm damage to home," *Maine Sunday Telegram*, 3 November 1991, pp. 1B and 12B.
5 McTernan and Koenig, *Israel: Blessing or Curse*, 63-64.
6 *Ibid.*, 64.
7 *Ibid.*, 66-67.
8 *Ibid.*, 103-4.
9 *Ibid.*, 151.
10 *Ibid.*, 93.
11 *Ibid.*, 94-95.
12 *Ibid.*, 100.
13 *Ibid.*, 99-100.

CHAPTER 2
Goldenah Medinah

1 Peter S. Ruckman, *Israel: A Deadly Piece of Dirt* (Pensacola, Fla.: Bible Baptist Bookstore, 2001), 497.
2 *Ibid.*, 124-28.
3 *Ibid.*, 217.
4 *Ibid.*, 26-27.
5 *Ibid.*, 374-75.
6 *Ibid.*, 75.
7 William Manchester, *A World Lit Only By Fire* (Boston: Little, Brown and Company, 1992), 54.
8 Barbara W. Tuchman, *A Distant Mirror* (New York: Alfred A. Knopf, Inc., 1978), 106-07.
9 Manchester, *World Lit By Fire*, 57.
10 *Ibid.*, 45.

11 Tuchman, *Distant Mirror*, 177.
12 Manchester, *World Lit By Fire*, 73.
13 *Ibid.*
14 *Ibid.*, 3.
15 Peter S. Ruckman, *The Bible: A Deadly Book* (Pensacola, Fla.: Bible Baptist Bookstore, 2003), viii.
16 Ruckman, *Israel: Deadly Dirt*, 287.
17 *Ibid.*, 301-02.
18 *Ibid.*, 293.
19 *Ibid.*, 429.
20 *Ibid.*, 337-38.
21 John McTernan and Bill Koenig, *Israel: The Blessing or The Curse* (Oklahoma City, Okla.: Hearthstone Publishing, 2001), 108.
22 Ruckman, *Bible: Deadly Book*, 82-83.
23 *World Book Encyclopedia*, 2003 ed., vol. P, *s.v.* "Palestine."
24 McTernan and Koenig, *Israel: Blessing or Curse*, 108-09.
25 Ruckman, *Israel: Deadly Dirt*, 476-77.
26 McTernan and Koenig, *Israel: Blessing or Curse*, 112-23.
27 Ruckman, *Israel: Deadly Dirt*, 449.
28 *Ibid.*, 293.
29 Ruckman, *Bible: Deadly Book*, 92.
30 McTernan and Koenig, *Israel: Blessing or Curse*, 186-87.
31 *Ibid.*, 187.
32 *Ibid.*, 188.
33 *Ibid.*, 188-89.
34 *Ibid.*, 157.
35 *Ibid.*, 126.
36 *Ibid.*, 174.

CHAPTER 3
The Fourfold Enlargement of Japheth

1 Carroll Quigley, *Tragedy and Hope: A History of the World in Our Time* (New York: The Macmillan Company, 1966), dust jacket.
2 Dennis Laurence Cuddy, *Secret Records Revealed: The Men, the Money, and the Methods Behind the New World Order* (Oklahoma City, Okla.: Hearthstone Publishing, Ltd., 1994), 7.
3 G. Edward Griffin, *The Creature from Jekyll Island* (Appleton, Wis.: American Opinion, 1994), 270.
4 Cuddy, *Secret Records Revealed*, 8.
5 Quigley, *Tragedy and Hope*, 130.
6 Alister E. McGrath, *In the Beginning: The Story of the King James Bible and How It Changed a Nation, a Language, and a Culture* (New York: Doubleday, 2001), 304-05.
7 Merrill F. Unger, *Archaeology and the Old Testament* (Grand Rapids, Mich.: Zondervan Publishing House, 1970), 83.
8 *World Book Encyclopedia*, 1998, *s.v.* "Noah."

9   *Ibid.,* "Hamites."
10 *The Scofield Study Bible,* ed. C. I. Scofield (New York: Oxford University Press, 1945), 16.
11 Paul Kennedy, *The Rise and Fall of the Great Powers: Economic Change and Military Conflict from 1500 to 2000* (New York: Random House, 1987), 149-50.
12 Samuel P. Huntington, *The Clash of Civilizations and the Remaking of World Order,* (New York: Simon & Schuster, 1996), 81-82.
13 Peter S. Ruckman, *The Book of Genesis* (Pensacola, Fla.: Bible Believers Press Bookstore, 1969), 246.
14 *Scofield Study Bible,* 17.
15 Kennedy, *Rise and Fall of Great Powers,* 16.
16 *Ibid.,* 6.
17 *Ibid.,* 7.
18 *Ibid.,* 10-11.
19 *Ibid.,* 11.
20 *Ibid.,* 12-13.
21 *Ibid.,* 14-15.
22 *Ibid.,* 17.
23 *Ibid.,* 17 and 19.
24 *Ibid.,* 19-20.
25 *Ibid.,* 20.
26 *Ibid.,* 21-22.
27 *Ibid.,* 22.
28 *Ibid.,* 29.
29 *Ibid.,* 30.
30 McGrath, *In The Beginning,* 5.
31 Philip Schaff, *History of the Christian Church,* vol. 6, *The Middle Ages, from Boniface VIII, 1204, to the Protestant Reformation, 1517* (Grand Rapids, Mich.: Wm. B. Eerdmans Publishing Co., 1910), 722.
32 Kennedy, *Rise and Fall of Great Powers,* 10.
33 J. R. Green, *A Short History of the English People* (New York: Harper and Bros. Publishers, 1884), 455-57.
34 Quigley, *Tragedy and Hope,* 16.
35 Arnold Dallimore, *George Whitefield: The Life and Times of the Great Evangelist of the Eighteenth-Century Revival,* vol. 1, (Carlisle, Penn.: Banner of Truth Trust, 1970), 289-92.
36 James Gilchrist Lawson, *Deeper Experiences of Famous Christians* (Anderson, Ind.: Warner Press, 1972), 135.
37 Arnold Dallimore, *George Whitefield,* 2:160.
38 Antony C. Sutton, *Energy: The Created Crisis* (New York: Books in Focus, 1979), 13.
39 Kennedy, *Rise and Fall of Great Powers,* 204.
40 *Ibid.,* 147.
41 *Ibid.*
42 *Ibid.,* 151.
43 *Ibid.,* 205.
44 Quigley, *Tragedy and Hope,* 34.
45 National Rifle Association fact sheet.
46 Kennedy, *Rise and Fall of Great Powers,* 81.
47 *Ibid.,* 156.
48 *Ibid.,* 158.
49 *Ibid.,* 147.
50 Paul Lee Tan, *Encyclopedia of 7,700 Illustrations: Signs of the Times* (Rockville, Md.: Assurance Publishers, 1979), 421.
51 Huntington, *Clash of Civilizations,* 45.
52 Kennedy, *Rise and Fall of Great Powers,* 96.
53 *Ibid.,* 230.
54 *Ibid.,* 99.
55 *Ibid.,* 203.
56 *Ibid.,* 153.
57 Quigley, *Tragedy and Hope,* 67.
58 *Ibid.,* 125-26.
59 Kennedy, *Rise and Fall of Great Powers,* 98.
60 McGrath, *In the Beginning,* 301.
61 Tan, *7,700 Illustrations,* 1037.

62 Elizabeth Longford, *Queen Victoria: Born to Succeed* (New York: Harper and Row, 1964), 44.
63 Robert Green, *Queen Victoria* (New York: Franklin Watts, Inc., 1969), 17-18.
64 Monica Charlot, *Victoria: The Young Queen* (Cambridge, England: Blackwell Publishers, 1991), 225.
65 Christopher Hibbert, *Queen Victoria: A Personal History* (New York: Basic Books, 2000), 294.
66 Longford, *Queen Victoria: Born to Succeed,* 44.
67 Tan, *7,700 Illustrations,* 129-30.
68 N. A. Waychak, *Messiah: The Story of George Frideric Handel* (St. Louis, Mo.: Scripture Memory Fellowship International, 1995), 99.
69 Kennedy, *Rise and Fall of Great Powers,* 151.
70 *Ibid.,* 155.
71 *The Cambridge Illustrated History of the British Empire,* ed. P. J. Marshall (Cambridge, England: Cambridge University Press, 1996), 384-389.
72 Quigley, *Tragedy and Hope,* 159-60.
73 McGrath, *In the Beginning,* 24-25.
74 *Ibid.,* 2.
75 *Ibid.,* 257.
76 *Ibid.,* 258.
77 *Ibid.,* 289.
78 *Ibid.,* 290.
79 *Ibid.,* 256.
80 *Ibid.,* 300.
81 *Ibid.,* back of dust jacket.
82 *Ibid.,* 290.
83 Tan, *7,700 Illustrations,* 807.
84 *Ibid.*
85 *Cambridge Illustrated History,* 24.
86 Eugene Myers Harrison, *Giants of the Missionary Trail* (Fairfax, Va.: Fairy Baptist Temple, 1990), 51.
87 *Ibid.,* 59.
88 *Ibid.*
89 *Ibid.,* 51.
90 *Ibid.*
91 *Ibid.,* 52.
92 *Ibid.,* 53.
93 *Ibid.,* 62.
94 *Ibid.,* 63.
95 *Ibid.,* 64.
96 *Ibid.*
97 *Ibid.*
98 J.R. Graves and S. Adlam, *The First Baptist Church in America: Not Founded by Roger Williams* (Texarkana, Tex.: Bogard Press, 1995), 41.
99 E. Wayne Thompson and David L. Cummins, *This Day in Baptist History* (Greenville, S.C.: Bob Jones University Press, 1993), 148.
100 Rousas J. Rushdoony, *This Independent Republic* (Fairfax, Va.: Thoburn Press, 1978), 93-94.

CHAPTER 4
Soul Liberty

1   Henry C. Vedder, *A Short History of the Baptists* (Valley Forge, Penn.: Judson Press, 1907), 104.
2   John T. Christian, *A History of the Baptists,* vol. 1 (Texarkana, Ark.-Tex.: Bogard Press, 1922), 359.
3   *Ibid.*
4   *Ibid.*
5   *Ibid.,* 375.
6   *Ibid.*
7   William G. McLoughlin, *Soul Liberty: The Baptists' Struggle in New England, 1630-1833* (Hanover, N. H.: University Press of New England, 1991), 17.
8   *Ibid.,* 30.
9   Christian, *History of Baptists,* 1:369.

10 *Ibid.*
11 McLoughlin, *Soul Liberty,* 27.
12 J. R. Graves and S. Adlam, *The First Baptist Church in America: Not Founded by Roger Williams* (Texarkana, Tex.: Bogard Press, 1995), 17.
13 *Ibid.,* 208-09.
14 *Ibid.,* 47.
15 *Ibid.,* 31.
16 *Ibid.,* 32.
17 *Ibid.,* 51.
18 *Ibid.,* 163.
19 *Ibid.,* 176-77.
20 *Ibid.,* 158.
21 *Ibid.,* 133.
22 *Ibid.,* 134.
23 *Ibid.,* 140.
24 *Ibid.*
25 *Ibid.,* 136.
26 *Ibid.,* 39.
27 *Ibid.,* 160-61.
28 Wilbur Nelson, *The Hero of Aquidneck: A Life of Dr. John Clarke* (New York: Fleming H. Revell Co., 1954), 15-16.
29 Graves and Adlam, *First Baptist Church in America,* 54.
30 *Ibid.,* 169.
31 *Ibid.,* 58.
32 Nelson, *Hero of Aquidneck,* 26.
33 Graves and Adlam, *First Baptist Church in America,* 55-58.
34 *Ibid.,* 220-21.
35 *Ibid.,* 223.
36 *Ibid.*
37 William Cathcart, ed., *Baptist Encyclopedia,* vol. 1 (Philadelphia: Louis H. Everts, 1881), 228.
38 Graves and Adlam, *First Baptist Church in America,* 14-15.
39 *Ibid.,* 20.
40 Nelson, *Hero of Aquidneck,* 66-68.
41 *Ibid.,* 69-71.
42 *Ibid.,* 71.
43 Graves and Adlam, *First Baptist Church in America,* 92.
44 *Ibid.,* 93.
45 *Ibid.,* 95.
46 *Ibid.*
47 Nelson, *Hero of Aquidneck,* 82.
48 Graves and Adlam, *First Baptist Church in America,* 110.
49 Nelson, *Hero of Aquidneck,* 82.
50 *Ibid.,* 83.
51 Graves and Adlam, *First Baptist Church in America,* 173-75.
52 *Ibid.,* 111.
53 *Ibid.,* 112.
54 *Ibid.,* 117.
55 *Ibid.*
56 David Benedict, *A General History of the Baptist Denomination in America,* vol.1 (Gallatin, Tenn.: Church History Research and Archives, 1985), 374.
57 Nelson, *Hero of Aquidneck,* 59.
58 *Ibid.,* 55.
59 *Ibid.,* 60-61.
60 *Ibid.,* 62.
61 Christian, *History of Baptists,* 2:44.
62 Morris A. Gutstein, *The Story of the Jews of Newport: Two and a Half Centuries of Judaism 1658-1908* (New York: Bloch Publishing Co., 1936), 36.
63 William J. Federer, *America's God and Country Encyclopedia of Quotations* (Coppell, Tex.: Fame Publishing Co., 1994), front jacket flap.
64 *Ibid.,* 106.
65 Nelson, *Hero of Aquidneck,* 44-45.
66 Federer, *America's God and Country,* 618.
67 *Ibid.,* 532.
68 Cathcart, *Baptist Encyclopedia,* 1:227.
69 *Ibid.,* 229.

70 Nelson, *Hero of Aquidneck,* 93-94.
71 *Ibid.,* 93.
72 *Ibid.,* 94.
73 *Ibid.,* 30.
74 *Ibid.,* 93.
75 Cathcart, *Baptist Encyclopedia,* 1:229.
76 Gutstein, *Jews of Newport,* 340-42.
77 *Ibid.,* 26.
78 *Ibid.,* 29-30.
79 *Ibid.,* 50.
80 Geraldine Foster, *The Jews in Rhode Island: A Brief History* (Providence, R.I.: Rhode Island Heritage Commission and the Rhode Island Publication Society, 1985), 1.
81 Gutstein, *Jews of Newport,* 61.
82 *Ibid.,* 69.
83 *Ibid.,* 48.
84 *Ibid.,* 49.
85 *Ibid.,* 55.
86 *Ibid.,* 56.
87 *Ibid.,* 166.
88 *Ibid.,* 49.
89 *Ibid.,* 157.
90 *Ibid.,* 165.
91 *Ibid.,* 111-12.
92 *Ibid.,* 158.
93 *Ibid.,* 140.
94 *Ibid.*
95 Vedder, *Short History of Baptists,* 307.
96 Mitchell Wilson, *American Science and Invention* (New York: Bonanza Books, 1954), 3-4.
97 Peter Marshall and David Manuel, *The Light and the Glory* (Old Tappan, N. J.: Fleming H. Revell, Co., 1977), 73-74.
98 George Whitefield, *George Whitefield's Journals* (Carlisle, Penn.: The Banner of Truth Trust, 1960), 155.
99 Keith J. Hardman, *The Spiritual Awakeners: American Revivalists from Solomon Stoddard to D. L. Moody* (Chicago: Moody Press, 1983), 83.
100 Arnold Dallimore, *George Whitefield,* vol. 2 (Carlisle, Penn.: The Banner of Truth Trust, 1990), 497.
101 Whitefield, *Journals,* 452.
102 *Ibid.,* 453-55.
103 Arnold Dallimore, *George Whitefield,* vol. 1 (Carlisle, Penn.: The Banner of Truth Trust, 1990), 527-28.
104 Dallimore, *George Whitefield,* 1:296.
105 Whitefield, *Journals,* 361.
106 *Ibid.,* 473.
107 *Ibid.,* 419.
108 *Ibid.,* 372.
109 *Ibid.,* 389.
110 *Ibid.,* 376.
111 *Ibid.,* 377.
112 *Ibid.,* 378.
113 *Ibid.,* 379.
114 *Ibid.,* 423.
115 Benedict, *General History of Baptist Denomination,* 1:274.
116 E. Wayne Thompson and David L. Cummins, *This Day in Baptist History* (Greenville, S.C.: Bob Jones University Press, 1993), 532.
117 Morgan Edwards, *Materials Towards A History of the Baptists,* vol. 2 (Danielsville, Ga.: Heritage Press, 1984), 93.
118 Thomas Armitage, *A History of the Baptists,* vol. 2 (Watertown, Wis.: Baptist Heritage Press, 1988), 728.
119 Benedict, *General History of Baptist Denomination,* 2:38-39.
120 Virgil Bopp, *Confidently Committed* (Grand Rapids, Mich.: Regular Baptist Press, 1987), 103.
121 McLoughlin, *Soul Liberty,* 161.
122 *Ibid.,* 159.
123 William Cathcart, *Baptists and the Revolution* (Philadelphia: S. A. George and Co., 1876), 88.

124 Gordon S. Wood, *The Radicalism of American Revolution* (New York: Vintage Books, 1993), 419.
125 Cathcart, *Baptists and Revolution*, 60-61.
126 Christian, *History of Baptists*, 2:229.
127 William Cathcart, *Baptist Patriots* (Grand Rapids, Mich.: Guardian Press, 1976), 42.
128 Cathcart, *Baptists and Revolution*, 10.
129 *Ibid.*, 35-46.
130 *Ibid.*, 39-40.
131 Christian, *History of Baptists*, 1:234.
132 Cathcart, *Baptist Patriots*, 42.
133 Cathcart, *Baptists and Revolution*, 41-42.
134 Armitage, *History of Baptists*, 2:794.
135 Lemuel Call Barnes, D.D., "Was General Washington Baptized by Chaplain Gano?" *Religious Herald*, 23 March 1933, 6.
136 James R. Beller, *The Baptist History Workbook: A Work Text History of the Baptized Believers From the Time of Christ to the 20th Century* (Arnold, Mo.: Prairie Fire Press, 2002), 219.
137 Lemuel Call Barnes, D.D., "George Washington and Freedom of Conscience," *The Journal of Religion*, no. 4, October 1932, 524.
138 *Ibid.*, 520.
139 *Ibid.*, 509.
140 *Ibid.*, 506.
141 Catherine Millard, *The Rewriting of American History* (Camp Hill, Penn.: Horizon House Publishers, 1991), 61.
142 *The Book of Common Prayer and Administration of the Sacraments and Other Rites and Ceremonies of the Church* (n.p.: Seabury Press, 1979), 298.
143 *Ibid.*, 306.
144 James R. Beller, *America in Crimson Red: The Baptist History of America* (Arnold, Mo.: Prairie Fire Press, 2004), 298.
145 *Ibid.*, 299.
146 *Ibid.*, 295.
147 E. Wayne Thompson and David L. Cummins, *This Day in Baptist History* (Greenville, S.C.: Bob Jones University Press, 1993), 327-28.
148 James Norwood, Unpublished Prepared Pamphlet, "George Washington's Faithful Pastor," 1.
149 Barnes, "Washington Baptized," 6.
150 *Ibid.*
151 Lemuel Call Barnes, D.D., "The John Gano Evidence of George Washington's Religion," *Bulletin of William Jewell College*, 15 September 1926, Series No. 24, no. 1, 5.
152 *Ibid.*
153 Barnes, "Washington Baptized," 7.
154 Beller, *America in Crimson Red*, 301.
155 McLoughlin, *Soul Liberty*, 192.
156 Lewis Peyton Little, *Imprisoned Preachers and Religious Liberty in Virginia* (Gallatin, Tenn.: Church History Research and Archives, 1987), 124.
157 Armitage, *History of Baptists*, 2:733-34.
158 Barnes, "George Washington and Freedom of Conscience," 506-07.
159 Christian, *History of Baptists*, 2:273.
160 John Eidsmoe, *Christianity and the Constitution* (Grand Rapids, Mich.: Baker Books, 1995), 208.
161 Armitage, *History of Baptists*, 2:797.
162 Barnes, "George Washington and Freedom of Conscience," 507.
163 Eidsmoe, *Christianity and the Constitution*, 297.
164 Armitage, *History of Baptists*, 2:788.
165 L. H. Butterfield, *Elder John Leland, Jeffersonian Itinerant* (Worcester, Mass.: American Antiquarian Society, 1953), 168-69.
166 William B. Sprague, *Annals of the American Baptist Pulpit* (New York: Robert Carter & Brothers, 1860), 175.
167 *Dictionary of American Biography*, 1961 ed. *s.v.* "John Leland."
168 *Annual Report, House of Representatives, 57th Congress, First Session, Document # 702*, vol. 1 (Washington, D.C.: 1901), 167.
169 Christian, *History of Baptists*, 2:244-45.
170 Armitage, *History of Baptists*, 2:807.
171 Ralph Ketcham, *James Madison: A Biography* (New York: The MacMillan Company, 1971), 251.
172 William Lee Miller, *The Business of May Next: James Madison and the Founding* (Charlottesville, Va.: The University Press of Virginia, 1992), 194-95.
173 Butterfield, *Elder John Leland*, 155-88.
174 Samuel Chiles Miller, "James Madison and his Co-worker, John Leland," *Religious Herald*, 18 October 1934, 4.
175 Sprague, *Annals of the American Pulpit*, 178-79.
176 *Ibid.*, 179-80.
177 *Ibid.*, 180.
178 Gutstein, *Jews of Newport*, 179-80.
179 *Ibid.*, 180.
180 *Ibid.*, 177.
181 *Ibid.*, 364.
182 *Ibid.*, 178.
183 *Ibid.*, 110.
184 *Ibid.*, 13-14.
185 Armitage, *History of Baptists*, 2:738.
186 Printed Copy of Address Given By R. H. Pitts to Baptist Journal Association (Nashville, Tenn.: Sunday School Board of the Southern Baptist Convention, 1925), 3.

CHAPTER 5
Serpents in Paradise

1 Thomas Armitage, *A History of the Baptists*, vol. 2 (Watertown, Wis.: Baptist Heritage Press, 1988), 798.
2 Ralph Ketcham, *James Madison: A Biography* (New York: The MacMillan Company, 1971), 671.
3 William J. Federer, *America's God and Country Encyclopedia of Quotations* (Coppell, Tex.: Fame Publishing, 1994), 204-5.
4 William G. McLoughlin, *Soul Liberty: The Baptists' Struggle in New England, 1630-1833* (Hanover, N.H.: University Press of New England, 1991), 249.
5 William T. Still, *New World Order: The Ancient Plan of Secret Societies* (Lafayette, La.: Hunting House Publishers, 1990), 62.
6 Robert Flood, *The Rebirth of America*, ed. Nancy Leigh DeMoss (Philadelphia: Arthur S. DeMoss Foundation, 1986), 151.
7 Still, *New World Order*, 46.
8 *Ibid.*, 45.
9 *Ibid.*, 46.
10 Cotton Mather, *The Great Works of Christ in America*, vol.1 (Carlisle, Penn.: Banner of Truth Trust, 1979), 55.
11 Martin Hintz and Kate Hintz, *Kwanzaa: Why We Celebrate It the Way We Do* (Mankato, Minn.: Capstone Press, 1996), 5.
12 E.T. Kirby, "Masks," *Academic American Encyclopedia*, vol. 13 (Danbury, Conn.: Grolier Incorporated, 1998), 196.
13 Alan Dundes, "Mask," *World Book Encyclopedia*, vol. 13 (Chicago: World Book Incorporated, 2001), 263-64.
14 Deborah M. Newton-Chocolate, *Kwanzaa* (Chicago: Children's Press, 1990), 3.
15 Smita P. Nordwall, "Witch doctors get paid for national soccer victory," *USA Today*, 9 April 2002, sec. A, p. 4.
16 Anthony C. LoBaido, "Child-rape epidemic in South Africa," *WorldNetDaily*, 26 December 2001 (http://www.worldnetdaily.com/news/article.asp? ARTICLE_ID=25806).
17 Hintz and Hintz, *Kwanzaa*, 22.

18 David Brion Davis, "Slavery," *World Book Encyclopedia*, vol. 17 (Chicago: World Book Incorporated, 2001), 502.

19 Bill Ward, "Blacks Owned Slaves, Too," *Charlotte Observer*, 20 December 2002, 18A.

20 A. Ralph Epperson, *The Unseen Hand: An Introduction into the Conspiratorial View of History* (Tucson, Ariz.: Publius Press, 1985), 151.

21 *Ibid.*, 156.

22 Nathaniel Weyl, *The Negro in American Civilization* (Washington, D.C.: Public Affairs Press, 1960), 80.

23 James Ronald Kennedy and Walter Donald Kennedy, *The South Was Right* (Gretna, La.: n.p., 1994), 27.

24 Epperson, *The Unseen Hand*, 151.

25 Rousas J. Rushdoony, *The Nature of the American System* (Fairfax, Va.: Thoburn Press, 1978), 83.

26 Weyl, *Negro in Amercian Civilization*, 50.

27 Rousas J. Rushdoony, *This Independent Republic* (Fairfax, Va.: Thoburn Press, 1978), 73.

28 Weyl, *Negro in American Civilization*, 74.

29 Richard N. Current, *The Lincoln Nobody Knows* (New York: Hill & Wang, 1958), 233.

30 Weyl, *Negro in American Civilization*, 35.

31 Diane Hoyt-Goldsmith, *Celebrating Kwanzaa* (New York: Holiday House, 1993), 10.

32 *Catholic Encyclopedia*, 1912 ed., *s.v.* "Torquemada."

33 William Bradford, *Of Plymouth Plantation: 1620-1647* (New York: Random House, 1981), 1.

34 Edmond Paris, *The Vatican Against Europe*, trans. by A. Robson (London: Wickliffe Press, 1961), 75.

35 Epperson, *The Unseen Hand*, 79.

36 Wickliffe B. Vennard, Sr., *The Federal Reserve Hoax: The Age of Deception* (Palmdale, Calif.: Omni Publications, n.d.), 244.

37 John A. Garraty and Peter Gay, eds., *The Columbia History of the World* (New York: Harper and Row, 1972), 798.

38 Samuel F. B. Morse, *Imminent Dangers to the Free Institutions of the United States Through Foreign Immigration* (New York: Arno Press, 1969), 14.

39 R. W Thompson, *The Papacy and the Civil Power* (New York: Harper & Bros. Publishers, 1876), 29.

40 *Ibid.*, 38.

41 Charles Chiniquy, *50 Years in the "Church" of Rome* (Chino, Calif.: Chick Publications, 1985), 285.

42 Vennard, *Federal Reserve Hoax*, 234.

43 Samuel F. B. Morse, *Foreign Conspiracy Against the Liberties of the United States* (New York: Arno Press, 1977), 110.

44 Thompson, *The Papacy and the Civil Power*, 29.

45 Ray Allen Billington, *The Protestant Crusade* (Chicago: Quadrangle Books, 1964), 158.

46 John T. Christian, *Americanism or Romanism, Which?* (Louisville, Ken.: Baptist Book Concern, 1895), 160-61.

47 Billington, *Protestant Crusade*, 291.

48 *Ibid.*

49 Chiniquy, *50 Years*, 285.

50 *Ibid.*

51 Fred C. Ainsworth, Brig. Gen. and Joseph W. Kirkley, *The War of the Rebellion*, ser. 4, vol. 3 (Washington, D.C.: n.p., 1900), 401.

52 Samuel Eliot Morrison and Henry Steele Commager, *The Growth of the American Republic*, vol. 2 (New York: Oxford University Press, 1962), 768.

53 Thomas M. Harris, *Rome's Responsibility for the Assassination of Abraham Lincoln* (Los Angeles: Heritage Manor, 1960), vi.

54 *Ibid.*, 7-8.

55 *Ibid.*, 15.

56 *Ibid.*, 12-13.

57 *Ibid.*, 24.

58 *Ibid.*, 37.

59 *Ibid.*, 3.

60 Federer, *America's God and Country*, 311.

61 Billington, *Protestant Crusade*, 324.

62 *Ibid.*

63 *Ibid.*, 198.

64 William P. Grady, *What Hath God Wrought!: A Biblical Interpretation of American History* (Knoxville, Tenn.: Grady Publications, Inc., 1996), 523.

65 Epperson, *The Unseen Hand*, 323.

66 *Ibid.*, 428.

67 A. Ralph Epperson, *The New World Order* (Tucson, Ariz.: Publius Press, 1990), 32.

68 Nesta Webster, *World Revolution: The Plot Against Civilisation*, ed. Anthony Gittens (Palmdale, Calif.: Omni Publications, 1921), 13.

69 Nesta Webster, *Secret Societies and Subversive Movements* (Palmdale, Calif.: Omni Publications, 1924), 4.

70 Epperson, *New World Order*, 40-41.

71 Webster, *Secret Societies*, 31-32.

72 Webster, *World Revolution*, 162.

73 *Ibid.*, 161.

74 *Ibid.*, 286.

75 Epperson, *New World Order*, 119.

76 Vicomte Léon De Poncins, *Freemasonry and the Vatican: A Struggle for Recognition*, trans. by Timothy Tindal-Robertson (Palmdale, Calif.: Omni Christian Book Club, 1968), 73-74.

77 Webster, *Secret Societies*, 18-19.

78 *Ibid.*, 19.

79 *Ibid.*, 367.

80 Webster, *World Revolution*, 20-21.

81 *Ibid.*, 89-90.

82 *Ibid.*, 89.

83 *Ibid.*, 93.

84 Still, *New World Order*, 59.

85 *Ibid.*

86 *Ibid.*, 46.

87 Webster, *Secret Societies*, 119.

88 Still, *New World Order*, 47.

89 *Ibid.*

90 *Ibid.*, 50.

91 *Ibid.*, 58.

92 *Ibid.*

CHAPTER 6
Limbaugh's Kooks

1 Rousas J. Rushdoony, *The Nature of the American System* (Fairfax, Va.: Thoburn Press, 1965), 135.

2 A. Ralph Epperson, *The Unseen Hand: An Introduction into the Conspiratorial View of History* (Tucson, Ariz.: Publius Press, 1985), 6-7.

3 *Ibid.*, 7.

4 *Ibid.*

5 Antony C. Sutton, *America's Secret Establishment: An Introduction to The Order of Skull and Bones* (Billings, Mont.: Liberty House Press, 1986), 3.

6 Rushdoony, *Nature of the American System*, 136.

7 *Ibid.*, 140.

8 Rush H. Limbaugh III, *The Way Things Ought to Be* (New York: Pocket Books, 1992), 296.

9 *Ibid.*, 303-04.

10 Texe Marrs, *Circle of Intrigue: The Hidden Inner Circle of the Global Illuminati Conspiracy* (Austin, Tex.: Living Truth Publishers, 1995), 49.

11 Dennis Laurence Cuddy, *Secret Records Revealed: The Men, the Money, and the Methods Behind the New World Order* (Oklahoma City, Okla.: Hearthstone Publishing, Ltd., 1994), 5.

12 *Ibid.*
13 *Ibid.*
14 *Ibid.*
15 *Ibid.,* 135.
16 James Perloff, *The Shadows of Power: The Council on Foreign Relations and the American Decline* (Appleton, Wis.: Western Islands Publishers, 1988), 12.
17 Marrs, *Circle of Intrigue,* 35.
18 William T. Still, *New World Order: The Ancient Plan of Secret Societies* (Lafayette, La.: Huntington House Publishers, 1990), 94.
19 Wickliffe B. Vennard, *The Federal Reserve Hoax: The Age of Deception* (Palmdale, Calif.: Omni Publications, n.d.), 51.
20 Edmond Paris, *The Vatican Against Europe,* trans. A. Robson (London: Wickliffe Press, 1961), 75.
21 Epperson, *Unseen Hand,* 79.
22 *Ibid.,* 196.
23 A. Ralph Epperson, *The New World Order* (Tucson, Ariz.: Publius Press, 1990), 163-64.
24 Epperson, *Unseen Hand,* 134.
25 Epperson, *New World Order,* 164.
26 Still, *New World Order,* 148.
27 Thomas M. Harris, *Rome's Responsibility for the Assassination of Abraham Lincoln* (Los Angeles: Heritage Manor, 1960), vi.
28 Epperson, *Unseen Hand,* 162.
29 Epperson, *New World Order,* 164.
30 Epperson, *Unseen Hand,* 124.
31 Still, *New World Order,* 150.
32 Theodore R. Thoren and Richard F. Warner, *The Truth in Money Book,* 4th ed. (Chagrin Falls, Oh.: Truth in Money Publications, Inc., 1994), 96.
33 Vennard, *Federal Reserve Hoax,* 51.
34 *Ibid.,* 147-48.
35 Epperson, *Unseen Hand,* 257.
36 Cuddy, *Secret Records Revealed,* 83.
37 *Ibid.,* 125.
38 John F. McManus, *The Insiders: Architects of the New World Order* (Appleton, Wis.: John Birch Society, 1995), 4.
39 *Ibid.,* 5.
40 Epperson, *Unseen Hand,* 247.
41 Gary Allen, *Say "NO!" to the New World Order* (Seal Beach, Calif.: Concord Press, 1987), 233.
42 McManus, *The Insiders,* 60.
43 *Ibid.*
44 *Ibid.*
45 *Ibid.*
46 *Ibid.,* 61.
47 Cuddy, *Secret Records Revealed,* 189.
48 *Ibid.,* 187.
49 *Ibid.,* 183.
50 Marrs, *Circle of Intrigue,* 181.
51 *Anti-Masonic Pamphlets,* "An Investigation into Free Masonry by a Joint Committee of the Legislature of Massachusetts, Printed by Order of the House of Representatives, March 1834" (Boston: Dutton and Wentworth, 1834), 37.
52 Epperson, *Unseen Hand,* 173.
53 Vennard, *Federal Reserve Hoax,* 235.
54 *Ibid.,* 281.
55 Epperson, *Unseen Hand,* 174.
56 Vennard, *Federal Reserve Hoax,* 49-50.
57 *Ibid.,* 246.
58 *Ibid.,* 135.
59 *Ibid.,* 134.
60 *Ibid.,* 148.
61 *Ibid.,* 145.
62 Perloff, *Shadows of Power,* 4.
63 Epperson, *Unseen Hand,* 311.
64 *Ibid.*

65 Vennard, *Federal Reserve Hoax,* 56.
66 Cuddy, *Secret Records Revealed,* 125.
67 Marrs, *Circle of Intrigue,* 143.
68 Perloff, *Shadows of Power,* 14-15.
69 Senator Joseph Biden, *The Threshold of the New World Order: The Wilsonian Vision and American Foreign Policy in the 1990s and Beyond* (Maryland Heights, Mo.: Better Books, 1994), 9-63 [typed from the Congressional Record by Jeanne Billingsley, July 1994].
70 Marrs, *Circle of Intrigue,* 161.
71 Vennard, *Federal Reserve Hoax,* 284.
72 *Ibid.,* 169.
73 *Anti-Masonic Pamphlets,* 14.
74 Epperson, *Unseen Hand,* 77.
75 *Ibid.,* 376.
76 R. W. Thompson, *The Papacy and the Civil Power* (New York: Harper & Brothers Publishers, 1876), 29.
77 Cuddy, *Secret Records Revealed,* 226-27.
78 Epperson, *Unseen Hand,* 294.
79 Perloff, *Shadows of Power,* 3.
80 Vennard, *Federal Reserve Hoax,* 128.
81 Cuddy, *Secret Records Revealed,* 111.
82 *Ibid.,* 157.
83 James D. Sanders, et al., *Soldiers of Misfortune: Washington's Secret Betrayal of American POWs in the Soviet Union* (Washington, D.C.: National Press Books, 1992), 95.
84 Cuddy, *Secret Records Revealed,* 130.
85 Epperson, *Unseen Hand,* 330-31.
86 Perloff, *Shadows of Power,* 5.
87 *Ibid.,* 14.
88 *Ibid.,* 55.
89 *Ibid.,* 56.
90 Epperson, *Unseen Hand,* 151.
91 Harris, *Rome's Responsibility,* 3.
92 Vennard, *Federal Reserve Hoax,* 131.
93 John Toland, *Infamy: Pearl Harbor and its Aftermath* (New York: Doubleday and Company, 1982), 176-77.
94 George S. Patton, Jr., *War as I Knew It* (Boston: Houghton Mifflin Company, 1947), 389-90.
95 Epperson, *Unseen Hand,* 320-21.
96 Perloff, *Shadows of Power,* 91.
97 Vennard, *Federal Reserve Hoax,* 130.
98 *Ibid.,* 146.
99 Epperson, *Unseen Hand,* 197.
100 Antony C. Sutton, *Two Faces of George Bush* (Clackamas, Ore.: Emissary Publications, 1988), 86-92.
101 Cuddy, *Secret Records Revealed,* 155.
102 Nesta H. Webster, *Secret Societies and Subversive Movements* (Palmdale, Calif.: Omni Publications, 1924), 258-59.
103 Sutton, *America's Secret Establishment,* 124.
104 Dan Smoot, *The Invisible Government* (Dallas, Tex.: The Dan Smoot Report, 1962), iii-iv.
105 Cuddy, *Secret Records Revealed,* 173.
106 Marrs, *Circle of Intrigue,* 57.
107 Epperson, *Unseen Hand,* 8.
108 Marrs, *Circle of Intrigue,* 54.
109 Epperson, *Unseen Hand,* 8.
110 Vennard, *Federal Reserve Hoax,* 52.
111 Perloff, *Shadows of Power,* 3.
112 A. Ralph Epperson, *The New World Order* (Tucson, Ariz.: Publius Press, 1990), 32.
113 Dr. S. Ireneus Prime, *The Life of Samuel F. B. Morse* (New York: Arno Press, 1974), 729.
114 Nesta Webster, *World Revolution: The Plot Against Civilisation,* ed. Anthony Gittens (Palmdale, Calif.: Omni Publications, 1921), 93.
115 Cuddy, *Secret Records Revealed,* 202-03.
116 Still, *New World Order,* 146.
117 Epperson, *Unseen Hand,* 76-77.

118 Webster, *World Revolution*, 300.
119 Still, *New World Order*, 147.
120 Webster, *World Revolution*, 6.
121 *Ibid.*
122 Vennard, *Federal Reserve Hoax*, 239.
123 Epperson, *Unseen Hand*, 348.
124 *Ibid.*
125 Cuddy, *Secret Records Revealed*, 184.
126 *Ibid.*, 175-76.
127 *Ibid.*, 170.
128 Otto Eisenshiml, *The Hidden Face of the Civil War* (New York: The Bobbs-Merrill Company, 1961), 5.
129 Samuel F. B. Morse, *Foreign Conspiracy Against the Liberties of the United States* (New York: Arno Press, 1977), 110.
130 Epperson, *Unseen Hand*, 133.
131 Cuddy, *Secret Records Revealed*, 40.
132 Epperson, *Unseen Hand*, 126.
133 Perloff, *Shadows of Power*, 111.
134 *Ibid.*, 147-48.
135 Avro Manhattan, *Murder in the Vatican* (Springfield, Mo.: Ozark Books, 1985), 6.
136 Ray Allen Billington, *The Protestant Crusade* (Chicago: Quadrangle Books, 1964), 123.
137 Charles Chiniquy, *50 Years in the "Church" of Rome* (Chino, Calif.: Chick Publications, 1985), 285.
138 Morse, *Foreign Conspiracy*, 28-29.
139 Vicomte Léon De Poncins, trans. Timothy Tindal-Robertson, *Freemasonry and the Vatican* (Palmdale, Calif.: Omni/Christian Book Club, 1968), 82.
140 Cuddy, *Secret Records Revealed*, 108.
141 Epperson, *Unseen Hand*, 50.
142 "Pope Remembers a Child's Gift," *Fairbanks Daily News-Miner*, 2 May 1984, 3.
143 Vennard, *Federal Reserve Hoax*, 100-01.
144 *Ibid.*, 101.
145 Cuddy, *Secret Records Revealed*, 170.
146 Epperson, *Unseen Hand*, 238-39.
147 Cuddy, *Secret Records Revealed*, 85-86.
148 *Ibid.*, 163.
149 *Ibid.*, 179.
150 *Ibid.*, 167.
151 *Ibid.*, 181-82.

CHAPTER 7
They Knew Too Much

1 Carroll Quigley, *Tragedy and Hope: A History of the World in Our Time* (New York: The Macmillan Company, 1966), 950.
2 A. Ralph Epperson, *The Unseen Hand: An Introduction into the Conspiratorial View of History* (Tucson, Ariz.: Publius Press, 1985), 434.
3 Burke McCarty, *The Suppressed Truth About the Assassination of Abraham Lincoln* (Philadelphia: Burke McCarty, n.d.) 44.
4 *Dictionary of American Biography*, 1961 ed., *s.v.* "William Henry Harrison."
5 McCarty, *Suppressed Truth*, 46.
6 *Ibid.*, 44.
7 *Ibid.*, 47.
8 *Ibid.*, 15.
9 *Ibid.*, 96.
10 *Ibid.*, 98.
11 Thomas M. Harris, *Rome's Responsibility for the Assassination of Abraham Lincoln* (Los Angeles: Heritage Manor, 1960), 29.
12 Avro Manhattan, *Murder in the Vatican* (Springfield, Mo.: Ozark Books, 1985), 116-17.
13 *Ibid.*, 136.

14 *Ibid.*, 160.
15 Epperson, *Unseen Hand*, 166.
16 *Ibid.*, 263.
17 Wickliffe B. Vennard, *The Federal Reserve Hoax: The Age of Deception* (Palmdale, Calif.: Omni Publications, n.d.), 286.
18 Epperson, *Unseen Hand*, 304
19 *Ibid.*, 301.
20 *Ibid.*, 305.
21 *Ibid.*
22 *Ibid.*
23 *Ibid.*, 305-06.
24 *Ibid.*, 308.
25 *Ibid.*, 315.
26 *Ibid.*
27 *Ibid.*
28 *Ibid.*
29 *Ibid.*
30 *Ibid.*, 423.
31 Leonard G. Horowitz, *Emerging Viruses: AIDS and Ebola – Nature, Accident or Intention?* (Rockport, Mass.: Tetrahedron, Inc., 1997), 230.
32 *Ibid.*
33 *Ibid.*, 230-31.
34 *Ibid.*, 232.
35 G. Edward. Griffith, *The Creature from Jekyll Island: A Second Look at the Federal Reserve* (Appleton, Wis.: American Opinion, 1994), 268-69.
36 *Ibid.*, 269.
37 Dennis Laurence Cuddy, *Secret Records Revealed: The Men, the Money, and the Methods Behind the New World Order* (Oklahoma City, Okla.: Hearthstone Publishing, Ltd., 1994), 121.

CHAPTER 8
Freemasonry

1 William T. Still, *New World Order: The Ancient Plan of Secret Societies* (Lafayette, La.: Huntington House Publishers, 1990), 50.
2 *Ibid.*
3 *Encyclopedia of World Biography*, 2nd Edition, vol. 1 (Detroit: Gale Research, 1998), 424.
4 A. Ralph Epperson, *The New World Order* (Tucson, Ariz.: Publius Press, 1990), 148.
5 *Ibid.*
6 *Ibid.*, 163.
7 Nesta H. Webster, *Secret Societies and Subversive Movements* (Palmdale, Calif.: Omni Publications, 1924), 100.
8 *Ibid.*, 99.
9 *Ibid.*, 103.
10 *Ibid.*, 100.
11 *Ibid.*, 120.
12 *Ibid.*, 121.
13 Charles G. Finney, *The Character, Claims and Workings of Freemasonry* (Cincinnati, Oh.: Western Tract and Book Society, 1869), 1.
14 Epperson, *New World Order*, 165.
15 Gary H. Kah, *En Route to Global Occupation* (Lafayette, La.: Huntington House Publishers, 1991), 111.
16 "Report on the Abduction and Murder of William Morgan, and on the Conduct and Measures of the Masonic Fraternity to Prevent Convictions, &c. by a Mr. Whittlesey," *The Proceedings of the United States Anti-Masonic Convention, Held at Philadelphia, September 11, 1830* (Philadelphia: I. P. Trimble, 1830), 15.
17 Epperson, *New World Order*, 162.

18 Vicomte Léon De Poncins, trans. by Timothy Tindal-Robertson, *Freemasonry and the Vatican* (Palmdale, Calif.: Omni/Christian Book Club, 1968), 42.

19 Still, *New World Order*, 107.

20 Captain William Morgan, *Freemasonry Exposed* (Chicago: Ezra A. Cook, Inc., 1867), 15.

21 Epperson, *New World Order*, 164.

22 *Ibid.*

23 Morgan, *Freemasonry Exposed*, 21-22.

24 *Ibid.*, 52.

25 *Ibid.*, 75.

26 Nesta Webster, ed. Anthony Gittens, *World Revolution: The Plot Against Civilisation* (Palmdale, Calif.: Omni Publications, 1921), 191.

27 Epperson, *New World Order*, 152.

28 Kah, *En Route to Globalism*, 127.

29 Still, *New World Order*, 115.

30 *Ibid.*, 110.

31 Jack Hurst, *Nathan Bedford Forrest* (New York: Alfred A. Knopf, 1993), 173.

32 Still, *New World Order*, 109.

33 Epperson, *New World Order*, 182.

34 Still, *New World Order*, 107.

35 Alphonse Cerza, *Encyclopedia Americana*, vol. 18 (Danbury, Conn.: Grolier, Inc., 1993), 432.

36 *Anti-Masonic Pamphlets*, "An Investigation into Free Masonry by a Joint Committee of the Legislature of Massachusetts, Printed by Order of the House of Representatives, March 1834" (Boston: Dutton and Wentworth, 1834), 14.

37 Epperson, *New World Order*, 164.

38 De Poncins, *Freemasonry and the Vatican*, 65.

39 *Ibid.*, 66

40 Joseph Ritner, "Vindication of George Washington from the Stigma of Adherence to Secret Societies," *Anti-Masonic Pamphlets*, 18 September 1837, p. 26.

41 Dan Smoot, *The Invisible Government* (Dallas, Tex.: The Dan Smoot Report, Inc., 1962), face page.

42 Ritner, "Vindication of George Washington," 28.

43 Still, *New World Order*, 109.

44 Ritner, "Vindication of George Washington," 28.

45 *Ibid.*, 24.

46 *Ibid.*, iii.

47 *Ibid.*, 11.

48 Still, *New World Order*, 60.

49 Ritner, "Vindication of George Washington," 15-16.

50 *Ibid.*, 15.

51 *Ibid.*, 14.

52 *Ibid.*, 15.

53 *Ibid.*, 15-16.

54 *Ibid.*, 22-23.

55 Waldo P. Harris III and James D. Mosteller, *Georgia's First Continuing Baptist Church* (College Park, Ga.: N & R Printing, Inc., 1997), 182.

56 Webster, *World Revolution*, 22.

57 Still, *New World Order*, 116.

58 Webster, *Secret Societies*, 330.

59 *Ibid.*, 147.

60 A. Ralph Epperson, *The Unseen Hand: An Introduction into the Conspiratorial View of History* (Tucson, Ariz.: Publius Press, 1985), 127.

61 Epperson, *New World Order*, 122.

62 Webster, *World Revolution*, 183.

63 Epperson, *New World Order*, 122.

64 *Ibid.*, 274.

65 Webster, *Secret Societies*, 277.

66 Edith Starr Miller, *Occult Theocrasy*, vol.1 (Los Angeles: The Christian Book Club of America, 1933), 220-21.

67 Still, *New World Order*, 31-33.

CHAPTER 9
The Illuminati

1 Edith Starr Miller, *Occult Theocrasy*, vol.1 (Los Angeles: The Christian Book Club of America, 1933), 373.

2 Nesta H. Webster, *Secret Societies and Subversive Movements* (Palmdale, Calif: Omni Publications, 1924), 199.

3 *Ibid.*, 197-98.

4 *Ibid.*, 198.

5 Nesta Webster, *World Revolution: The Plot Against Civilisation*, ed. Anthony Gittens (Palmdale, Calif.: Omni Publications, 1921), 48.

6 *Encyclopedia Americana*, vol.10, *s.v.* "Encyclopedists."

7 Webster, *Secret Societies*, back cover.

8 *Ibid*, 162.

9 Marshall Cavendish, *Man, Myth and Magic: The Illustrated Encyclopedia of Mythology, Religion and the Unknown*, vol.10 (New York: Marshall Cavendish Corporation, 1995), 1303.

10 *Encyclopedia of World Biography*, 2nd ed., *s.v.* Louis Blanc.

11 Webster, *World Revolution*, 23.

12 John Robison, *Proofs of a Conspiracy* (Belmont, Mass.: Western Islands, 1967), viii.

13 *Ibid.*, 58.

14 William T. Still, *New World Order: The Ancient Plan of Secret Societies* (Lafayette, La.: Huntington House Publishers, 1990), 73.

15 Edmond Paris, *The Secret History of the Jesuits* (Chino, Calif.: Chick Publications, 1975), 27.

16 Robison, *Proofs of a Conspiracy*, 85.

17 Webster, *World Revolution*, 23.

18 Webster, *Secret Societies*, 196.

19 *Ibid.*, 205.

20 Webster, *World Revolution*, 36.

21 Robison, *Proofs of a Conspiracy*, 94.

22 Webster, *Secret Societies*, 208-09.

23 Webster, *World Revolution*, 18.

24 *Ibid.*, 23-24.

25 Robison, *Proofs of a Conspiracy*, 70.

26 *Ibid.*, 106.

27 Webster, *World Revolution*, 13-14.

28 A. Ralph Epperson, *The Unseen Hand: An Introduction into the Conspiratorial View of History* (Tucson, Ariz.: Publius Press, 1985), 79.

29 Webster, *World Revolution*, 34.

30 Webster, *Secret Societies*, 207.

31 A. Ralph Epperson, *The New World Order* (Tucson, Ariz.: Publius Press, 1990), 16.

32 Webster, *Secret Societies*, 220.

33 Robison, *Proofs of a Conspiracy*, 111-12.

34 Still, *New World Order*, 62.

35 Webster, *Secret Societies*, 218-19.

36 Robison, *Proofs of a Conspiracy*, 111.

37 *Ibid.*, 156.

38 *Ibid.*, 111.

39 Still, *New World Order*, 78.

40 Robison, *Proofs of a Conspiracy*, vi-xii.

41 *Ibid.*, 113.

42 Adam Smith, *The Wealth of Nations*, ed., Edwin Cannan (New York: Random House, 1937), 302.

43 G. Edward Griffin, *The Creature From Jekyll Island: A Second Look at the Federal Reserve* (Appleton, Wis.: American Opinion Publishing, Inc., 1994), 218.

44 Miller, *Occult Theocrasy*, 184.

45 *Ibid.*

46 Webster, *Secret Societies*, 222.

47 Robison, *Proofs of a Conspiracy*, 65.

48 Dusty Sklar, *The Nazis and the Occult* (New York: Dorsett Press, 1977), 1.
49 Robison, *Proofs of a Conspiracy*, 112.
50 Webster, *Secret Societies*, 188.
51 Robison, *Proofs of a Conspiracy*, 66-67.
52 *Ibid.*, 71.
53 *Ibid.*
54 *Ibid.*, 110.
55 Anonymous, *Light Bearers of Darkness* (Hawthorne, Calif.: The Christian Book Club of America, 1930), 3-4.
56 Still, *New World Order*, 74.
57 Webster, *Secret Societies*, 233.
58 Epperson, *New World Order*, 106.
59 Webster, *World Revolution*, 31.
60 *Ibid.*
61 *Ibid.*, 32.
62 Webster, *Secret Societies*, 129.
63 William Schnoebelen, *Masonry: Beyond the Light* (Chino, Calif.: Chick Publications, 1991), 60.
64 Vicomte Léon De Poncins, *Freemasonry and the Vatican: A Struggle for Recognition*, trans. Timothy Tindal-Robertson (Palmdale, Calif.: Omni/Christian Book Club, 1968), 6.
65 Schnoebelen, *Masonry*, 61.
66 Miller, *Occult Theocrasy*, 363-64.
67 Board of Custodians, *Tennessee Craftsmen or Masonic Textbook as Authorized by the Most Worshipful Grand Lodge of the State of Tennessee* (n.p.: n.p., 1989), 9.
68 De Poncins, *Freemasonry and the Vatican*, 85-86.
69 Robison, *Proofs of a Conspiracy*, 224.
70 *Ibid.*, 109.
71 Webster, *Secret Societies*, 324.
72 *Ibid.*, 348-49.
73 De Poncins, *Freemasonry and the Vatican*, 50-51.
74 William Guy Carr, *Pawns in the Game*, (n.p: n.p., n.d.), 35.
75 Robison, *Proofs of a Conspiracy*, 245.
76 Webster, *Secret Societies*, 343.
77 Webster, *World Revolution*, 44.
78 Webster, *Secret Societies*, 274.
79 Carr, *Pawns in the Game*, 105-07.
80 Miller, *Occult Theocrasy*, 247-49.
81 *Ibid.*, 249.
82 Still, *New World Order*, 126.
83 Webster, *Secret Societies*, iv.
84 Still, *New World Order*, 81.
85 Robison, *Proofs of a Conspiracy*, 84.
86 *Ibid.*, 112.
87 Webster, *World Revolution*, 37.
88 Webster, *Secret Societies*, 259-63.
89 Webster, *World Revolution*, 85.

CHAPTER 10
The Battle for Washington, D.C.

1 John Robison, *Proofs of a Conspiracy* (Boston: Western Islands, 1967), 185.
2 Bob Larsen, *Larsen's New Book of Cults* (Wheaton, Ill.: Tyndale House Publishers, 1989), 388.
3 Nesta Webster, *World Revolution: The Plot Against Civilisation*, ed., Anthony Gittens (Palmdale, Calif.: Omni Publications, 1921), 86.
4 *Ibid.*
5 Keith J. Hardman, *The Spiritual Awakeners: American Revivalists from Solomon Stoddard to D. L. Moody* (Chicago: Moody Press, 1983), 112.
6 *Ibid.*
7 *Ibid.*, 112-13.
8 *Ibid.*, 114.
9 A. Ralph Epperson, *The New World Order*, (Tucson, Ariz.: Publius Press, 190), 115-16.
10 David Ovason, *The Secret Architecture of Our Nation's Capital: The Masons and the Building of Washington, D.C.* (New York: HarperCollins Publishers, Inc., 1999), 64.
11 William J. Federer, *America's God and Country Encyclopedia of Quotations* (Coppell, Tex.: Fame Publishing, 1994), 311.
12 Texe Marrs, *Flashpoint*, May 1995, 1.
13 A. Ralph Epperson, *America's Secret Destiny: The Role of Subversive Secret Societies in Shaping a Dreadful Future for America* (Tucson, Ariz.: Publius Press, 1995), 5.
14 *Ibid.*, 47.
15 *Ibid.*, 33.
16 *Ibid.*, 39.
17 John Eidsmoe, *Christianity and the Constitution* (Grand Rapids, Mich.: Baker Books, 1995), 356.
18 Epperson, *America's Secret Destiny*, 115.
19 *Ibid.*, 15.
20 *Ibid.*, 121.
21 *Ibid.*, 119.
22 A. Ralph Epperson, *Masonry: Conspiracy Against Christianity* (Tucson, Ariz.: Publius Press, 1997), 347-51.
23 *Ibid.*, 342.
24 Peter Marshall and David Manuel, *The Light and the Glory* (Old Tappan, N.J.: Fleming H. Revell, Co., 1977), 73-74.
25 David Barton, *A Spiritual Heritage Tour of the United States Capitol* (Aledo, Tex.: WallBuilders, 2000), 56.
26 Catherine Millard, *The Rewriting of American History* (Camp Hill, Penn.: Horizon House Publishers, 1991), 215.
27 *New Catholic Encyclopedia*, 1967 ed., *s.v.* "Junipero Serra."
28 *Ibid.*, "Inquisition."
29 Millard, *Rewriting America's History*, 222.
30 *Ibid.*
31 *Ibid.*
32 *Ibid.*, 216-17.
33 Author's personal file.
34 Millard, *Rewriting America's History*, 220.
35 *Ibid.*
36 *Ibid.*, 221.
37 Epperson, *America's Secret Destiny*, 61.
38 *Ibid.*, 38.
39 *Ibid.*, 7.
40 Barton, *Spiritual Heritage*, 42.
41 Millard, *Rewriting America's History*, 387.
42 Barton, *Spiritual Heritage*, 33.
43 *Ibid.*, 87.
44 *Ibid.*, 91.
45 Millard, *Rewriting America's History*, 383.
46 Tom Peters and Jim Allison, "Where Do Moses and the 10 Commandments Appear in the Supreme Court Building?" (http://www.members.tripod.com/~candst/tnppage/arg8a.htm).
47 *Ibid.*
48 *Ibid.*
49 Ovason, *Secret Architecture*, 8.
50 *Ibid.*, 1.
51 *Ibid.*, 395.
52 *Ibid.*, 70.
53 Michael Baignet and Richard Leigh, *The Temple and the Lodge* (New York: Arcade Publishing, 1989), 261.
54 Ovason, *Secret Architecture*, 76.
55 *Ibid.*, 411.
56 Baignet and Leigh, *Temple and Lodge*, 261-62.
57 Ovason, *Secret Architecture*, 72.
58 *Ibid.*, 71.
59 *Ibid.*, 73.
60 *Ibid.*, 72-74.
61 *Ibid.*, 68.
62 *Ibid.*, 55.
63 *Ibid.*, 45-47.
64 *Ibid.*, 42-43.
65 *Ibid.*, 48.

66 *Ibid.*
67 *Ibid.*
68 Barton, *Spiritual Heritage,* 79.
69 Frederick Goodman, *Magic Symbols* (London: Brian Todd Publishing, 1981), 6.
70 Marshall Cavendish, *Man, Magic and Myth: The Illustrated Encyclopedia of Mythology, Religion and the Unknown,* vol. 14 (New York: Marshall Cavendish Corporation, 1995), 2002.
71 *Ibid.*
72 *Ibid.*
73 Ralph Woodrow, *Reckless Rumors, Misinformation, Doomsday Delusions* (Palm Springs, Calif.: Ralph Woodrow Evangelistic Association, Inc., 2000), 51.
74 *Ibid.,* 105.
75 *Ibid.,* 95-99.
76 Ovason, *Secret Architecture,* 9.
77 *Ibid.,* 222.
78 "Masonic Symbols of Power in Their Seat of Power–Washington, D.C.," *CuttingEdge.org,* n.d. (http://cuttingedge.org/n1040.html).
79 *Ibid.*
80 Ovason, *Secret Architecture,* 288.
81 Barton, *Spiritual Heritage,* 80.
82 *Ibid.*
83 *Ibid.*
84 *Encyclopedia Americana, s.v.* "Obelisk."
85 Ovason, *Secret Architecture,* 127.
86 *Ibid.,* 128.
87 *Ibid.,* 133.
88 *Ibid.,* 134.
89 *Ibid.,* 128-29.
90 Epperson, *New World Order,* 100.
91 *Ibid.,* 101.
92 *Ibid.*
93 Ovason, *Secret Architecture,* inside back flap of dust jacket.
94 Millard, *Rewriting America's History,* 463.
95 Ovason, *Secret Architecture,* 10.
96 *Ibid.,* 62.
97 *Ibid.,* 351.
98 *Ibid.,* 3.
99 *Ibid.,* 480.
100 *Ibid.,* 166-67.
101 *Ibid.,* 335.
102 *Ibid.,* 104.
103 *Ibid.,* 270.
104 *Ibid.,* 492.
105 *Ibid.*
106 *Ibid.,* 493.
107 *Ibid.*
108 *Ibid.,* 282.
109 *Ibid.,* 291-92.
110 *Ibid.*
111 *Ibid.,* 292-93.
112 Millard, *Rewriting America's History,* 341.
113 Ovason, *Secret Architecture,* 194.
114 *Ibid.,* 196.
115 *Ibid.,* 432.
116 *Ibid.,* 28-29.
117 *Ibid.,* 30.
118 *Ibid.,* 31.
119 *Ibid.*
120 *Ibid.,* 14.
121 Arthur Fenton Hort, *Life and Letters of Fenton John Anthony Hort* (London: Macmillan & Co., 1896), 1:141.
122 Barton, *Spiritual Heritage,* 35-36.
123 Ovason, *Secret Architecture,* 214.
124 *Ibid.,* 436.
125 *Ibid.,* 209-10.
126 *Ibid.,* 435.
127 *Ibid.,* 269.
128 *Ibid.,* 269-70.
129 *Ibid.,* 186.
130 *Ibid.,* 430.
131 *Ibid.,* 49.
132 *Ibid.,* 161.
133 Gary Aldrich, *Unlimited Access: An FBI Agent Inside the Clinton White House* (Washington, D.C.: Regnery Publishing, Inc., 998), 105-06.
134 Ovason, *Secret Architecture,* 153.
135 David Remnick, "The Situationist-Annals of Politics," *New Yorker,* 5 September 1994, 93.
136 William P. Grady, *What Hath God Wrought!: A Biblical Interpretation of American History* (Knoxville, Tenn.: Grady Publications, Inc., 1996), 14-15.
137 Ovason, *Secret Architecture,* 241.
138 *Ibid.,* 442.
139 *Ibid.*
140 *Ibid.,* 241.
141 *Ibid.,* 5.
142 *Ibid.,* 404.

CHAPTER 11
Skull and Bones

1 Alexandra Robbins, *Secrets of the Tomb: Skull and Bones, the Ivy League and the Hidden Paths of Power* (Boston: Little, Brown and Company, 2002), 48.
2 *Ibid.,* 50.
3 Antony C. Sutton, *America's Secret Establishment: An Introduction to The Order of Skull and Bones* (Billings, Mont.: Liberty House Press, 1986), 6-7.
4 Robbins, *Secrets of the Tomb,* 42.
5 *Ibid.,* 45.
6 *Ibid.*
7 *Ibid.,* 66.
8 *Ibid.,* 202.
9 Sutton, *America's Secret Establishment,* 11.
10 *Ibid.*
11 Rousas J. Rushdoony, *This Independent Republic* (Fairfax, Va.: Thoburn Press, 1978), 93-94.
12 Keith J. Hardman, *The Spiritual Awakeners: American Revivalists from Solomon Stoddard to D. L. Moody* (Chicago: Moody Press, 1983), 125.
13 *Ibid.,* 123.
14 Sutton, *America's Secret Establishment,* 14.
15 Robbins, *Secrets of the Tomb,* 60.
16 Sutton, *America's Secret Establishment,* 5.
17 Ron Rosenbaum, "The Last Secrets of Skull and Bones," *Esquire,* September 1977, 85.
18 *Ibid.,* 89.
19 *Ibid.,* 86.
20 *Ibid.,* 89.
21 *Ibid.,* 87.
22 Sutton, *America's Secret Establishment,* vii and 16.
23 *Ibid.,* 8.
24 *Ibid.,* 20.
25 *Ibid.,* 47.
26 *Ibid.,* 57.
27 Walter Isaacson and Evan Thomas, *The Wise Men: Six Friends and the World They Made* (New York: Simon and Schuster, 1986), 47-48.
28 Webster Griffin Tarpley and Anton Chaitkin, *George Bush: The Unauthorized Biography* (Washington, D.C.: Executive Intelligence Review, 1992), 91.
29 *Ibid.,* 92.
30 Sutton, *America's Secret Establishment,* 25.
31 *Ibid.,* 53.
32 *Ibid.,* 94.

33 *Ibid.*, 91.
34 *Ibid.*, 87.
35 Rosenbaum, "Last Secrets," 88.
36 Sutton, *America's Secret Establishment*, 91.
37 *Encyclopedia Americana*, vol. 9, *s.v.* John Dewey.
38 Sutton, *America's Secret Establishment*, 102.
39 *Ibid.*, 103.
40 *Ibid.*
41 *Ibid.*, 104.
42 *Ibid.*
43 *Ibid.*, 105.
44 *Ibid.*
45 *Ibid.*, 27.
46 *Dictionary of American Biography*, 1959 ed., *s.v.* "Timothy Dwight."
47 Sutton, *America's Secret Establishment*, 107.
48 *Ibid.*, 43.
49 *Ibid.*, 62.
50 *Ibid.*
51 Isaacson and Thomas, *The Wise Men*, 430.
52 James Perloff, *The Shadows of Power: The Council on Foreign Relations and the American Decline* (Appleton, Wis.: Western Island Publishers, 1988), 81.
53 Isaacson and Thomas, *The Wise Men*, 68.
54 *Ibid.*, 27-28.
55 *Ibid.*, 28.
56 *Ibid.*, 72-73.
57 *Ibid.*, 25.
58 *Ibid.*, 81.
59 *Ibid.*, 19.
60 *Ibid.*, 25.
61 *Ibid.*, 29.
62 Robbins, *Secrets of the Tomb*, 10.
63 *Ibid.*, 162.
64 *Ibid.*, 10.
65 *Ibid.*
66 *Ibid.*, 175.
67 George W. Bush, *A Charge to Keep: My Journey to the White House* (New York: HarperCollins Publishers, 1999), 47.
68 Robbins, *Secrets of the Tomb*, 102.
69 *Ibid.*, inside dust jacket.
70 *Ibid.*, 10-11.
71 *Ibid.*, 9.
72 *Ibid.*
73 *Ibid.*, 8.
74 *Ibid.*, 163.
75 *Ibid.*, 189.
76 *Ibid.*, 84.
77 *Iibd.*, 115.
78 *Ibid.*
79 *Ibid.*, 78.
80 *Ibid.*, 87-88.
81 *Ibid.*, 56.
82 *Ibid.*, 194.
83 *Ibid.*
84 *Ibid.*, 92.
85 *Ibid.*, 119-121.
86 *Ibid.*, 134-35.
87 Bush, *A Charge to Keep*, 47.
88 Robbins, *Secrets of the Tomb*, 188.
89 *Ibid.*, 171.
90 Alex Jones, *9-11: Descent Into Tyrrany: The New World Order's Dark Plans to Turn Earth Into A Prison Planet* (Austin, Tex.: AEJ Publishing, 2002), 56.
91 Robbins, *Secrets of the Tomb*, 177-78.
92 *Ibid.*, 180.
93 *Ibid.*, 181-82.
94 Bush, *A Charge to Keep*, 19.
95 *Ibid.*, 136.

96 *Ibid.*
97 *Ibid.*
98 Nancy Gibbs and Richard N. Ostling, "God's Billy Pulpit," *Time*, 15 November 1993, 74.
99 Kevin Phillips, *American Dynasty: Aristocracy, Fortune and the Politics of Deceit in the House of Bush* (New York: Viking, 2004), 234.
100 Richard Land, "President Bush, Faith Convictions, and Media Cynicism: Christians and Muslims do not worship the same 'God'," *Beliefnet* (http://www.beliefnet.com/story/136/story_13644_1.html).
101 Mark Ellis, "Bush Worship at Shinto Temple Troubles Christians in Japan and U.S.," *Worthynews.com*, 18 February 2002 (http://www.worthynews.com/news-features-3/bush-shinto-temple.html).
102 Robbins, *Secrets of the Tomb*, 198.
103 *Ibid.*, 49.
104 *Ibid.*, 47.
105 *Ibid.*, 191.
106 *Ibid.*, 191-92.
107 *Ibid.*, 103.
108 *Ibid.*, 199-200.
109 *Ibid.*, 200.
110 *Ibid.*
111 *Ibid.*, 205-06.
112 *Ibid.*, 199-200.
113 *Webster's New Universal Unabridged Dictionary*, 1996 ed., *s.v.* "conspiracy."
114 Robbins, *Secrets of the Tomb*, 206.
115 *Ibid.*, 182.

CHAPTER 12
The Group

1 Jean Schiflet, *Victoria and Her Times* (New York: Henry Holt & Company, Inc., 1996), 45.
2 Robert Green, *Queen Victoria* (New York: Franklin Watts, Inc., 1969), 33.
3 Paul Kennedy, *The Rise and Fall of the Great Powers: Economic Change and Military Conflict from 1500 to 2000* (New York: Random House, 1987), 158.
4 *Ibid.*, 151-52.
5 Charles Haddon Spurgeon, *C. H. Spurgeon Autobiography*, vol. 1, *The Early Years* (Carlisle, Penn.: The Banner of Truth Trust, 1973), 533.
6 *Ibid.*, 534.
7 Charles Haddon Spurgeon, *The New Park Street Pulpit*, vol. 3 (Pasadena, Tex.: Pilgrim Publications, 1975), 380-87.
8 John William Burgon, B.D., *The Revision Revised* (Paradise, Penn.: Conservative Classics, 1883), 507.
9 David Otis Fuller, D.D., ed., *Which Bible?*, 5th ed., rev. (Grand Rapids, Mich.: Grand Rapids International Publications, 1975), 290.
10 Burgon, *Revision Revised*, 109.
11 Stanley Weintraub, *Victoria* (New York: Truman Talley Books, 1987), 357-58.
12 Burgon, *Revision Revised*, 515.
13 *Ibid.*, 312.
14 Hannah Pakula, *An Uncommon Woman* (New York: Simon & Schuster, 1995), 352.
15 Kennedy, *Rise and Fall of Great Powers*, 229-30.
16 Carroll Quigley, *Tragedy and Hope: A History of the World in Our Time* (New York: The Macmillan Company, 1966), 211.
17 Carroll Quigley, *The Anglo-American Establishment: From Rhodes to Cliveden* (New York: Books in Focus, 1981), 70.
18 *Ibid.*, 10.
19 *Ibid.*

20 Dennis Laurence Cuddy, *Secret Records Revealed: The Men, the Money, and the Methods Behind the New World Order* (Oklahoma City, Okla.: Hearthstone Publishing, Ltd., 1994), 115.
21 William Jasper, *Global Tyranny...Step By Step* (Appleton, Wis.: Western Island Publishers, 1993), 53.
22 Quigley, *Anglo-American Establishment*, 3.
23 Cuddy, *Secret Records Revealed*, 13.
24 Quigley, *Anglo-American Establishment*, vii.
25 Quigley, *Tragedy and Hope*, 950.
26 G. Edward Griffin, *The Creature From Jekyll Island: A Second Look at the Federal Reserve* (Appleton, Wis.: American Opinion Publishing, Inc., 1994), 268-69.
27 *Ibid.*, 269.
28 Quigley, *Anglo-American Establishment*, 3.
29 *Ibid.*, x.
30 *Ibid.*, 41.
31 *Ibid.*, 320.
32 Quigley, *Tragedy and Hope*, 326-27.
33 Quigley, *Anglo-American Establishment*, 33.
34 *Ibid.*, 34.
35 *Ibid.*, 35.
36 *Ibid.*, 34.
37 *Ibid.*, 35-36.
38 *Ibid.*, 36.
39 *Ibid.*
40 *Ibid.*, 319.
41 *Ibid.*
42 *Ibid.*, 49.
43 *Ibid.*
44 *Ibid.*, 86.
45 *Ibid.*, 15.
46 *Ibid.*, 197.
47 *Ibid.*, 21.
48 *Ibid.*
49 *Ibid.*, 22.
50 *Ibid.*, 98-99.
51 *Ibid.*, 99.
52 *Ibid.*, 151.
53 *Ibid.*, 104.
54 *Ibid.*, 108.
55 *Ibid.*, 113.
56 *Ibid.*, 116.
57 *Ibid.*, 74-75.
58 *Ibid.*, 134.
59 *Ibid.*, 129-30.
60 *Ibid.*, 126.
61 Quigley, *Tragedy and Hope*, 133.
62 *Ibid.*, 141.
63 *Ibid.*, 147.
64 *Ibid.*, 141-42.
65 *Ibid.*, 155.
66 John Eidsmoe, *Christianity and the Constitution* (Grand Rapids, Mich.: Baker Books, 1995), 381.
67 Quigley, *Tragedy and Hope*, 146.
68 Quigley, *Anglo-American Establishment*, 130-31.
69 *Ibid.*, 133.
70 *Ibid.*, 126-27.
71 *Ibid.*, 169.
72 Quigley, *Tragedy and Hope*, 246.
73 *Ibid.*, 247.
74 Quigley, *Anglo-American Establishment*, 172.
75 *Ibid.*
76 Peter S. Ruckman, *Israel: A Deadly Piece of Dirt* (Pensacola, Fla.: Bible Baptist Bookstore, 2001), 255.
77 Quigley, *Anglo-American Establishment*, 171.
78 *Ibid.*
79 *Ibid.*, 172.
80 *Ibid.*
81 *Ibid.*

82 *Ibid.*, 173.
83 *Ibid.*, 174.
84 *Ibid.*, 174-75.
85 Quigley, *Tragedy and Hope*, 951-52.
86 Quigley, *Anglo-American Establishment*, 114-15.
87 Quigley, *Tragedy and Hope*, 952.
88 James Perloff, *The Shadows of Power: The Council on Foreign Relations and the American Decline* (Appleton, Wis.: Western Islands Publishers, 1988), 37.
89 Dan Smoot, *The Invisible Government* (Dallas, Tex.: The Dan Smoot Report, Inc., 1962), 4.
90 Perloff, *Shadows of Power*, 6.
91 *Ibid.*
92 John F. McManus, *The Insiders: Architects of the New World Order* (Appleton, Wis.: John Birch Society, 1995), 9.
93 Perloff, *Shadows of Power*, 10.
94 *Ibid.*, 7.
95 *Ibid.*, 11.
96 *Ibid.*
97 *Ibid.*
98 *Ibid.*, 7.
99 Gary Allen, *The Rockefeller File* (Seal Beach, Calif.: '76 Press, 1976), 119.
100 Walter Isaacson and Evan Thomas, *The Wise Men: Six Friends and the World They Made* (New York: Simon & Schuster, 1986), 22.
101 Perloff, *Shadows of Power*, 7.
102 McManus, *The Insiders*, 96-97.
103 Isaacson and Thomas, *Wise Men*, 29.
104 Cuddy, *Secret Records Revealed*, 9-10.
105 *Ibid.*, 67.
106 *Ibid.*, 10.
107 *Ibid.*, 10-11.
108 *Ibid.*, 84.
109 *Ibid.*, 11.
110 *Ibid.*, 83.
111 *Ibid.*, 96.
112 *Ibid.*, 76-77.
113 *Ibid.*, 75.
114 *Ibid.*, 37.
115 *Ibid.*, 105.
116 *Ibid.*, 110.
117 *Ibid.*, 159-60.
118 Texe Marrs, *Circle of Intrigue: The Hidden Inner Circle of the Global Illuminati Conspiracy* (Austin, Tex.: Living Truth Publishers, 1995), 183.
119 *Wall Street Journal*, 29 March, 1992, 1.
120 Cuddy, *Secret Records Revealed*, 152-53.
121 *Ibid.*, 153-54.
122 *Ibid.*, 154.
123 McManus, *The Insiders*, 76.
124 Gary Aldrich, *Unlimited Access: An FBI Agent Inside the Clinton White House* (Washington, D.C.: Regnery Publishing, Inc.; 1998),191.
125 *Ibid.*, 137-38.
126 Lt. Col. Robert "Buzz" Patterson, USAF (Ret.), *Dereliction of Duty: The Eyewitness Account of How Bill Clinton Compromised America's National Security* (Washington, D.C.: Regnery Publishing, Inc., 2003), 56-58.
127 Cuddy, *Secret Records Revealed*, 14.
128 *Ibid.*, 149-50.
129 Isaacson and Thomas, *Wise Men*, 19.

CHAPTER 13
Attitude Check

1 James Perloff, *The Shadows of Power: The Council on Foreign Relations and the American Decline* (Appleton, Wis.: Western Islands Publishers, 1988), 204.

2 Antony C. Sutton, *America's Secret Establishment: An Introduction to The Order of Skull and Bones* (Billings, Mont.: Liberty House Press, 1986), 23.

3 Nesta H. Webster, *Secret Societies and Subversive Movements* (Palmdale, Calif.: Omni Publications, 1924), 236.

4 Texe Marrs, *Circle of Intrigue: The Hidden Inner Circle of the Global Illuminati Conspiracy* (Austin, Tex.: Living Truth Publishers, 1995), back cover.

5 William T. Still, *New World Order: The Ancient Plan of Secret Societies* (Lafayette, La.: Huntington House Publishers, 1990), 145.

CHAPTER 14
Bey Shang We

1 Ethel Ellis Birch, Unpublished Personal Memoir: John Morrison Birch (Macon, Ga.: n.p., n.d.), 1.

2 James Hefley and Marti Hefley, *The Secret File On John Birch* (Wheaton, Ill.: Tyndale House Publishers, Inc., 1980), 76.

3 *Ibid.*, 99.

4 Gen. James H. "Jimmy" Doolittle, *I Could Never Be So Lucky Again* (New York: Bantam Books, 1991), 257.

5 Claire Lee Chennault, *Way of a Fighter* (Tucson, Ariz.: James Thorvardson & Sons, 1949), 258.

6 Hefley and Hefley, *Secret File*, 125.

7 Chennault, *Way of a Fighter*, 6.

8 *Ibid.*, 259.

9 *Ibid.*

10 Robert H. W. Welch, Jr., *The Life of John Birch: In the Story of One American Boy, the Ordeal of His Age* (Boston: Western Islands Publishers, 1960), 32.

11 Hefley and Hefley, *Secret File*, 144.

12 Welch, *Life of John Birch*, 51.

13 Hefley and Hefley, *Secret File*, 26.

14 *Ibid.*

15 Welch, *Life of John Birch*, 37.

16 Hefley and Hefley, *Secret File*, 25.

17 Clyde Walter, "The Man Who Buried John Birch: Story of a Man and a Crusade," reprint from *Amarillo Daily News*, 5 July 1962, n.p.

18 Hefley and Hefley, *Secret File*, 197.

19 Welch, *Life of John Birch*, 14.

20 *Ibid.*, 45.

21 Robert L. Scott, Jr., "What John Birch Had to Do He Had to Do Alone," *Orlando Sentinel*, 27 August 1961, 23-f and 25-f.

22 Private interview with Retired General Robert Lee Scott, Jr., Macon, Georgia.; transcript in author's private file.

23 Private interview with Retired Brigadier General David Lee "Tex" Hill, San Antonio, Texas; transcript in author's private file.

24 Hefley and Hefley, *Secret File*, 84.

25 *Ibid.*

26 *Ibid.*, 83-84.

27 *Ibid.*, 26.

28 *Ibid.*, 175.

29 *Ibid.*, 196.

30 *Ibid.*, 193.

31 Walter, *The Man Who Buried John Birch*, n.p.

32 A. Ralph Epperson, *The Unseen Hand: An Introduction to the Conspiratorial View of History* (Tucson, Ariz.: Publius Press, 1985), 215.

33 *Ibid.*, 216.

34 *Ibid.*, 217.

35 Hefley and Hefley, *Secret File*, 171.

36 *Ibid.*, 215.

37 *Ibid.*, 11.

38 *Ibid.*, 201.

39 Chennault, *Way of a Fighter*, 260.

40 Transcript of testimony of 1st Lieutenant Tung Chin-Sheng, 1.

41 *Ibid.*

42 *Ibid.*, 1-3.

43 Hefley and Hefley, *Secret File*, 133.

44 Testimony of Tung Chin-Sheng, 3-4.

45 Lieutenant General A. C. Wedemeyer, "Memorandum to His Excellency, The Generalissimo Chiang Kai-Shek," 7 December 1945, 2.

46 Hefley and Hefley, *Secret File*, 215.

47 *Ibid.*, 218.

48 Report by 1st Lieutenant William T. Miller, n.d., 5.

49 Copy of letter by 1st Lieutenant William T. Miller; in author's personal file.

50 Albert C. Grimes, Lieutenant Laird M. Ogle and Sergeant Albert C. Meyers, "Report on Death of Captain Birch and Detention of His Part, 24 August to 21 October," 7 November 1945, 6.

51 General Chu Teh, "Memorandum to General A. C. Wedemeyer," 15 September 1945, 1.

52 C. O. Lamp, *Gentle Tigress* (New York: Dorchester Publishing Company, Inc., 1980), 286-87.

53 Hefley and Hefley, *Secret File*, 14.

54 *Ibid.*

55 *Ibid.*, 14-15.

56 *Ibid.*, 20.

57 Chennault, *Way of a Fighter*, 260.

58 Interview with Retired Brigadier General David Lee "Tex" Hill.

59 *Ibid.*

60 Interview with Retired General Robert Lee Scott.

61 *Ibid.*

62 *Ibid.*

63 *Ibid.*

64 *Ibid.*

65 Hefley and Hefley, *Secret File*, 28.

66 *Ibid.*, 225.

67 *Ibid.*, 185.

68 S. C. Lyons, *His Name Was John Birch* (Dry Branch, Ga.: n.p., 1968), 24.

69 *Ibid.*, 17.

70 *Ibid.*

71 From copy of letter in author's personal file.

72 Robin Birch, Unpublished Paper, "John Birch," 18 April 1973, 21-22.

CHAPTER 15
KAL 007

1 Jeffrey St. John, "Essay on Character: Lawrence Patton McDonald (1935-1983)," *The New American*, 30 September 1985, (http://www.thenewamerican.com/focus/mcdonald/mcdonald.htm.)

2 Warren P. Mass, "Watchman on the Wall," *The New American*, 29 August 1988, (http://www.thenewamerican.com/focus/mcdonald/mcdonald2.htm).

3 Dr. Lawrence P. McDonald, *America's Spiritual Heritage* (Resaca, Ga.: Faith Baptist Camp, November 1982), audiocassette.

4 *Ibid.*

5 James Perloff, *The Shadows of Power: The Council on Foreign Relations and the American Decline* (Appleton, Wis.: Western Islands Publishers, 1988), 214.

6 *Ibid.*, 214-15.

7 Jeffrey St. John, *Day of the Cobra: The True Story of KAL 007* (Nashville, Tenn.: Thomas Nelson Publishers, 1984), 19.

8 St. John, "Essay on Character," n.p.

9 *Ibid.*

10 Mass, "Watchman on the Wall," n.p.
11 St. John, *Day of the Cobra*, 174.
12 *Ibid.*, 102.
13 *Ibid.*, 69.
14 Seymour M. Hersh, *"The Target is Destroyed": What Really Happened to Flight 007 and What America Knew About It* (New York: Random House, 1986), 31.
15 St. John, *Day of the Cobra*, 74-75.
16 *Ibid.*, 75.
17 *Ibid.*, 78.
18 *Ibid.*, 70.
19 Hersh, *"The Target is Destroyed,"* 103.
20 *Ibid.*, 128.
21 St. John, *Day of the Cobra*, 114.
22 *Ibid.*, 121-22.
23 *Ibid.*, 116-17.
24 St. John, "Essay on Character," n.p.
25 St. John, *Day of the Cobra*, 136.
26 *Ibid.*, 132.
27 *Ibid.*, 59.
28 James Mann, *Rise of the Vulcans: The History of Bush's War Cabinet* (New York: Viking, 2004), 159.
29 St. John, *Day of the Cobra*, 16.
30 *Ibid.*, 11.
31 *Ibid.*, 146.
32 *Ibid.*, 149.
33 *Ibid.*, 155.
34 *Ibid.*, 153.
35 *Ibid.*, 17.
36 *Ibid.*, 16.
37 *Ibid.*, 20.
38 From transcript of private interview with Tommy Toles, Jefferson, Ga.: 3 April 2003; in author's personal file.
39 Bert Schlossberg, "KAL 007, the U.S. 7th Fleet and the Great Russian Ruse, Part I–The Mirage," (http://www.rescue007.org./docs/TheGreatRussianRuse.pdf).
40 St. John, *Day of the Cobra*, 173.
41 *Ibid.*, 79.
42 Michel Brun, *Incident at Sakhalin: The True Mission of Flight KAL 007* (New York: Four Walls Eight Windows, 1995), 258.
43 Bert Schlossberg, *Rescue 007: The Untold Story of KAL 007 and Its Survivors* (Philadelphia: Xlibris Corporation, 2000), 13.
44 St. John, *Day of the Cobra*, 71-72.
45 *Ibid.*, 82.
46 *Ibid.*, 83.
47 Brun, *Incident at Sakhalin*, xxii.
48 Hersh, "The Target is Destroyed," 226.
49 *Ibid.*, 204.
50 St. John, *Day of the Cobra*, 84.
51 Alexander Dallin, *Black Box: KAL 007 and the Superpowers* (Berkeley, Calif.: University of California Press, 1985), 112.
52 *Ibid.*, 27.
53 *Ibid.*
54 St. John, *Day of the Cobra*, 80.
55 *Ibid.*, 81.
56 *Ibid.*, 30.
57 *Ibid.*, 69.
58 *Ibid.*
59 *Ibid.*, 87.
60 Interview, Tommy Toles.
61 Dallin, *Black Box*, 77.
62 "Top Secret/Codeword, CIA Report" *rescue007.org*, 77 (http://www.rescue007.org/docs/CIAReport.pdf).
63 *Ibid.*, 4.
64 *Ibid.*, 5.

65 Avraham Shifrin, "Analysis of the Top Secret Codeworded CIA Report on the Subject of the Mysterious Disappearance of the South Korean Boeing 747 (Flight 007), Its Crew and Passengers After Its 1983 Shooting Down Near the Shores of Island Sakhalin." (Jerusalem, Israel: Research Centre for Prisons, Psychprisons and Forced Labor Concentration Camps of the USSR), 1.
66 *Ibid.*, 2.
67 "Top Secret/Codeword," 43.
68 Jesse Helms, "Questions on Korean Airlines Flight KAL 007," *rescue007.org* (http://www.rescue007.org/helms_letter.htm).
69 Brun, *Incident at Sakhalin*, 4.
70 *Ibid.*
71 *Ibid.*
72 *Ibid.*, 5.
73 *Ibid.*
74 *Ibid.*
75 *Ibid.*
76 Hersh, *"The Target is Destroyed,"* 71.
77 "Congressman's flight reportedly forced to Soviet isle," *Rocky Mountain News,* 1 September 1983, p. 1.
78 Hersh, "The Target is Destroyed," 143.
79 *Ibid.*, 143-44.
80 Brun, *Incident at Sakhalin*, 6.
81 Fletcher Prouty, "The Last Flight of 007" from *The Collected Works of Colonel Fletcher L. Prouty,* Len Osanic, ed., CD-Rom.
82 Brun, *Incident at Sakhalin*, 7.
83 Shifrin, "Analysis of CIA Report," 9.
84 Hersh, *"The Target is Destroyed,"* 143.
85 Tommy Toles interview.
86 "Georgia Democrat on Flight," *The New York Times,* 1 September 1983, sec. D, p. 19.
87 Tommy Toles interview.
88 *Ibid.*
89 *Ibid.*
90 *Ibid.*
91 *Iibd.*
92 *Ibid.*
93 *Ibid.*
94 *Ibid.*
95 *Ibid.*
96 *Ibid.*
97 *Ibid.*
98 *Ibid.*
99 "Top Secret/Codeword," 47.
100 *Ibid.*, 49.
101 Press Release, *Research Centre for Prisons, Psychprisons and Forced Labor Concentration Camps of the USSR,* 11 July 1991 (http://www.rescue007.org/docs/shifrinPressRelease1991-07-11.pdf).
102 "Top Secret/Codeword," 48.
103 *Ibid.*, 55.
104 *Ibid.*, 55-58.
105 "Top Secret/Codeword," 65.
106 Press Release, Centre for Prisons, p. 2-3.
107 Brun, *Incident at Sakhalin*, 131-32.
108 *Ibid.*, 133.
109 Andrej Illesh, "The Mystery of the Boeing–747, Part VIII" *Izvestia,* issues 18-27, 1991 (http://www.royfc.com/kal007.html).
110 Letter to Avraham Shifrin from Rear Admiral Bud Nance, 11 February 1992 (http://www.rescue007.org/nance_letter.htm).
111 Illesh, "Mystery of Boeing–747, Part II."
112 *Ibid.*
113 Brun, *Incident at Sakhalin*, xxii-xxiii.
114 *Ibid.*, 18.
115 *Ibid.*, 19-20.
116 *Ibid.*, 23.

117 *Ibid.*
118 *Ibid.,* 39.
119 *Ibid.,* 39-40.
120 *Ibid.,* 40.
121 Dallin, *Black Box,* 100.
122 Brun, *Incident at Sakhalin,* 35.
123 *Ibid.,* 119.
124 *Ibid.,* 120.
125 *Ibid.,* 130.
126 *Ibid.,* 130-31.
127 *Ibid.,* 122.
128 *Ibid.,* 131.
129 James Oberg, "KAL 007: The Real Story," *American Spectator,* October 1993 (http://www.jamesoberg. com/russian/kal007.htm).
130 Dallin, *Black Box,* 44.
131 Peter Vincent Pry, *War Scare* (Atlanta, Ga.: Turner Publishing, Inc., 1997), 12.
132 *Ibid.,* 14-15.
133 *Ibid.,* 56.
134 Dallin, *Black Box,* 6.
135 *Ibid.,* 56.
136 Hersh, "The Target is Destroyed," 251.
137 Brun, *Incident at Sakhalin,* inside front and back dust jacket flaps.
138 *Ibid.,* back of dust jacket.
139 *Ibid.,* 110.
140 Hersh, *"The Target is Destroyed,"* 252.
141 Brun, *Incident at Sakhalin,* 195.
142 *Ibid.,* 187.
143 Hersh, *"The Target is Destroyed,"* 155-56.
144 "Destruction of Korean Air Lines Boeing 747 on 31 August 1983," Attachment B. Report by the International Civil Aviation Organization (ICAO), 1993, 62-72.
145 *Ibid.,* 21.
146 Colonel L. Fletcher Prouty, Len Osanic, ed., "Safe on Sakhalin: The Story of Korean Air Lines Flight KE 007" from the Collected Works of Colonel L. Fletcher Prouty on CD.
147 Dallin, *Black Box,* 53-54.
148 Brun, *Incident at Sakhalin,* 42.
149 *Ibid.,* 44.
150 *Ibid.,* 42.
151 *Ibid.,* 42-43.
152 *Ibid.,* 65.
153 *Ibid.,* 265.
154 *Ibid.,* 135.
155 *Ibid.,* 205.
156 *Ibid.,* 182-83.
157 *Ibid.,* 80.
158 Illesh, "The Mystery of the Boeing–747, Part IV."
159 Dallin, *Black Box,* 119.
160 Brun, *Incident at Sakhalin,* 162-63.
161 *Ibid.,* 170.
162 *Ibid.,* 228.
163 *Ibid.,* 67-68.
164 *Ibid.,* 87-88.
165 *Ibid.,* 89.
166 *Ibid.,* 109.
167 *Ibid.,* 153.
168 *Ibid.,* 315.
169 *Ibid.,* 252-53.
170 *Ibid.,* 253.
171 Prouty, "Safe on Sakhalin" from "Collected Works" CD.
172 Brun, *Incident at Sakhalin,* 223.
173 *Ibid.,* 239.
174 *Ibid.,* 242.
175 *Ibid.,* 247-48.
176 *Ibid.,* 247.
177 Prouty, "The Last Flight of 007" from "Collected Works" CD.
178 Dallin, *Black Box,* 49.
179 Illesh, "The Mystery of the Boeing–747, Part X."
180 *Ibid.,* Part XI.
181 Brun, *Incident at Sakhalin,* 171.
182 1993 ICAO Report, 35-36.
183 Brun, *Incident at Sakhalin,* 317.
184 *Ibid.,* 266.
185 *Ibid.,* 262.
186 *Ibid.,* xv-xvi.
187 *Ibid.,* 258.
188 *Ibid.,* 6.
189 "Destruction of Korean Air Lines Boeing 747 Over Sea of Japan, 31 August 1983." Report by the International Civil Aviation Organization (ICAO), December 1983, 40.
190 Private interview with Tommy Toles.
191 Clyde Haberman, "Korean Jetliner With 269 Aboard Missing Near Soviet Pacific Island," *The New York Times,* 1 September 1983, D-19.
192 Hersh, *"The Target is Destroyed,"* 65.
193 1983 ICAO Report, 38.
194 *Ibid.,* 37.
195 Hersh, *"The Target is Destroyed,"* 196.
196 Prouty, "Safe on Sakhalin" from "Collected Works" CD.
197 *Ibid.*
198 1993 ICAO Report, 45.
199 Brun, *Incident at Sakhalin,* 254.
200 *Ibid.,* 242.
201 *Ibid.,* 105.
202 St. John, *Day of the Cobra,* 70.
203 Aleksandr Shalnev, "The Mystery of the Korean Boeing-747, Report from the USA, Part VI," *Izvestia,* 1991 (http://www.royfc.com/kal007.html).
204 Private Interview with Tommy Toles.
205 St. John, *Day of the Cobra,* 171.
206 McDonald, "America's Spiritual Heritage," audiocassette.
207 St. John, *Day of the Cobra,* 26-27.
208 *Ibid.,* 153-54.

CHAPTER 16
Clash Equals Cash

1 Nesta Webster, *Secret Societies and Subversive Movements* (Palmdale, Calif.: Omni Publications, 1924), 243.
2 A. Ralph Epperson, *The Unseen Hand: An Introduction to the Conspiratorial View of History* (Tucson, Ariz.: Publius Publishers, 1985), 9
3 Texe Marrs, *Circle of Intrigue: The Hidden Inner Circle of the Global Illuminati Conspiracy* (Austin, Tex.: Living Truth Publishers, 1995), 55.
4 Epperson, *Unseen Hand,* 270.
5 Walter Isaacson and Evan Thomas, *The Wise Men: Six Friends and the World They Made* (New York: Simon & Schuster, 1986), 218.
6 Wickliffe B. Vennard, Sr., *The Federal Reserve Hoax: The Age of Deception* (Palmdale, Calif.: Omni Publications, n.d.), 229.
7 Isaacson and Thomas, *Wise Men,* 250.
8 William T. Still, *New World Order: The Ancient Plan of Secret Societies* (Lafayette, La.: Huntington House Publishers, 1990), 171.
9 Isaacson and Thomas, *Wise Men,* 287.
10 M. Stanton Evans, *The Theme is Freedom* (Washington, D.C.: Regency Publishing, 1994), 104.
11 *Ibid.,* 99.
12 *Ibid.,* 103.
13 *Ibid.,* 98.
14 Isaacson and Thomas, *Wise Men,* 218.
15 *Ibid.,* 249.

16 Ibid.
17 Ibid., 181.
18 Ibid., 320.
19 Ibid.
20 Evans, The Theme is Freedom, 99.
21 Epperson, Unseen Hand, 9.
22 Antony C. Sutton, America's Secret Establishment:
    An Introduction to The Order of Skull and Bones (Billings,
    Mont.: Liberty House Press, 1986), 119.
23 Alex Jones, 9-11: Descent Into Tyranny; The New World
    Order's Dark Plans to Turn Earth Into A Prison Planet
    (Austin, Tex.: AEJ Publishing, 2002), 11.
24 Isaacson and Thomas, Wise Men, 195.
25 Robert Welch, The Politician (Belmont, Mass.: Belmont
    Publishing Co., 1963), 109.
26 Ibid.
27 John F. McManus, The Insiders: Architects of the New
    World Order (Appleton, Wis.: John Birch Society,
    1995), 49.
28 Isaacson and Thomas, Wise Men, 430.
29 Sutton, Secret Establishment, 34.
30 Ibid., 119.
31 Rush Limbaugh, The Way Things Ought to Be, ed.
    Judith Regan (New York: Simon & Schuster, 1992),
    286.
32 Dennis Laurence Cuddy, Secret Records Revealed: The
    Men, the Money and the Methods Behind the New World
    Order (Oklahoma City, Okla.: Hearthstone Publishing, Ltd.,
    1994), 148.
33 Carroll Quigley, Tragedy and Hope: A History of the World
    in Our Time (New York: The Macmillan Company,
    1966), 73.
34 Ibid., 945.
35 Sutton, America's Secret Establishment, 115.
36 Cuddy, Secret Records Revealed, 175-76.
37 Antony C. Sutton, Wall Street and the Bolshevik
    Revolution (New Rochelle, N.Y.: Arlington House
    Publishers, 1974), 91.
38 William Guy Carr, Pawns in the Game (Clearwater, Fla.:
    Angriff Press, 1958), 97-98.
39 Epperson, Unseen Hand, 261.
40 Carroll Quigley, The Anglo-American Establishment:
    From Rhodes to Cliveden (New York: Books in Focus,
    Inc., 1981), 5.
41 Quigley, Tragedy and Hope, 269.
42 Ibid., 271.
43 Carr, Pawns in the Game, 101.
44 Ibid., 102-03.
45 Quigley, Anglo-American Establishment, 146.
46 Quigley, Tragedy and Hope, 272.
47 Epperson, Unseen Hand, 67.
48 James Perloff, The Shadows of Power: The Council on
    Foreign Relations and the American Decline (Appleton,
    Wis.: Western Islands Publishers, 1988), 31.
49 Quigley, Tragedy and Hope, 282.
50 Epperson, Unseen Hand, 261.
51 Ibid., 67.
52 Quigley, Anglo-American Establishment, 249.
53 Ibid., 251.
54 Ibid., 251-52.
55 Ibid., 255.
56 Ibid., 259.
57 Ibid., 254.
58 Vicomte Léon DePoncins, Freemasonry and the Vatican:
    A Struggle for Recognition, trans. by Timothy Tindal-
    Robertson (Palmdale, Calif.: Omni/Christian Book Club,
    1968), 51.
59 Ibid.
60 Ibid., 52.
61 Ibid.
62 Ibid., 55.

63 Ibid.
64 Jones, Descent Into Tyranny, 23.
65 Robert B. Stinnett, Day of Deceit: The Truth About FDR
    and Pearl Harbor (New York: Touchstone, 2000), 275.
66 David Cox, "U.S. Prisoners Claim Roosevelt Left Them
    In Philippines Deliberately," The Scotsman, 30 July 2002
    (http://www.news.scotsman.com).
67 Kevin Phillips, American Dynasty: Aristocracy, Fortune,
    and the Politics of Deceit in the House of Bush (New
    York: Viking, 2004), 308.
68 James Bamford, Body of Secrets: Anatomy of the Ultra-
    Secret National Security Agency From the Cold War
    Through the Dawn of a New Century (New York:
    Doubleday, 2001), back jacket cover.
69 Ibid., 82.
70 Ibid., 82-83.
71 The Joint Chiefs of Staff, Memorandum for the Secretary
    of Defense. 13 March 1962. Subject: Justification for US
    Military Intervention in Cuba (TS). Washington, D.C.:
    The Joint Chiefs of Staff, i.
72 Ibid., 5.
73 Ibid., 7-8.
74 Ibid., 8.
75 Ibis., 8-9.
76 Bamford, Body of Secrets, 83.
77 Ibid., 89.
78 Ibid., 90-91.
79 Ibid., 67.
80 Ibid., 82.
81 Ibid., inside back flap of dust jacket.

CHAPTER 17
Oklahoma City Bombing

1 Alex Jones, 9-11: Descent Into Tyranny; The New World
   Order's Dark Plans to Turn Earth Into a Prison Planet
   (Austin, Tex.: AEJ Publishing, 2002), 34.
2 Ibid., 35-36.
3 Ibid., 36.
4 Ibid.
5 The Oklahoma Bombing Investigation Committee, Final
   Report On the Bombing of the Alfred P. Murrah Federal
   Building April 19, 1995 (Oklahoma City, Okla.: The
   Oklahoma Bombing Committee, 2001), xvi.
6 Ibid., 189.
7 Ibid., 188.
8 Ibid., 514.
9 Ibid., 515.
10 Ibid., 182-83.
11 Ibid., 187.
12 Ibid., back dust jacket.
13 Ibid., 201.
14 Ibid., 253.
15 Ibid., 173.
16 Ibid., 524.
17 Ibid., 176.
18 Ibid., 202.
19 Ibid., 184.
20 Jayna Davis, The Third Terrorist: The Middle East
   Connection to the Oklahoma City Bombing (Nashville,
   Tenn.: WND Books, 2004), ix.
21 Ibid., x.
22 OBIC, Final Report, 289.
23 Davis, Third Terrorist, 36.
24 Ibid., 37.
25 Ibid.
26 Ibid.
27 Ibid., 3-7.
28 Ibid.
29 Ibid., 3.

30 *Ibid.*, 3-6.
31 *Ibid.*, 6.
32 *Ibid.*, 3.
33 *Ibid.*, 132-33.
34 *Ibid.*, 6.
35 *Ibid.*
36 *Ibid.*, 3-7.
37 *Ibid.*, 5.
38 *Ibid.*
39 OBIC, *Final Report*, 300.
40 *Ibid.*, 284.
41 *Ibid.*
42 *Ibid.*, 285.
43 *Ibid.*, 286.
44 *Ibid.*, 284.
45 Richard A. Clarke, *Against All Enemies: Inside America's War on Terrorism* (New York: Free Press, 2004), 127.
46 OBIC, *Final Report*, 283.
47 Jones, *Descent Into Tyranny*, 53.
48 OBIC, *Final Report*, 271.
49 Jones, *Descent Into Tyranny*, 42.
50 *Ibid.*, 52.
51 OBIC, *Final Report*, 271.
52 *Ibid.*
53 Davis, *Third Terrorist*, 159.
54 *Ibid.*, 282.
55 *Ibid.*
56 *Ibid.*, 290.
57 *Ibid.*
58 OBIC, *Final Report*, 343.
59 *Ibid.*
60 Davis, *Third Terrorist*, 256.
61 *Ibid.*, 254.
62 *Ibid.*, 255.
63 *Ibid.*, 256.
64 *Ibid.*, 257.
65 *Ibid.*, 258.
66 OBIC, *Final Report*, 282.
67 Davis, *Third Terrorist*, 37.
68 *Ibid.*
69 *Ibid.*, 38.
70 Yossef Bodansky, *Bin Laden: The Man Who Declared War on America* (Roseville, Calif.: Prima Publishing, 2001), 218.
71 *Ibid.*, 34.
72 Davis, *Third Terrorist*, 291.
73 Bodansky, *Bin Laden*, 152.
74 *Ibid.*, 306.
75 *Ibid.*, 270.
76 Davis, *Third Terrorist*, 210.
77 OBIC, *Final Report*, xvi.
78 Davis, *Third Terrorist*, 290-91.
79 *Ibid.*, 286.
80 *Ibid.*, 292.
81 *Ibid.*, 287.
82 *Ibid.*, x.
83 *Ibid.*, 299-300.
84 *Ibid.*, 310.

CHAPTER 18
9/11 – An Overview

1 James Bamford, *A Pretext For War: 9/11, Iraq, and the Abuse of America's Intelligence Agencies* (New York: Doubleday, 2004), 3-4.
2 *Ibid.*, 9.
3 James Mann, *Rise of the Vulcans: The History of Bush's War Cabinet* (New York: Viking, 2004), 299.
4 Bamford, *Pretext For War*, 39-40.
5 Jennifer Senior, "The Firemen's Friar," *NewYorkmetro.com*, 12 November 2001 (http://www.newyorkmetro.com/nymetro/news/sept11/features/5372).
6 *Ibid.*
7 "The Life of Father Mychal Judge – Part One," *SaintMychal.com*, n.d. (http://www.saintmychal.com/life01.htm).
8 Senior, "Firemen's Friar."
9 LaTonya Taylor, "Fire Department Chaplain Dies in the Line of Duty: 'Father Mike' is remembered for compassion and always being first on the scene," *Christianity Today*, 18 September 2001 (http://www.christianitytoday.com/ct//2001/138/24.0.htm).
10 *Ibid.*
11 Senior, "Firemen's Friar."
12 Bob Woodward, *Plan of Attack* (New York: Simon & Schuster, 2004), 434.
13 Richard A. Clarke, *Against All Enemies: Inside America's War on Terror* (New York: Free Press), 194.
14 Senator Bob Graham with Jeff Nussbaum, *Intelligence Matters: The CIA, the FBI, Saudi Arabia, and the Failure of America's War on Terror* (New York: Random House, 2004), xii.
15 *Ibid.*, inside front jacket flap.
16 Bamford, *Pretext For War*, 112-13.
17 Peter L. Bergen, *Holy War, Inc.: Inside the Secret World of Osama bin Laden* (New York: The Free Press, 2001), 118.
18 Michael Moore, *Dude, Where's My Country?* (New York: Warner Books, 2003), 16.
19 Bamford, *Pretext For War*, 184.
20 Yosseff Bodansky, *The High Cost of Peace: How Washington's Middle East Policy Left America Vulnerable to Terrorism* (Roseville, Calif.: Prima Publishing, 2002), 214.
21 *Ibid.*, 122.
22 *Ibid.*, 418.
23 *Ibid.*, 357.
24 Craig Unger, *House of Bush, House of Saud: The Secret Relationship Between the World's Two Most Powerful Dynasties* (New York: Scribner, 2004), 237.
25 *Ibid.*
26 *Ibid.*
27 *Ibid.*, 238.
28 *Ibid.*
29 Bamford, *Pretext For War*, 242-44
30 John W. Dean, *Worse Than Watergate: The Secret Presidency of George W. Bush* (New York: Little, Brown and Company, 2004), 105.
31 Mann, *Rise of the Vulcans*, 255.
32 Clarke, *Against All Enemies*, 229.
33 Bamford, *Pretext For War*, 247.
34 *Ibid.*
35 *Ibid.*
36 David Ray Griffin, *The New Pearl Harbor: Disturbing Questions About the Bush Administration and 9/11* (Northampton, Mass.: Olive Branch Press, 2004), 85.
37 Graham, *Intelligence Matters*, 37.
38 Clarke, *Against All Enemies*, 235.
39 Bamford, *Pretext For War*, 245.
40 *Ibid.*, 248.
41 Clarke, *Against All Enemies*, 237.
42 *Ibid.*, 238.
43 Bamford, *Pretext For War*, 40.
44 Griffin, *New Pearl Harbor*, 60.
45 *Ibid.*
46 Bamford, *Pretext For War*, 37.
47 Griffin, *New Pearl Harbor*, 60.
48 Bamford, *Pretext For War*, 118.
49 Griffin, *New Pearl Harbor*, 60.
50 *Ibid.*, 61.

51 *Ibid.*, 8.
52 Bamford, *Pretext For War*, 51.
53 *Ibid.*
54 *Ibid.*, 16.
55 *Ibid.*, 61.
56 *Ibid.*, 18.
57 *Ibid.*, 33.
58 *Ibid.*, 39.
59 *Ibid.*, 78.
60 *Ibid.*, 79.
61 *Ibid.*, 57.
62 Clarke, *Against All Enemies*, 21.
63 Bamford, *Pretext For War*, 62.
64 Dean, *Worse Than Watergate*, 37.
65 *Ibid.*
66 *Ibid.*
67 *Ibid.*, 38.
68 Bamford, *Pretext for War*, 83.
69 *Ibid.*
70 *Ibid.*, 86-87.
71 *Ibid.*, 89.
72 *Ibid.*, 91.
73 *Ibid.*, 92.
74 *Ibid.*
75 Clarke, *Against All Enemies*, 24.
76 Woodward, *Plan of Attack*, 296.
77 Mann, *Rise of the Vulcans*, 221.
78 Jean-Charles Brisard and Guillaume Dasquié, trans. by Lucy Rounds with Peter Fifield and Nicholas Greenslade, *Forbidden Truth: U.S.-Taliban Secret Oil Diplomacy and the Failed Hunt for Bin Laden* (New York: Nation Books, 2002), xxiv.
79 Mann, *Rise of the Vulcans*, 288.
80 Griffin, *New Pearl Harbor*, 70.
81 David Wastell and Phillip Jacobson, "Israeli security issued urgent warnings to CIA of large-scale terror attacks," *news.telegraph.com*, 16 September 2001 (www.portal.telegraph.co.uk/news/main.jhtml?xml=%2F news%2F2001%2F09%2F16%2Fwcia16.xml).
82 Alex Jones, *9-11: Descent Into Tyranny; The New World Order's Dark Plans to Turn Earth Into a Prison Planet* (Austin, Tex.: AEJ Publishing, 2002), 80.
83 James Bamford, *Body of Secrets: Anatomy of the Ultra-Secret National Security Agency From the Cold War Through the Dawn of a New Century* (New York: Doubleday, 2001), xiii.
84 Jones, *Descent Into Tyranny*, 80-81.
85 Clarke, *Against All Enemies*, 218.
86 Graham, *Intelligence Matters*, 22.
87 James Perloff, *The Shadows of Power: The Council on Foreign Relations and the American Decline* (Appleton, Wis.: Western Islands Publishers, 1988), 66-67.
88 Griffin, *New Pearl Harbor*, 130.
89 Jones, *Descent Into Tyranny*, 57.
90 *Ibid.*, 58.
91 *Ibid.*, 57-58.
92 Griffin, *New Pearl Harbor*, vii.
93 *Ibid.*, ii.
94 *Ibid.*, i.
95 *Ibid.*, xxi-xxii.
96 *Ibid.*, xxii.
97 Kevin Phillips, *American Dynasty: Aristocracy, Fortune, and the Politics of Deceit in the House of Bush* (New York: Viking, 2004), 318.
98 *Ibid.*, 315.
99 Griffin, *New Pearl Harbor*, 120.
100 *Ibid.*, 20.
101 Jones, *Descent Into Tyranny*, 95-96.
102 Bamford, *Pretext For War*, 36.
103 Griffin, *New Pearl Harbor*, 63.
104 Bamford, *Pretext For War*, 36-37.

105 Jones, *Descent Into Tyranny*, 79.
106 Greg Gordon, "Senator Dayton charges FAA and NORAD part of 911 cover-up," *Star Tribune*, 3 August 2004 (http://bellaciao.org/en/article.php3?id_article=2387).
107 Jones, *Descent Into Tyranny*, 75.
108 *Ibid.*, 97-98.
109 *Ibid.*, 64-65.
110 Clarke, *Against All Enemies*, 236-37.
111 Griffin, *New Pearl Harbor*, 164.
112 *Ibid.*, 164-65.
113 Clarke, *Against All Enemies*, 245.
114 Mike Allen, "Bush Seeks to Restrict Hill Probes of Sept. 11," *Washington Post*, 30 January 2002, Edition F, A-4.
115 *Ibid.*
116 Dean, *Worse Than Watergate*, 3.
117 Brisard and Dasquié, *Forbidden Truth*, xxviii-xxix.
118 Unger, *House of Bush, House of Saud*, 4.
119 *Ibid.*, 277.
120 Robert Baer, *Sleeping with the Devil: How Washington Sold Our Soul for Saudi Crude* (New York: Crown Publishers, 2003), 21.
121 Brisard and Dasquié, *Forbidden Truth*, 50.
122 Unger, *House of Bush, House of Saud*, 272.
123 Griffin, *New Pearl Harbor*, 78.
124 *Ibid.*
125 Jones, *Descent Into Tyranny*, 65.
126 Griffin, *New Pearl Harbor*, 111.
127 Clarke, *Against All Enemies*, 33-34.
128 Jones, *Descent Into Tyranny*, 66.
129 Brisard and Dasquié, *Forbidden Truth*, 20.
130 *Ibid.*, 21.
131 *Ibid.*, xxviii.
132 *Ibid.*, 47-48.
133 *Ibid.*, 43.
134 Dan Briody, *The Iron Triangle: Inside the Secret World of the Carlyle Group* (Hoboken; N.J.: John Wiley & Sons, Inc., 2003), xxv.
135 Unger, *House of Bush, House of Saud*, 157.
136 Daniel Golden, James Bandler and Marcus Walker, "Bin Laden Family Is Tied to U.S. Group," *Wall Street Journal*, 27 September 2001, A3-A6.
137 Jones, *Descent Into Tyranny*, 67.
138 Unger, *House of Bush, House of Saud*, 156.
139 Briody, *Iron Triangle*, 139-40.
140 Unger, *House of Bush, House of Saud*, 249.
141 Briody, *Iron Triangle*, 141-42.
142 *Ibid.*, 142.
143 *Ibid.*, 143-44.
144 *Ibid.*, 144-46.
145 *Ibid.*, xxviii.
146 Unger, *House of Bush, House of Saud*, 36.
147 *Ibid.*, 9.
148 *Ibid.*, 252.
149 *Ibid.*, 7.
150 Graham, *Intelligence Matters*, 106.
151 Unger, *House of Bush, House of Saud*, 9.
152 *Ibid.*, 254.
153 *Ibid.*, 10.
154 *Ibid.*, 257.
155 *Ibid.*, 6.
156 *Ibid.*, 257-58.
157 Graham, *Intelligence Matters*, 106.
158 Unger, *House of Bush, House of Saud*, 130.
159 *Ibid.*, 152.
160 *Ibid.*, 152-53.
161 *Ibid.*, 145.
162 *Ibid.*, 188.
163 Daniel Kurtzman, "Bush Trades Jokes With Ozzy Osbourne: President Plays Role of Comedian in Chief," *Political Humor* (http://politicalhumor. about.com//library/weekly/aa050502a.htm).

164 Unger, *House of Bush, House of Saud,* 217.
165 *Ibid.,* 206.
166 *Ibid.,* 206-07.
167 *Ibid.,* 208.
168 *Ibid.,* 209.
169 *Ibid.,* 215-16.
170 *Ibid.,* 15-16.
171 *Ibid.,* 263.
172 *Ibid.,* 5.
173 *Ibid.,* 263.
174 *Ibid.,* 210.
175 *Ibid.,* 5.
176 *Ibid.,* 202.
177 *Ibid.,* 198.
178 *Ibid.,* 11.
179 Woodward, *Plan of Attack,* 324.
180 Unger, *House of Bush, House of Saud,* 264.
181 *Ibid.,* 265-66.
182 *Ibid.,* 266.
183 *Ibid.,* 267.
184 *Ibid.,* 267-68.
185 *Ibid.,* 268.
186 *Ibid.*
187 *Ibid.*
188 *Ibid.,* 268-69.
189 Thomas H. Kean, et al., *The 9/11 Commission Report: Final Report of the National Commission on Terrorist Attacks Upon the United States* (New York: W. W. Norton & Co., Inc., 2004), 330.
190 Unger, *House of Bush, House of Saud,* 269.
191 FEMA Report # 403, *World Trade Center Building Performance Study: Data Collection, Preliminary Observations, and Recommendations,* May 2002, 1, 4, 5-1 (http://www.fema.gov/library/wtcstudy.shtm).
192 *Ibid.*
193 Griffin, *New Pearl Harbor,* 12.
194 *Ibid.,* 13.
195 *Ibid.*
196 *Ibid.,* 14-15.
197 *Ibid.,* 17.
198 *Ibid.,* 16.
199 *Ibid.*
200 *Ibid.,* 17.
201 *Ibid.,* 15.
202 Kean, et al., *9/11 Commission Report,* 291.
203 Griffin, *New Pearl Harbor,* 18.
204 *Ibid.,* 19.
205 *Ibid.,* 179.
206 Bamford, *Pretext for War,* 58-59.
207 "United in Courage: New York City," *People.com,* 12 September 2001 (http://propagandamatrix.com/louie_cacchioli.htm).
208 Harvey Leifert, "Damage to Buildings Near World Trade Center Caused by Falling Debris and Air Pressure Wave, Not by Ground Shaking, Columbia Seismologist's Report in November 20 Issue of *Eos,*" *Earth Institute News,* 16 November 2001 (http://www.earth.columbia.edu/news/story11_16_01.html).
209 *Ibid.*
210 Griffin, *New Pearl Harbor,* 19.
211 Mann, *Vulcans,* 307.
212 Dave vonKleist, *911 In Plane Site* produced by Dave vonKleist, 70 minutes, 2004, videocassette.
213 Griffin, *New Pearl Harbor,* 160.
214 Unger, *House of Bush, House of Saud,* 4.
215 Dean, *Worse Than Watergate,* 198.
216 "US Leadership Had Foreknowledge of Impending 9-11 Attacks," *Zogby.com,* 31 August 2004 (http://www.zogby.com/news/ReadNews.dbm?ID=855).
217 *Ibid.*
218 Kean, et al., *9/11 Commission Report,* 305.

219 FEMA Report, Section 5.7, 31.
220 *Ibid.*
221 Griffin, *New Pearl Harbor,* 20-21.
222 Scott Loughrey, "WTC-7: The Improbable Collapse," 10 August 2003 (http://globalresearch.ca/aricles/LOU308A.html).
223 *America Rebuilds: A Year At Ground Zero* produced by Seth Kramer and Daniel A. Miller, narrated by Kevin Spacey, 90 minutes, 2002, videocassette.
224 Alex Jones, "Professional Demolition of World Trade Center Building 7" (http://www.prisonplanet.com/011904wtc7.com).
225 Donn de Grand Pré, *The Viper's Venom* (Madison, Va.: Grand Pré Books, 2002), 54.
226 Donn de Grand Pré, *The Rattler's Revenge* (Madison, Va.: Grand Pré Publishers, Ltd., 2003), 550-51.
227 Griffin, *New Pearl Harbor,* 41.
228 *Ibid.*
229 *Ibid.*
230 Graham, *Intelligence Matters,* 26.
231 Griffin, *New Pearl Harbor,* 40.
232 Alex Jones, "Transcript: Alex Jones Interviews Col. Donn de Grand-Pre, U.S.Army (ret.): Explosive New 9/11 Revelations and Explanations," *Prison Planet.com* (http://www.prisonplanet.com/022904degrand.html).
233 Jim Heikkila, "Planes of 911 Exceeded Their Software Limits," 17 August 2002, handout available from Grand Pré Publishers, Ltd.
234 De Grand Pré, *Rattler's Revenge,* 551.
235 De Grand Pré, *Viper's Venom,* 56.
236 *Ibid.,* 56-57.
237 Kean, et al., *9/11 Commission Report,* 285-86.
238 Griffin, *New Pearl Harbor,* 26.
239 *Ibid.,* 29-30.
240 Kean, et al., *9/11 Commission Report,* 313.
241 Griffin, *New Pearl Harbor,* 33.
242 *Ibid.,* 34.
243 *Ibid.*
244 *Ibid.,* 35.
245 *Ibid.,* 3-4.
246 *Ibid.,* 48.
247 Bamford, *Body of Secrets,* 85-86.
248 *Pentagon Building Performance Report* (Reston, Va.: American Society of Civil Engineers, 2003), 13.
249 *Ibid.,* 35- 39.
250 James L. Melton, *Satan's New World Order: How World Leaders are Building the Kingdom of Antichrist* (Martin, Tenn.: Bible Baptist Church, 2004), 4-5.
251 Unger, *House of Bush, House of Saud,* 242-45.

CHAPTER 19
"Bring It On"

1 John W. Dean, *Worse Than Watergate: The Secret Presidency of George W. Bush* (New York: Little, Brown and Company, 2004), 74.
2 *Ibid.*
3 Robert Flood, *The Rebirth of America,* ed. Nancy Leigh DeMoss (Philadelphia, Penn.: Arthur S. DeMoss Foundation, 1986), 151.
4 Dean, *Worse Than Watergate,* 74.
5 Bob Woodward, *Plan of Attack* (New York: Simon & Schuster, 2004), 249.
6 James Bamford, *A Pretext for War: 9/11, Iraq, and The Abuse of America's Intelligence Agencies* (New York: Doubleday, 2004), n.p.
7 Dean, *Worse Than Watergate,* 233.
8 Yossef Bodansky, *The Secret History of the Iraq War* (New York: HarperCollins Publishers, 2004), 177.
9 *Ibid.,* 338.

10 *Ibid.,* 502.
11 *Ibid.,* 422.
12 *Ibid.,* 286.
13 *Ibid.,* 444.
14 *Ibid.,* 426.
15 *Ibid.,* 378.
16 Michael Moore, *Dude, Where's My Country?* (New York: Warner Books, Inc., 2003), 74.
17 Yossef Bodansky, *Bin Laden: The Man Who Declared War on America* (Roseville, Calif.: Prima Publishing, 2001), 264.
18 Peter L. Bergen, *Holy War, Inc.: Inside the Secret World of Osama bin Laden* (New York: The Free Press, 2001), 109.
19 Bodansky, *Secret History,* 285.
20 *Ibid.,* 269.
21 *Ibid.,* 270.
22 *Ibid.,* 271.
23 John Eidsmoe, *Christianity and the Constitution* (Grand Rapids, Mich.: Baker Books, 1995), 381.
24 Bodansky, *Secret History,* 481-82.
25 *Ibid.,* 444.
26 *Ibid.,* 445.
27 *Ibid.*
28 *Ibid*
29 *Ibid.,* 254.
30 *Ibid.,* 495.
31 *Ibid.,* 530.
32 *Ibid.,* 385.
33 *Ibid.*
34 *Ibid.,* 432.
35 *Ibid.,* 385.
36 Woodward, *Plan of Attack,* 276.
37 Bodansky, *Bin Laden,* xv.
38 Moore, *Dude,* 72.
39 Bodansky, *Bin Laden,* 296-97.
40 *Ibid.,* xii.
41 Bodansky, *Secret History,* 242.
42 Toby Dodge, *Inventing Iraq: The Failure of Nation Building and a History Denied* (New York: Columbia University Press, 2003), xi-xii.
43 *Ibid.,* 30.
44 *Ibid.,* 24.
45 *Ibid.,* inside back jacket flap.
46 *Ibid.,* 38.
47 *Ibid.,* xiv.
48 Bodansky, *Bin Laden,* 19.
49 Dodge, *Inventing Iraq,* xi.
50 Bodansky, *Secret History,* 493-94.
51 Samuel P. Huntington, *The Clash of Civilizations and the Remaking of World Order* (New York: Simon & Schuster, 1996), 209; 217-18.
52 Woodward, *Plan of Attack,* 113.
53 Dodge, *Inventing Iraq,* 157.
54 Huntington, *Clash of Civilizations,* 39.
55 Robert Baer, *Sleeping With the Devil: How Washington Sold Our Soul for Saudi Crude* (New York: Crown Publishers, 2003), 83.
56 Jean-Charles Brisard and Guillaume Dasquié, *Forbidden Truth: U.S.-Taliban Secret Oil Diplomacy and the Failed Hunt for Bin Laden,* trans. by Lucy Rounds with Peter Fifield and Nicholas Greenslade (New York: Nations Books, 2002), 69-70.
57 Baer, *Sleeping With the Devil,*75.
58 Bodansky, *Bin Laden,* xiii-xiv.
59 *Ibid.,* xiv.
60 Craig Unger, *House of Bush, House of Saud: The Secret Relationship Between the World's Two Most Powerful Dynasties* (New York: Scribner, 2004), 83.
61 Bodansky, *Bin Laden,* xiv.
62 Unger, *House of Bush, House of Saud,* 28.
63 Baer, *Sleeping With the Devil,* 48-50.

64 *Ibid.,* 60.
65 Unger, *House of Bush, House of Saud,* 87.
66 *Ibid.,* 85-86.
67 Huntington, *Clash of Civilizations,* 116.
68 Yossef Bodansky, *The High Cost of Peace: How Washington's Middle East Policy Left America Vulnerable to Terrorism* (Roseville, Calif.: Forum, 2002), 6-7.
69 *Ibid.,* 163-64.
70 *Ibid.,* 8.
71 *Ibid.,* 71.
72 *Ibid.,* 9-10.
73 *Ibid.,* 10.
74 *Ibid.,* 9.
75 *Ibid.,* 11.
76 *Ibid.,* 137.
77 *Ibid.,* 92.
78 *Ibid.,* 109.
79 Unger, *House of Bush, House of Saud,* unnumbered picture page.
80 *Ibid.,* 68-69.
81 *Ibid.,* 79.
82 Kevin Phillips, *American Dynasty: Aristocracy, Fortune, and the Politics of Deceit in the House of Bush* (New York: Viking, 2004), 303.
83 *Ibid.*
84 *Ibid.,* 264.
85 Bodansky, *Bin Laden,* 10.
86 *Ibid.*
87 Brisard and Dasquié, *Forbidden Truth,* ix-xii.
88 Unger, *House of Bush, House of Saud,* 135.
89 *Ibid.,* 135.
90 *Ibid.*
91 *Ibid.,* 138.
92 *Ibid.,* 139.
93 Bodansky, *Bin Laden,* 191.
94 Susan Schmidt and Vernon Loeb, "Lynch kept firing until she ran out of ammo," *Washington Post,* 3 April 2003 (http://www.postgazette.com/nation/20030403rescuenat p3.asp).
95 *Ibid.*
96 John Kampfner, "Saving Private Lynch story 'flawed'," *BBC News,* 15 May 2003 (http://news.bbc.co.uk/1/hi/ programmes/correspondent/3028585.stm).
97 Colin L. Powell, *My American Journey* (New York: Random House, 1995), 460.
98 Bodansky, *Bin Laden,* 149.
99 Unger, *House of Bush, House of Saud,* 143-44.
100 *Ibid.,* 192.
101 Bodansky, *Bin Laden,* 33.
102 *Ibid.,* 295.
103 *Ibid., Ibid.,* 387.
104 *Ibid.,* 104.
105 Bodansky, *High Cost,* 334.
106 Bodansky, *Secret History,* 236.
107 *Ibid.,* 279.
108 *Ibid.,* 253.
109 *Ibid.,* 278.
110 Phillips, *American Dynasty,* 264-65.
111 *Ibid.,* 490.
112 *Ibid.,* back dust jacket.
113 Bodansky, *High Cost,* 455-56.
114 *Ibid.,* 405.
115 *Ibid.,* 504.
116 *Ibid.,* 505.
117 Woodward, *Plan of Attack,* 112.
118 Bodansky, *High Cost,* 506.
119 Bodansky, *Secret History,* 56.
120 *Ibid.,* 161.
121 *Ibid.,* 66-67.
122 Bodansky, *High Cost,* 493.
123 *Ibid.,* 436.

124 *Ibid.,* 454.
125 *Ibid.,* 466.
126 *Ibid.,* 480.
127 *Ibid.,* 483.
128 *Ibid.,* 530.
129 *Ibid.,* 531.
130 *Ibid.,* 550.
131 *Ibid.,* 553.
132 *Ibid.,* 537.
133 *Ibid.*
134 *Ibid.,* 491.
135 Bodansky, *Secret History,* 84.
136 *Ibid.,* 320.
137 *Ibid.,* 330.
138 *Ibid.,* 402.
139 Bodansky, *High Cost,* 210.
140 *Ibid.,* 535.
141 *Ibid.,* 332.
142 Phillips, *American Dynasty,* 254-55.
143 *Ibid.,* 226.
144 Bodansky, *Secret History,* 316.
145 *Ibid.,* 316-17.
146 Bamford, *Pretext for War,* 300.
147 Bodansky, *Secret History,* 52.
148 *Ibid.,* 53.
149 *Ibid.*
150 *Ibid.,* 51-54.
151 *Ibid.,* 342-43.
152 *Ibid.,* 259.
153 *Ibid.,* 231.
154 *Ibid.,* 138-39.
155 *Ibid.,* 146.
156 Woodward, *Plan of Attack,* 147.
157 *Ibid.,* 206.
158 Bodansky, *Secret History,* 222.
159 *Ibid.,* 224.
160 *Ibid.,* 225.
161 *Ibid.*
162 *Ibid.,* 237.
163 *Ibid.,* 230.
164 *Ibid.,* 228.
165 *Ibid.,* 281.
166 Woodward, *Plan of Attack,* 123.
167 *Ibid.,* 136.
168 *Ibid.,* 303.
169 James Mann, *Rise of the Vulcans: The History of Bush's War Cabinet* (New York: Viking Penguin, 2004), 361.
170 Dean, *Worse Than Watergate,* 50.
171 Daniel Golden, James Bandler and Marcus Walker, "Bin Laden Family Is Tied To U.S. Group," *Wall Street Journal,* 27 September 2001, pp. A3 and A6.
172 Brisard and Dasquié, *Forbidden Truth,* 38.
173 *Ibid.,* xxxiii.
174 Phillips, *American Dynasty,* 150.
175 *Ibid.,* 171.
176 *Ibid.,* 172-73.
177 Dan Briody, *The Halliburton Agenda: The Politics of Oil and Money* (Hoboken, N.J.: John Wiley & Sons, Inc., 2004), 185.
178 *Ibid.,* 221-22.
179 *Ibid.,* 186.
180 Phillips, *American Dynasty,* 171-72.
181 Briody, *Halliburton Agenda,* viii.
182 Phillips, *American Dynasty,* 172.
183 *Ibid.,* 174-75.
184 Briody, *Halliburton Agenda,* 228.
185 *Ibid.,* 230.
186 *Ibid.,* 228-29.
187 Phillips, *American Dynasty,* 171.
188 Briody, *Halliburton Agenda,* 214.
189 *Ibid.,* 235.
190 *Ibid.,* 205.
191 *Ibid.,* 66.
192 *Ibid.,* 114-16.
193 *Ibid.,* 117-18.
194 *Ibid.,* 164-68.
195 *Ibid.,* 145.
196 Dean, *Worse Than Watergate,* 97.
197 *Ibid.,* 98.
198 Bamford, *Pretext for War,* 262-63.
199 *Ibid.,* 263.
200 Unger, *House of Bush, House of Saud,* 263.
201 Thomas Donnelly, Donald Kagan and Gary Schmitt, *Rebuilding America's Defenses: Strategy, Forces and Resources For A New Century* (Washington, D.C.: Project for the New American Century, 2000), n.p.
202 Mann, *Rise of the Vulcans,* 316.
203 *Ibid.,* ix-x.
204 *Ibid.,* x.
205 Donnelly, Kagan and Schmitt, *Rebuilding America's Defenses,* iv.
206 *Ibid.,* 6.
207 Thomas P. M. Barnett, *The Pentagon's New Map: War and Peace in the Twenty-first Century* (New York: G. P. Putnam's Sons, 2004), front inside flap and back dust jacket.
208 *Ibid.,* back dust jacket.
209 *Ibid.,* front inside flap dust jacket.
210 *Ibid.,* 34.
211 *Ibid.*
212 *Ibid.,* 272.
213 Nedra Pickler, "No Rush to Bring Troops Home From Iraq: Bush Says U.S. Troops Will Return as Soon as Possible, Not Necessarily This Year," *AOL News Service,* 1 January 2005 (http://aolsvc.news.aol.com/article.adp?id=20050116002509990003).
214 Barnett, *Pentagon's New Map,* 178-79.
215 *Ibid.,* 205.
216 *Ibid.,* 231.
217 Donnelly, Kagan and Schmitt, *Rebuilding America's Defenses,* 51.
218 Barnett, *Pentagon's New Map,* 245.
219 *Ibid.,* 50.
220 Alex Jones, *9-11: Descent Into Tyranny; The New World Order's Dark Plans to Turn Earth Into a Prison Planet* (Austin: Tex.: AEJ Publishing, 2002), 7-8.
221 "United Nations' cartoon condoms: Global body unveils [expletive], [expletive] and [expletive] in TV ads pushing AIDS-prevention message," *WorldNetDaily,* 13 January 2005 (http://www.worldnetdaily.com/news/article.asp?ARTICLE_ID=42353).
222 Bamford, *Pretext for War,* 284.
223 *Ibid.,* 284-85.
224 *Ibid.,* 285-86.
225 Richard A. Clarke, *Against All Enemies: Inside America's War on Terror* (New York: Free Press, 2004), 32.
226 Bamford, *Pretext for War,* 286.
227 *Ibid.,* 260-61.
228 Clarke, *Against All Enemies,* 176.
229 Mann, *Rise of the Vulcans,* 250.
230 Bamford, *Pretext for War,* 261.
231 *Ibid.,* 267.
232 *Ibid.,* 268-69.
233 Woodward, *Plan of Attack,* 392.
234 Dean, *Worse Than Watergate,* 197.
235 Bodansky, *Secret History,* 432.

CHAPTER 20
Why America is Finished

1 Kevin Phillips, *American Dynasty: Aristocracy, Fortune, and the Politics of Deceit in the House of Bush* (New York: Viking, 2004), 137.
2 *Ibid.*, 47-48.
3 *Ibid.*, 296.
4 *Ibid.*, 87.
5 *Ibid.*, 345.
6 *Ibid.*, 147, 345-46.
7 *Ibid.*, 147.
8 John R. Rice, *Our God Breathed Book – the Bible* (Murfreesboro, Tenn.: The Sword of the Lord Publishers, 1969), 383.
9 David H. Sorenson, *Touch Not the Unclean Thing: The Bible Translation Controversy and the Principle of Separation* (Duluth, Minn: Northstar Baptist Ministries, 2001), back cover.
10 Ian R. K. Paisley, *My Plea For the Old Sword: The English Authorised Version (KJV)* (Greenville, S.C.: Emerald House, 1997), 102.
11 David Cloud, "Dr. Ian Paisley's Stand for the Old Bible," *Freepres.org*, n.d. (http://www.freepres.org/paisley.asp?paisley).
12 Lewis Lapham, *The Wish for Kings* (New York: Grove Press, 1993), 154-55.
13 John Dean, *Worse Than Watergate: The Secret Presidency of George W. Bush* (New York: Little, Brown and Company, 2004), 15.
14 William F. Still, *New World Order: The Ancient Plan of Secret Societies* (Lafayette, La.: Huntington House Publishers, 1990), 12.
15 *Ibid.*, 13.
16 *Ibid.*
17 *Ibid.*
18 Webster Griffin Tarpley and Anton Chaitkin, *George Bush: The Unauthorized Biography* (Washington, D.C.: Executive Intelligence Review, 1992), 370.
19 Phillips, *American Dynasty*, 284.
20 *Ibid.*, 285.
21 *Ibid.*, 286.
22 *Ibid.*, 289.
23 *Ibid.*, 288.
24 *Ibid.*, 53-54.
25 *Ibid.*, 54-55.
26 *Ibid.*, 58.
27 Carl Bernstein, "The Unholy Alliance," *Time*, 24 February 1992, 28.
28 Avro Manhattan, *The Vatican Moscow Washington Alliance* (Chino, Calif.: Chick Publications, 1986), 68.
29 Phillips, *American Dynasty*, 18-19.
30 Yossef Bodansky, *Bin Laden: The Man Who Declared War on America* (Roseville, Calif.: Prima Publishing, 2001), 278-79.
31 Phillips, *American Dynasty*, 17.
32 *Ibid.*, 59.
33 "Bill O'Reilly likes Bill Clinton for U.N. chief: FOX News star says he should replace Kofi Annan," *WorldNetDaily*, 5 January 2005 (http://www.worldnetdaily.com.com/news/article.asp?ARTICLE_ID=42247).
34 Joseph Farah, "The Ozzy and Dubya Show," *WorldNetDaily*, 13 May 2002 (http://www.worldnetdaily.com/news/article.asp?ARTICLE_ID=27597).
35 *Ibid.*
36 David Montgomery, "Great & Powerful Ozz: At the White House Correspondents' Dinner, a Heavy-Metal Taste of True Celebrity," *WashingtonPost.com*, 6 May 2002 (http://www.washingtonpost.com/ac2/wp-dyn/A37357-2002May5?language=printer).
37 Barton Gellman and Susan Schmidt, "Shadow Government Is at Work in Secret: After Attacks, Bush Ordered 100 Officials to Bunkers Away From Capital to Ensure Federal Survival," *WashingtonPost.com*, 1 March 2002 (http://www.washingtonpost.com/ac2/wp-dyn/A20584-2002Feb28?languageprinter).
38 Alex Jones, *9-11: Descent Into Tyranny; The New World Order's Dark Plans to Turn Earth Into a Prison Planet* (Austin, Tex.: AEJ Publishing, 2002), 99.
39 Dean, *Worse Than Watergate*, 101-02.
40 Jones, *Descent Into Tyranny*, 160.
41 John Eidsmoe, *Christianity and the Constitution* (Grand Rapids, Mich.: Baker Books, 1995), 381.
42 Dean, *Worse Than Watergate*, 96.
43 *Ibid.*, 96-97.
44 *Ibid.*, 97.
45 *Ibid.*, 77.
46 *Ibid.*, 78.
47 *Ibid.*, 80-82.
48 *Ibid.*, 185.
49 *Ibid.*, 186.
50 *Ibid.*, 185.
51 Peter S. Ruckman, *The Book of Genesis* (Pensacola, Fla.: Bible Believers Press, 1969), 182.
52 Montgomery, "Great & Powerful Ozz."
53 *Ibid.*
54 *Ibid.*
55 Joe Kovacs, "Denver backtracks on Christmas sign: But Christian church group still excluded from Parade of Lights," *WorldNetDaily*, 3 December 2004 (http://www.worldnetdaily.com/news/article.asp?ARTICLE_ID=41753).
56 Joe Kovacs, "Christmastime event is no-Christian zone: Santa, 'holy homosexuals' OK for parade, but no floats with direct religious themes," *WorldNetDaily*, 2 December 2004 (http://www.worldnetdaily.com/news/article.asp?ARTICLE_ID=41724).
57 *Ibid.*
58 Erin Curry, "Culture Digest: Carols sung after religion banned from parade; UCC sees rise in sales; liberals dominating colleges," *BPNews*, 8 December 2004 (http://www.bpnews.net/printerfriendly.asp?ID=19682).
59 Elisabeth Bumiller, "White House Letter; 'Pony Up' and Then 'Party On,' Inaugural Officials Say," *The New York Times*, 3 January 2005 (http://www.nytimes.com/2005/01/03/politics/03letter.html).
60 *Ibid.*
61 "Bush Twins Rock To Kid Rock," *Contactmusic.com*, 3 September 2004 (http://www.contactmusic.com/new/xmlfeed.nsf/mndwebpages/bush%20twins%20rock%20too%20kid%2020rock).
62 "Moral Values My [Expletive]," *Patridiots.com*, 4 January 2005 (http://www.patridiots.com/001368.html).
63 Ron Strom, "No Kid Rock at Bush concert: Committee backs off plan to feature rapper after pro-family Americans express outrage," *WorldNetDaily*, 12 January 2005 (http://www.worldnetdaily.com/news/article.asp?ARTICLE_ID_=42351).
64 Gil Kaufman, "Fuel Singer Shouts Obscenity At President's Bash – But Hilary Duff And JoJo Behave," *VH1.com*, 19 January 2005 (http://www.vh1.com/news/articles/1496000/20050119/fuel.jhtml?headlines=true
65 Jim VandeHei and Michael A. Fletcher, "Bush Says Election Ratified Iraq Policy: No U.S. Troop Withdrawal Date Is Set," *WashingtonPost.com*, 16 January 2005 (http://www.washingtonpost.com/ac2/wp-dyn/A12450-2005Jan15.html?sub=AR).
66 Jim VandeHei and Michael A. Fletcher, "Bush Upsets Some Supporters: President Is Urged to Press Ban on Same-Sex Marriage," *WashingtonPost.com*, 19 January 2005 (http://www.washingtonpost.com/wp-dyn/articles/A19167-2005Jan18.html).

67 Susan Page, "Cheney says he opposes marriage amendment," *USATODAY.com*, 24 August 2004 (http://www.usatoday.com/news/politicselections/nation/president/2004-08-24-cheney_x.htm).

68 "Put Jerry on Your Desk," *National Liberty Journal*, November 2004 (http://www.nljonline.com/nov04/put_jerry_on_your_desk.html).

69 Sara Lesley, "Liberty University Dedicates Helms School of Government," *National Liberty Journal*, October 2004 (http://www.nljonline.com).

70 Paul Smith, "Billy Graham: World Is Facing A 'Final Shaking': Belmont Abbey Confers Honorary Degree," *Gastonia Gazette*, 22 November 1967, A1.

71 *Ibid.*

72 Transcript of Tony Snow interview with Billy Graham on FOX News' *The Tony Snow Show*, 2 January 2000.

73 James Warren, "Nixon, Billy Graham make derogatory comments about Jews on tape," *Chicago Tribune: Internet Edition*, 28 February 2002 (http://www.fpp.co.uk/online/02/02/Graham_Nixon.html).

74 *Ibid.*

75 "Passing the Baton," transcript of Larry King interview with Dr. Billy Graham on *Larry King Live*, 21 December 2000.

76 Alex Johnson, "Bush – born again, or not?: The president has never clarified his conversion narrative," *MSNBC.com*, 28 September 2004 (http://www.msnbc.msn.com/id/6115719/).

77 Stephen Mansfield, *The Faith of George Bush* (Lake Mary, Fla.: Charisma House, 2003), 161.

78 Donn de Grand Pré, *Barbarians Inside the Gates: The Black Book of Bolshevism* (San Pedro, Calif.: GSG & Associates, 2000), 386.

79 de Grand Pré, *Barbarians*, 383-83.

80 *Ibid.*, 385.

81 William J. Federer, *America's God and Country Encyclopedia of Quotations* (Coppell, Tex.: Fame Publishing, 1994), 204-05.

82 Sam Cohen, *Shame: Confessions of the Father of the Neutron Bomb* (n.p.: Xlibris Corporation, 2000), 303.

83 Jean Torkelson, "Parade prohibition puzzles preacher," *Rocky Mountain News*, 1 December 2004 (http://www.rockymountainnews.com/drmn/religion/article/0,1299,DRMN_61_3365940,00.html).

84 "Denver Mayor to Light Community Menorah (He's the 'Merry Christmas' Censor)," *Free Republic*, 4 December 2004 (http://www.209.157.64.200/focus/f-news/1292776/posts).

85 Cohen, *Shame*, 29.

86 *Ibid.*, 28.

87 *Ibid.*, 276.

88 *Ibid.*, 49-55.

CHAPTER 21
The Little Bitty Baby

1 Sam Cohen and Joe Douglass, "The Nuclear Threat That Doesn't Exist—or Does It?" *Financial Sense Online*, 11 March 2003 (http://www.financialsense.com/editorials/douglass/2003/0311.htm).

2 Sam Cohen, *Shame: Confessions of the Father of the Neutron Bomb* (n.p.: Xlibris Corporation, 2000), 239.

3 Colin Powell, *My American Journey* (New York: Random House, 1995), 540.

4 Cohen and Douglass, "Nuclear Threat."

5 Cohen, *Shame*, 329-30.

6 " 'Sex bomb' snubbed by US military," *FairfaxDigital*, 17 January 2005 (http://smh.com.au/news/World/Make-love-not-war-US-turned-down-sex-bomb/2005/01/17/1105810802947.html?oneclick=true).

7 Yossef Bodansky, *Bin Laden: The Man Who Declared War on America* (Roseville, Calif.: Prima Publishing, 1999), 318.

8 *Ibid.*, 329-31.

9 Sam Cohen, *Shame*, 444-46.

10 *Ibid.*, 18.

11 *Ibid.*, 93.

12 *Ibid.*, 454-58.

13 *Ibid.*, 381.

14 Elise Labott, "Russia 'tests new missile systems,' " *CNN.com*, 17 November 2004 (http://www.cnn.com/2004/WORLD/europe/11/17/russia/putin).

15 Cohen, *Shame*, 89.

16 *Ibid.*, 79.

17 Thomas P. M. Barnett, *The Pentagon's New Map: War and Peace in the Twenty-first Century* (New York: G. P. Putnam's Sons, 2004), 287.

18 Samuel P. Huntington, *The Clash of Civilizations and the Remaking of World Order* (New York: Simon & Schuster, 1996), 103.

19 *Ibid.*, 231.

20 Cohen, *Shame*, 383.

21 Huntington, *Clash of Civilizations*, 188.

22 Barnett, *Pentagon's New Map*, 219-21.

23 Huntington, *Clash of Civilizations*, 240.

24 Barnett, *Pentagon's New Map*, 224.

25 Robert Baer, *Sleeping With the Devil: How Washington Sold Our Soul for Saudi Crude* (New York: Crown Publishers, 2003), xv-xvi).

26 Yossef Bodansky, *The High Cost of Peace: How Washington's Middle East Policy Left America Vulnerable to Terrorism* (Roseville, Calif.: Prima Publishing, 2002), 479.

27 Barnett, *Pentagon's New Map*, 224.

28 Marcia Dunn, "A Yen for Space," *Star Telegram*, 24 September 1999, 22A.

Bibliography

AINSWORTH, BRIG. GEN. FRED C. AND JOSEPH W. KIRKLEY. *The War of the Rebellion*. Series IV, Vol. III. Washington, D.C.: n.p., 1900.

ALDRICH, GARY. *Unlimited Access: An FBI Agent Inside the Clinton White House*. Washington, D.C.: Regnery Publishing, Inc., 1998.

ALLEN, GARY. *Say "NO!" to the New World Order*. Seal Beach, Calif.: Concord Press, 1987.

_____. *The Rockefeller File*. Seal Beach, Calif.: '76 Press, 1976.

ANONYMOUS. *Light Bearers of Darkness*. Hawthorne, Calif.: The Christian Book Club of America, 1930.

ARMITAGE, THOMAS. *A History of the Baptists*. Vol. 2. Watertown, Wis.: Baptist Heritage Press, 1988.

BAER, ROBERT. *Sleeping with the Devil: How Washington Sold Our Soul for Saudi Crude*. New York: Crown Publishers, 2003.

BAIGNET, MICHAEL AND RICHARD LEIGH. *The Temple and the Lodge*. New York: Arcade Publishing, 1989.

BAMFORD, JAMES. *A Pretext For War: 9/11, Iraq, and the Abuse of America's Intelligence Agencies*. New York: Doubleday, 2004.

_____. *Body of Secrets: Anatomy of the Ultra-Secret National Security Agency From the Cold War Through the Dawn of a New Century*. New York: Doubleday, 2001.

BARNETT, THOMAS P. M. *The Pentagon's New Map: War and Peace in the Twenty-first Century*. New York: G. P. Putnam's Sons, 2004.

BARTON, DAVID. *A Spiritual Heritage Tour of the United States Capitol*. Aledo, Tex.: WallBuilders, 2000.

BELLER, JAMES R. *America in Crimson Red: The Baptist History of America*. Arnold, Mo.: Prairie Fire Press, 2004.

_____. *The Baptist History Workbook: A Work Text History of the Baptized Believers From the Time of Christ to the 20th Century*. Arnold, Mo.: Prairie Fire Press, 2002.

BENNETT, DAVID A. *A General History of the Baptist Denomination in America*. Vols. 1 & 2. Gallatin, Tenn.: Church History Research and Archives, 1985.

BERGEN, PETER L. *Holy War, Inc.: Inside the Secret World of Osama bin Laden*. New York: The Free Press, 2001.

BILLINGTON, RAY ALLEN. *The Protestant Crusade*. Chicago: Quadrangle Books, 1964.

BODANSKY, YOSSEF. *Bin Laden: The Man Who Declared War on America*. Roseville, Calif.: Prima Publishing, 2001.

_____. *The High Cost of Peace: How Washington's Middle East Policy Left America Vulnerable to Terrorism*. Roseville, Calif.: Prima Publishing, 2002.

_____. *The Secret History of the Iraq War*. New York: HarperCollins Publishers, 2004.

BOPP, VIRGIL. *Confidently Committed*. Grand Rapids, Mich.: Regular Baptist Press, 1987.

BRADFORD, WILLIAM. *Of Plymouth Plantation: 1620-1647*. New York: Random House, 1981.

BRIODY, DAN. *The Halliburton Agenda: The Politics of Oil and Money*. Hoboken, N.J.: John Wiley & Sons, Inc., 2004.

_____. *The Iron Triangle: Inside the Secret World of the Carlyle Group*. Hoboken, N.J.: John Wiley & Sons, Inc., 2003.

BRISARD, JEAN-CHARLES AND GUILLAUME DASQUIÉ. *Forbidden Truth: U.S.-Taliban Secret Oil Diplomacy and the Failed Hunt for Bin Laden*. Translated by Lucy Rounds with Peter Fifield and Nicholas Greenslade. New York: Nation Books, 2002.

BRUN, MICHEL. *Incident At Sakhalin: The True Mission of Flight KAL 007*. New York: Four Walls Eight Windows, 1995.

BURGON, JOHN WILLIAM, B.D. *The Revision Revised*. Paradise, Penn.: Conservative Classics, 1883.

BUSH, GEORGE W. *A Charge to Keep: My Journey to the White House*. New York: HarperCollins Publishers, 1999.

BUTTERFIELD, L. H. *Elder John Leland, Jeffersonian Itinerant*. Worcester, Mass.: American Antiquarian Society, 1953.

CARR, WILLIAM GUY. *Pawns in the Game*. N.p.: n.p., n.d.

CATHCART, WILLIAM, ed. *Baptist Encyclopedia*. Vol. 1. Philadelphia: Louis H. Everts, 1881.

_____. *Baptist Patriots*. Grand Rapids, Mich.: Guardian Press, 1976.

_____. *Baptists and the Revolution*. Philadelphia: S. A. George and Co., 1876.

CHARLOT, MONICA. *Victoria: The Young Queen.* Cambridge, England: Blackwell _Publishers, 1991.

CHENNAULT, CLAIRE LEE. *Way of A Fighter.* Tucson, Ariz.: James Thorvardson & Sons, 1949.

CHINIQUY, CHARLES. *50 Years in the "Church" of Rome.* Chino, Calif.: Chick Publications, 1985.

CHRISTIAN, JOHN T. *A History of the Baptists.* Vols. 1 & 2. Texarkana, Tex.: Bogard Press, 1922.

_____. *Americanism or Romanism, Which?* Louisville, Ken.: Baptist Book Concern, 1895.

CLARKE, RICHARD A. *Against All Enemies: Inside America's War on Terrorism.* New York: Free Press, 2004.

COHEN, SAM. *Shame: Confessions of the Father of the Neutron Bomb.* N.p.: Xlibris Corporation, 2000.

CUDDY, DENNIS LAURENCE. *Secret Records Revealed: The Men, the Money, and the Methods Behind the New World Order.* Oklahoma City, Okla.: Hearthstone Publishing, Ltd., 1994.

CURRENT, RICHARD N. *The Lincoln Nobody Knows.* New York: Hill & Wang, 1958.

DALLIMORE, ARNOLD. *George Whitefield: The Life and Times of the Great Evangelist of the Eighteenth-Century Revival.* Vols. 1 & 2. Carlisle, Penn.: Banner of Truth Trust, 1970.

DALLIN, ALEXANDER. *Black Box: KAL 007 and the Superpowers.* Berkeley, Calif.: University of California Press, 1985.

DAVIS, JAYNA. *The Third Terrorist: The Middle East Connection to the Oklahoma City Bombing.* Nashville, Tenn.: WND Books, 2004.

DE GRAND PRÉ, DONN. *Barbarians Inside the Gates: The Black Book of Bolshevism.* San Pedro, Calif.: GSG & Associates, 2000.

_____. *The Rattler's Revenge.* Madison, Va.: Grand Pré Publishers, Ltd., 2003.

_____. *The Viper's Venom.* Madison, Va.: Grand Pré Books, 2002.

DE PONCINS, VICOMTE LÉON. *Freemasonry and the Vatican: A Struggle for Recognition.* Translated by Timothy Tindal-Robertson. Palmdale, Calif.: Omni/Christian Book Club, 1968.

DODGE, TOBY. *Inventing Iraq: The Failure of Nation Building and a History Denied.* New York: Columbia University Press, 2003.

DONNELLY, THOMAS, DONALD KAGAN AND GARY SCHMITT. *Rebuilding America's Defenses: Strategy, Forces and Resources For A New Century.* Washington, D.C.: Project for the New American Century, 2000.

DOOLITTLE, GEN. JAMES H. "JIMMY". *I Could Never Be So Lucky Again.* New York: Bantam Books, 1991.

EDWARDS, MORGAN. *Materials Towards A History of the Baptists.* Vol. 2. Danielsville, Ga.: Heritage Press, 1984.

EIDSMOE, JOHN. *Christianity and the Constitution.* Grand Rapids, Mich.: Baker Books, 1995.

EISENSHIML, OTTO. *The Hidden Face of the Civil War.* New York: The Bobbs-Merrill Company, 1961.

EPPERSON, A. RALPH. *America's Secret Destiny: The Role of Subversive Secret Societies in Shaping a Dreadful Future for America.* Tucson, Ariz.: Publius Press, 1995.

_____. *Masonry: Conspiracy Against Christianity.* Tucson, Ariz.: Publius Press, 1997.

_____. *The New World Order.* Tucson, Ariz.: Publius Press, 1990.

_____. *The Unseen Hand: An Introduction into the Conspiratorial View of History.* Tucson, Ariz.: Publius Press, 1985.

EVANS, M. STANTON. *The Theme is Freedom.* Washington, D.C.: Regnery Publishing, 1994.

FEDERER, WILLIAM J. *America's God and Country Encyclopedia of Quotes.* Coppell, Tex.: Fame Publishing, 1994.

FINNEY, CHARLES G. *The Character, Claims and Workings of Freemasonry.* Cincinnati, Oh.: Western Tract and Book Society, 1869.

FLOOD, ROBERT. *The Rebirth of America.* Nancy Leigh DeMoss, ed. Philadelphia: Arthur S. DeMoss Foundation, 1986.

FOSTER, GERALDINE. *The Jews in Rhode Island: A Brief History.* Providence, R.I.: Rhode Island Heritage Commission and the Rhode Island Publication Society, 1985.

FULLER, DAVID OTIS, D..D., ed. *Which Bible?* 5th ed., rev. Grand Rapids, Mich.: Grand Rapids International Publications, 1975.

GARRATY, JOHN A. AND PETER GAY, eds. *The Columbia History of the World.* New York: Harper and Row, 1972.

GOODMAN, FREDERICK. *Magic Symbols.* London: Brian Todd Publishing, 1981.

GRADY, WILLIAM P. *What Hath God Wrought!: A Biblical Interpretation of American History.* Knoxville, Tenn.: Grady Publications, Inc., 1996.

GRAHAM, SENATOR BOB WITH JEFF NUSSBAUM. *Intelligence Matters: The CIA, the FBI, Saudi Arabia, and the Failure of America's War on Terror.* New York: Random House, 2004.

GRAVES, J. R. AND S. ADLAM. *The First Baptist Church in America: Not Founded by Roger Williams.* Texarkana, Tex.: Bogard Press, 1995.

GREEN, J. R. *A Short History of the English People.* New York: Harper and Bros. Publishers, 1884.

GREEN, ROBERT. *Queen Victoria.* New York: Franklin Watts, Inc., 1969.

GRIFFIN, DAVID RAY. *The New Pearl Harbor: Disturbing Questions About the Bush Administration and 9/11.* Northampton, Mass.: Olive Branch Press, 2004.

GRIFFIN, G. EDWARD. *The Creature from Jekyll Island: A Second Look at the Federal Reserve*. Appleton, Wis.: American Opinion Publishing, Inc., 1994.

GUTSTEIN, MORRIS A. *The Story of the Jews of Newport: Two and a Half Centuries of Judaism 1658-1908*. New York: Bloch Publishing Co., 1936.

HARDMAN, KEITH J. *The Spiritual Awakeners: American Revivalists from Solomon Stoddard to D. L. Moody*. Chicago: Moody Press, 1983.

HARRIS, THOMAS M. *Rome's Responsibility for the Assassination of Abraham Lincoln*. Los Angeles: Heritage Manor, 1960.

HARRIS, WALDO P. AND JAMES D. MOSTELLER. *Georgia's First Continuing Baptist Church*. College Park, Ga.: N & R Printing, Inc., 1997.

HARRISON, EUGENE MYERS. *Giants of the Missionary Trail*. Fairfax, Va.: Fairy Baptist Temple, 1990.

HEFLEY, JAMES AND MARTI HEFLEY. *The Secret File on John Birch*. Wheaton, Ill.: Tyndale House Publishers, Inc., 1980.

HERSH, SEYMOUR M. *"The Target is Destroyed": What Really Happened to Flight 007 and What America Knew About It*. New York: Random House, 1986.

HIBBERT, CHRISTOPHER. *Queen Victoria: A Personal History*. New York: Basic Books, 2000.

HINTZ, MARTIN AND KATE HINTZ. *Kwanzaa: Why We Celebrate It the Way We Do*. Mankato, Minn.: Capstone Press, 1996.

HOROWITZ, LEONARD G. *Emerging Viruses: AIDS and Ebola – Nature, Accident or Intention?* Rockport, Mass.: Tetrahedron, Inc., 1997.

HORT, ARTHUR FENTON. *Life and Letters of Fenton John Anthony Hort*. Vol. 1. London: Macmillan & Co., 1896.

HOYT-GOLDSMITH, DIANE. *Celebrating Kwanzaa*. New York: Holiday House, 1993.

HUNTINGTON, SAMUEL P. *The Clash of Civilizations and the Remaking of World Order*. New York: Simon & Schuster, 1996.

HURST, JACK. *Nathan Bedford Forrest*. New York: Alfred A. Knopf, 1993.

ISAACSON, WALTER AND EVAN THOMAS. *The Wise Men: Six Friends and the World They Made*. New York: Simon and Schuster, 1986.

JASPER, WILLIAM. *Global Tyranny...Step By Step*. Appleton, Wis.: Western Islands Publishers, 1993.

JONES, ALEX. *9-11: Descent Into Tyranny; The New World Order's Dark Plans to Turn Earth Into A Prison Planet*. Austin, Tex.: AEJ Publishing, 2002.

KAH, GARY H. *En Route to Global Occupation: A High Ranking Government Liaison Exposes the Secret Agenda for World Unification*. Lafayette, La.: Huntington House Publishers, 1991.

KEAN, THOMAS H., ET AL. *The 9/11 Commission Report: Final Report of the National Commission on Terrorist Attacks Upon the United States*. New York: W. W. Norton & Co., Inc., 2004.

KENNEDY, PAUL. *The Rise and Fall of the Great Powers: Economic Change and Military Conflict from 1500 to 2000*. New York: Random House, 1987.

KENNEDY, JAMES RONALD AND WALTER DONALD KENNEDY. *The South Was Right*. Gretna, La.: n.p., 1994.

KETCHAM, RALPH. *James Madison: A Biography*. New York: The Macmillan Company, 1971.

LAMP, C. O. *Gentle Tigress*. New York: Dorchester Publishing Company, Inc., 1980.

LAPHAM, LEWIS. *The Wish for Kings*. New York: Grove Press, 1993.

LARSEN, BOB. *Larsen's New Book of Cults*. Wheaton, Ill.: Tyndale House Publishers, 1989.

LAWSON, JAMES GILCHRIST. *Deeper Experiences of Famous Christians*. Anderson, Ind.: Warner Press, 1972.

LIMBAUGH, RUSH H., III. *The Way Things Ought to Be*. New York: Pocket Books, 1992.

LITTLE, LEWIS PEYTON. *Imprisoned Preachers and Religious Liberty in Virginia*. Gallatin, Tenn.: Church History Research and Archives, 1987.

LONGFORD, ELIZABETH. *Queen Victoria: Born to Succeed*. New York: Harper and Row, 1964.

LYONS, S. C. *His Name Was John Birch*. Dry Branch, Ga.: n.p., 1968.

MANCHESTER, WILLIAM. *A World Lit Only By Fire*. Boston: Little, Brown and Company, 1992.

MANHATTAN, AVRO. *Murder in the Vatican*. Springfield, Mo.: Ozark Books, 1985.

_____. *The Vatican Moscow Washington Alliance*. Chino, Calif.: Chick Publications, 1986.

MANN, JAMES. *Rise of the Vulcans: The History of Bush's War Cabinet*. New York: Viking, 2004.

MANSFIELD, STEPHEN. *The Faith of George Bush*. Lake Mary, Fla.: Charisma House, 2003.

MARRS, TEXE. *Circle of Intrigue: The Hidden Inner Circle of the Global Illuminati Conspiracy*. Austin, Tex.: Living Truth Publishers, 1995.

MARSHALL, PETER AND DAVID MANUEL. *The Light and the Glory*. Old Tappan, N.J.: Fleming H. Revell, Co. 1977.

MARSHALL, P. J., ed. *The Cambridge Illustrated History of the British Empire*. Cambridge, England: Cambridge University Press, 1996.

MATHER, COTTON. *The Great Works of Christ in America*. Vol. 1. Carlisle, Penn.: Banner of Truth Trust, 1979.

MCCARTY, BURKE. *The Suppressed Truth About the Assassination of Abraham Lincoln.* Haverhill, Mass.: Arya Varta Publishing Co., 1924.

MCGRATH, ALISTER E. *In the Beginning: The Story of the King James Bible and How it Changed a Nation, a Language, and a Culture.* New York: Doubleday, 2001.

MCLOUGHLIN, WILLIAM G. *Soul Liberty: The Baptists' Struggle in New England, 1630-1833.* Hanover, N.H.: University Press of New England, 1991.

MCMANUS, JOHN F. *The Insiders: Architects of the New World Order.* Appleton, Wis.: The John Birch Society, 1995.

MCTERNAN, JOHN AND BILL KOENIG. *Israel: The Blessing or The Curse.* Oklahoma City, Okla.: Hearthstone Publishing, 2002.

MELTON, JAMES L. *Satan's New World Order: How World Leaders are Building the Kingdom of Antichrist.* Martin, Tenn.: Bible Baptist Church, 2004.

MILLARD, CATHERINE. *The Rewriting of American History.* Camp Hill, Penn.: Horizon House Publishers, 1991.

MILLER, EDITH STARR. *Occult Theocrasy.* Vol. 1. Los Angeles: The Christian Book Club of America, 1933.

MILLER, WILLIAM LEE. *The Business of May Next: James Madison and the Founding.* Charlottesville, Va.: The University Press of Virginia, 1992.

MOORE, MICHAEL. *Dude, Where's My Country?* New York: Warner Books, Inc., 2003.

MORGAN, CAPTAIN WILLIAM. *Freemasonry Exposed.* Chicago: Ezra A. Cook, Inc., 1867.

MORRISON, SAMUEL ELIOT AND HENRY STEELE COMMAGER. *The Growth of the American Republic.* Vol. 2. New York: Oxford University Press, 1962.

MORSE, SAMUEL F. B. *Foreign Conspiracy Against the Liberties of the United States.* New York: Arno Press, 1977.

_____. *Imminent Dangers to the Free Institutions of the United States Through Foreign Immigration.* New York: Arno Press, 1969.

NELSON, WILBUR. *The Hero of Aquidneck: A Life of Dr. John Clarke.* New York: Fleming H. Revell Co., 1954.

NEWTON-CHOCOLATE, DEBORAH M. *Kwanzaa.* Chicago: Children's Press, 1990.

OVASON, DAVID. *The Secret Architecture of Our Nation's Capital: The Masons and the Building of Washington, D.C.* New York: HarperCollins, 1999.

PAISLEY, IAN R. K. *My Plea for the Old Sword: The English Authorised Version (KJV).* Greenville, S.C.: Emerald House, 1997.

PAKULA, HANNAH. *An Uncommon Woman.* New York: Simon & Schuster, 1995.

PARIS, EDMOND. *The Secret History of the Jesuits.* Chino, Calif.: Chick Publications, 1975.

_____. *The Vatican Against Europe.* Translated by A. Robson. London: Wickliffe Press, 1961.

PATTERSON, COL. ROBERT "BUZZ". *Dereliction of Duty: The Eyewitness Account of How Bill Clinton Compromised America's National Security.* Washington, D.C.: Regnery Publishing, Inc., 2003.

PATTON, GEORGE S., JR. *War as I Knew It.* Boston: Houghton Mifflin Company, 1947.

Pentagon Building Performance Report. Reston, Va.: American Society of Civil Engineers, 2003.

PERLOFF, JAMES. *The Shadows of Power: The Council on Foreign Relations and the American Decline.* Appleton, Wis.: Western Islands Publishers, 1988.

PHILLIPS, KEVIN. *American Dynasty: Aristocracy, Fortune and the Politics of Deceit in the House of Bush.* New York: Viking, 2004.

POWELL, COLIN L. *My American Journey.* New York: Random House, 1995.

PRIME, S. IRENEUS. *The Life of Samuel F. B. Morse.* New York: Arno Press, 1974.

QUIGLEY, CARROLL. *The Anglo-American Establishment: From Rhodes to Cliveden.* New York: Books in Focus, Inc., 1981.

_____. *Tragedy and Hope: A History of the World in Our Time.* New York: The Macmillan Company, 1966.

RICE, JOHN R. *Our God Breathed Book – The Bible.* Murfreesboro, Tenn.: The Sword of the Lord Publishers, 1969.

ROBBINS, ALEXANDRA. *Secrets of the Tomb: Skull and Bones, the Ivy League and the Hidden Paths of Power.* Boston: Little, Brown and Company, 2002.

ROBISON, JOHN. *Proofs of a Conspiracy.* Belmont, Mass.: Western Islands, 1967.

RUCKMAN, PETER S. *Israel: A Deadly Piece of Dirt.* Pensacola, Fla.: Bible Baptist Bookstore, 2001.

_____. *The Book of Genesis.* Pensacola, Fla.: Bible Believers, Press, 1969.

RUSHDOONY, ROUSAS J. *The Nature of the American System.* Fairfax, Va.: Thoburn Press, 1978.

_____. *This Independent Republic.* Fairfax, Va.: Thoburn Press, 1978.

SANDERS, JAMES D., MARK A. SAUTER AND R. CORT KIRKWOOD. *Soldiers of Misfortune: Washington's Secret Betrayal of American POWs in the Soviet Union.* Washington, D.C.: National Press Books, 1992.

SCHAFF, PHILIP. *History of the Christian Church.* Vol. 6, *The Middle Ages, from Boniface VIII, 1204, to the Protestant Reformation, 1517.* Grand Rapids, Mich.: Wm. B. Eerdmans Publishing Co., 1910.

SCHIFLET, JEAN. *Victoria and Her Times.* New York: Henry Holt & Company, Inc., 1996.

SCHLOSSBERG, BERT. *Rescue 007: The Untold Story of KAL 007 and Its Survivors*. Philadelphia: Xlibris Corporation, 2000.

SCHNOEBELEN, WILLIAM. *Masonry: Beyond the Light*. Chino, Calif.: Chick Publications, 1991.

SKLAR, DUSTY. *The Nazis and the Occult*. New York: Dorsett Press, 1977.

SMITH, ADAM. *The Wealth of Nations*. Edited by Edwin Cannan. New York: Random House, 1937.

SMOOT, DAN. *The Invisible Government*. Dallas, Tex.: The Dan Smoot Report, 1962.

SPRAGUE, WILLIAM P. *Annals of the American Baptist Pulpit*. New York: Robert Carter & Brothers, 1860.

SORENSEN, DAVID H. *Touch Not the Unclean Thing: The Bible Translation Controversy and the Principle of Separation*. Duluth, Minn.: Northstar Baptist Ministries, 2001.

SPURGEON, CHARLES HADDON. *C. H. Spurgeon Autobiography*. Vol.1, *The Early Years*. Carlisle, Penn.: The Banner of Truth Trust, 1973.

_____. *The New Park Street Pulpit*. Vol. 3. Pasadena, Tex.: Pilgrim Publications, 1975.

ST. JOHN, JEFFREY. *Day of the Cobra: The True Story of KAL 007*. Nashville, Tenn.: Thomas Nelson Publishers, 1984.

STILL, WILLIAM T. *New World Order: The Ancient Plan of Secret Societies*. Lafayette, La.: Hunting House Publishers, 1990.

STINNETT, ROBERT B. *Day of Deceit: The Truth About FDR and Pearl Harbor*. New York: Touchstone, 2000.

SUTTON, ANTONY C. *America's Secret Establishment: An Introduction to The Order of Skull and Bones*. Billings, Mont.: Liberty House Press, 1986.

_____. *Energy: The Created Crisis*. New York: Books in Focus, 1979.

_____. *Two Faces of George Bush*. Clackamas, Ore.: Emissary Publications, 1988.

_____. *Wall Street and the Bolshevik Revolution*. New Rochelle, N.Y.: Arlington House Publishers, 1974.

TAN, PAUL LEE. *Encyclopedia of 7,700 Illustrations: Signs of the Times*. Rockville, Md.: Assurance Publishers, 1979.

TARPLEY, WEBSTER GRIFFIN AND ANTON CHAITKIN. *George Bush: The Unauthorized Biography*. Washington, D.C.: Executive Intelligence Review, 1992.

The Book of Common Prayer and Administration of the Sacraments and Other Rites and Ceremonies of the Church. N.p.: Seabury Press, 1979.

THE OKLAHOMA BOMBING INVESTIGATION COMMITTEE. *Final Report On the Bombing of the Alfred P. Murrah Federal Building April 19, 1995*. Oklahoma City, Okla.: The Oklahoma Bombing Committee, 2001.

THOMPSON, E. WAYNE AND DAVID L. CUMMINS. *This Day in Baptist History*. Greenville, S.C.: Bob Jones Press, 1993.

THOMPSON, R. W. *The Papacy and the Civil Power*. New York: Harper & Bros. Publishers, 1876.

THOREN, THEODORE R. AND RICHARD F. WARNER. *The Truth in Money Book*. 4th edition. Chagrin Falls, Oh.: Truth in Money Publications, Inc., 1994.

TOLAND, JOHN. *Infamy: Pearl Harbor and its Aftermath*. New York: Doubleday and Company, 1982.

TUCHMAN, BARBARA W. *A Distant Mirror*. New York: Alfred A. Knopf, Inc., 1978.

UNGER, CRAIG. *House of Bush, House of Saud: The Secret Relationship Between the World's Two Most Powerful Dynasties*. New York: Scribner, 2004.

UNGER, MERRILL F. *Archaeology and the Old Testament*. Grand Rapids, Mich.: Zondervan Publishing House, 1970.

VEDDER, HENRY C. *A Short History of the Baptists*. Valley Forge, Penn.: Judson Press, 1907.

VENNARD, WICKLIFFE B., SR. *The Federal Reserve Hoax: The Age of Deception*. Palmdale, Calif.: Omni Publications, n.d.

WAYCHAK, N. A. *Messiah: The Story of George Frideric Handel*. St. Louis, Mo.: Scripture Memory Fellowship International, 1995.

WEBSTER, NESTA. *Secret Societies and Subversive Movements*. Palmdale, Calif.: Omni Publications, 1924.

_____. *World Revolution: The Plot Against Civilisation*. Edited by Anthony Gittens. Palmdale, Calif.: Omni Publications, 1921.

WEINTRAUB, STANLEY. *Victoria*. New York: Truman Talley Books, 1987.

WELCH, ROBERT H. W., JR. *The Life of John Birch: In the Story of One American Boy, the Ordeal of His Age*. Boston: Western Islands Publications, 1960.

_____. *The Politician*. Belmont, Mass.: Belmont Publishing Co., 1963.

WEYL, NATHANIEL. *The Negro in American Civilization*. Washington, D.C.: Public Affairs Press, 1960.

WHITEFIELD, George. *George Whitefield's Journals*. Vol. 2. Carlisle, Penn.: The Banner of Truth Trust, 1960.

WILSON, Mitchell. *American Science and Invention*. New York: Bonanza Books, 1954.

WOOD, GORDON, S. *The Radicalism of American Revolution*. New York: Vintage Books, 1993.

WOODROW, RALPH. *Reckless Rumors, Misinformation, Doomsday Delusions*. Palm Springs, Calif.: Ralph Woodrow Evangelistic Association, Inc., 2000.

WOODWARD, BOB. *Plan of Attack*. New York: Simon & Schuster, 2004.

Index

George Town

Presidents House

PO'TO'MAK RIV[...]

38: 53, N.